# The American South

## Volume II

# Clio Bibliography Series No. 22

Pamela R. Byrne, Executive Editor
Suzanne R. Ontiveros, Managing Editor

# The American
# South

## A Historical Bibliography

### Volume II

Introduction by John B. Boles

Jessica S. Brown
Editor

ABC-CLIO

Santa Barbara, California
Oxford, England

**Library of Congress Cataloging-in-Publication Data**
Main entry under title:

The American South.

(Clio bibliography series ; no. 21-22)
Includes indexes.
1. Southern States—History—Abstracts. 2. Southern
States—History—Bibliography. I. Brown, Jessica S.
II. ABC-Clio Information Services. III. Series.
F209.A45  1985        016.975        85-19938
ISBN 0-87436-464-7 (set)
ISBN 0-87436-451-5 (v. 1)
ISBN 0-87436-457-4 (v. 2)

ABC-Clio, Inc.
2040 Alameda Padre Serra, Box 4397
Santa Barbara, California

Clio Press Ltd.
55 St. Thomas Street
Oxford, England

Printed and bound in the United States of America.

# TABLE OF CONTENTS

# GENERAL CONTENTS

VOLUME I

*The Major Periods in Southern History*

VOLUME II

*The Search for Southern History*

*Society, Culture, Politics, and Economy of
the South: Multiperiod*

*Indians in Southern History*

# INTRODUCTION

Since the rise of history as a professional discipline in American graduate schools around the turn of this century, there has been great interest in southern history. This has not been an area of interest confined to the former Confederate states, and in fact two of the founders of southern historical scholarship, William A. Dunning and Ulrich B. Phillips, taught at Columbia and Yale respectively; Harvard, Chicago, Wisconsin, Berkeley, and Stanford, along with geographically southern institutions such as Johns Hopkins and the University of North Carolina, have long been major training centers for historians of the region. In 1934 the Southern Historical Association was formed to underwrite the *Journal of Southern History* and sponsor an annual scholarly meeting, and today its over 2,500 individual members and almost 1,700 library subscribers represent all fifty states and twenty-nine foreign countries. Why this national, even international, fascination with the history of the South?

The perception of the South as a region different from the rest of the nation predates the rise of professional history by approximately a century. The causes of this perceived differentness of the South have long been debated and have been attributed to factors ranging from climate to economics, from the presence of blacks to the presence of Celts. It has been argued that the region represents the concentrated essence of the evils of the nation as a whole—it is simply more racist, more violent, and so on. Another interpretation suggests that the South's history itself sets it apart from the national experience—the South has been a land of poverty in a nation of plenty, a region that has tasted defeat in a nation that has mostly known success, a captive of guilt in an empire of innocence. Still others point to the people of the South, their folk culture, and posit that a unique relationship there of people to people and to the land has produced a distinct regional character. The precise sources of this Dixie difference remain unknown, and the quest for explanatory factors is complicated by the manifest diversity of the region even as scholars search for a central theme.

In a real sense, as David M. Potter once suggested, the South has been a sort of Sphinx on the American soil. Some have celebrated its difference, others have attacked it. In the mid-nineteenth century certain northern opponents of their incipient industrial revolution held up the South's presumed virtues to critique developments in their own region, even as in the 1920s a group of self-styled southern agrarians arose to defend their region's older ways against the onslaught of industrial modernity. The South has always meant different things to different observers, but it has been the great "other" in the American past. For that reason it has attracted interpreters of all kinds and for all purposes. It has been America's most exotic region, a mysterious land of romance and tragedy, whose climate, people—black and white, slave and free—and institutions have provoked curiosity and an urge to understand. The central event of American history, the Civil War, was of course integrally related to southern history, as was the nation's central dilemma of slavery and persisting racism. Hence, any complete understanding of the American past and character is tied in with that of its most distinctive region. Whether portrayed as America's bête noire or as a wholesome counterculture, the South has stood on the American landscape as a kind of interpretative Mount Everest that had to be scaled. For generations many of the nation's most skilled historians have analyzed the southern historical experience, and they have produced a magnificent body of scholarship unrivaled by that on any other region of the United States.

By the mid-1960s one might have expected this outpouring of historical writing to exhaust most topics of investigation. A landmark historiographical volume, *Writing Southern History,* Arthur S. Link and Rembert W. Patrick, eds., (Baton Rouge: Louisiana State University Press, 1965), contained seventeen detailed chapters that perceptively surveyed the rich body of work. But in part as a result of a process described by David M. Potter in a famous essay entitled "Depletion and Renewal in Southern History" (in Edgar T. Thompson, ed., *Perspectives on the South: Agenda for Research* Durham: Duke University Press, 1967), the very extent and sophistication of the scholarship completed suggested new areas for study and revealed deeper levels of complexity that required still further research and analysis. Moreover, developments in the larger society—the ongoing civil rights revolution, for example, and later the women's movement and the spurt of southern economic growth that gave rise to the misleading phrase "Sunbelt"—posed new questions for historians. Scholars discovered new sources—the slave narratives, for example—and new ways of utilizing familiar data like manuscript census returns. Borrowing from the *annales* school of French social historians, investigators began to explore archival materials like wills and demographic records with hitherto unheard of sophistication—and unexpectedly exciting results. On topics as diverse as the colonial Chesapeake and antebellum free blacks, postbellum sharecropping and late-nineteenth-century agrarian radicalism, there has been in the last decade and a half a veritable explosion of research.

Familiar topics like slavery and Reconstruction have been transformed in recent years by innovative research methodologies; by asking different kinds of questions and utilizing fresh evidence—some of it made comprehensible by new sampling and statistical techniques—these two aspects of the region's history bear little resemblance to interpretations widely held a generation ago. Social, cultural, and intellectual history are now common approaches to the region, with the result that, for example, a new understanding of the Old South is emerging. The role of ideas and ideologies in the region is currently being explored, and the mentalité of the common folk as well as the planter aristocrats is under subtle investigation. Slave culture has been explicated with a skill that makes that subfield of southern history one of the glories of American historical scholarship, and similar techniques are now being applied to the history of the southern yeomen, the majority of all southerners. The history of women has also been discovered, and some of the most fruitful work on the South is focused on recovering the role of gender—along with race and class—in southern history. The history of religion in the South has within the past decade and a half become a major subdiscipline of the field. Scholars are researching the development of science and medicine in the South, along with urban and ethnic history. More traditional topics have been invigorated by the rise of the "new" political and economic history, which is alert to the social, cultural, ethnic, and demographic dimensions of the subjects being studied. The secession crisis—both why and how the South seceded—has again attracted attention, and the Civil War, its military, political, and social history, continues to be a fertile ground of scholarship ranging far afield from the older bugles and swords approach. From the Populist revolt to the New Deal, from Progressivism to the Dixiecrats, southern political history remains a steady source of scholarship. The impact of the New Deal on southern agricultural poverty is a topic of much study, and World War II's role in transforming the rural, racist, impoverished South into today's so-called Sunbelt is generating fascinating comparative history; scholars now are moving beyond a moral tale of victims and violators and probing the economic and social origins and results of racism. In fact, every aspect of southern history is in a phase of constant revisionism, which makes it one of the most creative fields of American historical scholarship.

Much of the ongoing work is self-consciously methodological and interdisciplinary, with quantification and anthropological perspectives increasingly employed along with a comparative approach. The recent scholarship as a whole is far more interpretative, with practically no trace of the defensiveness that marred some of the writing as late as the 1940s. Even the familiar chronological boundaries have been blurred. For years southern colonial history was slighted, and "history of the South" courses began about 1800 or 1820. The recent work in demography and slavery in particular have pushed back the beginning of the courses almost two centuries. Slavery was often discussed as though it ended in 1861, but now the institution is traced through the Civil War and followed as it evolved into sharecropping. Reconstruction formerly "began" in 1865 when the war was over, but new work begins the process of Reconstruction in early 1862 when the first southern regions fell into Union hands. The long-running debate over how major a divide in the history of the South the Civil War was continues, with those who hold for greater continuity than discontinuity now in the ascendency, but interesting recent work suggests that World War II may have been an even more important watershed.

Clearly southern history is a vigorous field, with more practitioners, employing more sophisticated methodologies, incorporating a broader perspective than ever before on the past. Because of the volume and quality of the scholarship, it has become impossible for any one scholar to keep abreast of the writing across the whole spectrum of the field, especially the periodical literature where often the newest interpretations are first broached and better established views are tested in different regions and for different groups. The landmark historiographical volume *Writing Southern History* will be updated in 1986 with a similar cooperative volume entitled *Interpreting Southern History* (Baton Rouge: Louisiana State University Press), but like its predecessor it will emphasize books.

For the experienced researcher as well as the student, for the expert and the novice, this two-volume work, *The American South: A Historical Bibliography,* with its almost 8,900 abstracts and annotations of articles drawn from an international list of over 500 periodicals dealing with history and related disciplines published between 1974 and 1984 will prove an absolutely indispensable guide to the literature. In Volume I, the 4,775 entries are arranged alphabetically by author within five major chronological categories. Beginning with the colonial and revolutionary periods, the volume covers the early national and antebellum periods, the Confederate States of America and the Civil War, Reconstruction and the late nineteenth century, and the twentieth century. Within the five major categories, the entries are divided further into topical and chronological subcategories. In Volume II, the 4,118 abstracts and annotations are arranged topically and cover such major areas of study as images of the South and southern self-image, art and culture, education, southern economy, politics, and law, and Indians in southern history. Entries from Volume I are not duplicated in Volume II. In both volumes, the abstracts are properly more descriptive than interpretative, but they have enough substance in nearly all cases to enable a researcher to know if he needs to refer to the original article. If so, the bibliographical citation is complete enough to make that referral easy, even if via interlibrary loan.

The whole is indexed by author and subject, the latter the versatile ABC-SPIndex that is based on key subject terms linked with the historical dates to form a complete profile of the article. Each set of index terms is rotated alphabetically so that the complete profile appears under each of the subject terms. Thus, the accuracy and specificity of subject access is enhanced as compared to conventional, hierarchical indexes. A large number of cross-references has been included to ensure fast and thorough searching. The explanatory note at the beginning of the subject index provides further information for using ABC-SPIndex. A list of the periodicals covered in this volume follows the subject and author indexes.

These volumes represent the combined efforts of a skilled and diverse group. Pamela R. Byrne, Executive Editor, had overall responsibility for the creation of the bibliography and provided guidance essential to its production. Data Base Products Managing Editor Jessica S. Brown had responsibility for conceptualization of and final organization of the material. Electronic Publishing Group Managing Editor Suzanne R. Ontiveros oversaw all major editorial work on the abstracts and indexes in these volumes. Assistant Editor Susan K. Kinnell helped select entries from the data base and participated in the creation of the subject index. The Data Processing Services Department, under the supervision of Ken Baser, Director, and Deborah Looker, Production Supervisor, ably manipulated the data to meet the technical specifications of the editors. David R. Blanke, Applications Programmer, provided critical support to assure high quality photocomposition. Terri Wright MacRae, Graphics Production Staff Supervisor, and Tanya Cullen were responsible for essential paste-up corrections and book design.

Richly documenting the veritable explosion of research and the magnificent body of scholarship that has been produced over the last decade and a half, *The American South: A Historical Bibliography,* volumes I and II, is the most complete, accessible and up-to-date bibliography on Southern history available, and its enormous usefulness places all students of the field in debt to ABC-CLIO. It will facilitate the ongoing renewal of southern history.

*Rice University*                                                                                                              JOHN B. BOLES

*John B. Boles, Professor of History at Rice University and Managing Editor of the* Journal of Southern History, *is the author of* The Great Revival, 1787–1805: Origins of the Southern Evangelical Mind *(1972),* Religion in Antebellum Kentucky *(1976), and* Black Southerners, 1619–1869 *(1983), and editor of* America: The Middle Period *(1973),* Maryland Heritage *(1976),* Dixie Dateline: A Journalistic Portrait of the Contemporary South *(1983), and co-editor with Evelyn T. Nolen of* Interpreting Southern History *(1986).*

# LIST OF ABBREVIATIONS

*A.* .............. Author-prepared Abstract
*Acad.* ............ Academy, Academie, Academia
*Agric.* ........... Agriculture, Agricultural
*AIA* ............. Abstracts in Anthropology
*Akad.* ........... Akademie
*Am.* ............. America, American
*Ann.* ............. Annals, Annales, Annual, Annali
*Anthrop.* .......... Anthropology, Anthropological
*Arch.* ............. Archives
*Archaeol.* ......... Archaeology, Archaeological
*Art.* ............. Article
*Assoc.* ........... Association, Associate
*Biblio.* ........... Bibliography, Bibliographical
*Biog.* ............ Biography, Biographical
*Bol.* ............. Boletim, Boletin
*Bull.* ............ Bulletin
*c.* ................ century (in index)
*ca.* ............... circa
*Can.* ............ Canada, Canadian, Canadien
*Cent.* ............ Century
*Coll.* ............ College
*Com.* ............ Committee
*Comm.* ........... Commission
*Comp.* ............ Compiler
*DAI* ............. Dissertation Abstracts International
*Dept.* ............ Department
*Dir.* ............. Director, Direktor
*Econ.* ............ Economy, Econom-.
*Ed.* .............. Editor, Edition
*Educ.* ............ Education, Educational
*Geneal.* ........... Genealogy, Genealogical, Genealogique
*Grad.* ............ Graduate
*Hist.* ............. History, Hist-.
*IHE* ............. Indice Historico Espanol

*Illus.* ............. Illustrated, Illustration
*Inst.* ............. Institute, Institut-.
*Int.* ............. International, Internacional, Internationaal, Internationaux, Internazionale
*J.* ................ Journal, Journal-prepared Abstract
*Lib.* ............. Library, Libraries
*Mag.* ............ Magazine
*Mus.* ............ Museum, Musee, Museo
*Nac.* ............. Nacional
*Natl.* ............ National, Nationale
*Naz.* ............. Nazionale
*Phil.* ............. Philosophy, Philosophical
*Photo.* ........... Photograph
*Pol.* ............. Politics, Political, Politique, Politico
*Pr.* ............. Press
*Pres.* ............ President
*Pro.* ............. Proceedings
*Publ.* ............ Publishing, Publication
*Q.* .............. Quarterly
*Rev.* ............ Review, Revue, Revista, Revised
*Riv.* ............. Rivista
*Res.* ............. Research
*RSA* ............ Romanian Scientific Abstracts
*S.* ............... Staff-prepared Abstract
*Sci.* ............. Science, Scientific
*Secy.* ............ Secretary
*Soc.* ............. Society, Societe, Sociedad, Societa
*Sociol.* ........... Sociology, Sociological
*Tr.* .............. Transactions
*Transl.* ........... Translator, Translation
*U.* .............. University, Universi-.
*US* ............. United States
*Vol.* ............. Volume
*Y.* ............... Yearbook

Abbreviations also apply to feminine and plural forms.
Abbreviations not noted above are based on *Webster's Third New International Dictionary*
and the *United States Government Printing Office Style Manual*.

# THE SEARCH FOR SOUTHERN HISTORY

## General Historiography, Methodology, History Teaching, Sources, Preservation, and Work in Related Disciplines

1. Abraham, Mildred K. THE LIBRARY OF LADY JEAN SKIPWITH: A BOOK COLLECTION FROM THE AGE OF JEFFERSON. *Virginia Mag. of Hist. and Biog. 1983 91(3): 296-347.* Reared in Virginia and Great Britain, Lady Skipwith developed her fondness for reading and book collecting while a resident of Edinburgh. At age 40, when she married Sir Peyton Skipwith and moved to Mecklenburg County, she continued the pursuit of her favorite pastime. At her death she left a collection of 850 volumes (384 titles) emphasizing literature, travel, history, and biography. Jean Skipwith's collection is unique in that it was hers; most women did not own their own books. It also provides a rare glimpse at the reading habits of an educated 18th-century woman. Based on the Skipwith Papers (College of William and Mary), checklists of colonial libraries, and the Skipwith Papers at the Valentine Museum in Richmond; 82 notes, 2 photos, 2 tables, appendix.
D. J. Cimbala

2. Adams, Emily S. MEMORIAL TO A TIMELESS MAN. *Alabama Hist. Q. 1982 44(1-2): 9-17.* The life and contributions of Milo Barrett Howard, Jr. (1933-81), director of the Alabama Department of Archives and History, are reviewed. Based mostly on newspaper articles; 39 notes.
E. E. Eminhizer

3. Agnew, Brad. AROUND TAHLEQUAH COUNCIL FIRES: THE LIFE OF OKLAHOMA HISTORIAN T. L. BALLENGER. *Chronicles of Oklahoma 1982 60(3): 310-321.* After graduating from Ouachita Baptist College in 1905, Tom Lee Ballenger accepted a number of short-term teaching assignments that he alternated with work on a graduate degree. He completed the doctorate at the University of Oklahoma in 1939 and returned to Northeastern State Teachers College in Tahlequah, where he had been teaching since 1914. Ballenger has received praise as a superb teacher, but his main contribution to scholarship is his collecting of Cherokee archival materials and writing about local history topics. Based on interviews and Ballenger's unpublished manuscripts; 4 photos, 26 notes.
M. L. Tate

4. Allin, Jean. PLEASE DON'T BURY THE RECORDS. *Tampa Bay Hist. 1979 1(1): 67-75.* Excerpts from the daily journal of Jean Allin, March 1977-March 1979, relate her successful efforts (and those of many others) to save local county records of Manatee County, Florida, from destruction, to organize and house the records, and finally to establish a local historical library.

5. Almaráz, Félix D., Jr. CARLOS E. CASTAÑEDA'S RENDEZVOUS WITH A LIBRARY: THE LATIN AMERICAN COLLECTION, 1920-27—THE FIRST PHASE. *J. of Lib. Hist. 1981 16(2): 315-328.* Discusses the career of Carlos Eduardo Castañeda. He was born in 1896 in Mexico, and then attended school in Texas. He was regional director of President Franklin D. Roosevelt's Committee on Fair Employment Practices, librarian of the Benson Latin American Collection at the University of Texas at Austin, and a first-rate historian of the Borderlands. This article discusses the first phase of Castañeda's involvement with the library, which began in 1920 and concluded in 1927, when he assumed responsibility for the Latin American Collection. Personal correspondence; 38 notes.
J. Powell

6. Almaráz, Félix D., Jr. CARLOS EDUARDO CASTAÑEDA, MEXICAN-AMERICAN HISTORIAN: THE FORMATIVE YEARS, 1896-1927. *Pacific Hist. R. 1973 42(3): 319-334.* A biography of Carlos Eduardo Castañeda, Texas historiographer best known for *The Mexican Side of the Texas Revolution and Our Catholic Heritage in Texas, 1519-1936.* "No Mexican American historian in this century has approximated his solid publishing record of twelve books and seventy-eight articles." Born on 11 November 1896 in a small Mexican border town, Castañeda surmounted the difficulties inherent in his ethnic background, financial position, and geographic setting to establish himself as a scholar of the first rank, teacher, and librarian of the Latin American collection of the University of Texas. 42 notes.
B. L. Fenske

7. Almaráz, Félix D., Jr. "THE MAKING OF A BOLTONIAN: CARLOS E. CASTAÑEDA OF TEXAS—THE EARLY YEARS." *Red River Valley Hist. R. 1974 1(4): 329-350.* Spans Carlos E. Castañeda's early scholastic career (1921-36) as a historian of Spanish Texas, and his affiliation with Herbert Eugene Bolton, founder of borderlands history.

8. Arana, Luis Rafael. NOTES ON FORT MATANZAS NATIONAL MONUMENT. *Escribano 1981 18: 45-73.* Discusses the history, condition, construction, and repairs on Fort Matanzas National Monument near St. Augustine, Florida, 1820-1965.

9. Armstrong, Thomas F. and Fennell, Janice C. HISTORICAL AND GENEALOGICAL GOLD MINE: AN INDEX PROJECT FOR A SMALL-TOWN NEWSPAPER. *RQ 1982 22(2): 140-145.* Access to the information of small-town newspapers is limited by both availability of the papers and the lack of suitable indexes. In an effort to solve these problems, the authors have started an index-abstract, obtained funding, and are computerizing the index for the Milledgeville *Southern Recorder,* in Georgia. The project and its successor newspapers (1820-present) will be of value to librarians, historians, genealogists, and public officials.
J/S

10. Baehr, Theodore, Jr. and Wetherington, Mark V., comp. A TOPICAL BIBLIOGRAPHY OF ARTICLES FROM PUBLICATIONS NO. 1-50. *East Tennessee Hist. Soc. Publ. 1979 51: 163-178.* A bibliography of articles from the first 50 volumes of the *East Tennessee Historical Society's Publications;* the articles are divided into 18 topical categories covering political, social, archival, and other subjects.
D. A. Yanchisin

11. Bartley, Numan V. IN SEARCH OF THE NEW SOUTH: SOUTHERN POLITICS AFTER RECONSTRUCTION. *Rev. in Am. Hist. 1982 10(4): 150-163.* Examines historiography emphasizing the similarities between the antebellum Old South and the post-Reconstruction New South.

12. Becnel, Thomas. REPORT OF THE SIXTEENTH ANNUAL MEETING. *Louisiana Hist. 1974 15(3): 285-289.* Discusses papers read at the Louisiana Historical Association meeting in 1974.

13. Bennett, Patrick. GOLDEN AGE OF TEXAS HISTORIANS: AN INTERVIEW WITH RUPERT N. RICHARDSON. *Southwest Rev. 1982 67(1): 33-43.* With Walter Prescott Webb, J. Frank Dobie, Carl Coke Rister, and William Curry Holden, Rupert N. Richardson established the golden age of Texas historical research during the 1920's; Richardson believes that, along with local and regional history, a good subject for research would be man and the horse, tracing that history from the Carthaginians to the present.

14. Berrigan, Joseph R. MILTON W. HUMPHREYS, AN APPALACHIAN ODYSSEUS. *Southern Humanities Rev. 1977 11(Special Issue): 27-32.* Discusses the academic career of Milton W. Humphreys, a southern classicist, 1860-1919. One of six articles in this issue on classical traditions in the South.

15. BeVard, Ginger. SEARCHING FOR YOUR UPPER OHIO VALLEY ANCESTORS IN THE WEST VIRGINIA AND REGIONAL HISTORY COLLECTION. *Upper Ohio Valley Hist. Rev. 1983 13(1): 21-27.* Describes genealogy sources available in the West Virginia and Regional History Collection of the West Virginia University Library.

16. Bickel, Minnette. THE GEORGIA TRUST FOR HISTORIC PRESERVATION, INC. *Georgia Hist. Q. 1979 63(1): 22-27.* Describes the genesis in 1969, the founding in 1973, and the recent accomplishments, of the Georgia Trust for Historic Preservation, a citizen's organization that complements state government preservation efforts. Illus., 3 notes.                      G. R. Schroeder

17. Birdwhistell, Terry L. and Allen, Susan Emily. THE APPALACHIAN IMAGE REEXAMINED: AN ORAL HISTORY VIEW OF EASTERN KENTUCKY. *Register of the Kentucky Hist. Soc. 1983 81(3): 287-302.* Oral history has helped break some of the stereotypical images of life in Appalachia. Several oral history projects have revealed the mountain people to be hard workers who take pride in their work and independence. Other myths studied have included those associated with education, guns, feuds, violence, and moonshine. Sources include interviews; 44 notes.
                                                   J. F. Paul

18. Bowden, Thomas A. GUIDE TO PRE-1900 SOURCES FOR ECONOMIC AND SOCIAL HISTORY IN THE DELAWARE STATE ARCHIVES. *Working Papers from the Regional Econ. Hist. Res. Center 1977 1(2): 1-30.* Presents research sources in social history and economic history available through the Delaware state archives; includes imprints, graphics, wealth, land, demographic information, business, labor, and courts.

19. Bowers, Beth. DAUGHTER OF THE AMERICAN REVOLUTION MUSEUM. *Texana 1973 11(4): 362-373.* The museum has been at Texas Woman's University in Denton, Texas, since its founding in 1940.

20. Braden, Waldo W. and Eubanks, Ralph T. DALLAS C. DICKEY: PIONEER OF THE CRITICAL STUDY OF SOUTHERN PUBLIC ADDRESS. *Southern Speech Communication J. 1979 44(2): 119-146.* Professional and academic study during 1938-57 by Dallas C. Dickey (1904-57) in southern public address at Louisiana State University and the University of Florida lent credence to the field and helped establish it as an academic discipline.

21. Braden, Waldo W. and Mixon, Harold D. SOUTHERN PUBLIC ADDRESS: A BIBLIOGRAPHY OF THESES AND DISSERTATIONS, CONTINUED. *Southern Speech Communication J. 1983 48(3): 296-301.* Continued from a previous article (see entry in this bibliography). State-by-state listing of studies, 1975-82, of prominent southern speakers.

22. Brown, Dorothy M. and Duncan, Richard R. A SELECTED BIBLIOGRAPHY OF ARTICLES ON MARYLAND HISTORY IN OTHER JOURNALS. *Maryland Hist. Mag. 1974 69(3): 300-316.* "There is a serious need for an updated and wide-ranging bibliography of journal articles on Maryland for both the scholar and general reader." Thirty journals were culled to compile this listing, which shows that research has been concentrated in the colonial and early national period of Maryland's history, while the late 19th and the 20th centuries "are rich but largely neglected fields of study of the Old Line State." The list is not to be regarded as definitive. Secondary sources.              G. J. Bobango

23. Brown, Douglas Summers. LEWIS PRESTON SUMMERS: HISTORIAN OF THE VIRGINIA HIGHLANDS. *Virginia Cavalcade 1975 25(2): 52-57.* Discusses the historical writings about Washington County, Virginia, by lawyer Lewis Preston Summers, 1890-1943.

24. Brown, James S. AN APPALACHIAN FOOTNOTE TO TOYNBEE'S *A STUDY OF HISTORY*. *Appalachian J. 1978 6(1): 29-32.* Discusses D. C. Somervell's abridgement of Arnold J. Toynbee's *A Study of History*, and comments on Toynbee's superficial impressions of Appalachia.

25. Brown, Richard Maxwell. THE FORTIETH ANNUAL MEETING. *J. of Southern Hist. 1975 41(1): 59-88.* Summary of the meeting of the Southern Historical Association held in Dallas, Texas, 6-9 November 1974. Describes subject matter, speakers, audience responses, and anecdotes from the 47 regular sessions, 27 of which focused on Southern history, including the antebellum South, the Civil War and its aftermath, aspects of the New South, slavery, black history and racism, and women in the South.

26. Brown, Walter L. THE HELENA MEETING OF THE ARKANSAS HISTORICAL ASSOCIATION. *Arkansas Hist. Q. 1976 35(3): 292-298.* The 35th annual meeting of the Arkansas Historical Association was held in Helena, 22-24 April 1976, on the campus of Phillips County Community College. Mentions historical papers and meeting activities.                    T. L. Savitt

27. Brown, Walter L. THE JONESBORO MEETING OF THE ARKANSAS HISTORICAL ASSOCIATION. *Arkansas Hist. Q. 1975 34(4): 361-367.* At the 34th annual meeting of the Arkansas Historical Association (24-26 April 1975) papers were read on subjects including prison reform in the 1960's, medical conditions in Arkansas during the Civil War and the 1930's and 1940's, local history, historical artifacts in Arkansas, and a quantitative look at the first Reconstruction legislature in Arkansas. 2 illus.
                                                   T. L. Savitt

28. Bush, Robert D. and Touchstone, Blake. A SURVEY OF MANUSCRIPT HOLDINGS IN THE HISTORIC NEW ORLEANS COLLECTION. *Louisiana Hist. 1975 16(1): 89-96.* Describes the principal manuscript holdings of the Historic New Orleans Collection, which includes many items of interest for New Orleans and Louisiana history from the colonial period to 1966. Especially notable holdings are 11 Spanish land grants and other Spanish colonial documents (particularly for the administration of Bernardo de Gálvez), numerous financial records of the early 19th century, records relating to slavery and the Civil War, papers relating to late 19th-century industrial expansion, and the papers of New Orleans composer and pianist Louis M. Gottschalk. Photo.
                                                   R. L. Woodward, Jr.

29. Campbell, Mrs. Paul M. NORTH LOUISIANA HISTORICAL ASSOCIATION'S OLDEST MEMBER: "MISS LUCILE." *North Louisiana Hist. Assoc. J. 1975 6(3): 123-130.* "Miss Lucile" is 99-year-old Mrs. Robert Augustus Perryman (*nee* Melvill Lucile Martin) of Minden, Louisiana. She was born on Roslyn Plantation in the Flat Lick area of Claiborne Parish, one of several plantations owned by the Martin family. Describes her early years, her marriage on 16 August 1900 to Robert Augustus Perryman (1868-1930) of Coushatta, her son Robert Shelley Perryman, and her later years. Photo, 17 notes.                   A. N. Garland

30. Capers, Charlotte. RICHARD AUBREY MC LEMORE, 1903-1976. *J. of Mississippi Hist. 1976 38(4): 329-331.* A summary of the contributions of Richard Aubrey McLemore (1903-76) to the Mississippi Department of Archives and History, with which he was associated in several capacities, 1950-76.          J. W. Hillje

31. Carleton, Don E. A COOPERATIVE URBAN ARCHIVES PROGRAM: THE HOUSTON METROPOLITAN RESEARCH CENTER. *Midwestern Arch. 1982 6(2): 177-195.* Discusses the development, aims, and resources of the Houston Metropolitan Research Center from its beginnings as the Houston Metropolitan Archives and Research Center in 1974 until 1982, focusing on the contribution of various Houston civic organizations to its structure.

32. Carleton, Don E. and Adams, Katherine J. "A WORK PECULIARLY OUR OWN": ORIGINS OF THE BARKER TEXAS HISTORY CENTER, 1883-1950. *Southwestern Hist. Q. 1982 86(2): 197-230.* On 27 April 1950, University of Texas officials

dedicated the Eugene C. Barker Texas History Center. This center brought together the university's archives and the Texas Library Collection. Although the university made its first collection of Texana material in 1897, Barker, who served as chairman of the Department of History during 1910-25, gave the most important organizational direction and support to the development of this major Texana collection. Barker was so successful that the Texas Collection soon outgrew its space in the library, and, in 1945, the university agreed to establish a separate library for the collection. Based on university records at the Eugene C. Barker Texas History Center in Austin; 2 photos, 76 notes.          R. D. Hurt

33. Carnahan, Frances. APPALACHIAN HERITAGE. *Early Am. Life 1977 8(4): 28-31.* Marguerite Estep Carson has spent her life tracing the history of Appalachia through folk art, furniture, architecture, and farm implements; discusses her personal collection, dating from the late 17th century.

34. Carter, Dan T. THE FORTY-THIRD ANNUAL MEETING. *J. of Southern Hist. 1978 44(1): 67-92.* Reports on the annual meeting of the Southern Historical Association in New Orleans, Louisiana, 9-12 November 1977. Presents synopses of the 43 sessions, approximately half of which dealt with southern history.          M. S. Legan

35. Cash, William M. PROGRAM OF THE 1978 ANNUAL MEETING OF THE MISSISSIPPI HISTORICAL SOCIETY. *J. of Mississippi Hist. 1978 40(3): 253-256.* The 1978 meeting of the Mississippi Historical Society, held in Starkville, Mississippi, 2-4 March had as its theme local history. Speakers with expertise in local history were invited to present papers before the general sessions as well as the noon luncheon and the annual banquet. Session one was entitled "Aspects of Local History"; session two, "Grassroots History: Where It All Begins," and session three, "One Hundred Years of Higher Education in Mississippi." The convention concluded with the annual business meeting of the Society.          M. S. Legan

36. Cashin, Edward J. WILL THE REAL GEORGIA HISTORY RISE AND BE RECOGNIZED? *Georgia Hist. Q. 1981 65(1): 1-6.* Discussion of the "popular" history of Georgia as revealed by a small random survey.          G. R. Schroeder

37. Caudill, Harry M. EASTERN KENTUCKY AND THE HISTORY OF OUR COMMONWEALTH. *Register of the Kentucky Hist. Soc. 1979 77(4): 285-293.* This annual Boone Day lecture briefly summarizes Kentucky history, stresses the richness of that state's heritage, and suggests topics that need exploration. Covers ca. 1790-1979. Illus.          J. F. Paul

38. Cawthon, William Lamar, Jr. THE CLINTON CONSERVATION EFFORT. *Georgia Hist. Q. 1979 63(1): 124-128.* The Old Clinton Historical Society and the Clinton Foundation have joined together to try to preserve the early 1800's small town atmosphere of Clinton, Jones County, Georgia. 3 illus., 4 notes.          G. R. Schroeder

39. Chapman, Berlin Basil. OKLAHOMA TERRITORY AND THE NATIONAL ARCHIVES: A HISTORIAN'S PARADISE. *Chronicles of Oklahoma 1982-83 60(4): 400-411.* Berlin Basil Chapman recalls his arrival at Oklahoma State University in 1927 as a brand new assistant professor, and his quick discovery that Oklahoma history offered virgin territory for researchers. This led Chapman into the National Archives from which he extracted materials for a study of federal land management in Oklahoma Territory, a series of articles on Indian land claims, and a book on Otoe and Missouria treaty rights for the Indian Claims Commission. Similar trips to the National Archives during the 1960's revealed that new rules had been established which consumed more of the researcher's money and time, as well as reducing access to the stacks. 3 photos, 7 notes.          M. L. Tate

40. Clark, Georgia H. and Parham, R. Bruce, comp. ARKANSAS COUNTY AND LOCAL HISTORIES: A BIBLIOGRAPHY. *Arkansas Hist. Q. 1977 36(1): 50-84.* This bibliography lists all Ar-

kansas county and local histories published in books, journals, historical society series, and some genealogies and reminiscences. It excludes histories which appeared in magazines or newspapers, as well as transcripts of censuses, birth, marriage and death registers, gravestone inscriptions, family genealogies, and unpublished materials.          T. L. Savitt

41. Clark, Thomas D. REUBEN T. DURRETT AND HIS KENTUCKIANA INTEREST AND COLLECTION. *Filson Club Hist. Q. 1982 56(4): 353-378.* Provides the historical context in which Reuben Thomas Durrett collected a large number of books, documents, and manuscripts on the early history of Kentucky. Durrett was not only a collector, but he was also an amateur historian whose best known work was *John Filson, First Historian of Kentucky* (1884). In addition, Durrett was the primary person responsible for the founding of the Filson Club. He also served as a research source for many prominent historians of the period including J. Franklin Jameson, Theodore Roosevelt, and Frederick Jackson Turner. The author also details the lack of interest in the Durrett collection in Kentucky that led to it being housed outside of the state. Documentation comes primarily from the Durrett Papers at the Filson Club, Louisville, Kentucky; 2 photos, 70 notes.          G. B. McKinney

42. Cook, Philip C. AFFAIRS OF THE ASSOCIATION: REPORT OF THE SEVENTEENTH ANNUAL MEETING. *Louisiana Hist. 1975 16(3): 299-301.* The 1975 Annual Meeting of the Louisiana Historical Association was held at Baton Rouge. The first session was devoted to colonial Louisiana administration; the second, to pioneer efforts in black higher education in Louisiana; the third was concerned with antebellum press opinion of two wars, the Mexican War and the Crimean War; and the fourth revolved around three particularly colorful, militant conservatives of Louisiana.          E. P. Stickney

43. Cooksey, Gordon L. TWENTY-SEVENTH ANNUAL MEETING OF THE ALABAMA HISTORICAL ASSOCIATION. *Alabama R. 1974 27(4): 282-286.* Proceedings of the annual meeting held in Mobile, 25-27 April 1974, including listing of papers presented and the election of new officers.          J. F. Vivian

44. Couto, Richard A. POLITICAL SCIENCE AND APPALACHIA. *Appalachian J. 1978 5(1): 116-124.* Examines recent political science scholarship on Appalachia, focusing on economic conditions, political power, and economic, political, and social inequalities, 1960's-70's.

45. Coutts, Brian E. and Whitley, Merna. AN INVENTORY OF SOURCES IN THE DEPARTMENT OF ARCHIVES AND MANUSCRIPTS, LOUISIANA STATE UNIVERSITY, FOR THE HISTORY OF SPANISH LOUISIANA AND SPANISH WEST FLORIDA. *Louisiana Hist. 1978 19(2): 213-250.* Lists 172 collections of manuscripts and records containing material pertinent to the history of Spanish Louisiana and Spanish West Florida.          R. L. Woodward, Jr.

46. Cox, Lynn and Zinkham, Helena. PICTURE RESEARCH AT THE MARYLAND HISTORICAL SOCIETY: A GUIDE TO THE SOURCES. *Maryland Hist. Mag. 1981 76(1): 1-21.* Mentions basic picture research techniques and the collections of artifacts found at the Maryland Historical Society, and provides an annotated guide to the visual sources collections under the headings of General Library, Prints & Photographs Division, Manuscripts Division, Gallery, and the George Radcliffe Maritime Museum holdings. Gives quantities, inclusive dates, indexes, specific finding aids, and hours of operation for each division. Three appendixes list bibliographies for Society pictorial materials. 9 illus.          G. J. Bobango

47. Cox, Richard J., comp. A BIBLIOGRAPHY OF ARTICLES AND BOOKS ON MARYLAND HISTORY, 1976. *Maryland Hist. Mag. 1977 72(2): 288-314.* Lists about 375 popular and scholarly works under all categories, both primary and secondary in nature. Items dealing with more than one subject heading are cross-referenced.          G. J. Bobango

48. Cox, Richard J. A BIBLIOGRAPHY OF ARTICLES, BOOKS, AND DISSERTATIONS ON MARYLAND HISTORY, 1977. *Maryland Hist. Mag. 1978 73(3): 280-290.* Fourth in a series of annual bibliographies, including for the first time dissertations, and excluding genealogical works except those of broad importance such as compilations of census and newspaper records.
G. J. Bobango

49. Cox, Richard J. A BIBLIOGRAPHY OF ARTICLES, BOOKS, AND DISSERTATIONS ON MARYLAND HISTORY, 1978. *Maryland Hist. Mag. 1979 74(4): 358-366.* Lists 192 works on Maryland's history, with cross references, under the following categories: General and Bibliography; Archives and Library; Architecture and Historic Preservation; Art and Decorative Arts; Biography, Autobiography, and Reminiscences; Black History; County and Local; Economic and Business; Education; Ethnic History; Genealogy and Family History; Geography; Legal; Maritime; Military; Politics; Religion; Science and Technology; Social and Cultural; Sports; and Women's History.
C. B. Schulz

50. Cox, Richard J. A BIBLIOGRAPHY OF ARTICLES, BOOKS, AND DISSERTATIONS ON MARYLAND HISTORY, 1981. *Maryland Hist. Mag. 1982 77(3): 279-290.* The 8th annual bibliography lists alphabetically more than 200 books, articles, and bibliographies relative to all facets of Maryland history, from archaeology, to ethnic history, to women's history.
G. J. Bobango

51. Cox, Richard J. A BIBLIOGRAPHY OF ARTICLES, BOOKS, AND DISSERTATIONS ON MARYLAND HISTORY, 1980. *Maryland Hist. Mag. 1981 76(3): 286-295.* Annual alphabetical listing by authors of approximately 150 entries organized by categories, including archaeology, biography, black history, genealogy, maritime, urban, and women's history.
G. J. Bobango

52. Cox, Richard J. A BIBLIOGRAPHY OF ARTICLES, BOOKS, AND DISSERTATIONS ON MARYLAND HISTORY, 1979. *Maryland Hist. Mag. 1980 75(3): 238-249.* Baltimore City Archivist and Records Management Officer Richard J. Cox continues his annual bibliographies of Maryland history, with more than 150 listings, alphabetically arranged within each subdivision, under headings ranging from Archaeology to Black History to Economics and Business, to Ethnic Studies to Science and Technology, and concluding with Urban and Women's History.
G. J. Bobango

53. Cox, Richard J. A BIBLIOGRAPHY OF ARTICLES AND BOOKS ON MARYLAND HISTORY, 1975. *Maryland Hist. Mag. 1976 71(3): 449-464.* Presents the second annual bibliography, including more than 270 popular and scholarly publications. Changes from 1974's listing include combining the "county" section under an "urban, town, county, and local" category, and an alphabetical rather than a chronological arrangement. Genealogy and Heraldry is by far the largest section, with Military and Politics also sizable.
G. J. Bobango

54. Cox, Richard J. A BIBLIOGRAPHY OF ARTICLES AND BOOKS ON MARYLAND HISTORY, 1974. *Maryland Hist. Mag. 1975 70(2): 211-223.* Few bibliographies have been compiled on Maryland history; this is the first of what is to be an annual listing in the magazine. Includes both popular and scholarly works arranged alphabetically, chronologically, and by county or town, depending on the subject. Headings include Archaeology, Architecture, Art, Archives and Library, Biography, Black and Indian, Genealogy, Military, etc.
G. J. Bobango

55. Cox, Richard J. A CENTURY OF FRUSTRATION: THE MOVEMENT FOR A STATE ARCHIVES IN MARYLAND, 1811-1935. *Maryland Hist. Mag. 1983 78(2): 106-117.* The failure of early efforts to create a state archives in Maryland was due largely to "the consistent apathy of public officials over three centuries." These officials, however, were never hard-pressed by public concern, and most 19th-century efforts were by individuals or very small groups of citizens working with little public support. The Maryland Hall of Records was finally established after the Maryland Tercentenary Commission was formed in 1927. The Hall of Records quickly secured a reputation as one of the preeminent state archival institutions in the country. Based on the Maryland Archives and other primary sources and secondary works; 91 notes.
G. J. Bobango

56. Cox, Richard J. THE HISTORICAL DEVELOPMENT OF THE MANUSCRIPTS DIVISION OF THE MARYLAND HISTORICAL SOCIETY. *Maryland Hist. Mag. 1974 69(4): 409-417.* The increasing care of Maryland's documents, "probably unequaled in age, completeness, and historical interest by those of any of the original thirteen states," is a microcosm of national development. Colonial care of records was almost nil, and political squabbles and incompetent officials threatened their very survival, until well into the 19th century. State Librarian David Ridgely's efforts at preservation climaxed in the founding of the Maryland Historical Society in 1844. Efforts to gather papers from all over the state, catalog, index, and purchase collections were slow but steady until 1904 when the Public Records Commission was authorized by the state. Many of the founders' goals have been reached after a century and a half of effort, although lack of funds remains critical and much remains to be done to complete the microfilming projects and manuscripts guides begun in 1969-70. Based on the Minutes of the Society meetings, and on primary and secondary sources; 3 illus., 54 notes.
G. J. Bobango

57. Cox, Richard J. THE PLIGHT OF AMERICAN MUNICIPAL ARCHIVES: BALTIMORE, 1729-1979. *Am. Archivist 1979 42(3): 281-292.* Minimal care was given the Baltimore city archives until 1874 when they became one of several responsibilities of the city librarian. From 1874 to 1927, the attention the archives received depended largely upon the interests of each librarian and his ability to secure support from municipal officials. From 1927 to 1978, under the Bureau of Archives, the archives "disintegrated into a morass through mishandling and lack of direction." With the hiring of a professional archivist in 1978 and the strengthening of archival legislation the outlook for the Baltimore city archives is positive. 4 fig., 61 notes.
G.-A. Patzwald

58. Cox, Richard J. and Vanorny, Patricia M. THE RECORDS OF A CITY: BALTIMORE AND ITS HISTORICAL SOURCES. *Maryland Hist. Mag. 1975 70(3): 286-310.* The "slow appreciation of the significance of urban history" is reflected in the lack of care and attention paid to preserving Baltimore's historical documents. Despite progress earlier in this century, the historian of Baltimore today faces the same disorganization as 100 years ago, and still no separate records building with modern research and storage facilities has been erected. Provides a lengthy checklist, divided into private papers and public records, of Maryland depositories holding Baltimore City records. Most entries are annotated, with brief introductory comments on the history of the collections. Public Records are further subdivided. Based on diverse archival manuals, catalogs, and secondary works; 44 notes.
G. J. Bobango

59. Cox, Richard J. RESOURCES AND OPPORTUNITIES FOR RESEARCH AT THE BALTIMORE CITY ARCHIVES. *Working Papers from the Regional Econ. Hist. Res. Center 1981 4(1-2): 1-18.* Reports on Baltimore's municipal archives, kept haphazardly from 1796 until a professional archivist was hired in 1978 to preserve and catalog the important records; and lists records that were processed or partially processed as of March 1980.

60. Cox, Richard J. UNDERSTANDING THE MONUMENTAL CITY: A BIBLIOGRAPHICAL ESSAY ON BALTIMORE HISTORY. *Maryland Hist. Mag. 1982 77(1): 70-111.* Reviews the history of historical research and writing on Baltimore since 1824. Lists and annotates over 500 studies on all aspects of Baltimore and its past. The encouraging renaissance of local history is evidenced by the fact that two-thirds of the list has been published in the past decade. Includes bibliographies, research guides, general histories, and categories from architecture to religion. Lists recommended basic readings. Maryland Historical Society collections.
G. J. Bobango

61. Crawford, Charles W. THE DEVELOPMENT OF ORAL HISTORY RESEARCH IN TENNESSEE. *West Tennessee Hist. Soc. Papers 1975 29: 100-108.* Defines oral history as "a new discipline involving cooperative effort by a participant in history, a historian, and a machine." After succinctly describing seven programs active in Tennessee in oral history interviewing, the author then suggests some of the needs for oral history research in Tennessee: the country music industry; the culture and folklore of the Cumberland Plateau; notable events in recent Tennessee history; the post-World War II "war" at Athens; the experience of minorities who have been separated from the majority of the state's population; and the amount and kind of change occurring in selected Tennessee communities. Based on primary and secondary sources; 22 notes.
H. M. Parker, Jr.

62. Crocker, Ruth Hutchinson. ULRICH PHILLIPS: A SOUTHERN HISTORIAN RECONSIDERED. *Louisiana Studies 1976 15(2): 113-130.* Ulrich Bonnell Phillips (1877-1934), long considered the foremost American historian of the antebellum South, has been severely criticized by revisionist historians for his sympathetic treatment of slavery and the plantation, especially in his two most famous works, *American Negro Slavery* (1918) and *Life and Labor in the Old South* (1929). His work is typical of the Progressive era in which it was written; he was racist and his view of blacks never changed. However, his use of primary sources and analysis of the social and economic institutions of the South are still significant. Important insights still stand, such as the unique combination of blacks and whites in plantation society and the special role of the plantation aristocracy as the chief power in the antebellum South. Primary and secondary sources; 81 notes.          J. Buschen

63. Crowe, Charles. TIME ON THE CROSS: THE HISTORICAL MONOGRAPH AS A POP EVENT. *Hist. Teacher 1976 9(4): 588-630.* Provides a critical summary of the appearance of, and reactions to, Robert William Fogel and Stanley L. Engerman's *Time on the Cross* (1974). The book appeared amidst a massive public relations campaign, and the initial reactions were favorable. Gradually, criticisms began to appear, and these were elaborated by scholars such as Martin Duberman, John W. Blassingame, Winthrop D. Jordan, and Herbert G. Gutman. Accepts the critics' position; *Time on the Cross* aided conservative values and failed to accomplish a "cliometric revolution." Based on primary sources; 10 illus., 43 notes.          P. W. Kennedy

64. Currie, James T. THE RECONSTRUCTION CENTENNIAL: AN HISTORIOGRAPHICAL COMMEMORATION *Mississippi Q. 1977-78 31(1): 133-145.* Discusses nine recent historical studies (1973-76) on the effects of Reconstruction in the South during 1865-83.

65. Dameron, J. Lasley et al. BIBLIOGRAPHY: A CHECKLIST OF SCHOLARSHIP ON SOUTHERN LITERATURE FOR 1980. *Mississippi Q. 1981 34(2): 153-277.* Bibliography published by The Society for the Study of Southern Literature, prepared by the Society's Committee on Bibliography, of works published in 1978-80 on subject matter from 1607 to 1980; continues a previous bibliography.

66. Davis, David Brion. SLAVERY AND THE POST-WORLD WAR II HISTORIANS. *Daedalus 1974 103(2): 1-16.* Since 1956, five major turning points have occurred in the historiography of slavery: Kenneth Stampp's *Peculiar Institution* (New York: Alfred A. Knopf, 1956) demonstrated the topic's "peculiar urgency", Stanley Elkins' *Slavery* (Chicago: University of Chicago Press, 1959) questioned the cruelty or humaneness of American slavery, Conrad and Meyer's "The Economics of Slavery in the Ante-Bellum South" in Alfred Conrad and John Meyer, *The Economics of Slavery and Other Econometric Studies* (Chicago: Aldine, 1964) opened the "Cliometric Revolution", Philip D. Curtin's *The Atlantic Slave Trade: A Census* (Madison: University of Wisconsin Press, 1969) expanded the demography of slave trade hemispherically. Direct evidence from slaves has recently become available. The conflict and convergence of this historiography show in Eugene Genovese's

*Roll Jordan Roll* (1974) and Robert W. Fogel and Stanley L. Engerman's *Time on the Cross* (Boston: Little Brown, 1974). Secondary sources; 21 notes.          E. McCarthy

67. Dean, Michael P. W. J. CASH'S *THE MIND OF THE SOUTH:* SOUTHERN HISTORY, SOUTHERN STYLE. *Southern Studies 1981 20(3): 297-302.* Wilbur Joseph Cash's *The Mind of the South* (1941) has remained popular and useful, not only as a compendium of facts, but because of his unique Southern style, that of the hospitable storyteller. He used first person narration and rhetorical devices to achieve a very readable, personable work. 10 notes.          J. J. Buschen

68. Debo, Angie. A DEDICATION TO THE MEMORY OF CAROLYN THOMAS FOREMAN, 1872-1967. *Arizona and the West 1974 16(3): 214-218.* Carolyn Thomas was raised in the home of an Illinois congressman who became a federal judge in Indian Territory. She married Grant Foreman, a young law partner of her father. By the 1920's Foreman was well enough established to give up law. The Foremans devoted the rest of their lives to historical scholarship—collecting, research, and writing on Oklahoma and the Southwest. They produced more on the early history of Oklahoma, especially Indians, than all other scholars combined. Mrs. Foreman contributed articles to several journals, 87 to the *Chronicles of Oklahoma* alone, and wrote several books. Illus., biblio.          D. L. Smith

69. Dees, Anthony R. THE GEORGIA HISTORICAL SOCIETY IN HISTORIC PRESERVATION. *Georgia Hist. Q. 1979 63(1): 143-146.* Although the Georgia Historical Society (founded 1839) does not participate directly in architectural preservation efforts, its collections serve as valuable resources for preservation researchers.
G. R. Schroeder

70. Degler, Carl N. RETHINKING POST-CIVIL WAR HISTORY. *Virginia Q. Rev. 1981 57(2): 250-267.* Uses recent historiography of the post-Civil War Era to indicate that the rewriting of history advances knowledge and understanding of the past. For example, Roger L. Ransom and Richard Sutch's *One Kind of Freedom* (1977) indicates free blacks increased both their income and leisure after the war. More leisure, rather than the war's destructiveness, may explain postwar Southern economic backwardness. Robert Higgs's *Competition and Coercion* (1977) argues sharecropping was a partial victory for former slaves and that land distribution would not have worked. Several recent historians (William J. Cooper, Jonathan Wiener, Dwight B. Billings, Jr., and Roger L. Hart) question C. Vann Woodward's long accepted view that the New South was not built by the old planter class.

O. H. Zabel

71. Dennis, Frank Allen. RECENT MANUSCRIPT ACQUISITIONS AT MISSISSIPPI UNIVERSITY AND COLLEGE LIBRARIES—1976. *J. of Mississippi Hist. 1976 38(4): 371-373.* The first of a new series of regular reports on manuscripts recently acquired by Mississippi university and college libraries, this report briefly describes 11 collections acquired during 1976.

J. W. Hillje

72. Dennis, Frank Allen. A BIBLIOGRAPHY OF THESES AND DISSERTATIONS RELATING TO MISSISSIPPI, 1974. *J. of Mississippi Hist. 1975 37(2): 209-215.* Compilation of 39 theses and dissertations completed in 1974 and 32 in progress dealing with Mississippi history and literature.          J. W. Hillje

73. Dennis, Frank Allen. A BIBLIOGRAPHY OF THESES AND DISSERTATIONS RELATING TO MISSISSIPPI, 1975. *J. of Mississippi Hist. 1976 38(1): 85-93.* A compilation of 78 theses and dissertations completed in 1975, and 20 in progress, dealing with Mississippi history and literature.          J. W. Hillje

74. Dennis, Frank Allen, comp. A BIBLIOGRAPHY OF THESES AND DISSERTATIONS RELATING TO MISSISSIPPI, 1982. *J. of Mississippi Hist. 1982 44(1): 83-88*. Lists 22 titles relating to Mississippi history and 37 titles relating to Mississippi literature and authors. Notes works in progress.                    M. S. Legan

75. Dennis, Frank Allen, comp. A BIBLIOGRAPHY OF THESES AND DISSERTATIONS RELATING TO MISSISSIPPI, 1981. *J. of Mississippi Hist. 1981 43(1): 65-71*. This 24th annual compilation of theses and dissertations relating to Mississippi history and literature lists 68 titles. Also includes works in progress but not completed. Citations were obtained through questionnaires sent to 130 academic institutions and a search in *Dissertation Abstracts International: The Humanities and Social Sciences* (1979-80).
                                                           M. S. Legan

76. Dennis, Frank Allen, comp. A BIBLIOGRAPHY OF THESES AND DISSERTATIONS RELATING TO MISSISSIPPI, 1978. *J. of Mississippi Hist. 1979 41(1): 99-105*. This 22d-annual compilation of completed theses and dissertations and works in progress contains 76 references. Introduction suggests that there may be a resurgence of graduate interest in Mississippi history and Mississippi literature since the 1978 list includes 25 more works than the 1977 bibliography. Citations are obtained from *Dissertation Abstracts International* as well as questionnaires mailed to approximately 115 US academic departments offering graduate work in these fields.
                                                           M. S. Legan

77. Dennis, Frank Allen, comp. A BIBLIOGRAPHY OF THESES AND DISSERTATIONS RELATING TO MISSISSIPPI, 1977. *J. of Mississippi Hist. 1978 40(1): 73-77*. Continues the series begun by Willie D. Halsell with this 21st annual list which includes 37 completed theses and dissertations and 17 currently in progress. The compilation is divided into two basic categories, Mississippi history and literature, and then subdivided between the works completed and those still in process. Data were compiled from mailed questionnaires and from *Dissertation Abstracts International: The Humanities and Social Sciences* (1976-77).          M. S. Legan

78. Dennis, Frank Allen. A BIBLIOGRAPHY OF THESES AND DISSERTATIONS RELATING TO MISSISSIPPI, 1976. *J. of Mississippi Hist. 1977 39(1): 75-81*. Lists 62 completed theses and dissertations and 19 ones in progress which relate to Mississippi history and Mississippi literature.          J. W. Hillje

79. Dennis, Frank Allen. PROGRAM OF THE 1975 MEETING OF THE MISSISSIPPI HISTORICAL SOCIETY. *J. of Mississippi Hist. 1975 37(3): 283-290*. Describes the program of the 1975 meeting of the Mississippi Historical Society. Sessions were devoted to women, country music, genealogy, ethnic groups, natural disasters, and history and fiction.          J. W. Hillje

80. Dennis, Frank Allen, comp. RECENT MANUSCRIPT ACQUISITIONS AT MISSISSIPPI UNIVERSITY AND COLLEGE LIBRARIES, 1980. *J. of Mississippi Hist. 1980 42(4): 378-380*. This fifth compilation lists 33 manuscript collections that have been acquired in the libraries of the University of Southern Mississippi, Mississippi State University, the University of Mississippi, and Tougaloo College since 1 August 1979.          M. S. Legan

81. Dennis, Frank Allen, comp. RECENT MANUSCRIPT ACQUISITIONS AT MISSISSIPPI UNIVERSITY AND COLLEGE LIBRARIES: 1979. *J. of Mississippi Hist. 1979 41(4): 383-386*. Collections acquired by the five university and college libraries in Mississippi during August, 1978 and August, 1979 are listed. This is the fourth such compilation for researchers interested in the fields of Mississippi or southern history.          M. S. Legan

82. deTreville, Virginia. SOME CEMETERIES IN RICHMOND AND NEARBY COUNTIES: A SELECTED BIBLIOGRAPHY OF PRINTED SOURCES. *Richmond County Hist. 1980 12(2): 32-48*. Partial list of books on tombstone inscriptions in the library of the Georgia Genealogical Society; 1817-1946.

83. Dickens, Roy S., Jr. and Bowen, William R. PROBLEMS AND PROMISES IN URBAN HISTORICAL ARCHAEOLOGY: THE MARTA PROJECT. *Hist. Archaeol. 1980 14: 42-57*. Using the Metropolitan Atlanta Rapid Transit Authority Project (MARTA) as an example, discusses some of these problems and promises in urban archaeology. Survey, testing, and mitigation procedures are described and evaluated. Also, consideration is given to the potential uses of the urban archaeological resource, with examples of hypothesis testing, pattern delineation, identification of formation processes, and public education. Covers 1962-79.          J/S

84. Dinwiddie, Robert C. and Hough, Leslie S. THE SOUTHERN LABOR ARCHIVES. *Labor Hist. 1982 23(4): 502-512*. Chronicles the creation and collecting history of the Southern Labor Archives at Georgia State University in Atlanta. The archives collects the records of all labor organizations in the southeastern United States at the international, state, and local levels. The collections, for which detailed descriptions are provided, include the records of the United Textile Workers of America, District Four of the International Woodworkers of America, Stanton E. Smith, Atlanta Typographical Union Number 48, and the Atlanta lodge of the International Association of Machinists.          L. F. Velicer

85. Dobbins, Charles G. OLD ALABAMA BOOKS: A COLLECTOR'S NOTES. *Alabama R. 1976 29(1): 49-71*. Book collection and preservation has matured slowly in Alabama. As a result, many first editions of "Alabamiana," notably histories and reminiscences, are now true collector's items. The deficiency is being remedied by the State Department of Archives and History and the major universities, but the committed, resourceful bibliophile can still discover surprises in unlikely places. Primary and secondary sources; 56 notes.          J. F. Vivian

86. Dorsey, James E., comp. GEORGIA HISTORY IN 1982: A BIBLIOGRAPHY. *Georgia Hist. Q. 1983 67(4): 512-545*. Lists books and articles on Georgia history and genealogy published in 1982.          G. R. Schroeder

87. Dorsey, James E., comp. GEORGIA HISTORY IN 1979: A BIBLIOGRAPHY. *Georgia Hist. Q. 1980 64(4): 492-516*. Provides an annotative sentence if the title of any of these articles and books published during 1979 is unclear.          G. R. Schroeder

88. Dorsey, James E., comp. GEORGIA HISTORY IN 1980: A BIBLIOGRAPHY. *Georgia Hist. Q. 1981 65(4): 356-380*. Bibliography of articles and books on Georgia history (including local history and genealogy) published during 1980. Some are briefly annotated.          G. R. Schroeder

89. Dorsey, James E., comp. GEORGIA HISTORY IN 1981: A BIBLIOGRAPHY. *Georgia Hist. Q. 1982 66(4): 514-548*. Bibliography of books and articles on Georgia history and genealogy published in 1981.          G. R. Schroeder

90. Dorsey, James E., comp. THESES AND DISSERTATIONS IN GEORGIA HISTORY: A SUPPLEMENT. *Georgia Hist. Q. 1978 62(4): 322-331*. A listing intended to fill a bibliographical gap between 1971-74 and to include items prior to 1970 omitted from Dorsey's *A Bibliography of the Writings on Georgia History, 1900-1970*.          G. R. Schroeder

91. Doster, James E. TUSCALOOSA HISTORIANS. *Alabama Rev. 1974 27(2): 83-100*. Bibliographic and anecdotal review of academic, journalistic, and private persons in Tuscaloosa who have made significant contributions to Alabama history either through publications or manuscript, archival, and genealogical collections. The University of Alabama has long supported historical research, institutions, and organizations. Most local history is contained in private memoirs, newspaper articles, and reminiscences. Based on primary and secondary sources; 28 notes, biblio.
                                                           J. F. Vivian

92. Drake, Richard B. THE STRUGGLE IN APPALACHIAN STUDIES, 1950-1981. *Appalachian J. 1982 9(2-3): 191-194*. Traces the trends in Appalachian Studies both before and after the 1960's

War on Poverty, focusing on the threat to the Council of the Southern Mountains in 1970, and the survival of the unique Appalachian culture despite efforts by "missionaries" to achieve economic development and end poverty, and by members of "the Appalachian Studies Industry."

93.  Duke, John T. ARKANSAS LISTINGS IN THE NATIONAL REGISTER. *Arkansas Hist. Q. 1980 39(1): 64-65.* Illustrates and briefly describes three Arkansas houses on the National Register of Historic Places: Bozeman House (Clark County), Ferguson-Caldarera House (Fort Smith) and Frederick Hanger House (Little Rock). 3 photos.                                      G. R. Schroeder

94.  Duncan, Richard R.; Brown, Dorothy M.; and Nurnberger, Ralph D. THESES AND DISSERTATIONS ON VIRGINIA: A SUPPLEMENTARY BIBLIOGRAPHY. *Virginia Mag. of Hist. and Biog. 1975 83(3): 346-367.* In an attempt to update a compilation of theses and dissertations on Virginia history published in the *Virginia Magazine of History and Biography* in January 1971, additional schools were surveyed. The list includes research conducted in history, education, economics, political science, library science, and English departments.                            R. F. Oaks

95.  Durden, Robert F. THE AMERICAN REVOLUTION AS SEEN BY SOUTHERNERS IN 1861. *Louisiana Hist. 1978 19(1): 33-42.* Samples attitudes of southerners toward the American Revolution as the Civil War began. Opinions varied widely among both high-ranking Confederate leaders and ordinary folk, but a high degree of ambivalence was present among both. Few repudiated the Revolution. Although they often resented "its full equalitarianism," most "clung to the libertarian heritage." Based on published primary sources; 18 notes.                             R. L. Woodward

96.  Dure, Ann. THE ATHENS-CLARKE HERITAGE FOUNDATION. *Georgia Hist. Q. 1979 63(1): 83-89.* The Athens-Clarke Heritage Foundation was formed in 1967 to preserve and restore historically and architecturally important buildings in Athens and Clarke County, Georgia. The Foundation's projects, including the acquisition and restoration of the Church-Waddel-Brumby house, are described. 3 illus.                              G. R. Schroeder

97.  Egerton, John. SOUTHERN BOOKS AT HOME ON CAMPUS. *Southern Exposure 1983 11(1): 53-57.* Discusses the recent trend toward publication of commercial books on Southern subjects by university presses, and briefly reviews 12 examples of the genre dealing with Appalachia, regional culture, 19th- and 20th-century Southern female writers, society and politics, and blacks' struggles during the 1960's.

98.  Einstein, Frank H. THEORY *SÍ* PRACTICE *NO!* APPALACHIAN STUDIES COMES FULL CIRCLE. *Appalachian J. 1982 9(2-3): 195-201.* Because Appalachian Studies remained on the periphery of the standard college curriculum during the past decade, there was reason to think the program would survive where others might fail, but because of government cuts and a trend toward vocational training, Appalachian Studies is being "encouraged only in the celebration of a superficial culture severed from its political and economic roots."

99.  Eller, Ronald D. APPALACHIAN ORAL HISTORY: NEW DIRECTIONS FOR REGIONAL RESEARCH. *Appalachian J. 1977 4(4): 2-7.* The importance of saving Appalachian history through the collection of oral records is discussed with the problems, potentials, and need to research community and social structure, religion, race relations, and social history of the textile, coal and lumber industries.

100.  Eller, Ronald D. TOWARD A NEW HISTORY OF THE APPALACHIAN SOUTH. *Appalachian J. 1978 5(1): 74-81.* Assesses the historiography of Appalachia, 1930's-70's; gaps in intellectual, literary, economic, social, and political history still exist, and new areas, such as the effects of out-migration, need to be studied; the traditional "static" theory of Appalachia may be discarded.

101.  Ellis, L. Tuffly and Stockley, Barbara J., comps. and eds. A CHECKLIST OF THESES AND DISSERTATIONS IN TEXAS STUDIES, 1964-1974. *Southwestern Hist. Q. 1974 78(2): 183-198, (3): 313-324, (4): 447-463, 1975 79(1): 69-90, (2): 205-219, 1976 79(3): 317-332, (4): 441-460, 80(1): 79-94, (2): 201-214.* Includes works about any aspect of Texas, regardless of field. Responses were solicited from all graduate schools throughout the country covering theses and dissertations completed or to be completed between May 1964 and May 1974. The list commences with the Texas graduate schools, listing in alphabetical order by schools and by students from the respective institutions. Part I. Covers Abilene Christian College and Baylor University. Part II. Covers East Texas State U., Hardin-Simmons U., Incarnate Word Coll., Lamar U., and Midwestern U. Part III. Covers North Texas State U. Part IV. Covers Our Lady of the Lake Coll., Prairie View A & M Coll., St. Mary's U., and Sam Houston State U. Part V. Covers Southern Methodist U., Southwest Texas State U., Stephen F. Austin U., and Sul Ross State U. Part VI. Covers Texas A & I U. and part of Texas A & M U. Part VII. Completes Texas A & M and covers Texas Christian U. Part VIII. Covers part of Texas Southern U. Part IX. Completes Texas Southern and covers part of Texas Tech U. Article to be continued.                                               S

102.  Ellis, L. Tuffly and Stockley, Barbara J., eds. A CHECKLIST OF THESES AND DISSERTATIONS IN TEXAS STUDIES, 1964-1974. *Southwestern Hist. Q. 1977 80(3): 302-322; (4): 417-424; 81(1): 73-90; (2): 191-214.* Continued from a previous article (see entries in this chapter). Part X. Lists dissertations and theses on Texas subjects completed at Texas Tech University and Texas Women's University, 1964-74. Part XI. Lists theses and dissertations on Texas subjects completed during 1964-74 at Trinity University. Part XII. List of theses and dissertations on Texas subjects completed at the University of Houston and the University of Texas at Arlington, 1964-74. Part XIII. List of theses and dissertations on Texas subjects completed at the University of Texas at Austin, 1964-74. Article to be continued.           J. H. Broussard

103.  Ellis, L. Tuffly and Stockley, Barbara J., eds. A CHECKLIST OF THESES AND DISSERTATIONS IN TEXAS STUDIES, 1964-1974. *Southwestern Hist. Q. 1978 82(2): 173-192.* This last installment (see entries in this chapter) consists of works from graduate schools in the United States and Canada. Based on secondary material.                                          J. L. B. Atkinson

104.  Ellis, L. Tuffly and Stockley, Barbara J., ed. A CHECKLIST OF THESES AND DISSERTATIONS IN TEXAS STUDIES, 1964-1974. *Southwestern Hist. Q. 1978 81(3): 299-322.* Continued from a previous article (see entries in this chapter). Part XIV. Lists theses and dissertations on Texas subjects completed at the University of Texas at Austin. Article to be continued.

J. H. Broussard

105.  Ellis, L. Tuffly and Stockley, Barbara J., comps. A CHECKLIST OF THESES AND DISSERTATIONS IN TEXAS STUDIES, 1964-1974. *Southwestern Hist. Q. 1978 81(4): 427-450.* Concluded from a previous article (see entries in this chapter). A list of dissertations and theses on Texas subjects written at the University of Texas (Austin), the University of Texas (El Paso), the University of Texas Medical Branch (Galveston), West Texas State University, William Marsh Rice University, and addenda from previously listed schools. Covers works submitted 1964-74.          J. H. Broussard

106.  Evans, Margaret B. THOMASVILLE LANDMARKS, INC. *Georgia Hist. Q. 1979 63(1): 188-191.* Thomasville Landmarks, Inc. was formed in 1964 for historical and architectural preservation in Thomasville, Georgia. Describes accomplishments of the organization. Illus.                                          G. R. Schroeder

107.  Fisher, Steve; Foster, Jim; and Harnish, Mary. FROM NONSENSE TO GOOD SENSE: A COLLECTIVE REFLECTION ON APPALACHIA AND APPALACHIAN STUDIES. *Appalachian J. 1982 9(2-3): 149-161.* Appalachian Studies should be "liberating, facilitating, transcendent, grounded, historical, visionary, and committed."

108. Fisher, Steve. A SELECTIVE BIBLIOGRAPHY FOR APPALACHIAN STUDIES. *Appalachian J. 1982 9(2-3): 209-242.* Lists works published during the 20th century, dealing specifically with Appalachia in 13 subdivided sections.

109. Flaherty, David H. A SELECT GUIDE TO THE MANUSCRIPT COURT RECORDS OF COLONIAL VIRGINIA. *Am. J. of Legal Hist. 1975 19(2): 112-137.* Lists the bound volumes of Order and Minute Books for Virginia county courts that are available on microfilm in the Archives Division of the Virginia State Library in Richmond. Includes information about most of the Virginia counties founded before 1790, except those now in Kentucky and West Virginia. Lists manuscript court records, microfilms, and suit papers. Until the complete inventory of the extant county records for each Virginia county is completed (several years from now), scholars may gain some information about extant suit papers from this guide and the incomplete Works Progress Administration guide. Arranged in alphabetical order by counties; emphasizes pre-1790 records. 7 notes.                              R. V. Ritter

110. Folmar, J. Kent. TWENTY-EIGHTH ANNUAL MEETING OF THE ALABAMA HISTORICAL ASSOCIATION. *Alabama Rev. 1975 28(4): 276-281.* Reports on the annual meeting of the Alabama Historical Association held in Huntsville, Alabama on 25-26 April 1975. Professional and amateur historians presented 24 papers and addresses. Includes the business meeting, plans, and membership matters.                              J. F. Vivian

111. Fowler, Robert H. BEHIND THE LINES: IN MEMORIAM. *Civil War Times Illus. 1980 19(4): 13.* Historian Bell Irvin Wiley, who died on 4 April 1980, at age 72, was a prolific Civil War scholar, effective teacher (at Emory University and elsewhere), advocate of racial justice, and missionary in the cause of popularizing American history for the intelligent layman.          D. P. Jordan

112. Frantz, Joe B. SOLILOQUY ON STATE HISTORY. *Western Hist. Q. 1978 9(3): 315-322.* The author's *Texas: A Bicentennial History* is one of The States and the Nation Series in commemoration of the bicentennial. Describes his experience with writing the volume and gives his own estimate of its contribution and worth.                              D. L. Smith

113. Friend, Llerena. A DEDICATION TO THE MEMORY OF GEORGE PIERCE GARRISON, 1853-1910. *Arizona and the West 1975 17(4): 304-308.* George Pierce Garrison (1853-1910) was intimately associated in many capacities with the University of Texas at Austin. He established an institutional structure for professional historical study, helped launch the state historical society, and served as editor of its journal. His research and writing concerned the Anglo American and Hispanic American borderland people and cultures. Illus., biblio.                  D. L. Smith

114. Fuller, Justin. THIRTY-SECOND ANNUAL MEETING OF THE ALABAMA HISTORICAL ASSOCIATION. *Alabama Rev. 1979 32(4): 273-279.* Summarizes the proceedings of and papers presented at the 32d annual meeting of the Alabama Historical Association at Troy during 27-29 April 1979.         J. F. Vivian

115. Gamble, Robert A. and Green, George. LABOR ARCHIVES AT THE UNIVERSITY OF TEXAS AT ARLINGTON. *Labor Hist. 1982 23(4): 526-527.* Provides a brief introduction to the Texas Labor Archives at the University of Texas at Arlington and lists the major collections or groups of collections held by the archives.                              L. F. Velicer

116. Garrett, Franklin M. A SHORT ACCOUNT OF THE ATLANTA HISTORICAL SOCIETY. *Georgia Hist. Q. 1979 63(1): 100-108.* Describes the development and facilities of the Atlanta Historical Society, 1926-79. 3 illus., 13 notes.
G. R. Schroeder

117. Gatewood, Willard B., Jr. LAST HOPE, OR HOPEFUL AT LAST? RECENT VIEWS OF THE AMERICAN SOUTH. *Georgia Rev. 1978 32(1): 199-207.* Reviews two books on the South. Morton Sosna's *In Search of the Silent South: Southern Liberals and the Race Issue* indicates that the ultimate test of a white southern liberal was "his willingness or unwillingness to criticize racial mores." White liberals displayed remarkable continuity and Christian evangelicalism was a strong motivation for their actions. Daniel Leon Chandler's *The Natural Superiority of Southern Politicians: A Revisionist History* has a penchant for preemptive claims, and ignores the flaw of race prejudice in southern politics. Secondary sources; 5 notes.                              M. B. Lucas

118. Gaventa, John. APPALACHIAN STUDIES FROM AND FOR SOCIAL CHANGE. *Appalachian J. 1977 5(1): 23-30.* Examines the status of Appalachian studies; surveys economic power areas involving land use, energy resources, resorts, mining operations, agriculture, and manufacturing; scholars must learn to use local resources and opinions rather than strictly scholarly orientations when studying and recommending social change.

119. Gaventa, John. INEQUALITY AND THE APPALACHIAN STUDIES INDUSTRY. *Appalachian J. 1978 5(3): 322-329.* In order to best serve the people of Appalachia, through dissemination of information and resultant social and economic control, Appalachian studies programs must be not strictly academic but also social and political.

120. Gibson, Arrell Morgan. INDIAN PIONEER LEGACY: A GUIDE TO OKLAHOMA LITERATURE. *Chronicles of Oklahoma 1978 56(1): 3-33.* Lists and discusses books and journal articles relevant to Oklahoma's history from the early 19th century to the present. Also appraises some of the major newspaper sources, bibliographies, and documents collections. 9 photos.      M. L. Tate

121. Gilbert, Gail R. MARGARET MORRIS BRIDWELL: A BIBLIOGRAPHY. *Filson Club Hist. Q. 1983 57(3): 305-314.* An annotated bibliography of the published and unpublished works of Kentucky historian Margaret Morris Bridwell.
G. B. McKinney

122. Gilmore, Jann Haynes. GEORGIA'S HISTORIC PRESERVATION BEGINNING: THE GEORGIA HISTORICAL COMMISSION (1951-1973). *Georgia Hist. Q. 1979 63(1): 9-21.* Details the accomplishments of the Georgia Historical Commission in the marking, acquisition, and preservation of Georgia historical sites and the promotion of education in state history from its foundation in 1951 until the reorganization of the state government in 1973 and the Commission's absorption into another agency. Based on minutes; 4 illus., 18 notes.              G. R. Schroeder

123. Goddard, John H., Jr. HISTORY OF THE GRIFFIN HISTORICAL AND PRESERVATION SOCIETY, INC. *Georgia Hist. Q. 1979 63(1): 147-151.* Describes the foundation in 1969 and subsequent activities of the Griffin Historical and Preservation Society, Griffin, Georgia. Illus.                              G. R. Schroeder

124. Gonzales, John Edmond. SOME FURTHER OBSERVATIONS ON THE RECENT WRITING OF MISSISSIPPI HISTORY. *J. of Mississippi Hist. 1979 41(1): 83-98.* Discusses significant events in Mississippi historiography detailing the two-volume *History of Mississippi*, the establishment of the University and College Press of Mississippi, and the publication of significant monographs, references, and articles. Also notes archival collections, the Mississippi Historical Society, the Bicentennial celebration, the Civil War Centennial, and the growing interest in Mississippi writers of fiction.                              M. S. Legan

125. Goodwin, Stephen. SAFEGUARDING THE SENATE'S GOLDEN AGE. *Hist. Preservation 1983 35(6): 18-23.* A description of the renovation of the US Senate chamber used from 1810 to 1859, which was closed to the public from 1935 until 1976 because congressional rivalries thwarted restoration funding.

126. Gould, Alan B. REPORT ON THE STATUS OF HISTORY IN [THE] SCHOOLS, WEST VIRGINIA. *J. of the West Virginia Hist. Assoc. 1977 1(1): 37-40; 1978 2(1): 67-72.* Part I. Excerpts a report to the Organization of American Historians discussing the state of history teaching in West Virginia, specifically, teacher quali-

fication, curriculum, and enrollment, 1969-74. Part II. Discusses history teaching and curricula in West Virginia, 1976-77, and comments on higher educational institutions, and the work by the National Center for Higher Education Management System and the National Coordinating Committee for the Promotion of History.

127. Graf, LeRoy P. HIGHLIGHTS AND FORGOTTEN TREASURES: A FIFTY-YEAR RETROSPECTIVE OF THE ETHS *PUBLICATIONS. East Tennessee Hist. Soc. Publ. 1979 51: 3-13.* The East Tennessee Historical Society has issued a journal for 50 years. This commemorative issue reprints some of the best writings from professional and amateur historians that have appeared in the journal. Illus., 6 notes.                    D. A. Yanchisin

128. Gray, R. J. CULTURAL TRUTHS, NECESSARY TRADITIONS, AND THE MYTHOLOGISING OF HISTORY: AN APPROACH TO ALLEN TATE. *Indian J. of Am. Studies [India] 1974 4(1/2): 36-52.* Allen Tate's sense of history as a relatively unchanging framework of value is central to his literary work (1922-41). In describing the Old South, Tate articulated what might have happened if its best energies had been realized. Tate consciously constructed a myth out of a historical fact. The myth-making takes place in scenes emphasizing action, for only in action can knowledge be gained of the human experience. 18 notes.

L. V. Eid

129. Green, Archie. REGIONALISM IS A FOREVER AGENDA. *Appalachian J. 1982 9(2-3): 172-180.* Examines the evolution of Appalachian Studies based on presentations at the University of Kentucky's conference on Appalachian Studies, 22 May 1981; covers 1969-81.

130. Guertler, John T. A BRIEF DESCRIPTION OF THE COLLECTIONS OF THE BALTIMORE REGION INSTITUTIONAL STUDIES CENTER. *Working Papers from the Regional Econ. Hist. Res. Center 1981 4(1-2): 19-23.* Brief description followed by a list of the Baltimore Region Institutional Studies Center's holdings at the University of Baltimore, tracing the social, economic, and political development of Baltimore and its environs since 1821.

131. Gurr, Steve. THE SUMTER HISTORIC PRESERVATION SOCIETY. *Georgia Hist. Q. 1979 63(1): 180-187.* Describes the activities and preservation successes of the Sumter Historic Preservation Society (founded 1972) which focus on the Americus, Georgia area. Based on society archival material; 2 illus., 33 notes.

G. R. Schroeder

132. Hall, Jacquelyn Dowd. DOCUMENTING DIVERSITY: THE SOUTHERN EXPERIENCE. *Oral Hist. Rev. 1976: 19-28.* Discusses the use of oral history "as a methodological approach to historical problems," and states that the South offers especially rich prospects for the use of oral history. The Southern Oral History Program established by the Department of History of the University of North Carolina at Chapel Hill is conducting three well-defined projects on southern women, southern labor history, and the emergence of the South from a preindustrial stage. 15 notes.

D. A. Yanchisin

133. Hall, Virginius Cornick, Jr. THE VIRGINIA HISTORICAL SOCIETY: AN ANNIVERSARY NARRATIVE OF ITS FIRST CENTURY AND A HALF. *Virginia Mag. of Hist. and Biog. 1982 90(1): 3-150.* Recounts the events, acquisitions, and personalities of the society since its founding in 1831.

134. Halsell, Willie D. A BIBLIOGRAPHY OF THESES AND DISSERTATIONS RELATING TO MISSISSIPPI, 1973. *J. of Mississippi Hist. 1974 36(1): 105-111.* Lists 50 theses and dissertations completed in or by 1973, and 25 in progress.          J. W. Hillje

135. Halsell, Willie D. A BIBLIOGRAPHY OF THESES AND DISSERTATIONS RELATING TO MISSISSIPPI, 1972. *J. of Mississippi Hist. 1973 35(1): 83-90.* An annual list of theses and disser-

tations and work in progress related to Mississippi that were submitted for graduate degrees in 1972, plus some earlier studies not previously listed.                    J. W. Hillje

136. Hamer, Collin Bradfield, Jr. RECORDS OF THE CITY OF JEFFERSON (1850-1870) IN THE CITY ARCHIVES OF THE NEW ORLEANS PUBLIC LIBRARY. *Louisiana Hist. 1976 17(1): 51-67.* Describes in some detail the group of records in 69 volumes from Jefferson City turned over to the city archives of New Orleans from 1870-1972. Several attempts at cataloging these records had been initiated by personnel of the city archives since 1870, including an inventory completed by a federal works project. 17 notes.

E. P. Stickney

137. Hancock, Harold, comp. BIBLIOGRAPHY OF DELAWARE HISTORY, 1977-1978. *Delaware Hist. 1979 18(4): 275-282.* Lists with occasional brief annotations more than 100 books, articles, pamphlets, reprints, and theses about Delaware and famous citizens of Delaware. The items are drawn from popular and scholarly journals and from vanity, commercial, government, private, and university presses. The bibliography omits genealogical works and works of poetry and fiction.                    R. M. Miller

138. Hancock, Harold, comp. BIBLIOGRAPHY OF DELAWARE HISTORY, 1979-1980. *Delaware Hist. 1981 19(4): 243-249.* The bibliography excludes genealogical works, poetry, and fiction.

R. M. Miller

139. Harlan, Louis R. and Smock, Raymond. THE BOOKER T. WASHINGTON PAPERS. *Maryland Historian 1975 6(1): 55-59.* Traces the trials and tribulations of the first project designed to edit the papers of a Negro, in this case the Booker T. Washington papers.                    G. O. Gagnon

140. Harris, Dwight. MANUSCRIPT ACQUISITIONS OF THE DEPARTMENT OF ARCHIVES AND HISTORY, 1975. *J. of Mississippi Hist. 1976 38(1): 95-102.* Lists 157 private manuscript collections, including title, inclusive dates, and quantity of material, "processed and accessioned into the holdings of the Mississippi Department of Archives and History" in 1975.          J. W. Hillje

141. Harrison, Lowell H. SIGNIFICANT BOOKS IN KENTUCKY HISTORY. *Filson Club Hist. Q. 1977 51(3): 276-279.* Reports on a reputational survey of historical works about Kentucky. Richard H. Collins' 1874 study *History of Kentucky* was selected as the best book written before 1960 and Harry M. Caudill's *Night Comes to the Cumberlands,* published in 1963, was voted the best book since 1960. 4 tables.                    G. B. McKinney

142. Hartwig, Paul B. PRESERVATION IN LOUISIANA. *North Louisiana Hist. Assoc. J. 1978 9(3): 165-170.* The Louisiana Historic Preservation Office was established by the state legislature in 1971 out of concern for preservation of the state's archaeological, architectural, and historic sites. Describes the Office and its functions. Louisiana now has more than 150 places listed in the National Register of Historic Places. Provides introductory guidelines on how to obtain grants from federal agencies for historic preservation.

H. M. Parker, Jr.

143. Harzoff, Elizabeth. THE ROLE OF A FOLKLORIST IN A GOVERNMENT-SPONSORED LIVING HISTORY MUSEUM. *Kentucky Folklore Record 1980 26(1-2): 79-82.* Describes the author's work as an intern in the cultural history interpretation section of the Tennessee Valley Authority's Land Between the Lakes, part of which is a living history farm museum called "The Homeplace-1850."

144. Havard, William C. and Dauer, Manning J. THE SOUTHERN POLITICAL SCIENCE ASSOCIATION: A FIFTY YEAR LEGACY. *J. of Pol. 1980 42(3): 664-686.* The Southern Political Science Association was founded in 1928 as one manifestation of a regional renaissance. It has published the *Journal of Politics* since 1939, thereby supporting excellence in research, teaching, and public administration. The association has been a leader in recognizing the rights of women and racial minorities, refusing to meet in loca-

tions where any conferees might suffer discrimination. It has consistently defended academic freedom, notably against the attacks of Senator Joseph McCarthy. The SPSA has reflected both the expansion and improvement of southern educational institutions and the recent academic retrenchment throughout the United States. Hence, it has transcended its regional base and attained national and international recognition. 15 notes.                    A. W. Novitsky

145. Hendrix, James P., Jr. FROM ROMANCE TO SCHOLARSHIP: SOUTHERN HISTORY AT THE TAKE-OFF POINT. *Mississippi Q. 1977 30(2): 193-212.* Focuses on the 1920's-30's.

146. Heyl, Edgar. [BIBLIOGRAPHY OF MARYLAND PUBLICATIONS].
BIBLIOGRAPHICAL NOTES: UNRECORDED PRE-1831 MARYLAND PUBLICATIONS. *Maryland Hist. Mag. 1975 70(4): 394-400.* Lists 47 unrecorded Maryland publications published during 1800-30. The publications, primarily pamphlets, are in the library of the Maryland Historical Society.
BIBLIOGRAPHIC NOTES: UNRECORDED PRE-1832 MARYLAND PUBLICATIONS. *Maryland Hist. Mag. 1976 71(4): 527-547.* Lists 201 unrecorded Maryland publications, primarily pamphlets, published during 1800-31. Includes an index covering both lists, giving printers, publishers, and places of publication. The great majority are from the 1820's.
                                                            G. J. Bobango

147. Higgs, Robert J. CONSCIOUSNESS AND APPALACHIA. *Appalachian J. 1982 9(2-3): 202-206.* A professor of literature discusses Appalachian Studies; 1969-81.

148. Hobson, Fred. GERALD W. JOHNSON: THE SOUTHERNER AS REALIST. *Virginia Q. Rev. 1982 58(1): 1-25.* To consider representative Southerners as "rural, conservative, religious, romantic," and antireformist is too limiting for it ignores the liberal-progressive aspects which the life and work of Gerald W. Johnson represents. Born a Southerner, and remaining one in many ways, Johnson considered himself a realist and as a journalist-historian-sociologist participated in, keenly observed, and wrote extremely well about events from 1930 to 1980. He attacked "romantic illusion, fraud, sham and hypocrisy...." Like Mencken and Cash, he opposed Southern agrarianism. In the events of the 1960's, in a way, he saw the South of his youth come North.
                                                            O. H. Zabel

149. Hodson, Daniel L. HISTORIC PRESERVATION AND THE COORDINATING AND DEVELOPMENT COUNCIL OF NORTHWEST LOUISIANA. *North Louisiana Hist. Assoc. J. 1978 9(3): 171-173.* Discusses the origin (1975), functions, policies, and goals of the Coordinating and Development Council of Northwest Louisiana, an agency for preservation in 10 parishes. Continuous work on the preservation of the state's remaining landmarks is essential if available remnants of its heritage are to be preserved. The Council now lists more than 300 historic sites; an additional 140 need to be surveyed.                    H. M. Parker, Jr.

150. Holmes, H. T. ORAL HISTORY IN THE MISSISSIPPI DEPARTMENT OF ARCHIVES AND HISTORY. *J. of Mississippi Hist. 1976 38(1): 111-117.* Describes the development of oral history in the Mississippi Department of Archives and History 1958-75, and describes 38 oral history interviews processed as of 1 December 1975.                    J. W. Hillje

151. Holmes, H. T. ORAL HISTORY IN THE MISSISSIPPI DEPARTMENT OF ARCHIVES AND HISTORY. *J. of Mississippi Hist. 1977 39(1): 83-88.* Describes 27 oral history interviews in the oral history collection of the Mississippi Department of Archives and History which became available for research in 1976. Entries include the primary subject and the number of pages in the transcript.                    J. W. Hillje

152. Holmes, Jack D. L. AN 1858 VIEW ON HISTORICAL PRESERVATION IN MOBILE. *Alabama Hist. Q. 1982 44(1-2): 123-124.* Historic preservation is a problem that is not peculiar to

the present, as is illustrated by an editorial in the Mobile *Weekly Advertiser,* 3 April 1858, concerning the destruction of a house remaining from the time of the Spanish occupation. 2 notes.
                                                            E. E. Eminhizer

153. Holmes, Tony. HENDERSON COUNTY TENNESSEE HISTORY: A BIBLIOGRAPHY. *West Tennessee Hist. Soc. Papers 1982 36: 91-116.* Henderson County was created by the Tennessee state legislature in 1821 and organized in 1822. Most of the pertinent records have been permanently damaged or destroyed, and others are scattered across the state and nation and cannot be found locally. The bibliography consists of 49 entries divided among eight subdivisions: history and early settlement, genealogy, Scotts Hill history and genealogy, county records, education and schools, churches and religion, and general miscellaneous. Each entry is thoroughly annotated and records where the document is located. 29 notes.                    H. M. Parker, Jr.

154. Holt, Michael F. IN SEARCH OF SOUTHERN NATIONALISM. *Rev. in Am. Hist. 1980 8(2): 234-239.* Review essay of John McCardell's *The Idea of a Southern Nation: Southern Nationalists and Southern Nationalism, 1830-1860* (New York: W. W. Norton, 1979).

155. Hoole, W. Stanley. TWENTY-SIXTH ANNUAL MEETING OF THE ALABAMA HISTORICAL ASSOCIATION. *Alabama Rev. 1973 26(4): 267-272.* About 350 persons attended the meeting held in Tuscaloosa 27-28 April 1973. 12 papers were presented.
                                                            J. F. Vivian

156. Howard, Milo B., Jr. ALABAMA MUSEUMS: EARLY EFFORTS. *Alabama Rev. 1982 35(2): 83-93.* Briefly describes the origins of the oldest museums in Alabama, including the Alabama Museum of Natural History, the United Daughters of the Confederacy museums, several university museums, and the Alabama Department of Archives and History. Based on reports, newspapers, and secondary sources; 33 notes.                    G. R. Schroeder

157. Howard, Milo B., Jr. THOMAS MC ADORY OWEN: ALABAMA'S GREATEST BIBLIOGRAPHER. *Alabama Rev. 1975 28(1): 3-15.* Thomas M. Owen compiled "A Bibliography of Alabama," *Annual Report of the American Historical Association, 1897* (1898), still the standard source for state history. Owen's labor of love started in 1887, persisted and matured despite a number of vicissitudes, and when completed proved remarkable in scope and accuracy. The Owen papers provide a poor understanding of the methodology used, but suggest that he was indefatigable in correspondence, even to the point of making himself a nuisance. Fire destroyed Owen's personal library, a byproduct of his work, in 1906. Based on primary and secondary sources; 39 notes.
                                                            J. F. Vivian

158. Humphreys, Hubert. ORAL HISTORY RESEARCH IN LOUISIANA: AN OVERVIEW. *Louisiana Hist. 1979 20(4): 353-371.* Many narratives were collected around the state in the late 1930's under the auspices of the WPA, but the first extensive use of tape-recorded interviews for historical research occurred between 1956 and 1959 in connection with three projects: T. Harry Williams's research for his *Huey Long,* John L. Loos's investigations for his *Oil On Stream,* and William R. Hogan's and Richard Allen's founding of a jazz archive at Tulane University. Since then many other research projects and archival collections have made use of this valuable technique. Presidential address to the Louisiana Historical Association. Based on taped interviews; 47 notes.
                                                            D. B. Touchstone

159. Jacobs, Roberta Tansman. A WOMAN'S PLACE: ELIZABETH AMBLER OF VIRGINIA, 1780-1823. *J. of Popular Culture 1977 11(1): 211-218.* Historians, using quantitative methods and models from other social sciences, have extended their sources significantly in recent years. This has not been the case in women's history in spite of calls to break away from traditional approaches. This case study, which uses a traditional source (the Elizabeth Am-

bler papers of 1780-1823), illustrates the understanding of the female experience that may accrue through a biographical analysis. Primary and secondary sources; 25 notes.                    D. G. Nielson

160. Javersak, David T. ONE PLACE ON THIS GREAT GREEN PLANET WHERE ANDREW CARNEGIE CAN'T GET A MONUMENT WITH HIS MONEY. *West Virginia Hist. 1979 41(1): 7-19.* In 1903, in Wheeling, West Virginia, as a bitter legacy of the Homestead Strike of 1892, the Ohio Valley Trades and Labor Assembly, which held Andrew Carnegie personally responsible for the violence of that strike, successfully opposed the bond issue necessary to raise the money needed for a matching grant for a Carnegie Library. In 1911, Wheeling built a library from its own resources. 55 notes.                    J. D. Neville

161. Jenkins, William H. HIGHWAY MARKERS IN ALABAMA. *Alabama Rev. 1978 31(3): 209-223.* Describes highway historical markers erected since 1978. Thirty-two markers were placed in 16 counties.                    J. F. Vivian

162. Jenkins, William H. HIGHWAY MARKERS IN ALABAMA. *Alabama Rev. 1978 31(2): 137-147.* Lists 24 historical markers erected on highways in eight Alabama counties since the original compilations published in the *Alabama Review* during 1961-73.
                    J. F. Vivian

163. Jensen, Oliver et al. WORKING WITH BRUCE CATTON. *Am. Heritage 1979 30(2): 44-51.* Jensen and other co-workers comment on the writing and editorial efforts of Civil War historian Bruce Catton during 1954-78. 12 illus.                    J. F. Paul

164. Johannsen, Robert W. THE FORTY-EIGHTH ANNUAL MEETING. *J. of Southern Hist. 1983 49(1): 73-98.* During the Southern Historical Association's 1982 meeting in Memphis, Tennessee, participants heard 50 sessions and workshops.
                    T. D. Schoonover

165. Johnson, Guion Griffis. MY EXPLORATION OF THE SOUTHERN EXPERIENCE. *North Carolina Hist. Rev. 1980 57(2): 192-207.* The author recounts her transition from Texas journalism teacher to social historian of the South. As one of the first female historians in the South, she encountered some difficulties during graduate training. She began her work at University of North Carolina in sociology under Howard Odum in 1924 but soon switched to history, receiving her PhD in 1927, having written a dissertation which was later expanded and published as *Ante-Bellum North Carolina.* She and her sociologist husband, Guy B. Johnson, have spent their professional lives researching and writing about southern social conditions. They wrote several reports for Gunnar Myrdal as he composed *An American Dilemma.* Based on personal letters, Odum Papers, and recollections; 7 illus., 29 notes.
                    T. L. Savitt

166. Johnston, Frontis W. THE NORTH CAROLINA LITERARY AND HISTORICAL ASSOCIATION, 1900-1975. *North Carolina Hist. R. 1976 53(2): 155-167.* The North Carolina Literary and Historical Association, in its early years, sponsored legislation fostering cultural and educational activities in North Carolina. It has always encouraged writing on literary and historical subjects, a matter which became a focus of attention during the late 1960's when the Association was under attack for mediocrity, conservatism, and lack of vigor. Some members attempted to rotate the meeting sites away from Raleigh and to drop "Literary" from the Association's name. These discussions continue today. Based on primary and secondary sources; 6 illus., 23 notes.                    T. L. Savitt

167. Jones, H. G. BOOKS ABOUT NORTH CAROLINA, 1973-1974. *Mississippi Q. 1975 28(2): 205-213.* Reviews 10 books on North Carolina history.

168. Jones, H. G. NORTH CAROLINA BIBLIOGRAPHY, 1980-1981. *North Carolina Hist. Rev. 1982 59(2): 172-191.* Includes all the books on North Carolina or written by North Carolinians published between 1 July 1980 and 30 June 1981. The bibliogaphy is arranged topically. Subjects analyzed include bibliography, educa-

tion, folklore, social sciences, institutional history, church history, science and nature, applied arts, fine arts, poetry, drama, fiction, history, travel, genealogy, biography, new editions, and reprints.
                    T. L. Savitt

169. Jones, H. G. NORTH CAROLINA BIBLIOGRAPHY, 1973-1974. *North Carolina Hist. R. 1975 52(2): 171-189.* Lists all nonfiction books dealing with North Carolina subjects or written by North Carolinians published during 1 July 1973-30 June 1974. Books are classified as follows: Bibliography and Libraries, Social Sciences, Philology, Science, Applied Science and Useful Arts, Fine Arts and Recreation, Poetry, Drama, Fiction, Other Literature, History and Travel, Genealogy, Biography, New Editions and Reprints.
                    T. L. Savitt

170. Jones, H. G. NORTH CAROLINA BIBLIOGRAPHY, 1975-1976. *North Carolina Hist. Rev. 1977 54(2): 192-216.* This bibliography lists books dealing with North Carolina subjects or by North Carolinians published between 1 July 1975 and 30 June 1976. Only a few serials and government documents are included. Classifications include: bibliography, history, description, and travel, church history, social sciences and institutional history, genealogy, autobiography and biography, and new editions and reprints.
                    T. L. Savitt

171. Jones, H. G. NORTH CAROLINA BIBLIOGRAPHY, 1978-1979. *North Carolina Hist. Rev. 1980 57(2): 208-226.* Includes all books (no articles) dealing with North Carolina subjects or written by North Carolinians published between 1 July 1978 and 30 June 1979. The bibliography is arranged topically. Subjects analyzed include: bibliography, education, social sciences, institutional history, science and nature, applied arts, fine arts, poetry, drama, fiction, history, travel, genealogy, biography, and reprints.
                    T. L. Savitt

172. Jones, H. G. NORTH CAROLINA BIBLIOGRAPHY, 1979-1980. *North Carolina Hist. Rev. 1981 58(2): 163-184.* Included in this bibliography are all books dealing with North Carolina subjects or written by North Carolinians published between 1 July 1979 and 30 June 1980. The bibliography is arranged topically. Subjects analyzed include bibliography, education, folklore, social sciences, institutional history, church history, science and nature, applied arts, fine arts, poetry, drama, fiction, history, travel, genealogy, biography, new editions, and reprints.                    T. L. Savitt

173. Jones, H. G. NORTH CAROLINA BIBLIOGRAPHY, 1974-1975. *North Carolina Hist. R. 1976 53(2): 193-214.* A bibliography of books dealing with North Carolina subjects or written by North Carolinians published during 1 July 1974-30 June 1975. Pertinent subject headings are "History and Travel," "Genealogy and Genealogical Sources," "Autobiography and Biography," and "New Editions and Reprints."                    T. L. Savitt

174. Jones, H. G. THE RAPE OF HISTORY. *North Carolina Hist. Rev. 1977 54(2): 158-168.* The increasing specialization of historians in the 1960's and 70's caused a decline in the teaching level of survey and other general history courses. As students ceased taking history and called it irrelevant, educators began lowering history requirements for teacher certification and decreasing the history content of social studies syllabi. Social scientists joined educators in substituting their disciplines for humanistic history courses. In North Carolina, the state government has officially downgraded the status of the Department of Archives and History over the past ten years. Based on personal experiences, newspaper accounts, and journal articles; 21 notes.                    T. L. Savitt

175. Jones, Loyal. CHASING HATS IN THE WINDS OF APPALACHIAN STUDIES. *Appalachian J. 1982 9(2-3): 188-190.* Discusses the problem of defining Appalachian Studies from the perspective of a scholar trying to stay on top of everchanging trends in the field in order to teach effectively.

176. Jones, William M. THE SOURCE OF BALLAST AT A FLORIDA SITE. *Hist. Archaeol. 1976 10: 42-45.* Seemingly anomalous materials reported cover a span of time from late Medieval

times until the later part of the nineteenth century. They include ceramic sherds, white clay pipe stems, glass, bricks, and gravels as well as clay deposits. The evidence points to their origin in the vicinity of the present Bankside Power Station on the south bank of the Thames between London and Blackfriars Bridges. The [Florida] area was a quarantine station after 1880 where ships were required to discharge ballast during the yellow fever months of the summers. The site illustrates the value of identifying whether or not artifacts in coastal or estuarine areas are of primary deposition. Ballast sites are common and their origins may present very diverse cultural contexts.                                                        J

177. Jordan, H. Glenn and Blackburn, Bob L. TO PRESERVE AND PERPETUATE THE HISTORY OF OKLAHOMA. *Chronicles of Oklahoma 1980 58(3): 256-263.* Organized in 1893, the Oklahoma Historical Society had difficulty in acquiring permanent facilities. Located initially at Kingfisher, it moved in 1895 to Norman and six years later to Oklahoma City. The state finally erected a building in Oklahoma City during 1929-30 which still serves as the headquarters of the organization. Eleven photographs show the earlier homes of the society and various construction stages for the current structure.                     M. L. Tate

178. Karp, Walter. "MY GAWD, THEY'VE SOLD THE TOWN." *Am. Heritage 1981 32(5): 84-95.* In 1926, the Reverend William A. R. Goodwin persuaded John D. Rockefeller, Jr., to finance the restoration of colonial Williamsburg, Virginia, but not until 1928 did Goodwin officially acknowledge Rockefeller as the city's benefactor. From the beginning, Williamsburg has had a split personality—partly historical re-creation and partly an aesthetic creation. 18 illus.                                            J. F. Paul

179. Kelley, Denise and Bobbitt, Randy. FUNERAL HOME RECORDS AND THEIR VALUE IN GENEALOGICAL RESEARCH. *Tampa Bay Hist. 1981 3(2): 84-87; 1982 4(1): 78-83.* Part 1. Provides a partial listing of funeral homes in Florida and explains their importance in documenting family relationships. Part 2. Continues a listing of funeral homes in Florida; records are listed in alphabetical order by county dating to the late 1800's.

180. Kelly, James C., comp. A BIBLIOGRAPHY OF THE WRITINGS OF STANLEY F. HORN. *Tennessee Hist. Q. 1981 40(4): 395-400.* Presents a bibliography of the published work of substance of Stanley F. Horn (1889-1980) who was long associated with the *Southern Lumberman* and authored many works on Tennessee history. Biblio.                                  W. D. Piersen

181. Kelly, James C. THE BICENTENNIAL AND TENNESSEE HISTORY. *Tennessee Hist. Q. 1977 36(2): 224-236.* The Bicentennial celebrations generated a tremendous number of projects in Tennessee. They fall into the categories of films, publications, restorations, and reenactments. Much, however, still needs to be done to take advantage of all the history opportunities Tennessee has to offer. Secondary sources; 8 notes.                     M. B. Lucas

182. Kesner, Richard M. A BIBLIOGRAPHIC SURVEY OF DISSERTATIONS DEALING WITH APPALACHIA. *Appalachian J. 1979 6(4): 277-309.* Provides an introduction discussing the trends in research on Appalachia, and lists 512 dissertations on Appalachia, written during 1913-79 and listed by subject, such as economics, education, and political science.

183. Key, Betty McKeever. ORAL HISTORY IN MARYLAND. *Maryland Hist. Mag. 1975 70(4): 379-384.* Reviews the inception and progress of oral history programs since the 1940's, to the establishment of an Office of Oral History at the Maryland Historical Society in 1971. Since then a state-wide workshop on the subject has been held and procedures and guidelines formalizing criteria for interviews, selection of interviewees (called "narrators"), and cataloging have been developed. Misconceptions about oral history are put to rest as well, such as "interviews are not done exclusively with the oldest inhabitants of any community," and is not necessarily confined to "name" people. In this latter aspect, "oral history helps democratize historical sources." Mentions common elements

in folklore and oral history, and notes that oral history is not material prepared for the stage, radio, or television—its focus "is scholarly inquiry, not entertainment."                     G. J. Bobango

184. Key, Betty McKeever. ORAL HISTORY PROJECTS IN THE STATE OF MARYLAND. *Maryland Hist. 1982 13(2): 53-54.* Reviews the compendia of extant and in progress oral histories in Maryland and briefly mentions the various related publications by the Maryland Historical Society.                     G. O. Gagnon

185. Kimbrough, Janet C. THE EARLY HISTORY OF THE ASSOCIATION FOR THE PRESERVATION OF VIRGINIA ANTIQUITIES: A PERSONAL ACCOUNT. *Virginia Cavalcade 1980 30(2): 68-75.* Surveys preservation activities of the Association for the Preservation of Virginia Antiquities (APVA) since its founding in 1889; the author is the granddaughter of Cynthia Coleman, one of the founders.

186. Kirby, Jack Temple. THE SOUTHERN EXODUS, 1910-1960: A PRIMER FOR HISTORIANS. *J. of Southern Hist. 1983 49(4): 585-600.* Historians have been aware of the massive migration of both blacks and whites out of the South in the 20th century, but have contributed almost nothing to its measurement or understanding. Sociologists, geographers, and economists have sought abstract "laws" and have collected data and produced analyses for policy formation. Actual narrative and analysis of what occurred and why is very scarce. Much of the record may be lost if oral historians do not gather the data from Southern emigrants. Based on census reports, other government publications, dissertations and theses, and social science literature; 3 tables, 3 graphs, 38 notes.
                                                        T. Schoonover

187. Kitchen, Mary M. and Boyer, Dorothy M. THE HISTORY AND PURPOSE OF THE FLORIDA SOCIETY FOR GENEALOGICAL RESEARCH, INC. *Tampa Bay Hist. 1979 1(1): 76-77.* Formed in 1972 in Pinellas Park, Florida, the Florida Society for Genealogical Research, Inc., seeks to promote the recording of family history, share genealogical experiences, provide instructional materials, and publish, through its journal, the *Quarterly,* primary records—birth, death, and baptismal material.

188. Klotter, James C. CLIO IN THE COMMONWEALTH: THE STATUS OF KENTUCKY HISTORY. *Register of the Kentucky Hist. Soc. 1982 80(1): 65-88.* Kentucky, a state with a rich heritage, needs more and better historical analyses. The author suggests areas of strengths and weaknesses in historical coverage of the state. The frontier era and the Civil War period are the most studied parts of Kentucky's past, but much remains to be explored in other aspects. Sources are published historical literature; 80 notes.
                                                        J. F. Paul

189. Kolchin, Peter. THE SOCIOLOGIST AS SOUTHERN HISTORIAN. *Rev. in Am. Hist. 1977 5(1): 21-27.* Review article prompted by Edgar T. Thompson's *Plantation Societies, Race Relations, and the South: The Regimentation of Populations. Selected Papers of Edgar T. Thompson* (Durham, N.C.: Duke U. Pr., 1975).

190. Kondayan, Betty Ruth. THE LIBRARY OF LIBERTY HALL ACADEMY. *Virginia Mag. of Hist. and Biography 1978 86(4): 432-446.* Discusses a list of 101 titles purchased to start the Library of the former Augusta Academy in Lexington, Virginia, a forerunner of Washington and Lee University, of which 41 titles survive. Compares this list with other Library lists in the colonial and early national period. Almost half the books in the collection are religious in content, with English literature second. 90% of the authors wrote in the 17th and 18th centuries. Lists the Library collection. Table, 39 notes.                     P. J. Woehrmann

191. Kozisek, Jeffrey L. MANUSCRIPT ACQUISITIONS OF THE DEPARTMENT OF ARCHIVES AND HISTORY, 1973. *J. of Mississippi Hist. 1974 36(1): 113-116.* Lists 76 manuscript collections processed and accessioned in 1973 by the Mississippi Department of Archives and History.                     J. W. Hillje

192. Kukla, Jon. TOUCHES OF SENTIMENT IN THE AFFAIRS OF OLD BOOKS. *Virginia Cavalcade 1978 28(2): 78-83.* Recounts stories about these items in the Virginia State Library: a copy of Frances Quarles's *Enchiridion* (London, 1856) given by Rollin L. Hart, a journal of the Fifth Virginia Convention given by David A. Randall, and a hand-illuminated testimonial, a gift by the merchants of Belfast to Consul James Donnan in 1880.

193. Lachance, Paul F. THE URBAN SOUTH IN HISTORICAL PERSPECTIVE. *Can. Rev. of Am. Studies [Canada] 1982 13(1): 53-60.* Reviews Gary Lawson Browne's *Baltimore in the Nation, 1789-1861* (1980), Blaine A. Brownell and David R. Goldfield, eds., *The City in Southern History* (1977), and Whitman H. Ridgeway's *Community Leadership in Maryland, 1790-1840* (1979). The volumes raise important questions about conventional historical interpretations of the Old South, particularly the characterizing of it as agrarian and culturally homogeneous. 10 notes.
H. T. Lovin

194. Lackey, Richard S. PETITION TO THE LEGISLATIVE COUNCIL BY INHABITANTS LIVING ON THE CHICKASAWHAY RIVER, 1808. *J. of Mississippi Hist. 1975 37(3): 279-282.* An 1808 petition of 77 people living on the Chickasawhay River in Washington County, Mississippi, asking the legislature to organize a new county for them, which it did by creating Wayne County. The list of names is valuable for researchers because courthouse fires destroyed the territorial records of Greene and Wayne counties. Based on records in the Mississippi Department of Archives and History; 8 notes.
J. W. Hillje

195. Lawson, Steven F. and Ingalls, Robert P. *TAMPA BAY HISTORY:* AN EXPERIMENT IN PUBLIC HISTORY. *Public Hist. 1981 3(2): 53-62.* Discusses the creation of a new local history journal, *Tampa Bay History,* by the University of South Florida in Tampa in the late 1970's, to unite the university and the community in preserving the past.

196. Levstik, Frank R. A BIBLIOGRAPHY OF CIVIL WAR ARTICLES: 1974. *Civil War Hist. 1975 21(4): 330-348.* This bibliography of 304 articles published in 1974 deals with slavery, abolition, nonslavery antebellum materials, the 1860 election, secession, the Civil War, and Reconstruction.
E. C. Murdock

197. Lewis, Helen M. APPALACHIAN STUDIES: THE NEXT STEP. *Appalachian J. 1982 9(2-3): 162-171.* Reprints an introduction to a 1970 social work program with an Appalachian focus at Clinch Valley College to show that Appalachian Studies was then trying to destroy Appalachian culture; examines the present goal of Appalachian Studies, the reorientation of "industrial technology" to serve basic human needs."

198. Lisenby, Foy. CHARLES HILLMAN BROUGH AS HISTORIAN. *Arkansas Hist. Q. 1976 35(2): 115-126.* Charles Hillman Brough resigned as professor of economics and sociology at the University of Arkansas in 1915 to run for governor of Arkansas. During his academic career he wrote a Ph.D. dissertation on irrigation problems in Utah and the development of Mormonism there, and articles on such subjects as the Clinton, Mississippi race riot of 1875 and the industrial history of Arkansas. He supported the work of the Mississippi state archives and the Arkansas Historical Association. Brough also taught at Mississippi College. Based on the Brough Papers, newspaper accounts, published primary and secondary sources; 41 notes.
T. L. Savitt

199. Lowe, John. ETHNICITY AND THE HARVARD ENCYCLOPEDIA. *Appalachian J. 1983 10(2): 177-181.* The *Harvard Encyclopedia of American Ethnic Groups* attempts to define and describe ethnic groups in America and includes a section on the Appalachians.

200. Lyon, Elizabeth R. GEORGIA'S HISTORIC PRESERVATION OFFICE: A BRIEF HISTORY. *Georgia Hist. Q. 1979 63(1): 28-38.* Describes the development of the Georgia Historic Preservation Office, begun in 1969, including changes in structure, functions and responsibilities. 2 notes.
G. R. Schroeder

201. Manarin, Louis H. A BUILDING FOR THE PRESERVATION OF THE PUBLIC RECORD. *Virginia Cavalcade 1974 24(1): 22-30.* Discusses the background to the 1747 decision to build the Public Records Office in Williamsburg, Virginia, "the oldest archival structure in the Western Hemisphere."

202. Mathis, Ray. THE TWO-NESS AND MYTH OF RECENT SOUTHERN HISTORY. *Mississippi Q. 1978 31(4): 631-650.* Discusses the theme of duality in recent Southern history in several books and essays by prominent southern historians.

203. Matlack, Carol. EUFAULA. *Am. Preservation 1978 2(1): 9-21.* Eufaula, once the thriving commercial center of southeastern Alabama's "Black Belt," suffered economic decline after World War I. Historic preservation efforts began in 1965 with the founding of Eufaula Heritage Association and the purchase of the neoclassic Shorter Mansion. Through privately raised funds, the Association purchases endangered structures for resale to those committed to historic preservation. The downtown business district has been renovated through voluntary restoration and construction guidelines. Today 72 Eufaula structures are listed on the National Register of Historic Places. 15 photos.
S. C. Strom

204. Maxa, Kathleen. GEORGETOWN. *Am. Preservation 1980 3(2): 42-57.* Describes the neighborliness and small-town feeling of Georgetown, District of Columbia, founded in 1751 as a tobacco port on the Potomac River, and efforts among the town's long-time residents to retain its 18th-century qualities.

205. McCay, Michael C. LOCATING AND PHOTOGRAPHING MARINE WRECKAGE: THE SCOTT CREEK PROJECT. *Chesopiean 1982 20(3-4): 5-12.* Relates the methodology employed in locating and photographing shipwrecks found in Scott Creek, located at Portsmouth, Virginia.

206. McCrank, Lawrence J. THE CENTENNIAL CELEBRATION OF THE FOUNDATION OF THE PEABODY LIBRARY, BALTIMORE, MARYLAND: A REPORT AND REVIEW. *J. of Lib. Hist. 1979 14(2): 183-187.* Describes festivities and publications celebrating the Peabody Library's centenary in 1978.

207. McCrary, Royce C. THE PUBLICATIONS OF KENNETH COLEMAN TO 1 SEPTEMBER 1976. *Georgia Hist. Q. 1976 60(3): 282-286.* A bibliography of the books, journal articles, and articles in collections of essays published by Georgia historian Kenneth Coleman, a retired professor from the University of Georgia, Athens.
G. R. Schroeder

208. McKay, John J., Jr. STORY OF THE MIDDLE GEORGIA HISTORICAL SOCIETY, INC. *Georgia Hist. Q. 1979 63(1): 156-160.* Describes the accomplishments of the Middle Georgia Historical Society, Inc. (founded 1964) in preserving historic structures in Macon. 2 illus.
G. R. Schroeder

209. McKenzie, Robert H. CLIO'S PARTNERS: THE SIGNIFICANCE OF ALABAMA HISTORY AND THE CONTRIBUTIONS OF ITS CONTEMPORARY HISTORIANS. *Alabama Rev. 1975 28(4): 243-259.* Overview of historical studies produced by both professional and amateur historians that have appeared in the *Alabama Review,* relating major local, state, regional, and national themes and topics. Contributions for the Civil War, Reconstruction, the Populist-Progressive eras, and the black experience predominate, while comparatively few deal with the Depression, World War II, and recent events. Secondary sources; 23 notes, biblio.
J. F. Vivian

210. McKenzie, Robert H. OPPORTUNITIES FOR RESEARCH IN ALABAMA BUSINESS HISTORY. *J. of the Alabama Acad. of Sci. 1973 44(2): 114-119.* Presents the value of the study of busi-

ness history (values to political history, to economic theory, and to development of regional economic potential). Encourages scholarly research into Alabama business history, indicating completed studies and additional sources of information. 4 notes, biblio.

Sr. A. Doyle

211. McMillan, Edward. PROGRAM OF THE 1982 ANNUAL MEETING OF THE MISSISSIPPI HISTORICAL SOCIETY. *J. of Mississippi Hist. 1982 44(3): 253-257.* Report on the 1982 meeting of the Mississippi Historical Society in Natchez. The convention's general theme was the tricentennial of LaSalle's exploration of the Lower Mississippi Valley. Individual sessions included French colonial history, oral history, and general papers on the Natchez Pilgrimage, Mobilian trade language, the settlement of English Bend below New Orleans, and other topics on the Lower Mississippi Valley.

M. S. Legan

212. McNeil, W. K. APPALACHIAN FOLKLORE SCHOLARSHIP. *Appalachian J. 1977 5(1): 55-64.* Scholarship on Appalachian folklore is fairly limited to studies dealing with material culture; professional folklorists need to concentrate on interpretation of available material.

213. McWhiney, Grady. THE THIRTY-EIGHTH ANNUAL MEETING OF THE SOUTHERN HISTORICAL ASSOCIATION. *J. of Southern Hist. 1973 39(1): 67-92.* The 1972 meeting of the Southern Historical Association in Hollywood-by-the-Sea, Florida, was attended by more than 1100 persons. Includes concise summaries of the 52 sessions.

I. M. Leonard

214. Meador, Patricia L. ARCHIVAL ANGLES. *North Louisiana Hist. Assoc. J. 1982 13(2-3): 82-88.* A brief discussion of the wealth of information available for the study of family history in northwestern Louisiana through use of personal manuscript collections housed in various local archives. Sources are personal collections in the Louisiana State University at Shreveport archives; 7 notes.

J. F. Paul

215. Meador, Patricia L. ARCHIVAL ANGLES. *North Louisiana Hist. Assoc. J. 1981 12(2-3): 82-85.* To encourage further research on 19th- and 20th-century northwest Louisiana, the author has summarized the opportunities and the sources available to the historian, discussing the politics, economics, and physiographics of the Red River, suggesting chief sources for further study, and noting that agriculture and plantation life are appropriate subjects for further inquiry. 3 notes. Article to be continued.

J. F. Paul

216. Meadows, Vicky. THE NATIONAL TRUST ANSWERS PRESERVATIONIST NEEDS LOCALLY. *North Louisiana Hist. Assoc. J. 1978 9(3): 159-162.* Describes the National Trust for Historic Preservation and some of the work it has cosponsored in Louisiana.

H. M. Parker, Jr.

217. Melnick, Ralph. COLLEGE OF CHARLESTON SPECIAL COLLECTIONS: A GUIDE TO ITS HOLDINGS. *South Carolina Hist. Mag. 1980 81(2): 131-153.* Traces the origins of the Special Collections of the College of Charleston Library to 1748, when the founders of the Charles Town Library Society included a provision for a library at the college they were attempting to found in Charleston; the materials in the Special Collections date to the mid-17th century.

218. Meyer, Mary K. GENEALOGICA MARYLANDIA: REVEREND LEWIS RICHARDS' MARRIAGE RECORDS, 1784-1790. *Maryland Hist. Mag. 1975 70(3): 311-314.* Manuscript 690 of the Maryland Historical Society is Reverend Lewis Richards's marriage ledger for the First Baptist Church of Baltimore, and contains listings of all marriages he performed from 1784 until his retirement in 1818. His successor, Reverend Stephen P. Hill, continued to keep the ledger for 1835-69, the last 15 years of which he spent in Washington. Transcribes only a small portion of these records, December 1784-31 December 1789.

G. J. Bobango

219. Miller, Jim Wayne. APPALACHIAN STUDIES HARD AND SOFT: THE ACTION FOLK AND THE CREATIVE PEOPLE. *Appalachian J. 1982 9(2-3): 105-114.* Characterizes "action folk" as political and "creative people" as literary and artistic, and discusses the need for the two groups to work together in the discipline of Appalachian Studies.

220. Miller, Jim Wayne. A CHECKLIST AND PURCHASE GUIDE FOR SCHOOL AND COMMUNITY LIBRARIES IN APPALACHIA. *Appalachian J. 1978 5(2): 274-287.* Bibliography of materials pertaining to Appalachia which serve as basic guides and surveys to social organization, culture, folklore, politics, economic conditions, literature, language, botany, arts and crafts, music, and periodicals.

221. Milligan, John D. THE TREATMENT OF AN HISTORICAL SOURCE. *Hist. and Theory 1979 18(2): 177-196.* Uses an archival letter of Colonel Charles Ellet dated 28 January 1863, charging top-level federal military officers with planning a coup against their government during the Civil War, to demonstrate, step-by-step, the methods which must be followed to critically handle primary sources for the writing of credible history. By a careful examination of all available external and internal evidence concludes that this letter, despite its unequivocal charges, cannot be used to support the idea of any proposed coup. But on the basis of it and all the related circumstances, other conclusions (or at least questions) can be raised about the methods of organization and administration in wartime. 37 notes.

R. V. Ritter

222. Moeller, Madelyn. PHOTOGRAPHY AND HISTORY: USING PHOTOGRAPHS IN INTERPRETING OUR CULTURAL PAST. *J. of Am. Culture 1983 6(1): 3-17.* Focuses on the family photographs of Howard Clifton Griswold, an amateur photographer of Louisville, Kentucky, and discusses the changes in photography from purely professional photography to amateur photography and changes in the social role of photography as it emerged from the studio and entered the home.

223. Moltke-Hansen, David. FROM THE SOCIETY: MICROFICHE REGISTER. *South Carolina Hist. Mag. 1981 82(3): 280-287.* Beginning in January 1980, the South Carolina Historical Society started microfilming its holdings and South Carolina materials belonging to others. The society produced microfiche for distribution. The register includes only manuscript materials.

R. H. Tomlinson

224. Moore, Marie D., comp. SELECTED BIBLIOGRAPHY OF COMPLETED THESES AND DISSERTATIONS RELATED TO NORTH CAROLINA SUBJECTS, 1974-1978. *North Carolina Hist. Rev. 1979 56(1): 64-107.* Subjects include anthropology, architecture, art, economics, education (the longest section), folklore (the shortest), geography, history (second longest), home economics, journalism, literature, music, political science, psychology, religion, sociology, and speech. Compiled from *Dissertations Abstracts International, Masters Abstracts,* and information from graduate offices and libraries of colleges in North Carolina and other states.

T. L. Savitt

225. Moore, Marie D. SELECTED BIBLIOGRAPHY OF COMPLETED THESES AND DISSERTATIONS RELATED TO NORTH CAROLINA SUBJECTS. *North Carolina Hist. Rev. 1981 58(1): 67-77.* Lists dissertations and theses on North Carolina subjects either completed since January 1978 or not listed in the previously published compilation (1974-78). Among the subject headings are: American Studies, Education, Fine Arts, Folklore, Geography, History, Political Science, Literature, Religion, and Sociology. Based on communications with graduate offices and libraries of North Carolina's universities, and secondary sources.

T. L. Savitt

226. Moore, Marie D. SELECTED BIBLIOGRAPHY OF COMPLETED THESES AND DISSERTATIONS RELATED TO NORTH CAROLINA SUBJECTS. *North Carolina Hist. Rev. 1982 59(1): 67-78.* Dissertations and theses on North Carolina subjects completed since, or not listed in, previously published compilations (1974-78 and supplements for 1979-80) are included. Among the

subject headings are: American Studies, Anthropology and Archaeology, Architecture, Economics, Education, Fine Arts, Music, Theater, Folklore, Geography, History and Political Science, Journalism, Literature, Religion, and Sociology. T. L. Savitt

227. Moore, Marie D. SELECTED BIBLIOGRAPHY OF COMPLETED THESES AND DISSERTATIONS RELATED TO NORTH CAROLINA SUBJECTS. *North Carolina Hist. Rev. 1983 60(1): 89-99.* Includes dissertations and theses on North Carolina subjects completed since, or not listed in, earlier compilations (1974-78 and supplements for 1979-81). Covers social sciences, the arts, journalism, history, folklore, and other subjects. Based on *Dissertation Abstracts International, Masters Abstracts, Journal of American Studies,* and communications with graduate programs and libraries of North Carolina universities.

229. Moore, Ray Nichols. MOLLY HUSTON LEE: A PROFILE. *Wilson Lib. Bull. 1975 49(6): 432-439.* Black librarian Molly Huston Lee singlehandedly was responsible for the establishment, maintenance, and growth of the Richard B. Harrison Library, which was especially for local blacks, in Raleigh, North Carolina, 1935-68.

230. Morgan, William. LOUISVILLE: CITY OF PARADOXES. *Hist. Preservation 1982 34(3): 38-45.* Discusses preservation efforts in the blue-collar, factory city of Louisville, Kentucky, since 1972, when over 50 local preservation groups formed the Preservation Alliance, fought a bitter battle a few years later with developers, and settled differences; preservation efforts are secure.

231. Moyne, Elizabeth E., comp. BIBLIOGRAPHY OF DELAWARE HISTORY, 1975-1976. *Delaware Hist. 1977 17(4): 295-308.* Lists with annotations almost 200 books, pamphlets, articles, and reprints dealing with Delaware and famous Delawareans. The items are drawn from popular and scholarly journals and from vanity, private, and university and commercial presses. Omits genealogical works, fiction, and poetry. R. M. Miller

232. Moyne, Elizabeth E., comp. BIBLIOGRAPHY OF DELAWARE HISTORY, 1973-1974. *Delaware Hist. 1975 16(4): 358-365.* Lists (alphabetically by author) books, pamphlets, theses, and articles dealing with Delaware or famous Delawareans. The bibliography does not include genealogical works or works of poetry and fiction. R. M. Miller

233. Moyne, Elizabeth E., comp. BIBLIOGRAPHY OF DELAWARE HISTORY, 1971-1972. *Delaware Hist. 1973 15(4): 312-319.* Lists (alphabetically by author) books, pamphlets, and articles relative to Delaware or famous Delawareans. Also lists recent reprints of older books relative to Delaware. Does not include genealogical works, unpublished dissertations or theses, materials in mimeograph form, or works of poetry and fiction.
R. M. Miller

234. Murrah, David J. WILLIAM CURRY HOLDEN. *West Texas Hist. Assoc. Year Book 1978 54: 92-101.* William Curry Holden (1896-1978) was a historian, archaeologist, anthropologist, and museum director at Texas Tech University.

235. Newsome, Jerry. "PRIMITIVE BAPTISTS": A STUDY IN NAME FORMATION OR WHAT'S IN A WORD. *Viewpoints 1978 6: 63-70.* Discusses the origin of the Primitive Baptists in Georgia, 1835-87.

236. Nichols, C. Howard. FIFTEENTH ANNUAL MEETING. *Louisiana Hist. 1973 14(3): 305-307.* Lists sessions, events, and minutes of the 15th annual meeting of the Louisiana Historical Association, 1973.

237. Nodyne, Kenneth R. A COMPILATION OF ARTICLES ABOUT WHEELING IN THE *UPPER OHIO VALLEY HISTORICAL REVIEW,* 1968-1981. *Upper Ohio Valley Hist. Rev. 1981 10(2): 27-32.* Covers 1570-20th century.

238. Obermiller, Phillip. APPALACHIANS AS AN URBAN ETHNIC GROUP: ROMANTICISM, RENAISSANCE, OR REVOLUTION? AND A BRIEF BIBLIOGRAPHICAL ESSAY ON URBAN APPALACHIANS. *Appalachian J. 1978 5(1): 145-152.* Examines current research on groups migrating from Appalachia to urbanized areas; Appalachians are best studied when considered as an ethnic group.

239. O'Brien, Michael. THE NINETEENTH-CENTURY AMERICAN SOUTH. *Hist. J. [Great Britain] 1981 24(3): 751-763.* Reviews recent publications (1978-80) on the South. Considers the use of modernization theory in American historiography in general, its recent use by Southern historians, and assesses the contribution of these new publications to the problems of society and politics.

240. O'Brien, Michael. W. J. CASH, HEGEL, AND THE SOUTH. *J. of Southern Hist. 1978 44(3): 379-398.* Long widely read and admired, Wilbur J. Cash's *The Mind of the South* has received strong criticism from Eugene D. Genovese and C. Vann Woodward. Although Cash had probably never read Georg Hegel, he is a flawed Hegelian (that is, a philsophical idealist). *The Mind of the South* is a clumsy Hegelian work, written within a dialectic framework, about the southern *Zeitgeist* and its ability to transform perception of individual and socioeconomic realities. Perhaps Cash's major error was permitting perception to control and define material reality. A critical on-going analysis of assumptions should accompany the documentation of historical events. Printed primary and secondary sources; 35 notes. T. D. Schoonover

241. Olmert, Michael. SAVING THE CHESAPEAKE'S LEGENDARY LORE. *Hist. Preservation 1983 35(1): 28-35.* Profiles the Chesapeake Bay Maritime Museum in St. Michaels, Maryland, and R. J. Holt, the director.

242. Otto, John S. and Gilbert, G. D. THE PLAIN FOLK OF THE AMERICAN SOUTH: AN ARCHEOLOGICAL PERSPECTIVE. *Pioneer Am. 1982 14(2): 67-80.* Discusses the use of archaeology due to the dearth of traditional sources, to study the daily lives of Southern middle-class whites during the 1880's-1930's; focuses on the archaeological investigations of the Edward Hoover family lands in Louisville, Kentucky.

243. Palmer, Bruce. THE ROOTS OF REFORM: SOUTHERN POPULISTS AND THEIR SOUTHERN HISTORY. *Red River Valley Hist. Rev. 1979 4(2): 33-62.* Traces Populism in the American South between the 1850's and the 1890's, and discusses the southern Populists' view of the history of the South.

244. Platt, Frederick. NEW CASTLE: LIVING WITH HISTORY. *Early Am. Life 1977 8(1): 56-58.* A brief history of New Castle, Delaware, during 1655-1881 and describes its preservation of historic sites and restorations.

245. Plotnik, Art. LIBRARY LIFE IN THE DEEP SOUTH. PART I: FLUX AND CONFLUX AT THE DELTA. *Wilson Lib. Bull. 1973 47(7): 584-597.* Impressions of libraries in Louisiana, Mississippi, Alabama and Georgia. PART II: THE HEART OF DIXIE. *Wilson Lib. Bull. 1973 47(9): 779-789.* Observations of libraries in Mississippi and Alabama.

246. Posey, Walter B. THE SOUTHERN HISTORICAL ASSOCIATION: ITS FOUNDING AND FIRST YEAR. *J. of Southern Hist. 1977 43(1): 59-72.* The action and participation of 20 people in early November 1934, created the Southern Historical Association. Within the first year the *Journal of Southern History* was successfully and solidly begun and the association's first convention in Birmingham, Alabama was well attended. Based on private papers; 25 notes. T. D. Schoonover

247. Powell, William S. NORTH CAROLINA BIBLIOGRAPHY, 1972-1973. *North Carolina Hist. R. 1974 51(2): 215-223.* Unannotated bibliography under the following headings: Bibliography and Libraries, Philosophy and Religion, Economics and Sociology, Philology, Science, Applied Science and Useful Arts, Fine Art, Poetry, Drama, Fiction, Other Literature, History and Travel, Genealogy, Autobiography and Biography, New Editions and Reprints. Includes books dealing with North Carolina or by North Carolinians published during the year ending 30 June 1973.

E. P. Stickney

248. Price, Eugenia. THE ST. AUGUSTINE HISTORICAL SOCIETY LIBRARY: MY SECOND HOME. *Escribano 1977 14: 39-44.* Author discusses her research on local characters in the St. Augustine Historical Society Library, 1972-77.

249. Prunty, Merle C. GEOGRAPHY IN THE SOUTH. *Ann. of the Assoc. of Am. Geographers 1979 69(1): 53-58.* Surveys the development of geography departments in colleges and universities throughout the South, 1940's-50's; from a special issue celebrating the 75th anniversary of the Association of American Geographers.

250. Purrington, Burton L. THE STATUS AND FUTURE OF ARCHEOLOGY AND NATIVE AMERICAN STUDIES IN THE SOUTHERN APPALACHIANS. *Appalachian J. 1977 5(1): 40-54.* Assesses the status of archaeology and Indian studies in southern Appalachia, including methodology and theory; lists various studies; lesser-known Indians should be studied and sites should be protected from nonprofessionals, dam-building, and urbanization.

251. Reap, James K. LEGAL ASPECTS OF HISTORIC PRESERVATION. *Georgia Hist. Q. 1979 63(1): 68-76.* Lists and briefly describes federal and Georgia laws since 1889 which are relevant to historic preservation. Based on laws; 29 notes, biblio.

G. R. Schroeder

252. Robertson, James I., Jr. VIRGINIA HISTORICAL SOCIETY: THE ENERGIES OF SOME FOR THE ENRICHMENT OF ALL. *Virginia Mag. of Hist. and Biog. 1978 86(2): 131-145.* Traces the history and surveys the holdings of the Virginia Historical Society. An address to the annual meeting of the Society. Based on secondary sources and on primary material in the VHS; 24 notes.

R. F. Oaks

253. Rogers, George C. THE LAURENS PAPERS: HALF-WAY. *Pro. of the South Carolina Hist. Assoc. 1977: 37-48.* Surveys material in the first nine volumes of the Henry Laurens Papers. Suggests areas of further research, such as Charleston's merchants, Quakers, social life, and shipbuilding industry. Based on the Henry Laurens Papers and the *South Carolina Gazette;* 20 notes.

J. W. Thacker, Jr.

254. Rohrs, Richard C. THE STUDY OF OKLAHOMA HISTORY DURING THE TERRITORIAL PERIOD: AN ALTERNATIVE METHODOLOGICAL APPROACH. *Chronicles of Oklahoma 1982 60(2): 174-185.* Researchers are often forced to rely upon impressionistic accounts of a region or of historical events, and this sometimes leads to mistaken interpretations. Scholars such as Frederick Jackson Turner, Merle Curti, and Stephen Thernstrom have demonstrated the value of local sources in reconstructing the past, and the new social history focus on "history from the bottom up" has added to this call. In the case of Oklahoma, local sources are abundant and extremely rich in detail for the period after 1890. Among the most usable sources are censuses, published county histories, church records, city directories, Oklahoma Tract Books, Indian Census Rolls, and Works Progress Administration inventories of county records. Based on analysis of these collections and methodological articles; 40 notes.

M. L. Tate

255. Roper, Jack. PROGRESS AND HISTORY: A SOUTHERN DIALECTIC ON RACE. *Southern Humanities Rev. 1983 17(2): 101-119.* Discusses the differences in the philosophy of Southern history of Ulrich B. Phillips (1877-1934), a racial conservative, and C. Vann Woodward, a liberal.

256. Roper, James H. WATERFORD. *Am. Preservation 1979 2(5): 47-58.* Waterford, Virginia, a small town near Washington, D.C., has a tradition of historic preservation which has included restoration and preservation of a strip of open space surrounding the village and known as the Waterford Corridor, 1937-79.

257. Roper, John Herbert. C. VANN WOODWARD'S EARLY CAREER: THE HISTORIAN AS DISSIDENT YOUTH. *Georgia Hist. Q. 1980 64(1): 7-21.* Describes the early career of C. Vann Woodward (b. 1908), noted Southern historian, including people who influenced him in his liberal radical stands against racism, concluding with the completion of his dissertation which was published as *Tom Watson: Agrarian Rebel* (1938). Based on interviews with Woodward; 10 notes.

G. R. Schroeder

258. Ross, Margaret. HUGH PARK. *Arkansas Hist. Q. 1974 33(4): 334-336.* Obituary notice of Hugh Park (1906-74), newspaper editor and publisher (Van Buren *Press Argus*), who was the first and only printer of the *Arkansas Historical Quarterly.* His interest in Arkansas history grew after assuming the printer's post in 1942, and he soon became an influential member of the Arkansas Historical Society and publisher of local historical books and newspaper articles. Illus.

T. L. Savitt

259. Rundell, Walter, Jr. GUIDES TO MARYLAND'S PAST: EIGHT SOCIETY MICROFILM PROJECTS. *Maryland Hist. Mag. 1975 70(1): 92-97.* A critical review and summation of eight *Guides to the Microfilm Editions . . .* written and compiled by various authors since 1970. Two of them were produced and marketed commercially, the *Papers of the Maryland State Colonization Society* and the *Guide to the Charles Carroll Papers,* while the other six resulted from grants from the National Historical Publications Commission. These include Guides to the Robert Goodloe Harper Family Papers, the David Bailie Warden Papers, the John Pendleton Kennedy Papers, those of the Lloyds of Wye, William Wirt, and the Calvert family. Certain volumes are less valuable then others. The Carroll pamphlet lacks any indication of the content of the 2,035 items on film, and gives no reel numbers, nor costs. The other guides are very thorough, giving summary statements, biographical sketches, descriptions of the papers, bibliographical essays, and roll lists, plus inclusive dates for correspondence. The Kennedy papers Guide contains elaborate roll-notes identifying entries by item, and locating each on one of the 27 rolls. A further step forward has been the numbering of each frame so that citation of microfilmed documents may be exact. Moreover, all are available to scholars through inter-library loan. Based on the *Guides,* and including brief sketches of the historical role of each individual upon whose papers the collections are based.

G. J. Bobango

260. Rundell, Walter, Jr. WALTER PRESCOTT WEBB AND THE TEXAS STATE HISTORICAL ASSOCIATION. *Arizona and the West 1983 25(2): 109-136.* Walter Prescott Webb served as secretary of the Texas State Historical Association and as editor of the *Southwestern Historical Quarterly* during 1938-46 and continued his service to the association for many years thereafter. His vigorous stewardship transformed the organization into active promotion of the study and teaching of the state's history and confirmed his conviction that history must reach beyond the academic world to prosper. He was particularly proud of his successes in launching the Junior Historian movement and the publication of the *Handbook of Texas.* 5 illus., 67 notes.

D. L. Smith

261. Salley, Coleen Cole. NINETEENTH CENTURY NEW ORLEANS IN BOOKS. *Southern Q. 1982 20(2): 177-185.* A 155 entry bibliography divided into 11 major subject categories and consisting of materials found in the Historic New Orleans Collection, the New Orleans Public Library, Tulane University, and the Library Sales and Service bookstore.

W. A. Wiegand

262. Saye, Albert B. A TRIBUTE TO ELLIS MERTON COULTER. *Georgia Hist. Q. 1981 65(3): 183-188.* Biographical information on and tribute to Dr. Ellis Merton Coulter (1890-1981), professor of Georgian and Southern history at the University of Georgia for many years. Photo.

G. R. Schroeder

263. Sequine, Arlene. THE ROLE OF ACADEMIA IN PERPETUATING FOLKLIFE IN THE PUBLIC SECTOR. *Kentucky Folklore Record 1980 26(1-2): 16-22.* "Attempts to identify the role of academia in perpetuating folklore in the public sector through cross-curricular disciplines which embody the folk performing arts (folk dance, folk music, and traditional folksong) as vehicles of investigation into folklife studies," focusing on the use of Labanotation, a dance script.

264. Shaver, Claude L.; Ritchey, David; and Gresdna, Doty, comps. SOUTHERN THEATRE HISTORY: A BIBLIOGRAPHY OF THESES AND DISSERTATIONS. *Southern Speech Communication J. 1977 42(4): 362-373.* Includes papers written 1935-76.

265. Sheppard, Peggy. LIFE IS JUST LIKE IT USED TO BE AT GEORGIA'S LIVING HISTORY MUSEUM. *Georgia Life 1979 6(1): 14-17.* Agrirama, located near Tifton, Georgia, is a 70-acre living history museum where demonstrations in basketry, grain gristing, steam power, spinning, baking, and farming techniques of the 19th and early 20th centuries may be seen.

266. Sheppard, Peggy and Corley, Kit. A SALUTE TO COLUMBUS: ON THE OCCASION OF HER SESQUICENTENNIAL. *Georgia Life 1978 5(1): 12-16.* Chronicles the economic growth and population growth of Columbus, Georgia, covering 1828-1978, and discusses restoration and preservation projects, 1960's-70's.

267. Shera, Jesse H. LOUIS ROUND WILSON (1876-1979): THE LAST OF THE PIONEERS. *J. of Lib. Hist. 1982 17(1): 65-77.* Louis Round Wilson's career as a librarian began in 1901 with his appointment as head of the University of North Carolina's library. After a distinguished career there, which included the founding of the University of North Carolina Press, he left in 1932 to head the University of Chicago Graduate School of Library Science at the urging of Chicago's president, Robert Maynard Hutchins. Wilson's considerable accomplishments at Chicago were based on his ability to provide direction and leadership for the talented faculty already assembled there. After his retirement from Chicago in 1942, Wilson returned to an active role at the University of North Carolina, which continued through 1975. Biblio.
J. S. Coleman

268. Silverman, Catherine. THE UNITED STATES: THE SOUTH IN THE 19TH CENTURY. *Trends in Hist. 1979 1(2): 147-158.* Surveys historiography of the 1970's.

269. Simpson, Robert R. THE ORIGIN OF THE ARKANSAS HISTORY COMMISSION. *Arkansas Hist. Q. 1973 32(3): 241-254.*

270. Simpson, William S., Jr. A COMPARISON OF THE LIBRARIES OF SEVEN COLONIAL VIRGINIANS, 1754-1789. *J. of Lib. Hist., Phil. and Comparative Librarianship 1974 9(1): 54-65.* Examines the library inventories of collections belonging to David Black (d. 1773), Dabney Carr (d. 1773), John Parke Custis (d. 1781), William Fleming (d. 1795), John Herbert (d. 1760), John Moncure (d. 1764), and John Waller (d. 1754). Literature and history titles made up much of each collection; the number of books on medicine, religion, and law fluctuated greatly; titles on philosophy and applied and pure sciences were not widely purchased. A core collection was identified; e.g., 12 titles appeared in four libraries. Collections evidenced high literary quality, balance, and taste appropriate to knowledgeable persons. Concludes with linking of related studies by Louis B. Wright and Richard Beale Davis. Based on primary and secondary sources; 4 tables, 25 notes.
D. G. Davis, Jr.

271. Sitton, Thad and Harrell, Claudette. THE CALDWELL COUNTY PROJECT: CREATING A USABLE PAST. *Public Hist. 1979 1(3): 41-50.* Discusses the creation of the Caldwell County Tri-Cultural Oral History Project in 1976 in Texas to fill the need for a community history of the area that would include the history of blacks, and Mexican Americans in addition to Anglos.

272. Skates, John Ray, Jr. PROGRAM OF THE 1976 MEETING OF THE MISSISSIPPI HISTORICAL SOCIETY. *J. of Mississippi Hist. 1976 38(3): 279-282.* Describes papers delivered.
J. W. Hillje

273. Sloan, Herbert and Onuf, Peter. POLITICS, CULTURE, AND THE REVOLUTION IN VIRGINIA: A REVIEW OF RECENT WORK. *Virginia Mag. of Hist. and Biog. 1983 91(3): 259-284.* A historiographic overview of scholarship produced in recent years on the subject of Virginia's character prior to, during, and after the American Revolution. New books on the economy, social structure, the war, and postwar Virginia have all appeared within the past decade. Many of them are revisionist treatments, but there is a need for further study of this period as a continuum, rather than breaking it into artificially assigned time periods. Based on official records, Virginia newspapers, 1736-80, papers of Virginians, and 20th-century historical studies of the period; 62 notes.
D. J. Cimbala

274. Smith, Frank E. BELL I. WILEY: MISSISSIPPIAN. *J. of Mississippi Hist. 1980 42(3): 252-253.* Tribute to Bell Irvin Wiley, who died on 4 April 1980. Sketches his Mississippi background. Wiley is best recognized for his evaluation of the role of the common soldier during the Civil War and as the first historian to give scholarly attention to the experience of blacks during that war. Finishing his PhD at Yale, Wiley became a member of the faculty at the State Teachers College in Hattiesburg, Mississippi, where he revised his doctoral thesis into the book, *Southern Negroes (1861-1865).* In 1938, Wiley moved to the University of Mississippi, where he taught courses on the Old South and the Civil War. During this period, he researched and wrote his best-known work, *The Life of Johnny Reb.* Leaving Mississippi in 1946, Wiley taught at Louisiana State University and subsequently at Emory until his retirement. Wiley's identification was primarily with Emory and Atlanta, but Mississippi and Mississippians played a significant role in launching his professional career.
M. S. Legan

275. Smith, Janet Welt. ALISTAIR COOKE AND OTHER SOUTHERNERS. *Worldview 1974 17(11): 19-24.* Argues that 20th-century historians such as Alistair Cooke have distorted Civil War and Reconstruction history by maintaining that northerners were motivated to subdue the South by economic goals and not by the prospect of emancipating the slaves.

276. Smith, John David. JAMES FORD RHODES, WOODROW WILSON, AND THE PASSING OF THE AMATEUR HISTORIAN OF SLAVERY. *Mid-America 1982 64(3): 17-24.* Contrasts the attitudes and methods of James Ford Rhodes and Woodrow Wilson as historians and more narrowly as interpreters of slavery and the South, largely through analysis of Wilson's anonymous review of Rhodes's *History of the United States from the Compromise of 1850.* Rhodes was the amateur, narrative historian, a neoabolitionist, heavily dependent on travel accounts amassed for his private library; Wilson was the professional, an apologist for the Old South and advocate of synthesizing multiarchival sources. Based on the Wilson Papers and Rhodes's letters from several manuscript collections; 23 notes.
P. J. Woehrmann

277. Smith, John David and Miller, Randall M. A SOUTHERN HISTORIAN ON TOUR: CLEMENT EATON'S TRAVELS THROUGH THE NEW SOUTH. *Southern Studies 1982 21(2): 163-207.* Clement Eaton (1898-1980) was a foremost modern Southern historian. Born in South Carolina, he studied at Harvard, where his views broadened and became more liberal and his scholarly attitudes developed. He wrote several important books on the South and taught at several colleges before spending 22 years at the University of Kentucky. Includes complete texts of three diaries Eaton kept while on trips to the lower South in 1935, 1946, and 1953 showing his fascination with all facets of Southern history and culture. Based on 3 Eaton diaries and other papers in the Clement Eaton Papers at the University of Kentucky Library; 127 notes.
J. J. Buschen

278. Sosna, Morton. TWO SONGS OF THE SOUTH IN DIFFERENT KEYS. *Rev. in Am. Hist. 1980 8(1): 92-97.* Review essay of Dewey W. Grantham's *The Regional Imagination: The South and Recent American History* (Nashville, Tenn.: Vanderbilt U. Pr., 1979), and Michael O'Brien's *The Idea of the American South, 1920-1941* (Baltimore, Md.: The Johns Hopkins U. Pr., 1979); 1870-1977.

279. Southern, David W. *AN AMERICAN DILEMMA* REVISITED: MYRDALISM AND WHITE SOUTHERN LIBERALS. *South Atlantic Q. 1976 75(2): 182-197.* Reviews interpretations concerning Gunnar Myrdal's *An American Dilemma* during the past three decades. The views of historians, journalists, ministers, judges, lawyers, politicians, and scholars are included. Such individuals as Ralph McGill, Howard W. Odum, C. Vann Woodward, and Lewis M. Killian are featured. Concludes that Myrdal's theories have declined in acceptance. 35 notes. R. W. Dubay

280. Spalding, Phinizy. ACCESSIONS REGISTRY, GEORGIA DEPOSITORIES. *Georgia Hist. Q. 1980 64(1): 64-83.* Lists the archival and manuscript additions to Georgia repositories during 1978 and 1979. G. R. Schroeder

281. Spalding, Phinizy. ELLIS MERTON COULTER. *Georgia Hist. Q. 1981 65(1): npp.* Obituary of Ellis Merton Coulter (1890-1981), Georgia and Southern historian, professor at the University of Georgia at Athens for almost 40 years, and editor of the *Georgia Historical Quarterly* for 50 years. Photo. G. R. Schroeder

282. Spalding, Phinizy. THE VARIETY OF GEORGIA HISTORY: SOME RECENT WORK IN THE FIELD. *Georgia Hist. Q. 1980 64(4): 484-491.* Notes on 14 recent publications about Georgia history not previously reviewed in the *Georgia Historical Quarterly.* G. R. Schroeder

283. Stagner, Stephen. EPICS, SCIENCE, AND THE LOST FRONTIER: TEXAS HISTORICAL WRITING, 1836-1936. *Western Hist. Q. 1981 12(2): 165-181.* Early histories of Texas are more promotion than history, liberally mixing travel narratives and advertising to create "boosterism in historical disguise," vindicating Anglo-American Texans' right to the land. "Halfway-house professionalism" began to appear in the latter half of the 19th century to erode "interpretations of moral grandeur" in histories of the state. The state's status as "vanguard of Anglo-American expansion" suffered when early 20th century specialized scientific histories began to investigate the importance of Texas as a Borderland of New Spain. After a century of historical writing, however, "the grandiosity of the Texas venture" was still present, because historians frequently build upon the foundations of their predecessors. The bottom layers of Texas history have not been cleansed by the "acids of skepticism" they deserve. 58 notes. D. L. Smith

284. Stephenson, John. POLITICS AND SCHOLARSHIP: APPALACHIAN STUDIES ENTERS THE 1980'S. *Appalachian J. 1982 9(2-3): 97-104.* Discusses the questions addressed at the 21-22 May 1981 conference, "Appalachian Studies: Its Roots, Its Current Contexts, Its Future," held at the University of Kentucky and sponsored by the University's Appalachian Center, the *Appalachian Journal,* and the Margaret I. King Library, with support from the National Endowment for the Humanities, describing the purpose of Appalachian Studies during the last decade, the research quality, and future research requirements.

285. Stephenson, John B. and Greer, L. Sue. ETHNOGRAPHERS IN THEIR OWN CULTURES: TWO APPALACHIAN CASES. *Human Organization 1981 40(2): 123-130.* Describes the kinship ties and social mores of two southern mountain communities, and the unique development of each, which is all but invisible except to totally unbiased ethnographic research.

286. Sullivan, Larry E. SOURCES FOR THE STUDY OF BALTIMORE HISTORY AT THE MARYLAND HISTORICAL SOCIETY. *Working Papers from the Regional Econ. Hist. Res. Center 1981 4(1-2): 24-64.* Brief description of the holdings at the Mary-

land Historical Society, founded in 1844, tracing Maryland's and especially Baltimore's history, and lists the collections, which include family papers, business papers, records from private organizations, clubs, and institutions, scrapbooks, and church records, 18th century-1980.

287. Summersell, Charles G. TWENTY-NINTH ANNUAL MEETING OF THE ALABAMA HISTORICAL ASSOCIATION. *Alabama Rev. 1976 29(4): 273-279.* Summarizes a meeting held in Montgomery in April-May 1976. Lists sessions held, papers read, and other activities. Separate section, following, contains financial report of the Association for the fiscal year ending March 1976. J. F. Vivian

288. Talley, Marcia D. MORRIS LEON RADOFF: THE MAN AND THE MONUMENT. *Am. Arch. 1981 44(4): 327-340.* In 1939, Morris Leon Radoff began his 35-year tenure as director of the then three-year-old Maryland Hall of Records. Radoff's pioneering efforts in records management, high quality archival repair, and promotion of copying of archival materials made the Hall of Records one of the premier repositories in the United States. Radoff was particularly adept at convincing custodians of Maryland public records to deposit material with his agency. Through his efforts, the Hall of Records acquired originals or copies of numerous archival estrays. Radoff also wrote extensively and encouraged scholarly use of archival materials. Based mainly on interviews of Morris Leon Radoff's associated and annual reports of the Maryland Hall of Records; 87 notes. G.-A. Patzwald

289. Teel, Cora P. MANUSCRIPTS COLLECTIONS IN THE SPECIAL COLLECTIONS DEPARTMENT, MARSHALL UNIVERSITY. *West Virginia Hist. 1982 43(4): 329-341.* The Special Collections Department of the James E. Morrow Library at Marshall University emphasizes items on West Virginia history and culture. Lists items in the collection and hours it is open. J. D. Neville

290. Thweatt, John H. JAMES PRIESTLEY: CLASSICAL SCHOLAR OF THE OLD SOUTH. *Tennessee Hist. Q. 1980 39(4): 423-439.* Chronicles the career of James Priestley (d. 1821). In 1774 Priestley was taken into the home of a Presbyterian minister, Reverend William Graham, where he impressed his teacher with his keen and receptive mind. He excelled in classical literature. During more than 40 years he conducted classical academies in Virginia, Maryland, and Kentucky and in 1809 was elected president of Cumberland College, one of the most prestigious schools in the West. His students remembered his deep learning, laborious habits and strict discipline. Although somewhat eccentric, he inspired his students with an unwavering devotion to the pursuit of knowledge. Primary sources; 67 notes. J. Powell

291. Todd, William B. THE AITKEN LIBRARY. *Lib. Chronicle of the U. of Texas at Austin 1974 7: 58-63.* The 3,500 volume library of George Atherton Aitken, strong in 18th-century English literature, was acquired by the University of Texas in 1921. Reprints an article on Aitken and his collection by H. F. B. Wheeler in a 1909 issue of *The Bibliophile.*

292. Tomlin, Ronald E. OFFICIAL RECORD ACQUISITIONS OF THE DEPARTMENT OF ARCHIVES AND HISTORY, 1975. *J. of Mississippi Hist. 1976 38(1): 103-109.* Lists and describes government records (provincial, state, county, federal, and municipal) "processed and accessioned into the holdings of the Mississippi Department of Archives and History" in 1975. J. W. Hillje

293. Towns, W. Stuart; Kable, June E.; and Kell, Carl. A BIBLIOGRAPHY OF COMMUNICATION IN THE SOUTH FOR THE YEAR 1981. *Southern Speech Communication J. 1983 48(4): 391-397.* Covers 19th- and 20th-century topics.

294. Towns, W. Stuart; Kable, June E.; and Kell, Carl L. A BIBLIOGRAPHY OF SPEECH, THEATRE, AND MASS COMMUNICATION IN THE SOUTH FOR THE YEAR 1977. *Southern*

*Speech Communication J. 1978 44(1): 93-102.* Lists journal articles under public address, theater, speech education, and mass communication.

295.  Towns, W. Stuart and Roberts, Churchill L. A BIBLIOGRAPHY OF SPEECH, THEATRE, AND MASS COMMUNICATION IN THE SOUTH FOR THE YEAR 1975. *Southern Speech Communication J. 1976 42(1): 68-77.*

296.  Tregle, Joseph G., Jr. ANOTHER LOOK AT SHUGG'S LOUISIANA. *Louisiana Hist. 1976 17(3): 245-281.* Reviews Roger Shugg's *Origins of Class Struggle in Louisiana* (originally published in 1939; reprinted 1968 by L.S.U. Pr.). Despite great and persistent praise of this book over the years, reexamination of it reveals that it "is in reality a grossly unreliable work, unsound in its historical methodology, untrustworthy in its documentation, and essentially useless as a guide to antebellum Louisiana." Details the work, its sources and methodology, and other current research on the demography, slavery, and class structure of antebellum Louisiana. It is impossible "to measure the mischief done by Shugg's wayward monograph," and "it is time for Louisiana historians to set Shugg aside." Based on primary and secondary sources; 3 tables, 35 notes.
R. L. Woodward

297.  Vanorny, Patricia M. RECORDS OF THE BALTIMORE JUDICIAL SYSTEM. *Working Papers from the Regional Econ. Hist Res. Center 1981 4(1-2): 65-74.* Provides a brief history of the judicial structure in Baltimore over the past 200 years, focusing on the court records, particularly of civil and equity cases, which provide historians and archivists with information about families, neighborhoods, "economic conditions, social structures, and human behavior."

298.  Viccars, Marion. THE FIRST ONE HUNDRED. *Manuscripts 1973 25(1): 26-33.* Announces the initial catalog ("The First One Hundred") of family papers and business records relating to Pensacola and West Florida and briefly identifies some of the more significant collections held by the manuscripts collection at the five-year-old University of West Florida Library. The collections "are rich in source material for the economic and social historian in this almost unexploited part of the South." Illus.
D. A. Yanchisin

299.  Waddell, Gene. SEVENTY-EIGHT VOLUMES. *South Carolina Hist. Mag. 1978 79(3): 240-244.* Summarizes the type of material and historical periods emphasized in the *South Carolina Historical Magazine*, 1900-77.

300.  Walls, David S. and Billings, Dwight B. THE SOCIOLOGY OF SOUTHERN APPALACHIA. *Appalachia J. 1978 5(1): 131-144.* Examines sociological studies on Appalachia, 1930's-70's, including theoretical works on social change and problems, ethnic and minority subcultures, and economic and political power.

301.  Walsh, Lorena S. THE HISTORIAN AS CENSUS TAKER: INDIVIDUAL RECONSTITUTION AND THE RECONSTRUCTION OF CENSUSES FOR A COLONIAL CHESAPEAKE COUNTY. *William and Mary Q. 1981 38(2): 242-260.* Details the process of reconstituting a census. By using available records—wills, deeds, inventories, local court records and the like—vital histories of resident families can be assembled, and from this endeavor calculations can be made that are representative of society as a whole. Charles County, Maryland, is the case in point. A 1705 census is constructed, including an age profile. The reconstituted census provides a means for studying the demographic history of the county, including measurement of behavior. Uses all kinds of local and provincial records, chiefly pertaining to Charles County; 4 tables, 49 notes.
H. M. Ward

302.  Wates, Wylma Anne. IN THE BEGINNING: SOUTH CAROLINA HIRES ITS FIRST ARCHIVIST. *South Carolina Hist. Mag. 1979 80(2): 186-191.* Offers a history of the South Carolina Department of Archives and History, established in 1905 and headed for 44 years by Alexander S. Salley, Jr., on the 75th anniversary of the Department's existence.

303.  Watson, Charles S. DE SOTO'S EXPEDITION: CONTRASTING TREATMENTS IN PICKETT'S *HISTORY OF ALABAMA* AND SIMMS'S *VASCONSELOS. Alabama Rev. 1978 31(3): 199-208.* Albert J. Pickett's *History of Alabama* (1851) treated the de Soto expedition in a factual, objective manner. William Gilmore Simms's *Vasconselos: A Romance of the New World* (1853) was a moralistic reaction, a historical novel laced with moral judgments. Simms represented the Romantic impulse; Pickett anticipated the critical school that guides historical studies today. Primary and secondary sources; 33 notes.
J. F. Vivian

304.  Webb, Max. THE SELF, FORTUNE, AND PROVIDENCE: ALLEN TATE ON STONEWALL JACKSON. *Mississippi Q. 1977 30(2): 249-258.* Addresses the artistic consciousness of Allen Tate through investigation of his biography of Thomas "Stonewall" Jackson, connecting it with Tate's agrarianism and focusing on the biography itself as historical writing, 1927-28.

305.  Weinstein, Fred and Gover, C. Jane. THE MIND OF THE SOUTH: PAST CONTRIBUTIONS, FUTURE PROSPECTS. *Psychohistory Rev. 1981 10(1): 33-58.* Reviews writings by John Dollard, Wilbur J. Cash, Stanley Elkins, William R. Taylor and Eugene D. Genovese and finds that while they were not explicit psychohistorical studies, they did incorporate many psychoanalytic theories in their studies. Their emphasis on the problem of integration of the self with society coincided with changes in psychoanalytic theory in the 20th century.
J. M. Herrick

306.  Westbrook, Robert B. C. VANN WOODWARD: THE SOUTHERNER AS LIBERAL REALIST. *South Atlantic Q. 1978 77(1): 54-71.* C. Vann Woodward's work can best be thought of as a unique liberal realism built upon his threefold commitment to his southern heritage, to the strain of agrarian populism in American liberalism, and to the social responsibility of the historian. To him the southern experience has been uniquely un-American: one of poverty rather than wealth, frustration, failure, and defeat rather than triumph and unbroken success. Southern history compromises innocence and shatters the illusion of progress. It must be continuously protected from romanticism and obscurantism. His interpretation of history stands in stark contrast to the conservative approach which he deems not only as not viable, but as an illusionary fiction. As a liberal he discounts any persistence of the past in Burkean terms and places considerable emphasis on the role of irony in history. His realism is seen in his emphasis on southern Populism: emotional, agrarian, and lower class. Based on Woodward's writings; 62 notes.
H. M. Parker, Jr.

307.  Whisnant, David E. SECOND-LEVEL APPALACHIAN HISTORY: ANOTHER LOOK AT SOME FOTCHED-ON WOMEN. *Appalachian J. 1982 9(2-3): 115-123.* Briefly discusses the mastery of Appalachian Studies research on the exploitation of coal, the land, the people, their music, literature, image, etc., and examines a second level of research that questions the generalizations and assumptions made already, using as an example "fotched-on" women, virtuous, principled and religious, who attempted to bring medical care, culture, and education to the people of Appalachia and "who have served as a frequent and convenient target for our recent anti-missionary, anti-middle class barbs."

308.  White, Helen and Sugg, Redding. A COLLOQUIUM WITH SHELBY FOOTE. *Southern Humanities Rev. 1981 15(4): 281-299.* Presents the text of a colloquium that brought together novelist and historian Shelby Foote and the authors to discuss Foote's *The Civil War*, a history, and his novels on the South.

309.  Winfrey, Dorman H. THE TEXAS STATE LIBRARY. *Lib. Chronicle of the U. of Texas 1973 (6): 78-79.*

310.  Wiser, Vivian. SELECT BIBLIOGRAPHY ON HISTORY OF AGRICULTURE IN MARYLAND. *J. of NAL Assoc. 1976 1(3): 55-85.* Lists, by alphabetical order of the author's last name, 19th- and 20th-century books, periodicals, articles, journals, theses, and guides to manuscripts and records, of the history of agriculture in Maryland since the 17th century.

311. Wolf, Edwin, II. MORE BOOKS FROM THE LIBRARY OF THE BYRDS OF WESTOVER. *Pro. of the Am. Antiquarian Soc.* 1978 88(1): 51-82. Adds 94 titles to his earlier list published in these *Proceedings* in 1958. Annotated, with locations indicated.
J. Andrew

312. Wolfe, Maxine G. WHERE MONROE PRACTICED LAW. *Am. Bar Assoc. J.* 1973 59(11): 1282-1284. The house where James Monroe practiced law in Fredericksburg, Virginia, is now the James Monroe Museum and Memorial Library, perpetuating the memory of the statesman and philosopher.

313. Wood, W. K. U. B. PHILLIPS, UNSCIENTIFIC HISTORI-AN: A FURTHER NOTE ON HIS METHODOLOGY AND USE OF SOURCES. *Southern Studies* 1982 21(2): 146-162. Ulrich Bonnell Phillips, Southern historian, has a reputation for accuracy, objectivity, and thoroughness in research as elements of his scientific-critical method. This view is inaccurate; he limited his studies to a small area of the South, believed in the inherent inferiority of blacks, and used sources incompletely and selectively. In *History of Transportation in the Eastern Cotton Belt to 1860* (1908), Phillips neglected important source materials, misused evidence to support his biases, and misinterpreted facts. He did not use the records of the actual railroad companies, the extensive evidence of the Augusta *Chronicle*, or the Augusta City Council minutes. Documents many sources unused or used inaccurately. Primary records; 2 appendixes, 30 notes.
J. J. Buschen

314. Woodress, James. THE USES OF BIOGRAPHY: THE CASE OF WILLA CATHER. *Great Plains Q.* 1982 2(4): 195-203. Because most fiction is autobiographical in some sense, biographers of authors may be able to use the fictive work to draw out valuable data; study of the author's life in turn will supply information on the inspiration for the novel; utilizes the life and novels of Willa Cather to demonstrate the methodology.

315. Woodward, C. Vann. THE FUTURE OF SOUTHERN HISTORY. Delzell, Charles F., ed. *The Future of History: Essays in the Vanderbilt University Centennial Symposium* (Nashville: Vanderbilt U. Pr., 1977): 135-149. Southern history is a new field, but owing to the academic prosperity of the 1960's it has produced an enormous volume of works. It has undergone a qualitative improvement as research has become more interpretive and less narrative. As the central place of the South in the history of the nation has been recognized, the field has become less parochial and isolated. Much interest was stimulated by the civil rights movement, which in particular spawned the great controversy over the economics of slavery. The South has been a fruitful field for cliometricians, revisionary Marxists, and northerners interested in novelty. 9 notes.
P. L. Solodkin

316. Woodward, Michael Vaughan. E. MERTON COULTER AND THE ART OF BIOGRAPHY. *Georgia Hist. Q.* 1980 64(2): 159-171. Historian Ellis Merton Coulter has written many articles and books, including 10 biographies of Georgians and other southern personalities: William G. Brownlow, Thomas Spalding, John Jacobus Flournoy, the Jones family of Wormsloe, James Barrow, James Monroe Smith, Joseph Vallence Bevan, William Montague Browne, Daniel Lee, and George Walton Williams. 32 notes.
G. R. Schroeder

317. Woodward, Michael Vaughan. THE PUBLICATIONS OF ELLIS MERTON COULTER TO 1 JULY 1977. *Georgia Hist. Q.* 1977 61(3): 268-278. Provides a bibliography of books and articles authored, coauthored and edited by Ellis Merton Coulter during 1912-77. His writings deal primarily with Southern history and Georgia history in particular. The list excludes book reviews and newspaper articles.
G. R. Schroeder

318. York, Maurice C. THE DIALECTIC AND PHILANTHROPIC SOCIETIES' CONTRIBUTIONS TO THE LIBRARY OF THE UNIVERSITY OF NORTH CAROLINA, 1886-1906. *North Carolina Hist. Rev.* 1982 59(4): 327-353. Until 1886 the libraries of the University of North Carolina's two student literary and debating societies, the Dialectic Society and the Philanthropic Society, far

surpassed the university's collections. This situation, typical of most American schools at that time, changed as the university modernized its curriculum to train professionals, businessmen, scientists, and farmers, and introduced seminar, laboratory, and graduate instruction. During 1886-1906 the "Di" and "Phi" assisted in the transformation of the university library by merging their collections with the university's, contributing funds for purchase of books and periodicals, helping administer the collections, and providing some library endowment funds. Based on archival records of the University of North Carolina and the two societies, personal papers of key librarians and faculty members, early histories of the university, school magazines, and newspapers; 25 illus., 59 notes.
T. L. Savitt

319. Zeeck, B. THE TEXAS TECH UNIVERSITY MUSEUM. *J. of the West* 1979 18(4): 104-106. The Museum of Texas Tech University sponsors research, publishes scholarly reports, and designs exhibits centered on the theme of arid and semi-arid environments, and man's adaptation to them. A full program of lectures, seminars, classes, and concerts provides education for students and the public. Two organizations, the West Texas Museum Association, and the Ranching Heritage Association operate within the museum. 5 photos.
B. S. Porter

320. —. ACCESSIONS LIST, WEST VIRGINIA COLLECTION, WEST VIRGINIA UNIVERSITY. *West Virginia Hist.* 1975 36(2): 159-176. Lists the archives, manuscripts, and books recently acquired by the West Virginia Collection of West Virginia University in Morgantown, including some 19th-century business records.
J. H. Broussard

321. —. ACCESSIONS REGISTRY, 1973. GEORGIA DEPOSITORIES. *Georgia Hist. Q.* 1973 58(1): 105-115. Covers libraries and archival depositories in Georgia. Includes institution, name of collection, dates covered, size and nature, and subjects covered.
D. L. Smith

322. —. ACCESSIONS REGISTRY, 1974: GEORGIA DEPOSITORIES. *Georgia Hist. Q.* 1975 59(1): 50-64. Presents sources for research material on Georgia history contained in the Atlanta Historical Society Archives, encompassing the 1774-1974 era.

323. —. [APPALACHIAN STUDIES BIBLIOGRAPHY AND DIRECTORY]. *Appalachian J.* 1978 5(1): 153-192. Comprises seven appendixes to a special issue on Appalachian studies: Bibliography, Guide to Resources, Guide to Current Periodicals, Appalachian Directory, Selected Bibliography of Unpublished Theses and Dissertations, and a Registers of Teachers, Scholars, Writers, and Disciplines, and Suggestions for Research.

324. —. A CHECKLIST OF SCHOLARSHIP ON SOUTHERN LITERATURE FOR 1977. *Mississippi Q.* 1978 31(2): 253-332. Alphabetical bibliography of research on southern authors during 1977.

325. —. DIRECTORY OF HISTORICAL AND GENEALOGICAL SOCIETIES IN ARKANSAS, 1977-1978. *Arkansas Hist. Q.* 1978 37(1): 84-87. Lists 70 societies including address, person to contact, and title of periodical publication, if any.
G. R. Schroeder

326. —. EDWIN ADAMS DAVIS: PROFILE OF AN EDITOR. *Louisiana Hist.* 1973 14(3): 308-309. Tribute to historian Edwin Adams Davis, editor of *Louisiana History* 1958-73.

327. —. FLORIDA HISTORY RESEARCH IN PROGRESS. *Florida Hist. Q.* 1973 51(3): 303-309. Lists, alphabetically by institution, 82 scholarly works in progress on Florida history. Includes M.A. theses, Ph.D. dissertations, and faculty projects, from 26 colleges and universities.
J. E. Findling

328. —. FLORIDA HISTORY RESEARCH IN PROGRESS. *Florida Hist. Q.* 1975 53(3): 332-342. Lists all Florida history research reported to the *Florida Historical Quarterly* as recently completed or in progress. Includes doctoral dissertations and masters

theses completed in 1974. Listed by name of school, includes sociology, anthropology, political science, archaeology, geography, and urban studies. R. V. Ritter

329. —. FLORIDA HISTORY IN PERIODICALS, 1973. *Florida Hist. Q. 1974 53(1): 74-78.* A selected bibliography including scholarly articles on Florida history, archaeology, geography, and anthropology published in state, regional, and national periodicals in 1973. Arranged alphabetically by author with full bibliographic information. R. V. Ritter

330. —. FLORIDA HISTORY IN PERIODICALS. *Florida Hist. Q. 1981 60(2): 204-207.* A list of 54 articles dealing with Florida history, geography, anthropology and archaeology, appearing in state, regional or national periodicals in 1980. N. A. Kuntz

331. —. FLORIDA HISTORY IN PERIODICALS. *Florida Hist. Q. 1977 56(1): 75-78.* This select bibliography lists 48 scholarly articles on Florida history, archeology, geography, and anthropology published in state, regional, and national journals in 1976. Not included in the listing are articles, notes, and documents which appeared in *Florida Historical Quarterly.* P. A. Beaber

332. —. FLORIDA HISTORY IN PERIODICALS. *Florida Hist. Q. 1983 62(1): 73-78.* Lists scholarly articles pertaining to Florida history, archaeology, geography, and anthropology published in 1982. N. A. Kuntz

333. —. FLORIDA'S HISTORY IN PERIODICALS. *Florida Hist. Q. 1975 54(1): 85-89.* A bibliography of scholarly articles in various branches of Florida studies, published in a variety of journals during the year 1974. Lists 61 articles, without annotation. J. E. Findling

334. —. INSTITUTE FOR SOUTHERN STUDIES REPORT: THE NEXT CHAPTER IN SOME OF OUR STORIES. *Southern Exposure 1979 7(4): 121-134.* Surveys some of the new material now available to fill out stories previously or currently run in *Southern Exposure.* In some instances gives an address where the printed material may be secured. Illus. R. V. Ritter

335. —. LABOR HISTORY BIBLIOGRAPHY. *Southern Exposure 1976 4(1-2): 160-169.* Lists books, articles, and dissertations on southern labor history, 1900-75.

336. —. LIBRARIES: THE HUMANITIES RESEARCH CENTER, UNIVERSITY OF TEXAS, AUSTIN. *Academe 1979 65(3): 205-208.* Traces the beginnings of the Humanities Research Center at the University of Texas, Austin, founded over 30 years ago by Harry Huntt Ransom, Pesident of the University of Texas, and describes the library's acquisitions and collections over the years of its existence.

337. —. "PIKE COUNTY ALABAMA TOMB RECORDS." *Alabama Hist. Q. 1973 35(1-4): i-416.* An alphabetized list compiled by the Pike County Historical Society of all tomb inscriptions of white cemeteries in Pike County, Alabama, started in September 1970 and completed in October 1973. There are about 15,400 names found in 126 cemeteries. The material is organized with the family name first, the code number for the cemetery, birth and death dates, and any inscriptions on the tomb. Map. E. E. Eminhizer

338. —. PROCEEDINGS OF THE VIRGINIA HISTORICAL SOCIETY IN ANNUAL MEETING, JANUARY 22, 1973. *Virginia Mag. of Hist. and Biog. 1973 81(2): 217-250.* Meeting elected Society's officers and then saw documentary film highlighting the career of Gen. George C. Marshall. Included are reports of the Finance, Library, Publications, Museum, Membership, and Buildings and Grounds committees and a Report of the President. R. F. Oaks

339. —. PROCEEDINGS OF THE VIRGINIA HISTORICAL SOCIETY IN ANNUAL MEETING, JANUARY 21, 1974. *Virginia Mag. of Hist. and Biog. 1974 82(2): 220-252.* Various committee reports including the Library Committee's 1973 acquisitions of manuscripts, books, newspapers, maps, and prints. R. F. Oaks

340. —. PROCEEDINGS OF THE VIRGINIA HISTORICAL SOCIETY IN ANNUAL MEETING, JANUARY 20, 1975. *Virginia Mag. of Hist. and Biog. 1975 83(2): 215-250.* Presents reports of the president and various committees of the Virginia Historical Society. Necrology and benefactors for 1974 are also reported. Vice Admiral Marmaduke Gresham Bayne, US Navy Commandant of the National War College, addressed the Society on "Seapower and Virginia." R. F. Oaks

341. —. SOUTHERN HISTORY IN PERIODICALS, 1975: A SELECTED BIBLIOGRAPHY. *J. of Southern Hist. 1976 42(2): 223-257.* Lists most scholarly articles in southern history published in 1975, and a few late articles published in 1974. Articles appear in alphabetical order under seven headings: General and Unclassified, Bibliography and Historiography, Economics, Negro and Slavery, Religion, Science and Medicine, and Social, Cultural, and Intellectual, and in chronological order under two other headings: Military and Naval, and Politics and Government. T. D. Schoonover

342. —. SOUTHERN HISTORY IN PERIODICALS, 1974: A SELECTED BIBLIOGRAPHY. *J. of Southern Hist. 1975 41(2): 201-232.* A bibliography of periodical articles on southern history published during 1974. Omitted are genealogical and descriptive articles of interest to few persons. Some 1973 writings are included. Arrangement is by topic, with authors listed alphabetically under each heading, except for the "Military and Naval" and "Politics and Government" categories, which are presented chronologically. V. L. Human

343. —. SOUTHERN HISTORY IN PERIODICALS, 1976: A SELECTED BIBLIOGRAPHY. *J. of Southern Hist 1977 43(2): 237-270.* Lists about 700 articles, most published during 1976, listed under nine categories: "General and unclassified," "Bibliography and historiography," "Blacks and slavery," "Economic," "Military and naval," "Politics and government," "Religion," "Science and medicine," and "Social, cultural, and intellectual." T. D. Schoonover

344. —. SOUTHERN HISTORY IN PERIODICALS, 1977: A SELECTED BIBLIOGRAPHY. *J. of Southern Hist. 1978 44(2): 233-267.* Includes articles published in 1977 (and some 1976 references which appeared too late for inclusion in last year's list). The bibliography is divided into the following classifications: general and unclassified, bibliography and historiography, blacks and slavery, economic, military and naval, politics and government, religion, science and medicine, and social, cultural, and intellectual. M. S. Legan

345. —. SOUTHERN HISTORY IN PERIODICALS, 1980: A SELECTED BIBLIOGRAPHY. *J. of Southern Hist. 1981 47(2): 227-257.* Lists about 650 articles published in 1980 (and a few delayed publications bearing earlier dates), classified under nine headings: General and Unclassified, Bibliography and Historiography, Blacks and Slavery, Economic, Military and Naval, Politics and Government, Religion, Science and Medicine, and Social, Cultural, and Intellectual. T. D. Schoonover

346. —. SOUTHERN HISTORY IN PERIODICALS, 1973: A SELECTED BIBLIOGRAPHY. *J. of Southern Hist. 1974 40(2): 245-278.* Lists about 675 articles, published either in 1973 or, in cases of late publication, 1972 or earlier. Articles appear in alphabetical order under seven headings, "General and Unclassified," "Bibliography and Historiography," "Economic," "Negro and

Slavery," "Religion," "Science and Medicine," and "Social, Cultural, and Intellectual," and in chronological order under two other headings, "Military and Naval," and "Politics and Government."

T. D. Schoonover

347. —. SOUTHERN HISTORY IN PERIODICALS 1978: A SELECTED BIBLIOGRAPHY. *J. of Southern Hist. 1979 45(2): 221-254.* About 750 articles published in 1978, except for a few in delayed 1977 publications, are classified under nine headings: General and Unclassified, Bibliography and Historiography, Blacks and Slavery, Economic, Military and Naval, Politics and Government, Religion, Science and Medicine, and Social, Cultural and Intellectual.

T. D. Schoonover

348. —. SOUTHERN HISTORY IN PERIODICALS, 1981: A SELECTED BIBLIOGRAPHY. *J. of Southern Hist. 1982 48(2): 225-259.* Lists about 680 articles published in 1981 (and a few late publications bearing earlier dates), classified under nine headings: General and Unclassified, Bibliography and Historiography, Blacks and Slavery, Economic, Military and Naval, Politics and Government, Religion, Science and Medicine, and Social, Cultural, and Intellectual.

T. Schoonover

349. —. SOUTHERN HISTORY IN PERIODICALS, 1979: A SELECTED BIBLIOGRAPHY. *J. of Southern Hist. 1980 46(2): 239-267.* Lists about 725 articles published in 1979 (and a few delayed publications bearing earlier dates), and classifies them under nine headings: General and Unclassified; Bibliography and Historiography; Blacks and Slavery; Economic, Military and Naval; Politics and Government; Religion; Science and Medicine; and Social, Cultural, and Intellectual.

T. D. Schoonover

350. —. SOUTHERN HISTORY IN PERIODICALS, 1982: A SELECTED BIBLIOGRAPHY. *J. of Southern Hist. 1983 49(2): 245-278.* A bibliography listing of about 690 articles, mostly published during 1982, under nine category headings: "General and Unclassified," "Bibliography and Historiography," "Blacks and Slavery," "Economic," "Military and Naval," "Politics and Government," "Religion," "Science and Medicine," and "Social, Cultural, and Intellectual"; 1600-1982.

T. Schoonover

351. —. SOUTHERN HISTORY IN PERIODICALS, 1972: A SELECTED BIBLIOGRAPHY. *J. of Southern Hist. 1973 39(2): 223-254.* A listing of scholarly articles on southern history published in periodicals in 1972. The list is reasonably complete, excluding genealogical and descriptive articles of limited interest. Includes late articles published in 1971. Arranges listings alphabetically by author beneath general headings, except for the "Military and Naval" and "Politics and Government" categories, which are chronologically arranged.

V. L. Human

352. —. TEXAS COLLECTORS: VII: MORRIS COOK. *Lib. Chronicle of the U. of Texas at Austin 1974 7: 102-104.* The University of Texas at San Antonio has recently acquired the J. Frank Dobie collection of Morris Cook, a collector of Texana since 1933.

353. —. THE THREE WOMEN PRESIDENTS OF THE SOUTHERN HISTORICAL ASSOCIATION. *Southern Studies 1981 20(2): 101-121.*
Bleser, Carol K. INTRODUCTION, *pp. 101-102.*
Cox, LaWanda. ELLA LONN, *pp. 102-110.*
Weaver, Blanche Clark. KATHRYN TRIMMER ABBY HANNA, *pp. 110-115.*
Heath, Frederick M. MARY ELIZABETH MASSEY, *pp. 116-121.* Since its inception in 1935 the Southern Historical Association has had three women presidents: Ella Lonn (1878-1962) in 1946, Kathryn Trimmer Abby Hanna (1895-1967) in 1953, and Mary Elizabeth Massey (1915-1974) in 1972. All three taught in women's colleges, were outstanding and meticulous scholars who did their research primarily on the South, and included in their publications subjects in social history that were then unusual, such as women, foreigners, deserters, and exiles. Primary sources; 46 notes.

J. J. Buschen

354. —. [TWO VIEWS OF CLASS, CULTURE, AND POLITICS IN APPALACHIAN STUDIES]. *Appalachian J. 1982 9(2-3): 134-148.*
Billings, Dwight B. APPALACHIAN STUDIES: CLASS, CULTURE, AND POLITICS: I, *pp. 134-140.* Describes the course taught at the University of Kentucky which presents Appalachian Studies without contributing "to the reproduction of the dominant system of institutional power and class relations operating in the region, the nation, and the world," and which examines "the complex motivations and social functions of romantic tales capitalizing on hillbilly quaintness or of reform efforts and institution-building by mountain missionaries."
Reid, Herbert G. APPALACHIAN STUDIES: CLASS, CULTURE, AND POLITICS: II, *pp. 141-148.* States that "a central task of political education for democratic change is questioning the hegemony of the American corporate state" and that "a fundamental purpose of Appalachian Studies should be to help reconstruct a public sphere through which people can participate in democratizing the structures of political economy and everyday life."

355. —. WILLIAM MUNFORD ELLIS RACHAL: A TRIBUTE. *Virginia Mag. of Hist. and Biog. 1981 89(2): 131-134.* Reports the death of Rachal and publishes the declaration of the Virginia Historical Society Board of Trustees on his life and work. Rachal (1910-80), was editor of publications and recently acting director of the Society. The trustees praise Rachal's efforts, particularly on the *Virginia Magazine of History and Biography,* and on the James Madison *Papers.* Photo.

P. J. Woehrmann

356. —. WOMEN IN THE SOUTH: A BIBLIOGRAPHY. *Southern Exposure 1977 4(4): 98-103.* Includes works of general theory on women's studies, general studies of the South and southern women, autobiographies, biographies and memoirs of southern women, and southern women in literature, 18th-20th centuries.

N. Lederer

# Southern Black History

357. Beck, Tom. BUILDING A NEW WORLD: BLACK LABOR PHOTOGRAPHS. *Southern Exposure 1983 11(4): 52-55.* Presents photographs of black laborers and craftsmen in the South, which are part of a 1983 exhibit at the University of Maryland, Baltimore County.

358. Berry, Mary Frances. LINCOLN AND CIVIL RIGHTS FOR BLACKS. *Papers of the Abraham Lincoln Assoc. 1980 2: 46-57.* In his policies toward blacks, Lincoln struck a successful balance between personal idealism and practical political considerations of the day.

359. Bonacich, Edna. ABOLITION, THE EXTENSION OF SLAVERY, AND THE POSITION OF FREE BLACKS: A STUDY OF SPLIT LABOR MARKETS IN THE UNITED STATES, 1830-1863. *Am. J. of Sociol. 1975 81(3): 601-628.* Using the "split labor market" theory of ethnic and racial antagonism, this paper analyzes race relations in the pre-Civil War United States. Both slaves and free blacks are found to have been lower-priced sources of labor than whites, to whom they therefore posed a threat of displacement. Slavery was a system which gave southern capitalists total control of a cheap labor force, permitting extensive displacement. It also put the South in conflict with northern capital, because the latter depended on higher-priced (white) labor. Abolition threatened to increase competition between black and white labor, spreading the problem to all regions and segments of the economy. But manumission also made blacks more vulnerable to counterattacks by white labor in the form of either exclusion or caste. The various class interests of the three parties to split labor markets are presented for the North, South, and West on the issues of abolition, the extension of slavery, and the position of free

blacks. It is argued that an understanding of the interests of the white working class and its power to implement them is of major importance for untangling race relations before the Civil War.

J

360. Borchert, James. HISTORICAL PHOTO-ANALYSIS: A RESEARCH METHOD. *Hist. Methods 1982 15(2): 35-44.* Using a photographic collection of black migrants in Washington, D.C., during the Depression as a case in point, advocates a methodology concerned with material culture and behavior. Validity and bias are highly significant. The use of space is also instructive. The ultimate value of photography is to balance the historian's excessive reliance on the written word. 4 photos, 42 notes.                    D. K. Pickens

361. Boston, Thomas D. CAPITALIST DEVELOPMENT AND AFRO-AMERICAN LAND TENANCY. *Sci. & Soc. 1982-83 46(4): 445-460.* Traces the shifting relationship of blacks to Southern land and land tenancy from slavery to the present, noting especially the social relations of production in the contract labor system and, later, sharecropping. Secondary sources; 38 notes.

R. E. Butchart

362. Bradford, M. E. A FIRE BELL IN THE NIGHT: THE SOUTHERN CONSERVATIVE VIEW. *Modern Age 1973 17(1): 9-16.* At present the most interesting implication of American history to southern conservatives is evidence that their ideas about millennialism were correct, because they had endured it in connection with blacks, even as blacks endured it with hasty and uncircumstanced emancipation. Because American southerners of all colors have had time to learn that race problems are too complex to be easily solved, that they can only be accommodated, there has developed an immunity to millennialism in a racial context. Based on secondary sources; 15 notes.                    M. L. Lifka

363. Bradley, Frank. PERSONAL PROPERTY TAXES IN VIRGINIA—A GENEALOGICAL GOLDMINE. *J. of the Afro-American Hist. and Geneal. Soc. 1982 3(3): 125-136.* Presents the Charles City County tax list for 1782-87, which includes the names of free heads of households, and three numerals indicating: 1) number of free males over 21, 2) number of Negro slaves over 16, and 3) number of Negro slaves under 16.

364. Campbell, Rex R.; Johnson, Daniel M.; and Stangler, Gary. RETURN MIGRATION OF BLACK PEOPLE TO THE SOUTH. *Rural Sociol. 1974 39(4): 514-528.*

365. Carter, Purvis M. THE NEGRO IN PERIODICAL LITERATURE, 1970-1972. *J. of Negro Hist. 1978 63(1): 87-91, (2): 161-189, (3): 262-306.* Part I. Annotated bibliography of periodical literature printed 1970-72 under the headings: Ante-bellum, Civil War, and Reconstruction. Part II. Continues under the following headings: education, intellect, international affairs, labor, Latin America, and legislation. Part III. Covers medicine, the military, race relations, religion, source material, and slavery.

366. Corzine, Jay; Creech, James; and Corzine, Lin. BLACK CONCENTRATION AND LYNCHINGS IN THE SOUTH: TESTING BLALOCK'S POWER-THREAT HYPOTHESIS. *Social Forces 1983 61(3): 774-796.* A review of past tests of Blalock's propositions predicting relationships between minority percentage and discrimination shows significant gaps. Lynching rates of blacks in Southern counties between 1889 and 1931 are used to test the power-threat hypothesis that minority concentration is positively related, with increasing slope, to level of discrimination. The hypothesis is supported in the total South, but separate analyses of the deep South and border South reveal subregional variation, with the predicted relationship found only in the deep South. Thus, the effect of minority percentage on discrimination is specific to particular cultural and/or socioeconomic contexts.                    J/S

367. Crowe, Charles. HISTORIANS AND "BENIGN NEGLECT": CONSERVATIVE TRENDS IN SOUTHERN HISTORY AND BLACK STUDIES. *Rev. in Am. Hist. 1974 2(2): 163-173.* The new conservative Southern History, which has attempted to revive the reputation of Ulrich Bonnell Phillips (1877-

1934) by overlooking his corrosive racism, reflects a new "benign neglect" of racial justice and a dwindling commitment to Black History. A review essay. 13 notes.                    W. D. Piersen

368. Culpepper, Betty M. GENEALOGICAL RESOURCES AT THE MOORLAND-SPINGARN RESEARCH CENTER. *J. of the Afro-American Hist. and Geneal. Soc. 1981 2(3): 93-98.* Brief history of Howard University, founded in 1867, and its Moorland-Spingarn Research Center, focusing on the center's purpose and rich resources for Afro-American genealogy.

369. Curtis, Janet A. GREEN SPRING CHURCH NEGRO CEMETERY, HARFORD COUNTY, MARYLAND. *J. of the Afro-American Hist. and Geneal. Soc. 1981 2(3): 116.* Lists the inscriptions from the Green Spring Church Negro Cemetery in Harford County, Maryland, that date from the late 19th century.

370. DuBois, W. E. B. BEHOLD THE LAND. *Freedomways 1975 15(3): 206-211.* Reprint of a speech made in 1946 characterizing life for Negroes in the South.

371. Dyer, Thomas G. AN EARLY BLACK TEXTBOOK: *FLOYD'S FLOWERS OR DUTY AND BEAUTY FOR COLORED CHILDREN. Phylon 1976 37(4): 359-361.* Floyd's Flowers or Duty and Beauty for Colored Children (1905), by Silas X. Floyd of Augusta, Georgia, deserves careful analysis as a rare text written for blacks by a black. Much of its content betrayed an orientation to conventional morality and the self-help philosophy, but it also offered black children a glimpse into their rich historical heritage. The book "mirrored the powerful urge toward racial consciousness and self-confidence which existed among American blacks during one of the most difficult periods in their history." 7 notes.

E. P. Stickney

372. Friedman, Lawrence J. LIFE "IN THE LION'S MOUTH": ANOTHER LOOK AT BOOKER T. WASHINGTON. *J. of Negro Hist. 1974 59(4): 337-351.* Examines the failure of the recent historians and biographers of Booker T. Washington to understand the black leader's constantly changing tactics and rhetoric, which were the result of increasing racist pressures and racial self-hate among faltering black leaders elsewhere. Based on primary sources in the Library of Congress and secondary sources; 64 notes.

N. G. Sapper

373. Gavins, Raymond. HANCOCK, JACKSON, AND YOUNG: VIRGINIA'S BLACK TRIUMVIRATE, 1930-1945. *Virginia Mag. of Hist. and Biog. 1977 85(4): 470-486.* George B. Hancock, Luther P. Jackson, and Plummer B. Young have not received enough attention for their part in shaping the goals and strategies of blacks in Virginia and throughout the South. During the Depression, New Deal, and World War II, they attempted to improve the plight of blacks and to enlist white support for reform. Though essentially moderate, they were the precursors of later civil rights activists. Based on primary sources, interviews, newspapers, and secondary works; 40 notes.                    R. F. Oaks

374. Gayle, Addison, Jr. STRANGERS IN A STRANGE LAND. *Southern Exposure 1975 3(1): 4-7.* The mass migration of Negroes to the North after the American Civil War was a cultural loss. Black authors, cut off from their roots in the South and their source of creative inspiration, wrote distorted views of Black life. Whites and middle-class blacks demanded that "the reality of the racial problem be fictionalized," but overlooked black writers such as Jean Toomer (1894-1967) and Zora Hurston (1901-60) who portrayed the strength, endurance, and survival of their people. Primary sources; illus.                    G. A. Bolton

375. Gillette, Michael L. THE RISE OF THE NAACP IN TEXAS. *Southwestern Hist. Q. 1978 81(4): 393-416.* The NAACP was revived in Texas in the late 1930's by Antonio Maceo Smith, a black Dallas insuranceman. Later, Lulu B. White of Houston and William J. Durham and Juanita Craft, both of Dallas, also joined the leadership. Helped by organizers from the national NAACP office, the Texas group challenged the exclusion of blacks from juries and Democratic primaries. By the late 1940's there were 104

branches and 30,000 members; the leaders were nearly all professionals and businessmen, with a few teachers. Primary and secondary sources; 9 illus., 48 notes.                    J. H. Broussard

376. Groff, Patrick. THE FREEDMEN'S BUREAU IN HIGH SCHOOL HISTORY TEXTS. *J. of Negro Educ.* 1982 51(4): 425-433. A good example of distortion of Afro-American history is the treatment of the Freedmen's Bureau in high school history textbooks. Of 36 currently used books, 7 failed to mention the bureau, 11 discussed the bureau in a superficial manner, 9 provided positive evaluations, 5 implied that the bureau was not altogether successful, and only 4 made historically accurate statements about the bureau and its shortcomings.                    A. G. Belles

377. Hawkins, Homer C. TRENDS IN BLACK MIGRATION FROM 1863 TO 1960. *Phylon* 1973 34(2): 140-152. An account of Negro migration, first to the southwest, then westward to Oklahoma Territory where blacks such as Edward Preston McCabe founded Langston, an all-black community, and finally moved northward to the larger metropolitan areas.

378. Henry, Aaron; Long, Worth, interviewer. AARON HENRY FROM CLARKSDALE. *Southern Changes* 1983 5(5): 9-12. Autobiographical recollections of Aaron Henry, sketching his youth and involvement in the movement for black civil rights in Mississippi.

379. Jackson, Juanita; Slaughter, Sabra; and Blake, J. Herman. THE SEA ISLANDS AS A CULTURAL RESOURCE. *Black Scholar* 1974 5(6): 32-39. The Sea Islands or Gullah Area (the islands off the coast of South Carolina and Georgia) represent some of the most outstanding opportunities to black scholars for research. The unique history and geography of the area have combined to produce one of the most distinctive reservoirs of African-American culture in the United States. The isolation of the islands and the large numbers of slaves meant that the influence of American white culture upon African and slave culture was minimal. Areas in need of further study include African survivals and slavery, black genealogy, and contemporary Gullah culture. Based on primary and secondary sources; 14 notes.                    M. M. McCarthy

380. Johnson, Jerah. MARCUS B. CHRISTIAN AND THE WPA HISTORY OF BLACK PEOPLE IN LOUISIANA. *Louisiana Hist.* 1979 20(1): 113-115. Referring to a previous article on the Louisiana Federal Writers' Project at Dillard University, discusses the efforts of the project's director, Marcus B. Christian (1898-1976), to compile and write the history of blacks in Louisiana. All of his note cards and poems, as well as his unfinished history, are now deposited in the archives of the University of New Orleans. The University is also presently establishing a Marcus B. Christian Lectureship in Christian's honor.                    L. N. Powell

381. Jones, Yvonne V. KINSHIP AFFILIATION THROUGH TIME: BLACK HOMECOMINGS AND FAMILY REUNIONS IN A NORTH CAROLINA COUNTY. *Ethnohistory* 1980 27(1): 49-66. Annual homecomings and family reunions have reinforced ties of kinship and affinity over time among the black residents of a rural hamlet in Montgomery County, North Carolina. These annual ceremonies show the status one holds as a resident of the hamlet, in opposition to other such hamlets in the country, one's status as a member of a specific kin unit within the hamlet vis-a-vis other such units, and one's status as an affine. Utilizes historical sources (census records, oral histories, and local church and family records), in addition to participant observation, to analyze the formation of kin units and their subsequent segmentation over time.
                    J/S

382. King, Andrew A. BOOKER T. WASHINGTON AND THE MYTH OF HEROIC MATERIALISM. *Q. J. of Speech* 1974 60(3): 323-327. This article suggests that the traditional view of Booker T. Washington as a clever diplomat with an astonishing ability to ignore the realities of racism is inadequate. Seen from the standpoint of the myth critic, Washington's rhetoric illuminates the way in which cultural scenarios shape and restrict perception.                    J

383. Koroleva, A. P. BUKERISM [Bookerism]. *Voprosy Istorii* [USSR] 1976 (7): 123-137. Examines the career, writings, and influence of Booker T. Washington and the Tuskegee Institute. Shows that ruling circles in the United States were prepared to buy off black leaders and cause divisions within the black community. In addition, Washington's principles of free competition and individualism, borrowed from classical economics, no longer corresponded with reality. Bookerism is the ideology of the bourgeois exploiting upper levels of the Afro-American population. Based on secondary sources; 81 notes.                    C. J. Read

384. Malval, Fritz J. THE ARCHIVES OF HAMPTON INSTITUTE, HAMPTON, VIRGINIA. *J. of the Afro-American Hist. and Geneal. Soc.* 1982 3(1): 14-17. Lists the 24 volumes of the *Guide to the Archives* prepared with a National Endowment for the Humanities grant in 1977; the Hampton Institute Archives originated in 1967 as an archive for materials on the history and culture of blacks and Indians in the United States.

385. Marable, Manning. GROUNDINGS WITH MY SISTERS: PATRIARCHY AND THE EXPLOITATION OF BLACK WOMEN. *J. of Ethnic Studies* 1983 11(2): 1-39. "The actual practice of the Black Power movement was the perpetuation of the structures of White patriarchy under the guise of 'blackness.'" The struggle to destroy slavery, and the economic and political battles of Reconstruction, coincided with the entrenchment of patriarchal relations within the black community, an inevitable outgrowth of a capitalist society dominated by whites. Surveys progressive black leaders who spoke out for equality for black women, including Ida B. Wells, Mary Church Terrell, and W. E. B. DuBois. Based on secondary sources and commentaries, including black women's poetry; 4 tables, 86 notes.                    G. J. Bobango

386. Martin, Tony. DID W. E. B. DU BOIS PLAGIARIZE? *Afro-Americans in New York Life and Hist.* 1982 6(1): 51-53. W. E. B. Du Bois either intentionally or inadvertently plagiarized from Charles H. Wesley's *Negro Labor in the United States, 1850-1925* (1927), in *Black Reconstruction in America, 1860-1880* (1935).

387. McMurry, Linda O. A BLACK INTELLECTUAL IN THE NEW SOUTH: MONROE NATHAN WORK, 1866-1945. *Phylon* 1980 41(4): 333-344. Monroe Nathan Work, a black sociologist, began his career in the early 20th century. Caught in the ideological struggle between Booker T. Washington and W. E. B. DuBois, he tried to discover where the talents of black people could best be used in the search for recognition and rights. He sought to win the support of southern whites for the black cause. Based on primary materials in the Tuskegee Institute Archives and the Library of Congress; 32 notes, biblio.                    J. V. Coutinho

388. Meier, August. BENJAMIN QUARLES AND THE HISTORIOGRAPHY OF BLACK AMERICA. *Civil War Hist.* 1980 26(2): 101-116. Discusses the work of black historian Benjamin Quarles (b. 1904), whose works, including *The Negro in the American Revolution* (1961), *Black Abolitionists* (1969), *The Negro in the Civil War* (1953), and *Lincoln and the Negro* (1962), are important studies focusing on the narrative aspects of history and on how Negroes affected their white allies. Based on interview with Quarles and Quarles's works; 56 notes.                    G. R. Schroeder

389. Mullen, Andrea Kirsten. THE HISTORIOGRAPHY OF BLACK TEXAS SETTLEMENTS: A SURVEY AND CRITIQUE. *Pioneer Am. Soc. Tr.* 1981 4: 75-85. Covers 1870's-1979.

390. Obadele, Imari Abubakari. THE STRUGGLE OF THE REPUBLIC OF NEW AFRICA. *Black Scholar* 1974 5(9): 32-41. Recounts the black struggle in Mississippi. In 1866 the freedmen settled on lands in the Mississippi Valley which had territorial status and were, therefore, free from US constitutional restraints. When the blacks took up arms against the United States in 1866, they were defending not only their personal farms but also their independent Negro governments, the first governments of the New African nation in North America. The major work of the Republic

of New Afrika now is the establishment of agricultural cooperatives across the state, owned by blacks in America's ghettoes as well as the people on the land.                    M. M. McCarthy

391. Rein, Martin and Elliot, Jeffrey M. "ROOTS": A NEW APPROACH TO TEACHING BLACK HISTORY. *Negro Hist. Bull. 1977 40(1): 664-667.* "The book, as well as the dramatizations, skillfully portray the realities of this historical period" is, perhaps, the key sentence in this article. The approach eminates from Miami-Dade Community College in Miami, Florida.
                    R. J. Jirran

392. Savage, Roaslind, comp. THE BLACK EXPERIENCE IN OKLAHOMA FROM TERRITORIAL STATUS TO 1980: A SELECTED BIBLIOGRAPHY. *Chronicles of Oklahoma 1980-81 58(4): 465-467.* A selected list of secondary books, articles, master's theses, and doctoral dissertations covering various aspects of Oklahoma's black history, ranging from early townbuilding to desegregation of public schools. Two television documentaries are also listed, including the Emmy Award winner "Through the Looking Glass Darkly" (1973).                    M. L. Tate

393. Scott, Patricia Bell. BLACK FOLKLORE IN TENNESSEE: A WORKING BIBLIOGRAPHY. *Tennessee Folklore Soc. Bull. 1978 44(3): 130-133.* A bibliography of 19th-20th-century black folklore, relating specifically to Tennessee as well as the South in general, printed 1940's-70's.

394. Shapiro, Herbert. EUGENE GENOVESE, MARXISM, AND THE STUDY OF SLAVERY. *J. of Ethnic Studies 1982 9(4): 87-100.* The work of Eugene Genovese is widely perceived within and beyond the historical profession as a product of creative Marxist scholarship, especially now that his *Roll, Jordan, Roll* has become for many reviewers "a definitive benchmark in the historiography of slavery." A full assessment of his scholarship is in order, due to the crucial questions Genovese raises, and close analysis of works such as *The Political Economy of Slavery* shows his greatest lacunae: the minimizing of the significance of black struggle and the magnifying of whatever elements of passivity can be found among blacks insofar as they actively participated in the Civil War. Accommodation and the plantation as community are overdone themes. Summarizes critiques of Genovese by King, Gutman, Woodward, and others. 67 notes.                    G. J. Bobango

395. Shatsillo, V. K. PROBLEMY ISTORII NEGROV S.SH.A. V ZHURNALE "THE CRISIS" [The history of American blacks in *Crisis* magazine]. *Voprosy Istorii [USSR] 1982 (11): 160-165.* The American journal, *Crisis*, was founded in 1910 by W. E. B. Du Bois, one of the greatest activists in the black liberation movement. It is now issued by the NAACP and has maintained its goal to improve blacks' sociopolitical position and to safeguard their rights strictly within the framework of the law. *Crisis* has paid special attention to the history of American blacks. In the past 70 years articles have regularly covered topics such as the role of blacks in the War of Independence and Civil War; abolition; the rise of racism and the Ku Klux Klan; racial discrimination in higher education; and blacks' economic plight. Note.                    J. Bamber

396. Sherer, Robert G., Jr. JOHN WILLIAM BEVERLY: ALABAMA'S FIRST NEGRO HISTORIAN. *Alabama R. 1973 26(3): 194-208.* Slave-born John William Beverly (d. 1924) wrote the *History of Alabama for Use in Schools and for General Reading* (1901), the only Alabama history text written by a Negro. A contemporary of Booker T. Washington, Beverly necessarily wrote of racial matters circumspectly, yet sought to present his people in positive and constructive light. Biographical details. Based on primary and secondary sources; 42 notes.                    J. F. Vivian

397. Sitton, Thad. BLACK HISTORY FROM THE COMMUNITY: THE STRATEGIES OF FIELDWORK. *J. of Negro Educ. 1981 50(2): 171-181.* Suggestions, drawn from a successful project in Caldwell County, Texas, for the creation of a public history proj-

ect, emphasizing oral history techniques and including excerpts from the Caldwell County experience. Personal experience and secondary sources; 23 notes.                    R. E. Butchart

398. Smith, John David. DUBOIS AND PHILLIPS: SYMBOLIC ANTAGONISTS OF THE PROGRESSIVE ERA. *Centennial Rev. 1980 24(1): 88-102.* Compares the thought and writings of W. E. B. Du Bois and Ulrich B. Phillips, the Progressive Era's foremost historians on slavery. Both men wrote numerous books and articles on slavery and southern topics. Du Bois stressed the injustice of slavery, the contributions of African culture to black life, and racial equality; Phillips wrote from the perspective of the white middle class, viewed blacks as inferior, and defended southern institutions. Both men could be harshly critical of other scholars, and their opposing viewpoints inevitably brought them into contention. Du Bois reviewed Phillips's work negatively and charged him with racism. In contrast, Phillips all but ignored Du Bois, probably because his southern outlook prevented him from taking black intellectuals seriously. Had Phillips held a broader social perspective, he might have benefited from Du Bois's viewpoints on slavery. 33 notes.
                    A. Hoffman

399. Smith, William David. THE BLACK SELF-CONCEPT: SOME HISTORICAL AND THEORETICAL REFLECTIONS. *J. of Black Studies 1980 10(3): 355-366.* Research on black self-image has been "varied and inconclusive," but recent research has showed positive self-concepts. Black reactions to slavery ranged from suicide and revolt to accommodation and submission. White attitudes and treatment of blacks during slavery and since put such pressures on blacks that they, "as a people, are not psychologically free." Eighteen propositions explain black self-concept, then 12 recommendations indicate ways of understanding and helping develop more positive black self-concepts.                    R. G. Sherer

400. Steirer, William F., Jr. EUGENE D. GENOVESE: MARXIST-ROMANTIC HISTORIAN OF THE SOUTH. *Southern Rev. 1974 10(4): 840-850.*

401. Strawn, John. BLACK HISTORY AND BLACK CULTURE: A REVIEW ESSAY. *J. of Ethnic Studies 1974 1(4): 99-108.* Review of John Blassingame's *The Slave Community: Plantation Life in the Ante-Bellum South* (New York: Oxford U. Press, 1972); George Rawick's *From Sundown to Sunup: The Making of the Black Community* (Westport, Connecticut: Greenwood Publishing Company, 1972); Peter Kolchin's *First Freedom: The Responses of Alabama's Blacks to Emancipation and Reconstruction* (Westport, Connecticut: Greenwood Press, Inc., 1972); William Warren Rogers' and Robert David Ward's *August Reckoning: Jack Turner and Racism in Post-Civil War Alabama* (Baton Rouge: Louisiana State U. Press, 1973). Finds that each addresses the historical problem of slave personality and culture. All provide insights, since narratives and autobiographical accounts are frequently used, but neither alone nor together do they provide a detailed account of the historical development of Black culture. Suggests that such a study should give a synthesis of Black history and assist in a better understanding of American history.                    T. W. Smith

402. Taylor, Henry L. TOWARD A HISTORIOGRAPHY OF BLACK URBAN HISTORY: A BOOK REVIEW ESSAY. *Afro-Americans in New York Hist. and Life 1980 4(2): 71-80.* Review essay of Lester Lemon's *Black Tennessean: 1900 to 1930* (Knoxville: U. of Tennessee, 1978); discusses the rise of southern urban black populations, ghetto formation, and interurban black community variation.

403. Uhlenberg, Peter. NONECONOMIC DETERMINANTS OF NONMIGRATION: SOCIOLOGICAL CONSIDERATIONS FOR MIGRATION THEORY. *Rural Sociol. 1973 38(3): 296-311.* To further understanding of migration determinants, I examine the experiences of three groupings in the U.S.: Negro movement from the South 1860-1920; Japanese-American migration from internment camps during World War II; and exodus from Southern Appalachia between 1930 and 1960. Each . . . illustrates the importance of noneconomic variables in determining migration and the worth to noting nonmigration to understand the migration process. I suggest

using a framework which examines motivation for and constraints upon migration for individuals as a starting point in developing migration theory. When migration is viewed within a social structure, dependence upon the local community and potential for assimilation elsewhere appear as critical determinants of whether motivation for migration becomes actual movement.... I encourage future migration research to avoid an overemphasis upon economic factors and to reject the argument that no generalization is possible.

A

404. Vickery, Kenneth P. "HERRENVOK" DEMOCRACY AND EGALITARIANISM IN SOUTH AFRICA AND THE U.S. SOUTH. *Comparative Studies in Soc. and Hist. [Great Britain] 1974 16(3): 309-328.* Treats racism in the South and in South Africa in the 19th and 20th centuries.

405. Walker, Clarence E. MASSA'S NEW CLOTHES: A CRITIQUE OF EUGENE D. GENOVESE ON SOUTHERN SOCIETY, MASTER-SLAVE RELATIONS, AND SLAVE BEHAVIOR. *Umoja: A Scholarly J. of Black Studies 1980 4(2): 114-130.* Criticizes the explanatory uses Eugene D. Genovese makes of Antonio Gramsci's concept of hegemony since the concept of hegemony is inadequate as a conceptual framework for the study of southern society, because it obscures more than it reveals and presents an interpretation of history that is at variance with the facts of southern life.

406. Winston, Michael R. SELECTED DOCUMENTS ILLUSTRATIVE OF SOME ASPECTS OF THE LIFE OF BLACKS BETWEEN 1774-1841. *J. of Negro Hist. 1976 6(1): 88-97.* The first document, signed by Patrick Henry, reflects the white colonists' determination to control persons of color in 1778 during the War for Independence. A deed of emancipation recorded in Virginia in 1798 illustrates the opposite side of slavery. A marriage permit for slaves, dated 1802, reveals slaves' lack of control over their lives. A letter from Abraham Byrd to John Morgan in 1838 protests a black woman's insistence that she be treated as a human being. The resolution of the Colored Citizens of Washington, D.C., concerning Liberia insists that free black people be given a free choice to oppose or support the program of the American Colonization Society. Documents were selected from the Manuscript Division of the Moorland-Spingarn Research Center.                    N. G. Sapper

407. Wright, George C. ORAL HISTORY AND THE SEARCH FOR THE BLACK PAST IN KENTUCKY. *Oral Hist. Rev. 1982 10: 73-91.* The study of black history poses a number of problems for the historian, particularly locating reliable sources of evidence. There are four major oral history projects in Kentucky that provide useful data about blacks: 1) the University of Louisville interviews of black Louisvillians; 2) the Louisville and Nashville Railroad oral histories at the University of Louisville; 3) the Lexington Urban League project of blacks; and 4) the black church in Kentucky. These interviews and the works of historians show the benefits and shortcomings of oral history research and its value to black history. Based on the Duke University doctoral theses, "Blacks in Louisville Kentucky, 1890-1930;" 28 notes.                    D. A. Yanchisin

408. Wynes, Charles E. THOMY LAFON: BLACK PHILANTHROPIST. *Midwest Q. 1981 22(2): 105-112.* Thomy Lafon, a 19th-century black philanthropist of New Orleans, contributed generously to various New Orleans charities during his life and in his will. A devout Catholic, he gave to charities of all denominations, without considering race, sex, or age. Several New Orleans institutions were named in his honor. Based on city directories, newspapers, and secondary sources; 15 notes, biblio.
M. E. Quinlivan

# SOCIETY, CULTURE, POLITICS, AND ECONOMY OF THE SOUTH: MULTIPERIOD

## Images of the South and Southern Society

**409.** Abbott, Shirley. SOUTHERN WOMEN AND THE INDIS-PENSABLE MYTH. *Am. Heritage 1982 34(1): 82-91.* White Southern women were not the fine ladies of *Gone With the Wind,* but were, themselves, often victims of the system. In turn, many Southern women were "closet abolitionists," sympathetic to the plight of the blacks but unable to do more than work quietly to alleviate the slaves' distress. 2 photos, 5 illus.　　　J. F. Paul

**410.** Adams, Frank. ADAMS' JOURNEY. *Southern Exposure 1978 6(3): 18-25.* Combines excerpts from oral interviews conducted by the author on a trip through the South for the Institute for Southern Studies. Dr. Lewis Jones, a retired black sociology professor from Tuskegee Institute, reveals his admiration of the principled stand taken by Judge James Edwin Horton when he presided over the trial of the Scottsboro Boys during the 1930's, a stand which resulted in community ostracism of the judge. Two inmates, confined in the Winona, Mississippi jail along with Mrs. Fanny Lou Hamer in the 1960's, reveal the manner in which they were coerced by their jailers to beat Mrs. Hamer. Gravediggers at Arlington National Cemetary, responsible for the interment of President John F. Kennedy, discuss the nature of their task and the situation existing at the grave of the dead President. Former Governor of Arkansas Orval Faubus discusses his early life, emphasizing his brief attendance at leftwing Commonwealth College in the 1930's, and the later political repercussions that this aspect of his life had during his gubernatorial campaigns.　　　N. Lederer

**411.** Adams, Michael. "HOW COME EVERYBODY DOWN HERE HAS THREE NAMES?": MARTIN RITT'S SOUTHERN FILMS. *Southern Q. 1981 19(3-4): 143-155.* Martin Ritt has directed as many films with Southern settings as anyone in recent years. The author briefly reviews Ritt's Southern films, *The Long Hot Summer* (1958), *The Sound and the Fury* (1959), *Sounder* (1972), *Conrack* (1974), *Casey's Shadow* (1978), *Norma Rae* (1979), and *Back Roads* (1981). While Ritt obviously loves the South he does not give his audience the insights into the region that he could. 2 photos, 20 notes.　　　B. D. Ledbetter

**412.** Alther, Lisa. INTO THE MELTING POT. *Mankind 1976 5(9): 8-10, 48-51.* Legally classified as nonwhites in the 19th century, the Melungeons of eastern Tennessee and southwest Virginia are mountaineers who have been described as descended from Portuguese explorers, medieval Welsh, or the white remnants of the Lost Colony of Sir Walter Raleigh. They are commonly viewed as a mixture of white, black, and Cherokee. Until recently the group remained isolated and extremely poor, but recently some members of the population entity have benefited from improved economic conditions in Appalachia and have moved to towns. Long disparaged and discriminated against, the Melungeons now exhibit a good deal of ethnic pride which is reaping benefits in tourism. The view of the Melungeons as a race is incorrect and should be replaced by one visualizing them as individuals.　　　N. Lederer

**413.** Armour, Robert A. HISTORY WRITTEN IN JAGGED LIGHTING: REALISTIC SOUTH VS. ROMANTIC SOUTH IN *THE BIRTH OF A NATION. Southern Q. 1981 19(3-4): 14-21.* Discusses filmmaker D. W. Griffith's motives behind his film *The Birth of a Nation* (1915). Griffith sincerely wanted to make a film depicting the truth about the Civil War as seen by the Southerner. However, his idealized view of the South, a view founded in his

Southern background, came into conflict with the documentary potential of the film, thus creating a highly controversial film. 13 notes.　　　B. D. Ledbetter

**414.** Austin, Wade. THE REAL BEVERLY HILLBILLIES. *Southern Q. 1981 19(3-4): 83-94.* Looks at a number of low-budget "hillbilly" films about life in the South made between 1935 and 1955. These films express the American myth that life is better in the country than in the city and that city slickers are no match for country dwellers. 2 photos, 14 notes.　　　B. D. Ledbetter

**415.** Barbera, Jack. TOMORROW AND TOMORROW AND *TOMORROW. Southern Q. 1981 19(3-4): 183-197.* Tomorrow was enthusiastically received by many film reviewers upon release in 1972. But the film never became the success that the reviewers said it would, probably because it was shot by an independent company that lacked adequate distribution plans and because it was shot in black and white. It is an excellent film about Southern life. Covers 1920-40. 2 photos, 12 notes.　　　B. D. Ledbetter

**416.** Bargainnier, Earl F. THE FALCONHURST SERIES: A NEW POPULAR IMAGE OF THE OLD SOUTH. *J. of Popular Culture 1976 10(2): 298-314.* Examination of the major elements and characters of the Falconhurst series of novels (1957-73) by Kyle Onstott (1887-1966) and Lance Horner (1903-70). The "moonlight and magnolias" image of the old South popularized in fiction particularly by the novels of Frank Yerby and *Gone With the Wind* (1936), has been replaced by this eight-volume series in which violence, sex, and miscegenation are the mainstays. Plots and subplots involving tensions surrounding the slave-breeding industry of Falconhurst, all contribute to the revised popular image. Primary and secondary sources; table, 4 charts, 13 notes.

D. G. Nielson

**417.** Bernheim, Mark. FLORIDA: THE PERMANENCE OF AMERICA'S IDYLL. *Modernist Studies [Canada] 1982 4: 125-145.* Assesses the extent to which the image, during the 1920's-30's, of Miami, Florida, as a "permanent idyll" mirrored the aspirations and values implicit in the American Dream; disillusionment reflected in Dos Passos's *The Big Money* and Theodore Dreiser's *Vanity Fair* pieces on Florida, set in when the symbol of Florida as idyll fell prey to urbanization, corruption, and the economic crisis of the Great Depression.

**418.** Birbalsingh, Frank M. W. ADOLPHE ROBERTS: CREOLE ROMANTIC. *Caribbean Q. [Jamaica] 1973 19(2): 100-107.* W. Adolphe Roberts (1886-1962), a Creole born in Jamaica where he became a journalist, emigrated to the United States in 1906 and became a noted historian, journalist, editor, lecturer, novelist, scholar, and poet. His novels, 1929-49, cover a variety of New World areas and subjects, but the most famous is his trilogy on Louisiana—*Royal Street, Brave Mardi Gras,* and *Creole Dusk.* All emphasize his fondness for Creole culture and his sadness at its passing. 5 notes.　　　R. L. Woodward, Jr.

**419.** Bohn, Thomas W. and Millichap, Joseph. FILM IMAGES OF OKLAHOMA. *Film & Hist. 1980 10(4): 83-89.* Attempts to identify, analyze, and evaluate feature-length narrative films from 1910 to 1970 which depict the physical, historical, and cultural images of Oklahoma, with special attention to the examination of tensions existing between Oklahoma's reality and its public image as created and communicated by these films.

**420.** Bradford, Ronald W. ALEXANDER BLACKBURN BRAD-FORD: A KNIGHT OF THE SOUTH (1799-1873). *J. of Mississippi Hist. 1981 43(1): 59-64.* A biographical sketch of Alexander Blackburn Bradford, reflecting the aristocratic nature of the Old

South. The chivalric traits of this "southern gentleman" are described in the areas of law, leadership, politics, and the military. The author discusses Bradford's service in the Second Seminole War against Osceola, his contributions in recruiting Tennesseeans to fight in the Texas Revolution, and his valor and leadership as third-in-command of the Mississippi regiment during the Mexican War. 23 notes.     M. S. Legan

421. Bruce, Dickson D., Jr. DEATH AS TESTIMONY IN THE OLD SOUTH. *Southern Humanities Rev. 1978 12(2): 123-131.* Mentions glorification of death scenes in southern literature and strong support for evangelism.

422. Brugger, Robert J. THE MIND OF THE OLD SOUTH: NEW VIEWS. *Virginia Q. Rev. 1980 56(2): 277-295.* Analyzes several recent studies as a basis for a new critical understanding of the thinking of the Old South, because "at first glance, little of antebellum Southern thought remains 'thinkable' to us." Using the thought of antebellum southerners and recent monographs, the author raises questions about the influence of futuristic views, evangelical piety, anxiety over the political structure, the tensions within antebellum society, and the personal intentions of individuals on southern society and action.     O. H. Zabel

423. Buckley, Thomas E., ed. THE DUTIES OF A WIFE: BISHOP JAMES MADISON TO HIS DAUGHTER, 1811. *Virginia Mag. of Hist. and Biog. 1983 91(1): 98-104.* In a letter written to his daughter, Susan Randolph, upon her 31 December 1811 marriage to Robert Scott, Episcopal Bishop James Madison (1749-1812) advised his daughter to be submissive, obedient, virtuous, and ladylike as a wife. Madison, a liberal who was President James Madison's second cousin, and a president of William and Mary College, expressed sentiments about women and marriage that were later echoed in the 19th-century's Feminine Ideal. Despite the male revolutionaries' love of independence, women's roles in the colonial period did not differ greatly from those that dominated the following century. Based on the original letter at the Virginia Historical Society, and secondary works on 19th-century female life; portrait, 11 notes.     D. J. Cimbala

424. Byrd, Edward L., Jr. THE OLD SOUTH AS MODERN MYTH. *Red River Valley Hist. Rev. 1974 1(1): 55-65.*

425. Campbell, Edward D. C., Jr. "BURN, MANDINGO, BURN": THE PLANTATION SOUTH IN FILM, 1958-1978. *Southern Q. 1981 19(3-4): 107-116.* The major films about the plantation South have reversed the stereotypes; the black rebellious slave is never condemned for his actions just as earlier films, including *The Birth of a Nation*, never condemned the white plantation owner. The film industry has gone from one extreme to the other. Photo, 10 notes.     B. D. Ledbetter

426. Chappell, Fred. THE IMAGE OF THE SOUTH IN FILM. *Southern Humanities Rev. 1978 12 (4): 303-311.* Whether portrayed as Eden or Hell, the South in films, 1920's-70's, has come to be represented as a mythologized and unrealistic place.

427. Connelly, Thomas L. THE IMAGE AND THE GENERAL: ROBERT E. LEE IN AMERICAN HISTORIOGRAPHY. *Civil War Hist. 1973 19(1): 50-64.* Analyzes the evolution of the image of General Robert Edward Lee from the end of the Civil War into the early 20th century when he became a national hero. Without detracting from the greatness of the man, one might question whether this process of deification has not led to distortions. Secondary sources; 25 notes.     E. C. Murdock

428. Cook, Robert Cecil. A MEMOIR: TWO UNCLES OF A LONG TIME AGO. *J. of Mississippi Hist. 1978 40(2): 167-181.* A memoir of the author's boyhood at Magowah Place near Columbus, Mississippi, in the early 20th century. Describes his two uncles, both Confederate veterans. Supplies anecdotes of the Civil War and the author's relationships with his aunt and several former slaves.     M. S. Legan

429. Corte, Robert S. THE CELEBRATED WHITE SULPHUR SPRINGS OF GREENBRIER: NINETEENTH CENTURY TRAVEL ACCOUNTS. *West Virginia Hist. 1981 42(3-4): 191-221.* The 19th-century travel accounts by Harriet Martineau, "Viator," John H. B. Latrobe, "Peregrine Prolix," and "Mark Pencil" chronicle the rise of White Sulphur Springs, West Virginia, from a remote place to a fashionable antebellum spa. Discusses its decline and notes the influence of the railroads, and of Henry Clay, James Calwell, Major Baylis Anderson, and Robert E. Lee.

    J. D. Neville

430. Cummings, Scott and Pinnel, Charles Wellford, III. RACIAL DOUBLE STANDARDS OF MORALITY IN A SMALL SOUTHERN COMMUNITY: ANOTHER LOOK AT MYRDAL'S AMERICAN DILEMMA. *J. of Black Studies 1978 9(1): 67-86.* Applying L. Kohlberg's methodology and theory of social psychology to a random sample of 241 white voters in a Virginia town produced results contradicting Gunnar Myrdal's conclusion that Americans face a dilemma in reconciling racism and the American Creed. Myrdal oversimplified morality by not defining it precisely and by assuming that Americans shared one type of morality which could be identified with the American Creed. He also overlooked the possibility that the creed contains internal contradictions which may allow racists to see no conflict between their beliefs and the creed. Primary and secondary sources; 2 tables, note, biblio.     R. G. Sherer

431. Curran, Trisha. *GONE WITH THE WIND:* AN AMERICAN TRAGEDY. *Southern Q. 1981 19(3-4): 47-57.* Almost four decades after its release, the American Film Institute voted *Gone With the Wind* the greatest American movie ever made. The overwhelming popularity of the film lies in the fact that it is the greatest American tragedy ever filmed. As the modern American tragedy, the film allows triumph over despair and such stories are very popular with the American public. Photo, 6 notes.

    B. D. Ledbetter

432. Drake, Robert. THE LEGACY OF ALLEN TATE. *Modern Age 1979 23(3): 272-275.* Discusses poet, critic, biographer, and novelist Allen Tate (1899-1979). Tate's unique contribution was in seeing the cause of the South as the same as that of Western civilization: traditional, conservative, religious, and ordered. Tate was a proponent of regionalism rather than provincialism. From the perspective of his southern heritage he looked out on the world for universal values.     C. A. D'Aniello

433. Eaton, Clement. THE ROLE OF HONOR IN SOUTHERN SOCIETY. *Southern Humanities Rev. 1976 (Special Issue): 47-58.* Discusses the role of the romantic concept of honor in the social stratification, social status, and values of the South, 1820-61.

434. Eaton, Richard Bozman. GEORGE W. CABLE AND THE HISTORICAL ROMANCE. *Southern Literary J. 1975 8(1): 82-94.* Discusses social realism in the 19th-century novels of George Washington Cable, emphasizing his depiction of racism in New Orleans, Louisiana.

435. Eidson, John Olin. RECOLLECTIONS OF FROST'S MANY VISITS TO GEORGIA. *Georgia Life 1977 4(3): 34-35.* Robert Frost spent the last 30 years of his life annually visiting the University of Georgia to discuss his work and give poetry readings, thus creating a special affinity between himself and the people of Georgia (1935-63).

436. Farley, Benjamin W. GEORGE W. CABLE: PRESBYTERIAN ROMANCER, REFORMER, BIBLE TEACHER. *J. of Presbyterian Hist. 1980 58(2): 166-181.* In the last 25 years there have been three biographies of George Washington Cable (1844-1925), Southern Presbyterian, ex-Confederate soldier, and author of Creole stories. All three acknowledge his Presbyterian roots, and examine the influence of his church and home on his life and work. Concentrates attention on Cable as a Presbyterian, and explores his life, stories, and reforming activities in light of his Calvinistic heritage. Emphasizes the influence of his early home and training on his work and habits, the role of New Orleans Presbyterianism in his development, and, as his career advanced and his vision matured,

how he drew upon and reacted against his Presbyterian heritage. Based on Cable's writings and studies about him, particularly the biography by Lucy Leffingwell Cable Biklè, *George W. Cable, His Life and Letters* (1928); illus., 65 notes. H. M. Parker, Jr.

437. Faucette, Shirley. CLINTON—YESTERDAY. *J. of Mississippi Hist. 1978 40(3): 215-230.* First presented at the 3 March 1978 meeting of the Mississippi Historical Society, this paper contains material drawn from antebellum reminiscences on the history of Clinton, Mississippi. The author excerpts from extant accounts which describe the people and their society and culture in and around the health resort of Mr. Salus (the original name of Clinton). Significant inhabitants discussed in depth include Gideon Fitz, an early settler, Walter Leake, who became governor and whose plantation was visited by his friend, Marquis de Lafayette, and Cowles Mead, who, as acting governor, was responsible for the arrest in Natchez of Aaron Burr for treason. Especially noteworthy are the brief accounts of local duels, the coming of the railroad, and the development of the community as an educational center for the State. M. S. Legan

438. Feinberg, Andrew. VERMONT'S AMBIVALENT SOUTHERNER. *Horizon 1981 24(5): 56-60.* Brief introductory biography of novelist Lisa Alther, born in Kingsport, Tennessee, who now lives in Hinesburg, Vermont, focusing on the success of her first novel, *Kinflicks* (1976), and discusses her second novel, *Original Sins* (1981), about the transition of the South in the past 25 years.

439. Ford, Oliver. ADA JACK CARVER: THE BIOGRAPHY OF A SOUTHERN TRADITIONALIST. *Southern Studies 1979 18(2): 133-178.* Ada Jack Carver's (1890-1972) short stories, novels, and plays in the 1920's, set in her native region of Natchitoches, Louisiana, were awarded literary prizes and enthusiastic public acclaim. Her reputation has not remained high because she was unable to transcend her own circumstances. Her works are suffused with southern romanticism, stock characters, and plots in which characters are unable to break out of their isolation or niche in society. She was unable to accept the realism in the literature of her time. Her stories concerned, for the most part, alienated or socially disenfranchised and aging women. Her most successful short story was "Redbone" in 1924. Based on Melrose Collection at Northwestern State U., Louisiana, and other primary sources; 76 notes. J. J. Buschen

440. Fox-Genovese, Elizabeth. SCARLETT O'HARA: THE SOUTHERN LADY AS NEW WOMAN. *Am. Q. 1981 33(4): 391-411.* In *Gone with the Wind* (1936), a novel ostensibly about the South in the 1860's, Margaret Mitchell used Atlanta, Georgia, to symbolize a national transition from rural to urban, agrarian to industrial civilization. Although Mitchell appears to have affirmed the bourgeois values that emerged in the 1860's and persisted to the 1930's, the confusion of her heroine, Scarlett O'Hara, about female sexuality, gender identity, and gender role reflected the early 20th-century crisis in the bourgeois family and undermined Mitchell's support for middle-class social attitudes. Primary sources; 22 notes. E. L. Keyser

441. French, Warren. INTRODUCTION: "THE SOUTHERN": ANOTHER LOST CAUSE? *Southern Q. 1981 19(3-4): 3-13.* Introduces the issue devoted to "The South and Film." The issue discusses some of the major film classics about the South, attempts to create a Southern film genre, considers female characters in the South, William Faulkner, and the difficulties of shooting film on regional locations in the South. Covers 1915-81. 4 photos. B. D. Ledbetter

442. Gardner, Lloyd. A NORTH CAROLINA YANKEE IN KING ARTHUR'S COURT. *Rev. in Am. Hist. 1979 7(1): 103-106.* Review article prompted by John Milton Cooper, Jr.'s *Walter Hines Page: The Southerner as American, 1855-1918* (Chapel Hill: The U. of North Carolina Pr., 1977).

443. Goodwyn, Frank. THE INGENIOUS GENTLEMAN AND THE EXASPERATING LADY: DON QUIXOTE DE LA MANCHA AND SCARLETT O'HARA. *J. of Popular Culture 1982 16(1): 55-71.* Although of different times and settings, Miguel de Cervantes's *Don Quixote de la Mancha,* and Margaret Mitchell's *Gone With the Wind,* have much in common beyond being noted literary successes. In similar political atmospheres, both essentially deal with the same theme of genteel tradition, the inequalities it perpetuates, and the disillusionments suffered as the protagonists of each novel move beyond the traditions into reality. 3 notes. D. G. Nielson

444. Hackney, Sheldon. THE SOUTH AS A COUNTERCULTURE. *Am. Scholar 1973 42(2): 283-293.* Today's counterculture focuses on the quality of life and the individual's right to determine his own direction. "There is a large area of agreement between the culture of the South as understood by the Agrarians and the contemporary counterculture." Discusses the limitations of this similarity. E. P. Stickney

445. Harwell, Richard B. RECENT ISSUES OF WRITINGS BY ERSKINE CALDWELL. *Georgia Hist. Q. 1978 62(2): 169-172.* Erskine Caldwell wrote several controversial novels during the 1930's dealing with the rural poor in Georgia. Discusses the response, especially to *Tobacco Road,* as the book has recently been reissued. *God's Little Acre, Trouble in July,* and *Recollections of a Visitor on Earth* have also been republished.

G. R. Schroeder

446. Hobson, Fred. JAMES MC BRIDE DABBS: ISAAC MC CASLIN IN SOUTH CAROLINA. *Virginia Q. Rev. 1977 53(4): 640-659.* The South has changed and James McBride Dabbs, who resembles William Faulkner's Isaac McCaslin, may be the last Southerner to have "the visceral need" to describe the South. Describes Dabbs' plea for racial understanding and his proclamation of God's role in southern history and the failure of southern Protestantism in *The Southern Heritage* (1958), *Who Speaks for the South?* (1964), and *Haunted by God* (1972). O. H. Zabel

447. Holditch, W. Kenneth. *THE GRANDISSIMES* AND THE FRENCH QUARTER. *Southern Q. 1980 18(4): 34-50.* George Washington Cable's most significant novel, *The Grandissimes* (1880), relies heavily on the French Quarter of New Orleans as Cable pictured it to exist in the early 19th century. Knowledge of the French Quarter is necessary to understand the fiction of Cable. 10 photos, (one of Cable's home and nine taken in the French Quarter), 3 notes. B. D. Ledbetter

448. Hollis, Daniel W., III. GROVER CLEVELAND HALL: THE ANATOMIZATION OF A SOUTHERN JOURNALIST'S PHILOSOPHY. *Alabama Hist. Q. 1980 42(1-2): 87-101.* Grover Cleveland Hall used his personal journalism in the early 20th century to enjoin and cajole Southern consciousness. Termed a "Southern progressive," his ideas were rooted in family heritage and early newspaper experience. He was most influential as editor of the Montgomery, Alabama, *Advertiser.* Primary sources; 57 notes. A. Drysdale

449. Jeter, Ida. *JEZEBEL* AND THE EMERGENCE OF THE HOLLYWOOD TRADITION OF A DECADENT SOUTH. *Southern Q. 1981 19(3-4): 31-46.* Before World War II, the South in films was generally viewed as a grand old South where genteel Southern customs prevailed. After the war, the South was generally viewed as a section of decadence and depravity. The film *Jezebel* (1938) although containing traces of the romanticized view of the South prefigured the post-World War II view of the section by exploring the moral decay of the South. Photo, 6 notes. B. D. Ledbetter

450. Keller, Mark. T. B. THORPE'S 'TOM OWEN, THE BEE-HUNTER': SOUTHWESTERN HUMOR'S 'ORIGIN OF SPECIES.' *Southern Studies 1979 18(1): 89-101.* Thomas Bangs Thorpe of Louisiana wrote the two most famous humorous short stories to come out of the 19th century Old Southwest: "The Big Bear of Arkansas" (1841) and "Tom Owen, the Bee-Hunter" (1839). Both appeared in the *Spirit of the Times,* a New York City newspaper. In 1859 Thorpe wrote an essay, "Reminiscences of Tom Owen the Bee Hunter," for the *Spirit of the Times;* it is reprinted here. The

essay describes the real Tom Owen, his backwoods life, several anecdotes about him, and how Thorpe came to write and publish the story. 15 notes.      J. J. Buschen

451. Klotter, James C. THE BLACK SOUTH AND WHITE APPALACHIA. *J. of Am. Hist. 1980 66(4): 832-849.* Examines the similarity in stereotypes applied to both black slaves and Appalachian whites, and in particular the origins of stereotypes for Appalachian whites after the Civil War. By 1900, most Northerners had become impatient with their efforts to improve blacks and had shifted their attention to Appalachian whites, whom they regarded as "true" or "pure" Anglo-Saxons. These Appalachian Anglo-Saxons replaced blacks in the national awareness; they were deemed worthy of saving and civilizing because they were backward, poor, and white. 64 notes.      T. P. Linkfield

452. Kreyling, Michael. NATIONALIZING THE SOUTHERN HERO: ADAMS AND JAMES. *Mississippi Q. 1981 34(4): 383-402.* Examines the treatment of the Southern hero and Southern society in the writings of Henry Adams and Henry James.

453. Lee, David D. APPALACHIA ON FILM: THE MAKING OF *SERGEANT YORK. Southern Q. 1981 19(3-4): 207-221.* *Sergeant York* was one of the most successful films of 1941. This is an account of how Jesse L. Lasky, a Hollywood motion picture producer fallen on hard times, produced the film. Receiving the blessing of Alvin York, a hero of World War I, to make the film was the most difficult of many tasks Lasky had. Photo, 26 notes.      B. D. Ledbetter

454. Maddex, Jack P., Jr. POLLARD'S *THE LOST CAUSE REGAINED*: A MASK FOR SOUTHERN ACCOMMODATION. *J. of Southern Hist. 1974 40(4): 595-612.* Although Ulrich B. Phillips used Edward A. Pollard's *The Lost Cause Regained* (1868) to sustain his theory that white supremacy bound the antebellum and postbellum South together, neither Pollard's career nor his book support Phillips' thesis. Pollard's antebellum career emphasized "the conflict between a southern nationalism rooted in slavery and a Unionism rooted in the free-labor system." Pollard's continued assertion of southern nationalism during the reconstruction left him outside the political debate. Reconciliation with his day came in the *Lost Cause*, in which he accepts unionism and dismisses slavery as a financial matter. Since it opened the central question of black equality, he considers emancipation important but views secession as a conspiracy of Deep South politicians greedy for office. The *Lost Cause* permitted former Confederates to forget their attachment to plantation slavery and to view the Confederacy as a stand for white supremacy and constitutional limitations. Based on published primary and secondary sources; 55 notes.

T. D. Schoonover/S

455. May, Robert E. DIXIE'S MARTIAL IMAGE: A CONTINUING HISTORIOGRAPHICAL ENIGMA. *Historian 1978 40(2): 213-234.* Examines the theme of southern militancy in the antebellum, the postbellum, and the modern periods. Possible periods are drawn between the southern penchant for violence and the section's martial spirit. Offers some exceptions to the South's martial image, and describes recent challenges to the long accepted premise of a militant South. Suggests some new avenues of research that should be explored to reach a consensus on this issue.      M. S. Legan

456. May, Robert E. *GONE WITH THE WIND* AS SOUTHERN HISTORY: A REAPPRAISAL. *Southern Q. 1978 17(1): 51-64.* Past critics, in evaluating the historical accuracy of Margaret Mitchell's *Gone With the Wind*, have condemned it completely. This reappraisal of the work divides it into three basic parts; before, during, and after the war. Parts of the book are highly inaccurate from a historical point of view, while other parts, especially the coverage of the South during the war, are highly accurate. Studying the book in parts results in a more valid appraisal of *Gone With the Wind*. 21 notes.      B. D. Ledbetter

457. Miller, Robert Moats. "THE MIND OF THE SOUTH": ONCE MORE WITH BOLDNESS. *Rev. in Am. Hist. 1983 11(3): 360-364.* Reviews Daniel Joseph Singal's *The War Within: From Victorian to Modernist Thought in the South, 1919-1945* (1982), which examines the transformation of Southern values.

458. Millichap, Joseph R. THE SOUTH ON THE SCREEN. *Mississippi Q. 1982 35(4): 439-445.* Reviews Edward D. C. Campbell, Jr.'s *The Celluloid South: Hollywood and the Southern Myth* (1981) and *The South and Film* (1981), edited by Warren French, examining their accuracy in discussing the representation of Southern culture in film.

459. Morrison, Joseph L. W. J. CASH: THE SUMMING UP. *South Atlantic Q. 1977 76(4): 508-517.* W. J. Cash discerned an essential consensus in the South during 1830-1940 to convince white southerners to accept positive social change. He saw the southern mind self-consciously defending itself from the yankee mind, the modern mind, and the Negro's presence. Cash played the moralist and prophet in coming to understand the social changes taking place around him. Despite his eloquence and imaginative history, a new definition of the South must be made in the wake of all he foresaw.      W. L. Olbrich

460. Norden, Martin F. BUSINESS AND LOVE IN THE POST-RECONSTRUCTION SOUTH: WARNER BROTHERS' *BRIGHT LEAF. Southern Q. 1981 19(3-4): 95-106.* Critiques *Bright Leaf* (1950). The film, set in the South after the Civil War, depicts the fall of Southern values and lifestyles as industrialization begins to come to the South. Photo, 9 notes.      B. D. Ledbetter

461. O'Brien, Matthew C. JOHN ESTEN COOKE, GEORGE WASHINGTON, AND THE VIRGINIA CAVALIERS. *Virginia Mag. of Hist. and Biog. 1976 84(3): 259-265.* Though novelist John Esten Cooke is usually associated with the Civil War, he also wrote several novels set in pre-Revolutionary Virginia. His themes included both a longing for the Cavalier past, embodied in men such as George Washington, and a democratic disdain for the evils of the aristocratic class system. 4 notes.      R. F. Oaks

462. O'Brien, Michael. C. VANN WOODWARD AND THE BURDEN OF SOUTHERN LIBERALISM. *Am. Hist. Rev. 1973 78(3): 589-604.* Sketches the traditional historiography of the southern liberal past, notes the modifications which C. Vann Woodward made to it during and after the 1930's, and briefly traces the influence of his particular "Populist" version of southern liberalism on his writings. A few general social reasons within the South's intelligentsia are suggested to explain the shift. Woodward's "Beardianism" made him resist the consensus historiography of the 1950's, although he relied upon it in his essays upon southern identity. By shifting the definition of the South from its politics to its mind, he ironically undercut the rationale of his earlier work. His definition of southern distinctiveness ignored the strongest tradition of southern liberalism, its desire to assimilate the South to the nation, a movement not away from but toward "innocence." It is suggested that the impulse to pursue an image of the South in Woodward's work may be more central to the southern experience than the definition itself.      A

463. O'Donnell, Victoria. THE SOUTHERN WOMAN AS A TIME-BINDER IN FILM. *Southern Q. 1981 19(3-4): 156-163.* The ability to span time through the use of symbols has been labeled "time-binding." Actresses have been cast in many films not only because they portray a certain type of character but also because they are good time-binders. *Gone With the Wind* (1939), *Cat on a Hot Tin Roof* (1958), and *Rachel, Rachel* (1969) exemplify this. 8 notes, photo.      B. D. Ledbetter

464. O'Kain, Dennis. DOCUMENTING THE DEEP SOUTH: WILLIAM E. WILSON, PHOTOGRAPHER. *Georgia Rev. 1979 33(3): 662-680.* Little is known about the life of William E. Wilson (d. 1905), a photographer who lived in Georgia and Alabama at the end of the 19th century, but a large collection of his documentary photographs has survived. Wilson was the first professional photographer to document a vanishing way of life in the Deep

South. His photographs of poor black sharecroppers, the cotton industry, and the commonplace realities of everyday life are an unsentimental record of southern society in the 1880's and 1890's. Based on state and local archives and the University of Georgia Library's Special Collections; 16 photos.    J. N. McArthur

465. Otto, John Solomon. ORAL TRADITIONAL HISTORY IN THE SOUTHERN HIGHLANDS. *Appalachian J. 1981 9(1): 20-31.* Oral history of the Blue Ridge Mountains, the Allegheny Cumberland Plateau, the Highland Rim, the Ozark Plateau and the Ouachita Ridge—the Southern highlands—gives the historian a more accurate depiction of the "plain folk," the slaveless farmers and the small slaveholders, than do the travelogues written by Southern planters or Northern visitors; descendants of the "plain folk" still maintain a lifestyle of self-sufficiency in the 20th century.

466. Plecki, Gerard. THE SOUTH IN THE FILMS OF ROBERT ALTMAN. *Southern Q. 1981 19(3-4): 134-142.* Southerners in Robert Altman's films, *M*A*S*H, Brewster McCloud, Thieves Like Us,* and *Nashville,* represent a cross section of American lifestyles and attitudes. The people of the South are proud, resilient, and forceful but are also prone to racial and regional biases, stubbornness, and greed. Altman finds and pictures the South as the locus of conservatism in the United States. Covers 1969-75. 2 photos.
B. D. Ledbetter

467. Powers, Evelyn B. REVOLUTION IN APPALACHIA. *Appalachian J. 1978 5(2): 246-255.* Examines the connection between social organization and personalities in Appalachia, 1800-1970's.

468. Preston, Robert M. THE GREAT FIRE OF EMMITSBURG, MARYLAND: DOES A CATASTROPHIC EVENT CAUSE MOBILITY? *Maryland Hist. Mag. 1982 77(2): 172-182.* Emphasizes the importance of studying small towns with populations below 2,500 to understand truly the experience of the American population in the 19th century, since 80% of the Americans lived in such communities. Analysis of the population mobility in Emmitsburg, Maryland, in the 12 years after the "Great Fire" of June 1863 shows that, despite conventional wisdom, "social and economic causes rather than the Great Fire were the dominant causes" of geographic mobility. Social position and property-owning status were more important factors in determining whether someone, despite personal tragedy or catastrophe, would remain in or leave one's home town. Census data, secondary sources; table, 8 illus., 17 notes.
G. J. Bobango

469. Rable, George C. BOURBONISM, RECONSTRUCTION, AND THE PERSISTENCE OF SOUTHERN DISTINCTIVENESS. *Civil War Hist. 1983 29(2): 135-153.* Attempts to determine the "southern mind," demonstrating that southern ideas such as racism, paternalism, nationalism, personal honor, and rigid constitutionalism continued from the antebellum period through Reconstruction. Based on correspondence, newspapers and secondary sources; 52 notes.    G. R. Schroeder

470. Reid, Herbert G. APPALACHIAN POLICY, THE CORPORATE STATE, AND AMERICAN VALUES: A CRITICAL PERSPECTIVE. *Policy Studies J. 1980-81 9(4): 622-633.* The work of Henry Shapiro, Lawrence Goodwyn, David Whisnant, and others suggests that the myth (developed during 1880-1930) of Appalachia as a static region apart, a tribute to cultural pluralism, has concealed the fact of Appalachia's exploitation by US corporate capitalism, an exploitation that continues today.

471. Rogers, Gayle J. THE CHANGING IMAGE OF THE SOUTHERN WOMAN: A PERFORMER ON A PEDESTAL. *J. of Popular Culture 1982 16(3): 60-67.* The old image of the Southern woman, symbolized by the metaphor of a lady on a pedestal, has been replaced by a transitional image as traditional and modern cultures merge. Modern Southern fiction demonstrates that a more apt metaphor is that of a "performer on a pedestal." 25 notes.
D. G. Nielson

472. Roland, Charles P. THE EVER-VANISHING SOUTH. *J. of Southern Hist. 1982 48(1): 3-20.* Changes, including urbanization, industrialization, and legalized racial equality, especially since 1945, have led some to believe that the South has lost its distinctiveness as a region. Yet much remains that makes the region distinctive. Noteworthy hallmarks are conservative Protestantism and the literary tradition that "places unusual emphasis on the very points most emphasized in southern life itself: family, history, race, religion, and a sense of place...." Other regional traits include the frequency of violence, speech patterns, and a homogeneity and folksiness that defy urbanization and industrialization. Presidential address at the 1981 meeting of the Southern Historical Society. 54 notes.

473. Rotberg, Robert I. TWO SOCIETIES, BOTH UNFREE. *Rev. in Am. Hist. 1982 10(1): 1-6.* Reviews George M. Fredrickson's *White Supremacy: A Comparative Study in American and South African History* (1981), which compares the American South and South Africa and traces the history of race relations in both locations from the 18th to the 20th centuries.

474. Saunders, William C. SEA ISLANDS: THEN AND NOW. *J. of Black Studies 1980 10(4): 481-492.* Although resigned to the inevitability of change, the author, a lifetime resident of Johns Island, describes and decries the passing of old customs and ways of life on the Sea Islands of Georgia and South Carolina. Most of the old customs, work habits, beliefs, and speech patterns are dying out, but the people on the islands are still conscious and proud of being islanders. Ref.    R. G. Sherer

475. Seidel, Kathryn L. THE SOUTHERN BELLE AS AN ANTEBELLUM IDEAL. *Southern Q. 1977 15(4): 387-401.* Critiques the role and image of southern women in pre-Civil War literature, with special reference to novels. Focuses on the writings of Thomas R. Dew, Sarah J. Hale, Caroline Lee Hentz, Harriett Beecher Stowe and John Pendelton Kennedy. Victorian characteristics that typify antebellum womanhood were produced by literary and social conditions. 20 notes.    R. W. Dubay

476. Sessions, Robert P. APPALACHIANS AND NON-APPALACHIANS: THE COMMON BOND. *Appalachian J. 1977 4(4): 92-99.* A sociologist shows similarities between mountain people and most Americans, particularly their attitudes toward land and nature, friends and family, faith and struggle.

477. Shapiro, Edward S. FRANK L. OWSLEY AND THE DEFENSE OF SOUTHERN IDENTITY. *Tennessee Hist. Q. 1977 36(1): 75-94.* Frank L. Owsley's southern identity did not emanate from a logical idea carried to a conclusion. Instead, southernism was a militant defense of southern ideas, which differed from time to time, but which currently were attacked by the North. Primary and secondary sources; 32 notes.    M. B. Lucas

478. Snyder, Bob. IMAGE AND IDENTITY IN APPALACHIA. *Appalachian J. 1982 9(2-3): 124-133.* Discusses the doubts of scholars of Appalachian Studies about the generalizations about classes and groups, identity and image, in Appalachia, and presents Kenneth Boulding's theory called "eiconics," which might be applied to Appalachia; 1970's-81.

479. Stevens, John D. THE BLACK REACTION TO *GONE WITH THE WIND. J. of Popular Film 1973 2(4): 366-372.* Describes the reaction of Negro organizations and publications, especially the National Association for the Advancement of Colored People, to the stereotypes of black slaves as depicted in the film *Gone With The Wind* (1939).    S

480. Telotte, J. P. THE HUMAN LANDSCAPE OF JOHN FORD'S SOUTH. *Southern Q. 1981 19(3-4): 117-133.* John Ford is known for his Western films. However, he did make a number of Southern films. The author reviews Ford's Southern films, especially *Judge Priest* and *Steamboat 'Round the Bend* to determine Ford's depiction of the South. Ford shows the strength of the individual Southern man and his human nature. Ford is sympathetic to

the Southern man who can stand up and cling to his ideals when the world around him is changing. Covers 1918-62. Photo, 17 notes.                                          B. D. Ledbetter

481.    Tidwell, Donavon Duncan. SAM HOUSTON, SOUTHERN GENTLEMAN. *Texana 1973 11(4): 321-327.* Examines the life and career, 1832-54, of Sam Houston, in light of the popular image of a "Southern gentleman." 13 notes.

482.    Tindall, George B. BEYOND THE MAINSTREAM: THE ETHNIC SOUTHERNERS. *J. of Southern Hist. 1974 40(1): 3-18.* Examines the old and often repeated canard about the "Vanishing South." Discusses ethnicity and change in the South's past. After a broad survey of groups, ideas, and institutions in the South, concludes that "southern historians will be overwhelmed by the marvelous discovery that their field of study is nothing more nor less than the formation of ethnic groups." Also points out that to change is not to disappear nor to lose one's identity; thus, while the South will change, it will neither lose its identity nor disappear. Based on published primary and secondary sources; 42 notes. Presidential address at the Southern Historical Association meeting in Atlanta, Georgia, on 8 November 1973.                    T. D. Schoonover

483.    Tyler, Pamela. THE IDEAL RURAL SOUTHERN WOMAN AS SEEN BY *PROGRESSIVE FARMER* IN THE 1930S. *Southern Studies 1981 20(3): 278-296.* Compares attitudes expressed in the popular magazine, *Progressive Farmer and Southern Ruralist,* concerning white women of the middle class married to farm owners in the 1930's with the attitude toward such women during 1820-60. In important ways there is little difference between the two periods. The woman was expected to have piety, purity, submissiveness, and domesticity. Changes included additions rather than deletions of qualities; in 1930 greater involvement in community affairs was expected. The woman was now expected to be both farm wife and lady. Based on various articles in *Progressive Farmer and Southern Ruralist;* 34 notes.                    J. J. Buschen

484.    Verschuure, Eric Peter. STUMBLE, BUMBLE, MUMBLE: TV'S IMAGE OF THE SOUTH. *J. of Popular Culture 1982 16(3): 92-96.* Negative stereotypes have characterized television's portrayal of the South for two decades and there is little prospect for improvement. Appendix, 6 notes.                    D. G. Nielson

485.    Wegner, Hart. A CHRONICLE OF SOIL, SEASONS AND WEATHER: JEAN RENOIR'S *THE SOUTHERNER. Southern Q. 1981 19(3-4): 58-69.* Jean Renoir, the internationally known French film director, made six films in the United States in the 1940's. With the exception of the limited praise of *The Southerner* (1945), his films were disappointments to both himself and his motion picture companies. *The Southerner* was a simple and sincere attempt to observe life in the South without passing judgment on the section. This appealed to the moviegoing public. Photo, 31 notes.                    B. D. Ledbetter

486.    Williams, C. Fred. THE BEAR STATE IMAGE: ARKANSAS IN THE NINETEENTH CENTURY. *Arkansas Hist. Q. 1980 39(2): 99-111.* Few people in the 19th century had been to Arkansas, and so those who had any knowledge of the place at all gained it from reading travel accounts. These pictured the state as primitive and lawless, an image which, though often inaccurate, continued to be the common view. Based mainly on secondary sources; 42 notes.                    G. R. Schroeder

487.    Williams, Cratis D. and Pipes, Martha H., ed. THE SOUTHERN MOUNTAINEER IN FACT AND FICTION. *Appalachian J. 1975 3(1): 8-62; 1976 3(2): 100-162, (3): 186-261, (4): 334-392.* Traces Appalachian culture and the southern mountaineer since the 18th century.                    S

488.    Williams, John Alexander. HENRY SHAPIRO AND THE IDEA OF APPALACHIA: A REVIEW/ESSAY. *Appalachian J. 1978 5(3): 350-357.* Review article prompted by Henry D. Shapiro's *Appalachia on Our Mind* (Chapel Hill: U. of North Carolina Pr., 1978), which deals with the social, political, economic, and traditional conception of Appalachia in native and national thought.

489.    Williamson, J. W. UNINVENTING APPALACHIA: A REVIEW ESSAY. *Southern Q. 1979 17(3-4): 230-238.* Henry Shapiro's *Appalachia on Our Mind: The Southern Mountains and Mountaineers in the American Consciousness, 1870-1920* (Chapel Hill: U. of North Carolina Pr., 1978) is important, controversial, and necessary for those who want to understand Appalachia as it has been and as it is.                    B. D. Ledbetter

490.    Wilson, Richard L. SAM JONES: AN APOSTLE OF THE NEW SOUTH. *Georgia Hist. Q. 1973 57(4): 459-474.* One of the leading exponents of the concept of the New South, Sam Jones promoted his ideas in sermons, interviews, and a weekly newspaper column. Jones called for an end to sectionalism. He believed blacks should have industrial education and economic opportunities but not social equality. He preached middle-class virtues of hard work, frugality, and piety, and he wanted the government to stay out of education and the economy. 28 notes.                    D. L. Smith

491.    Wolfe, Margaret Ripley. COMMENTARY: SOUTHERN WOMEN. *Working Papers from the Regional Econ. Hist. Res. Center 1982 5(2-3): 156-165.* Protests stereotypical descriptions and ideas about the American South and Southern women specifically, and discuses some of the experiences that Southern women and Northern women had in common during the 18th and 19th centuries.

492.    Wolfe, Margaret Ripley. THE SOUTHERN LADY: LONG SUFFERING COUNTERPART OF THE GOOD OLE' BOY. *J. of Popular Culture 1977 11(1): 18-27.* The image of the southern lady, one of America's most enduring myths, has yet to be portrayed in other than stereotypic characteristics. She remains frozen in her familiar traditional form in spite of flexible characterizations of her male counterpart, the southern gentleman. Primary and secondary sources; 31 notes.                    D. G. Nielson

493.    Wolfe, Ralph Haven. THERE WILL ALWAYS BE A TARA. *J. of Popular Film 1974 3(3): 264-267.* Reviews Gavin Lambert's *GWTW: The Making of Gone With The Wind* (Boston: Little, Brown, and Company, 1973).

494.    Woodward, Michael Vaughan. ELLIS MERTON COULTER: A CASE STUDY IN THE DEVELOPMENT OF CONSERVATIVE RACISM IN THE NEW SOUTH. *Midwest Q. 1979 20(3): 269-280.* Gives the biography of southerner Ellis Merton Coulter (b. 1890), and discusses his attitudes in the present-day South to understand paternalistic racism in southern history.

495.    Wyatt-Brown, Bertram. THE ANTEBELLUM SOUTH AS A "CULTURE OF COURAGE". *Southern Studies 1981 20(3): 213-246.* The "South" is characterized essentially not as the home of slavery and cotton, but as a family-centered, honor-bound culture, in which certain qualities of gender, age, racial appearance, and bloodlines were more prominently valued than professionally acquired skills, intellectual thought, or specialized study. Most important was honor, based on the sacredness of hierarchy in the maintenance of virtue. Owning slaves was not an end, but a means of showing one's superiority. 56 notes.                    J. J. Buschen

## Southern Society

496.    Abbott, Martin. MEMOIRS OF A MILLEDGEVILLE NATIVE, AUGUSTIN H. HANSELL. *Georgia Hist. Q. 1973 57(3): 430-438.* The memoirs of Augustin H. Hansell (1817-1909), herein reproduced, are concerned with society in middle Georgia for the first 44 years of his life. He practiced law, served in the state legislature, and was named a county judge. Note.                    D. L. Smith

497.    Akin, Edward N. THE CLEVELAND CONNECTION: REVELATIONS FROM THE JOHN D. ROCKEFELLER-JULIA D. TUTTLE CORRESPONDENCE. *Tequesta 1982 42: 57-61.* The

letters indicate Julia Tuttle's evolving commitment to Florida. She was known as the "Mother of Miami." Her father-in-law had been John D. Rockefeller's first employer, in Cleveland, Ohio.

H. S. Marks

498. Algeo, John and Algeo, Adele. BIBLE BELT ONOMASTICS REVISITED. *Names 1983 31(2): 103-116.* Using three lists of names, obtained principally from Georgian high school graduation lists, college graduation lists, and obituary notices for people over the age of 40, analyzes the naming of children; finds that imaginative naming is less common in recent decades, that women are more apt to have double first names, and that certain names can be found in all three generation lists as the most popular.

499. Allain, Mathé. LES ACADIENS AUX XXᵉ SIÈCLE [The Acadians in the 20th century]. *Rev. de Louisiane 1979 8(2): 143-152.* Examines the daily life of Acadians in Louisiana who have retained some of their traditions, customs, and culture, in spite of the automobile and television, and have revived some others to occupy the leisure time created by technological progress and modernization.

500. Anderson, George M. AN EARLY COMMUTER: THE LETTERS OF JAMES AND MARY ANDERSON. *Maryland Hist. Mag. 1980 75(3): 217-232.* James Wallace Anderson (1797-1881) and Mary, his wife, owned a farm called Vallombrosa in Montgomery County, two miles north of Rockville, Maryland. Working as an auditor in the US Post Office in Washington, D.C., 1854-61, James was able to go home only twice a month or so, and thus carried on a frequent correspondence with his wife. Their 400 or so letters, here discussed and quoted by their great-grandson, provide an unusually full picture of urban boarding house life in the capital and rural farm existence in the mid-19th century. Brief biographical details of the couple's eight children are also included, along with the history of the farm to 1960. 96 notes.                      G. J. Bobango

501. Baker, Vaughan. LES ACADIENS EN LOUISIANE AVANT LA GUERRE DE SÉCESSION: ÉTUDE D'ASSIMILATION CULTURELLE [The Acadians in Louisiana before the Civil War: a study of cultural assimilation]. *Rev. de Louisiane 1979 8(2): 101-115.* Studies the process of cultural assimilation of the Cajuns, descendants of the Acadians exiled from Nova Scotia to Louisiana in 1755, and stresses that, although conscious of ethnic differences, they had adapted to their new environment by 1860.

502. Ball, Lynn. THE VISITABLE PAST OF LAVINIA HARTWELL EGAN. *North Louisiana Hist. Assoc. J. 1978 9(1): 1-11.* Discusses Lavinia Hartwell Egan and her forebears who settled at Mount Lebanon, Louisiana, from 1835, when Martin Canfield was the first to settle in the area, to 1945, when Egan died.

503. Bankston, William B. and Allen, H. David. RURAL SOCIAL AREAS AND PATTERNS OF HOMICIDE: AN ANALYSIS OF LETHAL VIOLENCE IN LOUISIANA. *Rural Sociol. 1980 45(2): 223-237.* Studies lethal violence in Louisiana, based on research of the structural and cultural factors in 10 rural Louisiana counties; concludes that both cultural and sociodemographic structure affect patterns of lethal violence, but that it is unknown whether all or some Southerners operate under a value system "associated with the possession and carrying of lethal weapons, and, especially, the willingness to use them," that is different from the rest of the United States; 19th century-1979.

504. Barney, William L. PATTERNS OF CRISIS: ALABAMA WHITE FAMILIES AND SOCIAL CHANGE, 1850-1870. *Sociol. and Social Res. 1979 63(3): 524-543.* This essay focuses on a generation of Alabama whites, drawn from four distinctive ecological and cultural zones, who lived through the period of intensifying sectionalism, the Civil War, and its legacy of defeat and poverty. Such an examination of various contexts of white Southern community life permits the investigation of the impact on the Southern social order of two ongoing crises—the first related to the role of slavery as an agent of socio-economic change which precipitated a Southern version of a modernization crisis hitherto identified primarily with the North; and the second related to the traumatic ex-

perience of defeat in the Civil War. The essay seeks to demonstrate that the pattern of white responses to these crises was a function of the contrasting strengths and stabilities of regional cultures markedly different in family and household structures and in stages of economic development.

J

505. Bauman, Mark. ROLE THEORY AND HISTORY: THE ILLUSTRATION OF ETHNIC BROKERAGE IN THE ATLANTA JEWISH COMMUNITY IN AN ERA OF TRANSITION AND CONFLICT. *Am. Jewish Hist. 1983 73(1): 71-95.* Uses role theory and the examples of four leaders in the Atlanta Jewish community to understand what constitutes successful ethnic brokerage. Harold Hirsch, Ezra Tourial, and Morris Lichtenstein acted effectively as liaisons between Jewish and non-Jewish groups and among German, East European, and Sephardic Jews. Leon Eplan, uncompromising in his demand for equality, proved unsuccessful in the broker role. Community attitudes, as well as personal attributes, determined success or failure. Primary sources; 43 notes.                      R. A. Keller

506. Beck, Earl R. GERMAN TOURISTS IN FLORIDA: A TWO-CENTURY RECORD. *Florida Hist. Q. 1982 61(2): 162-180.* Germans have commented frequently on Florida, its climate, flora, and fauna. For 200 years Germans have traveled the state. Commentators in the late 19th century were interested in plant life as well as environmental management. In contemporary times Florida must compete with other warm climate markets for the German tourist money, and travel accounts no longer exist. Based on travelers' accounts and other sources; 91 notes, 2 fig.

N. A. Kuntz

507. Billings, Dwight. CULTURE AND POVERTY IN APPALACHIA: A THEORETICAL DISCUSSION AND EMPIRICAL ANALYSIS. *Social Forces 1974 53(2): 315-323.* The prevalent explanation for the persistence of poverty in Appalachia stresses the region's traditional culture which ill equips its population for participation in the modern world. This research casts doubt on the cultural explanation. A scale of "middle-class orientation" was produced from the secondary analysis of data gathered from several thousand respondents in North Carolina. Attitudinal differences between respondents from the Appalachian subregion of that state and from other regions including the urban, industrial piedmont were quite small and attributable to rurality. Analysis controlling for age suggests that attitudinal factors cannot be used to account for economic development as it occurred in the Appalachian region. An alternative approach for further research is discussed.        J

508. Bogardus, Carl R., Sr. BLACK MARRIAGES, GALLATIN COUNTY, KENTUCKY, 1866 TO 1913. *J. of the Afro-American Hist. and Geneal. Soc. 1981 2(3): 117-122, (4): 161-175.* Alphabetical list by bridegroom's last name of marriages from the "Record Book for Colored Marriages" in Gallatin County; includes a bride index and an index of people officiating.

509. Bonawit, Oby. HISTORY OF PINEWOOD (COCOPLUM) CEMETERY. *Tequesta 1978 38: 63-71.* Possibly as early as 1855, burials south of the Miami River (and Miami) were usually made in the area where Pinewood Cemetery is now located. The cemetery was officially created by 1896. It is now abandoned and in need of protection. Roster of 80 burials in the cemetery provided.

H. S. Marks

510. Boney, Francis Nash. THE SOUTHERN ARISTOCRAT. *Midwest Q. 1974 15(3): 215-230.* Despite his image in American history, the Southern aristocrat has always been in the mainstream of acquisitive, capitalistic America.                      S

511. Brindley, Esther E. ETHEL MAE BRINDLEY, BIOGRAPHICAL SKETCH. *Chronicles of Oklahoma 1981 59(2): 237-240.* Life on a turn of the century farm near Mustang, Oklahoma, proved hard but adventurous for Ethel Mae Brindley. The death of her husband in 1921 left Brindley without an income and she moved to Edmond, Oklahoma, to open a rooming house. During the 1920's she undertook several business ventures, including a very

successful role as one of Oklahoma's first women oil brokers. Always civic-minded and progressive, she still remains active in Mustang's community affairs.                                                     M. L. Tate

512. Brodie, Fawn M. THOMAS JEFFERSON'S UNKNOWN GRANDCHILDREN. *Am. Heritage 1976 27(6): 28-33, 94-99.* Thomas Jefferson, married only once, had two families. The second family, by his quadroon slave, Sally Hemings, numbered seven children, from a liaison lasting 38 years. Their disappearance and that of their progeny resulted from several factors, including Jefferson's desire that they eventually "escape" into white society. Much information has recently come to light concerning Jefferson's other family. Family lines are traced from each of the children. Based on primary and secondary sources; 2 illus., 36 notes.                     J. F. Paul

513. Brown, Catherine and Ganschow, Thomas. THE AUGUSTA, GEORGIA, CHINESE: 1865-1980. *West Georgia Coll. Studies in the Social Sci. 1983 22: 27-41.* Immediately after the Civil War, the concept of cheap Chinese labor was favored in Augusta, but discrimination took root by the 1880's and did not abate until the mid-20th century.

514. Brown, Douglas Summers. THE LEGENDARY HERMIT-HUNTER OF WHITE TOP MOUNTAIN: WILBURN WATERS. *Virginia Cavalcade 1977 27(1): 42-47.* Wilburn Waters (1832-75), a hermit and mountain man, lived in the area of White Top Mountain, Virginia, for most of his life.

515. Brugger, Robert. THE CRADLE OF TRUE PATRIOTS. *Psychohistory Rev. 1977-78 6(2-3): 52-67.* Sketches the family background and youth of Beverley Tucker (1784-1851), states' rights, proslavery, gentleman patriot of Virginia. Tucker's personal and intellectual development was significantly influenced by childhood experiences, particularly his mother's death and the family's move when he was four. Based on family diaries and letters, and secondary works; 26 notes.                                       J. B. Street

516. Bryant, Keith L., Jr. THE ROLE AND STATUS OF THE FEMALE YEOMANRY IN THE ANTEBELLUM SOUTH: THE LITERARY VIEW. *Southern Q. 1980 18(2): 73-88.* In the past historians have given little attention to middle-class white women in the antebellum South. Using literary sources, the author finds that these women occupied significant positions in the antebellum South. For example, they worked, made money for the family, raised the children, established the moral tone in the home, and became important in religious institutions. Their early role in southern history should not be underestimated. Primary sources; 60 notes.
                                                          B. D. Ledbetter

517. Burnett, Robert A. LOUISVILLE'S FRENCH PAST. *Filson Club Hist. Q. 1976 50(2): 5-27.* Concentrates on the contributions of individual French Americans in Louisville, Kentucky, in the 19th century. Special mention is made of Jean de Crevecoeur, John and Louis Tarascon, John J. Audubon, John Colmesnil, and Union General Lovell Harrison Rousseau. There is little analysis, but the author does note that the French were so well assimilated by 1850 that they were not targets of nativist hostility. Based on local histories and county records; 74 notes.                        G. B. McKinney

518. Callahan, Helen. A STUDY OF DUBLIN: THE IRISH IN AUGUSTA. *Richmond County Hist. 1973 5(2): 5-14.* Augusta had Irish residents before the Irish immigration which occurred nationally during and immediately after the potato famine of 1845-51. A number came during the early 1830's to work as railroad laborers. Historically Augusta's Irish took an active role in community affairs. Irishmen became important local politicians and prominent businessmen. One of six articles in this issue on Augusta. Based on newspapers, business directories, and secondary sources; 42 notes.
                                                          H. R. Grant

519. Campbell, Randolph B. POPULATION PERSISTENCE AND SOCIAL CHANGE IN NINETEENTH-CENTURY TEXAS: HARRISON COUNTY, 1850-1880. *J. of Southern Hist. 1982 48(2): 185-204.* The Harrison County population was as geographically stable as other rural areas during this time. The former plant-

ers were somewhat less persistent geographically than the general population, but quite persistent in retaining their upper-class economic status. The Civil War and Reconstruction did not destroy the social position of the planter class in the social structure of the county. Based on manuscripts and printed census records, Harrison county tax rolls, and other local documents; 27 notes, 5 tables.
                                                          T. Schoonover

520. Carver, Joan S. WOMEN IN FLORIDA. *J. of Pol. 1979 41(3): 941-955.* Large-scale immigration since World War II has made Florida atypical of the South. On feminist issues, northern Florida remains more conservative than the southern and central regions. Only since 1960 have women made dramatic progress as power shifted from the north. During 1915-1920, 23 municipalities granted women suffrage, but feminist agitation was limited to that issue. The gains of the last two decades are attributed to an increasingly female work force; higher levels of education, especially legal training; higher voting rates and greater activism by feminist groups. Covers 1890-1978. Map, 3 tables, 22 notes.
                                                          A. W. Novitsky

521. Caselli, Rob. MAKING IT IN AMERICA—THE ITALIAN EXPERIENCE. *Social Studies 1973 64(4): 147-153.* Discusses contributions of immigrant Italians in both eastern and western United States. Focuses on the place of Italians in California and Louisiana history. Explores the issue of assimilation versus pluralism in American culture.                                    E. P. Stickney and S

522. Cashin, Edward J. VANN WOODWARD'S *TOM WATSON*: AN INTERPRETATION. *Georgia R. 1974 28(3): 519-531.* That C. Vann Woodward's *Tom Watson* (Savannah: Beehive Press, 1973) deserves the outstanding praise it has received is indicated by a Georgia publishing house's production of a second edition. But the author might have analyzed in more detail the forces that produced Watson. A look into the culture of the earliest settlers who entered Georgia from Virginia and South Carolina would indicate more clearly why the forces which produced Tom Watson in the end defeated him. 5 notes.                         M. B. Lucas

523. Cawthon, John Ardis. A BRIEF HISTORY OF WINN PARISH BASED UPON A SAMPLING OF INSCRIPTIONS ON TOMBSTONES. *North Louisiana Hist. Assoc. J. 1975 6(2): 74-80.* Winn Parish was created in 1852 and was named for Walter O. Winn, a lawyer from Alexandria. Originally, it had been a part of Natchitoches Parish, and settlers had built homes in the area long before it became a parish. Among the early settlers in the parish were Michael Adam Gaar and the members of his family, John Cloud and his family, Dr. T. A. Wilkinson, Elisha O. McGinty, and Wilber Lee Gatlin. Three governors of the state have come from the parish—Huey Pierce Long, Jr., Oscar K. Allen, and Earl Kemp Long. The parents of two of the governors—Huey P. Long, Sr., and Caledonia Tison Long—are buried in the Winnfield cemetery, as is the former governor, O. K. Allen. The parish also "had its share of outlaws and bandits, the most notorious being the West-Kimbrell gang which operated in the vicinity of Atlanta, Louisiana," in the years immediately following the Civil War. Winn Parish has not only produced a large number of outstanding political leaders, it was also "the birthplace of Populism in the state and of Socialism as well." 12 notes; 6 photos.                     A. N. Garland

524. Cawthon, John Ardis. A BRIEF HISTORY OF BIENVILLE PARISH BASED UPON A SAMPLING OF INSCRIPTIONS ON TOMBSTONES. *North Louisiana Hist. Assoc. J. 1976 7(4): 140-149.* Bienville Parish came into being on 14 March 1848; it was "carved from 'old Claiborne Parish' which had originally been a part of Natchitoches Parish." In 1837 men and women from South Carolina founded the village of Mount Lebanon; they also organized the first permanent Baptist church in North Louisiana. The Baptist Convention of Louisiana was organized at Mount Lebanon and the first signer was George Washington Baines, great-grandfather of Lyndon Baines Johnson. In 1855 Mount Lebanon University was founded and many distinguished visitors and scholars came to preach in the vicinity and to teach at the university. Among the more prominent names in the parish have been Mathias and Henry Ardis; James and Margaret Brice; A. S. B. Prior; Earl

R. Hester; W. D. "Pol" Perritt; D. K. and Zachariah Thomas; and James Robert Head. Primary and secondary sources. 7 photos, 21 notes.                                                    A. N. Garland

525. Cawthon, John Ardis. A BRIEF HISTORY OF CLAIBORNE PARISH BASED UPON A SAMPLING OF INSCRIPTIONS ON TOMBSTONES. *North Louisiana Hist. Assoc. J. 1974 5(3): 103-113.* Traces the local history of Claiborne parish, established in 1828, through inscriptions on cemetery tombstones.
                                                                                S

526. Cawthon, John Ardis. A BRIEF HISTORY OF UNION PARISH BASED UPON A SAMPLING OF INSCRIPTIONS OF TOMBSTONES. *North Louisiana Hist. Assoc. J. 1974 5(2): 68-72.* Established on 13 March 1839, Union Parish was created from the northern part of Ouachita Parish, one of the original parishes in 1812 when Louisiana was made a state, with Farmerville as the parish seat of justice. There were chiefly Baptist and Wesleyan Methodist settlers in the area before Union became a parish. Four state governors—George W. Donaghay, Tom J. Terral, W. W. Heard, and Ruffin G. Pleasant—were born in the parish, although none are buried there. Other prominent names connected with Union Parish are those of Thomas H. Harris, L. M. and Emma Dawson Phillips, Stephen S. and Mary A. Heard, Earl R. Hester, and J. D. and Nancy Baughman. 2 photos, reproduction, 5 notes.
                                                                        A. N. Garland

527. Cawthon, John Ardis. A BRIEF HISTORY OF MOREHOUSE PARISH BASED UPON A SAMPLING OF THE INSCRIPTIONS ON TOMBSTONES. *North Louisiana Hist. Assoc. J. 1973 5(1): 10-13.* Discusses the early history of Morehouse Parish and its formal creation as a parish in 1844. Describes the old cemetery in the town of Bastrop and several of the markers therein "which tell of the westward movement of people from the eastern section of the country." Also tells of a ceremony conducted in 1957 "when the traditional key to the city of Bastrop was presented to Eulalio Guiterrez, *presidente municpal* of Saltillo" because "Baron de Bastrop is buried in a Saltillo cemetery." Photo, 8 notes.
                                                                        A. N. Garland

528. Cawthon, John Ardis. A BRIEF HISTORY OF JACKSON PARISH BASED UPON A SAMPLING OF INSCRIPTIONS ON TOMBSTONES. *North Louisiana Hist. Assoc. J. 1974 6(1): 12-21.* Jackson Parish, named after Andrew Jackson, was formed on 27 February 1845 from parts of Claiborne, Ouachita, and Union Parishes. Vernon, probably the earliest settlement in the parish, was selected as the parish seat. In 1911 the seat was moved to Jonesboro. Among the names noted on tombstones in the Vernon, Longstraw, Ebenezer, Mount Zion, and Jonesboro cemeteries, and at other burial places in the parish, are Elizabeth Ashley, the McLain family, Mary Lee Aswell, Mrs. James H. Davis, the Hargrove family, the Sims family, the Posey family, the Clinton-Kavanaugh families, and the Reverend C. E. Foster. All of these people were prominent in the history of the parish. 8 photos, 13 notes.
                                                                        A. N. Garland

529. Cawthon, John Ardis. A BRIEF HISTORY OF LINCOLN PARISH BASED UPON A SAMPLING OF INSCRIPTIONS ON TOMBSTONES. *North Louisiana Hist. Assoc. J. 1973 4(3): 90-94.* Tells of the early history of Lincoln Parish—it was organized in 1873 and named for Abraham Lincoln, although "much earlier in the century, settlers had begun to make homes" in the area—and the ongoing discussion about which family came first, the Stows or the Colvins. Describes the graves and various markers in the different cemeteries in the parish and points out that the "oldest marked grave in present-day Lincoln Parish is that of Sarah Colvin Johnson, who, with her parents, is buried at the Katy Cemetery." Suggests that "the 'Valhalla' of Ruston and of Lincoln Parish might be said to be Greenwood Cemetery, Ruston. Buried there were not only the soldiers of various wars, but also the other heroes who had had a part in maintaining the cultural aspect of Lincoln Parish which had been her pride." 5 photos, 7 notes.
                                                                        A. N. Garland

530. Cawthon, John Ardis. A BRIEF HISTORY OF DE SOTO PARISH BASED UPON A SAMPLING OF INSCRIPTIONS ON TOMBSTONES. *North Louisiana Hist. Assoc. J. 1979 10(1): 8-12.* Named for the explorer, De Soto Parish was a composite of Europeans, Virginians, South Carolinians, and others. 4 illus., 13 notes.
                                                                        J. F. Paul

531. Cawthon, John Ardis. A BRIEF HISTORY OF OUACHITA PARISH BASED UPON A SAMPLING OF INSCRIPTIONS ON TOMBSTONES. *North Louisiana Hist. Assoc. J. 1981 12(1): 42-49.* A brief study of names and inscriptions found on tombstones in Ouachita Parish. 4 illus., 14 notes.
                                                                        J. F. Paul

532. Cawthon, John Ardis. A BRIEF HISTORY OF SHREVEPORT, CADDO PARISH, BASED UPON A SAMPLING OF INSCRIPTIONS ON TOMBSTONES. *North Louisiana Hist. Assoc. J. 1975 6(4): 165-173.* Although Caddo Parish came into existence on 18 January 1838, Shreveport was not incorporated until 1839. The "Valhalla" of the city is Oakland Cemetery, "across the street from the Municipal Auditorium on the south side of Milam Street." It is here that "the forefathers of Shreveport sleep...the pioneer bankers, doctors, lawyers, merchants and soldiers—the rich and the poor." Mary D. C. Cane, who donated land to the city for the cemetery, is buried there. Among other prominent names to be found in the cemetery are Foster, Levy, Bercher, Kimble, Kelly, Hamilton and Munson. Other cemeteries in the area are the Hebrew Rest, the Greenwood, and the Forest Park Cemetery. In these three one can find the names Goldstein, Dreyfuss, Saenger, Hardin, and Irvine, all of which were also important in the development of this "metropolis of North Louisiana." 12 photos, 4 notes.
                                                                        A. N. Garland

533. Cawthon, John Ardis. THE DOYLE SAGA, 1843-1981. *North Louisiana Hist. Assoc. J. 1981 12(4): 147-155.* The first Doyle moved to Claiborne Parish, Louisiana, in 1843. For 140 years, the family has continued to make contributions to all phases of life in northern Louisiana. The article traces the family's lineage through those years. Primary and secondary sources, including census and school records; 4 illus., 22 notes.          J. F. Paul

534. Chalker, Fussell M. HIGHLAND SCOTS IN THE GEORGIA LOWLANDS. *Georgia Hist. Q. 1976 60(1): 35-42.* Many Scots left Scotland following the Battle of Culloden in 1746, migrating to America and settling in the lowlands of Southeastern Georgia. They were primarily cattle raisers who maintained many of their original cultural customs for years. They were distinguised by their traditional dress, language, music and ways, tending to isolate themselves from mainstream society. They were successful in their dealings with the Creek Indians and acquired much land, and also remained deeply committed to the Presbyterian Church of Scotland. By Civil War times, these Scots had become more integrated into Georgia life and responded to the call to arms by wearing the Confederate gray. Primary and secondary sources. 53 notes.
                                                                        M. R. Gillam

535. Chalmers, David. THE RISE AND FALL OF THE INVISIBLE EMPIRE OF THE KU KLUX KLAN. *Contemporary Rev. [Great Britain] 1980 237(1375): 57-64.* Discusses the Ku Klux Klan from its beginning during Reconstruction, to 1979, arguing that it has not been stamped out because it still expresses the social, economic, and racial anxieties of a minority.

536. Chalmers, David. RULE BY TERROR. *Am. Hist. Illus. 1980 14(9): 8-9, 44-48, (10): 28-37.* Part I. Traces the history of the Ku Klux Klan from its formation in 1868 by a group of ex-Confederate soldiers in Pulaski, Tennessee, who named their social club after the Greek kyklos, meaning circle, until 1880. Part II. Conclusion discussing the revival of the Ku Klux Klan from the release of D. W. Griffith's film, *The Birth of a Nation* in 1915 to the 1920's.

537. Chenoweth, Dean. J. MANSE PATTON, A CONCHO BANKER. *West Texas Hist. Assoc. Y. 1979 55: 81-86.* Relates incidents in the life and career of J. Manse Patton (1885-1962), a small town banker of considerable warmth, acumen, and fiscal independence.

538. Clarke, Caroline McKinney. DAYS OF OLD DECATUR. *Georgia Life 1980 6(4): 15-18.* Reprints the letters of Levi Willard written in 1876 to *The Weekly News* in Springfield, Ohio, describing life in Decatur, Georgia, where Willard lived and owned a store, 1826-64.

539. Clinton, Catherine. THE PLANTATION MISTRESS: HER WORKING LIFE. *Southern Exposure 1983 11(1): 58-63.* Describes the lives of mistresses of large plantations in the Deep South during 1780-1835.

540. Cohen, William. NEGRO INVOLUNTARY SERVITUDE IN THE SOUTH, 1865-1940: A PRELIMINARY ANALYSIS. *J. of Southern Hist. 1976 42(1): 31-60.* Even after the 13th amendment, bondage stubbornly persisted, sustained by state and local laws and custom which continued to extract labor from Negroes. Despite the bondage systems, blacks were permitted a fair amount of mobility. The apparent contradiction stems from the willingness of the white power structure to permit black movement from areas of surplus labor to areas in need of labor, even during good times, and to make virtually no effort to restrict black mobility during depressions. Legal structure gave legitimacy to the bondage system, but the system was rooted in whites' assumption of their right to use Negro labor as they wished to. Based on manuscripts and primary and secondary sources; 63 notes.      T. D. Schoonover

541. Coke, Fletch; Graham, Eleanor; and Shriver, Attie Gene. FIRST LADIES OF TRAVELLERS' REST. *Tennessee Hist. Q. 1978 37(3); 321-328.* Describes the domestic and social life of Mary McConnell (White) May (1782-1862), who married Judge John Overton in 1820, and of Harriet Maxwell (1832-99), who married their son John in 1862. Travellers' Rest was a mecca for leading Tennessee political figures in the 19th century, among whom were Andrew Jackson, whom Judge Overton supported, Sam Houston, and John Eaton, husband of Peggy Eaton. The second Mrs. Eaton was pro-Confederate, and both generations were devout Presbyterians. Based on the Overton Papers in the Claybrooke Collection and secondary sources; 16 notes.      H. M. Parker, Jr.

542. Coke, Fletch. PROFILES OF JOHN OVERTON: JUDGE, FRIEND, FAMILY MAN, AND MASTER OF TRAVELLER'S REST. *Tennessee Hist. Q. 1978 37(4): 393-409.* Tennessee judge John Overton (1766-1833) was a friend to many, including Andrew Jackson. He married late in life, but was a devoted family man. He operated the plantation at Traveller's Rest, which was close by Nashville, Tennessee. He grew cotton of a very fine quality and also operated a gin for the benefit of his plantation and his neighbors in addition to establishing a nursery for fruit trees. Based on numerous family archival depositories in the Tennessee State Library and Archives; 86 notes.      H. M. Parker, Jr.

543. Conrad, Glenn R. POTPOURRI FRANÇAIS: VARIETIES OF FRENCH SETTLERS IN LOUISIANA. *Louisiana Rev. 1981 10(1): 1-9.* A relation of the French heritage in Louisiana since 1700, centering on the successive groups of various Gallic subcultures that have formed a Louisiana amalgam.

544. Contee, Clarence G. MACON B. ALLEN: "FIRST" BLACK IN THE LEGAL PROFESSION. *Crisis 1976 83(2): 67-69.* Macon B. Allen is believed to have been the first black lawyer in the United States. Born in 1816 in Indiana as a non-slave, he studied law in Maine under an antislavery leader, Samuel Fessenden. He was passed into the Maine bar in 1844, and was later admitted to the Massachusetts bar. After the Civil War Allen moved to Charleston, South Carolina, where he became a judge. He died in 1894.      A. G. Belles

545. Coomes, Charles S. TOLOMATO CEMETERY. *Escribano 1976 13(4): 107-138.* Presents a history of burial plots and the persons entombed in Tolomato Cemetery in St. Augustine, Florida, 1704-1876.

546. Cooper, John Milton, Jr. WALTER HINES PAGE: THE SOUTHERNER AS AMERICAN. *Virginia Q. Rev. 1977 53(4): 660-676.* Walter Hines Page, "one of the first Southerners after Reconstruction" to advocate national reunion, is best known as ambassador to England during World War I. However, he was a journalist and edited the *Forum* and the *Atlantic* and started the *World's Work.* Cofounder of the publishing house, Doubleday, Page and Co., he made important contributions to "Southern affairs, race relations, politics, diplomacy, philanthropy, education, public health, agriculture, business, literature, book publishing, and journalism."      O. H. Zabel

547. Crockett, Bernice Norman. "NO JOB FOR A WOMAN." *Chronicles of Oklahoma 1983 61(2): 148-167.* Sallie Lewis Sturgeon came to Oklahoma in 1894 with her husband, and they soon established residence in Ardmore. There Mrs. Sturgeon became a reporter for the local newspaper and created a weekly "women's news column." She later began publishing *The Oklahoma Lady,* the first exclusively women's journal published in Oklahoma. Despite her own sense of independence in the business world, Mrs. Sturgeon campaigned against women's suffrage. In 1920, Governor J. B. A. Robertson appointed her as the first female member of the Oklahoma State Health Department's team of sanitary inspectors. She diligently carried out her inspector duties and won praise throughout the state. 6 photos, 47 notes.      M. L. Tate

548. Dabney, Virginius and Kukla, Jon. THE MONTICELLO SCANDALS: HISTORY AND FICTION. *Virginia Cavalcade 1979 29(2): 52-61.* Examines Thomas Jefferson's reputation and the validity of claims that the slave Sally Hemings bore his children.

549. Day, James M. BIG FOOT WALLACE IN TRANS-PECOS TEXAS. *West Texas Hist. Assoc. Y. 1979 55: 70-80.* Analyzes the Texas career of William Alexander Anderson Wallace (1817-99), stage driver, frontiersman, Indian and Mexican fighter, and folk hero.

550. deCambra, Fernando P. LOS CIEN AÑOS DEL KU KLUX KLAN [A hundred years of the Ku Klux Klan]. *Nuestro Tiempo [Spain] 1965 24(138): 684-693.*

551. DeGrummond, Jane Lucas. CAYETANA SUSANA BOSQUE Y FANQUI, "A NOTABLE WOMAN". *Louisiana Hist. 1982 23(3): 277-294.* Life of a noted New Orleans beauty, the second wife of the provisional governor of Louisiana and later US Senator William Charles Cole Claiborne and, after his death, wife of John R. Grymes, lawyer and former US district attorney for the Louisiana district. Includes information on the careers of her husbands and the marital adventures of her numerous offspring. Based on church and family records, letters, and newspapers; 51 notes.      R. E. Noble

552. Dehler, Katherine B. MT. VERNON PLACE AT THE TURN OF THE CENTURY: A VIGNETTE OF THE GARRETT FAMILY. *Maryland Hist. Mag. 1974 69(3): 279-292.* Describes the philanthropic and social activities of John Work Garrett (1820-84), dynamic president of the Baltimore and Ohio Railroad. In 1872 he bought the house at No. 11 Mt. Vernon Place in Baltimore for his son, Robert Garrett, and it became "the most magnificent and interesting private residence" in the city. Robert turned the house into a New York "brownstone" despite much opposition from his neighbors, with the renovation under Stanford White's direction. Robert's wife, Mary Frick Garrett (1851-1936), added an enormous art collection and became the social arbiter of Baltimore. The Garretts fully demonstrated the *noblesse oblige* of their class, creating endowments in their wills for numerous medical, educational, and cultural foundations, alongside their contributions to banking and commerce. Primary and secondary sources; 5 illus., 45 notes.      G. J. Bobango

553. Dickens, Gloria. CHILDHOOD SONGS FROM NORTH CAROLINA. *North Carolina Folklore J. 1973 21(1): 4-9.* Contains lyrics of North Carolina children's songs collected by a North Carolina State University student at Metcalf Dormitory on the university campus. R. N. Lokken

554. Dormon, James H. ASPECTS OF ACADIAN PLANTATION LIFE IN THE MID-NINETEENTH CENTURY: A MICROCOSMIC VIEW. *Louisiana Hist. 1975 16(4): 361-370.* Provides a case study in southern Louisiana plantation life. Petite Anne was primarily a sugar plantation. The life is revealed by a diary kept in the 1850's by one of the inhabitants. Dormon focuses on the ways in which "the residents, black and white, related to their all-too-rare moments of leisure." 26 notes. E. P. Stickney

555. Drummond, Miriam F. PAPA'S POCKETS. *North Louisiana Hist. Assoc. J. 1975 7(1): 20-22.* The author recalls her grandfather, Corneilius Emmett Foster, his life and times, and, particularly, his pockets—"pockets that smelled of fruits, candy, and tobacco; pockets that promised excitement." He was a "preacher" who had "the confidence of his fellow men." 4 notes. A. N. Garland

556. Dunlevy, James A. REGIONAL PREFERENCES AND MIGRANT SETTLEMENT: ON THE AVOIDANCE OF THE SOUTH BY NINETEENTH-CENTURY IMMIGRANTS. *Res. in Econ. Hist. 1983 8: 217-251.* The pronounced pattern of settling outside the South displayed by 19th-century immigrants to the United States has traditionally been attributed in large measure to a hostile Southern social climate. The empirical support for this conventional position is shown to be weakened and in some cases reversed when the traditional model is expanded to include mean temperature, percentage of the population black, percentage of the population urban, and land availability. An anti-South bias present in the mid- to late 1800's had effectively disappeared by the beginning of the 20th century. J/S

557. Durham, Walter T. TENNESSEE COUNTESS. *Tennessee Hist. Q. 1980 39(3): 323-340.* Tennessee-born Eugenia Bate Bass (1826-1906), widow of a wealthy Mississippi planter, dazzled Washington society in 1865 by marrying Count Giuseppe Bertinatti, the Italian envoy. She traveled between the United States and Italy, visiting frequently her family in Tennessee, while watching over her estates, especially Riverside Plantation in Mississippi. She eventually settled in Nashville, where she died. Based on the Bate Family Papers of the Tennessee State Library and Archives; 2 illus., 20 notes. W. D. Piersen

558. Dürr, W. Theodore. PEOPLE OF THE PENINSULA. *Maryland Hist. Mag. 1982 77(1): 27-53.* Chronicles the past 100 years of life in South Baltimore. The Peninsula was the center of a rich and teeming ethnic life, composed of the 600,000 immigrants who debarked from transatlantic ships at Locust Point, Baltimore's own Ellis Island, during 1870-1900, and who labored for McCormick Spices, Federal Tin, or Bethlehem Shipbuilding. The blacks in Sharp-Leadenhall, especially, struggled against one barrier after another until the 1970's, as slumlord and roadlord alike tried to carve up South Baltimore. Local organizations fought back and won with their Congress of Peninsula Organizations. Oral interviews, city directories, University of Baltimore archives; 2 notes. G. J. Bobango

559. Eaton, Clement. BREAKING A PATH FOR THE LIBERATION OF WOMEN IN THE SOUTH. *Georgia Rev. 1974 28(2): 187-199.* With chivalry and the Bible as its guide, the South placed enormous restraints on the rights of women. Neverless, a small group of women spoke out against the double standard applied to southern females. Leading the struggle for equal rights for women were Rebecca L. Felton, Ellen Glasgow, Gertrude T. Clanton, Belle Kearney, Kate Gordon, Laura Clay, and Kate Chopin, all of whom had a part in the liberation of women. M. B. Lucas

560. Elder, Harris J. HENRY KAMP AND CULTURAL PLURALISM IN OKLAHOMA CITY. *Chronicles of Oklahoma 1977 55(1): 78-92.* In 1906, young Henry Kamp left Germany for St. Louis, Missouri, where his family had previously settled. Intent on setting up his own business, he found bustling Oklahoma City a promising location, and within a few years had established a lucrative grocery business. Kamp, a strong supporter of immigrants maintaining ties with their cultural heritage, helped found the Germania German Club and the German Evangelical and Reform Church in Oklahoma City. Anti-German sentiment during both world wars forced many German Americans to leave the area, but the Kamp family remained and helped strengthen the German American community. Based on primary and secondary sources; 4 photos, 49 notes. M. L. Tate

561. Enstam, Elizabeth York. OPPORTUNITY VERSUS PROPRIETY: THE LIFE AND CAREER OF FRONTIER MATRIARCH SARAH HORTON COCKRELL. *Frontiers 1981 6(3): 106-114.* Sarah Horton Cockrell was a founder of Dallas, Texas, and became one of its richest and most socially prominent citizens, 1819-92.

562. Ernst, William. THOMAS HICKS WYNNE: HORATIO ALGER IN NINETEENTH-CENTURY RICHMOND. *Virginia Cavalcade 1978 27(4): 186-191.* Recounts the business and political career of Thomas Hicks Wynne (1820-75), a leading citizen of Richmond, Virginia, 1840's-75.

563. Ernst, William. WILLIAM BARTON ROGERS: ANTEBELLUM VIRGINIA GEOLOGIST. *Virginia Cavalcade 1974 24(1): 13-20.* Biography of William Barton Rogers (1804-82), famous Virginia geologist.

564. Ervin, Sam J., Jr. ENTRIES IN COLONEL JOHN ERVIN'S BIBLE. *South Carolina Hist. Mag. 1978 79(3): 219-227.* Reproduces the entries made by Colonel John Ervin (1754-1810) and others in his Bible, including marriages, births, deaths, and other facts of family historical interest, 1770's-1920's.

565. Fishman, Walda Katz and Zweigenhaft, Richard L. JEWS AND THE NEW ORLEANS ECONOMIC AND SOCIAL ELITES. *Jewish Social Studies 1982 44(3-4): 291-298.* Jews are well represented among the upper echelons of New Orleans's economic institutions, but tend to be on the boards of small companies, especially family-owned retail businesses with all Jewish directors. There are no Jewish members in the most exclusive luncheon clubs and the top Mardi Gras krewes. While Jews have not been fully accepted into the social elite, they do maintain social contact with upper-class gentiles. New Orleans has been less receptive to upper-class Jewish residents than many other American cities. 23 notes. J. D. Sarna

566. Foster, Robert L. and Barr, Alwyn. BLACK LUBBOCK. *West Texas Hist. Assoc. Year Book 1978 54: 20-31.* Surveys the origins, history, problems, culture, and accomplishments of the black population of Lubbock, Texas, from its founding in 1910 through the 1970's.

567. Fox-Genovese, Elizabeth. ANTEBELLUM SOUTHERN HOUSEHOLDS: A NEW PERSPECTIVE ON A FAMILIAR QUESTION. *Rev. (Fernand Braudel Center) 1983 7(2): 215-253.* Because it was a domestic formation within a capitalist world market, Southern slavery had special characteristics. The entire plantation household, rather than the sub-households of individual nuclear families, is the appropriate unit of scholarly analysis. Antebellum plantations revolved totally around the planting activities of the planter. His role eliminated any assurance of stable slave nuclear families, and thus slaves sought maximum support in extended kin and religious affiliation. 9 notes. L. V. Eid

568. Frantz, Joe B. IN MEMORIAM: FRED R. COTTEN. *Southwestern Hist. Q. 1975 78(4): 464-466.* Fred Rider Cotten (1894-1974) was born in Weatherford, Texas, attended Columbia University, and received a law degree from the University of Texas. He assumed ownership of his father's undertaking and furniture businesses, both of which prospered. Cotten was active in Texas

historical affairs, serving as President of the Texas State Historical Association during the years 1962-64. He built up a large personal collection of historical relics, documents, and books.

V. L. Human

569. Gadsden, Sam; Brown, Bubberson; and Lindsay, Nick. STORIES FROM EDISTO ISLAND AS TOLD BY SAM GADSDEN AND BUBBERSON BROWN TO NICK LINDSAY. *Southern Exposure 1982 10(3): 27-32.* Personal narratives by Sam Gadsden and Bubberson Brown on daily life on this South Carolina island; the worst disaster was the storm of 1893, but there was the earthquake in 1886, and the depression of 1917.

570. Gamio, Manuel. SEÑORA FLORES DE ANDRADE. Mora, Magdalena and DelCastillo, Adelaida R., ed. *Mexican Women in the United States: Struggles Past and Present* (Los Angeles: U. of California Chicano Studies Res. Center, 1980): 189-192. Provides a personal account of the life of Flores de Andrade, a Mexican immigrant who came to El Paso, Texas, in 1906. In 1909 she founded the Daughters of Cuauhtemoc, a women's secret organization allied with the Liberal Party in opposition to the dictatorship of Porfirio Diaz in Mexico. In 1911 she was nearly executed for her activities, but escaped. Reprinted from Manuel Gamio's *The Mexican Immigrant: His Life Story* (1931).

J. Powell

571. Garonzik, Joseph. THE RACIAL AND ETHNIC MAKE-UP OF BALTIMORE NEIGHBORHOODS, 1850-1870. *Maryland Hist. Mag. 1976 71(3): 392-402.* Analyzes the significant changes in Baltimore's economy and population and the effects on spatial patterns. Along with a great influx of immigrants after 1865, mainly of German stock, Baltimore had more blacks than any northern city, proximity according to ethnicity apparently having little to do with choice of residence. Occupational proximity was more important, and with the increasing differentiation of the city into a central industrial district and areas of specialized production, working class, commercial, and professional people grouped themselves accordingly. Residential analysis shows that by 1870 a householder's residence, occupation, and ethnic origin were more closely related than origin and residence alone. Baltimore remained a patchwork of nationalities with white natives, Germans, Irish, and blacks scattered throughout the "social quilt" in heterogeneous neighborhoods. Not until the "new immigration" arrived did the city lose this integrated character. From the author's 1974 thesis at SUNY, Stony Brook, and secondary works; 2 tables, 20 notes.

G. J. Bobango

572. Gass, W. Conrad. A FELICITOUS LIFE: LUCY MARTIN BATTLE, 1805-1874. *North Carolina Hist. R. 1975 52(4): 367-393.* During the long and distinguished career of her lawyer-judge husband, William Horn Battle, Lucy Martin Battle assumed much of the responsibility for managing his private affairs. Mrs. Battle served briefly as his amanuensis, and then ran the large household of children and slaves, first in Raleigh, then in Chapel Hill, during her husband's frequent and lengthy absences. Her success at these tasks permitted William Battle to participate fully in public life in antebellum North Carolina. Based primarily on the Battle Family Papers, as well as other manuscript collections, newspaper accounts, public documents, and secondary sources; 7 illus., 94 notes.

T. L. Savitt

573. Gaston, Kay Baker. THE REMARKABLE HARRIET WHITESIDE. *Tennessee Hist. Q. 1981 40(4): 333-347.* Harriet Leonora Straw Whiteside (1824-1903) became a dominant figure in Chattanooga, Tennessee, by marrying wealthy James A. Whiteside (1803-61), who built a turnpike to his new hotel on the scenic Point of Lookout Mountain. Mrs. Whiteside was penalized for Confederate sympathies during the Civil War, and spent many of her remaining years aggressively protecting the Whiteside estate. Based on the *Chattanooga Times* and other sources; illus., 56 notes.

W. D. Piersen

574. Gibson, Gail. COSTUME AND FASHION IN CHARLESTON, 1769-1782. *South Carolina Hist. Mag. 1981 82(3): 225-247.* Elkanah Watson related in his memoirs that the fire that destroyed much of Charleston, South Carolina caused him some embarrass-

ment: while in ragged clothes, he failed to obtain entrance into a home because the butler thought that he was of another "class." This pointed to the importance of clothes as a symbol of class in South Carolina. While Americans paid attention to European styles, the hot climate of Charleston did produce some American alterations. Based on contemporary newspapers, Elkanah Watson's memoirs, and secondary sources; 102 notes.

R. H. Tomlinson

575. Gilbert, Dee. PATCHWORK: ORAL HISTORIES OF GRANDMOTHERS. *Southern Exposure 1983 11(5): 54-59.* Reprints brief oral histories of Southern grandmothers who related events of their own lives and those of their mothers and grandmothers, some dating back to Civil War days.

576. Giliomee, Hermann B. THE MALADY OF AMERICAN RACISM: A SOUTH AFRICAN PERSPECTIVE. *Can. Rev. of Am. Studies 1974 5(2): 202-209.* Reviews George M. Fredrickson's *The Black Image in the White Mind: The Debate on Afro-American Character and Destiny, 1817-1914* (New York: Harper and Row, 1971); H. Shelton Smith's *In His Image, But... : Racism in Southern Religion, 1780-1910* (Durham: Duke University Press, 1972); and Bruce Clayton's *The Savage Ideal: Intolerance and Intellectual Leadership in the South, 1890-1914* (Baltimore: Johns Hopkins U. Press, 1972). The three writers condemn 19th century racist ideas and ideals in the American South.

H. T. Lovin

577. Giordano, Paolo. ITALIAN IMMIGRATION IN THE STATE OF LOUISIANA: ITS CAUSES, EFFECTS, AND RESULTS. *Italian Americana 1979 5(2): 160-177.* Climate and the cosmopolitan nature of New Orleans were among the factors that drew Italians to Louisiana, 1880-1920. Many immigrants became successful merchants in the fruit business, and their success fostered prejudice that culminated in the lynchings of the Hennessey affair.

578. Giraud, Marcel; Conrad, Glenn R., transl. and ed. GERMAN EMIGRATION. *Louisiana Rev. 1981 10(2): 143-157.* Many of the 4000 Germans who departed from the French port of Lorient, heading for Louisiana in 1721 died during the voyage.

579. Gobetz, Giles E. SLOVENIAN ETHNIC STUDIES. *J. of Ethnic Studies 1975 2(4): 99-103.* Surveys outstanding Slovenians in America from the settlements in Georgia of the 1730's to "the most thoroughly studied Slovenian immigrant," the bishop and scholar Frederick Baraga, to 20th-century notables such as Louis Adamic and Marie Prisland. Lists the major annual Slovenian almanacs and newspapers and notes the work of the Slovenian Research Center of America, Inc. 31 notes.

G. J. Bobango

580. Gold, Gérald L. LES RÉGIONS: LA PRAIRIE [The regions: the Prairie]. *Vie Française [Canada] 1980 34(7-9): 47-51.* A brief history of Louisiana's Southeastern Prairie, center of the survival of social, cultural and linguistic activities of Louisiana's French residents; 1911-80.

581. Goudeau, John; Goudeau, Loretta; and Zachert, Martha Jane K., ed. A NINETEENTH CENTURY LOUISIANA LIBRARY: THE LA RUE LIBRARY. *J. of Lib. Hist. 1975 10(2): 162-168.* Partial contents of the collection of the LaRue family of Louisiana. A brief history of the family and some history and description of the collection accompanies the inventory. Secondary sources; 4 notes.

A. C. Dewees

582. Hale, Douglas. EUROPEAN IMMIGRANTS IN OKLAHOMA: A SURVEY. *Chronicles of Oklahoma 1975 53(2): 179-203.* Traces the significant immigration patterns of Europeans within Oklahoma by focusing on the major ethnic groups, their origins, and population densities. This preliminary study is confined to immigrants from Germany, Russia, Poland, Austria-Hungary, Italy, Sweden, Ireland, and Britain during 1890-1920. Mentions subgroups such as Jews and Russian Mennonites and makes methodological

suggestions for future detailed studies of Oklahoma immigrants. Based on primary and secondary sources; 6 charts, 9 population maps, 56 notes.                                    M. L. Tate

583. Harvey, Diane. THE TERRI, AUGUSTA'S BLACK EN-CLAVE. *Richmond County Hist. 1973 5(2): 60-75.* Known as "The Terri" (short for "The Territory"), this all-black section of Augusta dates from the post-Civil War era. Discusses, *inter alia,* residents' work activities and housing conditions. One of six articles in this issue on Augusta. Based on newspapers and secondary sources; 46 notes.                                          H. R. Grant

584. Head, Constance. THE BOOTH SISTERS OF BEL AIR. *Lincoln Herald 1981 84[.e., 83](3[.e., 4]): 759-764.* Biographies of the two sisters of John Wilkes and Edwin Booth, Rosalie Booth (1823-89) and Asia Booth Clarke (1835-88) who grew up in Bel Air and Baltimore.

585. Heath, Frederick M. and Kinard, Harriet H. PROHIBITION IN SOUTH CAROLINA, 1880-1940: AN OVERVIEW. *Pro. of the South Carolina Hist. Assoc. 1980: 118-132.* Analyzes the background and motivation of the prohibitionists in South Carolina and the five referenda on prohibition between 1892 and 1940. After the prohibitionists won the 1892 referendum, Ben Tillman convinced the state legislature to adopt the dispensary system, whereby the state received the profits from the sale of liquor and tightly controlled it at the same time. Although the prohibition forces won subsequent referenda, the state was reluctant to close down the dispensary system because of the revenue it generated. Religious reasons as well as proximity to Charleston (the further away the country, the more likely it was to vote for prohibition), were the two major reasons for supporting prohibition in South Carolina. Based on government documents and published works; 52 notes.                                    J. W. Thacker, Jr.

586. Henry, Bill. ALEX STEWART: A PERSONAL REMINIS-CENCE. *Tennessee Folklore Soc. Bull. 1981 47(2): 48-66.* Author's remembrance of his friend, 90-year-old cooper Alex Stewart who lives in Hancock County, Tennessee, from their meeting in 1968, including Stewart's memories of growing up in East Tennessee since his birth in 1891.

587. Herring, Neill. THE CONSTANCY OF CHANGE. *Southern Exposure 1974 1(3/4): 211-216.* Reviews W. J. Cash's *The Mind of the South* (New York: Alfred A. Knopf, 1941). Cash's South mirrors the white, upper-class male view of society. The substance of the book is its "complex interaction" of social forces and the many contrasts in southern culture. The sole unifying theme in southern culture is its individualism. Illus.            G. A. Bolton

588. Holman, C. Hugh. *BARREN GROUND* AND THE SHAPE OF HISTORY. *South Atlantic Q. 1978 77(2): 137-145.* Ellen Glasgow said that as early as 1900 she had projected a series of novels that would form a social history of Virginia from the decade prior to the Confederacy, the intention of which was to trace the rise of the middle classes as the dominant force in Southern democracy. *Barren Ground* (1925) is set in Piedmont, Virginia during 1894-1924. It is an inquiry into how a writer whose imagination has a powerful historical dimension deals with a intensely personal, subjective, and psychologically precise character in a very lengthy narrative. She is embodied in the character of the heroine, Dorinda Oakley. Glasgow's social history gives her the structure of a plot as the land and landscape provide her a massive symbolic value for depletion, exhaustion, and renewal. In this she differs from Faulkner, for she did not view the rising Southern middle class as lacking hope or as purely materialistic and destructive of old values.                                        H. M. Parker, Jr.

589. Huffman, Frank J., Jr. TOWN AND COUNTRY IN THE SOUTH, 1850-1880: A COMPARISON OF URBAN AND RU-RAL SOCIAL STRUCTURES. *South Atlantic Q. 1977 76(3): 366-381.* Links of continuity between the Old and New South can be found in Southern towns. Athens, Georgia, achieved a mature and stable urban society before the Civil War which successfully resisted all the political and social upheavals of the period. Its flexi-

ble urban lifestyle provided better opportunities for all social classes and all races than the surrounding agricultural countryside. Primary and secondary sources; table, 18 notes.          W. L. Olbrich

590. Ireland, Robert M. HOMICIDE IN NINETEENTH CENTU-RY KENTUCKY. *Register of the Kentucky Hist. Soc. 1983 81(2): 134-153.* Kentucky's high rate of homicide during 1830-85 is attributable to drunkenness, the carrying of concealed weapons, and the region's code of honor. The murder rate was consistent with prevailing social customs in the South. 2 photos, illus., 29 notes.                                          J. F. Paul

591. Jaworski, Leon. KNIGHTS OF THE INVISIBLE EMPIRE. *Crisis 1981 88(6): 274-276.* The modern Ku Klux Klan recently gained control of Lorena, Texas. This klan has roots in the movement begun in the 1920's by white collar professionals, civic leaders, and church members.                          A. G. Belles

592. Jebsen, Harry, Jr. THE PUBLIC ACCEPTANCE OF SPORTS IN DALLAS, 1880-1930. *J. of Sport Hist. 1979 6(3): 5-19.* During the first decade of the 20th century, sports became acceptable to municipal leaders, who felt that it might be a positive force that could allay discontent. The history of sports in Dallas demonstrates that its advent was national, occurring in western and southern cities at the same time as in older cities. At an early stage, organized sports had been available only to the middle and upper classes, but by the 1920's sports were available to all. To civic leaders, sports created a better people and a finer city. Sports became a pragmatic outlet for energy, and a means of controlling the population. Sources include municipal records of Dallas and city newspapers; 40 notes.                                   M. Kaufman

593. Jobson, Robert C. GERMAN-AMERICAN SETTLERS OF EARLY JEFFERSON COUNTY, KENTUCKY. *Filson Club Hist. Q. 1979 53(4): 344-357.* Describes early German immigrants to the colonies and their spread into Kentucky, lists many of the early German Americans in the Louisville, Kentucky, area, and provides a short biographical sketch of each. Based on local government documents; 72 notes.                             G. B. McKinney.

594. Johnson, James P. DEATH, GRIEF AND MOTHERHOOD: THE WOMAN WHO INSPIRED MOTHER'S DAY. *West Virginia Hist. 1978 39(2-3): 187-194.* Anna Reeves Jarvis (1833-1905) of West Virginia inspired Mother's Day. The daughter of a Methodist minister, she married another and had 11 children, many of whom died young. She dealt with her grief by volunteer work in the community. Her daughter, Anna, organized church services on the theme of motherhood on the second anniversary of her death. Primary and secondary sources; 29 notes.               J. H. Broussard

595. Joy, Charles Austin, ed. "ON PEOPLE AND PLACES": A MEMOIR BY BERKELEY MINOR. *Virginia Mag. of Hist. and Biog. 1983 91(2): 191-218.* Thomas Nelson Berkeley Minor was a neighbor and contemporary of author Thomas Nelson Page. Both resided in St. Martin's Parish of Upper Hanover County, the neighborhood Page often used as a setting in his works. In 1918, Minor obtained a copy of a St. Martin's Parish register dating from 1825, and used the names and events recorded there to write a narrative of the Parish interspersed with his recollections. The memoir, presented here, is a detailed, factual, account of the close, family-oriented society depicted by Page in his writings on rural Virginia. Based on the works of Thomas Nelson Page, contemporary periodicals, genealogical records at the Virginia Historical Society, and St. Martin's Parish census rolls; 4 photos, 98 notes.

D. J. Cimbala

596. Kartman, Lauraine Levy. JEWISH OCCUPATIONAL ROOTS IN BALTIMORE AT THE TURN OF THE CENTURY. *Maryland Hist. Mag. 1979 74(1): 52-61.* Studies the immigrant Polish-Russian Jewish working class community of Baltimore between 1895 and 1916 as to country of origin, occupations, and demographic features, based on a local midwife's records for a 19-year period, and a Workmen's Circle Insurance Ledger Book, a source which included women in its tabulations. Evidence suggests that upward occupational and geographical mobility for the original immi-

grant generation were minimal. Heavy stress on education for Jewish children meant, however, that the second generation would fulfill the community's aspirations for upward socioeconomic mobility. 4 tables, 3 notes.                                G. J. Bobango

597. Keller, Frank V.; Bederman, Sanford H.; and Hartshorn, Truman A. MIGRATION PATTERNS OF ATLANTA'S INNER CITY DISPLACED RESIDENTS. *West Georgia Coll. Studies in the Social Sci. 1977 16: 49-58.* Aggressive urban renewal in early 1960's Atlanta under the Model Neighborhood Area program resulted in a gross loss of 19,000 housing units; displaced residents—95 percent black—relocated "within the territory of black ghetto space."

598. Kersey, Harry A., Jr. THE JOHN DUBOIS FAMILY OF JUPITER: A FLORIDA PROTOTYPE, 1887-1981. *Tequesta 1981 41: 5-22.* Since Harry DuBois began living in Jupiter, Florida, during the 1880's, the DuBois family has been an integral part of the area's social history. During the 1890's Harry DuBois purchased a tract of 18 acres, known as Stone's Point, on the Loxahatchee River. His home was constructed on a massive oyster-shell mound 20 feet high and over 600 feet long. His first child, John, born in 1899, still lives there. Based on oral history interviews and family papers; 25 notes.                                H. S. Marks

599. Kiser, John. SCION OF BELMONT. *Tennessee Hist. Q. 1979 38(1): 34-61.* William Hayes Ackland was born at the stately mansion at Belmont, two miles from Nashville, Tennessee, in September 1855. He was well-educated, traveled widely in Europe after the Civil War, and was highly respected. Covers 1855-67. Excerpted from Ackland's proposed autobiography which is now part of the Southern Historical Collection of the University of North Carolina. Secondary sources; illus., 22 notes. Article to be continued.
M. B. Lucas

600. Kiser, John, ed. SCION OF BELMONT. *Tennessee Hist. Q. 1979 38(2): 188-203.* Continued from a previous article. Part II. William Hayes Ackland's (1856-1940) edited memoirs offer interesting anecdotes of Nashville, New Orleans, Chicago, New York, and White Sulphur Springs, Virginia, in the 1870's. Belmont, the Ackland family estate in Nashville, Tennessee, was host to the visiting elite, and Ackland recalls many celebrated figures. 7 notes.
W. D. Piersen

601. Klotter, James C. SLAVERY AND RACE: A FAMILY PERSPECTIVE. *Southern Studies 1978 17(4): 375-397.* Examines racial attitudes within the upper class Breckenridge family of Kentucky for four generations. All were prominent citizens, politicians, newspaper publishers, clergymen, educators; they were progressive for their times. John Breckenridge (1760-1806) supported slavery, but his son Robert Jefferson Breckenridge (1800-71) was antislavery and an educational reformer. Robert's son William C. P. Breckenridge (1837-1904) became a Democrat and supported legal rights for blacks under a paternalistic system. William's son Desha Breckenridge (1867-1935) was for states' rights and opposed to rights for blacks, probably because he was nonreligious and feared for his political career. Primary and secondary sources; 68 notes.
J. J. Buschen

602. Kondert, Reinhart. THE GERMANS OF ACADIA PARISH. *Rev. de Louisiane 1977 6(1): 19-37.* Chronicles the immigration of Germans into the mainly French Acadia Parish in Louisiana, 1870's-1917.

603. Lachance, Paul. INTERMARRIAGE AND FRENCH CULTURAL PERSISTENCE IN LATE SPANISH AND EARLY AMERICAN NEW ORLEANS. *Social Hist. [Canada] 1982 15(29): 47-81.* The insularity of ethnic groups such as Acadians and French Canadians is often considered the key to their cultural survival. The French population of New Orleans, however, survived by allying themselves through marriage with immigrants from France and refugees from Saint Domingue. French remained the language of the majority of the white population until the 1830's, while non-white Creoles maintained their language and numbers in the face of an influx of English-speaking free blacks from other US states because

of a natural population increase, and the arrival of refugees from Saint Domingue. Based on marriage records in the Archives of the Archdiocese of New Orleans; 2 graphs, 10 tables, appendix, 78 notes.                                D. F. Chard

604. Lale, Max S. "BUT DAVIS IS A HUSTLER.... " *Red River Valley Hist. Rev. 1980 5(2): 43-54.* Elmer Ellsworth Davis (1861-1939), born in Maine, moved to Denison (Texas) in 1894, ran a livery stable, and became a successful automobile salesman in 1912, the same year he was elected street and fire commissioner of Denison.

605. Langhorne, Elizabeth. NANCY LANGHORNE ASTOR: A VIRGINIAN IN ENGLAND. *Virginia Cavalcade 1974 23(3): 38-47.* Nancy Langhorne of Virginia (1879-1964) became Waldorf Astor's wife and the first woman to sit in the British Parliament.

606. Lanza, Michael L. THE JONES-LIDDELL FEUD. *Red River Valley Hist. Rev. 1975 2(4): 467-480.* A feud between the Jones family and the Liddell family, in Catahoula Parish, Louisiana, 1848-70, supposedly was initiated over a disputed flock of geese.

607. Larouche, Alain. LES RÉGIONS: EN BAS DU BAYOU (LAFOURCHE) [The regions: Lower Bayou (Lafourche)]. *Vie Française [Canada] 1980 34(7-9): 40-46.* A brief sociological, economic, and ethnic history of Lafourche Parish in Eastern Louisiana since the end of the 18th century.

608. Lasker, Morris. LETTER FROM A TEXAS PIONEER—1909. *Western States Jewish Hist. Q. 1983 15(4): 305-316.* Reprints a letter by Morris Lasker, a well-known merchant and banker of Galveston, Texas, recounting his experiences as a young man trying to become established in business after the Civil War. He was a partner with the Sanger family in Milliken, Texas, in 1866 and retained strong personal ties with them after establishing his own business. The letter also describes the yellow fever epidemic of the 1860's. Photo, 2 notes.            B. S. Porter

609. Law, Eileen and Ken, Sally. A STUDY OF THE CHINESE COMMUNITY. *Richmond County Hist. 1973 5(2): 23-43.* Chinese first arrived in Augusta in 1873 to work on a local canal construction project. After completion of the canal a number of Chinese workers remained to become the nucleus of Augusta's Chinese community. By the turn of the century a majority of the local Chinese population had entered the grocery and laundry businesses. In 1970 more than 1,500 Orientals lived in Augusta. One of six articles in this issue on Augusta. Based on interviews with the local Chinese population and on published secondary sources; 77 notes.
H. R. Grant

610. Lee, David D., ed. JESSE WAUGH, WEST VIRGINIAN. *West Virginia Hist. 1974 35(2): 154-162.* Jesse Waugh's "A Brief History of My Life," a narrative written for his grandchildren, contains reminiscences of life in 19th century West Virginia and personal advice to his grandchildren. Waugh went to school at age 11, became a farmer, lumberman, teacher, and carpenter, and held minor local offices. He was a Baptist deacon for 30 years and his "History" stresses the importance of a religious life.
J. H. Broussard

611. Leon, Arnoldo de. WRESTING A COMPETENCE IN NINETEENTH CENTURY TEXAS: THE CASE OF THE CHICANOS. *Red River Valley Hist. Rev. 1979 4(4): 52-64.* Mexican Americans, "having to exist under terms dictated to them by white society, invented, manipulated, and improved upon endurance mechanisms to withstand a society where dependency relegated them to impoverishment."

612. Lepre, Jerome. A FAMILY PORTRAIT. *J. of Mississippi Hist. 1979 41(4): 373-382.* Discusses the pioneer families of the Mississippi Gulf Coast. Included in the discussion are the Boney, Delaunay, Fountain, LaFontaine, Moran, Lepre, Necaise, Ladner, Ryan, Fayard, Cuevas, and Saujon families. Lepre traces his main

line of ancestors and recounts the difficulties he encountered in seeking to resolve contradictions and disagreements in his family history.                                                    M. S. Legan

613. Levy, B. H. SAVANNAH'S OLD JEWISH COMMUNITY CEMETERIES. *Georgia Hist. Q. 1982 66(1): 1-20.* Discusses the establishment and use of the Jewish burial ground on the Savannah, Georgia, Town Common; the Levi Sheftall family burial plot; and the cemetery established in trust by Mordecai Sheftall in 1773 and in use until 1881. Based on primary and secondary sources; 3 photos, 60 notes.                                    G. R. Schroeder

614. Lewis, Bessie M. THE WIGGS OF SOUTH CAROLINA. *South Carolina Hist. Mag. 1973 74(2): 80-97.* Traces the history of the Wigg family in South Carolina from the first appearance of Richard Wigg in court records, 1705/1706. The name figures prominently in public affairs in the state until the Civil War, when the Wiggs dispersed. 112 notes.                                D. L. Smith

615. Lich, Glen Ernest. BALTHASAR LICH, GERMAN RANCHER IN THE TEXAS HILLS. *Texana 1974 12(2): 101-123.* Biographical sketches of Balthasar Lich (1834-88) and his wife Elisabeth Scholl Lich (1842-1921). Balthasar, who came to Texas in 1857, lived in Fredericksburg and Kerrville before settling on Cypress Creek, 10 miles east of Kerrville and nine miles west of Comfort. He was a successful independent freighter during the Civil War and purchased a large amount of land to become a rancher after the war. After his death in 1888, his wife remained at Cypress Creek until she moved to Comfort in 1906 where she died in 1921. Primary and secondary sources; 81 notes.              B. D. Ledbetter

616. Liggin, Edna. BERTHA PORTER BURNS—FROM THE NORTH CORNER OF SHILOH. *North Louisiana Hist. Assoc. J. 1975 6(2):81-84.* Bertha Porter Burns was born north of Shiloh on 24 October 1884. In 1974, she was the "living widow of the late M. V. Burns, country preacher... mother to six children" with "the courage to live alone in her house in Bernice." She taught school at Mt. Sterling, Salem, and Mt. Patrick, all Baptist church-schoolhouses, and married the Reverend Marion Van Burns on 5 December 1905. They lived first in Oakland (Louisiana) and then in Shiloh, before moving to Bernice in 1922. "Generously and courageously, Bertha Burns shared with countless people the life of her husband." He died on 7 August 1965. 2 photos.

A. N. Garland

617. Liggin, Edna. CATHERINE COOK MABRY: MOTHER OF TWELVE, FROM THE WEST CORNER OF SHILOH. *North Louisiana Hist. Assoc. J. 1975 7(1): 23-25.* William Pierce Mabry and Catherine Cook were married in Alabama and lived for a time at Muscle Shoals, across the Dog River. They moved to Louisiana with two children and settled first at Patton Town, near present-day Lisbon. Later they moved to a farm about a mile northwest of the present town of Bernice and 10 more children were born to them; in all, they had 10 boys and 2 girls. In 1885, William Mabry was killed by bullets fired by four concealed gunmen. The four were captured and brought to trial, during which they claimed they had shot the wrong man. Catherine Cook Mabry continued to operate the farm and remained active until she was quite old. All except one of her children lived to be over 80 years of age. She eventually sold the farm and spent her remaining years with her children and grandchildren. Photo.                                    A. N. Garland

618. Liggin, Edna. MARGARET FULLER ELAM, SOLDIER'S DAUGHTER: FROM THE SOUTH CORNER OF SHILOH. *North Louisiana Assoc. J. 1975 6(4): 175-177.* Margaret Fuller Elam, now 100 years old, blind, and living in a nursing home in Bernice, was born 3 February 1874 "across Middlefork Creek, south of Shiloh." As a young girl she worked on her father's farm and during the summer went to Fellowship Church School. She married Henry Clay Elam, of Missouri, and bore four children, two of whom died at early ages. Her father, Alf Fuller, became famous

as a Civil War veteran and was the last surviving veteran of the Civil War in Lincoln Parish. Margaret Fuller Elam has been a member of the Fellowship Baptist Church for 87 years. Photo.

A. N. Garland

619. Liggin, Edna. MARY EDMUNDS TABOR LEE—FROM THE EAST CORNER OF SHILOH. *North Louisiana Hist. Assoc. J. 1975 6(3): 133-135.* Mary Edmunds Tabor Lee was born in Georgia but moved with her family to settle in Union Parish, west of Farmerville, in the 1840's. On 4 December 1852, 15-year-old Mary married George Tabor, and they lived in a house on property given them by her father some three miles east of Shiloh. They had five children during 1852-61, when George went off to war. He died, apparently in 1863, in Holly Springs, Mississippi. Mary married Dan Lee, about whom little is known, in 1866; he disappeared in 1871, after having fathered three children. From time to time thereafter Mary was "involved in litigation that complicated her life." She never married again and eventually "gained a reputation as a 'medicine woman,' and was sent for wherever there was sickness." Mary died 22 January 1926 and was buried at Shiloh.

A. N. Garland

620. Logan, Virginia Watson. IN MEMORIAM: JOSEPH IOOR WARING, 1897-1977. *South Carolina Hist. Mag. 1978 79(1): 71.* Joseph Ioor Waring was President of the South Carolina Historical Society during 1961-63 and editor of the *South Carolina Historical Magazine* during 1963-67.

621. Magarian, Horen Henry. THE FOUNDING AND ESTABLISHMENT OF THE ARMENIAN COMMUNITY OF RICHMOND, VIRGINIA. *Armenian R. 1975 28(3): 265-271.* Gives a history of the early Armenian community in Richmond, Virginia 1887-1910, based on the recollections of the author's uncle Manuel Vranian, a member of the original party.

622. Margario, Anthony V. and Molyneaux, J. Lambert. RESIDENTIAL SEGREGATION OF ITALIANS IN NEW ORLEANS AND SELECTED AMERICAN CITIES. *Louisiana Studies 1973 12(4): 639-648.*

623. Massey, Mary Elizabeth. THE MAKING OF A FEMINIST. *J. of Southern Hist. 1973 39(1): 3-22.* Ella Gertrude Clanton Thomas's journal of 41 years, 1848-89, is "among the most revealing records to come from the Civil War generation." It is "especially valuable for showing how and why a southern lady, reared in the tradition of the Old South, came to question its teachings and eventually to play a part in overturning many of its time-honored concepts." 81 notes.                              I. M. Leonard

624. McDonald, Forrest. THE ETHNIC FACTOR IN ALABAMA HISTORY: A NEGLECTED DIMENSION. *Alabama Rev. 1978 31(4): 256-265.* Argues that the predominant ethnic influence in Alabama (and possibly the South) is not WASP, but Celtic. Alabama history has been affected by inherent resistance to change, a tendency towards political as opposed to legal action, and a deep-seated antipathy to other ethnic groups, notably Germans. Primary and secondary sources; 5 notes.                          J. F. Vivian

625. McGinty, Garnie W. MARY JANE CONLY LESHE: PIONEER WOMAN OF BIENVILLE PARISH (1849-1932). *North Louisiana Hist. Assoc. J. 1976 7(2): 61-63.* Mary Jane Conly was the third child of Cullen Thomas Conly, of Savannah, Georgia. When she was about 20 she married Usir Leshe (1839-1934) and moved with him to Bienville Parish. She bore 14 children; one died in infancy, 13 reached adulthood. "The Leshe family were fervent patriots" and Mary Jane Leshe promoted "education and patriotism, instilling frugality, thrift, and industry in her descendants." She was a "deeply religious woman" and "a loyal and devoted member of the Baptist Church." Photo, 4 notes.

A. N. Garland

626. McGovern, James R. "SPORTING LIFE ON THE LINE": PROSTITUTION IN PROGRESSIVE ERA PENSACOLA. *Florida Hist. Q. 1975 54(2): 131-144.* In the first few decades of the 20th century Pensacola, Florida's police and city officials succeeded in

confining prostitution and saloons to a restricted area of the city rather than trying to eliminate the problems entirely. Confining prostitution to a specific area afforded both safety and economy to the rest of the city. In addition, the city received revenue in fines from occasional crackdowns. Changing morals and attitudes brought an end to the district of brothels by the beginning of World War II. Based on primary and secondary works; illus., 73 notes.

P. A. Beaber

627. McLemore, S. Dale. THE ORIGINS OF MEXICAN AMERICAN SUBORDINATION IN TEXAS. *Social Sci. Q. 1973 53(4): 656-670.* Tests the applicability of Noel's general theory of the origin of ethnic stratification.... . Finds that the theory offers a parsimonious yet complete explanation of the development of the subordinate status of this group.

J

628. Meeker, Edward. MORTALITY TRENDS OF SOUTHERN BLACKS, 1850-1910: SOME PRELIMINARY FINDINGS. *Explorations in Econ. Hist. 1976 13(1): 13-42.* Life expectancy at birth was in the low 30's between 1850 and 1860. It declined sharply between 1860 and 1880, and rose again between 1880 and 1910. Blacks were not held economically stagnant between the end of Reconstruction and the beginning of World War I. Based on published census reports and secondary accounts; 58 notes, appendix, biblio.

P. J. Coleman

629. Middleton, DeWight R. THE ORGANIZATION OF ETHNICITY IN TAMPA. *Ethnic Groups 1981 3(4): 281-306.* Examines the emergent, dynamic qualities of ethnic identity as it responds to changing local and exogenic contexts, and the adaptations of non-black ethnic groups in the urban South. Draws principally on archival and secondary sources to describe and analyze shifting ethnic group relations in different socioeconomic contexts over nearly a century of Tampa's urban development.

J

630. Miller, M. Sammye. LAST WILL AND TESTAMENT OF ROBERT REED CHURCH, SENIOR (1839-1912). *J. of Negro Hist. 1980 65(2): 156-163.* Robert Reed Church, Sr., was the most successful black businessman in Memphis, Tennessee, by the time of his death in 1912. He was one of the wealthiest Afro-Americans of his generation, and his children distinguished him as well. 8 notes.

N. G. Sapper

631. Mills, Gary B. COINCOIN: AN EIGHTEENTH-CENTURY "LIBERATED" WOMAN. *J. of Southern Hist. 1976 42(2): 205-222.* Documents the Louisiana legend of the exceptional black woman Coincoin. Freed when she was 46 years old and given about 80 acres of unimproved land, she managed to increase her estate to about 1000 acres, owned 16 slaves, and had purchased freedom for all of her children and grandchildren before dying at 75. Within a generation after her death, the family estate in Metoyer, Louisiana had increased to some 15,000 acres with over 400 slaves. This was an exceptionally impressive record for a black woman and her descendants in the antebellum South. Based on primary and secondary sources; 62 notes.

T. D. Schoonover

632. Mills, Gary B. and Mills, Elizabeth Shown. THE FORGOTTEN PEOPLE. *Family Heritage 1979 2(3): 78-81.* Originating from the marriage of a black slave named Marie Thérèse Coincoin and a Frenchman named Claude Thomas Pierre Metoyer, ca. 1767, a free mixed-blood colony of Creoles developed in Natchitoches on Louisiana's Cane River, persisting as an integrated and self-sustained community until the Civil War; after that the land was gradually sold and the family's unique social status was greatly altered by changing race relations into the 20th century.

633. Mitchell, Louis D. AARON MCDUFFIE MOORE: HE LED HIS SHEEP. *Crisis 1980 87(7): 248-257.* Aaron McDuffie Moore (1863-1923) was a medical doctor, philanthropist, educator, businessman, and religious leader in Durham, North Carolina. After graduating from Shaw University and Leonard Medical School, he settled in Durham. He was largely responsible for founding the North Carolina Mutual Life Insurance Company, Lincoln Hospital, Mechanics and Farmers Bank, and White Rock Baptist Church. He

attracted Duke and Rosenwald money for education and social reform. He served the federal government during World War I. He was a visionary who served the black community.

A. G. Belles

634. Mitchell, Robert D. CONTENT AND CONTEXT: TIDEWATER CHARACTERISTICS IN THE EARLY SHENANDOAH VALLEY. *Maryland Historian 1974 5(2): 79-92.* An acculturation study of the heterogeneous population of the Shenandoah Valley as it was affected by the Tidewater population ca. 1700-1820. Tidewater socio-economic traits combined with Tidewater political dominance to create a population which resembled Tidewater society but had significant differences. Based on primary and secondary sources; map, 33 notes.

G. O. Gagnon

635. Molnar, David Albert. WEST LIBERTY CEMETERY: REFLECTIONS ON THE VALUES OF OUR PAST. *Upper Ohio Valley Hist. Rev. 1981 10(2): 22-26.* Reprints the epitaphs on the four legible grave markers from the 18th century (1786, 1793, 1793, and 1799) and the five 20th-century legible markers (1903, 1919, 1922, 1926, and 1946) of the 150 remaining markers, in the West Liberty cemetery located off Route 88 and the West Liberty-Harvey Road.

636. Mormino, Gary and Pozzetta, George E. IMMIGRANT WOMEN IN TAMPA: THE ITALIAN EXPERIENCE, 1890-1930. *Florida Hist. Q. 1983 61(3): 296-312.* Italian women played a significant role in the cigar industry of Tampa, Florida. The Italian family structure was able to adjust to New World conditions. Italian women demonstrated frugality, hard work, and a retention of family bonds in coping with the new conditions of Florida. Based on personal interviews and other sources; 4 fig., 57 notes.

N. A. Kuntz

637. Mormino, Gary. "WE WORKED HARD AND TOOK CARE OF OUR OWN": ORAL HISTORY AND ITALIANS IN TAMPA. *Labor Hist. 1982 23(3): 395-415.* Italian immigrants migrated to Tampa, Florida, from three Sicilian villages in the southwestern province of Agrigento. The Italians first worked as cigar makers (as did Spanish and Cuban immigrants), though many more Italians later became owners of small stores and fruit stands than did the Spaniards or Cubans. The impact of migration was mitigated by mutual aid societies and a close family structure, but the surprisingly few Catholic churches in Ybor City, the Italian section of Tampa, attest to the anticlericalism of these immigrants. Based on interviews with Tampa's Italian immigrants and their children, contemporary newspaper accounts, and other primary sources; 3 tables, 70 notes.

L. F. Velicer

638. Murrah, Bill. LLANO COOPERATIVE COLONY. *Southern Exposure 1974 1(3/4): 87-104.* A group of socialists moved from California to Vernon Parish, Louisiana, to build a socialist community in 1917. Because of internal dissent over leadership and the external pressure of neighbors, the experiment ended in receivership in 1938 after several successful years. Based on interviews with participants and local residents; 13 illus., 4 notes, biblio.

G. A. Bolton

639. Nash, June. THE COST OF VIOLENCE. *J. of Black Studies 1973 4(2): 153-183.* The 1898 race riot in Wilmington, North Carolina, resulted in extensive property damage and more than 20 blacks being killed. Describes the riot and the reactions of both whites and blacks and compares it with the 1971 race riots in Wilmington. Primary sources; 2 notes, biblio.

K. Butcher

640. Owen, Polly. IS IT TRUE WHAT THEY SAY ABOUT THE IRISH? *West Tennessee Hist. Soc. Papers 1978 (32): 120-132.* Examines Irish-born men over age 20 in various occupations in the first three wards of Memphis in 1850, 1860, 1870, and 1880, and denies that Irish immigrants were less valuable, less sober, or less ingenious than their German counterparts. Points out positive quali-

ties of the Irish-born as a group and as individuals to the economic development of Memphis and the South. Based largely on US Census statistics and Memphis histories; 4 charts, 52 notes.

H. M. Parker, Jr.

641. Pérez, Louis A., Jr. CUBANS IN TAMPA: FROM EXILES TO IMMIGRANTS, 1892-1901. *Florida Hist. Q. 1978 57(2): 129-140.* Cuban cigarworkers in Tampa supported the Cuban independence cause in the 1880's and 1890's. The end of the war in 1898 marked a major shift in the cigarworkers' energies. Most reconciled themselves to permanent residence in the United States. Based mainly on secondary sources; 34 notes. P. A. Beaber

642. Pessen, Edward. IN FURTHER PURSUIT OF THE ANTEBELLUM SOUTHERN SOCIAL STRUCTURE. *Rev. in Am. Hist. 1978 6(3): 348-352.* Review article prompted by Randolph B. Campbell and Richard G. Lowe's *Wealth and Power in Antebellum Texas* (College Station: Texas A. & M. U. Pr., 1977).

643. Peterson, Peter L. A NEW OSLO ON THE PLAINS: THE ANDERS L. MORDT LAND COMPANY AND NORWEGIAN MIGRATION TO THE TEXAS PANHANDLE. *Panhandle-Plains Hist. Rev. 1976 49(1): 25-54.* Anders L. Mordt's 1907 establishment of Oslo in Hansford County, Texas marked the first Norwegian town in the Texas Panhandle. Rather than seeking immigrants directly from Norway, Mordt aimed his promotional literature at Norwegian communities throughout the Midwest. A small but steady stream of settlers took up sites during the initial years, but after 1912 the migration slowed. A sustained drought and a bitter dispute with the editor of its chief promotional newspaper undercut confidence in the scheme which went bankrupt by 1914. Despite this, about 30 families remained and built a stable community. Based on primary and secondary sources; 4 photos, table, 57 notes.

M. L. Tate

644. Pinsky, Mark. ASSIMILATED IN MILLTOWN. *Present Tense 1978 5(3): 35-39.* Studies the socioeconomic patterns of several Jewish families in "Milltown" (not the real name), an average-sized city in the American South, from the 1890's to the present, as representative of the individual goals and attitudes of southern Jews.

645. Poe, William A. NORTH LOUISIANA SOCIAL LIFE AS REFLECTED IN THE MINISTRY OF GREEN W. HARTSFIELD, 1860-96. *North Louisiana Hist. Assoc. J. 1981 12(1): 1-11.* Green W. Hartsfield (b. 1833) entered the Baptist ministry at the age of 26. Known as "the peoples' pastor" during his three decades of ministry, he served numerous churches in northern Louisiana. His ministry to blacks and whites, his aversion to revelry, and his and the area's concern with high infant mortality, are all reflected in the article. Based on census records, diaries, and parish records; illus., 51 notes. J. F. Paul

646. Pozzetta, George E. FOREIGN COLONIES IN SOUTH FLORIDA, 1865-1910. *Tequesta 1974 (34): 45-56.* Immigrant colonies were sought by land promoters in south Florida, for large tracts of land could be sold and prices on remaining tracts would be enhanced. Many of the transactions were clouded because of nefarious activities by promoters, but the Florida East Coast Railway and Henry Flagler were honest in their relations with immigrant colonists. Discusses the Scottish colony at Sarasota, the Danish colony of White City in St. Lucie County, Dania and Hallendale (designed for Swedish immigrants) in Dade County, and a Japanese settlement near Boca Raton in Broward County. Based on primary and secondary sources; 21 notes. H. S. Marks

647. Pozzetta, George E. FOREIGNERS IN FLORIDA: A STUDY OF IMMIGRATION PROMOTION, 1865-1910. *Florida Hist. Q. 1974 53(2): 164-180.* For many years following the Civil War much attention was given to attracting settlers as a means of building the economy of the state. Convinced that blacks were undependable as a labor force, Florida looked hopefully to immigrants. Various methods were used to attract them, but in the early

20th century, the tide of sentiment changed to opposition largely because of changes produced by southern Europeans in such areas as politics, religion, and culture. 2 photos, 45 notes.

R. V. Ritter

648. Pozzetta, George E. IMMIGRANTS AND RADICALS IN TAMPA, FLORIDA. *Florida Hist. Q. 1979 57(3): 337-348.* Reprints five articles from Italian-language newspapers revealing a rich cultural and intellectual life for Italian immigrants in Tampa, Florida. The immigrant workers were influenced in Sicily by "worker leagues." Such sotialistic or anacharistic concepts were influencial in the development of Tampa. Primary and secondary sources; 14 notes. N. A. Kuntz

649. Pozzetta, George E. and Kersey, Harry A., Jr. YAMATO COLONY: A JAPANESE PRESENCE IN SOUTH FLORIDA. *Tequesta 1976 36: 66-77.* In 1904 an effort was made to establish a Japanese colony in South Florida, just north of present-day Boca Raton. Failure at pineapple production and anti-Japanese sentiment caused the demise of the colony. During World War II all remaining physical evidence of the Yamato colony was removed when the US government purchased the site. However, those few Japanese remaining were not relocated as in the West Coast; they were restricted, however, to the county they were in. Based on primary and secondary sources; 31 notes. H. S. Marks

650. Prévos, André. [ACADIANS AND CAJUNS]. *Rev. d'Hist. de l'Amérique Française [Canada] 1980 34(1): 95-98.* Reviews Steven Del Sesto and Jon L. Gibson, ed., *The Culture of Acadiana* (Lafayette: U. of Southwestern Louisiana, 1975) and Glenn Conrad, ed., *The Cajuns* (Lafayette: U. of Southwestern Louisiana, 1978). Recent research on the Cajuns has dispelled many myths about the displaced Acadians. R. Aldrich

651. Pruden, George B., Jr. HISTORY OF THE CHINESE IN SAVANNAH, GEORGIA. *West Georgia Coll. Studies in the Social Sci. 1983 22: 13-25.* Although there were earlier visitors, Savannah's first Chinese resident arrived in 1872 and the few that followed were treated as unsavory curiosities until the 20th century, when they began to gain prominence.

652. Purvis, Thomas L. THE ETHNIC DESCENT OF KENTUCKY'S EARLY POPULATION: A STATISTICAL INVESTIGATION OF EUROPEAN AND AMERICAN SOURCES OF EMIGRATION, 1790-1820. *Register of the Kentucky Hist. Soc. 1982 80(3): 253-266.* An attempt to ascertain the ethnic background of the population of Kentucky. The newcomers of English-Welsh ancestry came largely from the eastern parts of Virginia and North Carolina, and the increase in German population suggests movement into Kentucky from Pennsylvania and Maryland. Based on the 1790 county tax lists, the 1820 federal census and other primary and secondary sources; 3 tables, 37 notes. J. F. Paul

653. Pyle, David. THE ETHNOGRAPHIC PHOTOGRAPHY OF W. D. SMITHERS. *Lib. Chronicle of the U. of Texas at Austin 1982 (19): 148-165.* Reproduces and describes the work of photojournalist W. D. Smithers, whose photographic work, although amateurish, was an honest depiction of Mexican-American life in Texas.

654. Quinn, Jane. NUNS IN YBOR CITY: THE SISTERS OF ST. JOSEPH AND THE IMMIGRANT COMMUNITY. *Tampa Bay Hist. 1983 5(1): 24-41.* The Sisters of St. Joseph, originally from France, came to Ybor City, Florida, and set up a teaching mission for the poor, 1891-1943.

655. Radford, John. THE CHARLESTON PLANTERS IN 1860. *South Carolina Hist. Mag. 1976 77(4): 227-235.* Examines the impact which planters who came to Charleston in the nonplanting season for the social atmosphere had on the social history and social geography of the area.

656. Reed, John Shelton. GETTING TO KNOW YOU: THE CONTACT HYPOTHESIS APPLIED TO THE SECTIONAL BELIEFS AND ATTITUDES OF WHITE SOUTHERNERS. *Social*

*Forces 1980 59(1): 123-135.* It seems reasonable to suppose that interaction between members of different groups will reduce stereotyping only in those cases where there are preexisting stereotypes. There is some evidence to indicate that American southerners without experience outside the region are unlikely to have firm regional stereotypes. Analysis of survey data from a sample of white North Carolinians reveals that, indeed, the initial effect of exposure to nonsoutherners is to produce conventional regional stereotypes (which suggests that those stereotypes reflect genuine cultural differences). Additional exposure, however, supports the "contact hypothesis"—i.e., it reduces stereotyping. The relation between exposure and hostility toward nonsoutherners, however, is monotonic and negative. Exposure evidently reduces hostility by some mechanism other than the elimination of derogatory stereotypes. J

657. Rhoads, Edward J. M. THE CHINESE IN TEXAS. *Southwestern Hist. Q. 1977 81(1): 1-36.* Chinese Americans in Texas have concentrated in four counties: Robertson (1870-90), El Paso (1880-1920), Bexar (1910-50), and Harris (1950-present). They have been mostly urban dwellers, in the laundry, grocery, and restaurant businesses. Until nearly 1940 they were mostly bachelor adult males who developed a strong community spirit in the face of hostility from white society. Since 1940 a new immigrant wave has divided Texas Chinese into an old-stock American-born group of South China peasant origin, and a newer foreign born group of North China elite origin. Primary and secondary sources; 8 illus., 3 tables, 62 notes. J. H. Broussard

658. Ruffin, Thomas F. THE FULLER-MURRELL CEMETERY. *North Louisiana Hist. Assoc. J. 1974 5(4): 148-153.* The Fuller-Murrell cemetery in Minden, Louisiana, is typical of many early-day cemeteries. "Within its fences lies the story of a pioneer North Louisiana family." The marriage of Elizabeth Rebecca Fuller to Isaac Murrell in 1853 brought together two influential families and together they "carried on the family tradition of civic endeavor." Map, 12 notes. A. N. Garland

659. Salmon, Marylynn. WOMEN AND PROPERTY IN SOUTH CAROLINA: THE EVIDENCE FROM MARRIAGE SETTLEMENTS. *William and Mary Q. 1982 39(4): 655-685.* Common law and equity conflicted regarding women's status. Under the former, women could not own property in marriage, but they could under the latter. Expands on the work of Richard B. Morris and Mary R. Beard as to equity protecting women's rights. Discusses trust estates. Marriage settlements tended to benefit wives more than husbands. Examines the status of couples who used trust estates and marriage settlements, using as criteria the values of settled property and occupations of husbands. Increasingly husbands and wives shared control of estates. Comments on the form and restrictions of agreements. Also notes descent of settlement property. As time passed, more women insisted on administration of their own property. Uses court records; 5 tables, 4 fig., 55 notes. H. M. Ward

660. Salomone, Jerome J. CAJUN SPARE TIME. *Rev. de Louisiane 1980 9(1): 20-26.* Discusses Louisiana Cajuns and their spare time, focusing on visiting friends and relatives, gardening, and church activities; and points out the difference between spare time and leisure time for Cajuns, and historical factors that have affected their spare time.

661. Santos, Richard G. CHICANOS OF JEWISH DESCENT IN TEXAS. *Western States Jewish Hist. Q. 1983 15(4): 327-333.* Spanish-speaking immigrants in Texas have come primarily from the Mexican states that comprised the old Spanish colony of Nuevo Reyno de León. The colony was settled partly by people of Sephardic Jewish origin. Despite their isolation from Jewish cultural centers and their assimilation into the dominant Hispanic culture, they retained some of their Jewish culture in food items, butchering methods, myths, and even religion. Reprinted from the *San Antonio Express,* 2 July 1973. B. S. Porter

662. Sarna, Jan. MARCHE, ARKANSAS: A PERSONAL REMINISCENCE OF LIFE AND CUSTOMS. *Arkansas Hist. Q. 1977 36(1): 31-49.* Marche, Arkansas, ten miles north of Little Rock, was for many years a thriving community consisting primarily of Polish immigrants and their descendants. Originally called Warren, in 1877 the town began to be a place for Poles to settle if they were dissatisfied with life in large cities like Chicago. They were also able to maintain their old country customs and heritage among friends. The author's family provides a typical history of an immigrant family. Primary and secondary sources; 7 illus., 23 notes. T. L. Savitt

663. Scarpaci, Jean. A TALE OF SELECTIVE ACCOMMODATION: SICILIANS AND NATIVE WHITES IN LOUISIANA. *J. of Ethnic Studies 1977 5(3): 37-50.* Narrates the harsh, unjust treatment of Sicilian immigrants in Louisiana parishes, and the gradual *modus vivendi* between them and southern native whites during 1871-1905. Whites stereotyped the Sicilians in the same categories as they did blacks, and attributed to them criminal involvement and intragroup violence. These suspicions produced episodes of lynching throughout the 1890's. Whites also were convinced that the "Dagoes" were primary carriers of yellow fever. Finally the Louisiana business community resented the large sums of money sent back to Italy by the immigrant laborers, funds which blacks would spend in the local economy. As Italians experienced upward economic mobility, however, behavioral changes forced by the desire for social acceptance took place, and they came to identify with the dominant white class attitudinally, yet retained strong group cohesiveness by extending *campanilismo* beyond their kinship groups. Primary and secondary sources; chart, 53 notes. G. J. Bobango

664. Sewell, Ernestine P. THE REAL ANABASIS OF CAPTAIN ROBSON: PIONEER EDITOR AND TOWN BUILDER. *Chronicles of Oklahoma 1973 51(2): 177-184.* Biography of George W. Robson (1837-1918), "one of the most influential men in Northwest Texas," editor of *Frontier Echo* and other Texas publications, and contributor to the growth of Caldwell, Kansas, and Medford, Oklahoma.

665. Shaffer, Janet. NARCISSA AND ROBERT OWEN: THE POINT OF HONOR YEARS. *Virginia Mag. of Hist. and Biog. 1981 89(2): 153-169.* Describes this Tennessee and Lynchburg, Virginia family headed by Robert Owen, who was president of the strategically important Virginia and Tennessee Railroad during the Civil War, focusing on the Lynchburg years. The family moved from the Point of Honor homestead to Norfolk in 1873 when the patriarch died. The widow managed to provide educations for the couple's two sons. William went into military medicine, and Robert into politics, ultimately as US Senator helping to write the Federal Reserve Bank Bill of 1913. The Lynchburg homestead is being restored. Based on Mrs. Owen's 1913 *Memoirs* and secondary sources. 76 notes. P. J. Woehrmann

666. Shankman, Arnold. THE SOUTH CAROLINA COUNCIL FOR THE COMMON GOOD. *Pro. of the South Carolina Hist. Assoc. 1982: 90-99.* Describes the history of the South Carolina Council for the Common Good, a women's organization founded in 1935 by Mrs. C. Fred Laurence to better the living conditions of South Carolina. During its 42-year existence the council advocated many social reforms, especially in the areas of educational reform, and women's rights. It voted to disband in 1977 due to declining membership. Based primarily on council records; 24 notes. J. W. Thacker, Jr.

667. Sherman, Joan R. DANIEL WEBSTER DAVIS: A BLACK VIRGINIA POET IN THE AGE OF ACCOMMODATION. *Virginia Mag. of Hist. and Biog. 1973 81(4): 457-478.* Daniel Webster Davis, educator, poet, and black leader of the late 19th and early 20th centuries, is often criticized as an "Uncle Tom" with a childlike longing for an unreal past. A closer examination of Davis' writings, however, especially his unpublished poetry, reveals his race-proud and militant attitudes. Perhaps moderate by today's standards, Davis won admiration from both races during his lifetime and made substantial contributions to the black community in Richmond. Based on Davis' published writings and unpublished manuscripts in the Virginia Historical Society; 33 notes, biblio., photo. R. F. Oaks

668. Shirk, George H. HENRY B. BASS. *Chronicles of Oklahoma 1975 53(2): 266-269.* Honors Oklahoma native son Henry B. Bass (1897-1975), an Enid businessman with state-wide recognition. A beneficiary of numerous awards and honorary degrees, Bass devoted much of his life to public service activities, authored four books, and served on the Board of Directors of the Oklahoma Historical Society. Photo.                                        M. L. Tate

669. Showalter, Grace I. THE VIRGINIA MENNONITE RHODES FAMILIES. *Pennsylvania Mennonite Heritage 1980 3(2): 15-22.* History of the Rhodes family and Rhodes descendants of Virginia since the late 1770's and early 1780's, when the first of the Mennonite Rhodes family migrated to Virginia from eastern Pennsylvania, until 1900.

670. Slusser, Cathy. WOMEN OF TAMPA BAY: A PHOTO ESSAY. *Tampa Bay Hist. 1983 5(2): 47-63.* Presents photographs of women at everyday tasks in the Tampa Bay area.

671. Smith, Douglas C. RACE RELATIONS AND INSTITUTIONAL RESPONSES IN WEST VIRGINIA: A HISTORY. *West Virginia Hist. 1977 39(1): 30-48.* In 1960 blacks made up 5% of West Virginia's population. They held more than 9% of state government jobs, nearly all unskilled or semi-skilled. Half or more of the state's public facilities were segregated. A Human Rights Commission was created in 1961 to work against discrimination and by 1966 open discrimination in education, health, and public facilities was ended. Primary and secondary sources; 2 maps, 5 charts.
                                        J. H. Broussard

672. Sowell, A. J. RANGER RELATES ADVENTURES OF A TEXAS FRONTIERSMAN. *Texana 1973 11(2): 188-196.* Relates the adventures of George W. Evans and his life on the Texas frontier, 1849-1907.

673. Spitzer, Nicholas R. "SOUTH OF THE SOUTH": COASTAL LOUISIANA. *Southern Exposure 1982 10(3): 56-59.* Reviews Cajun and Creole culture in coastal Louisiana.

674. Steelman, Lala Carr. THE LIFE-STYLE OF AN EASTERN NORTH CAROLINA PLANTER: ELIAS CARR OF BRACEBRIDGE HALL. *North Carolina Hist. Rev. 1980 57(1): 17-42.* Elias Carr (1839-1900), a wealthy planter, agricultural political leader, democrat, and North Carolina governor (1892-96), maintained a graceful, prosperous, satisfying lifestyle before and after the Civil War on his Edgecombe County estate, Bracebridge Hall. Unlike others of similar antebellum social and economic position, Carr managed to avoid the pitfalls of one-crop farming, sharecropping, labor unrest, and financial failure by diversifying his farming operations, employing workers at good wages, using fair labor practices, and using the latest scientific farming techniques. Based on recently discovered Elias Carr Papers at East Carolina University and published Carr genealogy records; 18 illus., 102 notes.
                                        T. L. Savitt

675. Stephanides, Marios. THE GREEK COMMUNITY IN LOUISVILLE. *Filson Club Hist. Q. 1981 55(1): 5-26.* The Greek community in Louisville has always been small, but it has developed many of the attributes of other immigrant groups. The first Greeks settled in Louisville in 1910, but they were not numerous enough to erect an Orthodox church until 1925. After the first generation, the native language and the church as the center of the community began to decline in significance. The desire to return to Greece also disappeared as the immigrants came to terms with American life and often anglicized their names. Generally, the individuals and families prospered in small businesses—particularly restaurants. Based on interviews; 54 notes.                  G. B. McKinney

676. Stevens, M. James. BILOXI'S LADY LIGHTHOUSE KEEPER. *J. of Mississippi Hist. 1974 36(1): 39-41.* A brief note and letter regarding three women who served as Biloxi's lighthouse keepers, 1854-61 and 1867-1929.
                                        J. W. Hillje

677. Suggs, H. Lewis. BLACK STRATEGY AND IDEOLOGY IN THE SEGREGATION ERA: P. B. YOUNG AND THE NORFOLK *JOURNAL AND GUIDE*, 1910-1954. *Virginia Mag. of Hist. and Biog. 1983 91(2): 161-190.* Political biography of Plummer Bernard Young, editor and publisher of the Norfolk *Journal and Guide,* which became the largest black weekly newspaper in the South. Like his fellow black editors, including Marcus Garvey, Robert Abbott, Robert Vann, and others, Young wielded substantial political power during the first half of the 20th century. Originally a Republican and Booker T. Washington supporter, Young became a Democrat by the late 1920's. He was always cautious in racial politics, never directly confronting the segregation issue. Significantly, two organizations to which Young belonged, the NAACP and the Southern Regional Council, later became outspokenly desegregationist. Based on the Norfolk *Journal and Guide* and other newspapers, and on the Booker T. Washington Papers and the NAACP Papers at the Library of Congress; photo, 88 notes.
                                        D. J. Cimbala

678. Tanks, Annie C. ABSALOM MARTIN: SOLDIER, SURVEYOR, SETTLER. *Upper Ohio Valley Hist. Rev. 1983 12(2): 2-14.* Details the life of Absalom Martin from his service in the American Revolution to his involvement in the surveying of the Northwest Territory and his settling eventually in an area near Wheeling, West Virginia.

679. Taylor, Jerome G., Jr. UPPER CLASS VIOLENCE IN NINETEENTH CENTURY TENNESSEE. *West Tennessee Hist. Soc. Papers 1980 (34): 28-52.* Three members of Tennessee's upper class in the 19th century committed a total of four criminal assaults and three homicides: Sam Houston, Nathan Bedford Forrest, and Joseph A. Mabry. They were men of strong, aggressive personalities, not habitually violent; yet violence seems to have played a larger role in their lives than in the lives of others. The causes of their violence were related generally to their professions. After 1850 Tennessee society as a whole became more critical of this type of behavior, requiring that to be successful, politicians had to be responsive to public opinion. Biographical, newspaper, and other secondary studies; 109 notes.               H. M. Parker, Jr.

680. Tsai, Shih-shan Henry. THE CHINESE IN ARKANSAS. *Amerasia J. 1981 8(1): 1-18.* Traces the history of Chinese Americans in Arkansas from the 1860's to the 1970's. There were some contract labor Chinese in the 1870's, but the majority of the current Chinese population is descended from individuals who came to Arkansas in the early 1900's as merchants in small, dominantly black communities. Based on secondary sources and a questionnaire. 4 tables, 33 notes.                 E. S. Johnson

681. Uhler, Margaret Anderson. "FLORIDA WHITE," SOUTHERN BELLE. *Florida Hist. Q. 1977 55(3): 299-309.* Ellen Adair White Beatty (1801-84), wife of Florida congressman Joseph M. White, enjoyed popularity and admiration in prominent social circles both here and abroad. She also figured in the Adair family genealogy. Based mainly on MS. and newspaper sources; 2 illus., 37 notes.                              P. A. Beaber

682. Utz, Dora Doster. WEST PALM BEACH. *Tequesta 1973 33: 51-68.* A personal reminiscence (written in 1956) of the author's life in early West Palm Beach.             H. S. Marks

683. Vlach, John Michael. THE CRAFTSMAN AND THE COMMUNAL IMAGE, PHILIP SIMMONS: CHARLESTON BLACKSMITH. *Family Heritage 1979 2(1): 14-19.* Describes the philosophy and work of Philip Simmons, a 20th century blacksmith in Charleston, South Carolina, who was born a slave in 1855.

684. Waddell, Eric. LES PEUPLES: LES CADJINS [The people: the Cajuns]. *Vie Française [Canada] 1980 34(7-9): 16-20.* A brief study of the Cajun subculture in Louisiana; 18th-20th centuries.

685. Waddell, Eric. LES PEUPLES: LES CRÉOLES DE COULEUR [The people: the Creoles]. *Vie Française [Canada] 1980 34(7-9): 31-34.* Relates briefly the history of the very small group of Creoles, descendants of Louisiana free blacks and mixed mar-

riages with French, German, Spanish, slaves and Indians; they lost their place in society after the Civil War and became scattered over the United States; 1860-1980.

686. Watriss, Wendy. "IT'S SOMETHING INSIDE YOU." *Southern Exposure 1977 4(4): 76-81.* Anna Mae Dickson emerged as a black community leader in east Texas during the 1950's and became especially active in school affairs. Compelled at an early age to labor as a cotton fieldhand, Dickson later engaged in domestic service. This experience provided her with considerable insight into the white community. Her present role as community activist rests on her belief that it is important to maintain links between the black and white communities and to have black representation in community organizations. Based on oral interviews.
N. Lederer

687. Weaver, Bill L. and Thompson, James A. WOMEN IN MEDICINE AND THE ISSUE IN LATE NINETEENTH-CENTURY ALABAMA. *Alabama Hist. Q. 1981 43(4): 292-314.* Indicates the arguments against and for female physicians. The arguments against ranged from the view that medicine was not a female career to the belief that women did not have the mental and emotional ability to cope in the field. 61 notes.
E. E. Eminhizer

688. Wesson, Kenneth R. THE SOUTHERN COUNTRY STORE REVISITED: A TEST CASE. *Alabama Hist. Q. 1980 42(3-4): 157-166.* A detailed look at the ledger of John C. H. Jones General Store in Fairfield, Alabama, in 1873, reveals information about rural Southerners, their financial problems, social habits, and diet. Primary source; 34 notes.
A. Drysdale

689. Westfall, Loy Glenn. IMMIGRANTS IN SOCIETY. *Américas (Organization of Am. States) 1982 34(4): 41-45.* Reviews the reasons for the formation of societies by ethnic groups to provide social and medical programs for immigrants during the 19th century; specifically treats those of Spanish or Cuban origin in Florida, some of which still exist.

690. Whear, Nancy V. A WEST VIRGINIA ORIGINAL: STELLA LAWRENCE FULLER, 1883-1981. *J. of the West Virginia Hist. Assoc. 1983 6(1): 11-26.* Discusses the career of social worker Stella Lawrence Fuller, including her work with the Salvation Army during 1916-43, and her administration of the Stella Fuller Settlement in Huntington, West Virginia.

691. Whitten, Dolphus, Jr. TRIBUTE TO GEORGE H. SHIRK. *Chronicles of Oklahoma 1977 55(3): 339-341.* Honors George Shirk (1913-77), former mayor of Oklahoma City and promoter of Oklahoma's heritage. He was a regular contributor to *Chronicles of Oklahoma,* published *Oklahoma Place Names,* and served as president of the Oklahoma Historical Society.
M. L. Tate

692. Wilkins, Woodrow W. CORAL GABLES: 1920'S NEW TOWN. *Hist. Preservation 1978 30(1): 6-9.* Discusses recent historic preservation efforts in Coral Gables, Florida, a completely planned city developed in 1921 by George E. Merrick and chartered in 1925. Discusses the design roles of architects Phineas E. Paist, AIA, and George H. Fink, landscape architect Frank M. Button, and artists Denman and Robert Fink. 7 photos.
R. M. Frame III

693. Woodman, Harold D. CLASS, SOCIAL CHANGE, AND FAMILY HISTORY. *Rev. in Am. Hist. 1983 11(2): 233-237.* Reviews *The Hammonds of Redcliffe* (1981), edited by Carol Bleser, a collection of letters written by members of the Hammond family of South Carolina from the early 19th to mid-20th centuries that provides insights into social change and the attempts of Southern plantation owners to adapt to this change.

694. Wubben, H. H. ["MOLLY" MASON REMEY].
MOLLY MASON: NEARLY EVERYBODY'S DARLING. PART I: THE CIVIL WAR ERA. *Ann. of Iowa 1977 43(8): 593-614.* Mary Josephine "Molly" Mason Remey (1845-1938) was the daughter of Charles Mason, Iowa's first Chief Justice and one-time head of the US Patent Office. A Civil War belle in the

nation's capital and later the wife of George Remey, the first Rear Admiral born west of the Mississippi River, Molly saw or met most presidents from Pierce to Taft. A product of a traditional upbringing, Molly blazed no new trails for women. Her life in Washington during the Civil War was one of visiting, partying, concert going, and church activities. Despite her family's southern sympathies and loyalty to the Democratic Party, Molly had many admirers amng Union officers stationed in the capital. Primary sources; 3 illus., 37 notes.
MOLLY MASON REMEY: "MY HEART IS SET ON MY CHILDREN." PART II: MOTHER AND NAVY WIFE. *Ann. of Iowa 1977 44(1): 52-67.* Molly Mason married George Remey, who was later an Admiral and commander of the US fleet in Asia during the Boxer Rebellion and the Philippine Insurrection. A conventional, 19th-century wife and mother, Molly subordinated herself to the needs of her children and to her husband's naval career. Primary sources; photo, 30 notes.
P. L. Petersen

695. —. [AUGUSTA ARSENAL CEMETERY]. *Richmond County Hist. 1980 12(1): 12-24.*
Pfadenhauer, Ruby Mabry McCrary. U.S. ARSENAL CEMETERY, AUGUSTA COLLEGE CAMPUS, *pp. 12-18.* Describes the Augusta Arsenal cemetery, 1826-1980.
—. LIST OF BURIALS IN THE OLD AUGUSTA ARSENAL CEMETERY, *pp. 18-24.* Known dates of death or burials of individuals interred during 1841-1948.

696. —. [WALKER CEMETERY: HISTORY AND BURIAL LIST]. *Richmond County Hist. 1980 12(1): 25-40.*
Callahan, Helen. THE WALKER CEMETERY: THE FIRST SEVENTY YEARS, *pp. 25-38.* Briefly describes Freeman Walker and his family, owners of the private Walker family cemetery on the grounds of Augusta College, and the federal government's acquisition of the property for use as an arsenal in 1826; until 1878.
Dumont, Louise M. WALKER CEMETERY: AN ALPHABETICAL LIST, *pp. 38-40.* Compiled in 1972.

697. —. WAR AND PEACE ON THE SUNCOAST: A PHOTO ESSAY. *Tampa Bay Hist. 1981 3(2): 40-57.* A collection of photographs depicting "the area of central and southwest Florida during war, peace, and recovery of the 1940's."

## The Southern Self-Image

698. Bargainnier, Earl F. THE MYTH OF MOONLIGHT AND MAGNOLIAS. *Louisiana Studies 1976 15(1): 5-20.* The idyllic picture of Southern life before the Civil War is a conscious creation of writers after the Civil War, especially Thomas Nelson Page (1853-1922) and Joel Chandler Harris (1848-1908), creator of the Uncle Remus tales. Sentimental treatment of the period compensated for the loss of the war, and reconciliation between the warring parties was promoted within the societal framework depicted. Stock characters and scenes were established. Twentieth-century works such as Margaret Mitchell's *Gone With the Wind* (1936) accept but enlarge upon the romantic myth. Based on literary works and secondary sources; 37 notes.
J. Buschen

699. Beckwith, James P., Jr. "A SHORT HISTORY OF THE A.E. O.C." BY THOMAS PINCKNEY RUTLEDGE. *South Carolina Hist. Mag. 1976 77(2): 97-109.* In 1835, three years after he helped found the A.E.O.C., Thomas P. Rutledge wrote a brief history of the organization which allowed southerners attending Harvard University to retain their southern identity and defend their region. Discusses student rebellion and election of officers. Primary sources; 45 notes.
R. H. Tomlinson

700. Black, Merle and Reed, John Shelton. BLACKS AND SOUTHERNERS: A RESEARCH NOTE. *J. of Pol. 1982 44(1): 165-171.* Since 1964, both whites and blacks in the South have exhibited warmer feelings for Southerners than have whites and blacks in other regions. In the 1960's, Southern blacks were sub-

stantially cooler than Southern whites, virtually equaling nonsouthern whites. By 1976, the gap between black and white attitudes had closed in the South and reversed outside the region. The change was uniform throughout age, education, and size-of-place categories for all blacks, except those in small Southern towns, and reflected social and political changes since the mid-60's. Southern blacks have both reevaluated whites and appropriated the label "Southerner." White Southerners have not manifested a similar change in attitude toward Southern blacks. Graph, 9 notes.
                                                                A. W. Novitsky

701. Bolsterli, Margaret Jones. THE VERY FOOD WE EAT: A SPECULATION ON THE NATURE OF SOUTHERN CULTURE. *Southern Humanities Rev. 1982 16(2): 119-127.* Comments on the influence of the black heritage upon Southern culture as exemplified by the Southern diet.

702. Boney, F. N. THE SOUTHERN ARISTOCRAT. *Midwest Q. 1979 21(1): 140-156.* First published in *Midwest Quarterly* in 1974; examines the prerequisites for admission into the ranks of the southern elite. White skin was essential, although Indian genes were sometimes tolerated. The southern culture, congenial to elites, was realistic and opportunistic, favoring those adept at making money. Apparently unique, the southern aristocracy in fact shared the nation's materialism. Select bibliography.                    R. V. Ritter

703. Coltharp, Lurline H. DUAL INFLUENCES ON CHICANO NAMING PRACTICES. *Names 1981 29(4): 297-302.* Studies the preferences of members of the El Paso, Texas, community for naming children to determine the influence of English and Spanish on Mexican Americans.

704. Current, Richard N. TARHEELS AND BADGERS: A COMPARATIVE HISTORY OF THEIR REPUTATIONS. *J. of Southern Hist. 1976 42(1): 3-30.* The "quality of life" rating game played by journalists, reformers, and social scientists assigns a moderate rating for Wisconsin and a low rating for North Carolina, but the author, differing from the most recent and elaborate rating system, would rate North Carolina and Wisconsin near the top. Observing that the reputation of each state has gone up and down over the years, and recounting the fate of the national reputations of Wisconsin and North Carolina over the years, he observes that North Carolinians are most convinced that they have the best state, which perhaps hinders them from making a "better" state. Presidential address delivered at the Southern Historical Association meeting in 1975. Based on printed sources; 59 notes.               T. D. Schoonover

705. Davis, Archie K. THE VEIL OF HUMILITY. *North Carolina Hist. Rev. 1974 51(2): 201-214.* Finds the Carolinian concern for humility to be a product of the past. Quotes at length a report from 1904 on the greatness of the state that has produced three great presidents: Andrew Jackson, James K. Polk, and Andrew Johnson who all "turned only temporarily to Tennessee while on their way to the White House." Enumerates the many achievements of the state. "The North Carolina troops were the last to lay down arms at Appomattox. No state can compare when it comes to commanding the loyalty of her citizens, either individual or corporate." Illus., table.                                            E. P. Stickney

706. Davis, Stephen. EMPTY EYES, MARBLE HAND: THE CONFEDERATE MONUMENT AND THE SOUTH. *J. of Popular Culture 1982 16(3): 2-21.* Initially raised as icons of Southern consciousness and later to instruct the public as to the correctness of the Southern cause, the Confederate monuments found throughout the South today are artifacts of the cultural changes that occurred as the New South emerged from the Old. 4 plates, 41 notes.
                                                                D. G. Nielson

707. Degler, Carl N. THE FOUNDATIONS OF SOUTHERN DISTINCTIVENESS. *Southern Rev. 1977 13(2): 225-239.* Most of the South did not want a separate Confederacy (as shown by the fear of a popular referendum in all southern states but Texas), and the differences in the South and North both before and after the Civil War cannot simply be attributed to slavery, but to a much deeper concept of region and world view, 1850's-70's.

708. Downing, Marvin. MEMORIAL TRIBUTES TO DAVID ("DAVY") CROCKETT IN TRENTON. *West Tennessee Hist. Soc. Papers 1979 33: 81-94.* From 1923 to 1968, Trenton, Tennessee, has become host to three monuments to Davy Crockett (1786-1836), each one surpassing its predecessor in visibility and utility. Each was designed to commemorate different facets of the life of this famous frontiersman and politician. Each tribute was made possible by citizens of Trenton and Gibson County, by state contributions in two instances, and by federal aid in one. Describes the three memorials and the actions leading up to each: a highway marker inscription (1923), a bronze bust of Crockett on the county courthouse lawn (1950), and the Crockett Room in the Gibson County Memorial Library (1968). Based on the files of the committees who did the work to make each memorial possible; 5 illus., map, 29 notes.                                        H. M. Parker, Jr.

709. Fullerton, Eula. THE OKLAHOMA STATE FLAG. *Chronicles of Oklahoma 1975 53(2): 270-273.* Examines the evolution of a state flag for Oklahoma to replace the one created in 1911. By 1924 the Oklahoma Historical Society and the State Chapter of the Daughters of the American Revolution created enough sentiment for a new flag that a design campaign was launched. The design offered by Mrs. George Fluke was accepted by the state legislature in March 1925. The pattern remained unchanged until 1941 when the word "Oklahoma" was added along the bottom border. Photo.                             M. L. Tate

710. Higgs, Robert J. VERSIONS OF "NATURAL MAN" IN APPALACHIA. *Appalachian J. 1977 4(4): 159-168.* Of the three types of "natural men" reflected in the literary heroes of Appalachia, the Jeffersonian-Thoreauvian "natural aristocrat" most accurately conveys the cultural identity of the Appalachian.

711. Knox, Ella-Prince. PAINTING IN THE SOUTH. *Virginia Cavalcade 1983 33(1): 20-29.* The 1983 exhibition, "Painting in the South: 1564-1980," held in Richmond, Virginia, reflects the South's changing self-image.

712. Kolodny, Annette. "STRIPT, SHORNE AND MADE DEFORMED": IMAGES ON THE SOUTHERN LANDSCAPE. *South Atlantic Q. 1976 75(1): 55-73.* Southern authors from John Smith to William Gilmore Simms, including the Southern Agrarians and William Faulkner have articulated the relationship Southerners have with their land. The Southerner sees the land "not as an object of domination and exploitation, but as a quintessentially feminine ambience, enclosing the individual in an environment of receptively, repose, and painless and integral satisfaction." However, the maternally generous southern landscape produced so much abundance as to produce and maintain the psychological utopian fantasy of the plantation system. This all-embracing repose is slightly tempered with Christian responsibility, and it is this responsibility which can save the southern environment today. Based on primary and secondary sources; 36 notes.                    W. L. Olbrich

713. Lewis, Henry W. HORSES AND HORSEMEN IN NORTHAMPTON BEFORE 1900. *North Carolina Hist. R. 1974 51(2): 125-148.* During 1762-1900 in the Northampton country, horses were a primary source of income for breeders and sport for those who raced or put their money on the horses. Gives concrete evidence of how these men recited the pedigrees of their horses with pride and accuracy. Illus., 132 notes.              E. P. Stickney

714. Lojek, Helen. THE SOUTHERN LADY GETS A DIVORCE: "SANER FEMINISM" IN THE NOVELS OF AMÉLIE RIVES. *Southern Literary J. 1979 12(1): 47-69.* Discusses the changing literary characters of Amélie Rives (1863-1945), which parallel the author's evolution from archetypical southern belle to moderate feminist.

715. McKinney, Gordon B. THE POLITICAL USES OF APPALACHIAN IDENTITY AFTER THE CIVIL WAR. *Appalachian J. 1980 7(3): 200-209.* Discusses how regional identity associated with the mountain people of Appalachia was exploited by politicians, particularly Republicans, during 1860-99, citing the 1860-61 secession crisis and the Civil War as cases in point.

716. Opie, John. A SENSE OF PLACE: THE WORLD WE HAVE LOST. *Appalachian J. 1977 4(4): 113-119.* The intimate relationship Appalachians feel with the land they live on, and the sense of belonging, is discussed in connection with the immigration of Lowland Scots into Appalachia during the 18th century.

717. Pena, Manuel H. FOLKSONG AND SOCIAL CHANGE: TWO CORRIDOS AS INTERPRETIVE SOURCES. *Aztlán 1982 13(1-2): 13-42.* Contrasts two famous Mexican-American corridos (ballads) in the context of their times. "El Corrido de Gregorio Cortez" depicted a heroic Mexican who overcame enormous odds in fighting the injustice done to him, in effect reversing the status of Anglo and Mexican in Texas in 1901. In contrast, "Discriminación a un Martir" portrayed Felix Longoria, a Mexican American killed in World War II, as a martyr when his hometown of Three River, Texas, refused to receive his body in the town funeral home, an incident that galvanized Mexican Americans nationwide. In both corridos, Mexicans were victimized by a vicious Anglo system. Where Cortez fought back on a legendary heroic level, Longoria became famous as a symbol of protest for a minority growing politically aware of its rights. Both types of corrido continue to be popular, and the genre continues to reflect the desire of Chicanos for political and social equality. 44 notes.                                A. Hoffman

718. Rumble, John W. A CAROLINA SQUIRE IN THE OLD SOUTH AND THE NEW: THE PAPERS OF JAMES F. SLOAN. *South Atlantic Q. 1982 81(3): 323-337.* South Carolinian James F. Sloan was a former Confederate captain whose life bracketed the Civil War. His newspaper memoirs, published at the turn of the century, are valuable historical sources, but his diaries are essential for viewing his experience as it evolved. Because of their broad coverage and their detail, the squire's journals are excellent vehicles for understanding a man who was grounded in traditions of agriculture, family loyalty, Presbyterian piety, and local organization. Altogether, his papers help to recreate the conservatism of one Southerner amid the transformations that war, emancipation, industrialization, and political conflict brought into his region in the four decades after 1860. Based on papers and a scrapbook in private possession; 25 notes.                                H. M. Parker, Jr.

719. Seawright, Sandy. TEN "GREATEST TENNESSEANS"—A REAPPRAISAL. *Tennessee Hist. Q. 1976 35(2): 222-224.* A comparison of two polls of the 10 greatest Tennesseans, living or dead. The first poll was conducted in 1931 by a newspaper, using the general public as an opinion source; the second poll, by the same newspaper, surveyed members of a historical society in 1976. The two sets of results have much in common, but some conspicuous differences occur. Some differences come from persons whose careers followed the period of the first poll, but others seem to reflect changing values, although no conclusions are drawn. 2 notes.
                                V. L. Human

720. Simms, L. Moody, Jr. THE GEORGIA BACKGROUND OF WILL N. HARBEN'S FICTION (WITH REPRINT OF HARBEN'S ESSAY "GEORGIA"). *Am. Literary Realism, 1870-1910 1978 11(1): 71-79.* Offers a biography of Will N. Harben and reprints his essay "Georgia" which appeared in *The Bookman,* 1913 38(4): 186-192; offers insight into his literary inspiration, his background, and the significance of his Georgia upbringing to his literature.

721. Smith, Sam B. WILMA DYKEMAN—*TENNESSEE: A BICENTENNIAL HISTORY*—AN ESSAY REVIEW AND APPRECIATION. *Tennessee Hist. Q. 1976 35(1): 95-103.* In her history, Wilma Dykeman illuminates what was "distinctly Tennessean," as well as "characteristically American," in the state's past. In doing so, she skillfully reduces the role of larger-than-life figures. The author herself embodies the best qualities of Tennessee's heritage. Her 10 previously published novels and essays, concerned with Tennessee history, civil rights, and human freedom, illustrate a profound reverence for life in the Albert Schweitzer tradition.
                                W. R. Hively

722. Smith, Stephen A. THE OLD SOUTH MYTH AS A CONTEMPORARY SOUTHERN COMMODITY. *J. of Popular Culture 1982 16(3): 22-29.* Tourism in the South, as state and private promotional literature demonstrate, capitalizes on historical misinterpretation and myths. The wealthy planter, the Southern belle, white-columned mansions, and monuments to the Confederate soldiers who "gave their lives in a just and holy cause," are typical of the elements used to market the myth of the "Old South." 3 fig., 33 notes.
                                D. G. Nielson

723. Stowe, Stephen M. THE "TOUCHINESS" OF THE GENTLEMEN PLANTER: THE SENSE OF ESTEEM AND CONTINUITY IN THE ANTE-BELLUM SOUTH. *Psychohistory Rev. 1979 8(3): 6-15.* Planters' subjective perceptions of their own behavior reveal pervasive feelings of self-doubt coupled with a sense of self-worth and power. Resultant tensions produced uneasy self-identity that resulted in questioning of the legitimacy of their power. Examines the code of honor among planters, their sense of esteem, and the use of deference in society and politics. Most planters were able to master the tensions and anxieties raised by doubt and threats to their self-esteem. 48 notes.
                                J. M. Herrick

724. Wright, R. Lewis. EDWARD BEYER IN AMERICA: A GERMAN PAINTER LOOKS AT VIRGINIA. *Art & Antiques 1980 3(6): 72-77.* German painter Edward Beyer came to America in 1848 or 1849, painted romantic scenes of Virginia, which reminded him of the Rhineland, from 1854 to 1857, and issued them in his *Album of Virginia.*

# Non-Southern Images of the South

725. Boney, F. N. THE SOUTH'S PECULIAR INTUITION. *Louisiana Studies 1973 12(4): 565-579.* Discusses optimistic attitudes in the South since the 17th century.

726. Chouillet, Jacques. MANON EN AMERIQUE [Manon in America]. *French-American Rev. 1982 6(2): 189-195.* The depiction of Louisiana in the Abbé Prévost's *Manon Lescaut* was highly inaccurate. Errors in topography and in calculation of distances to the nearest English settlements betray a limited knowledge of New Orleans. Many of the incorrect details were clearly included solely for literary effect. Variations in the narrative in the 1731 edition indicate alterations in Prévost's views of the themes of liberty, equality, virtue, virgin land, and the opportunity for new beginnings in America. 9 notes.
                                A. W. Novitsky

727. Crouthamel, James L. TOCQUEVILLE'S SOUTH. *J. of the Early Republic 1982 2(4): 381-401.* During their nine-month stay in America, 1831-32, Alexis de Tocqueville and Gustave Auguste de Beaumont de la Bonniniéré spent only nine weeks traversing the South. The descriptions of the region which appeared in Tocqueville's *Democracy in America* were not the judicious observations of an unbiased chronicler. Prior to their excursion, Tocqueville filled his travel notebooks with the observations of itinerants, businessmen, and politicians who expounded on the debilitating effects of slavery on the southern character. While Tocqueville intuitively grasped the problems presented by the sectional struggle for balance of power and by Indian removal and slavery, his apparent bias toward democracy in the free states, his lack of interest in the South as a region, and his failure to observe slavery first hand flaw his study of American democracy. 54 notes.
                                G. A. Glovins

728. Donaldson, Scott. SCOTT FITZGERALD'S ROMANCE WITH THE SOUTH. *Southern Literary J. 1973 5(2): 3-18.* F. Scott Fitzgerald's attitudes toward the American South were shaped by the two most important relationships of his life: those with his wife, Zelda Sayre of Alabama, and those with his father, Edward Fitzgerald of Maryland. From his father he inherited a tendency to glamorize the South which he never lost, and his spiritual home remained Maryland all his life. His fascination with Zelda and with the southern belle as a type culminated in the symbolic marriage of his brilliant northern success with her golden southern beauty.

That fascination steadily waned, however, as evidenced by his fiction, until his eventual realization that he and Zelda were locked in a struggle for survival. 36 notes.    J. L. Colwell

729. Eaton, Clement. CHARLES DARWIN AND CATHERINE HOPLEY: VICTORIAN VIEWS OF PLANTATION SOCIETIES. *Plantation Soc. in the Americas 1979 1(1): 16-27.* During his *Beagle* voyage of 1831-36, Charles Darwin observed "waning patriarchal" slavery on the Brazilian frontier. After tutoring on Virginia and Florida plantations, 1860-62, Catherine Hopley published her views of slavery and southern society. Both writers opposed slavery before seeing it, but they considered the plantation masters' hospitality and courtesy to be positive elements. Darwin condemned slavery's cruelty, but Hopley strove to correct what she saw as Englishmen's false stereotypes of southerners. 29 notes.
R. G. Sherer

730. Ehrenpreis, Anne Henry, ed. A VICTORIAN ENGLISHMAN ON TOUR: HENRY ARTHUR BRIGHT'S SOUTHERN JOURNAL, 1852. *Virginia Mag. of Hist. and Biog. 1976 84(3): 333-361.* When Henry Arthur Bright of Liverpool visited the United States in 1852, he kept a diary of his tour. Because it was intended for private use only, the diary contains candid observations of the Englishman's impressions. The portion published covers his visit to Washington, D.C., where Bright met President Millard Fillmore and other leaders; and his travels through Virginia. Edited from a typescript copy of the lost original; 123 notes.    R. F. Oaks

731. Fanning, Michael. NEW ORLEANS AND SHERWOOD ANDERSON. *Southern Studies 1978 17(2): 199-207.* Sherwood Anderson (1876-1941), a Midwestern writer, traveled to the South on several trips during 1920-26. He found New Orleans especially significant as offering an alternative style of life to the American values of materialism, Puritanism, and industrialization, which Anderson had come to criticize. His view of New Orleans was romantic; he found the people "civilized," openly sensual, leisurely, frank, and having a mixture of commendable European and black attitudes. The metaphor of the river, based on the Mississippi, became a favored motif; it was dark, ruthless, invigorating, powerful, spontaneous. Based on *Letters of Sherwood Anderson* and secondary sources; 22 notes.    J. Buschen

732. Feldman, Paula R. LETTERS UNRAVEL THE MYSTERY OF TRELAWNY'S AMERICAN YEARS. *Manuscripts 1980 32(3): 169-183.* Edward John Trelawny left little evidence of his stay in America, but a gathering of letters addressed to him clearly reveal his acquaintances and itineraries in America. Expecting war to erupt because of the Nullification Crisis, Trelawny left England for the United States in January 1833. He stayed in South Carolina until July 1835. While in America, Trelawny met Fanny Kemble, Catherine Stith, James Barbour, John Beaufair Irving, Emma Blake, and Christian Edward Detmold, among others. 5 illus., 29 notes.
D. A. Yanchisin

733. Fetherling, Doug. THE ECONOMY OF EARLY WHEELING AS SEEN THROUGH EUROPEAN EYES. *Upper Ohio Valley Hist. Rev. 1981 10(2): 3-8.* Reprints excerpts from the travel journals of Europeans on their observations of Wheeling, West Virginia's early economy: French botanist François-Andre Michaux in 1802, Frenchman Edouard de Montule in 1817, Englishman William Cobbett in 1816, Charles Dickens in 1842, Mrs. Frances Trollope in 1827, and English traveler Charles Augustus Murray in 1834.

734. Gerster, Patrick and Cords, Nicholas. THE NORTHERN ORIGINS OF SOUTHERN MYTHOLOGY. *J. of Southern Hist. 1977 43(4): 567-582.* America has long been receptive to and protective of its myths. The South especially has been active in American imagination and mythology. Southern myths have found proponents and even originators in the North, a section usually eager to believe anything about the South. This northern role in conception and preservation of southern myths may stem from

fascination in aristocracy, in lost causes, in the South's embodiment of the agrarian myth, or as a device to manipulate the North's own racial myth. Secondary sources; 47 notes.    T. D. Schoonover

735. Keeter, Larry G. MAX WEBER'S VISIT TO NORTH CAROLINA. *J. of the Hist. of Sociol. 1981 3(2): 108-114.* Reconstructs the details of German sociologist Max Weber's visit to the United States in 1904.

736. Martin, Ged, ed. THE BRITISH AND KENTUCKY, 1786. *Register of the Kentucky Hist. Soc. 1975 73(3): 288-290.* Letter reprinted from the London *Daily Universal Register* of 25 August 1786. Gives an account of a traveler's impressions of Kentucky in the 1780's, which viewed it as a rich land, capable of serving as a check on the spread of the United States. Primary and secondary sources; 8 notes.    J. F. Paul

737. Mixon, Wayne. THE UNFULFILLED DREAM: CHARLES W. CHESNUTT AND THE NEW SOUTH MOVEMENT. *Southern Humanities R. 1976 (Special Issue): 23-33.* Discusses the themes of the New South and racial stereotypes in the novels of Charles W. Chesnutt.

738. Neville, John Davenport. OSCAR WILDE: AN APOSTLE OF AESTHETICISM IN THE OLD DOMINION. *Virginia Cavalcade 1978 28(2): 62-69.* Describes Oscar Wilde's lecture tour to the South in 1882 and the response given his espousal of the artistic movement, aestheticism.

739. Newcomb, Horace. APPALACHIA ON TELEVISION: REGION AS SYMBOL IN AMERICAN POPULAR CULTURE. *Appalachian J. 1979-80 7(1-2): 155-164.* Examines the popular stereotypes of Appalachians on television which distort the values, attitudes, and culture of Appalachian inhabitants, focusing on such shows as *The Beverly Hillbillies, Hee Haw, Green Acres,* and others; 1960's-70's.

740. O'Brien, Dennis H. A KING OF FRANCE IN APPALACHIA. *West Virginia Hist. 1980 41(3): 245-256.* Emigrés from the French Revolution, Louis Philippe d'Orleans (later King Louis Philippe) and his brothers the Duke of Montpensier and the Count of Beaujolais came to America, where in 1797 they passed through West Virginia (then Virginia) on their way to New Orleans. Louis Philippe kept a journal and Montpensier painted watercolors. They visited Harper's Ferry, Charles Town, and later Wheeling. Based on Louis-Philippe d'Orleans, *Diary of My Travels in America;* 3 illus., 36 notes.    J. D. Neville

741. Prior, Linda T. RALPH WALDO EMERSON AND SOUTH CAROLINA. *South Carolina Hist. Mag. 1978 79(4): 253-263.* Chronicles Ralph Waldo Emerson's steadfast distaste for Southerners, because of his abolitionism, juxtaposed with his numerous friends and associates in South Carolina, 1817-71.

742. Remini, Robert V., ed. A NEW YORK "YANKEE" IN TENNESSEE, 1821. *Tennessee Hist. Q. 1978 37(3): 278-292.* J. D. Steele of New York made several business trips in the 1820's through the western and northeastern states. His journal records his reactions to many aspects of frontier living, providing a number of glimpses into Tennessee life at different levels of society in 1821. Little is known about him, but he was apparently educated, upper middle class, knowledgeable in French, and an avid reader of Sir Walter Scott. This portion of the journal covers a trip made in 1821 as he entered Tennessee through the Cumberland Gap on 9 January through 3 March when he left Nashville for Kentucky. 16 notes.    H. M. Parker, Jr.

743. Smith, Frasier. WHEELING IN 1806: A SUMMARY OF A PORTION OF THE BOOK *TRAVELS IN AMERICA* BY THOMAS ASHE, ESQ., PUBLISHED IN LONDON IN 1808, PERTAINING TO THE WHEELING AREA. *Upper Ohio Valley Hist. Rev. 1982 12(1): 18-22.*

744. Smith, James M. THOMAS HUXLEY IN NASHVILLE. *Tennessee Hist. Q. 1974 33(2): 191-203; (3): 322-341*. Part I. In September of 1876, Thomas Huxley arrived in Nashville for a visit with his sister, Lizzie Huxley Scott, who was living in the city. Despite attempting to make the visit a quiet one, news of Huxley's visit was voiced around Nashville, creating great interest. The Nashville Huxley visited was one in which the intellectual community still looked to England and Europe for cultural leadership. Secondary sources; 3 notes. Part II. Thomas Huxley's trip to Tennessee in 1876, originally intended as a vacation with his sister, Lizzie Huxley Smith, virtually became an official visit to Nashville. A meeting with the governor was followed by meetings with the Superintendent of Instruction, the Commissioner of Agriculture, and visits to the State Library, Fisk University, and Vanderbilt University. Leading citizens then called upon Huxley, and he agreed to deliver his first public lecture in America. Secondary sources; 36 notes.     M. B. Lucas

745. Thompson, Lawrence S. HISPANIC TRAVELLERS IN THE SOUTH SINCE THE CIVIL WAR. *Inter-Am. Rev. of Biblio. 1975 25(3): 256-270*. Spanish and Latin American travelers in the southern United States during 1865-1950 generally wrote about the racial situation, the cities, and agriculture. Major Hispanic travel writers are discussed. Annotated biblio.     B. D. Johnson

746. Trautmann, Frederic, ed. MARYLAND THROUGH A TRAVELER'S EYES: A VISIT BY SAMUEL LUDVIGH IN 1846. *Maryland Hist. Mag. 1983 78(1): 67-71*. Translates the section on Maryland from Samuel Ludvigh's travel book of 1848, *Licht und Schattenbilder... in den Vereinigten Staaten von Nord-Amerika*. Ludvigh was atheistic and anticlerical, a zealous rationalist, and a "tireless missionary of free thought" intent on spreading his views. He published a radical journal *Die Fackel* [The Torch] between 1843 and his death in 1869, and took subscriptions for it on his many lecture tours. One of his most important travel books came from his tour of the United States in 1846-47. The passages on his journey from Baltimore to Frederick to Cumberland are excellent period pieces laced with his renowned skepticism. "In America, everything that begins with prayer ends with money" and "well-behaved and obedient children are unusual in this country" are good examples. 15 notes.     G. J. Bobango

747. Viccars, Marion. A SWEDISH WRITER VISITS THE DEEP SOUTH IN 1851. *Alabama Hist. Q. 1976 38(1): 30-43*. Miss Fredrika Bremer, a noted novelist from Sweden, visited America during 1849-51. Describes her visit to the South in 1851, listing persons she met and indicating some of her impressions of places visited. Quotes at length from letters to her sister, Agathe (published as *The Home of the New World*). 3 illus., 10 notes.     E. E. Eminhizer

748. Weber, Bernard C. A NOTE ON THE SEVENTH EARL OF CARLISLE AND HIS VISIT TO NEW ORLEANS. *Louisiana Studies 1975 14(2): 198-200*. Contains two paragraphs taken from George William Frederick Howard, the Seventh Earl of Carlisle (1802-64), *Two Lectures, on the Poetry of Pope, and on His Own Travels in America* (1850). The Earl of Carlisle traveled in the United States in 1841 and wrote his impressions of the places he stayed. His remarks on New Orleans are brief and not very favorable. Based on *Two Lectures*; 2 notes.     B. A. Glasrud

749. Wesson, Kenneth R. TRAVELERS' ACCOUNTS OF THE SOUTHERN CHARACTER: ANTEBELLUM AND EARLY POSTBELLUM PERIOD. *Southern Studies 1978 17(3): 305-318*. Emphasizes how visitors regarded common southerners rather than wealthy planters or merchants. Most typical was the farmer who was poor, practiced ruinous agricultural techniques, owned a few mangy animals, and lived in a one room cabin. He ate and dressed very simply, did not practice gracious hospitality, but did honor women, had a high honor code and followed some kind of Christianity. He was often lawless, violent, drunk, and lazy, used tobacco freely, loved hunting, and was generally illiterate, using peculiar variants of the English language. Based on travel accounts by visitors to the South, 1850-70; 75 notes.     J. Buschen

750. Wetta, Frank J. AN ENGLISH GENTLEMEN'S SOUTHERN TOUR: THE RECOLLECTIONS AND REFLECTIONS OF JOHN GEORGE DODSON, FIRST BARON MONK BRETON. *Southern Studies 1978 17(3): 291-303*. John George Dodson (1825-97) spent six months in 1853-54 visiting the southern states, recording his observations in a diary and notes intended for the basis of four articles: "The South," "Three Days in New Orleans in January, 1854," "Slavery as Practised," and "Slavery as a System." These articles reflect the race and class prejudices of a Victorian gentlemen, but Dodson was an unimpassioned, intelligent, better than average observer. New Orleans bustled with economic activity; slavery, while sometimes appearing benign, was actually repressive; familiarity with slavery bred acceptance. Based on the First Baron Monk Bretton MSS in the Bodleian Library, Oxford.     J. Buschen

751. Williams, Leonard. LINGERING IN LOUISVILLE: IMPRESSIONS OF AN EARLY VISITOR. *Filson Club Hist. Q. 1978 52(2): 191-205*. Reproduces six articles about Louisville, Kentucky, during 1839-42, by Charles F. M. Noland for the New York *Spirit of the Times*. Covers horse racing and social matters. Based on the New York *Spirit of the Times;* 28 notes.     G. B. McKinney

752. Wynes, Charles E. THE RACE QUESTION IN THE SOUTH AS VIEWED BY BRITISH TRAVELERS, 1865-1914. *Louisiana Studies 1974 13(3): 223-240*. Surveys the opinions of British visitors to America regarding American race relations in the South. The effectiveness of black labor and the shift to white labor for the more skilled jobs and trades were noted. Segregation was rather general though not universal, but it was often indicated that the crux of the problem lay in the fear of intermarriage and assimilation. As time passed, the accounts of the Negro became more and more stereotyped, thereby reducing their significance, including as sophisticated an observer as James Bryce. 65 notes.     R. V. Ritter

753. Zagel, Hermann and Weiss, Richard A., transl. THE GRETNA-ALGIERS RAILROAD, A PICTURE FROM THE SUNNY SOUTH OF THE UNITED STATES. *Louisiana Hist. 1976 17(4): 458-463*. Translates Hermann Zagel's *Reisebilder aus den Vereinigten Staaten* [Pictures from Travels in the United States] (St. Louis: Louis Lange, 1907), a humorous narrative describing the railway built by Captain Pickles in 1883 that connected Gretna with Algiers, Louisiana. Originally utilizing steam Dummy locomotives, the line on the west bank of the Mississippi River opposite New Orleans soon resorted to mules to pull the cars between the two towns.     R. L. Woodward

# Art and Culture

## General

754. Austin, James C. and Pike, Wayne. THE LANGUAGE OF BILL ARP. *Am. Speech 1973 48(1-2): 84-97*. The Bill Arp letters, published mainly in southern newspapers from 1861 to 1903, were the literary creations of Georgia humorist Charles Henry Smith. Since they are considered a source of authentic language and lore of northwestern Georgia, the letters were examined for their linguistic features. Lists more than 1000 definitions and annotations of words. Biblio., word list.     P. A. Beaber

755. Barron, Hal Seth. A CASE FOR APPALACHIAN DEMOGRAPHIC HISTORY. *Appalachian J. 1977 4(3/4): 208-215*. Delineates the major demographic trends in 19th-century Appalachia and discusses the broader implications of those trends for the development of a distinctive mountain subculture.     M. T. Wilson

756. Batteau, Allen. AN AGENDA FOR IRRELEVANCE: MALCOLM CHAPMAN'S *THE GAELIC VISION IN SCOTTISH CULTURE*: A REVIEW ESSAY. *Appalachian J. 1981 8(3): 212-216*. Compares Malcolm Chapman's romantic notion of Gaelic culture in his *The Gaelic Vision in Scottish Culture* (1978) with the romantic notion of Appalachian culture.

757. Batteau, Allen. APPALACHIA AND THE CONCEPT OF CULTURE: A THEORY OF SHARED MISUNDERSTANDINGS. *Appalachian J. 1979-80 7(1-2): 9-31.* Discusses Appalachian culture in terms of the region itself, viewing culture as "contingent, negotiated, and politically constituted" rather than in terms of popular and academic definitions of culture.

758. Branch, Edgar M. A NEW CLEMENS FOOTPRINT: SOLEATHER STEPS FORWARD. *Am. Lit. 1982 54(4): 497-510.* An early literary effort by Mark Twain is a humorous sketch by "Soleather," published in the *New Orleans Crescent* on 21 July 1859. Clemens wrote the sketch as a letter to a "Mr. Baker" and infused it with vernacular humor. It represents one of Twain's early literary experiments while he was pursuing actively a career on the Mississippi River. The "Soleather" piece is printed in full; 20 notes.
T. P. Linkfield

759. Brinkman, Leonard W. HOME MANUFACTURES AS AN INDICATION OF AN EMERGING APPALACHIAN SUBCULTURE, 1840-1870. *West Georgia Coll. Studies in the Social Sci. 1973 12: 50-58.* One of seven articles in this issue on "Geographic Perspectives on Southern Development."
S

760. Bruce, D. D., Jr. PLAY, WORK, AND ETHICS IN THE OLD SOUTH. *Southern Folklore Q. 1977 41: 33-52.* Leisure in southern social organization instills cultural values in children; covers 18c-20c.

761. Bruce, Dickson D., Jr. HUNTING: DIMENSIONS OF ANTEBELLUM SOUTHERN CULTURE. *Mississippi Q. 1977 30(2): 259-282.* Examines hunting in the South as a sport and as a statement of Southern society and culture.

762. Degler, Carl N. A SOUTHERN ECCENTRIC. *Rev. in Am. Hist. 1980 8(3): 339-343.* Review essay of Robert Dawidoff's *The Education of John Randolph* (New York: W. W. Norton, 1979); ca. 1750's-84.

763. Fasold, Ralph W. THE RELATION BETWEEN BLACK AND WHITE SPEECH IN THE SOUTH. *Am. Speech 1981 56(3): 163-189.* Analyzes the linguistic differences between black and white speech in the South. Concludes that although the two groups differ in their grammar and phonology, such differences are relatively few and subtle due to decreolization. 6 tables, 12 notes, ref.
L. Moore

764. Gibson, George H., ed. WILLIAM P. BROBSON DIARY, 1825-1828. *Delaware Hist. 1973 15(4): 295-311.* Concluded from a previous article (see *Delaware Hist.* 1972 15(1): 55-84, (2): 124-155, (3): 195-217). Part IV. Covers January 1825 to August 1828. Brobson continues to reveal "the world of an educated public man in the early years of the republic." The diary details his reading habits, "his entertainments, and above all, the social and political issues which his bursting national pride could not resolve." The diary includes Brobson's observations on Quakers and the Elias Hicks controversy, his reaction to current historical literature, the impact of the death of Thomas Jefferson, a witty description of Hezikiah Niles and his bride honeymooning in Wilmington, his reflections on the party battles of the John Quincy Adams administration, and his sundry remarks on the explosion at the Garesche powder mill, a Walter Scott letter, the death and significance of Victor Marie duPont (1767-1827), the Maelzel automata in Philadelphia, and the place of the revived *American Quarterly Review* in literature. 34 notes.
R. M. Miller

765. Gohdes, Clarence, ed. OLD VIRGINIA GEORGICS. *Southern Literary J. 1978 11(1): 44-53.* Discusses interest in European tradition and respect for the classics among members of the landed gentry of the Old South.

766. Hoffecker, Carol E. CHURCH GOTHIC: A CASE STUDY OF REVIVAL ARCHITECTURE IN WILMINGTON, DELAWARE. *Winterthur Portfolio 1973 (8): 215-231.* Analyzes the reasoning and circumstances that led to the erection of two Gothic revival churches in Wilmington: St. John's Episcopal (1858) and

Grace Methodist (1867). The construction of St. John's reflected the congregation's desire, expressed through church leaders, to adhere to the theological statement of the Camden Society of Cambridge University. Gothic revival style was not chosen for social reasons or trends, but reflected developments of the entire Anglican Communion. Grace Methodist, on the other hand, was dressed up with Gothic trappings but lacked the symbols of sacramentalism that had provoked the Anglican Gothic revival. Grace Methodist indicates that the revival had come to symbolize "good taste." Based on primary and secondary sources; 18 illus., 34 notes.
N. A. Kuntz

767. Holmes, Nicholas H., Jr. THE CAPITOLS OF THE STATE OF ALABAMA. *Alabama Rev. 1979 32(3): 163-171.* Survey of Alabama capitol buildings constructed during 1819-1912 at Cahaba, Tuscaloosa, and Montgomery. Discusses architectural plans, completed features, and aesthetics. 22 notes.
J. F. Vivian

768. King, Richard H. MOURNING AND MELANCHOLIA: WILL PERCY AND THE SOUTHERN TRADITION. *Virginia Q. Rev. 1977 53(2): 248-264.* Examines William A. Percy's novel, *Lanterns on the Levee.* Concludes that Percy yearned "for a world which was irretrievable, if it ever had existed, and which stood now under the sign of the fathers and of death."
O. H. Zabel

769. Kulikoff, Allan. THE COLONIAL CHESAPEAKE: SEEDBED OF ANTEBELLUM SOUTHERN CULTURE? *J. of Southern Hist. 1979 45(4): 513-541.* After a long period of neglect, recent scholarly works reveal revived interest in Chesapeake history. "Linking long-term trends in population growth, land exploitation, and staple prices and production to social events" best explains social development in the Chesapeake Bay area. Even if the demographic and economic patterns revealed in Chesapeake are only partly accurate, they lead to important questions regarding the years 1790 to 1860 when the most dramatic spatial expansion of the South took place. Based chiefly on printed secondary materials; 41 notes.
T. D. Schoonover

770. Marsden, Peter V. and Reed, John Shelton. CULTURAL CHOICE AMONG SOUTHERNERS: SEVEN PATTERNS. *Am. Behavioral Sci. 1983 26(4): 479-492.* Discusses seven patterns of cultural choice isolated as part of a 1977 survey of leisure activities in the South, and isolates the social demographic correlates of each pattern.

771. McBath, James H. JAMES MILTON O'NEILL (1881-1970). *Southern Speech Communication J. 1982 47(2): 108-115.* Biographical sketch of James Milton O'Neill, first president of the Southern Speech Communication Association and first editor of the *Quarterly of Public Speaking* during 1916-20.

772. McNeil, W. K. and Nicol, Kathy. FOLK NARRATIVES OF JESSIE HUBERT WILKES. *Tennessee Folklore Soc. Bull. 1982 48(3): 68-82.* Presents excerpts from 1978 interviews with Jessie Hubert Wilkes, an Ozark Mountains storyteller from Cave City, Arkansas.

773. Miller, Jim Wayne. APPALACHIAN LITERATURE. *Appalachian J. 1978 5(1): 82-91.* Appalachian literature has only recently been studied by scholars and contributed to the study of regional literature and folklore.

774. Miller, Jim Wayne. REGIONS, FOLK LIFE, AND LITERARY CRITICISM. *Appalachian J. 1980 7(3): 180-187.* Discusses the ostensibly limiting aspect of regionalism and folklife, a prejudice of writers which has been perpetuated by literary critics in the highbrow tradition, and stresses the need for "an eclectic criticism" able to analyze Appalachian and other regional literature both in highbrow and lowbrow traditions; 1812-1979.

775. Ney, James W. RACISM, ELITISM AND THREE CURRENT VIEWS OF ENGLISH SPELLING. *Western R. 1973 10(1): 47-54.* English-speaking peoples often correlate spelling ability and general intelligence. Possibly, a defective English spelling system has reinforced elitism and racism in society. English orthography is

an unfair obstacle to disadvantaged speakers of a nonstandard Negro dialect of English and to speakers of many southern dialects. Most experts have found English spelling in need of reform. 5 notes.                                                    W. J. Furdell

776. Oatman, Russell Swinton. HOUSE IN NEWCASTLE, DELAWARE, C. 1790. *Early Am. Life. 1977 8(5): 50-51.* Reprints blueprints for and describes historic building in New Castle, Delaware.

777. O'Brien, Michael, ed. A CORRESPONDENCE: 1923-1958, EDWIN MIMS AND DONALD DAVIDSON. *Southern Rev. 1974 10(4): 904-922.* Discusses the agrarian movement in southern literature through the correspondence between Edwin Mims and Donald Davidson.

778. O'Brien, Michael. EDWIN MIMS: AN ASPECT OF THE MIND OF THE NEW SOUTH CONSIDERED. *South Atlantic Q. 1974 73(2): 199-212, (3): 324-334.* Part I. Discusses definitions of the South. Takes Edwin Mims as a case study in southern intellectual history, especially his 1926 book *The Advancing South.* To him, personalities were the key to social change. The most notable achievements he discussed were either in literature, or depended upon private philanthropy. He believed that the South should avail itself of the experiences of other sections and nations. 42 notes. Part II. Mims was influenced by Emersonian New England and Victorian Great Britain. He never fully understood the South, but more nearly approached that ideal than most writers. He recognized that much in the South must be retained, but insisted on superimposing a sort of New England on it. He always viewed the South with optimism, but offered no real solutions to its problems. 88 notes.
E. P. Stickney and V. L. Human

779. O'Cain, Raymond K. and Hopkins, John R. THE SOUTHERN MOUNTAIN VOCABULARY IN THE LOW COUNTRY OF SOUTH CAROLINA AND GEORGIA. *Appalachian J. 1977 4(4): 215-223.* Investigates the appearance of southern Appalachian mountain words in the coastal regions of South Carolina and Georgia, using the methods employed in Hans Kurath's research on American dialects.

780. Pudaloff, Ross. "A CERTAIN AMOUNT OF EXCELLENT ENGLISH": THE SECRET DIARIES OF WILLIAM BYRD. *Southern Lit. J. 1982 15(1): 101-119.* Discusses the motivations of William Byrd in keeping diaries written in code, which were banal and of little literary interest.

781. Rehin, George F. HARLEQUIN JIM CROW: CONTINUITY AND CONVERGENCE IN BLACKFACE CLOWNING. *J. of Popular Culture 1975 9(3): 682-701.* Reviews the history of and writings on 19th-century American minstrel shows and appearances of blackface characters in England from the 14th century. T. D. Rice's "Jump, Jim Crow" act swept England in the 1830's as it had America. The popularity of minstrelsy suggests that it had universal qualities and motivations rather than uniquely American ones. This is further demonstrated by minstrelsy's relation to other forms of popular theater, especially the *commedia dell'arte,* and Jim Crow's similarity to Harlequin and the clown of English pantomime. But the "belief that minstrels were the true national poets of America is almost as old as minstrelsy itself" and has become a conventional historical judgment. 40 notes.          J. D. Falk

782. Reid, Loren. JAMES A. WINANS (1872-1956). *Southern Speech Communication J. 1982 47(2): 115-123.* Biographical sketch of James A. Winans, second president of the Southern Speech Communication Association.

783. Saxon, John D. CONTEMPORARY SOUTHERN ORATORY: A RHETORIC OF HOPE, NOT DESPERATION. *Southern Speech Communication J. 1975 40(3): 262-274.* Contemporary southern oratory is "characterized by an aversion to the past rhetoric of desperation and lost causes, by a spirit of renewal, and with a focus which is decidedly futuristic."

784. Wilson, Gordon, Sr. ORIGINS OF THE PEOPLE OF THE MAMMOTH CAVE REGION AS SHOWN BY THEIR SURNAMES AND REGIONAL WORDS. *Kentucky Folklore Record 1973 17(1): 10-18.* Part I. A linguistic study of the Mammoth Cave region and a classification of language area origins based on taped interviews and the use of *Linguistic Atlas* and Wisconsin tests. Article to be continued.                                    J. C. Crowe

785. —. [THE GULLAH DIALECT]. *J. of Black Studies 1980 10(4): 417-435.*
Johnson, Guy B. THE GULLAH DIALECT REVISITED: A NOTE ON LINGUISTIC ACCULTURATION, *pp. 417-424.* The major weaknesses of the Melville J. Herskovits-Lorenzo D. Turner thesis are 1) not placing trait diffusion into context, 2) not providing an index of relative significance of specific items, 3) not assessing the white man's extreme dominance in the United States, and 4) not maintaining historical and cultural perspective. On several of the Georgia and South Carolina Sea Islands, the Gullah dialect virtually disappeared between 1940 and 1965. To improve American race relations, we should give Afro-Americans "a taste of self-confidence and an expectation of reward for honest effort," instead of trying to explain how black speech patterns represent African cultural survivals.
Baird, Keith E. GUY B. JOHNSON REVISITED: ANOTHER LOOK AT GULLAH, *pp. 425-435.* Guy B. Johnson's books and 1967 speech before the American Anthropological Association basically misunderstand the Gullah dialect of the Sea Islanders by treating it as an American English dialect instead of a language in its own right. It is an example of creole languages that exist throughout the world. Johnson's Eurocentric view of Gullah also ignores African adaptive and creative capability. Biblio.                              R. G. Sherer

# Intellectual Culture, Fine Arts, and Science

786. Agee, James and Evans, Walker. "EMMA" FROM *LET US NOW PRAISE FAMOUS MEN. Southern Exposure 1979 7(1): 8-17.* Excerpt from James Agee and Walker Evans's *Let Us Now Praise Famous Men* (1934) on the South during the Depression, which tells the story of a white sharecropping family in Alabama, particularly one member, Emma Gudger McCloud, then 18.

787. Aiken, Charles S. FAULKNER'S YOKNAPATAWPHA COUNTY: A PLACE IN THE AMERICAN SOUTH. *Geographical Rev. 1979 69(3): 331-348.* William Faulkner's fictional Yoknapatawpha County often is interpreted as the South in microcosm. This idea is refuted by examining the county's relationship to the Upland and Lowland Souths and to the rural and urban Souths. Faulkner imagined Yoknapatawpha to have a definite location in the Lowland South. Characters of the fictional place have ties to portions of the Upland South and to other areas of the Lowland. Although differences between the Yoknapatawpha countryside and small-town Jefferson are presented by Faulkner, principal rural-urban contrasts are between Yoknapatawpha and Memphis which lies beyond the county's boundaries. Because Faulkner's main purpose was to tell stories of the universal, mutual experiences of people rather than to depict the South, Yoknapatawpha County should be accepted as a universal place that is interconnected with all other places. 3 photos, 5 maps, 54 notes.                   J

788. Aiken, Charles S. THE TRANSFORMATION OF JAMES AGEE'S KNOXVILLE. *Geog. Rev. 1983 73(2): 150-165.* A prose poem, "Knoxville: Summer of 1915," and an autobiographical novel, *A Death in the Family,* by James Agee are set in a neighborhood near the central business district of Knoxville, Tennessee. In 1915 the neighborhood comprised single-family houses in which lived young couples with children. Beginning with the depression of 1929, the neighborhood was transformed through social filtering and the growth of the nearby University of Tennessee. The area is now an inner-city location where many houses have been converted to apartments for university students. Various groups of residents contend against each other to establish an identity for the neighborhood.                                            J/S

789. Allen, William Rodney. ALL THE NAMES OF DEATH: WALKER PERCY AND HEMINGWAY. *Mississippi Q. 1982-83 36(1): 3-19.* Ernest Hemingway was a major influence on the novels of Southerner Walker Percy, as both authors confronted issues of suicide and death in their lives and fiction.

790. Arms, Valarie Meliotes. WILLIAM STYRON AND THE SPELL OF THE SOUTH. *Mississippi Q. 1980-81 34(1): 25-36.* Directs attention to the ambiguity toward the South which characterizes the work of William Styron (his writings have been both praised for their southern characteristics and damned for the lack of them) and advances the view that, given the esteem which his novels are accorded abroad, Styron's work represents the expansion of the southern tradition into an international literature.

791. Arner, Robert D. JOHN SMITH, THE "STARVING TIME," AND THE GENESIS OF SOUTHERN HUMOR: VARIATIONS ON A THEME. *Louisiana Studies 1973 12(1): 383-390.* Analyzes John Smith's (1570?-1631) *General Historie of Virginia, New-England, and the Summer Isles* (1624) for its traces of humor. The main core of this humor appeared in the writings of other Southern colonials, including George Alsup, Ebenezer Cooke, and William Byrd, II, and was kept alive and enlarged by later writers such as A. B. Longstreet and Samuel L. Clemens. 18 notes.
G. W. McGinty

792. Arnold, Marilyn. WILLA CATHER'S NOSTALGIA: A STUDY IN AMBIVALENCE. *Res. Studies 1981 49(1): 23-34.* Agrees with those who see in Willa Cather's later work a stubborn prejudice against the present in favor of the past, but makes clear that there is in her work an almost equally strong counterthrust against nostalgia which qualifies her veneration of the past and renders her both a nostalgic and a severe critic of nostalgia.

793. Athas, Daphne. WHY THERE ARE NO SOUTHERN WRITERS. *Southern Rev. 1982 18(4): 755-766.* Recollections of living in Chapel Hill, North Carolina in the 1940's, the Southern social and cultural environments, with special attention to the Southern conception of womanhood, and the effects of the Southern way of life on Southern authors.

794. Baird, Reed M. OPIE READ: AN AMERICAN TRAVELER. *Tennessee Hist. Q. 1974 33(4): 410-428.* Opie Read was a southern regionalist writer who had the artistic detachment which precluded the sentimentality pervading the work of most postwar southerners. The foundations for his "character" novels were laid in the 1870's when Read led a vagabond life through Tennessee and Kentucky. A popular writer who reached his peak in the 1890's and early 1900's, this folk philosopher wrote for general audiences composed of the plain people of America. Secondary sources; 27 notes.
M. B. Lucas

795. Barge, Laura. AN ELIZABETH SPENCER CHECKLIST, 1948-1976. *Mississippi Q. 1976 29(4): 569-590.* Bibliography of works by and about Elizabeth Spencer, 1948-76.

796. Beauchamp, Virginia Walcott. LETTERS AS LITERATURE: THE PRESTONS OF BALTIMORE. *Maryland Hist. Mag. 1982 77(3): 213-221.* The extensive correspondence between Baltimore attorney William P. Preston and his wife Madge Preston during 1847-70 shows the possibilities for serious literary achievement in epistolary form. Among surviving correspondence is a lengthy exchange of letters with their only child, May, who attended St. Joseph's Academy at Emmitsburg, and became "an accomplished artist herself in the epistolary form." The self-portrait revealed in the letters, the concreteness of detail, the self-conscious literary stances of the husband's writing set beside the sheer entertainment value of his wife's style, raise the letters to the class of literature and are invaluable for social history. Based on manuscripts and secondary sources; 24 notes.
G. J. Bobango

797. Bendixen, Alfred. CABLE'S *THE GRANDISSIMES*: A LITERARY PIONEER CONFRONTS THE SOUTHERN TRADITION. *Southern Q. 1980 18(4): 23-33.* Before the appearance of George Washington Cable's *The Grandissimes* in 1880, prominent southern fiction perpetuated the plantation myth in the South. Refusing to go along with the plantation myth, he started a new trend in southern writing that was committed to exposing moral issues of the present and past in the South. Primary sources; 16 notes.
B. D. Ledbetter

798. Bennett, James D. A TRIBUTE TO LOUIS H. HAST, LOUISVILLE MUSICIAN. *Filson Club Hist. Q. 1978 52(4): 323-329.* Louis H. Hast, an immigrant from Germany, was a dominant figure in establishing a strong musical tradition in Louisville, Kentucky. In 1878 Hast became organist and choir director for Christ Church Cathedral and introduced classical music to church functions. He also started the Philharmonic and *La Reunion* Musicale and contributed to the Public Library. Newspapers and secondary works; 24 notes.
G. B. McKinney

799. Bennett, S. M. ORNAMENT AND ENVIRONMENT: USES OF FOLKLORE IN WILLA CATHER'S FICTION. *Tennessee Folklore Soc. Bull. 1974 40(3): 95-102.*

800. Benson, Robert G. THE EXCELLENCE OF JOHN DONALD WADE. *Mississippi Q. 1976 29(2): 233-239.* Discusses the fiction of southern author John Donald Wade, 1930's-60.

801. Berkove, Lawrence I. THE FREE MAN OF COLOR IN *THE GRANDISSIMES* AND WORKS BY HARRIS AND MARK TWAIN. *Southern Q. 1980 18(4): 60-73.* Soon after Reconstruction ended in 1877, the South's three most noted literary figures wrote significant works around the free man of color in the South: George Washington Cable's *The Grandissimes* (1880), Joel Chandler Harris's "Free Joe and the Rest of the World" (1884), and Mark Twain's *Huckleberry Finn* (1884). All three authors were critical of the South's treatment of the freedmen and pessimistic about the future of blacks in the South. Primary sources; 37 notes.
B. D. Ledbetter

802. Black, Ann McMurry. OLD-TIMEY FIDDLER. *Appalachian J. 1978 5(2): 256-267.* Discusses the fiddle playing of James "Buster" Russell, a native of Claiborne County, Tennessee; examines folk music of Appalachia and its origins in Renaissance, British, and Irish country music.

803. Bloomer, John W. "THE LOAFERS" IN BIRMINGHAM IN THE TWENTIES. *Alabama Rev. 1977 30(2): 101-107.* "The Loafers" was the name a group of aspiring fiction writers gave themselves in the 1920's. The leading personality was Octavus Roy Cohen in whose Birmingham apartment the group usually met. Most members were journalists, who concentrated on light stories and used the weekly gathering to hatch or develop plots and resolve literary problems. Several achieved national fame through major prizes or sensitive analyses of contemporary southern themes. Primary and secondary sources.
J. F. Vivian

804. Blotner, Joseph. THE FALKNERS AND THE FICTIONAL FAMILIES. *Georgia Rev. 1976 30(3): 572-592.* A thorough study of a representative selection of William Faulkner's writings indicates clearly that he drew heavily from the lives of friends and members of his family in his writings. The personalities and places presented, however, are far more than the simple lifting of characters he had known in toto. His people are a deft blending of history, people he knew, and his own philosophical leanings.
M. B. Lucas

805. Blotner, Joseph. WILLIAM FAULKNER'S ESSAY ON THE COMPOSITION OF *SARTORIS*. *Yale U. Lib. Gazette 1973 47(3): 121-124.* Introduces a previously unpublished Faulkner note regarding the composition of "Flags in the Dust," published in 1929 as *Sartoris*. Its editing by Faulkner and Ben Wasson led to Faulkner's discovery of the imaginary world he used in later works.
D. A. Yanchisin

806. Bonner, Judith Hopkins. GEORGE DAVID COULON: A NINETEENTH CENTURY FRENCH LOUISIANA PAINTER. *Southern Q. 1982 20(2): 41-61.* French-born George David Coulon was New Orleans's best-known, most prolific painter of the 19th

century. In an age when art provided no certain sustenance for its creators, Coulon was able to live comfortably by painting scores of landscapes and portraits, and by accepting commissions to decorate buildings and stage settings. Other members of his immediate family were also successful, though less renowned, artists. Coulon taught art during most of his adult life. 5 illus.                W. A. Wiegand

807.   Bonner, Thomas, Jr. CHRISTIANITY AND CATHOLICISM IN THE FICTION OF KATE CHOPIN. *Southern Q.* 1982 20(2): 118-125. An analysis of Kate Chopin's fiction demonstrates not only a heavy reliance on the culture of French Louisiana, but also the influence of the Roman Catholic and Christian environment in which she was raised. While she accepted the former, she was ambivalent about the latter, as is evident in her novel, *The Awakening,* and several short stories.                W. A. Wiegand

808.   Boozer, William, ed. JESSE STUART TO WILLIAM BOOZER: A DECADE OF SELECTED LETTERS, 1968-1978. *Register of the Kentucky Hist. Soc.* 1982 80(1): 1-64. Excerpts from letters written by Kentucky author Jesse Stuart to William Boozer. Stuart's feelings about his place as a literary figure, his interest in people, and in his and others' writings are covered. 5 illus., 121 notes.
                J. F. Paul

809.   Bosha, Francis J. WILLIAM FAULKNER AND THE EISENHOWER ADMINISTRATION. *J. of Mississippi Hist.* 1980 42(1): 49-54. After receiving the Nobel Prize in Literature for 1949, William Faulkner was asked by the State Department to travel abroad as a goodwill ambassador on four occasions between 1954 and 1961. His national service included a stateside phase: in June 1956, President Dwight D. Eisenhower requested that Faulkner serve as chairman of the Writers' Group of the People-to-People Program. The State Department also asked Faulkner to address the Seventh National Conference of the US National Commission for UNESCO in Denver, Colorado, on 2 October 1959. Describes the effort of Maxwell M. Rabb, Eisenhower's executive assistant campaign manager and future associate counsel to the president, to bring the southern writer's name to the attention of the Eisenhower administration. Discusses the opposition of minority groups to the appointment of Faulkner to work with a Civil Rights Commission and the People-to-People Program.                M. S. Legan

810.   Bourdon, David. WASHINGTON REVISITED. *Art in Am.* 1978 66(4): 95-99. Reminisces about the art scene in Washington, D.C., covering 1972-77, and lists the number of Washington artists who have moved to New York City.

811.   Bradford, M. E. THE ANOMALY OF FAULKNER'S WORLD WAR I STORIES. *Mississippi Q.* 1983 36(3): 243-262. Examines William Faulkner's fiction about World War I and the manner in which he expressed his disgust for the war as a tragic waste.

812.   Bradford, M. E. THE OTHER REPUBLIC: *ROMANITAS* IN SOUTHERN LITERATURE. *Southern Humanities Rev.* 1977 11(Special Issue): 4-14. Roman and southern literature accent dedication to society and state and pay attention to conduct rather than sensibility. One of six articles in this issue on classical traditions in the South.

813.   Brans, Jo. STRUGGLING AGAINST THE PLAID: AN INTERVIEW WITH EUDORA WELTY. *Southwest Rev.* 1981 66(3): 255-266. A 1980 interview with Pulitzer Prize-winning author Eudora Welty, focusing on her writing and the characters in her works, 1930's-80.

814.   Brantsaeter, Per L. TENNESSEE WILLIAMS OG DRONNINGEN AV ENGLAND [Tennessee Williams and the Queen of England]. *Samtiden [Norway]* 1977 86(5): 310-314. Reviews Tennessee William's *Memoirs* (New York, 1975), seeing it as an epilogue to the description of his sister Rose in his play *The Glass Menagerie* (1945).

815.   Bresnahan, Roger J. WILLIAM GILMORE SIMMS' REVOLUTIONARY WAR: A ROMANTIC VIEW OF SOUTHERN HISTORY. *Studies in Romanticism* 1976 15(4): 573-588. Examines the literature of William Gilmore Simms and his romantic attitude toward the American Revolution, 1830's-70's.

816.   Broadwell, Elizabeth Pell and Hoag, Ronald Wesley. A CONVERSATION WITH ELIZABETH SPENCER. *Southern Rev.* 1982 18(1): 111-130. In this 1980 interview, novelist Elizabeth Spencer discusses the Southern roots of her fiction and how she develops her plots and characters.

817.   Broadwell, Elizabeth Pell and Hoag, Ronald Wesley. "A WRITER FIRST": AN INTERVIEW WITH ERSKINE CALDWELL. *Georgia Rev.* 1982 36(1): 82-101. Erskine Caldwell, author of *Tobacco Road, God's Little Acre, Journeyman,* and other works, discusses his life, his career as a writer, and his view of the American South.                D. J. Cimbala

818.   Brodsky, Louis D. WILLIAM FAULKNER: POET AT LARGE. *Southern Rev.* 1982 18(4): 767-775. Reviews William Faulkner's poetic career between 1921 and 1924.

819.   Brooks, Cleanth. FAULKNER AND THE MUSE OF HISTORY. *Mississippi Q.* 1975 28(3): 265-279. William Faulkner's preoccupation with southern culture and history inspired his fiction during 1929-42.

820.   Bruccoli, Matthew J. "AN INSTANCE OF APPARENT PLAGIARISM": F. SCOTT FITZGERALD, WILLA CATHER, AND THE FIRST *GATSBY* MANUSCRIPT. *Princeton U. Lib. Chronicle* 1978 39(3): 171-178. Reprints a letter from F. Scott Fitzgerald to Willa Cather to explain an apparent plagiarism in his first draft of *The Great Gatsby* in 1925, which seemed to echo a passage from Cather's novel, *A Lost Lady,* which Fitzgerald had not read.

821.   Bryce, Lynn. SILENT CONFLUENCE: EASTERN AND WESTERN THEMES IN THE ADAMS' MONUMENT AT ROCK CREEK CEMETERY. *North Dakota Q.* 1983 51(2): 84-93. Describes Henry Brooks Adams's attempt to combine Oriental and Western religious concepts of contemplation and compassion in the memorial statue at Rock Creek Cemetery in Washington, D.C., which he commissioned after the death of his wife, Marion.

822.   Buffington, Robert. ALLEN TATE: SOCIETY, VOCATION, COMMUNION. *Southern Rev.* 1982 18(1): 62-72. Episodes in the life of poet, novelist, and editor Allen Tate demonstrate his complete absorption in his vocation as a way of life.

823.   Bush, Robert. GRACE KING: THE EMERGENCE OF A SOUTHERN INTELLECTUAL WOMAN. *Southern Rev.* 1977 13(2): 272-288. Examines the literature of Grace King, 1885-1932, and assesses her effect on other southern women intellectuals and the general culture of the South during the period.

824.   Butterworth, A. K. et al. BIBLIOGRAPHY: A CHECKLIST OF SCHOLARSHIP ON SOUTHERN LITERATURE FOR 1979. *Mississippi Q.* 1980 33(2): 167-287. Lists publications during 1979 on southern literature since 1607.

825.   Calhoon, Robert M. LITERARY HISTORY, INTELLECTUAL LIFE, AND THE CULTURE OF THE COLONIAL SOUTH. *Rev. in Am. Hist.* 1979 7(3): 331-337. Review article prompted by Richard Beale Davis's *Intellectual Life in the Colonial South, 1585-1763* (Knoxville: U. of Tennessee Pr., 1978); touches on the importance of literature in the colonial South, the image of Indians, and slavery's impact (or lack of it) on southern literary culture, 1585-1763.

826.   Calkin, Carleton I. JAMES CALVERT SMITH: HISTORIAN WITH A PAINT BRUSH. *Escribano* 1979 16: 33-42. Discusses the career of James Calvert Smith (1879-1962) and his famous depiction of the ceremony in which Florida was transferred from Spain to the United States on 10 July 1821; includes illustrations.

827.   Calkin, Carleton I. MARTIN JOHNSON HEADE: PAINTER OF FLORIDA. *Escribano 1977 14: 35-38.* Martin Johnson Heade (1819-1904), a landscape painter, came to Florida in 1883 and painted there until his death.

828.   Capers, Charlotte. THE NARROW ESCAPE OF "THE PETRIFIED MAN": EARLY EUDORA WELTY STORIES. *J. of Mississippi Hist. 1979 41(1): 25-32.* Discusses Eudora Welty's efforts to get her short story, "The Petrified Man," published. In an oral interview with Miss Capers in 1976, Welty recalled how, after "The Petrified Man" had made the rounds of the publishers and met rejection everywhere, she destroyed the manuscript in 1938. When Robert Penn Warren, editor of *The Southern Review,* later in the year requested another reading of the story, Miss Welty reconstructed it from memory. Her rewrite has since become one of her best-known short stories. Welty papers in the Mississippi Department of Archives and History.                                   M. S. Legan

829.   Chico, Beverly B. TWO AMERICAN FIRSTS: SARAH PEALE, PORTRAIT PAINTER, AND JOHN NEAL, CRITIC. *Maryland Hist. Mag. 1976 71(3): 349-359.* Establishes the identity of the author "of the earliest extant detailed art criticisms in the United States" as John Neal, impetuous, robust, and aggressive member of The Delphian Club of raconteurs. His series of 10 anonymous articles in the Baltimore *American and Commercial Daily Advertiser,* 19-31 October 1822, included discussion of five paintings by Sarah Peale, then in a large exhibition at her cousin Rembrandt Peale's Museum. Discusses and reproduces the two 1823 portraits of Neal done by Sarah, and his theories of color and glazing, which advice she seems to have taken seriously, for her work greatly improved in later years. Neal saw the critic's role as intended not to demean the artist, but to correct defects and perform a service to art, and as "Old Brush" he wrote a series of criticisms also in the *Federal Gazette and Baltimore Daily Advertiser* in 1823, urging Americans to emulate Sir Thomas Lawrence, and discussing Saran Peale's "Portrait of Mrs. H. Birckhead." Neal's 1829 Boston criticisms can now be seen as mere extensions of his earlier Baltimore efforts. Primary and secondary works; 2 illus., 30 notes.                                                   G. J. Bobango

830.   Christian, Garna L. IT BEATS PICKING COTTON: THE ORIGINS OF HOUSTON COUNTRY MUSIC. *Red River Valley Hist. Rev. 1982 7(3): 37-50.* Chronicles the origins and growth of country music in the Houston, Texas, area during the 1920's-50's, portraying early successes of performers and recording stars, and precursors of the country music of the 1970's.

831.   Clark, William Bedford. THE SERPENT OF LUST IN THE SOUTHERN GARDEN. *Southern R. 1974 10(4): 805-822.* Traces the theme of miscegenation in southern literature.

832.   Clausen, Christopher. GRECIAN THOUGHTS IN THE HOME FIELDS: REFLECTIONS ON SOUTHERN POETRY. *Georgia Rev. 1978 32(2): 283-305.* The lyric and narrative poetry of the South has never been as impressive as the region's fiction. Southern poets have inevitably felt more alienated from the region about which they are attempting to write than have the novelists. They have had no cultural heritage or even geographical capitol to look to, resulting in their isolation.                       M. B. Lucas

833.   Clements, William M. "COLLECTING BIRDSKINS": A ROLE FOR THE NONFICTION REGIONALIST. *Southern Q. 1978 17(1): 5-14.* Discusses the nonfiction works of three regionalists of the Ozark Mountains; Vance Randolph, Charles Morrow Wilson, and Otto Ernest Rayburn. Focusing on their interpretation of their role as regionalists, the author also develops his own concept of regionalism. All three writers believe that they are obligated to illustrate the unique character of the Ozarks, showing how it differs from every other region. All regionalists should follow their example. 14 notes.                                   B. D. Ledbetter

834.   Cohen, Blanche Klasmer. BENJAMIN KLASMER'S CONTRIBUTION TO BALTIMORE'S MUSICAL HISTORY. *Maryland Hist. Mag. 1977 72(2): 272-276.* Records the important role played by Benjamin Klasmer in bringing music to Baltimore for over 30 years, first as a cofounder of the Baltimore Symphony Orchestra, in 1916, and then as conductor of the Jewish Educational Alliance Symphony Orchestra in the 1920's. Throughout his career, Klasmer was the "leading musical director of pit orchestras" furnishing accompaniment to silent movies and vaudeville acts at the New Theater, the Garden and Rivoli Theaters, and the Hippodrome until his death in 1949. The tradition which he began is continued today by the Jewish Community Center and other groups. Perhaps his most popular renown, however, comes from his coauthorship of the theme song of the Baltimore Colts. 3 illus.        G. J. Bobango

835.   Colwill, Stiles Tuttle. TOWN & COUNTRY: THE SMALLER, GREENER BALTIMORE OF FRANCIS GUY. *Am. Heritage 1981 32(2): 18-27.* Francis Guy (1760-1820) decided to become an artist in 1799. His paintings of Baltimore, on display at the Maryland Historical Society, are illustrated in this article. 8 illus.                                                   J. F. Paul

836.   Cone, Edward T. THE MISS ETTA CONES, THE STEINS, AND M'SIEU MATISSE. A MEMOIR. *Am. Scholar 1973 42(3): 441-460.* Recalls the author's association with his aunts, Claribel and Etta Cone of Baltimore, famous art collectors. Describes the Cone collection and recounts experiences in Europe with Aunt Etta in 1933. Describes Etta's relationships with Gertrude Stein and her brothers, and with the painter Henri Matisse.        J. B. Street

837.   Conway, Cecelia and Thompson, Tommy. TALKING BANJO. *Southern Exposure 1974 2(1): 63-66.* Discusses the banjo, an instrument brought from Africa by Negro slaves, and interviews James Phillips "Dink" Roberts; a pre-blues musician in Alamance County, North Carolina.

838.   Cook, Martha E. A LITERARY FRIENDSHIP: ALLEN TATE AND DONALD DAVIDSON. *Southern Rev. 1982 18(4): 739-754.* Explores the literary friendship between American authors Allen Tate and Donald Davidson between 1921 and 1968.

839.   Core, George. ALLEN TATE AND THE SOUTH. *Southern Rev. 1976 12(4): 767-775.* Discusses Allen Tate's changing attitude toward his native land, the South, 1918-45, and the influence which the South had on his literature.

840.   Cowser, R. L., Jr. KINGFISH OF AMERICAN OPERA: AN INTERVIEW WITH CARLISLE FLOYD. *Southern Q. 1982 20(3): 5-18.* Interview with Carlisle Floyd, opera composer of *Willie Stark,* which was based on Robert Penn Warren's *All the King's Men.* Floyd relied on intuition for inspiration in writing his operas. They also reflect his ideas on the state of contemporary opera in the South and in the United States. 4 photos.
                                                   W. A. Wiegand

841.   Crider, Bill. SONS OF *TOBACCO ROAD:* "BACKWOODS" NOVELS. *J. of Popular Culture 1982 16(3): 47-59.* Discusses Southern "backwoods" variety paperback novels, which capitalized on the phenomenally successful paperback sales of Erskine Caldwell's *Tobacco Road* and *God's Little Acre* in the late 1940's. 16 illus.                                             D. G. Nielson

842.   Crouse, David L. ALLEN D. CARDEN: EARLY TENNESSEE MUSICIAN. *Tennessee Hist. Q. 1980 39(1): 11-15.* A brief biography of Allen D. Carden (1796-1859), who conducted singing schools in Nashville. He also published three tunebooks for frontier churches, to maintain "a uniform system of music—that there may be a little more harmony of the different churches": *The Missouri Harmony* (1820), *The Western Harmony* (1824), and *United States Harmony* (1829). The first went through 22 editions during 1820-59. 14 notes.                                   H. M. Parker, Jr.

843.   Cruse, Irma R. BERT HENDERSON: DEEP SOUTH PHILOSOPHER. *Alabama Hist. Q. 1982 44(1-2): 70-91.* Elbert Calvin (Bert) Henderson, Alabama's third poet laureate, is memorialized in a short biography, along with the publication of several of his better known poems. 30 notes.                       E. E. Eminhizer

844. Cullison, William R. TULANE'S RICHARD KOCH COLLECTION: A VISUAL SURVEY OF HISTORIC ARCHITECTURE IN THE MISSISSIPPI DELTA. *Louisiana Hist. 1977 18(4): 453-471.* The photographic collection of New Orleans architect Richard Koch (1889-1971) contains more than 5,000 pieces, the most important of which are photographs of historic buildings in the Mississippi River delta region of Louisiana and Mississippi. The collection is in Tulane University Library. 11 photos, 48 notes.
R. L. Woodward, Jr.

845. Dahl, James. WILLIAM FAULKNER ON INDIVIDUALISM. *West Georgia Coll. Rev. 1973 6: 3-9.*

846. Dale, Corinne. WILLIAM GILMORE SIMMS'S PORGY AS DOMESTIC HERO. *Southern Literary J. 1980 13(1): 55-71.* The character Porgy, who appears in four of William Gilmore Simms's seven Revolutionary romances (1835-55) set in the South, was a comical soldier, inept businessman, braggart, and fool, but also a domestic hero who exhibited his skills in the military camp and on his plantation.

847. David, Beverly R. VISIONS OF THE SOUTH: JOEL CHANDLER HARRIS AND HIS ILLUSTRATORS. *Am. Literary Realism, 1870-1910 1976 9(3): 189-206.* Discusses the illustrations of Arthur Burdett Frost for the stories of Joel Chandler Harris, the creator of the stories of Uncle Remus, 1880-95.

848. Davis, Thadious M. JASON COMPSON'S PLACE: A REASSESSMENT. *Southern Studies 1981 20(2): 137-150.* Jason, the middle Compson son, in William Faulkner's *The Sound and the Fury* (1929), is the character who helps place the entire work in its societal, cultural, and historical perspectives. His complex characterization reveals the nexus of familial and societal relationships that give meaning to the novel. He reveals a desperate search for a place in the Southern tradition, because his precise relationship to family, community, and himself is tortured and complex. Jason views himself as both victim and self-made man, but he is neither all villain nor all hero. Ultimately Jason appears to be a little man existing in a small world. 15 notes.
J. J. Buschen

849. Delcourt, Hazel R. ROLAND MCMILLAN HARPER: RECORDER OF EARLY TWENTIETH-CENTURY LANDSCAPES IN THE SOUTH. *Pioneer Am. 1978 10(2): 36-50.* Roland M. Harper (1878-1966) occupies a unique position in history among southern naturalists. His many publications, including maps and photographs of early 20th-century landscapes of the South, are of lasting value to students of both vegetation and cultural history. As an innovator in the field of plant geography, he employed what were then unorthodox techniques—the use of quantitative data—to the study of vegetation. Secondary sources and a selected bibliography of Roland M. Harper; 8 photos, map, table, fig., 10 notes.
C. R. Gunther, Jr.

850. Devlin, Albert J. JACKSON'S WELTY. *Southern Q. 1982 20(4): 54-91.* The relationship Eudora Welty developed with her native Jackson, Mississippi, is evident in the themes, characters and structure of her fiction. Not only does the Jackson scenery and its environment show up repeatedly in her work, but Welty also uses the Jackson mythos to develop her characters. 13 photos.
W. A. Wiegand

851. Devlin, Albert P. EUDORA WELTY'S HISTORICISM: METHOD AND VISION. *Mississippi Q. 1977 30(2): 213-234.* Eudora Welty's use of historical personages in her fiction reflects southern history, 1800-30.

852. Dewsnap, James W. WILLIAM GILMORE SIMMS' CAREER AS A PLAYWRIGHT. *Mississippi Q. 1976 29(2): 147-166.* Though William Gilmore Simms, a southern fiction writer, claimed that his forte was as a playwright, his plays never met with dramatic success, and during his career, 1824-76, only one was produced for a three-day run.

853. Dillon, Richard T. SOME SOURCES FOR FAULKNER'S VERSION OF THE FIRST AIR WAR. *Am. Literature 1973 44(4): 629-637.* Discusses the derivation of William Faulkner's material about combat aviation in World War I. The fiction of Elliot White Springs and James Warner Bellah may have influenced Faulkner's choice of topics.
H. M. Burns

854. Donald, David Herbert. PROMISED LAND OR PARADISE LOST: THE SOUTH BEHELD. *Georgia Rev. 1975 29(1): 184-187.* *Jericho: The South Beheld* (1974) by Herbert Shuptrine and James Dickey is one of the most beautiful books ever published about the South. It depicts through painting, poetry, and prose a place where one's spirit can be at ease, yet the authors lament the passing of this way of life.
M. B. Lucas

855. Duke, Maurice. CABELL'S AND GLASGOW'S RICHMOND: THE INTELLECTUAL BACKGROUND OF THE CITY. *Mississippi Q. 1974 27(4): 375-392.* One of a series of three papers on Richmond, Virginia, and southern writing.
S

856. Ellsworth, Linda V. GEORGE WASHINGTON SULLY. *Mag. Antiques 1983 123(3): 600-605.* Reproduces several of Sully's paintings of the western coast of Florida and New Orleans, 1829-39.

857. Evitts, William J. THE SAVAGE SOUTH: H. L. MENCKEN AND THE ROOTS OF A PERSISTENT IMAGE. *Virginia Q. Rev. 1973 49(4): 596-611.* "The basis of the modern motif of the savage South was laid in the 1920's." While H. L. Mencken did not create it single-handed, he was the most responsible and his South was a "complex creation made out of contradictory ideas, old myths and secret hopes."
O. H. Zabel

858. Ewan, Joseph. JOSIAH HALE, M.D., LOUISIANA BOTANIST, RAFINESQUE'S PUPIL. *J. of the Soc. for the Biblio. of Natural Hist. [Great Britain] 1977 8(3): 235-243.* Summarizes the life of Josiah Hale (ca. 1791-1856), a little-remembered figure in American natural history.

859. Farley, Benjamin W. ERSKINE CALDWELL: PREACHER'S SON AND SOUTHERN PROPHET. *J. of Presbyterian Hist. 1978 56(3): 202-217.* The Reverend Ira Sylvester Caldwell, father of the American novelist Erskine Caldwell, spent his entire ministry as pastor of the Associate Reformed Presbyterian Church, Wrens, Georgia. He placed greater emphasis on the ethical aspects of religion than the theological, a ministry which made a great impression on his son, Erskine. An examination of Erskine Caldwell's novels evidences a much more positive view on religion than is normally assumed. In a prophetic stance he has denounced the deep, engrained religion which is basically pietistic escapism, and the economic-agrarian system. His protest against Anglo-Saxon Protestantism in the South and southern indifference to the victims of sharecropping has been both noble and warranted. Based largely on Caldwell's novels and his correspondence with the author; photo, 53 notes.
H. M. Parker, Jr.

860. Farrell, David. POETRY AS A WAY OF LIFE: AN INTERVIEW WITH ROBERT PENN WARREN. *Georgia Rev. 1982 36(2): 314-331.* Poet and novelist Robert Penn Warren discusses his life and career since childhood. He describes his years at Vanderbilt University as a student member of the Fugitive Group, and his acquaintance with John Crowe Ransom, Allen Tate, Donald Davidson, Ralph McGill and others. Highlighted, too, are the effects on his life and work of a visual handicap, and time he spent living and writing in Italy. Warren does not consider his work a profession; rather, he sees it as a need, a way of life. Based on conversations held in 1980 and 1981; portrait.
D. J. Cimbala

861. Farrell, David. ROBERT PENN WARREN: A CONVERSATION ON POETRY. *South Atlantic Q. 1981 80(3): 272-280.* An oral interview of 1978 with Robert Penn Warren, who defines poetry as a way of life, "a way of living, of being open to experience, a way of existing meaningfully, as much of your time as possible." Discussion centers around the evolution of Warren's poetry from

his earliest collection to his last poem. Conversation reveals much of the writer's personal life and experiences and how these inspired much of his poetry. At the same time some of Warren's methodology for poetic writing is revealed, in addition to a certain amount of "inspiration" required to engage in composing this kind of literature. H. M. Parker, Jr.

862. Faulkner, William. THE REJECTED MANUSCRIPT OPENING OF *FLAGS IN THE DUST*. *Mississippi Q. 1980 33(3): 371-383*. Reprints the first seven pages from William Faulkner's rejected manuscript for *Flags in the Dust* and discusses their reincorporation into the later, accepted text.

863. Faulkner, William. THE UNCUT TEXT OF FAULKNER'S REVIEW OF *TEST PILOT*. *Mississippi Q. 1980 33(3): 385-389*. Reprints the text of a review which William Faulkner did for the *American Mercury* of Jimmy Collins's 1935 novel, *Test Pilot*.

864. Faust, Drew Gilpin. A SOUTHERN STEWARDSHIP: THE INTELLECTUAL AND THE PROSLAVERY ARGUMENT. *Am. Q. 1979 31(1): 63-80*. The writings of Southern intellectuals, rather than the polemical defenses offered by men such as John C. Calhoun, provide the best understanding of proslavery arguments. Their defense of the peculiar institution rested upon moral and philosophical assumptions not peculiar to the South but widely shared in mid-19th-century America. Biblically based in large part, their arguments also encompassed history and the new "scientific racism," and sought to further ideas of change and reform. Chart, 33 notes. D. G. Nielson

865. Fienberg, Lorne. COLONEL NOLAND OF THE *SPIRIT*: THE VOICES OF A GENTLEMAN IN SOUTHWEST HUMOR. *Am. Literature 1981 53(2): 232-245*. Analyzes the contributions of Charles Fenton Mercer Noland of Arkansas to William T. Porter's *Spirit of the Times*, a magazine devoted to cultivating the spirit of the ideal gentleman in antebellum America. Noland's letters to the *Spirit* parodied the values of Southern gentlemen he associated with and became stylistic models for other writers of Old Southwest humor. Covers 1836-44. 9 notes. T. P. Linkfield

866. Fine, Elsa Honig. SOUTHERN SUPPORT OF THE VISUAL ARTS: FOCUSING ON WOMEN. *Southern Q. 1981 19(2): 1-9*. The South has a strong literary tradition but lacks a strong visual arts tradition. The South is changing. The tempo of life in the region is significantly faster than it has been pictured. If visual art does catch on, as many female southern artists believe it will, the South's art will reflect the new character of contemporary life. 19 notes. B. D. Ledbetter

867. Fitzgerald, Sally. A MASTER CLASS: FROM THE CORRESPONDENCE OF CAROLINE GORDON AND FLANNERY O'CONNOR. *Georgia Rev. 1979 33(4): 827-846*. The nine pages of commentary that novelist Caroline Gordon (b. 1895) wrote to the young Flannery O'Connor (1925-64) after reading the manuscript of O'Connor's first novel, *Wise Blood*, are reprinted here, with excerpts from the correspondence between the two writers. Gordon served as O'Connor's mentor, commenting on every story and novel that the younger writer produced thereafter. Covers 1951-64. Based on Flannery O'Connor's files.
J. N. McArthur

868. Fitzgerald, Sally. ROOT AND BRANCH: O'CONNOR OF GEORGIA. *Georgia Hist. Q. 1980 64(4): 377-387*. Brief history of the Georgia ancestry of author Flannery O'Connor. Includes material on the development of Catholicism in the state as it relates to family members. From a talk delivered at the meeting of the Georgia Historical Society at Milledgeville in October 1980.
G. R. Schroeder

869. Flanary, Sara E. Lewis. WILLIAM EDWARD WEST IN NEW ORLEANS AND MISSISSIPPI. *Mag. Antiques 1983 124(5): 1010-1015*. A painter of society and literati portraits in Europe and America, William E. West also painted portraits early in his career

of some of the most prominent families of planters, merchants, and professionals in New Orleans and southwestern Mississippi; reproduces eight of these early paintings.

870. Flanders, Jane. KATHERINE ANNE PORTER AND THE ORDEAL OF SOUTHERN WOMANHOOD. *Southern Literary J. 1976 9(1): 47-60*. Examines Katherine Anne Porter as a Southern woman writer through her characters (women) and attempts to explain the reasons that her work has never been seriously considered; taking into account her early life in the South and the failure of love and death of the heart which is constant in all her characters, maintains that this is her own downfall and consequently the explanation for her difficulty in becoming properly recognized in literary criticism, 1935-62.

871. Floyd, William Barrow. GILBERT STUART'S FAVORITE PUPIL. *Horizon 1980 23(5): 44-47*. Southern portraitist Matthew Jouett (1788-1827), nicknamed "Kentucky" by his teacher Gilbert Stuart, saw his influence spread from Kentucky to the other Mississippi River plantation states during his short professional career (1815-27).

872. Flusche, Michael. THOMAS NELSON PAGE: THE QUANDARY OF A LITERARY GENTLEMAN. *Virginia Mag. of Hist. and Biog. 1976 84(4): 464-485*. Thomas Nelson Page, who turned to writing novels as a means of supplementing his income as a lawyer, quickly became the best known Southern author and the champion of the "Lost Cause." His appeal was to both Southerners and Northerners, lamenting past glories and unable to accept the changing values of an increasingly industrialized and urbanized society of the late 19th century. For Page and many other Americans, the fall of the Old South symbolized the uneasy transition to the modern world. Drawn partly from the Page Collection, University of Virginia, Page's published works, and the Page Collection, Duke University; illus., 70 notes. R. F. Oaks

873. Folks, Jeffrey J. WILLIAM FAULKNER AND THE SILENT FILM. *Southern Q. 1981 19(3-4): 171-182*. As a youngster, William Faulkner often attended silent films in his hometown of Oxford, Mississippi. His early writings indicate that he was knowledgeable of and interested in silent films. Many of Faulkner's attitudes and fictional motifs can be traced to his views of silent films, which reflected the conventions of popular culture. Covers 1910-40. 19 notes. B. D. Ledbetter

874. Forkner, Ben and Schricke, Gilbert. AN INTERVIEW WITH WILLIAM STYRON. *Southern R. 1974 10(4): 923-934*.

875. Foster, Gaines M. MIRAGE IN THE SAHARA OF THE BOZART: *THE LIBRARY OF SOUTHERN LITERATURE*. *Mississippi Q. 1974/75 28(1): 3-19*. Examines the contents of the 17-volume collection of southern literature, and discusses what its publication reveals about southern culture around the turn of the century.

876. Gage, Duane. WILLIAM FAULKNER'S INDIANS. *Am. Indian Q. 1974 1(1): 27-33*. William Faulkner included Indian characters in many of his writings. He took liberty with historical facts, but artistically his Indian stories are valid. He presented a primitive people who had been treated unjustly. Based on primary and secondary sources; 15 notes. G. L. Olson

877. Garrison, Gail L. TWO EARLY ROMANTIC PAINTINGS AT THE BALTIMORE CO-CATHEDRAL. *Maryland Hist. Mag. 1977 72(2): 253-265*. Describes the acquisition of two paintings, in 1820 and 1826, by the Baltimore Cathedral. One was a gift of King Louis XVIII of France and was acquired through the efforts of Archbishop of Baltimore Ambrose Maréchal and French Minister to the United States, Baron Hyde de Neuville. The earlier work was an unexpected present from the Comte de Menou. On the north wall is Baron Charles de Steuben's "Saint Louis Burying His Plague Stricken Troops Before Tunis AD 1270," while the south wall holds Jean-Baptiste Paulin-Guérin's "The Dead Christ in the Lap of the Virgin," or "Pietà," wrongly attributed until now to another artist. Examines letters from the Archives Nationales showing

the responses of French government officials to de Neuville's requests, provides biographical sketches of the two artists and shows the influence of Antoine-Jean Gros' style on their work, and notes the appropriateness of the Saint Louis painting for Baltimore at a time when the city was stricken with a yellow fever scourge. Primary and secondary sources; 4 photos, 34 notes.

G. J. Bobango

878. Gatton, John Spalding. "ONLY FOR GREAT ATTRACTIONS": LOUISVILLE'S AMPHITHEATRE AUDITORIUM. *Register of the Kentucky Hist. Soc. 1980 78(1): 27-38.* Opening in September 1889, Louisville's Amphitheatre Auditorium boasted the second largest stage in the United States. Developed by Captain William F. Norton, Jr. (alias "Daniel Quilp"), the theater was part of the city's cultural hub. It was sold at auction in 1904 and was immediately razed. 2 illus., 39 notes.                    J. F. Paul

879. Geist, Christopher D. VIOLENCE, PASSION, AND SEXUAL RACISM: THE PLANTATION NOVEL IN THE 1970S. *Southern Q. 1980 18(2): 60-72.* Studies more than 200 plantation novels written since 1955. Such novels are very popular, with hundreds of millions being sold. Almost all of the novels contain strong and vivid exploitation of sexual racism. Their popularity, in large part, results from the continuing fascination with fear of black sexuality by the white reader. 19 notes.                    B. D. Ledbetter

880. Gidley, M. FAULKNER'S LIVES. *J. of Am. Studies [Great Britain] 1981 15(2): 239-247.* Review article prompted by *Faulkner's Career* (1979) by Gary Lee Stonum, *William Faulkner: A Life on Paper* (1980) by A. L. Bezzerides, *Faulkner: The Transfiguration of Biography* (1980) by Judith Bryant Wittenberg, and *William Faulkner: His Life and Work* (1981) by David Minter. Two of the volumes essentially amass factual details about novelist William Faulkner; the others focus on interpretation of his writings. 35 notes.                    H. T. Lovin

881. Gifford, George, Jr. and Smallwood, Florence B. AUDUBON'S "VIEW OF BALTIMORE." *Maryland Hist. Mag. 1977 72(2): 266-271.* Identifies the background view of Baltimore in Plate 301, "The Canvass-Backed Duck," of Audubon's *Birds of America* as "almost certainly drawn" by George Lehman in October 1831. Lehman, a young Swiss from Pittsburgh, did numerous other backgrounds for the great naturalist; and it appears that Audubon sometimes pasted his bird drawings over the landscape scenes, thus creating collages to send to his engraver. Audubon added the view of Baltimore in deference to his patrons and in appreciation for an indemnity given him by the state of Maryland in 1836. Primary and secondary sources; illus., 20 notes.

G. J. Bobango

882. Gillespie, Dorothy. OVERCOMING BARRIERS: THE WOMAN ARTIST IN THE SOUTH. *Southern Q. 1979 17(2): 80-86.* The women artists in the South face many barriers. These obstacles might be overcome or at least reduced if they could find a local support system and gain access to a network to keep informed about what artists across the nation are doing.

B. D. Ledbetter

883. Goode, James M. OUTDOOR SCULPTURE: WASHINGTON'S OVERLOOKED MONUMENTS. *Historic Preservation 1973 25(1): 4-14.* Drawing on his book, *Open-Air Sculpture of Washington, D.C.: An Historical Guide* (1974), the author discusses many examples of Washington's 600 open-air sculptures. They range from the 1809 Lenthall Monument, the city's oldest, to the large abstract sculpture collection recently acquired by the Smithsonian Institution. Types represented include statues, equestrian statues, relief panels, aluminum and bronze doors, fountains, architectural sculpture, pediments, and animal, cemetery, and abstract sculpture. 13 photos.                    R. M. Frame III

884. Gray, Richard. SIGNS OF KINSHIP: THOMAS WOLFE AND HIS APPALACHIAN BACKGROUND. *Appalachian J. 1974 1(4): 309-319.*

885. Greene, Clarence H. THE DEAL FAMILY: CAROLINA GOSPEL SINGERS. *JEMF Q. 1983 19(69): 9-11.* The Deals received 30 dollars for each of the 24 selections they recorded for the Columbia Records Company during 1927-29.

886. Gretlund, Jan Nordby. AN INTERVIEW WITH EUDORA WELTY. *Southern Humanities Rev. 1980 14(3): 193-208.* In this interview, Eudora Welty expresses her views on a variety of subjects and discusses her approach to writing.

887. Gretlund, Jan Nordby. KATHERINE ANNE PORTER AND THE SOUTH: A CORRECTIVE. *Mississippi Q. 1981 34(4): 435-444.* Discusses inaccuracies in several biographical compilations about Katherine Anne Porter, and suggests more reliable source materials, especially concerning her early life and her later relationship to the South.

888. Gretlund, Jan Nordby. MADISON JONES: A BIBLIOGRAPHY. *Bull. of Biblio. 1982 39(3): 117-120.* Presents a brief background on Southern novelist Madison Jones, known as a spokesman for agrarian ideals, followed by a bibliography of primary and secondary sources published since the appearance of his first article in 1952.

889. Gronberg, Douglas C. THE PROBLEM OF THE PSEUDONYM AND THE FICTIONAL EDITOR IN RICHARD HENRY WILDE'S *HESPERIA: A POEM. Georgia Hist. Q. 1982 66(4): 549-554.* Discusses the efforts of Georgia lawyer and politician Richard Henry Wilde (d. 1847) to disguise the authorship of his lengthy poem *Hesperia: A Poem* since literary works were not appreciated in the antebellum South. Based on manuscripts, *Hesperia*, and secondary sources; 15 notes.                    G. R. Schroeder

890. Groos, Seymour and Murphy, Rosalie. FROM STEPHEN CRANE TO WILLIAM FAULKNER: SOME REMARKS ON THE RELIGIOUS SENSE IN AMERICAN LITERATURE. *Cithara 1977 16(2): 90-108.* Traces the important role of the religious sense in American literature even in a secular age, from Stephen Crane to William Faulkner.

891. Guilds, John C. SIMMS'S USE OF HISTORY: THEORY AND PRACTICE. *Mississippi Q. 1977 30(4): 505-511.* Examines William Gilmore Simms' use of history, particularly in his Revolutionary romances, 1834-69.

892. Guttenberg, Barnett. RUBIN ON THE FUGITIVES. *Mississippi Q. 1979 32(2): 291-299.* Review article prompted by Louis D. Rubin, Jr.'s, *The Wary Fugitives* (Louisiana State U. Pr., 1978), which discusses the careers of four southern writers, John Crowe Ransom, Allen Tate, Donald Davidson, and Robert Penn Warren, who collaborated on two works, *The Fugitive* (1922) and *I'll Take My Stand* (1930).

893. Hahn, H. George. TWILIGHT REFLECTIONS: THE HOLD OF VICTORIAN BALTIMORE ON LIZETTE WOODWORTH REESE AND H. L. MENCKEN. *Maryland Hist. 1980 11(1): 29-37.* Describes the influence of Baltimore and its environs on the literary work of Lizette Woodworth Reese and H. L. Mencken. Based on the authors' autobiographies and secondary sources; 27 notes.                    G. O. Gagnon

894. Haley, Kenneth C. A NINETEENTH CENTURY PORTRAITIST AND MORE: JAMES ALEXANDER SIMPSON. *Maryland Hist. Mag. 1977 72(3): 401-412.* Evaluates the work of James A. Simpson (1805-80). Discusses three early views of Georgetown College, painted during 1831-33; four portraits; and a copy of Gilbert Stuart's "Stephen Decatur" from 1846. Simpson excelled in his history paintings, one of which, "George Shoemaker Inspecting Wheat," is pictured here. It exemplifies "Simpson's consumate skill as genre painter." Simpson moved from Washington to Baltimore in 1860 and did many scriptural paintings in his last years, none of which have been uncovered to date. Primary and secondary sources; 10 reproductions, 17 notes.

G. J. Bobango

895. Hall, H. Gaston. NEW ORLEANS'S FIRST COMEDY: CELEBRATIONS IN 1764. *Theatre Survey 1980 21(2): 186-188.* Summarizes the history of the play *L'Amant auteur et valet* [The lover, author, and servant] and describes the circumstances of its performance in New Orleans in 1764, referred to in a manuscript copy of the journal of the new Director-General, d'Abbadie.

896. Hambrick, Keith S. THE SWEDISH NIGHTINGALE IN NEW ORLEANS: JENNY LIND'S VISIT OF 1851. *Louisiana Hist. 1981 22(4): 387-417.* Describes the enthusiastic reception Jenny Lind received during her 13-concert visit 7 February-10 March, providing information on the programs offered, the critics' reactions, the financial arrangements, the effects of local merchants to cash in on Lind's popularity, and her business relations with her manager, P. T. Barnum. Based primarily on newspaper accounts; 151 notes.                                                    R. E. Noble

897. Hanes, Frank Borden. LOOKING FOR PEIRSON RICKS. *North Carolina Hist. R. 1974 51(2): 190-200.* After writing three short stories, two hardbacked books, and a book review, Peirson Ricks of Winston-Salem, discouraged by the failure of his novel *The Hunter's Horn* (Scribners', 1947), committed suicide in 1950. Illus., note.                                    E. P. Stickney

898. Hanna, Archibald and Reese, William S. A TEXAS RARITY. *Yale U. Lib Gazette 1977 51(4): 213-217.* Although Thomas W. Streeter had conjectured the existence of a first edition (1838) of *Rachel Plummer's Narrative*, a Texas captivity tale, a copy had not been seen until a Texas bookseller turned one up in 1975. The book was purchased for the Streeter Texas Collection at Yale University. A facsimile of 400 copies is in press and is to be released by the Jenkins Publishing Company with an introduction by William S. Reese which reviews the bibliographic history of the book. Illus.                                                    D. A. Yanchisin

899. Harris, Michael H. *INTELLECTUAL LIFE IN THE COLONIAL SOUTH: A REVIEW ESSAY. J. of Lib. Hist. 1980 15(2): 201-204.* Calls the three-volume *Intellectual Life in the Colonial South, 1585-1763* by Richard Beale Davis (Knoxville: U. of Tennessee Pr., 1978) less interpretive than Perry Miller's works. Although Davis's assembly of facts and his bibliographic scope are impressive, his analysis lacks depth and his narrative requires coherence. His lack of thesis results in a work affording most value as a reference tool, perhaps the best available on southern cultural history to 1763.                                    D. J. Mycue

900. Havard, William C. THE JOURNALIST AS INTERPRETER OF THE SOUTH. *Virginia Q. Rev. 1983 59(1): 1-21.* The Southern Literary Renaissance was accompanied, especially during the 1940's-60's, by a journalistic renaissance. The best-known example is *The Mind of the South* by Wilbur J. Cash. Three other examples "provide a rough sketch of socio-political types among Southern journalists." Hodding Carter, Jr., somewhat paternalistic, mildly progressive, and somewhat egalitarian, "led the fight against extreme segregationists." P. D. East "was a radically individualistic Populist type" with a poor white background. James J. Kilpatrick, now known as a syndicated columnist, was "a legal abstractionist, a social conservative," and "an economic libertarian."

O. H. Zabel

901. Havard, William C. THE POLITICS OF *I'LL TAKE MY STAND. Southern Rev. 1980 16(4): 757-775.* The longevity of the Agrarians' vision, to which its publishing history since 1930 attests, indicates that their several views of practical politics collected in *I'll Take My Stand* cohere because of a shared understanding of the moral man leading a creative life in a good society; essentially theoretical, related to classical values, their publication fused literary and political movements.

902. Havard, William C. PRIDE AND FALL: A NEW SOURCE FOR INTERPRETING SOUTHERN EXPERIENCE. *Southern Rev. 1974 10(4): 823-839.* Evaluates the contribution of *Children of Pride: A True Story of Georgia and the Civil War* (New Haven:

Yale U. Press, 1972), a collection of letters written by the Charles Colcock Jones family from 1854-68, to the southern literary tradition.                                                    S

903. Hawkins, Peter S. FAITH AND DOUBT FIRST CLASS: THE LETTERS OF FLANNERY O'CONNOR. *Southern Humanities Rev. 1982 16(2): 91-103.* Reviews Sally Fitzgerald, ed., *Flannery O'Connor: The Habit of Being* (1979) stressing revelations gained about the author's personality and about her deep concern for the religious aspects of her friends' lives.

904. Hayhoe, George F. WILLIAM FAULKNER'S *FLAGS IN THE DUST. Mississippi Q. 1975 28(3): 370-386.* Presents evidence to substantiate the claim that the two available editions of William Faulkner's *Flags in the Dust*, Douglas Day's 1973 Random House edition and Vintage Books' 1974 edition, are rife with editorial negligence and inconsistency.

905. Heaney, Howell J. "THE RAVEN" REVISITED. *Manuscripts 1973 25(2): 87-95.* In January 1959 Colonel Richard Gimbel organized a major exhibition "to commemorate the 150th anniversary of the birth of Edgar Allan Poe" (1809-49). The catalog Gimbel prepared, published in the *Yale University Library Gazette* (April 1959), was composed largely of items from his own collection. Reviews some of the major items in the collection and its history. The collection, which now belongs to the Free Library of Philadelphia, includes a number of items related to "The Raven," the bird that inspired the poet, and the only known manuscript copy of the poem. Illus.                        D. A. Yanchisin

906. Hedin, Raymond. UNCLE REMUS: PUTTIN' ON OLE MASSA'S SON. *Southern Lit. J. 1982 15(1): 83-90.* Discusses the apparent contradiction between framework and the substance of the tales in the collections of Uncle Remus tales of Joel Chandler Harris.

907. Herndon, Jerry A. FAULKNER'S NOBEL PRIZE ADDRESS: A READING. *South Atlantic Q. 1982 81(1): 94-104.* In 1950 William Faulkner received the Nobel Prize for Literature. He responded to the honor by reading a 553-word paper. Opinions differ as to the interpretation of that address. Some see it as a definition of the writer's function, but it was a definition of man himself that insisted on the necessity of universal values and standards to define the quality and significance of human life, thus challenging the cult of moral relativism that characterizes the present age. 27 notes.                                    H. M. Parker, Jr.

908. Hitchcock, Bert. REDISCOVERING ALABAMA LITERATURE: THREE WRITERS OF LAFAYETTE. *Alabama Rev. 1983 36(3): 175-194.* Brief biographies and discussions of the work of Catharine Towles, Robert Wilton Burton, and George W. Hooper. Secondary sources; 13 notes.                        G. R. Schroeder

909. Hobson, Linda Whitney. THE STUDY OF CONSCIOUSNESS: AN INTERVIEW WITH WALKER PERCY. *Georgia Rev. 1981 35(1): 51-60.* Novelist Walker Percy discusses the influence of his southern upbringing on his work; his most recent novel, *The Second Coming;* and his interest in semiotics. Percy's current work-in-progress, *Novum Organum,* is based on his belief that scientific progress has failed to address the question of what it is to be a human being and how to deal with human predicaments. Illus.

J. N. McArthur

910. Hollis, Daniel W., III. THE HALL FAMILY AND TWENTIETH-CENTURY JOURNALISM IN ALABAMA. *Alabama Rev. 1979 32(2): 119-140.* The Hall family established itself in Alabama journalism in 1908. It continues so to the present, either as publishers, editors, business managers, or reporters. Some members are notable for their defense of civil liberties, one for winning the Pulitzer prize, and all for a commitment to their trade and the vitality of the human spirit. Primary and secondary sources; 75 notes.

J. F. Vivian

911. Holloway, Lou; Harrison, Alferdteen, interviewer. WE WERE PROFESSIONALS: LOU HOLLOWAY INTERVIEWED. *Southern Exposure 1980 8(3): 18-21.* Brief history of the female jazz band, the Rays of Rhythm, at Piney Woods School, founded in 1909 near Jackson, Mississippi, for black students; focusing on the experiences of Lou Holloway who joined the Rays of Rhythm in the early 1940's and traveled with the group when they went on tour to raise money for the school; 1940-49.

912. Holman, C. Hugh. ANOTHER LOOK AT NINETEENTH-CENTURY SOUTHERN FICTION. *Southern Humanities Rev. 1980 14(3): 235-245.* Discusses the style and themes of such 19th-century southern writers as Edgar Allan Poe.

913. Holman, C. Hugh. SIMMS' CHANGING VIEW OF LOYALISTS DURING THE REVOLUTION. *Mississippi Q. 1976 29(4): 501-513.* Examines William Gilmore Simms' evolving view of Loyalists in his cycle of novels concerning the American Revolution in South Carolina, 1780-83.

914. Holman, C. Hugh. THE SOUTHERN NOVELIST AND THE USES OF THE PAST. *Southern Humanities R. 1976 (Special Issue): 1-11.* Discusses the themes of the Civil War, Reconstruction, and slavery in novels of the South from the 1850's to the 20th century, emphasizing the works of William Faulkner and Robert Penn Warren.

915. Hoopes, James. MODERNIST CRITICISM AND TRANSCENDENTAL LITERATURE. *New England Q. 1979 52(4): 451-466.* Ivor Armstrong Richards's (b. 1893) language theory and his modernist literary criticism detrimentally influenced James Agee's (1909-55) *Let Us Now Praise Famous Men*. Agee was led to attempt to give an illusion of embodiment, rather than to address the subject itself. Discusses the style of Agee's prose. Based on Agee's writing; 29 notes.                    J. C. Bradford

916. Horsford, Howard C. LETTERS OF CAROLINE GORDON TATE TO SALLY WOOD KOHN, 1925-1937. *Princeton U. Lib. Chronicle 1982 44(1): 1-24.* These letters illuminate the early years of novelist Caroline Gordon's marriage to Allen Tate, her financial and moral support of Tate, their dedication to their literary careers and their literary friends, and their attitudes toward the South and its people.

917. Howell, Elmo. EUDORA WELTY AND THE CITY OF MAN. *Georgia Rev. 1979 33(4): 770-782.* Like Jane Austen (1775-1817), whose work she admires, Eudora Welty (b. 1909) ignores history and social themes to concentrate on the pattern formed by the lives of ordinary people. The South in which she sets her stories is a social order where certain principles are commonly held and where living itself is considered an art. Welty's characters grow and develop through their functional connections with each other and the place in which they live.                    J. N. McArthur

918. Howell, Elmo. KATE CHOPIN AND THE CREOLE COUNTRY. *Louisiana Hist. 1979 20(2): 209-219.* Long considered merely a local colorist, Kate Chopin (1851-1904) has as a result of the feminist movement received new and well-deserved attention. Elmo Howell considers her second novel, *The Awakening*, one of the most nearly perfect fictions in American literature. Her use of female characters and her careful depiction of south Louisiana ably buttress her greatest strength—examining universal themes and the complex responses which they elicit from the human soul. 22 notes.                    D. B. Touchstone

919. Howell, Elmo. SOUTHERN FICTION AND THE PATTERN OF FAILURE: THE EXAMPLE OF FAULKNER. *Georgia Rev. 1982 36(4): 755-770.* Mississippi author William Faulkner was a "freak genius," a product of his native South, and, by his own definition, a failure. Faulkner defined success as the ability to "risk failure" by attempting new forms in writing. According to this definition, Faulkner was never a successful novelist: his works, viewed as a whole, are repetitious, often reiterating themes and story lines. His fiction, like some works of fellow Southerners Mark Twain and Eudora Welty, tends to be fragmented and aimless, though not

without artistic merit. Their work is flawed because the South encourages a strong sense of community, making it difficult for the region's authors to write consistently good modern fiction, which stresses introspection and soul-searching. Based on Faulkner's novels, and Joseph Blotner's biography of the author.
                    D. J. Cimbala

920. Hübner, Jürgen. WILLIAM GILMORE SIMMS: SECTIONALISM AND POPULARITY. *Southern Studies 1979 18(1): 33-50.* The historical romances which William Gilmore Simms (1806-70) wrote during 1830-70 attempted to give the South a respectable regional literature and to promote intellectual development in the South. His most important works were *Martin Faber* (1833), *The Wigwam and the Cabin* (1845), *Katherine Walton* (1851), and *The Cassique of Kiawah* (1859). His depiction of southern aristocrats, slaves, poor whites, men, and women became the stock characters of Southern literature. His works were criticized in the 1830's when the reading audience was elite and conservative; but with the rise of a female middle class audience in the late 1840's, Simms's works became popular in both the North and the South and critical reviews echoed the new popularity. Based on 19th century book reviews and secondary sources; 28 notes.          J. J. Buschen

921. Inge, M. Thomas. THE CONTINUING RELEVANCE OF *I'LL TAKE MY STAND*. *Mississippi Q. 1980 33(4): 445-460.* According to those who have studied it carefully, including Cleanth Brooks, Richard J. Calhoun, Joseph K. Davis, Madison Jones, William Pratt, Edward S. Shapiro, Lewis P. Simpson, Floyd C. Watkins, and Thomas Daniel Young, the southern Agrarians' *I'll Take My Stand* (1930) is an increasingly relevant attack on the "Gospel of Progress," a prophetic document the foresight of which is now revealed.

922. Inge, M. Thomas. RICHMOND, VIRGINIA, AND SOUTHERN WRITING: INTRODUCTION. *Mississippi Q. 1974 27(4): 371-373.* Introduces three papers on the importance of Richmond, Virginia, in the careers of Ellen Glasgow and James Branch Cabell, and their relationship to the Southern Literary Renaissance.
                    S

923. Jacobs, Robert D. REPUBLICS OF LETTERS, NORTH AND SOUTH. *Mississippi Q. 1974/75 28(1): 93-102.* Reviews Lewis P. Simpson's *The Man of Letters in New England and the South* (Baton Rouge: Louisiana State U. Press, 1973).

924. James, A. Everette, Jr.; James, A. Everette, III; and Thomason, Elizabeth Williams. AN INTRODUCTION TO EUGENE HEALAN THOMASON: THE "ASHCAN ARTIST" WHO CAME TO THE MOUNTAINS. *Appalachian J. 1983 10(3): 276-285.* Discusses Eugene Healan Thomason, his artistic portrayal of the rural inhabitants of North Carolina, and his creation of a composite fictional family, the "Hankins," to represent these people without compromising their rights to privacy.

925. Jeffrey, David K. and Noble, Donald R. MADISON JONES: AN INTERVIEW. *Southern Q. 1983 21(3): 5-26.* Madison Jones, author of *The Innocent* (1957), *Forest of the Night* (1960), *A Buried Land* (1963), *An Exile* (1967), *A Cry of Absence* (1971), *Passage through Gehenna* (1978), and *Season of the Stranger* (1982) responds to questions about characters, themes, and fictional situations in his novels. He reflects on experiences of his childhood that show up in his fiction, describes the methods he uses to write, and discusses writers who most influenced his own work.
                    W. A. Wiegand

926. Johnson, Glen M. *BIG WOODS*: FAULKNER'S ELEGY FOR WILDERNESS. *Southern Humanities Rev. 1980 14(3): 249-258.* Discusses the thematic structure of William Faulkner's anthology *The Big Woods*, published in 1955.

927. Johnson, Robert L. WILLIAM FAULKNER, CALVINISM AND THE PRESBYTERIANS. *J. of Presbyterian Hist. 1979 57(1): 66-81.* Pursues William Faulkner's connections with Presbyterianism in three dimensions: his personal exposure to Presbyterian influence, the critical studies of Faulkner as a literary Calvinist, and *Light in*

*August,* which is treated as Faulkner's most detailed treatment of Calvinism. Admits that Faulkner was far from being a consistent, thorough-going Calvinist, but does give interesting vignettes which reflect Faulkner's propensity for a Calvinistic view, and demonstrates his philosophy through overarching themes in Faulkner's writings and thoughts. Based on Faulkner's writings and works of literary critics; 39 notes.              H. M. Parker, Jr.

928. Jones, Alfred Haworth. JOEL CHANDLER HARRIS: TALES OF UNCLE REMUS. *Am. Hist. Illus. 1983 18(3): 34-39.* Chronicles the life, career, and writings of Joel Chandler Harris during 1864-1907.

929. Justus, James H. ON THE RESTLESSNESS OF SOUTH-ERNERS. *Southern Rev. 1975 11(1): 65-83.* Examines southern writers' use of the national image of mobility and restlessness; one of six essays in this issue on Self and Society.

930. Justus, James H. SOME SOUTHERN TALENTS AND THEIR TRADITION. *Southern Literary J. 1978 10(2): 180-186.* Review article prompted by Richard Gray's *The Literature of Memory: Modern Writers of the American South* (Baltimore: The Johns Hopkins U. Pr., 1977).

931. Justus, James H. SOUTHERN POETS: THEN AND NOW. *Mississippi Q. 1980 33(4): 479-488.* The poets anthologized in *Contemporary Southern Poetry: An Anthology,* edited by Guy Owen and Mary C. Williams, have, for 50 years, written in reaction to the brittle, dry, ironic poetry of the Fugitives, who in turn were reacting against the excessive romanticism of the poets anthologized by Addison Hubbard in *The Lyric South* (1928).

932. Kennedy, Richard S. THOMAS WOLFE AND ELIZABETH NOWELL: A UNIQUE RELATIONSHIP. *South Atlantic Q. 1982 81(2): 202-213.* Much of the success of Thomas Wolfe can be traced to the editorial labors of Elizabeth Nowell, who first began working with Wolfe in 1933. At that time he was struggling with *Of Time and the River.* She drastically cut and altered Wolfe's stories and novels, which were usually far too lengthy for publication. It was a tribute to Nowell's tact that they could continue their association. Her assistance went beyond the literary into the area of publication. She spent so much time with his works because she was grateful that Wolfe had stuck with her when she was first starting out on her own; she also had a keen appreciation for his creative genius. She continued her loyalty even after his death, getting some unpublished articles into print. Based largely on Wolfe's letters in the Houghton Library, Harvard University; 13 notes.
              H. M. Parker, Jr.

933. King, Mitchell L. JAMES W. NICHOLSON: CLAIBORNE PARISH MATHEMATICIAN. *North Louisiana Hist. Assoc. J. 1976 8(1): 31-36.* James W. Nicholson (1844-1917) was educated at the Cane Ridge and Forest Grove schools, and at age 14 entered nearby Homer College. In 1861 he joined the Confederate Army and served throughout the Civil War in Company B, 12th Louisiana Infantry. He reentered Homer College in 1865, later became an instructor in mathematics there, and in 1876 accepted the chair of mathematics at Louisiana State University. He remained at that university for the remainder of his life, serving twice as its president. He considered his most notable accomplishment the invention of the trigonometric circle, "a simple memoric device for learning the trigonometric functions." Secondary sources; 25 notes.
              A. N. Garland

934. Klug, Michael A. WILLA CATHER: BETWEEN RED CLOUD AND BYZANTIUM. *Can. Rev. of Am. Studies [Canada] 1981 12(3): 287-299.* Writing early in the 20th century, American novelist Willa Cather (1876-1947) was troubled by the same spiritual and aesthetic contradictions that have frustrated 20th-century artists more recently. On the broadest level, Cather shares with her literary successors the conflicts inherent in the artistic desire for

freedom and personal success and artists' opposite impulses to make social equality and human brotherhood paramount. Based on Cather's writings and secondary sources; 12 notes.
              H. T. Lovin

935. Kreyling, Michael. THE RENAISSANCE OF THE SOUTHERN RENAISSANCE. *Mississippi Q. 1980-81 34(1): 60-67.* Reviews the literature which argues that the intellectual productions of the Southern Renaissance (ca. 1920-60) are directly attributable to social and historical factors unique to the South, factors which made for the thematic and stylistic distinctiveness of southern writing.

936. Landess, Thomas H. THE ACHIEVEMENT OF JULIA PETERKIN. *Mississippi Q. 1976 29(2): 221-232.* Discusses the fiction of Julia Peterkin, a Pulitzer Prize-winning southern author during the 1920's-30's.

937. Lanier, Doris. THE DEATH OF PAUL HAMILTON HAYNE. *Georgia Hist. Q. 1973 57(4): 579-584.* Editorial tribute from the *Macon Telegraph* to Paul Hamilton Hayne (1830-86), Georgia poet. 9 notes.              D. L. Smith

938. Lanier, Doris. JAMES WHITCOMB RILEY, "BILL" NYE, AND HARRY STILWELL EDWARDS: A LECTURE TOUR. *Georgia Hist. Q. 1973 57(2): 256-264.* Reports on the 1888 lecture tour of Hoosier poet James Whitcomb Riley, Maine humorist Edgar Wilson "Bill" Nye, and Georgia local color short story writer Harry Stillwell Edwards throughout Georgia. The lyceum movement was more than an educational movement in post-Civil War America; it was also designed to help reunify the country and to encourage support for public libraries. 35 notes.              D. L. Smith

939. Lanier, Doris. OSCAR WILDE TOURS GEORGIA: 1882. *Georgia Hist. Q. 1981 65(4): 329-340.* In 1882 Oscar Wilde, the British author and aesthetic, lectured on "Decorative Arts" in Columbus, Macon, Atlanta, Savannah and Augusta, Georgia. Because of his peculiar attire and mannerisms he was not well received, except in Atlanta. Based on newspapers and secondary sources; 37 notes.              G. R. Schroeder

940. Lawson, Lewis. HIGHLY RECOMMENDED SOUTHERN TOURS. *Southern Lit. J. 1981 14(1): 72-77.* Reviews J. V. Ridgelt's *Nineteenth-Century Southern Literature* (1980), Anne E. Rowe's *Enchanted Country* (1978), Wayne Mixon's *Southern Writers and the New South Movement, 1865-1913* (1980), and Richard H. King's *Southern Renaissance* (1980), which collectively provide in-depth treatment of the major movements in Southern literature.

941. LeQuire, Louise. EDMONDSON'S ART REFLECTS HIS FAITH, STRONG AND PURE. *Smithsonian 1981 12(5): 50-55.* Assesses the sculptures of Tennessean William Edmondson made between 1932 and his death in 1951 as expressions of his Baptist faith and examples of native American art.

942. Light, Kathleen. UNCLE REMUS AND THE FOLKLOR-ISTS. *Southern Literary J. 1975 7(2): 88-104.* Ethnologists and their racial theories so harassed Joel Chandler Harris that he abandoned writing his Uncle Remus stories and Negro folklore.

943. Lipscomb, Mance; Myers, A. Glenn; and Gardner, Don, ed. OUT OF THE BOTTOMS AND INTO THE BIG CITY. *Southern Exposure 1980 8(2): 4-11.* An excerpt from the forthcoming autobiography of Mance Lipscomb (1895-1976). Lipscomb, a black, was a Texas blues musician and played in many folk festivals after he was "discovered" in 1960. The excerpt tells how and why he brought his family to Houston in 1956 and portrays him as one example of the many who migrated to the southern urban centers in the 1950's. 8 photos.

944. Lodwick, Michael. REVIEW OF DREW GILPIN FAUST, *A SACRED CIRCLE: THE DILEMMA OF THE INTELLECTUAL IN THE OLD SOUTH, 1840-1860. Plantation Soc. in the Americas 1979 1(1): 73-76.* Drew Gilpin Faust's *A Sacred Circle* is an "unexampled ... collective portrait" of the Southern proslavery writers,

James H. Hammond, George Frederick Holmes, Edmund Ruffin, William Gilmore Simms, and Nathaniel Tucker. To Faust, these men were not primarily defending slavery or the South, but establishing their self-identity as intellectuals in an anti-intellectual culture. Scholars should avoid such anachronistic application of current, popular psychology to historic figures; but psychology, properly used, may be helpful in understanding the past. Secondary sources.

R. G. Sherer

945. Lornell, Kip. SPATIAL PERSPECTIVES ON THE FIELD RECORDING OF TRADITIONAL AMERICAN MUSIC: A CASE STUDY FROM TENNESSEE IN 1928. *Tennessee Folklore Soc. Bull. 1981 47(4): 153-159.* A demographic and sociological study exploring the recording of traditional country blues music on location by artist and repertory men and recording engineers using portable equipment in Tennessee in 1928, one of the attempts during the 1920's to aurally preserve traditional American music.

946. Lovering, Joseph P. THE FRIENDSHIP OF WILLA CATHER AND DOROTHY CANFIELD. *Vermont Hist. 1980 48(3): 144-154.* From their collaboration in writing a prize short story in 1894 until Cather's death in 1947, the two authors corresponded with and visited each other, except for a decade of unexplained coolness between them from about 1905 to early 1916. The hiatus perhaps relates to the elder woman's direct rise from frontier Nebraska, with less social status or grace than Canfield, but earlier literary success.

T. D. S. Bassett

947. Lowe, David. MARY CASSATT. *Am. Heritage 1973 25(1): 10-21, 96-100.* Discusses Cassatt's (1845-1926) life. 14 illus.

948. Luker, Ralph E. LIBERAL THEOLOGY AND SOCIAL CONSERVATISM: A SOUTHERN TRADITION 1840-1920. *Church Hist. 1981 50(2): 193-204.* James Warley Miles, an Episcopal priest and College of Charleston professor, was among the founders of a Southern intellectual tradition that found further expression in the thought of William Porcher DuBose and social reformer Edgar Gardner Murphy. This tradition sought to adopt religious ideas to modern culture, but theological assumptions were undercut because Miles, DuBose, and Murphy were viewed as spokesmen for the embattled southern social elite. 45 notes.

M. D. Dibert

949. MacDonald, Edgar. GLASGOW, CABELL, AND RICHMOND. *Mississippi Q. 1974 27(4): 393-414.* Examines the importance of Richmond in the writing of Ellen Glasgow and James Branch Cabell and asserts that "art is preeminently provincial." One of a series of three papers.

S

950. MacDonald, Edgar E. THE FRAGMENTED CABELL. *Southern Literary J. 1976 9(1): 104-111.* Review article prompted by editor Edward Wagenknecht's *The Letters of James Branch Cabell* (Norman: U. of Oklahoma Pr., 1975); the fragmented offerings add nothing to the need for an overall look at this minor literary figure, 1920's-58.

951. MacDonald, Edgar E. HENRY SYDNOR HARRISON: SOUTHERN FEMINIST. *Southern Literary J. 1980 13(1): 42-54.* Henry Sydnor Harrison's (1880-1930) novels were sympathetic to feminism; mentions *Queed* (1911), *V. V.'s Eyes* (1913), *Angela's Business* (1915), *Saint Teresa* (1922), *Andrew Bride of Paris* (1925), and the posthumously published *The Good Hope* (1931).

952. Maland, Charles. AGEE: A FILM. *Southern Q. 1981 19(3-4): 225-228.* Agee (1979) which won the Blue Ribbon for literature at the 1980 American Film Festival, is a documentary on the life of author James Agee. The film begins with Agee's childhood in Tennessee, continues with his years at Harvard and early adulthood in New York, through his publication of *Let Us Now Praise Famous Men* (1941) and concludes with his involvement in movies as a screenwriter. 3 notes.

B. D. Ledbetter

953. Martin, Jay. "THE WHOLE BURDEN OF MAN'S HISTORY OF HIS IMPOSSIBLE HEART'S DESIRE": THE EARLY LIFE OF WILLIAM FAULKNER. *Am. Literature 1982 53(4):*

*607-629.* Utilizes psychoanalytic methods to explain William Faulkner's early development as a writer. In his late 20's, repressed elements of Faulkner's personality emerged, thus allowing the writer to develop a double image of himself: the secret Faulkner and the public mask. It is this secret, but genuine, side of Faulkner that provided the inspiration for his best work. 51 notes.

T. P. Linkfield

954. Mathis, Ray. MYTHOLOGY AND THE MIND OF THE NEW SOUTH. *Georgia Hist. Q. 1976 60(3): 228-238.* There seems to be a consensus among historians that post-Civil War southern intellectual history is underdeveloped. Closely related to this deficiency is the myth that the South is distinctive. Discusses Michael O'Brien's "C. Vann Woodward and the Burden of Southern Liberalism," W. J. Cash's *The Mind of the South*, C. Vann Woodward's "The Elusive Mind of the South," George B. Tindall's "Mythology: A New Frontier in Southern History," Mark Schorer's "The Necessity of Myth," Richard M. Weaver's "Aspects of Southern Philosophy," and Paul B. Gaston's *The New South Creed* in light of their use of this myth. 23 notes.

G. R. Schroeder

955. McCane-O'Connor, Mallory. WOMEN ARTISTS IN THE SOUTHEAST: A NORTH FLORIDA SAMPLING. *Southern Q. 1979 17(2): 69-74.* The author prepared a questionnaire to investigate feelings of female artists in northern Florida about frustration, isolation, and solutions. Although the response was small, the author analyzed the feedback and made a number of recommendations to help solve problems faced by female artists.

B. D. Ledbetter

956. McCarthy, Kevin M. HISTORICAL ST. AUGUSTINE IN FICTION. *Escribano 1978 15: 61-72.* Discusses 20th-century fiction which uses St. Augustine, Florida, as a locale.

957. McCluskey, John. AMERICANISMS IN THE WRITINGS OF THOMAS NELSON PAGE. *Am. Speech 1982 57(1): 44-47.* Lists a glossary of 42 terms and phrases taken from the works of Southern author Thomas Nelson Page, most of which are not found in other references. Includes quotations from *The Novels, Stories, Sketches and Poems of Thomas Nelson Page* (1908).

L. Moore

958. McDonald, W. U., Jr. AN UNWORN PATH: BIBLIOGRAPHICAL AND TEXTUAL SCHOLARSHIP ON EUDORA WELTY. *Southern Q. 1982 20(4): 101-108.* By presenting a survey of the literature published about Eudora Welty, one must come to the conclusion that scholarship on this Southern woman writer is still in the developing stages. Other than Noel Polk's two published checklists *Mississippi Quarterly* (1973) and *American Book Collector* (1981), and his forthcoming descriptive bibliography, "the path has yet to be worn." The Mississippi Department of Archives and History and the Humanities Research Center at the University of Texas contain most of her primary materials.

W. A. Wiegand

959. McKenzie, Barbara. FLANNERY O'CONNOR AND "THE BUSINESS OF THE PURIFIED MIND." *Georgia Rev. 1979 33(4): 817-826.* Summarizes the life and work of Flannery O'Connor (1925-64), Georgia-born novelist and short story writer. O'Connor denied that the autobiographical element was prominent in her work: the "business of the purified mind," she wrote, was to exclude elements of the personality not germane to the subject. Based on published correspondence; 4 photos, 5 notes.

J. N. McArthur

960. Meadows, Eddie S. JAZZ ANTECEDENTS. *Freedomways 1977 17(2): 93-99.* The West African influence on the music of New Orleans contributed to the formation of modern jazz through the Congo Square ceremonies, where slaves could participate without inhibition, and through the fusion of West African and Catholic religious ceremonies in secret societies employing black bands. Later the close of the Civil War was significant to the development of jazz, as disbanding military units sold their band instruments cheaply or abandoned them on the battle fields.

961. Meeks, Elizabeth. REFLECTIONS OF THE MILIEU IN NAMES OF WILLIAM FAULKNER'S CHARACTERS. *Southern Studies 1981 20(1): 91-96.* In his works, William Faulkner (1897-1962) named his characters to reflect their personalities or local habitation. They were also typical and realistic names of the areas in which he set his works. The names placed characters in their class. He frequently used ancient Greek names, which is a Southern tradition. Satiric and comic names were also used for those purposes. 29 notes.                                      J. J. Buschen

962. Meese, Elizabeth A. TELLING IT ALL: LITERARY STANDARDS AND NARRATIVES BY SOUTHERN WOMEN. *Frontiers 1977 2(2): 63-67.* Oral history can broaden the context of the literature produced by southern women and blacks; part of a special issue on women's oral history.

963. Meindl, Dieter. A REAPPRAISAL OF MARGARET MITCHELL'S *GONE WITH THE WIND. Mississippi Q. 1981 34(4): 414-434.* Examines the contemporary and subsequent critical appraisal of Mitchell's famous work, and suggests that despite its great popular appeal it has seldom been given proper credit as a work of real literary or historical merit.

964. Meriwether, James B. AUGUSTUS BALDWIN LONGSTREET: REALIST AND ARTIST. *Mississippi Q. 1982 35(4): 351-364.* Discusses the contributions of Augustus Baldwin Longstreet to American literature through his *Georgia Scenes* (1835), a collection of humorous sketches of Georgia life.

965. Meriwether, James B. THE BOOKS OF WILLIAM FAULKNER. *Mississippi Q. 1982 35(3): 265-281.* Lists new editions of existing works by William Faulkner, as well as previously unpublished works and newly edited collections that have appeared since 1977.

966. Meriwether, Rebecca. THE COPYRIGHT OF FAULKNER'S FIRST BOOK. *Mississippi Q. 1983 36(3): 263-287.* Examines copyright law for its relevance to a 1921 work by William Faulkner, of which the author distributed a few handwritten copies, but which was copyrighted only after the author's death.

967. Meyers, Jeffrey. THE DEATH OF RANDALL JARRELL. *Virginia Q. Rev. 1982 58(3): 450-467.* The death of poet Randall Jarrell as the result of being struck by an automobile has "been surrounded by mystery." Officially it was called an accident, but many thought it suicide. The facts about his death are now known because of his certificate of death, coroner's report, and autopsy report. There is little doubt that it was suicide. The causes are uncertain but probably include his unhappy childhood, earlier excessive drinking, diminution of his poetic powers, unfavorable reviews, worry about health, a nervous breakdown, and other factors.                                      O. H. Zabel

968. Meyers, Jeffrey. RANDALL JARRELL: A BIBLIOGRAPHY OF CRITICISM, 1941-1981. *Bull. of Biblio. 1982 39(4): 227-234.* Unannotated bibliography on poet Randall Jarrell, including only substantial reviews and significant references in books and newspapers.

969. Michael, Marion C. SOUTHERN LITERATURE IN ACADEME. *Mississippi Q. 1978-79 32(1): 3-12.* Discusses the preparation of the revised, updated, and published (1979) supplemental bibliography by the author and O. B. Emerson to Clyde H. Cantrell's and Waton R. Patrick's edition of *Southern Literary Culture* (1955) and further research into Southern literature, 1948-79; from a special issue on Southern literary culture, 1969-75.

970. Michelson, Bruce F. RICHARD WILBUR: THE QUARREL WITH POE. *Southern Rev. 1978 14(2): 245-261.* Examines Richard Wilbur's study (1959) of Edgar Allan Poe and Wilbur's interpretations of Poe's symbolism.

971. Millgate, Michael. AMERICAN LITERATURE IN AMERICAN HISTORY. *Can. R. of Am. Studies 1973 4(1): 113-116.* Reviews Bert James Loewenberg's *American History in American*

*Thought: Christopher Columbus to Henry Adams* (New York: Simon and Schuster, 1972) and F. Garvin Davenport, Jr.'s *The Myth of Southern History: Historical Consciousness in Twentieth-Century Southern Literature* (Nashville: Vanderbilt U. Press, 1970). Both works are histories of ideas in America. Loewenberg's book, the first of a projected multivolume undertaking, treats the subject chronologically. Davenport places southern writers "in a national context"; he contends that southern writers were not essentially regionalists but wrestled with issues of national significance.                                      H. T. Lovin

972. Milum, Richard A. FAULKNER AND THE CAVALIER TRADITION: THE FRENCH BEQUEST. *Am. Literature 1974 45(4): 580-589.* Discusses the French cavalier tradition in literature as found in the works of William Faulkner.

973. Minter, David. FAULKNER AND THE USES OF BIOGRAPHY. *Georgia R. 1974 28(3): 455-463.* Reviews Joseph Blotner's *Faulkner: A Biography* (New York: Random House, 1974), and discusses the influence that William Faulkner's own life had on what he wrote. Suggests that his novels were influenced more by what he heard, observed, or felt than by what he had done. Faulkner creatively combined the actuality with the imaginary, and then evaluated his characters in the light of the ideal.                                      M. B. Lucas

974. Montgomery, Marion. SOUTHERN LETTERS IN THE TWENTIETH CENTURY: THE ARTICULATION OF A TRADITION. *Modern Age 1980 24(2): 121-133.* Since Southern literature, like the South, is such a various creature that one is ill-advised to pronounce dogmatically upon it, the author limits attention to a particular kind of southern writer who may be distinguished from a variety of his kinsmen, in and out of the South. In so doing he makes numerous comparisons with Flannery O'Connor. Discusses some of the literary characteristics of the Southern model, how he differs in his concept of reality, and his views on religion, evil, and ethics. 5 notes.                                      H. M. Parker, Jr.

975. Montgomery, Marion. SOUTHERN REFLECTIONS ON SOLZHENITSYN. *Modern Age 1975 19(2): 190-198.* " 'What has given the South her identity.' says Southern novelist Flannery O'Connor, 'are those beliefs and qualities which she has absorbed from the scriptures and from her own history of defeat and violation: a distrust of the abstract, a sense of human dependence on the grace of God, and a knowledge that evil is not simply a problem to be solved, but a mystery to be endured." When the "Southern writer" recognizes the point, one of the things he may write is the *Gulag Archipelago.* . . . Solzhenitsyn, like Flannery O'Connor, is a reactionary. . . . He wants to turn the clock back. . . . All the way back to Bethlehem."

976. Moore, Evelyn L. and Blunt, Ruth H. COMPOSITION, COLOR, AND SOMETIMES HUMOR: ARTIST BERNHARD GUTMANN OF LYNCHBURG. *Virginia Cavalcade 1982 31(4): 206-215.* Biography of German-born artist Bernhard Gutmann (1869-1936), who settled in Lynchburg, Virginia, in 1892 and became the first supervisor of drawing in the public schools there; paintings were known for their "humor and sense of design."

977. Moore, John R. LOUISIANA PLAYWRIGHT: PAUL T. NOLAN, A BIBLIOGRAPHY, PART II. *Louisiana Studies 1975 14(4): 422-426.* Continues a bibliography of the plays of Paul T. Nolan which was compiled by Beverly Matherne for the winter 1971 issue of *Louisiana Studies.* At that time the bibliography of Nolan's works included 81 drama entries. Provides an annotated listing of the more than two dozen more plays published since publication of that bibliography. Based on primary and secondary sources; 5 notes.                                      B. A. Glasrud

978. Moore, Rayburn S. THE ABSURDEST OF CRITICS: HAYNE ON HOWELLS. *Southern Literary J. 1979 12(1): 70-78.* Discusses the rather volatile relationship between Paul Hamilton Hayne, southern poet, and William Dean Howells, who edited the *Atlantic Monthly,* 1871-81.

979. Moorman, Charles. THERE ARE NO CHI OMEGAS AT PURDUE. *Southern Q. 1975 13(3): 181-187.* Discusses why the state of Mississippi has not produced a significant poet. Among the answers put forth are the "yarn spinning" tradition of the state's literary climate, the impact of the Civil War, and the life-style of the people. 2 notes. R. W. Dubay

980. Moss, William M. VINDICATOR OF SOUTHERN INTELLECT AND INSTITUTIONS: THE *SOUTHERN QUARTERLY REVIEW*. *Southern Literary J. 1980 13(1): 72-108.* The *Southern Quarterly Review*, published in Charleston, New Orleans, and other southern cities, and founded by Daniel K. Whitaker, defended slavery and states' rights from 1842 to 1857, and made a brief comeback in 1879-80.

981. Mugleston, William F. SOUTHERN LITERATURE AS HISTORY: SLAVERY IN THE ANTEBELLUM NOVEL. *Hist. Teacher 1974 8(1): 17-30.* Discusses slavery as reflected in southern novels. Early authors questioned the institution, while later ones increasingly came to its defense, or at least tolerated it. Generally, southern authors had no solution for the problem of slavery. They were ambivalent in their attitudes and frequently merely advocated respect and toleration. Primary and secondary sources; 29 notes. P. W. Kennedy

982. Neighbours, Kenneth F. JESSE WALLACE WILLIAMS: MAN, TEACHER AND WRITER. *West Texas Hist. Assoc. Year Book 1980 56: 49-57.* Remembrance dedicated to teacher and writer Jesse Wallace Williams, who taught at Midwestern State University in Wichita Falls, Texas, and wrote *Big Ranch Country*.

983. Newberger, Eli H. THE DEVELOPMENT OF NEW ORLEANS AND STRIDE PIANO STYLES. *J. of Jazz Studies 1977 4(2): 43-71.* Discusses piano playing styles of New Orleans jazz artists Jelly Roll Morton, Dink Johnson, Lil Hardin, Frank Melrose, Paul Lingle, Clarence Williams, James P. Johnson, Luckey Roberts, Eubie Blake, Fats Waller, Art Tatum, Willie "The Lion" Smith, Wally Rose, and Ralph Sutton, 1920's-40's.

984. Newcomb, William W., Jr. GERMAN ARTIST ON THE PEDERNALES. *Southwestern Hist. Q. 1978 82(2): 149-172.* Treats primarily the life and artistic contributions of Richard Petri, brother-in-law of Hermann Lungkwitz, also a Texas immigrant artist. This family bought a small farm on the Pedernales River in Texas in 1852. Until his death in 1857, Petri produced industriously an invaluable record of the people and life in this frontier community. Archival and secondary material; 36 illus., 27 notes. J. L. B. Atkinson

985. Newton, Scott. DAVID MCDOWELL ON JAMES AGEE. *Western Humanities Rev. 1980 34(2): 117-130.* Discusses the friendship between publisher David McDowell and author James Agee from 1936 until Agee's death in 1955, and reproduces McDowell's account of that friendship and of Agee's work.

986. Noble, Donald R. A CENTURY HENCE: GEORGE TUCKER'S VISION OF THE FUTURE. *Virginia Cavalcade 1976 25(4): 184-191.* Discusses the futuristic novels of Virginia lawyer, congressman, and political economist George Tucker, *A Voyage to the Moon* and *A Century Hence; or A Romance of 1941*, 1795-1861, including his views on slavery, overpopulation, feminism, and technology.

987. O'Brien, Matthew C. WILLIAM FAULKNER AND THE CIVIL WAR IN OXFORD, MISSISSIPPI. *J. of Mississippi Hist. 1973 35(2): 167-174.* Compares the Civil War in the fictional town of Jefferson and Yoknapatawpha County created by William Faulkner (1897-1962), and in the town of Oxford and Lafayette County, their counterparts in reality. Faulkner drew occasionally on actual events, but did not depend on them for subject matter, nor did he stress the material damage suffered by the town. Faulkner "is less concerned with a literal depiction of the war than he is with the 'moral' causes and effects of the conflict." Published sources; 6 notes. J. W. Hillje and S

988. Olds, Frederick A. HISTORIANS AND ART: AN OKLAHOMA CASE STUDY. *Chronicles of Oklahoma 1974 52(2): 196-206.* Oklahoma historians, like most American historians, have neglected art as a window on the past. Much can be discerned about Indian culture through studying paintings. Benjamin West did not concern himself with Indian portrayal, while Charles Marion Russell caught the essence of the Indian-horse culture in Oklahoma. Both Russell and Frederic Remington created factual representations of Indian life. Discusses Oklahoma artist Augusta Metcalf. Illus., 19 notes. E. P. Stickney

989. O'Leary, Beth Lokey. WASHINGTON BOGART COOPER, 1802-1888: THE INFLUENCES ON HIS WORK. *Tennessee Hist. Q. 1978 37(1): 68-75.* Washington Bogart Cooper was the most popular portrait artist in 19th-century Nashville. Self-taught, he painted about 35 portraits a year. Secondary sources; 21 notes. M. B. Lucas

990. Olson, Steven E. GREAT CIRCLE: CONRAD AIKEN'S AUTOPLASTIC JOURNEY INTO CHILDHOOD. *Southern Q. 1982 21(1): 38-63.* By tracing the periods 1900-01 and 1926-32 in Conrad Aiken's life, one can come to a better understanding of his novel, *Great Circle*. The first period manifests a childhood happiness evident in the Duxbury section of the novel and the second serves as a foundation for the adult world of the novel's chief character, Andrew Cather. 5 illus. W. A. Wiegand

991. Overstreet, Robert. SARAH BERNHARDT IN SAVANNAH. *Western Speech 1975 39(1): 20-25.* Sarah Bernhardt gave two performances in Savannah: *Camille* and *La Tosca* in 1892 and *Camille* again in 1906. S

992. Owens, William S. THE GOLDEN AGE OF TEXAS SCHOLARSHIP: WEBB, DOBIE, BEDICHEK, AND BOATRIGHT. *Southwest Rev. 1975 60(1): 1-14.* Examines the life and work of four authors who lived in and wrote about Texas (1927-70): J. Frank Dobie, Roy Bedichek, Walter Prescott Webb, and Mody C. Boatright.

993. Ownbey, Ray. DISCUSSIONS WITH WILLIAM STYRON. *Mississippi Q. 1977 30(2): 283-296.* In this interview Styron discusses his fiction, 1951-76, and the fiction of other southern writers, the South as a cultural entity, and his feelings about Negroes.

994. Park, Clara Claiborne. CRIPPLED LAUGHTER: TOWARD UNDERSTANDING FLANNERY O'CONNOR. *Am. Scholar 1982 51(2): 249-257.* Analyzes Flannery O'Connor and her fiction and concludes that her grotesque and ugly characters are no more depraved than the rest of fallen man and tell us a great deal about ourselves. F. F. Harling

995. Patton, Louise. THE SHREVEPORT ART CLUB: A BRIEF HISTORY. *North Louisiana Hist. Assoc. J. 1982 13(1): 15-26.* Organized in 1922, the Shreveport Art Club is credited with much of the success of the arts in the city since the club's founding. From seven founding members, the club grew to over 200 members by the 1950's, although experiencing many trying times and frustrations. Based on secondary sources, newspapers, and interviews; 37 notes. J. F. Paul

996. Petesch, Donald A. FAULKNER ON NEGROES: THE CONFLICT BETWEEN THE PUBLIC MAN AND THE PRIVATE ART. *Southern Humanities R. 1976 10(1): 55-63.* Public statements of William Faulkner about Negroes and school integration in the 1950's-60's were often contradictory and reflect the conflict between the artist and the public man.

997. Phillips, Bill. PIEDMONT COUNTRY BLUES. *Southern Exposure 1974 2(1): 56-62.* Discusses the musical style originated in the 1930's in Durham, North Carolina, by Gary Davis and Blind Boy Fuller.

998. Piacentino, Edward J. NO MORE "TREACHY SENTIMENTALITIES": THE LEGACY OF T. S. STRIBLING TO THE SOUTHERN LITERARY RENAISSENCE. *Southern Studies 1981*

*20(1): 67-83.* Thomas Sigismund Stribling (1881-1965) of Tennessee was a minor southern writer whose subject matter and treatment of the South helped stimulate the southern renaissance of literature and influenced the major writers of that movement. His earthy and realistic trilogy, *The Forge* (1931), *The Store* (1932), and *The Unfinished Cathedral* (1934) helped liberate modern southern literature from romanticism and introduced social realism. His seven novels represented a new departure in their blatantly realistic delineation of southern life. He used the middle class and poor whites as serious subject matter for the first time. 33 notes.

J. J. Buschen

999. Polk, Noel. WILLIAM FAULKNER'S "HONG LI" ON *ROYAL STREET. Lib. Chronicle of the U. of Texas 1980 (13):* 27-30. Analyzes William Faulkner's sketch "Hong Li," part of the pamphlet *Royal Street: New Orleans* bound in 1926, in a biographical context.

1000. Powell, Lawrence Clark. LETTER FROM THE SOUTHWEST. *Westways 1975 67(3): 18-21.* Notes several citizens—librarian Maud Sullivan, humanist C. L. Sonnichsen, writer Tom Lea, printer Carl Hertzog, and illustrator Jose Cisneros—who have helped make El Paso a center of Southwest culture.

1001. Pratt, Linda Ray. IMAGINING EXISTENCE: FORM AND HISTORY IN STEINBECK AND AGEE. *Southern R. 1975 11(1): 84-98.* One of six essays in this issue "On Self and Society."

1002. Presley, Delma Eugene. CARSON MC CULLERS AND THE SOUTH. *Georgia R. 1974 28(1): 19-32.* Presents a biographical sketch of Carson McCullers and an analysis of her relationship with the South as seen in her two most famous novels, *The Heart Is A Lonely Hunter* (1939) and *The Member of the Wedding* (1946). McCullers struggled to displace the burden of being a Southerner. Yet her early success came when she lived in the South and her later failure can be attributed to her flight northward. Her search was a quest for identity.

M. B. Lucas

1003. Prideaux, Tom. THE MAN BEHIND WASHINGTON'S KENNEDY CENTER. *Smithsonian 1979 9(10): 57-63.* Concentrates on the professional life of Washington's Kennedy Center Chairman Roger L. Stevens, who turned from real estate enterprises to theater productions where he became a prominent power, and was given charge of setting up a cultural center in Washington. Today, under his chairmanship, Washington's Kennedy Center has become a prosperous and vigorous performing arts organization benefiting the community. 11 illus.

G. P. Cleyet

1004. Prince, William S. ST. GEORGE TUCKER: BARD ON THE BENCH. *Virginia Mag. of Hist. and Biog. 1976 84(3):* 267-282. St. George Tucker, jurist and law professor, is seldom remembered as a Virginia poet of the Revolutionary and early National periods, even though he left several manuscript volumes with more than 200 poems. Fearing that his poetry might detract from his reputation as a legal scholar, Tucker published few of his poems. Yet he deserves to be remembered as one of the major poets of his era. Based largely on the Tucker-Coleman Coll., Swem Library, College of William and Mary; illus., 19 notes.

R. F. Oaks

1005. Putzel, Max. FAULKNER'S MEMPHIS STORIES. *Virginia Q. Rev. 1983 59(2): 254-270.* William Faulkner, although noted especially for his novels, also wrote short stories, which he found difficult but educationally rewarding. Some of these neglected short stories, particularly those connected with Memphis, Tennessee, were inspired partly by Faulkner's great aunt, Mrs. Walter B. McLean. Although these stories are quite ordinary, the criticism and advice they engendered from Alfred Dashiell of *Scribner's* and other magazine editors, such as H. L. Mencken and George Horace Lorimer, were responsible for some of the artistry Faulkner attained in his novels.

O. H. Zabel

1006. Pyron, Darden Asbury. THE INNER WAR OF SOUTHERN HISTORY. *Southern Studies 1981 20(1): 5-19. Gone with the Wind* (1936) by Margaret Mitchell has generally been interpreted as describing the ideal southern plantation legend with courtly men, gracious ladies, faithful retainers, pillared mansions, and high quality life. Actually Mitchell was attempting to describe the society of north Georgia with its yeoman farmer population living simple, rough lives. The novel clearly distinguishes between the weak, ineffectual, and effete men of the mansions as compared to the strong, productive small farmer. The novel is a classic case study of the differences among southerners: upper South vs. lower, seaboard vs. transmontaine, coast vs. delta, big city vs. all the rest. 20 notes.

J. J. Buschen

1007. Pyron, Darden Asbury. MARGARET MITCHELL: FIRST OR NOTHING. *Southern Q. 1982 20(3): 19-34.* A brief but careful look at the life of Margaret Mitchell, author of *Gone With the Wind,* to fill a gap between scholarly neglect and existing popular myths. Mitchell's statement that "If I can't be first, I'd rather be nothing," suggests the sources of her creative energy and demonstrates the impact of the problems she encountered as a woman in tradition-bound Southern society. Based on the Mitchell Papers at the University of Georgia.

W. A. Wiegand

1008. Rafert, Stewart. JAMES CURTIS BOOTH: DELAWARE'S FIRST GEOLOGIST. *Delaware Hist. 1976 17(2): 139-146.* Describes the life and career of James Curtis Booth, 1810-88, who studied medicine, chemistry, mineralogy, and geology in the United States and Europe. In 1836 he established what may be the first teaching chemistry laboratory in America and throughout his life was a dogged advocate of practical chemistry. In 1837 he started the Delaware geological survey and concluded that the main features of Maryland and New Jersey geology continued in Delaware. He located mineral resources, educated farmers in the use of minerals, and wrote a durable report, *Memoir of the Geological Survey of Delaware* (1841). 34 notes.

R. M. Miller

1009. Ragan, David Paul. "BELONGING TO THE BUSINESS OF MANKIND": THE ACHIEVEMENT OF FAULKNER'S *BIG WOODS. Mississippi Q. 1983 36(3): 301-317.* Discusses the theme of William Faulkner's *Big Woods* (1955), in which stories previously published were revised and joined to make a statement about the interaction of men and environment.

1010. Ragan, Sam. REMEMBERING STALWARTS. *North Carolina Hist. Rev. 1982 59(2): 139-146.* In 1980 and 1981, eight important writers in North Carolina died. Hugh T. Lefler (*The Growth of North Carolina* and *The History of a Southern State*), was the only historian in the group. Jonathan Daniels, (*Tar Heels* and *A Southerner Discovers the South*), and Harry Golden, (*Only in America* and *For 2 Cents Plain*) were newspapermen. Hugh Holman was a literary critic (*The Southerner as American: Thomas Wolfe* and *Southern Fiction Today*). Thad Stem (*Picture Poems* and *Entries from Oxford*), Paul Green (*In Abraham's Bosom* and *The Lost Colony*), Guy Owen (*Season of Fear* and *The Ballad of the Flim-Flam Man*), and James L. Person, poet laureate of North Carolina, were literary writers. Presented at annual meeting of the North Carolina Literary and Historical Association, 20 November 1981; 8 photos, 5 notes.

T. L. Savitt

1011. Ragan, Sam. THEY STRUCK SPARKS AND LIT LITERARY LANTERNS. *North Carolina Hist. Rev. 1978 55(2): 181-188.* A number of small literary magazines have been published in North Carolina in the last 150 years. Most survived for only a few issues, but others, like the *South Atlantic Quarterly, Southern Poetry Review,* and *Carolina Quarterly,* grew over the years, both in size and reputation, and have been publishing for years. The first literary magazine in the state was the *North Carolina Magazine,* published in 1813 at Salisbury. Many villages and towns have supported, at some time, such a literary magazine. Based on materials in the North Carolina Collection, University of North Carolina, Chapel Hill.

T. L. Savitt

1012. Ramage, James A. THOMAS HUNT MORGAN: FAMILY INFLUENCES IN THE MAKING OF A GREAT SCIENTIST. *Filson Club Hist. Q. 1979 53(1): 5-25.* Thomas Hunt Morgan was a Nobel Prize winner for biology in 1933. He developed the famous fruit fly experiments that confirmed much of the theoretical work of Charles Darwin and Gregor Johann Mendel. Much of the article deals with Morgan's namesake uncle, the famous Confederate raider, his father Charlton, and his uncle Basil Duke. The remainder of the account consists of anecdotes about Morgan as a scholar, teacher, father, and husband. Based on the Hunt-Morgan Papers at the University of Kentucky; 58 notes.

G. B. McKinney

1013. Raymond, Helen Marbury. MARIANNE MARBURY SLAUGHTER: MY AUNT, THE WRITER. *North Louisiana Hist. Assoc. J. 1979 10(1): 1-7.* Marianne Marbury Slaughter (1838-1928) wrote about plantation and small town life, folklore, gardening, and regional (southern) history. Illus., 9 notes.

J. F. Paul

1014. Reed, Richard. THE ROLE OF CHRONOLOGY IN FAULKNER'S YOKNAPATAWPHA FICTION. *Southern Literary J. 1974 7(1): 24-48.* A clear understanding of the chronology used by William Faulkner in his fictional Yoknapatawpha County helps the reader understand Faulkner's artistic sequence.

1015. Reid, Richard S. GARI MELCHERS: AN AMERICAN ARTIST IN VIRGINIA. *Virginia Cavalcade 1979 28(4): 154-171.* American artist Gari Melchers (1860-1932) first gained fame as a painter in Europe; then, beginning in the mid-1890's, he received acclaim in the United States as an artist in the impressionist style.

1016. Reinecke, George. ALFRED MERCIER, FRENCH NOVELIST OF NEW ORLEANS. *Southern Q. 1982 20(2): 145-176.* Alfred Mercier was born near New Orleans, immigrated to France in his teens, and earned a medical degree there. In 1865 he returned to New Orleans, set up a medical practice, and followed literary pursuits as an avocation. His novels include *Le Fou de Palerme* (1873), *Lidia* (1873), *La Fille du Prêtre* (1877-78), *L'Habitation Saint-Ybars* (1881), and *Johnelle* (1891). The contents of all are summarized and analyzed as contributions to New Orleans literature.

W. A. Wiegand

1017. Rhodes, Carolyn. GAIL GODWIN AND THE IDEAL OF SOUTHERN WOMANHOOD. *Southern Q. 1983 21(4): 54-66.* Gail Godwin, born in Alabama in 1937 and author of five novels, devotes much of her fictional attention to exploring the conservative feminine myth surrounding the Southern woman. She decries its insistence upon selflessness, and enumerates the limitations such conduct and social customs impose on self-discovery. Ultimately, her characters demonstrate to readers that the modern Southern woman can satisfactorily lead an orderly life with roots to the past as long as she insists on maintaining self-creativity. W. A. Wiegand

1018. Richardson, Thomas J. HONORÉ GRANDISSIME'S SOUTHERN DILEMMA: INTRODUCTION. *Southern Q. 1980 18(4): 1-12.* With the exception of Mark Twain, George Washington Cable was the most significant artist in the late 19th-century South. *The Grandissimes* (1880) was his most important work, but other works, both novels and essays on civil rights, have gained him a place of distinction in southern history. Primary sources; 15 notes.

B. D. Ledbetter

1019. Riggio, Thomas P. UNCLE TOM RECONSTRUCTED: A NEGLECTED CHAPTER IN THE HISTORY OF A BOOK. *Am. Q. 1976 28(1): 56-70.* An important link in the history of the reception to and impact of *Uncle Tom's Cabin* is found in its role in Southern Reconstruction fiction, especially in the novels of Thomas Dixon. In *The Leopard's Spots*, he achieved a direct and complete metamorphosis of Stowe's books through his characterizations. Dixon replaced Stowe's language of evangelical humanism with a rhetoric of white manifest destiny in which all except Negroes would be united in a new bond.

N. Lederer

1020. Ritchey, David. ROBERT DE LAPOUYADE: THE LAST OF THE LOUISIANA SCENE PAINTERS. *Louisiana Hist. 1973 14(1): 5-20.* Robert de Lapouyade was the leading set designer and scene painter for the most popular theaters in New Orleans, 1902-27. With the decline of the legitimate theater his profession became obsolete and he turned to designing department store windows and Mardi Gras floats. Based on newspapers, interviews, and the Robert de Lapouyade Collection at Louisiana State University; 9 photos, 25 notes.

R. L. Woodward

1021. Robinson, Jo Ann. LILLIAN SMITH: REFLECTIONS ON RACE AND SEX. *Southern Exposure 1977 4(4): 43-48.* The work and writings of Lillian Smith were primarily concerned with the entwined themes of race and sex in southern life. As director of a southern girls' camp she raised female consciousness and espoused racial equality. In her books she broke taboos on race and sex. With *Killers of the Dream* Smith was systematically ostracized by southern liberal newspapers and by the New York literary establishment. In her personal life female friends were most supportive of her endeavors and most perceptive of what she was attempting to accomplish. Primary sources.

N. Lederer

1022. Rogers-Price, Vivian and Griffin, William W. JOHN ABBOT: PIONEER ARTIST-NATURALIST OF GEORGIA. *Mag. Antiques 1983 124(4): 768-775.* Supporting his family by selling his exquisite graphite and watercolor illustrations, English-born John Abbot studied and depicted Savannah Valley natural history.

1023. Rouse, Blair. GONE WITH THE WIND: BUT NOT FORGOTTEN. *Southern Literary J. 1978 10(2): 173-179.* Review article prompted by *Margaret Mitchell's "Gone With The Wind" Letters, 1936-1949,* edited by Richard Harwell (New York: Macmillan Co., 1976), concerned with the writing and publishing of the book, its film version, and the changes it brought to Margaret Mitchell's life.

1024. Rovit, Earl. FAULKNER, HEMINGWAY, AND THE AMERICAN FAMILY. *Mississippi Q. 1976 29(4): 483-497.* Examines the childhood in middle-class rural homes which both Ernest Hemingway and William Faulkner shared, and the effect which this had on their world views, 1900-50.

1025. Roy, Roberta Teague. LAND AND THE SOUTHERN APPALACHIAN WOMAN: SENSUAL OR POETIC? *Kentucky Folklore Record 1979 25(3-4): 68-74.* American literary stereotypes call southern Appalachian men exploiters and destroyers of the land, and Appalachian women synthesizers with a transcendental, cosmic vision of the land, as discussed by Annette Kolodny and Susan Griffin, contemporary feminist writers who examine Ralph Waldo Emerson's essay *Nature*, and several books by 20th-century writers.

1026. Rubin, Louis D., Jr. THE MOCKINGBIRD IN THE GUM TREE: NOTES ON THE LANGUAGE OF AMERICAN LITERATURE. *Southern Rev. 1983 19(4): 785-801.* The problem that early American writers faced, that of using realistic vernacular speech without losing the expressive power of more formal language, was overcome by Mark Twain, Ernest Hemingway, and William Faulkner, who managed to combine both.

1027. Rubin, Louis D., Jr. SCHOLARSHIP IN SOUTHERN LITERATURE: ITS HISTORY AND RECENT DEVELOPMENTS. *Am. Studies Int. 1983 21(2): 3-34.* Traces southern literary criticism from its beginnings around 1890 through the split between historical scholarship (which concentrated on earlier literature) and criticism (which dealt with modern literature), and finally to the rapprochement after World War II, which focused critical insight on both early and modern literature, recognized the writings of black Southerners, and brought about an explosion of scholarship. Discusses modern critical studies of Southern literature since colonial times. Southern literary criticism in the 20th century moved from sectional defense and uncritical eulogy to disciplined understanding. 3 illus., biblio., 14 notes.

R. E. Noble

1028. Rubin, Louis D., Jr. A STUDY IN PASTORAL AND HISTORY. *Georgia Hist. Q. 1975 59(4): 442-454.* Review article prompted by Lewis P. Simpson's *Pastoral and History in Southern Literature* (Athens, Georgia: U. of Georgia Pr., 1975).

1029. Rubin, Louis D., Jr. THOMAS WOLFE AND THE PLACE HE CAME FROM. *Virginia Q. R. 1976 52(2): 183-202.* Thomas Wolfe is a southern author even though he may not resemble Faulkner, Warren, or others. He is a southern writer not only because he came from the South, but because in books such as *Look Homeward, Angel*, he wrote autobiographically. His "passionate moral involvement in a time and place... constitutes Thomas Wolfe's relationship with the South.... And the place he came from is Asheville, North Carolina." O. H. Zabel

1030. Rubin, Louis D., Jr. UNCLE REMUS AND THE UBIQUITOUS RABBIT. *Southern R. 1974 10(4): 787-804.* Of all his writings, Joel Chandler Harris' Uncle Remus stories depict most successfully the reality of Negroes' daily life in the South during the late 19th and early 20th century.

1031. Rubinstein, Stanley and Farley, Judith. ENOCH PRATT FREE LIBRARY AND BLACK PATRONS: EQUALITY IN LIBRARY SERVICES, 1882-1915. *J. of Lib. Hist. 1980 15(4): 445-453.* Discusses the availability of library services to Negroes in Baltimore, Maryland, especially the services of the Enoch Pratt Free Library, from its founding in 1886 until 1915. Baltimore in 1882 had an enormous black population, and educational facilities for blacks were inadequate. In order to balance this inequity, Enoch Pratt, a Baltimore philanthropist, established his library, open to blacks and whites, so that all might have equal opportunities in the field of continuing education, despite efforts to segregate the institution in the second decade of the 20th century. Primary sources; 37 notes. J. Powell

1032. Rutledge, John. MADISON CAWEIN AS AN EXPONENT OF GERMAN CULTURE. *Filson Club Hist. Q. 1977 51(1): 5-16.* Madison Julius Cawein, a Kentucky regional poet, played a leading role in introducing German poetry into America. Cawein was able to win some personal recognition as an interpreter of mountain scenery and nature. In addition, he used his German family background to translate the works of Nicolas Lenau, Ludwig Uhland, Emmanuel Geibel, Friedrich Bodenstedt, Heinrich Heine, and Johann Wolfgang von Goethe. Primarily based on the Cawein Papers at the Filson Club, Louisville, Kentucky, and his published works; 43 notes. G. B. McKinney

1033. Ryan, Steven T. FAULKNER AND QUANTUM MECHANICS. *Western Humanities Rev. 1979 33(4): 329-339.* Faulknerian literary method, which aimed at ever growing knowledge of and introspection into characters (with the express understanding that perfect knowledge was impossible), is compared with similar thought in contemporary quantum mechanics theory which realized the ever growing capacity for understanding without complete or perfect knowledge, 1920's-30's.

1034. Salmon, Emily J. DUNCAN SMITH: AN ARTIST REDISCOVERED. *Virginia Cavalcade 1981 30(4): 186-191.* Traces the career of Duncan Smith (1877-1934), a Virginia-born artist who specialized in murals, and is well-known in American art circles for his portraits of faculty members of the University of Virginia and for his paintings based upon the works of Edgar Allan Poe.

1035. Salmon, Emily J. and Salmon, John S. GENERAL LEE'S PHOTOGRAPHER: MICHAEL MILEY, OF LEXINGTON. *Virginia Cavalcade 1983 33(2): 86-96.* After establishing his Lexington, Virginia, studio in 1866, Michael Miley became Robert E. Lee's principal photographer; he specialized in portraits and outdoor scenes and successfully experimented with color photography and dry-plate negatives.

1036. Saunders, Frances W. EQUESTRIAN WASHINGTON FROM ROME TO RICHMOND. *Virginia Cavalcade 1975 25(1): 4-13.* Discusses the planning, erection, and unveiling of statues and monuments of George Washington in Richmond 1784-1868, emphasizing the sculpture of Thomas Crawford.

1037. Saunders, Sara Bradford. PORTRAITS AT EVERGREEN. *Daughters of the Am. Revolution Mag. 1976 110(1): 26-34, 63.* Discusses the history of the Weakley family portraits at Evergreen Place farm in Nashville, Tennessee, 1764-1892.

1038. Scarlett, Charles, Jr. A TALE OF RATIOCINATION: THE DEATH AND BURIAL OF EDGAR ALLAN POE. *Maryland Hist. Mag. 1978 73(4): 360-374.* Reconstructs Poe's arrival and death at Washington College Hospital in Baltimore, 3-7 October 1849, sorting through conflicting accounts and the mythology surrounding his final illness. Testimony of eyewitnesses, including gravediggers, also leads to the conclusion that Poe's remains were not moved in 1875 to the northwest corner of Westminster Yard cemetery and placed under a large monument erected by a "self-styled" society. The committee exumed the wrong body, being uncertain of the precise location of Poe's grave, and actually reburied young private Philip Mosher Jr., a veteran of 1812. Edgar Allan Poe remains the man of mystery to the very end. Primary and secondary accounts; note. G. J. Bobango

1039. Schafer, William J. GOOD-BAD (APPALACHIAN) NOVELS. *Appalachian J. 1982 9(4): 302-305.* Review article of Mike Henson's *Ransack* (1981) and Jack Welch's *Life at an Early Age* (1981); novels dealing with Appalachia that are not good literature but are powerful "cultural voices."

1040. Schafer, William J. MARY LEE SETTLE'S BEULAH QUINTET: HISTORY DARKLY, THROUGH A SINGLE-LENS REFLEX. *Appalachian J. 1982 10(1): 77-86.* Mary Lee Settle's five novels, covering over 200 years in the Appalachian coal-mining districts, embody four overriding images: the prison, the heritage of war, the complex family structure, and the transmuted land.

1041. Schafer, William J. THOUGHTS ON JAZZ HISTORIOGRAPHY: "BUDDY BOLDEN'S BLUES" VS. "BUDDY BOTTLEY'S BALLOON." *J. of Jazz Studies 1975 2(1): 3-14.* Describes the difficulty in finding accurate sources of information concerning early jazzmen, using the controversy over Buddy Bolden's New Orleans jazz band, circa 1895, and Buddy Bartley, a Negro balloonist living in New Orleans at approximately the same time, as an example. S

1042. Schmidt, Martin Frederick. THE KENTUCKY STOCK BOOK: A SEARCH FOR THE ELUSIVE. *Filson Club Hist. Q. 1974 48(3): 217-227.* Discusses efforts by Kentucky farmers and artists including Edward Troye, Thomas Campbell, and Colin Milne, to produce a book of prints and pedigrees for some of the state's livestock. The effort failed because of a lack of financing in 1838, but many prints had already been produced and a list of those that have been located is included. Documentation from contemporary newspapers; 2 photos, 23 notes. G. B. McKinney

1043. Schwartz, Lawrence. MALCOLM COWLEY'S PATH TO WILLIAM FAULKNER. *J. of Am. Studies [Great Britain] 1982 16(2): 229-242.* Early in the 1940's, Malcolm Cowley abandoned the radical literary activities and politics in which he was immersed in the 30's. Among his post-1940 roles, he became an important but apolitical literary critic. He contributed leadership toward regenerating interest in the writings of novelist William Faulkner. Based on Cowley's published writings and his private papers in the Newberry Library; 32 notes. H. T. Lovin

1044. Scura, Dorothy. GLASGOW AND THE SOUTHERN RENAISSANCE: THE CONFERENCE AT CHARLOTTESVILLE. *Mississippi Q. 1974 27(4): 415-434.* The Southern Writers Conference in Charlottesville, Virginia, on 23-24 October 1931. One of three papers. S

1045. Scura, Dorothy M. HOMAGE TO CONSTANCE CARY HARRISON. *Southern Humanities Rev. 1976 (Special Issue): 35-46.* Discusses the themes of plantation life and the Civil War in the novels of Constance Cary Harrison, 1863-1911.

1046. Scura, Dorothy McInnis. THE SOUTHERN LADY IN THE EARLY NOVELS OF ELLEN GLASGOW. *Mississippi Q. 1977-78 31(1): 17-32.* Examines the female characters in the novels of Ellen Glasgow during 1898-1913, as a representation of mythical Southern womanhood.

1047. Segrest, M. LINES I DARE TO WRITE: LESBIAN WRITING IN THE SOUTH. *Southern Exposure 1981 9(2): 53-55, 57-62.* Assesses lesbian fiction and poetry in the South from the first wave of the 1920's-50's, with the works of Angelina Weld Grimké, Carson McCullers, and Lillian Smith, to the lesbian-feminist cultural revolution of the 1960's and 70's.

1048. Shapiro, Henry D. APPALACHIA AND THE IDEA OF AMERICA: THE PROBLEM OF THE PERSISTING FRONTIER. *Appalachian J. 1977 4(4): 43-55.* Growth of the conception of Appalachia as an "other" America, now ingrained into the mainstream of American consciousness, has been developed since 1870 by writers depicting picturesque conditions of mountain life, moonshining, feuding, violence, and lawlessness of the region.

1049. Shapiro, Henry D. JOHN F. DAY AND THE DISAPPEARANCE OF APPALACHIA FROM THE AMERICAN CONSCIOUSNESS. *Appalachian J. 1983 10(2): 157-164.* Reissue of John Day's *Bloody Ground* (1941) which described the dilemma arising from the glorification of Appalachia as truly American, and the reality of poverty and repression in that area.

1050. Sharma, P. P. WILLIAM FAULKNER'S SOUTH AND THE OTHER SOUTH. *Indian J. of Am. Studies [India] 1977 7(1): 79-93.* Contrasts William Faulkner's view of the South with the views of Thomas Nelson Page and Eudora Welty. Faulkner portrays a land gripped by a moral chaos, Page portrays an idealized or romanticized South, and Welty portrays a land unconcerned with disturbing issues. Faulkner's view has become dominant because, while it is firmly anchored to the clearly recognizable reality of Mississippi, it is a microcosm of the modern world and a symbol of man's plight in it. 34 notes.                    L. V. Eid

1051. Shellenberger, Jack H. WILLIAM FAULKNER—STAG (SHORT TERM AMERICAN GRANTEE). *Foreign Service J. 1977 54(1): 10-11, 30.* Relates the author's experiences as a member of the US Information Service making a documentary film on novelist William Faulkner's impressions while travelling through Japan in 1955.

1052. Shelton, Frances and McBride, Lucia. A TRIPTYCH OF COLONIAL MUSIC. *Daughters of the Am. Revolution Mag. 1980 114(3): 304-315, 327.* Discusses the colonial music of the New England colonies, the Southern colonies, and the Middle colonies, 17th-18th centuries.

1053. Shelton, Frank W. HARRY CREWS: MAN'S SEARCH FOR PERFECTION. *Southern Literary J. 1980 12(2): 97-113.* Discusses Harry Crews's eight novels published during 1968-76, his nonfiction collection, *Blood and Grits* (1979), and his autobiography, *A Childhood* (1978), focusing on the grotesque characters and the human search for perfection in an imperfect world, akin to the tradition of Erskine Caldwell and Flannery O'Connor, and his use of the theme of "the problem of encroachment of modernism on the traditional Southern ways of life."

1054. Shillingsburg, Miriam J. THE SOUTHRON AS AMERICAN: WILLIAM GILMORE SIMMS. *Studies in the Am. Renaissance 1980: 409-423.* Discusses the career of writer and editor William Gilmore Simms during 1824-56. At a time when American art was coming into maturity, Simms failed to mature as a serious artist because of the "insularity of his subject matter" and his staunch defense of the endangered pride of the South. His interests centered around South Carolina. In 1849 he took up the editorship

of the *Southern Quarterly Review.* His lecture tour to New York in the autumn of 1856 was a failure, forcing him to turn inward and to see the South as his domain, and the eventual decline of his stature as an American, rather than a Southern writer. Based on letters, other primary sources, and journal articles; 31 notes.
                    J. Powell

1055. Shillingsburg, Miriam J. WILLIAM GILMORE SIMMS AND THE MYTH OF APPALACHIA. *Appalachian J. 1979 6(2): 111-120.* William Gilmore Simms wrote on Appalachia during 1847-50 as a region of magnificence, grandeur, and violence, adding to the area's myth.

1056. Short, Julee. WALTER S. CAMPBELL: OKLAHOMA WRITER. *Chronicles of Oklahoma 1973/74 51(4): 473-486.* Biographical sketch of Walter S. Campbell (1887-1957) (pseud. Stanley Vestal), who wrote about the Southwest and its mountain men and Indians.

1057. Silver, James W. FAULKNER'S SOUTH. *Southern Humanities Rev. 1976 10(4): 301-311.* Discusses personal feelings about the writings of William Faulkner and Faulkner's relation to the South and to history in general.

1058. Simms, L. Moody, Jr. CORRA HARRIS ON THE DECLINE OF SOUTHERN WRITING. *Southern Studies 1979 18(2): 247-250.* Corra Harris (1869-1935), a Georgian, in the 1900's wrote that southern writing of her time was in decline because the works of too many southern authors were characterized by extreme defensiveness, devotion to the glories of the Old South, and worship at the tomb of the Lost Cause of the Civil War. Her outspoken criticism was not typical of southern writers of her day. Based on Harris's articles in the *Independent,* 1903-1908; 11 notes.
                    J. J. Buschen

1059. Simms, L. Moody, Jr. CORRA HARRIS, WILLIAM PETERFIELD TRENT, AND SOUTHERN WRITING. *Mississippi Q. 1979 32(4): 641-650.* Reprints Corra Harris's "Southern Writers," which originally appeared in *The Critic* (1905), and which analyzes the region's authors, 17c-1890's, denouncing "patriotic literary criticism," particularly William Peterfield Trent's book, *Southern Writers* (1905).

1060. Simms, L. Moody, Jr. EDWARD CALEDON BRUCE: VIRGINIA ARTIST AND WRITER. *Virginia Cavalcade 1974 23(3): 30-37.* Considers the artistic and reporting skills of Edward Caledon Bruce in Virginia, 1847-1901.

1061. Simms, L. Moody, Jr. JOHN BLENNERHASSETT MARTIN, WILLIAM GARL BROWN AND FLAVIUS JAMES FISHER: THREE NINETEENTH-CENTURY VIRGINIA PORTRAITISTS. *Virginia Cavalcade 1975 25(2): 72-79.* Discusses the oil paintings of portraitists John Blennerhassett Martin, William Garl Brown and Flavius James Fisher in Virginia, 1817-1905.

1062. Simms, L. Moody, Jr. MARGARET JUNKIN PRESTON: SOUTHERN POET. *Southern Studies 1980 19(1): 94-100.* Margaret Junkin Preston (1820-97), housewife, was a good, although not great, poet. She contributed to the revival of southern letters after the Civil War. The epitome of suffering, southern womanhood persevering under adversity, she most successfully created dramatic monologues, sonnets, and ballads, especially character portraits. Literary tastes changed; today her works seem rhetorical and sentimental. 15 notes.                    J. J. Buschen

1063. Simms, L. Moody, Jr. MAURICE THOMPSON RECALLS PAUL HAMILTON HAYNE. *Southern Studies 1977 16(1): 91-97.* James Maurice Thompson (1844-1901) was an Indiana writer and correspondent of the Southern poet Paul Hamilton Hayne (1830-1886). In 1881, Thompson visited Hayne at the latter's home at Copse Hill in Groveton, Georgia. Thompson's report of the visit, "The Last Literary Cavalier," appeared in the *Critic* in April 1901, and is reprinted here. Thompson viewed Hayne as the embodiment of the Southern literary tradition in the late 19th century. In 1881 Hayne lived in a simple wood shanty. He was a charming host, delightful raconteur, and had known most of the prominent figures in southern literature before and after the Civil War. His work lies at the juncture between the literature of the Old South and the New South; he was the end of an era. 8 notes.    J. Buschen

1064. Simms, L. Moody, Jr. NINETEENTH CENTURY VIRGINIA PORTRAITURE: GENNARO PERSICO, JAMES W. FORD, AND LOUIS M. D. GUILLAUME. *Southern Q. 1978 17(1): 15-28.* These portraitists are important not so much for their many existing portraits, but for being "representative of those Virginia portraitists who recorded the likeness of generation after generation of nineteenth-century Virginians." 34 notes.
B. D. Ledbetter

1065. Simms, L. Moody, Jr. PHILIP ALEXANDER BRUCE ON LITERATURE: ONE SOUTHERNER'S OPINIONS. *Southern Studies 1977 16(3): 329-334.* In 1889 Philip Alexander Bruce (1856-1933), a social commentator and historian of 17th-century Virginia, wrote a literary column for the Richmond *Times* in which he expressed in personal terms his views, as an intelligent and well-educated southerner, of contemporary literature. He saw depravity, obscenity, and immorality running rampant in American literature and disapproved of it. It was caused by wealth, widespread education, and the American emphasis on practicality. He offered a list of 91 exemplary literary works, only 24 by Americans. 7 notes.
J. Buschen

1066. Simms, L. Moody, Jr. TOWARD NORMS: THE FINE ARTS IN THE AMERICAN SOUTH, 1900-1960. *Southern Q. 1983 21(2): 29-67.* For most of the 20th century the South trailed the rest of the nation in cultural achievements. This poor showing can partly be traced to the South's emphasis of the practical over the aesthetic, its rural economic and population base, and its willingness to imitate the North. Jazz represents the South's sole unique contribution to American culture.    W. A. Wiegand

1067. Simpson, Joel. NEW ORLEANS' NEW JAZZMEN. *Horizon 1982 25(6): 34-39.* Discusses the musicians and their styles in the new generation of jazz stars in New Orleans since the mid-1970's, including pianist Ellis Marsalis, his sons Wynton and Branford, saxophonist Tony Dagradi, bassist and cellist Ramsey McLean, saxophonist Edward "Kidd" Jordan, pianist and composer James Drew, saxophonist Paul McGinley, and guitarist Steve Masakowski.

1068. Simpson, Lewis P. THE ART OF THOUGHT IN VIRGINIA. *Early Am. Literature 1979-80 14(3): 253-268.* By the late 18th century, Virginia's intellectual consciousness had developed a diverse model based on rationality and secular morality. the process began with Captain John Smith and culminated with Thomas Jefferson, who harmonized with the tone and temper of his age. Depends heavily upon two seocndary works by Richard Beale Davis: *Intellectual Life in Jefferson's Virginia, 1780-1830* (1964); and *Intellectual life in the Colonial South, 1585-1763* (1978). Based on an essay presented to the Modern Language Association, 30 December 1978; 18 notes.    T. P. Linkfield

1069. Simpson, Lewis P. A NECROLOGY OF MODERN SOUTHERN FICTION. *Southern Literary J. 1977 9(2): 150-159.* Examines the blend of subjects and psychologies which combine to make the fiction of the South unique; examines the literary techniques of various southern authors, 19th-20th centuries.

1070. Skaggs, Merrill M. SOUTHERN COMPOST. *Southern Literary J. 1978 10(2): 155-160.* Review article prompted by William L. Frank's *Sherwood Bonner (Catherine McDowell)* (Boston: Twayne Publishers, 1976), discussing her contribution to southern literature, 1864-83.

1071. Skaggs, Merrill Maguire. WILLA CATHER'S EXPERIMENTAL SOUTHERN NOVEL. *Mississippi Q. 1981-82 35(1): 3-14.* Willa Cather "returned to the scenes of her childhood in order first to assault standard literary assumptions about antebellum

Southern life, then to challenge the widely accepted stereotype of the Southern lady, and finally to try out a new and, for her, radically different, narrative form."

1072. Smith, Allan. THE PSYCHOLOGICAL CONTEXT OF THREE TALES BY POE. *J. of Am. Studies [Great Britain] 1973 7(3): 279-292.* Analyzes three works—"The Black Cat," "Berenice," and "The Murders in the Rue Morgue"—by Edgar Allen Poe (1809-49). Poe drew upon scientific postulations of contemporary psychologists George Combe (1788-1858), Frederick Rauch, (1806-41), and Thomas Upham (1799-1872). Their theories significantly influenced Poe. Based on secondary sources; 60 notes.
H. T. Lovin

1073. Smith, C. Michael. THE SURPRISING POPULARITY OF ERSKINE CALDWELL'S SOUTH. *J. of Popular Culture 1982 16(3): 42-46.* Some of the popularity of Erskine Caldwell's depiction of the South in *Tobacco Road* (1932) and *God's Little Acre* (1933) stems from the obscenity charges that were leveled against both novels. However, Caldwell's fictional South was popular also because it fed northern interests in the South, and provided a glimpse of the seamy side of Southern life that "counteracted the moonlight-and-magnolias stereotype" of the times. 18 notes.
D. G. Nielson

1074. Smith, Gerald J. JOHN DONALD WADE: A BIBLIOGRAPHICAL NOTE. *Mississippi Q. 1976 29(2): 241-244.* Presents a bibliography of books, poems, and articles of southern fiction writer John Donald Wade, 1910-55.

1075. Smith, Lillian. THE OLD DAYS IN JASPER: A REMINISCENCE. *Virginia Q. Rev. 1982 58(4): 677-686.* Lillian Smith, author of *Strange Fruit* and *Killers of the Dream,* describes youthful experiences in Jasper, Florida that influenced her writing career. Some of her memories included her friend, listener, and collaborator in youthful dreams, Marjorie White, picnics at Shaky Pond with its trembling earth raising questions of reality, and funerals causing a youthful consideration of time and eternity. These concerns and memories among others, were "what maybe turned me into a writer." Note.    O. H. Zabel

1076. Smith, Margaret Denton. CHECKLIST OF PHOTOGRAPHERS WORKING IN NEW ORLEANS, 1840-1865. *Louisiana Hist. 1979 20(4): 393-430.* Demonstrates the growth and variety of photography in New Orleans during this dynamic period in the city's history. Lists more than 100 daguerreotypists and photographers. Most entries include some biographical data, the location of studios, and the years in which activity can be documented. Based on contemporary newspapers, city directories, and census records; note.    D. B. Touchstone

1077. Snell, Susan. WILLIAM FAULKNER, PHIL STONE, AND KATRINA CARTER: A BIOGRAPHICAL FOOTNOTE TO THE SUMMER OF 1914. *Southern Lit. J. 1983 15(2): 76-86.* Discusses the little-known influence of William Faulkner by Katrina Carter herself and by her introduction of Faulkner to Phil Stone; covers 1914-60.

1078. Snyder, Bob. COLONIAL MIMESIS AND THE APPALACHIAN RENASCENCE. *Appalachian J. 1978 5(3): 340-349.* Cultural development, as represented by contemporary Appalachian poetry, is blocked by four transactions which confuse conceptual and social forces in regional literature: regional/provincial; folk; social science; and political.

1079. Soderbergh, Peter A. THE SOUTH IN JUVENILE SERIES BOOKS, 1907-1917. *Mississippi Q. 1974 27(2): 131-140.*

1080. Speer, Jean Haskell. CULTURE AS BARTER. *Appalachian J. 1983 10(4): 366-371.* Reviews Mark Dawidziak's *The Barter Theater Story: Love Made Visible* (1982), a popular history of the Barter Theater in Abingdon, Virginia, which was founded in 1932.

1081. Steakley, Bobbie Eubanks. COLORADO CITY OPERA HOUSES. *Permian Hist. Ann. 1981 21: 59-65.* Traces the history of two opera houses in Colorado City, Texas: the Frenkel Opera House, dedicated in 1884 and destroyed by a storm in 1896, and the Colorado Opera House, built in 1900 and restored as a theater playhouse in 1969-71; describes their role in the cultural life of the city.

1082. Strickland, Betty Jo. THE SHORT FICTION OF WILLIAM GILMORE SIMMS: A CHECKLIST. *Mississippi Q. 1976 29(4): 591-608.* Bibliography of William Gilmore Simms' writings, spanning the period 1825-70.

1083. Sullivan, Clayton. THE CRAWFORD MANUSCRIPT BY MAGGIE TATE LEA (1867-1893) OF AMITE COUNTY. *J. of Mississippi Hist. 1978 40(4): 341-352.* The Crawford Manuscript was written by Maggie Tate Lea around 1890. She was born in Amite County, Mississippi, in 1867 and died there in 1893. The manuscript is an unpretentious story written for the entertainment of children and concerns the activities of Margaret Muse Clay, born in Chesterfield County, Virginia, in 1737. A major episode in the narrative is an account of a public whipping of Baptists for their religious beliefs in Chesterfield County (1773?). The manuscript also contains some examples of folk medicine used by "Grandmother Clay," after she moved to Mississippi about 1802.

M. S. Legan

1084. Swift, Mary Grace. DANCING BELLES AND BEAUX OF OLD NEW ORLEANS. *Rev. de Louisiane 1978 7(1): 49-63.* Offers a history of theatrical dance, primarily ballet, in New Orleans, 1803-22.

1085. Swift, Mary Grace. DANCING BELLES AND BEAUX OF OLD NEW ORLEANS. *Rev. de Louisiane 1979 8(2): 135-142.* Continued from previous article. Traces dance appearances and ballet performances in New Orleans from 1829, when Madame Claude Labasse, formerly Mademoiselle Hutin, appeared in the opera *Le Macon* in New Orleans, until the 1840's, when *Giselle* was performed; discusses the success of ballet performed for both French- and English-speaking audiences.

1086. Taylor, Helen. THE CASE OF GRACE KING. *Southern Rev. 1982 18(4): 685-702.* Discusses the work of Southern writer Grace King, with special attention to the influence of her ideology of womanhood.

1087. Taylor, Welford Dunaway. JULIUS JOHN LANKES: VIRGINIA WOODCUT ARTIST. *Virginia Cavalcade 1976 26(1): 4-19.* Discusses Julius John Lankes (1908-58), a Virginia artist, began work in woodcuts when a wind storm blew down some of the trees in his father's apple orchard; discusses the woodcuts used as illustrations and Lankes's books of renderings.

1088. Tebbetts, Dianne. TRADITIONAL HOUSES OF INDEPENDENCE COUNTY, ARKANSAS. *Pioneer Am. 1978 10(1): 36-55.* Analyzes house types in Independence County, Arkansas to reveal the heritage of its earlier settlers. Due to a scarcity of written accounts of the region, houses were studied to comprehend the personality and culture of the inhabitants. Six modes of construction were used, but the major types were log, frame, and box. These traditional house types were further divided into styles. The simplest form was the single-pen house, but the most widespread was the double-pen house with two front doors. Dogtrot houses were among other common types which may have been modified. The traditional architecture agrees with written record in that the owners have always been open, unselfconscious people living in harmony with their surroundings. Based on field work, unpublished Ph.D. dissertation, and secondary sources; 7 photos, 41 notes.

C. R. Gunter, Jr.

1089. Tedford, Barbara Wilkie. FLANNERY O'CONNOR AND THE SOCIAL CLASSES. *Southern Literary J. 1981 13(2): 27-40.* Discusses the social stratification in southern culture reflected in the short stories of Flannery O'Connor, the first of which appeared in 1946, and the last of which appeared in 1965.

1090. Tentarelli, Ronda Cabot. THE LIFE AND TIMES OF THE *SOUTHERN REVIEW*. *Southern Studies 1977 16(2): 129-151.* Robert Penn Warren (b. 1905) and Cleanth Brooks (b. 1906) began publication of the *Southern Review* in 1935 from Louisiana State University. Partly as a reaction to the Scopes trial publicity of 1925 and partly as a result of the work of the Nashville Agrarians, a group of young southern poets, the *Review* provided a vehicle for scholarly, political, and economic essays, fiction of the highest quality, literary articles emphasizing the "new criticism," poetry, and book reviews. The journal ceased publication in 1942, basically for internal political reasons. The *Review* was especially important as an expression of the Southern Renaissance and the New Criticism. Based on an unpublished doctoral thesis, interviews with Brooks, and secondary sources; 52 notes.

J. Buschen

1091. Tharpe, Jac. INTERVIEW WITH ERSKINE CALDWELL. *Southern Q. 1981 20(1): 64-74.* Part of an interview with Erskine Caldwell at the University of Southern Mississippi in August 1971. Caldwell discusses 20th-century US authors.

B. D. Ledbetter

1092. Thomas, James W. LYLE SAXON'S STRUGGLE WITH *CHILDREN OF STRANGERS*. *Southern Studies 1977 16(1): 27-40.* Lyle Saxon was an established reporter for the New Orleans *Times-Picayune*. He wrote four nonfictional works on regional Louisiana history during 1927-30, but his great desire was to write a novel about plantation life. An opportunity to reside at Melrose plantation provided him with the time and atmosphere, but the novel took seven years to complete *Children of Strangers* (1937). A distinguished regional novel, it was the only significant work Saxon published. A combination of alcoholism, procrastination, involvement with the Works Progress Administration, laziness, and excessive socializing contributed to his failure to achieve more. Based on Saxon letters at Northwestern State University of Louisiana, other primary and secondary sources; 44 notes.

J. Buschen

1093. Toth, Emily. KATE CHOPIN AND LITERARY CONVENTION: "DÉSIRÉE'S BABY". *Southern Studies 1981 20(2): 201-208.* Kate Chopin (1851-1904), Southern writer, was noted for handling conventional material in creative ways. She recognized the artistic value of social and literary conventions. She believed a shrewd author could lead readers beyond convention to new insights on life. Many authors used the Tragic Mulatto or Tragic Octoroon, the character of mixed blood. In Chopin's short story, "Désirée's Baby" (1893), the foundling Désirée marries the plantation owner, Armand. When their child appears to be not totally white, Armand accuses Désirée of a tainted ancestry and drives her off. Ultimately it is revealed that it is Armand who had a black mother. Thus to rely on appearances or convention can mislead and enchain. 27 notes.

J. J. Buschen

1094. Trotman, C. James. GEORGE W. CABLE AND TRADITION. *Texas Q. 1976 19(3): 51-58.* In 1879 the publication of *Old Creole Days* made George Washington Cable famous, though today few people read his work. Cable fit into the local color tradition, but he fit the romantic mold, too. In later years he dropped social criticism from his work, a price he paid for success. Based on primary and secondary sources; 8 notes.

R. H. Tomlinson

1095. Tucker, Edward L. PHILIP PENDLETON COOKE AND *THE SOUTHERN LITERARY MESSENGER*: SELECTED LETTERS. *Mississippi Q. 1973/74 27(1): 79-99.* The letters indicate, *inter alia*, Cooke's association with the first editor, Edgar Allan Poe.

S

1096. Turner, Arlin. GEORGE W. CABLE'S USE OF THE PAST. *Mississippi Q. 1977 30(4): 512-516.* Examines the literature of George Washington Cable, who employed his knowledge of New Orleans regional history in his novels, 1870's-90's.

1097. Turner, Arlin. WILLIAM FAULKNER: THE GROWTH AND SURVIVAL OF A LEGEND—A REVIEW ESSAY. *Southern Humanities Rev. 1975 9(1): 91-97.* Review of Joseph Blotner's *Faulkner: A Biography* (New York: Random House, 1974).

1098. Turner, Frederick. CONGO SQUARE. *Am. Heritage 1982 33(2): 86-95.* Beauregard Square, or Congo Square as it was known to the city's 60,000 black residents, gave birth to New Orleans Jazz in 1895 when Buddy Bolden ("King" Bolden thereafter) improvised a chorus of blues. 9 illus. J. F. Paul

1099. Turner, Frederick. A MUSIC OF THE STREETS. *Massachusetts Rev. 1977 18(3): 555-556.* Nathan (Jim) Robinson (1892-1976) was a black trombonist in New Orleans, Louisiana. Includes detailed description of his funeral. Based on personal observations of and conversations with Robinson during their long friendship. E. R. Campbell

1100. Tuthill, Burnet Corwin. RECOLLECTIONS OF A MUSICAL LIFE, 1888-1973. *West Tennessee Hist. Soc. Papers 1977 31: 77-108.* Autobiographical sketch by one of America's best-loved musicians, who for three decades was associated with the choral program at Southwestern College, Memphis, Tennessee. Covers his personal life and training as a musician. He participated in the Shrivenham American (Army) University in England after World War II, and at Southwestern developed an outstanding choral group. He was acquainted with numerous musicians from both America and Europe. Illus. H. M. Parker, Jr.

1101. Vandenberg, Laura Lieberman. SOUTHERN HISTORIES, CONTEMPORARY OPINIONS: THREE ATLANTA WOMEN ARTISTS. *Southern Q. 1979 17(2): 52-68.* Presents edited interviews with three Atlanta women artists—Anne Emanuel, Alyson Pon, and Scribenne Stone. They were selected because they were typical of southern female artists' views of their work. Tapes of their interviews were presented in an exhibition at the Atlanta Art Workers Coalition gallery, 7 September-27 October 1978. 3 fig. B. D. Ledbetter

1102. VanNoppen, Martha. A CONVERSATION WITH EUDORA WELTY. *Southern Q. 1982 20(4): 7-23.* Previously unpublished interview with Eudora Welty, which took place in Jackson, Mississippi, on 9 August 1978. Welty discusses at length the character of Laurel in her novel, *The Optimist's Daughter,* and the function of "memory," which runs through the work. Welty also defines the role of the critic and reflects upon her experiences as a Southern woman writer. W. A. Wiegand

1103. Volkman, Arthur G. LAUSSAT RICHTER ROGERS: ARTIST AND CONSERVATOR. *Delaware Hist. 1980 19(2): 59-63.* Examines the life and work of Laussat Richter Rogers (1866-1957), a product of American schools of law, architecture, and design and of French art schools, who settled in Delaware in 1903 to work as an architect. Rogers achieved modest distinction for his murals and paintings and also for his architectural work, principally on the Immanuel Episcopal Church and related properties in New Castle, Delaware. No public display or collection of Rogers's work exists, but many of his portraits remain in private hands. 11 notes. R. M. Miller

1104. Wages, Jack D. and Andrews, William D., comps. SOUTHERN LITERARY CULTURE: 1969-1975. *Mississippi Q. 1978-79 32(1): 13-215.* Bibliography of theses and dissertations pertaining to Southern literary culture under major headings: authors, general culture, education, folklore, history, journalism, libraries, linguistics, music, politics, religion, and speech and theater, 1969-75.

1105. Wagner, Frederick. SIMMS' EDITING OF *THE LIFE OF NATHANAEL GREENE. Southern Literary J. 1978 11(1): 41-43.* William Gilmore Simms's "editing" of *The Life of Nathanael Greene, Major-General in the Army of the Revolution* (New York, 1849) actually was an abridgment and paraphrasing of William P. Johnson's 1822 biography of Greene.

1106. Walser, Richard. BIBLIO-BIOGRAPHY OF SKITT TALIAFERRO. *North Carolina Hist. Rev. 1978 55(4): 375-395.* Hardin Edwards Taliaferro (1811-75) was a Baptist minister, writer, and editor of the *South Western Baptist,* who was born and raised in Surry County, North Carolina, but lived most of his life in Tuskegee, Alabama. He wrote two very different books within three

years, one deeply religious, the other humorous. The second, *Fisher's River (North Carolina) Scenes and Characters* (1859), has won him acclaim as a regional literary humorist. Little had been known or written about him until recently though his work was well known to antebellum southerners. Based on contemporary articles in the *South Western Baptist,* proceedings of state Baptist conventions, records of church schools, and manuscript census entries; 5 illus., 2 maps, 158 notes. T. L. Savitt

1107. Walser, Richard. ON FAULKNER'S PUTTING WOLFE FIRST. *South Atlantic Q. 1979 78(2): 172-181.* In a 1947 summer workshop at Oxford, Mississippi, William Faulkner was asked to rank his contemporary American authors in order of their importance. He then named Thomas Wolfe, John Dos Passos, Ernest Hemingway, Willa Cather, and John Steinbeck. His rationale was that since neither he nor his contemporaries had succeeded, he would rank them in accordance to the grandeur of their failure. He then inserted himself between Wolfe and Dos Passos. The news release that followed the announcement failed to mention failure as the criterion for ranking. There were unhappy reactions. Through the years he changed the order of the names, but Wolfe's was always at the top because Faulkner believed that he had extended his capacities, however humanly limited, to the ultimate—something neither his contemporaries nor he had the energy, desire, or ability to do. Based on newspaper reports, edited collections of Faulkner's and Wolfe's works, and secondary sources; 13 notes. H. M. Parker, Jr.

1108. Ward, Barry J. COAGULATING INTO CLANS: POETRY AND IDENTITY IN A MIXED BLOOD COMMUNITY. *Kentucky Folklore Record 1983 29(1-2): 39-46.* The angry and satiric poetry of William A. Norris is obsessed with identity and freedom from bigotry for his extended, mixed-blood clan of Guineas, residents of northcentral West Virginia since the late 1700's.

1109. Ward, W. H. THE RUSH TO FIND AN APPALACHIAN LITERATURE. *Appalachian J. 1978 5(3): 330-334.* Discusses current literature about Appalachia by Appalachians, 1970's; explores academic and cultural aspects of the writing and speculates on the emergence of a regional literature.

1110. Watson, Charles S. SIMMS AND THE BEGINNINGS OF LOCAL COLOR. *Mississippi Q. 1981-82 35(1): 25-39.* At the end of his long career as the dominant literary force in the antebellum South, William Gilmore Simms helped initiate the first literary movement of the postbellum South, the local color movement, which was to enlist the talents of Mary Noailles Murfree, George Washington Cable, Mark Twain, and Joel Chandler Harris; ca. 1860's-80's.

1111. Watson, Charles S. SIMMS' ANSWER TO *UNCLE TOM'S CABIN*: CRITICISM OF THE SOUTH IN *WOODCRAFT. Southern Literary J. 1976 9(1): 78-90.* Discusses William Gilmore Simms' view of the South as it is brought out in one of his novels, *Woodcraft,* 1852.

1112. Watson, James G. LITERARY SELF-CRITICISM: FAULKNER IN FICTION ON FICTION. *Southern Q. 1981 20(1): 46-63.* A modernist writer can be judged by the self-criticism evident in his work. T. S. Eliot, James Joyce, and Ezra Pound show this, as does William Faulkner. Faulkner's self-criticism greatly contributed to his development. 30 notes. B. D. Ledbetter

1113. Weeks, Christopher. PRESERVING AN OLD-WORLD HERITAGE. *Hist. Preservation 1981 33(6): 30-35.* Like their father and grandfather before them, John and Bob Giannetti restore and recreate plaster ornaments in the District of Columbia area; their commissions include such projects as changing the direction of the eagle's gaze on the Presidential Seal and restoring the east front of the Capitol for John F. Kennedy's inauguration.

1114. Welch, Jack. A SOCIOLOGICAL RATIONALE FOR THE EXISTENCE OF APPALACHIAN LITERATURE. *Appalachian J. 1976 3(2) 168-180.* Defines Appalachian literature and relates its values to the social and cultural life of the area.

1115. Welty, Eudora. LOOKING BACK AT THE FIRST STORY. *Georgia Rev. 1979 33(4): 741-755.* In writing her first published story, "Death of a Traveling Salesman," the author (b. 1909) was inspired by the tales and traveling life of a neighbor in Jackson, Mississippi, in the 1930's. Like all of her stories, its generative force came from real life and was influenced by the fairy tales and myths that she read as a child.     J. N. McArthur

1116. Werner, Craig. TELL OLD PHARAOH: THE AFRO-AMERICAN RESPONSE TO FAULKNER. *Southern Rev. 1983 19(4): 711-735.* Discusses the attitudes of James Baldwin and other black American writers, as expressed in their own work, to the race-related points of view exposed in William Faulkner's novels.

1117. Wernick, Robert. ATLANTA'S NEW HIGH ART MUSEUM IS A JEWEL FOR A QUEENLY CITY. *Smithsonian 1984 14(10): 38-47.* Traces the development of the High Museum of Art, located in Atlanta, Georgia, focusing on the contributions of Mrs. Joseph M. High and Coca-Cola Company magnate Robert Winship Woodruff.

1118. White, Chappell. THE ARTS ARE ALIVE AND REASONABLY WELL UNDER ATLANTA'S BUSINESS-BRED ALLIANCE. *Southern Voices 1974 1(1): 71-74.* Activities of the Atlanta Memorial Arts Center since its opening in October 1968. The Atlanta Arts Alliance is now composed of four institutions: the Atlanta Symphony, the High Museum of Art, the Atlanta College of Art, and the Alliance Theatre Company. The alliance has concentrated power, administrative skill, and a staff of professionals.
    D. D. Cameron

1119. Whitt, Lena M. CHESNUTT'S CHINQUAPIN COUNTY. *Southern Literary J. 1981 13(2): 41-58.* Discusses Charles W. Chesnutt's fictional Chinquapin County, based on his formative years in Fayetteville, North Carolina, described in 30 stories and three novels dealing with life in the Reconstruction Period from 1865-1900 and the antebellum period.

1120. Williams, Benjamin B. NINETEENTH CENTURY MONTGOMERY AUTHORS. *Alabama Hist. Q. 1975 37(2): 136-145.* Gives bibliographical data on and synopsizes the published work of Samuel Clarke Oliver (1799-1848), Henry Washington Hilliard (1808-92), John Dennis Phelan (1810-79), William Falconer (b. ca. 1822), Julia Louisa Hentz Keyes (1828-79), Rosalie Miller Murphey (1842-1900?), Thaddeus Constantine Willis Brewer (1844-1912), Clifford Anderson Lanier (1849-1908), Kate Slaughter McKinney (1859-1939), and Francis Banton Lloyd (1861-97). 7 notes.     E. E. Eminhizer

1121. Williams, Ernest P. WILLIAM STYRON AND HIS TEN BLACK CRITICS: A BELATED MEDITATION. *Phylon 1976 37(2): 189-195.* In their *William Styron's Nat Turner: Ten Black Writers Respond* (Boston; 1968), the contributors contend that in his widely acclaimed novel, *The Confessions of Nat Turner,* Styron failed to recreate Nat Turner in his proper context. Styron rejected the idea of persistent slave unrest and was unjustly condemned for not making Nat Turner more violently militant and less encumbered by thought. However, the writers are "justified in denouncing Styron's insistence on promoting the line that blacks were essentially satisfied being enslaved and that they were too docile and spiritless to protest." Styron and his 10 critics all failed by "advancing views not supported by known facts."     E. P. Stickney

1122. Williams, Mary C. NEW VOICES IN SOUTHERN POETRY. *North Carolina Hist. Rev. 1980 57(2): 160-168.* Southern, and in particular, North Carolina poetry cannot, anymore, be casually pigeonholed as in earlier days. Now poets include black men (T. J. Reddy, Lance Jeffers, Gerald Barrax) and women, black and white (Julia Fields, Kathryn Stripling Byer, Ann F. Deagon). Stereotypes, even of the traditional white male country poet, have broken down. Diversity and versatility are now the rule. 5 illus., 10 notes.     T. L. Savitt

1123. Williamson, J. W. APPALACHIAN POETRY: THE POLITICS OF COMING HOME. *Southern Exposure 1981 9(2): 69-74.* Describes the politics and writing of three Appalachian poets, Jim Webb, Jim Wayne Miller, and Gurney Norman and their embracing of their mountain identity as part of the recent wave of positive cultural and ethnic identification in America.

1124. Willig, Charles. BERRY FLEMING: NOVELIST IN POLITICS. *Richmond County Hist. 1977 9(2): 30-38.* Discusses the literature of Berry Fleming, a politician from Augusta, Georgia, 1930-76.

1125. Wills, J. Robert. PREVAILING SHADOWS: THE PLAYS OF LEE PENNINGTON. *Southern Q. 1981 20(1): 25-34.* Lee Pennington, author of over 1,000 poems, has written seven dramas. These have not received the attention that they deserve. Set in the southern Appalachians, all reflect Pennington's understanding of that regional culture. 16 notes.     B. D. Ledbetter

1126. Wiltshire, Susan Ford. INTRODUCTION: THE CLASSICAL TRADITION IN THE SOUTH. *Southern Humanities Rev. 1977 11(Special issue): 1-3.* Tendencies toward studies in Greek, Latin, and classical disciplines in the South come about through a basic sense of history, personalism, sense of place, commitment to the land, respect for nature, religious awe, and closeness to the affective side of human consciousness. Introduction to five papers in this issue on classical traditions in the South.

1127. Wimsatt, Mary Ann. REALISM AND ROMANCE IN SIMMS'S MIDCENTURY FICTION. *Southern Literary J. 1980 12(2): 29-48.* William Gilmore Simms wrote from 1825 to 1870, and changed his style due to changes in the historical romance tradition beginning in the early 19th century, which led him to combine elements of realism and satire with romance.

1128. Wimsatt, Mary Ann. SIMMS'S WAR NOVELS. *Mississippi Q. 1977 30(2): 297-304.* A review article prompted by *The Revolutionary War Novels of William Gilmore Simms* (Spartanburg, South Carolina: Reprint Company, 1975), an eight-volume set of all of Simms' historical novels dealing with the American Revolution, 1775-82.

1129. Windham, Wyolene. HUDDIE "LEADBELLY" LEDBETTER: SOME REMINISCENCES OF HIS COUSIN, BLANCHE LOVE. *North Louisiana Hist. Assoc. J. 1976 7(3): 96-100.* The author recounts the conversation she had recently with Blanche Love, a cousin of Huddie "Leadbelly" Ledbetter, the black folk and blues singer-composer who died in 1949 and who is buried in Shiloh Cemetery near Longwood, where he was born on the Jeter place in the 1880's. She remembers that "Huddie always had music—'it was born in him' "; that he was not a regular churchgoer; and that, despite his prison record, "he never meddled nobody, he never stole anything, and he never started no fuss. He just wouldn't take nothing off nobody, so if anybody tried to start something with him, he lit right into them; it didn't make no difference if they was black or white." 2 photos, 4 notes.
    A. N. Garland

1130. Wittenberg, Judith Bryant. FAULKNER AND EUGENE O'NEILL. *Mississippi Q. 1980 33(3): 327-341.* The presence of Eugene O'Neill's works in William Faulkner's personal library, Faulkner's interest in drama, and the pair's interest in the same authors indicate that O'Neill influenced Faulkner's writing, especially with a model for classic tragedy which his "Mourning Becomes Electra" provided for Faulkner's 1931 novel, *Absalom, Absalom!*

1131. Woodress, James. WILLA CATHER AND HISTORY. *Arizona Q. 1978 34(3): 239-254.* Cather's historical fiction, especially *Death Comes for the Archbishop,* was written because of disillusionment with the present and growing preference for eras and characters she could empathize with in the last two decades of her life.     D. S. Schmidt

1132. Woodward, C. Vann. WHY THE SOUTHERN RENAISSANCE? *Virginia Q. Rev. 1975 51(2): 222-239.* Defines the Southern Renaissance as literary in the four decades after 1929, identifying it with William Faulkner and numerous other writers. Explores the "defensive" and "backward-glance" hypotheses, but concludes "the historian had best concentrate on 'necessary conditions' and leave causation and explanation to non-historians...."
O. H. Zabel

1133. Wright, R. Lewis. JAMES WARRELL: ARTIST AND ENTREPRENEUR. *Virginia Cavalcade 1973 22(3): 5-19.* With eight paintings by Warrell (1780?-1854).

1134. Yardley, Jonathan. CHRONICLE OF SOUTHERN NOVELS. *Partisan Rev. 1973 40(2): 286-293.* Reviews 15 recent southern novels. Calder Willingham's *Eternal Fire* (New York: Vanguard, 1962) was a turning point in the literary history of the South because it was a parody of Southern Gothic. The new novelists are concerned with continuity. They deal with myth and symbol in an urban or surrealistic context, but the old form of a humility before the lessons of history still challenges their artistic abilities. This blending should provide the next literary development.
D. K. Pickens

1135. Young, Thomas Daniel and Hindle, John, ed. ALLEN TATE AND JOHN PEALE BISHOP: AN EXCHANGE OF LETTERS, 1931. *Southern Rev. 1980 16(4): 879-906.* Brief background to the friendship between Allen Tate and John Peale Bishop from their first meeting in 1925 until Bishop's death in 1944, focusing on a series of letters to each other in 1931 offering encouragement and critiques of their respective writing.

1136. Young, Thomas Daniel. A NEW BREED: WALKER PERCY'S CRITICS' ATTEMPTS TO PLACE HIM. *Mississippi Q. 1980 33(4): 489-498.* Walker Percy has denied being a Southern writer, but, as Cleanth Brooks has shown, critics must take Percy's traditional southern background into account if they are to assess and understand his work; ca. 1940-79.

1137. Young, Thomas Daniel. WITHOUT RANK OR PRIMACY. *Mississippi Q. 1974 27(4): 435-446.* John Crowe Ransom taught high school in Taylorsville, Mississippi, to earn tuition for his education at Vanderbilt University.

1138. Zender, Karl. FAULKNER AT FORTY: THE ARTIST AT HOME. *Southern Rev. 1981 17(2): 288-302.* Draws parallels between Roth Edmonds, the protagonist of *Go Down, Moses,* and William Faulkner at the time he wrote it: both are about 40, both live in the same location, both have similar personal relationships, and most importantly, both have similar dominant emotional states.

1139. —. CATAWBA CHRONICLE. *Am. Heritage 1982 33(5): 100-105.* Paintings by Barry G. Huffman that depict the history of a North Carolina county. 9 illus.
J. F. Paul

1140. —. A CHECKLIST OF SCHOLARSHIP ON SOUTHERN LITERATURE FOR 1974. *Mississippi Q. 1975 28(2): 219-261.*

1141. —. A CHECKLIST OF SCHOLARSHIP ON SOUTHERN LITERATURE FOR 1981. *Mississippi Q. 1982 35(2): 138-238.* Colonial, antebellum, postbellum, contemporary, and general categories organize 804 entries on literature of the South.

1142. —. FAULKNER 1980: A SURVEY OF RESEARCH AND CRITICISM. *Mississippi Q. 1981 34(3): 343-366.* Evaluates books and articles on William Faulkner's work, 1974-80.

1143. —. FAULKNER 1981: A SURVEY OF RESEARCH AND CRITICISM. *Mississippi Q. 1982 35(3): 313-336.* Describes studies of William Faulkner in 1980-81.

1144. —. [JOHN BANVARD'S MISSISSIPPI]. *Am. Hist. Illus. 1982 17(7): 30-39.*

Hanners, John. JOHN BANVARD'S MISSISSIPPI PANORAMA, *pp. 30-31, 36-39.* Describes the career of 19th-century American painter John Banvard, focusing on his monumental work, "Mississippi Panorama," which he exhibited in London during 1849-50.
—. PORTFOLIO: BANVARD'S RIVER SCENES, *pp. 32-35.* Additional Mississippi River scenes by Banvard as they looked in the 19th century.

1145. —. THE ONDERDONKS...A FAMILY OF TEXAS PAINTERS. *Southwestern Art 1976 5(1): 32-43.* Discusses the painting of the members of the Onderdonk family, Robert Jenkins (1852-1917), Robert Julian (1882-1922), and Eleanor Rogers (1884-1964).

1146. —. PAINTING IN THE SOUTHLAND. *Am. Heritage 1983 34(4): 28-41.* Presents examples of Southern painting included in the "Painting in the South, 1564-1980," exhibition organized by the Virginia Museum in Richmond. 14 illus.
J. F. Paul

1147. —. [PERIODICAL CONTRIBUTIONS OF JOEL CHANDLER HARRIS].
Strickland, William Bradley. A CHECK LIST OF PERIODICAL CONTRIBUTIONS OF JOEL CHANDLER HARRIS (1848-1908). *Am. Literary Realism, 1870-1910 1976 9(3): 207-230.* Lists contributions in periodicals including fiction, poetry, reviews, letters, essays, articles and editorials, by Joel Chandler Harris, southern folklorist and author, 1862-1908.
Bickley, R. Bruce, Jr. and Strickland, William Bradley. A CHECKLIST OF PERIODICAL CONTRIBUTIONS OF JOEL CHANDLER HARRIS: PART II. *Am. Literary Realism, 1870-1910 1978 11(1): 139-140.* Supplements the above bibliography with additional works by Harris.

1148. —. THE VANISHED TEXAS OF THEODORE GENTILZ. *Am. Heritage 1974 25(6): 18-27.* Paintings of 19th-century San Antonio, Texas, by Theodore Gentilz, taken from *Theodore Gentilz: Artist of the Old Southwest,* by Dorothy Steinbomer Kendall and Carmen Perry (University of Texas Press, 1974).

# Southern Architecture, Buildings, Monuments

1149. Alder, Gale Shipman. 1785: ARCHITECT AND IMAGE-MAKER JULES HENRI DE SIBOUR. *Hist. Preservation 1979 31(3): 12-13.* Biography of Jules Henri de Sibour (1872-1938), the architect who designed the luxury apartment at 1785 Massachusetts Avenue in Washington, D.C., in 1906 and 1907.

1150. Alexander, Robert L. BALTIMORE ROW HOUSES OF THE EARLY NINETEENTH CENTURY. *Am. Studies 1975 16(2): 65-76.* Row housing became predominant in the industrial age and characterized most major urban centers. Surveys the rise and cost of such housing throughout the early 19th century. The chaos of style reflected the sociopolitical structure and conflict of those years. Speculation led to increasing density, and builders strove primarily for profits. Primary and secondary sources; 4 illus.; 2 maps, 17 notes.
J. Andrew

1151. Alexander, Robert L. NICHOLAS ROGERS, GENTLEMAN-ARCHITECT OF BALTIMORE. *Maryland Hist. Mag. 1983 78(2): 85-105.* Colonel Nicholas Rogers, a fourth-generation Baltimorean and heir to a mercantile fortune, collaborated with Robert Cary Long, Sr., to create many classical additions to Maryland's architectural heritage. Describes several buildings that were products of the Rogers and Long partnership, including Druid Hill, the Baltimore Dancing Assembly, the County Jail, Holliday Street Theater, and St. Paul's Church. 28 notes, 15 illus.
G. J. Bobango

1152. Allcott, John V. ROBERT DONALDSON, THE FIRST NORTH CAROLINIAN TO BECOME PROMINENT IN THE ARTS. *North Carolina Hist. R. 1975 52(4): 333-366.* Robert Donaldson (1800-72), a Fayetteville, North Carolina, native, promoted architecture and landscaping throughout his life, much of which was spent in New York. Independently wealthy, Donaldson built a showpiece home, Blithewood-on-the-Hudson, and became a patron of the arts. He furthered the career of his friend, Alexander Jackson Davis, by recommending him to design and landscape several buildings at the University of North Carolina. Based on manuscript collections and published primary material, newspaper accounts, and secondary sources; 17 illus., 122 notes.

T. L. Savitt

1153. Allcott, John V. SCHOLARLY BOOKS AND FROLIC-SOME BLADES: A. J. DAVIS DESIGNS A LIBRARY-BALLROOM. *J. of the Soc. of Architectural Historians 1974 33(2): 145-154.* Presents and discusses plans for Smith Hall at the University of North Carolina by architect Alexander Jackson Davis (1850-52).

1154. Anderson, Annette. WHAT WE'VE FORGOTTEN. *Southern Exposure 1980 8(1): 65-67.* Why is it that 200 years after ordinary people designed and built homes, towns, and plantations across the South, most people today need design assistance to build a good playground or a clinic? Once, most men knew how to build. Few became adults without working in construction of some kind, whether it be a house or a cupboard. This situation no longer obtains. One of the purposes of Community Design Centers in the South is to encourage full participation of local people in designing their own structures instead of having outsiders do it for them. Outlines how design centers function and interact with a community organization. 2 photos.

H. M. Parker, Jr.

1155. Ash, Stephen V. THE SAM HOUSTON SCHOOLHOUSE: A MIRROR OF ITS CHANGING PAST. *Tennessee Hist. Q. 1978 37(4): 375-392.* A historical site may serve as a sort of mirror of its past, reflecting in its own story the changing history of its community, state, and nation. Such is the case of the Sam Houston Schoolhouse, located in Blount County, near Maryville, Tennessee. According to oral tradition, Sam Houston (1793-1863) taught at the school some time between 1809 and 1812, for one or two terms. Yet regarding this connection, only two facts can be established: the schoolhouse did stand in 1812 and Sam Houston did teach about that same time. Discusses the role of the "open field" school in frontier history, describes the structure of the building and traces its history to the present, when in 1972 it was placed on the National Register of Historical Places and was also selected as a National Historic Site. Based on Blount County records, oral interviews and secondary sources; 2 photos, 47 notes.

H. M. Parker, Jr.

1156. Ayers, Edward L. NORTHERN BUSINESS AND THE SHAPE OF SOUTHERN PROGRESS: THE CASE OF TENNESSEE'S "MODEL CITY." *Tennessee Hist. Q. 1980 39(2): 208-222.* Kingsport, Tennessee, was by most material standards one of the more attractive small towns in the South in the early part of this century. But the progress had its price. Southern towns such as Kingsport traded their autonomy for paternalistic development. Their futures depended upon the needs and desires of companies owned and controlled in the North. Kingsport became the Model City because those needs and desires were thoroughly planned and coordinated. Other southern communities became traditional hard-luck company towns because their northern creators did not plan their domination so thoroughly. Newspapers and secondary studies; 50 notes.

H. M. Parker, Jr.

1157. Bacot, H. Parrott. HISTORY IN HOUSES: MAGNOLIA MOUND PLANTATION HOUSE IN BATON ROUGE, LOUISIANA. *Mag. Antiques 1983 123(5): 1054-1061.* Describes the architecture, interior furnishings, and land of the Magnolia Mound Plantation House in Baton Rouge, Louisiana; discusses previous owners.

1158. Baer, Evelyn D. COWNES: A REMINISCENCE. *Virginia Cavalcade 1982 32(1): 30-39.* From the time the author was 2 or 3 in the early 1920's until the 1930's, he spent summers at Cownes, an estate built in 1846 in King William County, Virginia, and owned by his grandmother, who had established a girls' school there in 1894.

1159. Barnwell, John. MONTICELLO: 1856. *J. of the Soc. of Architectural Historians 1975 34(4): 280-285.* Presents a letter from 1856 describing Monticello, Thomas Jefferson's estate, near Charlottesville, Virginia.

1160. Bartlett, Ellen. MIAMI BEACH BETS ON ART DECO. *Hist. Preservation 1981 33(1): 8-15.* Discusses Miami Beach's Art Deco Historic District, a one-square-mile area of 800 houses, apartment buildings, and hotels built during the 1920's, 1930's, and early 1940's, in the National Register of Historic Places since 1979, and restoration there.

1161. Baumstein, Paschal. VARIATIONS IN HERALDIC INSIGNIA AT MARYHELP ABBEY. *Am. Benedictine Rev. 1983 34(1): 62-73.* Reviews the development of Maryhelp Abbey, known commonly as Belmont Abbey, and Belmont Abbey College in North Carolina by studying the three heraldic insignia used throughout the abbey's history. 3 fig., 23 notes.

J. H. Pragman

1162. Bishir, Catherine W. JACOB W. HOLT: AN AMERICAN BUILDER. *Winterthur Portfolio 1981 16(1): 1-31.* Jacob W. Holt (d. 1880) was a notable architect in southern Virginia and central North Carolina. His design was practical, fitting the needs and desires of middle-class Americans. Holt did not represent an elite section, nor did his work fall into the category of folk architecture. He was able to combine traditional design with changing fashion. Based on county records, on-site inspections, family papers, and other sources; 44 illus., 56 notes.

N. A. Kuntz

1163. Bjornseth, Dick. NO-CODE COMFORT. *Reason 1983 15(3): 43-47.* Unincorporated areas near Houston, Texas, have experienced rapid growth since 1975, but despite the absence of both zoning and building codes there has been no reduction in the quality of construction.

1164. Bowman, David. BEALE STREET BLUES. *Southern Exposure 1977 5(1): 75-79.* The effort to convert the once-bustling black business area of Beale Street, in Memphis, Tennessee, into a tourist attraction has been underway since 1963. Public and private agencies have obtained millions of federal tax dollars for that purpose. Viable businesses have been forcibly relocated, sound buildings have been condemned and torn down, and residents have been relocated. Schemes for updating Beale Street have not resulted in anything of merit and the neighborhood today is in a shambles.

N. Lederer

1165. Bowman, David. MEMPHIS, TENNESSEE: HOW TO STOP DEVELOPERS. *Southern Exposure 1976 3(4): 18-24.* Examines a fight between Memphis citizens and local planning agencies over the plan of James Rouse, Boyle Investments, and the First Tennessee National Corporation to develop 5,000 acres of public lands into a city-within-a-city, 1971-76.

1166. Brigance, Fred W. THE HERMITAGE TOMB: ITS CONSTRUCTION AND PRESERVATION. *Tennessee Hist. Q. 1982 41(4): 326-336.* Traces the history of the tomb of Rachel and Andrew Jackson, located at their Tennessee estate, the Hermitage, from its construction in 1829 to its restoration in 1976. 2 illus., 24 notes.

W. D. Piersen

1167. Broward, Robert C. JACKSONVILLE: SOUTHERN HOME FOR THE PRAIRIE SCHOOL. *Hist. Preservation 1978 30(1): 16-19.* Jacksonville, Florida, burned in 1901 and was almost totally rebuilt by 1917. Describes a number of buildings designed by Prairie School architect Henry John Klutho (1873-1964). 2 illus.

R. M. Frame III

1168. Brown, David J. THE WINDSOR HOTEL IN AMERICUS. *Georgia Hist. Q. 1980 64(1): 35-49.* Describes the planning, construction and furnishings of the Windsor Hotel in Americus, Georgia, during 1890-92. Gottfried L. Norrman (d. 1909) was the architect of this Victorian showplace. Also mentions changes that occurred up until its closing in 1974. It is now being restored. Based mainly on newspaper articles; 3 photos, 62 notes.

G. R. Schroeder

1169. Brown, Kenny L. and Fischer, LeRoy H. OLD CENTRAL: A PICTORIAL ESSAY. *Chronicles of Oklahoma 1977-78 55(4): 403-423.* The forerunner of today's Oklahoma State University in Stillwater opened its doors in 1894 with the single building called Old Central. Funded by bond issues and partly built by students, it served the campus for many decades, but as early as the 1920's many persons favored its replacement with a larger and safer building. During 1971 the Oklahoma Legislature appropriated money for Old Central's restoration because of its historic value. Primary and secondary sources; 22 photos, 19 notes.

M. L. Tate

1170. Browning, Denise. THE E. W. MARLAND MANSION AND ESTATE. *Chronicles of Oklahoma 1978 56(1): 40-72.* In 1928 Ernest W. Marland built a $2,500,000 mansion in Ponca City, Oklahoma, from the great fortune that he had amassed in the oil industry. Marland's company eventually failed. His property passed into the hands of several owners until 1975, when Ponca City bought the mansion. Floor plans and descriptions of each of the major rooms are given. Primary sources; 4 illus., 10 photos, 64 notes.

M. L. Tate

1171. Bryant, Keith L., Jr. CATHEDRALS, CASTLES, AND RO-MAN BATHS: RAILWAY STATION ARCHITECTURE IN THE URBAN SOUTH. *J. of Urban Hist. 1976 2(2): 195-230.* During 1890-1920 Southern cities built railroad stations which became important economic and cultural centers. Southern cities did not lag behind their larger Northern counterparts in physical maturation or technology. 10 figs., 72 notes.

T. W. Smith

1172. Bryant, Keith L., Jr. THE RAILROAD STATION AS A SYMBOL OF URBANIZATION IN THE SOUTH, 1890's-1920. *South Atlantic Q. 1976 75(4): 499-509.* The railroad station represented urban maturity to American cities. In the South, the sheer physical growth of railroad traffic alone would have justified large stations, but the civic boomers also saw in the monumental stations a tangible "symbol of corporate prosperity, urban expansion, and anticipated economic growth." All large urban centers in the South indulged in constructing huge terminals in the central business district. Even smaller cities, such as Meridian, Mississippi, built imposing edifices. Primary and secondary sources; 40 notes.

W. L. Olbrich

1173. Bryant, Keith L., Jr. RAILWAY STATIONS OF TEXAS: A DISAPPEARING ARCHITECTURAL HERITAGE. *Southwestern Hist. Q. 1976 79(4): 417-440.* Texas has a large number of railway stations, of many different architectural styles. The most common small depots were wood, brick, or stucco, built to a standardized plan, but a few big stations are outstanding. Gives details on building the M-K-T station in San Antonio (1917), Union Station in Houston (1909-11), and Union Station in Dallas (1915-16). Based on primary and secondary sources; illus., 31 notes.

J. H. Broussard

1174. Buckner, Gladys. WOMAN'S LIB—1853. *Daughters of the Am. Revolution Mag. 1976 110(2): 192-195.* Discusses the life of Ann Pamela Cunningham (1816-1875), founder of the Mount Vernon Ladies' Association which in 1858 acquired George Washington's home, Mount Vernon, in Virginia, and has operated it since as a national shrine.

1175. Bull, Elias B. STORM TOWERS OF THE SANTEE DEL-TA. *South Carolina Hist. Mag. 1980 81(2): 95-101.* Describes brick storm towers, 20-30 feet in diameter and 20 feet high, built to house field slaves during storm-caused floods on the Santee Delta in South Carolina in the late 18th century and the early 19th; five of the towers are known to the author.

1176. Burkhardt, Sue Pope. THE PORT OF PALM BEACH: THE BREAKERS PIER. *Tequesta 1973 33: 69-74.* A history of the Breakers Pier at Palm Beach, used to embark passengers from Palm Beach to south Florida, Nassau, and Cuba. Based on primary and secondary sources; 3 notes.

H. S. Marks

1177. Burton, Marda Kaiser. NATCHEZ: NO LONGER YOUR TYPICAL SOUTHERN BELLE. *Hist. Preservation 1980 32(6): 8-15.* Discusses preservation efforts in Natchez, Mississippi, particularly the annual Natchez Pilgrimage, during which preserved homes are opened for public tours, and gives a brief history of this Mississippi River landing town since the early 18th century.

1178. Burton, Tommye S. COURTHOUSE OF PRINCE WIL-LIAM COUNTY. *Virginia Cavalcade 1978 28(1): 34-47.* Chronicles the locations and structures of the courthouses serving Prince William County, Virginia, 1722-1978.

1179. Bushong, William B. WILLIAM PERCIVAL, AN EN-GLISH ARCHITECT IN THE OLD NORTH STATE, 1857-1860. *North Carolina Hist. Rev. 1980 57(3): 310-339.* William Percival, an English architect about whose life little is known, left a number of reminders of his presence in North Carolina, 1857-60. He appeared in Richmond, Virginia, in 1855 as an engineer and architect, moved to Raleigh, North Carolina, in 1857, and departed in early 1860. No record of his life before or after this has yet been found. While in North Carolina Percival designed 13 ecclesiastical, public, and domestic structures, including the Caswell County courthouse in Yanceyville, churches in Hillsborough, Tarboro and Raleigh, and two dormitory-classroom buildings at the University of North Carolina. Many still stand. Based primarily on contemporary newspaper articles, and scattered letters in various families' papers; 32 illus., table, 64 notes.

T. L. Savitt

1180. Butler, Jeanne F. COMPETITION 1792: DESIGNING A NATION'S CAPITOL. *Capitol Studies 1976 4(1): 7-96.* Presents a biography and analysis of plans for each participant in the 1792-93 competition for the architectural design of the Capitol Building.

1181. Cable, Mary. BUILDINGS FOR SALE: UNEXPECTED BEAUTY FROM A CITY ARCHIVE. *Am. Heritage 1979 30(5): 66-77.* Pictorial essay of watercolor drawings of New Orleans architecture. As buildings were sold at public auction, 1802-1918, a drawing was required. These were kept; and from the city's holdings the author has compiled a forthcoming book, *Lost New Orleans.* 10 illus.

J. F. Paul

1182. Cable, Mary and Prager, Annabelle. THE LEVYS OF MONTICELLO. *Am. Heritage 1978 29(2): 30-39.* After Thomas Jefferson's death in 1826, Monticello was sold in 1831 and quickly fell into disrepair. Purchased by Uriah Philips Levy in 1836, little was done to preserve the home. Levy's will left the property to the United States but with too many strings attached. One of Levy's nephews, Jefferson Monroe Levy, bought the property in 1879 and began to restore it. By the turn of the century, the house was sound again, and public clamor to make it a national shrine mounted and in 1923, the Thomas Jefferson Memorial Association bought the property. In 1954, the house underwent a complete renovation. But for J. M. Levy, the house might have been lost to history. 14 illus.

J. F. Paul

1183. Calhoun, Charles. ADDISON MIZNER: GOLD COAST ARCHITECT. *Art & Antiques 1981 4(4): 72-75.* Brief biography of architect Addison Mizner, focusing on the Mediterranean-style homes, shops, and buildings he designed in Palm Beach, Florida, 1918-31.

1184. Campbell, Thomas Lorraine. THE STORY OF A MINDEN HOUSE. *North Louisiana Hist. Assoc. J. 1979 10(2): 29-35.* Summary of the building and rebuilding of a house, originally built in 1841, which is soon to become a museum. Drury H. Murrell's home in Minden burned in 1879 but was promptly replaced by a less elegant house. That replacement, with structural changes made by later owners, including a funeral home, was moved to its new location as a museum in 1978-79. 2 illus.                    J. F. Paul

1185. Cantrell, Brent. TRADITIONAL GRAVE STRUCTURES ON THE EASTERN HIGHLAND RIM. *Tennessee Folklore Soc. Bull. 1981 47(3): 93-103.* Describes the traditional grave structures along the Cumberland Plateau-Highland Rim in central Tennessee, which date from 1811 to 1964.

1186. Capitman, Barbara Baer. RE-DISCOVERY OF ART DE-CO. *Am. Preservation 1978 6(6): 30-41.* Old Miami Beach, where 72% of the residents are defined as elderly, may become the country's youngest historic district with a preponderance of Spanish and Art Deco buildings dating 1920-35. The resurgence of Art Deco in New York design circles has led to a reappraisal of the 293 Art Deco structures of Miami Beach. The Miami Design Preservation League has worked with state and federal agencies to survey the buildings and obtain funding for rehabilitation. Designed by such young innovators as Henry Hohauser and Murray Dixon, the unique exteriors of the apartments and small hotels have survived in excellent condition. Supporters hope that the new appreciation will preserve the human scale of the area for its elderly residents and discourage large-scale resort redevelopment. 10 photos.
                                                                 S. C. Strom

1187. Carson, Cary; Barka, Norman F.; Kelso, William M.; Stone, Garry Wheeler; and Upton, Dell. IMPERMANENT ARCHITEC-TURE IN THE SOUTHERN AMERICAN COLONIES. *Winterthur Portfolio 1981 16(2-3): 135-196.* An analysis of vernacular architecture of 17th-century Virginia and Maryland. There are few remaining examples of colonial life on the Chesapeake. Recent studies, dating from 1968, demonstrate the need to reevaluate previous interpretations of earthfast buildings in colonial America and in England. Based on archaeological studies, excavations; 16 fig., 170 notes, 3 appendixes.                    N. A. Kuntz

1188. Carson, Cary. THE "VIRGINIA HOUSE" IN MARY-LAND. *Maryland Hist. Mag. 1974 69(2): 185-196.* Describes two houses illustrative of vernacular architecture in Maryland, buildings designed according to local custom to meet individuals' personal requirements. "Polite" architecture conforming to standard or imported designs gave way to buildings appropriate to tobacco culture. The Holly Hill House at Friendship, Anne Arundel County, contained two older timber-framed houses encased inside the brick walls, dating to the last third of the 17th century. The Sarum House, Newport, Charles County, holds beneath its 18th-century exterior "the nearly intact timber-framed skeleton of a one-story dwelling," built during 1662-80, the earliest fully developed "Virginia style" house extant in Maryland or Virginia. Sarum conformed to the prototype in every detail: a one-story, frame building with two rooms on the ground floor, the "whole being covered with unpainted riven clapboards," with exterior gable and chimneys. Primary sources; 5 illus., glossary, 7 notes.
                                                                 G. J. Bobango

1189. Carter, Thomas. THE JOEL COCK HOUSE: 1885—MEADOWS OF DAN, PATRICK COUNTY, VIRGINIA. *Southern Folklore Q. 1975 39(4): 329-340.* Discusses the history and architecture of the Joel Cock farm in Meadows of Dan, Patrick County, Virginia, from 1830-85, emphasizing log building techniques and barn styles.

1190. Chappell, Edward A. ACCULTURATION IN THE SHEN-ANDOAH VALLEY: RHENISH HOUSES OF THE MASSANUT-TEN SETTLEMENT. *Pro. of the Am. Phil. Soc. 1980 124(1): 55-89.* Swiss and German immigrants who moved from Pennsylvania to Virginia's Shenandoah Valley in the 18th century carried a Rhenish culture which distinguished them from neighboring Scots-Irish and English groups. One component part of this culture was a basic house model. Near the end of the 18th century, these folk experienced increased acculturation pressures from the dominant Anglo-Saxon group. Reaction to this pressure was the suppression of certain evidence of ethnic background, e.g., traditional house forms and language. As a result, public use of the German lan-

guage declined and the Rhenish house was changed at first in response to new concepts of aesthetics and domestic functions, and later abandoned in favor of an Anglo-American form. Based on numerous monographs in architectural history; 63 fig., internal documentation.                    H. M. Parker, Jr.

1191. Cizek, Eugene D. THE CREOLE ARCHITECTURE OF NINETEENTH CENTURY NEW ORLEANS. *Southern Q. 1982 20(2): 62-86.* Residential architecture in 19th-century New Orleans demonstrates a quality unique to the Creole origins of the city. A combination of Spanish-Latin, French, American, and Caribbean influences with the environmental conditions imposed by the prevailing geography distinguished Creole residential architecture from any other. 20 drawings.                    W. A. Wiegand

1192. Clayton, LaReine Warden. THE IRISH PEDDLER-BOY AND OLD DEERY INN. *Tennessee Hist. Q. 1977 36(2): 149-160.* After selling trinkets and notions in Ireland, William Deery (d. 1845) came to America where he purchased a trading post at Blountville, Tennessee in 1795. Deery made two additions to the building from hewn logs and chiseled stone, brought in stagecoaches, and backed steamboat ventures into the area. The building still stands and is a major landmark in East Tennessee. Primary and secondary sources; 2 illus., 8 notes.                    M. B. Lucas

1193. Cohen, Richard Bowen. ONCE THERE WAS LIGHT: A HISTORY OF VIRGINIA'S LIGHTHOUSES. *Virginia Cavalcade 1977 27(1): 4-19.* Covers 1718-1963.

1194. Connell, Mary Ann Strong. THE FIRST PEABODY HO-TEL: 1869-1923. *West Tennessee Hist. Soc. Papers 1975 29: 38-54.* Memphis' strategic location on the Mississippi and as a railroad terminus prompted Robert Campbell Brinkley to erect a luxurious hotel there, equal to any in the South. The hotel was formally opened 5 February 1869. Costing $60,000, it contained 75 rooms with private baths, ballroom, saloon and lobby. It quickly became the locale for Memphis social life. Dignitaries made it their headquarters when in Memphis. In 1906, a huge, 200-room addition was constructed, costing $350,000. The famous hotel was closed 28 August 1923 as a result of proposed city alterations. Based on primary sources; photo, 68 notes.                    H. M. Parker, Jr.

1195. Connelly, John Lawrence. OLD NORTH NASHVILLE AND GERMANTOWN. *Tennessee Hist. Q. 1980 39(2): 115-148.* Traces the history of North Nashville since its first log cabin. Describes important families, business, churches, migrants, and ethnic societies in the community. Based on newspaper accounts, interviews, and secondary material; 4 illus., 73 notes.
                                                                 H. M. Parker, Jr.

1196. Cook, Philip C. A CASE STUDY OF FUNCTIONAL PRESERVATION: THE KIDD-DAVIS HOUSE OF RUSTON AS MUSEUM AND COMMUNITY CENTER. *North Louisiana Hist. Assoc. J. 1978 9(3): 149-153.* Describes the restoration of the Kidd-Davis House, Ruston, Louisiana, which was built in 1885. Its historic significance is in the kind of architectural forms it represents—how Americans modified late Victorian with the styles of the early 20th century. The building now houses the Ruston Chamber of Commerce, the Lincoln Parish Museum, and the Lincoln Visitors Bureau. 2 photos.                    H. M. Parker, Jr.

1197. Coomes, Charles S. THE BASILICA-CATHEDRAL OF ST. AUGUSTINE, ST. AUGUSTINE, FLORIDA, AND ITS HISTO-RY. *Escribano 1983 20: 32-44.* Describes the construction and architectural features of the Catholic cathedral of St. Augustine, Florida.

1198. Cooney, Deborah. ADELICIA'S HOUSE: TROPHIES OF A WEEKEND COLLECTOR. *Nineteenth Cent. 1979 5(4): 49-51.* Introduces a find of seven stereographs of the Nashville mansion Belmont, and describes the history, architecture, and interior decoration of this huge Italianate villa, built in 1850 for Adelicia Hayes Franklin Ackland.

1199. Cooper, Patricia Irvin. POSTSCRIPT TO "A QUAKER-PLAN HOUSE IN GEORGIA." *Pioneer Am. 1979 11(3): 142-150.* Discusses the architectural nature of the Gilmer House, a Quaker-plan house built in 1800 in Oglethorpe County, Georgia, recently moved to Washington, Wilkes County, Georgia.

1200. Cooper, Patricia Irvin. A QUAKER-PLAN HOUSE IN GEORGIA. *Pioneer Am. 1978 10(1): 14-34.* Describes the Thomas Gilmer House, built in 1800 in Oglethorpe County, Georgia, from the standpoint of the artisanry; proposes a source of its Quaker-plan, angle fireplaces, and craftsmen, and suggests an explanation for the plan's appearance in Piedmont, Georgia. Based on archival material in the manuscript collection, University of Georgia Libraries, Athens, personal interviews, and secondary sources; 6 photos, 2 fig., 32 notes. C. R. Gunter, Jr.

1201. Corley, Florence Fleming. THE OLD MEDICAL COLLEGE AND THE GOVERNOR'S MANSION: TWO EARLY GREEK REVIVAL PUBLIC BUILDINGS IN GEORGIA. *Richmond County Hist. 1976 8(2): 5-22.* Discusses the popularity which Greek revival architecture enjoyed in Georgia in the 1820's-30's, and discusses two specific buildings in Augusta, Georgia, designed by Charles B. Cluskey, the Governor's Mansion and the Medical College.

1202. Cornwell, Ilene J. DEVON FARM: HARPETH LANDMARK. *Tennessee Hist. Q. 1975 34(2): 113-129.* Devon Farm, with its large brick structure, is located on the Little and Big Harpeth Rivers in Davidson and Williamson counties. John Davis, who arrived in middle Tennessee in 1788, received a grant for the land from North Carolina, and expanded his holdings rapidly. The joining of his family by marriage with that of James Robertson produced many of the leaders of Tennessee over the past seven generations. Chart, 33 notes. M. B. Lucas

1203. Craig, Yvonne L. THE JOHN JAY FRENCH HOUSE, BEAUMONT, TEXAS. *Mag. Antiques 1983 123(1): 237-241.* Describes the history and design of the oldest house in Beaumont, 1845.

1204. Crocker, Mary Wallace. ASHER BENJAMIN AND AMERICAN ARCHITECTURE: ASHER BENJAMIN: THE INFLUENCE OF HIS HANDBOOKS OF MISSISSIPPI BUILDINGS. *J. of the Soc. of Architectural Hist. 1979 38(3): 266-270.* The handbooks of Asher Benjamin were designed principally for the use of those builders who resided at such a distance from cities that they could not have the assistance of a regular architect. Mississippi is such a place. Benjamin designs occurred at every level of domestic architecture from the Greek Revival Cottage to some of the finest 19th century mansions. 6 fig., 7 notes, appendix with a list of the instances of use of Asher Benjamin's books in Mississippi. The Appendix has three columns; Title of Book and Place; Location and Name of Building; Field Notes. R. J. Jirran

1205. Crutchfield, James A. PIONEER ARCHITECTURE IN TENNESSEE. *Tennessee Hist. Q. 1976 35(2): 162-174.* Early architecture in Tennessee consisted primarily of stockades, blockhouses, and log cabins. The first two disappeared when the Indians did, but the log cabin survived for more than a century. Stockades were simply high wooden fences surrounding a cluster of houses. They were very effective against Indian attacks, their only weakness being fire. The blockhouse also was wooden, had two stories, had gun ports which permitted defense from any direction, and was usually part of a stockade. Log cabins arose from the necessity of using materials at hand. They were small or large, simple or elaborate, but generally were roughly finished and strongly built. 22 notes. V. L. Human

1206. Cullison, William R. ARCHITECTURAL RECORDS: RECENT ACQUISITIONS AT TULANE. *Louisiana Hist. 1980 21(2): 196-200.* Lists and briefly describes six large collections of architectural construction drawings, renderings, photographs, correspondence, and related items. The approximately 240,000 pieces in these collections document the construction of many important buildings in Louisiana. Examination of six collections in the Special Collection Division, Tulane University Library, New Orleans; note. D. B. Touchstone

1207. Curtis, James R. LAMENT FOR AN ART DECO LANDMARK. *Landscape 1983 27(1): 40-47.* Documents the destruction in 1981 in Miami Beach, Florida, of the New Yorker Hotel, a fine example of Art Deco architecture that was built in 1940.

1208. Damaris, Gypsy. THE COLUMBIA RESTAURANT. *North Louisiana Hist. Assoc. J. 1978 9(1): 43-46.* Discusses the Columbia Restaurant in Shreveport, Louisiana, from around 1900 until the restaurant was sold in 1969.

1209. Daniels, Maygene. DISTRICT OF COLUMBIA BUILDING PERMITS. *Am. Archivist 1975 38(1): 23-30.* National Archives Record Group 351 consists of District of Columbia building permits issued during 1877-1949. The records are useful for economic, social, demographic, and architectural studies as well as for guiding restoration of historic areas. Because the procedures and forms remained unchanged during the period, uniform quantifiable data is readily available. Based on primary sources; 2 illus., 14 notes. J. A. Benson

1210. Darst, Maury. TEXAS LIGHTHOUSES: THE EARLY YEARS, 1850-1900. *Southwestern Hist. Q. 1976 79(3): 301-316.* A photographic essay on the various types of lighthouses built on the Texas coast before 1900, showing the difficulties and delays involved in appropriations and construction. Based on primary sources; illus., 23 notes. J. H. Broussard

1211. Davidson, Faye Tennyson. THE AMES PLANTATION, GRAND JUNCTION. *Tennessee Hist. Q. 1979 38(3): 267-276.* Traces the history of the Ames Plantation near Grand Junction, Tennessee, in three stages: as the 19th-century farm of the Micajah Clark Moorman (1775-1826) family and their descendants, as the early 20th-century hunting lodge of New England industrialist Hobart C. Ames, and finally since 1950 as a model farm of the College of Agriculture of the University of Tennessee. Primary sources; 21 notes. W. D. Piersen

1212. Dickinson, W. Calvin. FRONTIER SPLENDOR: THE CARTER MANSION AT SYCAMORE SHOALS. *Tennessee Hist. Q. 1982 41(4): 317-325.* The Carter Mansion in Elizabethton, Tennessee, sequentially housed the influential families of John Carter and his son Landon. The six-room house, apparently built in the 1780's, is one of the oldest in the state and has architectural features typical of the 17th through 19th centuries. Based on an unpublished 1974 report prepared for the Tennessee Historical Commission, Nashville; 2 illus., 26 notes. W. D. Piersen

1213. Dixon, Caroline Wyche. THE MILES BREWTON HOUSE: EZRA WAITE'S ARCHITECTURAL BOOKS AND OTHER POSSIBLE DESIGN SOURCES. *South Carolina Hist. Mag. 1981 82(2): 118-142.* Standing at 27 King Street, Charleston, is the Miles Brewton House, an example of English Palladianism in American architecture. Comparing the house's design and ornamentation with architectural books in the library of Ezra Waite, who played a major role in the design and execution of the house, reveals support for the contention that Palladian taste dominated Charleston's architecture in the last half of the 18th century. Based on primary sources found in South Carolina Department of Archives and History; 11 plates, 42 notes. R. H. Tomlinson

1214. Dougherty, J. P. BAROQUE AND PICTURESQUE MOTIFS IN L'ENFANT'S DESIGN FOR THE FEDERAL CAPITAL. *Am. Q. 1974 26(1): 23-36.* L'Enfant's proposed and partially executed plan (1791) combined a gridiron design with coordinates varying in frequency and a system of radiocentric avenues derived from the two main foci of the President's House and the Capitol. His scheme derived from his concept of a strong nationally elected executive balancing a locally elected house of legislators. His emphasis on broad vistas was better suited for the capital of an empire rather than for a republic, while his awareness of scenic backdrops for his projected public buildings indicated the influence of the English cult of the picturesque.                            N. Lederer

1215.  Drago, Edmund and Melnick, Ralph. THE OLD SLAVE MART MUSEUM, CHARLESTON, SOUTH CAROLINA: REDISCOVERING THE PAST. *Civil War Hist. 1981 27(2): 138-154.* Traces the origin, ownership, and uses of the building now known as the Old Slave Mart Museum in Charleston, South Carolina, determining that the building (or parts of it) was in fact used for slave trading and does deserve to be designated in the National Register of Historic Places. Based on deeds, newspapers, and other primary and secondary sources; 64 notes.          G. R. Schroeder

1216.  Durham, Walter T. WYNNEWOOD. *Tennessee Hist. Q. 1974 33(2): 127-156.* Wynnewood was built at Bledsoe's Lick in 1828 with the idea of making it a stagecoach inn and hotel. Constructed of hardwood logs, the main two story building contained 10 rooms, eight with fireplaces. Changes in the travel routes resulted in business failure for those initially involved, whereupon A. R. Wynne became the sole owner. The Wynne family resided there until the state acquired the property in 1971. The well preserved log cabin, one of the largest in existence in Tennessee, became a National Historic Landmark in 1973. Primary and secondary sources; illus., 3 photos, 56 notes. Article to be continued.
                                                    M. B. Lucas

1217.  Evans, E. Raymond. THE STRIP HOUSE IN TENNESSEE FOLK-ARCHITECTURE. *Tennessee Folklore Soc. Bull. 1976 42(4): 163-166.* Examines the construction of strip houses, homes lived in by poor Negroes during the early 20th century.

1218.  Faust, Patricia L. SAVANNAH: A CITY RECLAIMED. *Early Am. Life 1978 9(4): 20-23, 52.* Discusses a program of historic preservation of buildings and houses in Savannah, Georgia, dating from colonial times, through the aid of a local banker, Lee Adler, 1961-77.

1219.  Fazio, Michael. ARCHITECTURAL PRESERVATION IN NATCHEZ, MISSISSIPPI: A CONCEPTION OF TIME AND PLACE. *Southern Q. 1980 19(1): 136-149.* In Natchez, architectural preservation has developed into a major industry. By studying the Natchez Pilgrimage of Homes, the author relates how this small town has used its historic architecture to promote its economic wellbeing. Other similar US small towns could do the same. 23 notes.
                                                    B. D. Ledbetter

1220.  Ferguson, Henry N. THE MAN WHO SAVED MONTICELLO. *Am. Hist. Illus. 1980 14(10): 20-27.* Discusses the design and construction of Thomas Jefferson's Virginia home, Monticello, which he designed and built in 1809, and traces the estate's history from Jefferson's death in 1826 and Uriah Phillips Levy's acquisition and renovation of it in 1836, to its present upkeep by the Thomas Jefferson Memorial Foundation.

1221.  Fischer, LeRoy H. THE FAIRCHILD WINERY. *Chronicles of Oklahoma 1977 55(2): 135-156.* Surveys the history of Oklahoma City's Fairchild Wine Vault which in 1975 was named to the National Register of Historic Places. Built in 1893 by Edward B. Fairchild to process and store wine produced from his orchards, it served the local market until Oklahoma legislated prohibition in 1907. Its unique architectural design and distinction as one of Oklahoma City's oldest structures insured its restoration by the state. Based on interviews and primary sources; 12 photos, 33 notes.
                                                    M. L. Tate

1222.  Fischer, LeRoy H. THE HISTORIC PRESERVATION MOVEMENT IN OKLAHOMA. *Chronicles of Oklahoma 1979 57(1): 3-25.* Efforts to identify, mark, and preserve Oklahoma landmarks began with Professor Joseph B. Thoburn's work on prehistoric sites during the early 20th century. Muriel H. Wright expanded the inventory of sites during the following 50 years and published short histories of many of them in the *Chronicles of Oklahoma.* She received much support from Oklahoma's first State Historic Preservation Officer, George H. Shirk, who created the

state's most comprehensive preservation plan and coauthored the book, *Mark of Heritage: Oklahoma Historical Markers* (1958, 1976). Since 1960, financial aid from the state legislature and matching funds from the federal government have helped expand Oklahoma's historic preservation movement. Secondary sources; 17 photos, 22 notes.                                    M. L. Tate

1223.  Frisbie, Louise K. "COME IN AND BE OUR GUEST": HISTORIC HOTELS ALONG THE SUNCOAST. *Tampa Bay Hist. 1983 5(2): 42-55.* Photographs of 24 hotels, some no longer in existence, in the 15 counties surrounding Tampa, Florida, 1880's-1983.

1224.  Frost, Roon. WATERFORD'S 250 YEARS. *Early Am. Life 1983 14(5): 38-41.* The Virginia village of Waterford is a showcase of early Americana; most of the buildings erected since its 1733 settlement by Pennsylvania Quakers are still in good repair.

1225.  Gamble, Robert. THE WHITE-COLUMN TRADITION: CLASSICAL ARCHITECTURE AND THE SOUTHERN MYSTIQUE. *Southern Humanities Rev. 1977 11(Special Issue): 41-59.* Greek-style architecture, sporting colonnades and porticos, aided South's drift toward classical Greek society, complete with slavery within democracy and an unrealistic mystique surrounding its ersatz aristocracy, 1820's-50's. One of six articles in this issue on classical traditions in the South.

1226.  Ganong, Overton G. THE PESO DE BURGO-PELLICER HOUSES. *Escribano 1975 12(3): 81-99.* Discusses the history of the buildings erected by Francisco Pellicer and José (Pepino) Peso de Burgo, Minorcan immigrants to the colony of New Smyrna, Florida, 1780-1831.                                                S

1227.  Garner, H. Hal. HISTORIC RESTORATION IN NORTHEAST LOUISIANA: BOSCOBEL COTTAGE. *North Louisiana Hist. Assoc. J. 1978 9(3): 125-129.* The Boscobel Cottage in Ouachita Parish, Louisiana, was built in 1820. Describes the restoration of the house in recent years and the methodology employed to ascertain the dates of architectural innovations in the original plantation structure. Illus.                              H. M. Parker, Jr.

1228.  Graham, Thomas. FLAGLER'S MAGNIFICENT HOTEL PONCE DE LEON. *Florida Hist. Q. 1975 54(1): 1-17.* Discusses the origins, construction, and use of the Hotel Ponce de Leon in St. Augustine, Florida. Built in 1887 by oil magnate Henry Morrison Flagler (1830-1913), the hotel was designed by architect Bernard Maybeck in Spanish Renaissance style, and decorated by Louis Tiffany. For several years, the hotel was perhaps the country's most fashionable resort. A decline set in, brought on by such diverse causes as the depression of the 1890's, bad freezes in St. Augustine, and increasing interest in South Florida. Nevertheless, the Ponce de Leon continued to operate as a hotel until 1967, and is now the campus for Flagler College. Based on manuscript, newspaper, and secondary sources, and interviews; 9 illus., 75 notes.
                                                    J. E. Findling

1229.  Grant, H. Roger and Hofsommer, Donovan L. "KATY" DEPOTS OF OKLAHOMA: A PICTORIAL HISTORY. *Chronicles of Oklahoma 1974 52(3): 331-341.* Briefly describes the architecture of Oklahoma depots of the Missouri, Kansas and Texas ("Katy") Railroad. Stations are classified into three categories with distinctions made between rural and urban: Late Victorian (ca 1870-1910), Early Modern (ca 1910-25), and Modern (ca 1925 to present). 10 photos, map, plan, 6 notes.           N. J. Street

1230.  Greenberg, Mike. THE WATCHFUL WARRIORS. *Hist. Preservation 1983 35(3): 42-45.* Describes the efforts of the San Antonio Conservation Society to save historic buildings in San Antonio, Texas, since the 1970's.

1231.  Greenwalt, Mary Burgner. WAR CORRESPONDENTS' MEMORIAL: GATHLAND STATE PARK WASHINGTON COUNTY, MARYLAND. *Daughters of the Am. Revolution Mag. 1978 112(5): 408-410.* Describes the origins of Maryland's Gathland State Park's War Correspondents' Memorial, conceived and designed by Civil War correspondent George Alfred Townsend, and its erection in 1895.

1232. Grider, Sylvia Ann. THE SHOTGUN HOUSE IN OIL BOOMTOWNS OF THE TEXAS PANHANDLE. *Pioneer Am. 1975 7(2): 47-55.* Singles out the shotgun house, a cheap and quickly-built form of housing associated in this instance with the oil boomtowns of the Texas Panhandle during the mid-1920's. The shotgun house as a type is one room wide with the rooms end to end and the front and back doors in the gable ends. Construction techniques were so simple that a skilled carpenter and a helper could complete one of these buildings in one and one-half to two days. The origin of this house is obscure, but evidence suggests that the shotgun house spread from western Louisiana to Texas via rig builders, gamblers, drug pushers, and other "boom chasers." Although not built for permanence, many have remained remarkably durable. Based on field research, including interviews, and secondary sources; 2 photos, fig., 23 notes.                C. R. Gunter, Jr.

1233. Hagy, James William. COURTHOUSE OF RUSSELL COUNTY. *Virginia Cavalcade 1973 22(4): 12-17.*

1234. Hagy, James William. COURTHOUSES OF WASHINGTON COUNTY. *Virginia Cavalcade 1975 25(2): 80-85.* Discusses the construction and architecture of courthouses in Washington County, Virginia, 1777-1868.

1235. Halverson, Delia. THE FOUR SIDES OF THE PINK PALACE: THE MARBLE MANSION, OR THE TATE HOMESTEAD. *Georgia Life 1979 6(3): 18-21.* Describes the architecture of the pink marble Tate homestead and its changes since it was built in the mid-1920's by Colonel Sam Tate at a cost of $400,000 in Pickens County, Georgia.

1236. Harden, John. RESTORATION OF TRYON PALACE. *Curator 1975 18(4): 287-295.* Gives an illustrated account of the restoration of Tryon Palace in New Bern, North Carolina, which was built in 1767-70, showing the completed house and gardens which are now a State Historical Site.

1237. Harnsberger, Douglas. "IN DELORME'S MANNER..." *APT Bull. [Canada] 1981 13(4): 2-8.* Discusses an x-ray probe of the dome of Thomas Jefferson's Monticello; conducted in 1981, the probe revealed that the construction of the dome followed the method of prominent 16th-century French architect Philibert Delorme.

1238. Harper, Robert W., III. DECORATIVE ARTS AT THE XIMENEZ-FATIO HOUSE: FURNISHINGS USED TO INTERPRET THE PAST. *Escribano 1979 16: 59-75.* Relates the history of the Ximenez-Fatio house, 1798-1970's, and describes the refurbishing of its rooms in the mid-1970's in the style of frontier St. Augustine; includes plates.

1239. Harris, Sally. COURTHOUSES OF SMYTH COUNTY. *Virginia Cavalcade 1980 30(1): 30-37.* Traces the establishment of Smyth County, Virginia, 1832, and the design and construction of its two capitol buildings in 1834 and 1905.

1240. Hayward, Mary Ellen. URBAN VERNACULAR ARCHITECTURE IN NINETEENTH-CENTURY BALTIMORE. *Winterthur Portfolio 1981 16(1): 33-63.* The Federal Hill district in Baltimore, Maryland, stands as a model of how high-style architecture was modified to provide inexpensive houses for the working class. An analysis of such architecture indicates that there was a constant relationship in architecture between upper-class and working-class housing. Based on town records and other sources; 30 illus., 49 notes.                N. A. Kuntz

1241. Hazlett, Thomas. THEY BUILT THEIR OWN HIGHWAY... AND OTHER TALES OF PRIVATE LAND-USE PLANNING. *Reason 1983 15(7): 22-30.* Since 1940, the Houston

Planning Department has coordinated public and private activities which, without public zoning, have created a city that is more workable than its tightly-zoned counterparts.

1242. Heisner, Beverly. HARRIET MORRISON IRWIN'S HEXAGONAL HOUSE: AN INVENTION TO IMPROVE DOMESTIC DWELLINGS. *North Carolina Hist. Rev. 1981 58(2): 105-123.* Harriet Morrison Irwin (1828-97) of Charlotte, North Carolina, was the first woman in the United States to patent an architectural design. Irwin's hexagonal house plan, patented in 1869, expressed her desire for an efficient but open home, with easy access to nature. Her novel, *The Hermit of Petraea* (1871), dedicated to the English writer, John Ruskin, author of popular books on architecture, contains discussions of Irwin's views on the relationship between humans, their homes, and the natural environment. Irwin's own needs as an invalid also influenced her architectural designs. James Patton Irwin (1820-1903), Harriet's husband, advertised her designs in regional magazines. Several homes may have been built according to her designs. Based on genealogical materials, private family papers, US Patent Office Records, Irwin's novel, county property records, and secondary sources on local history. 19 illus., 2 architectural plans, reproduction of Irwin's Letters Patent; 58 notes.

T. L. Savitt

1243. Herman, Bernard L. and Orr, David G. PEAR VALLEY ET AL.: AN EXCURSION INTO THE ANALYSIS OF SOUTHERN VERNACULAR ARCHITECTURE. *Southern Folklore Q. 1975 39(4): 307-327.* Discusses the folk architecture of houses in rural settlements of Virginia from the 17th to the 19th centuries, emphasizing Georgian styles.

1244. Hoagland, Alison K. DEER PARK HOTEL. *Maryland Hist. Mag. 1978 73(4): 340-351.* The popularity of the summer resort in late 19th century America, as symbolic of the search for the wilderness and a longing to escape industrial civilization, is epitomized in B & O president John Garrett's Deer Park Hotel in Garrett County, Maryland, opened in 1873. Designed by architect Ephraim Baldwin in Swiss Alpine style, by 1884 it included also five large cottages, one of them used by Grover Cleveland on his honeymoon. Deer Park, with its elitist appeal and integration of buildings into the landscape, was the finest example of the indigenous Shingle Style of architecture, perfected by Henry Hobson Richardson and popularly called Queen Anne. Its escapist nature and rapport with its surroundings are a most fitting commentary on the late 19th century. Primary and secondary sources; 6 illus., 38 notes.

G. J. Bobango

1245. Howett, Catherine M. BARNSLEY GARDENS: THE FACTS BEHIND THE FABLES. *Georgia Hist. Q. 1980 64(2): 172-189.* Discusses the design and construction of "Woodlands," also known as Barnsley Gardens, the "rural villa" home of English gentleman and amateur architect Godfrey Barnsley. Located near Kingston, Georgia, the estate was based on the landscape principles of Andrew Jackson Downing, and was under construction, though never completed, during ca. 1840-70. Based on the Barnsley papers and secondary sources; 2 illus., 2 photos, map, 41 notes.

G. R. Schroeder

1246. Howett, Catherine M. A SOUTHERN LADY'S LEGACY: THE ITALIAN "TERRACES" OF LA GRANGE, GEORGIA. *J. of Garden Hist. [Great Britain] 1982 2(4): 343-360.* Sarah Coleman Ferrell created and maintained during 1840-1903 elaborate European-influenced gardens at her home, "The Terraces," as an opportunity for horticultural display and religious piety.

1247. Howland, Richard H. PORTFOLIO: CAMDEN. *Nineteenth Cent. 1979 5(4): 40-44.* Describes the history, architecture, and interior decoration of Camden, a well-preserved house near Port Royal, Virginia, completed in 1859 by architect Norris G. Starkwether and now owned by and lived in by Richard Turner Pratt, the son of William C. Pratt, who commissioned it.

1248. Hulan, Richard H. MIDDLE TENNESSEE AND THE DOGTROT HOUSE. *Pioneer Am. 1975 7(2): 37-46.* Presents documentary and graphic evidence relating to four early Middle Tennessee dogtrot houses. Each house can be dated between 1780 and 1810, which is somewhat earlier than Henry Glassie's tentative date of 1825 for the development of this house type. It is speculated that further research may reveal the presence of this house type in earlier settlement areas, especially in Kentucky. Secondary sources; illus., 2 photos, map, fig., 39 notes.　　　C. R. Gunter, Jr.

1249.　Huth, Tom. SHOULD CHARLESTON GO NEW SOUTH? *Hist. Preservation 1979 31(3): 32-38.* Discusses issues facing preservationists in Charleston, South Carolina, particularly a proposal to build a modern hotel-conference-shopping complex downtown amid Victorian and other historical architectural styles; 1970's.

1250.　Jeane, D. Gregory. THE UPLAND SOUTH CEMETERY: AN AMERICAN TYPE. *J. of Popular Culture 1978 11(4): 895-903.* Cemeteries in the Upland South are distinguished by their hilltop locations, small size, preferred vegetation, unique decorations, and traditional ceremonies of piety.

1251.　Jennings, J. L. Sibley, Jr. ARTISTRY AS DESIGN: L'ENFANT'S EXTRAORDINARY CITY. *Q. J. of the Lib. of Congress 1979 36(3): 225-278.* Discusses the design of the capital city of the United States attributed to French émigré architect-engineer Pierre Charles L'Enfant (1754-1825) and the confusion of this design with that of another design by American surveyor Andrew Ellicott. The background history for planning a federal city and the choice of L'Enfant to design it is given. L'Enfant is traced back to his birthplace Paris to demonstrate the influence of his past on his design for the capital. Statements made by L'Enfant do not agree with the design motives attributed to him. The city he designed would be totally different from what we have today if his plan was the accepted one. Intensive study of the document in the Library of Congress raises doubts as to whether this is L'Enfant's final 1791 plan or the Ellicott plan of 1792. Based on correspondence, National Archives Records, L'Enfant Papers, and maps; 11 illus., 11 photos, 5 maps, 114 notes.　　　M. A. Kascus

1252.　Johnson, Janis. GOOD TIMES AND BAD FOR ART DECO ON MIAMI BEACH STRIP. *Smithsonian 1982 13(9): 58-67.* Describes the efforts and problems of preserving some of the better Art Deco buildings of the 1930's in Miami Beach.

1253.　Jones, Elizabeth F. and Kinsman, Mary Jean. UNKNOWN WIGHT DESIGNS IN LOUISVILLE, KENTUCKY. *Nineteenth Cent. 1980 6(4): 57-60.* Reproduces and describes the original drawings and elevations of the High Victorian Gothic house designed by New Yorker Peter Bonnett Wight (1838-1925) for Louisvillian Thomas Prather Jacob and built in 1869.

1254.　Jordan, Terry G. A FOREBAY BANK BARN IN TEXAS. *Pennsylvania Folklife 1980-81 30(2): 72-77.* The Hamic family barn of Chalk Mountain, Texas, shares three features found in Pennsylvania German barns: 1) the two-level floor plan, 2) the banked ramp entrance to the upper level, and 3) the projecting forebay on the barnyard side of the structure; the barn seems misplaced in Texas, raising questions of the antecedence of American barn types and cultural diffusion.

1255.　Jordan, Terry G. LOG CORNER-TIMBERING IN TEXAS. *Pioneer Am. 1976 8(1): 8-18.* Seeks to increase knowledge of the diffusion process of the log construction culture by concentrating on corner-notching, an easily identifiable element which also displays pronounced areal variation. Texas provides a useful laboratory in which to test the influence of various causal factors in log construction. Field observations in upper southern counties of Texas reveal that the type of wood and type of structure are strongly correlated to notch type. Most builders knew how to fashion more than one type of notch. Builders also selected notch types according to the type of wood available. Based on extensive field research and secondary sources; 5 maps, 8 photos, 6 tables, 10 notes.　　　C. R. Gunter, Jr.

1256.　Kay, Jane Holtz. MIZNER'S EDEN. *Am. Preservation 1982 4(2): 35-48.* Describes the architecture of Palm Beach, Florida, designed by flamboyant architect Addison Mizner and developed by Paris Singer.

1257.　Kemp, Emory L. IRON, ENGINEERS AND THE WHEELING SUSPENSION BRIDGE. *Upper Ohio Valley Hist. Rev. 1982 11(2): 2-11.* Focuses on iron smelting with coke after 1709, and on the Wheeling Suspension Bridge.

1258.　Kerber, Stephen. WILLIAM EDWARDS AND THE HISTORIC UNIVERSITY OF FLORIDA CAMPUS: A PHOTOGRAPHIC ESSAY. *Florida Hist. Q. 1979 57(3): 327-336.* The buildings designed by William A. Edwards on the University of Florida campus during 1905-25 are in danger of destruction. Modern growth and needs threaten many of the Collegiate Gothic structures. The future of Edwards' buildings has not been decided. Primary and secondary sources; 8 photos, 39 notes.　　　N. A. Kuntz

1259.　Kilgore, Sherry J. A BRIEF SURVEY OF FRONTIER ARCHITECTURAL CHARACTERISTICS IN ROBERTSON AND SUMNER COUNTIES. *Tennessee Folklore Soc. Bull. 1978 44(3): 116-126.* Describes rural architecture in Tennessee during the 18th and 19th centuries.

1260.　Klepper, Bobbie Jean. THE WHITE-POOL HOUSE IN ODESSA, TEXAS. *Permian Hist. Ann. 1980 20: 3-19.* Traces the history of the White-Pool House, the oldest existing structure in Odessa, Texas, from its construction in 1887 as the residence of Charles White (1824-1905) and his wife Lucy Haughton White (1830-1920), to its designation as a historical monument in 1978.

1261.　Laska, Shirley Bradway; Seaman, Jerrol M.; and McSeveny, Dennis R. INNER-CITY REINVESTMENT: NEIGHBOURHOOD CHARACTERISTICS AND SPATIAL PATTERNS OVER TIME. *Urban Studies [Great Britain] 1982 19(2): 155-165.* Examines housing renovation in old New Orleans, 1971-78. The physical remnants of the 19th-century city had more effect on the popularity of renovation than did their current social characteristics. Gentrification shows that the wealthy may find many desirable locations within the urban area but the renovation movement brings into question assumptions about the importance of the neighborhood's social characteristics to middle-income home buyers. Based on census data; 4 tables, fig., biblio., 13 notes.　　　D. J. Nicholls

1262.　Lawrence, Henry W. SOUTHERN SPAS: SOURCE OF THE AMERICAN RESORT TRADITION. *Landscape 1983 27(2): 1-12.* The Southern antebellum style of constructing hot-spring resorts, that of a central building flanked by wings of individual cottages, was adopted nationally after the Civil War and has continued to influence vacation-resort design.

1263.　Lay, K. Edward and Pawlett, Nathaniel Mason. ARCHITECTURAL SURVEYS ASSOCIATED WITH EARLY ROAD SYSTEMS. *APT Bull. [Canada] 1980 12(2): 3-36.* Discusses research on metal truss bridges in Virginia, and the history of roads in Virginia, specifically in Albemarle County from 1725 to 1816, the beginning of the turnpike era, and the architectural surveys of the buildings along these roads.

1264.　Lees, William Bennett. THE HISTORICAL DEVELOPMENT OF LIMERICK PLANTATION, A TIDEWATER RICE PLANTATION IN BERKELEY COUNTY, SOUTH CAROLINA, 1683-1945. *South Carolina Hist. Mag. 1981 82(1): 44-62.*

1265.　Levin, Alexandra Lee. COLONEL NICHOLAS ROGERS AND HIS COUNTRY SEAT, "DRUID HILL." *Maryland Hist. Mag. 1977 72(1): 78-82.* Colonel Nicholas Rogers (1753-1822), Revolutionary War officer and Baltimore city father, acquired the sizable property known as Druid Hill through his marriage to Eleanor Buchanan. About 1796, he erected a mansion "so compact and commodious as to outvie most of the buildings in the vicinity of Baltimore." The grounds were in the best English landscape gardening style. When the house burned shortly after completion, a second dwelling, two-story and square with carefully balanced windows and doors, replaced it, by 1801. The colonel's son bequeathed the property, complete with the family burial plot, to the city of Baltimore in 1860. The present Druid Hill Park still reflects the artistry of Rogers' planning. Primary and secondary sources; 8 notes.

G. J. Bobango

1266. Lewis, Monnie. THRONATEESKA HERITAGE FOUNDATION. *Georgia Hist. Q. 1979 63(1): 78-82.* The Thronateeska Heritage Foundation, founded in 1974 by the merger of two other organizations, is developing Heritage Plaza, in Albany, Georgia, focusing on the restoration of the old railroad depot and several other buildings which will serve as museums on transportation and Southwest Georgia history and culture. Based on newspaper clippings and interviews; illus. G. R. Schroeder

1267. Lewis, Wilber H. ARTISTS OF SAINT ANNE'S ROCK CHAPEL. *North Louisiana Hist. Assoc. J. 1976 7(2): 64-67.* Saint Anne's Chapel was built in 1891 by Carmelite monks on the grounds of Saint Joseph's Monastery in northern DeSoto Parish. It was "a tiny, one-room chapel of stone—the last of several religious buildings to be erected" at the Monastery. Since 1891, "artists have sketched Saint Anne's Chapel in charcoal or pen and ink, and have painted it with oils, watercolors, and pastels." The Chapel "was forsaken about 1910," and it was not until 1959 that an effort was made to restore it. Restoration was completed in 1961 under the leadership of Father William Kwaaitaal, but when the latter was transferred soon after, again the Chapel deteriorated. In 1975, Father Leger Tremblay began to restore the Chapel and "has definite plans for Saint Anne's rock chapel." 3 photos, line drawing, 10 notes. A. N. Garland

1268. Llewellyn, Robert, photog. A NEW VIEW OF MONTICELLO. *Hist. Preservation 1983 35(5): 48-51.* Presents photographs of Thomas Jefferson's Monticello estate near Charlottesville, Virginia.

1269. Lounsbury, Carl. THE DEVELOPMENT OF DOMESTIC ARCHITECTURE IN THE ALBEMARLE REGION. *North Carolina Hist. Rev. 1977 54(1): 17-48.* The changing vernacular architecture of farmhouses in Gates, Perquimans, and Pasquotank counties during 1660-1860 reflected evolving living standards of rural North Carolinians. As concerns of privacy, comfort, style, and display of wealth grew, the architectural forms of these farmhouses altered to fit the new demands. Houses became more formal and specialized, permitting a greater variety of household activities. A wide variation in housing conditions arose based on class distinctions in society. Based on manuscript county records and family papers, contemporary newspapers, primary published records, and secondary sources; 6 illus., map, 13 figs., 57 notes.

T. L. Savitt

1270. Lupold, John S. HISTORIC COLUMBUS FOUNDATION, 1966-1978. *Georgia Hist. Q. 1979 63(1): 129-137.* The restoration of the Springer Opera House was the impetus for the organization of the Historic Columbus Foundation. Describes the activities of this foundation which have resulted in improvements in nearly one quarter of the remaining original city buildings. Based on interviews; 3 illus., 9 notes. G. R. Schroeder

1271. Lupold, John S. REVITALIZING FOUNDRIES, HOTELS AND GRIST MILLS IN COLUMBUS. *Georgia Hist. Q. 1979 63(1): 138-142.* Describes several specific successful restoration projects in Columbus, Georgia, during the 1970's, including Rankin Square and the Iron Works, and their commercial viability. Based on interviews and magazine articles; 2 illus., 4 notes.

G. R. Schroeder

1272. Lyle, Royster, Jr. COURTHOUSES OF ROCKBRIDGE COUNTY. *Virginia Cavalcade 1976 25(3): 118-125.* Discusses the construction and architecture of courthouses in Rockbridge County, Virginia, 1778-1897.

1273. Lyle, Royster, Jr. and Paxton, Matthew W., Jr. THE V. M. I. BARRACKS. *Virginia Cavalcade 1974 23(3): 14-29.* Describes construction of Virginia Military Institute in Lexington and includes architectural plans and sketches by Alexander Jackson Davis.

1274. Maddox, Dawn. THE BUILDINGS AND GROUNDS OF JEFFERSON COLLEGE IN THE NINETEENTH CENTURY. *J. of Mississippi Hist. 1973 35(1): 37-53.* Describes the planning, construction, and repair of the buildings and grounds of Jefferson College near Natchez, 1802-95. Based on the Jefferson College Papers; 28 notes. J. W. Hillje

1275. Manucy, Albert. CHANGING TRADITIONS IN ST. AUGUSTINE ARCHITECTURE. *Escribano 1982 19: 1-28.* Impact of English building practices and neoclassicism on construction in St. Augustine, Florida, during the last quarter of the 1700's.

1276. Manucy, Albert. THE CITY GATE OF ST. AUGUSTINE. *Escribano 1973 10(1): 1-13.* Concluded from a 1964 article.

S

1277. Manucy, Albert. TOWARD RE-CREATION OF 16TH CENTURY ST. AUGUSTINE. *Escribano 1977 14: 1-4.* The St. Augustine Restoration Foundation promotes historical preservation so that past architecture, history, and culture will be available to contemporary history students.

1278. Martin, Charles E. HEAD OF HOLLYBUSH, RECONSTRUCTING MATERIAL CULTURE THROUGH ORAL HISTORY. *Pioneer Am. 1981 13(1): 3-16.* Briefly traces the growth of the head of Hollybush, an eastern Kentucky farming community abandoned in 1960, focusing on the largely isolated community's architectural history from the 1880's to the 1950's as determined by the oral history accounts of residents.

1279. Martin, Charles E. HOWARD ACREE'S CHIMNEY: THE DILEMMA OF INNOVATION. *Pioneer Am. 1983 15(1): 35-49.* Presents a brief biography of Howard Acree and describes the design and construction of the fireplace he built in his four-room frame house in eastern Kentucky in 1934.

1280. Martin, F. Lestar. MT. LEBANON'S HISTORIC HOUSES: A PRESENTATION BY LOUISIANA TECH UNIVERSITY'S SCHOOL OF ARCHITECTURE. *North Louisiana Hist. Assoc. J. 1978 9(3): 115-124.* Brief histories and descriptions of six dwellings and a church of the antebellum vintage in and around the village of Mt. Lebanon, Louisiana. Provides floor plans and front elevation of each structure. H. M. Parker, Jr.

1281. Martin, F. Lestar. "SYLVAN RETREAT": A RESTORATION PROJECT. *North Louisiana Hist. Assoc. J. 1978 9(3): 135-142.* The author-preserver discusses the renovation of Sylvan retreat, a Bienville Parish, Louisiana, farm house erected in 1848. The history of the house is described in three periods, each of which ushered in architectural changes to the original structure and the immediate grounds. 7 illus. H. M. Parker, Jr.

1282. Matlack, Carol. SAVANNAH. *Am. Preservation 1979 2(3): 9-25.* The rhythmic progression of squares planned by James Oglethorpe in 1733 and the subsequent cottom boom made Savannah architecturally unique. The late 19th-century economic crises led to a 100 year decline in the center city. The turning point was in 1954 when efforts to save the City Market Square and Davenport House led to the creation of Historic Savannah Foundation which buys threatened properties and resells them to preservationists. Two square miles of downtown were designated an historic district in 1966. Preservation has brought rising property values, tourism, and new business opportunities. Since 1967, the displacement problem has been addressed by Savannah Landmark which restores buildings for low income rental. 18 photos. S. C. Strom

1283. Matthews, Janet Snyder. MANATEE VILLAGE HISTORICAL PARK. *Tampa Bay Hist. 1979 1(1): 31-36.* Efforts by the Heritage of Manatee's Environment (HOME), 1974-76, resulted in a preservation movement which saved two historic buildings of Manatee Village: the United Methodist Church (built in 1889) and the original county courthouse (built in 1859).

1284. Maxa, Kathleen. KEY WEST: A TINY FLORIDA IS-LAND WHERE DIVERSITY IS AS PRIZED AS 19TH CENTU-RY ARCHITECTURE. *Am. Preservation 1980 3(3): 9-23.* Examines unique 19th-century architectural styles such as Bahamian, New England, Creole, and Victorian, in Key West, Florida, and recent attempts to retain Key West's diversity.

1285. McAllister, James L., Jr. ARCHITECTURE AND CHANGE IN THE DIOCESE OF VIRGINIA. *Hist. Mag.of the Protestant Episcopal Church 1976 45(3): 297-323.* Ecclesiastical architectural form follows function. Traces the architectural changes which occurred in the structures of early Virginia Episcopal edifices as the function of preaching under the earlier evangelical bishops was replaced by emphasis on the sacraments. Instead of the pulpit occupying the center of the front of the church, it was replaced by the altar and chancel, which had not existed in the original structures. Most contemporary Virginia Episcopalians have no idea that many of the buildings in which they now worship were originally erected to emphasize and enhance the importance of preaching in public worship. Based on secondary sources; 5 illus., 83 notes.
H. M. Parker, Jr.

1286. McCabe, Carol. MR. JEFFERSON'S GARDEN. *Early Am. Life 1983 14(3): 44-49.* Discusses the restoration of the original gardens and orchards at Monticello, the Virginia home of Thomas Jefferson; includes excerpts from Jefferson's correspondence regarding gardens and gardening.

1287. McCants, Sister Dorothea Olga. OLD ST. VINCENT ACADEMY. *North Louisiana Hist. Assoc. J. 1973 5(1): 25-27.* The "old St. Vincent Academy structure located at Southern and St. Vincent Avenues, landmark in Shreveport for over half a century, is .... being torn down by workmen engaged by the owners, The Daughters of the Cross." Many people in Shreveport will remember the old building because "salvaged materials of the old building are being put to other use in various areas in and around Shreveport," and because "the two side-altars of handcarved carara marble that once served in the chapel now grace the sanctuary of Shreveport's ... Holy Trinity Church on Marshall Street." Discusses the role of Louis G. Sicard, Jr., and his wife in preserving the memory of the building through the creation of many mementos and souvenirs. 4 photos.
A. N. Garland

1288. McClure, Dennis and McClure, Pam. THE OLD COVERED BRIDGES OF GEORGIA. *Georgia Life 1977 4(3): 24-27.* Discusses and depicts seven color photographs of old covered bridges in Georgia, most built in the 19th century, many now relocated and restored.

1289. McCue, George. AIRPORT ARCHITECTURE: THE DAL-LAS-FORT WORTH SOLUTION. *Art in Am. 1974 62(1): 74-77.*

1290. McCue, George. THE OCTAGON—TOWN HOUSE THAT PRECEDED THE TOWN. *Historic Preservation 1974 26(2): 27-31.* The Octagon was built in 1800 as a town house for Colonel John Tayloe of Virginia when Washington, D.C. was still a "marshy woodland." Designed for its "sharp-cornered site" by Dr. William Thornton, it is "one of the great prototypes" of the Federal style. Since 1902 it has been the headquarters of the American Institute of Architects. 2 illus., 6 photos.
R. M. Frame III

1291. McDowell, Peggy. NEW ORLEANS CEMETERIES: AR-CHITECTURAL STYLES AND INFLUENCES. *Southern Q. 1982 20(2): 9-27.* The great age of funerary architecture in New Orleans lasted for most of the 19th century and into the first three decades of the 20th. Toward the latter part of this period, the architecture became increasingly elaborate, reflecting the influence of Jacques Nicholas Bussiere de Pouilly. Tombs, monuments, and mausoleums reflect the cultural and artistic values of the society in which they exist, and in New Orleans provide a particularly interesting case

study because most are above ground, even though the development of proper drainage eventually rendered this unnecessary. 12 illus.
W. A. Wiegand

1292. McMurtry, R. Gerald. THE HARDIN THOMAS HOUSE. *Lincoln Herald 1974 76(1): 4-6.* Describes the Hardin Thomas double log cabin that Thomas Lincoln, the father of Abraham Lincoln, built. As a joiner, Thomas Lincoln did fine and lasting work. The house is being restored as part of Valley Creek City Park, Elizabethtown, Kentucky. Based on genealogical research; 2 photos.
A. C. Aimone

1293. McNabb, William Ross. WESTCLIFF: MR. FULTON'S MANSION. *East Tennessee Hist. Soc. Publ. 1977 49: 93-97.* Among those great palatial mansions in the Mediterranean mode blending the fantasy and magnificence of the 1920's was Knoxville's Westcliff, which was built for Weston M. Fulton in 1929. 13 notes, 6 illus.
D. A. Yanchisin

1294. Mellown, Robert O. THE PRESIDENT'S MANSION AT THE UNIVERSITY OF ALABAMA. *Alabama Rev. 1982 35(3): 200-229.* Describes the construction and renovation of a Greek Revival mansion. Based on university records; 86 notes.
G. R. Schroeder

1295. Miller, Theodora R. A VICTORIAN HOME RESTORED. *Georgia Life 1978 4(4): 31-36.* Describes restoration of a 1906 Victorian house in Monroe, Georgia, 1972-78.

1296. Mitchell, William R., Jr. A LOOK AT HISTORIC PRES-ERVATION AND AMERICAN ARCHITECTURE, EMPHASIZ-ING GEORGIA. *Georgia Hist. Q. 1979 63(1): 39-52.* Discusses the development of the relationship between architectural history and historic preservation during the 20th century, especially as they pertain to Georgia. 2 illus., 47 notes.
G. R. Schroeder

1297. Montequin, François-Auguste de. EL PROCESO DE UR-BANIZACION EN SAN AGUSTIN DE LA FLORIDA, 1565-1821: ARQUITECTURA CIVIL Y MILITAR [The urbanization process in St. Augustine, Florida, 1565-1821: civilian and military architecture]. *Anuario de Estudios Americanos [Spain] 1980 37: 583-647.* Although St. Augustine was founded to perform civilian, religious, and military functions, its architecture reflects principally the last activity. 98 notes, 4 photos.
J. A. Lewis

1298. Moore, John Hammond. THAT "COMMODIOUS" AN-NEX TO JEFFERSON'S ROTUNDA: WAS IT REALLY A NA-TIONAL MAUSOLEUM? *Virginia Cavalcade 1980 29(3): 114-123.* The Annex added to Thomas Jefferson's Rotunda at the University of Virginia between 1851 and 1853 was destroyed by fire along with the Rotunda in 1895 and never restored; describes its designer, architect Robert Mills (1781-1855), and some of his other buildings. The Rotunda was restored in the 1970's to Jefferson's original floor plan.

1299. Morrow, Sara Sprott. ADOLPHUS HEIMAN'S LEGACY TO NASHVILLE. *Tennessee Hist. Q. 1974 33(1): 3-21.* Adolphus Heiman arrived in Nashville from his native Prussia in 1836 at the age of 27. Though first employed as a stone cutter, he was most successful in architecture, including college buildings, bridges, and churches. Traces the history of his most famous work, the College Building, originally designed for the University of Nashville in 1853 and subsequently used by several other colleges. Illus., 4 photos, 21 notes.
M. B. Lucas

1300. Morrow, Sara Sprott. THE CHURCH OF THE HOLY TRINITY; ENGLISH COUNTRYSIDE TRANQUILITY IN DOWNTOWN NASHVILLE. *Tennessee Hist. Q. 1975 34(4): 333-349.* Describes the origins and development of the Holy Trinity Episcopal Church which began as a mission church in South Nashville during the 1840's. The church, an excellent example of Gothic Revival architecture, was completed in 1853, survived use as a powder magazine during the Civil War, and is being restored under direction of the Tennessee Historical Commission. Secondary sources; 2 illus., 18 notes.                                    M. B. Lucas

1301. Morrow, Sara Sprott. ST. PAUL'S CHURCH, FRANKLIN. *Tennessee Hist. Q. 1975 34(1): 3-18.* In 1827 the Episcopal church had its beginning in Tennessee when James Hervey Otey organized St. Paul's Church in Franklin. The 40 by 80 foot structure with its 18 to 24 inch walls was completed in 1834, a year before Otey was elected the first bishop of Tennessee. During the Civil War the church suffered much damage, but in later years, with the addition of its famed Tiffany stained-glass windows, its appearance improved. Based on primary and secondary sources; illus., 25 notes.
                                                      M. B. Lucas

1302. Muckelroy, Duncan G. RANCHING HISTORY OF THE AMERICAN WEST: REVITALIZED THROUGH THE PRESERVATION OF ITS ARCHITECTURE. *Pioneer Am. 1974 6(2): 34-42.* Interprets 20 restored and reconstructed architectural types at Texas Tech University, which were selected to exemplify the ranching history of the American West. These buildings came from diverse locations in Texas, and an effort has been made to utilize plant materials and shaped terrains indigenous to the original location. Based on interviews and on primary and secondary sources; 6 photos, fig., 10 notes.                        C. R. Gunter, Jr.

1303. Murray, Ruth C. THE ABSALOM AUTREY LOG HOUSE: LINCOLN PARISH, LOUISIANA. *Pioneer Am. 1982 14(3): 137-140.* Presents the settlement of land in Lincoln Parish by Absalom Autrey and his family; describes the log house built by Autrey in 1849.

1304. Neff, Merry. TIDEWATER HOUSE. *Early Am. Life. 1983 14(1): 33-38.* History and photographs of the Gilbert Leigh House, built in 1759 in Edenton, North Carolina, and recently restored.

1305. Nesbitt, Martha C. TO FAIRFIELD WITH LOVE: A RURAL MARYLAND HOUSE AND HOUSEHOLD. *Maryland Hist. Mag. 1975 70(1): 68-89.* Emphasizes the "almost human attributes of character and personality" represented by certain old homes of Montgomery County and chronicles the building and family history of *Fairfield*, home of the Pierce-Iddings-Willson Family for 115 years, and located in present-day Brighton community. Built by Edward Pierce for his father and sister Ann in 1856, the house also became his home after his marriage to Sophia Kummer from the Moravian Female Seminary of Bethlehem, Pennsylvania. The strong Quaker heritage of the area was enriched by Sophie's musical enthusiasm. The Pierces' daughter Fanny married William Iddings in 1894 and they inaugurated a carpet, rug, and mat-weaving business into the family homestead, which continued through the 1960's. Deborah Alice Iddings (1896- ) lived at Fairfield until its sale in 1968. A re-roofing job in the 1950's uncovered a cache of letters and an 1817 diary of one of the Kummer sisters which shed new light on the early Moravian community and its personnel. The author knew Fanny Pierce Iddings personally and much of this article consists of her personal reminiscences and writings. Longevity seems inherent in the Fairfield clan, for all the principals lived into their late eighties and nineties. Based on family Day Books, diaries, letters, interviews by the author, and secondary sources; 5 illus., 28 notes.                                              G. J. Bobango

1306. Netherton, Nan and Netherton, Ross. COURTHOUSES OF FAIRFAX COUNTY. *Virginia Cavalcade 1977 27(2): 86-95.* Discusses the sites and buildings of Fairfax County courthouses, 1742-1966.

1307. Newton, Ada L. K. THE ANGLO-IRISH HOUSE OF THE RIO GRANDE. *Pioneer Am. 1973 5(1): 33-38.* Documents evidence of Irish settlement along the Rio Grande in both Texas and Mexico from distinctly North Irish house types. Colonization by northern Europeans, especially those who were cattle raisers by tradition, was encouraged by Mexico after 1821, and Texas after 1836. In their first state of development these houses were usually constructed of native rock, conglomerate, sandstone, or caliche, and consisted of one room (14 to 18 feet by 24 feet). Several diagnostic

traits are examined, and it is apparent that no house type in either Mexico or Spain was its ancestor. Only further study will complete the story of diffusion. Presently, one can only speculate concerning related matters—how Mexican are the people? or how much did the Irish contribute to the southwestern cattle tradition? Based on interviews, secondary sources, and the author's unpublished master's thesis; 4 photos, map, 2 figs., 15 notes.
                                                    C. R. Gunter, Jr.

1308. Newton, Milton B., Jr. and Pulliam-DiNapoli, Linda LOG HOUSES AS PUBLIC OCCASIONS: A HISTORICAL THEORY. *Ann. of the Assoc. of Am. Geographers 1977 67(3): 360-383.* Pioneer log houses of Anglo Louisiana incompletely fit some of the more common theories used to explain Southern folk houses. Slight modifications of some of these theories can be reconciled with observed houses if we radically change the conception of the type from an imposed model to an instance of man's public life. This reformulation of the ontogenic status of the house, checked against comparisons of several hundred houses, allows us to find the place of the Louisiana log houses.                                    J

1309. Nolen, Laura Bryant. COURTHOUSES OF GRAYSON COUNTY. *Virginia Cavalcade 1976 25(4): 158-163.* Discusses the construction and architecture of courthouses in Grayson County, Virginia, 1792-1909, emphasizing the role of the Virginia state government.

1310. Norton, Paul F. THE ARCHITECT OF CALVERTON. *Maryland Hist. Mag. 1981 76(2): 113-123.* The country mansion and estate called Calverton near Baltimore, created by wealthy merchant Dennis A. Smith after his purchase in 1815, became the County Alms House and then the "Hebrew Orphan Asylum," until its complete destruction by fire early in the 1870's. Credit was long given to Robert Cary Long, Sr., as the original architect, but thorough study of existing evidence shows that Long was only "the builder and modifier," who used the plans of Joseph Jacques Ramée for both the landscape and the mansion. Ramée returned to Europe shortly after 1816, and Baltimore mapmakers and chroniclers associated only Long's name with the project by the 1820's. Based on correspondence and secondary works; 19 notes.
                                                      G. J. Bobango

1311. O'Loughlin, John and Munski, Douglas C. HOUSING REHABILITATION IN THE INNER CITY: A COMPARISON OF TWO NEIGHBORHOODS IN NEW ORLEANS. *Econ. Geography 1979 55(1): 52-70.* Housing rehabilitation and restoration of historic homes in the Lower Marigny and Algiers Point neighborhoods of New Orleans, 1950-70, was influenced by the attraction of historic buildings and the proximity of urban services.

1312. O'Malley, James R. and Rehder, John B. THE TWO-STORY LOG CABIN IN THE UPLAND SOUTH. *J. of Popular Culture 1978 11(4): 904-915.* Cultural change, architectural development, and spatial needs caused the development of two-story log cabins in the upland South, 18th-20th centuries.

1313. Oppel, Mary Cronan. PARADISE LOST: THE STORY OF CHAUMIÈRE DES PRAIRIES. *Filson Club Hist. Q. 1982 56(2): 201-210.* Describes the construction of the house and gardens of David Meade, located nine miles from Lexington, Kentucky. Meade, a member of the Virginia elite, was forced by financial difficulties to resettle in Kentucky in 1800. The house was built on a modified Georgian plan with a large separate kitchen nearby. The gardens were based on the English tradition. The estate was abandoned soon after Meade's death in 1830. Based on the Webb-Prentiss Papers at the University of Virginia, Charlottesville, Virginia; 29 notes, photo.                               G. B. McKinney

1314. Orr-Cahall, Christina. PALM BEACH: THE PREDICAMENT OF A RESORT. *Hist. Preservation 1978 30(1): 10-15.* The important architectural heritage of Palm Beach, Florida, from the 1920's and the 1960's, which has been preserved over the years "by its wealthy, privacy seeking residents," is now endangered "precisely because of those same residents' laissez-faire isolationist attitudes." There must be community-wide preservation organization and legal action. 5 photos.                                    R. M. Frame III

1315. Oszuscik, Philippe. FRENCH CREOLE HOUSING ON THE GULF COAST: THE EARLY YEARS. *Pioneer Am. Soc. Tr. 1983 6: 49-58.* Discusses the folk house style, French creole housing, found along the Gulf Coast that dates from the late 1600's; this basic creole cottage plan can be traced to Haiti.

1316. Page, Thomas More. LLOYD TILGHMAN AND SHERWOOD MANOR. *Maryland Hist. Mag. 1979 74(2): 152-174.* Traces the family background, education, probable adult activities, and court property settlement (when he died intestate) of Lloyd Tilghman (1749-1811), second son of revolutionary activist Matthew Tilghman (1718-90). Lloyd lived and died in relative obscurity, carefully managing his father's and then his own extensive landholdings in Talbot County, Maryland. His principal historical legacy is his dwelling, Sherwood Manor, still in existence and on the National Register of Historic Places. Concludes with a detailed architectural description and ownership record of Sherwood Manor. Based on contemporary correspondence, census records, tax lists, wills, land records, and court proceedings of Talbot County, Maryland; 2 illus., 114 notes.                                    C. B. Schulz

1317. Pastier, John. AFTER THE ALAMO. *Hist. Preservation 1983 35(3): 40-42, 46-47.* Describes the efforts since the 1920's of preservationists in San Antonio, Texas, to preserve and restore historic buildings.

1318. Patrick, James. THE ARCHITECTURE OF ADOLPHUS HEIMAN.
PART I: CS *Tennessee Hist. Q. 1979 38(2): 167-187.* Adolphus Heiman (1809-62) was a successful architect in Nashville, Tennessee. Working as an architect, stonemason, and delineator, he designed the Baptist Church in 1837, helped plan the ill-fated suspension bridge over the Cumberland, then designed the Adelphi Theater, the Tennessee Hospital for the Insane, the Davidson County Jail, several buildings for the University of Nashville, Hume High School, and three other buildings. Primary sources; 2 illus., photo, 116 notes.
PART II. ROMANTIC CLASSICISM, 1854-1862. *Tennessee Hist. Q. 1979 38(3): 277-295.* Heiman celebrated the flowering southern culture with elegant Grecian, castellated, and Italianate design. Mentions buildings possibly designed by Heiman, who was best known for his design of the Belle Monte in Nashville. 4 illus., 72 notes.                   W. D. Piersen

1319. Patrick, James. ECCLESIOLOGICAL GOTHIC IN THE ANTEBELLUM SOUTH. *Winterthur Portfolio 1980 15(2): 117-138.* An analysis of Ecclesiological Gothic architecture and its acceptance by the Protestant Episcopal Church. Architects Richard Upjohn and Frank Wills were the most prominent designers in the field. Ecclesiological Gothic became controversial when it challenged the Puritan concept that religious architecture led to idolatry. Based on autobiographies, society reports, religious newspapers and other sources; 3 illus., 15 photos, 2 building plans, 76 notes.
                                    N. A. Kuntz

1320. Peebles, Robert H. THE GALVESTON HARBOR CONTROVERSY OF THE GILDED AGE. *Texana 1974 12(1): 74-83.* Focuses on the internal bickering and the engineering problems which had to be solved before Galveston harbor could be converted into a deep-water port. After much controversy in the 1880's, it was agreed that the cost would be so great that the federal government would be needed to underwrite the expense. It was also agreed that Galveston would be the best commercial harbor between the Rio Grande and the Mississippi River. With this settled, in 1890 Congress chose Galveston to receive federal funds for the project. Based on primary and secondary sources; 46 notes.
                                    B. D. Ledbetter

1321. Peterson, Anne E. FRANCES B. JOHNSTON: THE CRUSADER WITH A CAMERA. *Hist. Preservation 1980 32(1): 17-20.* Frances B. Johnston's photographic survey of old buildings in Fred-

ericksburg, Virginia, in 1929 attracted the attention of several illustrious bodies, including the Carnegie Corporation, which in 1933 provided the first of a series of grants. These grants enabled Johnston to document the early architecture of nine southern states. Her 10,000 photos insure the photographic, if not physical, survival of early American architecture. Frances Johnston's straightforward technique, praised by experts in construction, among others, alerted the public to the cause of architectural preservation long before such causes became popular. 5 photos.

1322. Pickens, Buford. MR. JEFFERSON AS REVOLUTIONARY ARCHITECT. *J. of the Soc. of Architectural Historians 1975 34(4): 257-279.* Discusses Thomas Jefferson's architectural designs for buildings in Virginia between 1769 and 1809.

1323. Pond, Neil. TENNESSEE'S TYREE SPRINGS: THE MOST CELEBRATED WATERING PLACE IN THE STATE. *Kentucky Folklore Record 1978 24(3-4): 64-73.* Richard C. Tyree developed Sumner County's first commercial vacation and resort hotel in 1822, and in little more than 10 years it became the most celebrated spa in Tennessee; after destruction in the Civil War, the hotel and spa were rebuilt during the 1880's or 1890's and operated by a Mrs. Cartwright until her death in 1925; the hotel was destroyed by fire in 1940.

1324. Priddy, Benjamin, Jr. OLD CHURCHES OF MEMPHIS. *West Tennessee Hist. Soc. Papers 1975 29: 130-161.* Discusses three antebellum and seven postbellum churches in Memphis which reflect 19th-century church architecture. No church structures erected before 1840 survive. In 1844 the first permanent church was erected of brick—a representation of the earliest effort of Memphis congregations to create permanent religious housing. Based on primary and secondary sources; 9 photos, 92 notes.
                                    H. M. Parker, Jr.

1325. Rasmussen, William M. S. DESIGNERS, BUILDERS, AND ARCHITECTURAL TRADITIONS IN COLONIAL VIRGINIA. *Virginia Mag. of Hist. and Biog. 1982 90(2): 198-212.* Few men in 18th-century Virginia were trained as architects. Many landowners designed their own homes and outbuildings, often with the help of popular how-to articles and books on structure and proportion. Designs were similar to those found in England, but they were modified to suit the conditions of Virginia plantation life. The buildings often were constructed by indentured servants, craftsmen imported from England to perform the work. Various contractual arrangements were devised to provide payment to the workers and their supervisors, and to insure against destruction of partially completed buildings. 68 notes.                   D. J. Cimbala

1326. Rasmussen, William M. S. SABINE HALL, A CLASSICAL VILLA IN VIRGINIA. *J. of the Soc. of Architectural Hist. 1980 39(4): 286-296.* Attempts to establish and analyze the several building campaigns that went into Sabine Hall, an early Georgian mansion in Virginia, and so to recover the appearance of the house in the early 18th century. 21 fig., 41 notes.                   R. J. Jirran

1327. Reece, Ray. GALVESTON. *Am. Preservation 1977 1(1): 42-55.* Galveston, Texas, a prosperous seaport during 1840-1900, is a city of distinguished and opulent Victorian architecture. One of its notable neighborhoods is the East End which was allowed to deteriorate during 1910-60. Since 1960, the East End has been a focus of concern for preservationists. The Galveston Historical Foundation succeeded in establishing the East End Historical District in 1972. Led by a citizen's governing panel, the East End Historical District Board, residents are restoring homes and a new spirit of community pride is evident. With rising prices and fashionability, have come disputes over aesthetics, increased density, new construction, and the displacement of low-income residents which the Board is working to resolve. 14 photos.                   S. C. Strom

1328. Reed, Helen Scott Townsend. AGECROFT HALL, RICHMOND, VIRGINIA. *Mag. Antiques 1983 123(2): 392-398.* Recounts the history of Agecroft Hall, an Elizabethan manor moved to Richmond, Virginia, in 1926 that was filled with period furnishings providing a unique example of 16th- and 17th-century English domestic architecture and lifestyle.

1329. Reiter, Beth Lattimore and Adler, Leopold, II. RESTORATION OF SAVANNAH'S VICTORIAN DISTRICT. *Georgia Hist. Q. 1979 63(1): 164-172.* The Savannah Landmark Rehabilitation Project, Inc. was formed in 1974 to rehabilitate the Victorian District of Savannah, not only to preserve the architecture, but also to improve living conditions for the inhabitants. The history of the area and the progress of this project are described. Primary and secondary sources; 3 illus., 19 notes.                    G. R. Schroeder

1330. Reynolds, Ann Vines. NASHVILLE'S CUSTOM HOUSE. *Tennessee Hist. Q. 1978 37(3): 263-277.* Describes the acquisition of the land, the erection of the Pointed Gothic stone structure, the later additions to the edifice, and the many government agencies which occupied the Nashville Custom House, the cornerstone of which was laid by President Rutherford B. Hayes on 19 September 1877. In 1972 the structure was listed in the National Register of Historic Places, and in 1976 it was declared surplus property and given to the city of Nashville. It has now been restored to its original condition, both interior and exterior. Government sources and secondary works; 2 photos, 39 notes.            H. M. Parker, Jr.

1331. Reynolds, Kris. MAJOR SKINNER AND THE SKINNER HOUSE. *Richmond County Hist. 1978 10(1): 5-13.* Provides a fragmentary biography of William Skinner, 1767-1820, and a history of the house standing on the family land, 1773-1966, located in Augusta, Georgia.

1332. Rhangos, Audrey Dunn. HISTORIC SAVANNAH FOUNDATION. *Georgia Hist. Q. 1979 63(1): 173-179.* Describes the activities of the Historic Savannah Foundation (formed 1955) to interest and educate citizens of Savannah, Georgia in preserving their architectural heritage. Many successes are reported and Savannah has become a national example for its preservation programs. 3 illus.                    G. R. Schroeder

1333. Rhoads, William B. FRANKLIN D. ROOSEVELT AND THE ARCHITECTURE OF WARM SPRINGS. *Georgia Hist. Q. 1983 67(1): 70-87.* Discusses the participation of Franklin D. Roosevelt in the design of his home and the buildings of the Georgia Warm Springs Foundation in Warm Springs, Georgia, during the late 1920's. Architect Henry J. Toombs worked closely with Roosevelt throughout the period of construction. Based on correspondence and other primary and secondary sources; 3 photos, 5 fig., 46 notes.                    G. R. Schroeder

1334. Ricci, James M. THE BUNGALOW: A HISTORY OF THE MOST PREDOMINANT STYLE OF TAMPA BAY. *Tampa Bay Hist. 1979 1(2): 6-13.* Discusses the evolution and inherent philosophy of bungalow architecture, 1840's-1930, and the role it played in the development of Tampa Bay from 1910 to 1930.

1335. Ristow, Walter W. ROBERT MILL'S ATLAS OF SOUTH CAROLINA. *Q. J. of the Lib. of Congress 1977 34(1): 52-66.* Robert Mills designed private and public buildings, including the Washington Monument, in Philadelphia, Baltimore, and the District of Columbia. Some remain as monuments to his architectural genius. He served in the War of 1812 and became a major in the US Corps of Topographical Engineers before becoming a civil and military engineer for South Carolina. His 1825 *Atlas of South Carolina* was the first atlas of a separate state. Mills' "dedicated and self-sacrificing personal effort" to complete the compilation and publication of the atlas gave impetus to local and regional cartography in the early 19th century. Illus., 25 notes.        E. P. Stickney

1336. Robinson, Willard B. COLONIAL RANCH ARCHITECTURE IN THE SPANISH-MEXICAN TRADITION. *Southwestern Hist. Q. 1979 83(2): 123-150.* The architecture of ranches in the Spanish-Mexican Southwest (specifically, southern Texas) illustrates the use of local building materials and the functional need for defense. Ranch headquarters were usually located on high ground near water, fuel, and shade trees. Many houses were primitive as

late as 1900, but the patron usually had at least one great stone house with plaster walls, minimal furniture, and gun loopholes rather than windows. 17 illus., 37 notes.            J. H. Broussard

1337. Robinson, Willard B. HOUSES OF WORSHIP IN NINETEENTH-CENTURY TEXAS. *Southwestern Hist. Q. 1982 85(3): 235-298.* In Texas, the values, customs, and characteristics of 19th-century society are reflected in church and chapel architecture. That architecture ranges from the simplicity of the fundamentalist sects' clapboard structures to the ornate Gothic revival of the liturgical faiths, and from the influence of Northern Europe to the Near East. The design and location of the churches also reflects the role of the church in the community, and church architecture provides a visual history that can be read as profitably as any document for knowledge about the US past. 72 notes; 51 photos.                    R. D. Hurt

1338. Robinson, Willard B. TEMPLES OF KNOWLEDGE: HISTORIC MAINS OF TEXAS COLLEGES AND UNIVERSITIES. *Southwestern Hist. Q. 1974 77(4): 445-480.* Examines the establishment of colleges and universities in Texas, especially the architectural features of their original buildings, called "old mains" or "temples of knowledge." Although they expressed the cultural values of their builders, the college mains lost prestige with the next generations. Further along, frequently, there is renewed appreciation for the earlier structural styles. 26 illus., 51 notes.                    D. L. Smith

1339. Roper, James E. PADDY MEAGHER, TOM HULING AND THE BELL TAVERN. *West Tennessee Hist. Soc. Papers 1977 31: 5-32.* Reassesses the roles of Paddy Meagher, the most colorful citizen of early Memphis, Tennessee, his son-in-law Tom Huling, and the Bell Tavern which Meagher operated for a short time. The article reconstructs the life of Meagher, traces the history of the Bell Tavern until it was torn down in 1918, and examines the various land transactions connected with Meagher. Based on the Thomas B. Huling Papers in the University of Texas Archives and the Shelby County, Tennessee, Register of Warranty Deeds; picture, 132 notes.                    H. M. Parker, Jr.

1340. Roper, James H. EUTAW. *Am. Preservation 1979 2(6): 49-59.* Describes the restoration of the Kirkwood house, an example of Greek Revival architecture in Eutaw, Alabama; 1972-79.

1341. Roper, James H. NATCHITOCHES: WHERE A STRONG PRESERVATION ORDINANCE PROTECTS VALUABLE BUILDINGS. *Am. Preservation 1980 3(4): 49-57.* Briefly traces efforts to preserve historical buildings in Natchitoches, Louisiana, the oldest permanent settlement (1714) in the Louisiana Purchase, to 1945 when the Lemee House, built in the 1830's, was saved and restored, to the creation of the Natchitoches Historic District in the early 1970's, and particularly the recent preservation ordinance which prohibits demolitions in the city's historic district.

1342. Ruffin, Thomas F. THE BRIDGE THAT LINKED NORTH LOUISIANA. *North Louisiana Hist. Assoc. J. 1973 4(3): 84-89.* "Nine bridges have been built across the Red River to connect Caddo and Bossier Parishes" and "one more is in the planning stage . . . but the most venerable is the old Vicksburg, Shreveport, and Pacific (now Illinois Central) Railroad Bridge—the bridge that completed the last link in rail service across North Louisiana." Discusses the importance of such a bridge, steps to have the bridge built, and construction of the bridge. Mentions the rules adopted for the bridge's use, the duties of the toll collectors, the flood of 1892 which destroyed the bridge's eastern span, and other events until the dismantling of the bridge in 1968. Originally in the *Shreveport Magazine*, Volume 26, November 1971. 33 notes.                    A. N. Garland

1343. Rumore, Samuel A., Jr. NOTEWORTHY BIRMINGHAM FIRES. *Alabama Rev. 1978 31(1): 65-71.* Provides brief accounts of historic fires in Birmingham: Caldwell House hotel, 1894; City Hall, 1925 and 1944; Loveman's department store, 1934. Primary and secondary sources; 4 notes.            J. F. Vivian

1344. Salmon, Myrene. L'ENFANT AND THE PLANNING OF WASHINGTON, D.C. *Hist. Today [Great Britain] 1976 26(11): 699-706.* Examines the role which Pierre Charles L'Enfant played in the design and layout of Washington, D.C., 1796-1825.

1345. Schuetz, Mardith. PROFESSIONAL ARTISANS IN THE HISPANIC SOUTHWEST: THE CHURCHES OF SAN ANTONIO, TEXAS. *Americas (Acad. of Am. Franciscan Hist.) 1983 40(1): 17-71.* Skilled masons and other craftsmen were brought from Mexico and Europe to build mission churches in the San Antonio area. Some craftsmen were eventually trained in Texas, as well. San José Mission features a particularly outstanding baroque church, but other churches also display a high degree of professional workmanship. Based on documents in ecclesiastical and local archives; table, 32 fig., 48 notes.          D. Bushnell

1346. Scott, Gary. HISTORIC CONCRETE PRESERVATION PROBLEMS AT FORT WASHINGTON, MARYLAND. *APT Bull. [Canada] 1978 10(2): 122-131.* Gun batteries at Fort Washington, Maryland, dating from the 1880's are in need of restoration (which includes removal of laitence and sealing of water-caused cracks with some form of flexible epoxy) if they are to remain as historical landmarks.

1347. Seeliger, Edward. ARLINGTON CEMETERY: A HISTORIC LANDMARK OF HOMER, LOUISIANA, 1910-1982. *North Louisiana Hist. Assoc. J. 1982 13(4): 139-141.* Discusses the "new" cemetery in Homer and the dilapidated building currently housing tools which once was probably a cemetery chapel. Interviews with local residents; 2 photos, 7 notes.          J. F. Paul

1348. Segrest, Eileen. INMAN PARK: A CASE STUDY IN NEIGHBORHOOD REVITALIZATION. *Georgia Hist. Q. 1979 63(1): 109-117.* Inman Park, Atlanta's first garden suburb, was planned in the 1880's and many elegant Victorian homes were built there. The area declined until a group of preservationists bought homes there and in 1970 founded Inman Park Restoration, Inc. Projects have included court cases against the highway department, nomination of the area to the National Register of Historic Places, rezoning, and restoration of many homes. Based mainly on interviews; 3 illus., 3 notes, biblio.          G. R. Schroeder

1349. Shashaty, Andre. SWEET VICTORY—AT LAST! *Hist. Preservation 1984 36(1): 46-51.* Highlights the history of preservation efforts in saving the Old Post Office, Washington, D.C.

1350. Sherman, Philip. BALTIMORE'S 104TH MEDICAL REGIMENT ARMORY. *Maryland Hist. Mag. 1975 70(3): 275-278.* The red sandstone structure originally opened in 1858 as the Western Female High School on West Fayette near Paca Street. "One of the most spacious, commodious, and beautiful edifices in the City," the building served as a school until 1896, when turrets and battlements were added and it became a Maryland National Guard Armory. Briefly chronicles the various military units which were quartered in the building, redesignated as the 104th Medical Regiment Armory after World War I. The armory served "many civic, athletic, and veteran organizations as a meeting place and was host to many of Baltimore's most lavish functions, being known locally as "The Baltimore Garden." The 104th continued to use it until 1962, when expansion plans of the University of Maryland caused its demolition. The final military formation in the 104-year-old hall was impressive and emotional. Secondary sources; 8 notes.
          G. J. Bobango

1351. Simpson, Pamela H. THE MOLDED BRICK CORNICE IN THE VALLEY OF VIRGINIA. *APT Bull. [Canada] 1980 12(4): 29-33.* Describes the molded brick cornice used on buildings during the 1790's-1870's in Virginia's Shenandoah Valley and especially in Rockbridge County; a style most likely brought to this country by Scotch, Irish and German immigrants.

1352. Sinwell, Marion Parsons. CHESTNUTWOOD, 1694-1978. *Maryland Hist. Mag. 1980 75(3): 198-202.* The property bought in May 1978 by the Roland Park Country School for its new campus has a long and interesting history. From the original "Fox Hall"

or "Vauxhall" in a 1694 patent for 200 acres on the north side of the Patapsco River in the woods, the site held the famous Evans' Church of the Methodist circuit for some 90 years, and in 1853 began to change hands through a series of owners, which included Jerome Napoleon Bonaparte and his sons. Purchased by Edward H. Bouton, manager of the Roland Park Company in 1892, the main building by 1906 was in the hands of Dr. Alfred R. L. Dohme, Board Chairman of the fledgling Roland Park Country School. The house is little changed in 100 years. Original land records, patents, and wills; 35 notes.          G. J. Bobango

1353. Smathers, Mike. THE SEARCH FOR THE GARDEN. *Southern Exposure 1980 8(1): 57-63.* An in-depth comparison of the 250 homes built between 1934 and 1938 as part of the Cumberland Homesteads, a New Deal resettlement project on Tennessee's Cumberland Plateau, and the contemporary (1970 ff.) development of Fairfield Glade, a private undertaking in the same vicinity. Particularly important is the contrast in the entire sociology related to both projects. The Homesteaders represented a traditional genre of southerners; the Glade residents represent people from the Midwest with urban sympathies. 6 photos, map.
          H. M. Parker, Jr.

1354. Snell, David. "HUBBUB" OF HOUSTON, THE RICE HOTEL, GOES TO THE GREAT CONVENTION IN THE SKY. *Smithsonian 1975 6(4): 48-59.* Offers colorful anecdotes of Jesse Holman Jones and his Rice Hotel, from its use as the Texas capitol in 1837 to its demise in 1974.

1355. Snodgrass, Dena. THE CITY GATE TABLET. *Escribano 1973 10(1): 14-18.* A plaque for the dedication of the City Gate of St. Augustine, Florida.          S

1356. Snow, Nan. COLUMBUS. *Am. Preservation 1981 4(1): 44-58.* Discusses preservationists' efforts in saving historic buildings and areas in Columbus, Georgia, beginning in 1964 when a drive was launched to save the Springer Opera House from being razed; 1820's-1981.

1357. Somerville, Mollie. THE UNITED STATES CAPITOL. *Daughters of the Am. Revolution Mag. 1976 110(6): 893-897, 930.* Discusses the history of the Capitol Building from its design (1792) through its construction, including descriptions of the statuary and frescoes.

1358. Spalding, Phinizy. NEIGHBORHOOD CONSERVATION, OR, GETTING IT ALL TOGETHER IN COBBHAM. *Georgia Hist. Q. 1979 63(1): 90-99.* Cobbham, first suburb of Athens, Georgia, was settled in 1834. Many fine Victorian homes in the area have recently been demolished. In 1972 the Cobb-Hill Street Community Association was formed in protest, succeeded by the Historic Cobbham Foundation in 1977. Actions, successes, and problems of these two groups are described. Based on the files of the Historic Cobbham Foundation; 3 illus., 29 notes.
          G. R. Schroeder

1359. Spalding, Phinizy. THE RELEVANCE OF LOCAL HISTORY: AUGUSTA AND SACRED HEART. *Richmond County Hist. 1979 11(1): 5-10.* The author discusses his interest in local history, particularly in Georgia, and urges the preservation of Sacred Heart Church in Augusta.

1360. Spears, James E. THE WOOLDRIDGE MONUMENTS: "STRANGE PROCESSION WHICH NEVER MOVES." *Kentucky Folklore Record 1976 22(1): 2-10.* A statuary garden depicting the immediate family and favorite domestic animals of Henry C. Wooldridge stands in the cemetery plot in which Wooldridge was buried in 1899 in Mayfield, Kentucky. 6 photos, 18 notes.

1361. Stephenson, Richard W. THE DELINEATION OF A GRAND PLAN. *Q. J. of the Lib. of Congress 1979 36(3): 207-224.* Discusses the story of French émigré Pierre Charles L'Enfant's (1754-1825) proposed plan for the design of the capital of his adopted country. The passage of "An Act for establishing the temporary and permanent seat of the Government of the United

States" 16 July 1790 led to the establishment of a federal territory and its designated location on the Potomac River. L'Enfant expressed his interest in being involved in the design of the new city to President George Washington, and he was later appointed by him as engineer of the undertaking. L'Enfant was later dismissed from responsibility for the design, but the plan that he presented to the President on 28 August 1791, entitled "Plan of the City," is thought to be the manuscript design of the city preserved in the Library of Congress. Based on Digges-L'Enfant-Morgan Papers, records of the Office of Public Buildings and Grounds, correspondence, newspapers, and manuscripts; 3 illus., 3 maps, 75 notes.

M. A. Kascus

1362. Stickann, Richard and Stickann, Catherine. THOMAS USTICK WALTER: ARCHITECT OF THE CAPITOL. *Daughters of the Am. Revolution Mag. 1979 113(5): 506-511.* Thomas Ustick Walter (1804-1887), the fourth professional architect on the Capitol, worked there from 1851 to 1865, when he retired.

1363. Stoner, Paula. EARLY FOLK ARCHITECTURE OF WASHINGTON COUNTY. *Maryland Hist. Mag. 1977 72(4): 512-522.* Examines the adaptation of German, Scotch-Irish, and English building traditions to the environmental materials in Washington County, Maryland, during the latter 18th and early 19th centuries, as seen in houses, arch bridges, farm walls, barns, and gristmills. The abundance of wood and limestone strongly influenced durability and styles, which ranged from log cabins to weatherboarded log houses to formal Georgian-style stone mansions. The number of these buildings still standing testifies to the harmony possible between people and nature. Based on the "Conogochegue Manor" Survey of 1767 and the 1798 Pennsylvania tax lists for nearby Franklin County; 13 illus.

G. J. Bobango

1364. Stuck, Goodloe. HISTORICAL PRESERVATION IN SHREVEPORT: SIX YEARS OF STRUGGLING AND EDUCATING. *North Louisiana Hist. Assoc. J. 1978 9(3): 131-133.* Because Shreveport lacked buildings 'over a hundred years old." it was difficult for the Historic Preservation of Shreveport Committee to persuade the public that there were buildings worth saving. The group thus began the task of educating groups and individuals in Shreveport about the value of historic preservation. The committee has renovated some Victorian houses of the late 19th century. Recounts how the committee established its goals for further preservation in the city. 2 photos.

H. M. Parker, Jr.

1365. Stuck, Goodloe. RESTORING A LOG HOUSE IN DE SOTO PARISH. *North Louisiana Hist. Assoc. J. 1978 9(3): 143-146.* Describes the many difficulties in restoring and preserving a log cabin, from the time the cabin was purchased through its removal and the various stages of preservation. Covers 1960-78. 3 photos.

H. M. Parker, Jr.

1366. Terrell, David. OAKLAND CEMETERY. *Am. Preservation 1979 2(6): 41-48.* Amid urban renewal and modern construction, the Historic Oakland Cemetery, Inc., group of Atlanta, Georgia, seeks to restore and preserve the Oakland Cemetery (begun in 1850), which has representative forms of southern architecture and is one of the few historic landmarks remaining in Atlanta; 1975-79.

1367. Terrell, I. L. COURTHOUSES OF ROCKINGHAM COUNTY. *Virginia Cavalcade 1973 23(2): 42-47.* Describes, using photos, the five courthouses erected on the same site in Harrisonburg.

1368. Thomas, James C. SHAKER ARCHITECTURE IN KENTUCKY. *Filson Club Hist. Q. 1979 53(1): 26-36.* Shaker colonies at Pleasant Hill and South Union, Kentucky, provide an excellent example of that sect's early 19th-century interior and exterior architecture. The buildings were constructed in a style called "Shaker Georgian" that emphasized simplicity and practicality. Based on records at Pleasant Hill and on printed memoirs; 4 photos, 25 notes.

G. B. McKinney

1369. Thomas, Samuel W. AN ENDURING FOLLY: THE JEFFERSON COUNTY COURTHOUSE. *Filson Club Hist. Q. 1981 55(4): 311-343.* Traces the planning, construction, and preservation of the courthouse in Louisville, Kentucky. It was designed in 1835 by Gideon Shryrock in a classical style and was altered and completed by architects Albert Fink and Brinton Davis in 1860. Its most arresting feature is a large rotunda that houses statues of Thomas Jefferson and Henry Clay. Despite modifications required by natural disasters, the integrity of the building has been preserved to the present. Recently, the courthouse has been recognized as one of Louisville's architectural treasures. Based on unpublished city records; 3 photos, 2 illus.

G. B. McKinney

1370. Thompson, Alan S. THE CASPIANA "BIG HOUSE": HISTORY AND RESTORATION. *North Louisiana Hist. Assoc. J. 1978 9(3): 107-114.* Chronicle of the "Big House" of the Caspiana Plantation of the William Joseph Hutchinson family, and a description of the restoration efforts of the Junior League of Shreveport, Louisiana, and the Social Sciences Department of Louisiana State University in Shreveport to prepare it for use in the Pioneer Heritage Program. The house was originally built in 1856. Provides "before" and "after" photographs of the restoration project. Based on Hutchinson family archives, records of the Caspiana Plantation, and secondary newspaper accounts; 5 illus., 15 notes.

H. M. Parker, Jr.

1371. Tippett, Cindy. SPRING LAKE PLANTATION. *North Louisiana Hist. Assoc. J. 1976 7(2): 56-60.* The Spring Lake Plantation was built in the 1860's near Homer, Louisiana by Ambrose Augustus Phillips, who brought his family to north Louisiana from Hogansville, Georgia in 1860. Other owners were the Kerr family, J. B. McFarland, the J. W. Allison family, and J. R. Kennedy. The house burned in 1924. Today, the land belongs to the Wideman-Watson Estate, and "only the tile spring house remains of all the buildings that were on the place." 2 photos, 6 notes.

A. N. Garland

1372. Treadway, Sandra Gioia. POPES CREEK PLANTATION: BIRTHPLACE OF GEORGE WASHINGTON. *Virginia Cavalcade 1982 31(4): 192-205.* History of Popes Creek plantation, 60 miles downriver from Mount Vernon, from 1656-57, when Washington's great-grandfather John Washington settled nearby, until the present, including the reconstruction of the home.

1373. Turman, Nora Miller. *TROMPE L'OEIL* IN ACCOMAC: ST. JAMES EPISCOPAL CHURCH. *Virginia Cavalcade 1974 23(4): 5-9.* Discusses the history and architecture of the St. James Episcopal Church in Accomac, Virginia, 1838-1969.

1374. Turner, Paul Venable. FRANK LLOYD WRIGHT'S OTHER LARKIN BUILDING. *J. of the Soc. of Architectural Hist. 1980 39(4): 304-306.* The First Larkin Company building designed by Frank Lloyd Wright was the Buffalo headquarters; the "other" building was the exhibition pavillion for the 1907 Jamestown Ter-Centennial Exposition at Norfolk, Virginia. Based on *The Official Blue Book of the Jamestown Ter-Centennial Exposition,* published in 1909 at Norfolk; 3 fig., 10 notes.

R. J. Jirran

1375. Turner, Suzanne Louise. PLANTATION PAPERS AS A SOURCE FOR LANDSCAPE DOCUMENTATION AND INTERPRETATION: THE THOMAS BUTLER PAPERS. *APT Bull. [Canada] 1980 12(3): 28-45.* Discusses the documents of a 19th-century Louisiana plantation-owning family, the Thomas Butler Family Collection at Louisiana State University, which describe the landscape of the plantation from 1768 to 1900.

1376. Upshur, Eleanor Walton. EARLY HOUSES OF VIRGINIA'S EASTERN SHORE. *Virginia Cavalcade 1974 23(4): 38-47.* Discusses the construction and architecture of houses on the Eastern Shore of Virginia, 1638-1843.

1377. Upton, Dell. TOWARD A PERFORMANCE THEORY OF VERNACULAR ARCHITECTURE: TIDEWATER VIRGINIA AS A CASE STUDY. *Folklore Forum 1979 12(2-3): 173-196.* Drawing on sociolinguists' models, asserts that, rather than a distillation or diffusion of "higher" forms of architecture, folk architecture is morphologically predictable, represents community standards, and is readily adaptable to change and increasing community complexity and growth; covers 1640's-1850's. One of four articles in this issue on the study of material aspects of American folk culture.

1378. Upton, Dell. VERNACULAR DOMESTIC ARCHITECTURE IN EIGHTEENTH-CENTURY VIRGINIA. *Winterthur Portfolio 1982 17(2-3): 95-119.* Tradition states that vernacular architecture in Virginia was overwhelmed in the 18th century by new and popular concepts. The end result was the eradication of local architectural forms. Recent studies indicate that local builders in Virginia "systematically dismembered" the new concepts and combined them into local patterns. Resulting buildings reflected the close relationships between local and "extralocal" impulses in vernacular design. Based on on-site inspection, architectual plans and journals, and other sources; 25 fig., 43 notes.     N. A. Kuntz

1379. Vlach, John Michael. THE SHOTGUN HOUSE: AN AFRICAN ARCHITECTURAL LEGACY. *Pioneer Am. 1976 8(1): 47-56, (2): 57-70.* Part I. Attempts to unravel previous interpretations of Afro-American material contributions to America, especially that of the shotgun house type, an Afro-American artifact that was adopted by whites and incorporated into popular building practices. Most students of folk architecture have not attempted to seek the origins of this house type. Frequent occurrences of shotgun subtypes in the New Orleans vicinity dating to the mid-1880's suggest that this house type had had time to develop and become standardized. During the first decade of the 19th century many free Negroes came to New Orleans from Haiti. Due to a housing shortage, Negroes who were financially able to do so developed their own architectural environment—the shotgun house type. Based on documents found in the New Orleans Notarial Archives and in the Tulane University Library, Special Collection Division, two unpublished Ph.D. dissertations, and secondary works; illus., 5 photos, 5 figs., 34 notes. Part II. Traces the history of the shotgun house type from West Africa (Nigeria) to Louisiana via Haiti. Fieldwork in Haiti and New Orleans indicates that their shotgun houses are similar not only in type but also in specific detail. These architectural relations are complicated by the occurrence of similar housing constructed by the Arawak Indians, who were indigenous to Haiti. The slave trade, which reached its peak in the 1780's, is responsible for bringing Yoruba-related peoples of West Africa to Haiti. The Yoruba solution to the problem of plantation housing in Haiti reflects a form and philosophy of architecture which resembles a pattern derived from their African antecedents. Based on extensive field work in New Orleans, Haiti, and West Africa, one unpublished Ph.D. dissertation, and secondary works; 2 illus., 5 photos, 14 figs., 17 notes.     C. R. Gunter, Jr.

1380. Vrugt, Ellen van de. WASHINGTON D.C., EEN OPMERKELIJK STEDEBOUWDUNDIG ONTWERP? [Washington, D.C.: a remarkable townplanning design?]. *Spiegel Hist. [Netherlands] 1981 16(3): 152-156.* Discusses the planning and political considerations involved in building a new capital city upon territory of its own. The dominant influence in the planning was Pierre Charles L'Enfant, who adapted the grand architecture of prerevolutionary Europe (Versailles, Schonbrunn, Karlsruhe) to the political principles of the new American republic. In this he was influenced by Nicholson's work on Annapolis. Primary sources; 4 illus.
    C. W. Wood, Jr.

1381. Watson, Thomas D. and Wilson, Samuel, Jr. A LOST LANDMARK REVISITED: THE PANTON HOUSE OF PENSACOLA. *Florida Hist. Q. 1981 60(1): 42-50.* William Panton made his fortune through the Indian trade. He constructed an imposing three-story brick mansion near Pensacola in 1796. A recent archaeological investigation gives some idea of the size of the house and the materials used. Further research and analysis is needed before authentic reconstruction can take place. Based on archaeological studies and other sources; 23 notes, appendix.     N. A. Kuntz

1382. Welles, Edward O., Jr. GEORGE WASHINGTON SLEPT HERE... AND HERE'S HOW IT REALLY LOOKED. *Hist. Preservation 1982 34(3): 22-27.* Describes how scientific analysis was

used to determine colors originally used to paint the interior of George Washington's Mount Vernon in order to restore the interiors; surprisingly, the colors were quite bright.

1383. Wells, Carol. EARLIEST LOG CABINS OF NATCHITOCHES. *North Louisiana Hist. Assoc. J. 1975 6(3): 117-122.* Not until 1795 was a log cabin mentioned in the legal records of Natchitoches, although "judging by American names and English fences, log cabins probably were built about 10 years before their first mention in official records." The log cabins that were built "had already assumed a French character." In effect, "Natchitoches log cabins looked like Natchitoches *bousillage*-panelled framed houses. They were built in the same shape and size, had similar rooflines, galleries, chimneys, probable additions, and interior partition." Includes a table comparing three cabin contracts. 10 notes.
    A. N. Garland

1384. Welsh, Frank S. and Granquist, Charles L. RESTORATION OF THE EXTERIOR SANDED PAINT AT MONTICELLO. *APT Bull. [Canada] 1983 15(2): 2-10.* Describes the restoration of the house's original sanded-paint surfaces.

1385. Wenger, Mark R. THE ARCHITECTURE OF THE GOVERNOR'S PALACE AT WILLIAMSBURG. *Virginia Cavalcade 1981 31(1): 12-19.* The design and construction of the Governor's Palace at Williamsburg, Virginia, 1705-22, was based on the Dutch Palladian style; discusses the building's reconstruction between 1931 and 1934.

1386. Wernick, Robert. THE GREATEST SHOW ON EARTH DIDN'T COMPARE TO HOME. *Smithsonian 1981 12(6): 62-71.* Describes the landmark mansion built for Circus King John Ringling and his wife Mable in the early 1920's on Florida's Sarasota Bay; designed by architect Dwight James Baum, it combined replicas of the facades of the Doge's Palace in Venice and Madison Square Garden in New York City. It was called Ca' d'Zan, Venetian dialect for the house of John, and was occupied by John until his death in 1936.

1387. White, Richard D., Jr. WHEN LIGHTSHIPS WATCHED OVER VIRGINIA WATERS. *Virginia Cavalcade 1980 30(1): 38-47.* Lightships, vessels equipped with warning beacons, served as floating lighthouses and were common in Virginia waters, 1819-1965.

1388. White, Roger B. WHITHER THE URBAN HISTORY EXHIBIT? THE PEALE MUSEUM'S "ROWHOUSE." *Technology and Culture 1983 24(1): 76-90.* "A welcome addition to the new wave of urban history exhibits," Rowhouse, opened in 1981, treats four phases in the history of the average Baltimorean's habitat: The Booming Port, 1800-1860; Streets, Alleys and Workingmen, 1850-1900; Beauty and Bathrooms for Everyone, 1890-1915; and Daylight Suburbs, 1915-1955. 3 illus.     C. O. Smith

1389. Whitwell, W. L. SAINT ANDREW'S ROMAN CATHOLIC CHURCH: ROANOKE'S HIGH VICTORIAN GOTHIC LANDMARK. *Virginia Cavalcade 1975 24(3): 124-133.* History and architectural description of Saint Andrew's Church in Roanoke, Virginia.

1390. Williams, Douglas, Jr. BRESTON PLANTATION HOUSE. *North Louisiana Hist. Assoc. J. 1979 10(4): 122-128.* It is not certain when the Breston Plantation House, on the east bank of the Ouachita River near Columbia, Louisiana, was built, though guesses range from 1790 to 1838. Acquisition and ownership of the property by the family of Jean Bres is discussed, as is the family's loss of the property in 1866. 2 illus., 15 notes.     J. F. Paul

1391. Wilson, Samuel, Jr. PIETRO CARDELLI, SCULPTOR OF THE CABILDO'S EAGLE. *Louisiana Hist. 1981 21(4): 399-405.* Discusses the steps taken and money paid to place the coat of arms of New Orleans on the Cabildo in Jackson Square. Since the building had Spanish "armorial bearings," the city wanted them replaced with the city's. In 1821, Pietro Cardelli contracted for the sculptural work and completed the work in that year. Based on newspapers of the time and records of the City Council of New Orleans; 23 notes.                                                              R. H. Tomlinson

1392. Wilson, Samuel, Jr. RELIGIOUS ARCHITECTURE IN FRENCH COLONIAL LOUISIANA. *Winterthur Portfolio 1973 (8): 63-106.* The original intent of French colonization in Louisiana was religious. That intention, however, was subordinated to France's military and political objectives. The building of religious structures was relegated to state officials and carried out by military engineers. Church construction was therefore subordinated to more worldly needs. Early missionaries were left to their own devices as the first churches were constructed inside forts. Early designs for New Orleans were attempts to translate the concepts of Sebastien Le Prestre, Marechal de Vauban (1633-1707), to New World conditions. Concepts of French architecture influenced Spanish design long after Spain took control of the territory. Based on primary and secondary sources; 39 illus., 122 notes.                N. A. Kuntz

1393. Witsell, Charles, Jr. WAVERLEY. *Am. Preservation 1978 1(2): 64-72.* Waverly, a classic Greek Revival plantation house near West Point, Mississippi, was completed in 1852 by George Hamilton Young. The house was abandoned during 1913-62, when it was purchased by Mr. and Mrs. Robert Snow. The house has been painstakingly restored. Its most notable feature is an octagonal central hall extending 52 feet upward to a large cupola. Original brass, lighting fixtures, brass window cornices, "marblized" woodwork, and Venetian glass sidelights and transom around the front door all survived to make this one of the most interesting and least-publicized major homes in the country. 10 photos.
                                                             S. C. Strom

1394. Wood, Adriane. THE MACON HERITAGE FOUNDATION. *Georgia Hist. Q. 1979 63(1): 152-155.* The Macon Heritage Foundation was formed in 1975 to prevent the destruction of historically and architecturally important buildings in Macon, Georgia. Goals and activities of the foundation are discussed.
                                                         G. R. Schroeder

1395. Woods, H. Merle. HISTORICAL PRESERVATION WHICH OCCURRED IN EL RENO AND ST. LOUIS 75 YEARS AGO. *Chronicles of Oklahoma 1979-80 57(4): 446-450.* During the World's Fair, or Louisiana Purchase Exposition (St. Louis, 1904), officials from Oklahoma Territory constructed an elaborate two-story stucco building to display Oklahoma's agricultural, mineral, and industrial products. To save the building from destruction at the end of the Fair, the Elks Lodge in El Reno, Oklahoma, paid for its removal to their home town. The structure was rebuilt at El Reno and became the social center of the city. 2 photos.
                                                             M. L. Tate

1396. Woodward, Anne. 1785: A LANDMARK FOR THE NATIONAL TRUST. *Hist. Preservation 1979 31(3): 2-7.* The National Trust for Historic Preservation has moved into and restored a former luxury apartment built in the Beaux-arts style in 1906-07 at 1785 Massachusetts Avenue in Washington, D.C.; mentions tenants of the building and details its restoration.

1397. Yetter, George Humphrey. STANFORD WHITE AT THE UNIVERSITY OF VIRGINIA: SOME NEW LIGHT ON AN OLD QUESTION. *J. of the Soc. of Architectural Hist. 1981 40(1): 320-325.* The rector, W. C. N. Randolph, not White, was chiefly responsible for fouling Jefferson's original plan. White has been unduly berated. Based on a newly discovered letter from W. C. N. Randolph to White in the Manuscripts Department of the University of Virginia Library.                                    R. J. Jirran

1398. Yorke, Douglas A., Jr. KENTUCKY FRIED DESIGN. *Southern Exposure 1980 8(1): 70-73.* Increasingly ubiquitous in the South franchise architecture spreads its blandness freely, creating environments oblivious to local traditions and regional flavors. But now the national franchises are acknowledging local and regional characteristics in their architecture. Often fast food merchandisers are required to make structural adaptations reflecting local and regional characteristics before moving into an area. The three major

elements of classical architecture (base, column and capital) are compared to the modern architecture of the fast food industry. 11 photos.                                                        H. M. Parker, Jr.

1399. Zimmer, Edward F. and Scott, Pamela J. ALEXANDER PARRIS, B. HENRY LATROBE, AND THE JOHN WICKHAM HOUSE IN RICHMOND, VIRGINIA. *J. of the Soc. of Architectural Hist. 1982 41(3): 202-211.* The Wickham House, built during 1811-12 by Alexander Parris, revealed the influence of B. Henry Latrobe and was a clear forerunner of the Boston Sears House, 1819-21; Saint Paul's Church, 1819; and Faneuil Hall Market, 1824. 17 fig., 33 notes.                                            R. J. Jirran

1400. —. BEFORE THE WATERS COME: PHOTOGRAPHS BY DENNIS O'KAIN. *Georgia Rev. 1981 35(2): 319-336.* A portfolio of 16 of the 250 photographs by Dennis O'Kain of sites constructed from 1793 to 1927 that are subject to flooding by the construction of the Richard B. Russell Dam on the Savannah River. The photographs are part of a Historic American Building Survey (HABS) project analyzing and recording approximately 571 archaeological and historical sites scheduled for relocation or flooding.
                                                         P. D. Hinnebusch

1401. —. [DESIGN IN THE GULF AREA].
Wilson, Samuel, Jr. ARCHITECTURE IN EIGHTEENTH-CENTURY WEST FLORIDA. Proctor, Samuel, ed. *Eighteenth-Cent. Florida and Its Borderlands* (Gainesville: U. of Florida, 1975): pp. 102-139. A review of 18th-century architecture in West Florida. Few buildings of the period remain; plans and specifications for some others are extant. The early French and Spanish settlers essentially used wood construction. An early Spanish fort became a model for most later efforts. As colonization took hold in earnest, a number of brick buildings appeared. Wood remained the primary construction medium for private homes, which were usually elevated to provide protection against the elements. Disastrous fires caused new regulations designed to discourage all-wood construction. 21 photos, 53 notes.

Poesch, Jessie J. COLONIAL PAINTING AND FURNITURE IN A FLORIDA BORDERLAND. Proctor, Samuel, ed. *Eighteenth-Cent. Florida and Its Borderlands* (Gainesville: U. of Florida, 1975): pp. 140-153. Reviews colonial painting and furniture in West Florida. Furniture remains are few and none are absolutely authenticated. Overall, a French influence predominates, but little else can be said with certainty. Slender evidence suggests the presence of cabinetmakers, but the extant pieces may have been manufactured elsewhere. The few existing paintings are at least generally authenticated. Benjamin Henry Latrobe was an early watercolorist. Joseph Salazar de Mendoza was the most important artist. Edmund Brewster was a later artist. The finer arts did survive in the hostile and sparsely-settled land, but natural disasters and changes of regimes have caused few of their products to survive. 7 photos, 21 notes.

vanRavenswaay, Charles. COMMENTARY. Proctor, Samuel, ed. *Eighteenth-Cent. Florida and Its Borderlands* (Gainesville: U. of Florida, 1975): pp. 154-157. "As both Mr. Wilson and Dr. Poesch have suggested, the history of design in the Gulf area must be studied in relation to its political and social history as well as to the construction and making of furniture in other parts of the Spanish and French colonies in North America."
                                                          V. L. Human/S

1402. —. METICULOUS MR. MEIGS. *Am. Hist. Illus. 1980 15(7): 34-37.* Discusses Montgomery Cunningham Meigs's participation in the construction of the Capitol building dome in Washington, D.C., as supervisor of public works, beginning in 1853, and reprints a letter to Congressman J. Glancy Jones of Reading, Pennsylvania, describing the construction and strength of the dome in 1858.

1403. —. NEW ORLEANS. *Am. Preservation 1978 1(3): 51-56.* The Coliseum Square Association was responsible for saving the historically valuable Lower Garden district of New Orleans, Louisi-

ana, from demolition to allow a new bridge. The group's most significant contribution was establishment of the New Orleans Historic District Landmarks Committee in the face of city indifference. Illus.
J. Tull

1404. —. POLITICS LINKED TO HISTORY. *Am. Preservation 1978 1(3): 36-44.* Thomasville, Georgia, flourished as a winter health resort during 1870-1900's and still attracts distinguished visitors. President William McKinley (1843-1901) spent time there as did Dwight D. Eisenhower (1890-1969) after his heart attack in 1956. There are many Victorian homes being restored by Thomasville Landmarks, Inc., in an ambitious project. Illus.     J. Tull

1405. —. TEXAS WINDOWS: THE RESTORATION AT HENKEL SQUARE. *Early Am. Life 1984 15(1): 24-31.* Illustrates log cabins preserved at Henkel Square in Round Top, Texas; prints excerpts from letters of German immigrants who settled the community.

## Popular Culture, Folk Art, and the Media

1406. Abrams, W. Amos. BRINGING IN THE SHEAVES. *Appalachian J. 1977 4(4): 169-185.* Presents the text and background history of a collection of previously unpublished Appalachian folk songs collected and written down in the late 19th century.

1407. Abrams, W. Amos. DELLA ADAMS BOSTIC: SWEET SINGER OF OLD SONGS. *North Carolina Folklore J. 1973 21(3): 132-146.* Tells of the discovery in 1937 of a bound manuscript of 22 folksongs, originally owned by Moses Adams in the early 19th century, and the recording in 1938 of tunes sung by Mrs. Della Adams Bostic (1866-1962), a descendant of Moses Adams. Reprints the lyrics of seven folksongs.     R. N. Lokken

1408. Abrams, W. Amos. PURE COINCIDENCE—IF NOT, WHY NOT? *North Carolina Folklore J. 1973 21(4): 177-180.* Tells of another version of the "Sweet Sally" ballad found in a Lunenburg County (Virginia) manuscript dated 1825, contemporaneous with the "Sweet Sally" ballad in the Adams Manuscript collection of handwritten songs which the author discussed in the September 1973 *North Carolina Folklore Journal* (see abstract 11A:2969). The article contains the entire Lunenburg County version of the ballad.
R. N. Lokken

1409. Adamson, June. FROM BULLETIN TO BROADSIDE: A HISTORY OF BY-AUTHORITY JOURNALISM IN OAK RIDGE, TENNESSEE. *Tennessee Hist. Q. 1979 38(4): 479-493.* The Oak Ridge *Journal* was developed under the authority of the Army Corps of Engineers to serve the atomic energy project at Oak Ridge, Tennessee. Because the project was top secret, the paper carried mainly news of stores, public health clinics, churches, and innocuous local events. Covers 1943-49. Based on personal interviews, letters, and the *Journal;* 31 notes.     W. D. Piersen

1410. Agee, Hugh. GHOST LORE FROM SEVIER COUNTY, TENNESSEE. *Tennessee Folklore Soc. Bull. 1973 39(1): 8-10.* Ruth Maples Whaley, a native of Sevierville, Tennessee, who now resides in Nakina, North Carolina, related several accounts of ghosts and the appearance of mysterious lights. Based on an interview with Mrs. Whaley.     L. Russell

1411. Alexander, Robert L. NEOCLASSICAL WROUGHT IRON IN BALTIMORE. *Winterthur Portfolio 1983 18(2-3): 147-186.* Wrought iron in the 19th century reveals interrelations of style, technique, and economics. The role of the blacksmith aided in the art form's particularization. The wrought iron work preserved in pictures defines the neoclassicism of Baltimore. Mass production and the social changes of the 1850's eliminated the independent craftsmen. Based on primary and secondary sources; 58 fig., 53 notes, appendix.     N. A. Kuntz

1412. Allain, Mathé and Ancelet, Barry Jean. FEU DE SAVANE: A LITERARY RENAISSANCE IN FRENCH LOUISIANA. *Southern Exposure 1981 9(2): 4-10.* Describes the revival of Cajun folk music since 1948 and, following the state legislature's 1968 declaration of Louisiana as a bilingual state, the general rebirth of French language and literature.

1413. Allen, Margaret Sheffield. PETROLEUM: THE DEVIL'S FUEL. *Kentucky Folklore Record 1976 22(2): 33-38.* Discusses folklore surrounding oil and the first drilling of oil in Kentucky, 1829; draws conclusions between evil and the devil and oil in folklore.

1414. Allen, Ruby. MOONSHINING AS A FINE ART ON A KENTUCKY CREEK. *Kentucky Folklore Record 1975 21(2): 34-40.* Describes creekside locations of moonshining stills, with methods and recipes for various forms of liquor.     S

1415. Alsobrook, David E. MOBILE'S FORGOTTEN PROGRESSIVE: A. N. JOHNSON, EDITOR AND ENTREPRENEUR. *Alabama Rev. 1979 32(3): 188-202.* Andrew N. Johnson (1865-1922) was a reform-minded black businessman, newspaper editor, and civic leader in Mobile (Alabama) and Nashville (Tennessee). An active Republican, he opposed Alabama's lily-white faction, unsuccessfully tried to persuade President Theodore Roosevelt to remove Jim Crow proponents from patronage positions, and supported the National Negro Business League. Primary and secondary sources; 51 notes.     J. F. Vivian

1416. Alvey, R. Gerard. THE STORY WOMAN. *Kentucky Folklore Record 1977 23(3-4): 66-71.* Henrietta Ellery Child, though originally from Boston, moved to the Appalachian Mountains in Kentucky and spent the majority of her life, (1912-68) teaching at Berea College and in the small backwoods schools where she gained her reputation in storytelling.

1417. Anderson-Green, Paula Hathaway. "THE LORD'S WORK": SOUTHERN FOLK BELIEF IN SIGNS, WARNINGS, AND DREAM-VISIONS. *Tennessee Folklore Soc. Bull. 1977 43(3): 113-127.* Examines Biblical roots for the belief in premonitions and visions, and the folklore surrounding such occurrences in the South, 20th century.

1418. Andrews, Nathalie and Larson, Eric. CHILD OF THE LORD: INTERVIEW WITH BILL LIVERS. *Southern Exposure 1978 6(1): 14-19.* A lifelong tenant farmer in Owens County, Kentucky, Livers achieved local prominence as a musician-fiddler and renowned storyteller. His reminiscences include obtaining groundhogs as food, how to prepare groundhog meat, his mother and her work as a domestic servant, his involvement in music, experiences driving an automobile in the 1920's, and involvement in bootlegging.     N. Lederer

1419. Ansley, Fran; Bell, Brenda; and Reece, Florence. "LITTLE DAVID BLUES"/AN INTERVIEW WITH TOM LOWRY. *Southern Exposure 1974 1(3/4): 137-143.* The folk song "Little David Blues" was written by coal miner Tom Lowry during the 1932 Davidson-Wilder strike in Tennessee. The song tells of the miners' poor working and living conditions. Lowry relates how he came to compose the song. Based on oral interview; 4 illus.
G. A. Bolton

1420. Anthony, Allen. PLEASANT GROVE SCHOOL: A REFLECTION OF EARLY RURAL KENTUCKY FOLK CULTURE. *Kentucky Folklore Record 1983 29(1-2): 1-14.* Basic curricula and simple disciplinary measures changed little in the small, rural Kentucky elementary school during 1840-1949.

1421. Asbury, Eslie. KENTUCKY WIT AND HUMOR. *Filson Club Hist. Q. 1981 55(1): 27-39.* There is no professional analysis of Kentucky wit and humor, but the author includes a sample of several styles of Kentucky tall stories, newspaper commentary, and insults.     G. B. McKinney

1422. Ashby, Rickie Zayne. THE POSSUM HUNTERS IN THE ORAL TRADITION. *Kentucky Folklore Record 1975 21(2): 56-61.* Presents two folksongs and one poem about a vigilante group, the Possum Hunters, in Ohio County, Kentucky.                                    S

1423. Auman, Dorothy Cole and Zug, Charles G., III. NINE GENERATIONS OF POTTERS: THE COLE FAMILY. *Southern Exposure 1977 5(2-3): 166-174.* The Cole family has been involved in pottery manufacture in North Carolina for 200 years. The family's pottery making tradition has been traced back to 18th-century England, and some family members may have made pottery during the early 17th century in Jamestown. For most of the 19th and early 20th centuries, the Coles manufactured simply designed, utilitarian pottery for local and regional use and sale. During the 1920's-30's, a greater variety of designs was introduced along with pottery aimed at tourism, garden use, and artistic forms. Despite some modern innovations, pottery making still retains many ties to traditional modes of manufacture. Based on participant observation.

N. Lederer

1424. Ball, Donald B. NOTES ON THE SLANG AND FOLK SPEECH OF KNOXVILLE, KNOX COUNTY, TENNESSEE. *Tennessee Folklore Soc. Bull. 1978 44(3): 134-142.* Using 15 informants, aged 30-80, compiles an alphabetical listing of slang and folk speech common to Knoxville, Tennessee, 1974-75.

1425. Ball, Donald B. SOCIAL ACTIVITIES ASSOCIATED WITH TWO CEMETERIES IN COFFEE COUNTY, TENNESSEE. *Tennessee Folklore Soc. Bull. 1975 41(3): 93-98.* Discusses family gatherings held at local cemeteries as "folkgatherings," usually celebrated on Decoration Day to commemorate the family's dead relations.

1426. Bargainnier, Earl F. TIN PAN ALLEY AND DIXIE: THE SOUTH IN POPULAR SONG. *Mississippi Q. 1977 30(4): 527-564.* Examines images of the South as portrayed in popular music, 1890's-1950's; includes a bibliography of songs written during the period.

1427. Barnett, C. Robert. RECREATIONAL PATTERNS OF THE COLONIAL VIRGINIA ARISTOCRAT. *J. of the West Virginia Hist. Assoc. 1978 2(1): 1-10.* Recreational activities in Virginia, 1640's-1775, restricted by the plantation economy, were spurred by the desire to emulate English country gentlemen, and largely were centered around gambling, billiards, cards, bowling, cockfighting, and horse racing.

1428. Baxley, Bennett. EARLY ARTISANS, THE GORDONS OF BLACK MINGO. *South Carolina Hist. Mag. 1980 81(2): 122-130.* Describes the furniture pieces and crafts of metal, wood, horn, leather, and ivory made by brothers James (1815-65) and David (1816-75) Gordon of Black Mingo, South Carolina, whose work was quite refined considering that the period art is characteristically crude and uncreative; also gives a brief ancestral background of the brothers dating to 1757.

1429. Berryman, Jack W. JOHN S. SKINNER'S *AMERICAN FARMER:* BREEDING AND RACING THE MARYLAND "BLOOD HORSE," 1819-1929. *Maryland Hist. Mag. 1981 76(2): 159-173.* Few men did more to establish the "Sport of Kings" in Maryland and America than did John Stuart Skinner, editor, agriculturist, breeder, and publisher of the famous Baltimore-based *American Farmer.* Skinner and his magazine were instrumental in encouraging the systematic breeding of thoroughbred horses and the subsequent formalized recording system for their pedigrees. Moreover, his constant support for horse racing as the only true test of fine breeding served to promote and disseminate the sport throughout the eastern United States. The "stock farm" that he started with Robert Oliver and Major Isaac McKim in 1821 was "the first American attempt to improve domestic animals on a settled and permanent plan." Based on the *American Farmer* and secondary literature; 89 notes.                       G. J. Bobango

1430. Bezou, James F. HISTORIQUE DU JOURNALISME D'EXPRESSION FRANCAISE EN LOUISIANE [History of French-language journalism in Louisiana]. *Rev. de Louisiane 1977 6(1): 39-44.* Discusses the first French-language newspapers in Louisiana, including their popularity, growth, readership, publishers, and editors, 1794-1860.

1431. Birdwhistell, Terry L. WHAS RADIO AND THE DEVELOPMENT OF BROADCASTING IN KENTUCKY, 1922-1942. *Register of the Kentucky Hist. Soc. 1981 79(4): 333-353.* Kentucky's first radio station, WHAS, went on the air from Louisville in July of 1922. Underwritten financially by newspapers, the station was not seen as a means of making money. Soon, however, the lure of commercials would be too strong to resist. In 1926, the station affiliated with NBC, but switched to CBS in 1932. In 1929, educational programming began. With 50,000 watts of transmission power after 1933, the station became known widely. Its impact on the state and region was large, although its educational efforts were generally ineffective. Primary and secondary sources, including interviews and information from the WHAS Oral History project; 5 illus., 79 notes.                       J. F. Paul

1432. Blaustein, Richard. "FURTHERING THE FOLK ARTS IN TENNESSEE": REPORT ON A SYMPOSIUM. *Tennessee Folklore Soc. Bull. 1979 45(3): 112-115.* Report of the "Furthering the Folk Arts in Tennessee" symposium held at East Tennessee State University on 2-4 November 1978.

1433. Blaustein, Richard. FURTHERING THE FOLK ARTS IN TENNESSEE: SOME OBSERVATIONS. *Kentucky Folklore Record 1980 26(1-2): 4-7.* Reports on the symposium, Furthering the Folk Arts in Tennessee, sponsored by the Tennessee Folklore Society and East Tennessee State University's Institute for Appalachian Affairs, held 3-4 November 1979. Covers 1934-79.

1434. Blaustein, Richard. THE OLD TIME COUNTRY RADIO REUNION: A DIFFERENT KIND OF FOLK FESTIVAL. *Tennessee Folklore Soc. Bull. 1980 46(4): 105-118.* Discusses the author's participation in the organization of an Old Time Country Radio Reunion in 1979 in Tennessee's oldest town, Jonesboro, as an alternative to the conventional folk festival which is often contradictory and artificial, in a celebration of the history of country music on radio in upper East Tennessee.

1435. Blaustein, Richard. THE SOUR M*A*S*H SYNDROME: A SURVIVOR'S VIEW OF THE FOLKLIFE FESTIVAL AT THE 1982 WORLD'S FAIR. *Tennessee Folklore Soc. Bull. 1983 49(1): 7-11.* Many performers and employees of the Stokely Van Camp Folklife Festival at the World's Fair in Knoxville, Tennessee, managed to cope by joking and teasing.

1436. Blaustein, Richard. TRAVELING WITH CLINT HOWARD: THE ROLE OF OUTSIDERS IN APPALACHIAN STUDIES. *Appalachian J. 1982 9(2-3): 183-187.* Between ca. 1960-81 the author became interested in old-time mountain music; he attended a meeting of the Folk Arts Panel of the Tennessee Arts Commission with old-time musician Clint Howard to discuss maintaining the cultural heritage of the Southern Appalachians, particularly that of Johnson County, Tennessee.

1437. Boswell, George W. and Pullen, Thomas M. MISSISSIPPI FOLK NAMES OF PLANTS. *Kentucky Folklore Record 1976 22(3): 64-69.* Lists folk names, common names, and scientific names for 103 native plants of Mississippi collected by WPA archives workers and Folk Literature students, 1930's-70's.

1438. Boswell, George W. A NOTE ON THE BARRING OF 3/2 TUNES. *Kentucky Folklore Record 1973 19(1): 11-14.*

1439. Boswell, George W. OLE MISS JOKES AND ANECDOTES. *Tennessee Folklore Soc. Bull. 1976 42(2): 72-82.* Discusses types of jokes and anecdotes popular among university students in Mississippi, 1950's-70's, including ethnic "humor', riddles and "sick" jokes.

1440. Boswell, George W. THE OPERATION OF POPULAR ETYMOLOGY IN FOLKSONG DICTION. *Tennessee Folklore Soc. Bull.* 1973 39(2): 37-58. Detailed classification of folk etymology including pronunciation, morphology, and syntax in the texts of the author's Middle Tennessee collection of 859 ballads and songs.
                                                              L. Russell

1441. Boswell, George W. A SONG TO SING: *ROSE MARY AND TIDE. Kentucky Folklore Record* 1973 19(4): 117-118.

1442. Bowers, Thomas A. 'PRECISION JOURNALISM' IN NORTH CAROLINA IN THE 1800'S. *Journalism Q.* 1976 53(4): 738-740. In 1810 the Raleigh *Star*, under the editorship of Thomas Henderson, Jr., and Dr. Calvin Jones, conducted a "survey" to gain information which might help to promote communications between the eastern and western areas of the state, but responses were long in arriving and the results of the survey were never published by the *Star*.

1443. Bowles, Stephen E. *CABARET* AND *NASHVILLE*: THE MUSICAL AS SOCIAL COMMENT. *J. of Popular Culture* 1978 12(3): 550-556. Examines two films, *Cabaret* (1972) and *Nashville* (1975), as historical documents as each reflects the values and cultural milieu of a particular historical period; the former, Berlin during the 1930's, the latter, Nashville, Tennessee, and the country-western music scene during the 1970's.

1444. Bradford, Danelle and Winters, John D. SEVENTY-EIGHT YEARS OF FOOTBALL AT LOUISIANA TECH. *North Louisiana Hist. Assoc. J.* 1980 11(3): 11-22. A history of football at Louisiana Tech University since 1901. Based on yearbooks and newspapers; 19 notes.
                                                              J. F. Paul

1445. Brandmeyer, Gerard A. BASEBALL AND THE AMERICAN DREAM: A CONVERSATION WITH AL LOPEZ. *Tampa Bay Hist.* 1981 3(1): 48-73. Brief introduction followed by an interview with veteran baseball player and manager Al Lopez, originally of Ybor City, Florida, focusing on Lopez's professional baseball career from 1925 to 1969 and his early life as the son of a Spanish-born cigar selector in the cigar industry.

1446. Bulger, Peggy A. DEFINING FOLK ARTS FOR THE WORKING FOLKLORIST. *Kentucky Folklore Record* 1980 26(1-2): 62-66. Describes the author's experience as the coordinator for a folklife/folk arts program for the Division of Cultural Affairs and consultant to the Fine Arts Council of Florida, particularly her difficulty in defining folk arts, concluding that "historic, nostalgic, and entertaining characteristics" are not "definitive to folk arts"; 1976-79.

1447. Bulger, Peggy A. LITTLE HAVANA: FOLK TRADITIONS OF AN IMMIGRANT ENCLAVE. *Kentucky Folklore Record* 1983 29(1-2): 15-23. Social customs such as the Afro-Catholic religion of Santeria, the debutante's Fiesta de Quinze, and voodoo thrive in Miami's "Little Havana," the home of Cuban refugees and, outside Havana, the largest Cuban community.

1448. Burkette, Alice Gaillard. TOMBSTONE INSCRIPTIONS AT WALNUT GROVE PLANTATION CEMETERY. *South Carolina Hist. Mag.* 1976 77(3): 189-193.

1449. Burrison, John A. AFRO-AMERICAN FOLK POTTERY IN THE SOUTH. *Southern Folklore Q.* 1978 42(2-3): 175-199. Focuses on recent research into Afro-American folk pottery and potters in the South, particularly the Afro-American potters concentrated in the Edgefield District of South Carolina, and specifically the slave potter named Dave (1780-1863), the most prominent of the Edgefield District potters; also discusses the Afro-American pottery decorated with applied stylized faces; ca. 1795-1909.

1450. Burrison, John A. ALKALINE-GLAZED STONEWARE: A DEEP-SOUTH POTTERY TRADITION. *Southern Folklore Q.* 1975 39(4): 377-389. Discusses folk pottery in the South, concentrating on alkaline-glazed stoneware, 1830-1910, and emphasizing chemical oxidizing techniques in kilns.

1451. Burrison, John A. CLAY CLANS: GEORGIA'S POTTERY DYNASTIES. *Family Heritage* 1979 2(3): 70-77. Georgia pottery communities developed along the Piedmont Plateau in the early 19th century, involving entire families who have carefully guarded secrets and intermarried to maintain family lines, as exemplified by the Ferguson and Hewell families.

1452. Bush, John. *THE TENSAS GAZETTE*: A BRIEF SKETCH. *North Louisiana Hist. Assoc. J.* 1974 5(4): 135-137. The *Tensas Gazette*, the second oldest newspaper in Louisiana, was established as a weekly at St. Joseph in 1852 by Andrew Manschalk. Its name was changed in 1870 to *The North Louisiana Journal*, but in 1886, it reverted. Among the paper's more prominent owners and editors have been T. W. Castleman, W. E. Dixon, R. H. Snyder, Hugh Tullis, and Josiah Scott. 16 notes.        A. N. Garland

1453. Camp, Charles and Whisnant, David E. A VOICE FROM HOME: SOUTHERN MOUNTAIN MUSICIANS ON THE MARYLAND-PENNSYLVANIA BORDER. *Southern Exposure* 1977 5(2-3): 80-89. Since the late 1930's and early 1940's, the Maryland-Pennsylvania border area has been an important source of country music performers as well as a region supplying large audiences of country music listeners. The area was settled by Southerners migrating for economic reasons from North Carolina and Virginia, including members of important musical families such as the Campbells, Lundys, Woods, De Busks, and Graybeals. Country musicians have been able to find auditors through engagements at local amusement parks as well as through local radio stations featuring country music. Based on extensive interviews, primary and secondary sources.                    N. Lederer

1454. Carvajal, Christa J. GERMAN ETHNIC THEATRE IN TEXAS: THE NINETEENTH CENTURY. *Theatre Survey* 1982 23(2): 163-176. Recounts the establishment of theater associations by German-American immigrants in Texas during the 1850's-70's.

1455. Casey, Naomi Taylor. MISS EDITH JOHNSON: PIONEER NEWSPAPER WOMAN. *Chronicles of Oklahoma* 1982 60(1): 66-73. Edith Johnson began her 50-year newspaper career in 1908 when she was hired as a reporter for the *Daily Oklahoman*. Within 10 years she had passed the stages of beat reporting to writing her own column. The Republic Syndicate eventually carried her Sunday advice column to a host of newspapers throughout the nation. As a champion of the expanding roles of women, she published *Women of the Business World* in 1923 and used her column to encourage women into enterprises previously reserved for men. Based on interviews and the writings of Edith Johnson; 2 photos.
                                                              M. L. Tate

1456. Cashin, Edward J. THOMAS W. LOYLESS, RESPONSIBLE JOURNALIST. *Richmond County Hist.* 1977 9(1): 18-28. Thomas W. Loyless edited the *Augusta Chronicle*, 1903-26.

1457. Cawthon, John Ardis. MAKE A JOYFUL NOISE: SELECTED NORTH LOUISIANA MUSICIANS. *North Louisiana Hist. Assoc. J.* 1978 9(1): 29-35. Covers 1812-1977.

1458. Chenoweth, Dean. HOUSTON HARTE: JOURNALISTIC GIANT. *West Texas Hist. Assoc. Year Book* 1981 57: 107-117. Houston Harte, a young Missouri newspaperman who arrived in West Texas in the early 1900's, bought the *Texas Standard* after World War I and continued buying other newspapers until by 1972 he owned 19; he was an important and active community leader in San Angelo, Texas.

1459. Claypool, Gerald B. JESSE HAYCRAFT. *Kentucky Folklore Record* 1976 22(3): 71-73. Discusses the musical career, both instrumental and vocal, of Jesse Robert Haycraft, an inhabitant of Grayson County, Kentucky, 1935-76.

1460. Cobb, James C. FROM MUSKOGEE TO LUCKENBACH: COUNTRY MUSIC AND THE "SOUTHERNIZATION" OF AMERICA. *J. of Popular Culture 1982 16(3): 81-91.* Popular acceptance of country music in the 1970's is a phenomenon linked to the "Southernization" of America. Social, economic, political, and demographic changes led to a more favorable assessment of the South in the 1960's, despite the region's distinct and traditional cultural ambience. 32 notes.          D. G. Nielson

1461. Cochran, Martha and Cochran, Bob. AN INTERVIEW WITH BRICE TYLER—BIRD CARVER. *New York Folklore Q. 1973 29(1): 21-37.*

1462. Cochran, Robert; Cochran, Martha; and Pierle, Christopher. THE PREPARATION AND USE OF BEAR GRASS ROPE: AN INTERVIEW WITH ROBERT SIMMONS, MISSISSIPPI FOLK CRAFTSMAN. *New York Folklore Q. 1974 30(3): 185-196.*

1463. Colmant, Berta. FOUR PREACHER TALES FROM WEST CENTRAL GEORGIA. *Tennessee Folklore Soc. Bull. 1976 42(3): 125-128.* Discusses and presents 19th- and 20th-century humorous folktales involving white and Negro rural preachers from the west central region of Georgia.

1464. Comeaux, Malcolm L. ORIGIN AND EVOLUTION OF MISSISSIPPI RIVER FISHING CRAFT. *Pioneer Am. 1978 10(1): 72-97.* Folk boats in the Mississippi River system illustrate how culture, environment, and technology interact in determining which boats are abandoned and which evolve and are successful. Analyzes major types of fishing craft: the skiff, the flatboat, and the canoe. Also summarizes differing traditions of the fishing industry as associated with watercraft in the upper Mississippi River system, in Appalachian streams, and in the Atchafalaya Swamp of Louisiana. Based on field work made possible by a Faculty Research Grant from Arizona State University, two unpublished Ph.D. dissertations, government documents, and secondary sources; illus., 13 photos, map, 2 fig., 30 notes.          C. R. Gunter, Jr.

1465. Cone, Carl B. SPORTS HISTORY WITH A KENTUCKY BOUQUET. *Register of the Kentucky Hist. Soc. 1979 77(4): 275-284.* Notes the recent success of sports history as a facet of social history and suggests that the existing abundant documentation makes the history of sport a legitimate research subject. Kentucky has a rich sports heritage, particularly in the equestrian sports. 4 illus.          J. F. Paul

1466. Cooper, Patricia Irvin. SOME STRANGE NORTH GEORGIA TOMBSTONES. *Pioneer Am. Soc. Tr. 1982 5: 27-36.* Describes housetombs and freestanding, discoidal headstones.

1467. Cothran, Kay L. MAGAZINE TRAVEL ACCOUNTS OF PINEY WOODS FOLKLIFE. *Tennessee Folklore Soc. Bull. 1973 39(3): 80-86.* Discusses the problem of using nonethnographic sources as data in evaluating 19th-century folklife, specifically the descriptions of behavior biased by lack of understanding of cultural differences.          L. Russell

1468. Cothran, Kay L. TALKING TRASH IN THE OKEFENOKEE SWAMP RIM, GEORGIA. *J. of Am. Folklore 1974 87(346): 340-356.* "Talking Trash" is a male leisure-time social activity of lower Georgia's "cracker culture." Small talk, personal experience, whoppers, tall tales, relations of practical joking, and tales of killings and lynchings evaluate human relationships and behavior and offer a character-strutting fantasy realm which sneers at middle-class values. Women enjoy hearing of foolish males, but find the wild pranks disconcerting. Based on fieldwork and secondary sources; 17 notes.          W. D. Piersen

1469. Daniel, Wayne W. THE GEORGIA OLD-TIME FIDDLERS' CONVENTION: 1920 EDITION. *JEMF Q. 1980 16(58): 67-73.*

1470. Daniel, Wayne W. TEX FOREMAN AND CURLEY COLLINS REMEMBER POP ECKLER AND HIS YOUNG'UNS. *JEMF Q. 1980 16(59): 132-139.* Tex Forman and Curley Collins describe their experiences as members of the unrecorded, pioneer country music group, Pop Eckler and His Young'uns, heard on radio station WSB broadcast from Atlanta, Georgia, from 1936 to 1942, and also, briefly, on stations WGST and WAGA.

1471. Daniels, William G. THE EPWORTH JUBILEE COMMUNITY ARTS CENTER OF KNOXVILLE, TENNESSEE: COMMUNITY ARTS IN AN URBAN APPALACHIAN CENTER. *Arts in Soc. 1975 12(1): 24-31.* The primary purposes of the Epworth Jubilee Community Arts Center is to encourage appreciation of the Appalachian heritage by those who have moved to the city, away from their cultural roots, and to encourage emerging artists who represent Appalachian culture to remain in the area and develop their art.

1472. Davis, Junetta. MIRROR TO THE WORLD: TWENTY-FIVE YEARS OF *OKLAHOMA TODAY. Chronicles of Oklahoma 1980-81 58(4): 412-419.* In 1956 Governor Raymond Gary helped initiate *Oklahoma Today* as a means of promoting a positive image of the state to outsiders and residents alike. Initially the magazine operated on a small budget and with a small staff that solicited articles from public-spirited citizens. Beautiful photographs eventually became its chief attraction, thus documenting the geographical diversity of the state and increasing tourism. 4 photos.          M. L. Tate

1473. Deahl, William E., Jr. BUFFALO BILL'S WILD WEST SHOW IN NEW ORLEANS. *Louisiana Hist. 1975 16(3): 289-290.* During the winnter of 1884-85 Buffalo Bill's Wild West wintered in New Orleans where, despite 44 days of rain, it attracted an enthusiastic audience. To offset the effects of the weather, Cody formed a drama company in which he starred in a western melodrama, *Prairie Wolf,* which was well received by large audiences. Illus., 27 notes.          E. P. Stickney

1474. Deen, Jeannie. A YOUNG GIRL'S FANCY. *Southern Q. 1979 18(1): 169-172.* The author was in elementary school in Mississippi when rock and roll singer Elvis Presley (1935-77) made it to the top. When a teenager, she dreamed of meeting him. She once visited Graceland, his home in Memphis, Tennessee. In 1976, the author saw him in a concert in Jackson, Mississippi, and was disappointed in her earlier fancy for him.          B. D. Ledbetter

1475. DelSesto, Steven L. ROLES, RULES, AND ORGANIZATION: A DESCRIPTIVE ACCOUNT OF COCKFIGHTING IN RURAL LOUISIANA. *Southern Folklore Q. 1975 39(1): 1-14.* Describes the social background of cockfighting in the 20th century, including the roles of the owners and bettors, rules of the fight, and the actual fight situation.          S

1476. deMetz, Kaye. DANCE DUELS ON NEW ORLEANS STAGES DURING THE NINETEENTH CENTURY. *Southern Speech Communications J. 1976 41(3): 278-289.* Discusses the social background of dance competitions in minstrel shows in New Orleans, Louisiana in the 1840's and 50's, emphasizing their ideological relationship to traditional US individualism.

1477. DeMetz, Kaye. MINSTREL DANCING IN NEW ORLEANS' NINETEENTH CENTURY THEATERS. *Southern Q. 1982 20(2): 28-40.* Southerners took a hedonistic view of their culture and institutions and sought to romanticize them. When abolitionists attempted to persuade the nation to end slavery, Southerners responded in part by romanticizing the institution and depicting the life of the black slave as idyllic. The minstrel dance was one manifestation of that response. In New Orleans, audiences most often watched Thomas Dartmouth Rice and John Diamond in performances of *Oh! Hush!* and *Bone Squash.* The minstrel dance later provided a foundation for vaudeville and burlesque, contributed to the development of tap dancing, and left large contributions in the areas of folk music and dance. On occasion, it also served as a conduct for black performers to enter white society.          W. A. Wiegand

1478. DeMetz, Kaye. THEATRICAL DANCING IN NINE-TEENTH-CENTURY NEW ORLEANS. *Louisiana Hist. 1980 21(1) 23-42.* Describes the touring and local artists who danced for enthusiastic audiences in antebellum New Orleans. Many theaters flourished in the Crescent City during this era. Their varied bills frequently included performances such as ballet, character dancing, minstrel dances, gymnastic demonstrations, and even novelty pieces between acts. Based on newspapers; 52 notes.

D. B. Touchstone

1479. Downs, Fane. FANDANGLE: MYTH AS REALITY. *West Texas Hist. Assoc. Year Book 1978 54: 3-9.* Analyzes the origins and themes of the annual Fort Griffin fandangle since 1938 which is viewed as a collective celebration of the mythical and, to a lesser extent, the realistic folk past.

1480. Downs, Virginia. FOLK POETRY IN GRAVESTONE VERSE. *Kentucky Folklore Record 1979 25(1-2): 28-36.* Examines folk poetry on tombstones, based on the author's study of six cemeteries in Virginia that date from the mid-19th century to the early 20th century.

1481. Doyle, Charles Clay. THE POWER OF NOT THINKING: A JOCULAR TOOTHACHE CURE. *Kentucky Folklore Record 1983 29(1-2): 24-29.* The rural Alabama cure for toothaches requires some ritual while concentrating on not thinking about the pain; mentions numerous variations of the cure, some dating from 16th-century England.

1482. Dunbar, G. S. HENRY CLAY ON KENTUCKY BLUE-GRASS, 1838. *Agric. Hist. 1977 51(3): 520-523.* The term "Kentucky bluegrass" was used at least as early as 1838, although the grass originated in Europe. A letter by Henry Clay, printed here, throws light on its culture and use. 7 notes. D. E. Bowers

1483. Dunn, Durwood. THE FOLK CULTURE OF CADES COVE, TENNESSEE. *Tennessee Folklore Soc. Bull. 1977 53(2): 67-86.* Chronicles growth of the culture, 1865-1975.

1484. Dykeman, Wilma. APPALACHIA IN CONTEXT. *Appalachian J. 1977 4(4): 28-42.* Comparing Appalachia with the Old South, industrial America between 1865 and the 1930's, and the Third World, helps clarify Appalachia's relative isolation and questions the putative poverty of its culture.

1485. Edmonds, Katharine Spicer. IN THE REALM OF HOSPITALITY: COOKBOOKS OF THE EASTERN SHORE. *Virginia Cavalcade 1974 23(4): 10-17.* Discusses cookbooks and recipes published by Bessie Gunter and her descendants in the eastern shore, Virginia, 1889-1935.

1486. Edwards, Katharine Bush. BUSH HILL CEMETERY. *South Carolina Hist. Mag. 1977 78(2): 148-149.* Records epitaphs from gravestones in the Bush Hill Cemetery, formerly on the property of the Bush Home but later removed to Williston when the AEC purchased the land; gravestones show dates, 1835-1905.

1487. Edwards, Katharine Bush. INSCRIPTIONS FROM THE MT. BETHEL BAPTIST AND EBENEZER METHODIST CHURCH CEMETERIES, ANDERSON COUNTY. *South Carolina Hist. Mag. 1978 79(2): 138-147.* Lists alphabetically the names and attached birth and death dates on gravestones in the Mount Bethel Baptist Church and the Ebenezer Lutheran Church cemeteries in Anderson County, South Carolina, from 1856-1978.

1488. Eiler, Lyntha Scott; Eiler, Terry; and Fleischauer, Carl. PEOPLE OF THE BLUE RIDGE: A PHOTOGRAPHIC PORTRAIT. *Q. J. of the Lib. of Congress 1981 38(3): 134-143.* In 1978 the American Folklife Center at the Library of Congress, working in cooperation with the National Park Service, conducted the Blue Ridge Parkway Folklife Project, designed to provide information for the Blue Ridge Parkway's cultural program demonstrating the relationship between the national park and the people who live near it. The documentary archive created by the project includes tapes, photographs, field notes, video recordings, and architectural drawings. The project produced a phonograph record *Children of the Heav'nly King* and a book of photographs, *Blue Ridge Harvest.* The article contains photographs selected from the latter, portraying three of the region's families: the Severts, the Brims, and the Keiths. J. Powell

1489. Ezell, Macel D. EARLY ATTITUDES TOWARD ALCOHOLIC BEVERAGES IN THE SOUTH. *Red River Valley Hist. Rev. 1982 7(1): 64-70.* Traditions brought from Europe contained customs and attitudes including frequent consumption of alcoholic beverages; however, as the frontier faded and town-life developed, temperance movements found considerable support among the populous South.

1490. Feintuch, Burt. DANCING TO THE MUSIC: DOMESTIC SQUARE DANCES AND COMMUNITY IN SOUTHCENTRAL KENTUCKY (1880-1940). *J. of the Folklore Inst. 1981 18(1): 49-68.* Oral history interviews with dancers, callers, and musicians in 11 Kentucky counties indicates that domestic square dances once helped participants to define a sense of community and to develop social cohesion. The dances were held as early as 1815, but oral sources and the sparse documentation available suggest that their primary importance dates from 1880. These events, which were held in private homes, centered on a closely knit neighborhood characterized by its "closed" nature and stability. After about 1940, the domestic square dances in southcentral Kentucky gave way to more public affairs, which were held in commercial centers such as Bowling Green. This shift probably represents an altered concept of community. Based on fieldwork; map, 39 notes. C. D. Geist

1491. Feintuch, Burt. EXAMINING MUSICAL MOTIVATION: WHY DOES SAMMY PLAY THE FIDDLE? *Western Folklore 1983 42(3): 208-215.* Family tradition, role models, community acceptance, and expectations are determining factors in the decision to learn and play musical instruments in southern Kentucky. Based on interviews; 16 notes. R. E. Goerler

1492. Feintuch, Burt. THE FIDDLE IN THE UNITED STATES: AN HISTORICAL OVERVIEW. *Kentucky Folklore Record 1983 29(1-2): 30-38.* Fiddles were brought to America by 1620 and were used for minor dances and contests until the recording and radio booms of the 1920's brought mass popularity.

1493. Figh, Margaret Gillis and Kirkpatrick, Margaret B. THE DEVELOPMENT OF AN ALABAMA FOLKTALE. *Southern Folklore Q. 1974 38(2): 109-120.*

1494. Finger, Bill. BASCOM LAMAR LUNSFORD: THE LIMITS OF A FOLK HERO. *Southern Exposure 1974 2(1): 27-37.* Describes Bascom Lamar Lunsford's folksongs which reflect social conditions in North Carolina's Appalachia.

1495. Fisher, Stephen L. FOLK CULTURE OR FOLKTALE: PREVAILING ASSUMPTIONS ABOUT THE APPALACHIAN PERSONALITY. *Appalachian J. 1977 4(4): 14-25.* Recent scholarship on Appalachian folk culture suggests that the accepted model of Appalachia's subculture is a distorted description which inhibits meaningful social change within the region.

1496. Forman, William H., Jr. WILLIAM P. HARPER AND THE EARLY NEW ORLEANS CARNIVAL. *Louisiana Hist. 1973 14(1): 40-47.* William Poynot Harper played a major role in the development of the Mistick Krewe of Comus and celebration of Mardi Gras in New Orleans 1866-72. Based on the author's collection; 8 photos. R. L. Woodward

1497. Forrester, Rebel C., ed. THE MAKING OF A COUNTRY EDITOR: JAMES M. BRICE AND THE *NEWS-BANNER* OF TROY, TENNESSEE. *West Tennessee Hist. Soc. Papers 1981 35: 103-117.* James Moffatt Brice was a newspaper editor in Obion County for 33 years when he penned his recollections in 1925, a year before he died. Through his eyes one enters a world of a bygone past and walks the streets of Troy, a small, rural West Tennessee town. The portions selected constitute but a fraction of Brice's manuscript. 4 illus.                                      H. M. Parker, Jr.

1498. Foster, Elizabeth Pyburn. THE SILOAM CAMP GROUND: A MEMOIR OF ELIZABETH PYBURN FOSTER. *North Louisiana Hist. Assoc. J. 1977 8(5): 203-206.* Throughout North Louisiana during the late 19th century, camp ground meetings were quite popular. The author tells of a meeting that lasted a week and was held at the Old Siloam Camp Ground. Describes the living and cooking arrangements, the religious services, and some attendees. Illus., 2 notes.                                          A. N. Garland

1499. Freedman, Alex S. THE PASSING OF THE ARKANSAS GRANNY MIDWIFE. *Kentucky Folklore Record 1974 20(4): 101-103.*

1500. Geary, Helen Brophy. AFTER THE LAST PICTURE SHOW. *Chronicles of Oklahoma 1983 61(1): 4-27.* Lawrence William Brophy arrived in Oklahoma during November 1907 and soon opened his first movie theater in Chandler. During the following two decades, he operated 21 theaters across Oklahoma, Arkansas, and Missouri. Presenting both motion pictures and vaudeville acts, Brophy offered the most recent movies in the most comfortable of buildings. Along with other theater managers he resisted church opposition to Sunday showings and excessive censorship. In 1915 he was elected first vice-president of the Motion Picture Theatre Exhibitors' League, but 11 years later he sold all of his buildings and turned to other successful business ventures. Based on newspapers; 8 photos, 41 notes.                                          M. L. Tate

1501. George, Angelo I. THE LEGEND OF ELEVEN JONES' CAVE, JEFFERSON COUNTY, KENTUCKY. *Filson Club Hist. Q. 1974 48(4): 342-359.* Relates a number of legends about Eleven Jones' Cave near Louisville, Kentucky, including one that maintains that it was an outlaw sanctuary. Also describes two recent survey trips into the cave which help explain some of the legends. Documented by newspapers and personal correspondence; 2 illus., 52 notes.                                          G. B. McKinney

1502. Gernes, Sonia. ARTISTS OF COMMUNITY: THE ROLE OF STORYTELLERS IN THE TALES OF THE SOUTHWEST HUMORISTS. *J. of Popular Culture 1982 15(4): 114-128.* Surveys numerous humorous, violent, and often scatological tales of the Old Southwest to demonstrate the narrative techniques used by storytellers to establish their rights to belong to a community, protect it, enhance their position in it, or form a community where one did not exist before. 20 notes.                                          D. G. Nielson

1503. Gordon, Robert. "HUNTING LIES AND FISHY STORIES" FROM BEDFORD COUNTY. *Tennessee Folklore Soc. Bull. 1977 43(1): 23-26.* Records the hunting stories and fish stories of four informants in Bedford County, Tennessee, 1977.

1504. Graves, Oliver Finley. THE BED-OF-SNAKES MOTIF IN SOUTHERN FOLKLORE: THE LEGENDS OF THE HAPLESS WATERSKIER, AND THE INCAUTIOUS SWIMMER, AND THE UNWITTING FISHERBOY. *Southern Folklore Q. 1978 42(4): 337-359.* Discusses three stories popular in the southeastern states that involve a bed of snakes, a waterskier, a swimmer, or a fisherboy, focusing on the tellers of the stories, the reasons for the telling, and the irony of the deaths of the innocent victims; 1976.

1505. Green, Archie. OLD DAN TUCKER. *JEMF Q. 1981 17(62): 85-94, 106.* Brief biography of Daniel Decatur Emmett, who wrote the hit song "Old Dan Tucker" for the Virginia Minstrels, a group formed in January 1843 with Emmett, Billy Whitlock, Dick Pelham, and Frank Brower; focuses on the song's wide appeal and its publication in music books with illustrations of Dan Tucker.

1506. Green, Henry D. FURNITURE OF THE GEORGIA PIEDMONT BEFORE 1820. *Art & Antiques 1982 5(1): 80-87.* Describes the style of furniture and architecture that emerged from the workshops of the mostly Scotch-Irish settlers of the Georgia Pied-

mont toward the end of the 18th century, made largely from pine, walnut, birch, maple, and cherry, by itinerant cabinetmakers whose unique huntboards and cellarets, among other furniture, were decorated with inlay and "has a solid, honest style, good proportions, and nice moldings."

1507. Greene, Robert B. HENRY L. BANDY: "THE OLD-TIME FIDDLER." *Kentucky Folklore Record 1972 18(4): 99-102.* Biographical sketch of an Allen County musician who gained fame as a fiddler in the early days of the Grand Ole Opry.

                                                   J. C. Crowe

1508. Guthrie, Charles S. HOG LORE OF THE CUMBERLAND VALLEY. *Kentucky Folklore Record 1977 23(3-4): 79-86.* Discusses hog raising and feeding practices of the Cumberland River Valley area of Kentucky and the role of pigs in folklore and folklife of the area during 1900-50's.

1509. Guy, Duane F. AN AMPHITHEATER FOR THE PANHANDLE. *Panhandle-Plains Hist. Rev. 1978 51: 179-193.* Beginning in 1934, some citizens in the Texas Panhandle launched efforts to construct an amphitheater in Palo Duro Canyon. In 1960 the effort was revived by business and civic promoters from the nearby town of Canyon who wished to draw tourists to outdoor theatrical performances. The amphitheater was completed three years later and soon evolved into the scene for the celebrated pageant "Texas," which since then has been presented every summer against the picturesque backdrop of the canyon. Based on interviews; 27 notes.

                                                   M. L. Tate

1510. Gwinn, Erna Ottl. THE LIEDERKRANZ IN LOUISVILLE, 1848-1877. *Filson Club Hist. Q. 1975 49(3): 276-290.* The Liederkranz, a German-American music society, played an important role in the integration of the German community into the life of Louisville, Kentucky. Started in 1848, the organization was strengthened by the arrival of German liberals after the failure of the revolution of that year. By the mid-1850's the Germans formed one-third of Louisville's population and faced nativist hostility organized in the Know-Nothing movement. Violent demonstrations forced the chorus to suppress publicity of its performances that included works by composer Richard Wagner. The Liederkranz suspended operations during the Civil War, but afterward grew rapidly and was able to build a large auditorium by 1873. An audience of 8,000 that attended a performance in 1877 demonstrated that the Germans were an accepted part of Louisville life. Based on German language histories and Louisville newspapers; 71 notes.          G. B. McKinney

1511. Gwinn, Erna Ottl. THE LIEDERKRANZ IN LOUISVILLE, 1877-1959. *Filson Club Hist. Q. 1981 55(1): 40-59.* Continued from a previous article (see entry in this chapter). Despite the title, deals almost solely with the years before 1918. The Liederkranz was one of several German singing societies in Louisville. As the German community became better integrated into Louisville life after 1877, the Liederkranz had a difficult existence. A perpetual lack of funds and a fire that destroyed the society's hall made it impossible for the Liederkranz to enjoy any sustained period of success. Several of its traditional activities including the annual *Stiftungsfest* at New Year's were enjoyed by all Germans in Louisville. Misguided patriotism concerning German-American cultural activities during World War I had a devastating impact. Based on local newspapers in both German and English; 2 photos, 107 notes.          G. B. McKinney

1512. Haden, Courtney. DIXIE ROCK: THE FUSION'S STILL BURNING. *Southern Exposure 1977 5(2-3): 37-43.* Over the past 30 years, southern rock music has gone through several cycles of emergence, persistence, decline, and revival. Sam Phillips, Memphis record producer of Sun Records, was instrumental in the first appearance of Southern rock which featured black musical expressions aimed at a predominantly white audience. He recorded Elvis Presley, Jerry Lee Lewis, and other prominent Southern rock performers. After a decline in the late 1950's, the Southern rock reemerged through performers such as Booker T. and the MGs, Otis Redding, and the "Muscle Shoals sound," shaped by producer Rick Hall and highlighted in the revival of the career of Aretha Franklin. Duane Allman epitomizes a more recent manifestation of Southern rock music. Based on personal observation.          N. Lederer

1513. Halan, Y. C. THE FOLKLORE OF THE APPALA-CHIANS. *Indian J. of Am. Studies [India] 1977 7(1): 28-40.* The Appalachian region is one of America's most richly folkloristic places. Their folklore reflects the Scotch Irish background of the early settlers, as well as the socioeconomic conditions of the region. Their folk music, ballads, tales, riddles, beliefs, and hymns retained an old, often British, flavor because the region's isolation permitted the preservation and development of a strong folk culture. Today the old ways of entertainment have been almost forgotten. 61 notes.          L. V. Eid

1514. Hale, Tony. GRASSROOTS BLUEGRASS IN MEMPHIS: THE LUCY OPRY. *Tennessee Folklore Soc. Bull. 1983 49(2): 51-64.* Describes the Lucy Opry, both an indoor formal concert and an outdoor (parking lot) session, where townsfolk and musicians gather; no admission is charged nor fees paid.

1515. Hale, Tony. LUCY OPRY AS A CONSERVATIVE TRA-DITION. *Tennessee Folklore Soc. Bull. 1983 49(3): 120-128.* Even new bluegrass music is played in the old way at the Lucy Opry concert hall in Memphis, Tennessee, because the young musicians want to preserve tradition and the older ones dislike change.

1516. Hample, Judy. WILLIAM WIRT'S FAMILIAR ESSAYS: CRITICISM OF VIRGINIA ORATORY. *Southern Speech Communication J. 1978 44(1): 25-41.* William Wirt attempted to popular-ize classical and 18th-century theories of rhetoric and public speaking in the face of what he considered a decline in eloquence in 19th-century Virginia.

1517. Hancock, Harold B. FURNITURE CRAFTSMEN IN DEL-AWARE RECORDS. *Winterthur Portfolio 1974 (9): 175-212.* The Hall of Records in Dover, Delaware, reveals new and important in-formation concerning wood craftsmen in the state prior to 1850. Some 200 previously unknown craftsmen have now been identified along with 150 apprentices. The purpose of listing the names of such craftsmen is to stimulate further research into the furniture makers and their products. Based on primary and secondary sources; 6 photos, 18 notes, 7 appendices.          N. A. Kuntz

1518. Hancock, Joyce. APPALACHIAN WELCOME: A PHOTO-GRAPHIC ESSAY. *Appalachian J. 1981 8(3): 188-195.* Photo-graphic essay of people in Appalachia who exhibit the "qualities of intelligence, creativity, humor, and heart."

1519. Harper, Jared and Hudson, Charles. IRISH TRAVELER CANT IN ITS SOCIAL SETTING. *Southern Folklore Q. 1973 37(2): 101-114.*

1520. Harper, Robert W., III. SOUVENIRS OF THE ANCIENT CITY. *Escribano 1981 18: 33-44.* Describes and illustrates the sou-venirs, especially ceramics, available in St. Augustine, Florida, dur-ing 1840-1920.

1521. Harrison, Bill and Wolfe, Charles. SHOOTING THE AN-VIL. *Tennessee Folklore Soc. Bull. 1977 43(1): 1-13.* Gives the his-tory of a folk custom used at public celebrations throughout the South known as the anvil shoot, 1890's-1977.

1522. Hartsfield, Mariella G. THE GRADY COUNTY DUMB-BULL. *Tennessee Folklore Soc. Bull. 1979 45(3): 107-110.* Traces the presence of the "dumb-bull" device (used for practical jokes in Grady County, Georgia, during the 1900's); it has links to Asia, Africa, Australia and New Guinea, and to European tradition, and may be traced to Paleolithic times.

1523. Hayden, Dolores and Marris, Peter. THE QUILTMAKER'S LANDSCAPE. *Landscape 1981 25(3): 39-47.* Examines "quilt ico-nography, as a detailed record of American women's experiences of our landscape and buildings," focusing on Elizabeth Roseberry Mitchell's Kentucky Coffin Quilt, made in 1839, showing a plan of

a cemetery with a family burial plot in the center, Virginia Ivey's quilt showing the Russellville, Kentucky, fairgrounds in 1856, Mrs. Mahikoa's schematic plan of the island of Hawaii on a quilt made in 1904, and others.

1524. Head, Faye E. THE BIRTH AND DEATH OF THE TU-LANE AND THE CRESCENT: TWIN-THEATRES OF NEW ORLEANS, LOUISIANA. *Louisiana Studies 1976 15(3): 294-303.* In 1896 Marc Klaw (1858-1936) and Abraham Lincoln Erlanger (1860-1930) formed a Theatrical Syndicate to facilitate scheduling of touring shows by combining theaters and shows under the con-trol of a single agent. In New Orleans in 1898 they built opulent twin theaters, the Tulane and the Crescent, to put on the shows they controlled. The theaters were created to monopolize theatrical productions in New Orleans and also to house the large touring companies of the day. Seating about 1,500 each and designed in Louis XV style, they were eminently successful for 20 years. They succumbed to changing fashions in entertainment and were demol-ished in 1937. Based on contemporary newspaper accounts and sec-ondary sources; 46 notes.          J. Buschen

1525. Hedges, James S. MRS. YARDLEY'S QUILT PATTERNS. *Tennessee Folklore Soc. Bull. 1975 41(4): 145-150.* Discusses the art of quilting as practiced by the mountaineers of the Knoxville, Tennessee area during the 18th century.

1526. Henry, Susan L. TERRA-COTTA TOBACCO PIPES IN 17TH CENTURY MARYLAND AND VIRGINIA: A PRELIMI-NARY STUDY. *Hist. Archaeol. 1979 13: 14-37.* Terra-cotta tobac-co pipes similar in style and decoration to English white clay pipes are occasionally recovered from 17th-century European sites. Colo-nists may have made their own tobacco pipes of local clay when English goods were more expensive during the several economic de-pressions of the 17th century. The terra-cotta pipes recovered from St. John's, a dwelling in St. Mary's City, Maryland, were analyzed using the criteria of bowl shape, manufacturing scars, and decora-tive motifs, resulting in a distinction between aboriginal handmade pipes and colonial mold-made pipes. The results of the analysis al-so show that datable occurrences of the St. John's mold-made ter-ra-cotta tobacco pipes bracket at least two of the major economic depressions in the last half of the 17th century.          J

1527. Herzog, Harold and Cheek, Pauline B. GRIT AND STEEL: THE ANATOMY OF COCKFIGHTING. *Southern Exposure 1979 7(3): 36-40.* Cockfighting enjoys its greatest popularity in rural communities in the United States ranging from Virginia to New Mexico. Although illegal in most areas, the sport enjoys a great de-al of audience interest and flourishes owing to lax law enforcement and low visibility to the general public. The most common type of organized cockfighting match held today is the "derby" in which cocks fight in a round robin with the winner taking the pot. Cock-fights end when a handler concedes the fight, when a cock does not adhere to the second's count in forms of attack called "pit-tings," or when a cock dies. Cockfights attract blacks and whites, men and women. Generally considerable gambling takes place around the pit. Based largely on interviews and personal observa-tion.          N. Lederer

1528. Hicks, Ronald G. and Gordon, Avishag. FOREIGN NEWS CONTENT IN ISRAELI AND U.S. NEWSPAPERS. *Journalism Q. 1974 51(4): 639-644.* In a study of three Israeli newspapers and the New Orleans *Times-Picayune* "ethnocentrism, elitism and news distance are seen as more important in determining news content than the factor of physical distance between nations."          S

1529. Hilliard, Addie Suggs. ON SWALLOWING PUNKIN SEED. *Tennessee Folklore Soc. Bull. 1974 40(4): 119-121.* Discuss-es superstitions and folklore surrounding pregnancy and childbirth in Chester County, Tennessee.

1530. Hilliard, Addie Suggs. WHAT'LL WE GIVE THE BABY-O? *Tennessee Folklore Soc. Bull. 1974 40(2): 41-46.* Folk medicine for new-born infants.

1531. Hilliard, Elbert R. and Gonzales, John E. THE FIRST FORTY YEARS: EDITORS OF THE *JOURNAL,* 1939-1979. *J. of Mississippi Hist.* 1979 41(1): 1-3. Chronicles editors of the *Journal of Mississippi History* during its first 40 years. The founding editor of the *Journal*, during 1939-56, was William D. McCain, and the present editor, since 1963, is John Edmond Gonzales. Also lists the editors-in-chief, associate editors, editorial associates, managing editors, and assistant editors.                                    M. S. Legan

1532. Holditch, W. Kenneth. THE SINGING HEART: A STUDY OF THE LIFE AND WORK OF PEARL RIVERS. *Southern Q.* 1982 20(2): 87-117. Eliza Jane Poitevent Holbrook Nicholson (1849-96), better known as Pearl Rivers, her pseudonym as a poet, spent a sheltered childhood on a southern Mississippi plantation. Shortly after the death of her first husband, Colonel Alva Morris Holbrook, she took over his position as publisher of the New Orleans *Daily Picayune* and turned it into a successful venture. She did this by creating a women's page and providing something of interest for all ages and sexes. As Pearl Rivers, she was also an accomplished poet who reached the creative maturity evident in *Hagar* shortly before her death.                                    W. A. Wiegand

1533. Hudelston, Jesse. *THE BALLAD OF THE BRASWELL BOYS:* A PUTNAM COUNTY INCIDENT. *Tennessee Folklore Soc. Bull.* 1980 46(1): 25-30. The Ballad of the Braswell Boys, from the Upper Cumberland region and still sung today, tells of the execution by hanging of George (Teak) and Joe Braswell on 27 March 1878 for the murder of Russell and John Allison on 29 November 1875.

1534. Husted, Margaret. MARY RANDOLPH'S *THE VIRGINIA HOUSEWIFE:* AMERICA'S FIRST REGIONAL COOKBOOK. *Virginia Cavalcade* 1980 30(2): 76-87. Recounts the life and cooking of Mary Randolph (1762-1828); includes copies of some of her recipes.

1535. Inge, M. Thomas. THE APPALACHIAN BACKGROUNDS OF BILLY DE BECK'S SNUFFY SMITH. *Appalachian J.* 1977 4(2): 120-132. Discusses cartoonist Billy De Beck's research into the works of Mary Noailles Murfree, George Washington Harris, and other Appalachian folk humorists in devising the hillbilly dialect of comic character Snuffy Smith in his comic strip *Barney Google and Snuffy Smith* 1934-42.

1536. Inglesby, Charlotte. TOMBSTONE INSCRIPTIONS, MAY RIVER PLANTATIONS. *South Carolina Hist. Mag.* 1973 74(1): 31-36. Copies the tombstone inscriptions found in the burial grounds of the Montpelier, Moreland, Octagon, Longworth, and Theus plantations. Mentions other genealogical data. 23 notes.
                                    D. L. Smith

1537. Ivey, Saundra Keyes. ASCRIBED ETHNICITY AND THE ETHNIC DISPLAY EVENT: THE MELUNGEONS OF HANCOCK COUNTY, TENNESSEE. *Western Folklore* 1977 36(1): 85-107. Using an outdoor drama, "Walk Toward the Sunset," as a focus, the author presents an in-depth study of the origins and history of the Melungeon people and examines the myths and legends relating to this "mysterious" ethnic group. Based on primary and secondary sources and interviews; 64 notes.    S. L. Myres

1538. Ivey, Saundra Keyes. AUNT MAHALA MULLINS IN FOLKLORE, FAKELORE, AND LITERATURE. *Tennessee Folklore Soc. Bull.* 1975 41(1): 1-8. Discusses fact and fiction about Mahala Mullins (ca. 1824-95), a moonshiner in Hancock County, Tennessee, known for her liquor and her immense weight.

1539. Jammes, Jean-Marie. COMMENT ET POURQUOI NOUS POUVONS ET NOUS DEVONS SAUVER LE FRANCAIS EN ACADIANA [How and why we can and must save French in Acadiana]. *Rev. de Louisiane* 1977 6(2): 101-134. Relates the use of French in Acadiana (the southern sectors of Louisiana) and prescribes saving the French language in this area.

1540. Jarman, Brenda Sudduth. "AILIN' ANIMALS": FOLK TREATMENTS COLLECTED IN RUTHERFORD COUNTY, TENNESSEE. *Tennessee Folklore Soc. Bull.* 1978 44(2): 55-64. Discusses folk medicine practiced on farm and domestic animals in Rutherford County, Tennessee, 1976-77.

1541. Jarrett, Walter. [NEW ORLEANS].
NEW ORLEANS: THE CITY THAT CARE FORGOT. PART I: UNDER FRENCH AND SPANISH FLAGS. *Mankind* 1974 4(7): 16-23, 48-51. Traces the early history of New Orleans until the Louisiana Purchase.
DOWN THE RIVER TO NEW ORLEANS, PART II: UNDER AMERICAN AND CONFEDERATE FLAGS. *Mankind* 1974 4(8): 18-25, 58-59. Describes New Orleans from 1803, when Louisianna was purchased from France by Thomas Jefferson, to about 1900.

1542. Jarrott, Emory. TOMBSTONE INSCRIPTIONS AT STROBHAR AND DUPONT CEMETERIES, PURRYSBURG. *South Carolina Hist. Mag.* 1978 79(1): 60-62. Lists inscriptions on tombstones in two Purrysburg, South Carolina graveyards, Strobhar Cemetery and DuPont Cemetery, with sites dated 1736-1872.

1543. Johnson, Geraldine N. "PLAIN AND FANCY": THE SOCIOECONOMICS OF BLUE RIDGE QUILTS. *Appalachian J.* 1982 10(1): 12-35. Blue Ridge quilts of North Carolina and Virginia are closely tied to the region in which they are created, are basically used for warmth, and differ both in design and in technique from the Pennsylvania-German traditions in quilting.

1544. Johnson, James D. AN INSTANCE OF TOASTS AMONG SOUTHERN WHITES. *Western Folklore* 1981 40(4): 329-337. Examines the oral literature of toasts ("short narrative rhymes... characterized by obscene words and explicit sexual references") among Southern white males. Analyzes the text of four such toasts and shows that they are not, as some have thought, an "exclusively black phenomenon" but are also told by whites, often with modifications of black texts. Based on oral interviews; 19 notes.
                                    S. L. Myres

1545. Johnson, Robert Foster. HENRY COUNTY CEMETERIES. *Filson Club Hist. Q.* 1978 52(3): 280-303, (4): 340-362. Part I. Lists information on tombstones in Henry County, Kentucky, 1770-1966. Part II. Covers 1811-1970.    G. B. McKinney

1546. Jolley, Clyde W. FAMOUS GEORGIA WOMEN: CORRA HARRIS. *Georgia Life* 1980 6(4): 22-23. Corra White Harris (1869-1935) wrote 24 book-length manuscripts and over 250 articles for *The Saturday Evening Post, Pictorial Review, American Magazine, Cosmopolitan, The Independent, Ladies' Home Journal, Harpers,* and others, 20 of which were published in book form.

1547. Jones, Loyal. JEAN RITCHIE, TWENTY-FIVE YEARS AFTER. *Appalachian J.* 1981 8(3): 224-229. Reviews Jean Ritchie's *Singing Family of the Cumberlands* (1955), the story of her Appalachian 16-person singing family with 19th century values, and Jean Ritchie's record, *High Hills and Mountains* (1979).

1548. Jones, Michael Owen. THE USEFUL AND THE USELESS IN FOLK ART. *J. of Popular Culture* 1973 6(4): 794-818. Explores the question of the aesthetics of folk art as conceived by folklorists and by the people, using rural whites of Appalachia, especially chairmakers, as examples.                                    S

1549. Jordan, James William. AN AMBIVALENT RELATIONSHIP: DOG AND HUMAN IN THE FOLK CULTURE OF THE RURAL SOUTH. *Appalachian J.* 1975 2(3): 238-248. Examines attitudes toward dogs in the rural South.

1550. Jordan, Terry G. "THE ROSES SO RED AND THE LILIES SO FAIR": SOUTHERN FOLK CEMETERIES IN TEXAS. *Southwestern Hist. Q.* 1980 83(3): 227-258. Southern folk cemeteries in Texas are a mixture of cultural origins. From Africa comes the bare "scraped-earth ground and the placing of broken crockery on graves; from pagan Britain come the grave mounds and the cedar or juniper plantings.'' Shells on the graves, rose bushes and flowers, the use of tombstones, and dove and pomegranate inscriptions derive from pagan Southern Europe. Of Christian British origin are the burial with feet to the east, the wife's position on the left of the husband, and the use of unsanctified ground with fence and lichgate. The use of gravehouses probably originated with the American Indians. Based on personal observation and other primary sources; 15 illus., 2 maps, table, 35 notes.

J. H. Broussard

1551. Joyner, Charles W. DULCIMER MAKING IN WESTERN NORTH CAROLINA: CREATIVITY IN A TRADITIONAL MOUNTAIN CRAFT. *Southern Folklore Q. 1975 39(4): 341-359.* Discusses the craft of dulcimer making in the Blue Ridge Mountains of western North Carolina in the 1960's and 70's, emphasizing the work of Frank Hodges, Stanley Hicks, Leonard Glenn and Edd Presnell.

1552. Joyner, Charles W. THE REPERTORY OF NANCY JONES AS A MIRROR OF CULTURE IN SCOTLAND COUNTY. *North Carolina Folklore J. 1973 21(3): 89-97.* Analyzes the folksongs of Miss Nancy Jones of Scotland County, "in the hope of casting some illumination on the role of the individual folksinger in sustaining tradition, on the role of tradition in shaping the culture in which the individual lives, and on the interrelations between the three.'' The "tragic sense of life, rooted in hardship and defeat,'' which "underlies all Southern folk culture'' is mirrored in Miss Jones' folksong repertory.

R. N. Lokken

1553. Lancaster, R. Kent. GREEN MOUNT: THE INTRODUCTION OF THE RURAL CEMETERY INTO BALTIMORE. *Maryland Hist. Mag. 1979 74(1): 62-79.* Civic pride, and the opening of Boston and Philadelphia's urban "rural cemeteries,'' caused Baltimore to respond to Samuel D. Walker's appeals by the late 1830's by creating Green Mount on the northern boundary of the city on some 60 acres of the country estate of the merchant prince Robert Oliver. Primarily the work of Baltimore's premier architect, Robert Cary Long, Jr., Green Mount in its pure and natural setting reflected the changing 19th-century concept of death—not the terrible extinction of the past, but a rest or sleep. The author's necrogeographic analysis of Section Q of the cemetery demonstrates the distribution of wealth and social fluidity, as well as changing styles in grave markers, of more than a century of Baltimore's residents, and sees the cemetery as almost a museum, a disappearing archive undeserving of its present neglect. Primary sources; 3 tables, 33 notes.

G. J. Bobango

1554. Lancaster, R. Kent. OLD ST. PAUL'S CEMETERY, BALTIMORE. *Maryland Hist. Mag. 1983 78(2): 129-142.* St. Paul's Cemetery was the fashionable place to be buried in late 18th-century Baltimore, but the opening of Green Mount in 1839 eclipsed the historic burial ground where rest the remains of numerous founding fathers of Baltimore, and the nation. Even in 1875, neglect of the cemetery was notorious, and rumors that the city intended to appropriate the land resulted in the transfer of the graves of whole families to newer cemeteries. Vandalism reached an extreme state by the 1950's. A section of the cemetery was sold to the city for the East-West Expressway in 1974. The sad chronicle of St. Paul's points to the central issue of whether a church, a city, and citizens have responsibility to the dead of generations long past, especially when the creators of the city are among the deceased. Based on newspapers, Allen's *Sketches of St. Paul's Parish* (1855), and secondary works; 29 notes.

G. J. Bobango

1555. Lane, Patricia G. BIRTH, MARRIAGE, AND DEATH: PAST AND PRESENT CUSTOMS IN EAST TENNESSEE. *Tennessee Folklore Soc. Bull. 1982 48(2): 53-60.* Discusses the changes in beliefs and rituals regarding birth, marriage, and death, concluding that some elements of the old traditions survive in current practices.

1556. Lanier, Doris. BILL NYE IN THE SOUTH. *Ann. of Wyoming 1974 46(2): 253-262.* Discusses an 1888 lecture tour through the South by renowned humorists Edgar Wilson ("Bill'') Nye and James Whitcomb Riley. Excerpted newspaper accounts of their engagements in Virginia and Georgia reflect their wide popularity. Touring under the auspices of the Redpath Lyceum Bureau, they helped to reunify national feeling following the Civil War. Much of their humor is captured in short newspaper vignettes. Also appearing with them in some of the speaking engagements was Harry Stillwell Edwards, a Georgia short-story writer, celebrated for his use of local southern themes. 20 notes.

M. L. Tate

1557. Lawrence, Keith. ARNOLD SCHULTZ: THE GREATEST(?) GUITAR PICKER'S LIFE ENDED BEFORE PROMISE REALIZED. *JEMF Q. 1981 17(61): 2-8.* Presents a biography of Arnold Schultz (1886-1931), thought by many to be the best guitar picker in the western Kentucky coalfields and a major influence on Bill Monroe, creator of the bluegrass sound a number of years after poisoned whiskey killed Schultz.

1558. Leich, Jean. A HISTORY OF NEWSPAPERS IN LINCOLN PARISH, 1873-1923. *North Louisiana Hist. Assoc. J. 1977 8(2): 81-86.* Lincoln Parish came into existence in 1873, and newspapers "have been part of the history of Lincoln Parish since its inception.'' The first paper in the parish was the *Vienna Sentinal,* edited by Sidney McCranie. The paper was moved in 1885 to Ruston, the new parish seat, and renamed the *Ruston Calligraph.* Other newspapers published in the parish over the years were the *Baptist Chronicle,* the *Ruston Daily Times,* the *Ruston Leader,* and the *Progressive Age.* The *Leader* was a successor to the *Calligraph* and the only daily paper being published in the parish in the 1920's. 17 notes.

A. N. Garland

1559. Lightfoot, William E. THE BALLAD "TALT HALL'' IN REGIONAL CONTEXT. *Southern Folklore Q. 1978 42(4): 361-373.* Presents several versions of the American folk ballad "Talt Hall,'' which tells the story of notorious 19th-century murderer Talt Hall of Kentucky.

1560. Locke, Louis G. ANTIQUE FURNITURE OF THE SHENANDOAH VALLEY. *Virginia Cavalcade 1975 24(3): 108-115.* Illustrated essay tracing the history of cabinetmaking in the Shenandoah Valley from 18th century colonial settlements to the early 19th century.

1561. Loftin, Bernadette K. A WOMAN LIBERATED: LILLIAN C. WEST, EDITOR. *Florida Hist. Q. 1974 52(4): 396-410.* Lillian Carlisle West (1884-1970) was editor of the weekly Panama City (Florida) *Pilot* during 1917-37. She also managed two other newspapers during this time and operated a land company and a publishing house. Her professional involvement gave her a position of community leadership equalled by few women of her time. West succeeded her husband in these positions but, once on her own, staked out strongly independent editorial positions until she sold her newspaper and retired from public life in 1937. Based on interviews, newspaper, census, and secondary sources; 73 notes.

J. E. Findling

1562. Lornell, Kip. "SOD'' ROGERS: TIPTON COUNTY HERBALIST. *Tennessee Folklore Soc. Bull. 1982 48(2): 61-65.* Biography of Tennessee herbalist Sod Rogers, born in 1911, now residing in Tipton County, focusing on his wariness of the medical profession and his reliance on common sense to treat physical complaints.

1563. Lowe, Robert A. and Menard, Montana X. MOZART PARK AND THE INCLINE. *Upper Ohio Valley Hist. Rev. 1981 11(1): 10-16.* Describes the founding and development of Mozart Park in south Wheeling, West Virginia, the dream of Henry Schmulbach, which opened in 1893, and discusses activities at the park, focusing on the construction of an inclined railroad to the park, which operated until 1907; the park closed in 1917-18.

1564. Ludden, Keith J. "IF IT'S ON THE RADIO, WHY BOTHER'': A STUDY OF TWO SOUTH-EAST BARREN COUNTY BALLAD SINGERS. *Kentucky Folklore Record 1978 24(2): 54-60.* Discusses the balladry and lives (ca. 1930-77) of Clorine Jones Lawson and Gladys Jones Pace.

1565. Maguire, Robert. LES CRÉOLES ET L'UTILISATION DE LANGUE CRÉOLE DE LA PAROISSE ST-MARTIN [Creoles and creole language use in St. Martin Parish, Louisiana]. *Cahiers de Géographie du Québec [Canada] 1979 23(59): 281-302.* Surveys the origins and uses of the Creole language in the south central and southeast regions of Louisiana from the early 19th century to the present.

1566. Malone, Bill C. ELVIS, COUNTRY MUSIC, AND THE SOUTH. *Southern Q. 1979 18(1): 123-134.* The style of rock and roll singer Elvis Presley (1935-77) came from earlier country music. His success came from his charismatic ability to combine his sensuality and his energy with the appearance of a bad southern boy tapping a new young audience. Teenagers in the mid-50's demanded young role models for heroes, and Presley best filled that role.
B. D. Ledbetter

1567. March, Stephen and Holt, David. CHASE THAT RABBIT. *Southern Exposure 1977 5(2-3): 44-47.* Clog dancing is divided into two primary forms, precision clogging, and traditional, or freestyle, clogging. It is an influential and popular artform in western North Carolina. Clogging as a dance technique has been influenced by traditional Cherokee Indian dancing and probably by transplantation of similar dances from England. Its effective performance requires talent, a keen sense of rhythm, and much practice. The log dancers are vitally aware of the close connections between their performances and their folk heritage. Based on interviews and personal observation.
N. Lederer

1568. Margavio, Anthony V. THE REACTION OF THE PRESS TO THE ITALIAN AMERICAN IN NEW ORLEANS, 1880 TO 1920. *Italian Americana 1978 4(1): 72-83.* Mirroring the national pattern of discrimination, the New Orleans press tended to use stereotypes of Italian Americans as criminals.

1569. Marshall, Howard W. and Vlach, John M. TOWARD A FOLKLIFE APPROACH TO AMERICAN DIALECTS. *Am. Speech 1973 48(3/4): 163-191.* The interaction between folklife and dialect is shown for three areas: Pennsylvania and the Valley of Virginia, the deep South, and southern Indiana. The folklife approach to dialects can be useful in explaining dialect boundaries, dialect overlapping, and the presence of lexical items. Because folklife and dialect are subject to the same historical and cultural influences, folklorists and dialect scholars can work together for mutual assistance and understanding. Table, 22 figs., 7 notes, biblio.
P. A. Beaber

1570. Marshall, Howard Wight. "KEEP ON THE SUNNY SIDE OF LIFE": PATTERNS AND RELIGIOUS EXPRESSION IN BLUEGRASS GOSPEL MUSIC. *New York Folklore Q. 1974 30(1): 3-43.*

1571. Marshall, John. EARLIE BOTTS. *Kentucky Folklore Record 1978 24(3-4): 81-88.* Describes the career (1946-77) of Earlie Botts (of Monroe County, Kentucky), "one of the few traditional 'standing hand' banjo players left in an area where that method of playing was once prevalent."

1572. Martin, Charles E. DECORATING THE APPALACHIAN HOUSE. *Appalachian J. 1982 10(1): 42-52.* Papering the walls with newspaper or magazine pages was the most common way to decorate cabins in Appalachia.

1573. Martin, Charles E. "MAKE 'EM FAST AND SHED 'EM QUICK": THE APPALACHIAN CRAFTSMAN REVISITED. *Appalachian J. 1981 9(1): 4-19.* Irvin Messer, an Appalachian craftsman, demonstrates the continued adaptability of culture and tradition when given new values and expectations that affect builders as well as users of his homemade chairs and baskets.

1574. Matthews, Nancy Torrance. THE DUEL IN NINETEENTH CENTURY SOUTH CAROLINA: CUSTOM OVER WRITTEN LAW. *Pro. of the South Carolina Hist. Assoc. 1979: 78-84.* Despite strong antidueling laws in South Carolina, duels continued until 1880 because respectable members of society approved

of them as means of redressing personal insults. The Cash-Shannon duel in 1880 was the culmination of a gradual shift away from support of the duel since the Civil War. The tremendous displacement in the society, politics, and economics of the state after the Civil War contributed to the decline of dueling. Published works; 60 notes.
J. W. Thacker, Jr.

1575. McCracken, Robert D. CULTURAL DIFFERENCES IN FOOD PREFERENCES AND MEANINGS. *Human Organization 1982 41(2): 161-167.* Compares food preferences and the reasons given for such preferences by black and white high school students on the basis of a survey conducted in Memphis, Tennessee, and describes how cultural differences between the two groups are mirrored in their food likes and dislikes.

1576. McGinty, Brian. "THIS CORDIAL JULEP." *Early Am. Life 1978 9(2): 26-28, 63.* History of the famous southern drink, mint julep, 1660-1949; discusses its association with horse races and recipe variations from the notes of famous Americans.

1577. Melchor, Marilyn. RAISED-PANEL FURNITURE OF VIRGINIA'S EASTERN SHORE, 1730-1830. *Art & Antiques 1982 5(6): 84-91.* Chronicles a century of distinctive cupboards and chests whose regional style changed little during the decades of its production.

1578. Mellinger, Marie B. THE SPIRIT IS STRONG IN THE ROOT, WITH A BRIEF MOUNTAIN HERBAL. *Appalachian J. 1977 4(3,4): 242-254.* A complete guide to medicinal plants in the Appalachian region, discussing their original use by the Cherokee Indians in 1540.
M. T. Wilson

1579. Menig, Harry. WOODY GUTHRIE: THE OKLAHOMA YEARS, 1912-1929. *Chronicles of Oklahoma 1975 53(2): 239-265.* Popular folksinger and journalist Woody Guthrie grew up in Okemah, Oklahoma, an oil boom town which had a lasting effect upon his life and music. A close attachment to his parents made him a life-long advocate of strong family ties, and his small town upbringing made him conscious of the rights of the common man. From Okemah's black community he also developed an appreciation of the blues which became an integral part of his ballad style. Deeply affected by the calamitous Dust Bowl and Great Depression, Guthrie represented a national voice for the dispossessed and their search for self-respect. Based on primary sources; interviews, 3 photos, 53 notes.
M. L. Tate

1580. Miller, Edna Clark. HISTORIC BRANDS OF BORDEN COUNTY. *Permian Hist. Ann. 1980 20: 67-87.* Describes and reproduces historic cattle brands found in Borden County, West Texas, during the 19th century; comments on the history of the ranches that used them and on the difficulties of the cattlemen during cattle drives.

1581. Miller, George L. A TENANT FARMER'S TABLEWARE: NINETEENTH-CENTURY CERAMICS FROM TABB'S PURCHASE. *Maryland Hist. Mag. 1974 69(2): 197-210.* Tenant farmers could not afford to buy matched sets of tableware even were they available.

1582. Miller, Terry E. OLD TIME SHAPE-NOTE SINGING SCHOOLS IN EASTERN KENTUCKY. *Southern Q. 1981 20(1): 35-45.* Francis Marion Tackett, 77 years old, appears to be the last shape-note singing teacher in eastern Kentucky. He still teaches as he did 50 years ago. Primary sources; 5 notes.
B. D. Ledbetter

1583. Milspaw, Yvonne J. WITCHCRAFT IN APPALACHIA: PROTECTION FOR THE POOR. *Indiana Folklore 1978 11(1): 71-86.* Folktales collected in West Virginia indicate that persons who claimed to be witches were usually elderly, eccentric women who functioned as manipulators of public fear in order to gain material goods necessary for survival and to command community respect.

1584. Mizell, Terrence A. GETTING SNOOKERED IN THE HORSE BUSINESS. *Tennessee Folklore Soc. Bull. 1978 44(4): 197-200.* A lighthearted description of horse trading in Tennessee based on personal experiences.

1585. Montell, Lynwood. "MY MOTHER SLEW ME: MY FATHER ATE ME." *Kentucky Folklore Record 1973 19(2): 42-44.*

1586. Moore, J. Roderick. EARTHENWARE POTTERS ALONG THE GREAT ROAD IN VIRGINIA AND TENNESSEE. *Mag. Antiques 1983 124(3): 528-537.* Discusses a school of Southern pottery that came from the potters along the main route from Virginia west to Kentucky and Tennessee.

1587. Moore, Willard B. THE WRITTEN AND ORAL NARRATIVES OF SARA COWAN. *Indiana Folklore 1977 10(1): 7-91.* Sara Cowan, a native of Greensboro, Kentucky, wrote a column in the Greensboro *Weekly Courier* on folklore and local history (through her reminiscences), 1968-72, and compiled a series of folklore tape recordings for the author, 1974.

1588. Morazan, Ronald R. "QUADROON" BALLS IN THE SPANISH PERIOD. *Louisiana Hist. 1973 14(3): 310-315.* Reproduces documents concerning public dances held by quadroons in New Orleans, 1792-1800.

1589. Moser, Joan. FRIDAY AT PARHAMS': CONTEMPORARY APPALACHIAN MUSIC IN CONTEXT. *Appalachian J. 1977 4(4): 206-214.* Description of one family's get-togethers demonstrates how traditional Appalachian folk culture and folk songs are preserved through informal gatherings, creating a complex educational process for its participants.

1590. Moser, Mabel Y. CHRISTIAN HARMONY SINGING AT ETOWAH. *Appalachian J. 1974 1(4): 263-270.* Describes the history and present expressions of Christian harmony singing.

1591. Moyers, Bill. THE ADVENTURES OF A RADICAL HILLBILLY: AN INTERVIEW WITH MYLES HORTON. *Appalachian J. 1982 9(4): 248-285.* Reprints the text of the interview between Bill Moyers and hillbilly organizer Myles Horton, founder of the Highlander Folk School, union organizer, and civil rights activist in the Chattanooga area of Tennessee, during 1932-81.

1592. Mullen, Patrick. TEXAS GULF COAST FISHING LORE. *Southern Exposure 1977 5(2-3): 134-139.* The sea and bay fishermen ply their crafts along the Texas Gulf Coast. Each has an individual and distinctive tradition dating back to the 19th century. The sea fishermen, confronted with the dangers of the open seas, have a host of superstitions, customs and legends. The bay fishermen's tradition is replete with tall tales, local character stories, and buried treasure legends. Based on interviews and personal observation.
N. Lederer

1593. Mullen, Patrick B. THE FOLK IDEA OF UNLIMITED GOOD IN AMERICAN BURIED TREASURE LEGENDS. *J. of the Folklore Inst. 1978 15(3): 209-220.* Examines the concept of unlimited good in American legends of buried treasure based on Gerald T. Hurley's and Alan Dundes's analyses of buried treasure legends throughout America's history, and provides several examples of legends collected by the article author in 1967 and 1971 on the Texas Gulf Coast.

1594. Musick, Ruth Ann. WITCHCRAFT AND THE DEVIL IN WEST VIRGINIA. *Appalachian J. 1974 1(4): 271-276.* Tales of the evil eye and the devil told to the author, 1950-67.

1595. Muth, Bell Rowan Stuart. PLACE NAMES ON A FAMILY FARM. *Kentucky Folklore Record 1978 24(1): 15-17.* Discusses language as folklore; the Stewart family of Warren and Butler Counties, Kentucky, is an example of the survival of personal identity for more than 100 years.

1596. Neal, Julia. THE ALLAN M. TROUT COLLECTION. *Kentucky Folklore Record 1973 19(2): 32-35.* A folklore collection given to Western Kentucky University.     S

1597. Norcini, Marilyn J. JOHN JANVIER SR., DELAWARE CABINETMAKER. *Mag. Antiques 1983 123(5): 1062-1068.* Describes various pieces created by John Janvier, Sr., who made cabinets, chairs, and coffins, in 18th-century Odessa, Delaware.

1598. O'Brien, Lucy Fulghum. THE *TRIBUNE'S* FIRST WOMAN REPORTER. *Tampa Bay Hist. 1982 4(1): 50-68.* The author's first job after graduating with a degree in journalism from Florida State College for Women in Tallahassee in 1935 was with the Tampa *Tribune* as a news reporter in 1936; she worked for the paper intermittently until the late 1950's.

1599. O'Connell, Barry. DOCK BOGGS, MUSICIAN AND COAL MINER. *Appalachian J. 1983-84 11(1-2): 44-57.* Profiles the financial and emotional turmoil in the life of Appalachian banjo player Dock Boggs, of West Norton, Virginia; discusses his brief recording career in 1927, which seemed to offer an escape from a life of coal mining, and describes his rediscovery during the folk revival of the 1960's.

1600. Olmert, Michael. IN WINTERTHUR'S SPLENDID ROOMS, FURNISHING IS ART. *Smithsonian 1983 14(2): 98-111.* Henry Francis du Pont's collection, 1923-69, of the best of American furniture, arts, and crafts, 1640-1840, is displayed in the 196 period rooms of Winterthur Museum in Delaware.

1601. Osthaus, Carl R. FROM THE OLD SOUTH TO THE NEW SOUTH: THE EDITORIAL CAREER OF WILLIAM TAPPAN THOMPSON OF THE *SAVANNAH MORNING NEWS*. *Southern Q. 1976 14(3): 237-260.* An historical overview of Georgia newspaperman William Tappan Thompson. Explores his views and actions relating to such major Southern issues as sectionalism, the Confederacy, Reconstruction, and the emergence of Southern industry. As reflected in his writings, Thompson personified the dominant Southern position concerning race relations, slavery, economic attitudes and the Civil War. 104 notes.    R. W. Dubay

1602. Otto, John S. and Burns, Augustus M. BLACK AND WHITE CULTURAL INTERACTION IN THE EARLY TWENTIETH CENTURY SOUTH: RACE AND HILLBILLY MUSIC. *Phylon 1974 35(4): 407-417.* Twentieth-century folk music can be a valuable tool in understanding the acculturation of Afro- and Euro-Americans. Documentary evidence is plentiful, and needs to be explored fully by a cooperative effort of scholars. Written sources, phonograph records, interviews, and participant observations are all useful and in need of further investigation. Informants can furnish evidence about the intensity of interracial social contacts at home and at work, about the circumstances in which participants learned to play and where they earned their money, about radio listening and record purchasing habits, and about attitudes toward associating with members of another race. Existing evidence indicates that some musical interchange did occur. Music frequently became the common interest which drew whites and blacks together. Musicians mentioned in the study include Jimmy Rodgers, Charley Patton and the Mississippi Sheiks, W. C. Handy, Bill Monroe, Bill Broonzy, Blind Lemon Jefferson, and Willie "Sonny Boy" Williamson. Based on primary and secondary sources; 68 notes.    B. A. Glasrud

1603. Oukada, Larbi. THE TERRITORY AND POPULATION OF FRENCH-SPEAKING LOUISIANA. *Rev. de Louisiane 1978 7(1): 5-34.* Twentieth-century studies of French-speakers in Louisiana contain social, demographic, political, and linguistic biases; suggests criteria for an interdisciplinary study of the extent of the French community in the 20th century.

1604. Oursler, Loree. THE COLLIER MEMOIR. *North Louisiana Hist. Assoc. J. 1974 6(1): 33-35.* In August 1971, the author received a letter from Ruby Eddins Collier, a resident of Shreveport, Louisiana, in which she mentioned Monterey, Texas, "a thriving busy town one hundred and ten years ago . . . located five miles from Vivian, Louisiana," about which "there have been lots of very interesting tales.'' The author visited Ruby Collier, who talked extensively about past events and the local folklore of Monterey, where both her father and grandfather had lived.

A. N. Garland

1605. Ousley, Stanley. THE KENTUCKY IRISH AMERICAN. *Filson Club Hist. Q. 1979 53(2): 178-195.* The *Kentucky Irish American,* a Louisville newspaper, was founded in 1898. Until the end of World War I it centered its attention on ethnic and nationalist themes. After 1900 the paper increasingly was "Catholic in orientation and outlook." After 1930 the *Irish American* strongly supported the programs of the Democratic Party. The paper was forced to shut down in 1968. 69 notes.                    G. M. McKinney

1606. Owen, Guy. THE LYING CONTEST. *Tennessee Folklore Soc. Bull. 1974 40(1): 17-22.* A fictional but accurate representation of tall-tale telling in rural Cape Fear County, North Carolina.

1607. Oxrieder, Julia Woodbridge. ELMIRA HUDSON NEW: FRIEND AND INFORMANT: FOLKLORE FROM ANSON COUNTY, NORTH CAROLINA. *Kentucky Folklore Record 1975 21(1): 3-12.* Gives examples of folklore collected by Elmira Hudson New (1900's to the present) in Anson County, North Carolina, including folk ballads and songs, folk medicines and superstitions.

1608. Paredes, Américo. TEXAS-MEXICAN CANCIONERO: FOLKSONGS OF THE LOWER BORDER. *Southern Exposure 1982 10(4): 50-57.* The stories and meaning behind the folksongs of the border Mexican-Americans of the Rio Grande Valley.

1609. Parker, David B. BILL ARP AND BLACKS: THE FORGOTTEN LETTERS. *Georgia Hist. Q. 1983 67(3): 336-349.* Discusses the letters of Bill Arp, pen name for Charles Henry Smith, humorous Southern social commentator, which he wrote weekly for the Atlanta *Constitution.* Smith's attitude toward blacks changed in about 1890 from paternal tolerance to fear. Based on Arp's unpublished letters and on secondary sources; 73 notes.

G. R. Schroeder

1610. Parramore, Thomas C. FORGING THE TREMULOUS LINK: THE FIRST HALF-CENTURY OF THE *NORTH CAROLINA HISTORICAL REVIEW. North Carolina Hist. R. 1974 51(4): 361-378.* Provides a synopsis of the history of the *North Carolina Historical Review.* The journal is financed with state money, but at first had few readers and contributors. The Great Depression severely strained its financial resources, and World War II caused a reduction of literary contributions. The postwar period brought changes; contributions and subscribers increased markedly. The journal reached into new areas of exploration and soon became a mainstream publication in its field. 8 photos, 77 notes.

V. L. Human

1611. Patterson, Daniel W. A WOMAN OF THE HILLS: THE WORK OF MAUDE MINISH SUTTON. *Southern Exposure 1977 5(2-3): 105-113.* Maude Minish Sutton was an assiduous collector of folklore and folklife survivals in western North Carolina during the 1920's-30's. Her findings were incorporated in a dispersed fashion in the Frank C. Brown Collection of North Carolina Folklore. Her writings on life in the Blue Ridge Mountains are valuable, although marked by a view for the quaint, sentimental, and romantic conceptions of mountain scenery. Sutton based some of her writings on her acquaintanceship with Ann Coffey, a mountain woman whose mannerisms and view of life were incorporated in the main character of the four sketches appended to the article. Primary and secondary sources.

N. Lederer

1612. Pearsall, Erin Anne. THE LEGEND OF SWANN'S CUT. *North Carolina Folklore J. 1973 21(2): 64-69.* Analyzes a legend of the Cape Fear region of North Carolina which has persisted as an oral tradition since the early 19th century. Explains the reasons for its continued popularity in that part of the state. The legend purports to explain the digging of a canal called Swann's Cut on Northeast Cape Fear River as a trick to win a boat race around 1800. Map.

R. N. Lokken

1613. Pederson, Lee. THE RANDY SONS OF NANCY WHISKEY. *Am. Speech 1977 52(1-2): 112-121.* There remains extensive investigation and research to be done in the genealogy and the development of the American cousins of Nancy Whiskey. There is a treacherous gamut awaiting young scholars who are willing to take on the language of southern moonshining as can be observed in a brief review of the problem. 10 notes.

D. A. Yanchisin

1614. Pennington, Lee and Pennington, Joy. TWO TALES FROM BLOODY HARLAN. *Appalachian J. 1973 1(2): 139-142.* Presents two folk tales. "Monster on Black Mountain" preserves the aura of dark mystery that surrounds Kentucky's largest mountain. "The Giant Man" speaks of one who straddles Highway 119 and hoofs it up hillsides 50 feet at a stride.

D. M. Dean

1615. Perret, J. John. STRANGE TRUE STORIES OF LOUISIANA: HISTORY OR HOAX? *Southern Studies 1977 16(1): 41-53.* *Strange True Stories of Louisiana* (1889) by George W. Cable began with three stories acquired from the Louisiana French writer Ms. Sidonie de la Houssaye. They are fanciful creations which deceived the careless Cable who later, in articles in *Century Magazine,* attempted to explain the errors as oversights. This was simply false, as research proves that the stories are pure fabrications. Overwhelming internal evidence, such as false and contradictory dates, purposeful creation or mingling of characters, arbitrary use of locations, and the character of Ms. Houssaye, shows the three stories, "The Young Aunt with White Hair," "The Adventures of Françoise and Suzanne," and "Alix de Morainville," to be hoaxes. Primary and secondary sources; 16 notes.    J. Buschen

1616. Perry, Clay. JOHN P. MITCHELL, VIRGINIA'S JOURNALIST OF REFORM. *Journalism Hist. 1977-78 4(4): 142-147, 156.* Examines the life and work of John P. Mitchell (1863-1929), editor of the Richmond *Planet,* and concentrates on his fight against racial discrimination.

1617. Pieroth, Doris Hinson. THE ONLY SHOW IN TOWN: ELLEN WHITMORE MOHRBACHER'S SAVOY THEATRE. *Chronicles of Oklahoma 1982 60(3): 260-279.* A daughter of Oklahoma pioneers, Ellen Whitmore Mohrbacher raised a family and maintained a flourishing movie theater business following her husband's death in 1918. She purchased the failing Savoy Theatre in Prague, Oklahoma, during 1921 and transformed it into a regal entertainment center, complete with all the latest equipment and movies. Mohrbacher personally booked all films and refused those she considered to be of questionable moral value. In 1943, her theater hosted the world premier of *Hangmen Also Die.* Business gradually declined in the 1950's due to competition from television, and the theater was sold in 1958. Based on a 1981 interview with Ellen Mohrbacher; 5 photos, 53 notes.

M. L. Tate

1618. Pitchford, Anita. THE MATERIAL CULTURE OF THE TRADITIONAL EAST TEXAS GRAVEYARD. *Southern Folklore Q. 1979 43(3-4): 277-290.* Details traditional arrangements and artifacts observed in 20th-century cemeteries in Cass County, Texas, revealing the region's Southern culture.

1619. Plater, Ormonde. THE LOVINGOOD PATRIARCHY. *Appalachian J. 1973 1(2): 82-93.* Newspaper yarns of the Old Southwest often dealt with erotic slapstick. Sut Lovingood, created by George Washington Harris, was flagrantly erotic. Discusses the nudity and other forms of obscene revelation in five stories about the Lovingood family. 2 illus., 26 notes.    D. M. Dean

1620. Poston, Glenda. TALL TALES FROM PERQUIMANS COUNTY. *North Carolina Folklore J. 1973 21(1): 40-47.* Two fantastic tales from Perquimans County.    R. N. Lokken

1621. Pratt, Linda Ray. ELVIS, OR THE IRONIES OF A SOUTHERN IDENTITY. *Southern Q. 1979 18(1): 40-51.* Elvis Presley (1935-77) was the most popular entertainer in the world when he died in 1977, but he was more popular in the South, where he was born, than anywhere else. Outside the South, he was always viewed in his 50's image; in the South he evolved and was at the center of southern rock at the time of his death.

B. D. Ledbetter

1622. Presley, Delma E. THE CRACKERS OF GEORGIA. *Georgia Hist. Q. 1976 60(2): 102-116.* "Cracker" is a term which has been used, often in a derogatory way, to describe Georgia residents since colonial times. Demonstrates the term's use with examples from contemporary journals and other writings and analyzes the term's linguistic background. The resulting definition of a "Cracker" is a "proud pioneer." Primary and secondary sources; 36 notes.

G. R. Schroeder

1623. Pusateri, C. Joseph. RADIO BROADCASTERS AND THE CHALLENGE OF TELEVISION: A NEW ORLEANS CASE. *Business Hist. Rev. 1980 54(3): 303-329.* Radio station operators faced a difficult decision in the late 1940's, whether to seek television channel grants from the FCC or to confine their activities to the proven profitability of AM broadcasting. New Orleans' WWL, a major southern station and a CBS affiliate, internally debated the issue during 1947 and 1948. A relatively conservative ownership feared jeopardizing AM profits by investing in the extremely costly and speculative venture of television. Finally, under pressure from outside expertise and the fear of being frozen out of the limited channel grants available, WWL filed for television. The WWL experience demonstrates the risk-taking aspect of technological innovation. Based mainly on WWL station records; 5 tables, 62 notes.

A

1624. Pusateri, C. Joseph. THE STORMY CAREER OF A RADIO MAVERICK, W. K. HENDERSON OF KWKH. *Louisiana Studies 1976 15(4): 389-407.* During 1925-33, William Kennon Henderson (1880-1945) owned and ran radio station KWKH in Shreveport, Louisiana. By arbitrarily increasing his kilowatt power and by his provocative attacks on William K. Skelly of KVOO in Tulsa while trying to maintain his broadcasting license, Henderson provoked the federal government to pass the Radio Act of 1927 and the Davis Amendment of 1928. Henderson's final attack on chain stores was less successful, and economic problems brought on by the Depression and poor management led to the selling of the station in 1933. Henderson used a flamboyant style and what some called profanity to develop a nationwide audience that contributed considerable sums of money and wrote thousands of letters in his support. Based on primary sources in archives of Federal Radio Commission, Louisiana newspapers, KWKH Archives, and others, and on secondary sources; 46 notes.

J. Buschen

1625. Reidenbaugh, Lowell. MARY ANNA MORRISON JACKSON. *Lincoln Herald 1983 85(2): 100-108.* Mary Anna Morrison Jackson, widow of Lieutenant General Thomas "Stonewall" Jackson, was a public figure of sentimental devotion after the Civil War, particularly for Southerners, and attended many memorial occasions.

1626. Reyna, José R. NOTES ON TEJANO MUSIC. *Atzlán 1982 13(1-2): 81-94.* Traces the development of Chicano music in Texas, a process which has produced a distinctive style of popular bicultural music. Tejano music falls into two categories: *conjunto,* a musical group consisting of accordion, *bajo sexto* guitar, bass, and drums, which evolved from the Mexican culture for over a century to achieve maturity in the 1940's and 1950's; and *bandas,* larger bands based on the Anglo bands of the Big Band era. Both types have experimented with different instruments (such as organs and six-string guitars) to achieve their distinctive sounds. Many individuals in the groups have gained prominence in the world of professional popular music. Tejano music continues as an identifiable yet flexible musical form firmly grounded in cultural traditions. Based on secondary sources, interviews, and recordings.

A. Hoffman

1627. Reynolds, George. OPOSSUM HUNTING IN SOUTHWESTERN VIRGINIA. *Kentucky Folklore Record 1974 20(4): 99-100.*

1628. Rickels, Patricia. LE FOLKLORE DES ACADIENS [The Acadians' folklore]. *Rev. de Louisiana 1978 7(2): 101-115.* Studies Acadian folklore in Louisiana since the 18th century and mentions social customs still alive.

1629. Riedl, Norbert F. and Buckles, Carol K. HOUSE CUSTOMS AND BELIEFS IN EAST TENNESSEE. *Tennessee Folklore Soc. Bull. 1975 41(2): 47-56.* Poses and attempts to answer questions in four broad categories: building a house, entering and leaving a house, life crises and the house, and housecleaning.

1630. Riess, Steven A. THE BASEBALL MAGNATE AND URBAN POLITICS IN THE PROGRESSIVE ERA. *J. of Sport Hist. 1974 1(1): 41-62.* Baseball is supposed to exemplify the best in American society: competition, honesty, and diligence. During the Progressive era 17 of the 18 major-league teams were operated by men who "typified some of its worst aspects." They had political connections, and the owners included political bosses and friends of professional gamblers. Examines the situation in Atlanta, Chicago, and New York. 65 notes.

M. Kaufman

1631. Riley, Sam G. A SEARCH FOR THE CULTURAL BIGFOOT: FOLKLORE OR FAKELORE? *J. of Popular Culture 1976 10(2): 337-387.* Examination of the mass of southeastern US folklore indicates that the Bigfoot stories of the sea island areas of South Carolina and the coastal areas of Georgia are Southeastern States "fakelore" adopted from the Sasquatch folklore of the Pacific Northwest. Primary and secondary sources. Table, 37 notes.

D. G. Nielson

1632. Ritchie, Jean. LIVING IS COLLECTING: GROWING UP IN A SOUTHERN APPALACHIAN "FOLK" FAMILY. *Appalachian J. 1977 4(4): 188-198.* The author's personal remembrances of Jason Ritchie are combined with the texts of some of his unpublished folklore and folk songs.

1633. Roach, Fred, Jr. WILL ROGERS' YOUTHFUL RELATIONSHIP WITH HIS FATHER, CLEM ROGERS: A STORY OF LOVE AND TENSION. *Chronicles of Oklahoma 1980 58(3): 325-342.* Presents a sociological-psychological assessment of the relationship between Will Rogers and his father during the former's boyhood and teenage years. The father, Clem Rogers, had high expectations for his son and always demanded success from him. Will was more easygoing and oriented toward the loving affection offered by his mother rather than the harshness of his father. The personality clash increased after the mother's death, and young Will went from one venture to another with little success. Only after Will won acclaim in vaudeville did the rift begin to heal, but Clem's untimely death in 1911 prohibited the full reconciliation. 5 photos, 45 notes.

M. L. Tate

1634. Robbins, Peggy. WHERE CARNIVAL IS KING. *Am. Hist. Illus. 1979 13(10): 4-11, 46-49.* Discusses Mardi Gras celebrations in New Orleans, 1718-1978.

1635. Robe, Stanley L. A BORDER *CANCIONERO* AND A REGIONAL VIEW OF FOLKSONG. *New Scholar 1977 6: 257-268.* Reviews Americo Paredes's *A Texas-Mexican Cancionero: Folksongs of the Lower Border* (Urbana: U. of Illinois Pr., 1976). The cultural change accelerated by World War II has affected the content and style of border ballads. Traditional folk songs are out of style with the younger generation who increasingly accept Anglo norms in music. Part of the special issue, "New Direction in Chicano Scholarship." 9 notes.

D. K. Pickens

1636. Rowland, A. R. PICTURE POST CARDS: GLIMPSES OF AUGUSTA'S PAST. *Richmond County Hist. 1983 15(1): 5-8.* Reproduces six picture postcards showing views of Augusta, Georgia, ca. 1900-25, and sketches the history of the picture postcard since 1869.

1637. Salem, Jim. COON DOG GRAVEYARD. *Southern Exposure 1979 7(3): 27-29.* Key Underwood Memorial Park in Tennessee Valley, Alabama, is a graveyard for coon dogs. Elaborate and simple memorials installed by the owners of deceased animals indicate the intense attachment of hunters to their dogs. Only after the dogs have proven themselves do owners become attached to them. The coon hunter ordinarily is so addicted to the sport that its practice takes precedence over virtually every other aspect of life. Based on interviews and personal observations.

1638. Sammons, Jeffrey T. BOXING AS A REFLECTION OF SOCIETY: THE SOUTHERN REACTION TO JOE LOUIS. *J. of Popular Culture 1983 16(4): 23-33.* The career of boxer Joe Louis demonstrates that sport heroes reflect contemporary public moods and beliefs. Despite his successes, Louis throughout his career was subject to the dictates of Southern racial etiquette. Based on contemporary Southern newspapers; 41 notes. D. G. Nielson

1639. Sasson, Diane Hyde. "THE STONE": VERSIONS OF A CAMP-MEETING SONG COLLECTED IN NORTH CAROLINA. *Southern Folklore Q. 1978 42(4): 375-384.* Reprints several versions of the religious folk hymn "The Stone," known in North Carolina and sung for the author in 1971 and 1972 by people who remembered hearing it as far back as the 1930's.

1640. Saxton, Alexander. BLACKFACE MINSTRELSY AND JACKSONIAN IDEOLOGY. *Am. Q. 1975 27(1): 3-28.* Blackface minstrelsy during 1854-75 was a white product expressing class identification and hostility, ethnic satire, social and political commentary, and sexual attitudes. Thomas Rice, Dan Emmett, E. P. Christy, and other minstrels were largely urban products employing the image of a romantic South to symbolize the rural origins of their audiences. The non-humanity of Negroes depicted emphasized the desire of the minstrels to create white egalitarianism. N. Lederer

1641. Schulman, Steven A. HOWESS DEWEY WINFREY: THE REJECTED SONGMAKER. *J. of Am. Folklore 1974 87(343): 72-84.* The satiric songs of Howess Dewey Winfrey were never accepted into the traditional balladry of Cumberland County, Kentucky, because the community disapproved of his social criticism and sense of humor. However, Winfrey's songs should be considered part of the area's folklore. Analyzes five song and two speech texts. Primary and secondary sources; 32 notes. W. D. Piersen

1642. Seroff, Doug. POLK MILLER AND THE OLD SOUTH QUARTETTE. *JEMF Q. 1982 28(67-68): 147-150.* Discusses the career of Polk Miller and the Old South Quartette of Richmond, Virginia, who, from 1899 to 1912, sang songs evoking Southern plantation life.

1643. Simms, L. Moody, Jr. RICHARD MALCOLM JOHNSTON ON RURAL LIFE IN MIDDLE GEORGIA. *Georgia Hist. Q. 1974 58(Supplement): 181-192.* Middle Georgia was composed of Putman county and those surrounding it. It was an area composed of immigrants from western Europe except Britain. The culture of the area was rustic, and the humor unique. Although slavery was practiced, it did not inhibit a positive relationship between slave and master which led to an extension of the regional humor. The rural humor and careless speech patterns of the area erroneously led outsiders to assume that middle Georgians were ignorant, but the misconception was more likely due to a failure to understand the culture of the region. Primary and secondary sources; 5 notes. M. R. Gillam

1644. Smith, Betty N. THE GAP IN ORAL TRADITION. *Appalachian J. 1977 4(4): 199-205.* Laments the present failure of most Appalachian children to learn traditional folk songs from their elders and emphasizes the value of efforts made for their preservation.

1645. Smith, L. Allen. TOWARD A RECONSTRUCTION OF THE DEVELOPMENT OF THE APPALACHIAN DULCIMER: WHAT THE INSTRUMENTS SUGGEST. *J. of Am. Folklore 1980 93(370): 385-396.* The Appalachian dulcimer seems to have evolved from the Pennsylvania German zither after the sound box was enlarged, and the instrument was lengthened, narrowed, and

given fewer strings but more frets. Covers 1800-1940. Based on a field census of pre-1940 fretted zithers in the upland South; 10 illus., 14 notes. W. D. Piersen

1646. Smith, Ralph A. THE CRUCIAL ROLE OF PRAIRIE COAL. *West Texas Hist. Assoc. Year Book 1981 57: 3-33.* Discusses the importance of cow dung, or "Old Chips," for use as fuel on the West Texas frontier because no other fuel source was available; in 1541 Francisco Vazques Coronado a Carlos first wrote about using chips to cook, but in the 1930's coal and kerosene replaced chips except for special situations.

1647. Smyth, Willie J. EARLY KNOXVILLE RADIO (1921-41): WNOX AND THE *MIDDAY MERRY GO-ROUND. JEMF Q. 1982 28(67-68): 109-115.* Discusses the content and personnel of Knoxville, Tennessee's WNOX country music radio station from 1921 to 1941, especially the program *Midday Merry Go-Round.*

1648. Soileau, Jeanne. CHILDREN'S CHEERS AS FOLKLORE. *Western Folklore 1980 39(3): 232-247.* Presents a series of cheers collected from a south Louisiana public school and at a Camp Fire Girls camp in Baton Rouge. Discusses the differences in the cheering styles of black, white, and integrated cheering squads and briefly analyzes cheering activities among young girls who are not members of official cheering squads. Field observations and secondary sources; 10 notes. S. L. Myres

1649. Stanley, David H. THE GOSPEL-SINGING CONVENTION IN SOUTH GEORGIA. *J. of Am. Folklore 1982 95(375): 1-32.* The annual singing conventions of Southern Protestant churches and communities are a declining tradition whose origins go back to singing school competitions and a blending of gospel and popular music. As community recreational events, the conventions unite sacred and secular realms giving scope to individual and group participation through new-book music using shape-note notation. Based on the American Folklife Center's South-Central Georgia Folklife Project of 1977; 5 fig., 14 notes, biblio.

W. D. Piersen

1650. Stansel, David B., Jr. UNIQUE EXPERIENCES AT THE MACO LIGHT. *North Carolina Folklore J. 1973 21(1): 18-22.* Stories told by North Carolina State University students about a legendary ghost-light at the scene of a 19th-century railroad accident at Maco, near Wilmington, North Carolina. R. N. Lokken

1651. Stem, Thad, Jr. ABSENT WITH LEAVE, OR HOW MUSTY FILES CAME ALIVE. *North Carolina Hist. R. 1974 51(2): 170-182.* North Carolina was among the last of the original colonies to get a printing press. Distant news was given priority for many decades on the theory that readers of newspapers already knew the local news. The subscriber had to pick up his copy at the shop since Congress extended special mailing privileges only in 1879. Recounts the story of many local papers and their editors. Illus. E. P. Stickney

1652. Stewart, David Marshall. WILLIAM T. BERRY AND HIS FABULOUS BOOKSTORE: NASHVILLE'S LITERARY EMPORIUM WITHOUT PARALLEL. *Tennessee Hist. Q. 1978 37(1): 36-48.* Berry's Bookstore, the best west of the Allegheny Mountains, existed from 1835 to 1876. It was the general meeting place of leading politicians. Its reading room served primarily as a gentleman's club for years. Berry's strong Union stand at the outbreak of the Civil War, however, heralded the beginning of the decline of his bookstore. Secondary material; 3 notes. M. B. Lucas

1653. Stone, William J., Jr. TEXAS' FIRST CHURCH NEWSPAPER: THE TEXAS PRESBYTERIAN, 1846-1865. *Texana 1973 12(3): 239-247.* In 1846 at Victoria, A. J. McGown began publishing the *Texas Presbyterian.* McGown, an ordained Cumberland Presbyterian Church minister, had his problems from the outset. Problems during the 10 years of publication included poor financing, few subscribers, poor mail service, no adequate place to print the paper (he moved from Victoria to Houston and then to Huntsville and threatened other moves), and few qualified correspondents. He ceased publication in 1856 and returned to an active preaching ministry. Primary and secondary sources; 18 notes.

B. D. Ledbetter

1654. Stricklin, David. NOTHING FORCED OR FANCY. *Southern Exposure 1980 8(4): 46-51.* Discusses the revitalization of Bob Wills and the Texas Playboys in the mid-1970's when progressive country music rose in popularity, and provides a biography of Bob Wills and a history of the Playboys since the 1920's.

1655. Strohfeldt, Thomas A. JACOB RIZER: A BARDSTOWN RIFLEMAKER. *Filson Club Hist. Q. 1974 48(1): 5-15.* Provides a brief biography of riflemaker Jacob Rizer and discusses the way his designs combined practical and artistic features. Each Kentucky long rifle reflected unique attributes of both the maker and the person who commissioned the work. Rizer's style was distinctive but not highly original. Documentation from county records and secondary works; 5 illus., 46 notes.

G. B. McKinney

1656. Struna, Nancy L. THE NORTH-SOUTH RACES: AMERICAN THOROUGHBRED RACING IN TRANSITION: 1823-1850. *J. of Sport Hist. 1981 8(2): 28-57.* North-South horse racing began in 1822 with the challenge by a Virginia breeder, James J. Harrison, to New York's Charles Van Ranst for a match race between the Virginia champion, Sir Charles, and the New Yorker's American Eclipse. From that first race through the 1840's, North-South races were important to both the agricultural orientation of American society and to the American image. The last major race was held in 1843. Sectionalism seemingly had become the biggest enemy of the races, as once friendly rivalry could no longer bear the intense political friction of the time. Also, unfavorable economic conditions had eroded the financial base upon which the races had developed. The original value system which spawned the races had changed. Based upon newspapers and magazines of the period; 90 notes.

M. Kaufman

1657. Sturdevant, Lynda M. GIRL SCOUTING IN STILLWATER, OKLAHOMA: A CASE STUDY IN LOCAL HISTORY. *Chronicles of Oklahoma 1979 57(1): 34-48.* Though first organized in 1927, Girl Scouting in Stillwater, Oklahoma, did not attach itself to the national organization until 1937. Fundraising projects dominated the following years as the local organizers attempted to attract new members and expand activities. Stillwater businesses contributed significant aid to the local chapter and helped build a lodge in the late 1930's. During the 1950's the Stillwater Council fought a losing battle with the national Girl Scout organization which merged several administrative districts. Still the local chapter was able to continue with its own goals and has been a major asset to the community. Newspapers and interviews; 5 photos, 50 notes.

M. L. Tate

1658. Sweezy, Nancy. TRADITION IN CLAY: PIEDMONT POTTERY. *Historic Preservation 1975 27(4): 20-23.* Relates the history of pottery making on North Carolina's Piedmont plateau (Moore and Randolph counties) and describes processes "which have remained essentially the same for 235 years." 6 photos.

R. M. Frame III

1659. Swisher, Bob. GERMAN FOLK ART IN HARMONY CEMETERY. *Appalachian J. 1978 5(3): 313-317.* Photos of 11 tombstones found in Jane Lew, West Virginia, at the Harmony Methodist Church Cemetery show decorative folk symbols representative of local German settlers, 1827-55.

1660. Taylor, Deborah. TRADITIONAL TALES FROM SALTER PATH. *North Carolina Folklore J. 1973 21(1): 10-14.* Four folk tales of Salter Path, a village in Carteret County, North Carolina, as told to the author by David Merle, a native of Salter Path. Glossary.

R. N. Lokken

1661. Tharp, Mel. ICE CREAM SUPPER. *Kentucky Folklore Record 1975 21(3): 74-76.* Presents recollections of the early ice cream supper in the rural counties of McLean and Hopkins in Kentucky during the 1930's and 1940's.

1662. Tharp, Mel. JOHNSON RODS, HORSESHOE BREAD, AND OTHER TENNESSEE COLLOQUIALISMS. *Tennessee Folklore Soc. Bull. 1983 49(2): 74-77.* Describes attempts to discover the origins of such quaint colloquial expressions as "being drunker'n a light bread hog" in Tennessee and Kentucky.

1663. Thompson, Lawrence S. THE LORE OF LIGHTNING IN KENTUCKY. *Kentucky Folklore Record 1974 20(1): 14-17.*

1664. Thompson, Lawrence S. THE MOON IN KENTUCKY AND ELSEWHERE. *Kentucky Folklore Record 1973 19(1): 7-10.*

1665. Thompson, Lawrence S. WHISKEY IN KENTUCKY FOLK BELIEF. *Kentucky Folklore Record 1974 20(2): 35-38.*

1666. Thornell, Fran. "THE HANDKERCHIEF STORY" AND "THE HANTED HOUSE": TWO MIDDLE TENNESSEE GHOST STORIES. *Tennessee Folklore Soc. Bull. 1978 44(2): 71-75.* Recounts two folktales involving ghosts, told by Pearl Oliver Miller, 1977.

1667. Thurman, Kelly. BRADLEY KINCAID: MUSIC FROM THE MOUNTAINS IN THE 1920S. *Register of the Kentucky Hist. Soc. 1982 80(2): 170-182.* Bradley Kincaid was an able representative of the culture of his native Kentucky. On the radio, in concerts, and in his publishing, Kincaid helped make popular the music of Appalachia and the mountain people of Kentucky. After his start with station WLS, he left Chicago and worked with many other stations for the next 20 years. Although he left radio in the 1950's, his interest in collecting and publishing country music continues in the 1980's. Interviews and secondary sources; 10 notes, 3 photos.

J. F. Paul

1668. Thurman, Kelly. FONTAINE FOX: KENTUCKY'S FOREMOST CARTOONIST. *Register of the Kentucky Hist. Soc. 1979 77(2): 112-128.* Biography of Kentucky cartoonist Fontaine Fox (b. 1884), focusing on his career as a cartoonist beginning in 1904, while a student at Indiana University, until 1955, when he drew his last cartoon strip; focuses on 1920-21.

1669. Tidwell, Donavon Duncan. SAM HOUSTON: FREEMASON. *Texana 1973 11(3): 260-274.* Discusses Sam Houston's affiliation with the Order of Freemasons in Texas, 1817-65. 74 notes.

1670. Tolman, Donald K. THROUGH THE ETHER: THE BIRTH OF RADIO IN CENTRAL OKLAHOMA. *Chronicles of Oklahoma 1983 61(2): 130-147.* Surveys the growth of radio stations in central Oklahoma from the 1921 inauguration of Oklahoma City's WKY to the diverse stations of the early 1930's. The new invention found enough immediate success among advertisers and the public that it was soon able to offer specialized programs that included live bands, news broadcasts, educational shows, religious services, and even remote live broadcasts. Based on newspapers and interviews; 8 photos, 51 notes.

M. L. Tate

1671. Trudeau, Nancy B. SAWYER DOWNS: "RIGHT PLACE, WRONG TIME." *North Louisiana Hist. Assoc. J. 1983 14(1): 41-50.* Sawyer Downs, a horse racing track in Bossier Parish, south of Benton, Louisiana, opened in 1965, but was plagued from the start by many problems and opponents. Politics, religion, and rumors of involvement with organized crime all played a part in the delays and ultimate demise of Earl Sawyer's dream. Another track, the successful Louisiana Downs, was luckier as the political climate had changed by the time it sought permission to build in Bossier Parish. Based on Sawyer Downs Collection (LSU-Shreveport) and secondary sources; 69 notes.

J. F. Paul

1672. Tucker, Stephen R. PENTECOSTALISM AND POPULAR CULTURE IN THE SOUTH: A STUDY OF FOUR MUSICIANS. *J. of Popular Culture 1982 16(3): 68-80.* Brief biographical sketches of James Blackwood, Johnny Cash, Jerry Lee Lewis, and Tammy Wynette illustrate the important influence of pentecostalism on Southern popular music from gospel to rockabilly. Based on interviews; 55 notes.

D. G. Nielson

1673. Tucker, Steve. THE LOUISIANA HAYRIDE, 1948-1954. *North Louisiana Hist. Assoc. J.* 1977 8(5): 187-202. After World War II, country music became quite popular throughout the country. Although the Grand Ole Opry in Nashville, Tennessee, was considered country music's focal point, many regional radio variety programs similar to the Opry came into being. The most successful and important of these was the Louisiana Hayride, broadcast over radio station KWKH in Shreveport. It soon became known as the "Cradle of the Stars," because many of the men and women who performed for the Hayride eventually moved to Nashville and the Opry. In 1954, the Hayride brought Elvis Presley, and the impact of his songs and singing was devastating to both the Hayride and country music. When he left, the Hayride began to decline, and it went off the air in 1962. Today, the Hayride is back as a showcase for new country music performers. Primary and secondary sources; 72 notes.                                    A. N. Garland

1674. Tullos, Allen. "THE DEAD BE BURIED HERE": IRISH JOKES OF TOMMIE BASS. *Southern Folklore Q.* 1977 41: 81-96. Discusses "jokes" denigrating the Irish character which were fostered in Great Britain and the United States, 16th-19th centuries; reprints a series which the author collected from Tommie Bass, a herbalist in Leesburg, Alabama, 1973.

1675. VanOsdol, Scott, photog., and Dickey, Dan W. LA MUSICA NORTEÑA: A PHOTOGRAPHIC ESSAY. *Southern Exposure* 1983 11(1): 38-41. Portrays the popularity of Norteña, a blend of 19th-century dances and 20th-century Latin Caribbean rhythms, within the Spanish community of San Antonio, Texas, since the 1930's.

1676. Wallis, Michael. NEW TRAILS FOR OLD-TIME BOOTS. *Am. West* 1981 18(1): 38-47, 64-65. The true cowboy boot with a reinforced arch and a higher heel first appeared in the 1870's. There have been some evolutionary changes since then, always functional. Bootmaking is a craft that is handed down from generation to generation in family companies. Boots are still an integral part of cowboys' equipment. Today fashion has made them a coveted item for others as well. Although bootmaking and outlets are widespread, Texas continues to be the heart and soul of cowboy boot country. 14 illus.                          D. L. Smith

1677. Ward, Barry J. ITALIAN-AMERICAN FOLK POETRY. *West Virginia Hist.* 1982 43(4): 285-302. Italian Americans Roy and Reginia D'Aritano have helped record the folk songs of Italian immigrants to West Virginia. Many of the songs are tributes to the saints and the Virgin Mary. Others deal with experiences of immigrants in their new country and with Christopher Columbus as an Italian national hero. 26 notes.                      J. D. Neville

1678. Ward, W. H. WATSON OF DEEP GAP: A RETROSPECTIVE. *Appalachian J.* 1975 2(2): 102-110. Reviews recording of Arthel "Doc" Watson, rural guitarist from Deep Gap, North Carolina.

1679. Weatherford, Sally E. PROFILE OF A MURFREESBORO QUILTMAKER AND HER CRAFT. *Tennessee Folklore Soc. Bull.* 1978 44(3): 108-114. Offers a biographical sketch of Nellie Virge, 1880's-1970's, focusing on her quilting, and describing 12 of her patterns.

1680. Weldy, Mary Helen and Taylor, David L. GONE BUT NOT FORGOTTEN: THE LIFE AND WORK OF A TRADITIONAL TOMBSTONE CARVER. *Keystone Folklore* 1976-77 21(2): 14-33. Focuses on the life of tombstone carver Christopher Carson Hancock (1878-1936) of Allen County, Kentucky; his work, described here, is found in Allen County, other surrounding counties, and Tennessee.

1681. Wells, E. D. DUCHE, THE POTTER. *Georgia Hist. Q.* 1957 41(4): 383-390. Studies the life and art of Georgia potter Andrew Duche (b. 1709) and narrates the story of 20th-century efforts to locate samples of his work.

1682. Welsh, Jack. THE BELL WITCH. *Kentucky Folklore Record* 1973 19(4): 112-116. Stories of Kate Bell, a witch in 19th-century Tennessee.

1683. Western, John. SOCIAL GROUPS AND ACTIVITY PATTERNS IN HOUMA, LOUISIANA. *Geographical R.* 1973 63(3): 301-321. The city of Houma, in the bayou country of southern Louisiana, was once a sequestered fishing, trapping, and sugarcane- and oyster-producing area where Cajun French was the dominant language. Since World War II, however, a surge in oilfield activity has almost tripled the population of Houma. The growth has brought the superimposition of a third social group, immigrant anglophone Texans, on the two principal local groups, the blacks and the Cajun whites. A simple model is constructed to describe the relationships of each group to the others, and the activitiy patterns of each group on neighborhood, city, North American, and world scales are delineated. Cajuns are found to be acculturated into the exogenous white system more rapidly than blacks are, and several intermediate social groups emerge.                          J

1684. Whisnant, David. THICKER THAN FIDDLERS IN HELL: ISSUES AND RESOURCES IN APPALACHIAN MUSIC. *Appalachian J.* 1978 5(1): 103-115. Examines studies in Appalachian music; future studies must focus on the origins and regional character of Appalachian music, which has unified the area's folk culture, 1880's-1977.

1685. Whisnant, David E. FINDING THE WAY BETWEEN THE OLD AND THE NEW: THE MOUNTAIN DANCE AND FOLK FESTIVAL AND BASCOM LAMAR LUNSFORD'S WORK AS A CITIZEN. *Appalachian J.* 1979-80 7(1-2): 135-154. The Mountain Dance and Folk Festival began in 1928 under the direction of Bascom Lamar Lunsford as part of the Asheville (North Carolina) Rhododendron Festival, and is still an annual affair.

1686. Wiggins, Gene. FLAT CREEK REVISITED: JAMES MARLOWE PROPES. *JEMF Q.* 1981 17(63): 132-138. Presents the reminiscences of James Marlowe Propes, born in 1900, a member of the Flat Creek Sacred Singers of the Flat Creek Baptist Church in Gainesville, Georgia, who began singing at the age of five or six and was also a member of the Propes Quartette beginning in about 1924.

1687. Wiggins, Gene. THE SOCIO-POLITICAL WORKS OF FIDDLIN' JOHN AND MOONSHINE KATE. *Southern Folklore Q.* 1977 41: 97-118. John Carson and eventually his daughter, Kate Carson, wrote and sang political songs during 1900-49 which championed poor, working, and rural people in Georgia and lambasted "big city" politics.

1688. Wigginton, Eliot. APPALACHIAN FOLK CULTURE. *Historic Preservation* 1973 25(1): 23-27. Comments by the staff of *Foxfire* magazine, high school students from Rabun Gap, and the editor, a teacher. Discuss their attempts to record and preserve the local Appalachian mountain peoples' way of life. Illus., 5 photos.                          R. M. Frame III

1689. Wilgus, D. K. "ROSE CONNOLEY": AN IRISH BALLAD. *J. of Am. Folklore* 1979 92(364): 172-195. An analysis of the texts of the ballad "Rose Connoley" suggests that it originated in Ireland in the early 19th century but was popularized in the southern Appalachian region of the United States where the first examples were recorded. An index of 71 American performances is included. Based on song texts; 28 notes, index.

W. D. Piersen

1690. Wilhelm, Gene, Jr. FOLK CULTURE HISTORY OF THE BLUE RIDGE MOUNTAINS. *Appalachian J.* 1975 2(3): 192-222. Describes the geography and early inhabitants of the Blue Ridge Mountains from 1730 to 1800 and the culture produced by the interaction between man and land.

1691. Wilhelm, Gene, Jr. FOLK SETTLEMENTS IN THE BLUE RIDGE MOUNTAINS. *Appalachian J. 1978 5(2): 204-245.* Discusses types of folk settlements in the Blue Ridge Mountains of Virginia, 1740's-1970's, including gap, hollow, cove, ridge, and meadow settlements.

1692. Williams, Brett. THE SOUTH IN THE CITY. *J. of Popular Culture 1982 16(3): 30-41.* Examines the phenomenon of "Southernness" in popular culture—especially music, dance, dress, and sports—in defining individual and shared "place" in predominately black neighborhoods in Washington, D.C., and Champaign-Urbana, Illinois. 29 notes.　　　　D. G. Nielson

1693. Williams, Cratis. BALLAD COLLECTING IN THE 1930'S. *Appalachian J. 1979-80 7(1-2): 33-36.* The author discusses his interest in Appalachian ballads and his research on and collection of ballads in the 1930's.

1694. Williamson, Billie. FUN AND GAMES OF MOUNTAIN CHILDREN. *Kentucky Folklore Record 1975 21(2): 43-55.* Describes songs and children's games common in eastern Kentucky.　　　　S

1695. Willingham, Calder. TRUE MYTH-MAKER OF THE POST-BELLUM SOUTH. *Georgia Hist. Q. 1975 59(2): 243-247.* Discusses Erskine Caldwell (*Tobacco Road, God's Little Acre*) as a creator of folk legends in post-Civil War southern literature.

1696. Wilson, Janice Crabtree. THE *GENERAL MAGAZINE, AND IMPARTIAL REVIEW:* A SOUTHERN MAGAZINE IN THE EIGHTEENTH CENTURY. *Southern Literary J. 1979 11(2): 66-77.* Describes the *General Magazine, and Impartial Review,* an 18th-century Southern publication which was a collection of stories, essays, poems, and information covering a wide range of subjects.

1697. Winans, Robert B. THE FOLK, THE STAGE, AND FIVE-STRING BANJO IN THE NINETEENTH CENTURY. *J. of Am. Folklore 1976 89(354): 407-437.* Studies the interchange between folk, popular, and art traditions by tracing banjo playing from early 19th-century black folk traditions to its arrival on the minstrelsy stage by 1840 from where it moved to the Appalachian mountain white folk style sometime after 1865. Classical banjo style, in turn, modified minstrelsy style during the 1870's and affected white mountain playing by 1890. Based on secondary sources; 10 figs., 123 notes.　　　　W. D. Piersen

1698. Wittliff, William D. VAQUERO: GENESIS OF THE TEXAS COWBOY. *Lib. Chronicle of the U. of Texas 1973 (6): 76-77.* Photograph and commentary about a Mexican vaquero.

1699. Wolf, Edward C. THE WHEELING SAENGERFEST OF 1906. *Upper Ohio Valley Hist. Rev. 1982 11(2): 18-29.* Account of the third Saengerfest held in Wheeling, West Virginia, on 21-23 August 1906, a music festival that was sponsored by the German singing society, the Central Ohio Singing District, and hosted by Wheeling's Arion, Beethoven, and Mozart societies, whose histories are traced to 1855.

1700. Wolf, Edward C. WHEELING'S GERMAN SINGING SOCIETIES. *West Virginia Hist. 1980-81 42(1-2): 1-56.* Discusses the 11 German Singing Societies—Maennerchor, Harmonie, Liedertafel, Beethoven, Concordia, Liederkranz, Germania, Teutonia, Harmonie-Maennerchor, Arion, and Mozart—from the organization of the first one in 1855 until the dissolution of the last one in 1961. An important aspect of Wheeling social life, these societies reflected various social classes and enjoyed great popularity until anti-German sentiments during World War I and changing social values dealt them a death blow. Newspaper accounts, scrapbooks, and interviews with individuals; 10 photos, 42 notes.　　　　J. D. Neville

1701. Wolfe, Charles. COUNTY RECORDS AND BLUE RIDGE MUSIC. *Appalachian J. 1980 7(3): 234-238.* Describes the album collection called *Fiddling by the Hearth,* released by County Re-cords in Floyd County, Virginia, in fall, 1980, part of County Records' 700 series which began in 1964, and briefly traces the history of recording Blue Ridge tunes since the 1920's.

1702. Young, Chester Raymond. THE OBSERVANCE OF OLD CHRISTMAS IN SOUTHERN APPALACHIA. *Appalachian J. 1977 4(4): 147-158.* Social customs and ballads from Appalachian Christmas celebrations are the direct result of resistance to the 1753 adaptation of the Gregorian calendar in England, which created the celebration of "Old Christmas" on 5 January.

1703. Zacharias, Dianna. THE GORDON WILSON COLLECTION. *Tennessee Folklore Soc. Bull. 1974 40(3): 82-94.* Describes the Gordon Wilson archives on folklore and linguistics in Edmonson County, Kentucky.　　　　S

1704. Zug, Charles G., III. JUGTOWN REBORN: THE NORTH CAROLINA FOLK POTTER IN TRANSITION. *Pioneer Am. Soc. Tr. 1980 3: 1-24.* Traces the history and developments of the folk pottery made in North Carolina in three areas all known at some point as Jugtown: the eastern Piedmont in Randolph, Moore and Chatham counties, the western Piedmont along the border between Lincoln and Catawba counties, and other areas in the Piedmont.

1705. —. [HILLBILLY ARTISTS JOHN MCGHEE AND FRANK WELLING]. *JEMF Q. 1981 17(62): 57-74.*
Tribe, Ivan M. JOHN MCGHEE AND FRANK WELLING: WEST VIRGINIA'S MOST-RECORDED OLD-TIME ARTISTS, pp. 57-63.
Tribe, Ivan M. A WELLING AND MCGHEE DISCOGRAPHY, pp. 64-74. Biographies of John Leftridge McGhee (1882-1945) and Frank Welling (1900-57) who began recording together in 1927 and became the most-recorded old-time musicians in West Virginia, followed by a discography of their recordings from 1927 to ca. 1949.

1706. —. MOUNTAIN LEGEND IN EASTERN KENTUCKY. *Kentucky Folklore Record 1973 19(3): 58-78.*
Bianchi, Diane. MOUNTAIN LEGEND IN EASTERN KENTUCKY, pp. 58-71.
Jansen, William Hugh. COMMENTARY, pp. 72-78.
Collection of 19 legends recorded in 1972 in Evarts.　　　　S

1707. —. RAILROADING ON THE GULF COAST: A CONVERSATION WITH E. A. "FROG" SMITH. *Tampa Bay Hist. 1980 2(2): 41-60.* Interview with E. A. "Frog" Smith, born in 1896 in Pinebloom, Georgia, on life as a steam railroader.

# Black Culture

1708. Anderson, Solena. BACK IN 'DEM DAYS: A BLACK FAMILY REMINISCES. *J. of Mississippi Hist. 1974 36(2): 179-185.* Describes "the folkways of blacks living in the Homochit-to River Valley of southwestern Mississippi," including home cures, superstitions, and miscellaneous social customs. Based on the author's interviews with relatives.　　　　J. W. Hillje

1709. Andrews, William L. THE SIGNIFICANCE OF CHARLES W. CHESNUTT'S "CONJURE STORIES." *Southern Literary J. 1974 7(1): 78-99.* Discusses the significance of the works of Charles W. Chesnutt, who came into prominence during the late 19th century in North Carolina as the first important black American fiction writer.

1710. Andrews, William L. WILLIAM DEAN HOWELLS AND CHARLES W. CHESNUTT: CRITICISM AND RACE FICTION IN THE AGE OF BOOKER T. WASHINGTON. *Am. Lit. 1976 48(3): 327-339.* "An understanding of the way Howells and Chesnutt viewed each other can reveal something of the complexity of Howells's approach to Afro-American literature, while in Chesnutt's case, the experience with Howells underlines the central problem Chesnutt as a black writer faced at the turn of the century: how to get a hearing for an increasingly vigorous expression of protest from a white reading audience, which, if listening at all, was already attuned to the more soothing message of Booker T. Washington."

1711. Aptheker, Bettina. THE SUPPRESSION OF THE *FREE SPEECH*: IDA B. WELLS AND THE MEMPHIS LYNCHING, 1892. *San José Studies 1977 3(3): 34-40.* Discusses the violent suppression of the *Free Speech,* a black newspaper in Memphis, Tennessee, whose condemnation in editorials by its publisher, Ida B. Wells, of race-related lynchings in 1892, resulted in the closure of the paper by members of the white community.

1712. Aronson, David. JAZZ: A MUSIC IN EXILE. *Int. Social Sci. J. [France] 1982 34(4): 583-598.* Describes the evolution of jazz music in the United States during the 1920's-70's and the lingering prejudice against both jazz as an art form and black musicians.

1713. Ashdown, Ellen A. CHESTER L. WILLIAMS: BLACK SCULPTOR IN THE SOUTH. *Crisis 1979 86(4): 129-132.* The life of black sculptor Chester L. Williams is full of paradoxes. He believes that living in the South is professional suicide; he lives there anyway. He believes that artists are visionaries; he would like to make big money in the art business. He believes that an artist is an artist; yet, for Williams, black art is his life. He teaches at Florida A & M University with exhilaration and zest. His work reflects his own black heritage. He is an experimenter and likes to push his sculpture to the "tenth degree," toward ugliness, so that he can look back and know for sure the best stage. Williams takes risks and does work he is not particularly close to if, in the long run, it provides him space to make the move that really counts.
A. G. Belles

1714. Baldwin, Brooke. THE CAKEWALK: A STUDY IN STEREOTYPE AND REALITY. *J. of Social Hist. 1981 15(2): 205-218.* This black dance form originated as a plantation satire of white behavior, not, as whites chose to claim publicly, a poor mimicry of a higher culture. Focuses on the control whites managed to exercise over it and its commercial development as it became more widely known in the 1890's. 49 notes.
C. M. Hough

1715. Baldwin, Lewis V. FESTIVITY AND CELEBRATION: A PROFILE OF WILMINGTON'S BIG QUARTERLY. *Delaware Hist. 1981 19(4): 197-211.* Describes the character and development of the Big Quarterly in Wilmington, Delaware, a black religious festival inaugurated in 1814 by Peter Spencer. Popular in the 19th century, the festival attracted as many as 10,000 persons for religious services and social intercourse. It offered slaves an opportunity to escape to freedom. The Union Church of African Members, followers of Spencer, benefitted from the gathering which also served as a general conference. Some blacks opposed the festival after the Civil War because they disliked the shouting and dancing, which they thought was undignified, and in the 20th century other critics decried the growing commercialism attending the festival. The Big Quarterly survived until 1981, when different religious habits among young people, commercialism, and the Civil Rights Movement drew away supporters. 57 notes.
R. M. Miller

1716. Biola, Heather. THE BLACK WASHERWOMEN IN SOUTHERN TRADITION. *Tennessee Folklore Soc. Bull. 1979 45(1): 17-27.* Analyzes historical ideals, folklore images, and literary characterizations of laundry and black laundresses as a folklore image in southern tradition, 17th-20th centuries.

1717. Brown, Robert L. CLASSICAL INFLUENCES ON JAZZ. *J. of Jazz Stud. 1976 3(2): 19-35.* Examines the influence and use of classical music in traditional New Orleans jazz improvisations and composition, 1897-1970's.

1718. Caffey, H. David. THE MUSICAL STYLE OF LOUIS ARMSTRONG, 1925-29. *J. of Jazz Studies 1975 3(1): 72-96.* Discusses jazz styles explored by Louis Armstrong and his groups the Hot Five and the Hot Seven from 1925-29, emphasizing blues music.

1719. Cavin, Susan. MISSING WOMEN: ON THE VOODOO TRAIL TO JAZZ. *J. of Jazz Studies 1975 3(1): 4-27.* Discusses the role of voodoo women and black magic cults in the evolution of jazz music in the 19th century, emphasizing the Negro culture of New Orleans.

1720. Cayer, David A. BLACK AND BLUE AND BLACK AGAIN: THREE STAGES OF RACIAL IMAGERY IN JAZZ LYRICS. *J. of Jazz Studies 1974 1(2): 38-71.* Analyzes the lyrics of 20th century Negro jazz.

1721. Cimbala, Paul A. FORTUNATE BONDSMEN: BLACK "MUSICIANERS" AND THEIR ROLE AS AN ANTEBELLUM SOUTHERN PLANTATION ELITE. *Southern Studies 1979 18(3): 291-303.* Slave instrumentalists, called "musicianers" by fellow blacks, had special social status in the antebellum South. Such musicianers were common and enjoyed special freedoms, especially of movement, and could pick up independent income. They were liked and respected by blacks because they provided relief from the drudgery of work and transmitted black culture. Whites liked them because they provided entertainment for white social gatherings and because it was believed they kept the other blacks docile and contented. Based especially on the collection of Federal Writers' Project ex-slave narratives, *The American Slave: A Composite Autobiography;* 62 notes.
J. J. Buschen

1722. Clayton, Ronnie W. FEDERAL WRITERS' PROJECT FOR BLACKS IN LOUISIANA. *Louisiana Hist. 1978 19(3): 327-335.* On the initiative of Lyle Saxon, the director of the Louisiana Federal Writers' Project, a black writers' project was formed at Dillard University in New Orleans for the purpose of writing a Negro history in Louisiana. The information they gathered was included in the publications of the Louisiana Writers' Project, guidebooks for Louisiana and New Orleans, and, more especially, in the folkloric *Gumbo Ya-Ya* (Boston, 1945). The Dillard group's projected Negro history, however, differed markedly from the interpretation of Louisiana's past as found in *Gumbo Ya-Ya,* but it was never published, despite Saxon's efforts. The records were deposited at Dillard University, but they have since disappeared, only the outline and prospectus being preserved in the Saxon papers at Tulane University, on which this article is based. 34 notes.
R. L. Woodward, Jr.

1723. Cortinovis, Irene E. JAZZ ON THE RIVERBOATS, THE WAY A PIANO PLAYER TELLS IT. *J. of Jazz Studies 1974 1(2): 72-78.* Interviews Gus Perryman, a Negro jazz musician in the South, 1910-30.

1724. Cowley, John. SHACK BULLIES AND LEVEE CONTRACTORS: STUDIES IN THE ORAL HISTORY OF A BLACK PROTEST SONG TRADITION. *JEMF Q. 1980 16(60): 182-193.* Describes black protest songs from the 1920's, which tell the story of the shack bully, the man responsible for waking blacks working on the levees along the Mississippi River, first built by the French in 1718.

1725. Craven, Martha Jacquelyn. A PORTRAIT OF EMILY TUBMAN. *Richmond County Hist. 1974 6(1): 4-10.* Presents a short biography of Emily Tubman, 1818-85, following her life as it coincided with events in Georgia and the South, and examines her efforts to aid in the establishment of Liberia. Reproduction, 27 notes.

1726. Current, Gloster B. "LOVE YOU MADLY"—DUKE ELLINGTON. *Crisis 1974 81(6): 197-200.* Biography of Edward Kennedy "Duke" Ellington, 1899-1974, the jazz musician.

1727. Current, Gloster B. SCOTT JOPLIN. *Crisis 1975 82(6): 219-221.* The works of Scott Joplin are enjoying a revival and the music industry is making money with the compositions of a black musician who died disappointed and broke. Joplin (1868-1917) be-

came known as the king of ragtime. He composed 53 pieces for piano, 10 songs, and the opera *Treemonisha*. Joplin married Lottie
Stokes in 1909 and settled in New York City until he died.

A. G. Belles

1728. David, Thadious M. ALICE WALKER'S CELEBRATION
OF SELF IN SOUTHERN GENERATIONS. *Southern Q. 1983
21(4): 38-53.* Alice Walker, who was born in Georgia in 1944, has
written a biography, three novels, and several collections of poetry
and short stories. Throughout her works she uses her own experiences as a black woman growing up in the South as a backdrop
for the tales she is telling. Her major accomplishment as a writer
is her ability to explore the Southern black woman's contradictory
response between self-destruction and self-affirmation.

W. A. Wiegand

1729. Davis, Ronald L. EARLY JAZZ: ANOTHER LOOK.
*Southwest Rev. 1973 58(1): 1-13, (2): 144-154.* Part I. Traces the
three main elements in the New Orleans jazz scene after the Civil
War. One element was the Creole blacks who had access "to musical instruments early, had learned to read music, and played in a
style essentially derived from Europe." A second group was the uptown blacks who obtained instruments much later and played a
"rougher, blues-colored music." The Creole black preferred the
clarinet, but the uptown black used the cornet. The third unit was
the white jazz tradition known as Dixieland. Among the individual
musicians mentioned were John Robichaux, Charles (Buddy) Bolden, Manuel Perez, and George V. (Papa Jack) Laine. Another facet to New Orleans music was the development separately but
parallel to the early jazz bands of the barrelhouse piano, a movement strongly influenced by the blues. The star of New Orleans pi-
anists was Ferdinand "Jelly Roll" Morton. The presence of
multiple traditions and the eventual intermingling of styles makes
the study of New Orleans music much more complicated than previous writers have indicated. Part II. Traces the spread of jazz from
the South (especially New Orleans) northward in the early 20th
century. The first jazz band to play in the North was Tom Brown
with his five-piece Dixieland combination in Chicago in 1914, not
the Original Dixieland Jazz Band which played first in New York
in 1917. Surprisingly, the music played in New Orleans had never
been called jazz; the name was first used in Chicago. Many other
groups quickly followed Brown into the North, especially after the
closing of Storyville during World War I. The movement to the
North prompted many changes—unionization, new instruments,
commercialization. Based on taped interviews in the Jazz Archives
at Tulane University.

D. F. Henderson

1730. Dent, Tom. OCTAVE LILLY, JR.: IN MEMORIAM. *Crisis
1976 83(7): 243-244.* Octave Lilly was a successful black insurance
executive as well as a southern black writer and poet. He worked
for the WPA Federal Writers Project in the late 1930's. His poems
were published in *Opportunity* and the *Crisis*. He did not write
again until the late 1960's, at the age of 60. He died while some
of his work was being published. Through his poetry he fought for
economic survival and artistic expression for Negroes.

A. G. Belles

1731. Dews, Margery P. A GEORGIAN BROUGHT PIZZAZZ
TO JAZZ. *Georgia Life 1978 4(4): 25, 30.* Georgia's Fletcher Henderson, who developed the jazz orchestra in the 1920's, was a talented musician and bandleader and greatly influenced the evolution
of jazz.

1732. Evans, David. FIELDWORK WITH BLUES SINGERS:
THE UNINTENTIONALLY INDUCED NATURAL CONTEXT.
*Southern Folklore Q. 1978 42(1): 9-16.* Discusses methodology and
problems in collecting folklore of the blues; focuses on the author's
study of Afro-American folk blues songs to understand the processes of learning and composition; 1960's-70's.

1733. Ferris, William. BLACK FOLK ARTS AND CRAFTS: A
MISSISSIPPI SAMPLE (PHOTO ESSAY). *Southern Folklore Q.
1978 42(2-3): 209-241.* Personal accounts of Mississippi blacks and

their arts and crafts such as basketmaking, fifemaking, quiltmaking,
wood carving, etc., including pictures of the craftspeople and their
projects; 20th century.

1734. Gaffney, Floyd. THE FREE SOUTHERN THEATRE: NOT
JUST SURVIVAL. *Crisis 1978 85(1): 20-23.* The Free Southern
Theatre has served the black community since 1963, despite many
problems. It has attempted to change the cultural mythology by
portraying the black man realistically. Located in New Orleans, the
Free Southern Theatre has offered significant drama relevant to
black audiences, permitted post-performance discussions to evaluate
the aesthetic experience, and established a physical and financial
base for the future.

A. G. Belles

1735. Giles, James R. RICHARD WRIGHT'S SUCCESSFUL
FAILURE: A NEW LOOK AT *UNCLE TOM'S CHILDREN.*
*Phylon 1973 34(3): 256-266.* Discusses Negro novelist Richard
Wright's *Uncle Tom's Children* (1938).

1736. Guillaume, Alfred J., Jr. LOVE, DEATH, AND FAITH IN
THE NEW ORLEANS POETS OF COLOR. *Southern Q. 1982
20(2): 126-144.* Restrictions placed on Creoles of color in antebellum New Orleans did not totally prevent several of them from writing and publishing poetry. A signal accomplishment was the
publication of *Les Cenelles* (1845), a collective effort of 17 poets.
Because the climate of the times militated against addressing the
oppression evident in social and political reality, these poets stuck
generally to safe themes like love and death. Not until the Civil
War and after did they use the columns of two newspapers, *Union*
(1862-64) and *Tribune de la Nouvelle Orleans* (1864-69), where
they more directly addressed the environment in which they wrote.

W. A. Wiegand

1737. Harris, M. Roy. *LES CENELLES:* MEANING OF A
FRENCH AFRO-AMERICAN TITLE FROM NEW ORLEANS.
*Louisiana Rev. 1982 11(2): 179-196.* Discusses the possible mean-
ings of the title of a collection of poetry, *Les Cenelles: Choix de
Poésies Indigènes,* published in New Orleans in 1845, and contain-
ing 85 poems by 17 free black men.

1738. Helbling, Mark. ALAIN LOCKE: AMBIVALENCE AND
HOPE. *Phylon 1979 40(3): 291-300.* Analyzes the philosophical position of Alain Locke, professor of philosophy at Howard University
in Washington, D.C., who influenced many young black writers of
the Harlem Renaissance (1920's and 1930's). Based on Locke's
writings and on secondary sources; 32 notes.

G. R. Schroeder

1739. Hemenway, Robert. FOLKLORE FIELD NOTES FROM
ZORA NEALE HURSTON. *Black Scholar 1976 7(7): 39-46.* Zora
Neale Hurston (1901-60) wrote four novels, two collections of folklore, numerous short stories and essays, and an autobiography. As
a member of the Florida Federal Writers' Project, she began editing a book on Negroes in Florida but left the project in 1939, never completing the book. Included are some of the notes, never
published before, on her projected volume. Primary and secondary
sources; 11 notes.

B. D. Ledbetter

1740. Hentoff, Nat. THE POLITICAL ECONOMY OF JAZZ.
*Social Policy 1976 6(5): 53-56.* Discusses Negro jazz musicians' attitudes toward white jazz musicians, 1920's-70's, emphasizing jazz
as an extension of Negro culture.

1741. Hill, Patricia Liggins. "BLUES FOR A MISSISSIPPI
BLACK BOY": ETHERIDGE KNIGHT'S CRAFT IN THE
BLACK ORAL TRADITION. *Mississippi Q. 1982-83 36(1): 21-33.*
Etheridge Knight's written and oral poetry, 1968-80, bridges Afri-
can spirituality and musical form and the blues and oral traditions
of blacks in the South.

1742. Hill, Patricia Liggins. FRANCES W. HARPER'S AUNT
CHLOE POEMS FROM *SKETCHES OF SOUTHERN LIFE:* AN-
TITHESIS TO THE PLANTATION LITERARY TRADITION.
*Mississippi Q. 1981 34(4): 403-413.* Discusses the content and style

of Frances W. Harper's "Aunt Chloe" poems to support her consideration as one of the most important black women writers of the 19th century.

1743. Huber, Leonard V. REFLECTIONS ON THE COLORFUL CUSTOMS OF LATTER-DAY NEW ORLEANS CREOLES. *Louisiana Hist. 1980 21(3): 223-235.* New Orleans Creoles, "native Louisianians of French or Spanish ancestry or both," kept their distinct culture intact, along with and in part thanks to their almost exclusive use of the French language, up to the turn of the present century. Between 1900 and 1939, dilution of Creole culture was reflected by an almost complete exodus from the French Quarter. Launcelot Harris, who closely observed Creole life in the 1890's, and Roger Baudier, who in the 1930's wrote a regular column on the subject, have left a detailed picture of Creole customs. Discusses some humorous Creole expressions, as well as social customs in the areas of marriage, social and cultural life, religion, and education.
L. Van Wyk

1744. Hull, Gloria T. ALICE DUNBAR-NELSON: DELAWARE WRITER AND WOMAN OF AFFAIRS. *Delaware Hist. 1976 17(2): 87-103.* Presents a biography of Alice Dunbar-Nelson, who was active in black educational and philanthropic enterprises and community affairs in Wilmington. Her poetry and prose writing, dominated by themes of love and war, bridged the distance separating her husband, Paul Laurence Dunbar, and the dialect writers of the Harlem Renaissance. Dunbar-Nelson used regionalism and local color, and, unlike other black writers, she attempted the short story as her main prose medium, helping create a black short story tradition. Based on Dunbar-Nelson's writings and her unpublished diary; 3 illus., 18 notes.
R. M. Miller

1745. Jackson, Blyden. GEORGE MOSES HORTON, NORTH CAROLINIAN. *North Carolina Hist. R. 1976 53(2): 140-147.* George Moses Horton (ca. 1797-1884), an early slave poet, lived near Chapel Hill. He began, as a young man, spending Sundays on the University of North Carolina campus and was soon spending more time in town than on his master's farm. Horton wrote poetry, both for himself (three books) and for students (love poems to send to sweethearts), and thereby earned enough money to support himself and satisfy his master. He moved to Philadelphia after the Civil War, where he died in obscurity. 3 illus.
T. L. Savitt

1746. Lenz, Günter H. SOUTHERN EXPOSURES: THE URBAN EXPERIENCE AND THE RE-CONSTRUCTION OF BLACK FOLK CULTURE AND COMMUNITY IN THE WORKS OF RICHARD WRIGHT AND ZORA NEALE HURSTON. *New York Folklore 1981 7(1-2): 3-39.* Describes black literature in America from the 1920's to the 1970's as a reflection of the experiences of US blacks.

1747. Lornell, Kip. BLACK MATERIAL FOLK CULTURE. *Southern Folklore Q. 1978 42(2-3): 287-294.* Bibliography of publications on black material folk culture published during 1842-1976, including manuscripts in preparation in 1976.

1748. MacLeod, Bruce A. QUILLS, FIFES, AND FLUTES BEFORE THE CIVIL WAR. *Southern Folklore Q. 1978 42(2-3): 201-208.* Discusses numerous references to the quills, fifes, and flutes, drums, fiddles, and banjos played by blacks in the South before the Civil War, in the slave narratives collected under the direction of the Federal Writers' Project of the 1930's.

1749. Markus, Julia. ROMARE BEARDEN'S ART DOES GO HOME AGAIN—TO CONQUER. *Smithsonian 1981 11(12): 70-77.* Traces the cultural background and examines some of the collages of black American artist Romare Bearden, whose work is presently being exhibited in four major southern cities.

1750. Mason, Julian. BLACK WRITERS OF THE SOUTH. *Mississippi Q. 1978 31(2): 169-184.* Literary anthologies of southern authors lack material on black writers; examines blacks in southern literature and the basic ignorance surrounding the study of black literary tradition of the South; covers 18th-20th centuries.

1751. McGinty, Brian. JAZZ: RED HOT AND COOL. *Am. Hist. Illus. 1979 14(8): 8-11, 42-46.* Part I. Chronicles forms of black music popular during 17th-19th centuries and surveys the evolution of jazz, 1890's-1920's, highlighting better-known musicians such as Charles "Buddy" Bolden, Joe "King" Oliver, Louis Armstrong, Jelly Roll Morton, and Jack "Papa" Laine. Part II. Discusses "The Jazz Age" of the 1920's, particularly jazz musicians such as the Original Dixieland Jazz Band formed in 1917, Paul Whiteman, known as the "King of Jazz," Leon (Bix) Beiderbecke, Louis Armstrong, Ethel Waters, and others.

1752. McNeil, W. K. THE FIRST AMERICAN COLLECTORS OF AFRICAN FOLKLORE. *Kentucky Folklore Record 1982 28(3-4): 40-47.* Among the first missionaries to study African native languages, habits, and folklore thoroughly are Thomas Jefferson Bowen, a Southern Baptist Convention minister who worked in Nigeria, Lewis Grout, a Congregational minister who worked among the South African Zulu tribes, and Swiss-American Heli Chatelain, who worked in Luanda as pioneer and linguist for Bishop William Taylor's African missions, and who wrote *Folk-Tales of Angola* (1894), which became a source to document the African origins of several Negro tales from Georgia.

1753. Meadows, Eddie S. BLUES: A MUSICAL AND SOCIOLOGICAL ANALYSIS. *Freedomways 1976 16(1): 60-64.* Examines the historical roots of blues (coming from west Africa) and the sociological aspects of the creation of blues music; warns against criticizing blues in light of traditional western music.

1754. Moore, Janie Gilliard. AFRICANISMS AMONG BLACKS OF THE SEA ISLANDS. *J. of Black Studies 1980 10(4): 467-480.* The author's contacts with Africans at the Interdenominational Theological Center in Atlanta, Georgia, made her aware of similarities between the cultures of Africa and the South Carolina and Georgia Sea Islands where she grew up. Among the similarities are the islanders' Gullah dialect, the role of the traditional healer or root doctor, and the islanders' beliefs in hags whose spirits leave their bodies to torment other people, in people's spirits leaving their bodies while they sleep, in the intervention of the dead into the affairs of the living, and in thunder as God talking. African practices and beliefs on the islands probably have African theological implications. Biblio., appendix of terms.
R. G. Sherer

1755. Morgan, Gordon D. and Kunkel, Peter. ARKANSAS' OZARK MOUNTAIN BLACKS: AN INTRODUCTION. *Phylon 1973 34(3): 283-288.* A study of Negroes living in the Ozark Mountains, specifically those living in Ruddell Hill, an enclave near Batesville in Independence County, Arkansas.
S

1756. Morris, Kelso B. THE WILEY COLLEGIANS: REMINISCENCES OF A BLACK COLLEGE BANDLEADER, 1925-35. *Ann. Rev. of Jazz Studies 1982 1: 17-20.* Kelso B. Morris describes his experiences as both a member and a leader of a black college jazz band in the 1920's-30's; Wiley College in Marshall, Texas, was just one of many black schools with dance bands of professional caliber.

1757. O'Neal, John. THE FREE SOUTHERN THEATRE: LIVING IN THE DANGER ZONE. *Black Scholar 1979 10(10): 11-13.* Discusses the Free Southern Theatre's fusion of politics and art, and its part in the struggle to end oppression against black Americans and fight against imperialism and to improve the quality of life, 1960's-70's.

1758. Ostendorf, Berndt. MINSTRELSY AND EARLY JAZZ. *Massachusetts Rev. 1979 20(3): 574-602.* According to legend, the birth of jazz occurred in New Orleans around 1900. American popular culture had then turned into a polyethnic hybrid. Ralph Ellison (b. 1914) stated that the culture is "jazz-shaped," and built on black folklore. The foremost attraction of blackface minstrelsy was economic. Secondly, it lay in gamesmanship. Minstrelsy's cultural results are: 1) the Euro-American cultural tradition, 2) the black-white adaptive culture, and 3) the minstrel culture. Early jazz leaned on minstrelsy's melodic tradition. New Orleans jazz began when blacks imitated western brass music's pomp and added dance. Today the black-inflected American musical vernacular has become the inspiration for the international youth culture. Based on autobiographies and newspapers; 45 notes.                    E. R. Campbell

1759. Otto, John Solomon and Burns, Augustus M. "TOUGH TIMES": DOWNHOME BLUES RECORDINGS AS FOLK HISTORY. *Southern Q. 1983 21(3): 27-43.* Transcriptions of thousands of songs in a musical genre called "downhome blues" that were recorded between 1924 and the present represent a largely untapped body of historical evidence about black life. Lyrics in many of these songs reflect the values of working-class blacks from rural backgrounds. Although historians have often lamented that poor blacks generally left no written sources for scholars to study, the words contained in these songs may provide a means to understand their place in the historical record.                    W. A. Wiegand

1760. Peek, Phil. AFRO-AMERICAN MATERIAL CULTURE AND THE AFRO-AMERICAN CRAFTSMAN. *Southern Folklore Q. 1978 42(2-3): 109-134.* Discusses scholars' works on African material culture in the United States, focusing on arts and crafts, musical instruments, and Afro-American craftsmen and artists from slave-trading times (1619-1850's) until the early 20th century.

1761. Pettis, Joyce. THE BLACK HISTORICAL NOVEL AS BEST SELLER. *Kentucky Folklore Record 1979 25(3-4): 51-59.* Discusses the black characters in Alex Haley's *Roots* (New York: Doubleday and Co., 1976), Margaret Walker's *Jubilee* (Boston: Houghton, Mifflin Co., 1966), and Ernest Gaines's *The Autobiography of Miss Jane Pittman* (New York: Bantam Books, Inc., 1971); these historical novels, written by black authors, span slavery, Reconstruction, and the 20th century.

1762. Rabun, Josette Hensley and Blakemore, Robbie G. LEWIS S. BUCKNER, BLACK ARTISAN (C. 1856-1924) OF SEVIERVILLE, TENNESSEE. *Tennessee Folklore Soc. Bull. 1982 48(1): 1-10.* Biography of cabinetmaker and carpenter Lewis S. Buckner (ca. 1856-1924), with photographs of some of his work.

1763. Raley, Joyce Reid. PRESENTING FIVE BLACK ARTISTS. *Georgia Life 1979 6(3): 24-27.* Briefly discusses the work and artistic careers of southern black artists Allen Omar Rasheed, an oil painter who began his career in 1961; Gary King, an art instructor; Jim Alexander, photographer; Javon Brothers, painter and sculptor; and John Riddle, sculptor.

1764. Reagon, Bernice. THE LADYSTREETSINGER. *Southern Exposure 1974 2(1): 38-41.* Portrays the life of Flora Molton, a black woman, who has sung her folk songs on the streets of the District of Columbia since the 1930's.                    S

1765. Render, Sylvia Lyons. AFRO-AMERICAN WOMEN: THE OUTSTANDING AND THE OBSCURE. *Q. J. of the Lib. of Congress 1975 32(4): 306-321.* Discusses the lives of three Afro-American women residents of the District of Columbia. The first was Anna Murry Douglass, relatively obscure, but whose influence upon her husband, Frederick Douglass, should not be minimized. The second woman was the outstanding Mary Church Terrell, 1863-1954. She represented Negro women abroad on a number of occasions, and was a pioneer in attacking segregation in Washington. The third woman, the obscure Ruth Anna Fisher, 1886-1975, spent most of her life copying foreign documents for the Library of Congress. Illus., 24 notes.                    E. P. Stickney

1766. Rich, Carroll Y. BORN WITH THE VEIL: BLACK FOLKLORE IN LOUISIANA. *J. of Am. Folklore 1976 89(353): 328-331.* Folk beliefs about the special powers of children "born with the veil" still found among Bienville Parish, Louisiana, blacks are dying out among the younger generation. Based on field interviews and secondary sources; 7 notes.                    W. D. Piersen

1767. Rowley-Rotunno, Virginia. SCOTT JOPLIN: RENASCENCE OF A BLACK COMPOSER OF RAGTIME AND GRAND OPERA. *Negro Hist. Bull. 1974 37(1): 188-193.* Scott Joplin, the black composer of ragtime, "led the vanguard of American popular music in the early part of the twentieth century." His

grand opera, *Treemonisha,* never produced in his lifetime, created a musical sensation with its premiere in Atlanta in 1972. "He certainly presaged the women's lib movement of the 1970's by having a heroine as the leader of the oppressed black race." Details his life and enumerates and evaluates his works. Illus., 64 notes.
                    E. P. Stickney

1768. Sapper, Neil. BLACK CULTURE IN URBAN TEXAS: *A LONE STAR RENAISSANCE. Red River Valley Hist. Rev. 1981 6(2): 56-77.* Discusses the trickle-down effects of the Harlem Renaissance movement on the efforts of black Texans to develop outlets for black artistic expression in Texas, 1930-54.

1769. Starks, George L., Jr. SINGING 'BOUT A GOOD TIME: SEA ISLAND RELIGIOUS MUSIC. *J. of Black Studies 1980 10(4): 417-424.* The importance of music in the Georgia and South Carolina Sea Islands can be best appreciated in religious services. Although standard rituals and hymns are changing the services, traditional music and dance are still important, especially during the offering and at prayer meetings. After members of the congregation walk to the table at the front of the church to make their offerings, the choir and ushers march or dance to the table, never letting one foot cross the other. Prayer meeting testimonies end with traditional songs. Traditional spirituals are still sung in many churches, along with hymns and gospel songs, many of which are sung in the a cappella style of the spirituals. Based on personal observation; biblio.                    R. G. Sherer

1770. Suggs, Henry Lewis. P. B. YOUNG OF THE NORFOLK *JOURNAL AND GUIDE:* A BOOKER T. WASHINGTON MILITANT, 1904-1928. *J. of Negro Hist. 1979 64(4): 365-376.* Plummer B. Young became a disciple of Booker T. Washington in 1904 and upheld self-help and economic advancement throughout the 1920's. Despite the accommodating and ingratiating tone in Young's public statements, his felicitous manner of expression masked the protest quality of his thought and bridged the contradictions in his philosophy. Based on the Washington papers and the NAACP papers in the Library of Congress, and on the Norfolk *Journal and Guide;* 62 notes.                    N. G. Sapper

1771. Titon, Jeff Todd. INTRODUCTION [TO AN ISSUE ON THE BLUES]. *Southern Folklore Q. 1978 42(1): 1-8.* Defines blues, synopsizes each article, and provides a bibliography of articles, periodicals, and books on the subject.

1772. Twining, Mary A. AFRICAN-AFRO-AMERICAN ARTISTIC CONTINUITY. *J. of African Studies 1975-76 2(4): 569-578.* Studies the extent of African cultural retention among the slaves transported to North America. It appears that there was much more retention than has been claimed. This is illustrated in arts and crafts by examining basketry, bedquilts, brooms, fish nets, and wood carvings. Concludes that "belief systems and folk culture from the African past were used wherever practical by the slaves, freemen, and freedmen." 17 notes.                    R. V. Ritter

1773. Twining, Mary A. DAMAS AND TWO SEA ISLAND POETS: A BRIEF COMPARISON IN LIGHT OF THE PHILOSOPHY OF NEGRITUDE. *J. of Black Studies 1980 10(4): 449-460.* Two black poets of the South Carolina and Georgia Sea Islands, James Jenkins and an anonymous writer, express the same feelings of negritude as does Leon Damas as they move from recognition to acceptance to responsible action. Jenkins's "What is de Hour?" is a conversation with a preacher that condemns the preacher's religion and calls for black power. In "Orangeburg Massacre," an anonymous writer condemns white murder and oppression of blacks and Indians, concluding that if whites do not change, "WE WILL ALL DIE TOGETHER!" Ref.                    R. G. Sherer

1774. Twining, Mary A. and Baird, Keith E. INTRODUCTION TO SEA ISLAND FOLKLIFE. *J. of Black Studies 1980 10(4): 387-416.* The relative isolation of Afro-Americans on the Georgia-South Carolina Sea Islands has made their culture more similar to that of Afro-Caribbeans and Africans than the cultures of other North American Afro-Americans. Improved transportation and communications since the 1930's have weakened the unique island culture, as have literacy campaigns and other self-help efforts of the islanders. Even so, the islanders still retain distinctive African cultural patterns in education, economic activities (farm labor), language (Gullah), voluntary associations, world view, kinship patterns, and religion. Based on personal communications and observations and on folklore collections; biblio. R. G. Sherer

1775. Twining, Mary A. and Baird, Keith E. PREFACE: THE SIGNIFICANCE OF SEA ISLAND CULTURE. *J. of Black Studies 1980 10(4): 379-386.* A wide variety of writers, from members of 19th-century planters' families to modern scholars, have noted African cultural survivals on the Georgia and South Carolina Sea Islands. Melville J. Herskovits showed that survivals were weaker there than in the Caribbean, but stronger than in the rest of the United States. Recent field research reveals even stronger survivals than Herskovits described. The Sea Islands are "a prime living laboratory of African cultural survivals" despite the corrosive influence of modern transportation and communications. Based on folklore collections and a plantation diary; biblio. R. G. Sherer

1776. Twining, Mary Arnold. SOURCES IN THE FOLKLORE AND FOLKLIFE OF THE SEA ISLANDS. *Southern Folklore Q. 1975 39(2): 135-149.* Reports on sources available on the folklore of the Sea Islands, with regard to Afro-American culture.

1777. Vlach, John. GRAVEYARDS AND AFRO-AMERICAN ART. *Southern Exposure 1977 5(2-3): 161-165.* Many Afro-American graves in rural southern areas are decorated with artifacts similar to graves in Africa. There is little difference between African and Afro-American religious beliefs about death and how death should be treated by the living. African-style grave decoration dating back to the 1880's still persists in certain black cemeteries in the South, and even on Staten Island. Broken bottles, pots, and other objects of daily use are placed on the graves. Primary and secondary sources. N. Lederer

1778. Vlach, John Michael. AFRO-AMERICAN FOLK CRAFTS IN NINETEENTH CENTURY TEXAS. *Western Folklore 1981 40(2): 149-161.* Points out the strong southern heritage of Texas and the Afro-American contributions to Texas traditions, pleading for "a more detailed black Texan history." Textile arts and carpentry, two important crafts practiced by black Texans, are examined. Based on Works Projects Administration interviews with ex-slaves and other primary sources; 72 notes. S. L. Myres

1779. Walling, William and Shatzkin, Roger. IT AIN'T THE BLUES: BILLIE HOLIDAY, SIDNEY FURIE AND KITSCH. *J. of Jazz Studies 1973 1(1): 21-33.* Discusses the music of Billie Holiday in the 1930's and the rendition of her life and jazz style in the 1972 film by Sidney Furie, *Lady Sings the Blues.*

1780. White, John. VEILED TESTIMONY: NEGRO SPIRITUALS AND THE SLAVE EXPERIENCE. *J. of Am. Studies [Great Britain] 1983 17(2): 251-263.* The literature on Negro slavery in America includes substantial collections of black spirituals, and many scholars have analyzed this material. These interpreters cite the spirituals as evidence that the slaves' folk culture successfully insulated slaves from the dehumanizing aspects of bondage. However, the spirituals often allude to slavery's most dehumanizing effects and, in any event, offer imprecise evidence for assessing the slaves' culture. Based on printed collections of spirituals and secondary sources; 37 notes. H. T. Lovin

1781. Wiggins, Gene. LAODICEAN GOSPELEER: EMORY PECK. *Tennessee Folklore Soc. Bull. 1981 47(4): 165-172.* Biography of Emory Speer Peck (1893-1975), born in Lumpkin County, Georgia, instrumentalist, singer, piano tuner, professor at Brenau College, and gospel music writer, who has been described as being rather uninterested in his gospel music, similar to "what St. Paul called the church at Laodicea—'lukewarm.' "

1782. Wood, Peter H. WHETTING, SETTING AND LAYING TIMBERS: BLACK BUILDERS IN THE EARLY SOUTH. *Southern Exposure 1980 8(1): 3-8.* Negroes were not the only builders in the colonial South, but for the first 200 years they did much of the major construction work there. However, precise knowledge about early black craftsmen and their built environment is as crude today as the general understanding of Afro-American music and language was 50 years ago. Many brought their skills with them from Africa and passed them on through their descendants. They were especially experts in the handling and treating of lumber. The creation of numerous and varied types of buildings in the South reflect the ability of the blacks to retain, assert, and even teach certain ancestral styles and values. 9 photos, 3 notes. H. M. Parker, Jr.

1783. Wynes, Charles E. JOHN HENRY SMYTH: SOUTHERNER, AMERICAN, BLACK NATIONALIST. *Southern Studies 1978 17(4): 427-432.* John Henry Smyth (1844-1908), a black from Virginia, achieved success as an artist, lawyer, bank official, US minister to Liberia, businessman, newspaper writer, and educator. He proclaimed that a black could be proud of his African roots while succeeding in American life. He had considerable influence and many prominent, powerful friends. Secondary sources; 11 notes. J. J. Buschen

# Education in the South

## General

1784. Alsobrook, David E. MOBILE V. BIRMINGHAM: THE ALABAMA MEDICAL COLLEGE CONTROVERSY, 1912-1920. *Alabama Rev. 1983 36(1): 37-56.* Describes the attempts of various Birmingham promoters to have the medical school transferred there from Mobile. The results of this competition were lower quality medical education in both places and finally, both schools being closed due to insufficient financial support. Based on correspondence and other primary and secondary sources; 58 notes. G. R. Schroeder

1785. Bailey, Fred A. CASTE AND THE CLASSROOM IN ANTEBELLUM TENNESSEE. *Maryland Hist. 1982 13(1): 39-54.* Class was largely determined by parental class, and educational institutions played a role in perpetuating the caste system. The author's thesis is an antidote to Frank Owsley's claims for interclass mobility through education. Based on Civil War veteran data and secondary sources; map, 9 tables, 40 notes. G. O. Gagnon

1786. Baker, Liva. GEORGE WYTHE: FIRST PROFESSOR OF LAW AND POLICE AT THE COLLEGE OF WILLIAM AND MARY. *Virginia Cavalcade 1973 22(4): 31-35.*

1787. Bardsley, Beverly J. STATE EDUCATION AGENCIES AND URBAN SCHOOL DISTRICTS: A CASE STUDY IN TEXAS. *Educ. and Urban Soc. 1981 13(3): 309-331.* Describes the involvement of the Texas Education Agency with urban school districts since the early 1970's, whose various urban committees, while they have provided some advances in equalization aid, aid for compensatory education, and transportation funding, have not yet effected major beneficial changes in legislation for urban schools.

1788. Barone, Thomas. THINGS OF USE AND THINGS OF BEAUTY: THE SWAIN COUNTY HIGH SCHOOL ARTS PROGRAM. *Daedalus 1983 112(3): 1-28.* Art teacher Donald Forrister has developed a successful high school arts program at Swain County High School, in an impoverished rural area of North Carolina; he combines vocational and aesthetic training into a framework in which students learn purposeful self-expression.

1789. Barr, Susan M. OUR GEM ON GUNTER MOUNTAIN: KATE DUNCAN SMITH DAR SCHOOL. *Daughters of the Am. Revolution Mag. 1973 107(7): 644-646, 648-651, 766.*

1790. Benario, Herbert W. THE CLASSICS IN SOUTHERN HIGHER EDUCATION. *Southern Humanities Rev. 1977 11(Special Issue): 15-20.* Discusses higher education in the South, 1693-

1924, focusing on propensity for study in classics and outstanding students. One of six articles in this issue on classical traditions in the South.

1791. Bevins, Ann B. SISTERS OF THE VISITATION: 100 YEARS IN SCOTT COUNTY, MT. ADMIRABILIS AND CARDOME. *Register of the Kentucky Hist. Soc. 1976 74(1): 30-39.* Surveys the origins and development of the educational efforts of the Sisters of the Visitation in Scott County, Kentucky. The first academy, Mount Admirabilis, opened in 1875. In 1896, the nuns moved to Cardome, the Georgetown home of former governor James Fisher Robinson. Based on primary and secondary sources; 30 notes.
         J. F. Paul

1792. Bixler, Ray H. THE PSYCHOLOGY DEPARTMENT AT THE UNIVERSITY OF LOUISVILLE, 1907-1953. *Filson Club Hist. Q. 1983 57(3): 253-269.* Account of the early history of the Psychology Department at the University of Louisville. Ellis Freeman, the only member of the department during 1929-37, was a fine scholar, but he was also quite controversial and was forced to resign after instituting a libel suit against prominent local citizens. Based on published and unpublished University of Louisville records; 56 notes, 4 photos.
         G. B. McKinney

1793. Black, Watt L. EDUCATION IN THE SOUTH FROM 1820 TO 1860 WITH EMPHASIS ON THE GROWTH OF TEACHER EDUCATION. *Louisiana Studies 1973 12(4): 617-630.*

1794. Blazek, Ron. LIBRARY IN A PIONEER COMMUNITY: LEMON CITY, FLORIDA. *Tequesta 1982 42: 39-55.* A community library was created in Lemon City by the Lemon City Library Association, but not until 1904. Contrary to popular belief, Coconut Grove had the earliest library and library association in South Florida. Opened in December 1904, the library was a single-story frame structure, and it outlived the city itself. In 1925 Lemon City became a part of Miami, but it was not until 1942 that the library was joined to the Miami Public Library System. Largely based on contemporary newspaper accounts.
         H. S. Marks

1795. Brittain, James E. and McMath, Robert C., Jr. ENGINEERS AND THE NEW SOUTH CREED: THE FORMATION AND EARLY DEVELOPMENT OF GEORGIA TECH. *Technology and Culture 1977 18(2): 175-201.* Intended by its founders as an instrument of industrialization for the New South, Georgia Tech opened in 1888 with a curriculum modeled upon the shop culture tradition of Worcester Free Institute. Although more scientific courses were added later, the practical tradition continued strong into the 20th century. Career patterns of graduates show that even though many worked outside the state, the school "contributed significantly to the pool of technically trained people needed to build the industrial New South." Matriculation records show that Tech "remained beyond the reach of most of Georgia's poor and rural youths." 9 tables; 73 notes.
         C. O. Smith

1796. Buckley, Cathryn. THE EVERETT INSTITUTE. *North Louisiana Hist. Assoc. J. 1977 8(3): 119-124.* Everett Institute was founded in 1893 by the Everett Baptist Association and was located at Spearsville, in Union Parish. Its purpose was to offer the first two years of college courses to prepare its students to enter the state's larger colleges as juniors. George Mason was the Institute's first principal and served during 1894-98. The driving force behind the school's establishment was J. V. B. Waldrop, pastor of the Spearsville Baptist Church. The Institute's name honored John Pickney Everett, one of the founders of the Everett Baptist Association. Although it closed its doors in 1908 the Institute had earned a good reputation in north Louisiana. Primary and secondary sources; 36 notes.
         A. N. Garland

1797. Bush, Robert. DR. ALDERMAN'S SYMPOSIUM ON THE SOUTH. *Mississippi Q. 1973-74 27(1): 3-19.* Twenty American intellectuals contribute ideas on the progress of education in the South and the role of the South in the development of the nation.
         S

1798. Carleton, Don E. MC CARTHYISM IN HOUSTON: THE GEORGE EBEY AFFAIR. *Southwestern Hist. Q. 1976 80(2): 163-176.* Dr. George Ebey became deputy superintendent of the Houston Independent School District in 1952 just as the city was going through a stage of militant anti-Communism and anti-liberalism led by the Minute Women and school business manager Hubert L. Mills. Ebey had worked for liberal social causes in California and Oregon in the 1940's and the Minute Women accused him of Communist associations. A board investigation did not prove the charges but did show Ebey's background as too liberal for the board's conservative majority, which terminated his contract in 1953. Primary sources; 32 notes.
         J. H. Broussard

1799. Casdorph, Paul D. CLARENCE W. MEADOWS, W. W. TRENT AND EDUCATIONAL REFORM IN WEST VIRGINIA. *West Virginia Hist. 1980 41(2): 126-141.* Governor Clarence W. Meadows and State Superintendent of Schools W. W. Trent struggled over educational reform. In his study of West Virginia schools, George D. Strayer commended its county unit system but recommended that the state superintendent be appointed rather than elected. Trent, however, successfully opposed this change, which came only after he was no longer in office. The West Virginia Education Association was also involved in the controversy. Covers 1932-58. Based on West Virginia Government documents and on newspaper accounts; 38 notes.
         J. D. Neville

1800. Cashin, Mary Ann. CUMMING PAPERS, 1794 TO 1954. *Richmond County Hist. 1983 15(2): 4-7.* Documents covering more than 150 years of the activities of the Cumming family of Augusta, Georgia, have been donated to Reese Library of Augusta College.

1801. Cavallo, Dominick. KINDERGARTEN PEDAGOGY: A REVIEW ESSAY. *Hist. of Educ. Q. 1978 18(3): 365-368.* Review article prompted by Rebecca Murray's *History of the Public School Kindergarten in North Carolina* (New York: Mss Information Corp., 1974) and Elizabeth Dale Ross's *The Kindergarten Crusade* (Athens, Ohio: Ohio U. Pr., 1976); covers 19th-20th centuries.

1802. Cawthon, John Ardis. DOYLINE SCHOOL, 1905. *North Louisiana Hist. Assoc. J. 1977 8(5): 185-186.* In 1905, the 32 students of Doyline School in Webster Parish posed for a picture with their teacher, Mary Lou Richardson. Only six of those students are living today, but so is their teacher, who married Robert M. Sibley in 1907. The Doyline School, which existed 1903-37, was considered to have "the finest schoolhouse and the best equipment in North Louisiana," and was also the first consolidated school in North Louisiana outside of Caddo Parish. Primary sources; photo, 3 notes.
         A. N. Garland

1803. Chitty, Arthur Ben. WOMEN AND BLACK EDUCATION: THREE PROFILES. *Hist. Mag. of the Protestant Episcopal Church 1983 52(2): 153-165.* Brief vignettes of three women who made significant contributions to black higher education in the Protestant Episcopal Church. Anna Haywood Cooper (ca. 1858-1965) was only the fourth Negro woman to earn a doctorate from the Sorbonne—and at the age of 65. She became second president of Frelinghuysen University in Raleigh, North Carolina. While her forte was adult education, she never neglected the social and educational needs of children and youth. Isabella Gibson Robertson (1892-1976) was a financially comfortable white woman who was vitally concerned with supporting Saint Augustine College in Raleigh, North Carolina, a school she never saw but to which she contributed large sums. Mary Niven Alston (1918-81) was another white Episcopal woman who befriended black Episcopal schools. In her will she left $50,000 to Vorhees College in Denmark, South Carolina, a school she had never visited, but one of the numerous institutions she assisted in higher education. 3 photos.
         H. M. Parker, Jr.

1804. Christianson, Eric H. THE CONDITIONS FOR SCIENCE IN THE ACADEMIC DEPARTMENT OF TRANSYLVANIA UNIVERSITY, 1799-1857. *Register of the Kentucky Hist. Soc. 1981 79(4): 305-325.* The teaching of science at Transylvania University from 1799 until the demise of the university after 1857 was a qualified success. The presence of a renowned medical department both helped and hindered the attempt of the academic department to develop a reputation for excellence in science. By the 1820's, the study of science was an important part of the effort by the academic department. Primary and secondary sources, including records of Transylvania University; 6 illus., 62 notes.

J. F. Paul

1805. Cobb, William H. FROM UTOPIAN ISOLATION TO RADICAL ACTIVISM: COMMONWEALTH COLLEGE, 1925-1935. *Arkansas Hist. Q. 1973 32(2): 132-147.*

1806. Cook, Philip C. MT. LEBANON UNIVERSITY IN PEACE AND WAR. *North Louisiana Hist. Assoc. J. 1978 9(2): 55-63.* Mt. Lebanon University (for men), established in 1835, was the first institution of higher learning in North Louisiana. In addition there was a Female College and a preparatory school. The schools were established by Baptists who had migrated from around Abbeville, South Carolina. At the beginning of the Civil War the university was flourishing; however, the war altered the function of both the university and the college. The former's facilities were converted into a Confederate hospital; the latter's into a medical laboratory. The college never reopened after the war; the university did, but by the end of the century it had closed. Primary and secondary sources; 38 notes.          H. M. Parker, Jr.

1807. Cordle, Charles G. TRUSTEES OF THE ACADEMY OF RICHMOND COUNTY 1783-1863. *Richmond County Hist. 1980 12(2): 4-29.* Biographical sketches of the trustees of the Academy of Richmond County from 1783 to 1863, listed in chronological order; an appendix to Charles G. Cordle's master's thesis, *An Antebellum Academy: The Academy of Richmond County 1783-1863,* written in 1935.

1808. Coulter, E. Merton. BENJAMIN BRASWELL, GEORGIA PIONEER PHILANTHROPIST. *Georgia Hist. Q. 1981 65(2): 67-81.* Benjamin Braswell (d. 1817), Morgan County, Georgia, plantation owner about whom little else is known, left his estate to be used for the education of Morgan County orphans. Describes the growth and uses of this trust fund to about 1960. Based on court and foundation records; 57 notes.          G. R. Schroeder

1809. Cox, Dwayne. HOW OLD IS THE UNIVERSITY OF LOUISVILLE? *Register of the Kentucky Hist. Soc. 1983 81(1): 59-76.* The University of Louisville was probably started in 1837 even though university officials attempted to link its beginnings to the Jefferson Seminary, chartered in 1798. In 1837 the first full-scale city plans were made for an all-purpose university, and the course of the university's history since was probably unaffected by the existence earlier of the seminary. 5 photos, 29 notes.

J. F. Paul

1810. Daniel, Walter C. *THE CRISIS* AND *OPPORTUNITY* VS. WASHINGTON, D.C., BOARD OF EDUCATION. *Crisis 1978 85(6): 205-207.* In the spring of 1936, *The Crisis* and *Opportunity* were banned from the approved reading list of the public schools in the District of Columbia. Members of the Board of Education believed that the magazines contained reading matter objectionable because it was militant propaganda. Antisubversive hysteria and the American reaction to the rise of fascism fostered this repressive climate. The Board also objected to the use of the word "nigger" in the magazines. The editors of both magazines failed to get the decision reversed for several years.          A. G. Belles

1811. DeVane, F. Arthur. BIRDWOOD JUNIOR COLLEGE: TWO DECADES, 1954-1974. *Viewpoints: Georgia Baptist Hist. 1974 4: 87-98.*

1812. Evans, Frank B. CARLO BELLINI AND HIS RUSSIAN FRIEND FEDOR KARZHAVIN. *Virginia Mag. of Hist. and Biog. 1980 88(3): 338-354.* Traces through meager sources the career of Carlo Bellini (d. 1805) of the College of William and Mary, who was the first professor of modern languages in North America. Patronized by Phillip Mazzini, who sheltered him when he came to Virginia in 1773, and by Thomas Jefferson, who apparently secured him a clerkship as Virginia legislature translator, and his academic

post, Bellini served in the latter capacity to 1803. Given to exaggerated statements and perhaps not well grounded in any foreign language other than Italian, Bellini did not prosper financially or academically. Fedor Karzhavin, a Russian adventurer and Bellini's acquaintance, had similar unfulfilled hopes to use his linguistic skills. 65 notes.          P. J. Woehrmann

1813. Everman, H. E. EARLY EDUCATIONAL CHANNELS OF BOURBON COUNTY. *Register of the Kentucky Hist. Soc. 1975 73(2): 136-149.* Reports on education in Bourbon County, Kentucky. Education was provided in the home or in religious-oriented private schools until 1846 when public education came into being. Primary and secondary sources; 50 notes.          J. F. Paul

1814. Franklin, Robert L. GEORGIA BAPTIST STUDENT UNION POWER: DAVID BASCOM NICHOLSON III. *Viewpoints: Georgia Baptist Hist. 1974 4: 67-85.* Examines the activities (1925-52) of David Bascom Nicholson, III, educator, religious leader, and first secretary of the Baptist Student Center in Athens, Georgia.          S

1815. Gardner, Robert G. WOODLAND FEMALE COLLEGE. *Viewpoints: Georgia Baptist Hist. 1978 (6): 71-82.* History of Woodland Female College in Cedartown, Georgia, associated with the Baptist Church in that state, 1851-87.

1816. Green, Joe L. THE EDUCATIONAL SIGNIFICANCE OF HUEY P. LONG. *Louisiana Studies 1974 13(3): 263-277.* Studies the influence of Huey P. Long on education. What was "the meaning of his leadership as a phenomenon of culture in his native Louisiana, the residual effects of which have extended into the present?" Based on a schematic model of "the hero in history," concludes that "his appeal to the people was through actions which sought to rectify the deplorable educational situation" in which the economic elite exploited the ignorance of the masses. "His aim... was was to liberate the oppressed masses through better and more accessible education." Diagram, 41 notes.          R. V. Ritter

1817. Griffin, Keith H. THE LIGHT THAT FAILED: A RHETORICAL ANALYSIS OF WALTER HINES PAGE AS A CEREMONIAL ORATOR. *Southern Speech Communication J. 1981 46(3): 228-250.* From 1889 to 1914 Walter Hines Page and other educational reformers in the South attempted to reconcile their Southern heritage which taught the inferiority of the Negro with their beliefs in the Jeffersonian principle of equal opportunity for all; Page and his colleagues failed, however, because of their disdain for Southern myth and their failure to glorify the antebellum South and its struggle against the North.

1818. Harrison, Lowell. BEREA: AN EXPERIMENT IN EDUCATION. *Am. Hist. Illus. 1981 15(10): 8-17.* Berea College in Madison County, Kentucky, founded in 1858 by John G. Fee, John A. R. Rogers, and Fee's cousin John G. Hanson, all farmers and ministers, on Christian principles opposing "sectarianism, slaveholding, caste, and every other wrong institution or practice," had not changed its essential character through 1979.

1819. Hay, Melba Porter, ed. MEMOIRS OF CHARLES HENRY DAILY. *Register of the Kentucky Hist. Soc. 1978 76(2): 133-152.* Charles Henry Daily (1847-1932), a teacher and farmer, completed a handwritten memoir at the age of 84. Discusses his childhood, youth, and experiences as a teacher in Kentucky. 9 notes.

J. F. Paul

1820. Head, Ronald B. THE DECLENSION OF GEORGE W. BLAETTERMANN: FIRST PROFESSOR OF MODERN LANGUAGES AT THE UNIVERSITY OF VIRGINIA. *Virginia Cavalcade 1982 31(4): 182-191.* Saxony-born George W. Blaettermann (1782-1850) immigrated to the United States in 1824, began teaching at the University of Virginia, and quickly established a reputation as a poor teacher and a "rude, cantankerous, arrogant, and spiteful" person who whipped his wife (Elizabeth) twice in public and was terminated from the university in 1840 because of it.

1821. Henry, Inez. FAMOUS GEORGIA WOMEN: MARTHA BERRY. *Georgia Life 1979 6(2): 30-32.* Martha Berry (1866-1942) of Oak Hill, Georgia, founded four Sunday schools, four day schools, the Boy's Industrial School (changed in 1909 to the Berry Schools, with the addition of a girl's school), and a Junior College.

1822. Holmes, Jack D. L. EDUCATIONAL OPPORTUNITIES IN SPANISH WEST FLORIDA, 1781-1821. *Florida Hist. Q. 1981 60(1): 77-87.* The legend of Spanish incompetence in terms of educational opportunities does not withstand examination. An analysis of official reports, diaries, and memoirs indicates surprising educational opportunities in West Florida. Based on family letters, military records, and other sources; 46 notes.          N. A. Kuntz

1823. Horton, Bill. IMAGES OF CLASSLESSNESS AND BEREA COLLEGE. *Appalachian J. 1983-84 11(1-2): 58-66.* Criticizes Berea College's attempts to promote classlessness, as described in the Kentucky college's anniversary publications, *Berea's First 125 Years* (1982), and *Berea's First Century 1855-1955* (1955).

1824. Hunt, Carolyn. THE EARLY SCHOOLS OF MINDEN. *North Louisiana Hist. Assoc. J. 1978 9(2): 97-100.* Discusses the evolution of schools in Minden, Louisiana, since 1838. The early years of private and public education in Minden laid the foundation of a sound school system which has successfully met the many problems it has faced. Secondary sources; 26 notes          H. M. Parker, Jr.

1825. Jackameit, William P. THE EVOLUTION OF PUBLIC HIGHER EDUCATION GOVERNANCE IN WEST VIRGINIA: A STUDY OF POLITICAL INFLUENCE UPON EDUCATIONAL POLICY. *West Virginia Hist. 1975 36(2): 97-130.* Radical Republicans began West Virginia's higher education system and Democrats extended it in the 1870's. When Republicans returned to power in the 1890's they divided school regents and employees equally between the parties and created new schools as well. By 1907 there were six separate boards of regents which were then consolidated, but within 20 years a separate board for the state University was re-created. When Democrats came to power in the state after 1930 they fired some Republicans (including the president of Marshall College, causing a student strike) but failed in an attempt to oust the president of West Virginia University. After several false starts, a single Board of Regents for all colleges was created in 1969. Based on primary and secondary sources; 127 notes.          J. H. Broussard

1826. Johnson, Kenneth R. FLORENCE UNIVERSITY FOR WOMEN. *Alabama Hist. Q. 1976 38(4): 305-311.* Traces the history of Florence University for Women from its beginning in 1890 as the Southern Female University until a fire destroyed the building in 1910. 22 notes.          E. E. Eminhizer

1827. Johnson, Kenneth R. FLORENCE UNIVERSITY FOR WOMEN. *Alabama Hist. Q. 1976 38(2): 137-143.* Describes the founding, operation, and failure of a women's college at Florence, Alabama. Covers 1890-1911. 22 notes.          E. E. Eminhizer

1828. Johnson, Kenneth R. THE PEABODY FUND: ITS ROLE AND INFLUENCE IN ALABAMA. *Alabama Rev. 1974 27(2): 101-126.* Boston philanthropist George Peabody created a trust of two million dollars in 1867 to promote education within the poorer sections of the South. Distribution of monies in Alabama went largely to public schools until 1876, to normal schools until 1892, and to rural education haphazardly thereafter until 1914, when the trust was liquidated. The fund aided and popularized education, but did not influence educational trends, independently improve the quality of instruction, or challenge existing racial prejudices. Based on primary and secondary sources; tables, charts, 55 notes.          J. F. Vivian

1829. Johnson, Kenneth R. URBAN BOOSTERISM AND HIGHER EDUCATION IN THE NEW SOUTH: A CASE STUDY. *Alabama Hist. Q. 1980 42(1-2): 40-58.* In the 19th century, business and town officials often used many inducements to persuade institutions of higher education to locate in their community,

hoping for prestige and economic strength. A study is made of the events surrounding one such institution in Florence, Alabama, the Southern Female University. The school originated and thrived on religious discontent and business promoters' dreams of profit. Primary sources; 37 notes.          A. Drysdale

1830. Kennedy, William Bean. HIGHLANDER PRAXIS: LEARNING WITH MYLES HORTON. *Teachers Coll. Record 1981 83(1): 105-119.* Quotes and analyzes the remarks of Myles Horton, founder of the Highlander Folk School in Tennessee, as a basis for developing guidelines for movement education. As practiced at Highlander, movement education focuses on students' specific problems, stresses group self-education, and is strongly action oriented. Based on an interview with Myles Horton; bibliography.          E. C. Bailey, Jr.

1831. Kilgore, William J. ACADEMIC FREEDOM IN TEXAS. *AAUP Bull. 1979 65(3): 177-185.* Covers the past 50 years.

1832. Klibaner, Irwin. THE TRAVAIL OF SOUTHERN RADICALS: THE SOUTHERN CONFERENCE EDUCATION FUND, 1946-1976. *J. of Southern Hist. 1983 49(2): 179-202.* The Southern Conference Education Fund was not a membership organization, but a goal-directed body aimed at interracial education and health services. Most successful and active in the early and mid-1960's, it fell to the conflict between black power advocates and liberal, interracial advocates. Although the Southern Conference Education Fund collapsed in the 1970's, popular front liberals and radicals had made an important contribution to the contemporary South. Based on the Braden Papers, State Historical Society of Wisconsin, the Southern Conference Education Fund Papers, Tuskegee Institute Library, A. W. Williams Papers, Franklin Roosevelt Library, and newspapers; 58 notes.          T. Schoonover

1833. Lauderdale, William B. THE HOLTVILLE SCHOOL: A PROGRESSIVE EDUCATION EXPERIMENT. *Alabama Hist. Q. 1978 40(1-2): 62-76.* The Holtville School at Holtville, Alabama, was one of the better known progressive schools after World War II. Describes the development of its program and evaluates its results. Covers 1920's-present. 38 notes.          E. E. Eminhizer

1834. Lauderdale, William B. A PROGRESSIVE ERA FOR EDUCATION IN ALABAMA, 1935-1951. *Alabama Hist. Q. 1975 37(1): 38-67.* The progressive education movement reached its peak just before World War II. Alabama became one of the most important states in the progressive movement. The first educational innovations were introduced by Dr. C. B. Smith, Director of the Division of Instruction, who developed a problem-centered approach to education. He was followed by W. Morrison McCall. Peabody College consultants aided curriculum development. The practical application of the new ideas and their effect on the community is illustrated by a case study of the schools at Cold Springs and Fairview. World War II had a negative effect, and in 1951 a conservative was elected State Superintendent. 39 notes.          E. E. Eminhizer

1835. Liggin, Edna M. ROOTS OF THE VINE AND JOHN LEWIS LIGGIN: MASTER TEACHER. *North Louisiana Hist. Assoc. J. 1980 11(2): 18-26.* John Lewis Liggin (1881-1959) taught for 51 years, mostly in parish schools in north Louisiana. Educated at Mount Lebanon Baptist College and Louisiana State University, Liggin served as teacher and administrator in several schools, retiring at the age of 70. 2 illus.          J. F. Paul

1836. Lyon, Ralph M. THE EARLY YEARS OF LIVINGSTON FEMALE ACADEMY. *Alabama Hist. Q. 1975 37(3): 192-205.* Lists the four types of schools in the United States in the antebellum period; the academy was a popular form in the South. Details the founding and operation of the Livingston Female Academy, a Presbyterian institution, to 1907. 60 notes.          E. E. Eminhizer

1837. Mathis, Ray. WALTER B. HILL AND THE SAVAGE IDEAL. *Georgia Hist. Q. 1976 60(1): 23-34.* Walter B. Hill accepted the chancellorship of the University of Georgia in 1899 following several unsuccessful attempts in being elected to the federal judiciary. He had previously been in law practice as the representative of railroad interests. His positions on social issues were not consistent with generally held southern views. His efforts at the University of Georgia were to bring the institution to a position of financial stability and academic freedom for the faculty. He made some progress in both areas but was unable to break many long standing traditions of rule by the trustees. He spoke out on such issues as racism, women's rights, and prohibition. Primary and secondary sources; 23 notes.

M. R. Gillam

1838. Mathis, Ray. WALTER B. HILL, A NEW CHANCELLOR FOR THE UNIVERSITY OF GEORGIA. *Georgia Hist. Q. 1973 57(1): 76-84.* Describes the conditions that forced one chancellor from office and the election of a new one to head the University of Georgia. Walter B. Hill was a layman, a Georgian, and an alumnus as well as a good leader. The crisis that peaked in 1897 was over in 1901. The Methodists and Baptists were conciliated, agricultural instruction was vitalized, the alumni were organized, enrollment increased, and the state legislature made an appropriation. From the author's doctoral dissertation. 12 notes.

D. L. Smith

1839. Mayfield, Chris. LIVING WITH DAY CARE. *Southern Exposure 1980 8(3): 22-33.* Traces the history of day care since the Depression, when day nurseries were established as part of the Works Progress Administration program, focusing on day care since the 1960's in Jacksonville, Florida; Swainsboro, Georgia; and Durham, North Carolina.

1840. McClary, Ben Harris. THE FIRST PROFESSORSHIP OF ENGLISH LITERATURE IN AMERICA. *Georgia Hist. Q. 1973 57(2): 274-276.* Traces the history and occupants of the first professorship of English literature in the United States. It was established by Wesleyan Female College, Macon, Georgia, in 1844. The chair has since been endowed and is called the Cobb Alumnae Professorship of English Literature. 11 notes. D. L. Smith

1841. McCrimmon, Barbara. JOHNS HOPKINS UNIVERSITY'S SECOND PROFESSOR. *Manuscripts 1981 33(3): 173-184.* Eccentric, disorganized, often dissatisfied, and the original absent-minded professor, James Joseph Sylvester was also a brilliant mathematician. Despite any trepidations that Daniel Coit Gilman must have suffered in recruiting Sylvester, contributed to by Sylvester's unfortunate stay at the University of Virginia, the mathematician was an inspiring teacher and a productive scholar during his tenure at Johns Hopkins University. Covers 1825-84. Based on original correspondence; 2 illus. D. A. Yanchisin

1842. Meriwether, Robert W. GALLOWAY COLLEGE: THE EARLY YEARS, 1889-1907. *Arkansas Hist. Q. 1981 40(4): 291-337.* Discusses the development of and difficulties experienced by the Southern Methodist Galloway Female College, Searcy, Arkansas, from its founding in 1889 to 1907, when it ceased to be, in effect, a secondary school and actually became a college. Based on college records, newspapers, and other primary and secondary sources; 10 photos, 140 notes. G. R. Schroeder

1843. Miller, Jim Wayne. APPALACHIAN EDUCATION: A CRITIQUE AND SUGGESTION FOR REFORM. *Appalachian J. 1977 5(1): 13-22.* Criticizes traditional education methods in Appalachia; educational reform is necessary so that higher education in the region can provide students with the ability to critically assess their background and become involved in local secondary schools and local government.

1844. Montgomery, James R. JOHN R. NEAL AND THE UNIVERSITY OF TENNESSEE: A FIVE PART TRAGEDY. *Tennessee Hist. Q. 1979 38(2): 214-234.* After graduation from the University of Tennessee in 1893, John R. Neal (1876-1959) remained associated with that school for most of his life. He supported the university as a member of the state legislature and taught law there from 1909 until his release in 1923 for eccentric behavior (*not* for his defense of evolution, as is commonly assert-

ed). Neal then sought revenge against the university's administrators—he opened his own competing law school. Based on university papers, interviews, and other sources; 99 notes.

W. D. Piersen

1845. Nelms, Jack. THE DALLAS ACADEMY: BACKBONE OF THE PERMANENT SCHOOL SYSTEM IN SELMA. *Alabama Rev. 1976 29(2): 113-123.* Provides a brief history of the Dallas Academy in Selma from its inception in 1836 until its closing in 1961. The school thrived during 1839-53, closed during the Civil War, and reopened in 1868, partly with aid from the George Peabody fund. Growth of a tax-supported school system, notably after 1913, and changing residential patterns eventually rendered the institution unnecessary. Based on primary and secondary sources; 27 notes. J. F. Vivian

1846. Noble, Fraser. WILLIAM SMITH AND THE COLONIAL SCOTTISH CONNECTION: AN ADDRESS COMMEMORATING THE 200TH ANNIVERSARY OF WASHINGTON COLLEGE, CHESTERTOWN, MARYLAND, 11 OCTOBER 1981. *Hist. Mag. of the Protestant Episcopal Church 1982 51(3): 241-250.* Traces the academic career and contributions of the Anglican William Smith from his Scottish experience at Aberdeen's King's College in 1743, to the University of Pennsylvania in 1754, thence to his founding of Washington College, Chestertown, Maryland in 1781. Smith was also one of the founders of the American Philosophical Society and was equally active in the field of natural philosophy. He carried to Washington College the high ethical principles with which King's College had imbued him. 6 photos. H. M. Parker, Jr.

1847. Numbers, Ronald L. and Numbers, Janet S. SCIENCE IN THE OLD SOUTH: A REAPPRAISAL. *J. of Southern Hist. 1982 48(2): 163-184.* Although the South produced some noted scientists, it did not keep up with the North. A survey of various factors, such as religion, climate, educational institutions, and educational values (stress upon classics and disparagement of science), suggests demographic and environmental factors rather than slave-related mental attributes shaped the South's inability to keep pace with the North. Based on printed memoirs, correspondence, biographical collections, contemporary journals, and printed American Association for the Advancement of Science materials; 65 notes, 10 tables.

T. Schoonover

1848. Oldschue, Jerry C. HISTORICAL ARCHAEOLOGY ON THE UNIVERSITY OF ALABAMA CAMPUS. *Alabama Rev. 1977 30(4): 266-275.* Discovery of a well in 1972 prompted systematic excavation of the University of Alabama's campus in order to determine more clearly the configuration and remains of the original, pre-Civil War institution. Since then, a number of dormitories have been sited; and tools, hardware, and artifacts have been uncovered. Excavation continues. Primary and secondary sources; 9 notes. J. F. Vivian

1849. Orser, W. Edward. MORRIS R. MITCHELL (1895-1976): SOCIAL AND EDUCATIONAL VISIONARY. *Appalachian J. 1977 4(2): 100-104.* Elaborates on the sociopolitical overtones in the teaching career and progressive educational theory of southern educator Morris R. Mitchell, for whom community and cooperation were the focus in life and in education.

1850. O'Steen, Neal. PIONEER EDUCATION IN THE TENNESSEE COUNTRY. *Tennessee Hist. Q. 1976 35(2): 199-219.* The earliest educators in Tennessee were missionaries. Not until 1780 was the first true school established. The early schools were located in forts, and teaching was loose and unstructured. Religious schools were soon opened, all education was originally permeated with religion, but interest in practical subjects soon started the move to secularization. The first college was established in 1795. The old ideal of education for all was still only a dream when Tennessee became a state; governments paid more lip service to education than to actual financial aid. 72 notes. V. L. Human

1851. Peden, Creighton. A PIONEER MODEL: LAWTON B. EV-ANS. *Richmond County Hist. 1977 9(2): 5-13.* Discusses the role played by Lawton B. Evans in the establishment of the Augusta and Evans County, Georgia, public schools system, 1882-1934.

1852. Plank, David N. and Peterson, Paul E. DOES URBAN RE-FORM IMPLY CLASS CONFLICT? THE CASE OF ATLANTA'S SCHOOLS. *Hist. of Educ. Q. 1983 23(2): 151-173.* The class-conflict model dominates the explanation of Progressive educational reform. The 1897 reform of the Atlanta schools was, in many ways, a classic reform movement: the school board size was reduced, the superintendent's power was increased, economies were made and Progressive curricular innovations instituted. However, close exami-nation of the Atlanta experience demonstrates the inadequacy of the dominant explanatory model. The reforms did not merely serve class interests but were necessary to maintain growth of a complex educational system. In addition, the reforms were instituted by mid-dle-class professionals equally antagonistic to the traditional busi-ness elites and to working-class groups. Based on contemporary newspaper accounts and school records; 57 notes.
J. T. Holton

1853. Pryor, Elizabeth Brown. AN ANOMALOUS PERSON: THE NORTHERN TUTOR IN PLANTATION SOCIETY, 1773-1860. *J. of Southern Hist. 1981 47(3): 363-392.* Between graduation and a professional career young Northerners out of financial neces-sity accepted positions as plantation tutors in the South. A study of 80 male and 10 female tutors between 1773 and 1860 suggests that the tutors enjoyed relatively high salaries and light duties and that their employers, out of an esteem for learning, were willing to dis-regard the tutors' background and welcome them as valued mem-bers of the family. Despite these advantages, many tutors isolated themselves, suffering from what they considered to be intemper-ance, impiety, and shallowness of conversation, from their discom-fort with the institution of slavery, and, above all, from their undefined social status. Primary sources; 66 notes, appendix.
E. L. Keyser

1854. Racine, Phillip N. A PROGRESSIVE FIGHTS EFFICIEN-CY: THE SURVIVAL OF WILLIS SUTTON, SCHOOL SUPER-INTENDENT. *South Atlantic Q. 1977 76(1): 103-116.* While Superintendent of Atlanta Public Schools during 1921-43, Willis Sutton fought City Hall and big business to save public education. Confronted with a financial crisis, the city tried to eliminate "frills" such as free textbooks, teachers' benefits, public elections to the School Board, Negro night schools, and music, art, and physical ed-ucation courses. Sutton had initiated or improved most of these pro-grams. Atlanta businessmen offered to bail out the schools if these programs were cut and Sutton fired. However, Sutton's allies, which included organized labor, Atlanta teachers, and the National Edu-cation Association, kept him and his programs working. 29 notes.
W. L. Olbrich

1855. Riesman, David. NEW COLLEGE. *Change 1975 7(4): 34-43.* The sixties saw the emergence of a number of remarkable, innovative colleges, including Florida's New College and Florida Presbyterian, later renamed Eckerd. Both have recently engaged in negotiations with the state: New College and the state's board of regents agreed on its acquisition by the University of South Florida on July 1 of this year. Eckerd had proposed a public-private cam-pus-sharing venture, somewhat similar to that operating at Cornell University. Those negotiations have been terminated. New College now becomes an upper-division campus of USF in return for a state expenditure of slightly under $4 million for plant, debt ser-vice, and interim operations. The present economic circumstances make New College's practical continuation in any form rather un-likely, though a newly organized New College Foundation hopes to raise sufficient private funds to carry on New College's remarkable program. David Riesman here describes the unique history of New College. In a later issue, George Bonham will profile the interesting development of Eckerd College.
J

1856. Rosen, F. Bruce. THE INFLUENCE OF THE PEABODY FUND ON EDUCATION IN RECONSTRUCTION FLORIDA. *Florida Hist. Q. 1977 55(3): 310-320.* The Peabody Fund encour-aged public elementary education through financial support. Its most significant influence was to encourage Florida's racially segre-gated and unequal school system. The Fund's policy of less aid for black schools was justified on the grounds that funds for the educa-tion of black children came from the Freedmen's Bureau, charitable organizations, and the state. Primary and secondary works; 57 notes.
P. A. Beaber

1857. Rottier, Catherine M. ELLEN SPENCER MUSSEY AND THE WASHINGTON COLLEGE OF LAW. *Maryland Hist. Mag. 1974 69(4): 361-382.* The path to legal education for women was a slow and difficult one until 1898, "when the Washington College of Law, a school established 'primarily for women,' was founded by two pioneer female attorneys, Ellen Spencer Mussey and Emma M. Gillett." Surveys women's attempts to remove restrictive charter provisions of law schools, and gain bar recognition. The school's early years are described, and progress under various deans until 1949 when it merged with American University. Mrs. Mussey's ex-tensive involvement in the women's rights movement and the work of the Red Cross, the Grand Army of the Republic, and temper-ance groups is also detailed, and the College's graduates are traced in their careers. Primary and secondary works; 11 illus., 47 notes.
G. J. Bobango

1858. Saladin, Kenneth S. SIXTY YEARS OF CREATIONISM IN GEORGIA. *Society 1983 20(2): 17-25.* Reviews the periodic re-sumption of polemics and political statements against the teaching of evolution and the expected reactions of anticreationists; finds that these arenas are usually in the South and focuses on the con-troversy in Georgia, 20th century.

1859. Salmond, John A. "THE GREAT SOUTHERN COMMIE HUNT": AUBREY WILLIAMS, THE SOUTHERN CONFER-ENCE EDUCATIONAL FUND, AND THE INTERNAL SECUR-ITY SUB COMMITTEE. *South Atlantic Q. 1978 77(4): 433-452.* A detailed account of the Senate Internal Security Subcommittee, headed by Eastland of Mississippi, and the hearings held in New Orleans in March 1954 at which time Aubrey W. Williams, presi-dent of the Southern Conference Educational Fund Inc., was que-ried and harassed regarding Communists in the SCEF. The hearing emphasized that in the McCarthy era the pursuit of subversion too easily turned into the harassment of domestic dissenters; in this in-stance it was the uncompromising advocates of integration in a re-gion girding itself for the battle against what would be the most serious challenge yet to its social structure, the anticipated Supreme Court decision outlawing public school segregation. Suggests that Eastland had very much in his mind the need to destroy the credi-bility of those white southerners who opposed the prevailing sys-tem. Based on two collections of Aubrey Williams's papers—one in the Roosevelt Library, the other in the possession of Mrs. Anita Williams—, contemporary newspaper accounts and interviews; 43 notes.
H. M. Parker, Jr.

1860. Scarpaci, J. Vincenza. LOUIS H. LEVIN OF BALTIMORE: A PIONEER IN CULTURAL PLURALISM. *Maryland Hist. Mag. 1982 77(2): 183-192.* Louis H. Levin of Baltimore was a journalist, charity worker, and educator active at the turn of the century. At a time when Horace Kallen was formulating and expounding the ideal of cultural pluralism in America, Levin, in his newspaper the *Jewish Comment,* in papers delivered at national conferences, in a series of lectures at Goucher College on "Immigration," and at Johns Hopkins University on the immigrant experience, taught of the enrichment of American society by citizens of diverse back-grounds. Covers 1889-1923. Extracted from Levin's class notes and writings; illus., 33 notes.
G. J. Bobango

1861. Sewell, Diamond. JAMES BENJAMIN ASWELL: EDUCA-TOR AND STATESMAN. *North Louisiana Hist. Assoc. J. 1974 5(4): 118-129.* Short biography of James B. Aswell (1869-1931), who has been called "the father of the modern educational pro-gram in Louisiana." Aswell began teaching in Louisiana in 1893, established the first high school in Calhoun Parish, and taught at the Louisiana Industrial Institute in Ruston and at Louisiana State Normal in Natchitoches. In 1900 he became president of the Rus-ton school, and in 1904 was elected State Superintendent of Education. Soon after his reelection in 1908, Aswell resigned to become president of the Normal college. An unsuccessful candidate for governor in 1912, he was elected to Congress in 1912, and served continuously until his death. Photo, 57 notes.

A. N. Garland and S

1862. Shannon, Samuel H. LAND-GRANT COLLEGE EDUCATION AND BLACK TENNESSEANS: A CASE STUDY IN THE POLITICS OF EDUCATION. *Hist. of Educ. Q. 1982 22(2): 139-157.* The Morrill Act (US, 1862) established both the land-grant college and a role for the federal government in higher education in addition to revolutionizing the conception of the college in a scientific and technological society. The land-grant college in the South was only for whites. The story of the political struggle of black citizens and educators to gain an appropriate share of land-grant education in Tennessee is also the history of Tennessee State University (for blacks) and the University of Tennessee (for whites) from 1869 to 1977, when a federal judge ordered the dismantling of Tennessee's dual system of higher education. Based on legislative archives, contemporary newspaper accounts, and letters from contemporaries; 58 notes.

J. T. Holton

1863. Sherwood, Dolly. HISTORICAL GOODIES CRAMMED INTO OLD CAMELBACK TRUNKS. *Smithsonian 1977 8(3): 106-113.* The West Virginia Heritage Trunk project of the state's Department of Education, travels to all the schools to enrich the eighth grade social studies curricula. The artifacts are copies of the contents of trunks from the first decade of West Virginia's history, 1863-73, and are used for roleplaying by an entire classroom. Besides clothing, there are dulcimers, puppets, quilts, toys, and other items. The 36 roles were grouped into six families for roleplaying. Illus.

E. P. Stickney

1864. Steele, Max. THE ADIDAS GENERATION: REFLECTIONS ON STUDENT WRITING. *Southern Exposure 1981 9(2): 75-77.* Assesses student writing of the late 1960's and early 1970's at the University of North Carolina as it reflects the breakdown of the traditional family structure and of a strict moral code in the wake of the so-called permissive society.

1865. Taggart, Robert J. THE MODERNIZATION OF DELAWARE'S SCHOOL TAX SYSTEM DURING THE 1920'S. *Delaware Hist. 1979 18(3): 153-179.* Changes in the state's tax structure, removing most school revenue obligations from local districts and centralizing revenue collection, a shift to corporate and income taxes as primary sources of tax revenue, and the modernization of the state tax office after 1925 by Pierre S. duPont, created a large revenue surplus, even during the Depression. The state used the money to rebuild its school system. Based on the duPont papers, newspaper accounts, and government reports; 4 tables, 115 notes.

R. M. Miller

1866. Tate, Roger D., Jr. FRANKLIN L. RILEY AND THE UNIVERSITY OF MISSISSIPPI (1897-1914). *J. of Mississippi Hist. 1980 42(2): 99-111.* Born in Simpson County, Mississippi, in 1868, Franklin L. Riley completed his undergraduate education at Mississippi College and his Ph.D. in history at Johns Hopkins University in 1896. Shortly after returning home, Riley was invited by Chancellor Robert Burwell Fulton to become the University of Mississippi's first professor of history. Describes Riley's 17-year career at Mississippi. Enumerates Riley's scholarly accomplishments and the controversies surrounding him as a devotee of the new "scientific history." Discusses university problems with the state's political leaders and Riley's analyses of them. After Riley's invitation to noted historian Albert Bushnell Hart to speak at the 10th anniversary of the Mississippi Historical Society was denounced by State Archivist Dunbar Rowland in 1908 and after Governor Earl L. Brewer in 1911 fired five university professors and cut Chancellor Andrew Armstrong Kincannon's salary, the native son sought another position outside the state. In 1913, he joined the faculty of Washington and Lee in Lexington, Virginia. He taught there until his death in 1929 at age 61.

M. S. Legan

1867. Tate, Roger D., Jr., ed. A LETTER FROM CLEO HEARON TO WILLIAM E. DODD [1910]. *J. of Mississippi Hist. 1980 42(2): 153-154.* Presents a letter to her University of Chicago mentor, William E. Dodd, by the first Mississippi woman to obtain a doctorate and an able practitioner of scientific history. Cleo Hearon, who published a monograph on Mississippi's reaction to the nullification crisis and another on the state's role in the Compromise of 1850, describes her continuing research.

M. S. Legan

1868. Taylor, Cecil G. et al. PAUL MERRILL SPURLIN. *French-American Rev. 1982 6(2): 139-146.* Spurlin graduated from Emory University in 1925, did postgraduate work at the University of Lyon, and taught at Birmingham-Southern, Emory, and Johns Hopkins, receiving his doctorate from the latter in 1936. He then taught at Louisiana State University, where he was an active participant in the Maison Française from 1936 to 1944, and at the University of Michigan from 1946 to the present. His arrival at Louisiana State University occurred during a period of dynamic growth for that school and the Maison Française became a symbol of the state's French heritage, adding depth to the campus French studies program. Spurlin has specialized in 18th-century French literature and French-American intellectual relations, participating in various scholarly programs and organizations. Provides a chronological list of Spurlin's published works. 2 illus., biblio.

A. W. Novitsky

1869. Thigpen, Richard. THE FOUR PUBLIC BUILDINGS OF THE UNIVERSITY OF ALABAMA TO SURVIVE THE CIVIL WAR. *Alabama Rev. 1981 34(1): 50-58.* Traces the history of the four structures on the University of Alabama campus at Tuscaloosa that survived the Civil War. Several undocumented stories are told about campus personalities who attempted to save the university's physical plant. Each of the buildings has a unique history, but the most outstanding building architecturally is the President's Mansion, a Greek Revival structure built in the 1840's. The remaining survivals include the Gorgas House, said to be the first permanent building on the campus, the Observatory, and the Round House (also named the Jason Shrine). Based on University of Alabama Records, 1820-1921; 19 notes.

C. R. Gunter, Jr.

1870. Towns, W. Stuart. THE FLORIDA CHAUTAUQUA: A CASE STUDY IN AMERICAN EDUCATION. *Southern Speech Communications J. 1977 42(3): 228-245.* Traces the evolution of the Florida Chautauqua in DeFuniak Springs as a focal point for cultural events, lectures, educational events, conferences, and social gatherings, 1899-1935.

1871. Vinovskis, Maris A. and Bernard, Richard M. BEYOND CATHARINE BEECHER: FEMALE EDUCATION IN THE ANTEBELLUM PERIOD. *Signs 1978 3(4): 856-869.* Proposes a less elitist approach to the study of antebellum education, especially in the South. Data from the censuses of 1840-60 show that most female education was on the elementary level. Further exploration of a number of issues is needed, including: regional variation in the amount of general interest in education, a high illiteracy rate for white southern women and its general influence on southern society, and the practice and the philosophy of segregation by sex. Based on US census data and on secondary sources; 3 tables, 23 notes.

S. P. Conner

1872. Vossler, Kathryn Babb. WOMEN AND EDUCATION IN WEST VIRGINIA, 1810-1909. *West Virginia Hist. 1975 36(4): 271-290.* West Virginia schools in the 19th century educated women only in their traditional roles as homemakers, mothers, and moral guardians of society. Several private academies took women students before the Civil War, and the public school system also served females, but not with the same variety of courses open to males. Industrialization improved the position of women, and by the 1890's schools offered new opportunities, especially in the prosperous coal counties. Based on local records and secondary sources; 6 tables, 69 notes.

J. H. Broussard

1873. Walzel, Diana Lynn. BASIL LANNEAU GILDERSLEEVE: CLASSICAL SCHOLAR. *Virginia Cavalcade 1976 25(3): 110-117.* Discusses the classical scholarship and teaching of Basil Lanneau Gildersleeve (1831-1924) at the University of Virginia in Charlottesville (1856-76); also discusses his Greek studies, 1845-1924.

1874. Warford, Malcolm L. THE MAKING AND UNMAKING OF A RADICAL TRADITION: BEREA COLLEGE, 1855-1904. *Encounter 1977 38(2): 149-161.* Berea College was a religious college founded by John Gregg Fee, a Presbyterian missionary, in Kentucky, 1855-1904; emphasizes the abolitionist stance of its founders.

1875. Watterson, William Collins. HIS MASTER'S VOICE. *Virginia Q. Rev. 1984 60(1): 134-153.* Personal reminiscences about Mr. Simcott, a schoolmaster at Peddie Academy until his sudden death in 1972. Simcott—authoritarian, fastidious, and a committed teacher personally interested in his charges—tried to introduce his students to the finer things in life.    O. H. Zabel/S

1876. Weaver, Bettie Woodson. NINETEENTH-CENTURY EDUCATION IN WESTERN CHESTERFIELD COUNTY. *Virginia Cavalcade 1975 25(1): 38-47.* Discusses state government programs to enhance the public school system in western Chesterfield County 1796-1870, emphasizing the problem of illiteracy.

1877. Wells, Carol. KIND AND GENTLE ADMONITIONS: THE EDUCATION OF A LOUISIANA TEACHER. *Louisiana Hist. 1976 17(3): 283-297.* Born in South Carolina in 1847, Hattie Lake came with her father to Caddo Parish, Louisiana, when she was six. Educated on Louisiana plantations and at Mansfield Female College and Greenville Baptist Female College, she graduated from the latter in 1867. She made little use of the classical education she received at college, however, until 1878 when she was invited to teach in East Baton Rouge Parish, a job she received after some opposition from those who believed only men should be employed to teach. Based principally on correspondence and memoirs of Hattie Lake; photo, 36 notes.    R. L. Woodward

1878. Weyant, Jane G. THE DEBATE OVER HIGHER EDUCATION IN THE SOUTH, 1850-1860. *Mississippi Q. 1976 29(4): 539-558.* Discusses higher education in the South, 1850-60, emphasizing evolution in thought to include instruction in liberal arts as well as classics and the belief on the part of many elitist-minded reformers that reform in higher education would eventually diffuse to secondary and elementary levels, thus precluding the need for reform in mass public education.

1879. Whitehead, John S. CAUGHT BETWEEN TWO WORLDS: *MR. JEFFERSON'S UNIVERSITY* AND THE LITERATURE OF AMERICAN HIGHER EDUCATION. *South Atlantic Q. 1983 82(2): 206-215.* Reviews Virginius Dabney's *Mr. Jefferson's University* (1981). After tracing the contemporary historiography of American higher education, expresses disappointment with the parochial presentation of Dabney's history of the University of Virginia. 4 notes.    H. M. Parker, Jr.

1880. Wiley, Bell I. THE SPURNED SCHOOLTEACHERS FROM YANKEEDOM. *Am. Hist. Illus. 1980 14(10): 14-19.* Discusses the antagonism toward northern schoolteachers in the South, including threats of abuse and lynching, in the years prior to the outbreak of the Civil War, and briefly traces the presence of northern schoolteachers in the South since the 1770's.

1881. Willard, Julia L. REFLECTIONS OF AN ALABAMA TEACHER, 1875-1950. *Alabama Hist. Q. 1976 38(4): 291-304.* Supplies excerpts from the records of Orlena Harper McClesky and an interview with her niece, Alice Harper Strickland.
   E. E. Eminhizer

1882. Williams, Linda. SHORT-CHANGING EQUAL EDUCATION. *Southern Exposure 1979 7(2): 103-106.* Discusses underallocation of funds to public schools that serve areas of primarily minority population, throughout the South.

1883. Willie, Charles V. THE EDUCATION OF BENJAMIN ELIJAH MAYS: AN EXPERIENCE IN EFFECTIVE TEACHING. *Teachers Coll. Record 1983 84(4): 955-962.* The educational career of Benjamin Elijah Mays, former president of Morehouse College, illustrates the importance of providing with kindly support, accepting them initially as they are, and allowing for different temporal learning patterns. Mays's early schooling progressed slowly and he had difficulty initially at Bates College. Encouraged by his professors, however, he graduated and went on to earn his doctorate. 5 notes.    E. C. Bailey, Jr.

1884. Woods, H. Ted. EARLY EDUCATION IN CALDWELL PARISH. *North Louisiana Hist. Assoc. J. 1975 6(2): 85-87.* Two months before the parish became a separate governmental unit in 1838, "the first organized effort to provide higher education for the children of Caldwell Parish was begun" when the Pine Grove Academy was established two miles southwest of Columbia. In that same year, the state legislature incorporated the Academy and appropriated monies to construct a building. It "did not prove to be a successful educational venture" although it did remain in operation "until the early Reconstruction period." Almost all of the schools in the parish closed during the Civil War. After the war, at least until 1879, the parish had few public education facilities. Among the schools which are remembered from those years are the Little Star school (the first school in the parish to be called a high school), the Triune Church school, the Dirt Bridge Church school, the Welcome Home school, the Grayson school, and the Columbia school. Among the early school superintendents were N. M. Davis, J. W. McGinnis, C. P. Thornhill, and A. B. Hundley. The superintendents "were employed at a salary of from $200 to $300 annually, to keep the records of the school board and were not employed to supervise instruction."    A. N. Garland

## Educational Institutions

1885. Bailey, Fred A. OLIVER PERRY TEMPLE AND THE STRUGGLE FOR TENNESSEE'S AGRICULTURAL COLLEGE. *Tennessee Hist. Q. 1977 36(1): 44-61.* The prime creator of the University of Tennessee's Agricultural College was Oliver Perry Temple. In 1869 the faculty and board were divided over agricultural and classical education policy, but after two decades of bitter controversy the agricultural curriculum was firmly established. Primary and secondary sources; 46 notes.    M. B. Lucas

1886. Baker, Eugene W. UNION UNIVERSITY BUILDING UPON THE PAST TAKES GIANT STEP INTO THE FUTURE. *West Tennessee Hist. Soc. Papers 1975 29: 64-70.* One of two articles in this issue which deal with Union University in Jackson, Tennessee, which celebrated its Sesquicentennial in 1975. Discusses the college's past, and describes the school's decision to move its campus to a new location on the edge of Jackson. The new campus will cost $10 million and will permit an "innovative, modern, and flexible" program. Based on secondary sources; photo.
   H. M. Parker, Jr.

1887. Barrett, Clifton Waller. THE STRUGGLE TO CREATE A UNIVERSITY. *Virginia Q. R. 1973 49(4): 494-506.* Details Thomas Jefferson's planning and development of the University of Virginia which finally opened in 1825, the year before his death. Serious planning, complicated by personal family and financial problems, began in 1809; and 1814 was "the beginning of twelve years of unceasing struggle" to create a fine university.
   O. H. Zabel

1888. Bettersworth, John K. "THE COW IN THE FRONT YARD": HOW A LAND-GRANT UNIVERSITY GREW IN MISSISSIPPI. *Agric. Hist. 1979 53(1): 62-70.* Recounts the founding and development of Mississippi A. & M. College, noting especially the work of its board member Colonel W. B. Montgomery, and Stephen D. Lee, its first president. A major contribution was the recruiting of Frank A. Gully of Michigan A. & M. as head of the agriculture department and Robert Kedzie, also from Michigan, in chemistry. Vigorous programs of experimentation and extension were continued by their successors in what became Mississippi State University. Although the old-time small farmer is practically extinct and the curriculum has been greatly proliferated, "the cow is still in the front yard (of the University), but we make sure it does not kick over the art student's easel." 49 notes. R. V. Ritter

1889. Bettersworth, John K. MISSISSIPPI STATE UNIVERSITY: A CENTENNIAL SKETCH. *J. of Mississippi Hist. 1979 41(1): 33-52*. A historical overview of Mississippi State University by emeritus professor of history and vice-president for academic affairs at that institution. Discusses the movement to establish an agricultural college as well as the debate over its location. Significant developments and key individuals in the historical panorama of the University between its founding and its centennial celebration in 1978 are surveyed. Topics include student life, enrollment, presidents, development of curricula, and the effects of Mississippi politics on university affairs. M. S. Legan

1890. Brabham, Robin. DEFINING THE AMERICAN UNIVERSITY: THE UNIVERSITY OF NORTH CAROLINA, 1865-1875. *North Carolina Hist. Rev. 1980 57(4): 427-455*. The University of North Carolina (UNC), along with a number of other major universities, struggled through a period of reform and redefinition as America's educational needs changed during the latter 19th century. A university now had to be more than a larger version of a country college; it had to offer more applied and advanced courses, and in areas to fit an increasingly business and technology oriented society. UNC, a successful, traditional, antebellum state school, failed to meet its constituents' curricular needs in the immediate postwar years. President David Lowry Swain began the reform process with Morrill Land Grant funds and some new ideas proposed by the trustees and faculty. Before the latter plans could be implemented, federal Reconstruction Acts caused a reorganization of the state education system, including selection of Republican-leaning trustees and president Solomom Pool. Enrollment dropped, enmity rose, and the trustees closed the school from 1871 to 1875. A new board and President Kemp P. Battle reorganized the university into six colleges leading to degrees of Bachelor of Arts, Bachelor of Science, Bachelor of Agriculture, and Master of Arts. UNC Papers and Trustee Minutes, and secondary sources; 13 illus., 73 notes. T. L. Savitt

1891. Chepesiuk, Ron. THE WINTHROP COLLEGE ARCHIVES AND SPECIAL COLLECTIONS: SELECTED RESOURCES FOR THE STUDY OF WOMEN'S HISTORY. *South Carolina Hist. Mag. 1981 82(2): 143-172*. Winthrop College, founded in 1886, by the 1920's was one of the largest women's colleges in the country. Although Winthrop became coeducational in 1974, it retains its interest in collecting material important in the study of women's education. The current collection includes letters, diaries, scrapbooks, photobooks, speeches, and yearbooks totaling over 700 linear feet and 1,300 bound volumes. By acquiring papers and records of women's organizations not related to the college, Winthrop's collection became important for the study of South Carolina as well as Winthrop College. Based on primary sources in Winthrop College Archives and Special Collections; 2 notes. R. H. Tomlinson

1892. Chitty, Arthur Ben. SEWANEE: THEN AND NOW. *Tennessee Hist. Q. 1979 38(4): 383-400*. The collegiate gothic architecture of the University of the South at Sewanee, Tennessee, reflects the Anglican origins of a campus where learning and religion are joined. Between 1875-1915 nine major stone buildings were constructed and historical restoration has kept the campus a place of pilgrimage for many Episcopalians. Based primarily on the Sewanee Archives and personal interviews; 3 illus., 54 notes. W. D. Piersen

1893. Cresswell, John W. CHARACTER BUILDING AT KINGFISHER COLLEGE, 1890-1922. *Chronicles of Oklahoma 1977 55(3): 266-281*. Founded in 1890 by Congregationalists, Kingfisher College grew rapidly under its resourceful president J. T. House, who attracted funding from eastern philanthropists. The school's commitment to "character building" stressed the classics and earned it a commendable academic reputation. Declining enrollments during World War I, a shrinking endowment, and investment

losses forced the college to close in 1922. Its legacy continued through its highly successful graduates and through the Kingfisher College Chair in the University of Oklahoma's Department of Philosophy. Primary and secondary sources; 3 photos, 3 charts, 51 notes. M. L. Tate

1894. Crowson, E. T. SAMUEL STANHOPE SMITH: A FOUNDER OF HAMPDEN-SYDNEY COLLEGE. *Virginia Cavalcade 1974 24(2): 52-61*. Hampden-Sydney College was founded by Presbyterian educator Samuel Stanhope Smith six months before the Declaration of Independence was signed, and he went on to make outstanding contributions to early education in America.

1895. Daniel, W. Harrison. THE GENESIS OF RICHMOND COLLEGE, 1843-1860. *Virginia Mag. of Hist. and Biog. 1975 83(2): 131-149*. When Virginia Baptist Seminary was transformed into Richmond College, the new institution faced many problems. In the early years the trustees developed a curriculum, established rules of behavior for students and faculty, and raised funds to keep the college operating. By the 1850's many problems had been solved. The faculty and student body had increased, and financially the college was flourishing. The Civil War destroyed the gains of the previous decades, however, and rebuilding had to begin after Appomattox. Based largely on the minutes of the Board of Trustees and newspaper accounts; 57 notes. R. F. Oaks

1896. Daniel, W. Harrison. OLD LYNCHBURG COLLEGE, 1855-1869. *Virginia Mag. of Hist. and Bio. 1980 88(4): 446-477*. Narrates the birth, decline, and death of the college. Begun in 1850 by the Methodist Protestant Church as Madison College at Uniontown, Pennsylvania, the school, beset by sectional pressures, in effect in 1855 decamped to what was considered by most administrators, faculty, and students the more congenial social climate of Lynchburg, Virginia. The original college closed in 1858. Although the college was nominally supported by the Southern Conferences of the Church, tangible aid was small, and most disappointingly so from the Lynchburg area. During the Civil War, classes were suspended because most of the college community left for the Confederate military. The school did not reopen, and trustees sold the property in 1869. 113 notes. P. J. Woehrmann

1897. Dugger, Ronnie. THE UNIVERSITY OF TEXAS: THE POLITICS OF KNOWLEDGE. *Change 1974 6(1): 30-39, 60-61*. UT stood on the threshold of greatness—until a power clash rent it asunder. J

1898. Durden, Robert F. JAMES B. DUKE AND THE LAUNCHING OF DUKE UNIVERSITY. *South Atlantic Q. 1975 74(2): 143-163*. A review of the creation and early years (1924-30) of Duke University, Durham, North Carolina. The university was the brainchild of James Duke, wealthy industrialist, who set up an endowment to finance construction and operation. The university replaced Trinity College, was built of local stone, and sought excellence rather than size. Reports of its wealth were both fabulous and erroneous; in fact, the new university had to cut back both construction plans and operating programs in order to make ends meet. The death of Duke at the beginning of the construction period worsened the financial situation. 42 notes. V. L. Human

1899. Durden, Robert F. THE ORIGINS OF THE DUKE ENDOWMENT AND THE LAUNCHING OF DUKE UNIVERSITY. *North Carolina Hist. Rev. 1975 52(2): 130-146*. In 1890 Washington Duke paid for Trinity College's move from Randolph County to Durham, North Carolina. Thus began the Duke family's long and close affiliation with Trinity. When the college fell into financial difficulty in 1892, Duke's son Benjamin N. interceded with cash. Benjamin and his brother James B. Duke then poured time and money into Trinity, culminating in the establishment, in 1924, of the Duke Endowment, used partly to build a new University named Duke. Based on personal manuscripts and university papers, published reports and secondary sources; 13 illus., 20 notes. T. L. Savitt

1900. Egerton, John. THE RISE OF THE SOUTHERN STAR: DUKE UNIVERSITY. *Change 1973-74 5(10): 28-35.* Up to very recently, the quality of Southern education was thought to be considerably below that of much of the rest of the country. But several Southern universities are rapidly achieving first-rank status and international reputations, with Duke University among the leaders. Under the energetic presidency of Terry Sanford, Duke has now joined that very small group of America's most prestigious research universities.                    J

1901. Ellis, L. Tuffly. THE UNIVERSITY'S CENTENNIAL: A COMMEMORATION. *Southwestern Hist. Q. 1982 86(2): 125-134.* An introductory essay for a special issue in recognition of the centennial of the University of Texas. This article provides a brief overview of the university's development and summarizes the eight articles in the issue. Secondary sources; 2 photos, 9 notes.
                    R. D. Hurt

1902. Everhart, Frances B. THE SOUTH CAROLINA COLLEGE LIBRARY. *J. of Lib. Hist. 1968 3(3): 221-241.* Records the origins and vicissitudes of the South Carolina College Library, the plans of which were approved in 1802. Although the library had a promising beginning, it had become neglected by the 1830's. In the 1840's, it was relocated and the library earned a reputation for its handsome building and excellent collection of books, the rarest of which are listed here. Although the college closed during the Civil War, 1862-66, the library escaped destruction. Primary and secondary sources; 98 notes.                    M. Feingold

1903. Ferguson, Anne Williams. CARRY ME NOT, REPEAT NOT, BACK TO OLE VIRGINNY: A BOARDING SCHOOL CHRONICLE OF THE 40'S. *Virginia Q. R. 1976 52(2): 243-248.* Presents a humorous description of experiences at Chatham Hall, an Episcopalian boarding school in Virginia in the 1940's. From examining her daughter's experience at another school, the author concludes that the prudery and snobbishness of the 40's has been somewhat reduced, but not entirely eliminated.    O. H. Zabel

1904. Fischer, LeRoy H. "INSTRUCTION, RESEARCH, AND EXTENSION": THE HISTORY DEPARTMENT AT OKLAHOMA STATE UNIVERSITY. *Chronicles of Oklahoma 1983 61(1): 48-67.* The Oklahoma State University History Department faced an uphill battle in gaining credibility, financial support, and professional staff. University presidents Angelo Scott (1899-1908) and Bradford Knapp (1923-1928) stressed the need for history and additional social sciences, but other presidents saw the school's mission in terms of agriculture and science. Real growth came after World War II with the return of veterans and a state requirement of American history for all students. By 1968 a successful doctoral program was in place, and with it came an expansion of faculty and a dedication to research. Based on interviews and records at Oklahoma State University; 11 photos, 27 notes.    M. L. Tate

1905. Fletcher, Charlotte. 1784: THE YEAR ST. JOHN'S COLLEGE WAS NAMED. *Maryland Hist. Mag. 1979 74(2): 133-151.* Since 1870, the name of St. John's for the college in Annapolis, Maryland, was believed to have been taken from the college of the same name in Cambridge University, honoring the Evangelist. The Maryland college was named in honor of the Evangelist, but for other reasons. Discussion of the 1784 Charter of the college originated in the Assembly on 27 December, the feast day of St. John the Evangelist. The name of St. John had a special meaning for many of those promoting the college, because of its associations with Freemasonry. The name may also have been chosen to honor George Washington, a Mason. Based on newspapers, official records of the Maryland Assembly, letters, Masonic archival materials; 2 illus., 55 notes.                    C. B. Schulz

1906. Goodman, George J. and Lawson, Cheryl A. THE BOTANICAL ITINERARIES OF A. H. VAN VLEET. *Chronicles of Oklahoma 1978 56(3): 322-330.* While head of the University of Oklahoma Biology Department, Dr. Albert H. Van Vleet (1861-1925) conducted several important botanical explorations in Oklahoma Territory. These yielded valuable plant specimens which were transferred to the university for further study. Several fires during the early 20th century destroyed portions of these collections, but Van Vleet continued collecting and successfully worked toward creating the university's graduate program. Primary and secondary sources; photo, 3 maps, 14 notes.                    M. L. Tate

1907. Gray, Ricky Harold. CORONA FEMALE COLLEGE (1857-1864). *J. of Mississippi Hist. 1980 42(2): 129-134.* Corona Female College, established by L. B. and Susan P. (Moore) Gaston on 15 July 1857 in Corinth, Mississippi, enjoyed a brief existence. Although one of the first accredited colleges in the state and one of the first woman colleges in the United States, the Civil War ended its academic life in 1861. Describes the use of the college building as a Union hospital during the war and its final destruction by fire in 1864.                    M. S. Legan

1908. Griffin, Roger A. TO ESTABLISH A UNIVERSITY OF THE FIRST CLASS. *Southwestern Hist. Q. 1982 86(2): 135-160.* On 11 February 1858, Governor Hardin R. Runnels signed a bill which appropriated $100,000 in US bonds for the creation of the University of Texas. The state legislature also provided a tenth of the public lands which originally had been reserved to support railroad expansion for the development of a university. The Civil War, Reconstruction, and Texas politics, however, delayed construction for 25 years, and the first class did not enroll until the autumn of 1883. Based on gubernatorial and legislative documents; 4 photos, chart, 47 notes.                    R. D. Hurt

1909. Grob, Alan. INVASION IN AUSTIN. *AAUP Bull. 1975 61(1): 5-12.* Ronnie Dugger's *Our Invaded Universities* (New York: Norton, 1974), warns about meddlesome regents and mentions the University of Texas.

1910. Hagerman, Edward. BLACK MOUNTAIN BREAKDOWN. *Can. Rev. of Am. Studies [Canada] 1976 7(2): 220-224.* Review article prompted by Martin Duberman's *Black Mountain: An Exploration in Community* (New York, 1975), largely an intellectual history of Black Mountain College in North Carolina 1933-56.
                    H. T. Lovin

1911. Hall, Lark. V. L. PARRINGTON'S OKLAHOMA YEARS, 1897-1908: "FEW HIGH LIGHTS AND MUCH MONOTONE." *Pacific Northwest Q. 1981 72(1): 20-28.* In 1897 Vernon L. Parrington assumed a position as instructor of English and modern languages at the University of Oklahoma. During the following eleven years he performed a host of duties, ranging from organizing an English Department to coaching football. His hard work earned few plaudits, and in 1908 he was unfairly dismissed due to pressures from religious groups who wanted all "immoral faculty" fired. From there he went on to a distinguished academic career at the University of Washington. Photo, 23 notes.                    M. L. Tate

1912. Heuvel, Lisa. "THE PEAL THAT WAKES NO ECHO": BENJAMIN EWELL AND THE COLLEGE OF WILLIAM AND MARY. *Virginia Cavalcade 1978 28(2): 70-77.* Traces the presidency of Benjamin Stoddert Ewell at the College of William and Mary, 1854-88, highlighting his leadership through two fires, the attempted relocation to Richmond from Williamsburg, and financial disaster.

1913. Hockman, Dan M. WILLIAM DAWSON: MASTER AND SECOND PRESIDENT OF THE COLLEGE OF WILLIAM AND MARY. *Hist. Mag. of the Protestant Episcopal Church 1983 52(3): 199-214.* William Dawson had a profound impact on the College of William and Mary during its formative years, 1729-52—first as master and later as president. From the very onset he played a prominent role in selecting faculty, obtaining financial support, upgrading the quality of the library, encouraging emphasis on classical studies, and promoting religious instruction for blacks, Indians, and indigent whites. Dawson's impressive accomplishments reveal much about his personality and character. The salient feature of his tenure as president was the absence of serious dissent among faculty and between faculty and the Visitors. Based on a microfilm copy of the Fullham Palace manuscript at the University of Illinois, Champaign-Urbana, on the faculty journal of the College of William and Mary, and the Dawson manuscript; 70 notes.

H. M. Parker, Jr.

1914. Holder, Ray. CENTENARY: ROOTS OF A PIONEER COLLEGE (1838-1844). *J. of Mississippi Hist.* 1980 42(2): 77-98. Present-day Centenary College in Shreveport, Louisiana, had its genesis in an antebellum educational renaissance among Mississippi Methodists. The Mississippi Conference, seeking the advantage of an institution of higher learning in closer proximity to its ministerial endeavors, was stimulated by the Wesley Centennial (1838-39) to launch such an enterprise. Discusses the college's Mississippi period before it was removed to Jackson, Louisiana, in 1845. Describes its founders, administrators, faculty, students and student life. Examines controversial issues, particularly the debate over the initial location of the institution in Brandon Springs and its subsequent relocation in the facilities of state-owned Louisiana College which the Methodists acquired. Prominent individuals in the history of Centenary during 1838-44 included: William Winans, David O. Shattuck, Edward McGehee, Thomas C. Thornton, and Charles K. Marshall.

M. S. Legan

1915. Holley, Edward. INSIDE OUR SCHOOLS: CHAPEL HILL. *Wilson Lib. Bull.* 1981 56(2): 128-132. Traces the foundation in 1931 of the University of North Carolina at Chapel Hill's library education program, funded during its first five years by a $100,000 grant from the Carnegie Corporation announced in 1929, focusing on the program's curriculum, special programs offered, enrollment, and early leaders, including Louis Round Wilson and Susan Grey Akers.

1916. Holliman, Glenn N. THE WEBB SCHOOL JUNIOR ROOM: THE SYMBOL OF A SCHOOL. *Tennessee Hist. Q.* 1977 36(3): 287-304. Though the Junior Room of the Webb School of Bell Buckle, Tennessee, was not constructed until 1886, it symbolized the philosophy of the school and its founder, William R. "Sawney" Webb. For it was in the Junior Room that Webb conducted his famous Latin classes where he developed his instructional method known as "trapping," or going to the front of the class upon delivering a superior performance. The school is in its 108th year. Secondary sources; 4 illus., 3 notes.

M. B. Lucas

1917. Hollow, Elizabeth Patton. DEVELOPMENT OF THE BROWNSVILLE BAPTIST FEMALE COLLEGE: AN EXAMPLE OF FEMALE EDUCATION IN THE SOUTH, 1850-1910. *West Tennessee Hist. Soc. Papers* 1978 (32): 48-59. The West Tennessee Baptist Female College, Brownsville, Tennessee, was chartered in 1850 and was dissolved in 1910. Higher education was available to women in the South before accredited colleges for women were established and before public coeducation was accepted or available. Based largely on the *Proceedings* of the West Tennessee Baptist Convention, publications of the Brownsville Female College, and secondary sources; 4 illus., 61 notes.

H. M. Parker, Jr.

1918. Lamon, Lester C. THE BLACK COMMUNITY IN NASHVILLE AND THE FISK UNIVERSITY STUDENT STRIKE OF 1924-1925. *J. of Southern Hist.* 1974 40(2): 225-244. Discusses Fisk University students' struggle to obtain freedom from paternalistic control of their clubs, publications, and dress codes and to secure student participation in school administration through a student council, student publications, and an athletic association. With the white administration unwilling to make any appreciable concessions, the resultant friction and confrontation moved the struggle into the community. The administration sought support from the whites in Nashville, while the students sought support from the black community in Nashville. With solid local and national black support, Fisk President Fayette Avery McKenzie was forced to resign in 1925. Although not replaced with a black, the new president granted most of the students' previous demands. Based on manuscripts and printed primary and secondary sources; 46 notes.

T. D. Schoonover

1919. Lewis, Leon. BLACK MOUNTAIN COLLEGE: A STRANGE SPOT IN A STRANGE SPOT. *Appalachian J.* 1973 1(2): 115-118. A discussion of the history of Black Mountain College and a critique of Martin Duberman's *Black Mountain, An Exploration in Community*.

D. M. Dean

1920. Lewis, Wilber Helen. MANSFIELD FEMALE COLLEGE REUNION—1974. *North Louisiana Hist. Assoc. J.* 1974 6(1): 30-32. Mansfield Female College, the first college for women west of the Mississippi River, was founded in 1844 and closed in 1930. "College spirit has not waned," however, and a large number of alumnae return biennially for a school reunion. The 1974 gathering of 93 alumnae and their friends had representatives from the classes of 1914-30, and the principal speaker was Dr. Walter Lowrey of Centenary College. 3 illus., 5 photos.

A. N. Garland

1921. Malone, E. T., Jr. THE UNIVERSITY OF NORTH CAROLINA IN EDWIN FULLER'S 1873 NOVEL, *SEA-GIFT*. *North Carolina Hist. Rev.* 1976 53(3): 288-302. Edwin Wiley Fuller (1847-76), a student at the University of North Carolina 1864-66, portrayed student and city life in Chapel Hill between 1843 and 1868 in his 1873 novel, *Sea-Gift*. Romance, duelling, the sin of pride, freshman hazing, and social classes are among the topics Fuller touches on. *Sea-Gift* never received widespread acclaim, though its reviewers generally viewed it with favor. Based on private papers, newspaper and periodical articles, and secondary sources; 6 illus., 44 notes.

T. L. Savitt

1922. Mayo, Janet. THE AUTHORITY TO GOVERN AND THE RIGHT TO DANCE ON CAMPUS AT CENTENARY COLLEGE. *North Louisiana Hist. Assoc. J.* 1978 9(4): 205-218. Describes the controversy which developed over a dancing resolution passed in 1941 by the Board of Centenary College, a Methodist-controlled college, and the effect it had on the division of power between the Board, the faculty, and the Methodist Church. The major issue that finally emerged was not whether dancing could be permitted on the campus, but rather who possessed the power to govern the college. In the end the Board became the sole authority with the power to govern and operate the college. Through action of the Board, the faculty gained the power to establish curriculum, maintain discipline, and regulate student life. Thus an insignificant controversy over dancing established the policy whereby Centenary College would be governed and operated in the future. Based on minutes of the Board of Trustees of Centenary College, publications and records of the Louisiana Conference of the Methodist Church, South, contemporary newspaper accounts and oral interviews; 67 notes.

H. M. Parker, Jr.

1923. Meade, C. Wade. EDWIN WHITFIELD FAY: NORTH LOUISIANA'S CONTRIBUTION TO CLASSICAL STUDIES. *North Louisiana Hist. Assoc. J.* 1974 5(2): 45-49. Edwin Whitfield Fay was born in Minden, Louisiana, on 1 January 1865 and received all of his early formal education at home. In 1890 he received his Ph.D. degree from Johns Hopkins University, graduating with Phi Beta Kappa honors as a classical scholar. He eventually joined the faculty of the University of Texas in Austin in 1899 and remained there until his death in 1920. He was considered an international scholar in the field of comparative Indo-European philology, and his bibliography contains 193 entries. Fay helped build the Classics department at the University of Texas into one of the best in the world. Illus., 21 notes.

A. N. Garland

1924. Monroe, Margaret Towers. A SHORT SKETCH OF MRS. ANNA CALHOUN SMITH'S VERNON SCHOOL, 1885-1901. *North Louisiana Hist. Assoc. J.* 1976 7(3): 104-109. Anna Calhoun Smith's school, established at Vernon in 1885, was "the primary instrument of education for the children of the entire community." Among her students were "future ministers, teachers, presidents of three Louisiana colleges, and a United States Senator." Prior to her marriage to Judge Newton McKay Smith in 1885, Anna Calhoun had been "presiding teacher of Minden Female College at Minden." Descended from "a long line of Presbyterian teachers and preachers," she had been "largely educated by her mother." She started her school in Vernon primarily to instruct her stepchildren, and emphasized reading, writing, arithmetic, and Latin. The school was closed before Judge and Mrs. Smith moved to Ruston in 1901. Condensed from a more detailed article in the Prescott Memorial Library at Louisiana Tech University. Contains a list of students who attended Mrs. Smith's Vernon school. Photo, 9 notes.

A. N. Garland

1925. O'Steen, Neal. THE UNIVERSITY OF TENNESSEE: EVOLUTION OF A CAMPUS. *Tennessee Hist. Q. 1980 39(3): 257-281.* The architectural variety of the University of Tennessee, Knoxville is a reflection of the school's changing mission. Greek Revival lecture halls of the small liberal arts campus made way after 1869 for the Collegiate Gothic science and technology buildings, which served the university's new land grant status. Since the 1960's, new modes of financing have produced a major campus of some 115 structures. Today contemporary architecture mirrors the research orientation of our present decade. Primary sources; 4 illus., 74 notes.

W. D. Piersen

1926. Peterson, Owen. FORUM DEBATING: 150 DEBATES LATER. *Southern Speech Communication J. 1982 47(4): 435-443.* Traces the history and development of audience participation debates, called the LSU Forum, which has been sponsored by the Louisiana State University Department of Speech during the last 18 years; discusses how they are organized, operated, and their values and limitations.

1927. Pohl, James W. THE BIBLE DECADE AND THE ORIGIN OF NATIONAL ATHLETIC PROMINENCE. *Southwestern Hist. Q. 1982 86(2): 299-320.* The University of Texas began its rise to national athletic prominence in 1937 when Dana X. Bible became football coach. Bible instituted an effective player recruitment program, improved the athletic facilities, and hired an excellent coaching staff. When he retired in 1946, the University of Texas had a winning football tradition, and Texans had come to expect victory on the football field. Based on university records at the Eugene C. Barker Texas History Center in Austin; 2 photos, 42 notes.

R. D. Hurt

1928. Poole, David R., Jr. EDUCATIONAL WORK AT WHITEFIELD'S ORPHAN SCHOOL IN GEORGIA. *Methodist Hist. 1977 15(3): 186-195.* George Whitefield established a school near Savannah, Georgia in 1738 to provide an education for orphans and the children of the poor. By 1771 it became a school not only for these but for others who could afford to pay for education. The curriculum was not exceeded even in some exclusive academies in America. It was an outstanding example of American colonial education influenced and shaped by the Great Awakening and its reforming thrust. 58 notes.

H. L. Calkin

1929. Posner, Bruce G. JOINING THE MAINSTREAM: TOUGALOO DEBATES ITS COURSE. *Change 1975/76 7(10): 14-17.* Discusses the history of Tougaloo College in Jackson, Mississippi, from its founding in 1869 as a school for freed slaves to 1975, emphasizing current problems with financing and with the ROTC program.

1930. Pusey, William Webb, III. LEXINGTON'S FEMALE ACADEMY. *Virginia Cavalcade 1982 32(1): 40-47.* Discusses parental interest in forming a school for the girls of Lexington, Virginia; which resulted in the founding of the Ann Smith Academy in October 1807; traces the academy's history through its demise in 1910.

1931. Putney, Martha S. THE BALTIMORE NORMAL SCHOOL FOR THE EDUCATION OF COLORED TEACHERS: ITS FOUNDERS AND ITS FOUNDING. *Maryland Hist. Mag. 1977 72(2): 238-252.* Shows that, contrary to statements in present and past school catalogues, today's Bowie State College was not the result of a legacy of Nelson Wells of Baltimore, a black man who died in 1843. Some of the Wells Fund, which had supported the Nelson Wells Free School during 1845-69, was used to help establish the Baltimore Normal School in 1871; and one of Wells' trustees, John Needles, was a founding officer of this body. Surveys the history of the Normal School and reports on the first three anniversary meetings of its directors, the Baltimore Association for the Mo-

ral and Educational Improvement of Colored People. Instrumental in the school's existence were the New England Freedmen's Aid Society, the Philadelphia Friends Association, and the Federal Freedmen's Bureau, along with the efforts of such individuals as Joseph M. Cushing and Libertus Van Bokkelen to gain state support for black education. Clarifies certain problems about where the first school building was located and when the first classes convened. Primary sources; 43 notes.

G. J. Bobango

1932. Putney, Martha S. THE BALTIMORE NORMAL SCHOOL CASH BOOK: THE FUNDING AND MANAGEMENT OF A BLACK MISSION SCHOOL, THE PREDECESSOR OF BOWIE STATE COLLEGE. *J. of the Afro-American Hist. and Geneal. Soc. 1981 2(2): 65-74.* Discusses the receipts and expenditures as listed in the Baltimore Normal School Cash Book and maintained by John A. Needles and his successor F. Henry Boggs, from 7 October 1870 to 21 September 1908; the Baltimore Normal School for the Education of Colored Teachers was started in 1866 by the Baltimore Association for the Moral and Educational Improvement of Colored People and was run by the state beginning in 1908; it became Bowie State College.

1933. Putney, Martha S. THE FORMATIVE YEARS OF MARYLAND'S FIRST BLACK POSTSECONDARY SCHOOL. *Maryland Hist. Mag. 1978 73(2): 168-179.* In 1908 the trustees of the Baltimore Normal School for the Education of Colored Teachers donated their establishment and its assets to the state on condition that Maryland maintain a permanent school for the training of black teachers. Discusses the first six formative years of the public existence of the new institution created by the state school board and Superintendent Dr. M. Bates Stephens, the Maryland Normal and Industrial School near Bowie in Prince George's County. Not only did the state strongly revise the curriculum to an industrial and training orientation, but it never provided adequate funding for housing and training the students. Free daily labor was required of students, the administrators had multiple job assignments at less than equitable pay, and absence of funds for any but manual training courses contrasted sharply with Maryland's generous treatment of its white normal school at Towson. Primary and secondary materials; 26 notes.

G. J. Bobango

1934. Requardt, Cynthia Horsburgh. ALTERNATIVE PROFESSIONS FOR GOUCHER COLLEGE GRADUATES, 1892-1910. *Maryland Hist. Mag. 1979 74(3): 274-281.* Seventy-two percent of the women who graduated from Goucher College before 1910 worked at some time, primarily in education and social work. Inspired by the first president, Rev. John F. Goucher, who stressed womanly careers of service, the graduates willingly chose these careers, where they could continue in environments dominated by women and advance to high occupational levels without male competition. College volunteer experience in the Charity Organization Society of Baltimore, the College Settlements Association, and the YWCA, helped determine career choice and ease the transition. Based on Goucher College records, student newspaper files; 36 notes.

C. B. Schulz

1935. Rogers, Lorene et al. IN MEMORIAM: HARRY HUNTT RANSOM. *Texas Q. 1976 19(4): 167.* On 4 May 1976 friends and colleagues remembered Harry Huntt Ransom, Chancellor Emeritus of the Texas university system. Besides praising his work at the University of Texas and noting his efforts in founding the *Texas Quarterly,* the speakers recalled his desire to help people make the most of their talents.

R. Tomlinson

1936. Rogers, Tommy Wayne. OAKLAND COLLEGE, 1830-1871. *J. of Mississippi Hist. 1974 36(2): 143-60.* Traces the history of Oakland College, a small Presbyterian school near Rodney, Mississippi, from its founding in 1830 to its closing in 1871. Established to provide an educated clergy, by 1856 the school had an enrollment of 100 students and in 1860 was the oldest college in the state in continuous operation. Based on various published sources; 91 notes.

J. W. Hillje

1937. Roper, James E. SOUTHWESTERN AT MEMPHIS, 1848-1981. *Tennessee Hist. Q. 1982 41(3): 207-223.* The solid stone architecture of Southwestern at Memphis College belies the liberal arts college's hand-to-mouth struggle for survival and then excellence. America's great wars brought crucial challenges to Southwestern in 1861, 1917, 1941, and the 1960's necessitating several vital changes regarding ties to the Presbyterian Church, higher academic standards, admission of females, relocation to Memphis, an impressive record of construction, new interdisciplinary emphasis, and less rigid curriculum. Based on the *Southwestern News* and other sources; 2 illus., 84 notes.

W. D. Piersen

1938. Roth, Gary G. WAKE FOREST COLLEGE AND THE RISE OF SOUTHEASTERN BAPTIST THEOLOGICAL SEMINARY, 1945-1951. *Baptist Hist. and Heritage 1976 11(2): 69-79.* During 1925-50 Southern Baptist membership had increased 67 percent. For the Southern Baptist Convention, the establishment of a seminary in the southeast would help to meet the increasing demand for trained ministers. For Wake Forest College, the seminary's establishment could serve to meet other, more immediate needs, because the College would be leaving Wake Forest, North Carolina, to go to Winston-Salem. The sale of the college campus to the Southern Baptist Convention for the site of Southeastern Baptist Theological Seminary quieted those critics who objected to moving the college to Winston-Salem. With the seminary utilizing the college's former campus, such usage would be in keeping with the founders' intentions. The availability of the campus was a factor in the establishment of a much-needed seminary. Chronicles the establishment of the seminary at Wake Forest. Based largely on annual reports of the Southern Baptist Convention and the North Carolina Southern Baptist Convention; 31 notes.

H. M. Parker, Jr.

1939. Rowe, Frederick B. and Murray, Frank S. A NOTE ON THE TITCHENER INFLUENCE ON THE FIRST PSYCHOLOGY LABORATORY IN THE SOUTH. *J. of the Hist. of the Behavioral Sci. 1979 15(3): 282-284.* The psychology laboratory at Randolph-Macon Woman's College was the first to be established in the South. The influence of E. B. Titchener on the founder, Celestia S. Parrish, and the other members of the early psychology department at Randolph-Macon Woman's College is briefly presented. 12 notes.

J

1940. Sharp, Madora Hall. JEFFERSON COLLEGE. *Daughters of Am. Revolution Mag. 1975 109(7): 748-750, 789.* Discusses the history of Jefferson College, founded in 1802 near Natchez.

1941. Smith, Gerald J. AUGUSTUS BALDWIN LONGSTREET AND SOUTH CAROLINA COLLEGE. *Methodist Hist. 1979 17(3): 200-202.* Augustus Baldwin Longstreet (1790-1870) was a Georgia lawyer, Methodist minister, horticulturist, author, and president of the University of Mississippi and Emory, Centenary, and South Carolina Colleges. At South Carolina College, where he went in 1858, he was faced with rebuilding a tottering administration and revitalizing the faculty. Because of his erratic behavior, Longstreet gained a reputation among the students of "being 'cracked' mentally." A letter written in 1850 by a student, Robert de Treville Lawrence, is published to illustrate this attitude. 3 notes.

H. L. Calkin

1942. Smith, Kay Riser. LOUISIANA'S TWO CHAUTAUQUAS. *North Louisiana Hist. Assoc. J. 1974 5(4): 138-142.* The Louisiana Chautauqua Society was formed in 1890 in Ruston and was "the first summer school for teachers in the state." In 1906, blacks from Allen Greene (now Grambling), Louisiana, formed a Chautauqua for Negroes, "to improve, gratify and benefit the colored teachers of Louisiana, and advance the colored people in our state." 52 notes.

A. N. Garland

1943. Spurr, Stephen H. "FIRED WITH ENTHUSIASM." *Change 1976 8(4): 42-47.* The University of Texas has had 20 presidents in 80 years and not one of them remained until retirement. The latest refugee from the office tells his story. J

1944. Stephenson, William E. THE DAVISES, THE SOUTHALLS, AND THE FOUNDING OF WESLEYAN FEMALE COLLEGE, 1854-1859. *North Carolina Hist. Rev. 1980 57(3): 257-279.* In March 1855 Methodists of the Murfreesboro, North Carolina area established Wesleyan Female College, thereby answering the region's Baptists, who had founded Chowan Female College in 1848. About 100 young women annually from southern Virginia and northern North Carolina attended the school, studying music and other subjects, learning social skills, making new friends, and maturing both mentally and physically. Behind the scenes personal and political stresses occurred regularly among those in charge of Wesleyan, particularly the families of the school's president (Joseph H. Davis), and the trustees' president (John Wesley Southall). This infighting finally resulted in the Davis's departure in 1859. Based primarily on the Beale and Davis Family Papers at the University of North Carolina; 9 illus., 71 notes.

T. L. Savitt

1945. Sweig, Donald M. "VERT A COLLEDGE... ": A STUDY OF THE COAT-OF-ARMS AND SEALS OF THE COLLEGE OF WILLIAM AND MARY IN VIRGINIA. *Virginia Mag. of Hist. and Biog. 1976 84(2): 142-165.* The College of William and Mary is the only American college granted a coat of arms by the College of Arms in London. William and Mary has used three different coats of arms in its history. The first, dating from the 1690's, was superseded in the years after the Revolution and long forgotten. In the 1920's, when a document bearing the original coat of arms was discovered, the college adopted a third coat of arms, still in use, which, though an attempt to reproduce the original, differs in several respects. Based upon documents in the Swem Library, College of William and Mary, Virginia State Library, and Library of Congress; 4 illus., 61 notes.

R. F. Oaks

1946. Tarter, Brent. THE MAKING OF A UNIVERSITY PRESIDENT: JOHN LLOYD NEWCOMB AND THE UNIVERSITY OF VIRGINIA, 1931-1933. *Virginia Mag. of Hist. and Biog. 1979 87(4): 473-481.* Recounts the process whereby John Lloyd Newcomb, the acting president following the 1931 death of the nationally recognized Edwin A. Aldermann, became president. The University Board of Visitors, highly valuing political and social accomplishment, but low on educational experience, searched in vain for two years, mainly among politicians, attorneys, and financiers, for a successor. Finally pressure for a decision, and endorsement of Newcomb, sometime Dean of the Engineering School and Aldermann's assistant, by faculty, alumni and student groups, with a final boost from the Harry Byrd interests, resolved the board on Newcomb as the best available man for the conservative course desired. Newcomb, who did not promote his candidacy, served competently if not to Aldermann's standard, until his 1947 retirement. 17 notes.

P. J. Woehrmann

1947. Tenery, Saphronia Jane and Torbet, Mary. A NEW LOOK AT SOME OLD SCHOOLS OF CLAIBORNE PARISH. *North Louisiana Hist. Assoc. J. 1979 10(3): 111-119, (4): 148-155.* Part I. THE ACADEMIES. Discusses the origin and growth of the academy movement in Claiborne Parish. Beginning about 1833, the movement caught on quickly. Describes academies at Athens, Summerfield, Arizona, Lisbon, and Eureka. Part II. Discusses additional schools. The Homer Male College, founded in 1885, and the Homer Female Masonic Institute, founded in 1857, merged in 1855 and became the first public school in 1900. 74 notes.

J. F. Paul

1948. TeSelle, Eugene. THE NASHVILLE INSTITUTE AND ROGER WILLIAMS UNIVERSITY: BENEVOLENCE, PATERNALISM, AND BLACK CONSCIOUSNESS, 1867-1910. *Tennessee Hist. Q. 1982 41(4): 360-379.* In 1867, Welsh-born Daniel W. Phillips opened the Nashville Institute (later Roger Williams University) in Nashville, Tennessee, to train black ministers. A series of mysterious fires and a compromise between the school's three constituencies—Southern blacks, benevolent Northern whites, and Nashville whites—led the school to move from its valuable real estate next to Vanderbilt University and to set up north of town under black leadership. Based on materials in the American Baptist Historical Society, Rochester, New York, and other primary sources; illus., table, 84 notes.      W. D. Piersen

1949. Thelin, John R. LOOKING FOR THE LONE STAR LEGACY: HIGHER EDUCATION IN TEXAS. *Hist. of Educ. Q. 1977 17(2): 221-229.* Review article prompted by Mary Thomas's *Southern Methodist University: Founding and Early Years* (Dallas: Southern Methodist U. Pr., 1974) and Jane G. Rushing and Kline A. Nall's *Evolution of a University: Texas Tech's First Fifty Years* (Austin, Texas: Madrona Pr., 1975). Local needs and goals dominated both universities in their early years. They are both Texas-style booster colleges. Sideshow activities such as football games, homecoming ceremonies, ties to the local merchants, and alumni boosterism were often central to the life of the universities, contrary to the high ideals of their faculty. 9 notes.      L. C. Smith

1950. Thomas, James H. and Hurt, Jeffry A. SOUTHWESTERN NORMAL SCHOOL: THE FOUNDING OF AN INSTITUTION. *Chronicles of Oklahoma 1976/77 54(4): 461-467.* Originally established as a teacher training school in Weatherford, Southwestern State Normal School, grew, 1902-39, to become Southwestern State University.

1951. Thoroughman, Thomas V. VALUES AND ISSUES: THE HUMANITIES PROGRAM AT WOFFORD COLLEGE. *Liberal Educ. 1979 65(1): 98-110.* Wofford College, Spartanburg, South Carolina, already established as a liberal arts college, widened its humanities curriculum by adding flexibility, emphasizing communication and advising skills, modifying foreign language requirements, adding reading and writing labs, and originating issues and values seminars as well as cultural and interdisciplinary majors, 1971-79. One of nine articles in this issue on the humanities in transition.

1952. Thrasher, Sue. FIFTY YEARS WITH HIGHLANDER. *Southern Changes 1982 4(6): 4-9.* Highlander Research and Education Center, founded in 1932 in Grundy County, Tennessee, as an Appalachian folk school, became a training center for labor activists in the 1930's and 40's and for civil rights activists in the 1950's-70's, was closed briefly by the state of Tennessee in 1961, and currently focuses its educational efforts on issues relating to Appalachian communities and to minorities in the Deep South.

1953. Uzee, Philip D. A QUARTER'S WORTH OF NICHOLLS. *Louisiana Hist. 1973 14(2): 156-164.* Francis T. Nicholls Junior College, a branch of Louisiana State University and Agricultural and Mechanical College, was established in 1944 at Thibodaux. Nicholls opened four years later with a student body of 161 and a faculty of 15. The institution became Francis T. Nicholls State College in 1956, when it was transferred from the L.S.U. Board of Supervisors to the Louisiana State Board of Education. The name was changed to Nicholls State University in 1970. During its quarter-century of existence Nicholls State grew to a student enrollment of 5,701, a faculty of 220, and a physical plant of 31 buildings. 11 photos.      R. L. Woodward, Jr.

1954. Vaughn, William P., ed. "SOUTH CAROLINA UNIVERSITY—1876" OF FISK PARSONS BREWER. *South Carolina Hist. Mag. 1975 76(4): 225-233.* Arriving at the University of South Carolina to teach the classics in 1873, the year when Negroes first enrolled, Fisk Parsons Brewer assisted in the integration of higher education. In 1876, just prior to the collapse of reconstruction, Brewer wrote an essay extolling the virtues of the university and his preparatory program for blacks and whites. He urged the state to continue integrated education; in addition, he suggested that the college hire teaching assistants (recent college graduates) to assist experienced instructors. Primary sources; 7 notes.      R. H. Tomlinson

1955. Vincent, Charles. LAYING THE CORNERSTONE AT SOUTHERN UNIVERSITY. *Louisiana Hist. 1976 17(3): 335-342.* Southern University in New Orleans was established for Negroes by the Louisiana Constitutional Convention of 1879 and a legislative act of 1880. After beginning classes in the Hebrew Girls' School on Calliope Street, it moved to its own new building at

Soniat and Magazine Streets in 1887. The cornerstone for that building was laid on 8 May 1886 with a ceremony that included both blacks and whites and was conducted in Masonic ritual. Theophile T. Allain gave the principal address, with other speeches by Douglas Burrell, Thomas A. Cage, Henry Demas, and F. L. Richardson. Music was by the Excelsior Brass Band. Based on primary sources; illus., 20 notes.      R. L. Woodward

1956. Ward, Richard Hiram. UNION UNIVERSITY AND ITS PREDECESSORS: HISTORICAL HIGHLIGHTS. *West Tennessee Hist. Soc. Papers 1975 29: 55-63.* Describes the Centennial/Sesquicentennial Celebration of Union University, Jackson, Tennessee, and presents the school's involvement in the history and development of West Tennessee. Beginning as Jackson Male Academy, the school was incorporated 4 February 1826. In 1844 the legislature chartered West Tennessee College in Jackson. In 1848 Union College was established in Murphreesboro. In 1874 the Tennessee Baptist Association accepted an offer to relocate Union in Jackson, and the school was then called Southwestern Baptist University. After meeting certain conditions, the trustees of West Tennessee College conveyed their campus and buildings to the trustees of Southwestern Baptist University. In 1907 the name of the institution was changed to Union University. One of two articles in this issue about Union University. Based on primary sources; 17 photos, 12 notes.      H. M. Parker, Jr.

1957. Wernick, Robert. THINKING BIG AND BETTER, TOO, AT THE UNIVERSITY OF TEXAS. *Smithsonian 1983 14(8): 140-151.* Discusses the fortunes of the University of Texas at Austin, which expanded rapidly after money earned from oil strikes on university lands enabled it to attract the best minds and art and library collections; the university has become a national center for fusion theory, and the home of the Clayton Foundation Biochemical Institute, the Performing Arts Center, and the University of Texas Longhorns.

1958. Wilkins, S. A. CADDO PARISH WANTS A JUNIOR COLLEGE. *North Louisiana Hist. Assoc. J. 1983 14(2-3): 103-110.* Traces efforts of Caddo Parish to establish a junior college as permitted by a Louisiana law passed in 1928. Opposition to the move came from Centenary College in Shreveport and from the Shreveport Real Estate Board, which indicated that it opposed a proposed property tax levy but not the junior college itself. Even Huey Long opposed the effort. The voters of the parish rejected the proposed tax levy in 1937 and it would be 32 years before a branch of Louisiana State University would be established in Shreveport. 30 notes.      J. F. Paul

1959. Wilkins, S. A. DODD COLLEGE: A BRIEF HISTORY. *North Louisiana Hist. Assoc. J. 1980 11(3): 29-34.* Dodd College opened in 1927 in Shreveport, Louisiana, the result of efforts by Dr. Monroe E. Dodd, Sr. Sponsored by the Louisiana Baptist Convention, the college was started to prepare girls for womanhood. Some 2,000 students attended during the college's 15-year history. Based on college sources and newspapers; illus., 26 notes.      J. F. Paul

1960. Wilkins, S. A. DODD COLLEGE, SHREVEPORT, LOUISIANA: NORTHWEST LOUISIANA JUNIOR COLLEGE OF LSU? *North Louisiana Hist. Assoc. J. 1983 14(1): 13-20.* In 1937, citizens of Shreveport sought to create a junior college branch of LSU by having the Parish School Board acquire the private Dodd College. Dodd's trustees decided instead to embark upon a renewal program for the Baptist college. 30 notes.      J. F. Paul

1961. Wodehouse, Lawrence. KOCHER AT BLACK MOUNTAIN. *J. of the Soc. of Architectural Hist. 1982 41(4): 328-332.* A. Lawrence Kocher designed the Studies Building on the campus of Black Mountain College, an innovative educational experiment in western North Carolina. 6 photos, 25 notes.

1962. —. [ST. JOHN'S]. *Change 1974 6(4): 28-36, 62-63.*
Grant, Gerald and Riesman, David. ST. JOHN'S AND THE GREAT BOOKS, *pp. 28-33, 36, 62-63.*

Barr, Stringfellow. A RETROSPECTIVE ON ST. JOHN'S, *pp. 35, 63.*
A small [Maryland] liberal arts college rejects education "despoiled by barbarians" and clings to a nineteenth-century intellectual ideal.                                          J

# Black Education and Educational Segregation

1963. Abney, Everett E. A COMPARISON OF THE STATUS OF FLORIDA'S BLACK PUBLIC SCHOOL PRINCIPALS, 1965-66/1975-76. *J. of Negro Educ. 1980 49(4): 398-406.* School integration in Florida has resulted in a marked decline in the number of black principals since 1964, despite growth in the system during the same period. Secondary sources; table, 3 notes.          R. E. Butchart

1964. Abney, Everett E. THE STATUS OF FLORIDA'S BLACK SCHOOL PRINCIPALS. *J. of Negro Educ. 1974 43(1): 3-8.* A 1964-65 survey in Florida showed that with the consolidation of black and white schools, 40% of the black respondents and 20% of the white respondents were no longer principals. Black principals were generally given lesser posts, whereas the whites were generally promoted to central office positions. Table, 4 notes.
                                                      B. D. Johnson

1965. Adams, David W. PHILANTHROPISTS, PROGRESSIVES, AND SOUTHERN BLACK EDUCATION. *Hist. of Educ. Q. 1983 23(1): 99-111.* Reviews Robert Francis Engs's *Freedom's First Generation: Black Hampton, Virginia, 1861-1890* (1979), *Resurgent Politics and Educational Progressivism in the New South: North Carolina, 1890-1913* (1979) by H. Leon Prather, Sr., and *The Jeanes Story: A Chapter in the History of American Education, 1908-1968* (1979) by Mildred M. Williams et al., which examine the role of Northern missionaries and philanthropists in establishing educational opportunities and policy for poor Southern blacks. 22 notes.                                          J. T. Holton

1966. Anderson, James D. NORTHERN FOUNDATIONS AND THE SHAPING OF SOUTHERN BLACK RURAL EDUCATION, 1902-1935. *Hist. of Educ. Q. 1978 18(4): 371-396.* A study of the initiation and development of northern industrialists' philanthropy in southern, black, rural education revealed programs which emphasized industrial rather than academic curricula and goals, sometimes contrary to the Negroes' interests. The philanthropists "were primarily motivated by practical interests in the relationship of black industrial education to the development of Southern agriculture and national industrial life." They sought a politically stable Southern agricultural economy without any disruption of the Southern racial hierarchy. 41 notes.          R. V. Ritter

1967. Arnez, Nancy L. IMPLEMENTATION OF DESEGREGATION AS A DISCRIMINATORY PROCESS. *J. of Negro Educ. 1978 47(1): 28-45.* Although ostensibly implemented to end educational discrimination, desegregation has in practice been highly discriminatory, resulting in high incidence of discipline against black students, demotions and dismissals for black educators, and ability grouping inimical to blacks. The desegregation efforts in Louisville, Kentucky, are analyzed as a case study. Newspapers, NEA and HEW documents, and other primary and secondary sources; 38 notes.                                          R. E. Butchart

1968. Beezer, Bruce. NORTH CAROLINA'S RATIONALE FOR MANDATING SEPARATE SCHOOLS: A LEGAL HISTORY. *J. of Negro Educ. 1983 52(3): 213-226.* The North Carolina Supreme Court never challenged segregated schools or tried to make them equal before the US Supreme Court's 1954 desegregation decision. Viewing segregation as natural, it carefully kept children with any black ancestry out of white schools; but to support a state constitutional requirement for uniform application of taxes, it also kept school districts from applying property taxes from whites only to white schools and property taxes from blacks to black schools. Based on North Carolina and US Supreme Court decisions; 51 notes.                                          R. G. Sherer

1969. Bellamy, Donnie D. JAMES H. TORBERT: ANOTHER FORGOTTEN BENEFACTOR OF BLACK PEOPLE. *Negro Hist. Bull. 1976 39(3): 549-553.* James H. Torbert (1868-1911) joined the Fort Valley High and Industrial School staff in 1897. By the time of Torbert's accidental death in 1911, the Georgia school had grown from a shanty on four acres to seven modern buildings on 40 acres. Due largely to his efforts, it is now recognized as one of the most important industrial schools for Negroes in the South. 50 notes.                                          W. R. Hively

1970. Bellamy, Donnie D. WHITES SUE FOR DESEGREGATION IN GEORGIA: THE FORT VALLEY STATE COLLEGE CASE. *J. of Negro Hist. 1979 64(4): 316-341.* Hunnicutt et al. v. Burge et al, the legal action initiated in 1972 and aimed at Fort Valley State College in Peach County, Georgia, was grounded in white resentment of the political power held by students at that historically black college. Seeking the dissolution of Fort Valley State College as a segregated institution which discriminated against whites, the lawsuit was an expression of white backlash against the idea of sharing political power with blacks. Based on court records and primary materials; 91 notes.          N. G. Sapper

1971. Bishop, David W. THE CONSENT DECREE BETWEEN THE UNIVERSITY OF NORTH CAROLINA SYSTEM AND THE U.S. DEPARTMENT OF EDUCATION, 1981-1982. *J. of Negro Educ. 1983 52(3): 350-361.* The NAACP Legal Defense Fund sued North Carolina and other states in 1972 and 1977 to force them to desegregate their colleges and universities. To avoid having to meet Judge John H. Pratt's stringent requirements, including taking specific steps to strengthen "traditionally black institutions," North Carolina in 1979 sued the Department of Health, Education and Welfare in a North Carolina District Court. This court accepted a much milder plan devised in secret meetings between North Carolina and the Department of Education. This plan, embodied in a consent decree, will severely damage black higher education in the state. Based on legal memoranda and briefs, court decisions, and interviews; 28 notes.          R. G. Sherer

1972. Braithwaite, Roland. A MINORITY PERCEPTION OF LIBERAL EDUCATION: THE EXAMPLE OF TALLADEGA COLLEGE. *Liberal Educ. 1981 67(3): 219-232.* Even though black liberal arts colleges and their curriculum do not specifically advocate preserving black cultural tradition, these colleges, like Talladega College, Talladega, Alabama, achieve this unwritten goal through their music groups, their preservation of folklore, and, more importantly, the knowledge gained at the college which develops blacks' awareness of their own culture; covers 1875-1980.

1973. Branton, Wiley A. LITTLE ROCK REVISITED: DESEGREGATION TO RESEGREGATION. *J. of Negro Educ. 1983 52(3): 250-269.* Describes legal action over school integration in Little Rock, Arkansas, from the school board's 1955 integration plan, through the 1957 crisis involving Governor Orvil E. Faubus and President Eisenhower, to the successful suit to reopen the city's public schools in 1959. Tragically, school desegregation litigation was still in progress in the city in 1982. Based on court cases and Branton's personal files; 18 notes.          R. G. Sherer

1974. Burns, Augustus M., III. GRADUATE EDUCATION FOR BLACKS IN NORTH CAROLINA, 1930-1951. *J. of Southern Hist. 1980 46(2): 195-218.* From Thomas R. Hocutt's attempt to enter the University of North Carolina's pharmacy school in 1933 until the final legal battle over the Harold Thomas Epps and Floyd B. McKissick suits in 1951, many North Carolina white leaders sought to block black efforts to enter graduate and professional training, both out of conscience and because they found it expedient to have the onus of desegregation passed on to the federal government. Based on the University of North Carolina Archives, private collections, court records, newspapers, and other sources; 73 notes.                                          T. D. Schoonover

1975. Butler, Johnny S. BLACK EDUCATORS IN LOUISIANA—A QUESTION OF SURVIVAL. *J. of Negro Educ. 1974 43(1): 4-24.* Studies the fates of black Louisiana educators since 1964, using legal records of the Louisiana Educational Association, interviews with displaced black educators, and published data. Hiring and firing was in the hands of segregationists, and blacks were displaced. Few black educators are being hired today in Louisiana. 3 tables, 29 notes.                              B. D. Johnson

1976. Carter, Doris Dorcas. ALICE GRUNDY BLALOCK: A PORTRAIT OF LOVE. *North Louisiana Hist. Assoc. J. 1982 13(4): 131-138.* Alice Grundy Blalock was a leader in the struggle to eliminate illiteracy in the black communities of Louisiana. Prior to beginning her long career as a teacher-trainer at Louisiana Normal and Industrial Institute (now Grambling State University) in 1929, she taught successfully in several public schools. She worked hard to make Grambling a reputable institution of higher learning and earned a reputation as a "master teacher." 40 notes.

J. F. Paul

1977. Carter, Doris Dorcas. CHARLES P. ADAMS AND GRAMBLING STATE UNIVERSITY: THE FORMATIVE YEARS (1901-1928). *Louisiana Hist. 1976 17(4): 401-412.* Black settlers in the vicinity of Grambling, Louisiana, organized the North Louisiana Colored Agricultural Relief Association Union in 1896 behind the leadership of Lafayette Richmond. In 1899 that organization decided to establish a coeducational industrial school at Grambling, and in 1901 they asked Booker T. Washington of Tuskegee Institute to send someone to organize the school. Washington sent Charles P. Adams, who organized the school and led it through its difficult early years. Disputes with the Agricultural Relief Organization over the nature of the school and Adams' appeals to whites for assitance led to establishment of a new school in Grambling by Adams in 1905, known as North Louisiana Agricultural and Industrial School. It began to receive Lincoln Parish funds in 1912 and became completely Parish-supported in 1918, when its name was changed to Lincoln Parish Training School. In 1928, through the efforts of Gov. Huey P. Long and State Senator Robert B. Knott, the school became a state school. Based principally on unpublished M.A. thesis by Earl Maxie, "The Development of Grambling College" (Tuskegee Institute, 1950), interviews with Maxie, and unpublished papers at Grambling University; 39 notes.

R. L. Woodward

1978. Clark, Septima Poinsett. CITIZENSHIP AND GOSPEL. *J. of Black Studies 1980 10(4): 461-466.* The Southern Christian Leadership Conference's Citizenship Education Program at Dorchester Center, McIntosh, Georgia, is providing basic literacy, citizenship, and community leadership training for black Americans who failed to receive adequate education in the separate and unequal schools of the South. Anyone from 17 to 70 who can read aloud well and write legibly may teach in the school. By 1964, more than 500 people from nine southern states received this training.                                          R. G. Sherer

1979. Cochran, A. B. and Uhlman, Thomas M. BLACK POPULATIONS AND SCHOOL INTEGRATION—A RESEARCH NOTE. *Phylon 1973 34(1): 43-48.* Based on a study on school integration in North Carolina, 1967-68, discusses school integration and the percentage of Negroes in the area.

1980. Collier-Thomas, Bettye. THE IMPACT OF BLACK WOMEN IN EDUCATION: AN HISTORICAL OVERVIEW. *J. of Negro Educ. 1982 51(3): 173-180.* Since the 1890's black women have been a major force in Southern education despite barriers of racism and sexism which often confined them to low salaries in rural schools. Even in the 20th century, black women hold most teaching positions up to the secondary level and most administrative slots in kindergartens and elementary schools, but few teaching or administrative posts above these levels. There is a need for more studies of black women educators. Based on census reports; table, 6 notes.                                          R. G. Sherer

1981. Cook, James F. THE EUGENE TALMADGE-WALTER COCKING CONTROVERSY. *Phylon 1974 35(2): 181-192.* Reviews the disagreement between Governor Eugene Talmadge of Georgia and Walter Cocking of the University of Georgia. By request of his supervisors, Cocking drafted a report on the higher education of Negroes in Georgia, in which he found the current

system lacking and advocated improvements. Talmadge was incensed; he accused Cocking of advocating the integration of schools. The Governor determined to get rid of Cocking, and finally did so by means of a packed Board of Regents. There followed a general academic purge which seriously damaged the state's intellectual reputation. Covers the period 1937-43. 69 notes.

V. L. Human

1982. Cooper, Algia R. BROWN V. BOARD OF EDUCATION AND VIRGIL DARNELL HAWKINS: TWENTY-EIGHT YEARS AND SIX PETITIONS TO JUSTICE. *J. of Negro Hist. 1979 64(1): 1-20.* Chronicles the battle waged by Virgil Darnell Hawkins, 1949-76, in the Florida courts, to be admitted first to law school at the University of Florida and eventually to the Florida Bar.

1983. Crain, Robert L. and Mahard, Rita E. THE CONSEQUENCES OF CONTROVERSY ACCOMPANYING INSTITUTIONAL CHANGE: THE CASE OF SCHOOL DESEGREGATION. *Am. Sociol. Rev. 1982 47(6): 697-708.* Community conflict early in the desegregation process is associated with lower racial tension and black student alienation a few years later in the South. This is because conflict creates stronger cohesion within the black community and greater support for school desegregation among blacks, which in turn lead to less tension in the schools. Based on a survey of students and teachers in biracial high schools.

J/S

1984. Crosthwait, D. N., Jr. THE FIRST BLACK HIGH SCHOOL IN NASHVILLE. *Negro Hist. Bull. 1974 37(4): 266-268.* Describes the organization of Meigs High School (1886) for Negroes under its first principal, D. N. Crosthwait.

1985. Cunningham, George K. and Husk, William L. WHITE FLIGHT: A CLOSER LOOK AT THE ASSUMPTIONS. *Urban Rev. 1980 12(1): 23-30.* The authors look at a series of studies by Armor, Coleman, Farley and Rossel in relation to the inevitability of white flight in the face of school desegregation. The authors studied school desegregation and its effect on white flight in Jefferson County, Kentucky. They came to the same conclusion as the other studies: that "the decision made by these parents to send their children to non-public schools was clearly related to the implementation of the desegregation plan."      R. J. Wechman

1986. Dews, Margery P. F. H. HENDERSON AND HOWARD NORMAL SCHOOL. *Georgia Hist. Q. 1979 63(2): 252-263.* For 62 years Fletcher Hamilton Henderson (1857-1943) was a teacher and principal at Howard Normal School, later known as Randolph County Training School, a very successful black high school in Cuthbert, Georgia. Primary and secondary sources; 31 notes.

G. R. Schroeder

1987. Dinnerstein, Leonard. SOUTHERN JEWRY AND THE DESEGREGATION CRISIS, 1954-1970. *Am. Jewish Hist. Q. 1973 62(3): 231-241.* Despite the participation of many Jews in the civil rights movement, the level of commitment varied widely. Southern Jews, many of them merchants dependent upon the goodwill of their neighbors, were circumspect in their allegiance to equal rights, except in a few areas like Atlanta and among some college groups. In the early 1960's, perhaps six to 10 rabbis in the South worked for the cause, including Jacob Rothschild, Emmet Frank, Perry Nussbaum, and Charles Mantninband. Based on correspondence of southern rabbis at the American Jewish Archives; 32 notes.

F. Rosenthal

1988. Dixon, Blase. THE CATHOLIC UNIVERSITY OF AMERICA AND THE RACIAL QUESTION, 1914-1918. *Records of the Am. Catholic Hist. Soc. of Philadelphia 1973 84(4): 221-224.* The refusal to matriculate Charles H. Wesley in 1914 was the first known instance of racial discrimination at the Catholic University of America. Exclusion of Negroes became a policy in 1919 and the bar was not completely lifted until 1948. 10 notes.

J. M. McCarthy

1989. Dozier, Richard K. FROM HUMBLE BEGINNINGS TO NATIONAL SHRINE: TUSKEGEE INSTITUTE. *Hist. Preservation 1981 33(1): 40-45.* Brief history of Tuskegee Institute, built in 1881 in Macon County, Alabama; focuses on recent interest in preserving it by architects, builders, and preservationists in the black community, especially since it was designated a National Historic Landmark District in 1965.

1990. Egerton, John. A GENTLEMEN'S FIGHT. *Am. Heritage 1979 30(5): 56-65.* The struggle for school integration in Prince Edward County, Virginia, began in earnest in 1951. The 1954 decision of the Supreme Court led to massive resistance throughout the South. In 1959, officials in Prince Edward County closed their schools. Segregation continues, despite a 1964 court order to the contrary. Yet, as earlier, the county has escaped the violence that occurred elsewhere. 7 illus.                                J. F. Paul

1991. Elusche, Michael. ANTISLAVERY AND SPIRITUALISM: MYRTILLA MINER AND HER SCHOOL. *New-York Hist. Soc. Q. 1975 59(2): 149-172.* Founded in 1851, the Miner School for Negro Girls in Washington D.C., offered one of the few opportunities in the nation to young black girls seeking an education. Miss Miner, a sickly, intense, pious native of upstate New York, was able to establish and continue the school despite limited resources and much opposition. For a decade the school limped along until she left suddenly in 1861 for California where she became absorbed in spiritualism. Three years later she died, still hoping for the millennium. The school she founded eventually (1955) became part of the District of Columbia Teachers College, while her name is preserved on a District of Columbia elementary school. Primary and secondary sources; 4 illus., 45 notes.            C. L. Grant

1992. Falk, William W. and Cosby, Arthur G. SCHOOL DESEGREGATION AND THE EDUCATIONAL PROJECTIONS OF RURAL, BLACK YOUTH. *Rural Sociol. 1974 39(1): 28-41.* Investigates the effects of school desegregation on the attitudes of young Negroes in rural Texas; based on interviews 1966-72.

1993. Fleming, Cynthia Griggs. THE PLIGHT OF BLACK EDUCATORS IN POST-WAR TENNESSEE, 1865-1920. *J. of Negro Hist. 1979 64(4): 355-364.* Tennessee's black teachers were forced to maintain a balance among the dictates of the whites who controlled public funds, the welfare of their black students, and the integrity of their profession. The pursuit of a line of least resistance expended an inordinate amount of the skills and energies of the black teachers of Tennessee. Based on public records in Tennessee; 37 notes.                                N. G. Sapper

1994. Fleming, Cynthia Griggs. A SURVEY OF THE BEGINNINGS OF TENNESSEE'S BLACK COLLEGES AND UNIVERSITIES. *Tennessee Hist. Q. 1980 39(2): 195-207.* A broad survey of the founding of schools for black Tennesseans from immediately after the Civil War to 1920. While religious denominations were eager to establish schools for the freedmen, few of the latter understood what was involved in obtaining a college education. Lack of funding hounded both students and institutions. It was not until 1912 that Tennessee established a normal school for its black residents. During 1876-1909, only 525 students had graduated from the church-related black colleges and universities. Moral development as well as intellectual was stressed in the church schools, yet most white missionaries did not feel that black graduates could hold responsible positions within the general society. Yet, with all their shortcomings, the denominational institutions provided the only local opportunities for the state's blacks to receive any college or professional training between 1865 and 1920. Secondary sources; 45 notes.                                H. M. Parker, Jr.

1995. Frazier, Kitty and Simmons, Diana. FANNIE COBB CARTER (1872-1973). *J. of the West Virginia Hist. Assoc. 1983 6(1): 1-10.* Summarizes the career of black educator Fannie Cobb Carter and the education of black youth in West Virginia.

1996. Freeman, Richard B. POLITICAL POWER, DESEGREGATION, AND EMPLOYMENT OF BLACK SCHOOL TEACHERS. *J. of Pol. Econ. 1977 85(2): 299-322.* Examines the impact of de jure desegregation on education in the South and of increased black voting power on the demand for black schoolteachers in the United States. Because changes in the black share of voters in the post-World War II South are due largely to "exogenous" national laws (the Voting Rights Act of 1965, in particular), the paper provides a unique test of the impact of changes in political power on public decisionmaking. The main finding is that increased black voting power appears to have raised demand for black schoolteachers in the 1960's. There is additional suggestive evidence that black voting power operated in part through election of black officials. The increase in demand due to the changes in voting offset most of the reduction in demand due to desegregation of schooling in the South, averting the potential dire effects of desegregated education on employment of black teachers. Instead of declining, relative employment of blacks in teaching was maintained, and relative incomes rose in the 1950's and 1960's. These results are consistent with the broad "governmental discrimination" hypothesis that much of the economic progress or retrogression of blacks in the United States is explicable in terms of black political power and resultant governmental activity.                                J

1997. Gardner, Bettye. ANTE-BELLUM BLACK EDUCATION IN BALTIMORE. *Maryland Hist. Mag. 1976 71(3): 360-366.* "On the eve of the Civil War Baltimore had the largest free black community in the nation." About 15 schools for blacks were operating. From Sabbath schools operated by Methodists, Presbyterians, and Quakers, black education expanded through the efforts of the African Methodist Episcopal Church under Daniel Coker, and the Oblates' Academy "for young girls of color." William Watkins' Academy was perhaps the most prestigious private school for blacks, while the school run by William Lively offered a comprehensive curriculum and "showed the seriousness with which... blacks pursued the education of the whole person." All black schools were self-sustaining, receiving no state or local government funds, and whites in Baltimore generally opposed educating the black population, continuing to tax black property holders to maintain schools from which black children were excluded by law. Baltimore's black community, nevertheless, was one of the largest and most cohesive in America due to this experience. From Baltimore City Records, and secondary materials; 25 notes.

G. J. Bobango

1998. Gardner, Booker T. THE EDUCATIONAL CONTRIBUTIONS OF BOOKER T. WASHINGTON. *J. of Negro Educ. 1975 44(4): 502-518.* Reviews the educational theories (1881-1915) of Booker T. Washington, who stressed practical skills for economic survival, giving rise to the charge that his principles kept blacks in menial positions.

1999. Giles, Michael W. RACIAL STABILITY AND URBAN SCHOOL DESEGREGATION. *Urban Affairs Q. 1976 12(4): 499-510.* Studies Florida's Jacksonville area to test the assumption that school desegregation produces white withdrawal and resegregation. Desegregation was ordered in 1963 and began in 1972, when a court ordered plan was implemented. Initial white withdrawal was evident in previously all black public schools, but was not apparent when blacks were integrated into previously all white schools. An increased but stable percentage of students are sent to private schools. Expansion of the ghetto explains why some schools have shown a five percent or more increase in black students since 1972. Desegregation can be attained without substantial resegregation. Primary and secondary sources; 2 tables, 7 notes, biblio.

L. N. Beecher

2000. Giles, Micheal W. BLACK CONCENTRATION AND SCHOOL DISTRICT SIZE AS PREDICTORS OF SCHOOL SEGREGATION: THE IMPACT OF FEDERAL ENFORCEMENT. *Sociol. of Educ. 1975 48(4): 411-419.* In the years up to 1968 little progress was made toward implementing school desegregation. Numerous studies during this period attempted to link socioeconomic variables to school segregation. In these studies, black concentration consistently emerged as an important determinant of school segregation. The results of the present study indicate that federal enforcement of desegregation between 1968 and 1970 produced a dramatic decline in the level of school segregation in the South and virtually eliminated the well established relationship between the concentration of black people and school segregation in that region.

J

2001.   Gillette, Michael L. BLACKS CHALLENGE THE WHITE UNIVERSITY. *Southwestern Hist. Q. 1982 86(2): 321-344.* The University of Texas inadvertently admitted its first black student in October 1938. Although the student was soon forced to withdraw, the incident served as the first challenge to segregated higher education in Texas. Subsequently during the 1940's, the NAACP sought to desegregate the university's law, medical and graduate schools. The university was found unable to provide separate but equal facilities, and in 1950 was ordered by the US Supreme Court to admit students who could not find training at the black colleges in the state. Desegregation proceeded slowly, and blacks were not admitted to undergraduate study until 1956. Segregated dormitories existed until the 1960's. Based on university records at the Eugene C. Barker Texas History Center in Austin and NAACP records in Houston; 2 photos, 52 notes.        R. D. Hurt

2002.   Gilpin, Patrick J. CHARLES S. JOHNSON AND THE SOUTHERN EDUCATIONAL REPORTING SERVICE. *J. of Negro Hist. 1978 63(3): 197-208.* Though it sought to report on the developments in southern education stemming from the Supreme Court decision outlawing segregation in public schools, the Southern Educational Reporting Service was established and virtually completely staffed by whites, including its founder, Charles S. Johnson, 1954-60's.

2003.   Gilpin, Patrick J. CHARLES S. JOHNSON AND THE RACE RELATIONS INSTITUTES AT FISK UNIVERSITY. *Phylon 1980 41(3): 300-311.* The annual Race Relations Institutes at Fisk University in Nashville, Tennessee, were the first truly interracial meetings held in the South during the age of Jim Crow. These meetings on race relations made significant contributions to the struggle for racial justice. Covers 1942-56. Based on the Charles S. Johnson Papers at Fisk University; 40 notes.

N. G. Sapper

2004.   Goodenow, Ronald K. PARADOX IN PROGRESSIVE EDUCATIONAL REFORM: THE SOUTH AND THE EDUCATION OF BLACKS IN THE DEPRESSION YEARS. *Phylon 1978 39(1): 49-65.* Progressive educational reforms in the South seemingly functioned to serve modernization, but paradoxically maintained racist patterns which were contradictory to progressive ideology. White educators emphasized occupational training for blacks at the expense of academic preparation and also advocated a biracial, segregated South. Black criticism of progressive education has called for testing the democratic ideology against the real conditions of oppression. Primary and secondary sources; 74 notes.        J. Moore

2005.   Guy-Sheftall, Beverly. BLACK WOMEN AND HIGHER EDUCATION: SPELMAN AND BENNETT COLLEGES REVISITED. *J. of Negro Educ. 1982 51(3): 278-287.* Provides a list of black women's colleges focusing on Bennett College in Greensboro, North Carolina, and Spelman College in Atlanta, Georgia. Discusses outstanding Spelman and Bennett alumnae, black women administrators at the colleges, the need for continuing such schools, and presents a five-page selected bibliography on black women and higher education. Secondary sources; 9 notes.        R. G. Sherer

2006.   Hall, Leon. THE IMPLEMENTORS' REVENGE. *Southern Exposure 1979 7(2): 122-125.* Southern public schools have been physically desegregated, but more subtle methods—intelligence testing, tracking, ability grouping, and segregated academies—deprive blacks of equal opportunity.

2007.   Harley, Sharon. BEYOND THE CLASSROOM: ORGANIZATIONAL LIVES OF BLACK FEMALE EDUCATORS IN THE DISTRICT OF COLUMBIA, 1890-1930. *J. of Negro Educ. 1982 51(3): 254-265.* The sense of a special responsibility which only they could fulfill pulled black women teachers into the women's club movement during 1890-1930. Black club women, deriving their status more from "moral and cultural stature" than from their edu-

cation, refused to bring working-class women into the elite clubs or to associate with them socially. The clubs also sought to demonstrate their members' culture and refinement to whites. As women got the vote and municipal agencies began charity work by 1920, black women's organizations became more political and open to all classes. Based on census and other governmental agencies' reports, periodicals, archives, and black organizations' published reports and directories; 29 notes.        R. G. Sherer

2008.   Higgins, Renelda. TUSKEGEE: 100 YEARS LATER. *Crisis 1981 88(6): 268-273.* Tuskegee Institute celebrated Founder's Day on 4 July 1981, marking 100 years of existence. Booker T. Washington believed that home economics and agriculture could solve the problems of rural blacks. Today, 3,600 students study not only trades and industrial education but also the arts and sciences. The second century for Tuskegee begins with the installation of the school's 4th president, Dr. Benjamin Payton.        A. G. Belles

2009.   Hine, Darlene Clark. FROM HOSPITAL TO COLLEGE: BLACK NURSE LEADERS AND THE RISE OF COLLEGIATE NURSING SCHOOLS. *J. of Negro Educ. 1982 51(3): 222-237.* Segregation and the shift from hospital to collegiate nursing education by the 1940's threatened to exclude black nurses from high level and administrative positions. To meet this challenge, the General Education Board helped several outstanding black women start programs for nursing education at black colleges. Rita E. Miller at Dillard University in New Orleans, Louisiana, (1942) and Mary Elizabeth Lancaster Carnegie at Florida A. & M. College in Tallahassee (1945) were two such women. Miller had to develop a program new to black colleges, but Carnegie also had to fight entrenched opposition at her school. Based on General Education Board Archives; 39 notes.        R. G. Sherer

2010.   Hines, Linda O. GEORGE W. CARVER AND THE TUSKEGEE AGRICULTURAL EXPERIMENT STATION. *Agric. Hist. 1979 53(1): 71-83.* Booker T. Washington's securing of George Washington Carver for his agricultural work at Tuskegee Institute was of major importance. Carver's goal was to improve the quality of life among black farmers, thus making them self-sufficient and economically independent. His dream was never realized, largely because the whole movement of agriculture through the efforts of the USDA was toward larger agribusiness units. Yet it was the combination of Washington's ambition and consummate skill in political barbaining and Carver's advanced agricultural training applied to the staples of scientific agriculture which placed Tuskegee Institute in the mainstream, and sometimes the forefront, of early agricultural research and education. 33 notes. Comment by Irvin May, pp. 102-104.        R. V. Ritter

2011.   Hobson, Julius, Jr. EDUCATIONAL POLICY AND THE COURTS: THE CASE OF WASHINGTON, D.C. *Urban Rev. 1978 10(1): 5-19.* Agencies conducting Washington, D.C.'s public schools, 1804-1974, failed to provide equal education for black students despite studies which provided information on discrimination. Since 1910, D.C. residents have sought judicial relief from the "malpractice and negligence" of school officials. Although the courts have corrected many educational abuses, Washington furnishes a case study of the courts' inability to formulate and execute nondiscriminatory educational policy throughout the United States. Equal education depends upon educational agencies' fulfillment of their responsibilities. Based on published government documents and secondary studies; biblio.        R. G. Sherer

2012.   Hoffius, Steve. I EXPECT I'LL GET A PLAQUE. *Southern Exposure 1979 7(2): 74-76.* Septima Clark began her teaching career in South Carolina in 1916, but lost her position in 1956 because of her known membership in the National Association for the Advancement of Colored People (NAACP); after that, she became a teacher in Citizenship schools (preparing blacks to register to vote) and an active member of the Southern Christian Leadership Conference.

2013.   Hornsbey, Alton, Jr. THE "COLORED BRANCH UNIVERSITY" ISSUE IN TEXAS—PRELUDE TO SWEATT VS. PAINTER. *J. of Negro Hist. 1976 6(1): 51-60.* Texas long evaded the charge of its constitution to establish a separate but equal "university of the first class" for black Texans. After nearly three-quarters of a century (1876-1947), the state managed to establish a "branch university for colored youth" in only a few months when the black people of Texas began to seek redress in the federal courts. Despite the attempts to evade an idea whose time had come, the University of Texas was ultimately integrated as a result of the campaign. Based on primary and secondary sources; 42 notes.                                                         N. G. Sapper

2014. Howard, Victor B. THE STRUGGLE FOR EQUAL EDUCATION IN KENTUCKY, 1866-1884. *J. of Negro Educ. 1977 46(3): 305-328.* Documents the efforts of blacks and whites in Kentucky to secure education for black children. State funding for black schools was eventually brought into parity with white schools, but legal precedents were established to assure segregation. Primary (including archival) and secondary sources; 94 notes.
R. E. Butchart

2015. Hubbell, John T. SOME REACTIONS TO THE DESEGREGATION OF THE UNIVERSITY OF OKLAHOMA, 1946-1950. *Phylon 1973 34(2): 187-196.*

2016. Hunter, Tera. THE CORRECT THING: CHARLOTTE HAWKINS BROWN AND THE PALMER INSTITUTE. *Southern Exposure 1983 11(5): 37-43.* After only one year of college training, Charlotte Hawkins Brown founded the Alice Freeman Palmer Memorial Institute in Sedalia, North Carolina, in 1902 and raised this young black women's school to national prominence despite the social barriers that faced all black women.

2017. Ivey, Saundra Keyes. FINANCIAL PRESSURES AND DESEGREGATION SUIT ARE TENNESSEE CONCERNS. *Change 1981 13(8): 46-48.* Details the financial concerns facing Tennessee's public colleges and universities during 1981-82, and the possibility of new desegregation hearings since the filing of a segregation lawsuit in 1968.

2018. Jackameit, William P. A SHORT HISTORY OF NEGRO PUBLIC HIGHER EDUCATION IN WEST VIRGINIA, 1890-1965. *West Virginia Hist. 1976 37(4): 309-325.* West Virginia created two Negro colleges in the 1890's (now West Virginia State College and Bluefield State College). Only 5 percent of the state's population was black, but the Negro colleges received more than 10 percent of public higher education funds, and by the 1950's West Virginia State College had a national reputation in Negro education. However, rapid desegregation after 1954 brought a flood of local white students to both schools, and by 1960 they served chiefly their home counties as commuter schools. Based on primary and secondary sources; 2 tables, 51 notes.          J. H. Broussard

2019. Jackson, John S., III. ALIENATION AND BLACK POLITICAL PARTICIPATION. *J. of Pol. 1973 35(4): 849-885.* Examines the "dimensions of alienation" among black college students in Tennessee and Arkansas during 1968-69. From general concepts of alienation three dependent variables were derived: political efficacy, political cynicism, and personal anomie. The author's "informed speculation" is that while many young blacks are highly cynical they also possess high morale and a strong sense of political efficacy. The cynicism of these blacks led them to expect little in the way of response from government; therefore they did not have the explosive tendencies exhibited elsewhere. Southern blacks seemed to be "caught in their own cultural lag." The crucial factor for the future will be the political system's responsiveness; this remains a subject of lasting contention in the South. 10 tables, 86 notes, appendix.                                                          A. R. Stoesen

2020. Jenkins, Robert L. THE DEVELOPMENT OF BLACK HIGHER EDUCATION IN MISSISSIPPI (1865-1920). *J. of Mississippi Hist. 1983 45(4): 272-286.* Sketches the history of black colleges in Mississippi as they developed from Reconstruction into the 20th century. Black religious denominations were important in establishing Rust College, Tougaloo College, Jackson State University, and Mississippi Industrial College. Describes the growth of Alcorn State University, which until 1940 was the only black school

operating as a fully public-supported institution. Black institutions were essentially places to receive vocational training or the basic rudiments, and these limited functions retarded black Mississippi colleges in their slow evolution toward a true collegiate basis. Still, the institutions played a vital educational role as they fulfilled an insatiable desire for learning among Mississippi blacks and molded many of the state's black leaders. Based on government documents, college catalogs, and secondary materials; 36 notes.
M. S. Legan

2021. Jones, Allen W. THE ROLE OF TUSKEGEE INSTITUTE IN THE EDUCATION OF BLACK FARMERS. *J. of Negro Hist. 1975 60(2): 252-267.* Discusses the role of Booker T. Washington as a leader of the rural life activities of black people. Washington and the agriculture faculty of Tuskegee Institute educated and influenced black farmers with the Annual Negro Conferences, the Tuskegee Experiment Station, the Agricultural Short Course, the Farmers' Institutes, the Farmers' County Fairs, the Movable School, and the numerous newspapers and other publications. Based on primary materials in both the Library of Congress and the Tuskegee Institute Archives; 48 notes.          N. G. Sapper

2022. Jones, H. Lawrence. PHILLIP REED: PROMINENT BLACK EDUCATOR OF WHEELING. *Upper Ohio Valley Hist. Rev. 1983 13(1): 4-9.* Traces the career of black educator Phillip Nathanial Reed and briefly outlines education for blacks in Wheeling, West Virginia, emphasizing the role of Lincoln School.

2023. Kelley, Don Quinn. IDEOLOGY AND EDUCATION: UPLIFTING THE MASSES IN NINETEENTH CENTURY ALABAMA. *Phylon 1979 40(2): 147-158.* Discusses education for blacks in Alabama, 1870's-90's, detailing black frustrations, disappointments, and the success of industrial training schools run by blacks for blacks, such as Booker T. Washington's Tuskegee Institute. 41 notes.                                                         G. R. Schroeder

2024. Kennedy, Thomas C. SOUTHLAND COLLEGE: THE SOCIETY OF FRIENDS AND BLACK EDUCATION IN ARKANSAS. *Arkansas Hist. Q. 1983 42(3): 207-238.* Chronicles the history of Southland College, a project of the Indiana Yearly Meeting of the Society of Friends for the education of blacks, located near Helena, Arkansas. Based on periodicals, Indiana Yearly Meeting records, and interviews; 4 photos, 109 notes, 4 appendixes.
G. R. Schroeder

2025. Keubler, Edward J. THE DESEGREGATION OF THE UNIVERSITY OF MARYLAND. *Maryland Hist. Mag. 1976 71(1): 37-49.* A study of the case of Donald G. Murray, the first black since the passage of the "separate but equal" doctrine to enter a southern university. After the exchange of a typical pattern of form letters with the admissions officials of the University of Maryland, Murray was denied entrance to the School of Law and referred to the all-Negro Morgan College and a virtually nonexistent black scholarship fund. The NAACP, with Thurgood Marshall coordinating the case, challenged the university in the Maryland courts in June 1935, and a writ of mandamus ordered Murray's admission. In the following year this writ was upheld in the Court of Appeals. Murray himself was watched carefully by the NAACP, tutored in his studies, and guided in legal procedures by Marshall and Charles H. Houston of Howard University. Winning acceptance by his classmates and graduating in 1938, Murray passed his bar exam and devoted himself to a simple life of public service in Baltimore, not seeking notoriety. His case, however, set the precedent for the NAACP to continue its fight against unequal education for blacks, even though full desegregation was a long time away. Primary sources; 82 notes.                                    G. J. Bobango

2026. Kluger, Richard. THE QUEST FOR SIMPLE JUSTICE. *Southern Exposure 1979 7(2): 6-17.* In 1948, blacks in Clarendon County, South Carolina, with the aid of the National Association for the Advancement of Colored People (NAACP), sued the county public schools for racist and unequal treatment of black children; this and four similar suits were heard before the Supreme Court in *Brown* v. *Board of Education* (US, 1954).

2027. Kousser, J. Morgan. PROGRESSIVISM—FOR MIDDLE CLASS WHITES ONLY: NORTH CAROLINA EDUCATION, 1880-1910. *J. of Southern Hist. 1980 46(2): 169-194.* Quantitative analysis of tax, income, property value and education expenditure data bears out C. Vann Woodward's picture of a dramatic increase in racial discrimination around the turn of the century. As a result of disenfranchisement, progressive-era North Carolina produced education only for middle-class whites. 12 tables, fig., 36 notes, appendix.                                    T. D. Schoonover

2028. Kunstel, Marcia. BREAKING THE CONSPIRACY OF SILENCE. *Southern Exposure 1979 7(2): 77-83.* Working through a small group known as Mississippians for Public Education, dedicated white women spoke at community and club meetings to encourage the integration of southern public schools, 1960's.

2029. Leffall, Doris C. and Sims, Janet L. MARY MC LEOD BETHUNE—THE EDUCATOR; ALSO INCLUDING A SELECTED ANNOTATED BIBLIOGRAPHY. *J. of Negro Educ. 1976 45(3): 342-359.* Presents a brief biography of Mary McLeod Bethune, the daughter of former slaves and founder of the school in Daytona Beach, Florida which became Bethune-Cookman College. Includes a 15 page annotated bibliography of related materials. 2 notes.                                    B. D. Johnson

2030. Lewis, Ronald L., ed. REVEREND T. G. STEWART AND "MIXED" SCHOOLS IN DELAWARE, 1882. *Delaware Hist. 1980 19(1): 53-58.* Publishes an account of a speech delivered in Wilmington in 1882 by Theophilous G. Stewart, pastor of Bethel African Methodist Episcopal Church in Wilmington. In the speech Stewart attacked the early efforts to impose segregation in post-Civil War Delaware and demanded access to public schools for blacks, who were taxpayers and citizens of the community and the nation. 9 notes.                                    R. M. Miller

2031. Lewis, Ronald L. REVEREND T. G. STEWART AND THE EDUCATION OF BLACKS IN RECONSTRUCTION DELAWARE. *Delaware Hist. 1981 19(3): 156-178.* Describes the career of Theophilus Gould Steward, a minister in the African Methodist Episcopal Church, who became a forceful advocate of educational rights and integration for blacks. In Delaware, Steward's integrationist approach caused rifts in the Republican Party and among blacks and failed to impress public policy. Segregation triumphed in education, as elsewhere, although Steward's insistence on state support for black education contributed to Delaware providing public support to blacks for the first time. The author also follows Steward's public career in Gouldtown, New Jersey; Phildelphia, Pennsylvania; Haiti; and Brooklyn, New York. Based on Steward's writings, newspapers, and manuscripts; 43 notes.

R. M. Miller

2032. Lightfoot, Sara Lawrence. PORTRAITS OF EXEMPLARY SECONDARY SCHOOLS: GEORGE WASHINGTON CARVER COMPREHENSIVE HIGH SCHOOL. *Daedalus 1981 110(4): 17-37.* Discusses the progress of George Washington Carver Comprehensive High School, a primarily black school in Atlanta, Georgia, from the late 1970's, when the school was nearly closed because of violence, poverty, and the other blights of the inner city, to 1981, when Carver High School proved to be an example of how urban schools can be revitalized; concentrates on Carver's community outreach and vocational programs and on the role of Norris Hogans, the principal, and of Alonzo Crim, the superintendent of the Atlanta public schools in the rebirth of Carver.

2033. Long, Larry H. and Hansen, Kristin A. SELECTIVITY OF BLACK RETURN MIGRATION TO THE SOUTH. *Rural Sociol. 1977 42(3): 317-331.* The probability of black moving from the South has been directly related to years of school completed. Of those who leave, the most highly educated are the most likely to return. This and other evidence fails to support the hypothesis that return of the least capable migrants accounts for why southern-born blacks in the North earn more than northern-born blacks. Other implications are explored. The rate of black migration from the South appears to be declining at almost every educational level, and return migration seems to be rising at almost every educational

level. The degree of selectivity of black outmigration and return migration did not appreciably change between the 1950's and the 1960's.                                    J

2034. Lord, J. Dennis and Catau, John C. THE SCHOOL DESEGREGATION-RESEGREGATION SCENARIO: CHARLOTTE-MECKLENBURG'S EXPERIENCE. *Urban Affairs Q. 1981 16(3): 369-376.* Based on enrollment data since 1969, determines the degree of resegregation (schools again becoming racially imbalanced after initial desegregation). The data reveals that, after desegregation in 1970, the system experienced resegregation as early as 1973, and that the district since then has undergone an integration-resegregation cycle on three year intervals. The data suggests resegregation is a product of residential changes, not private school flight. Desegregation is a continuing struggle, not a onetime event. Table, biblio.                                    L. N. Beecher

2035. Lowry, Mark, II. SCHOOLS IN TRANSITION. *Ann. of the Assoc. of Am. Geographers 1973 63(2): 167-180.* The geography of schools in Mississippi has undergone four phases of change during the past three decades, and there are indications that a fifth phase is in the offing. Through all phases, racial segregation in schools and patterns of resistance to change have been influenced significantly by residential segregation at the local level and by the racial composition of the population at broader scales. The impending fifth phase, which is likely to be a return to some form of dual school system, has been prompted by a movement of white people to private schools and other bold reactions. Such reactions resulted from Federal Government orders to desegregate schools contrary to residential segregation, a most fundamental facet of the spatial structure of the society.                                    J

2036. Margo, Robert A. RACE DIFFERENCES IN PUBLIC SCHOOL EXPENDITURES: DISFRANCHISEMENT AND SCHOOL FINANCE IN LOUISIANA, 1890-1910. *Social Sci. Hist. 1982 6(1): 9-34.* Between 1890 and 1910 public education in the South improved dramatically in terms of expenditure per student, length of term, and enrollment rates. This improvement affected mostly white students; the gap between black and white students widened substantially. An econometric model of school board behavior suggests that disfranchisement of black voters was a major factor in growing inequalities in school finance in Louisiana during this period. Disfranchisement facilitated shifting state subsidies for all children to white students and the lowering of local school support taxes. Based primarily on the Biennial Reports of the State Superintendent of Public Education (Louisiana); 5 tables, 14 notes, biblio.                                    L. K. Blaser

2037. Martin, Sandy Dwayne. THE AMERICAN BAPTIST HOME MISSION SOCIETY AND BLACK HIGHER EDUCATION IN THE SOUTH, 1865-1920. *Foundations 1981 24(4): 310-327.* Discusses and evaluates the role and philosophy of the American Baptist Home Mission Society toward the higher education of former slaves. Mentions Virginia Union University in Richmond and Spelman College in Atlanta, Georgia. Black contributions are stressed. Based on annual minutes of the American Baptist Home Mission Society; 42 notes.                                    E. E. Eminhizer

2038. McGinty, Doris E. GIFTED MINDS AND PURE HEARTS: MARY L. EUROPE AND ESTELLE PINCKNEY WEBSTER. *J. of Negro Educ. 1982 51(3): 266-277.* Biographical sketches of two black music teachers in Washington, D.C., Mary Lorraine Europe (1882-1947) and Estelle Etelka Pinckney Webster (ca. 1895-1966). Europe was music teacher and accompanist for music teachers in the black divisions of Washington's public schools, 1903-16, and music teacher at M Street (later Dunbar) High School, 1916-44. After teaching briefly in several schools, Webster conducted a private studio and sang professionally, 1921-25, before becoming a music teacher at Armstrong Manual Training High School, 1926-58. Based on interviews, newspapers, and private papers; 23 notes.                                    R. G. Sherer

2039. McMillan, George. BEAUFORT ACADEMY—"NONE EVER APPLIED." *Southern Changes 1982 4(6): 3-4.* A bond issue for support of public schools in Beaufort, South Carolina, was opposed unsuccessfully during 1974-80 by a citizens' group, some of whose members may have been supporters of Beaufort Academy, a local private school that since its founding in 1966 has never had a black student.

2040. Messner, William F. BLACK EDUCATION IN LOUISIANA, 1863-1865. *Civil War Hist. 1976 22(1): 41-59.* Explains why the Union Army played a more central role in the education of freedmen in Louisiana than elsewhere in the South. General Nathaniel Prentiss Banks, Commander of the Department of the Gulf, was concerned primarily with establishing firm control over the freedmen and sought to do this through a closely supervised free labor system. He quickly learned, however, that the blacks desired an education above all else. Banks modified his policy and, in 1863, created a school system that was carefully monitored by the army. Economic reconstruction and political reliability both were to be served. Although the project was troubled by white opposition and inadequate financing, it worked well and proved fundamental to whatever improvement in status Louisiana blacks enjoyed in the postwar years.                                        E. C. Murdock

2041. Middleton, Ernest J. THE LOUISIANA EDUCATION ASSOCIATION, 1901-1970. *J. of Negro Educ. 1978 47(4): 363-378.* The Louisiana Colored Teachers Association, predecessor to the all-black Louisiana Education Association (LEA), was formed by concerned black educators such as J. B. LaFarque in 1901. It consistently fought for equality in Louisiana education, first within the framework of segregation, and then in the difficult years of white resistance to the national demand for integration. In 1969, the National Education Association disaffiliated the all-white Louisiana Teachers Association for refusal to integrate, and the LEA became the sole recognized teacher association in the state. Primary sources, including interviews, Association convention minutes, and manuscript material; 52 notes.                             R. E. Butchart

2042. Miracle, Andrew W., Jr. FACTORS AFFECTING INTERRACIAL COOPERATION: A CASE STUDY OF A HIGH SCHOOL FOOTBALL TEAM. *Human Organization 1981 40(2): 150-154.* Data gathered during 1972-76 at a southern high school show that interaction increased among black and white members of the football team when directly involved with the game, while more traditional patterns of segregation reemerged off the field.

2043. Molnar, Joseph J.; Dunkelberger, John E.; and Salter, Dannis A. AGRICULTURAL EDUCATION IN THE SOUTH: A COMPARISON OF STUDENT CHARACTERISTICS AT LAND GRANT INSTITUTIONS. *J. of Negro Educ. 1981 50(1): 26-40.* Enrollments in agricultural education have risen sharply in recent years, due to increased awareness of agriculture's centrality in a time of scarcity, and due to increasing white-collar occupations in agribusiness. After discussing southern black and white land grant colleges (founded in 1890 and 1862, respectively, as a result of two Morrill Land Grant College Acts), the authors present the results of a large survey of agriculture students at those colleges. They found that students attracted to agriculture education include substantial proportions of females and minorities. The students were more likely to be from urban than rural homes, except for black students. Aspirations differed between black and white students. Original research, secondary sources; 6 tables, 21 notes.
                                                        R. E. Butchart

2044. Muller, Mary Lee. NEW ORLEANS PUBLIC SCHOOL DESEGREGATION. *Louisiana Hist. 1976 17(1): 69-88.* The *Brown* decision of 1954 prohibiting school segregation was a much resented intrusion of federal authority in local New Orleans affairs. The integration issue divided the white community into two opposing camps. The city's leadership sanctioned the fight against court-ordered desegregation by shunning acceptance of the order. When finally compelled to implement desegregation, the school board chose to limit racial mixing through pupil placement in the ninth ward, seemingly the course of least liability—politically, economically, and socially. 88 notes.                          E. P. Stickney

2045. Nelson, Paul David. EXPERIMENT IN INTERRACIAL EDUCATION AT BEREA COLLEGE, 1858-1908. *J. of Negro Hist. 1974 59(1): 13-27.* The interracial program of Berea College upheld the total equality of Negroes while maintaining a 50-50 ratio of black and white students, 1858-92. In the later years, William G. Frost, the newly inaugurated president of Berea, placed greater emphasis upon the educational needs of white southerners. By 1908 the interracial program had been renounced for the education of white mountain youth. Based on primary materials in the Berea College Archives and on secondary sources; 60 notes.
                                                        N. G. Sapper

2046. Neverdon-Morton, Cynthia. SELF-HELP PROGRAMS AS EDUCATIVE ACTIVITIES OF BLACK WOMEN IN THE SOUTH, 1895-1925; FOCUS ON FOUR KEY AREAS. *J. of Negro Educ. 1982 51(3): 207-221.* Describes four self-help programs during 1895-1925 led by Margaret M. Washington in Tuskegee, Alabama; Lizzie A. Jenkins in Virginia; Lugenia Hope in Atlanta, Georgia; and Ida A. Cummings in Baltimore, Maryland. These programs were typical of programs throughout the South led by other educated black women who clearly identified the problems facing black Americans. These women established meaningful, enduring, and successful programs that united black communities to deal with the problems and that challenged racist attitudes while working within the system and winning white support. Based on reports in black college and university archives and secondary sources; 21 notes.                                            R. G. Sherer

2047. Nevin, David and Bills, Robert. THE SCHOOLS THAT FEAR BUILT. *Southern Exposure 1979 7(2): 110-113.* Parents' fear of having their children exposed to integration has brought about the establishment of dozens of private schools throughout the South, many adhering to evangelical Protestantism, 1970's.

2048. Noblit, George W. and Collins, Thomas W. SCHOOL FLIGHT AND SCHOOL POLICY: DESEGREGATION AND RESEGREGATION IN THE MEMPHIS CITY SCHOOLS. *Urban Rev. 1978 10(3): 203-212.* Current debate on "white flight" after desegregation of public schools is based on quantitative studies of city school systems, such as O. Z. Stephens's 1976 report on Memphis schools. Ethnographic case studies of specific schools are also needed to understand the impact of desegregation. For white parents who removed their children from one Memphis public school the main "pull" factor was the establishment of white, private academies, usually in congregational Protestant churches. The main "push" factors were the parents' desires for "quality" education, i.e. discipline and a flexible curriculum offering advanced or honors courses, and for control of the schools' student organizations. Primary and secondary sources; 3 notes, biblio.              R. G. Sherer

2049. Parker, Everett C. THE SCANDAL OF THE WILMINGTON TEN. *Crisis 1977 84(1): 29-32.* New evidence uncovered in August 1976 should convince impartial observers that nine young black men and a white woman have been railroaded into prison by the North Carolina criminal justice system. The case grew out of a 1971 school desegregation situation in Wilmington. Black students and parents were faced with opposition from the Ku Klux Klan and the Rights of White People. Crowds and protests accompanied the formal grievance procedures. A white man was shot near a black church that had been the constant target of night-riding firestarters. The Wilmington Ten were arrested for attempted murder and arson. So much evidence has been suppressed that a new trial seems justified.                                          A. G. Belles

2050. Parker, Gail and Smith, Marlin. BIBLIOGRAPHY ON SCHOOL DESEGREGATION AND THE SOUTH, 1954-1979. *Southern Exposure 1979 7(2): 156-160.* Alphabetically lists books, articles, dissertations, and reports about desegregation in the public schools.

2051. Patton, June O. MOONLIGHT AND MAGNOLIAS IN SOUTHERN EDUCATION: THE BLACK MAMMY MEMORIAL INSTITUTE. *J. of Negro Hist. 1980 65(2): 149-155.* Athens, Georgia, was the seat of a unique expression of nostalgia for the black cook-housekeeper: an evening school for prospective black cooks in white homes. 15 notes. N. G. Sapper

2052. Pearson, Ralph L. REFLECTIONS ON BLACK COLLEGES: THE HISTORICAL PERSPECTIVE OF CHARLES S. JOHNSON. *Hist. of Educ. Q. 1983 23(1): 55-68.* Charles S. Johnson, the first black president of Fisk University (1946-56), was a principal spokesman for black higher education from 1928 to his death in 1956. Johnson, by training a sociologist, developed his philosophy pragmatically out of hard empirical data and recognized the vocational responsibilities of black colleges and universities. He also recognized the black cultural heritage and the role of the black colleges in sustaining this heritage. Thus Johnson's work provides a historical perspective on the dilemmas faced by a society that must deal with the fact of two societies, one black and one white. Based on Johnson's publications and public addresses; 37 notes.
J. T. Holton

2053. Perry, B. L. BLACK COLLEGES AND UNIVERSITIES IN FLORIDA: PAST, PRESENT AND FUTURE. *J. of Black Studies 1975 6(1): 69-78.* A historical survey of the establishment and growth of black colleges in Florida. K. Butcher

2054. Pinsky, Mark. FINANCES: DOUBLE DEALING IN PLAINS, GEORGIA. *Southern Exposure 1979 7(2): 98-102.* To avoid integration, county officials and school board members of Sumter County, Georgia, resisted renovation of extant buildings (serving primarily black populations), sold newer ones as "surplus" to private white academies, and juggled funds to white areas, 1960's-75.

2055. Putney, Martha S. THE BLACK COLLEGES IN THE MARYLAND STATE COLLEGE SYSTEM: QUEST FOR EQUAL OPPORTUNITY, 1908-1975. *Maryland Hist. Mag. 1980 75(4): 335-343.* Explores Maryland's record of compliance with laws and court orders on access to educational opportunities for Negroes in the state college system, a part of the state's postsecondary schools, and the efforts of blacks to improve the quality of education provided by this system, in a state which was the next to the last to provide public facilities for blacks beyond high school. Enrollments by racial composition, integration of faculties, annual expenditures per student, have all improved as a result of black agitation, Health, Education and Welfare intervention, and key court decisions which produced the 1974 *Maryland Plan for... Desegregation of the Public Postsecondary Education Institutions in the State.* State Board of Education Minutes, Trustee Reports, secondary studies; 33 notes. G. J. Bobango

2056. Putney, Martha S. NELSON WELLS AND HIS LEGACY. *Negro Hist. Bull. 1976 39(7): 642-647.* Reviews the will of Nelson Wells, a successful Negro drayman who invested wisely and built up a modest fortune. His will stipulated that the money was to be used to educate the free Negro children of Baltimore. Trustees of the fund established a school for that purpose which endured until after the Civil War, when a court challenge reduced the fund. The remainder was given to a school to educate Negro teachers; the funds lasted until 1908. 5 photos, 24 notes. V. L. Human

2057. Ramsey, B. Carlyle. THE UNIVERSITY SYSTEM CONTROVERSY REEXAMINED: THE TALMADGE-HOLLEY CONNECTION. *Georgia Hist. Q. 1980 64(2): 190-203.* Georgia Governor Eugene Talmadge began his third term in 1941 with an effort to rid the Georgia University system of individuals promoting racial equality. His particular focus was Dr. Walter D. Cocking, Dean of the College of Education at the University of Georgia, who was dismissed in July 1941. In these endeavors, Talmadge was supported by Joseph Winthrop Holley, the black president of Georgia Normal College in Albany, to the disgust of other blacks. Based on interviews, newspapers and other sources; 62 notes.
G. R. Schroeder

2058. Rector, Theresa A. BLACK NUNS AS EDUCATORS. *J. of Negro Educ. 1982 51(3): 238-253.* Discusses the black schools conducted by the three black, Roman Catholic, religious communities

of nuns in the United States—the Oblate Sisters of Providence, Baltimore, Maryland; the Congregation of the Sisters of the Holy Family, New Orleans, Louisiana; and the Franciscan Handmaids of Mary, Savannah, Georgia; covers 1829-1982. Based on interviews and questionnaires from the archivists of the three black religious communities of nuns and secondary sources; 51 notes, 3 tables.
R. G. Sherer

2059. Richardson, Joe M. FRANCIS L. CARDOZO: BLACK EDUCATOR DURING RECONSTRUCTION. *J. of Negro Educ. 1979 48(1): 73-83.* Cardozo was a freeborn South Carolina mulatto who obtained a European education before the Civil War. In 1865 he returned to Charleston, South Carolina, to direct a school under the auspices of the American Missionary Association for the newly freed blacks. His school quickly became the premier freedmen's school of South Carolina. His strong leadership abilities led him toward politics; he left his school in 1868 to serve in the state constitutional convention, and subsequently was elected to two major state offices. 37 notes. R. E. Butchart

2060. Rodgers, Harrell R., Jr. CIVICS CURRICULA AND SOUTHERN SCHOOLCHILDREN: THE IMPACT OF SEGREGATED AND INTEGRATED SCHOOL ENVIRONMENTS. *J. of Pol. 1973 35(4): 1002-1007.* Black students in integrated schools gain greater knowledge and interest in politics than those in segregated schools, probably as a result of "better instruction." At the same time, blacks experience a decrease in "anticipated political participation" resulting from a "more realistic appraisal of restrictions on black participation and citizen participation in general." Civics courses "have little impact on the political attitudes and knowledge of white high school students." 2 tables, 12 notes.
A. R. Stoesen

2061. Rosenthal, Joel. SOUTHERN BLACK STUDENT ACTIVISM: ASSIMILATION VS. NATIONALISM. *J. of Negro Educ. 1975 44(2): 113-129.* The tension between aspiration for white middle-class status and race pride has underscored student activism in southern black colleges and universities since before 1900. The growth of southern black student activism prior to 1960 laid the groundwork for the sit-in movement, the growth of SNCC, the rise of Stokely Carmichael, and the turn to black nationalism. The violent stage of activism ended with the series of student deaths such as those at Jackson State College, 1970, and Southern University, 1972. The underlying tension has not been resolved. Primary and secondary sources; 87 notes. R. E. Butchart

2062. Rosenthal, Steven J. SYMBOLIC RACISM AND DESEGREGATION: DIVERGENT ATTITUDES AND PERCEPTIONS OF BLACK AND WHITE UNIVERSITY STUDENTS. *Phylon 1980 41(3): 257-266.* A survey of 383 whites and 136 blacks enrolled at Old Dominion University in Norfolk, Virginia, in 1978 revealed that blacks overwhelmingly reject the symbolic racist beliefs held by many whites. Afro-Americans continue to perceive themselves as victims of racism and inequality. The white opposition to further desegregation of Old Dominion University and the Virginia system of public higher education dispels claims that the racist views of whites have dramatically declined. 8 tables, 12 notes.
N. G. Sapper

2063. Rothschild, Mary Aickin. THE VOLUNTEERS AND THE FREEDOM SCHOOLS: EDUCATION FOR SOCIAL CHANGE IN MISSISSIPPI. *Hist. of Educ. Q. 1982 22(4): 401-420.* The aim in 1964 of the 45 Freedom Schools in Mississippi was to bring about social change in the "closed society" of the state by educating black 10th and 11th graders. During the first summer an estimated 2,500-2,700 black Mississippians had attended at least some classes where the curriculum was a mixture of academic courses and politics. At best, the schools provided a model for integrated education and for political action based on that education. By 1965, the black activist founders had turned their energies to direct political action. Based on interviews and papers of participants; 43 notes.
J. T. Holton

2064. San Miguel, Guadalupe, Jr. THE STRUGGLE AGAINST SEPARATE AND UNEQUAL SCHOOLS: MIDDLE CLASS MEXICAN AMERICANS AND THE DESEGREGATION CAMPAIGN IN TEXAS, 1929-1957. *Hist. of Educ. Q. 1983 23(3): 343-359.* Educational discrimination against Mexican Americans in Texas was challenged primarily by the ideologically liberal League of United Latin American Citizens and the G.I. Forum. Both organizations were dominated by middle-class Mexican Americans. These organizations established the illegality of discrimination against Mexican-American pupils, encouraged the Mexican community to take advantage of public schools, and maintained the spirit of resistance to discrimination. The liberal political outlook of these organizations, however, prevented them from examining the sources of social inequality and from developing "revolutionary strategies" to eliminate them. Based on the records of the League of Latin American Citizens and the G.I. Forum, and on letters and interviews; 73 notes.            J. T. Holton

2065. Schab, Fred. ATTITUDES OF GEORGIA HIGH SCHOOL STUDENTS TOWARD INTEGRATION, 1965 AND 1980: A COMPARATIVE NOTE. *J. of Negro Educ. 1982 51(1): 73-75.* Surveys of the attitudes of black and white Georgia high school students toward integration showed that white students' attitudes shifted to favor integration (6.5% to 36.9% for; 67.8% to 26.4% against) while black students' approval of integration remained about the same (56.8% to 56.7%), but their disapproval drastically increased (7.2% to 25.8%). Other variables included in this analysis were the sex of respondents, seniors (by race), and the academic standing of responding students. Table, 6 notes.
            R. G. Sherer

2066. Scott, Charlotte H. COLLEGE DESEGREGATION: VIRGINIA'S SAD EXPERIENCE. *Virginia Q. Rev. 1982 58(2): 221-235.* In 1980 Virginian higher education actually remained segregated in spite of federal court decisions and the Virginia Plan for Equal Opportunity. One reason is that black high school seniors tend to prepare for college, not by studying college preparatory courses, but by emphasizing vocational or general programs. Based on two surveys of Virginian high school seniors.
            O. H. Zabel

2067. Scott, Hugh J. DESEGREGATION IN NASHVILLE: CONFLICTS AND CONTRADICTIONS IN PRESERVING SCHOOLS IN BLACK COMMUNITIES. *Educ. and Urban Soc. 1983 15(2): 235-244.* Examines community reaction to desegregation and school closings in Nashville, Tennessee; includes a review of relevant litigation since 1955.

2068. Sewell, George. MORRIS BROWN COLLEGE: LEGACY OF WESLEY JOHN GAINES. *Crisis 1981 88(3): 133-136.* In 1881, a group of blacks led by Reverend Wesley John Gaines decided to open the first black-supported college in Atlanta. Clarke College, Morehouse College, and Atlanta University had been founded on white financial backing. Morris Brown College, named after the second bishop of the African Methodist Episcopal Church, opened its doors in November 1885. In 1932, Morris Brown became the undergraduate college of Atlanta University.
            A. G. Belles

2069. Sherer, Robert G., Jr. WILLIAM BURNS PATERSON: "PIONEER AS WELL AS APOSTLE OF NEGRO EDUCATION IN ALABAMA". *Alabama Hist. Q. 1974 36(2): 121-150.* William Burns Paterson (1849-1915) was a Scot who became interested in classical education for Negroes. A contemporary of Booker T. Washington, he disagreed with Washington's stress on manual arts training. Paterson in 1878 became president of Alabama State College (Negro), a post he held until his death in 1915. He attempted to bring into this school, which was oriented primarily to teacher training, as much traditional college work as possible. Described also is his work with the Alabama State Teachers Association. 68 notes.            E. E. Eminhizer

2070. Sherman, Joel D. FINANCING LOCAL SCHOOLS: THE IMPACT OF DESEGREGATION. *Policy Studies J. 1979 7(4): 701-706.* White flight to private educational academies in the face

of forced desegregation in South Carolina's public schools brought about disparities in tax rates and local revenues for school districts, 1965-75.

2071. Shick, Tom W. SCHOOLING FOR FREEDMEN. *Rev. in Am. Hist. 1981 9(2): 186-189.* Review essay of Ronald E. Butchart's *Northern Schools, Southern Blacks, and Reconstruction: Freedmen's Education, 1862-1873* (1980) and Jacqueline Jones's *Soldiers of Light and Love: Northern Teachers and Georgia Blacks, 1862-1875* (1980).

2072. Sigelman, Lee and Karnig, Albert K. BLACK EDUCATION AND BUREAUCRATIC EMPLOYMENT. *Social Sci. Q. 1977 57(4): 858-863.* Nonparametric (tau) correlations of six educational variables with the ratios of black bureaucratic employment for 38 states do not indicate a direct relationship between educational attainment and employment. Separation of the data into Southern and non-Southern states suggests that the positive correlations may be spuriously high reflections of a regional racial atmosphere; employment correlates more closely with education in the South, but bureaucratic representation there is proportionately the lowest. Black educational attainment and bureaucratic employment apparently are both dependent on some more enduring and less manipulative sociopolitical factors. Based on government statistics; 2 tables, biblio.            W. R. Hively

2073. Silverman, Irwin and Shaw, Marvin E. EFFECTS OF SUDDEN MASS DESEGREGATION ON INTERRACIAL INTERACTION AND ATTITUDES IN ONE SOUTHERN CITY. *J. of Social Issues 1973 29(4): 133-142.* "The extent to which blacks and whites interacted socially on school grounds and their attitudes toward each other were ascertained across time during the first semester of an integration program in three southern secondary schools. Interracial interactions remained sparse throughout the semester and over time showed no increases approaching significance though attitudes did become more tolerant. Several effects on both variables related to race, sex, and grade level are reported."
            J

2074. Smith, Elsie J. THE CAREER DEVELOPMENT OF YOUNG BLACK FEMALES: THE FORGOTTEN GROUP. *Youth & Soc. 1981 12(3): 277-312.* A review of the scanty literature on black female career development shows conflicting results. Black adolescents and college women show little awareness of occupational opportunities, choosing sex-role stereotyped careers. They seem to have no higher aspirations than white women of the same age, and seem no more socialized for higher job and educational aspirations than black men. Since the mid-1960's, education and career aspirations of Southern black women seem to have declined. Biblio.
            J. H. Sweetland

2075. Smitherman, Geneva. "WHAT GO ROUND COME ROUND": *KING* IN PERSPECTIVE. *Harvard Educ. Rev. 1981 51(1): 40-56.* Discusses *Martin Luther King Junior Elementary School Children* v. *Ann Arbor School District Board* (Michigan, 1979), in which the plantiffs successfully sued to improve the instruction of standard English, and its implications for public policy and black community development in light of the reality of white racism and class contradictions among Negroes in the United States.

2076. Southern, David W. BEYOND JIM CROW LIBERALISM: JUDGE WARING'S FIGHT AGAINST SEGREGATION IN SOUTH CAROLINA, 1942-52. *J. of Negro Hist. 1981 66(3): 209-227.* After being elevated to a federal judgeship at age 61, South Carolina's Judge Julius Waties Waring began to destroy Jim Crow. He was an unusual white Southerner surprising many on the bench. He encouraged Thurgood Marshall and the NAACP to attack segregated schools in South Carolina in 1950.
            A. G. Belles

2077. Sowell, Thomas. BLACK EXCELLENCE: THE CASE OF DUNBAR HIGH SCHOOL. *Public Interest 1974 (35): 3-21.* An account of one of the most successful all-Negro schools, Dunbar High School in Washington, D.C., during 1870-1955. "The first black general (Benjamin O. Davis), the first black federal judge (William H. Hastie), the first black Cabinet member (Robert C. Weaver), the discoverer of blood plasma (Charles Drew), and the first black Senator (Edward W. Brooke) were all Dunbar graduates.... The founders of the school intended it to be an institution solely devoted to preparing black students for college and in that special role it was unsurpassed." 8 notes.      D. D. Cameron

2078. Spivey, Donald. THE AFRICAN CRUSADE FOR BLACK INDUSTRIAL SCHOOLING. *J. of Negro Hist. 1978 63(1): 1-17.* Industrial arts education was utilized in the maintenance of subordination and exploitation of black people in the US South and in Africa. It was a negative aspect of the Pan-African movement. Both white Europeans and white Southerners put industrial schooling to effective use in pursuing a world order based upon white rule. Primary materials in the Rockefeller archives and domestic and foreign secondary materials; covers 1879-1940. 82 notes.

N. G. Sapper

2079. Spivey, Donald. CRISIS ON A BLACK CAMPUS: LANGSTON UNIVERSITY AND ITS STRUGGLE FOR SURVIVAL. *Chronicles of Oklahoma 1981-82 59(4): 430-447.* Modern Langston University owes its inception to Edward P. McCabe, a prominent black leader who utilized some old-fashioned politicking to establish the black college in 1896. Most citizens of Langston, Oklahoma, espoused a separatist philosophy and opposed the accommodationist ideas of Booker T. Washington. Worsening economic conditions during the 1930's forced school leaders to compromise and accept a larger percentage of white funding and outside control. Racially discriminatory practices in the issuance of state funds hindered Langston University's mission through the 1960's, and national desegregation activities during the 1970's somewhat undercut its enrollment. Based on newspapers and General Education Board Files; 3 photos, 44 notes.      M. L. Tate

2080. Stewart, Joseph, Jr. and Bullock, Charles S., III. IMPLEMENTING EQUAL EDUCATION OPPORTUNITY POLICY: A COMPARISON OF THE OUTCOMES OF HEW AND JUSTICE DEPARTMENT EFFORTS. *Administration & Soc. 1981 12(4): 427-446.* The desegregation efforts of both the Health, Education, and Welfare Department and the Justice Department in Arkansas, Georgia, Louisiana, and Texas between 1968 and 1974 failed to achieve equal opportunity in education; touches on the problem in defining and implementing policy.

2081. Stuart, Reginald. BUSING AND THE MEDIA IN NASHVILLE. *New South 1973 28(2): 79-87.*

2082. Taggart, Robert J. PHILANTHROPY AND BLACK PUBLIC EDUCATION IN DELAWARE, 1918-1930. *Pennsylvania Mag. of Hist. and Biog. 1979 103(4): 467-483.* Gifts of Pierre du Pont improved black education, particularly in the building of schools. A side-effect was more viable segregation, yet du Pont's philanthropy ensured the rights of blacks to a decent schooling. Based on Longwood MS. and others, Eleutherian Mills Historical Library, official records, newspapers, and secondary works; 51 notes.      T. H. Wendel

2083. Terjen, Kitty. CRADLE OF RESISTANCE: PRINCE EDWARD COUNTY TODAY. *New South 1973 28(3): 18-27.* Prince Edward County, with successful private schools, continues to have school segregation.

2084. Thomas, Bettye C. PUBLIC EDUCATION AND BLACK PROTEST IN BALTIMORE, 1865-1900. *Maryland Hist. Mag. 1976 71(3): 381-391.* Reviews the efforts of the Baltimore Association for the Moral and Educational Improvement of the Colored People led by such as Isaac Myers, and Brotherhood of Liberty formed by Harvey Johnson and other Baptist ministers, to acquire public schools, have black teachers hired, secure additional school facilities, and initiate industrial education for black children. Blacks found themselves forced to support Jim Crow legislation and urge all black teachers for the colored schools because the Board of School Commissioners would not allow blacks and whites to teach in the same schools. From 1867 to 1900 black schools grew from

10 to 27 and enrollment from 901 to 9,383. The Mechanical and Industrial Association achieved success only in 1892 with the opening of the Colored Manual Training School. Black leaders were convinced by the Rev. William Alexander and his paper, the *Afro American*, that economic advancement and first-class citizenship depended on equal access to schools, and thus zealously pursued their goals in the face of a white city commission which yielded step-by-step and only very reluctantly. Primary and secondary works; 45 notes.      G. J. Bobango

2085. Timberlake, C. L. THE EARLY STRUGGLE FOR EDUCATION OF THE BLACKS IN THE COMMONWEALTH OF KENTUCKY. *Register of the Kentucky Hist. Soc. 1973 71(3): 225-252.* Before the Civil War, education for black children was limited to private religious instruction. A general school law of 1837 did not even mention blacks. The first provision for financial support of black education came in 1866, and the first black high school was founded in that year. Berea College and Simmons University offered further opportunities. The Kentucky Negro Education Association, formed in 1877, led the fight for Normal Schools for blacks. State institutions for blacks were established, beginning in Frankfort in 1886. The Day Law (1904), aimed primarily at Berea, prohibited desegregated private educational institutions. Efforts to reopen opportunities for blacks succeeded most notably in the Brown decision of the Supreme Court in 1954. Based on primary and secondary sources; 39 notes.      J. F. Paul

2086. Urban, Wayne R. RECONSTRUCTING RECONSTRUCTION: A PROBLEM FOR EDUCATIONAL HISTORIANS. *Hist. of Educ. Q. 1975 15(1): 119-126.* Review article prompted by William Preston Vaughn's *Schools for All: The Blacks and Public Education in the South* (Lexington: U. Pr. of Kentucky, 1974) and Donald R. Warren's *To Enforce Education: A History of the Founding Years of the United States Office of Education* (Detroit: Wayne State U. Pr., 1974).

2087. Waller, Robert L. TEACHING ETHNIC STUDIES IN SELECTED MEMPHIS CITY JUNIOR HIGH SCHOOLS. *J. of Negro Educ. 1978 47(3): 290-297.* Analysis of the results of ethnic studies for black junior high school students in Memphis, Tennessee public schools indicates raised consciousness, increased awareness of ethnic and cultural differences, and increased pride in ethnicity; 1973-74.

2088. Ware, Gilbert. *HOCUTT*: GENESIS OF *BROWN*. *J. of Negro Educ. 1983 52(3): 227-233.* Despite the opposition of local blacks and state black leaders, including C. C. Spaulding and Dr. James E. Shepard, attorneys Conrad O. Pearson and Cecil A. McCoy filed suit to get Thomas R. Hocutt admitted to the all-white, University of North Carolina School of Pharmacy. At the attorneys' request, the National Association for the Advancement of Colored People sent attorney William Henry Hastie to assist in the case. Hocutt lost, but the case, especially Judge M. V. Barnhill's suggestions about how the petition should have been filed, laid the basis for the 1954 *Brown* v. *Board of Education* case. Based on interviews and on the William Henry Hastie Papers; 33 notes.

R. G. Sherer

2089. Wennersten, John R. THE BLACK SCHOOL TEACHER IN MARYLAND—1930'S. *Negro Hist. Bull. 1975 38(3): 370-373.* During the 1930's black teachers in Maryland grappled with limited intellectual preparation, job opportunities, and salary. In 1938 the black teachers association joined with the National Association for the Advancement of Colored People to bring salary equalization before the state court. These court cases, leading to salary equalization, were an essential part of the black teacher's experience.      M. J. Wentworth

2090. Wennersten, John R. and Wennersten, Ruth Ellen. SEPARATE AND UNEQUAL: THE EVOLUTION OF A BLACK LAND GRANT COLLEGE IN MARYLAND, 1890-1930. *Maryland Hist. Mag. 1977 72(1): 110-117.* Relates the troubled history of Princess Anne Academy, near Somerset on the lower Eastern Shore, which became a land-grant school after the second Morrill Act in 1890. Relations between the black Academy and the local white populace were not cordial. The state kept the institution in a state of relative pauperism, refusing year after year to make adequate and mandated appropriations. Illiteracy rates were so high among Maryland blacks, and there were so few black high schools outside of Baltimore, that the Academy spent most of its energies and programs providing secondary courses. Only a tenth of its students did college level work. School authorities were inexperienced in accounting and record management. The Academy's trustees were also those of Morgan College, and they ran the school to Morgan's advantage, even siphoning off funds. The land-grant mission of a full curriculum for Princess Anne remained an ideal rather than a fact. Because many believed that both the school and the surrounding region were hopelessly backward, there seemed little point in expanding its resources to serve an inhospitable environment. Only since 1935 has its fate improved, but the travail of the early years produced a lasting influence. Primary and secondary sources; 27 notes.

G. J. Bobango

2091. West, Earle H. THE HARRIS BROTHERS: BLACK NORTHERN TEACHERS IN THE RECONSTRUCTION SOUTH. *J. of Negro Educ. 1979 48(2): 126-138.* Discusses the teaching careers of the Harris brothers, Robert, William, and Cicero, and compares them with those of white Northern teachers who moved to the South after the Civil War to teach. The motivations of the Harris brothers were similar to those of the whites. They both wanted to teach in the South for humanitarian and religious purposes. Their activities regarding teaching were also similar. The Harris brothers spent more time with black families during their spare hours than did whites, who were more politically active. Primary sources; 65 notes.

J. Powell

2092. Wheeler, Elizabeth L. ISAAC FISHER: THE FRUSTRATIONS OF A NEGRO EDUCATOR AT BRANCH NORMAL COLLEGE, 1902-1911. *Arkansas Hist. Q. 1982 41(1): 3-50.* Details the difficulties encountered by Tuskegee graduate Isaac Fisher, Negro principal at Branch Normal College (now the University of Arkansas) at Pine Bluff. Although Fisher was apparently a good teacher and much respected by the students, he had virtually no administrative power as he was hampered by the machinations of William Stephen Harris—the school's white treasurer and head of the mechanical department, the college trustees, and the blacks of Pine Bluff who resented the displacement of Fisher's predecessor Joseph Carter Corbin. Based on newspapers, correspondence with Booker T. Washington, and other primary sources; 5 illus., 188 notes.

G. R. Schroeder

2093. White, Arthur O. STATE LEADERSHIP AND BLACK EDUCATION IN FLORIDA, 1876-1976. *Phylon 1981 42(2): 168-179.* Negroes sought to maintain some free public schools in Florida. Segregationist policies and administrators made the process difficult. Funds often came from outside the state. Black teachers and parents often found themselves in court seeking fairness in education. Busing and school closings are only recent obstacles in the century-old struggle.

A. G. Belles

2094. Williams, Randall. LAFAYETTE'S TWO SCHOOL SYSTEMS. *Southern Exposure 1979 7(2): 107-109.* Dissatisfaction over integration of the public schools in Lafayette, Alabama, led white parents to withdraw their children and to establish private schools, leading to two school systems, a public one for the blacks and a private one for the whites, 1966-70's.

2095. Wolfe, Karl. GREAT MAN—DR. LAURENCE JONES. *J. of Mississippi Hist. 1976 38(2): 199-212.* The author, an artist, describes several conversations he had in 1954 with Dr. Laurence Jones, a black educator, while painting his portrait. Reveals details of Jones' life and his establishment of Piney Woods School in Mississippi.

J. W. Hillje

2096. Wright, George C. THE FAITH PLAN: A BLACK INSTITUTION GROWS DURING THE DEPRESSION. *Filson Club. Hist. Q. 1977 51(4): 336-349.* Describes the successful efforts of J. Mansir Tydings and Whitney M. Young to keep Lincoln Institute in Kentucky from being closed during the depression of the 1930's. The two men saved the black school by encouraging outside dona-

tions, upgrading the school farm, and attracting new students. By 1937 faculty salaries were increased, library holdings were enlarged, and student activities were broadened. Based on interviews with Tydings and Young and school records; 71 notes.

G. B. McKinney

2097. Wright, George C. THE FOUNDING OF LINCOLN INSTITUTE. *Filson Club Hist. Q. 1975 49(1): 57-70.* In 1904, state Representative Carl Day persuaded the Kentucky state legislature to make it illegal for any institution in the state to be racially integrated. The bill was aimed at Berea College, racially integrated since 1863, which challenged the legislation in the courts, but in 1908 the US Supreme Court ruled against the school. President William Frost and the board of trustees were determined not to desert their Negro students, purchasing a site in the western part of Kentucky with the help of a large gift from Berea trustee Andrew Carnegie. The newly created Lincoln Institute opened in 1912 and was patterned after Booker T. Washington's Tuskegee Institute, which led some black leaders to criticize the new college. Documentation from newspapers and manuscripts in the Berea College library. 87 notes.

G. B. McKinney

2098. Yancy, Dorothy Gowser. WILLIAM EDWARD BURGHARDT DU BOIS' ATLANTA YEARS: THE HUMAN SIDE: A STUDY BASED UPON ORAL SOURCES. *J. of Negro History 1978 63(1): 59-67.* W. E. B. DuBois was a complex individual in the recollections of students, colleagues, critics, and friends during his tenure at Atlanta University. The humanity of DuBois has been ignored by most of the writers who have examined his life and work. Based on interviews with 10 persons who were associated with DuBois as either students or colleagues; 62 notes.

N. G. Sapper

2099. —. A CONFLICT OF CULTURES. *Southern Exposure 1979 7(2): 126-128.* Discriminatory use of discipline leading to suspension of black students has been used throughout the South to resist mandatory school integration, 1968-73.

2100. —. [LITTLE ROCK]. *Southern Exposure 1979 7(2): 38-47.*
Eckford, Elizabeth. LITTLE ROCK, 1957: THE FIRST DAY, *pp. 38-39.* Elizabeth Eckford recalls the events of 3 September 1957, when, following a desegregation decree, she attempted to attend Central High School in Little Rock, Arkansas.
Mayfield, Chris. LITTLE ROCK, 1957-1960: "THE MIDDLE GROUND TURNS TO QUICKSAND," *pp. 40-44.* Public opinion in Little Rock swung between reactionary to moderate during attempted integration of the public schools and resulted in the closure of all public schools by Governor Faubus rather than accepting submission to desegregation, 1957-60.
Egerton, John. LITTLE ROCK, 1976: "GOING BACK WOULD BE UNTHINKABLE," *pp. 45-46.* Traces changes occurring since integration in the areas of enrollment, discipline, parental participation, and in-school segregation, 1976.
Masterson, Mike. LITTLE ROCK, 1979: "THERE HAVE BEEN CHANGES," *pp. 46-47.* Contrasts attitudes on desegregation within the community, the school administration, and the student body 1957 and 1979.

2101. —. [NEW ORLEANS]. *Southern Exposure 1979 7(2): 55-63.*
—. NEW ORLEANS, 1960-1979, *pp. 55-56.* Though known as an oasis of racial tolerance in the South, New Orleans, Louisiana, reacted violently against federally-ordered integration in 1960.
Coles, Robert. NEW ORLEANS, 1960: "AS BAD AS THEY MAKE IT, THE STRONGER I'LL GET," *pp. 57-60.* Relates the reactions of the mother and grandmother of Tessie Provost, one of three black children picked to be "integrated" into New Orleans all-white public schools, 1960.
Jupiter, Clare. NEW ORLEANS, 1979: "IT WAS WORTH IT," *pp. 61-62.* Interview with Tessie Provost, her mother Dorothy Provost, and her grandmother, Dora Provost, recalls what the initial integration period, 1961-63 was like for all three.

—. NEW ORLEANS, 1960: "THE VILEST SORT OF ABUSE," *p. 63.* Psychological and physical threats were used against the three white families which persisted in allowing their children to attend integrated schools in New Orleans, 1960.

2102. —. [PRINCE EDWARD COUNTY]. *Southern Exposure 1979 7(2): 64-71.*
Smith, R. C. PRINCE EDWARD COUNTY, 1979: "JUST SAY THAT WE REMEMBER," *pp. 64-67, 70-71.* Rather than accept integration, public schools in Prince Edward County, Virginia, closed their doors, generating a spate of "activity centers," "free schools," and home-based classrooms which ended by federal order in 1964.
—. PRINCE EDWARD, 1954-1959: "OUR WHITE CASE IS LOST," *pp. 68-69.* County officials in Prince Edward County, Virginia, resisted federally-ordered integration of public schools 1954-59, culminating in closure of schools due to failure to fund.

# Medicine and Health

2103. Agogino, George A. and Ferguson, Bobbie. *CURANDERISMO:* THE FOLK HEALER IN THE SPANISH-SPEAKING COMMUNITY. *Masterkey 1983 57(3): 101-106.* Discusses the importance of *curanderos* in Mexican-American culture and gives a detailed account of the famous Don Pedrito Jaramillo, *curandero* of Los Almos, Texas, who used prayer and very simple cures to heal patients.

2104. Arbuckle, H. C., III. DON JOSÉ AND DON PEDRITO. *Southwest Rev. 1974 59(2): 189-194.* Don José C. Lozano describes a 19th-century South Texas folk healer, Pedrito Jaramillo, and relates stories of some of his cures.

2105. Baird, Nancy D. [ASIATIC CHOLERA].
ASIATIC CHOLERA'S FIRST VISIT TO KENTUCKY: A STUDY IN PANIC AND FEAR. *Filson Club Hist. Q. 1974 48(3): 228-240.* Traces the devastating impact of cholera on Kentucky in 1832-33. In several areas more than 10 per cent of the population was killed by the disease. General ignorance of the cause of cholera and lack of medical resources led to widespread panic and disruption of life throughout the state, particularly in Lexington. Documentation by contemporary newspapers and journals; 51 notes.
ASIATIC CHOLERA: KENTUCKY'S FIRST PUBLIC HEALTH INSTRUCTOR. *Filson Club Hist. Q. 1974 48(4): 327-341.* Cholera epidemics in Kentucky during 1848-53, 1866, and 1873 were primary factors in improved public health in the state. Louisville, Covington, and Lexington were particularly active in the campaign to clean up the streets and residential areas. Yet by 1873, scientific understanding of the disease still had not advanced to the point where the initial outbreak could be isolated and prevented from spreading. 50 notes.
G. B. McKinney

2106. Baird, Nancy D. A KENTUCKY PHYSICIAN EXAMINES MEMPHIS. *Tennessee Hist. Q. 1978 37(2): 190-202.* Dr. Lunsford Pitts Yandell of Louisville, Kentucky, began practicing medicine in Memphis two years before the Civil War. Financially unsuccessful in private practice, Yandell attempted to supplement his income by resurrecting the virtually defunct Memphis Medical College. With the aid of his father, also a physician, who moved from Louisville, the medical school opened in the fall of 1860. Yandell's relatives were apprised of his activities and given a picture of society in Memphis regularly by letters. South Carolina's secession and the outbreak of the Civil War ended Yandell's career in Memphis. He joined the Confederate Army as a surgeon, and served until the end of the war. Primary and secondary sources; 29 notes.
M. B. Lucas

2107. Baird, Nancy D. THE "SPANISH LADY" IN KENTUCKY, 1918-1919. *Filson Club Hist. Q. 1976 50(3): 290-301.* An account of the influenza epidemic in Kentucky in the fall and winter of 1918 and 1919. The initial outbreak took place at Camp Taylor near Louisville, where 1,500 soldiers died. The disease also ravaged the civilian population, which was vulnerable because so many doctors were serving in the military. More than 15,000 died of the flu in Kentucky before the spring of 1919. Based on contemporary newspapers; 2 tables, 25 notes.
G. B. McKinney

2108. Bauer, Mary. GULFPORT'S AND BILOXI'S HOSPITALS: THEIR FIRST FIFTY YEARS. *J. of Mississippi Hist. 1977 39(4): 317-337.* Describes the development of hospitals in Gulfport and Biloxi, Mississippi during 1907-63 and focuses on a few controversies and financial problems, and especially on the gradual expansion and improvement of physical facilities. Based on newspapers, interviews, and unpublished manuscripts; 85 notes.
J. W. Hillje

2109. Beardsley, E. H. MAKING SEPARATE EQUAL: BLACK PHYSICIANS AND THE PROBLEMS OF MEDICAL SEGREGATION IN THE PRE-WORLD WAR II SOUTH. *Bull. of the Hist. of Medicine 1983 57(3): 382-396.* Before World War II, Southern black physicians were excluded from medical organizations, hospitals, and state and local health departments. This segregation drove away needed practitioners, and helped to destroy the professionalism of those who chose to remain in the South. Some black physicians, however, such as Henry R. Butler, Clyde Donnell, Pierce S. Moton, and L. W. Long, did not accept prevailing conditions and sought to upgrade their profession as well as the health and medical care of their race. Their efforts were aided by Northern black physicians who in some cases had national standing and professional contacts and thus were able to extend the local influence of these few Southern black physicians to the entire region. These Northern black physicians included M. O. Bousfield, Peter M. Murray, Hildrus Poindexter, and Paul Cornely. Based on unpublished correspondence and on medical and public health journals; 53 notes.
M. Kaufman

2110. Breeden, James O. BODY SNATCHERS AND ANATOMY PROFESSORS: MEDICAL EDUCATION IN NINETEENTH-CENTURY VIRGINIA. *Virginia Mag. of Hist. and Biog. 1975 83(3): 321-345.* The study of anatomy, recognized as essential to medical education in the 19th century, was hampered by state laws prohibiting the legal acquisition of cadavers. Medical schools relied on grave robbers, who developed their profession into an art, to supply the needed bodies. At the University of Virginia in the 1850's, anatomy professor John A. G. Davis went to great lengths to secure the 20 to 25 corpses he needed each year. His task was all the more difficult because of competition from the Medical College of Virginia in Richmond, though in the decade before the Civil War the two schools agreed to cooperate in a joint effort which proved relatively successful. Drawn primarily from the John S. Davis Papers at the University of Virginia and secondary sources; 65 notes.
R. F. Oaks

2111. Breeden, James O. THOMSONIANISM IN VIRGINIA. *Virginia Mag. of Hist. and Biog. 1974 82(2): 150-180.* Thomsonianism, a sectarian form of medical practice, presented a serious challenge to the medical profession, achieving wide popularity during the 1820's-30's, and continuing to receive support until the Civil War. The shortcomings of traditional medicine in the first half of the 19th century enabled Samuel Thomson to popularize his theory of disease and to promote his cures based on the "wonder drug" lobelia, steambaths, and enemas. The struggle for recognition and acceptance in Virginia reflects the nationwide growth and eventual decline of the movement. Primary and secondary sources; 123 notes.
R. F. Oaks

2112. Brown, D. Clayton. HEALTH OF FARM CHILDREN IN THE SOUTH, 1900-1950. *Agric. Hist. 1979 53(1): 170-187.* Incomplete and inaccurate record-keeping makes usable statistics available for no earlier than the 1930's and even these were seriously limited. Analyzes the available data covering the major communicable diseases, health impairments, and mortality. The farm child of the South had relatively poorer health with the attendant results: low school achievement and high mortality. By 1950 the worst conditions had disappeared. 2 tables, 43 notes. Comment by Donald Holley, pp. 203-205.                    R. V. Ritter

2113. Carroll, Kenneth L., ed. DEATH COMES TO A QUAKERESS. *Quaker Hist. 1975 64(2): 96-104.* Sarah Taylor (ca. 1798-1823), second of nine children of Mary Alexander (Alvord) (1770-1820) and Thomas Tylor (1752-1829), died in Baltimore, a member of Northwest Fork Monthly Meeting, Caroline County, on the Eastern Shore of Maryland, of an operation to remove a large tumor on her neck aand shoulder. Copies of two letters from the patient and two from attending friends describing her trip to Baltimore, her condition and the operation, are in a privately owned family record. Family, friends, and the 13 physicians are identified in 23 notes and the introduction.      T. D. S. Bassett

2114. Casey, Powell A., comp. REGISTERED PHYSICIANS AND SURGEONS OF NORTH LOUISIANA, JANUARY 31, 1886. *North Louisiana Hist. Assoc. J. 1976 7(4): 165-175.* In 1882, the Louisiana State legislature passed an act that required, as of 1 January 1883, the registration and certification of all physicians and surgeons then practicing in the State. The Act required each practicing physician and surgeon, except those who had been practicing medicine in Louisiana without a diploma for five years prior to the passage of the act, to file an affidavit with the State Board of Health showing the individual's full name, the date and place of his birth, the date of his diploma, the name and place of the medical school in America or Europe issuing it, and the names of the places where he may have previously practiced medicine. The act also excluded "females practicing midwifery." Contains the names, locations, and educational qualifications (or other qualifications) of the practicing physicians and surgeons in North Louisiana in early 1886. Compiled from data in the *Baton Rouge Capitolian* dated 20 March 1886.                    A. N. Garland

2115. Chitwood, W. R. GOVERNOR JOHN FLOYD, PHYSICIAN. *Virginia Cavalcade 1976 26(2): 86-95.* Examines the medical practice, 1802-36, of Virginia governor (1830-34) John Floyd; discusses his experimentation and the state of medical practice in Virginia and elsewhere.

2116. Cooke, R. C.; Hamner, E. D.; and Lumpkin, Ben Gray. REMEDIES. *Tennessee Folklore Soc. Bull. 1976 42(2): 65-69.* Discusses folk medicine and the use of herbs in the treatment of illnesses and diseases in humans and animals in Tennessee in the 19th century.

2117. Coreil, Jeannine and Marshall, Patricia A. LOCUS OF ILLNESS CONTROL: A CROSS-CULTURAL STUDY. *Human Organization 1982 41(2): 131-138.* A comparative study of rural Haitian and southern Appalachian health beliefs, focusing on differing attitudes to the cure or prevention of illness among the two groups; 1978-79.

2118. Courtwright, David T. THE HIDDEN EPIDEMIC: OPIATE ADDICTION AND COCAINE USE IN THE SOUTH, 1860-1920. *J. of Southern Hist. 1983 49(1): 57-72.* Opiate addiction in the South was linked to endemic infectious and parasitic diseases and to the lingering trauma of the Civil War. It was more prevalent among whites than blacks because blacks lacked access to professional medical care and had partial immunity to malarial diseases. Later, when blacks moved to northern cities, they encountered opiates in larger numbers. Based upon the Kolb Papers, US National Library of Medicine, manuscripts at the Tulane University School of Medicine, in the Treasury Department Files, and in various other holding journals, and printed primary sources; 48 notes, 4 tables.                    T. D. Schoonover

2119. Crowe-Carraco, Carol. MARY BRECKINRIDGE AND THE FRONTIER NURSING SERVICE. *Register of the Kentucky Hist. Soc. 1978 76(3): 179-191.* Personal tragedies led Mary Breckinridge to work for a family centered health care system in frontier Kentucky areas. From the mid-1920's until her death 40 years later, Breckinridge and the Frontier Nursing Service provided assistance in midwifery, general family care, and disease prevention.

From small beginnings, the FNS network grew to cover an area of almost 700 square miles. Primary and secondary sources; 2 illus., 51 notes.                    J. F. Paul

2120. Cullen, Joseph P. CHIMBORAZO HOSPITAL: "THAT CHARNAL HOUSE OF LIVING SUFFERERS." *Civil War Times Illus. 1981 19(9): 36-42.* Under the leadership of Dr. James Brown McCaw (1823-1906), this installation in Richmond, Virginia, surmounted many obstacles and became "one of the best administered hospitals in the country, as well as one of the largest."

D. P. Jordan

2121. Duffy, John. NINETEENTH CENTURY PUBLIC HEALTH IN NEW YORK AND NEW ORLEANS: A COMPARISON. *Louisiana Hist. 1974 15(4): 325-338.*

2122. Duffy, John. PHARMACY IN FRANCO-SPANISH LOUISIANA. Bender, George A. and Parascandola, John, eds. *American Pharmacy in the Colonial and Revolutionary Periods* (Madison, Wisconsin: American Inst. of the Hist. of Pharmacy, 1977): 15-26. Examines medical availability and the practice of pharmacy (including the legal aspects of it) during the French (1717-69), Spanish (1769-1803), and US (1803-52) jurisdictions in Louisiana; sketches individuals involved.

2123. Eberson, Frederick. A GREAT PURGING—CHOLERA OR CALOMEL? *Filson Club Hist. Q. 1976 50(2): 28-35.* Presents a biographical sketch of a 19th-century Kentucky physician named John Esten Cooke. Cooke taught at Transylvania University Medical School during 1828-37 and during 1837-44 at the Louisville Medical Institute. Cooke was the author of a three-volume text *Treatise of Pathology and Therapeutics* and was the editor of the *Transylvania Journal of Medicine.* He was a firm follower of the theory that the blood had to be purged with the use of Calomel to reduce fever. His dosages were often excessive although he was regarded as a good doctor by his contemporaries. He risked his life treating victims of the cholera epidemic of 1833. Based on contemporary medical journals and books; 20 notes.

G. B. McKinney

2124. Eberson, Frederick W. KENTUCKY BIOGRAPHICAL NOTEBOOK: DR. FREDERICK RIDGELY, 1757-1824. *Filson Club Hist. Q. 1983 57(2): 223-225.* Dr. Frederick Ridgely, despite no formal training, served as a medical officer in the American army during the Revolutionary War. After the war, he practiced medicine in Lexington, Kentucky, and was Professor of Medicine at Transylvania University from 1799 to 1822. Secondary sources.

G. B. McKinney

2125. Engelhardt, H. Tristram, Jr. THE DISEASE OF MASTURBATION: VALUES AND THE CONCEPT OF DISEASE. *Bull. of the Hist. of Medicine 1974 48(2): 234-248.* Examines 19th-century medical theories of masturbation and utilizes annual reports of the Charity Hospital of Louisiana in New Orleans to show hospitalizations and diagnoses of masturbation. Read at the 46th annual meeting of the American Association for the History of Medicine, Cincinnati, Ohio, 5 May 1973.                    S

2126. Falk, Leslie A. A CENTURY OF SERVICE: MEHARRY MEDICAL COLLEGE. *Southern Exposure 1978 6(2): 14-18.* The founding of Meharry Medical College in Nashville, Tennessee, in 1876 was intended to produce quality physicians and leaders of the black community rather than lower level medical personnel and licensed practical nurses. Meharry was one of the few black medical colleges to remain open following the report on American medical education by Abraham Flexner in 1910. The college became deeply involved in the civil rights struggle during the 1950's-60's. The school became a leader in providing innovative health service delivery and medical education with the inauguration of Dr. Lloyd Elam as college president. Projects of the Meharry faculty and students include: the Neighborhood Health Center, an on-campus Comprehensive Health Center, the Poor People's Health Clinic, as well as supporting the Indian Health Service and the Waverly-Belmont Clinic in Nashville. Secondary sources and personal observations.

N. Lederer

2127. Gifford, G. Edmund, Jr. THE CHARLESTON PHYSI-CIAN-NATURALISTS. *Bull. of the Hist. of Medicine 1975 49(4): 556-574.* Studies the physician-naturalists of Charleston during the 18th and 19th centuries. In the 18th century, the leader was Dr. Alexander Garden (1725-1791), a native of Scotland who settled in South Carolina. Details his relations with European scientists. From 1840 to the Civil War, the South Carolina naturalists reached their high water mark, with the publication of numerous important works which achieved international fame. Among those mentioned are Edmund Ravenel (1797-1871), J. J. Audubon, and Louis Agassiz. The Charleston physician-naturalists maintained contacts with their colleagues of Boston and Philadelphia, but the Civil War destroyed the economic base for scientific research, and the work of the naturalists ceased. The work of the physician-naturalists demonstrates the close ties between medicine and natural history during the period. 67 notes, illustrated.

M. Kaufman

2128. Gill, Harold B., Jr., ed. DR. DE SEQUEYRA'S "DISEAS-ES OF VIRGINIA." *Virginia Mag. of Hist. and Biog. 1978 86(3): 295-298.* Late in his 50-year career of practicing medicine in Williamsburg, Dr. John de Sequeyra (1712-95) wrote a short essay summarizing the ailments of Virginians in the last half of the 18th century. Edited from the manuscript in the Galt Collection, Colonial Williamsburg; 3 notes.

R. F. Oaks

2129. Gilliand, Evelyn. THE LEGALIZATION OF CHIROPRAC-TIC IN THE STATE OF LOUISIANA. *North Louisiana Hist. Assoc. J. 1981 12(2-3): 104-110.* Louisiana was the last state to legalize chiropractic. Although chiropractors had practiced in the state since at least 1921, not until 1947 was their work legalized. In the interim, several practitioners were fined and/or jailed. Based on interviews and newspaper accounts; 30 notes.

J. F. Paul

2130. Goldfield, David R. THE BUSINESS OF HEALTH PLANNING: DISEASE PREVENTION IN THE OLD SOUTH. *J. of Southern Hist. 1976 42(4): 557-570.* Natural and social features such as the lack of a germ theory of disease, rapid urbanization, and the general climatic state of southern cites—late or no frosts, hot, humid summers—made southern cities particularly susceptible to epidemic disease. However, the cost-benefit mentality of urban business-government leaders with regard to urban public services represent a major factor in making the epidemics as deadly as they were. Street cleaning contracts let on a political reward basis without concern for performance, and quarantine laws which were not enforced because of the hostility of the business community were supplemented by city governments and public news media which denied the existence of epidemics out of competitive desire to prevent other cities from taking commercial advantage of their cities' misfortunes. Only slowly did immigrants, a growing, articulate working class, and advances in medical science produce an active public health service which could use sanitation and quarantine to effectively fight disease.

T. Schoonover

2131. Green, Edward C. MODERN APPALACHIAN FOLK HEALER. *Appalachian J. 1978 6(1): 2-15.* Discusses folk healing in Central Appalachia; Clarence Gray of West Virginia is a healer and mail-order herbalist.

2132. Gurr, Steve. CONTRIBUTIONS TO SOCIAL HISTORY BY SOME GEORGIA PHYSICIANS. *Georgia Hist. Q. 1973 57(3): 421-429.* Antebellum southern society can be better understood through biographical studies of its physicians. Georgia doctors were involved in political, economic, religious, and other cultural interests of their communities. They were also interested in upgrading of the education of doctors. Other fertile fields of research include the history of medical journalism and black physicians. 35 notes.

D. L. Smith

2133. Harvey, Katherine A. PRACTICING MEDICINE AT THE BALTIMORE ALMSHOUSE, 1828-1850. *Maryland Hist. Mag. 1979 74(3): 223-237.* Established in 1773, the Baltimore Almshouse was legally required to allot some funds to medical care of the poor, including free blacks and immigrants. Provided by 6-10 resident medical students supervised by one or two attending physicians, this included chronic care for the aged, insane, and tubercular; lying-in and surgical procedures; and treatment of over 350 diseases. Cupping, blistering, and treatment of pain, alcoholism, and insanity with opium and whiskey were routine procedures. Treatment also included attention to diet, and experimental use of new medical techniques and theories. Only 12.5% of 2,000 patients per year died in hospital. All patients received care comparable to that given at the University Hospital. Based on hospital records and reports, medical journal publications of almshouse physicians, contemporary medical literature; 101 notes.

C. B. Schulz

2134. Hassler, William W. DR. HUNTER HOLMES MCGUIRE: SURGEON TO STONEWALL JACKSON, THE CONFEDERA-CY, AND THE NATION. *Virginia Cavalcade 1982 32(2): 52-61.* Details the life of Dr. McGuire from his medical training and war work to his private practice and work in medical education in Virginia, 1855-1900.

2135. Hildreth, Peggy Bassett. EARLY RED CROSS: THE HOWARD ASSOCIATION OF NEW ORLEANS, 1837-1878. *Louisiana Hist.1979 20(1): 77-92.* Founded in 1837 and incorporated in 1842, xtheHowardAssociationof New Orleans was a nonsectarian, philanthropic organization that performed medical and social work for the indigent victims of yellow fever and cholera epidemics. During its active service it cared for nearly 130,000 patients, black and white, in 11 epidemics, raised and dispensed over $750,000, and fostered 29 similar organizations in 9 states. It performed its last service in 1878, and thereafter was superseded by municipal, state, and federal health agencies. The Howard Association helped engender the national public health movement and the Public Health Service. Printed reports and secondary sources; table, 159 notes.

L. N. Powell

2136. Hill, Carole E. BLACK HEALING PRACTICES IN THE RURAL SOUTH. *J. of Popular Culture 1973 6(4): 849-853.* Based on interviews with 20 healers and 27 clients over a 15-month period.

2137. Hodge, Robert A. SOME MADSTONES OF VIRGINIA. *Pioneer Am. 1973 5(1): 1-8.* Identifies several madstones, a term associated with a variety of natural or manufactured objects superstitiously believed to have the power of adhering tightly to a wound made by a venomous animal. Once the poison has been sucked from the wound the stone drops free. Documented case histories exist for many madstones used for treatment during the 19th and 20th centuries. The belief in the madstone was not limited to Virginia since there are records of their existence or use in at least 22 states. Many depositions are found in court records, but there is no rational explanation for the behavior of the stones. Based on interviews and secondary sources; 3 photos, table, 38 notes.

C. R. Gunter, Jr.

2138. Hoffius, Steve. HEALING WATERS. *Southern Exposure 1978 6(2): 54-58.* Many Southerners have relied on the presumed curative effects of thermal springs, artesian wells, and other water sources to treat ailments. Throughout the region, such sources of water have gained attention for their medicinal qualities. The artesian well water of Charleston, South Carolina, has long been locally famous for its healthful qualities as has the Healing Springs', near Blackville, South Carolina. The thermal springs of Virginia constituted the basis for an extensive tourist business in the 19th century, often featuring exclusive resorts and hotels catering to upper class whites desiring to benefit from treatment at the spas. White Sulphur Springs is among the most famous of these spas.

N. Lederer

2139. Honley, Steven Alan. A HISTORY OF THE 1873 YELLOW FEVER EPIDEMIC IN SHREVEPORT, LOUISIANA. *North Louisiana Hist. Assoc. J. 1982 13(2-3): 90-96.* An epidemic of yellow fever, lasting for 10 weeks between August and November 1873, claimed at least 759 lives in Shreveport. In addition, untold numbers of others permanently left the city and region. Newspapers and other primary sources; 47 notes.        J. F. Paul

2140. Jones, Gordon W. MEDICINE IN VIRGINIA IN REVOLUTIONARY TIMES. *J. of the Hist. of Medicine & Allied Sci. 1976 31(3): 250-270.* In Revolutionary Virginia, there was a low life expectancy and poor health, especially among the young. Tuberculosis and typhoid were endemic, along with the deadly "bloody flux," probably a type of dysentery. Smallpox was sporadic in Virginia, due to the isolation of the settlements. Treatments were vigorous; patients were purged and bloodletting was practiced in an effort to get rid of the noxious humors thought to be the cause of disease. There were about 500 physicians in the state, but only about 55 held M.D.'s or had some training in medical schools. The rest were trained by apprenticeship. The apprenticeship-trained physicians settled in rural areas, while the university-educated practitioners tended to settle in towns. Five of the physicians were busy with professional research and writing: John Tennant, John Mitchell, John Leigh, James McClurg, and William Brown. Planters treated their own slaves. The first Lunatic Asylum in America was established in 1773 in Williamsburg. 45 notes.        M. Kaufman

2141. Keating, Bern. THE EPIDEMIC HUNTERS NOW USE STATISTICS AS MUCH AS DRAMATIC DETECTIVE WORK. *Smithsonian 1973 3(11): 34-42.* Scientists from the Center for Disease Control in Atlanta, Georgia, attempt to locate and eradicate diseases.        S

2142. Kerson, Toba Schwaber. ALMSHOUSE TO MUNICIPAL HOSPITAL: THE BALITMORE EXPERIENCE. *Bull. of the Hist. of Medicine 1981 55(2): 203-220.* The history of the Baltimore City Hospital began in 1772 with the construction of the County Almshouse. In 1794, during the yellow fever epidemic, the almshouse was used as a hospital, and when the epidemic passed, the city erected its first separate institution for the indigent sick and lunatics of Baltimore. By 1816, the city had expanded to the gates of the almshouse, and in 1820 the inmates were moved to a new site two miles outside the city limits. After the move, the Almshouse became more oriented toward illness and disease. In 1840, Dr. William Power as resident physician introduced the scientific method into health care. The institution was transformed from almshouse to asylum and then to general hospital. Based on manuscripts at the Maryland Historical Society, and upon newspapers and other sources; 121 notes.        M. Kaufman

2143. King, Arthur G. THE LEGEND OF JESSE BENNET'S 1794 CAESARIAN SECTION. *Bull. of the Hist. of Medicine 1976 50(2): 242-250.* In 1929 an article in the *Virginia Medical Monthly* caused a stir by claiming that Jesse Bennet performed the first cesarean section in the United States in 1794, and that he also performed the first oophorectomy. An analysis of all the sources indicates that this legend is based on hearsay, and that there is no evidence that Bennet was more than a successful shopkeeper who sold medications and who performed some bloodletting and blistering for his customers. 29 notes.        M. Kaufman

2144. Legan, Marshall Scott. THE DISAPPEARANCE OF BRONZE JOHN IN MISSISSIPPI. *J. of Mississippi Hist. 1976 38(1): 33-46.* Describes the search for the cause of yellow fever, especially by the Reed Commission, 1900-01, and Harris A. Gant of the Mississippi State Board of Health; and the 1905 yellow fever epidemic in Mississippi and government efforts to combat it. Based on primary and secondary sources; 35 notes.        J. W. Hillje

2145. Linder, Suzanne G. PIONEER PHYSICIANS IN MARLBORO COUNTY, 1760-1824. *South Carolina Hist. Mag. 1980 81(3): 232-244.* Discusses the nature of medicine, its practitioners, and their impact upon this area of rural South Carolina.

2146. Marshall, John. THE MADSTONE: ITS ORIGINS AND APPLICATION IN BARLOW, BALLARD COUNTY, KENTUCKY. *Kentucky Folklore Record 1978 24(2): 42-48.* Discusses the medicinal use and folklore of madstones, particularly the madstone of Mr. Vivian J. Barlow of Barlow, Kentucky, used by his family, ca. 1695-1901.

2147. McCurley, Edward B. FROM TROUBLESOME CREEK TO SOLDIER: THE MAKING OF A LOCAL PRACTITIONER. *Tennessee Folklore Soc. Bull. 1978 44(2): 76-83.* J. D. "Dock" Patton's (1857-1932) folk knowledge and practical experience in medicine earned him a job as a local medical practitioner in Breathitt County, Kentucky, 1879-1920, even though he had no real medical training.

2148. McKee, James W. MEDICAL PRACTICE IN THE OLD SOUTH: DR. MITCHELL TATE SENDS A BILL TO GENERAL FRANCIS PRESTON. *Virginia Mag. of Hist. and Biog. 1973 81(2): 151-156.* This bill for medical services performed during 1815-21 for the family and workers of General Francis Preston, owner of a salt works in Washington County, Virginia, helps one to understand the practice of medicine in the early 19th century. Document in possession of Dr. Tate's descendants; 7 notes.        R. F. Oaks

2149. Middleton, Stephen E. LUTHER LONGINO, MEDICAL DOCTOR AND WRITER. *North Louisiana Hist. Assoc. J. 1976 7(2): 48-55.* Luther Longino was born in Palmetto, Georgia on 21 January 1857. One of seven children born to James W. and Jerusha Wilkinson Longino, he lived on the family farm until after the Civil War, when the family moved to Louisiana and settled near Haynesville in Claiborne Parish. Interested in medicine, he graduated in 1883 from the Missouri Medical College in St. Louis, did postgraduate work in New Orleans; and studied at Mayo Institute in Minnesota and hospital schools in Chicago, New York, and New Orleans. He began his practice in the western part of Claiborne Parish, moved to Homer, and in 1897 he went to Minden where he remained for 51 years until his death in 1948. Interested in many fields, Longino's writings "are of great interest to the serious student of north Louisiana literature and history." An appendix contains a partial Longino family tree. Photo, 18 notes.        A. N. Garland

2150. Miller, Marc. DYING FOR DOLLARS. *Southern Exposure 1978 6(2): 105-113.* For generations the South has suffered under the worst health care in the nation. Federal programs have not alleviated the high rates of industrial injuries, lowest life expectancy in America, few physicians, lack of outpatient services, and low wages and poor working conditions for health care employees; they have instead exacerbated the condition of health care delivery by subsidizing profit making enterprise and fee-for-service physician reimbursement. The Southern health care delivery system is characterized by many proprietary hospitals seeking profits through cutting services and consequently costs as much as possible. Insurance and pharmaceutical companies and proprietary hospitals have joined in generating a system providing Southerners with high costs and inadequate health care.        N. Lederer

2151. Moore, George and Moll, Wilhelm. CHANGING PRACTICES AND DISEASE PATTERNS AT THE UNIVERSITY OF VIRGINIA HOSPITAL SINCE 1907. *Bull. of the Hist. of Medicine 1978 52(4): 571-578.* A comparison of medical records at the University of Virginia Hospital covering the years 1907-11 and February through December 1973 demonstrates historical trends in hospital treated diseases and conditions. Length of hospitalization has decreased by almost 44% and the hospital death rate has been reduced by half. The number of surgical cases also decreased from 70% to 42%. The percentage of private patients (not supported by public charity) increased from 20% in 1907-11 to 48.8% in 1973. This category also included those who did not have their own private physician on the staff. 10 notes.        M. Kaufman

2152. Moores, Russell R. "EXEGIT MOMENTUM AERE PERENNIUS": MILTON ANTONY, M.D. *Richmond County Hist. 1977 9(1): 10-17.* Biography (1800-39) of Milton Antony, an Augusta doctor responsible for establishing the Medical College of Georgia.

2153. Morris, James P. AN AMERICAN FIRST: BLOOD TRANSFUSION IN NEW ORLEANS IN THE 1850'S. *Louisiana Hist. 1975 16(4): 341-360.* The French-speaking group of New Orleans doctors reflected developments in Paris medicine. The first recorded transfusion of blood into a human patient at Charity Hospital in New Orleans in 1854 was influenced by the work of French physicians. Dr. Samuel Choppin soon after he returned from abroad decided to perform a transfusion operation, using those instruments that he himself had seen successfully employed there. Describes a successful transfusion in 1858 by Dr. N. B. Benedict who noted that the experimental procedure had been tried in Europe prior to 1853 only 21 times, all but two of which were successful. Illus., 34 notes.                E. P. Stickney

2154. Murphy, Robert L. and Nodyne, Kenneth R. THE HEALING SCIENCE IN THE MOUNTAIN STATE: SOME NOTABLE MEDICAL PERSONALITIES OF WEST VIRGINIA. *West Virginia Hist. 1981 42(3-4): 285-306.* Brief biographical sketches of leading physicians and dentists in West Virginia since 1769. Secondary sources.                J. D. Neville

2155. Ochsner, Alton. THE HISTORY OF THORACIC AND VASCULAR SURGERY IN THE NEW ORLEANS AREA DURING THE FIRST HALF OF THE TWENTIETH CENTURY. *Bull. of the Hist. of Medicine 1977 51(2): 169-187.* Alton Ochsner and his associates built on the rich heritage of vascular surgery in the New Orleans area that developed partly because Charity Hospital provided a large amount of clinical material and principally because of Rudolph Matas, the father of vascular surgery. During 1927-52 100 publications on thoracic and vascular surgery came out of New Orleans, 26 on venous thrombosis, 24 on cancer of the lung, 11 on bronchiectasis, 13 on diseases of the esophagus, 4 on surgical treatment of tuberculosis, 3 on the heart and pericardium, etc. In 1948 Ochsner was president of the American Association of Thoracic Surgery and appointed a committee to organize the Board of Thoracic Surgery, established a founders group, appointed an examining committee, and set up requirements for training and certification. 129 notes.                M. Kaufman

2156. Parascandola, John. JOHN J. ABEL AND THE EARLY DEVELOPMENT OF PHARMACOLOGY AT THE JOHNS HOPKINS UNIVERSITY. *Bull. of the Hist. of Medicine 1982 56(4): 512-527.* John Jacob Abel (1857-1938) was the first professor of pharmacology at Johns Hopkins University Medical School. His laboratory provided training of many pharmacologists who were required for academic, industrial, and governmental positions. He contributed greatly to the professionalization of pharmacology through his role as a founder of the first national pharmacology society and journal in America. In 1908, he invited 18 men interested in pharmacology to establish the American Society for Pharmacology and Experimental Therapeutics, and at the organizational meeting he announced that he was establishing the *Journal of Pharmacology and Experimental Therapeutics.* Based on documents in the Chesney Archives at Johns Hopkins and published sources; 64 notes, 3 illus.                M. Kaufman

2157. Pearce, George F. TORMENT OF PESTILENCE: YELLOW FEVER EPIDEMICS IN PENSACOLA. *Florida Hist. Q. 1978 56(4): 448-472.* Throughout the 19th century yellow fever plagued Pensacola. The epidemics caused a high mortality rate, disrupted business and economic life, and bitterly divided the community over solutions. By 1906, shortly after the discovery of the cause and transmission of the disease, Pensacola at last reported no cases of yellow fever. Based on newspapers, government reports, and secondary sources; 4 illus., 106 notes.                P. A. Beaber

2158. Peyton, Rupert. A WEBSTER PARISH COUNTRY DOCTOR'S RECORD. *North Louisiana Hist. Assoc. J. 1979 10(3): 103-110.* Johnathan Singleton Cheshire, M.D. (1830-91), left a diary which omitted all references to his medical practice. Later, however, a secret record was found that detailed his experiences, his patients, and his trials and tribulations during 1882-88. The author, Cheshire's grandson, opened the record in spite of the doctor's earlier wishes.                J. F. Paul

2159. Peyton, Westmore. TENDER LOVING CARE: A STUDY OF THE DOCTORS, THEIR MEDICINES AND MEDICAL TREATMENT DURING THE AMERICAN CIVIL WAR ERA. *Lincoln Herald 1982 84(2): 106-113.* Describes the medical training of doctors, the medicines they used, the diseases and injuries encountered, and the facilities for care of the sick and injured during the Civil War.

2160. Plotkin, Robert. LOUISIANA STATE HOSPITAL: THE DARK AT THE END OF THE TUNNEL. *New South 1973 28(3): 28-36.* East Louisiana State Hospital's mental ward cannot provide adequate service for its patients.                S

2161. Plummer, Betty L. DOCUMENT: LETTERS OF JAMES DURHAM TO BENJAMIN RUSH. *J. of Negro Hist. 1980 65(3): 261-269.* James Durham, born a slave in 1762 in Philadelphia, had several physicians as owners. Robert Dow, a New Orleans doctor, granted Durham his freedom in 1783. Durham had already learned enough medicine to be considered one of the first black physicians in the United States. His friendship with the prominent Benjamin Rush resulted in a regular exchange of letters from 1789 to 1802 which contain information about medicine, patients, and Louisiana.                A. G. Belles

2162. Posey, Darrell A. ENTOMOLOGICAL CONSIDERATIONS IN SOUTHEASTERN ABORIGINAL DEMOGRAPHY. *Ethnohistory 1976 23(2): 147-160.* Insects are one of the most important ecological factors affecting man and yet they have been largely ignored in anthropological studies. In the Southeastern U.S.A. Amerind groups recognized the importance of insects and adapted their own behavior through a sophisticated knowledge of insect behavior. Insects and insect products were used and traded extensively, and were imbedded in myth and lore, especially that concerning disease. Depletion of Amerind populations may be closely correlated with the transport from the Old World of typhus and plague.                J

2163. Pullen, John J. GENTLEMEN, THIS IS NO HUMBUG. *Am. Heritage 1979 30(5): 80-96.* By 1840, the only widely used anesthetic was opium. During the 1840's, breakthroughs occurred in medicine's attempts to conquer pain. Crawford Long, in Georgia, noted the effect of nitrous oxide when used in "happy hours" and began using it surgically in 1842. In 1844, dentist Horace Wells tried nitrous oxide and concluded that it could be used in tooth extractions. Others began to use ether at about the same time. By the Civil War, many surgical procedures were rendered tolerable, thanks to these discoveries. 16 illus.                J. F. Paul

2164. Raichelson, Richard M. BELIEF AND EFFECTIVITY: FOLK MEDICINE IN TENNESSEE. *Tennessee Folklore Soc. Bull. 1983 49(3): 103-119.* Tennessee folk medicine, partly learned from Indians, contains a magico-religious component but also employs naturally occurring compounds found in scientific medicine; includes a list of folk remedies.

2165. Robinson, Henry S. ROBERT AND RODERICK BADGER, PIONEER GEORGIA DENTISTS. *Negro Hist. Bull. 1961 24(4): 77-80* Provides biographies of Robert (1829-?) and Roderick (1834-90) Badger, half-brothers, and two of the first black dentists in the United States; also provides their respective families' genealogies until 1958.

2166. Savitt, Todd L. JAMES E. COPELAND: A COUNTRY DOCTOR IN AN AGE OF MEDICAL CHANGE. *Virginia Cavalcade 1973 23(1): 10-17.*

2167. Spears, John and Sydenham, Diane. THE EVOLUTION OF MEDICAL PRACTICE IN TWO MARGINAL AREAS OF THE WESTERN WORLD, 1750-1830. *Hist. Reflections [Canada] 1982 9(1-2): 195-212.* Examines changes in medical practice in the southern French Alps and South Carolina during 1750-1830. While access to medical care improved in the French case, rural South Carolina, in particular, remained ill-served, although Charleston did have a number of doctors and some were highly qualified. Under the French centralizing administration, however, the Hautes-Alpes department was ready for the later and more successful extension of scientific medicine than was the American colony. Archival, primary and secondary sources; table, 54 notes.

M. Schumacher

2168. Spinks, Martha. "HOLLOW-TAIL": FOLK OPERATION FOR A FOLK DISEASE. *Kentucky Folklore Record 1974 20(1): 3-8.* Folk medicine for a cattle disease.          S

2169. Stephens, Lester D. OF MERCURY, MOSES, AND MEDICINE: VIEWS OF DR. JOHN M. B. HARDEN. *Georgia Hist. Q. 1975 59(4): 402-415.* Examines the studies which a Georgia doctor, John M. B. Harden, made of the effects of mercury on human beings and the effects which this had on his medical practices, 1810-48.

2170. Straight, William M., M.D. JAMES M. JACKSON, JR., MIAMI'S FIRST PHYSICIAN. *Tequesta 1973 33: 75-86.* Biography of the first physician to reside in Miami, for whom Jackson Memorial Hospital was named in 1924. Based on primary and secondary sources; 16 notes.

H. S. Marks

2171. Streitmatter, Rodger. JOHN BLAIR RADFORD OF ARNHEIM: NEW RIVER VALLEY DOCTOR AND BUSINESSMAN. *Virginia Cavalcade 1979 28(4): 180-185.* Disputes the myth that Southern gentlemen led a life of leisure, by providing a biography of the energetic and hard-working doctor and businessman, John Blair Radford (1813-72).

2172. Stuart, Jesse. REMEDIES THAT STAND OUT IN MEMORY. *Kentucky Folklore Record 1976 22(3): 59-63.* Describes folk medicine remedies used by the inhabitants of Greenup County, Kentucky, 20th century.

2173. Turner, Charles W. LETTERS (1790-1800) OF JOHN JOHNSTON, ROCKBRIDGE MEDICAL STUDENT AND DOCTOR. *J. of the Hist. of Medicine and Allied Sci. 1959 14(2): 191-196.* Letters of Dr. John Johnston (1764-1815) to his father relating his medical studies, financial difficulties, and the course of his career.

2174. Vermeer, Donald E. and Frate, Dennis A. GEOPHAGY IN A MISSISSIPPI COUNTY. *Ann. of the Assoc. of Am. Geographers 1975 65(3): 414-424.* Discusses the phenomenon of earth-eating by Negro women and children in Holmes County, Mississippi (1975).

2175. Walters-Bugbee, Chris. "AND NONE OF THEM LEFTHANDED": MIDWIFE FROM PLAINS. *Southern Exposure 1977 5(1): 4-12.* An interview with Gussie Jackson, 78, a black midwife from southwest Georgia, reveals the manner in which until recently midwives faithfully and efficiently served the black rural community in the South. They were trained to practice by the state and through working with experienced midwives. The women delivered the babies upon referral by doctors. Midwives were rigorously taught to observe birth as a natural process and ordinarily practiced extensive patience in waiting for the birth process to proceed along its normal course. Medical benefits under welfare and the movement of people off the farms and into southern cities have caused midwifery to be almost entirely replaced by hospital delivery of babies.

N. Lederer

2176. Waring, Joseph I. CHARLESTON MEDICINE, 1800-1860. *J. of the Hist. of Medicine & Allied Sci. 1976 31(3): 320-242.* In 1789 a group of physicians established the Medical Society of South Carolina, and they began to establish a library, adopt a fee bill, and advise municipal authorities on matters of medicine and public health. In 1823-24, due to the work of the society, the Medical College of South Carolina was established; it opened in 1824. Discusses the history of medical licensing; the conflict between the Thomsonians and the orthodox physicians played a major role in events. Describes medical literature and the diseases and treatments of the period. Illus., charts, 72 notes.

M. Kaufman

2177. Warner, John Harley. A SOUTHERN MEDICAL REFORM: THE MEANING OF THE ANTEBELLUM ARGUMENT FOR SOUTHERN MEDICAL EDUCATION. *Bull. of the Hist. of Medicine 1983 57(3): 364-381.* Many Southern physicians argued that Southern medical practice was distinctive and that Southern physicians ought to be trained only in Southern schools. The argument for Southern medical education was used by Southern physicians with intellectual aspirations as the best way to elevate the profession in the South, by promoting medical schools and their related medical journals. In this way, they hoped to reform medical institutions in the South. Based on the writings of Southern physicians in journals and unpublished correspondence in Southern archives; 59 notes.

M. Kaufman

2178. Weisert, John J. DR. ANTHONY HUNN: FROM STORM AND STRESS TO TEMPEST AND SUNSHINE. *Filson Club Hist. Q. 1982 56(2): 211-224.* A biographical sketch of Anton Christian Hunnius. Born in Weimar, Germany, he spent his early-adult years trying to achieve fame as a poet, actor, and dramatist. His most successful play was a comedy *Der Taubstumme.* Dissatisfied with the lifestyle of the theater, Hunnius prepared a rigorous personal study program that facilitated attending and graduating from medical school. Soon thereafter, he immigrated to Kentucky where he immediately established a successful medical practice. Shortening his name to Hunn, the new American also became a newspaper editor who was involved in disputes with Henry Clay and American nativists. In 1829, Hunn published *The Medical Friend of the People* which was a newspaper about his experiences as a doctor. He died in Kentucky in 1834. Secondary materials in German and contemporary Kentucky newspapers; 30 notes.

G. B. McKinney

2179. Wood, Peter. PEOPLE'S MEDICINE IN THE EARLY SOUTH. *Southern Exposure 1978 6(2): 50-53.* Alternative traditions of medical care and disease treatment have existed for centuries in the South to an extent greater than in any other section of the country. Black and white Southerners have benefited from comparatively equal treatment of maladies available at low cost through easily obtainable herbal remedies. Many of the methods of treatment of sickness were derived from Indian medicine which as early as the 17th century were adopted by whites. Afro-Americans also early gained reputations for their effective use of herbal medicine. Afro-Americans were under suspicion during the period of slavery owing to their knowledge of poisons which, whites feared, would be used against the master class. Even given the scientific advances in medicine in the 19th century, Southerners continued to rely on home remedies for many ailments.

N. Lederer

2180. Wynes, Charles E. DR. JAMES DURHAM, MYSTERIOUS EIGHTEENTH-CENTURY BLACK PHYSICIAN: MAN OR MYTH? *Pennsylvania Mag. of Hist. and Biog. 1979 103(3): 325-333.* In spite of scholarship to the contrary, James Durham did practice medicine in New Orleans. His correspondence with Benjamin Rush ceases after 1802 when there is no further record of him. Based on Rush collection, Hist. Soc. of Pennsylvania and secondary works; 29 notes.

T. H. Wendel

# Religion in the South

2181. Abernathy, Mollie C. SOUTHERN WOMEN, SOCIAL RECONSTRUCTION, AND THE CHURCH IN THE 1920'S. *Louisiana Studies 1974 13(4): 289-312.* Southern radical social feminists comprised a special group of southern women who combined extreme or hard-core feminism and a social reconstructionist program. Despite significant changes in the decades before World War I, the evolution of women's organizations in the South was a decade behind that of their northern sisters, though many southern women served in the Y.W.C.A. "Without the radical social feminists spurring on ordinary southern club and church-women to action little progress pertaining to women would have been accomplished during the reactionary decade of the 1920's." 60 notes.

E. P. Stickney

2182. Agonito, Joseph. ST. INIGOES MANOR: A NINE-TEENTH CENTURY JESUIT PLANTATION. *Maryland Hist. Mag. 1977 72(1): 83-98.* St. Inigoes in St. Marys County, Maryland, is "the most ancient Jesuit establishment in the United States, and probably the oldest in the world... in the possession of the Society." Surveys the history of the plantation and its manor house and church, ravaged by time and twice attacked by the British. Emphasizes the management of Brother Joseph Mobberly during 1806-20 and his handling of the slave population on the estate. Details food, clothing, health care, and the problem of finding capable overseers. The Jesuit regulation of slave marriages was serious and conscientious. Mobberly found managing the Society's 43 slaves frustrating, and he came to believe that free white labor would be as productive and more profitable. By the late 1830's the Jesuits sold off all their slaves. Still in the Society's hands, St. Inigoes has lost ground to the St. Mary's River and a Navy air base. The original manor house burned in 1872. The present church of St. Ignatius was restored in the 1950's and is a reminder of a rich, historic past. Primary sources, including Mobberly's diary; 3 illus., 3 maps, 72 notes.                                          G. J. Bobango

2183. Alvis, Joel L., Jr. RACIAL TURMOIL AND RELIGIOUS REACTION: THE RT. REV. JOHN M. ALLIN. *Hist. Mag. of the Protestant Episcopal Church 1981 50(1): 83-96.* The involvement of John M. Allin, Bishop Coadjutor of the Episcopal Diocese of Mississippi (1961-66) and Bishop of the Diocese (1966-74) poses a problem in interpreting the role of the Southern moderate in the civil rights crisis. As a participant in an indigenous attempt to respond to racial violence he was perceived by many fellow Mississippians, especially those outside the Episcopal Church, as a liberal. As an official of a denomination in the National Council of Churches which questioned the procedures and attitudes of Council activity in his own diocese, however, he appeared as a defender of the status quo. Based largely on the archives of the Diocese of Mississippi, particularly the Committee of Concern File, St. Andrew's Cathedral, Jackson, Mississippi; 80 notes.          H. M. Parker, Jr.

2184. Ammerman, Nancy T. THE CIVIL RIGHTS MOVEMENT AND THE CLERGY IN A SOUTHERN COMMUNITY. *Sociol. Analysis 1980 41(4): 339-350.* Seventy-two of Tuscaloosa, Alabama's white clergymen were interviewed regarding the civil rights movement and integration in their community. Civil rights activism was shown to be the strongest predictor of decreased localism, mediating the effects of education and urban backgrounds. For the minority of these clergymen who were active in the movement, a supportive reference group of clergy colleagues and mainline denominations was important. This countered their isolation from the rest of the religious community and lack of agreement with their laity. This minority represents an important alternative definition of the Southern religious world.                                          J/S

2185. Armentrout, Donald S. THE BEGINNINGS OF THEOLOGICAL EDUCATION AT THE UNIVERSITY OF THE SOUTH: THE ROLE OF JOHN AUSTIN MERRICK. *Hist. Mag. of the Protestant Episcopal Church 1982 51(3): 253-267.* John Austin Merrick was an Episcopal priest who combined two dominant concerns in the 19th century—education and missions. As a High Churchman, he stressed the discipline, doctrine, and worship of the church as expressed in the *Book of Common Prayer*. For less than a year he was associated with the Diocesan Training School at Sewanee, Tennessee. Discusses far more the varied ministerial labors of Merrick than his work at Sewanee. However it is quite obvious that he fit in well with the parameters for theological education as it developed at the new theological seminary at Sewanee: Catholic and faithful to tradition without being slavish; connected with the past but open to the present; liturgical without being ritualistic; and unified in defined doctrine and liberty of opinion. Based on *Journals* of numerous dioceses and studies in American Episcopal history; 3 photos, 78 notes.                   H. M. Parker, Jr.

2186. Armour, Rollin S. SIDELIGHTS ON FLORIDA BAPTIST HISTORY: THE WINTER ASSEMBLY AT UMATILLA AND A CONNECTION WITH THE ASSASSINATION OF PRESIDENT LINCOLN. *Baptist Hist. and Heritage 1973 8(4): 225-231.* Two

notes; one about the establishment of Southern Baptist winter assembly grounds; the other about the son of a Baptist pastor, convicted for his part in the assassination of Lincoln.        S

2187. Ashdown, Paul G. SAMUEL RINGGOLD: A MISSIONARY IN THE TENNESSEE VALLEY, 1860-1911. *Tennessee Hist. Q. 1979 38(2): 204-213.* Samuel Ringgold (1825-1911) arrived in Bowling Green, Kentucky, as an Episcopal deacon in 1861, just in time to be caught in the middle of a loyalty controversy between the Confederate Episcopal Church and Union troops. Ringgold kept Christ Church (in Bowling Green) neutral and later kept wartime politics out of his church in Knoxville. There Ringgold later became the foremost churchman in eastern Tennessee. Based on copies of Ringgold correspondence and on other sources; 74 notes.

W. D. Piersen

2188. Baer, Hans A. BLACK SPIRITUAL CHURCHES: A NEGLECTED SOCIO-RELIGIOUS INSTITUTION. *Phylon 1981 42(3): 207-223.* The black Spiritual churches have been neglected as a fascinating socioreligious institution. The movement seems to have originated with Mother Anderson after she moved to New Orleans in 1918. Most black Spiritual churches incorporate elements from many religious traditions and lack well-defined formal creeds. The storefront settings lend themselves to the dynamic process of the community. Many services include a prophecy session, hymn singing, shouting, and messages. They often provide the means for lower-class victims of the social order to cope with the temporal world.                                          A. G. Belles

2189. Bailey, Kenneth K. THE POST CIVIL WAR RACIAL SEPARATIONS IN SOUTHERN PROTESTANTISM: ANOTHER LOOK. *Church Hist. 1977 46(4): 453-475.* There was a drastic contrast between the remarkably fixed, remarkably unified, harshly separatist racial opinions that developed in the popular white southern churches in the 1880's and 1890's and the more flexible outlooks that earlier seemed ascendant. Racial tendencies in religion were interdenominational, and regionally peculiar. Biracial denominationalism was for a time a viable prospect. Color separations can be attributed to white rather than black initiatives. Based on Conference notes and religious newspaper accounts; 25 notes.

M. D. Dibert

2190. Bailey, Kenneth K. PROTESTANTISM AND AFRO-AMERICANS IN THE OLD SOUTH: ANOTHER LOOK. *J. of Southern Hist. 1975 41(4): 451-472.* A review of the well-established view that antebellum southern Protestant churches simply served as ecclesiastical arms of secular slavery. It is true that many of the charges are justified, but the other side of the coin has been poorly exposed. Negroes served in all religious capacities from lay offices to full clerical ordination. There were some mixed congregations and white congregations with black pastors. Black clergy were never numerous, but their influence was great. The beginning of the Reconstruction era found many former slaves competent to teach the gospel. 32 notes.                   V. L. Human

2191. Bailey, Raymond C. POPULAR PETITIONS AND RELIGION IN EIGHTEENTH-CENTURY COLONIAL VIRGINIA. *Hist. Mag. of the Protestant Episcopal Church 1977 46(4): 419-428.* While in form the vestry, comprised of the social elite, controlled the parish government of the established church in 18th-century Virginia, in practice the petitions of local parishioners to the House of Burgesses played a major role in creating new parishes or altering their boundaries and in reversing arbitrary or unpopular decisions of the vestry. As a result, despite the theoretically undemocratic features of parish government at that time, the public interest was safeguarded and considerable popular participation was encouraged. In religious matters, as in many others, colonial Virginians used petitions to play a major role in influencing public policy. *House Journals, Executive Journals of the Council of Colonial Virginia,* and the author's doctoral dissertation in addition to other primary and secondary sources; table, 24 notes.

H. M. Parker, Jr.

2192. Baker, Robert A. THE CONTRIBUTIONS OF SOUTH CAROLINA BAPTISTS TO THE RISE AND DEVELOPMENT OF THE SOUTHERN BAPTIST CONVENTION. *Baptist Hist. and Heritage 1982 17(3): 2-9, 19.* Traces the beginnings of Baptists in South Carolina from the 1680's, when a Baptist group immigrated from Great Britain to what is now Charleston, where, in 1696, a congregation led by William Screven, from Kittery, Maine, joined them; discusses the importance of the South Carolina Baptists in the development of the Southern Baptist Convention, of their missionary work, and of their ministerial education program.

2193. Baker, Robert A. THE MAGNIFICENT YEARS (1917-1931). *Baptist Hist. and Heritage 1973 8(3): 144-157, 167.* A progressive era for the Southern Baptist Convention.

2194. Baker, Robert A. REFLECTIONS ON THE SOUTHERN BAPTIST CONVENTION AND ITS PEOPLE, 1607-1972. *Baptist Hist. and Heritage 1974 9(4): 223-229.*

2195. Barnes, Robert. GENEALOGICA MARYLANDIA: SOMERSET PARISH RECORDS. *Maryland Hist. Mag. 1974 69(4): 418-425.* Somerset Parish was one of the original parishes established in 1692 in Maryland, its first church probably built during 1694-97 on the Elzy estate known as Almodington. The parish register is one of the few not already transcribed by Lucy H. Harrison. The church register records births, marriages, baptisms, according to surnames, alphabetically during 1696-1805. Includes comments such as "negro slave girl" or "Eligitimate child of... " and occasionally a death date. Entries range from 1696 through 1805. Based on the original register; note.        G. J. Bobango

2196. Bauman, Mark K. HITTING THE SAWDUST TRAIL: BILLY SUNDAY'S ATLANTA CAMPAIGN OF 1917. *Southern Studies 1980 19(4): 385-399.* Billy Sunday's revival meetings in Atlanta, Georgia, in 1917 were his first activities in the South. Reaction to the event was generally highly enthusiastic; political, civic, business, and religious leaders united in their support of the event. A general religious revival was taking place in the South, and extensive preparation and committee work was done across denominational lines. However, segregated meetings were similar to those in other parts of the country. Based on reports in Atlanta newspapers; 31 notes.        J. J. Buschen

2197. Bauman, Mark K. JOHN T. SCOPES, LEOPOLD AND LOEB, AND BISHOP WARREN A. CANDLER. *Methodist Hist. 1978 16(2): 92-100.* Warren A. Candler (1857-1941), bishop of the Methodist Episcopal Church, South, offered a conservative analysis of the Scopes trial. Candler opposed liberals and rallied conservatives. He was opposed to the idea of evolution and believed the Leopold-Loeb trial brought the evils of the liberal modernist persuasion into bold relief. Based on Candler's writings; 21 notes.        H. L. Calkin

2198. Bauman, Mark K. and Shankman, Arnold. THE RABBI AS ETHNIC BROKER: THE CASE OF DAVID MARX. *J. of Am. Ethnic Hist. 1983 2(2): 51-68.* Examines the role of Rabbi David Marx (1872-1962) as an ethnic broker for Atlanta's Jews. "The ethnic broker model of the Southern Reform rabbinate differed in meaningful ways from the roles played by Southern Orthodox rabbis and Northern counterparts." 38 notes.        N. C. Burckel

2199. Beeth, Howard. THE SOUTH AND THE OUTSIDER: ORIGIN OF A PARTNERSHIP. *Southern Humanities Rev. 1975 9(4): 345-357.* Discusses the concept of the Outsider (someone or thing which is not native to a specific area) in specific terms of the South and the Society of Friends during the 19th century.

2200. Berman, Myron. RABBI EDWARD NATHAN CALISH AND THE DEBATE OVER ZIONISM IN RICHMOND, VIRGINIA. *Am. Jewish Hist. Q. 1973 62(3): 295-305.* Rabbi Calish, who served the Richmond Jewish community 1891-1945, was a consistent foe of the Zionist movement, and thus shared the position of many southern Jews of his time and generation. He was one of the original founders of the American Council for Judaism.        F. Rosenthal

2201. Berry, Benjamin D., Jr. THE PLYMOUTH CONGREGATIONAL CHURCH OF LOUISVILLE, KENTUCKY. *Phylon 1981 42(3): 224-232.* The early years (1877-1930) of Plymouth Congregational Church illustrate the struggles black churches had providing spiritual and community leadership for the growing middle- and upper-class Negroes. The success of the church usually depended upon the personality of the minister. Some of the clergy emphasized the building, some the size of the congregation, some the program, and some tied together all three. The Plymouth church became a gathering place for black professionals and educators.        A. G. Belles

2202. Black, Margie. "OUR OWN LOTTIE MOON": THE STORY OF LOTTIE MOON AND HER RELATIONSHIP WITH CARTERSVILLE BAPTIST CHURCH. *Viewpoints: Georgia Baptist Hist. 1974 4: 5-16.*

2203. Blair, John L. A BAPTIST MINISTER VISITS KENTUCKY: THE JOURNAL OF ANDREW BROADDUS I. *Register of the Kentucky Hist. Soc. 1973 71(4): 393-425.* Reprints edited journal of Reverend Andrew Broaddus I (1770-1848) of a trip made into Kentucky, 9 October-29 November 1817 from the manuscript in the Virginia Baptist Historical Society, Richmond.        J. F. Paul

2204. Blauvelt, Martha Tomhave. SLAVES AND GENTLEMEN: RELIGION IN THE ANTEBELLUM SOUTH. *Rev. in Am. Hist. 1979 7(3): 350-355.* Review article prompted by E. Brooks Holifield's *The Gentlemen Theologians: American Theology in Southern Culture, 1795-1860* (Durham, North Carolina: Duke U. Pr., 1978) and Albert J. Raboteau's *Slave Religion: The "Invisible Institution" in the Antebellum South* (New York: Oxford U. Pr., 1978) discusses the impact of rationalism and evangelism and how southern religions accommodated to the institution of slavery.

2205. Blevins, Kent B. SOUTHERN BAPTIST ATTITUDES TOWARD THE VIETNAM WAR IN THE YEARS 1965-1970. *Foundations 1980 23(3): 231-244.* Discusses positions on the Vietnam War among Southern Baptists, seeks a Southern Baptist consensus about the war, and traces the evolution of Southern Baptist attitudes toward it. Concludes that Southern Baptist were concerned, but took little action as peacemakers. Based mostly on the *Baptist Messenger* and *Baptist Record;* 62 notes.        E. E. Eminhizer

2206. Boles, John B. RELIGION IN THE SOUTH: A TRADITION RECOVERED. *Maryland Hist. Mag. 1982 77(4): 388-401.* Three recent books on Southern religious history point to the current interest in a topic sadly neglected in scholarship until recently. After a historiographic review of reasons for this lag and milestone works of the period 1941-78, analyzes Anne C. Loveland's *Southern Evangelicals and the Social Order, 1800-1860* (1980), Charles Reagan Wilson's *Baptized in Blood: The Religion of the Lost Cause, 1865-1920* (1980), and Samuel S. Hill, Jr.'s, *The South and the North in American Religion* (1980). These, combined with forthcoming books, suggest that southern religion has become a tradition recovered. Primary and secondary sources; 26 notes.        G. J. Bobango

2207. Boling, T. Edward. SOCIAL FACTORS IN CHURCH EXTENSION: SOUTHERN BAPTISTS IN THE NORTH. *Foundations 1975 18(2): 146-152.* Southern Baptist extension in the north is seen as a continuation of rural southern religious patterns. Extended into urban areas, this pattern establishes identity for a minority ethnic group. The church, because of denominational organization, allows missionary personnel and programs to move into newly settled areas. 8 notes.        E. E. Eminhizer

2208. Boling, T. Edwin. DENOMINATIONAL SECTARIANS: PRESERVING THE MYSTIQUE. *Foundations 1978 21(4): 365-372.* As the Southern Baptists advance beyond their regional base where they are a dominant denomination, they move out as a pioneer mission producing groups appropriately termed *dynamic sects.* The combination of denominational support and a sect-type spontaneity suggests the term *denominational sectarians* as descriptive of Southern Baptist pioneer mission organizations. Focuses on some of the interpretive and explanatory characteristics present in this religious movement. As Southern Baptists move North and West they carry with them the mystique of their regional religious experience. Each new congregation is the attempt to confirm a southern mystique born of a historical sectionalism. The old-time religion, a link to the past, is at the same time a search for a comfortable, predictable future. Based on sociological studies; 19 notes.
H. M. Parker, Jr.

2209. Bolton, S. Charles and Ledbetter, Cal, Jr. COMPULSORY BIBLE READING IN ARKANSAS AND THE CULTURE OF SOUTHERN FUNDAMENTALISM. *Social Sci. Q. 1983 64(3): 670-676.* The Arkansas Bible Reading Act of 1930, an initiative measure that required daily Bible readings in the public schools, was passed as an expression of a southern religious tradition that dates from the antebellum period.

2210. Bosworth, Timothy W. ANTI-CATHOLICISM AS A POLITICAL TOOL IN MID-EIGHTEENTH-CENTURY MARYLAND. *Catholic Hist. Rev. 1975 61(4): 539-563.* During the 1750's there existed in Maryland a belief that Catholics were on the verge of subverting the colony's Protestant government and delivering it to the French. Investigates anti-Catholic propaganda, relying heavily upon the *Archives of Maryland* and the *Maryland Gazette.* The prospect of a war with Catholic France drew latent anti-Catholicism to the surface and produced a Catholic scare. Politicians then seized upon this fear of Catholics and used it to gain power over the proprietor. Protestants rationalized their actions in terms of the good Protestants defending the British Empire against its enemies, the Catholics.

2211. Branch, Harold T. IMPLICATIONS OF MULTIPLE AFFILIATION FOR BLACK SOUTHERN BAPTISTS. *Baptist Hist. and Heritage 1981 16(3): 41-48, 60.* Brief background of events leading up to the entrance of black churches into the Southern Baptist Convention in 1951, focusing on multiple affiliation (membership of a church in two separate conventions) beginning in Austin, Texas, in 1955, and the challenges and opportunities for such black Baptist churches.

2212. Branson, Branley Allan. THE STRENGTH OF SIMPLICITY. *Américas (Organization of Am. States) 1978 30(8): 38-43.* Discusses the United Society of Believers, or Shakers, and describes the restoration of Pleasant Hill, the largest of the Shaker communities, which was started in Kentucky in 1805.

2213. Bratton, Mary J. JOHN JASPER OF RICHMOND: FROM SLAVE PREACHER TO COMMUNITY LEADER. *Virginia Cavalcade 1979 29(1): 32-39.* Black minister John Jasper (1812-1901), who was born a slave on a Virginia plantation, joined the First African Baptist Church in 1842, and gained national attention in 1878 when he preached a sermon called, "The Sun Do Move."

2214. Breibart, Solomon. THE SYNAGOGUES OF KAHAL KADOSH BETH ELOHIM, CHARLESTON. *South Carolina Hist. Mag. 1979 80(3): 215-235.* Provides a brief history of Jews in South Carolina dating to 1695, and describes the synagogues of Kahal Kadosh Beth Elohim (Holy Congregation House of God), from 1749 until 1978, in Charleston; includes photographs and floor plans.

2215. Brewster, C. Ray. JESSE MERCER'S *CLUSTER.* *Viewpoints 1982 8: 33-49.* An analytical history of the 1813 hymnbook, *The Cluster of Spiritual Songs, Divine Hymns, and Sacred Poems,* also known as *Mercer's Cluster,* published in Georgia, that discusses its sources, arrangement, organization, and the criteria of selection and arrangement.

2216. Broach, Claude U. INTRODUCING SOUTHERN BAPTISTS. *Greek Orthodox Theological Rev. 1977 22(4): 367-375.* Describes the membership, beliefs, and policy procedures of contemporary Southern Baptists, focusing on President Jimmy Carter's church in Plains, Georgia.

2217. Brown, Douglas Summers. ELIZABETH HENRY CAMPBELL RUSSELL: PATRONESS OF EARLY METHODISM IN THE HIGHLANDS OF VIRGINIA. *Virginia Cavalcade 1980 30(3): 110-117.* Biography of Elizabeth Henry Campbell Russell (1749-1825), sister of Patrick Henry and wife first of William Campbell and then of William Russell, both Revolutionary War heroes, focusing on her evangelism for the Methodist Church, which she joined in 1788, in the Holston River Valley.

2218. Brown, Lawrence L. TEXAS BISHOP VETOES WOMEN COUNCIL DELEGATES IN 1921. *Hist. Mag. of the Protestant Episcopal Church 1979 48(1): 93-102.* At the Annual Council of the Episcopal Diocese of Texas in 1921 an amendment to the constitution which would have allowed women as delegates to the Council was adopted by lay and clerical votes, but was vetoed by Bishop George Herbert Kinsolving. Traces the drive for women's rights in the diocese, the origin of the power of the bishop to veto, and why the bishop vetoed the measure: he felt that the church was moving with secular trends, and not in harmony with apostolic precept. It was not until 1969 that the council authorized women as delegates, and the provision was made operative the next year. Based on the Journal of the Annual Council of the Diocese of Texas; 41 notes.
H. M. Parker, Jr.

2219. Brown, Lisle G. WEST VIRGINIA AND MORMONISM'S RAREST BOOK. *West Virginia Hist. 1978 39(2-3): 195-199.* The first printing of Joseph Smith's *Book of Commandments* was disrupted by an anti-Mormon mob that wrecked the printing office in Independence, Missouri, in 1833. A few copies of the book were saved, printed on paper furnished by William Lambdin of Wheeling, West Virginia. By 1968 a copy of the book brought $4500. Primary and secondary sources; illus., 16 notes.
J. H. Broussard

2220. Buice, David. WHEN THE SAINTS CAME MARCHING IN: THE MORMON EXPERIENCE IN ANTEBELLUM NEW ORLEANS, 1840-1855. *Louisiana Hist. 1982 23(3): 221-237.* New Orleans, where Roman Catholicism was strong and a hedonistic atmosphere prevailed, was never a fertile field for Mormon missionary activity; Mormon congregations there were tiny. But the city became the major entry point for Mormon immigrants from Europe, officially recommended by the church in 1846. From then until 1855, when rail connections between New York and Chicago provided a better route, Mormon immigrants braved the hardships of the long ocean voyage and the hostility and temptations of the New Orleans milieu to make their entry. Based primarily on diaries and journals of Mormon participants and on Mormon newspapers; 33 notes.
R. E. Noble

2221. Byars, Patti W. JONESBORO PRESBYTERIANS CELEBRATE CENTENNIAL. *Georgia Life 1979 6(2): 34-35.* The Presbyterian Church in Jonesboro, Georgia, was organized on 28 September 1879.

2222. Byrnside, Ron. TOWARD A HISTORY OF MUSIC IN GEORGIA. *Georgia Hist. Q. 1981 65(1): 16-21.* Discussion of the first hymnbook in colonial Georgia, John Wesley's *Collection of Psalms and Hymns* (1737), also called the *Charlestown Collection,* which contains the texts of psalm versions and hymns that were not approved by the Church of England. Based on the hymnbook and primary sources; 8 notes.
G. R. Schroeder

2223. Campbell, Will. THE CALL. *Southern Exposure 1976 4(3): 25-32.* The author reminisces about a Southern Baptist preacher, Thad Garner, whose unorthodox life and ministerial style might have led some to believe he was a nonbeliever.

2224. Campbell, Will D. COME. *Southern Voices 1974 1(1): 41-48.* Studies the use of serpents by one Appalachian revivalist folk religion as a method of conquering evil.                    S

2225. Cannon, William R. THE PIERCES: FATHER AND SON. *Methodist Hist. 1978 17(1): 3-15.* Lovick Pierce (1785-1879) was a Georgia minister in the Methodist Episcopal and later Methodist Episcopal South churches for nearly 75 years. George Foster Pierce (1811-84), his son, was a minister and later bishop of the Methodist Episcopal Church, South. Recounts biographical information for both and describes their contributions to the work of the church.
                                                             H. L. Calkin

2226. Carawan, Guy and Carawan, Candy. THAT HOLDING SPIRIT. *Southern Exposure 1976 4(3): 10-13.* Moving Star Hall, a black church on Johns Island, South Carolina, is the center of an evangelistic sect of Negroes still similar to 18th-century slave/ African-inspired religion.

2227. Card, Edith B. "SAINTS BOUND FOR HEAVEN": THE SINGING SCHOOL LIVES ON. *Southern Q. 1976 15(1): 75-87.* Concerns 19th century song writer William Walker, whose influence on church music in the American South is significant. Examples of his music, explanations relating to its meaning, and justifications for its existence are provided. 23 notes.              R. W. Dubay

2228. Carswell, W. J. MOSES N. MCCALL, JR., AND DAVID GONTO DANIELL. *Viewpoints: Georgia Baptist Hist. 1980 7: 35-45.* Biographies of Baptist ministers Moses N. McCall, Jr., teacher and president of Monroe Female (now Tift) College in 1884-85, and his father-in-law, missionary David Gonto Daniell (1808-84).

2229. Carter, James E. THE FRATERNAL ADDRESS OF SOUTHERN BAPTISTS. *Baptist Hist. and Heritage 1977 12(4): 211-218.* "The Fraternal Address of Southern Baptists," issued in 1919, was never officially adopted by the Southern Baptist Convention, although its major author was the influential Dr. E. Y. Mullins. Containing a succinct though incomplete doctrinal position, the purpose of the address was to open communications and cooperation with Baptist groups scattered throughout the world. It was mostly ignored, yet it stands as a statement of Baptist belief. Secondary sources; 43 notes.              H. M. Parker, Jr.

2230. Cartledge, Tony W. SAMUEL CARTLEDGE: COLONIAL "SAUL OF TARSUS." *Viewpoints 1982 8: 13-31.* Samuel Cartledge was a Baptist pastor in Georgia and South Carolina during 1790-1843; discusses his conversion and the style of his sermons.

2231. Carwardine, Richard. AMERICAN EVANGELICAL PROTESTANTISM AND THE REFORM IMPULSE. *J. of the United Reformed Church Hist. Soc. [Great Britain] 1980 2(5): 153-160.* Reviews the following works which address aspects of American evangelical Protestantism in the 19th century: Ronald Walters's *The Antislavery Appeal: American Abolitionism after 1830* (London: Johns Hopkins U. Pr., 1976), Marie Caskey's *Chariot of Fire: Religion and the Beecher Family* (London: Yale U. Pr., 1978), Donald G. Mathews's *Religion in the Old South* (London: U. of Chicago Pr., 1977), and James H. Moorhead's *American Apocalypse: Yankee Protestants and the Civil War* (London: Yale U. Pr., 1978). Each of these volumes develops and refines an understanding of the relationship between evangelicalism and the reform impulse.
                                                             S. C. Pearson, Jr.

2232. Chapman, Berlin B. A. M. GRIMES: COUNTRY TEACHER AND ITINERANT MINISTER. *West Virginia Hist. 1979 40(3): 287-292.* Addison McLaughlin Grimes (1863-1964), a Methodist Episcopal preacher of Webster County, West Virginia, kept a record of sermons, marriages, funerals, and other religious activities, 1895-1920. Based on newspapers; 3 illus.              J. H. Broussard

2233. Chrysler, Elizabeth. "ALL GLORY TO GOD." *North Louisiana Hist. Assoc. J. 1981 12(2-3): 62-66.* Sister Dorothea Olga McCants's *They Came to Louisiana,* (1970), and *With Valor They Serve,* translations of letters, tell the story of the Daughters of the Cross in Louisiana. Ten missionary nuns arrived from France in 1855. The letters were written between the nuns and their French correspondents. The first book ends with the return of the principle early figure, Mother Hyacinth, to France, and the second begins with 1882, and centers around the convent and academy at Shreveport. Records the publishing history of the books. Based on the letters.                                                  J. F. Paul

2234. Clark, Michael D. JONATHAN BOUCHER AND THE TOLERATION OF ROMAN CATHOLICS IN MARYLAND. *Maryland Hist. Mag. 1976 71(2): 194-204.* An Anglican minister of Queen Anne's Parish, Jonathan Boucher has been cited "as an exception to the almost universal anti-Catholicism of colonial Protestants, especially for his 1774 sermon 'On the Toleration of Papists.'" Others have noted his hypocrisy in holding out sympathy for Catholics only to enlist them in the Loyalist cause during the Revolution. Actually the more just verdict of him is "opportunism". A devotee of 18th-century paternalistic conservatism, with a "melioristic position," Boucher had an ecumenical disposition which urged the reunion of Catholic, Protestant Englishman, and Presbyterian, with the Anglican confession being the most fit "centre of union." Moreover, the collapse of Jacobitism after 1746 had removed much of the political rationale for Catholic-baiting. Though he urged freedom of religious conviction, Boucher remained fixed in his period's belief that such toleration did not extend to granting equality of political status to dissenters. Primarily extracted from Boucher's own writings and secondary sources; 39 notes.              G. J. Bobango

2235. Clayton, J. Glen. SOUTH CAROLINA SHAPERS OF SOUTHERN BAPTISTS. *Baptist Hist. and Heritage 1982 17(3): 10-19.* Examines the political and social climate of 17th-century South Carolina which allowed religious dissent and the formation of Baptist congregations; discusses some 17th- and 18th century Baptist leaders: William Screven, Oliver Hart, Philip Mulkey, Richard Furman, Hephzibah Jenkins Townsend, William Bullein Johnson, and Basil Manly, Sr.

2236. Clebsch, William A. SOUTHERN RELIGION RESURRECTED. *Rev. in Am. Hist. 1978 6(3): 337-339.* Review article prompted by Donald G. Mathews' *Religion in the Old South* (Chicago: U. of Chicago Pr., 1977).

2237. Clements, William. THE AMERICAN FOLK CHURCH IN NORTHEAST ARKANSAS. *J. of the Folklore Inst. 1978 15(2): 161-180.* Discusses folk religion in the United States, as revealed in the teachings, structures, and proceedings of Baptists and Pentecostals in northeastern Arkansas. These churches emphasize an orientation to the past, the literalism of the Scriptures, an awareness of providence, an emphasis on evangelism, a lack of formalism in their services, the presence of rich emotionalism, moral rigorism, sectarianism, member equality, and plant isolation. Folk churches tend to closely resemble American mainline churches of the turn of the century. Folk churches are distinctive and significant in American life, although they have been little studied. 46 notes, appendix.
                                                             V. L. Human

2238. Clements, William M. FAITH HEALING NARRATIVES FROM NORTHEAST ARKANSAS. *Indiana Folklore 1976 9(1): 15-40.* Describes the belief systems of one religious sect, the Pentecostals, and relates narratives of faith healing emanating from white Pentecostals in northeast Arkansas, 1937-73.

2239. Clemmons, William P. THE CONTRIBUTIONS OF THE SUNDAY SCHOOL TO SOUTHERN BAPTIST CHURCHES. *Baptist Hist. and Heritage 1983 18(1): 31-43.* The contributions include increasing lay involvement in the church, building an indigenous church, "creating the means for rural Baptists in the South to make the transition to urban, affluent, educated, and sophisticated mainline American Protestantism," and redefining the place of the professional church staff during the 20th century.

2240. Clemmons, William P. VOLUNTEER MISSIONS AMONG TWENTIETH CENTURY SOUTHERN BAPTISTS. *Baptist Hist. and Heritage 1979 14(1): 37-49.* A volunteer is not a career worker, receives no wages or honoraria, and has different responsibilities, preparation, and identification in the community than the career worker. The Southern Baptist Convention presently employs thousands of denominational employees, however all agencies and levels of the Church continue to be staffed by thousands of volunteers who give millions of hours each week to make possible the far-flung ministry of Southern Baptists. Examines voluntarism since the 1940's in five Southern Baptist denominational agencies: Women's Missionary Union, Brotherhood Commission, National Student Ministries, Home Missions, and Foreign Missions. Volunteer involvements help church members become more aware of missions by seeing what is going on first-hand. Based on official records of the Southern Baptist Convention; 84 notes.

H. M. Parker, Jr.

2241. Cobb, Buell E., Jr. FASOLA FOLK: SACRED HARP SINGING IN THE SOUTH. *Southern Exposure 1977 5(2-3): 48-53.* Sacred Harp singing began in the 1840's as a nondenominational form of religious music. Today it persists in Southern rural areas and among the Primitive Baptists. The music is based on the use of shaped notes found in collections of hymns. The singing is almost exclusively ensemble, characterized by the generation of large volumes of sound. Singing meetings or conventions are regularly held throughout the year in rural areas of Alabama, Mississippi, Georgia, Florida, Texas, and Tennessee. Teachers train people to sing in the Sacred Harp tradition, but most learning is acquired on the spot. Singing meets usually last all day, with periodic breaks and ample lunches. Several thousand people still participate in Sacred Harp singing on a regular basis. Primary research and interviews.

N. Lederer

2242. Coke, Fletch. CHRIST CHURCH, EPISCOPAL, NASHVILLE. *Tennessee Hist. Q. 1979 38(2): 141-157.* The Episcopal church was established in Tennessee during the 1820's by James Hervey Otey (1800-63). Christ Church in Nashville was organized in 1829 and solidified in Gothic-styled stone in 1831. A new Victorian Gothic structure was built for the church in 1894. The leadership of Christ Church is reflected in its eight rectors between 1890 and 1944 who were later made bishops. Based on the Christ Church Vestry Book and other primary sources; 84 notes.

W. D. Piersen

2243. Cook, Philip C. THE PIONEER PREACHERS OF THE NORTH LOUISIANA HILL COUNTRY. *North Louisiana Hist. Assoc. J. 1983 14(1): 1-12.* James Brinson and William Stevenson were Carolinians whose missionary impulses led them into the hill country of northern Louisiana. Both brought their followers with them. Brinson and his group founded the Pine Hills Baptist Church near Vienna in 1821, the first church of any kind in the hill country. Stevenson brought the Methodist faith to the area in 1824. These men were important in the development of the area and in the progress of their respective denominations in Louisiana. 51 notes.

J. F. Paul

2244. Cowett, Mark. RABBI MORRIS NEWFIELD AND THE SOCIAL GOSPEL: THEOLOGY AND SOCIETAL REFORM IN THE SOUTH. *Am. Jewish Arch. 1982 34(1): 52-74.* Morris Newfield was a Jewish counterpart of the progressive Christian ministers who preached a "social gospel" at the turn of the century. As rabbi of Temple Emanu-El in Birmingham, Alabama, Newfield had to develop a theology that would keep his congregants loyal and attentive, but not alienate the Christians in that city. In the late 1890's a spirit of ecumenism existed, and Newfield took advantage of it in making contacts with local Christians. Newfield put his social ideas into practice through extensive involvement with social agencies and as a social worker. Based on Temple Emanu-El's records, the Newfield Papers at the American Jewish Archives, and numerous primary and secondary sources; 42 notes, photo.

T. Koppel

2245. Cox, Richard J. STEPHEN BORDLEY, GEORGE WHITEFIELD, AND THE GREAT AWAKENING IN MARYLAND. *Hist. Mag. of the Protestant Episcopal Church 1977 46(3): 297-307.* Historians have commented little on the Great Awakening in Maryland. Presents a three-page letter by lawyer Stephen Bordley (1710-64) discussing George Whitefield's preaching in Annapolis in December 1739. The letter reveals the responses of upper-class

Anglicans in Maryland to the Great Awakening. Bordley faulted Whitefield's theology, but praised his excellent delivery. Based on primary and secondary sources; 33 notes.

H. M. Parker, Jr.

2246. Crawford, G. B. THE PREACHER'S LAMENT: SPIRITUAL COUNSEL FOR A SLAVE SOCIETY. *Rev. in Am. Hist. 1981 9(4): 487-491.* Reviews Anne C. Loveland's *Southern Evangelicals and the Social Order, 1800-1860* (1980), which examines the beliefs common among Southern Baptist, Methodist, and Presbyterian clergymen in the South.

2247. Crews, Clyde F. HALLOWED GROUND: THE CATHEDRAL OF THE ASSUMPTION IN LOUISVILLE HISTORY. *Filson Club. Hist. Q. 1977 51(3): 249-261.* Sketches the role of the Cathedral of the Assumption in the life of the Louisville, Kentucky, Catholic community since 1852. Based on newspapers and church records; 50 notes.

G. B. McKinney

2248. Daniel, Harry. CAREY H. ALLEN. *Filson Club Hist. Q. 1983 57(3): 315-318.* Relates the sparse details of the brief ministry of Carey H. Allen. Allen was ordained as Presbyterian minister in 1790. A very effective public speaker, he proved to be a popular preacher in rural Virginia and Kentucky. He died in 1795.

G. B. McKinney

2249. Daniel, W. Harrison. THE EFFECTS OF THE CIVIL WAR ON SOUTHERN PROTESTANTISM. *Maryland Hist. Mag. 1974 69(1): 44-63.* All branches of Protestantism were scarred and afflicted by the Civil War. All denominations carried on extensive activities to care for the wounded, orphans and widows of the Southern armies. Northern troops committed many unjustifiable outrages on Southern churches, while inflation brought serious financial problems to the clergy, many of whom took secular employment. Southern Presbyterians, Lutherans, and Episcopalians all split from their Northern brethren and formed separate organizations, but war brought no revival enthusiasm to the Southern churches as it did in the camps. Federal treatment of Southern clergymen was largely moderate and tolerant, but those who persisted in "political preaching" were punished. All denominations "faced a major rebuilding task in the spring of 1865." Primary and secondary sources; 6 illus., 79 notes.

G. J. Bobango

2250. D'Antoni, Blaise C. THE CHURCH RECORDS OF NORTH LOUISIANA. *Louisiana Hist. 1974 15(1): 59-67.* Outlines preservation efforts, 1930's-74, of colonial period Catholic records.

2251. Davis, Charles Thomas and Humphrey, Richard Alan. APPALACHIAN RELIGION: A DIVERSITY OF CONSCIOUSNESS. *Appalachian J. 1978 5(4): 390-399.* The traditional scientific-historical approach to the study of southern Appalachian religion, which emphasizes doctrine, is misleading, because the crux of religion for mountaineers is the daily repetition of archetypal patterns established by Christ in the New Testament, and the recitation of a personal story of conversion.

2252. Deibert, William E. THOMAS BACON, COLONIAL CLERGYMAN. *Maryland Hist. Mag. 1978 73(1): 79-86.* Surveys the American career of the Anglican priest Thomas Bacon (1700-68), rector of St. Peter's Parish, Talbot County, Maryland, and after 1758 of All Saints Church in Frederick. Though he was fundamentalist and conservative in religious and political beliefs, Bacon's ministry had a progressive social content, and he not only preached that slaves should be taught Christianity but also founded perhaps the first charity working school in Maryland. His project of publishing the laws of Maryland flung him into a four-year political battle (centered on inclusion or omission of the 1661 Tonnage Act) between the proprietary and antiproprietary parties in the General Assembly. Minister, musician, physician, educator, gardener, and student of law, he exemplified the 18th-century Renaissance man and achieved a prominence matched by few Maryland clergymen. Primary and secondary sources; illus., 65 notes.

G. J. Bobango

2253. DelPino, Julius E. BLACKS IN THE UNITED METHOD-IST CHURCH FROM ITS BEGINNING TO 1968. *Methodist Hist. 1980 19(1): 3-20.* Traces the experiences of blacks within the Methodist Church from 1769 to 1968. From 1794 to 1870 a number of separate black denominations started; they continue until today. Those who remained within the Methodist Episcopal Church and the Methodist Episcopal Church, South were racially and organizationally divided from the white churches until 1939. At that time a Central Jurisdiction was provided to include all black conferences. This was eliminated by 1968 when the blacks were merged into the white jurisdictions. Map, 38 notes.                    H. L. Calkin

2254. Deweese, Charles W. RELIEF FOR THE BAPTIST INFORMATION CENTER. *Baptist Hist. and Heritage 1974 9(2): 79-81.* Discusses Volume III of the *Encyclopedia of Southern Baptists,* 1971, which covers developments in Southern Baptist life since 1956.

2255. Deweese, Charles W. SOUTHERN BAPTISTS AND CHURCH COVENANTS. *Baptist Hist. and Heritage 1974 9(1): 2-15.* In 1853 J. Newton Brown published his personal revision of the 1833 New Hampshire Covenant which is used by most churches of the Southern Baptist Convention today.

2256. Deweese, Charles W. STATE BAPTIST HISTORICAL JOURNALS. *Baptist Hist. and Heritage 1978 14(4): 34, 36.* Lists periodicals published by Baptist historical societies in Alabama, Georgia, Kentucky, Oklahoma, South Carolina, and Virginia; one since the 1950's, three since the 1960's, and two since the 1970's.

2257. Dickinson, George E. CHANGING RELIGIOUS BEHAVIOR OF ADOLESCENTS 1964-1979. *Youth & Soc. 1982 13(3): 283-288.* Discusses the religious behavior of students at a northeastern Texas community high school during 1964-79, using frequency of church attendance, frequency of Bible reading, and whether grace is said at meals as dependent variables, and race, time, and sex as independent variables; religious involvement decreased during 1964-74 but trends indicate a possible reversal in 1979.

2258. Dickinson, George E. RELIGIOUS PRACTICES OF ADOLESCENTS IN A SOUTHERN COMMUNITY: 1964-1974. *J. for the Sci. Study of Religion 1976 15(4): 361-364.* Examines differences in church attendance and outward religiosity in Negroes and whites in a southern community; affiliation with established churches is declining among adolescents.

2259. Dickson, D. Bruce, Jr. RELIGION, SOCIETY AND CULTURE IN THE OLD SOUTH: A COMPARATIVE VIEW. *Am. Q. 1974 26(4): 399-416.* Discusses the religious life and its relationship with the antebellum Southern society of the "plain-folk" small farmers and the Negro slaves. Stresses the impact of evangelicalism upon Methodism and Baptism, and compares and contrasts the differing white and black concepts of religion as an alternative to the oppressions of this world. 48 notes.          C. W. Olson

2260. Dismukes, Camillus J., ed. THE WILLIAM HERVEY DAVIS MARRIAGE REGISTER, 1837-1880. *South Carolina Hist. Mag. 1976 77(1): 41-48.* Reverend William Hervey Davis served Presbyterian churches in South Carolina for 38 years: Wilmington Presbyterian Church and Hopewell Presbyterian Church. The register contains a list of marriages performed by Davis during his years in South Carolina as well as several he performed in Georgia after leaving South Carolina. Based on primary sources; 12 notes.
R. H. Tomlinson

2261. Dodd, Damon C. FREEWILL BAPTISTS IN GEORGIA. *Viewpoints: Georgia Baptist Hist. 1978 (6): 55-62.* Chronicles Freewill Baptists from 1727 in North Carolina to their expansion into South Carolina, Alabama, and Florida, focusing on the growth of the sect in Georgia, 1776-1977.

2262. Elifson, Kirk W. and Irwin, Joseph. BLACK MINISTERS' ATTITUDES TOWARD POPULATION SIZE AND BIRTH CONTROL. *Sociol. Analysis 1977 38(3): 252-257.* Attitudes toward ideal black population size and genocidal efforts by whites were assessed

in conjunction with a larger study of 154 black ministers in Nashville, Tennessee. A variety of demographic and experiential indicators which hypothetically should serve as predictors of the stance taken by the ministers were considered. While the demographic variables did not show any consistent relationship with the ministers' overall orientation to the issue of minority status, both attitudinal and experiential variables were of predictive value.          J

2263. Elkins, Nancy F. SEVENTH-DAY ADVENTISTS: A STUDY OF HOME MISSION WORK IN WESTERN NORTH CAROLINA. *Appalachian J. 1981 8(2): 119-125.* Contrasts the missionary approach employed by most northern denominations with that followed by the Seventh-day Adventists and suggests that the Adventists succeeded largely because it was their purpose not to change the mountain society into an imitation of the rest of America but rather to settle among the mountain people and reveal Adventist doctrine by applying it practically to everyday life; 1870-99.

2264. Ellis, William E. CATHOLICISM AND THE SOUTHERN ETHOS: THE ROLE OF PATRICK HENRY CALLAHAN. *Catholic Hist. Rev. 1983 69(1): 41-50.* Patrick Henry Callahan, son of Irish Catholic immigrants, endeavored to accommodate Catholicism to the Southern ethos, but also sought to uplift that character in crusades against religious and racial prejudices. He blended roles as manufacturer, profit-sharing pioneer, leader in the fight for tolerance, and prohibitionist into a busy life. During World War I, he directed a Knights of Columbus campaign against anti-Catholicism. In the interwar period he often stepped outside official Catholic circles and developed his own distinctive antiprejudice programs. Prior to World War II, Callahan served as a valuable independent critic of the Southern ethos.          A

2265. Ellis, William E. EDGAR YOUNG MULLINS AND THE CRISES OF MODERATE SOUTHERN BAPTIST LEADERSHIP. *Foundations 1976 19(2): 171-185.* Describes Edgar Young Mullins' (1860-1928) life down to his election as President of Southern Seminary, and discusses his leadership as a moderate in the Southern Baptist Convention. Mullins continually modified his position toward a more conservative position. He lost his place of leadership near the end of his life because of the evolution controversy which was prominent in the South. 61 notes.          E. E. Eminhizer

2266. Ellwanger, Walter H. LUTHERANISM IN ALABAMA AND OTHER PARTS OF THE SOUTH. *Concordia Hist. Inst. Q. 1975 48(2): 35-43.* Reviews the development of Lutheranism in the Deep South with comments on the impact of the religion on the region. The works of several prominent Lutherans, including Niles J. Bakke and Rosa J. Young, have been cited with Alabama emerging as the focal point. Mentions congregational development in Mississippi, Louisiana, and the Carolinas. The civil rights movement of the early 1960's witnessed the adjustment of the Lutheran Church to a more liberal position; the Alabama Lutheran Academy and College opened its doors to black students for ministerial and teacher training.          W. T. Walker

2267. Evans, Teddy H. THE BIG HATCHIE BAPTIST ASSOCIATION: 1828-1978: PART I 1828-1903. *West Tennessee Hist. Soc. Papers 1978 (32): 148-157.* Trenchant account of the first 75 years of the Big Hatchie Baptist Association, in connection with the Southern Baptist Convention. Emphasizes the work of missions and evangelism as well as the strong leadership of several early pastors. The Landmark movement began within the association, under the leadership of Dr. J. R. Graves. Traces divisions within the association which led to the establishment of other associations. To be continued.          H. M. Parker, Jr.

2268. Evans, Teddy H. THE BIG HATCHIE BAPTIST ASSOCIATION, 1903-1978. *West Tennessee Hist. Soc. Papers 1979 33: 95-102.* Continued from a previous article. Part II. Describes the Big Hatchie Baptist Association, located in Haywood, Lauderdale, and Tipton counties in West Tennessee. At present the Association consists of 32 congregations. In the 20th century the churches grad-

ually abandoned their adherence to Landmarkism and became more closely integrated into the missionary, educational, and benevolent ministries of the Tennessee and Southern Baptist Conventions.
H. M. Parker, Jr.

2269. Ferm, Lois. BILLY GRAHAM IN FLORIDA. *Florida Hist. Q. 1981 60(2): 174-185.* Billy Graham moved to Florida for health reasons and enrolled in the Florida Bible Institute (now Trinity Bible College) in Dunedin. While attending the institute, Graham came into contact with well-known evangelists including Gypsy Smith, William Evans and others. Success in the pulpit led Graham to baptism by immersion and ordination as an evangelist in the Baptist Church. Graham returned often to Florida. During his Tampa Crusade, in March 1979, 52,000 people attended the closing meeting. Based on oral history records and transcripts at the Billy Graham Center, Wheaton College, Wheaton, Illinois, and other sources; 4 fig., 34 notes.
N. A. Kuntz

2270. Feucht, Oscar E. ST. PAUL'S LUTHERAN CHURCH, WARTBURG, TENNESSEE. *Concordia Hist. Inst. Q. 1975 48(3): 67-86.* The history of St. Paul's Lutheran Church in Wartburg, Tennessee, dates from 1844 when George F. Gerding founded the town and donated land for the church. The church has steadily developed from the pastorates of John F. Wilkes, John L. Hirschmann, Carl A. Bruegemann, Otto Carl Praetorius, and others. The mission churches which developed out of St. Paul's were located in Deermont, Deer Lodge, and Oakdale, Tennessee. 27 photos, biblio.
W. T. Walker

2271. Fitch, James E. MAJOR THRUSTS IN SUNDAY SCHOOL DEVELOPMENT SINCE 1900. *Baptist Hist. and Heritage 1983 18(1): 17-30.* Chronicles the Sunday school movement among Southern Baptists.

2272. Fletcher, Jesse C. A HISTORY OF THE FOREIGN MISSION BOARD OF THE SOUTHERN BAPTIST CONVENTION DURING THE CIVIL WAR. *Baptist Hist. and Heritage 1975 10(4): 204-219.* Describes the difficulties that the Southern Baptist Convention encountered during the Civil War in supporting missionaries in such diverse places as China and Africa. Provides insight into a denomination's operations under adverse conditions. The Foreign Mission Board survived the war primarily because of its convictions regarding the worthiness of its efforts, the innovative procedures used by those supporting foreign missions, and the dedication and resiliency of the missionaries. Based on correspondence of the Board; 97 notes.
H. M. Parker, Jr.

2273. Flynt, J. Wayne. THE IMPACT OF SOCIAL FACTORS ON SOUTHERN BAPTIST EXPANSION, 1800-1914. *Baptist Hist. and Heritage 1982 17(3): 20-31.* Examines the elements contributing to Southern Baptist development: individualism, appeal to the common people, revivalism, and racial attitudes.

2274. Flynt, J. Wayne. SOUTHERN BAPTISTS: RURAL TO URBAN TRANSITION. *Baptist Hist. and Heritage 1981 16(1): 24-34.* Traces the transition from predominantly rural churches (almost 70% of Southern Baptists in the United States belonged to rural churches in 1922) to urban churches that dealt with city life, since the 19th century.

2275. Foster, Gaines M. BISHOP CHESHIRE AND BLACK PARTICIPATION IN THE EPISCOPAL CHURCH: THE LIMITATIONS OF RELIGIOUS PATERNALISM. *North Carolina Hist. Rev. 1977 54(1): 49-65.* Joseph Blount Cheshire, Jr. (1850-1932), Episcopal Bishop of North Carolina (1893-1932), held mid-19th-century paternalistic views toward Negroes at the time segregation was rapidly gaining acceptance in the South. As Church leaders attempted entirely to separate and remove black priests from the ruling hierarchy at century's end, Cheshire advocated active black participation. Paradoxically, his religious paternalism did not extend to the social sphere where he maintained a strong attitude of white supremacy and black subservience. Based on contemporary church publications, unpublished autobiographies, Blount manuscript papers, and secondary sources; 9 illus., 33 notes.
T. L. Savitt

2276. Franch, Michael S. THE CONGREGATIONAL COMMUNITY IN THE CHANGING CITY, 1840-70. *Maryland Hist. Mag. 1976 71(3): 367-380.* The relocation of white, English-language Protestant churches from Baltimore's central city area to newer outlying neighborhoods was due not only to a desire for more select surroundings, but also to urban demographic and economic changes and "the financial imperatives of the American system of voluntary support for religious institutions." Membership in Protestant congregations depended not on geographic residency but on voluntary association: churches regardless of theology were "gathered" organizations. Congregational cohesion depended on whether a church was "pewed" or free-seat, on the social and ethnic homogeneity of the neighborhood, and on members' physical proximity to the church. As economic change allowed members to buy new residences outside the core city area, the "downtown" churches faced bankruptcy and commercial encroachment on their properties. Thus "daughter" churches were founded in the new residential areas, while older core churches came to serve lower-status groups. Primary and secondary sources; 6 maps, 2 tables, 29 notes.
G. J. Bobango

2277. Freeze, Gary. LIKE A HOUSE BUILT UPON SAND: THE ANGLICAN CHURCH AND ESTABLISHMENT IN NORTH CAROLINA, 1765-1776. *Hist. Mag. of the Protestant Episcopal Church 1979 48(4): 405-432.* Of all the establishments of the Church of England in colonial America, North Carolina's was the weakest. To offset this, on the eve of the Revolution, Governor William Tryon energetically pushed for greater conformity in the colony. As a result, the Church became a symbol of royal despotism. Tryon's attempts to impose a more structured, hierarchical society gave colonists reason to revolt, because their principles of fair government and a just society had been violated. Examines Presbyterians and Baptists as dissenters in the colony. Based largely on *Colonial Records of North Carolina*, Clark's *State Records of North Carolina*, and secondary sources; 116 notes.
H. M. Parker, Jr.

2278. Gaddy, C. Welton. SIGNIFICANT INFLUENCES OF BAPTISTS ON POLITICS IN AMERICA. *Baptist Hist. and Heritage 1976 11(2): 27-38.* Baptists fought long and successfully to obtain religious freedom in America and to get the First Amendment into the Constitution. But their emphasis on individualism in the religious experience and life has hindered most Southern Baptists from contributing any positive influence on the later American political scene. As individuals and churches they will oppose liquor and gambling, but they will not participate in fights for better housing for the poor, fair labor practices, etc. No leader has appeared among Southern Baptists, as Walter Rauschenbusch did in the North, to interpret the meaning of social Christianity and to call forth concerted efforts on major social problems. Thus the prophetic pulpit is largely absent in Southern Baptist churches. Neither a word of help or hope is extended. Some Southern Baptists have contributed much as individuals to the body politic. Urges the development of the political clout of the Southern Baptist Convention, lest that power become more a myth and less a reality. Based largely on Annual Reports of the Southern Baptist Convention and secondary sources; 23 notes.
H. M. Parker, Jr.

2279. Gage, Patricia Anthony. THE SAWDUST TRAIL LIVES ON AT THE HUDSON CAMP MEETING. *North Louisiana Hist. Assoc. J. 1979 10(1): 23-25.* An account of the 1977 camp meeting, with a brief history of the Hudson Holiness Interdenominational Camp site which was established in 1899 in Winn Parish, Louisiana. 2 illus.
J. F. Paul

2280. Gann, Daniel H. HARRY CREWS: A BIBLIOGRAPHY. *Bull. of Biblio. 1982 39(3): 139-145.* Bibliography of primary and secondary sources of Southern writer Harry Crews from 1963, when his first piece of fiction was published, until 1981.

2281. Gardner, Robert G. LANDMARK BANNER AND CHEROKEE BAPTIST. *Viewpoints: Georgia Baptist Hist. 1974 4: 27-38.* Examines a Baptist church newspaper, the *Landmark Banner and Cherokee Baptist,* and its role (1859-64) in a religious controversy concerning the Cherokee Georgia Baptist Convention.          S

2282. Gardner, Robert G. PRIMARY SOURCES IN THE STUDY OF EIGHTEENTH-CENTURY GEORGIA BAPTIST HISTORY. *Viewpoints: Georgia Baptist Hist. 1980 7: 59-118.* Reprints texts from a collection on 18th-century Georgia Baptist history, including primary information about Morgan Edwards, Hezekiah Smith, Isaac Backus, John Asplund, Baptist associations, and local churches.

2283. Gardner, Robert G. SPENCER BIDWELL KING, JR. *Viewpoints: Georgia Baptist Hist. 1978 (6): 19-24.* Obituary of Spencer Bidwell King, Jr. (1904-77), discussing his contributions to the Baptist Church in Georgia as a historian of the church and the state, and his work as an educator in state church schools, 1930's-77.

2284. Gaw, Jerry L. REFUGE IN A WHITE WORLD: THE NEGRO CHURCH IN NORTH LOUISIANA DURING RECONSTRUCTION. *North Louisiana Hist. Assoc. J. 1980 11(4): 19-32.* Religion and politics mixed as various denominations attempted to meet the religious needs of the Negroes of Northern Louisiana. Racial separation in existing churches developed as white ministers often continued to champion the Confederate cause after the Civil War. Black churches, particularly Methodist and Baptist, often became the centers of religious and civil zeal. While Southern white churches resisted change, the black churches kept up the spirit of their members. 82 notes.          J. F. Paul

2285. Gerrard, Ginny. A HISTORY OF THE PROTESTANT EPISCOPAL CHURCH IN SHREVEPORT, LOUISIANA, 1839-1916. *North Louisiana Hist. Assoc. J. 1978 9(4): 193-203.* The Episcopal Church is the oldest Protestant Church in Louisiana and has the oldest congregation in Shreveport. Following a visit to northwestern Louisiana in 1838 by the young and newly-elected Bishop of Louisiana, Leonidas Polk, the first services were conducted in 1839. St. Paul's church was formally organized in 1845; its name was changed to St. Mark's in 1850. By 1916 the church had seen the services of 10 rectors and was the largest Episcopal church in Shreveport, thus fulfilling Polk's prophecy: "The place has a promising future." Based on the Polk Papers, Jesse duPont Library archives, University of the South, the Journal of the Diocese of Louisiana, files of St. Mark's church and secondary sources; 74 notes.          H. M. Parker, Jr.

2286. Gillespie, Paul and Head, Keith. GRANNY REED: A TESTIMONY. *Southern Exposure 1976 4(3): 33-37.* Interviews Granny Reed, a member of the Church of God in North Carolina, about practices such as faith healing and speaking in tongues, and about her own religious beliefs and interpretations of the Bible.

2287. Gilliam, Will D. ROBERT JEFFERSON BRECKENRIDGE, 1800-1871. *Register of the Kentucky Hist. Soc. 1974 72(3): 207-223, (4): 319-336.* Part 1. Breckenridge's public career as a lawyer, legislator, minister, editor, educator, and college president extended from the 1820's to his resignation as head of the Danville Theological Seminary in 1869. Breckenridge favored gradual emancipation and African colonization of freed slaves, and detested abolitionists. He believed in predestination and the authority of the Bible. He was influential in the establishment of Kentucky's public school system. Based on primary and secondary sources; illus., 27 notes. Part 2. Covers the period from 1832 and emphasizes Presbyterian Breckenridge's importance to his denomination. His views owed much to the writings of Samuel Miller, second professor elected to Princeton Theological Seminary. He endorsed a supernatural Christianity, and the infallibility of the Scriptures. The writings of his grandson, Benjamin Breckinridge Warfield, who was on the Princeton faculty 1887-1921, continued many of Breckenridge's arguments. Breckenridge had accepted his views on faith, but Warfield had a scholarly basis for his understanding. Includes

an account of Breckinridge's debate on slavery with George Thompson in Glasgow in 1836. Primary and secondary sources; 17 notes.          J. F. Paul

2288. Gizycki, Horst von. ALTERNATIVE LEBENSFORMEN (3): DIE CHRISTLICHE KOMMUNITÄT DER KOINONIA-PARTNER IN GEORGIA [Alternative life styles (3): the Christian community of the Koinonia Partners in Georgia]. *Frankfurter Hefte [West Germany] 1976 31(3): 35-42.* Discusses the philosophy and history of Koinonia Farm, a Christian commune founded in Georgia in 1942 by Clarence Jordan; covers 1942-60's.

2289. Golding, Gordon. "THAT OLD TIME RELIGION": PORTRAIT DE LA RELIGION TRADITIONNALISTE DES BLANCS DU SUD, 1950-1970 ["That old time religion": traditionalist religion for Southern whites, 1950-70]. *Rev. Française d'Études Américaines [France] 1981 6(12): 247-258.* Discusses the role of established Southern Protestant churches in the community life of the South in articulating as well as formulating opinion on issues ranging from the desegregation of public schools to support of US intervention in the Vietnam War and the Korean War.

2290. Gorman, Frederick J. E. and DiBlasi, Michael. GRAVESTONE ICONOGRAPHY AND MORTUARY IDEOLOGY. *Ethnohistory 1981 28(1): 79-98.* Examines 18th and early 19th century mortuary ideology in South Carolina and Georgia as it was conditioned by religious, social and economic factors. Hypotheses about mortuary concepts are derived from the ethnohistory of Euro-American religion, society and economy in these two colonies. The test implications of these hypotheses consist of expectations about the patterning of gravestone iconography which is assumed to be the material correlate of mortuary ideas during this era. Inference about various mortuary values is based upon statistical evaluation of the iconography of a sample of over three hundred gravestones in six southeastern colonial cemeteries. A comparison of these beliefs among South Carolinians and Georgians with the mortuary ideology of colonial New Englanders yields some surprising similarities and differences.          J

2291. Gravely, William B. A BLACK METHODIST ON RECONSTRUCTION IN MISSISSIPPI: THREE LETTERS BY JAMES LYNCH IN 1868-1869. *Methodist Hist. 1973 11(4): 2-18.* Reprints three letters of 1868-69 in the Matthew Simpson Papers at the Library of Congress from James Lynch (1839-72), black minister of the Methodist Episcopal Church, to Bishop Matthew Simpson (1811-84). Lynch discussed the need to extend the work of the Methodist Episcopal Church in Mississippi during Reconstruction, the need for educational facilities for blacks, and his own political and preaching career. The editor provides biographical data on Lynch and information on the activities of the Methodist Episcopal churches in the South after the Civil War. Based on Methodist periodicals; 46 notes.          H. L. Calkin

2292. Gravely, William B. THE SOCIAL, POLITICAL AND RELIGIOUS SIGNIFICANCE OF THE COLORED METHODIST EPISCOPAL CHURCH (1870). *Methodist Hist. 1979 18(1): 3-25.* In 1865 the Methodist Episcopal Church, South faced the problem of the status of its black members, no longer slaves. The freedmen's options were: membership in the African Methodist Episcopal or the African Methodist Episcopal Zion churches, the southern church, or in northern Methodist missions. In 1870 the decision was made to form a separate organization for blacks, the Colored Methodist Episcopal Church. Under conditions of religious liberty and voluntary choice in religious matters, racial segregation was established institutionally. Based on denominational publications of the period and secondary works; 83 notes.          H. L. Calkin

2293. Gray, Sally M. JOSEPH CARDEN'S "MOST PERFECT" CHURCH. *Chronicles of Oklahoma 1981 59(1): 73-82.* When Right Reverend Francis Key Brooke, first Episcopal bishop to Oklahoma, arrived at Ardmore in 1893, there was no church. By 1907, however, the congregation had grown to 85 members and gradual improvements were being added to the original wooden structure. St. Philip's Church received a major boost when Reverend Joseph Carden became rector and launched the crusade to build a permanent brick structure. With his new church finally completed in 1927, Carden retired from active ministry. Based on *The Oklahoma Churchman* (1925); 7 photos, 18 notes.

M. L. Tate

2294. Green, Jesse C., Jr. THE EARLY VIRGINIA ARGUMENT FOR SEPARATION OF CHURCH AND STATE. *Baptist Hist. and Heritage 1976 11(1): 16-26.* The struggle (ca. 1775-1810) of Virginia Baptists for the disestablishment of the state church and the privilege of freedom of religion for all men has had great implications for both the church and state in America. Three doctrines served as the foundation for the Baptist position: the nature of salvation, the nature of the church, and a belief in the necessity for the separation of civil and ecclesiastical authority. Baptists did not achieve separation of church and state alone (for the active aid of Jefferson and Madison was also a considerable factor), but did serve as a constant reminder of the necessity of securing what they believed to be the inalienable rights of men. Based largely on the writings of John Leland and other primary sources; 62 notes.

H. M. Parker, Jr.

2295. Gundersen, Joan R. THE SEARCH FOR GOOD MEN: RECRUITING MINISTERS IN COLONIAL VIRGINIA. *Hist. Mag. of the Protestant Episcopal Church 1979 48(4): 453-464.* Challenges the thesis that, in colonial Virginia, the Anglican Church failed to find good men to serve its churches, or lacked quality among its candidates. Focuses on how Virginians, including George Washington, did find enough suitable men for a greatly expanding church. By 1776, in contrast to 1726, the number of priests had increased to 109 from 42, and more than half were colonial-born, in contrast to none 50 years earlier. Based on author's doctoral dissertation; the Fulham Palace Manuscripts, Virginia Colonial Records Project microfilm; published collections of letters and secondary sources; 2 fig., 58 notes.

H. M. Parker, Jr.

2296. Gundersen, Joan Rezner. THE MYTH OF THE INDEPENDENT VIRGINIA VESTRY. *Hist. Mag. of the Protestant Episcopal Church 1975 44(2): 133-141.* In the 17th century the Virginia vestry kept close control of the right to hire and dismiss the parish parson. This situation changed drastically after 1700, and by mid-century the vestry had lost any effective control over the parish minister; some vestries were faced with frequent elections. The changed condition, which most historians fail to see, is traceable largely to Commissary James Blair, who worked very closely with the Virginia governors to protect the clergy on the one hand, and to check the high-handed vestry on the other. By 1750 it was all but impossible for the vestry to get rid of incompetent clergy. Based on primary sources; 33 notes.

H. M. Parker, Jr.

2297. Halbrooks, G. Thomas. CHURCH MEMBERSHIP TRENDS IN THE TWENTIETH CENTURY. *Baptist Hist. and Heritage 1981 16(1): 35-44.* Discusses the increase in Southern Baptists' membership particularly during the 1960's and 1970's, due to changing values, demographic and economic changes, and to institutional factors such as the Baptist theology of evangelism and missions, effective programs and structures, a sense of identity, and unity in diversity.

2298. Halbrooks, G. Thomas. GROWING PAINS: THE IMPACT OF EXPANSION ON SOUTHERN BAPTISTS SINCE 1942. *Baptist Hist. and Heritage 1982 17(3): 44-54.* Discusses the impact of the expansion of the Southern Baptist Convention into California, Oregon, Illinois, New Mexico, and Arizona during 1942-78.

2299. Hall, Bob. CASE STUDY: COCA-COLA AND METHODISM. *Southern Exposure 1976 4(3): 98-101.* Examines the Methodist Church in the South since the 1840's, aid from the shareholders of the Coca-Cola Company in 1898, and religious education in the form of Emory University and Vanderbilt University.

2300. Hamovitch, Mitzi Berger. MY LIFE I WILL NOT LET THEE GO EXCEPT THOU BLESS ME: AN INTERVIEW WITH JANET LEWIS. *Southern Rev. 1982 18(2): 299-313.* Presents an interview with Southern poet Janet Lewis in which she discusses her life and work, and those of other poets.

2301. Hancock, Harold B., ed. WILLIAM MORGAN'S AUTOBIOGRAPHY AND DIARY: LIFE IN SUSSEX COUNTY, 1780-1857. *Delaware Hist. 1980 19(1): 39-52, (2): 106-126.* Part 1. Publishes the diary and excerpts from the autobiography of a Methodist Protestant minister residing in Sussex County, Delaware. The diary and autobiography relate William Morgan's childhood and education, his conversion experience, revivals, descriptions of church services and political rallies, his involvement with the Sons of Temperance, Sussex County social life, medical history of the region, and farming practices. As a preacher, farmer, and physician, Morgan touched the lives and interests of most inhabitants of the county. Illus., 28 notes. Part 2. Entries from William Morgan's diary from 1829 until Morgan's death in 1857 recount the effort to introduce silk culture in Delaware, July 4th celebrations, the author's meetings with (and assessments of) various religious figures (principally Methodists) and politicians in Delaware, revivals, the Millerite movement, fishing, sharp dealings at the Cannon Ferry, shipbuilding and sailing, and Sussex County social life, medical practices, and farming. 65 notes.

R. M. Miller

2302. Harrington, Michael L. EVANGELICISM AND RACISM IN THE DEVELOPMENT OF SOUTHERN RELIGION. *Mississippi Q. 1974 27(2): 201-209.* Review essay on John B. Boles' *The Great Revival, 1785-1805: The Origins of the Southern Evangelical Mind* (Lexington: U. Press of Kentucky, 1972) and H. Shelton Smith's *In His Image, But...: Racism in Southern Religion* (Durham, N.C.: Duke U. Press, 1972).

2303. Harris, Waldo P., III. DANIEL MARSHALL: LONE GEORGIA BAPTIST REVOLUTIONARY PASTOR. *Viewpoints: Georgia Baptist Hist. 1976 5: 51-64.* Daniel Marshall, a convert to the Baptist Church, became a minister in that religion; examines his political stand during and following the American Revolution, and covers the period 1747-1823.

2304. Harris, Waldo P., III. LOCATIONS ASSOCIATED WITH DANIEL MARSHALL AND THE KIOKEE CHURCH. *Viewpoints: Georgia Baptist Hist. 1978 (6): 25-46.* Chronicles the settlement of land belonging to Daniel Marshall on Great Kiokee Creek in Richmond County, Georgia, 1784-1819, and discusses his work establishing the Kiokee Church, an all-black Baptist Church.

2305. Hartwell, Charles K., Mrs. MOBILE TO CHINA: A VALIANT WOMAN'S MISSION. *Alabama Rev. 1978 31(4): 243-255.* Describes Mary Horton Stuart's (1842-1926) early life in Mobile, Alabama, and the 39 years she spent as a Presbyterian missionary in Hangchow, Nanking, and Peking. Of her four sons, John L. Stuart became president of Yenching University and US ambassador to China, and Warren Stuart became president of Hangchow College. Primary and secondary sources; 48 notes.

J. F. Vivian

2306. Hays, Brooks. REFLECTIONS ON THE ROLE OF BAPTISTS IN POLITICS AND THE FUTURE OF AMERICA. *Baptist Hist. and Heritage 1976 11(3): 169-178.* The author, former president of the Southern Baptist Convention, gives his "authentic hopes" for the church on the threshold of America's third century: attitudinal conditioning for leadership in social and political action, working toward a better relationship with other religious bodies, pleading for help for the socially and economically deprived, accentuating concern for a strong public school system, and continuing efforts to strengthen the denomination's own educational structure.

H. M. Parker, Jr.

2307. Hennesey, James. ROMAN CATHOLICISM: THE MARYLAND TRADITION. *Thought 1976 51(202): 282-295.* Distinguishes between two Roman Catholic traditions, a distinctively Anglo-American Catholicism which survives well into the 19th century, and an ultramontane Catholicism which reflects the preoccupations of the European continent. Colonial Maryland played a part in the development of the first tradition's ideas concerning the freedom of conscience and the separation of Church and state.

J. C. English

2308. Herring, Reuben. SOUTHERN BAPTIST CONVENTION RESOLUTIONS ON THE FAMILY. *Baptist Hist. and Heritage 1982 17(1): 36-45, 64.* Reprints resolutions related to the family passed by the Southern Baptist Convention from 1863 to 1980, but mainly from the 1970's, on issues such as abortion, homosexuality, marriage and divorce, women's and children's rights, and sex education; discusses the Southern Baptist stand on other issues such as alcohol use, pornography, and television morality.

2309. Hertzberg, Steven. THE JEWISH COMMUNITY OF ATLANTA FROM THE END OF THE CIVIL WAR UNTIL THE END OF THE FRANK CASE. *Am. Jewish Hist. Q. 1973 62(3): 250-287.* Atlanta's Jewish community was by 1913 the largest in a South transformed by urbanization, industrialization, and Negro emancipation. There were more than 1,200 Jewish immigrants from Eastern Europe by 1910. Under the leadership of Rabbi David Marx (1872-1962) the established German Jews were led into classical Reform, while the East European and Levantine settlers maintained various forms of traditional Judaism. Thus two separate communities were created. Only in philanthropic activities did the two cooperate. In Atlanta and throughout the United States during this period, discrimination against even the established community of Western European Jews was increasing, setting the stage for the Leo M. Frank tragedy of 1913. 84 notes.          F. Rosenthal

2310. Hildebrand, Reginald F. METHODIST EPISCOPAL POLICY ON THE ORDINATION OF BLACK MINISTERS, 1784-1864. *Methodist Hist. 1982 20(3): 124-142.* Following the establishment of the Methodist Episcopal Church in 1784, some black preachers were ordained as deacons but were not permitted to perform the sacraments at that level in the hierarchy of ordained clergy. As a result many of them left to organize their own denominations. Various proposals were made to change this, and finally in 1864 blacks were permitted to organize a mission conference within the Methodist Episcopal Church. Their status was changed four years later to that of an annual conference, together with the ordination that they sought. Based on journals and other publications of the Methodist Episcopal Church; 53 notes.          H. L. Calkin

2311. Hill, A. Shrady. THE PARSON'S CAUSE. *Hist. Mag. of the Protestant Episcopal Church 1977 46(1): 5-35.* Salaries of colonial Virginia Anglican ministers were paid in tobacco. When the demand for tobacco was high, the clergy prospered; when low, they suffered. Prices were not stable, hence there was considerable uncertainty from year to year over what the clergy could expect in purchasing power. Treats not only the economic ramifications of the arrangement but also deals with the political aspects of a state-supported clergy in an area that was becoming increasingly hostile to Anglicanism. Patrick Henry earned some of his early honors by opposing state support to the established church. Even the courts openly defied the English government. At the same time, the indifference of the clergy toward the colonists failed to gain the support or the respect of the latter. Primary and secondary sources; 79 notes, 2 appendixes.          H. M. Parker, Jr.

2312. Hites, Margaret Ann. PETER DOUB, 1796-1869, HIS CONTRIBUTION TO THE RELIGIOUS AND EDUCATIONAL DEVELOPMENT OF NORTH CAROLINA. *Methodist Hist. 1973 11(4): 19-45.* Doub, a Methodist Episcopal preacher in North Carolina, was active in expanding the work of the church in that area, in developing educational facilities for women, and in the church controversy over slavery. Based on Doub's autobiography, journal, and letters in the Perkins Library, Duke University; 71 notes.          H. L. Calkin

2313. Holder, Ray. METHODIST BEGINNINGS IN NEW ORLEANS 1813-1814. *Louisiana Hist. 1977 18(2): 171-187.* Under orders from the Methodist General Conferences of 1812, itinerant preacher William Winans endeavored to establish Methodism in New Orleans, Louisiana, in 1813-14 with a school and church. He faced considerable opposition in New Orleans, and he believed he

did not accomplish much. Not until 1825 did "the continuous history of Methodism in New Orleans" begin. Based on Winans' unfinished autobiography and secondary sources; 80 notes.          R. L. Woodward, Jr.

2314. Holifield, E. Brooks. MERCERSBURG, PRINCETON, AND THE SOUTH: THE SACRAMENTAL CONTROVERSY IN THE NINETEENTH CENTURY. *J. of Presbyterian Hist. 1976 54(2): 238-257.* Delineates connections between John W. Nevin's Mercersburg mystical presence position on the Lord's Supper and its reception by John B. Adger of Columbia Seminary in South Carolina, and the reaction of Princeton's scion Charles Hodge and connections to Union Seminary in Richmond, Virginia, as represented by Robert L. Dabney. Based almost wholly on the writings of these four men, plus dissertations on Nevin and Hodge; 2 illus., 54 notes.          H. M. Parker, Jr.

2315. Holifield, E. Brooks. THOMAS SMYTH: THE SOCIAL IDEAS OF A SOUTHERN EVANGELIST. *J. of Presbyterian Hist. 1973 51(1): 24-40.* Thomas Smyth, a South Carolina pastor in the Presbyterian Church, 1831-70, was concerned with theological ideologies of social order and developed a theological rationale for social conservatism without entirely abandoning Lockean tradition.

2316. Holmes, David L. DEVEREUX JARRATT: A LETTER AND A REEVALUATION. *Hist. Mag. of the Protestant Episcopal Church 1978 47(1): 37-49.* A revisionist interpretation of the Virginia Episcopal priest, Devereux Jarratt (1733-1801), who was largely responsible for reviving the Episcopal Church in Virginia after the Revolution. Suggests that a closer analysis of his *Life* reveals layers of complexity as interesting for what it said as for what it left unsaid. The letter was written a few weeks before his death. It displays some of the characteristics of his career—an abiding fellowship for those with whom he agreed, a brotherly feeling for other evangelical denominations, a love for the Bible, a wide background in secular literature, a devotion to Reformation doctrine, a modified Calvinism, a sense of being out of place in his Church and the world, and a resultant striving to be "entirely abstracted from this world." Since few of Jarratt's writings have surfaced the letter is valuable. Based largely on Jarratt's *Life* and includes the letter which was found in the Archives and Historical Collections of the Episcopal Church; 45 notes.          H. M. Parker, Jr.

2317. Hoobler, James A. KARNAK ON THE CUMBERLAND. *Tennessee Hist. Q. 1976 35(3): 251-262.* Provides a narrative history of the First Presbyterian Church in Nashville, Tennessee, from its organization in 1814 to 1976. Mentions the church's ministers, architectural history, and more important worshippers; and discusses use of the church as a conference and community center. During the Civil War it was an Army hospital, and in 1907 it was the site of the national meeting of the Women's Christian Temperance Union. Based on primary and secondary sources; 2 illus., 20 notes.          A. E. Wiederrecht

2318. Hood, R. E. FROM A HEADSTART TO A DEADSTART: THE HISTORICAL BASIS FOR BLACK INDIFFERENCE TOWARD THE EPISCOPAL CHURCH 1800-1860. *Hist. Mag. of the Protestant Episcopal Church 1982 51(3): 269-296.* By examining the antebellum South where most slaves resided and where the Episcopal Church was quite strong (Virginia, North and South Carolina, and Georgia), two principal reasons emerge for the indifference of blacks toward the Episcopal Church: the Great Awakening, which accounted for large-scale conversions of blacks to the Baptist and Methodist churches, and the bafflement of white Episcopal clergymen as they encountered black religious piety. Negroes entered the Baptist and Methodist churches for three reasons: 1) the ministants of the Anglican clergy were unwilling to make adaptations to meet the religious needs and expressions of slaves; 2) the Episcopalians were slow to move into the new Southern frontiers; and 3) the church was unwilling to raise up in the South an indigenous black clergy to minister to blacks. These factors undermine the traditional view that blacks entered the Baptist and Methodist churches because they had an innate emotional nature that led

them to identify with those churches. Based on various Diocesan *Journals* and studies in the black American religious experience; 124 notes.
H. M. Parker, Jr.

2319. Hughes, Richard B. WILLIAM STUART RED, HISTORI-AN: APPRECIATION AND CRITICISM. *Southwestern Hist. Q. 1976 79(3): 296-300.* William Stuart Red (1857-1933), though not a professional historian, helped preserve important primary sources in Texas religious history and wrote on the role of religion in the 19th-century Texas frontier. Based on primary sources; 8 notes.
J. H. Broussard

2320. Hulan, Richard. JOHN ADAM GRANADE: THE "WILD MAN" OF GOOSE CREEK. *Western Folklore 1974 33(1): 77-87.* Traces the career of the noted American Methodist revivalist minister and camp meeting hymnist, John Adam Granade (d. 1807). Comments on his best-known hymns. Based on primary and secondary sources; 30 notes, appendix.
S. L. Myres

2321. Humphrey, Richard A. DEVELOPMENT OF RELIGION IN SOUTHERN APPALACHIA: THE PERSONAL QUALITY. *Appalachian J. 1974 1(4): 244-254.* The emphasis on personal religious experience which coincides with the life style of the mountain environment accounts for the predominance of Baptists and Methodists over Presbyterians.
S

2322. Hunter, Lloyd A. MARK TWAIN AND THE SOUTHERN EVANGELICAL MIND. *Missouri Hist. Soc. Bull. 1977 33(4): 246-264.* Analyzes the ways in which the South's particularistic "evangelical faith" influenced the life and thought of Mark Twain. Twain was unable to avoid the religious evangelistic spirit that prevailed on the southern frontier where he resided, though he increasingly disagreed with many aspects of southern evangelical pietism. He resisted those features that he considered intolerant of individual conscience or repressive to individual humanitarian impulses. Based on Clemens' writings and secondary sources; 5 pictures, 74 notes.
H. T. Lovin

2323. Igleheart, Glenn A. ECUMENICAL CONCERNS AMONG SOUTHERN BAPTISTS. *J. of Ecumenical Studies 1980 17(2): 49-61.* Begins with Southern Baptist openness to ecumenism before 1919. Between 1919 and 1964, Southern Baptists particularly feared that ecumenism was common denominator Christianity bent on the development of a super church. In the 1950's and 1960's, particularly at Southern Baptist theological seminaries, a warming trend toward ecumenism was evident. By 1964, a new period of openness in terms of communication and cooperation with other Christian groups was evident in Southern Baptist churches. What the new trend means in terms of local ecumenism, inter-Baptist cooperation, and interdenominational cooperation is described.
J. A. Overbeck

2324. Isaac, Rhys. EVANGELICAL REVOLT: THE NATURE OF THE BAPTISTS' CHALLENGE TO THE TRADITIONAL ORDER IN VIRGINIA, 1765 TO 1775. *William and Mary Q. 1974 31(3): 345-368.* Describes the rise of the Baptist Church in Virginia, with emphasis on evangelicalism and social life. Contrasts the austerity of the Baptists with the Anglican establishment. Baptist church discipline, mistaken by the gentry for radicalism, served to ameliorate disorder. Comments on the struggle for religious toleration and poses questions about the relation of religion to popular culture. Based chiefly on church records and contemporary journals; 60 notes.
H. M. Ward

2325. Isaac, Rhys. RELIGION AND AUTHORITY: PROBLEMS OF THE ANGLICAN ESTABLISHMENT IN THE ERA OF THE GREAT AWAKENING AND THE PARSONS' CAUSE. *William and Mary Q. 1973 30(1): 3-36.* Traces the internal problems of the church during the breaking up of the coordinate relationship between church and state in Virginia, including vestry disputes, the negative image and low status of the clergy, and clerical corporatist ambitions. Anticlericalism was dramatically abetted by the Parsons' Cause, the trial of the Reverend John Brunskill, and the dismissal of the Reverend Thomas Robinson from the College. The dissent-

ers' influence was growing; and as church power waned, so did the authority of the gentry establishment. Based on church and court records and on secondary sources; 2 tables, 134 notes.
H. M. Ward

2326. Jackson, Hermione Dannelly. WIFE NUMBER TWO: ELIZA G. SEXTON SHUCK, THE FIRST BAPTIST FOREIGN MISSIONARY FROM ALABAMA. *Baptist Hist. and Heritage 1973 8(2): 69-78.* Church history of a Baptist missionary to China.

2327. Jackson, Irene V. MUSIC AMONG BLACKS IN THE EPISCOPAL CHURCH: SOME PRELIMINARY CONSIDERATIONS. *Hist. Mag. of the Protestant Episcopal Church 1980 49(1): 21-35.* Discusses music among black Episcopalians from the antebellum period to 1975. In the first period blacks contributed to the growing body of Afro-American religious folksong, later to be known as spirituals. "Let us Break Bread Together on our Knees" originated at this time, and even organs appeared in black Episcopal churches. After the Civil War a black "cultivated" tradition appeared in contrast to "folk" or "vernacular" tradition. Now one group is making an effort to move from a hymnbook tradition to a strictly oral one, with music and text being so familiar to the people that they may enter into the worship service without being bound to the printed page. Author hopes the article will stimulate more studies in this field. Secondary sources; 45 notes.
H. M. Parker, Jr.

2328. Jentz, John. A NOTE ON GENOVESE'S ACCOUNT OF THE SLAVES' RELIGION. *Civil War Hist. 1977 23(2): 161-169.* Eugene D. Genovese's *Roll, Jordan, Roll* deserves critical attention, as in its argument that the slaves' religion was unconducive to millenarianism, hence to a revolutionary political tradition. Millenarianism, as shown in popular black movements, probably did exist; there were not such exaggerated differences between black and white Baptist or Methodist Christianity. Genovese's own account makes the planter regime so pervasively powerful that revolutionary solutions would have been suicidal. His argument "distorts his provocative interpretation of the slaves' religion." Based on secondary sources; 28 notes.
R. E. Stack

2329. Jobson, Robert C. JOHN CLARK BAYLESS, A KENTUCKY PRESBYTERIAN MINISTER, 1841-1875. *Filson Club Hist. Q. 1983 57(2): 188-206.* John Clark Bayless was educated at Centre College and Princeton Theological Seminary and entered the ministry. He served as pastor for Presbyterian churches in West Virginia, Indiana, and Kentucky. Despite poor health, Bayless proved to be an effective preacher and attracted many members to his congregations. Based on an unpublished family history and papers; 65 notes.
G. B. McKinney

2330. Jones, George Fenwick. JOHN MARTIN BOLTZIUS' TRIP TO CHARLESTON OCTOBER 1742. *South Carolina Hist. Mag. 1981 82(2): 87-110.* In October 1742, Pastor John Martin Boltzius,, a respected leader of the Lutheran Church in Georgia, met with Henry Melchoir Mühlenberg to familiarize Mühlenberg with America before he organized a Lutheran Church in Philadelphia. Although Boltzius had hoped to accompany Mühlenberg from Georgia to Philadelphia, poor health prevented Boltzius from going beyond Charleston, South Carolina. On the journey from Ebenezer, Georgia, to Charleston, Boltzius's diary recorded information on travel, slavery, and religious activities. 47 notes.
R. H. Tomlinson

2331. Jones, Loyal. OLD-TIME BAPTISTS AND MAINLINE CHRISTIANITY. *Appalachian J. 1977 4(4): 120-130.* Similarities and distinctions between the fundamentalism and practices of Appalachia's Baptist sects reflect an earlier age in American religious beliefs, and are combined with criticisms of mountain religion and several extended quotes conveying local attitudes toward religion.

2332. Jones, Loyal. STUDYING MOUNTAIN RELIGION. *Appalachian J. 1978 5(1): 125-130.* Annotated bibliography of studies of Protestantism in Appalachia, 1905-75; warns researchers against judgmentalism.

2333. Jordan, Terry G. FOREST FOLK, PRAIRIE FOLK: RURAL RELIGIOUS CULTURE IN NORTH TEXAS. *Southwestern Hist. Q. 1976 80(2): 135-162.* In Cooke and Denton Counties, Texas, fundamentalists from the upper South settled the "Cross Timbers" oak forest and German Catholics settled the prairie land. Rural church architecture shows the cultural differences in the stern, one-room white frame "folk chapel" and the elaborate German "cathedral." Cemetery arrangements and customs also are quite different; German orderliness, attention to family history, and sense of community contrast with the southern Protestant simplicity and emphasis on family. Primary and secondary sources; 18 illus., 2 tables, 28 notes.
J. H. Broussard

2334. Jordan, Terry G. A RELIGIOUS GEOGRAPHY OF THE HILL COUNTRY GERMANS OF TEXAS. Luebke, Frederick C., ed. *Ethnicity on the Great Plains* (Lincoln: U. of Nebraska Pr., for the Center for Great Plains Studies, 1980): 109-128. Provides a religious geography of the German Hill Country of south-central Texas. Reviews the history of the several denominations in the area—Lutherans, Evangelicals, Methodists, Catholics—and of freethinkers, from 1844 through 1910. Maps their locations and reveals varying patterns of residential segregation and spatial organization. Studies the distinctive architecture of German church buildings erected before 1910. Notes that in burial practice radical departures from European custom have occurred. Despite varying degrees of acculturation, much evidence of German ethnicity survives in the Hill Country today. Secondary sources; table, 9 fig., 20 notes.
J. Powell

2335. Juárez, José Roberto. LA IGLESIA CATÓLICA Y EL CHICANO EN SUD TEXAS, 1836-1911. [The Catholic Church and the Chicano in southern Texas, 1836-1911]. *Aztlán 1973 4(2): 217-255.*

2336. Kaganoff, Nathan M. AN ORTHODOX RABBINATE IN THE SOUTH: TOBIAS GEFFEN, 1870-1970. *Am. Jewish Hist. 1983 73(1): 56-70.* Tobias Geffen left his Lithuanian homeland after the 1903 Kishinev pogrom, served briefly as a rabbi in New York City and Canton, Ohio, and then for nearly 60 years was rabbi of the Congregation Shearith Israel of Atlanta, where, in addition to supporting community educational and charity enterprises, he established religious schools, helped make local food products kosher, served the needs of Jewish soldiers and prisoners, and deftly handled so many religious issues that for years he was recognized as the Orthodox authority for Southern Jews. Though not as unemotional as the typical Lithuanian rabbinic scholar, he epitomized the immigrant rabbi, whose Old World Orthodoxy could not survive into the second generation. Based on the Rabbi Tobias Geffen Papers in the American Jewish Historical Society and other primary sources; 34 notes.
R. A. Keller

2337. Kane, Steven M. HOLY GHOST PEOPLE: THE SNAKE-HANDLERS OF SOUTHERN APPALACHIA. *Appalachian J. 1974 1(4): 255-262.* Discusses the Pentecostal Holiness Church and George Went Hensley, 1909-73.
S

2338. Kane, Steven M. RITUAL POSSESSION IN A SOUTHERN APPALACHIAN RELIGIOUS SECT. *J. of Am. Folklore 1974 87(346): 293-302.* The possession trances of southern Appalachian serpent-handling sects are stylized, controlled, and conventional activities adopted by people well-adjusted to their Pentecostal religious environment. The "power" of these trances includes glossolalia, serpent and fire handling, strychnine drinking, miracle working, casting out devils, healing, prophecy, and discerning spirits. Based on fieldwork during 1972-74 and secondary sources; 9 notes.
W. D. Piersen

2339. Kariel, Audrey Daniels. THE JEWISH STORY AND MEMORIES OF MARSHALL, TEXAS. *Western States Jewish Hist. Q. 1982 14(3): 195-206.* Jews were among the pioneer settlers of Marshall, Texas, founded in 1842. Many of them came from Syracuse, New York, in the 1850's, including the Doppelmayer, Wolf, Exstein, Grossman, Bernstein, and Weisman families. By 1868, the Jewish community was large enough to organize a benevolent society. There followed a B'nai B'rith lodge in 1876 and Sab-

bath school in 1877; in 1887 the Moses Montefiore Congregation, Adath Israel, was organized. A declining Jewish population in the 1960's and 70's forced the congregation to merge with that of Longview, Texas. Based on newspaper articles and records in the Harrison County Historical Museum; 4 photos, 36 notes.
B. S. Porter

2340. Kessel, Elizabeth A. "A MIGHTY FORTRESS IS OUR GOD": GERMAN RELIGIOUS AND EDUCATIONAL ORGANIZATIONS ON THE MARYLAND FRONTIER, 1734-1800. *Maryland Hist. Mag. 1982 77(4): 370-387.* At the end of the 18th century, after three generations of German Lutheran, Reformed, and sectarian congregational life in Frederick County, Maryland, German spirituality on the frontier continued to be strong. Wars, intolerance, economic hardships, and pressures from the Anglican Church did not prevent German settlers from establishing and sustaining religious and educational institutions. Affected by colonial conditions, German churches in Frederick County were always a blend of the old and new, but were endowed with features which "became hallmarks of American Protestantism: voluntarism; congregationalism; denominationalism; independence from European churches; and adherence to separation of church and state." Archival and other primary sources; 2 tables; 76 notes.
G. J. Bobango

2341. King, Bernard D. THE TWO KINGS. *Viewpoints: Georgia Baptist Hist. 1980 7: 17-26.* Remembrance of Georgia Baptists Spencer B. King, Sr. (b. 1880), a preacher, and his son Spencer B. King, Jr. (b. 1904), who taught history at Mercer University through 1973.

2342. King, Spencer B., Jr. BAPTIST LEADERS IN EARLY GEORGIA POLITICS. *Viewpoints: Georgia Baptist Hist. 1976 5: 45-50.* Covers 1772-1823.

2343. Kirby, Rich. AND WE'LL SING TOGETHER. *Southern Exposure 1976 4(3): 4-9.* Discusses Southern mountain religious music, including beginnings in the 18th century, its use in revivalistic situations, and contemporary songbooks.

2344. Krebs, Sylvia. FUNERAL MEATS AND SECOND MARRIAGES: ALABAMA CHURCHES IN THE PRESIDENTIAL RECONSTRUCTION PERIOD. *Alabama Hist. Q. 1975 37(3): 206-216.* The division in the churches continued following the Civil War, and unification did not occur as some expected, except with the Episcopalians. The problems of the churches were many, but mostly economic, social, and morale-oriented. The factors causing a continuation of division are discussed, as well as the reasons for Episcopal reunion. 35 notes.
E. E. Eminhizer

2345. Kurtz, Ernest. THE TRAGEDY OF SOUTHERN RELIGION. *Georgia Hist. Q. 1982 66(2): 217-247.* Discusses the complex background and reasons for the inability of Southern white Christians to accept the position known as neoorthodoxy, with its focus on "human finitude" and the limitations inherent in the "human experience" during the 1930's. Secondary sources; 132 notes.
G. R. Schroeder

2346. Ledbetter, Patsy. DEFENSE OF THE FAITH: J. FRANK NORRIS AND TEXAS FUNDAMENTALISM, 1920-1929. *Arizona and the West 1973 15(1): 45-62.* Urban growth, loss of individualism, and increased industrialization were regarded as a threat to the traditional values of a predominantly rural nation. This and a backlash from the fervor of the European war years brought a wave of reaction to liberal and scientific thought throughout the country in the 1920's. Religious fundamentalism among the Protestant sects was one of the most important aspects of this reaction. It was basically a response to the attempt of liberal theology to reconcile modern science with Christianity. In Texas, a predominantly rural state with industrialization imminent, fundamentalist sentiment became especially intense in the 1920's. Textbook censorship, agitation in the state legislature, and disturbances in the Protestant churches affected all segments of the population. John Franklyn Norris (1877-1952), a Baptist evangelist known as the "Texas Tornado," led the crusade in the state against alcohol, gambling, Catholicism, Sunday movies, and religious modernism. 5 illus., 32 notes.                                                    D. L. Smith

2347. Lee, Jerry J. SEPARATION AND CRYSTALLIZATION OF NORTHWEST GEORGIA PRIMITIVE BAPTISTS. *Viewpoints: Georgia Baptist Hist. 1974 4: 39-53.*

2348. Letsinger, Norman H. THE STATUS OF WOMEN IN THE SOUTHERN BAPTIST CONVENTION IN HISTORICAL PERSPECTIVE. *Baptist Hist. and Heritage 1977 12(1): 37-44.* The status of women in Southern Baptist circles has improved from a time when women were forbidden to speak in church or serve in positions of leadership to the present where a woman has been elected to a top position of leadership in the Southern Baptist Convention. Although women have not achieved a position of leadership in the Convention concomitant with their role in the local churches and in proportion to their numbers, abilities, and experiences, they have become significantly more involved as messengers (delegates) to the Convention and as members of committees, boards and commissions of the Convention. Based on annual records of the Southern Baptist Convention and records and histories of associations; 62 notes.                          H. M. Parker, Jr.

2349. Liggin, Edna. A SHORT CONCISE HISTORY OF THE CONCORD BAPTIST ASSOCIATION. *North Louisiana Hist. Assoc. J. 1976 7(3): 101-103.* On 3 November 1832, 15 representatives from four of the eight Baptist churches then in existence between the Ouachita and Red Rivers in North Louisiana "met at Black Lake Church in what is now Webster Parish to constitute the Concord Missionary Baptist Association." The word "missionary" was later dropped from the association's name. These churches previously had belonged to the Louisiana Baptist Association, which was almost disrupted by the action of the original 15 "Concord Men." The association counted 17 member churches in 1845, the year the Southern Baptist Convention met for the first time. In 1846, the association was large enough to divide its territory, and by 1900, "the original Concord Association had expanded into at least twenty-three smaller associations." In 1972, after 140 years, the association represented 35 churches and had a membership of 14,447.                                                      A. N. Garland

2350. Lord, Clyde W. THE MINERAL SPRINGS HOLINESS CAMP MEETINGS. *Louisiana Hist. 1975 16(3): 257-277.* Soon after the Civil War the "National Camp Meeting Association for the Promotion of Holiness" was formed by a prominent group of Methodist clergymen. A rift between the holiness devotees and the Methodist conservative leadership developed and reached a crisis by the mid-1890's when several small holiness sects withdrew and formed the Church of the Nazarene. The camp meetings at Mineral Springs continued from 1903-26. By that time it had become evident that the defenders of Methodist conservatism were fighting a losing battle. Illus., 75 notes.                             E. P. Stickney

2351. Loveland, Anne C. PRESBYTERIANS AND REVIVALISM IN THE OLD SOUTH. *J. of Presbyterian Hist. 1979 57(1): 36-49.* Throughout the antebellum decades southern Presbyterians utilized the revival as an important source for ministerial candidates and as a way of encouraging support of benevolent programs. The revival was also considered a necessary safeguard of republicanism. Revivals were credited with improving the morality of the communities in which they were conducted. But above all, they were viewed as the chief means of adding members to the Presbyterian Church. Thus revivalism was an important and integral part of Presbyterian life in the Old South. Based on religious newspapers and publications and secondary sources; illus., 50 notes.
                                                          H. M. Parker, Jr.

2352. Loveland, Anne C. THE "SOUTHERN WORK" OF THE REVEREND JOSEPH C. HARTZELL, PASTOR OF AMES CHURCH IN NEW ORLEANS, 1870-1873. *Louisiana Hist. 1975 16(4): 391-407.* "Like most other Northern Methodist missionaries to the South, Hartzell saw no conflict in linking religious endeavors and Republican politics." Hartzell supervised three Methodist institutions for Negroes: Union Normal School, Thomson Institute, and

the Freedmen's Orphan Home which combined educational and missionary efforts. The response of Southern Whites to the educational and missionary work of the Northern Methodists among the freedmen was generally unsympathetic. Another reason for the loss of support was the Republicans ultimately abandoned the social and political goals of Reconstruction. Based largely on correspondence from the Hartzell and Baldwin Papers. Illus., 42 notes.
                                                          E. P. Stickney

2353. Mabee, Charles. THOMAS JEFFERSON'S ANTICLERICAL BIBLE. *Hist. Mag. of the Protestant Episcopal Church 1979 48(4): 473-481.* Thomas Jefferson's unpublished "scissors-and-paste" treatment of the gospels during 1813-20 reveals him as an American, not a Marcionite, and as a declericalizer rather than a demythologizer. In endeavoring to rid the scriptures of what he deemed to be priest-ridden interpretations, Jefferson inadvertently grasped one of the basic themes of the gospels: truth is not as it appears in this world. Demonstrates this by drawing attention to the positioning of the gospel passages in Jefferson's work. Thomas Jefferson thus emerges in the "prophetic and apologetic spirit of a true devotee of Jesus." Based on Jefferson's letters and secondary sources; 21 notes.                                         H. M. Parker, Jr.

2354. Maddex, Jack P. FROM THEOCRACY TO SPIRITUALITY: THE SOUTHERN PRESBYTERIAN REVERSAL ON CHURCH AND STATE. *J. of Presbyterian Hist. 1976 54(4): 438-457.* Challenges the premise that Southern Presbyterians embraced the doctrine of the spirituality of the Church before 1861. Claims that antebellum Southern Presbyterians did not teach consistently absolute separation of religion from politics, or even church from state. Most were proslavery social activists who worked through the church to defend slavery and reform its practice. Only during Reconstruction, in drastically altered circumstances, did they take up the cause of a non-secular church—borrowing the concept from the conservative Presbyterians in the border states, such as Stuart Robinson of Louisville. Based on official ecclesiastical documents, current church newspapers and secondary sources; 139 notes.
                                                          H. M. Parker, Jr.

2355. Maddex, Jack P., Jr. "THE SOUTHERN APOSTASY" REVISITED: THE SIGNIFICANCE OF PROSLAVERY CHRISTIANITY. *Marxist Perspectives 1979 2(3): 132-141.* Examines studies of religion in the South published between 1844 and 1977 and concludes that the hypothesis that proslavery Christianity was a conscientious religious expression of class ideology appears to accord with the ecclesiastical history of the Old South better than does the longstanding hypothesis that it was a superficial defensive argument devised by thelogians who, at heart, shared the "American" libertarian norms.

2356. Maguire, Marsha. CONFIRMING THE WORD. *Q. J. of the Lib. of Congress 1981 38(3): 166-179.* At the beginning of this century various fundamentalist sects in the rural regions of southern Appalachia pioneered the handling of poisonous snakes, handling of fire, and drinking of strychnine as demonstrations of their faith and the power of the Holy Spirit. These practices have since spread to urban industrial centers in Ohio, Indiana, Michigan, and California and have stimulated the interest of scholars in such disciplines as American studies, psychiatry, folklore, sociology, anthropology, social psychology, and various fields of medicine. While a few worshippers have died from snake bites, the incidence of being bitten while in a trance is remarkably low. Every Southern state except West Virginia has made snakehandling illegal. Secondary sources; 21 notes.                                                J. Powell

2357. Mariner, Kirk. THE NEGRO'S PLACE: VIRGINIA METHODISTS DEBATE UNIFICATION: 1924-1925. *Methodist Hist. 1980 18(3): 155-170.* In 1924 and 1925 a controversy arose in the Methodist Episcopal Church, South, regarding unification with the Methodist Episcopal Church (North). The real issue was race rather than unification since the southern Methodist Episcopal Church membership was almost totally white. In the ensuing debate in Virginia there was a great range of viewpoints on the racial issue. Without agreement on this issue, unification failed to be adopted at that time. Based on periodicals of the period and secondary sources; 78 notes.                                              H. L. Calkin

2358.   Martensen, Katherine A. REGION, RELIGION, AND SOCIAL ACTION: THE CATHOLIC COMMITTEE OF THE SOUTH, 1939-1956. *Catholic Hist. Rev. 1982 68(2): 249-267.* The Catholic Committee of the South (CCS) consisted of clerics and laymen who envisioned effecting social change in the modern South through the use of religious principles. The CCS grew out of two forces that blossomed in the 1930's: the maturation of the American Catholic social movement and the efforts by progressive Southerners to solve regional problems. During its 10 conventions, held from 1940 to 1953, the CCS confronted key Southern problems and offered often unpopular remedies. Victimized by the political and social fears that dominated much of the period, the CCS faded out of existence in the 1950's.                                              A

2359.   Martin, Junius J. GEORGIA'S FIRST MINISTER: THE REVEREND DR. HENRY HERBERT. *Georgia Hist. Q. 1982 66(2): 113-118.* Discusses what little is known about the career of the Reverend Henry Herbert (d. 1733), who came to Georgia with the first boatload of Oglethorpe's settlers, and demonstrates the possibility that the Anglican clergyman was the illegitimate son of Arthur Herbert (1647-1716), Earl of Torrington. 18 notes.
                                              G. R. Schroeder

2360.   Martin, Robert F. CRITIQUE OF SOUTHERN SOCIETY AND VISION OF A NEW ORDER: THE FELLOWSHIP OF SOUTHERN CHURCHMEN, 1934-1957. *Church Hist. 1983 52(1): 66-80.* The Fellowship of Southern Churchmen was founded in 1934 to provide a radical critique of 20th-century Southern civilization. This group was influenced by Reinhold Niebuhr's neoorthodoxy and Christian Socialism. Changing membership and political conditions led to the group's disbanding in 1957. 40 notes.
                                              M. D. Dibert

2361.   Martin, Robert F. THE HOLINESS-PENTECOSTAL REVIVAL IN THE CAROLINAS, 1896-1940. *Pro. of the South Carolina Hist. Assoc. 1979: 59-78.* In 1896, a holiness-pentecostal revival began in the Carolinas, causing catastrophic losses in the membership rolls of traditional denominations. Many of the new members were poor, but all classes and socioeconomic groups were affected. The holiness movement grew rapidly because it offered something missing from the more traditional churches. Published sources; 2 tables, 36 notes.                                              J. W. Thacker, Jr.

2362.   Martin, William. GOD WITH THE WENDS. *Concordia Hist. Inst. Q. 1981 54(3): 136-138.* Describes St. Paul's Church, the first Missouri Synod Lutheran Church in Texas founded in the 1850's in Serbin, and its members, Wends (or Sorbs), who fled Central Europe and Prussian oppression and settled in Central Texas beginning in 1854.

2363.   Mason, Zane. SOME THOUGHTS ON FRONTIER RELIGION IN TEXAS AFTER THE CIVIL WAR. *West Texas Hist. Assoc. Year Book 1981 57: 34-46.* Discusses the rapid growth of organized religion in Texas immediately after the Civil War, focusing on religious practices, church membership and attendance, the work of preachers, and revivalism, during 1870-80.

2364.   Mathews, Donald G. CHARLES COLCOCK JONES AND THE SOUTHERN EVANGELICAL CRUSADE TO FORM A BIRACIAL COMMUNITY. *J. of Southern Hist. 1975 41(3): 299-320.* Charles Colcock Jones, reformist clergyman of the antebellum period, was early disturbed by the slaveholding South in which he resided. He resolved to improve the lot of the Negro, but was sufficiently wise to recognize that any reform must enlist the support of whites. He appealed to the Christian religious conscience, hoping to remake the Negro in the white man's image. He avoided confrontation. Support was reluctantly forthcoming. Jones' personal life was exemplary, but he failed really to change anything. The future biracial Utopia he envisioned became a blueprint for postwar religious reformers. 50 notes.                             V. L. Human

2365.   Mathews, Donald G. RELIGION IN THE OLD SOUTH: SPECULATION ON METHODOLOGY. *South Atlantic Q 1974 73(1): 34-52.* Historical scholarship has ignored southerners' views of the Bible. Evangelical Protestantism in the South tried to Christianize the slaves and reform slavery from within, which in turn altered southern religion. 23 notes.              E. P. Stickney

2366.   May, Lynn E., Jr. THE EMERGING ROLE OF SUNDAY SCHOOLS IN SOUTHERN BAPTIST LIFE TO 1900. *Baptist Hist. and Heritage 1983 18(1): 6-15.* Covers 1790-1900.

2367.   Mayse, Edgar C. ERNEST TRICE THOMPSON: PRESBYTERIAN OF THE SOUTH. *J. of Presbyterian Hist. 1978 56(1): 36-46.* Interviews Ernest Trice Thompson, Southern Presbyterian seminary professor and former Moderator of the General Assembly. For more than 40 years at Union Theological Seminary, Richmond, Virginia, he taught in every major field. He has made major contributions in the area of church history, which he taught to men who were becoming pastors. He is interested in the past as it illuminates the present. Illus., 8 notes.                    H. M. Parker, Jr.

2368.   McBeth, Harry Leon. THE ROLE OF WOMEN IN SOUTHERN BAPTIST HISTORY. *Baptist Hist. and Heritage 1977 12(1): 3-25.* Reviews the role of women in early American Baptist life, then relates Southern Baptists' reluctant acceptance of women's organized participation in denominational life. Presents especially valuable material on the gradual movement of women into influential roles in the denomination and on the contributions of women to the growth of Southern Baptists. Based largely on Southern Baptist periodicals and weeklies of the 19th century and on other secondary materials; 98 notes.                    H. M. Parker, Jr.

2369.   McCall, Duke K. THE SOUTHERN BAPTIST THEOLOGICAL SEMINARY. *Baptist Hist. and Heritage 1977 12(4): 194-197.* Describes the oldest of the six Southern Baptist theological seminaries, which celebrated 100 years of service in Louisville, Kentucky, in 1977. It had been located in Greenville, South Carolina. Mentions leading personalities, critical events, and that current enrollment is about 3,000.                    H. M. Parker, Jr.

2370.   McCall, Emmanuel L. HOME MISSION BOARD MINISTRY IN THE BLACK COMMUNITY. *Baptist Hist. and Heritage 1981 16(3): 29-40.* Reduces a history of the Home Mission Board (HMB) of the Southern Baptist Convention in the black community to three periods: the "overtly paternal" period, 1845-1972; the "developing fraternal" period, 1972-75; and the "declared inclusivism" period, 1975-81.

2371.   McClellan, Albert. THE SHAPING OF THE SOUTHERN BAPTIST MIND. *Baptist Hist. and Heritage 1978 13(3): 2-11.* Contemporary Baptists are no longer a homogeneous people. The Baptist mind may not be as simple and closed as it once was, and it has doctrinal, organizational, and cultural dimensions. Yet there is still a fairly well-defined core of theological understanding common to most Southern Baptists, plus an organizational mind that is probably sanctioned as much by society as by doctrine. The cultural dimensions of Southern Baptist values are harder to perceive and define. Traces significant historical developments, controversies, and personalities which have helped to mold the Baptist mind. Secondary sources; 8 notes.                    H. M. Parker, Jr.

2372.   McElreath, Walter. MCEACHERN MEMORIAL METHODIST CHURCH. *Georgia Hist. Q. 1957 41(4): 365-382.* Narrates the story of the founding of what is now known as the McEachern Memorial Methodist Church by David Newton McEachern (1814-47); the history of this church is intimately bound up with the history of the community in which it is located; 1831-1951.

2373.   McKibbens, Thomas R., Jr. THE ROLE OF PREACHING IN SOUTHERN BAPTIST HISTORY. *Baptist Hist. and Heritage 1980 15(1): 30-36, 64.* Surveys the evolution, distinguishing characteristics, and the dominant role of preaching in the Southern Baptist Church, from 1707 to 1980.

2374. McKivigan, John R. THE AMERICAN BAPTIST FREE MISSION SOCIETY: ABOLITIONIST REACTION TO THE 1845 BAPTIST SCHISM. *Foundations 1978 21(4): 240-355.* Examines abolitionist relations with Northern Baptists, both before and after the 1845 schism. The American Free Baptist Mission Society was composed of those Baptists who would have no fellowship with Baptists who were in any way connected with the institution of domestic slavery—whether through slave-holding or in accepting contributions from those who held slaves. The group worked outside the normal lines of denominational missionary activity, supporting only missionaries who labored in free states. The persistence of abolitionist criticism of northern Baptists thus requires a reassessment of the denomination's pre-Civil War antislavery reputation. The number of northern Baptist associations renouncing fellowship with slaveholders steadily increased during the 1850's and helped sharpen sectional polarization, freeing northern Baptists to speak more agggressively against slavery. Based on the Annual Reports of the ABFMS and similar benevolent societies; 46 notes.

H. M. Parker, Jr.

2375. McLoughlin, William G. THE CHEROKEE BAPTIST PREACHER AND THE GREAT SCHISM OF 1844-45: A FOOTNOTE TO BAPTIST HISTORY. *Foundations 1981 24(2): 137-147.* The schism of 1844-45 among Baptists was caused by the abolitionist-slavery controversy. It has been the impression that Jesse Bushyhead, a Cherokee Baptist preacher, precipitated it. It has been held as a part of the history of this period that Bushyhead was a slaveholder. Investigates Bushyhead's place in the schism and his being a slaveholder. The charges aimed at Bushyhead by abolitionists were not true. Places Bushyhead in proper perspective insofar as his role in Baptist missions is concerned. Based on Baptist Board of Foreign Mission records and other sources; 25 notes.

E. E. Eminhizer

2376. McSwain, Larry and Shurden, Walter B. CHANGING VALUES OF SOUTHERN BAPTISTS, 1900-1980. *Baptist Hist. and Heritage 1981 16(1): 45-54.* Provides statistics, focusing on 1945-79 and concluding that in spite of their present less traditional and conservative image, Southern Baptists maintain a strong commitment to family values, have replaced a legalistic pietism by a social ethic, and have recently been confronted by a conservative minority of leaders who disagree with the changes.

2377. Measures, Royce. J. FRANK NORRIS: A FORERUNNER OF THE NEW RIGHT. *Fides et Hist. 1982 15(1): 61-70.* Analyzes the life of the controversial and enigmatic Texas Baptist minister, J. Frank Norris. A fundamentalist firebrand, Norris distinguished himself at Fort Worth's First Baptist Church where he preached for 43 years, much to the consternation of mainline Baptists. Through his influential newspaper, the *Baptist Standard,* Norris attacked the evils of racetrack betting and succeeded in getting the practice outlawed in 1908. His greatest political triumph came in 1928 when he waged a vigorous partisan attack against the Catholic Democratic presidential candidate, Al Smith, and helped in getting staunchly Democratic Texas to go for Hoover. His influence on the modern New Right religious movement is obscure and tangential at best. 30 notes.

G. A. Glovins

2378. Midgette, Nancy Smith. WILLIAM E. CRANE AND PASTORAL COUNSELING IN THE SOUTH. *J. of Presbyterian Hist. 1983 61(3): 353-371.* Focuses on the ministry of the Southern Presbyterian pastor, William E. Crane, and his relationships with the various congregations he served. A pioneer in the field of pastoral counseling, he sought new ways by which the church could speak to the people as they faced crises in their lives wrought by the rapidly changing social and economic environment. His advocacy of counseling, although not directly addressing the cultural conditions that led to personal problems, opened lines of communication between the fields of psychology and religion. Crane came to believe that, in addition to the healing powers of the Holy Spirit, a scientific understanding of human behavior could provide pastors with an effective tool for helping people adjust to stress-provoking situa-

tions. Based on the William E. Crane Collection, at the Historical Foundation of the Presbyterian and Reformed Churches; photo, 50 notes.

H. M. Parker, Jr.

2379. Miller, Randall M. BLACK CATHOLICS IN THE SLAVE SOUTH: SOME NEEDS AND OPPORTUNITIES FOR STUDY. *Records of the Am. Catholic Hist. Soc. of Philadelphia 1975 86(1-4): 93-106.* Catholic slaveholders as well as Catholic slaves await their historians. The why and how of the Church's function and its failure among blacks and whites of the Old South remain open questions which constitute the main agenda for research for serious students of Catholic Church history in the South. 36 notes.

J. M. McCarthy

2380. Miller, Robert Moats. ONE BIBLE BELT STATE'S ENCOUNTER WITH POPULISM AND "PROGRESSIVE" CAPITALISM. *Rev. in Am. Hist. 1976 4(4): 571-576.* Review article prompted by Frederick A. Bode's *Protestantism and the New South: North Carolina Baptists and Methodists in Political Crisis, 1894-1903* (Charlottesville: U. Pr. of Virginia, 1975); discusses the interaction of religion and politics in North Carolina.

2381. Miller, Rush G. JOHN G. JONES: PIONEER CIRCUIT RIDER AND HISTORIAN. *J. of Mississippi Hist. 1977 39(1): 17-39.* Describes the life and career of John Griffing Jones (1804-88), who was a Methodist "circuit rider, presiding elder, and noted historian" in Mississippi during 1824-88. Describes his experiences as a circuit rider and preacher, his view of slavery, and his writings. As a church historian he wrote many periodical articles, a history of Protestantism in the Old Southwest, and a two-volume history of Methodism in Mississippi. Based largely on Jones' journal; 58 notes.

J. W. Hillje

2382. Miltenberger, Stephan. "THE WAY WE WERE": 125 YEARS OF ST. ALPHONSUS PARISH, WHEELING. *Upper Ohio Valley Hist. Rev. 1983 12(2): 25-35.* Discusses the founding of a Catholic parish specifically for the German-American residents of Wheeling, West Virginia, in 1856 and its development and leadership during its 125-year history.

2383. Mitchell, Joseph. SOUTHERN METHODIST NEWSPAPERS DURING THE CIVIL WAR. *Methodist Hist. 1973 11(2): 20-39.* Analyzes the role of church newspapers in preserving the Methodist Episcopal Church, South, during the war and in reviving it afterwards. Describes the difficulties of publication in wartime. Articles and editorials dealt with general news, support of the South and slavery, the church's role in the war, attacks on the North, and avoidance of sins. Contemporary newspapers; 104 notes.

H. L. Calkin

2384. Moody, Dale. THE SHAPING OF SOUTHERN BAPTIST POLITY. *Baptist Hist. and Heritage 1979 14(3): 2-11.* Discusses how the congregation, association, and convention in the Southern Baptist Church have shaped its political organization through Campbellism, landmarkism, dispensationalism, fundamentalism, and conservatism since the 16th century.

2385. Moore, David O. THE WITHDRAWAL OF BLACKS FROM SOUTHERN BAPTIST CHURCHES FOLLOWING EMANCIPATION. *Baptist Hist. and Heritage 1981 16(3): 12-18.* Discusses black attendance at white churches, 1845-63; the desire by blacks to have their own leadership, their wish for the structured social life and higher status that separate churches provided, new ideas about black liberation that "called blacks to a crusade for their own freedom," and "the backlash of northern carpet-bagger politics."

2386. Moore, John S. THE STRUGGLE FOR FREEDOM IN VIRGINIA. *Baptist Hist. and Heritage 1976 11(3): 160-168.* The United States became the first nation in the world to insure religious freedom for all in its organic laws. The long struggle of Baptists to achieve this required nearly two centuries, involving much sacrifice and persecution. A large amount of credit must go to the tireless and persevering Virginia Baptists. Based largely on secondary sources; 25 notes.　　　　　　　　　　H. M. Parker, Jr.

2387. Moore, LeRoy. CRAZY QUILT: SOUTHERN BAPTIST PATTERNS OF THE CHURCH. *Foundations 1977 20(1): 12-35.* The Baptist view of the church has never been uniform. Traces the development of three historic positions: Connectional, which began with the Philadelphia Association in 1704; Localist, which evolved from the 18th-century awakenings; and Individualist, which came from Isaac Bachus and the Separate Baptist of New England. These major themes have been changed by centralization following 1845 and the beginning of the Southern Baptist Convention and Landmarkism in the early part of the 20th century. Points out the conflict between these historic positions and the statement of faith and message. Although Southern Baptists hold that they keep power at the local level, they have one of the most authoritarian religious structures in America. 105 notes.　　　　E. E. Eminhizer

2388. Morgan, David T. JOHN WESLEY'S SOJOURN IN GEORGIA REVISITED. *Georgia Hist. Q. 1980 64(3): 253-262.* Describes John Wesley's tenure as a minister in Georgia (1736-38), determining that the results were principally negative. Based on John Wesley's *Journal* and secondary sources; 26 notes.
　　　　　　　　　　　　　　　　G. R. Schroeder

2389. Morgan, David T. JUDAISM IN EIGHTEENTH-CENTURY GEORGIA. *Georgia Hist. Q. 1974 58(1): 41-54.* Traces the development of Judaism in Georgia until it achieved a permanent institutional form. The first group of Jewish immigrants met official opposition, but they freely observed their religion and remained until the War of Jenkins' Ear brought their departure. A second group arrived in 1762; they were forced out during the American Revolution. They returned after the peace. The state incorporated a Jewish congregation in 1790, evidence that religious freedom had become a reality. 34 notes.　　　　D. L. Smith

2390. Mounger, Dwyn M. HISTORY AS INTERPRETED BY STEPHEN ELLIOTT. *Hist. Mag. of the Protestant Episcopal Church 1975 44(3): 285-317.* Stephen Elliott (1806-66) was the first Episcopal bishop of Georgia. Through his sermons and voluminous writings he conceived of history from the traditional Christian point of view: the fulfillment of the divine will. He was one of the major apologists for the southern way of life. He viewed slavery as intricately woven into the fabric of southern life, decried abolitionism, led the way in evangelizing slaves, and favored the southern cause during the Civil War. Never wavering in his belief that God was on the side of the Stars and Bars, he anticipated Confederate victory down to the last battle. Even the defeat he accepted as the work of God, not of man. His greatest delusion in historical interpretation lay in his claim to be able to read the approval and condemnation of God in the events of history, despite the fact that on occasion he would admit that discernment was difficult. Only the Confederate defeat changed him from a strict Deuteronomist in history. Based largely on Elliott's writings; 117 notes.
　　　　　　　　　　　　　　　　H. M. Parker, Jr.

2391. Mulder, John M. JOSEPH RUGGLES WILSON: SOUTHERN PRESBYTERIAN PATRIARCH. *J. of Presbyterian Hist. 1974 52(3): 245-271.* Joseph Ruggles Wilson (1822-1903) was one of the founders of the southern Presbyterian Church and a powerful church official, preacher, and professor.　　　　　S

2392. Music, David W. J. R. GRAVES' *THE LITTLE SERAPH* (1874): A MEMPHIS TUNEBOOK. *West Tennessee Hist. Soc. Papers 1981 35: 40-50.* *The Little Seraph* was the first religious music book from Memphis. It was compiled by James Robinson Graves, one of the leaders in the formation of the Southern Baptist Sunday School Union and in the Landmark movement. The book employed a system of musical notation usually called "shape-note." The music was drawn from four church song traditions: English and American psalm and hymn tunes of the 17th and 18th centuries, the Mason-Hastings-Bradbury school of American composers, the gospel song, and American folk-hymn tunes. It was designed for both Sunday school and church service. It marks an important step in the transference of the folk hymn from the *fasola* collections to those of general appeal and provides an interesting juxtaposition of the gospel song, folk hymn, and other styles of church song. Secondary sources; 19 notes.　　　　　　　　　H. M. Parker, Jr.

2393. Nettles, Tom J. PATTERNS OF FINANCIAL GIVING FOR MISSION SUPPORT AMONG BAPTISTS. *Baptist Hist. and Heritage 1979 14(1): 27-36.* Investigates the extent of financial support for missionary organizations in the Southern Baptist Convention, examines tendencies toward increasing or decreasing support, and seeks to determine elements in the movement to which Baptists have responded either positively or negatively. Concludes that Southern Baptists will be slow to give if not thoroughly persuaded of the theological or biblical validity of an enterprise. Upon the conviction that those they are supporting are betraying them or are unbiblical, support will be withdrawn. Emphasis on the lostness of man, the reality of the judgment, the sufficiency of Christ, the necessity of hearing the word of truth, and the missionary imperative do much to support a strong mission thrust. Covers 1792-1976. Secondary sources; 2 tables, 30 notes.　　　　H. M. Parker, Jr.

2394. Nettles, Tom J. SOUTHERN BAPTISTS: REGIONAL TO NATIONAL TRANSITION. *Baptist Hist. and Heritage 1981 16(1): 13-23.* Discusses the presence of Southern Baptists in the south and southwestern United States during the 19th century, and the expansion of the Southern Baptists into all 50 states during the 20th century.

2395. Nettles, Tom J. THEMES FOR RESEARCH IN SOUTHERN BAPTIST HISTORY. *Baptist Hist. and Heritage 1979 14(2): 15-19.* Suggests possible topics for researching Southern Baptist history, 1607-1979.

2396. Newcomb, Horace. BEING SOUTHERN BAPTIST ON THE NORTHERN FRINGE. *Southern Exposure 1976 4(3): 66-72.* The author reminisces about what his membership in the Southern Baptists meant to his childhood, social development, and education, 1940's-70's.

2397. Newman, Harvey K. PIETY AND SEGREGATION: WHITE PROTESTANT ATTITUDES TOWARD BLACKS IN ATLANTA, 1865-1905. *Georgia Hist. Q. 1979 63(2): 238-251.* Following the Civil War, previously integrated Atlanta Protestant churches became segregated. In the interests of maintaining a social order with blacks at the bottom, white church members refused to cooperate with anything that might result in racial equality, even when suggested and exemplified by Bishop Gilbert Haven of the Methodist Episcopal Church. This paternalism and aloofness contributed to racial tensions which led to a tragic massacre in September 1906. Primary and secondary sources; 42 notes.
　　　　　　　　　　　　　　　　G. R. Schroeder

2398. Noon, Thomas R. THE ALABAMA BLACK LUTHERAN MISSION FIELD OF 1916-31: HOW IT LOOKS TODAY. *Concordia Hist. Inst. Q. 1979 52(3): 128-135.* Presents 1977-78 photographs of the 33 missions established to convert Alabama Negroes and discusses the missions' histories.

2399. Noon, Thomas R. BLACK LUTHERANS LICENSED AND ORDAINED (1865-1889). *Concordia Hist. Inst. Q. 1977 50(2): 54-63.* During the decades following the Civil War, the Lutheran Church had to adjust to the new status of the Blacks. The approaches varied slightly from one synod to another but the general movement was toward the creation of a black Lutheran clergy which would administer to the needs of the black people. The North Carolina Synod produced the most lasting results in this endeavor. Primary sources; 32 notes.　　　　W. T. Walker

2400. Noon, Thomas R. EARLY BLACK LUTHERANS IN THE SOUTH (TO 1865). *Concordia Hist. Inst. Q. 1977 50(2): 50-53.* Prior to the abolition of slavery, Lutherans split on the issue according to regional lines. Southern Lutherans defended slavery because of the economy. In the South, the Lutheran Church involved itself with the blacks; slave owners were urged to provide baptism and religious instruction to their slaves. As a result of this procedure and the nature of slavery, blacks in the South before 1865 became Lutherans because their owners were such and not by choice. 15 notes.                                                                    W. T. Walker

2401.  Owens, William A. ANGLO-TEXAN SPIRITUALS. *Southwestern Hist. Q. 1982 86(1): 31-48.* The spirituals of the white churches in Texas reflect the fundamentalist religion of the state. Although rudimentary in lyrics, notes, and meter, the poetry and music of those spirituals remain an important part of Anglo-Texan folk culture. Personal observations of the author.
                                                                    R. D. Hurt

2402.  Papageorge, Linda Madson. FEMINISM AND METHODIST MISSIONARY ACTIVITY IN CHINA: THE EXPERIENCE OF ATLANTA'S LAURA HAYGOOD, 1884-1900. *West Georgia Coll. Studies in the Social Sci. 1983 22: 71-77.* A devout Christian and feminist, Laura A. Haygood became a Methodist Episcopal Church (South) missionary in China and participated in feminist reforms of the missionary administration.

2403.  Parker, Harold M. THE NEW SCHOOL SYNOD OF KENTUCKY. *Filson Club Hist. Q. 1976 50(2): 52-89.* Details the division within the Presbyterian Church in Kentucky during 1837-58. Despite the claims of the author, the New School Synod was not a significant institution although it did produce several outstanding clergymen including Archer C. Dickerson, Joseph C. Stiles, and Thomas Cleland. The conflict was generated by ecclesiastical questions rather than doctrinal differences, and, as a result, the New School group rejoined the parent body in 1858. Documentation comes from contemporary tracts, newspapers, and histories; 121 notes.                                                   G. B. McKinney

2404.  Parker, Harold M., Jr. THE CASSVILLE CONVENTION: ABORTED BIRTH OF A SOUTHERN PRESBYTERIAN CHURCH. *Historian 1980 42(4): 612-630.* The 1837 rift between Old School and New School Presbyterians climaxed a tumultuous decade for the Presbyterian Church. In 1840 a convention met for four days in Cassville, Georgia, to establish a Southern Presbyterian Church. The developments that led up to the convention, the work it accomplished, and its ultimate failure are discussed. Basically, the Cassville Convention was alien to the spirit of American Presbyterianism which saw the church as a bond for the nation. Primary sources.                                                           R. S. Sliwoski

2405.  Parker, Harold M., Jr. A NEW SCHOOL PRESBYTERIAN SEMINARY IN WOODFORD COUNTY. *Register of the Kentucky Hist. Soc. 1976 74(2): 99-111.* Intertwined in the history of Presbyterianism in Kentucky were the themes of division and education. The Old School-New School division in the church in 1837 did not lead to a split in Kentucky until 1840. The slavery issue intruded into the Kentucky situation, and the small New School group had to rely on the North for financial support and for ministers. In 1849, the group accepted the offer of the Macedonia Church to erect a building for a seminary. Two years later, the effort collapsed because of financial difficulties, lack of leadership, and other problems. Primary and secondary sources; 26 notes.
                                                                    J. F. Paul

2406.  Parker, Harold M., Jr. A SCHOOL OF THE PROPHETS AT MARYVILLE. *Tennessee Hist. Q. 1975 34(1): 72-90.* In 1819 Dr. Isaac Anderson began the Southern and Western Theological Seminary in Maryville, Tennessee, with the idea of providing religious training for Presbyterian ministers in an area where there was a shortage. The seminary set a high intellectual standard, grew rapidly, and became a center of abolitionism. Failing financial support, divisions within the church, and agitation over slavery led to the demise of the seminary in the late 1850's. Secondary sources; 55 notes.                                                              M. B. Lucas

2407.  Parker, Harold M., Jr. SOUTHERN PRESBYTERIAN ECUMENISM: SIX SUCCESSFUL UNIONS. *J. of Presbyterian Hist. 1978 56(2): 91-106.* In the first 14 years of its history, the Southern Presbyterian Church successfully participated in six organic unions with the Independent Presbyterian Church, the United Synod of the South, the Presbytery of Patapsco, the Kentucky Pres-

bytery of the Associate Reformed Presbyterian Church, and the Old School Synods of Kentucky and Missouri. Discusses the impact of these unions in three categories: numerically, the Church gained members and congregations; geographically, it spread into the Border States and was also strengthened in the states of the old Confederacy; doctrinally, it accommodated its position to several groups. Challenges the premise of Southern Presbyterian purists who have insisted that in every instance the unions took place on the basis of perfect doctrinal affinity. Based on the author's earlier studies of the unions and primary sources; 2 tables, 41 notes.
                                                                    A

2408.  Paterwick, Stephen. THE EFFECT OF THE CIVIL WAR ON SHAKER SOCIETIES. *Hist. J. of Western Massachusetts 1973 2(1): 6-26.* The Civil War represented a watershed in Shaker history, separating a period of growth from one of decline. The Kentucky settlements suffered from plunder, arson, and the strenuous efforts to feed, clothe, and nurse soldiers on both sides. All settlements were faced with trade dislocation; and the sale of seeds, fruits, preserves, and livestock languished. The mood of the postwar years was one of crass materialism, and the Shaker population declined. Based on secondary sources; 2 illus., 19 notes.
                                                                    S. S. Sprague

2409.  Patterson, Michael S. THE FALL OF A BISHOP: JAMES CANNON, JR., *VERSUS* CARTER GLASS, 1909-1934. *J. of Southern Hist. 1973 39(4): 493-518.* Examines the fall of Methodist Bishop James Cannon, Jr., from power and political influence. The factors of his decline involved political struggles in Virginia and in the nation at large. Senator Carter Glass, his constant antagonist, sought to discredit Cannon in order to destroy his political influence. Glass, with the help of powerful friends, publicized Cannon's misuse of public, church, and political funds, and questionable stock transactions. Cannon was investigated by Congress, the Methodist Church, and the courts, and was removed from the political arena. Based on contemporary newspaper reports, US government documents, and primary and secondary sources; 92 notes.
                                                                    N. J. Street

2410.  Patterson, W. Morgan. BAPTIST GROWTH IN AMERICA: EVALUATION OF TRENDS. *Baptist Hist. and Heritage 1979 14(1): 16-26.* Attributes the growth of Southern Baptists since the 18th century, apart from sociological, demographic, and cultural influences, to religious factors: 1) heritage of the revival emphasis, 2) denominational pride growing out of Landmark exclusiveness, 3) development of efficient and adaptable denominational organizations, 4) sense of denominational loyalty, 5) massive program of tuition-free theological education, 6) dispersion of Southern Baptists across the United States, and 7) a gift for organizing and promoting programs and methods to share the gospel in a more effective way. Statistical materials and secondary sources; 3 tables, 36 notes.
                                                                    H. M. Parker, Jr.

2411.  Patterson, W. Morgan. THE INFLUENCE OF LANDMARKISM AMONG BAPTISTS. *Baptist Hist. and Heritage 1975 10(1): 44-55.* Identifies specific historical situations in which the Landmark movement influences the Baptist church. The greatest influence was and is among Baptists of the Old Southwest, largely due to the 50 year editorial ministry of James Robinson Graves in Nashville and Memphis. Seaboard Baptists were more settled, and thus less susceptible to the controversies which raged along the frontier and the newly settled lands. Landmarkism was responsible for the idea that the local church, not boards, should be responsible for the conduct and administration of missionary activity, which spawned the gospel missions concept. The Landmark theory of Baptist succession was challenged at the end of the last century, creating the Whitsitt Controversy. Landmarkism has peaked, but its final effects remain to be seen. Based largely on unpublished dissertations and secondary sources; 27 notes.         H. M. Parker, Jr.

2412.  Patterson, W. Morgan. THE SOUTHERN BAPTIST THEOLOGIAN AS CONTROVERSIALIST: A CONTRAST. *Baptist Hist. and Heritage 1980 15(3): 7-14.* Compares and contrasts the attitudes and outlooks of Southern Baptist James Robinson Graves (1820-93), founder of the Landmark movement, and Edgar Young

Mullins (1860-1928), who was involved in the fundamentalist-modernist controversy of the 1920's; and discusses the contributions of both men to the theology of Southern Baptists.

2413. Pearson, Fred Lamar, Jr. and Tomberlin, Joseph Aaron. JOHN DOE, ALIAS GOD: A NOTE ON FATHER DIVINE'S GEORGIA CAREER. *Georgia Hist. Q. 1976 60(1): 43-48.* George Baker (later, "Father Divine") was born in Savannah and grew up in the South. He became involved with Samuel Morris, "Father Jehovia," in Baltimore and assumed the title "The Messenger." The trinity was completed with the addition of St. John the Vine Hickerson. There was soon to be conflict over divinity, and Hickerson and "The Messenger" moved in independent directions. Baker went to Valdosta where he began to develop a following, mainly of black females. Eventually (1914) he was taken to court, and after a series of court battles, he was acquitted and left Valdosta with some of his followers. Primary and secondary sources; 29 notes.
M. R. Gillam

2414. Poe, William A. THE STORY OF A FRIENDSHIP AND A BOOK: W. E. PAXTON AND GREEN W. HARTSFIELD. *Louisana Hist. 1981 22(2): 167-182.* Discusses the friendship between Baptist ministers W. E. Paxton and Green W. Hartsfield. Paxton was instrumental in the formation of the Baptist Historical Society in 1860. He gathered data from all over Louisiana and by 1881 had completed a manuscript of some 500 pages, which was destined to become one of the most treasured books in Louisiana history. It was entitled *History of the Baptists of Louisiana from the Earliest Times to the Present.* Because of his untimely death in 1883, the book only saw print because of Hartsfield's attention to the project. Primary sources; 52 notes.
J. Powell

2415. Proctor, Emerson. BAPTIST CONFESSIONS OF FAITH AND GEORGIA PRIMITIVE BAPTISTS. *Viewpoints: Georgia Baptist Hist. 1976 5: 81-90.* Examines the history of the Baptist Church through confessions of faith, touching on the beginnings of the religion in Great Britain, 1633-80, and the various sects within the United States, including Regular, Orthodox, Separate, Particular, Missionary, and Primitive Baptists, and a small section on the Georgia Primitive Baptists, 1690-1900.

2416. Rainard, R. Lyn. CONFLICT INSIDE THE EARTH: THE KORESHAN UNITY IN LEE COUNTY. *Tampa Bay Hist. 1981 3(1): 5-16.* Describes the Koreshan Unity, a small utopian religious community in Lee County, Florida, during the late 19th and early 20th centuries, led by Cyrus Reed Teed (1839-1908), focusing on lawsuits against the group by private citizens that went unnoticed by officials in Lee County until the Koreshans tried to enter politics; with Teed's death the Koreshans disbanded.

2417. Redman, Barbara J. THE IMPACT OF GREAT REVIVAL RELIGION ON THE PERSONAL CHARACTERISTICS OF THE SOUTHERN APPALACHIAN PEOPLE. *Southern Studies 1981 20(3): 303-310.* Raises question of whether the theology of the Great Revival caused or adapted itself to the social and cultural context of Southern Appalachia. Great Revival preaching emphasized a theology of individualism, rather than church structure or hierarchy. Today relatively few people in the area are church members; the Bible is revered and taken literally but not often read; traditional views of human sinfulness are widely held; practices such as grace before meals are common. Great Revival theology significantly affected contemporary Appalachia through its personal implications. Biblio.
J. J. Buschen

2418. Reilly, Timothy E. SLAVERY AND THE SOUTHWESTERN EVANGELIST IN NEW ORLEANS (1800-1861). *J. of Mississippi Hist. 1979 41(4): 301-317.* Fundamentalism in New Orleans in the antebellum period produced mixed results. So desperate had Methodist and Baptist organizations become for converts that they were willing to proselytize among blacks and whites alike. Studies these protestant efforts, and especially some of the clergy's liberal racial philosophies which placed them outside the mainstream in the South's defense of slavery. Key figures in New Orleans protestantism considered include: William Winans, Benjamin M. Drake, Asa C. Goldsbury, Holland McTyeire, and William Cecil Duncan.

Concludes that New Orleans Catholicism and Protestantism were able to arrange a religious pluralism as the protestant clergy, with strong roots in the South's agrarian society, sought to create a religious culture which would be responsive to urban needs.
M. S. Legan

2419. Reilly, Timothy F. BENJAMIN M. PALMER: SECESSIONIST BECOME NATIONALIST. *Louisiana Hist. 1977 18(3): 287-301.* A Presbyterian minister from New Orleans, Benjamin Morgan Palmer (1818-1902) favored secession and championed the southern cause, but after the war he espoused reunion and consolidation of the nation. He remained a staunch racist until his death in 1902. Based principally on Palmer's published works and newspapers; photo, 45 notes.
R. L. Woodward, Jr.

2420. Reilly, Timothy. GENTEEL REFORM VERSUS SOUTHERN ALLEGIANCE: EPISCOPALIAN DILEMMA IN OLD NEW ORLEANS. *Hist. Mag. of the Protestant Episcopal Church 1975 44(4): 437-450.* The first Episcopal church in New Orleans was founded in 1805; the first Bishop of Louisiana, Leonidas Polk, was consecrated in 1838. His basic thrust among Negro slaves was in education. In response to the increasing sectional hostility between North and South, Polk also sought to establish a regional southern university, which was ultimately the University of the South at Sewanee, Tennessee. He was an advocate of gradual emancipation, and supported the efforts of the American Colonization Society up to the eve of the Civil War. He urged humanitarian treatment of slaves. His proselytizing efforts among them resulted in black communicants outnumbering whites in his diocese. He became a planter with slaves, and with the advent of the Civil War his program of genteel reform and educational development was considerably altered. His ministry terminated when he lost his life as a general in the Confederate Army. His religious career was governed by an emotionalism which was intermittently charged by a strong regional identification and an essential conservatism. Based on primary and secondary sources; 50 notes.
H. M. Parker, Jr.

2421. Reilly, Timothy F. PARSON CLAPP OF NEW ORLEANS: ANTEBELLUM SOCIAL CRITIC, RELIGIOUS RADICAL, AND MEMBER OF THE ESTABLISHMENT. *Louisiana Hist. 1975 16(2): 167-191.* "Unitarianism in antebellum New Orleans was among the most distinctive religious forces in the Old South. The Church was founded and shepherded by Parson Theodore Clapp, a New England native and former Presbyterian who continually challenged sacred dictums of Christian orthodoxy." Arriving in New Orleans in 1822 and remaining until 1856, Clapp opposed revivalism and theological concepts involving the Trinity, everlasting punishment, and predestination. He defended slavery "because he recognized the supremacy of the large business class in New Orleans and the rest of the South. Such a compromise... entitled him to a position of social respectability. Clapp valued the propagation of his radical theology above everything else." Primary and secondary sources; 3 photos, 68 notes.
R. L. Woodward

2422. Reily, Duncan A. REUNION SHENANIGAN: BISHOP WILLIAM CAPERS' "LETTER" OF 1854. *Methodist Hist. 1977 15(2): 131-139.* In 1875 the New York weekly newspaper *Christian Advocate* published a letter purportedly written by Methodist Bishop William Capers in 1854 on slavery and abolition, and its effect on the uniting of the north and south branches of the Methodist Church. Concludes that the letter was very probably a forgery, intended to influence the Methodist Episcopal Church, South to move toward reunion with the Methodist Episcopal Church. 7 notes.
H. L. Calkin

2423. Rennie, Sandra. THE ROLE OF THE PREACHER: INDEX TO THE CONSOLIDATION OF THE BAPTIST MOVEMENT IN VIRGINIA FROM 1760 TO 1790. *Virginia Mag. of Hist. and Biog. 1980 88(4): 430-441.* Traces the evolving role of the preacher in the Separatist Baptist Church. Many sinners were convicted and shepherded during the early period under the self-sustaining, dramatic, and personally forceful preachers. They claimed direct celestial guidance for their unprepared—and, unfortunately for historians, unprinted—sermons. The reputation of the "great preachers" eventually retarded the entry of new persons into the ministry. The increasingly distinctive doctrinal differences were indeed related to preacher rivalry. By the 1790's, the stress on formally stated beliefs led to the professional preacher educated at a theological academy, and salaried. 49 notes.

P. J. Woehrmann

2424. Rennie, Sandra. VIRGINIA'S BAPTIST PERSECUTION, 1765-1778. *J. of Religious History [Australia] 1982 12(1): 48-61.* During 1765-78 Baptists in Virginia experienced a persecution that manifested itself in mob demonstrations and harassment by civil authorities. Both regular Baptists, of English origin, and Separatist Baptists, originating from the Congregationalists of New England, were persecuted. The basis of the persecution was the fear of a slave revolt resulting from the impact of Baptist preaching. Primary sources; 83 notes.                   W. T. Walker

2425. Rensi, Ray C. THE GOSPEL ACCORDING TO SAM JONES. *Georgia Hist. Q. 1976 60(3): 251-263.* The 19th-century Georgia revivalist Sam Jones stressed the importance of self-reliance and opposed amusements such as dancing, card-playing, the theater, baseball, the use of cigarettes, and especially liquor. These views were representative of the rural South for which Jones spoke. Primary and secondary sources; 44 notes.      G. R. Schroeder

2426. Reynierse, Peter J. A HISTORY OF ST. JOHN'S CHURCH, VERSAILLES, KENTUCKY. *Hist. Mag. of the Protestant Episcopal Church 1976 45(1): 47-55.* Chronicles the history of St. John's Episcopal Church, Versailles, Kentucky, largely through its clergy from the earliest services in 1829 to the present. The parish was organized 29 June 1847, and the church was consecrated 10 May 1854. In the early years the shortage of Episcopal priests in Kentucky was the major problem confronting the church; in later years it was the brevity of their pastorates. Cites several anecdotes in the church's history, and describes the numerous improvements and additions to the church property and edifice. Based largely on primary sources, especially the church register; 25 notes.

H. M. Parker, Jr.

2427. Richardson, Fredrick. AMERICAN BAPTISTS' SOUTHERN MISSION. *Foundations 1975 18(2): 136-145.* American (Northern) Baptists began missions in the South among blacks as soon as possible following the war. The first were supported by the Freedmen's Fund. Discusses the foundation of Northern Baptist educational institutions in the South for blacks. These include Shaw University, started by Henry Tupper in 1865; Wayland Seminary, 1865; Richmond Institute, started by Nathaniel Colver, 1865; Nashville Institute, started by D. W. Phillips in 1866; Augusta Institute by William Jefferson White, 1867; Leland University by Holbrook Chamberlain, 1870; Benedict Institute, 1871; Natchez Seminary, 1877; Spelman Seminary, 1881; and Bishop College, 1881. 49 notes.                        E. E. Eminhizer

2428. Richardson, Joe M. THE AMERICAN MISSIONARY ASSOCIATION AND BLACK EDUCATION IN CIVIL WAR MISSOURI. *Missouri Hist. R. 1975 69(4): 433-488.* The American Missionary Association carried on antislavery work in Missouri before the Civil War, and educational programs during and after the war. In 1862 George Candee, the first educational representative, arrived in St. Louis. Real educational work did not begin until 1863 with the arrival of J. L. Richardson. After concentrating its work in St. Louis, the A.M.A. began to expand into other areas after 1864. After the war it continued modest support in Missouri but transferred most of its activities to the South. Most of the work to educate the 115,000 Negroes in Missouri fell to the blacks themselves, the state, and other benevolent societies, but they were able to build on a foundation already laid by the A.M.A. Based on primary and secondary sources; illus., 40 notes.      W. F. Zornow

2429. Richardson, Joe M. THE FAILURE OF THE AMERICAN MISSIONARY ASSOCIATION TO EXPAND CONGREGATIONALISM AMONG SOUTHERN BLACKS. *Southern Studies 1979 18(1): 51-73.* Thousands of blacks belonged to white Christian churches before the Civil War, but by 1865 almost all belonged to solely black congregations. The American Missionary Association

was founded in 1846 as an evangelical, abolitionist society, which in its first years promoted education, black suffrage, and full citizenship. Association schools held nondenominational prayer meetings and taught religion. The Association ultimately failed to attract permanent black members because of its ties to Congregationalism (which was alien to emotional black religious expression), because of its insistence on white ministers, and because of its paternalistic attitudes. Based on American Missionary Association Archives at Dillard U., New Orleans, and on primary and secondary sources; 71 notes.                                 J. J. Buschen

2430. Richardson, Joe M. "WE ARE TRULY DOING MISSIONARY WORK": LETTERS FROM AMERICAN MISSIONARY ASSOCIATION TEACHERS IN FLORIDA, 1864-1874. *Florida Hist. Q. 1975 54(2): 178-195.* The American Missionary Association led the way in aiding Florida's 62,000 freedmen by advocating full citizenship and by establishing schools throughout the state. Although few in number, American Missionary Association teachers instructed hundreds of students and with the aid of other benevolent societies and the Florida legislature, achieved an educational system for black people. Based on the Association's archives at the Amistad Reserach Center, Dillard University; 11 letters, 22 notes.

P. A. Beaber

2431. Robbins, Peggy. THE "LITTLE ADVENTURES" OF MADELEINE HACHARD. *Am. Hist. Illus. 1977 12(4): 36-42.* A group of Ursulines went from France to New Orleans in 1727 to teach female settlers, Indians, and Negroes; focuses on Sister Marie Madeleine of St. Stanislaus (d. 1760).

2432. Rogers, Ben. BLACK TEXAS BAPTIST CHURCH RECORDS. *J. of the Afro-American Hist. and Geneal. Soc. 1982 3(2): 65-66.* Lists in alphabetical order the minutes of Texas Negro Baptist associations in the archives of the Fleming Library of the Southwestern Baptist Theological Seminary during 1875 to 1941.

2433. Rogers, Tommy W. T. C. THORNTON: A METHODIST EDUCATOR OF ANTEBELLUM MISSISSIPPI. *J. of Mississippi Hist. 1982 44(2): 136-146.* Born in 1794 in Dumfries, Virginia, Thomas C. Thornton moved to Mississippi in 1841 after his appointment to the presidency of Centenary College at Brandon Springs. From 1841 until his death in 1860, Thornton continued as a pivotal figure in the development of denominational education in the state. The author sketches Thornton's affiliation with Centenary College, the College of Jackson, Brandon College, and Madison College, and traces the successes and failures experienced by these institutions under Thornton's direction. Also included is Senator Albert Gallatin Brown's praise of Thornton's defense of slavery entitled, *An Inquiry Into Slavery.* Brown's expression of appreciation for this Southern educator, who served as the "paragon of Methodist influence on behalf of higher education in antebellum Mississippi," may well have served as his eulogy. Based on primary materials and John G. Jones, *A Complete History of Methodism as Connected with the Methodist Episcopal Church, South;* 29 notes.

M. S. Legan

2434. Romo, Oscar I. ETHNIC SOUTHERN BAPTISTS: CONTEXTS, TRENDS, CONTRIBUTIONS. *Baptist Hist. and Heritage 1983 18(3): 3-10.* The rise of "ethnic sensitivity and awareness" since the 1940's requires that Southern Baptists affirm the legitimacy of ethnicity and multilingualism in church life.

2435. Rose, Royce A. THE RURAL CHURCH: NOT GONE, BUT FORGOTTEN? *Baptist Hist. and Heritage 1983 18(4): 44-46.* Examines the establishment of the Long-Range Rural Church Committee of the Southern Baptist Convention, which is active in supporting rural Baptist churches that face declining membership and resources.

2436. Rosenswaike, Ira. THE FOUNDING OF BALTIMORE'S FIRST JEWISH CONGREGATION: FACT VS. FICTION. *Am. Jewish Arch. 1976 28(2): 119-125.* Disputes the claim that Isaac Leeser's uncle Zalma Rehine was a founder of the Baltimore Hebrew Congregation. Writers of local history, he urges, "would do well not to rely on some of the hearsay evidence of their predecessors, who often lacked scholarly training."          J

2437. Rosenwaike, Ira. THE FIRST JEWISH SETTLERS IN LOUISVILLE. *Filson Club Hist. Q. 1979 53(1): 37-44.* By 1832 the Jewish population of Louisville was large enough to support the establishment of the Israelite Benevolent Society. Most of the community was highly mobile at this time; few of the early Jewish settlers remained in the city for more than a decade. Based on local government records and the federal census. 38 notes.

G. B. McKinney

2438. Ross, Edyth L. BLACK HERITAGE IN SOCIAL WELFARE: A CASE STUDY OF ATLANTA. *Phylon 1976 37(4): 297-307.* "An examination of the social welfare heritage of black Americans demonstrates their pioneer role in devising many forms of social intervention for promoting the social welfare of the group." The First Congregational Church, the first institutional church of the country, the largest and most progressive Negro church, developed a social welfare program the effectiveness of which is shown by the fact that the death rate in the church was one-third lower than that among the white population. The program played a large part in the restoration of the city's Negro community after the terrible race riot of 1906. Describes the development of the School of Social Service which became affiliated with Atlanta University. 20 notes.          E. P. Stickney

2439. Rothschild, Janice. PRE-1867 ATLANTA JEWRY. *Am. Jewish Hist. Q. 1973 62(3): 242-249.* The first Jewish family—Jacob and Jeanetta Hirsch Haas with their four children—came to Atlanta in 1845, soon followed by Henry Levi, Herman Haas, David Mayer, and others, mostly from southern Germany. Sketches family, business, and social activities. Mayer was instrumental in organizing the Hebrew Benevolent Society and a Jewish cemetery, and led the small community during the Civil War. Based on contemporary newspaper data and family recollections; 26 notes.          F. Rosenthal

2440. Routh, Porter. THE ROLE OF THE EXECUTIVE COMMITTEE OF THE SOUTHERN BAPTIST CHURCH. *Baptist Hist. and Heritage 1976 11(4): 194-203.* The Executive Committee of the Southern Baptist Church was formed in 1917 and strengthened in 1927. In 1976 a Committee of Seven, having completed a two-year study of the Executive Committee, returned an "Affirmative Appraisal" of the Committee's work to the Convention. Describes the role of the Executive Committee in the Southern Baptist Convention under the following topics: housekeeping, fiscal (with considerable detail), mediation, program statements, press relations, and general duties. Based on the *Annual* of the Southern Baptist Convention; 29 notes.          H. M. Parker, Jr.

2441. Rowatt, G. Wade, Jr. and Bertolino-Green, Dianne. FAMILY MINISTRIES AMONG SOUTHERN BAPTISTS. *Baptist Hist. and Heritage 1982 17(1): 13-25, 62.* Defines family ministry as "any specific Christian program or activity intended to rescue, instruct, and/or undergird a family group" and traces the history and development of family ministries among Southern Baptists from 1845 to 1960; discusses local church programs on family life, their achievements, and future areas of concern.

2442. Rutledge, Arthur B. LAYMEN IN SOUTHERN BAPTIST HOME MISSIONS HISTORY. *Baptist Hist. and Heritage 1978 13(1): 17-25.* Roots of Southern Baptist home missions appeared long before there was any national ecclesiastical organization in America. The Baptist laity opened their homes for worship services, witnessed to their neighbors, preached to ethnic minorities, served as lay preachers, contributed time and money, and were greatly instrumental in organizing new congregations and erecting new churches. Traces trends through the 19th and 20th centuries, underscoring the continuing role of the layman as the denomination has moved out of the South into almost every state. Secondary sources; 51 notes.          H. M. Parker, Jr.

2443. Saltzman, Rachelle. SHALOM Y'ALL. *Southern Exposure 1983 11(5): 28-36.* With American backgrounds varying from Revolutionary War origins to recent immigrants from the USSR, Jews in Memphis and throughout the South have benefited from Jewish organizations and American liberties.

2444. Santos Hernández, Angel. PRESENCIA MISIONERA EN LA ANTIGUA LUISIANA [Missionary presence in old Louisiana]. *Missionalia Hispanica [Spain] 1975 32(94): 77-101.* Sketches the history of old Louisiana, dealing with its earliest exploration and evangelization connected with the Canadian Indian missions of the Jesuits. The Franciscan Recollects from Paris and the Capuchins were later entrusted with some areas. There were problems of ecclesiastical jurisdiction during the successive French, Spanish, and American periods. In the 20th century the evangelization of several Indian tribes has been the work chiefly of the Jesuits. Based on secondary sources; 29 notes.          J. Correia-Afonso

2445. Sapp, W. David. SOUTHERN BAPTIST RESPONSES TO THE AMERICAN ECONOMY, 1900-1980. *Baptist Hist. and Heritage 1981 16(1): 3-12.*

2446. Saunders, Davis L. CHANGING CONCEPTS OF VOCATION IN SOUTHERN BAPTIST FOREIGN MISSIONS, 1845-1973. *Baptist Hist. and Heritage 1974 8(4): 213-219.* The development of the concept of foreign mission service among Southern Baptists.

2447. Schefski, Harold K. MARGARET MITCHELL: *GONE WITH THE WIND* AND *WAR AND PEACE. Southern Studies 1980 19(3): 243-260.* A number of critics have compared Margaret Mitchell's *Gone with the Wind* (1936) with Leo Tolstoy's *War and Peace* (1863-69), both being large works of broad scope highlighting individual fate in the midst of social upheaval. In addition, both are historical novels, family chronicles, and *Bildungromanen*. The theme of both is the glorification of a conquered but resisting and never-surrendering people. Both emphasize individual survival in the wake of public trauma and social chaos. A heroic city plays a role in each. There are similar characters, as Melanie and Princess Mary; there are frequent linkages among characters. Both authors wrote the last chapters first and then worked their way back. Thus there are similarities in genre, theme, character, and style. Based on Richard Harwell's *Margaret Mitchell's "Gone with the Wind" Letters* (1976); 39 notes.          J. J. Buschen

2448. Scott, P. G. JAMES BLAIR AND THE SCOTTISH CHURCH: A NEW SOURCE. *William and Mary Q. 1976 33(2): 300-308.* James Blair was a minister in the Church of Scotland before changing to the Church of England and coming to America as a bishop's commissary. In Virginia he became the founder and first president of the College of William and Mary. The minute book of the Presbytery of Dalkeith, Scotland, shows early development of Blair's traits, such as his financial high-handedness and political ability. It also proves his disputed ordination of 1679 in episcopal orders. Points out Blair's views on organization at parish and precinct levels. Compares Blair's Scottish activities with those in Virginia in 1699. In spite of receiving episcopal orders, Blair remained essentially a Scottish churchman. Based on the minutes and on miscellaneous church literature. 34 notes.          H. M. Ward

2449. Sessions, Gene A. MYTH, MORMONISM, AND MURDER IN THE SOUTH. *South Atlantic Q. 1976 75(2): 212-225.* Examines inhumane acts directed against members of the Church of Jesus Christ of Latter-day Saints from the post-Reconstruction period to the early 20th century for the purpose of understanding the broader question of violence in Southern history. Sociological and psychological explanations are analyzed in accounting for such mistreatment. Tennessee, Georgia and Alabama receive primary focus. 29 notes.          R. W. Dubay

2450. Sessions, Jim. A MIGHTY FORTRESS: PROTESTANT POWER AND WEALTH. *Southern Exposure 1976 4(3): 83-97.* Explores Protestant growth in the South, 1940-75, including corporate wealth and political power. In pp. 88-92, examines the extensive network of Southern Baptist churches, including wealth, various sects, investments, and political power. In pp. 92-95, discusses assets, educational opportunities, and church organization of the United Methodist Church, 1930's-70's. In pp. 96-98, examines church government, political power, and property of the Presbyterian Church.

2451. Shook, Robert W. ABRAHAM LEVI: FATHER OF VICTORIA JEWRY. *Western States Jewish Hist. Q. 1977 9(2): 144-154.* Victoria, Texas, was a trade and cattle center serving Texas and northern Mexico since before the Civil War. Abraham Levi (1822-1902) was among the earliest Jewish settlers in Victoria, arriving in 1848 or 1849. By the 1870's the Jewish community included 15 families and had organized a reform congregation. Levi operated a retail store, and engaged in land transactions and private banking. The Levi Bank and Trust Company (now the Victoria Bank and Trust) was franchised in 1910. Levi's activities in the community included serving as president of the Jewish congregation and as a city alderman. Primary and secondary sources; 3 photos, 26 notes.      B. S. Porter

2452. Short, Ron. THE OLD REGULAR BAPTIST CHURCH. *Southern Exposure 1976 4(3): 60-65.* The Old Regular Baptist Church exists primarily in Appalachia; discusses Appalachian community life.

2453. Shurden, Walter B. THE INERRANCY DEBATE: A COMPARATIVE STUDY OF SOUTHERN BAPTIST CONTROVERSIES. *Baptist Hist. and Heritage 1981 16(2): 12-19.* Compares the contemporary Inerrancy debate (referring to Scripture) within the Baptist Church with the three major debates which preceded it in the 20th century, and concludes that the Inerrancy debate differs from the others insofar as its supporters are seeking to force their point of view upon others through political maneuvering.

2454. Shurden, Walter B. THE PASTOR AS DENOMINATIONAL THEOLOGIAN IN SOUTHERN BAPTIST HISTORY. *Baptist Hist. and Heritage 1980 15(3): 15-22.* Discusses the changing role of Southern Baptist pastors as denominational theologians in three distinct periods: ca. 1700-1859, when "pastors were the primary denominational theologians"; 1859-1960, characterized by the founding of the Southern Baptist Theological Seminary and the professors' preeminence in denominationalism; and 1960-80, characterized by the pastors' resurgence.

2455. Shurden, Walter B. THE SOUTHERN BAPTIST SYNTHESIS: IS IT CRACKING? *Baptist Hist. and Heritage 1981 16(2): 2-11.* The Southern Baptist synthesis shaped in the 18th, 19th, and 20th centuries is beginning to crack because of stresses placed on it since World War II and can be maintained only through informed knowledge of the Baptist denominational heritage.

2456. Simms, L. Moody, Jr. THEODORE DU BOSE BRATTON, CHRISTIAN PRINCIPLES, AND THE RACE QUESTION. *J. of Mississippi Hist. 1976 38(1): 47-52.* Describes a 1908 speech by Theodore DuBose Bratton, the Episcopal Bishop of Mississippi, to the Conference for Education in the South. The speech illustrates the attitudes of many white southern Christian moderates who believed in Negro inferiority and "sought merely to neutralize the harshest aspects of white supremacy." Based on secondary sources; 15 notes.      J. W. Hillje

2457. Smith, Harold S. THE LIFE AND WORKS OF J. R. GRAVES (1820-1893). *Baptist Hist. and Heritage 1975 10(1): 19-27.* Although James Robinson Graves is best known for Baptists Landmarkism, the article emphasizes 50 years in which Graves was editor of the *Tennessee Baptist,* a weekly religious paper. Graves was insistent on an educated Baptist ministry, and was largely instrumental in founding the Southern Baptist Seminary in Greenville, South Carolina, in 1859. Based largely on the *Tennessee Baptist,* with a few references to Graves' works; 48 notes.

     H. M. Parker, Jr.

2458. Smith, Julia Floyd. MARCHING TO ZION: THE RELIGION OF BLACK BAPTISTS IN COASTAL GEORGIA PRIOR TO 1865. *Viewpoints: Georgia Baptist Hist. 1978 (6): 47-54.* Discusses black Baptist Churches in Georgia, 1750's-1830's.

2459. Smith, Sid. GROWTH OF BLACK SOUTHERN BAPTIST CHURCHES IN THE INNER CITY. *Baptist Hist. and Heritage 1981 16(3): 49-60.* Discusses the "Study of Black Southern Baptists" and the interaction between the Ethnic Liaison Unit of the Southern Baptist Sunday School Board and 350 black Southern Baptist leaders in the past two years, and presents some generalizations about the growth of black Southern Baptist churches in the inner city based on basic models such as the religious education model, the social service model, and the urban planning model; 1951-81.

2460. Smylie, James H. THE BIBLE, RACE AND THE CHANGING SOUTH. *J. of Presbyterian Hist. 1981 59(2): 197-218.* Examines the principal statements of the Presbyterian Church in the United States (the Southern Presbyterian Church) to ascertain what part the Bible played in shaping the mind of this Southern denomination on racial matters. After reference to the denomination's attitudes at its beginnings in 1861, it focuses on the period after the 1930's when Southern Presbyterians felt the mounting pressure to deal with societal problems as well as race relations. Based largely on the *Minutes* of the Presbyterian Church in the United States and historical studies; illus., 47 notes.      H. M. Parker, Jr.

2461. Snyder, Walter W. H. D. WACKER, BESUCHER, REISEPREDIGER, PASTOR IN FRONTIER TEXAS. *Concordia Hist. Inst. Q. 1980 53(2): 70-83.* Examines the meaning and duties of a *Besucher* or "visitor" and a *Reiseprediger* or "circuit rider" of the Missouri Synod of the Lutheran Church, formed during 1847-65, as part of a program to reach German Lutherans in the Western District. Discusses Hermann Dietrich Wacker (1867-1938) who served as a *Besucher, Reiseprediger,* and pastor for the Lutheran Church in parts of Texas and what is now Oklahoma.

2462. Sobel, Mechal. "THEY CAN NEVER BOTH PROSPER TOGETHER": BLACK AND WHITE BAPTISTS IN NASHVILLE, TENNESSEE. *Tennessee Hist. Q. 1979 38(3): 296-307.* The First Baptist Church of Nashville, Tennessee, initially welcomed black membership in the 1820's, although blacks' duties and privileges were circumscribed. By 1834, both whites and blacks began to move for greater black autonomy. This led to a separate black meeting in 1841, a black minister—Nelson Merry (1824-84)—and mission in 1853, and finally a separate church in 1865. Based on the Manuscript Minutes of the Southern Baptist Historical Commission, Nashville; 44 notes.      W. D. Piersen

2463. Stallings, Evelyn T. A HISTORY OF HOLLY GROVE METHODIST CHURCH. *North Louisiana Hist. Assoc. J. 1983 14(2-3): 82-102.* According to a state historical marker near Leesville, Louisiana, Methodist services began in the area in 1826, and the Holly Grove Methodist Church was organized in 1835. Traces the history of this church. 2 photos, 94 notes, appendix.

     J. F. Paul

2464. Standing, Herbert C. QUAKERS IN DELAWARE IN THE TIME OF WILLIAM PENN. *Delaware Hist. 1982 20(2): 123-147.* Describes the Quaker families and meeting groups in Delaware from the 1680's to 1710's, focusing on the organization, evolution, and membership patterns of meeting groups at Newark, Centre, New Castle, Duck Creek, Georges Creek, and in lower Delaware. Mostly primary sources; 112 notes.      R. M. Miller

2465. Stange, Douglas C. ABOLITIONISM AS MALEFICENCE: SOUTHERN UNITARIANS VERSUS "PURITAN FANATICISM": 1831-1860. *Harvard Lib. Bull. 1978 26(2): 146-171.* Southern Unitarians generally took a much more favorable view on slavery than their northern coreligionists. By examining the careers of prominent southern Unitarians, including Samuel Gilman of

Charleston, Richard Arnold of Savannah, and Theodore Clapp of New Orleans, presents the full range of southern Unitarian views on slavery and relations with northern Unitarians. Notes.

W. H. Mulligan, Jr.

2466. Starin, Mary M. THE REVEREND DOCTOR JOHN GORDON, 1717-1790. *Maryland Hist. Mag. 1980 75(3): 167-197.* Information already published about the Reverend John Gordon in secondary sources has, in almost every instance, proved to be incorrect. Despite diligent research, large gaps in the biography of this important clergyman of St. Michael's Parish in Talbot County, Maryland, remain unfilled. Active in secular affairs as well, a member of the famed Tuesday Club, Gordon was one of the many Anglicans who long opposed the establishment of an episcopate in this country, although the revolution caused him to reevaluate his position. His tenure (1749-90) at St. Michael's put him in the list of Maryland's first citizens. 103 notes.          G. J. Bobango

2467. Steele, David L. THE AUTOBIOGRAPHY OF THE REVEREND JOHN YOUNG, 1747-1837. *Methodist Hist. 1974 13(1): 17-40.* John Young was a Methodist clergyman ordained in 1819. This autobiography, written in 1818 or 1819, covers his early days in North Carolina and includes a statement of his doctrine. 45 notes.          H. L. Calkin

2468. Steely, John E. MINISTERIAL CERTIFICATION IN SOUTHERN BAPTIST HISTORY: ORDINATION. *Baptist Hist. and Heritage 1980 15(1): 23-29, 61.* Discusses the lack of change and absence of any standard interpretation in the practice of ordination, from 1677 through 1980, and suggests that the question of female ordination may cause this situation to change.

2469. Stein, Stephen J. THE CONVERSION OF CHARLES WILLING BYRD TO SHAKERISM. *Filson Club Hist. Q. 1982 56(4): 395-414.* Traces the religious ideas of Charles Willing Byrd. Byrd, the direct descendant of an aristocratic Virginia family, began his journey as an Anglican and then became successively a skeptic, an evangelical, and finally a Shaker. The author points out that Byrd's final conversion was much more rational and less spontaneous than historians had previously thought. Documentation comes from the Byrd Papers at the Indiana University Library; 64 notes.          G. B. McKinney

2470. Stern, Malcolm H. GROWING UP IN PIONEER SAVANNAH: THE UNFINISHED MEMOIR OF LEVI SHEFTALL (1739-1809). *Michael: On the Hist. of the Jews in the Diaspora [Israel] 1975 3: 15-22.* Levi Sheftall was a son of Benjamin Sheftall (1692-1765), a native of Prussia and one of the first Jews to settle in Georgia; he was half-brother to Mordecai Sheftall. Reprints the oldest known memoir of an American Jew and possibly the earliest description of life in pioneer Savannah. Starting from scratch, Levi Sheftall accumulated a large fortune, including many slaves, but eventually lost most of it. Imprisoned as a rebel during the American Revolution, he denied entertaining such sentiments. He was active in Jewish community life. 10 notes.          T. Sassoon

2471. Stewart, James Brewer. EVANGELICALISM AND THE RADICAL STRAIN IN SOUTHERN ANTISLAVERY THOUGHT DURING THE 1820'S. *J. of Southern Hist. 1973 39(3): 379-396.* Discusses southern antislavery sentiments during the 1820's among scattered groups of devout Evangelicals, located mostly in the northernmost parts of the South. These few "radicals" believed slavery to be a cause for the decline of religious piety, a contradiction of religious creeds, a crime against humanity, an erosive force on morality and traditional values, and a cause of the diffusion of corruption and civic decay. The Evangelicals attempted to spread their gospel to purify "churchly institutions," and in the process estranged themselves from southern society. Much of the later abolitionism of the North was similar to or built upon their ideas. Based on contemporary publications and addresses, and secondary sources; 63 notes.          N. J. Street

2472. Stokes, Durward T. JEREMIAH NORMAN, PIONEER METHODIST MINISTER IN AUGUSTA, AND HIS DIARY. *Richmond County Hist. 1978 10(1): 20-35.* Excerpts from the diary of Jeremiah Norman, an itinerant preacher for the Methodist Episcopal Church on the Augusta Circuit, describes his experiences in the ministry traveling from town to town to deliver his soap box evangelism, 1798-1801.

2473. Storey, John W. THE RHETORIC OF PATERNALISM: SOUTHERN BAPTISTS AND NEGRO EDUCATION IN THE LATTER NINETEENTH CENTURY. *Southern Humanities Rev. 1978 12(2): 101-108.* Southern Baptists, 1880's-90's, paternalistically supported black education, but soon even that became little more than rhetoric based on laissez-faire attitudes toward civil rights and economic betterment.

2474. Storey, John W. SOUTHERN BAPTISTS AND THE RACIAL CONTROVERSY IN THE CHURCHES AND SCHOOLS DURING RECONSTRUCTION. *Mississippi Q. 1978 31(2): 211-228.* Separation in Southern Baptist churches and opposition to equal education for blacks stemmed from the fear that equal voice in church and education would force Negroes out of "their place" in southern society and initiate a new generation of "uppity" blacks.

2475. Stritch, Thomas J. THREE CATHOLIC BISHOPS FROM TENNESSEE. *Tennessee Hist. Q. 1978 37(1): 3-35.* Much of the material about these three Catholic, Irish American bishops is reproduced from the author's memory. The three bishops, John Morris (1866-1946), John P. Farrelly (1856-1921), and Samuel A. Stritch (1887-1958), were all southerners whose lives were intertwined. They were wise, possibly great men who exhibited a tremendous influence on the South. Primary and secondary sources; 2 illus., 70 notes.          M. B. Lucas

2476. Stroupe, Henry S. "CITE THEM BOTH TO ATTEND THE NEXT CHURCH CONFERENCE": SOCIAL CONTROL BY NORTH CAROLINA BAPTIST CHURCHES, 1772-1908. *North Carolina Hist. R. 1975 52(2): 156-170.* Baptist church congregations in North Carolina have exercised direct control over the personal conduct of members since the 18th century. Until the early 20th century transgressors were made to fear for their souls and their social standing in the community. Churches excommunicated or suspended white and black congregants for adultery, drunkenness, thievery, lying, swearing, quarreling, etc. Following World War I the church began employing indirect methods for social control, such as the temperance movement and blue laws. Based on manuscript church records, and published primary and secondary sources; 4 illus., table, 37 notes.          T. L. Savitt

2477. Stubblefield, Jerry M. CREATIVE ADVANCEMENTS IN SOUTHERN BAPTIST SUNDAY SCHOOL WORK. *Baptist Hist. and Heritage 1983 18(1): 44-55.* Considers ecumenical aspects of Sunday school work, emphases given different age groups, curriculum expansion, leadership training, the Southern Baptist approach to Sunday schools, responses of Baptists in other countries to Southern Baptist methods, and the emergence of church staff leadership for Sunday schools.

2478. Sutherland, Hunter C. A BRIEF HISTORY OF THE BUSH RIVER FRIENDS MEETING OF HARFORD COUNTY, MARYLAND. *Maryland Hist. Mag. 1982 77(4): 365-369.* The first Quaker meeting house built north of Annapolis was on the old post road at the western edge of Bynum Run and known as the Bush River Quaker Meeting. Dating from 1706 in a house built by Aquila Paca, High Sheriff of Harford County, the Bush River Meeting's membership was never large and was in fact kept small by the practice of disownment for "marrying out" to a non-Quaker and for other infractions. Still the Bush River Meeting was the source of many leaders in Maryland such as Peter Bond, James Lee, Jacob Giles, and the descendants of John Lee Webster. By 1800 the meeting moved to a brick house on the east side of Abingdon and the Bush River Meeting was laid down in 1826. Maryland Historical Society archives and secondary works; 33 notes.

G. J. Bobango

2479. Sutton, Brett. IN THE GOOD OLD WAY: PRIMITIVE BAPTIST TRADITIONS. *Southern Exposure 1977 5(2-3): 97-104.* Folk revivalists have neglected the rich folk tradition of the Primitive Baptist Church of Appalachia. Church belief centers on predestination and is characterized by a stern, austere attitude toward the outside world. Primitive Baptists have a simple, honest concern with the trials and tribulations of the world, including a realistic approach to death. They do not believe in converting others to their faith and they reject the concept of church growth and expansion. The church relies on oral testimony and lay preaching. Church music is based on 18th- and early 19th-century hymns collected during the church's founding. Although there have been efforts to incorporate newer music into the church, this move has been resisted by many members. Based on participant observation in southwest Virginia.                                                         N. Lederer

2480. Taulman, James E. THE LIFE AND WRITINGS OF AMOS COOPER DAYTON (1813-1865). *Baptist Hist. and Heritage 1975 10(1): 36-43.* One of the "Great Triumvirate" of the Landmark movement, Dayton was the first Baptist in the South to write a religious novel. Seeking to disseminate Baptist doctrine through the medium of fiction, he defined the church in one of his novels as a "local" group, organized independently of Christian people—a definition of the church which became a major cornerstone of Landmarkism. Beginning as a Presbyterian, he became a Baptist in 1852, and launched his literary career the following year. He authored 13 volumes of fiction and theology and contributed nearly 1,000 articles to 20 different religious periodicals. Primary and secondary sources; 44 notes.                    H. M. Parker, Jr.

2481. Terrell, Thomas E., Jr. "SOME HOLSOM EXHORTATIONS": HENRY WHITE'S SEVENTEENTH-CENTURY SOUTHERN RELIGIOUS NARRATIVE IN VERSE. *Early Am. Lit. 1983 18(1): 31-44.* A poem by Quaker Henry White, written in the Albemarle region of North Carolina in 1698, is the earliest poem known to have been written in the Carolinas and the first Southern religious narrative. Depicting the fall of man and his eventual salvation, the poem was intended to instruct members of White's Quaker community. 7 notes.                    T. P. Linkfield

2482. Thomas, Arthur Dicken, Jr. REASONABLE REVIVALISM: PRESBYTERIAN EVANGELIZATION OF EDUCATED VIRGINIANS, 1787-1837. *J. of Presbyterian Hist. 1983 61(3): 316-334.* Virginia Presbyterian preachers led their constituencies into revival during the 2d Great Awakening by use of reasonable—rather than emotional—revivalism. They made effective use of Christian apologetics as a preparation for revival. A study of Presbyterian revivals in Virginia reveals that the era of Southern antebellum revivalism was "an age of reason," not a "flight from reason in reaction to the Enlightenment," as Sidney Mead has argued. Through an articulate defense of Christianity and a reasonable form of revivalism, the ministers captured the hearts and wills of Virginia intellectuals and public officials through a four-fold attack: they wrote and preached on the evidences of Christianity as a preparation for the Gospel, labored for revivals on college campuses, conducted revivals with decorum and reason, and worked to convert distinguished "infidels" to a well-reasoned orthodoxy. Based on the writings of Presbyterian leaders; 58 notes.                    H. M. Parker, Jr.

2483. Thomas, Samuel W. and Young, Mary Lawrence. THE DEVELOPMENT OF SHAKERTOWN AT PLEASANT HILL, KENTUCKY. *Filson Club Hist. Q. 1975 49(3): 231-255.* Traces the history of the Shaker community at Pleasant Hill, Kentucky. Taking advantage of the favorable climate of opinion created by the Great Revival, three Shaker missionaries settled in Kentucky in 1805 and began to convert some of the native population. Their efforts were successful and by the 1830's the community numbered 500. Describes the buildings constructed at Pleasant Hill and several contemporary accounts of Shaker life. Death, destruction brought by the Civil War, and the materialism of the Gilded Age caused a decline in the community. By 1910 creditors had taken control of the Shaker land and the group was forced to disband. Documentation comes from manuscripts at Case Western Reserve University and Shaker collections in Kentucky; 114 notes.                    G. B. McKinney

2484. Thompson, Ernest T. BLACK PRESBYTERIANS: EDUCATION AND EVANGELISM AFTER THE CIVIL WAR. *J. of Presbyterian Hist. 1973 51(2): 174-198.* Presbyterians' evangelization and Christian education of their former slaves after the Civil War.

2485. Thompson, J. Earl, Jr. SLAVERY AND PRESBYTERIANISM IN THE REVOLUTIONARY ERA. *J. of Presbyterian Hist. 1976 54(1): 121-141.* Throughout the Revolutionary epoch Presbyterians attempted to build an antislavery platform upon which the entire church could stand, to unify a young and fragile Christian community avoiding the disruption of schism which had plagued them before the Revolution, and to create a large and strong denomination. Their social goal was to maintain the tranquility, order, and racial homogeneity of white America by protecting the nation against an invasion of degraded freed blacks. They believed that they could reconcile their competing values of hostility toward slavery, fear of freedom, and loyalty to a united demonination and to a racially homogeneous America by embracing the ideology and program of gradualism. Traces the attitudes of Presbyterian leaders toward slavery—Samuel Davies, Dr. Bejamin Rush, Jacob Green, Samuel Stanhope Smith, Elias Boudinot, Samuel Miller, and David Rice. Based largely on writings of the leaders cited; 91 notes.                    H. M. Parker, Jr.

2486. Thompson, James J., Jr. SOUTHERN BAPTISTS AND ANTI-CATHOLICISM IN THE 1920'S. *Mississippi Q. 1979 32(4): 611-625.* Discusses the reasons for, and the nature of, anti-Catholicism among Southern Baptists who spearheaded the Protestant opposition to Roman Catholicism in the 1920's.

2487. Thompson, James J., Jr. SOUTHERN BAPTISTS AND THE ANTIEVOLUTION CONTROVERSY OF THE 1920'S. *Mississippi Q. 1975/76 29(1): 65-81.*

2488. Thompson, James J., Jr. SOUTHERN BAPTIST CITY AND COUNTRY CHURCHES IN THE TWENTIES. *Foundations 1974 17(4): 351-363.* In the 1920's Southern Baptists tried to combat the decline in rural church membership and the evils of urbanization in the South with evangelicalism.

2489. Thompson, James J., Jr. SOUTHERN BAPTISTS AND POST-WAR DISILLUSIONMENT 1918-1920. *Foundations 1978 21(2): 113-122.* Some feel there was disillusionment following World War I. Holds that this idea was not universally true. Examines the Southern Baptists' attitudes on the war and its meaning during 1918-20 as an example of a different view. 35 notes.                    E. E. Eminhizer

2490. Thompson, Roger M. THE DECLINE OF CEDAR KEY: MORMON LORE IN NORTH FLORIDA AND ITS SOCIAL FUNCTION. *Southern Folklore Q. 1975 39(1): 39-62.* Describes the presence of Mormons in the fishing village of Cedar Key and the folk legend which developed around a supposed instance in which they were run out of town.                    S

2491. Tillman, William M., Jr. PATTERNS IN FAMILY ETHICS IN BAPTIST LIFE. *Baptist Hist. and Heritage 1982 17(1): 26-35, 53.* Traces changes in family life patterns, particularly the dynamics of Puritan standards of behavior and cultural standards of behavior, and how they have affected family life among Southern Baptists.

2492. Toulouse, Mark G. A CASE STUDY IN SCHISM: J. FRANK NORRIS AND THE SOUTHERN BAPTIST CONVENTION. *Foundations 1981 24(1): 32-53.* Following an overview of J. Frank Norris's life (d. 1952), centers on his battle with the Southern Baptists. His separation from the church seems to have been caused more by his abusive methods and personality than his theology. Based on the Norris papers and published materials; 70 notes, biblio.                    E. E. Eminhizer

2493. Trotti, John Boone. THOMAS WOLFE: THE PRESBYTERIAN CONNECTION. *J. of Presbyterian Hist. 1981 59(4): 517-542.* Discusses the relationship of the American novelist Thomas Wolfe (1900-38) and the Presbyterian Church, particularly the First Presbyterian Church, Asheville, North Carolina, which he attended until he went away to college. There are numerous references to this congregation in his autobiographical novel, *Look Homeward, Angel* (1929). Although never a communicant member of the church, he nevertheless felt very close to its life. Also traces his religious connection through his student days and later years. The Calvinistic theology he imbibed through catechetical memorization remained with him and surfaces throughout his works. His own lifelong posture toward institutional Christianity was that of the inquirer, the listener, the critic, mildly amused, yet not fully committed. In a wistful way, he was attracted to the Christian faith and, in a personal way, to Presbyterianism. Based on oral interviews, archival records in the Historical Foundation, Montreat, North Carolina, and Wolfe's published works; 2 pictures, 153 notes.

H. M. Parker, Jr.

2494. Troy, Bill and Williams, Claude. THE PEOPLE'S INSTITUTE OF APPLIED RELIGION. *Southern Exposure 1976 4(3): 46-53.* The People's Institute of Applied Religion was established by Claude Williams and his wife Joyce Williams to train religious leaders of the cotton belt in labor unionism, 1940-75.

2495. Tull, James E. THE LANDMARK MOVEMENT: AN HISTORICAL AND THEOLOGICAL APPRAISAL. *Baptist Hist. and Heritage 1975 10(1): 3-18.* A balanced presentation of the Landmark movement among American Baptists. The central idea of Landmarkism is the authority of the local congregation in Baptist ecclesiology. Landmarkism is viewed as a doctrinal aberration from the English and early American Baptist theology and polity. Traces the movement from its 1851 beginning in Cotton Grove, Tennessee to its present flickering embers. In its extremity Landmarkism was sectarian in its emphasis on the role of the local church, its denial of the validity of "alien" immersion, an adherence to strict, local church communion, and a hostile response to the ecumenical movement—all of which are quite foreign to the ecclesiological traditions which had been developed by English and American Baptists in the 17th and 18th centuries. Based largely on religious newspapers and works written by James R. Graves; 31 notes.

H. M. Parker, Jr.

2496. Tyler, Lyon G. GOD AND MR. PETIGRU: EPISCOPAL ATTITUDES TOWARD FAITH AND DOCTRINE IN ANTEBELLUM SOUTH CAROLINA. *Hist. Mag. of the Protestant Episcopal Church 1983 52(3): 229-243.* Although not a communicant member of the Episcopal Church in Beaufort, South Carolina, James L. Petigru was nevertheless a member of the vestry—an ecclesiastical paradox not unusual in the Episcopal Church at that time. Although he had doubts about the effective value of revivalism, he did believe in a transcendent and personal God. In his letters he wrote of God, providence, Christianity, and the apostles, but seldom of Jesus Christ. For Petigru, renewal came to the church not simply through good works and good lives, but through the demonstration of the power of God. In his daily life he was a lawyer, serving for a time as the state attorney general. Based on the Vanderhorst Papers in the South Carolina Historical Society and on the Pettigrew Family Papers in the Southern Collection, University of North Carolina; illus., 57 notes.    H. M. Parker, Jr.

2497. Van Deburg, William L. FREDERICK DOUGLASS: MARYLAND SLAVE TO RELIGIOUS LIBERAL. *Maryland Hist. Mag. 1974 69(1): 27-43.* Young Frederick Douglass was convinced of the omnipotence of God and His role as "Supreme Judge of the Universe." By the 1840's, however, the influence of Reason, Transcendentalism, and Unitarianism convinced him that the abolition movement must be primarily a human enterprise. Despising the passive attitude displayed by many Negro ministers, Douglass even criticized Henry Ward Beecher's reliance on God to end slavery. Increasingly enlightenment terminology crept into Douglass' writings and speeches, and his move to a humanistic theology climaxed with his address in Philadelphia's Horticultural Hall on 26 April

1870 when he lauded Wendell Phillips, Elijah Lovejoy, John Brown, and Abraham Lincoln in celebrating the recently ratified 15th Amendment. Primary and secondary sources; 8 illus., 59 notes.

G. J. Bobango

2498. Vernon, Walter N. METHODIST PIONEERS ALONG THE GREAT BEND OF RED RIVER. *Red River Valley Hist. Rev. 1981 6(1): 46-57.* Discusses the work of Methodist circuit riders along the Great Bend of the Red River in Arkansas, Oklahoma, and Texas beginning as early as 1784 when Francis Asbury, who became bishop of the Methodists that year, began the westward push to preach to settlers in the west.

2499. Voth, M. Agnes. MOTHER M. BEATRICE RENGGLI, O.S.B.[:] FOUNDRESS OF THE AMERICAN OLIVETAN BENEDICTINE SISTERS[,] JONESBORO, ARKANSAS. *Am. Benedictine Rev. 1974 25(3): 389-409.* Presents a brief biography of Rose Renggli, foundress of the American Olivetan Benedictine Sisters, and a history of Roman Catholic missionary work in Arkansas during the late 19th and early 20th centuries. 15 notes.

J. H. Pragman

2500. Walker, Arthur L., Jr. THE MAJOR. *Baptist Hist. and Heritage 1974 9(1): 40-47, 54.* Biographical sketch of Harwell G. Davis, president of Howard College and a prominent Alabama Baptist.

S

2501. Walker, Charles O. THE COMMITTEE ON BAPTIST HISTORY, 1948-1978. *Viewpoints: Georgia Baptist Hist. 1978 (6): 83-96.* Formed in 1948, the Committee on Baptist History of the Georgia Baptist Convention has sought to identify and establish Baptist landmarks in Georgia, collect historical materials, sponsor a collective history of Georgia Baptists, and maintain a fund for ongoing historical studies.

2502. Walker, Charles O. GEORGIA BAPTIST HISTORY INTERESTS. *Viewpoints: Georgia Baptist Hist. 1974 4: 55-66.* Examines interest in Baptist church history among Georgia Baptists.

S

2503. Walker, Charles O. GEORGIA'S RELIGION IN THE COLONIAL ERA, 1733-1790. *Viewpoints: Georgia Baptist Hist. 1976 5: 17-44.* Examines Anglicans, Jews, Lutherans, Presbyterians, Congregationalists, Quakers, and Baptists in Georgia, 1733-90, taking into account the American Revolution and its effect on religious practices in the state.

2504. Walker, Charles O. SEARCY SLATON GARRISON. *Viewpoints: Georgia Baptist Hist. 1980 7: 5-16.* Searcy Slaton Garrison has served as executive secretary-treasurer of the Georgia Baptist Convention from 1955 through 1980, overseeing the Convention's projects and concerns.

2505. Walsh, James P. "BLACK COTTED RASKOLLS": ANTI-ANGLICAN CRITICISM IN COLONIAL VIRGINIA. *Virginia Mag. of Hist. and Biog. 1980 88(1): 21-36.* Colonial Virginia saw its Anglican clergy as lazy and irresponsible, or alternately as lustful for power. Having to serve geographically large parishes made the clergy appear neglectful. Traces the laity's discontent to clerical rebukes of their sins, and the problem of the clergy's social status. Clergymen complained too, particularly about tenure and salaries, but had opportunity for material improvement and security. Ministers looked to Great Britain, from whence they came, for support in their struggles with Virginians. 57 notes.

P. J. Woehrmann

2506. Walters, Jonathan. A REVOLUTIONARY MONASTERY. *Hist. Preservation 1980 32(4): 42-47.* Discusses the history of Wormeley Manor along the Shenandoah River in Virginia, and its 20th-century role for the Trappists as Holy Cross Abbey.

2507. Washburn, A. V. SUNDAY SCHOOL: A VEHICLE FOR CHURCH GROWTH. *Baptist Hist. and Heritage 1983 18(1): 56-64.* Considers the theological reasons for creating Sunday schools and examines the contributions of Southern Baptists to the Sunday school movement: relating the Sunday school to church outreach; providing a Bible-based, graded curriculum; providing lay leadership training; and developing a formula for building a Sunday school program; covers 1891-1980.

2508. Wasserman, Ira M. RELIGIOUS AFFILIATIONS AND HOMICIDE: HISTORICAL RESULTS FROM THE RURAL SOUTH. *J. for the Sci. Study of Religion 1978 17(4): 415-418.* Examines the relationship of religious affiliation to murder, comparing whites and blacks; based on information from a 1916 census department study and the 1920 murder rates in the rural South.

2509. Wasson, Margaret. TEXAS METHODISM'S OTHER HALF. *Methodist Hist. 1981 19(4): 206-223.* Women in Texas during the early 1830's acquired a role in the Methodist Church, hosting religious services and requesting missionaries. Their role has steadily increased. They have organized missionary societies, become missionaries, supported educational and other institutions and taught in religious organizations. It seems certain that laywomen will assume even more responsible positions, and clergywomen will find greater opportunities for Christian service. Based on secondary works; 48 notes.                                    H. L. Calkin

2510. Watson, Alan D. THE ANGLICAN PARISH IN ROYAL NORTH CAROLINA, 1729-1775. *Hist. Mag. of the Protestant Episcopal Church 1979 48(3): 303-319.* Through a study of two colonial Anglican parishes, St. Paul's (Chowan County) and St. John's (Carteret County), demonstrates ways the church in east North Carolina preached and met the needs of a substantial segment of the population. The parish remained a viable institution throughout the royal era. The assembly continually relieved the parish of its civil responsibilities, reflecting the inability of parishes to cope with such duties on the one hand as well as the increasing competence of county units of government on the other. Yet the parish did retain a competent taxing power which it used to support and enlarge the church establishment and an extensive system of poor relief. Based largely on the records of the two parishes and the two counties and North Carolina colonial and state records; 85 notes.                                    H. M. Parker, Jr.

2511. Watts, John D. W. HIGHER EDUCATION IN SOUTHERN BAPTIST FOREIGN MISSIONS. *Baptist Hist. and Heritage 1976 11(4): 218-229.* William Carey established the first Baptist institution of higher learning on the foreign mission field at Serampore, India, in 1826. He thus initiated a history of establishing colleges and seminaries on foreign fields which Southern Baptists have continued. Traces the development of institutions of higher learning among Southern Baptist foreign missions, with most emphasis placed upon theological seminaries. The greatest institutional growth has developed since World War II. Based on primary and secondary sources; 28 notes.                                    H. M. Parker, Jr.

2512. Weaver, C. Douglas. DAVID THOMAS AND THE REGULAR BAPTISTS IN COLONIAL VIRGINIA. *Baptist Hist. and Heritage 1983 18(4): 3-19.* Recounts the history of the Regular Baptists in Virginia until their unification with the Separate Baptists in 1787, focusing on the leadership role of David Thomas; Thomas later became established as a prominent Baptist preacher in Kentucky.

2513. Webb, Bernard L. LITTLE CHURCHES OF LONG AGO. *Georgia Life 1978 5(3): 21-31.* Discusses Georgia's churches built from 1751 to the 1900's; provides photographs.

2514. Weeks, Louis. STUART ROBINSON: KENTUCKY PRESBYTERIAN LEADER. *Filson Club Hist. Q. 1980 54(4): 360-377.* Stuart Robinson was minister of the Second Presbyterian Church of Louisville, Kentucky, from 1858 until his death in 1881. Born in Ireland in 1814, Robinson was educated at Amherst and Union Theological Seminary in Virginia. After short pastorates in Kentucky and Maryland, Robinson taught at Danville Seminary between 1856 and 1858. There he wrote the first of three theology texts. After he assumed the Louisville position, he became involved in Civil War controversies and spent most of the war in voluntary exile in Canada. During Reconstruction Robinson was the most ac-

tive leader in the movement to ally Kentucky Old School Prsbyterians with the southern branch of the church. Based on published church records and Robinson's personal scrapbook; photo, 77 notes.                                    G. B. McKinney

2515. Weeks, Louis. TERAH TEMPLIN: KENTUCKY'S FIRST PRESBYTERIAN PREACHER. *Filson Club Hist. Q. 1979 53(1): 45-60.* Terah Templin was the first Presbyterian minister in Kentucky in 1780. He helped organize many congregations, the Transylvania Presbytery, and the Synod of Kentucky. Based on published church minutes; 53 notes.                                    G. B. McKinney

2516. Weeks, Louis B. THE SCRIPTURES AND SABBATH OBSERVANCE IN THE SOUTH. *J. of Presbyterian Hist. 1981 59(2): 267-284.* Traces a history of the use of the Bible in focusing the matter of Sabbath observance for the Presbyterian Church in the United States (the Southern Presbyterian Church). Traces the evolution in doctrine from more legalistic and proscriptive formulations in the 19th century to those that offer more freedom in the 20th. Describes the various mechanisms southern Presbyterians have employed to discern the import of biblical teaching relative to the nature of the Sabbath for church and society. Explores the ecclesiastical pronouncements to learn more generally about religious authority and the relationships of Bible, creeds, and practice. Based almost wholly on the *Minutes* of the Presbyterian Church of the United States; 45 notes.                                    H. M. Parker, Jr.

2517. Weisheit, Eldon J. THE BLACK BELT REVISITED. *Concordia Hist. Inst. Q. 1975 48(2): 44-50.* A pictorial examination of the recent history of Lutheranism in the Deep South. Twelve photographs depict the development of Lutheranism with primary interest on Alabama.                                    W. T. Walker

2518. Weiskircher, Robert F. THE ROMAN CATHOLIC CHURCH IN WHEELING: EARLY HISTORY TO 1850. *Upper Ohio Valley Hist. Rev. 1982 11(2): 12-17.* Traces the history of the Roman Catholic Church in Wheeling, West Virginia, from 1749, when Father Joseph de Bonnecamps, a Jesuit priest, said the first Mass, until 1850, when the Diocese of Wheeling was created.

2519. Wheeler, Edward L. AN OVERVIEW OF BLACK SOUTHERN BAPTIST INVOLVEMENTS. *Baptist Hist. and Heritage 1981 16(3): 3-11, 40.* Black Southern Baptist involvements in the Southern Baptist Convention hardly existed until the last decade; 1845-1980.

2520. Whisenhunt, Donald W. RUFUS KITCHENS: A TWENTIETH CENTURY CIRCUIT RIDER. *West Texas Hist. Assoc. Year Book 1981 57: 47-54.* Rufus Kitchens was a Methodist Church minister who rode the circuit in West Texas during 1932-58, but was typical of 19th-century frontier circuit riders.

2521. Whitaker, Thomas. THE GASPER RIVER MEETING HOUSE. *Filson Club Hist. Q. 1982 56(1): 30-61.* The Gasper River Meeting House in Logan County, Kentucky, was the center of the frontier revival that became the Second Great Awakening. This Presbyterian congregation was served by James McGready and John Rankin, who were the earliest leaders of the camp meeting revivals. The emotionalism of the participants was rejected by the traditional Presbyterian leadership. The result was the formation of the Cumberland Presbyterian Church, even though McGready remained in the traditional church and Rankin joined a Shaker community. Primarily based on McGready's published autobiography and the manuscript autobiography of Rankin at Western Kentucky University; 78 notes.                                    G. B. McKinney

2522. White, Ronald C., Jr. BEYOND THE SACRED: EDGAR GARDNER MURPHY AND A MINISTRY OF SOCIAL REFORM. *Hist. Mag. of the Protestant Episcopal Church 1980 49(1): 51-70.* In November 1901 Edgar Gardner Murphy (1869-1913), Episcopal minister in Montgomery, Alabama, was invited to become executive secretary of the Southern Education Board. He had been long active in southern social reform movements. His decision to accept the invitation involved a profound religious and vocational decision. It required resigning his charge and also his vows as an

Episcopal priest. But it was very clear that he was not leaving his calling to the ministry; he was merely shifting his location from the parish ministry to a ministry of social reform. The impetus for his reform efforts had been nourished by a religious motivation expressed in social consciousness. His sense of ministry continued in and through the midst of changing responsibilities. Based on the Edgar Gardner Murphy and the Southern Education Board Papers, Southern Historical Collection, University of North Carolina (Chapel Hill), Booker T. Washington Papers (Library of Congress), and on lesser primary and secondary sources; 43 notes.

H. M. Parker, Jr.

2523. Williams, John R., ed. FRONTIER EVANGELIST THE JOURNAL OF HENRY BRYSON. *Alabama Hist. Q. 1980 42(1-2): 5-39.* Henry Bryson was a preacher for the Associate Reformed Presbyterian Church in South Carolina. During 1826 and 1827 he undertook an evangelistic mission through Georgia, Alabama, Tennessee, and Florida. A copy of the journal he kept during this trip is presented. Although incomplete, it both roughly traces his route and gives some insight into what his work entailed. Primary source; 69 notes.

A. Drysdale

2524. Wilson, Charles Reagan. BISHOP THOMAS FRANK GAILOR: CELEBRANT OF SOUTHERN TRADITION. *Tennessee Hist. Q. 1979 38(3): 322-331.* Episcopal Bishop Thomas Frank Gailor (1856-1935) of Tennessee was a great regional rhetorician of the Lost Cause and a southern liberal adamantly opposed to political equality for blacks. His personal childhood wartime experiences, reinforced by his relationship with the University of the South, led Gailor to emphasize the spiritual quality of the Confederacy's patriotism, self-sacrifice, and loyalty as a model for American nationalism. Based on the Thomas F. Gailor Personal Collection, DuPont Library, University of the South, Sewanee, Tennessee; 20 notes.

W. D. Piersen

2525. Wilson, Charles Reagan. THE RELIGION OF THE LOST CAUSE: RITUAL AND THE ORGANIZATION OF THE SOUTHERN CIVIL RELIGION, 1865-1920. *J. of Southern Hist. 1980 46(2): 219-238.* The importance of religion in the South has long been noted, but the ties between religion and culture are closer than has been suggested. The post-Civil War years witnessed the birth of a pervasive common civil religion heavy with mythology, ritual, and organization. Southerners have tried to defend on a cultural and religious level what defeat in 1865 made impossible on a political level. The Lost Cause—defeat in a holy war—has left southerners to face guilt, doubt, and the triumph of evil: in other words, to form a tragic sense of life. Base on the *Confederate Veteran*, other organizational publications, and other sources; 36 notes.

T. D. Schoonover

2526. Wilson, Charles Reagan. ROBERT LEWIS DABNEY: RELIGION AND THE SOUTHERN HOLOCAUST. *Virginia Mag. of Hist. and Biog. 1981 89(1): 79-89.* Analyzes the post-Civil War life of Robert Lewis Dabney, a Presbyterian theologian and philosopher at Union Seminary, Hampden-Sydney, Virginia. Dabney tried to preserve what remained of a perceived Southern ethic, and warned of moral dangers to a defeated people. Disgusted by 1881 with northern debauchery of the South, in declining health, he accepted a philosophy appointment at the new University of Texas. He taught there and helped found a seminary in Austin, but by 1890 was again disgusted by too many "Yankees" about him. In 1894 the University Regents forced him to resign because of small classes, an act likely precipitated by his enemies. He died in 1896, an example of a soul troubled by the fate of the postbellum South. 27 notes.

P. J. Woehrmann

2527. Wimsatt, Mary Ann. GYASCUTUS AND THE DEVIL'S FORK. *Mississippi Q. 1981 34(2): 123-134.* Review essay of *Gyascutus: Studies in Antebellum Southern Humorous and Sporting Writing,* edited by James L. W. West, III, *Costerus,* New Series, Vol. 5-6 (1978) and *Cavorting on the Devil's Fork: The Pete Whetstone Letters of C. F. M. Noland,* edited, with introduction, by Leonard Williams (1979), examples of antebellum southern or southwestern humor; mid-19th century.

2528. Winchester, Alice. SHAKERTOWN AT PLEASANT HILL. *Hist. Preservation 1977 29(4): 13-20.* Discusses efforts by Shakers to preserve Shakertown, Pleasant Hill, Kentucky. The commune was founded in 1805 by missionaries from New Lebanon, New York, and formally dissolved in 1910. Preservation efforts have been active since 1960 and include adaptive use of some of the 27 surviving buildings. 12 photos.

R. M. Frame, III

2529. Winter, R. Milton. JAMES A. LYON: SOUTHERN PRESBYTERIAN APOSTLE OF PROGRESS. *J. of Presbyterian Hist. 1982 60(4): 314-335.* The Reverend James A. Lyon (1814-82) was a forward-looking pastor of the Columbus, Mississippi, Presbyterian Church during and after the Civil War. In 1863 he was moderator of the Presbyterian Church in the Confederate States of America. He frequently stood alone in his convictions. He demonstrated a progressive spirit, particularly about education, slavery, national unity, and denominational reunion. Based on his "Journal" (Mitchell Memorial Library, Mississippi State University), his numerous newspaper and journal articles, and minutes of ecclesiastical judicatories; illus., 93 notes.

H. M. Parker, Jr.

2530. Wood, James E., Jr. THE NEW RELIGIOUS RIGHT AND ITS IMPLICATIONS FOR SOUTHERN BAPTISTS. *Foundations 1982 25(2): 153-166.* The New Right promotes bigger government through its support of more military spending, but it wants to curb government power in social areas. It also supports authoritarian religious institutions and has an affinity with authoritarian political institutions. The rise of the New Right in politics is attributable to Fundamentalist concern over a variety of social issues. There was a resurgence of Fundamentalism in the Southern Baptist Convention with the election of W. Owen White as president in 1964. The New Right appeals to many Southern Baptists concerned about the social revolution of recent decades. However, most Southern Baptists do not support the New Right out of hand. Based on the *Annual of the Southern Baptist Convention* and secondary sources; 33 notes.

E. E. Eminhizer

2531. —. [ISSACHAR J. ROBERTS]. *Pro. of the South Carolina Hist. Assoc. 1981: 28-55.*
Pruden, George B., Jr. ISSACHAR J. ROBERTS: A SOUTHERN MISSIONARY PIONEER IN CHINA, *pp. 28-52.* Examines the early missionary career of Issachar Jacob Roberts in China during 1837-47. In the latter year his floating mission was sunk by a mob of angry Chinese. Roberts's success as a Baptist missionary was limited by his difficult personality. Based on the papers of the Southern Baptist Missionary Board and published works; 64 notes.
Gettys, James W., Jr. COMMENTARY, *pp. 53-55.* Discussion of Roberts's earlier career as a farmer and his theology might help explain his differences with other missionaries.

J. W. Thacker, Jr.

2532. —. SOUTHERN BAPTIST CHURCHES 200 YEARS OLD OR OLDER. *Baptist Hist. and Heritage 1976 11(4): 232-234.* A compilation of 108 Baptist churches located in Virginia (59), North Carolina (25), South Carolina (20), Georgia (three), and Maryland (one), which are 200 years old or older. Lists each church according to date of founding, name, county in which it is located, and 1975 membership.

H. M. Parker, Jr.

# The Southern Economy

## General

2533. Abbott, Collamer M. CORNISH MINERS IN APPALACHIAN COPPER CAMPS. *Rev. Int. d'Hist. de la Banque [Italy] 1973 (7): 199-219.* Although they did not constitute a majority, Cornish miners represented a significant part of the work force in the copper mines of Appalachia, 1830-90. Sources for development in the mining regions, especially those for Orange County in Vermont and Polk County in Tennessee, indicate that mine owners looked to the Cornishmen for the skills necessary for hardrock, underground mining. They also were sought out as foremen. Both the methods of working the mines and the systems of payment reflected the traditional practices of the Cornish miners in the old country. Based on US Census, mining company records, newspapers, and secondary sources; 51 notes.                    D. McGinnis

2534. Adams, Donald R., Jr. ONE HUNDRED YEARS OF PRICES AND WAGES: MARYLAND, 1750-1850. *Working Papers from the Regional Econ. Hist. Res. Center 1982 5(4): 90-129.* Shows that rural Americans remained a powerful influence on total US expenditures throughout the antebellum period.

2535. Alford, John J. THE ROLE OF MANAGEMENT IN CHESAPEAKE OYSTER PRODUCTION. *Geographical R. 1973 63(1): 44-54.* Although the Chesapeake Bay is perhaps the world's greatest natural oyster fishery, production from these waters has dropped drastically in the last eighty years. Since the ecological base of the fishery remains largely intact, lack of proper management must be blamed for this decline. Recently, in an effort to increase production, Maryland and Virginia have begun to farm oysters intensively by planting large amounts of shell (to provide a suitable surface on which the larvae can settle) and of seed oysters. Private oystermen, who have long been gatherers of a wild crop, are becoming workers on the state farms. The program presents fiscal and tax problems, but preliminary results to date permit cautious optimism about the future of the fishery.                    J

2536. Anthony, Allen. STEAMBOAT 'ROUND KENTUCKY BEND: A GOLDEN ERA. *Register of the Kentucky Hist. Soc. 1979 77(1): 25-29.* Settlement of Kentucky Bend, the unattached portion of Fulton County which has remained isolated in a loop of the Mississippi River, in southwestern Kentucky, began shortly after 1812. The economy of the area was based on farming, and as landing sites developed, a "golden era" followed and lasted throughout the middle- and late-19th century. Primary and secondary sources; 9 illus., 21 notes.                    J. F. Paul

2537. Banks, Alan J. THE EMERGENCE OF A CAPITALISTIC LABOR MARKET IN EASTERN KENTUCKY. *Appalachian J. 1980 7(3): 188-198.* Traces the development of capitalist modes of production (CMP) in Kentucky, from the preindustrial, agricultural economy of 1787 through the 1890's, focusing on the labor and economic policies of Kentucky politicians.

2538. Bauer, Craig A. FROM BURNT CANES TO BUDDING CITY: A HISTORY OF THE CITY OF KENNER, LOUISIANA. *Louisiana Hist. 1982 23(4): 353-381.* Kenner, Louisiana, the sixth-largest city in the state, originated in 1717 as the French settlement of Cannes Brûlées. The first major growth came with the introduction of sugar planting in the late 18th century, and the Kenner family, with its modernized plantations, dominated the area until the Civil War. After the war, Kenner switched to truck farms, many of which were established by Italian immigrants. The major factors in 20th-century development were the direct rail link with New Orleans and the establishment of New Orleans International Airport. Rapid expansion, caused by the airport and an influx of city-dwellers from New Orleans, has virtually destroyed agriculture in Kenner. Based largely on manuscript sources at Tulane University, Jefferson Parish Court House, Louisiana State University, and the Kenner City Council; table, 70 notes.                    D. J. Nicholls

2539. Bell, Samuel E. and Smallwood, James M. ZONA LIBRE: TRADE & DIPLOMACY ON THE MEXICAN BORDER, 1858-1905. *Arizona and the West 1982 24(2): 119-152.* Mexico established the Zona Libre in 1858 to counteract the highly favorable trade conditions enjoyed by the American towns along the Texas-Tamaulipas border. It was subsequently extended to the Pacific Ocean. The Mexican towns had an unprecedented boom during the Civil War, siphoning European goods to the Confederacy. The trade balance shifted to the American side after the war. American border merchants protested the zone because it encouraged smuggling and it became a sore point in diplomatic relations between the two countries. Mexico, fearful of revolution along the border and disliking American bullying, continued the zone's existence be-

yond its economic usefulness. Its abolition in 1905 paved the way for improved relations between the two countries. Map, 6 illus., 84 notes.                    D. L. Smith

2540. Bender, Thomas. LAW, ECONOMY, AND SOCIAL VALUES IN JACKSONIAN AMERICA: A MARYLAND CASE STUDY. *Maryland Hist. Mag. 1976 71(4): 484-497.* The interaction of law, economy, and social values in Maryland, especially in relation to transportation, reveals a change in the working premises of the law favorable to the prodigious economic expansion occurring after 1840. During the 1820's-30's, there was a "significant shift in values" from a community-oriented, security-conscious, deferential, and slowly-paced society to a more individualistic, achievement-oriented, competitive, egalitarian, and dynamic one. The legal battles between the Baltimore and Ohio Railroad and the Chesapeake and Ohio Canal Company illustrate the conflict between the modern and the conservative forces. The victory of the theory of the purposive over the "status" contract as well as a view of eminent domain which rejected the old hierarchic, organic version of community and opted for competition over monopoly were embodied in an 1836 law. This law reserved states' right to alter or repeal a corporate charter at its pleasure. Modernizers sought a legal environment producing corporate egalitarianism in which entrepeneurs were left unprotected from the numerous failures of a competitive market. Primary and secondary sources; 46 notes.                    G. J. Bobango

2541. Bertho, Catherine. COCA-COLA, C'EST FOU! [Coca-Cola, that's crazy!]. *Histoire [France] 1983 (57): 88-91.* Describes the marketing and advertising of Coca-Cola from 1886-1967.

2542. Bethell, Thomas N. IN DEFENSE OF FREEDOM'S VICTORY!: THE ORDEAL OF THE FEDERATION OF SOUTHERN COOPERATIVES. *Southern Exposure 1982 10(5): 48-59.* Profiles the organization, goals, objectives, and legal problems of the Federation of Southern Cooperatives, which is headed by Charles Prejean.

2543. Billings, Dwight B. NEW WAYS OF TELLING THE NEW SOUTH STORY: NUMAN BARTLEY ON THE CREATION OF MODERN GEORGIA. *Georgia Hist. Q. 1983 67(4): 480-488.* Reviews Numan V. Bartley's *The Creation of Modern Georgia* (1983), stressing models of Southern development. Based on Bartley's book and secondary sources; 18 notes.                    G. R. Schroeder

2544. Blakely, Edward J. and Bradshaw, Ted K. THE IMPACT OF RECENT MIGRANTS ON ECONOMIC DEVELOPMENT IN SMALL TOWNS. *Southern Q. 1980 19(1): 30-49.* Traditionally, small towns and rural areas in the South during the 20th century have been considered depressed, isolated, and backward. This is changing. During the last decade many small towns and rural areas have had large population increases. The newcomers to these areas have substantial economic resources and are seeking a better quality of life than the urban areas can offer them. 5 tables, 27 notes.                    B. D. Ledbetter

2545. Blicksilver, Jack. KINSHIP AND FRIENDSHIP IN THE EMERGENCE OF A FAMILY-CONTROLLED SOUTHERN ENTERPRISE: LIFE INSURANCE COMPANY OF GEORGIA, 1891-1950. Greenfield, Sidney M.; Strickon, Arnold; and Aubey, Robert T., ed. *Entrepreneurs in Cultural Context* (Albuquerque: U. of New Mexico Pr., 1979): 89-121. Reviews the history of the Life Insurance Company of Georgia from its founding by a group of farm-bred white Georgians. The group of friends (Isham Mallie Sheffield, D. F. Owen, J. J. Carleton, and John Newton McEachern) began by selling burial and health insurance to the black community, and, as they expanded, kept control of the company in the hands of family members of the original group until 1975. 18 notes.                    S

2546. Bonnifield, Paul. ENERGY RESOURCES ON THE SOUTHERN GREAT PLAINS. *Chronicles of Oklahoma 1981 59(3): 345-359.* As the gold and silver mining frontier moved into the Denver area in 1859, the need for a cheap source of energy became critical for the first time on the Great Plains. Coal provided

that source, and, with the coming of the railroads, coal mining expanded to all areas of the West. By World War I wildcatting for oil and natural gas turned the southern Plains into a boom area, especially in western Oklahoma and the Texas Panhandle. The petroleum industry grew alongside the agricultural frontier, and, in the case of the 1930's Dust Bowl, it helped maintain some prosperity for communities that otherwise would have been economically devastated. Based on newspapers and secondary sources; 35 notes.
M. L. Tate

2547. Borchert, James. ALLEY LANDSCAPES OF WASHINGTON. *Landscape 1979 23(3): 3-10.* Contrasts the residents of Washington, D.C., alleys and alley housing from the 1850's when Virginia and Maryland blacks migrated to the alleys, to the restoration movement of the 1940's and 1950's when white-collar and professional workers (mostly white) moved in to replace the blacks.

2548. Borchert, James. ALLEY LIFE IN WASHINGTON. *Society 1981 18(5): 96-99.* Photo essay with text on the buildings in central Washington, D.C., called alley dwellings, and the people, black laborers, laundresses, and domestics who survived in these slums until "gentrification" overtook them.

2549. Borchert, James. URBAN NEIGHBORHOOD AND COMMUNITY: INFORMAL GROUP LIFE, 1850-1970. *J. of Interdisciplinary Hist. 1981 11(4): 607-631.* Focuses on black working-class migrants in Washington, D.C., who live in houses facing alleys. Sociologists, and more recently historians, have been revising earlier formulations about the impact of the city on folk migrants. The historical development of alley housing in Washington dates to the 1850's, when an expanding population led to more intensive land use. The reduction in the number of alley dwellings began in the 1890's. Although outsiders perceived the alley settlements negatively, those who lived there perceived themselves in a more positive way. Several levels of community organization in the alleys—family, neighborhood activity, and the alley church—helped to maintain social order and bind the community together. Secondary sources; photo, 2 maps, 36 notes. C. R. Gunter, Jr.

2550. Boulding, Kenneth E. THE PUZZLE OF THE NORTH-SOUTH DIFFERENTIAL. *Southern Humanities Rev. 1976 10(2): 119-130.* Reprints a speech delivered at Auburn University on 2 April 1975, reflecting on the inexplicable but consistent differential between the North and South in such areas as economic development and health.

2551. Boxerman, Burton Alan. THE EDISON BROTHERS, SHOE MERCHANTS: THEIR GEORGIA YEARS. *Georgia Hist. Q. 1973 57(4): 511-525.* Traces the history of the retail shoe store ventures of five sons of a Russian Jewish emigrant in Georgia and their merger into the Edison Brothers Company that became the largest chain of women's shoe stores in the nation. D. L. Smith

2552. Bragaw, Donald H. STATUS OF NEGROES IN A SOUTHERN PORT CITY IN THE PROGRESSIVE ERA. *Florida Hist. Q. 1973 51(3): 281-302.* Traces the growth, leveling off, and decline of proportionate Negro population in Pensacola between 1896 and the 1920's. Discusses occupational groups and residential patterns. The decline in the employment and economic status of Negroes began around 1906 with the exhaustion of nearby forests and resultant slacking of the lumber industry. Negro fortunes received another blow in 1910 with the temporary closing of the naval base. Its reopening as a naval air station in 1916 did not bring recovery. Based on census records, city directories, newspapers, interviews, and secondary sources; 59 notes. J. E. Findling

2553. Browne, Gary L. BUSINESS INNOVATION AND SOCIAL CHANGE: THE CAREER OF ALEXANDER BROWN AFTER THE WAR OF 1812. *Maryland Hist. Mag. 1974 69(3): 243-255.* Alexander Brown (1764-1834) of Baltimore, founder of Alex, Brown & Sons with its network of family firms in Liverpool, New York, and Philadelphia, was a forerunner of the later 19th-century businessman. Brown was a business innovator who observed social conditions carefully and was a transition figure to the era after 1819 when cash and short credits became the norms of

business relations. By concentrating his capital in small-risk ventures and acquiring ships and Bank of the United States stock during the Panic of 1819, he came to monopolize Baltimore's shipping trade with Liverpool by 1822. Brown next expanded into packet ships, extended his lines to Philadelphia, and began financing Baltimore importers, specializing in merchant banking from the late 1820's to his death in 1834. The emergence of a money economy and the growth of the Anglo-American cotton trade allowed him to escape Baltimore's declining position in trans-Atlantic trade. His most important innovation was the drawing up of his own bills of exchange. By 1830 his company rivaled the Bank of the United States in the American foreign exchange markets, and the transition from the "traditional" to the "modern" merchant was nearly complete. Primary and secondary sources; 3 illus., 18 notes.
G. J. Bobango

2554. Burns, Anna C. HENRY E. HARDTNER, LOUISIANA'S FIRST CONSERVATIONIST. *J. of Forest Hist. 1978 22(2): 78-85.* Henry Ernest Hardtner (1871-1935), a Louisiana lumberman of German ancestry, was the state's first advocate of forest conservation. Untrained in forestry, he nevertheless taught himself the rudiments of silviculture and developed a vision of reforestation as the economic salvation of the region's declining forest industries. Appointed chairman of the Louisiana Commission for the Conservation of Natural Resources in 1908, he worked in the political arena to establish a state forestry agency and related conservation legislation. Participation in regional and national trade, conservation, and forestry organizations, as well as instructive cooperation with the U.S. Forest Service and Yale School of Forestry, brought him deserved recognition as the "Father of Forestry in the South." His successful experiments and demonstrations on timberlands near Urania, dating from about 1904, influenced a generation of southern lumbermen to begin practicing forestry. Based on interviews, correspondence, and secondary sources; 6 illus., 32 notes.
R. J. Fahl

2555. Carson, Gerald. BOURBON: AMBER WAVES OF GRAIN—100 PROOF. *Am. Heritage 1974 25(2): 60-63, 95.* Early history (1802-62) of the liquor industry centered in Kentucky.
S

2556. Cassity, Michael J. SOUTHERN WORKERS AND SOCIAL CHANGE: CONCEPTS AND PROSPECTS. *Georgia Hist. Q. 1978 62(3): 200-212.* Histories of American labor have usually concentrated on the economic aspects and the labor unions. Suggests that many questions about the social implications of labor which have been asked by European labor historians should be applied to the American labor movement and particularly workers in the South. Secondary sources; 17 notes. G. R. Schroeder

2557. Clark, Thomas D. KENTUCKY LOGMEN. *J. of Forest Hist. 1981 25(3): 144-157.* Cutting and rafting timber provided an economic supplement for the subsistence farmers of Kentucky's Appalachian, Pennyroyal, and Mississippian Embayment regions. The skills, techniques, equipment, and dangers involved in rafting logs on Kentucky's unpredictable rivers are an important part of regional folklore. Based on state and federal reports, oral interviews, and secondary sources; 11 photos, 42 notes. R. W. Judd

2558. Cochrane, James L. and Griepentrog, Gary L. COTTON TEXTILE PRICES 1965-66: THE MICROECONOMICS OF MORAL SUASION. *Southern Econ. J. 1977 44(1): 74-84.* Examines the effect which the Johnson administration's attempt to limit increases in wage and price levels had on the South and the price of cotton textiles, 1965-66.

2559. Coclanis, Peter A. RICE PRICES IN THE 1720S AND THE EVOLUTION OF THE SOUTH CAROLINA ECONOMY. *J. of Southern Hist. 1982 48(4): 531-544.* Traditional claim of decline in South Carolina's economy in the 1720's does not correlate with the aggregate data which reveals a steadily expanding economy. The important sectors of naval stores and cattle ranching did decline, but rice production, for example, expanded quite extensively. What occurred was a structural change in South Carolina's economic system. Based on manuscript South Carolina court records and plantation account books, *Historical Statistics of the United States*, dissertations, and printed primary materials; 30 notes, 4 tables, fig.

T. D. Schoonover

2560. Cordes, Helen. ACADIAN DELIGHT BAKERY: A VENTURE INTO FRUITCAKE. *Southern Exposure 1983 11(6): 42-44.* The bakery, a black-owned cooperative business, was founded in 1963 in Lake Charles, Louisiana, by the Southern Consumers Cooperative, which sponsors other black economic development projects in the South, including education programs, a scholarship fund, a business information program, a minority business loan organization, and a co-operative farming subsidiary.

2561. Courson, Maxwell Taylor. THE CUP AND GUTTER EXPERIMENTS OF CHARLES HOLMES HERTY. *Georgia Hist. Q. 1980 64(4): 459-471.* Charles Holmes Herty (1867-1938), chemistry professor at the University of Georgia, devised a new method of collecting turpentine which spared the trees. During the 1930's he also demonstrated that satisfactory newsprint could be made from southern pine trees. Various commemorations of his accomplishments are mentioned. Based on correspondence, newspaper articles, and secondary sources; 27 notes.

G. R. Schroeder

2562. Cruickshank, Alistair B. DEVELOPMENT OF THE DEEP SOUTH: A REAPPRAISAL. *Scottish Geographical Mag. [Great Britain] 1980 96(2): 91-104.* Discusses the resilience of the economies of the Deep South states during the economic recession, 1970-77, in contrast with the stagnation of the commercial and industrial North, concentrating particularly on population change and industrial development. 2 tables, 4 fig., 45 notes.

2563. Dakin, Patricia L. A FRAGMENT OF AMERICANA: THE LAST MOSS GIN. *Louisiana Rev. 1981 10(2): 173-181.* Spanish moss, one of Louisiana's natural resources, was used in many products during 19c-1980, including bricks, horsecollars, saddle blankets, and mattresses.

2564. Daniel, Pete. THE TRANSFORMATION OF THE RURAL SOUTH, 1930 TO THE PRESENT. *Agric. Hist. 1981 55(3): 231-248.* A combination of government policies and mechanization has destroyed the traditional southern rural life based on tenant farming. New Deal agricultural subsidies encouraged landlords to get rid of sharecroppers. The Depression helped concentrate land ownership in the hands of insurance companies and cotton ginners who did not directly farm their land. The rice industry has been highly mechanized but neither rice nor tobacco was much affected by government programs. Cotton growing has been greatly changed by mechanization and has nearly disappeared from the Carolinas and Black Belt. Southern agriculture is now capital-intensive rather than labor-intensive. Based on National Archives records and other sources; 34 notes.

D. E. Bowers

2565. Davis, Steve. THE SOUTH AS "THE NATION'S NO. 1 ECONOMIC PROBLEM": THE NEC REPORT OF 1938. *Georgia Hist. Q. 1978 62(2): 119-132.* The National Emergency Council *Report on the Economic Conditions of the South*, principally drafted by Clark Howell Foreman, caused much discussion in 1938. Many people approved of pointing out southern economic weaknesses as a means of correcting them, but others opposed President Franklin D. Roosevelt's attempt to use the report to unseat political opponents. The influence of the report in improving southern economic conditions is undetermined. Primary sources; 26 notes.

G. R. Schroeder

2566. DeLeon, Arnoldo and Stewart, Kenneth L. LOST DREAMS AND FOUND FORTUNES: MEXICAN AND ANGLO IMMIGRANTS IN SOUTH TEXAS, 1850-1900. *Western Hist. Q. 1983 14(3): 291-310.* Analysis of migration into south Texas from Mexico and from the United States and Europe. Examines the historical forces that determined the destiny of the two groups in the area that promised an equal start but eventually developed into inequali-

ties. Mexican impoverishment was the result of historical conditions rather than any migratory impulse or any difficulty in living in an American context. 3 tables, 30 notes.

D. L. Smith

2567. DeMoss, Nettie; Crone, Norman, ed. INDIAN TERRITORY MEMORIES. *Chronicles of Oklahoma 1981 59(1): 106-110.* Recounts the author's reminiscences of homesteading near Peggs, Oklahoma from 1896 to 1915 and the fear of Indians. The family moved to Tahlequah in 1915 and soon thereafter to Sand Springs where the oil boom was underway. The author married and took a job with the City Welfare Department during the economic hard times of the 1920's and 1930's.

M. L. Tate

2568. Dreese, G. Richard. BANKS AND REGIONAL ECONOMIC DEVELOPMENT. *Southern Econ. J. 1974 40(4): 647-656.*

2569. Dunn, Hampton. "WISH YOU WERE HERE": A PHOTO ESSAY. *Tampa Bay Hist. 1982 4(1): 33-49.* Reproduces postcards of sites in the 15 counties of the Tampa Bay area from the 1890's, when tourists first began flocking to Florida, until 1981.

2570. Eason, Thomas. HISTORIC INSTITUTIONAL CHANGE IN THE MISSISSIPPI ECONOMY. *J. of Mississippi Hist. 1973 35(4): 345-359.* Examines the attitudes of Mississippians since the early 19th century regarding economic development, the relationship of the state to the rest of the nation, the reasons Mississippi's development has lagged behind that of Alabama and Louisiana, and similarities between Mississippi's development and problems of underdeveloped countries today. From the early 19th century through the 1930's Mississippi had an unbalanced colonial economy and was an economic colony of the Northeast. Based largely on secondary sources; 38 notes.

J. W. Hillje

2571. Einstein, Frank H. THINGS FALL APART IN APPALACHIA TOO: HUBERT SKIDMORE'S ACCOUNT OF THE TRANSITION TO CAPITALISM. *Appalachian J. 1983-84 11(1-2): 32-42.* Examines Hubert Skidmore's novels *I Will Lift Up Mine Eyes* (1936) and *Heaven Came So Near* (1938) as accounts of Appalachia's transition to capitalism, seen from the victims' rather than the capitalists' perspective.

2572. Ellis, L. Tuffly. THE NEW ORLEANS COTTON EXCHANGE: THE FORMATIVE YEARS, 1870-1880. *J. of Southern Hist. 1973 39(4): 545-564.* Describes the formation and development of the New Orleans Cotton Exchange during 1871-80, established as a means to revive and regulate the cotton market in that city. By 1880 the Exchange was the leading cotton market in the world and had set up a futures market. It was able to restore order to the local market, curb further decline of trade, and help improve communication and transport between the city and other areas, developing a "spirit of mutual cooperation among New Orleans traders." Based on reports of the New Orleans Cotton Exchange, US government documents, contemporary newspaper reports, and primary and secondary sources; 56 notes.

N. J. Street

2573. Engerman, Stanley L. MARXIST ECONOMIC STUDIES OF THE SLAVE SOUTH. *Marxist Perspectives 1978 1(1): 148-165.* Broad overview of Marxist interpretations of social and economic life in the South before the Civil War.

2574. Estall, Robert. THE CHANGING BALANCE OF THE NORTHERN AND SOUTHERN REGIONS OF THE UNITED STATES. *J. of Am. Studies [Great Britain] 1980 14(3): 365-386.* With cries of industrial piracy flung from the North, Northeast US economic development slowed dramatically in the 1970's while growth in the South escalated. These developments produced major changes, intensified regional conflicts, and had wide repercussions in both economic and political arenas. But the economic shifts appear unlikely to result in the Northeast losing its industrial hegemony or becoming economically and politically subordinate to the growing South. 3 maps, 3 tables, 22 notes.

H. T. Lovin

2575. Fairclough, Adam. THE PUBLIC UTILITIES INDUSTRY IN NEW ORLEANS: A STUDY IN CAPITAL, LABOR AND GOVERNMENT, 1894-1929. *Louisiana Hist. 1981 22(1): 45-65.*

Chronicles municipal efforts to regulate New Orleans's public utilities, and the efforts on behalf of transit workers of the Amalgamated Association of Street and Electric Railway Employees of America (AASEREA) from the 1894 founding of the Citizens' Protective Association to the AASEREA's decisive defeat in the transit strike of 1929. In 1902 all local transit, gas, and electric companies were consolidated as the New Orleans Railways Company which later became New Orleans Public Service Inc. (NOPSI). Also in 1902, the AASEREA won partial recognition through a strike which, despite some union violence, enjoyed much public support. During this period both city and union were handicapped in their dealings with NOPSI by the attitude of the courts. Contemporary press and secondary sources; 46 notes. L. Van Wyk

2576. Farbman, Michael. INCOME CONCENTRATION IN THE SOUTHERN UNITED STATES. *Rev. of Econ. and Statistics 1973 55(3): 333-340.*

2577. Fisher, Steve. POWER AND POWERLESSNESS IN APPALACHIA: A REVIEW ESSAY. *Appalachian J. 1981 8(2): 142-149.* John Gaventa's *Power and Powerlessness: Quiescence and Rebellion in an Appalachian Valley* (Oxford: Clarendon Pr.; and Urbana: U. of Illinois Pr., 1980) views Appalachia's quiescent acceptance of corporate exploitation not as a result of the apathetic and fatalistic nature of Appalachian culture but rather as a function of the very exploitative power relationships which continue in central Appalachia.

2578. Fitzgerald, Martha H. STEAMBOATS ON THE RIVER: LIFELINE OF TENSAS PARISH. *North Louisiana Hist. Assoc. J. 1976 7(4): 123-130.* For more than 60 years in the 19th century, steamboats were the lifeline of Tensas Parish to the outside world, and they provided the primary facilities for travel, communication, and entertainment, as well as for shipping goods to market and bringing supplies to the Parish's plantations and industries. The parish, in northeastern Louisiana, was incorporated in 1843 and produced cotton in abundance; it was one of the State's richest regions before the Civil War. "The last few years of the nineteenth century witnessed the highest development of the steamboat industry, along with the Tensas Parish front, as all along the Mississippi," and cotton remained the parish's principal product. When the railroad finally reached the parish in 1904, "the days of the steamboat were numbered." Primary and secondary sources; 26 notes. A. N. Garland

2579. Fleisig, Heywood. SLAVERY, THE SUPPLY OF AGRICULTURAL LABOR, AND THE INDUSTRIALIZATION OF THE SOUTH. *J. of Econ. Hist. 1976 36(3): 572-597.* This article assumes that the only effect of slavery was the relief of a labor constraint facing individual farmers, and shows the conditions under which slavery would increase the share of agriculture in total output, reduce the size of the market for, and the incentive to invent and innovate, new farm machinery. Two farm models are developed, one with a fixed labor-constraint, the other with a rising labor supply-curve; these are contrasted with a third model of an unconstrained farm. The constrained (free labor) and unconstrained (slave labor) models successfully predict several salient differences between northern and southern agriculture and industry. J

2580. Friedmann, Harriet. ECONOMIC ANALYSIS OF THE POSTBELLUM SOUTH: REGIONAL ECONOMICS AND WORLD MARKETS: A REVIEW ARTICLE. *Comparative Studies in Soc. and Hist. [Great Britain] 1980 22(4): 639-652.* Papers of the Chicago School's Edgar T. Thompson, collected in *Plantation Societies, Race Relations, and the South: The Regimentation of Populations* (Durham: Duke U. Pr., 1975), focus on the South as a social formation with the plantation its characteristic institution; Marxist Jay R. Mandle, in *The Roots of Black Poverty: The Southern Plantation after the Civil War* (Durham: Duke U. Pr., 1978), adopts Thompson's focus, contributes the idea that the South as a social formation was dependent upon its boundedness as a region of labor mobility, but fails to develop Thompson's insights into labor organization or to include external markets in his analysis; Gavin Wright, in *The Political Economy of the Cotton South: Households, Markets, and Wealth in the Nineteenth Century* (New

York: W. W. Norton & Co., 1978), supplies this lack by elaborating on Thompson's insights into the family as the unit of production and on the world economy as a condition for the emergence and continuation of the plantation system.

2581. Galenson, David. THE PROFITABILITY OF THE LONG DRIVE. *Agric. Hist. 1977 51(4): 737-758.* Uses a mathematical formula to determine the amount of profit that could be made trailing cattle from Texas to the railhead in Kansas during 1865-85. The mathematical formula includes: the market price of a steer in Texas, the number of cattle purchased, the cost of provisions, wages paid to the hired hands, the cost of horses, the number of cattle arriving in Kansas, and the market price of steers in Kansas. Based on primary and secondary sources; 6 tables, 45 notes. R. T. Fulton

2582. Gaventa, John. IN APPALACHIA: PROPERTY IS THEFT. *Southern Exposure 1973 1(2): 42-52.* Since the 1890's the coal mining industry has made large profits in Appalachia while the people live in poverty. S

2583. George, Paul S. PASSAGE TO THE NEW EDEN: TOURISM IN MIAMI FROM FLAGLER THROUGH EVEREST G. SEWELL. *Florida Hist. Q. 1981 59(4): 440-463.* The advent of Henry M. Flagler's Florida East Coast Railway into Miami in April 1896 marks the beginnings of unprecedented growth. Later promotion of Miami attractions was undertaken by Everest G. Sewell through the local chamber of commerce. By 1940 Miami represented the pinnacle of success. Flagler, Sewell, and others combined the area's assets with changing American lifestyles. Based on public reports, newspapers, and other sources; 100 notes. N. A. Kuntz

2584. Groth, Philip. PLANTATION AGRICULTURE AND THE URBANIZATION OF THE SOUTH. *Rural Sociol. 1977 42(2): 206-219.* It is widely recognized that the South has been and remains the most rural region of the nation. Two divergent historical interpretations of the rurality of the South have been offered—one which focuses on the political economy of the South and one which stresses a variety of socioeconomic, topographical, and climatic features of the region. In this research the author derived and tested several hypotheses in which the level of urbanization of counties and economic subregions of the South were related to their plantation, political economic, character. The tests of these hypotheses suggest that neither the political economic nor the eclectic theory offers a sound explanation of the rurality of the South. J

2585. Guermonprez, Jean H. LES "PACKETS" DU MISSISSIPPI [Packet boats of the Mississippi]. *Miroir de l'Hist. [France] 1958 (99): 322-328.* Packet boats, introduced in 1816 by Henry Shreve, played an important role in the 19th-century economic development of the region.

2586. Hair, William I. PLUNDERED LEGACY: THE EARLY HISTORY OF NORTH LOUISIANA'S OIL AND GAS INDUSTRY. *North Louisiana Hist. Assoc. J. 1977 8(5): 179-184.* In the early 20th century, huge oil and natural gas deposits were discovered in northwest Louisiana. In northeast Louisiana, little oil was discovered, but large natural gas deposits were unearthed. Unfortunately, much of the natural gas that was discovered in both sections of the state was wasted; the gas was either burned at the well or wasted by the carbon black industry. Controls were eventually established, but they were too late to stop the kind of waste that deprived future Louisianians and future Americans of the benefits of this most important natural resource. Primary and secondary sources; 18 notes. A. N. Garland

2587. Hall, Bob and Williams, Bob. CASE STUDY: WHO'S GETTING RICH IN THE NEW SOUTH. *Southern Exposure 1978 6(3): 92-95.* The South has recently been receiving an increasing share of the national wealth. However, it has not been reflected in an equitable distribution of income and power among all southern socioeconomic classes. Rather, the new wealth is being redistributed along the same lines of wealth and power which existed in the South prior to 1963 and the reforms of the 1960's which had the intent of changing economic conditions in the region. The richest fifth of the Southern population receives 40% of the income. Local and state taxing favors the economically well off at the expense of the poor and working class.　　　　　　　　　　N. Lederer

2588. Hansen, Niles. DOES THE SOUTH HAVE A STAKE IN NORTHERN URBAN POVERTY? *Southern Econ. J. 1979 45(4): 1220-1224.* Studies of poverty rates, education, and migration from 1959-70's show that migration from the South has not caused urban poverty in the North, as traditionally believed.

2589. Hanson Jones, Alice. AMERICAN PROBATE INVENTORIES: A SOURCE TO ESTIMATE WEALTH IN 1774 IN THIRTEEN COLONIES AND THREE REGIONS. *A. A. G. Bijdragen [Netherlands] 1980 23: 239-256.* Examines the character and contents of American probate inventories. The author discusses their adequacy for estimating the wealth of living wealthholders and describes the information not included in the inventories, such as the ownership of land and buildings, debts owed by the deceased, and the age of the deceased. The inventories were those of free persons only, and the author made use of a computer to analyze data. The South stands out as the richest region. Occupations heavily represented in the high wealth class were esquires, gentlemen, officials, merchants, and farmers who had side activities, such as milling. There was little distinction between the urban and rural distributions from lower to higher wealth. Based on probate inventories and secondary sources; 4 tables, 2 fig., 48 notes.
　　　　　　　　　　G. L. Neville

2590. Hart, John Fraser. LAND ROTATION IN APPALACHIA. *Geographical Rev. 1977 67(2): 148-166.* Much farmland in Appalachia has been cultivated until the soil was exhausted, then "abandoned" to pasture and second-growth woodland, and eventually cleared for cultivation once again after a period of rest under trees. This practice of land rotation may be a continuation of the Scottish tradition of intermittent cultivation of an "outfield." Although land rotation seems to be an effective technique for maintaining production from marginal agricultural land, it has received limited attention because land in rotation does not claim the professional interest either of agriculturalists or of foresters, because outsiders have wished to see the South in an unfavorable light, and because the national economic ethos has taught practitioners of land rotation to feel ashamed of a system of limited economic productivity.
　　　　　　　　　　J

2591. Haulman, C. A. CHANGES IN THE ECONOMIC POWER STRUCTURES IN DUVAL COUNTY, FLORIDA, DURING THE CIVIL WAR AND RECONSTRUCTION. *Florida Hist. Q. 1973 52(2): 175-184.* Compares the 1860 and 1870 census returns of Duval County, Florida. After discussing methodological problems, concludes that the upper class in 1870 was composed of substantially different families than in 1860, including higher percentages of merchant-businessmen and newly arrived Northerners. 3 tables, 25 notes.　　　　　J. E. Findling

2592. Haymans, Karen. THE DECLINE OF THE STEAMBOAT ON THE RED RIVER. *North Louisiana Hist. Assoc. J. 1977 8(2): 77-80.* For almost 70 years "steamboats inspired the growth and provided the sustenance of the Red River area in Louisiana." But numerous obstacles in the river, such as natural dams, sand bars, snags, and periods of low water during which navigation was prohibited, eventually "made transportation by rail increasingly popular." The steamer was at "its highest peak of glory in the 1870s," but the number of such boats operating on the Red River declined from 118 in that decade to 45 by the end of the century, and to 22 by 1910. Steamboat traffic simply could not compete with the railroads. 19 notes.　　　　　　　　A. N. Garland

2593. Hearden, Patrick J. AGRICULTURAL BUSINESSMEN IN THE NEW SOUTH. *Louisiana Studies 1975 14(2): 145-159.* Argues that, contrary to other studies, in the last three decades of the 19th century southern agricultural businessmen allied with urban entrepreneurs in calling for southern economic independence which would be based primarily on large scale textile manufacturing. This was especially the case in South Carolina, North Carolina, Georgia, Alabama, and Mississippi. Such agrarian support for the New

South of industrialization and manufacturing also came from major farm groups such as the Grange and the Farmers Alliance. Primary and secondary sources; 67 notes.　　　　　B. A. Glasrud

2594. Hertzberg, Steven. MAKING IT IN ATLANTA: ECONOMIC MOBILITY IN A SOUTHERN JEWISH COMMUNITY, 1870-1911. *Ann. of Jewish Social Sci. 1978 17: 185-216.* Studies the mobility of Atlanta's Jewish population during 1870-1911. The Jews more than any other group viewed America as the Promised Land. Therefore, a study of their mobility within a major southern city is of special significance.　　　　　　　R. J. Wechman

2595. Hindes, Ruthanna. DELAWARE SILVERSMITHS, 1728-1880: NEW DISCOVERIES. *Delaware Hist. 1981 19(3): 127-155.* Updates the information found in the author's "Delaware Silversmiths, 1700-1850," *Delaware History,* 12 (1967), by including silversmiths, shopkeepers, and dealers. Provides biographicals sketches of 81 such figures. 2 illus., 113 notes.　　　　R. M. Miller

2596. Humphrey, Lowin. A HISTORY OF CROSS LAKE: 1883-1926. *North Louisiana Hist. Assoc. J. 1979 10(3): 84-92.* In 1926, Cross Lake Reservoir became the source of water for the City of Shreveport. Traces the deliberations and negotiations leading to the development of the reservoir in 1926. Primary sources; illus., 78 notes.　　　　　　　　　　J. F. Paul

2597. Ingham, John N. BEATING PLOWS INTO BOND SHARES. *Can. Rev. of Am. Studies [Canada] 1980 11(3): 355-363.* Review article prompted by publication of Gabor S. Boritt's *Lincoln and the Economics of the American Dream* (Memphis, Tenn., 1978); John A. James's *Money and Capital Markets in Postbellum America* (Princeton, N.J., 1978); Jay R. Mandle's *The Roots of Black Poverty: The Southern Plantation after the Civil War* (Durham, N.C., 1978); Claude F. Oubre's *Forty Acres and a Mule: The Freedman's Bureau and Black Land Ownership* (Baton Rouge, La., 1978). Although dealing with disparate topics, the books in common analyze the impact of social and economic change in post-Civil War America.　　　　　H. T. Lovin

2598. Jolley, Clyde W. POLK COUNTY: A TALE OF TWO CITIES. *Georgia Life 1978 4(4): 12-15.* Describes Cedartown and Rockmart in Polk County, Georgia: their economic conditions, people, and points of interest.

2599. Jones, Walter B. ALABAMA OBSOLETE CURRENCY. *Alabama Rev. 1977 30(3): 213-226.* Discusses the numismatic content and quality of the "Mobile hoard," a box of notes uncovered in 1965, dating mostly from the Civil War. Collection includes bank, insurance, and railroad company scrip, as well as state and county government notes. Primary and secondary sources; note, lists.　　　　　　　　　　J. F. Vivian

2600. Kelly, Charles G. MEMORIES OF LONGSTRAW (1857-1900). *North Louisiana Hist. Assoc. J. 1974 5(4): 143-147.* Two miles south of Choudrant, Louisiana, and five miles southeast of Ruston, lies "the old and forgotten village of Longstraw." The village name derives from its location in one of the few areas of northern Louisiana where longleaf pine trees grow. The first church in the community was established on 31 August 1857. Although after 1865 more people began to move into the community, the construction of a railroad line north of the village halted its development. 4 photos, 6 notes.　　　　　A. N. Garland

2601. Khan, Mohammad Mohabbat. EVOLUTION OF MANAGEMENT-LABOUR RELATIONS IN TENNESSEE VALLEY AUTHORITY: AN OVERVIEW. *Dhaka U. Studies Part A [Bangladesh] 1979 (30): 70-77.* The Tennessee Valley Authority was created in 1933 to stimulate economic development in Appalachia. In 1935 the TVA Board of Directors issued the Employee Relationship Policy, which gave TVA employees the right to form unions and to negotiate collectively with the management. Responding to the policy, the American Federation of Labor organized the TVA workers along craft lines, a situation that has held since. In general, labor relations have tended to be harmonious and there has been an openness that operates even at the lowest levels in the TVA. Public documents and secondary works; 8 notes.

J. V. Groves

2602.  Killick, John. RISK, SPECIALIZATION AND PROFIT IN THE MERCANTILE SECTOR OF THE NINETEENTH CENTURY COTTON TRADE: ALEXANDER BROWN AND SONS 1820-80. *Business Hist. [Great Britain] 1974 16(1): 1-16.* Beginning in Baltimore in the linen trade in 1800, the firm Alexander Brown and Sons moved into cotton and, to a lesser extent, shipping. Branches were sited in Liverpool, Philadelphia, and New York. By mid-century it was the leading foreign exchange house in the United States. Late in the century it moved into investment banking. Based on primary sources; 2 tables, appendix.

B. L. Crapster

2603.  Kovac, George. ESCAPE TO FREEDOM: A YUGOSLAV IN NORTH LOUISIANA. *North Louisiana Hist. Assoc. J. 1980 11(3): 23-28.* The author's account (written ca. 1965) of his escape from the Austro-Hungarian army in 1913 and his life making railroad cross-ties in Texas and Louisiana and later farming in North Louisiana.

J. F. Paul

2604.  MacFie, David A. RICHMOND NAVAL AIR STATION, 1942-1961. *Tequesta 1977 (37): 38-50.* Richmond Air Force Base was established in 1942 as a lighter-than-air base 19 miles south of Miami, Florida. A hurricane in 1945 destroyed the dirigible hangars, which were the world's largest wooden structures. The University of Miami leased the base for 15 years, but relinquished control in 1970 to Dade County, which used the property as a cageless zoological park.

H. S. Marks

2605.  Mahoney, Betsy. THE FACTS BEHIND THE MYTHS. *Southern Exposure 1981 9(4): 5-8.* A statistical report on how the average Southern working woman has two full-time jobs—in the home and in the workplace—and she is not appropriately rewarded for either.

2606.  Malizia, Emil. ECONOMIC IMPERIALISM: AN INTERPRETATION OF APPALACHIAN UNDERDEVELOPMENT. *Appalachian J. 1973 1(2): 130-138.* Discusses types of imperialism and relates them to "The case of Central Appalachia." A relative equality exists between Central Appalachia and the United States with regard to capital value per worker, but a net outflow of economic surplus has occurred in the last 80 years. Appalachian development will not be realized until the residents appropriate their surplus and control its utilization.

D. M. Dean

2607.  Mandle, Jay R. THE ECONOMIC UNDERDEVELOPMENT OF THE POSTBELLUM SOUTH. *Marxist Perspectives 1978 1(4): 68-79.* Discusses two hypotheses about southern economic underdevelopment during 1865-70's and suggests additional reasons for the South's lag in income and productivity.

2608.  McCarthy, Joe. THE MAN WHO INVENTED MIAMI BEACH. *Am. Heritage 1975 27(1): 64-71, 100-101.* Carl Graham Fisher, the builder of the Indianapolis Speedway, gambled millions of dollars on Florida long before the boom started. Heavy investments, completion of a bridge, and the end of World War I led to financial gains with peace, prosperity, and increased automobile travel. As money came in, more was spent on hotels, golf courses, and other attractions. The boom of the 1920's led to discouragement and Fisher turned his interests to Montauk, New York, a project overrun by the depression. Fisher died in 1939 leaving a meager estate of $40,000. 16 illus.

J. F. Paul

2609.  McKenzie, Robert H; Moore, Warner O.; and Oldschue, Jerry C. BUSINESS SUCCESS AND LEADERSHIP IN ALABAMA: A PRELIMINARY INQUIRY. *Alabama Hist. Q. 1981 43(4): 259-287.* Consists of a brief description of the lives of the 26 persons selected to the Alabama Business Hall of Fame, with emphasis on their business lives. In examining the success of these men, the authors conclude that such a study does not reveal the "secret of success." These men were, however, of rural or small

town background; most were college educated, not active in politics, and affiliated with the major religious groups. They were also involved in civil and charitable activities. 26 notes.

E. E. Eminhizer

2610.  McKenzie, Robert H. POSTBELLUM ECONOMIC DEVELOPMENT IN THE SOUTH: CONSEQUENCES OF BELIEF. *Southern Studies 1982 21(1): 27-60.* Summarizes various views on economic developments in the South after the Civil War and poses questions yet to be answered. The traditional view is that the economy was devastated by the war and its aftermath. Another view is that the South maintained a backward, "colonial" economy in contrast to the newly industrialized North. Recently, some authors have maintained that Southern attitudes, values, and social institutions accounted for the backward economy. The true explanation involves aspects of all of these; one must avoid polarities in interpretation. 86 notes.

J. J. Buschen

2611.  McKnight, Joseph W. PROTECTION OF THE FAMILY HOME FROM SEIZURE BY CREDITORS: THE SOURCES AND EVOLUTION OF A LEGAL PRINCIPLE. *Southwestern Hist. Q. 1983 86(3): 369-399.* In 1829, the Texas legislature drew upon Spanish tradition to provide a debt moratorium to protect colonists from the loss of their land and chattel for prior debts. A decade later, the Texas Congress extended debtor protection when it exempted personal property and the family home from seizure. The Texas constitutions of 1845 and 1876 provided similar protection from loss of property to creditors. These precedents influenced the formulation of federal bankruptcy law and the concept of homestead in Spain and Mexico. Legal treatises and documents of Spain and Texas; 92 notes.

R. D. Hurt

2612.  McWhiney, Grady. SAVING THE BEST FROM THE PAST. *Alabama Rev. 1979 32(4): 243-272.* An appeal against permitting polluting industrialization and its concomitant population concentration from transforming the South, lest the "best" of agrarian culture be forever destroyed. Primary and secondary sources; 38 notes.

J. F. Vivian

2613.  Mercier, Laurie. THE BUSINESS HISTORY OF JACKSON, TENNESSEE. *West Tennessee Hist. Soc. Papers 1981 35: 95-102.* Comments on business in Jackson, which had an economy based on agriculture, the railroads, lumber, and major manufacturing firms. Because of the diversified economic base, Jackson moved through such crises as World War I and the Great Depression without suffering much adversity. Transition rather than stagnation marked the changes in the business climate. Based on some business house records and contemporary newspaper accounts; 38 pictures, 26 notes.

H. M. Parker, Jr.

2614.  Mills, Gary B. NEW LIFE FOR THE RIVER OF DEATH: DEVELOPMENT OF THE YAZOO RIVER BASIN, 1873-1977. *J. of Mississippi Hist. 1979 41(4): 287-300.* Examines flood control and navigation in the Yazoo Valley, Mississippi. Primary emphasis has been laid on flood control, especially as railroads began to make serious inroads into river transportation. Discusses the public's retreat from the principles of state rights and individual enterprise in favor of allowing the federal government to assume more responsibility and control. Attributes credit to US Representative Will M. Whittington for securing funding for the Yazoo Basin Development, and describes the construction of the four reservoirs and dams (Sardis, Arkabutla, Enid, Grenada) used to harness the region's headwaters. Discusses efforts to control the backwaters and the Sunflower River Basin. Concludes that national interest in the region as well as increased federal responsibility for coordinated water resource development has made a positive contribution to the economic and social life of the basin.

M. S. Legan

2615.  Mohl, Raymond A. CHANGING ECONOMIC PATTERNS IN THE MIAMI METROPOLITAN AREA, 1940-1980. *Tequesta 1982 42: 63-73.* The Miami metropolitan area has been a dynamic and changing urban region since World War II, developing a more diversified economy than just a tourist and retirement haven. Manufacturing, international trade and banking, a "free trade zone," and the influx of Cuban emigres have positively altered the Miami area. Based largely on newspaper accounts.     H. S. Marks

2616. Montgomery, Donald Ray. SIMON T. SANDERS: PUBLIC SERVANT. *Arkansas Hist. Q. 1980 39(2): 159-168.* Account of the life and service of Simon T. Sanders (1797-1882), county clerk and postmaster of Washington, Hempstead County, Arkansas. 22 notes.
    G. R. Schroeder

2617. Moore, Jamie W. THE LOWCOUNTRY IN ECONOMIC TRANSITION: CHARLESTON SINCE 1865. *South Carolina Hist. Mag. 1979 80(2): 156-171.* Describes the economic plans for Charleston, South Carolina, which were drawn up and implemented in order to insure maximum prosperity and trade between Charleston and the Indians, France, Britain, Spain, and the rest of the United States following the Civil War in 1865.

2618. Munn, Robert F. THE DEVELOPMENT OF STRIP MINING IN SOUTHERN APPALACHIA. *Appalachian J. 1975 3(1): 87-92.*

2619. Nanjundappa, G. OCCUPATIONAL DIFFERENTIALS AMONG BLACK MALE CROSS-REGIONAL MIGRANTS FROM AND TO THE SOUTH. *Phylon 1981 42(1): 52-59.* The 1967 Survey of Economic Opportunity of 1967 offers investigators a chance to study the occupational differentials among black male cross-regional migrants. Under study were men who either moved out of or into the South. More than two-thirds of those who moved out were semiskilled or unskilled blue collar workers or farmers. Less than one-third were highly skilled or white collar. As a whole, the South sustained a net loss of 878,000 workers.
    A. G. Belles

2620. Nugent, Walter. THE DISAPPEARANCE OF THE PRODUCING CLASSES. *Rev. in Am. Hist. 1981 9(2): 196-200.* Review essay of Bruce Palmer's *"Man Over Money": The Southern Populist Critique of American Capitalism* (1980), which focuses on the southern Populists' commitment to private property and the marketplace from 1890 to 1896.

2621. O'Dell, J. H. THE SOUTH SINCE MEMPHIS. *Freedomways 1982 22(2): 68-80.* Discusses the influx of capital into the Southern states, which has done little to alleviate poverty, especially among blacks; 1968-80.

2622. Olson, Mancur. THE SOUTH WILL FALL AGAIN: THE SOUTH AS LEADER AND LAGGARD IN ECONOMIC GROWTH. *Southern Econ. J. 1983 49(4): 917-932.* Discusses the economy of the South since the Civil War, and the rapid industrialization and economic growth since 1945, due to levels of cartelization of the labor force, wage differentials, and improved transportation; as economic conditions and labor and racial policies come to match those of the rest of the nation, its economic growth will slow.

2623. Olson, Sherry H. BALTIMORE IMITATES THE SPIDER. *Ann. of the Assoc. of Am. Geographers 1979 69(4): 557-574.* Examines the impact of geographical strategies of investments in Baltimore, Maryland on economic growth, income redistribution, social conflict, and social pathology, 1745-1950's.

2624. Parker, William N. THE SOUTH IN THE NATIONAL ECONOMY, 1865-1970. *Southern Econ. J. 1980 46(4): 1019-1048.* The underdevelopment of the American South in the 75 years after the Civil War was part of a national social, economic, and demographic pattern that could not be broken until technical and economic changes which occurred only in the 1930's and 1940's.

2625. Persky, Joseph. THE SOUTH: A COLONY AT HOME. *Southern Exposure 1973 1(2): 14-22.* Discusses the economic exploitation of the Southern states by the North since 1860.

2626. Pittman, Walter. CHEMICAL REGULATION IN MISSISSIPPI: THE STATE LABORATORY (1882- ). *J. of Mississippi Hist. 1979 41(2): 133-153.* Discusses the regulatory services of the Mississippi State Chemical Laboratory, located on the Mississippi State University campus, and its key leaders during the organization's 97 years. Traces the laboratory's close association with Mississippi agriculture as well as its expanded jurisdiction into pure food and drug regulation, petroleum and chemical analysis, and research. Important figures in the laboratory's history include: John A. Myers, W. L. Hutchinson, William Flowers Hand, M. P. Etheredge, and Doctor James P. Minyard, Jr. The evolution of the laboratory's administrative structure into its present four divisions is discussed. Several dramatic incidents, such as the discovery of the contamination of millions of Mississippi chickens by the pesticide Dieldrin in 1974, illustrate the invaluable service which the State Laboratory has long rendered.     M. S. Legan

2627. Poston, Dudley L., Jr. AN ECOLOGICAL ANALYSIS OF MIGRATION IN METROPOLITAN AMERICA, 1970-75. *Social Sci. Q. 1980 61(3-4): 418-433.* Examines population distribution between 1970-75 using an ecological perspective. An ecological premise presumes a reciprocal relationship between the size of population and the organizational complexity which services that population. Population should be treated as a dependent variable in organizational growth. Any shift in population is followed by a related shift in organizational complexity. The hypothesis was tested in the old cotton belt, including about 250 counties from South Carolina to Texas, using black migration data for 1940-50 and 1950-60. During those periods, the black population in the cotton belt's metropolitan areas increased more than elsewhere. The cotton belt is unlikely to lose its population to other states. Census Bureau data; 2 tables, 18 notes.     M. Mtewa

2628. Price, Jacob M. NEW TIME SERIES FOR SCOTLAND'S AND BRITAIN'S TRADE WITH THE THIRTEEN COLONIES AND STATES, 1740 TO 1791. *William and Mary Q. 1975 32(2): 307-325.* Traces the growth of record keeping of export and import statistics by the Inspectors General. Discusses avenues of trade, particularly with Virginia and Maryland, amounts of exports and imports, and official values for the trade. The Scottish data is most important in analyzing the trade of Virginia and Maryland. Lists official values of English trade with Virginia and Maryland, Scottish imports and exports (1740-91). Based on records of the Inspector-General of Exports and Imports, legislative records, and statistical studies; 2 tables, 35 notes, 4 appendixes.
    H. M. Ward

2629. Pritchett, B. Michael. NORTHERN INSTITUTIONS IN SOUTHERN FINANCIAL HISTORY: A NOTE ON INSURANCE INVESTMENTS. *J. of Southern Hist. 1975 41(3): 391-396.* A reanalysis of the old claim that the southern states were impoverished by the outflow of capital to northern insurance companies. The companies have issued statistics to suggest the opposite, but have selected their data. Comparison of total premiums paid with proportion of total investment received bears out the contention that the southern states' economies were dominated and impoverished by northern insurance companies during the years 1874-1900. 2 tables, 9 notes.     V. L. Human

2630. Ransom, Roger L. and Sutch, Richard. GROWTH AND WELFARE IN THE AMERICAN SOUTH OF THE NINETEENTH CENTURY. *Explorations in Econ. Hist. 1979 16(2): 207-236.* The authors of *One Kind of Freedom: The Economic Consequences of Emancipation* (1975) review the literature on growth and welfare and clarify and extend the argument presented in their book. Based on published statistics and reports and on secondary accounts; 4 tables, 2 fig., 41 notes, 53 ref.
    P. J. Coleman

2631. Rehder, John B.; Morgan, John; and Medford, Joy L. DECLINE OF SMOKEHOUSES IN GRAINGER COUNTY, TENNESSEE. *West Georgia Coll. Studies in the Social Sci. 1979 18: 75-83.* Describes the characteristics and functions of smokehouses in the county from 1785 to 1979, and attributes their decline to the local change from semisubsistence agriculture to a mixed economy.

2632. Royalty, Dale. BANKING AND THE COMMONWEALTH IDEAL IN KENTUCKY, 1806-1822. *Register of the Kentucky Hist. Soc. 1979 77(2): 91-107.* Traces "Kentucky's experience with banking (which) marks an important transition from commonwealth to nationalism" during a period when "the legislature was guided by the commonwealth ideal that the state had the responsibility of promoting the economic welfare of the people it represented."

2633. Ryant, Carl G. THE SOUTH AND THE MOVEMENT AGAINST CHAIN STORES. *J. of Southern Hist. 1973 39(2): 207-222.* The movement against chain stores began in the southern states because of a fear of absentee control, and a desire to keep a state's money within the state. The Great Depression caused a suspicion of big business and the movement became national. Discriminatory state taxes were passed. Efforts to establish a national anti-chain store tax aroused opposition. Unions, farmers, and consumer groups fought the tax. The measure failed to get out of committee, and World War II finally finished the movement. 27 notes.
V. L. Human

2634. Schene, Michael G. INDIAN KEY. *Tequesta 1976 36: 3-27.* Jacob Housman came to Indian Key sometime in the early 1820's and developed it into an important trading and salvage area. In 1838 Henry Perrine moved to the Key and began to develop tropical horticultural products, but the noted massacre at the Key by Indians on 7 August 1840 marked the beginning of the decline of Indian Key. Based on primary sources; 109 notes.
H. S. Marks

2635. Singal, Daniel Joseph. BROADUS MITCHELL AND THE PERSISTENCE OF NEW SOUTH THOUGHT. *J. of Southern Hist. 1979 45(3): 353-380.* While Broadus Mitchell should have been a modern intellectual leader in the development of social science in the South, the early influences of his father, a New South spokesman, and other New South leaders such as Daniel Augustus Tompkins, George Foster Peabody, and Thomas Nelson Page shaped Mitchell's life. Despite his turn to socialism, Mitchell remained bound to a 19th-century view of US economic history. Oral history tapes, manuscript and printed primary and secondary sources; 48 notes.
T. D. Schoonover

2636. Singal, Daniel Joseph. ULRICH B. PHILLIPS: THE OLD SOUTH AS THE NEW. *J. of Am. Hist. 1976 63(4): 871-891.* Ulrich B. Phillips (1877-1934) was a far more complicated thinker than his liberal detractors have depicted. Despite his bias toward the plantation system, Phillips deserves to be included among the New South school of historians. He desperately wanted antebellum planters to appear as forerunners of modern businessmen acceptable within the framework of New South values. Phillips unintentionally became the first major southern intellectual to challenge the Cavalier myth. He was not a true reactionary but a post-Victorian who was part of that sizable contingent of intellectuals caught in the transition from 19th- to 20th-century thought. Primary and secondary sources; 41 notes.
W. R. Hively

2637. Skelton, Lynda Worley. THE IMPORTING AND EXPORTING COMPANY OF SOUTH CAROLINA (1862-1876). *South Carolina Hist. Mag. 1974 75(1): 24-32.* As the Union blockade of southern ports became more effective, companies began to form on both sides of the Atlantic to handle the blockade running trade. The Importing and Exporting Company of South Carolina was the first and largest chartered by the state legislature. Such companies ensured continuation of Confederate military operations and gave the South manufactured civilian goods it could not get otherwise. I. and E. conducted a multimillion dollar business throughout the war and paid its final dividend in 1876. 31 notes.
D. L. Smith

2638. Smith, Miriam Jane. FORGOTTEN VIRGINIAN—FROM BRITISH MERCHANT TO PROMINENT CITIZEN: THOMAS RUTHERFOORD, 1755-1852. *West Virginia Hist. 1974 36(1): 50-62.* Thomas Rutherfoord (1776-1852) was born in Glasgow, worked for his brothers' mercantile firm, and settled at Richmond, Virginia in the 1780's. In the business boom after 1790 he started his own firm, developed suburban land, speculated in tobacco, and

later entered milling. A federalist, he feared war with Britain would be disastrous for America, and he opposed the 1807 Embargo. By 1811 he was the wealthiest man in Richmond, with assets over $110,000. After 1815 he made huge profits from land sales and retired, though continuing as a bank director and city councilman. Based largely on Rutherfoord's autobiography; 55 notes.
J. H. Broussard

2639. Smith, W. Calvin. UTOPIA'S LAST CHANCE? THE GEORGIA SILK BOOMLET OF 1751. *Georgia Hist. Q. 1975 59(1): 25-37.* Discusses the silk industry in Georgia in 1751, and its sponsorship by the Georgia Corporation Trustees.

2640. Spratt, John S. BANKING PHOBIA IN TEXAS. *Southwest Rev. 1975 60(4): 341-354.* Describes the history of banks and banking in Texas, from the chartering of the first Bank of Texas in 1835 by the Congress of the Republic, to the present.

2641. Stackhouse, H. H. THE MODEL LAND TRACT: THE DEVELOPMENT OF A RESIDENTIAL NEIGHBORHOOD. *Escribano 1979 16: 25-32.* Traces the origins and development of the Model Land Company tract, a residential section in St. Augustine, Florida, founded by Henry M. Flagler in 1885 and shaped by his company to the 1920's, determining its present character.

2642. Stapleton, Darwin H. A NOTE ON SOME SOURCES FOR DELAWARE BUSINESS, ECONOMIC, AND TECHNOLOGICAL HISTORY. *Delaware Hist. 1974 16(1): 73-78.* Describes 10 collections relating to business and economic history accessioned after 1949 and housed at the Historical Society of Pennsylvania. Includes supportive manuscript material references and annotation. The materials represented in the selection support the contention of Carol Hoffecker and John A. Munroe that Delaware "was an economic dependency of Philadelphia." The collections described are: Franks & Lewden Daybook, 1810-11; Gilpin Papers, 1727-1872; John Sergeant Papers, 1783-1897; Baltimore and Philadelphia Steamboat Company Papers, 1844-1936; Bush & Lobdell Carwheel Company Papers, 1817-1929; Cadwalader Collection, 1784-1878; Thomas P. Cope Collection, ca. 1790-1925; McCall Family Papers, 1739-1886; Samuel Morse Felton Papers, 1814-88; and James P. Faries Collection, 1800. 6 notes.
R. M. Miller

2643. Sternberg, Irma O. MEMPHIS MERCHANT FOR MORE THAN SIXTY YEARS: MY FATHER, "UNCLE" IKE OTTENHEIMER. *West Tennessee Hist. Soc. Papers 1981 35: 122-127.* Orphaned at the age of two, Ike Ottenheimer (1871-1963) grew up in the home of Jacob Goldsmith, who became one of Memphis's leading merchants. Ottenheimer, however, was the catalyst for the phenomenal growth of Goldsmith's, one of the leading department stores in the South. Among his merchandising innovations was a full-page ad in the first section of every edition of *The Commercial Appeal*, buying all the foreign-made merchandise he could when World War I began, conceiving the Goldsmith's Christmas Parade—a decade before Macy's, and insisting on good customer service based on the high quality of the merchandise. Secondary materials; 12 notes.
H. M. Parker, Jr.

2644. Wadlow, Ralph and Wadlow, Carroll; Bowden, Beryl, introd. PIONEERS IN PALMDALE, GLADES COUNTY. *Tampa Bay Hist. 1982 4(2): 61-76.* Ralph Wadlow tells of the hardships endured by his family when his parents moved to Palmdale in 1932 to settle on land purchased, unseen, by a relative; covers 1932-69.

2645. Walls, Edwina. THE INTRODUCTION OF PREPAYMENT MEDICINE TO ARKANSAS: THE TRINITY HOSPITAL EXPERIENCE. *Arkansas Hist. Q. 1983 42(1): 3-26.* Describes the organization and operation of Trinity Hospital in Little Rock during 1924-53, the first prepayment contract medical plan in Arkansas. Discusses the controversy with the Pulaski County Medical Society, which opposed contract medicine. Based on interviews, minutes, and other primary and secondary sources; 2 photos, 116 notes.
G. R. Schroeder

2646. Watters, Gary. THE RUSSIAN JEW IN OKLAHOMA: THE MAY BROTHERS. *Chronicles of Oklahoma 1975-76 53(4): 479-491.* Facing increased persecution in tsarist Russia, Hyman Madanic and his son Ben emigrated to the United States in 1889. After leaving Ellis Island, where their name was changed to Madansky, they took jobs in the sweatshop system of St. Louis' clothing industry. Hard work and frugality brought enough money to bring the rest of the family from Russia in 1893. Soon the family was Americanized and opened its own clothing store in Fairfield, Illinois. In 1908 they moved to the boomtown of Tulsa, Oklahoma, where their business proved successful enough to open branches in nearby towns. Following World War I, they changed their name to the May brothers and their business became widely known. The Great Depression undercut the family fortunes and closed the Tulsa store, but the branches survived. Primary and secondary sources; 3 photos, 21 notes.     M. L. Tate

2647. Whisnant, David E. CONTROVERSY IN GOD'S GREAT DIVISION: THE COUNCIL OF THE MOUNTAINS. *Appalachian J. 1974 2(1): 7-45.* History of the Council of Southern Mountain Workers, a group of social reformers, ministers, doctors, and agriculturalists who seek improvement of living standards in rural southern areas.     S

2648. Whitaker, Thomas. HISTORY OF THE UNITED STATES POST OFFICE, SOUTH UNION, LOGAN COUNTY, KENTUCKY 42283. *Filson Club Hist. Q. 1973 47(2): 145-160.* Chronicles the history of a post office in rural Kentucky and the impact the Civil War had on operations of the postal system. Established in 1826, the South Union Post Office served the Shaker community located in Union during the 19th century. Based primarily on unpublished Shaker journals at Western Kentucky University and the Shaker museum, Auburn, Kentucky; 9 notes.

G. B. McKinney

2649. Whitfield, Stephen J. COMMERCIAL PASSIONS: THE SOUTHERN JEW AS BUSINESSMAN. *Am. Jewish Hist. 1982 71(3): 342-357.* Illustrates and assesses the prominent role of the Jewish businessman in the South and of the Southern Jewish businessman in American life generally. Though a miniscule portion of Southern population, Jews found opportunities in shopkeeping more than in agriculture or intellectual pursuits, and exploited them to great success, though many of the most successful entrepreneurs subsequently left for other regions where opportunity was even greater. Jewish businessmen were more apt to trade and associate with blacks, and they helped modernize Southern mores and morals. Based on primary sources; 34 notes.     R. A. Keller

2650. Wiener, Jonathan M. CLASS STRUCTURE AND ECONOMIC DEVELOPMENT IN THE AMERICAN SOUTH, 1865-1955. *Am. Hist. Rev. 1979 84(4): 970-992.* The American South between the Civil War and World War II was neither an immature form nor an incomplete version of the North; its class relations constituted a fully formed system that was qualitatively different from the North's classic capitalism. The distinctiveness arose out of the labor-repressive nature of southern production and the direct participation of the state in enforcing restrictions on the mobility of labor. This system was based on a net of laws centering around debt peonage. Not until the Great Depression of the 1930's and World War II was the South's distinctive system of class relations shattered; beginning in the late 1940's, the South joined the North in classic capitalist development, based on agricultural mechanization and a labor force that was not tied to the land. This class analysis is contrasted to interpretations that regard the South as a growing free market economy, and as an evolving bourgeois society. (Following the body of the article Robert Higgs (pp. 993-997) and Harold D. Woodman (pp. 997-1001) provide a commentary on this interpretation of southern economic development, and I (pp. 1002-1006) then provide an analysis of their remarks).     A

2651. Willingham, John. GEORGE BARNARD: TRADER AND MERCHANT ON THE TEXAS FRONTIER. *Texana 1973 12(4): 305-334.* In the late 1830's George Barnard came to the Waco, Texas region from Hartford, Connecticut. Only 19 years of age at the time, he was the first white settler in the region. Becoming resident agent there at a post established by the firm of John F. Torrey and Brothers of Houston, he traded with the area Indians and invested heavily in land. By 1857 he was financially secure and went into semi-retirement, dying in 1883. Based on primary and secondary sources; 85 notes.     B. D. Ledbetter

2652. Wilson, Charles R. THE SOUTHERN FUNERAL DIRECTOR: MANAGING DEATH IN THE NEW SOUTH. *Georgia Hist. Q. 1983 67(1): 49-69.* History of the development of funeral directing as a business in the South during the 1880's-1930's. Based on funeral directors' publications; 36 notes.     G. R. Schroeder

2653. Wilson, Kenneth L. and Martin, W. Allen. ETHNIC ENCLAVES: A COMPARISON OF THE CUBAN AND BLACK ECONOMIES IN MIAMI. *Am. J. of Sociol. 1982 88(1): 135-160.* Compares the economic structure of the Cuban and black communities in Miami, Florida, during the 1920's-80, focusing on Cuban-owned and black-owned businesses; Cubans are successful while the blacks are not.

2654. Wimmer, Larry T. THE GOLD CRISIS OF 1869: STABILIZING OR DESTABILIZING SPECULATION UNDER FLOATING EXCHANGE RATES? *Explorations in Econ. Hist. 1975 12(2): 105-122.* Analyzes Jay Gould's effort in the New York gold market to raise the greenback price of gold. Shows that Black Friday might not have occurred had the government declared its neutrality more quickly and that in any event speculative capital flows would have stabilized exchange rates within a short time. Based on the records of the Erie Railroad, Cleveland, Ohio, published reports, financial periodicals, and secondary accounts.

P. J. Coleman

2655. Winkler, Elizabeth B. THE ECONOMIC CONSEQUENCES OF EMANCIPATION. *J. of European Econ. Hist. [Italy] 1980 9(3): 765-770.* A report of a symposium held at Duke University on 11 February 1978 to report the conclusions of the Southern Economic History Project. Six reports analyzing the development of economic institutions in the American South after the emancipation of the slaves were presented.     D. S. Rockwood

2656. Wren, Benjamin. THE RISING SUN ON THE MISSISSIPPI, 1900-1975. *Louisiana Hist. 1976 17(3): 321-342.* New Orleans' attitude toward the Japanese has varied since 1900, depending on international political events, but since 1945 Japanese trade relations have become increasingly important to New Orleans. By 1974 20% of all exports from the port of New Orleans were destined for Japan. Based on primary and secondary sources; 38 notes.

R. L. Woodward

2657. Wright, Gavin. THE STRANGE CAREER OF THE NEW SOUTHERN ECONOMIC HISTORY. *Rev. in Am. Hist. 1982 10(4): 164-180.* Surveys major themes in the history of Southern economy, emphasizing regional economic development and the role of blacks.

2658. Yelton, Susan. NEWNANSVILLE: A LOST FLORIDA SETTLEMENT. *Florida Hist. Q. 1975 53(3): 319-331.* Studies the rise and decline of Newnansville, made the county seat of Alachua County by legislative action 15 November 1828. A fort site during the Second Seminole War, it was a prosperous 19th-century settlement in one of the richest land belts in north-central Florida. However, it became isolated from other portions of the county and its final demise was insured when the Charlotte Harbor Railroad, which had been scheduled to connect Newnansville with Gainesville, passed a mile south of town. 47 notes.     R. V. Ritter

2659. Young, Otis E., Jr. THE SOUTHERN GOLD RUSH, 1828. *J. of Southern Hist. 1982 48(3): 373-392.* Gold discoveries and mining in the Appalachian Piedmont before the economic crisis of the late 1830's stimulated land speculation, canal building, and wildcat banking. It also served as a pilot experiment and educational experience for the later gold rushes. The technology developed in Virginia, North Carolina, and South Carolina were reapplied later in the West. Based on US Geological Survey reports and other printed primary materials; 54 notes. T. D. Schoonover

2660. —. [ANTEBELLUM SOUTHERN INCOME] *Explorations in Econ. Hist. 1975 12(1): 89-99, 101-102.*
Gallman, Robert E. SOUTHERN ANTE-BELLUM INCOME RECONSIDERED, *pp. 89-99.* A critique of and rejoinder to an article by Gerald Gunderson (Explorations in Econ. Hist. 1973 10(2): 151-176) on income estimates in the South in the 1840's.
Gunderson, Gerald. SOUTHERN INCOME RECONSIDERED: A REPLY, *pp. 101-102.* In answer to Gallman's critique, Gunderson explains and defends his original article.

2661. —. BUILDING RESEARCH. *Southern Exposure 1980 8(1): 101-118.* Criticizes contemporary corporations involved in the diverse areas of heavy construction, housing, landscaping, and building materials. American contractors are losing out in overseas construction to other nations. Particular interest is focused on Brown & Root, Inc., a subsidiary of Halliburton, concentrating on the South. Very poor housing has been erected in recent years, and very little in the rural areas where serious housing shortages exist. The culprit in every instance seems to be the multicorporation conglomerate. 3 photos, 16 tables, graph. H. M. Parker, Jr.

2662. —. [ECONOMIC DEVELOPMENT IN THE SOUTH, 1770-1900]. *Agric. Hist. 1975 49(2): 343-380.*
Engerman, Stanley L. A RECONSIDERATION OF SOUTHERN ECONOMIC GROWTH, 1770-1860, pp. 343-361. Recent studies have shown that the South was in a better economic position in 1860 than formerly thought. Southern agriculture was more efficient than that of the North, and manufacturing was not only growing rapidly, but was widespread (if one includes agricultural processing). In per capita income and distribution of wealth, the South remained only slightly behind the North and was ahead of most European countries. These interpretations suggest a new framework for the study of southern society. Table, 57 notes.
Rubin, Julius. THE LIMITS OF AGRICULTURAL PROGRESS IN THE NINETEENTH-CENTURY SOUTH, pp. 362-373. The growth of 19th-century agriculture in the lower South was limited by climate and soil as well as by institutional factors such as slavery and tenant farming. Heavy rain and acid soil made it difficult to grow the forage crops necessary to support high-quality livestock, which in turn would have improved the soil, while high temperatures lowered milk production and brought pests and diseases not found in the North. Scientific advances necessary to improve southern agriculture had to await the coming of the 20th century. 14 notes.
Woodman, Harold D. NEW PERSPECTIVES ON SOUTHERN ECONOMIC DEVELOPMENT: A COMMENT, pp. 374-380. Stanley Engerman's paper overestimates the prosperity of the antebellum South. Per capita income was lower than in the North when examined by region, increases in productivity were limited by the scarcity of plantation land and difficulty of mechanization, and the use of 1860 census data overstates the cotton crop. Julius Rubin's paper shows that dividing the region into lower South and upper South gives us new insights into southern agriculture. The growth of food production alongside that of cotton made the southern food market shallow and limited urbanization. Table, 4 notes.
D. E. Bowers

## Agriculture and the Plantation and Rural Economies

2663. Abel, Ernest L. WHEN TOBACCO WAS KING. *Am. Hist. Illus. 1977 11(10): 10-19.* Discusses the history of the cultivation of tobacco in Virginia, 1613-1732, and the important role which it played in the economy of that colony.

2664. Aiken, Charles S. THE EVOLUTION OF COTTON GINNING IN THE SOUTHEASTERN UNITED STATES. *Geographical Rev. 1973 63(2): 196-224.* Cotton ginning in the southeastern United States can be structured in terms of three 'revolutions' or periods of rapid technological change. The Eli Whitney gin was the principal contribution during the revolution that closed the eighteenth century and began the nineteenth. As a result of the second revolution, which followed the Civil War, building morphology changed, the number of gins decreased, and new business allied with ginning developed. In the 1940's mechanical harvesting of cotton initiated the third revolution. This revolution also caused building alterations, accelerated declines in the number of gins, and produced changes in the sizes of service areas. The present ginning industry is a product of continuing evolutionary processes that are influenced primarily by economic, technological, and political factors. J

2665. Aldrich, Mark. FLEXIBLE EXCHANGE RATES, NORTHERN EXPANSION, AND THE MARKET FOR SOUTHERN COTTON: 1866-1879. *J. of Econ. Hist. 1973 33(2): 399-416.* Although no single interest group was responsible, Charles Beard's explanation of prewar southern economic decline applies to the postwar period in at least one respect. Northern and western economic development reinforced the war's destruction by hampering southern recovery of cotton markets. The decision to return gold to its prewar price—implying a long period of flexible exchanges—coupled with foreign investments in the North and West, plus expanding western grain exports that drove down the price of gold, increased the cost of southern cotton to foreign buyers. Based on US Dept. of Commerce statistics and secondary sources; 3 tables, 43 notes. W. R. Hively

2666. Alston, Lee J. and Higgs, Robert. CONTRACTUAL MIX IN SOUTHERN AGRICULTURE SINCE THE CIVIL WAR: FACTS, HYPOTHESES, AND TESTS. *J. of Econ. Hist. 1982 42(2): 327-353.* In the South after 1865, workers and property owners employed a variety of contracts—wage payment, crop sharing, and land rental—to bring together cooperating resources in agricultural production. The contractual mix varied over time and space, depending on the relative resource endowments of the contracting parties, the prevailing risk conditions, and the costs of alternative contractural arrangements. To understand the contractual mix, certain empirical distinctions must be made, and the major hypothesess advanced to explain the mix must be seen as complementary rather than mutually exclusive. J/S

2667. Alston, Lee J. TENURE CHOICE IN SOUTHERN AGRICULTURE, 1930-1960. *Explorations in Econ. Hist. 1981 18(3): 211-232.* Analyzes the decline in agricultural tenant contracts in 10 southern states from Texas to the Carolinas during 1930-60. Mechanization and crop choice reduced supervision costs and the type of labor needed. Wage labor became more cost efficient, reducing tenancy contracts. 3 tables, app., 16 notes, 41 ref.

P. J. Coleman

2668. Anderson, James D. THE SOUTHERN IMPROVEMENT COMPANY: NORTHERN REFORMERS' INVESTMENT IN NEGRO COTTON TENANCY 1900-1920. *Agric. Hist. 1978 52(1): 111-131.* The Southern Improvement Company, holding land in Virginia and Alabama, was founded by northern reformers in 1900 to provide southern Negroes with the means to become independent farmers. The SIC was dissolved in 1917 because the black farmers found they couldn't operate at a profit under the company restrictions. Primary and secondary sources; 39 notes.

R. T. Fulton

2669. Argersinger, Peter H. ORGANIZING THE FARMERS' MOVEMENT. *Rev. in Am. Hist. 1976 4(4): 565-570.* Review article prompted by Robert C. McMath, Jr.'s *Populist Vanguard: A History of the Southern Farmers' Alliance* (Chapel Hill: U. of North Carolina Pr., 1975); discusses the social functions of the agricultural movement, 1870's-80's.

2670. Baker, T. Lindsay. WINDMILLS OF THE PANHANDLE PLAINS. *Panhandle-Plains Hist. Rev. 1980 53: 71-110.* Windmills first appeared in the arid Texas Panhandle in the mid-1880's. Within a decade steel windmills had replaced the original wooden structures. Eyewitness descriptions, and 20 action photographs, are reprinted. 25 notes.　　M. L. Tate

2671. Banks, Ann. TOBACCO TALK. *Southern Exposure 1980 8(4): 34-45.* Describes the Federal Writers' Project, part of the New Deal's national work relief program, focusing on four brief accounts from the FWP tobacco study on tobacco farming during the 1930's.

2672. Bartley, Numan V. ANOTHER NEW SOUTH? *Georgia Hist. Q. 1981 65(2): 119-137.* Discusses various historians' interpretations of the development of the New South after the Civil War, determining that plantation-oriented leadership continued to control the region until the breakdown of the agricultural economy due to various disasters in the 1920's. 52 notes.　　G. R. Schroeder

2673. Barton, Josef J. LAND, LABOR, AND COMMUNITY IN NUECES: CZECH FARMERS AND MEXICAN LABORERS IN SOUTH TEXAS, 1880-1930. Luebke, Frederick C., ed. *Ethnicity on the Great Plains* (Lincoln: U. of Nebraska Pr., for the Center for Great Plains Studies, 1980): 190-209. Discusses the similarities and contrasts between Czech farmers and Mexican laborers, and the relationships of land and family in Nueces County, Texas, early in the 20th century. Both groups were highly transient, but each was united by bonds of common origin and kinship. Whereas Czechs were linked by generational lines, Mexicans were united by lateral ties among kinfolk. Among the Czechs landownership quickly became the mode, but Mexican tenant farmers were reduced to a migrant, landless rural proletariat. Both groups attempted to use familiar forms as they faced new and altered circumstances. Out of such confrontations emerged ethnic cultures that shaped and sustained their lives. Religion became the bond of community in both groups, as cooperative efforts were transformed into institutions and ritual associations into resources for collective action. Secondary sources; 31 notes.　　J. Powell

2674. Bellamy, Donnie D. HENRY A. HUNT AND BLACK AGRICULTURAL LEADERSHIP IN THE NEW SOUTH. *J. of Negro Hist. 1975 60(4): 464-479.* Discusses the achievements of Henry Alexander Hunt during 1890-1938 in instituting and promoting programs of social change and economic reform among the black farmers of North Carolina and Georgia, in particular his foundation of the Forth Valley High Industrial School. Apart from introducing farmers to the notion of scientific farming, Hunt was successful in persuading them to join credit unions to buy their own land, in making them aware of goverment loan programs, and in establishing the Flint River farms in Macon County, Georgia, a farm cooperative. 49 notes.　　C. A. McNeill

2675. Bildner, Robert. SOUTHERN FARMS: A VANISHING BREED. *Southern Exposure 1974 2(2/3): 72-79.* Discusses economic difficulties of small farmers in the South in the 1970's, emphasizing problems in competing with agribusiness conglomerates.

2676. Bishko, Lucretia Ramsey. LAFAYETTE AND THE MARYLAND AGRICULTURAL SOCIETY: 1824-1832. *Maryland Hist. Mag. 1975 70(1): 45-67.* "All the latent patriotism of the last half century burst forth during Lafayette's year-long visit to the twenty-four states," during 1824-25, and Maryland was not to be outdone. The Maryland Agricultural Society, in its sixth year, postponed its fifth Agricultural Fair and Exhibition and launched "a splendid promotional scheme" under the lead of John S. Skinner, Postmaster of Baltimore, secretary of the Society, and editor of the *American Farmer.* Silver premium-prizes for the best farm produce and livestock were awarded personally by Lafayette at the fair, and became treasured heirlooms due to their inscriptions, "from the hands of Lafayette." Agriculture continued to dominate the nation's guest on his frequent stops in Baltimore, and detailed arrangements for transporting the copious amounts of livestock, seed, mechanical equipment, and plants bestowed on him to his estate in France, La Grange, are reported. The voyage was hard on the American tur-

keys, cows, oppossums, and partridges, and during 1826 "packet ship captains were... busy carrying presents back and forth across the Atlantic." Americans took pride in the awards given to Lafayette by French societies for his prize specimens sired from American stock. Primary and secondary sources; 2 illus., 86 notes.　　G. J. Bobango

2677. Bonnifield, Paul. THE OKLAHOMA PANHANDLE'S AGRICULTURE TO 1930. *Red River Valley Hist. Rev. 1978 3(1): 61-76.* Agriculture in the Oklahoma panhandle consisted primarily of field crops (grains) and was subject to annual weather cycles typical of the high plains semiarid environment, 1880-1930.

2678. Bowman, Shearer Davis. ANTEBELLUM PLANTERS AND *VORMÄRZ* JUNKERS IN COMPARATIVE PERSPECTIVE. *Am. Hist. Rev. 1980 85(4): 779-808.* Antebellum planters and *Vormärz* Junkers were comparable landed elites primarily because of similarities between plantations and *Rittergüter* (knights' estates) as capitalist agricultural enterprises and autocratic political communities. Thus, proslavery and Old Prussian thought manifested striking ideological parallels, particularly with respect to their reliance on the conservative ideas of Edmund Burke. Because of geographic, demographic, racial, and political differences between their regional societies, however, planters enjoyed a much higher level of popular approval in the South than did Junkers in East Elbia, although the Junkers exercised more flexible and durable influence over their central government. Regional differences also caused the tension between pragmatic and idealistic conservatives to have a less divisive impact on planters than on Junkers. Hence, planters in 1860-61 were much more united against northern challenges to slavery than were Junkers in 1848 against revolutionary attacks on the privileges of *Rittergut* owners. Primary sources, including agricultural periodicals, manuscript collections of planters, and published writings of ideologues; 2 illus., 84 notes.　　A

2679. Brewer, Krista, interviewer. THE GOOD LIFE ON A 25-ACRE FARM. *Southern Exposure 1983 11(6): 27-29.* Booker T. Whatley, a retired professor from Tuskegee Institute, believes in the future of small farms as profitable enterprises and has been involved in planning 25-acre model farms.

2680. Brown, William R. and Reynolds, Morgan O. DEBT PEONAGE RE-EXAMINED. *J. of Econ. Hist. 1973 33(4): 862-871.* Roger L. Ransom and Richard Sutch (see entry S:6712) suggest that a credit monopoly allowed Southern merchants to coerce farmers into "excessive" cotton production and to reap the profits of selling foodstuffs to the growers. Since only indirect evidence for this "debt peonage" is offered, the consistency of Southern agricultural activity with general market behavior theory puts their hypothesis on "tenuous ground." An alternative explanation is grounded in basic economic theory. When trade barriers are relaxed, as happened after the Civil War, specialization grows and wealth increases. 2 tables, 31 notes.　　W. R. Hively

2681. Buker, George E. ENGINEERS VS. FLORIDA'S GREEN MENACE. *Florida Hist. Q. 1982 60(4): 413-427.* The spread of water hyacinth is "fantastic"; it doubles every month of the growing season. From its introduction to Florida in 1884 to the present, state and local officials have attempted to control the plant. By 1982 a combination of underwater cutting, chemical spraying, and biological control has the plant in check. Based on Florida state records, records of the Army Corps of Engineers, personal interviews, and other sources; 29 notes.　　N. A. Kuntz

2682. Caron, Dewey M. THE ART OF BEEKEEPING IN MARYLAND: PAST AND PRESENT. *J. of NAL Assoc. 1976 1(3): 37-42.* History of beekeeping in Maryland after the colony was settled in 1634; discusses the teaching of apiculture at the University of Maryland since its founding in 1859.

2683. Caron, Dewey M. BEE CULTURE IN MARYLAND. *J. of NAL Assoc. 1976 1(1-2): 10-14.* History of honey bee culture in Maryland since the bees' introduction there in 1634; focuses on the second half of the 19th century and on current beekeeping at the University of Maryland.

2684. Carter, Betty W. MULES IN THE DELTA. *Am. Heritage 1976 28(1): 54-63.* The rich bottom land in Mississippi called the Delta was opened to cotton after the Civil War. Men and mules cleared and drained the land and raised the crops until after World War II when the tractor and the mechanized cotton picker took over. 6 illus.                                            B. J. Paul

2685. Carter, Dan T. NEW WINE IN OLD BOTTLES: THE DEBUNKING OF GEORGE WASHINGTON CARVER. *Rev. in Am. Hist. 1982 10(3): 408-412.* Reviews Linda O. McMurry's *George Washington Carver: Scientist and Symbol* (1981), which recounts Carver's career as a student, educator, and scientist; his famous agricultural experiments had few practical results, but the myth of Carver as scientist has served to spread his doctrine of self-help.

2686. Clemens, Paul G. E. THE OPERATION OF AN EIGHTEENTH-CENTURY CHESAPEAKE TOBACCO PLANTATION. *Agricultural Hist. 1975 49(3): 517-531.* Tobacco planters on Maryland's Eastern Shore found it difficult to support themselves from tobacco alone, as half of the amount which tobacco workers produced went for their maintenance. Large planters fared better than small ones but seldom made more than six percent on their investments. Because of low tobacco prices planters increasingly diversified into grain and livestock production, making tobacco areas less dependent on one crop than rice and sugar areas. Based on farm records, death inventories, tax lists, and land records. 9 tables, 18 notes.                                           D. E. Bowers

2687. Clift, Eleanor. BLACK LAND LOSS: 6,000,000 ACRES AND FADING FAST. *Southern Exposure 1974 2(2/3): 108-111.* Discusses attempts by Negroes and Southern Rural Action, Inc., to form agricultural cooperatives in rural settlements in the South, 1966-70's, including aspects of land tenure.

2688. Clifton, James M. CHARLES MANIGAULT'S ESSAY ON THE ECONOMICS OF MILLING RICE. *Agric. Hist. 1978 52(1): 104-110.* In a letter to his plantation overseer, and his son Louis, Charles Manigault in 1852 estimates the comparative costs of sending a rice crop to a miller for processing as opposed to milling the rice in his own facilities. Manigault computed a savings of nearly a third by milling the rice on his Georgia plantation. Primary and secondary sources; 11 notes.                              R. T. Fulton

2689. Clifton, James M. HOPETON, MODEL PLANTATION OF THE ANTEBELLUM SOUTH. *Georgia Hist. Q. 1982 66(4): 429-449.* Describes Hopeton, a large plantation on the Altamaha River in Glynn County, Georgia, focusing on its varied major crops: sea island cotton, sugar, and, most profitably, rice. Plantation records are extant from ca. 1818-52. Based on plantation records and other primary and secondary sources; 2 tables, 2 fig., 65 notes.                                       G. R. Schroeder

2690. Clifton, James M. THE RICE INDUSTRY IN COLONIAL AMERICA. *Agric. Hist. 1981 55(3): 266-283.* Rice culture in the southern colonies went through a longer period of experimentation than any other major colonial crop. Carolina planters drew more on the experience of African slaves than that of other New World rice planters. They tried various types of seed and attempted to grow rice on both dry and swamp lands. Gradually, rice growers discovered a sophisticated method of tidal irrigation but were slow to develop threshing and polishing machinery. From its beginnings in the late 17th century, rice became a very profitable crop by the mid-18th century and was responsible for many large southern fortunes. Table, 80 notes.                                  D. E. Bowers

2691. Clifton, James M. TWILIGHT COMES TO THE RICE KINGDOM: POSTBELLUM RICE CULTURE ON THE SOUTH ATLANTIC COAST. *Georgia Hist. Q. 1978 62(2): 146-154.* Gives statistics on the decline of rice production in North Carolina, South Carolina and Georgia and mentions the development of rice planting in Louisiana. Primary sources, census returns; 29 notes.
                                                    G. R. Schroeder

2692. Colbert, William W., Jr. WILLIAM WILLIAMS COLBERT: BIENVILLE PARISH PLANTER (1807-1890). *North Louisiana Hist. Assoc. J. 1973 5(1): 21-24.* William Williams Colbert was born in Georgia in 1807. He moved with his wife and children to Bienville Parish in 1849. He first purchased land—160 acres—from his brother, who had come to Bienville Parish a year before. Eventually, Colbert owned more than 2,400 acres and "Oak Lawn plantation, [which] with its house, servants and landscape, its gin and shop, its many types of livestock and fowl... provided all of the necessaries and comforts of plantation living." The Colberts had 10 children (four daughters and six sons); one son died in the Confederate Army. 13 notes.                             A. N. Garland

2693. Coleman, A. Lee and Hall, Larry D. BLACK FARM OPERATORS AND FARM POPULATION. 1900-1970: ALABAMA AND KENTUCKY. *Phylon 1979 40(4): 387-402.* Examines statistics to analyze the decline in black farm operators and farm population in Alabama and Kentucky from 1900-70. Based on census data; 2 maps, 5 tables, 4 notes.                        G. R. Schroeder

2694. Comeaux, Malcolm. LES ACADIENS LOUISIANAIS: L'IMPACT DE L'ENVIRONNEMENT [Louisiana Acadians: Impact of the environment]. *Rev. de Louisiane 1977 6(2): 163-178.* Discusses the impact of the land in Louisiana on the daily life, folk culture, and occupations of Acadians there; discusses farming, river culture, and swamp life, 18th-19th centuries.

2695. Cooke, J. W. STONEY POINT, 1866-1969. *Filson Club Hist. Q. 1976 50(4): 337-352.* Stoney Point is an unincorporated black community located in Warren County, Kentucky. Black ownership of the area began in 1848 with the death of a white plantation owner named William White. White freed at least six of his 50 slaves and provided them with part of his farm and the equipment to work the land. The Stoney Point Missionary Baptist Church, organized in 1866, became the focal point of the community. The church not only acted as a center of worship, but it regulated the social life of its members as well. In 1880 the church had about 250 members; the number has been declining ever since. Race relations with nearby whites were generally peaceful because many of the blacks were forced to work for white farmers to supplement their incomes. Based on government reports and personal interviews; 20 notes.                              G. B. McKinney

2696. Coon, David L. ELIZA LUCAS PINCKNEY AND THE REINTRODUCTION OF INDIGO CULTURE IN SOUTH CAROLINA. *J. of Southern Hist. 1976 42(1): 61-76.* When economic problems led to the decline of rice and the rise of indigo culture, little attention was given to the historical origins of that product into South Carolina. Only when indigo culture began to disappear was there an expressed interest in its introduction into Carolina. Although Eliza Lucas Pinckney is credited with first developing indigo culture in the 1740's, it was the result of various English and French individuals and connections from the indigo growing areas of the Caribbean, including Negro slaves coming from these indigo areas, who brought their skills with them. Based upon manuscript and primary and secondary printed sources; 49 notes.
                                                    T. D. Schoonover

2697. Cooper, William J., Jr. THE COTTON CRISIS IN THE ANTEBELLUM SOUTH: ANOTHER LOOK. *Agric. Hist. 1975 49(2): 381-391.* Southerners in the 1850's did not believe a crisis in cotton production was coming. Agricultural periodicals show an optimism that was borne out later in the century as production expanded greatly; yields per acre improved with the application of fertilizer, and prices held firm. 3 tables, 46 notes.
                                                    D. E. Bowers

2698. Coté, Joseph A. CLARENCE HAMILTON POE: THE FARMER'S VOICE, 1899-1964. *Agric. Hist. 1979 53(1): 30-41.* Coming to the staff of the *Progressive Farmer* in 1897 as "printer's devil," Clarence Hamilton Poe became editor in 1899. An aggressive spokesman for agrarian values, he viewed the farmers as the "guardians of the nation's heritage," and used the pages of his journal to propose reforms which would rejuvenate southern agriculture and end the expanding exodus from the farm. A major method which he advocated was the agricultural cooperative; however, his fertile mind and accurate analysis of problems reached out in many directions. Through his journal he championed agricultural reform measures, and brought hope and encouragement to southern farmers, including positive change. 48 notes. Comment by William Scarborough, pp. 60-61.      R. V. Ritter

2699. Coughenour, C. Milton. FARMERS, LOCATION, AND THE DIFFERENTIATION OF CROPS FROM LIVESTOCK IN FARMING. *Rural Sociol. 1980 45(4): 569-590.* Focuses on data from a survey of Kentucky farmers; 1973-74.

2700. Crook, Morgan R. and O'Grady, Patricia D. SPALDING'S SUGAR WORKS SITE, SAPELO ISLAND, GEORGIA. *Industrial Archaeol. [Great Britain] 1977 12(4): 318-350.* Reports the results of the 1976 archaeological investigations of the Thomas Spalding sugar works, provides an economic background for the development of sugar operations, and examines 19th-century sugar production.

2701. Crosby, Earl W. LIMITED SUCCESS AGAINST LONG ODDS: THE BLACK COUNTY AGENT. *Agric. Hist. 1983 57(3): 277-288.* In 1906, the Department of Agriculture began employing blacks as county extension agents to help black farmers in the South. Extension programs for blacks emphasized subsistence farming and improvement of living conditions rather than commercial farming, as in the white program. Although most black farmers were tenants, the black agents directed their attention mainly to landowning farmers; work with tenants depended heavily on cooperation by white landlords. The black extension program did little to help the poorest farmers but there were many individual success stories, including farmers who joined cooperative and livestock associations. Based largely on government documents; 3 tables, 24 notes.      D. E. Bowers

2702. Crosby, Earl W. THE ROOTS OF BLACK AGRICULTURAL EXTENSION WORK. *Historian 1977 39(2): 228-247.* The beginnings of black agricultural extension work may be credited to the efforts of Booker T. Washington at Tuskegee Institute of Tuskegee, Alabama. The first Tuskegee Negro Conference, in 1892, renewed interest in improving agricultural methods. The success and growth of this annual conference was followed by similar satellite conferences. A Department of Agriculture was founded at the Institute, with George Washington Carver as its first head. The efforts thus begun developed in various directions, such as demonstration wagon trips into rural communities and short courses at Tuskegee. More importantly, these efforts inspired similar efforts throughout the South, such as Seaman A. Knapp's programs, and the active support of John D. Rockefeller's General Education Board. 45 notes.      R. V. Ritter

2703. Dann, Martin. BLACK POPULISM: A STUDY OF THE COLORED FARMERS' ALLIANCE THROUGH 1891. *J. of Ethnic Studies 1974 2(3): 58-71.* Describes the efforts of post-Civil War blacks to break the deadlock of oppression and exploitation by organized action. The Colored Farmers' Alliance may have evolved out of secret rural societies, some of them founded by Knights of Labor organizers sent South during the 1880's. Reviews the career of Colonel R. M. Humphrey, and the spread of the Alliance from Texas into South Carolina under T. E. Pratt of Cheraw, and to Virginia under C. W. Macune. The turning point for the CFA came between the Ocala Convention and the Cincinnati Conference, when fears of whites increased in the face of cotton pickers' strikes and CFA support for a third political party. The failure of Humphrey's general strike call of September 1891 discredited the militant wing of the Alliance which generally encouraged the brutal repression of black labor agitation, forgetting the political expediency which had originally produced limited support for black agrarianism. Based on primary news accounts, periodicals, secondary works; 43 notes.      G. J. Bobango

2704. Davis, Ronald L. F. THE U.S. ARMY AND THE ORIGINS OF SHARECROPPING IN THE NATCHEZ DISTRICT: A CASE STUDY. *J. of Negro History 1977 62(1): 60-80.* Investigating the apparent contradiction between the war to end slavery and

the origins of sharecropping, examines the role of the US Army in the transition from slavery to sharecropping. In the Mississippi Valley and other areas it supervised the economic treatment of blacks as refugees and free men for six years or more in the 1860's. Although no official policy launched sharecropping, the Army and the Freedmen's Bureau contributed indirectly to its emergence, as demonstrated by the Natchez district experience. Based mainly on government records; 70 notes.      P. J. Taylorson

2705. Decanio, Stephen. COTTON "OVERPRODUCTION" IN LATE NINETEENTH-CENTURY SOUTHERN AGRICULTURE. *J. of Econ. Hist. 1973 33(3): 608-633.* Quantitative analysis of supply functions suggests that "southern cotton farmers were as flexible and as price-responsive as wheat farmers in the rest of the United States during the late nineteenth and early twentieth centuries." Southern growers were economically astute in rejecting the proposed panacea of diversification. "No evidence of alleged traditionalism, or of merchants' insistence on cotton" leading to overspecialization or overproduction can be found. The frequently expressed idea that cotton overproduction fueled the Populist movement of the 1890's must therefore be reexamined. Primary and secondary sources; 5 tables, 2 graphs, 29 notes.      W. R. Hively

2706. DeCanio, Stephen. PRODUCTIVITY AND INCOME DISTRIBUTION IN THE POST-BELLUM SOUTH. *J. of Econ. Hist. 1974 34(2): 422-446.* Tests alternative hypotheses concerning the exploitation of Southern farmers during 1880-1910. Southern farmers were not exploited by either merchants or large landowners. Cotton cannot necessarily be associated with a system of exploitation because cotton was the most profitable crop available. Whites were not uniformly more productive than blacks. Racial discrimination does not account for income and productivity differences among Southern farmers. Based on contemporary published accounts, official published documents, and secondary sources; 4 tables, 34 notes.      O. H. Reichardt

2707. Dethloff, Henry C.; Fite, Gilbert C. (commentary). THE COLONIAL RICE TRADE. *Agric. Hist. 1982 56(1): 231-248.* Rice production in South Carolina began in the late 1600's and expanded rapidly over the next century as technological improvements were introduced. British Navigation Acts had little adverse effect on the rice trade. Unlike planters in Virginia, South Carolina rice merchants became primarily urban dwellers who had increasingly close ties to New England merchants. By the American Revolution the rice trade had reached a level of sophistication comparable to the later antebellum cotton and rice industries. Comments, pp. 244-248; table, 29 notes.      D. E. Bowers

2708. Droze, W. H. TVA AND THE ORDINARY FARMER. *Agric. Hist. 1979 53(1): 188-202.* The Tennessee Valley Authority has brought extensive change to the farmers of the Tennessee Valley. An analysis of the economic, social, and technological changes, however, reveals great variation in the extent of benefit to the individual farm families. There have been many improvements in standard of living; however, "there are still many limited-resource farmers who have been bypassed by progress." 41 notes. Comment by Donald Holley, pp. 203-205.      R. V. Ritter

2709. Ellis, William E.; Lowitt, Richard, (commentary). ROBERT WORTH BINGHAM AND THE CRISIS OF COOPERATIVE MARKETING IN THE TWENTIES. *Agric. Hist. 1982 56(1): 99-121.* The organization of tobacco marketing cooperatives in the 1920's was spurred by the farmers' hostility to monopolistic tobacco companies and a disastrous price break in 1920. The two men most responsible for cooperatives were Robert Worth Bingham, a wealthy Louisville newspaper editor, and Aaron Sapiro, a San Francisco lawyer and cooperatives organizer. They helped set up two large cooperatives, one for burley tobacco (1921) and one for dark tobacco (1922) located in Kentucky and Tennessee; a third association was formed in Virginia and the Carolinas. At first, cooperatives succeeded in raising prices by holding tobacco off the market, but they soon succumbed to internal bickering, the reluctance of farmers to delay marketing, and the refusal of most large tobacco companies to buy cooperative tobacco. These cooperatives, however, did lay the foundation for the cooperative movement of the 1930's. Comments, pp. 117-121; 51 notes.    D. E. Bowers

2710. Ferleger, Louis. FARM MECHANIZATION IN THE SOUTHERN SUGAR SECTOR AFTER THE CIVIL WAR. *Louisiana Hist. 1982 23(1): 21-34.* Attributes the failure to mechanize sugar harvesting in Louisiana to the existence of a steady supply of cheap black labor maintained through legal restraints on black mobility, quick suppression of strikes, and the lack of alternative job opportunities for Negroes. This supports the thesis that "inducement mechanisms and focusing devices," such as labor shortages, are necessary catalysts for technological innovation. Mainly secondary sources; 26 notes.    R. E. Noble

2711. Fisher, James S. NEGRO FARM OWNERSHIP IN THE SOUTH. *Ann. of the Assoc. of Am. Geographers 1973 63(4): 478-489.* Rural Negroes achieved farm ownership in the southern United States after the Civil War. The number of Negro farm owners has declined substantially from a peak of more than 200,000 around World War I, yet they remain significant in some areas. The small size of Negro farms, and the limited capital of their owners, will make their survival difficult. Many of these landholdings now have greater social value than economic significance.    J

2712. Fisher, Steve. LAND REFORM AND APPALACHIA: LESSONS FROM THE THIRD WORLD. *Appalachian J. 1983 10(2): 122-133.*

2713. Fite, Gilbert C. SOUTHERN AGRICULTURE SINCE THE CIVIL WAR: AN OVERVIEW. *Agric. Hist. 1979 53(1): 3-21.* Surveys the changes and developments that have come into southern farm methods and life since the Civil War, taking into account the great variations between the different regions. These changes include diversification (from domination by cotton) systems of land tenure, movement into balancing crops with livestock, new and better methods, economic reforms, and the modernization of home life. 40 notes.    R. V. Ritter

2714. Fornari, Harry D. THE BIG CHANGE: COTTON TO SOYBEANS. *Agric. Hist. 1979 53(1): 245-253.* Soybean cultivation in the United States is comparatively recent, coming ultimately from China where soybean history goes back to 3000 B.C. After World War I they became a major source of feed and oil, the big boom coming during World War II. When the surplus of cotton became a major problem at the beginning of the Great Depression however, there was a push by the Agriculture Department to substitute beans in southern agriculture. Diversified uses for soybean products greatly spurred their replacement of cotton as the major staple crop. Table, 16 notes.    R. V. Ritter

2715. Foust, J. Brady and Vogeler, Ingolf. PROLEGOMENON TO FUTURE RESEARCH ON BLACK AGRICULTURE IN THE SOUTH. *West Georgia Coll. Studies in the Social Sci. 1979 18: 85-92.* Analyzes the demise of black agriculture, stressing 1954-64 and 1967-74, as a symptom of the larger societal processes and surveys the conservative, liberal, and radical viewpoints of it.

2716. Fox-Genovese, Elizabeth. FRANCE AND THE CHESAPEAKE: A HISTORY OF THE FRENCH TOBACCO MONOPOLY, 1674-1791. *J. of Modern Hist. 1974 46(4): 691-701.* Reviews Jacob Price's *France and the Chesapeake: A History of the French Tobacco Monopoly, 1674-1791, and its Relationship to the British and American Tobacco Trade,* 2 vols. (Ann Arbor: U. of Michigan Press, 1973). The book studies the tobacco monopoly, the *ancien regime,* the old colonial system, the Atlantic community, and the significance of the French Revolution. 15 notes.    P. J. Beck

2717. Gallman, Robert E. INFLUENCES ON THE DISTRIBUTION OF LANDHOLDINGS IN EARLY COLONIAL NORTH CAROLINA. *J. of Econ. Hist. 1982 42(3): 549-575.* The economy of North Carolina was agrarian. Analyzes the distribution of land by means of multiple regression models employing measures of the

principal life events of households. The data are drawn from an eastern community, Prequimans County, and refer to the late 17th and early 18th centuries.    J/S

2718. Gardien, Kent. THE SPLENDID FOOLS: PHILADELPHIA ORIGINS OF ALABAMA'S VINE AND OLIVE COLONY. *Pennsylvania Mag. of Hist. and Biog. 1980 104(4): 491-507.* William Lee helped organize the Colonial Society of French Emigrants, the intention of which was to found a town in the West, where the vine and olive might be cultivated, and for which federal support was received. Based on Girard Family Papers, American Philosophical Society, and other manuscripts, newspapers, and secondary works; 34 notes.    T. H. Wendel

2719. Gates, Paul W. FEDERAL LAND POLICIES IN THE SOUTHERN PUBLIC LAND STATES. *Agric. Hist. 1979 53(1): 206-227.* There has been a minimum of attention given by historians to the sale of public lands in Alabama, Arkansas, Florida, and Louisiana. Land sales in the South brought in far less than did such sales in the North. Surveys his earlier research on various aspects of the topic: "Southern Investments in Northern Lands Before the Civil War," (*J. of So. Hist. 1939 5*(May): 155-185) and "Private Land Claims in the South" (*J. of So. Hist. 1956 22*(May): 183-204). After surveying the social, economic, and political forces determining the outcome, concludes that there are striking contrasts "between the way federal land policies have worked out in the South and in the North." 37 notes, 5 tables.    R. V. Ritter

2720. Gatewood, Willard B., Jr. THE AGRARIANS FROM THE PERSPECTIVE OF FIFTY YEARS: AN ESSAY REVIEW. *Florida Hist. Q. 1983 61(3): 313-321.* A review essay of *I'll Take My Stand* (1930) along with recent commentary and publications on the South. Contemporary authors now champion the view of the 12 Southerners who protested materialism and spiritual disorder 50 years ago. Primary sources; note.    N. A. Kuntz

2721. Gilbert, Jess and Brown, Steve. ALTERNATIVE LAND REFORM PROPOSALS IN THE 1930S: THE NASHVILLE AGRARIANS AND THE SOUTHERN TENANT FARMERS' UNION. *Agric. Hist. 1981 55(4): 351-369.* The Nashville Agrarians and Southern Tenant Farmers' Union presented alternatives to the New Deal's farm programs that attacked corporate capitalism and urged land reform. The Nashville Agrarians, a group of southern writers and social scientists who wrote *I'll Take My Stand,* opposed industrialism and sought a return to the small, diversified, self-sufficient farms of the early republic. The Southern Tenant Farmers' Union, an Arkansas-based group with socialist roots, wanted the government to buy farmland and lease it to small farmers, tenants, and cooperatives. Neither organization was able to get a strong farm tenant law through Congress, and by the late 1930's the movement had subsided. 50 notes.    D. E. Bowers

2722. Gouger, James B. THE NORTHERN NECK OF VIRGINIA: A TIDEWATER GRAIN-FARMING REGION IN THE ANTEBELLUM SOUTH. *West Georgia Coll. Studies in the Social Sci. 1977 16: 73-90.* Although tobacco cultivation dominated antebellum Tidewater Virginia, the presence of knowledgable German immigrants and the availability of waterways had influenced a shift to grain production in the "Northern Neck" counties by 1790.

2723. Gracy, David B., II. IRRIGATION ON THE HIGH PLAINS—A PERSPECTIVE. *Red River Valley Hist. R. 1974 1(2): 127-131.* History of irrigation schemes on the Texas plains since the 1930's, and a view of future irrigation plans.

2724. Gracy, David B., II. SELLING THE FUTURE: A BIOGRAPHY OF WILLIAM PULVER SOASH. *Panhandle-Plains Hist. Rev. 1977 50: 1-75.* William Pulver Soash (1877-1961) during 1905-43 helped open the Texas Panhandle to agricultural settlement. His initial colonization efforts were thwarted by the drought of 1909-10, but Soash reorganized his efforts in the southern Panhandle by cooperating with the railroads and large ranchers. Combining humanitarianism with the businessman's instinct for profits, he defied the negative stereotype so often associated with land agents. Based on archival sources and interviews; 5 photos, 156 notes.                                          M. L. Tate

2725.  Grant, Philip A., Jr. SOUTHERN CONGRESSMEN AND AGRICULTURE, 1921-1932. *Agric. Hist. 1979 53(1): 338-352.* Analyzes five measures designed for rural relief and the reaction of Southern congressmen to them: the Cooperative Marketing Act (1922), the Intermediate Credit Act (1923), the Farm Relief (McNary-Haugen) bills (1927-28), and the Agricultural Marketing Act (US, 1929). The problems of US agriculture received much attention in Congress; most remained unsolved and were compounded by the 1929 financial crisis. However, southern congressmen were committed to concerted government action. 42 notes. Comment by John E. Lee, Jr., pp. 372-376.          R. V. Ritter

2726.  Graves, Gregory R. EXODUS FROM INDIAN TERRITORY: THE EVOLUTION OF COTTON CULTURE IN EASTERN OKLAHOMA. *Chronicles of Oklahoma 1982 60(2): 186-209.* During 1930-40, the population of Oklahoma's leading cotton-producing counties declined by more than 10%. Contrary to prevailing beliefs, this was not due to drought and dust bowl conditions, but rather to the long term change in the cotton culture. Farm tenancy has been declining since the mid-1920's, as had the need for cotton pickers who were being replaced by mechanization. Decreased demand for cotton and crop reduction programs of the Agricultural Adjustment Act further exacerbated the problems of farm tenants and sharecroppers who soon became the mobile "Okies" seeking jobs elsewhere. Based on government reports, newspapers, and secondary sources; 6 photos, 82 notes.          M. L. Tate

2727.  Halliday, James. BLAST AND COUNTERBLAST. *Blackwood's Mag. [Great Britain] 1975 317(1914): 327-338.* Elaborates on the demise of tobacco growing in Winchcombe, the attitude of the monarchy toward it, and the rise of the colony of Virginia as major world supplier of tobacco.

2728.  Hart, John Fraser. THE DEMISE OF KING COTTON. *Ann. of the Assoc. of Am. Geographers 1977 67(3): 307-322.* Cotton fields were associated closely with rolling plains and black people in the traditional South. Cotton acreage within the region has declined sharply from its peak in 1929, and the crop has become increasingly concentrated in favored areas. The demise of cotton is best described by a mini-atlas of comparable maps of cotton and its correlatives. The once close relationship between cotton and black people has weakened steadily since World War I. The long term effect of the boll weevil on cotton acreage may have been exaggerated.                                          J

2729.  Hart, John Fraser. LAND USE CHANGE IN A PIEDMONT COUNTY. *Ann. of the Assoc. of Am. Geographers 1980 70(4): 492-527.* Uses Carroll County, Georgia, as a microcosm of the southern Piedmont Plateau to analyze what has become of agricultural land formerly given over to the cultivation of cotton.

2730.  Hart, John Fraser and Chestang, Ennis L. RURAL REVOLUTION IN EAST CAROLINA. *Geographical Rev. 1978 68(4): 435-458.* Rural areas in eastern North Carolina have been revolutionized by the recent mechanization of flue-cured tobacco production. Field layouts have been changed, farm operations have been dispersed over large areas, and some farm operators have become sidewalk farmers. Farm workers released by mechanization have found jobs in large new factories that have been attracted to the area by the availability of labor. Many factory workers prefer to remain in the countryside, and they commute long distances to their jobs. Huge new rural factories, rows of new brick homes along rural roads, and batteries of new bulk-curing barns at the old farmsteads are among the most dramatic langscape manifestations of the rural revolution in eastern North Carolina.          J

2731.  Helms, Douglas. TECHNOLOGICAL METHODS FOR BOLL WEEVIL CONTROL. *Agric. Hist. 1979 53(1): 286-299.* Many methods of control have been tried, including early unsuccessful attempts at poisoning, using earlier developing varieties of cotton, and many "bug catcher" contraptions. The Agriculture De-

partment returned to the further testing and use of pesticides. These methods led to significant changes in southern agriculture: increased mechanization and the consolidation of farms. 68 notes.
                                          R. V. Ritter

2732.  Henry, Diana Mara. FUTURE FOOD? *Southern Exposure 1983 11(6): 22-26.* The Dart and Kraft Company's pavilion at the Experimental Prototype Community of Tomorrow in Walt Disney World, Orlando, Florida, displays the corporation's vision of American agriculture of the future, and the dominant place in it for corporations.

2733.  Herndon, G. Melvin. ELLIOTT L. STORY: A SMALL FARMER'S STRUGGLE FOR ECONOMIC SURVIVAL IN ANTEBELLUM VIRGINIA. *Agric. Hist. 1982 56(3): 516-527.* Virginia farming had declined by the early 19th century due to soil exhaustion and poor farm practices. But not all farmers followed the two most publicized alternatives of moving west or adopting scientific farming. The experience of Elliott L. Story of Southampton County is representative of many small farmers who did little to improve their farming and relied instead on outside work to supplement their incomes. During 1838-80 Story frequently taught school while employing hired hands to help him on the farm. Based on Story's diary; 46 notes.                                          D. E. Bowers

2734.  Herndon, G. Melvin. FROM ORPHANS TO MERCHANTS TO PLANTERS: THE GALT BROTHERS, WILLIAM AND JAMES. *Virginia Cavalcade 1979 29(1): 22-31.* William (1800-51) and James (1805-76) Galt, brothers orphaned in Scotland, arrived in Virginia in the early 19th century and became wealthy and well-known planters and humane slaveholders, and actively supported the Confederacy.

2735.  Herndon, G. Melvin. THE IMPACT OF THE AMERICAN REVOLUTION ON AGRICULTURE AND AGRARIAN LEADERSHIP IN THE SOUTH: AN INTERPRETATION. *Louisiana Studies 1976 15(3): 279-286.* In 1794 the English Board of Agriculture sent William Strickland (1787-1854) to the United States to observe farm practices and production, probably in response to an increase in emigration from England. Strickland visited parts of New England, New York, and Virginia and reported on land conditions, land prices, slavery, and agricultural techniques. He concluded that productivity of the soil in the southern states had been much greater before the Revolution; the decline was due to the demise of the landed aristocracy and to the growth of democracy. The author refutes Strickland's observations, claiming bias to discourage emigration. In reality production was increasing, as a result of new crops and expanding farm lands west of the mountains. Based essentially on secondary sources; 26 notes.          J. Buschen

2736.  Higgs, Robert. THE BOLL WEEVIL, THE COTTON ECONOMY, AND BLACK MIGRATION, 1910-1930. *Agric. Hist. 1976 50(2): 335-350.* Boll weevil infestation in the South was neither a necessary nor a sufficient condition underlying the Great Migration. The opening of numerous industrial employment opportunities for Negroes in the North during the war and differences in southern income levels largely determined which states would contribute most heavily to the exodus. Based on primary and secondary sources; 4 tables, 23 notes.          R. T. Fulton

2737.  Hiller, Sandra J. TRIAL AND ERROR: EARLY MARTIN COUNTY AGRICULTURE. *Permian Hist. Ann. 1981 21: 13-32.* Focuses on the experimental nature of the early settlers' attempts to adapt their farming practices to the region's arid climate.

2738.  Hilliard, Sam B. SITE CHARACTERISTICS AND SPATIAL STABILITY OF THE LOUISIANA SUGARCANE INDUSTRY. *Agric. Hist. 1979 53(1): 254-269.* Studies the peculiar situation in the Louisiana sugar cane country, and the factors that determined the location and the permanence of the industry. The crop requires ample moisture, well-drained soil, and a long, frost-free season. Covers the physical characteristics of the sites, the adaptation of the production units to fit the sites, the nature of cane growing and sugar making, and the stability of cane production.

The demands of the plant itself resulted in the natural levees being preferred, and, once established, these canefields have produced cane for many decades. Table, 9 fig., 6 notes. R. V. Ritter

2739. Huffman, Wallace E. BLACK-WHITE HUMAN CAPITAL DIFFERENCES: IMPACT ON AGRICULTURAL PRODUCTIVITY IN THE U.S. SOUTH. *Am. Econ. Rev. 1981 71(1): 94-107.* In the quality and quantity of public extension assistance to agriculture, black farmers have suffered. They have experienced poorer educational opportunities, which means lower levels of productivity. Covers 1945-64. 4 tables, 34 ref., 25 notes. D. K. Pickens

2740. Inglesby, Charlotte. SAVANNAH AND THE CAROLINA PLANTERS. *Georgia Hist. Q. 1978 62(1): 24-31.* Brief biographies of some of the rice planters of the Savannah River area of South Carolina who had townhouses in Savannah. Included are the Longworths, James Proctor Screven (1799-?), William Coffee Daniell (1792-ca.1860), Langdon Cheves (1814-63), Joseph Alston Huger (1816-98), and James Heyward Lynah (1848-1933).

G. R. Schroeder

2741. Jacobsen, Timothy C. JOSEPH BUCKNER KILLEBREW: AGRARIANISM IN THE NEW SOUTH. *Tennessee Hist. Q. 1974 33(2): 157-174.* Long before the better known leaders of the New South emerged, Joseph Buckner Killebrew, a frequent public servant in Tennessee, spoke vigorously in favor of developing the ideals of Thomas Jefferson and John Taylor in post-Civil-War southern agriculture. Killebrew advocated two themes: the yeoman farmer ideal, and the celebration of the fruitful earth itself. Primary and secondary sources; 48 notes. M. B. Lucas

2742. James, John A. THE WELFARE EFFECTS OF THE ANTEBELLUM TARIFF: A GENERAL EQUILIBRIUM ANALYSIS. *Explorations in Econ. Hist. 1978 15(3): 231-256.* Uses mathematical models to demonstrate that had the United States abandoned the tariff in 1859, the South would have benefited by rising cotton prices and higher returns on capital invested in cotton production. Published documents and secondary accounts; 6 tables, 30 notes, 56 ref. P. J. Coleman

2743. Jeffrey, Julie Roy. WOMEN IN THE SOUTHERN FARMERS' ALLIANCE: A RECONSIDERATION OF THE ROLE AND STATUS OF WOMEN IN THE LATE NINETEENTH CENTURY SOUTH. *Feminist Studies 1975 3(1/2): 72-91.* The Southern Farmers' Alliance was a major force in the 1880's and 1890's. Its goal was the revival of southern agriculture. The activities of the Alliance in North Carolina illustrate the organization's general attitude toward women. Rejecting the traditional female stereotype of pale fragile gentility, the Alliance encouraged female participation in its affairs and proposed education and economic equality for women. However, these goals for women existed within the framework of renewing southern agriculture. Women were to be coworkers on the farm, sharing agricultural tasks and prosperity rather than any equal status in the larger political world. The Alliance enlarged the traditional view of women, encouraged education and participation, but did not go further toward female equality outside farm life. Primary and secondary sources; 79 notes.

S. R. Herstein

2744. Jensen, Joan M. CHURNS AND BUTTER MAKING IN THE MID-ATLANTIC FARM ECONOMY, 1750-1850. *Working Papers from the Regional Econ. Hist. Res. Center 1982 5(2-3): 59-100.* Discusses the importance of cottage industries, such as butter making, done almost entirely by women, and describes different types of churns in southeastern Pennsylvania and northern Delaware.

2745. Johnson, William R. RURAL REHABILITATION IN THE NEW DEAL: THE ROPESVILLE PROJECT. *Southwestern Hist. Q. 1976 79(3): 279-295.* Ropesville, near Lubbock, Texas, was a successful example of the New Deal's rural rehabilitation communities. During 1934-43, over 300 people (all local poor farm families) were settled on small farms in housing built by the federal Resettlement Administration. Under the close guidance of government managers, the project's residents improved their standard of living

and developed good relations with the townspeople of Ropesville. The project ended in 1943 with the sale of the farms to the occupants. Based on primary sources; 49 notes. J. H. Broussard

2746. Jones, Allen W. THE SOUTH'S FIRST BLACK FARM AGENTS. *Agricultural Hist. 1976 50(4): 636-644.* In 1906 Thomas M. Campbell and John B. Pierce became the first black extension agents of the Agriculture Department. As the program expanded through World War I, Campbell and Pierce were placed in charge of hundreds of farm and home demonstration agents, although their work was under the control of white supervisors and subject to the availability of local funds. By demonstrating improved agricultural techniques directly to black farmers, extension agents helped improve the quality of southern agriculture. 22 notes.

D. E. Bowers

2747. Jones, Allen W. THOMAS M. CAMPBELL: BLACK AGRICULTURAL LEADER OF THE NEW SOUTH. *Agric. Hist. 1979 53(1): 42-59.* A record of the training, ideals, and methods used to improve agricultural techniques and personal attitudes of the black small farmers of Macon and the surrounding counties of Alabama. In 1906 Thomas M. Campbell was hired by the Agriculture Department as its first black farm agent to operate a traveling agricultural wagon and conduct farm demonstration work. His career spanned nearly half a century and established him as one of the most effective and highly recognized black agricultural leaders in the United States, coming ultimately to reach out in his influence to all of southern agriculture. He tried "to help the masses of black people in the South achieve economic independence, a higher standard of living, and a better home and family life." 58 notes. Comment by William Scarborough, pp. 60-61. R. V. Ritter

2748. Killick, J. R. THE TRANSFORMATION OF COTTON MARKETING IN THE LATE NINETEENTH CENTURY: ALEXANDER SPRUNT AND SON OF WILMINGTON, N.C., 1866-1956. *Business Hist. Rev. 1981 55(2): 143-169.* Major improvements took place in the system for marketing southern cotton internationally during 1880-1920. Alexander Sprunt and Son was probably the largest cotton exporting firm in the United States in that period and its history reflected those changes. Improvements included the installation of efficient cotton compresses to reduce the size of bales, a more sophisticated attitude toward futures trading, successful negotiation of special volume transportation rates, and the establishment of overseas branches. After World War I, the firm experienced a decline in part because of an aging management, family friction, and a failure to effectively expand activities into the trans-Mississippi cotton region. Based on company records; 4 tables, 50 notes. C. J. Pusateri

2749. Killick, John R. THE COTTON OPERATIONS OF ALEXANDER BROWN AND SONS IN THE DEEP SOUTH, 1820-1860. *J. of Southern Hist. 1977 43(2): 169-194.* Southern historiography has focused on the slave plantation system of the interior rather than on the commercial trader of the ports. This neglect of the interregional and international cotton trade organization is unfortunate, considering the importance of the Atlantic commerce to the cotton system. A study of the British-American firm of Alexander Brown and Sons reveals that, contrary to general belief, cotton trading firms were so competitive that they did not normally accumulate great profits. Furthermore the Civil War era saw the beginning of the end of British firms in this business on a major scale; in the postwar years they were replaced by domestic, often southern, firms. Based on mss. and printed primary and secondary sources; 4 tables, 38 notes. T. D. Schoonover

2750. Kindem, Gorham. SOUTHERN EXPOSURE: *KUDZU AND IT'S GRITS. Southern Q. 1981 19(3-4): 199-206.* The South's two most plentiful and fascinating agricultural products are kudzu and grits. They have been the subject of two documentaries, *Kudzu* (1976) and *It's Grits* (1978). The filmmakers inform and entertain the viewing public with facts and opinions about the soil conservation plant and the very popular ethnic food. Both films tell a great deal about Southern life as it is today and as it has been during the last few decades. 3 photos. B. D. Ledbetter

2751. King, J. Crawford, Jr. THE CLOSING OF THE SOUTH-ERN RANGE: AN EXPLORATORY STUDY. *J. of Southern Hist. 1982 48(1): 53-70.* The open range encouraged a leisurely method of raising livestock that increasingly came under attack after the Civil War. Though planters favored closing the range, their inability to achieve this goal quickly indicates that their control of the South was not as sure as is sometimes believed. Areas dominated by white farmers who owned their own farms and who were not ex-clusively tied to cotton growing remained open range longer than did other areas. "Open-range areas had larger farms and many more livestock, than did the stock-law areas," indicating that the quest to close the range was more than a battle between the haves and have-nots. Focuses on Alabama with reference to Georgia and, especially, Mississippi. 41 notes.                                S

2752. Kirby, Jack Temple. THE TRANSFORMATION OF SOUTHERN PLANTATIONS C. 1920-1960. *Agric. Hist. 1983 57(3): 257-276.* Examines the transformation of Southern planta-tions from the pattern of sharecropping and tenancy that developed after the Civil War into large, modern farms like those outside the South. Scarce capital and cheap labor had long kept planters from consolidating their farms. The boll weevil infestation of the 1910's-20's drove some tenants off the land, but not until the price-support programs of the New Deal did planters have the capital to make substantial changes. By 1934, sharecroppers and tenants were being evicted throughout the plantation area and were gradually re-placed by hired labor on centralized farms. By the mid-1950's, mechanization and the use of herbicides caused a sharp drop in ag-ricultural labor requirements. Planters deemphasized cotton produc-tion, favoring more diversified plantings, and enlarged their fields. 3 charts, 68 notes.                                          D. E. Bowers

2753. Kosarev, B. M. GENEZIS PLANTATSIONNOI RABOV-LADEL'CHESKOI SISTEMY V S.SH.A. [The genesis of the slave-owning plantation system in the U.S.A.]. *Voprosy Istorii [USSR] 1978 (5): 62-73.* The author investigates the rise and development of the slaveowning plantation system in the U.S.A. In the 17th-18th centuries the markets for the sale of tobacco and other export crops grown by the labour of Negro slaves were extremely unstable. The development of the plantation system in Britain's North American colonies proceeded at a relatively slow rate. The system of slavery which existed there constituted one of the economic forms. By the end of the 18th century the industrial revolution in the cotton pro-duction of England, which subsequently spread to a number of oth-er European countries and to North America, led to the emergence of a steadily expanding market for the sale of cotton—the chief product of slave labour; in the 19th century the slaveholding econo-my in the South of the U.S.A. became transformed into the planta-tion system proper.                                                   J

2754. Kulikoff, Allan. FARMING ON THE VIRGINIA FRON-TIER. *Rev. in Am. Hist. 1978 6(4): 459-464.* Review article prompted by Robert D. Mitchell's *Commercialism and Frontier: Perspectives on the Early Shenandoah Valley* (Charlottesville: U. Pr. of Virginia, 1977) which describes agricultural and economic development and settlement patterns in 18th-century Virginia.

2755. Kupp, Jan. DUTCH NOTARIAL ACTS RELATING TO THE TOBACCO TRADE OF VIRGINIA, 1608-1653. *William and Mary Q. 1973 30(4): 653-655.* Calls attention to documents in the Notarial Archives of Amsterdam and Rotterdam on the early com-mercial relations of Holland and Virginia. The Dutch notaries drew up many documents, much like the modern lawyer. Because of the Dutch-Virginia tobacco trade the documents provide much informa-tion on all aspects of shipping, controversies over quality and trad-ing practices, the financial position of leading colonists, international business, and attitudes of colonists toward the Dutch. Tells how to secure photocopies of the documents and a descriptive calendar from the University of Victoria, British Columbia.
                                                                H. M. Ward

2756. Kurokawa, Katsutoshi. JKYSEIKI AMERIKA NAMBU HAKUJIN SHŌNŌMIN NI TSUITE NO ICHIKŌSATSU: MIS-HISHIPPI SH O CHSHIN NI [White small farmers in the South of the United States in the latter part of the 19th century].

*Shakaikeizaishigaku (Socio-Economic Hist.) [Japan] 1975 41(1): 59-72.* Analyzes small farms in Mississippi after the Civil War, fo-cusing on the increase of cotton cultivation by white farmers, and the increase in white tenant farmers.

2757. LaGodna, Martin M. GREENS, GRIST AND GUERN-SEYS: DEVELOPMENT OF THE FLORIDA STATE AGRICUL-TURAL MARKETING SYSTEM. *Florida Hist. Q. 1974 53(2): 146-163.* Studies the steps taken to improve agricultural marketing and the programs initiated by the state government to further agri-cultural enterprises, beginning with the establishment of the Florida Marketing Bureau 1 July 1917, in Jacksonville. The efforts took on various forms, but the cooperatives and the "farmers' markets" were the most significant. Commissioner of Agriculture Nathan Mayo was the principal leader in marketing development, especially favoring the small producers. 47 notes; 2 photos.
                                                                R. V. Ritter

2758. Lale, Max S. and Campbell, Randolph B., ed. THE PLAN-TATION JOURNAL OF JOHN B. WEBSTER, FEBRUARY 17, 1858-NOVEMBER 5, 1859. *Southwestern Hist. Q. 1980 84(1): 49-79.* From 17 February 1858 to 5 November 1859, John B. Web-ster, a plantation owner in Harrison County, Texas, kept a daily journal. The original journal is located in the East Texas Baptist College Library, but this annotated selection of events from daily life presents a detailed account of slavery, particularly in connection with agriculture. Annotations based on primary sources; photo, 6 tables, 42 notes.                                                R. D. Hurt

2759. Lee, Susan Previant. ANTEBELLUM LAND EXPANSION: ANOTHER VIEW. *Agric. Hist. 1978 52(4): 488-502.* The first part of the article is based on the economic topography of cotton inter-ests for 1850 and 1860 based on estimates of the differential im-pact of expansion on factor payments and estimates of relative land/slave holdings. The topography does not suggest neat divisions of interest between the Southeast and the Old Southwest. While the Old Southwest was relatively land rich (more clearly in 1860), the simple east/west division masked a complex ordering of subregions. The second part of the study attempts to test the relationship be-tween this derived economic topography and congressional voting on two important land bills, using regression and logit analysis. The topography appears to explain voting behavior as well or better than traditional sectional divisions. Primary and secondary sources; 3 tables, 23 notes.                                            R. T. Fulton

2760. Leverett, William E., Jr. and Shi, David E. AGRARIAN-ISM FOR COMMUTERS. *South Atlantic Q. 1980 79(2): 204-218.* The Agrarians considered themselves the high priests of the tradi-tional southern faith based on subsistence agriculture, the family, community, historical culture, and belief in a stern God. They championed a return to a simpler society after World War I. How to live was more important than making a living. During the New Deal era, when many intellectuals were proposing various forms of collectivism, the Agrarians proposed self-sufficiency on the land as the proper economic means to the good life, as well as a good in itself. Leaders in the movement were Ralph Borsodi, Chauncey D. Stillman, and Herbert Agar, among others. Based on the many books and articles by Borsodi, Stillman and Agar and other writ-ings of the period; 35 notes.                            H. M. Parker, Jr.

2761. Lewis, Carolyn Baker. AGRICULTURAL EVOLUTION ON SECONDARY FRONTIERS: A FLORIDA MODEL. Savage, William W., Jr. and Thompson, Stephen I., ed. *The Frontier: Com-parative Studies,* vol. 2 (Norman: U. of Oklahoma Pr., 1979): 205-233. Florida was a secondary frontier, an area of marginal desir-ability passed over by the first waves of settlers, which ultimately became a commercial success. Perceived as a land of hostile Indi-ans, poor soil, and tropical climate, Florida was bypassed by most settlers before the Civil War. After the war, when prime farm land in the West seemed to have been claimed, farmers began to move in increasing numbers to Florida. The improved railroad systems opened up northern markets for fresh fruit, and Floridians experimented with grapes, pineapples, and citrus fruit. By 1910, citrus was the basis of commercial agriculture in Florida. 56 notes.

S

2762. Lewis, Robert Donald. RECOLLECTIONS OF AGRICULTURAL RESEARCH: 1946-1962. *Red River Valley Hist. Rev. 1978 3(1): 109-118.* The author reminisces about his directorship of the Texas Agricultural Experiment Station, 1946-62, and research which doubled crop yield at the Station.

2763. Littlefield, Daniel F., Jr. and Underhill, Lonnie E. KILDARE, OKLAHOMA TERRITORY: STORY OF AN AGRICULTURAL BOOM TOWN. *Great Plains J. 1975 15(1): 28-54.* Discusses Kildare, Oklahoma, created when the Cherokee Strip opened to settlement, to present a case study of an agricultural boom town. Like many other boom towns, Kildare, founded in 1893, was "sustained for a time by the enthusiasm generated in land openings, but . . . ultimately lost out." Primary sources; 5 illus., 3 maps, 77 notes.                          O. H. Zabel

2764. Lucas, Robert C. and Gilstrap, Lucille. HOMESTEADING THE STRIP. *Chronicles of Oklahoma 1973 51(3): 285-308.* Personal account of a homesteading family from 1889 to 1903 in the Cherokee Outlet in Indian Territory.

2765. Lusk, Sonia Marcel. WATER SOURCES IN EARLY WEST TEXAS. *Permian Hist. Ann. 1980 20: 55-65.* Discusses settlers' search for reliable sources of water in the West Texas frontier region from 1854 to 1915, focusing upon the increasing use of windmills and upon innovative techniques for drilling wells between 1882 and 1890.

2766. Lyson, Thomas A. ONLY A FEW: RECRUITMENT TO FARMING AMONG SOUTHERN BLACKS. *Phylon 1980 41(4): 379-389.* Examines the role played by predominantly black southern agricultural colleges in selecting and sorting talent for farm-related work roles; describes social factors and background conditions associated with a desire to farm, adacemic and extracurricular interests of farm-oriented blacks, and their career expectations. Based on data collected for the US Department of Agriculture Southern Regional Research Project S-114, 1977; 5 tables, 16 notes.
J. V. Coutinho

2767. MacKethan, Lucinda H. THOMAS NELSON PAGE: THE PLANTATION IS ARCADY. *Virginia Q. Rev. 1978 54(2): 314-332.* Using Thomas Nelson Page's works, particularly *In Ole Virginia* (1887), describes a romantic dream of the antebellum South. Uses "the plantation locale," especially the great house; "the image of the Southern gentleman; and most important, the 'old time' Negro . . . through whose voice the Old South achieves mystic status."                          O. H. Zabel

2768. MacKethan, Lucinda. I'LL TAKE MY STAND: THE RELEVANCE OF THE AGRARIAN VISION. *Virginia Q. Rev. 1980 56(4): 477-595.* In 1930, 12 southern writers published a symposium, *I'll Take My Stand: The South and the Agrarian Tradition,* which still is relevant in defining concerns of modern people, including southern writers. Donald Davidson, John Crowe Ransom, Allen Tate, Robert Penn Warren, and others were concerned about what science, technology, and the modern state were doing to civilized society. The author discusses their views under three headings: "A Certain Terrain" (need for a sense of continuity), "A Certain History" (need to relate the present to the past), and "A Certain Inherited Way of Living" (need for "faith in human dignity and worth.").                          O. H. Zabel

2769. Mackintosh, Barry. GEORGE WASHINGTON CARVER: THE MAKING OF A MYTH. *J. of Southern Hist. 1976 42(4): 507-528.* As in other areas of human endeavor, talented black American scientists have not obtained the recognition they deserve. George Washington Carver in reality possessed little scientific ability and a low level of achievement, but he has received great praise and recognition. Carver's work with the peanut and sweet potato transformed neither southern agrarian life nor agriculturally based

industrial life, nor did he leave behind scientific-technological works permitting his alleged work to be studied, verified, or implemented. It was his personality and character—soft-spoken, deferential, submissive, and pious—which prompted whites to accept him and to build myths around him. His reputation must rest more on his social and psychological utility than on his scientific achievement.
T. Schoonover

2770. Mackintosh, Barry. GEORGE WASHINGTON CARVER AND THE PEANUT: NEW LIGHT ON A MUCH-LOVED MYTH. *Am. Heritage 1977 28(5): 66-73.* The legend of George Washington Carver was helped by his appearance of humility, his race, and his field, agriculture. Encouraged by the *Reader's Digest* and other sources, the myth continues despite recent scholarly reassessments and efforts to downplay his scientific achievements. 9 illus.                          J. F. Paul

2771. Maguire, Jane. ED, A BLACK SHARECROPPER'S STORY. *Am. Heritage 1976 27(2): 8-13, 91-93.* Ed Brown, a black sharecropper from Georgia, told his story to the author. The white landowners sometimes took advantage of the sharecropper, lying about income from crops and not fulfilling verbal contracts. From the book *Ed* (W. W. Norton, 1976). Illus.                          B. J. Paul

2772. Mandle, Jay R. THE PLANTATION ECONOMY AND ITS AFTERMATH. *Rev. of Radical Pol. Econ. 1974 6(1): 32-48.* A plantation economy based upon share-cropping continued in the South after the Civil War, but from 1910 the labor demands of a dynamic northern capitalist society, intensified by the decrease in immigrants, opened industrial employment to Negroes. Although generally confined to low-income occupations, a substantial degree of upward mobility has occurred recently. The economic differences within the black population and occupational convergence of black and white laborers in the future may create a biracial working-class movement. Based on published official statistics and secondary works; 2 tables, fig., 20 notes.                          P. R. Shergold

2773. Mandle, Jay R. THE PLANTATION STATES AS A SUB-REGION OF THE POST-BELLUM SOUTH. *J. of Econ. Hist. 1974 34(3): 732-738.* Important regional differences may be obscured if the postbellum South is studied as a whole or divided into the subregions used by the Census Bureau. Statistics based on dividing the South into economically functional units indicate that the states in which plantation farming was most prominent differed significantly from the remainder of the South. Based on official statistics and secondary sources; 3 tables, 5 notes.                          O. H. Reichardt

2774. Marable, Manning. THE POLITICS OF BLACK LAND TENURE, 1877-1915. *Agric. Hist. 1979 53(1): 142-152.* For a time after the Civil War blacks were making remarkable progress in gaining an economic foothold through ownership and working of their small farms. This, however, had no permanence. A violent racism combined with political power made the "goal of black economic self-sufficiency a bitter illusion rather than a possibility." Black land tenure collapsed; this was not a failure of black people, but resulted from the lack of equal economic opportunity for all members of society. 32 notes.                          R. V. Ritter

2775. Massey, David Dyar. THE FEDERATION OF SOUTHERN COOPERATIVES: HARD TIMES AND HIGH HOPES. *Southern Exposure 1974 2(2/3): 38-51.* Discusses federal funding of the Federation of Southern Cooperatives in aiding poor Negroes and small farmers in rural settlements in the South, 1967-74.

2776. May, Irvin. AGRICULTURAL SCIENCE IN THE TEXAS PANHANDLE: THE TEXAS AGRICULTURAL EXPERIMENT STATION. *Panhandle-Plains Hist. Rev. 1980 53: 111-137.* Recounts the efforts of the Texas Agricultural Experiment Station to bring a more scientific approach to Panhandle farming. The major impetus to this scientific approach came during the Dust Bowl years when the Amarillo Station, under David Reid and Milburn Atkins, began to develop hardier wheat. By the 1950's the Amarillo Station was heavily involved in research on weed control, insect infestations and better irrigation techniques. Today, the US Department of Agriculture at Bushland continues its predecessor's work, serving the needs of Panhandle farmers. Primary sources; 70 notes.

M. L. Tate

2777. May, Irvin. J. H. CONNELL: AGGIE ADMINISTRATOR, THE TEXAS YEARS. *Red River Valley Hist. Rev. 1978 3(1): 93-108.* James H. Connell directed the Texas Agricultural Experiment Station, 1893-1902.

2778. May, Irvin. THE ORIGINS AND DEVELOPMENT OF THE TEXAS AGRICULTURAL EXPERIMENT STATION, 1888-1892. *Panhandle-Plains Hist. Rev. 1976 49(1): 55-79.* Part I. Traces the history of the Texas Agricultural Experiment Station (TAES) from 1888 to 1893 when it gained a broader acceptance within the state. As a component of Texas A & M College, TAES faced many crises brought on by a hostile *Texas Farm and Ranch* which branded the program an extravagant waste. The high caliber of TAES directors, including Frank Gulley and George Curtis, produced a viable teaching and research department, but the Texas Legislature refused economic support. Federal funds through the Hatch Act also proved insufficient for substations throughout the state. Important cotton and silage studies, plus TAES success in eradicating Texas fever from cattle, won converts who successfully helped promote the station after 1892. Based on primary and secondary sources; 43 notes. Article to be continued.

M. L. Tate

2779. McCann, Alison. THE LETTERBOOK OF ROBERT RAPER. *South Carolina Hist. Mag. 1981 82(2): 111-117.* Between 1759 and 1765, letters from Robert Raper of Charleston, descendant of a family which established a firm of solicitors in Chichester, informed clients about trade and the condition of their plantations. In detail he covered fluctuations in prices as well as the quality of goods sent to the plantations. When smallpox and raids by Cherokee Indians threatened local communities, he described these crises. Besides giving incidental information on local events, he provided data on events of national importance, such as the riots protesting the Stamp Act. Based on the letterbook of Robert Raper held in the West Sussex County Record Office in Chichester, England; 4 notes.

R. H. Tomlinson

2780. McCloud, Emma Gudger. "SO I SUNG TO MYSELF." *Southern Exposure 1979 7(1): 18-26.* Gives Emma Gugder McCloud's impressions of her life as a member of a poor white sharecropping family living in the South during the Depression; she had been portrayed in James Agee and Walker Evans's *Let Us Now Praise Famous Men* (1934).

2781. McColloch, Lacy Porter. ALFRED CLAY HALE, NATIVE SON AND MAN OF DESTINY. *Arkansas Hist. Q. 1976 35(3): 246-260.* Alfred Clay Hale (1895-1972) taught vocational agriculture at schools in Arkansas for 31 years. He left teaching in 1953 to enter the State Department as an agricultural expert assigned to underdeveloped countries. Following 11 years in Thailand, Ecuador, British Guiana, and Washington, D.C., Hale retired to his Arkansas home. Based on Hale's memoirs and records, information from Hale's family, and recollections of the author; 4 illus.

T. L. Savitt

2782. McCorkle, James L., Jr. MISSISSIPPI TRUCK CROPS: AN EXERCISE IN AGRARIAN ORGANIZATION. *Mississippi Q. 1979-80 33(1): 55-77.* History of the commercial vegetable industry, or truck farming in Mississippi, particularly in Copiah County, from the 1870's until the mid-1940's, and the organizations that were formed among producers to maintain a stable industry.

2783. McCorkle, James L., Jr. PROBLEMS OF A SOUTHERN AGRARIAN INDUSTRY: COOPERATION AND SELF-INTEREST. *Southern Studies 1978 17(3): 241-254.* During 1925-40 Mississippi and Texas commercial tomato and cabbage growers were unable to maintain satisfactory prices by voluntary controls through regional cooperative markets. Individual self-interest overrode general prosperity. Appeals were made to the federal government for tariff agreements with Mexico and Canada, and the Federal Surplus Commodities Corporation bought excess production

to maintain price stability. Only a regulated economy preserved these agricultural industries. Based on newspaper accounts; 51 notes.

J. Buschen

2784. McDean, Harry C. THE 'OKIE' MIGRATION AS A SOCIO-ECONOMIC NECESSITY IN OKLAHOMA. *Red River Valley Hist. Rev. 1978 3(1): 77-92.* Serious soil depletion in Oklahoma, 1921-30's, made it economically and agriculturally necessary for farmers to move.

2785. McDonald, Forrest and McWhiney, Grady. THE ANTEBELLUM SOUTHERN HERDSMAN: A REINTERPRETATION. *J. of Southern Hist. 1975 41(2): 147-166.* A reanalysis of the importance of stock-raising in the pre-Civil War southern United States. Later historians have underestimated the herdsman's importance because earlier historians overemphasized the significance of the plantation. Hogs created more wealth than cotton. Herdsmen were freer people, thus apparently indolent; much of their stock was fed by nature. Stock-raising declined after the war. The vast herds of cattle and hogs were depleted by northern armies and thereafter by Negro thievery. The southern character was probably predominantly shaped by the herdsmen. Table, 42 notes.

V. L. Human

2786. McDonald, Forrest and McWhiney, Grady. THE SOUTH FROM SELF-SUFFICIENCY TO PEONAGE: AN INTERPRETATION. *Am. Hist. Rev. 1980 85(5): 1095-1118.* In the antebellum South, Celtic peoples found an ideal geopolitical niche to carry on their traditional pastoral lifestyle. This required little work in comparison with tilling the land, and thus Southerners have been thought of as lazy, though their way of life gave them a certain self-sufficiency. After the Civil War, Northerners colonized the South, bringing about substantial changes. Landlords discouraged tenants from raising foodstuffs for their own consumption, for this was unprofitable to the landlords. Furthermore the capacity of the tenants to produce and transport their stock was undermined. This was devastating to the herders, and reduced their status to little better than slaves. Commentary follows, pp. 1150-1166. Primary sources; 5 fig. 52 notes.

J. Powell

2787. McGee, Leo and Boone, Robert. BLACK RURAL LAND DECLINE IN THE SOUTH. *Black Scholar 1977 8(7): 8-11.* In 1910, blacks owned 15 million acres of rural acreage; by 1974, they owned only five million acres. Blacks migrated to the North in large numbers during the last half-century. Now there is a reverse of that trend. If blacks can regain ownership of more southern land, they can become more secure and independent. Primary and secondary sources; 19 notes.

B. D. Ledbetter

2788. McGuire, Robert A. A PORTFOLIO ANALYSIS OF CROP DIVERSIFICATION AND RISK IN THE COTTON SOUTH. *Explorations in Econ. Hist. 1980 17(4): 342-371.* In recent years, 1973-77, scholars of the postbellum American South have disagreed on whether cotton or corn was the riskier crop, whether farmers displayed risk-averting or risk-taking behavior, and whether data and methods used to analyze acreage management decisions are appropriate. Evidence indicates that farmers preferring cotton over corn were not gamblers. 6 tables, 30 notes, 46 ref., appendix.

P. J. Coleman

2789. McWhiney, Grady. THE REVOLUTION IN NINETEENTH-CENTURY ALABAMA AGRICULTURE. *Alabama Rev. 1978 31(1): 3-32.* The Civil War and Reconstruction devastated the Alabama livestock industry. Thieving freedmen, northern dumping of commodities and its effect on prices and quality, pellagra, and the abandonment of antebellum husbandry practices, among other reasons, inhibited recovery. The Yankee work ethic was not an integral part of antebellum livestock raising, but the southern system was sufficient to meet population needs. Primary and secondary sources; 50 notes.

J. F. Vivian

2790. Mealer, W. Theodore, Jr. and Prunty, Merle C. OPEN-RANGE RANCHING IN SOUTHERN FLORIDA. *Ann. of the Assoc. of Am. Geographers 1976 66(3): 360-376.* Discusses the roles of land tenure and settlement in ranching and cattle raising in southern Florida from the 1840's to the 20th century, emphasizing recent developments in breeding and disease treatment.

2791. Menard, Russell R. A NOTE ON CHESAPEAKE TOBACCO PRICES, 1618-1660. *Virginia Mag. of Hist. and Biog. 1976 84(4): 401-410.* Though it is impossible to determine yearly fluctuations of tobacco prices for the early 17th century with the same accuracy as for the later decades of that century, there are some sources that indicate general price levels and provide a description of long-term trends, and enable researchers to distinguish good years from bad. 12 notes.                    R. F. Oaks

2792. Menard, Russell R. THE TOBACCO INDUSTRY IN THE CHESAPEAKE COLONIES, 1617-1730: AN INTERPRETATION. *Res. in Econ. Hist. 1980 5: 109-177.* Since tobacco dominated the export sector of Maryland and Virginia during the early colonial period, a description of that industry must stand at the center of any interpretation of the Chesapeake economy. This essay offers such a description and interpretation. It focuses on the interaction between secular trends and short-term movements in staple production in order to illuminate the process of expansion in the tobacco industry and the role of this central export in the develoment of the Chesapeake economy. It is intended as a case study of the growth of the export sector in colonial economies with, it is hoped, implications of more than merely local interest.                    J

2793. Menius, Arthur C., III. JAMES BENNITT: PORTRAIT OF AN ANTEBELLUM YEOMAN. *North Carolina Hist. Rev. 1981 58(4): 305-326.* James Bennitt, whose home on the Hillsborough-Durham road served as the place of General Joseph E. Johnston's surrender to Union General William T. Sherman in 1865, represents the typical antebellum Southern yeoman farmer. In debt and frequently sued for nonpayment as he attempted to establish a farm and family in the 1830's, Bennitt was able to purchase his own land in 1846. His account book for 1839-49 describes his sales, including excess food crops (little cotton), and expenditures, including labor at specific times of the year, new farm implements and repair of worn ones, magazines, newspapers, and books. Further study of "plain folks" records is needed to change long held misconceptions. Based primarily on the Bennitt Papers at Duke University, manuscript county records at the North Carolina Archives, and numerous secondary sources; 11 illus., 113 notes.                    T. L. Savitt

2794. Metzer, Jacob. RATIONAL MANAGEMENT, MODERN BUSINESS PRACTICES, AND ECONOMIES OF SCALE IN THE ANTE-BELLUM SOUTHERN PLANTATIONS. *Explorations in Econ. Hist. 1975 12(2): 123-150.* Examines the attitudes and practices of plantation owners as business managers; their basic objective was long-run profit maximization. They sought to achieve this through division of labor, functional specialization, resource allocation, and coordination of the managerial factor. Based on manuscripts at Louisiana State University, Baton Rouge, the Mississippi Department of Archives and History, Jackson, and the University of North Carolina, Chapel Hill, published records, and secondary accounts.                    P. J. Coleman

2795. Mills, Nicolaus. BROWN-LUNG COTTON-MILL BLUES. *Dissent 1978 25(1): 8-11.* Discusses the suppression of information on brown-lung, the occupational disease of cotton-mill workers, throughout the history of the American textile industry, and the progress in the late 1970's by the Carolina Brown Lung Association to eradicate the disease and bring the industry under control.

2796. Mitchell, Robert D. AGRICULTURAL CHANGE AND THE AMERICAN REVOLUTION: A VIRGINIA CASE STUDY. *Agric. Hist. 1973 47(2): 110-132.* The Revolution caused few qualitative improvements in the agriculture of the Shenandoah Valley, although some farm products underwent wartime adjustments of varying importance. Table, 30 notes.                    D. E. Brewster

2797. Molnar, Joseph J. and Dunkelberger, John E. THE EXPECTATION TO FARM: AN INTERACTION OF BACKGROUND AND EXPERIENCE. *Rural Sociol. 1981 46(1): 62-84.* Examines the background and experiences of agriculture students of the

1970's who expect to enter farming as an occupation, focusing on two samples of agriculture students at 1862 and 1890 land-grant universities in the South.

2798. Musoke, Moses S. MECHANIZING COTTON PRODUCTION IN THE AMERICAN SOUTH: THE TRACTOR, 1915-1960. *Explorations in Econ. Hist. 1981 18(4): 347-375.* The introduction of the tractor into the cotton industry in the American South resulted in modernization of agricultural processes and replaced sharecropping, the foundation of postbellum cotton production. In 1920 there were 36,500 tractors in the South. In 1940 there were 271,000; and during the next two decades the number rose to more than 1.4 million. This was accompanied by a decline of 90% in the number of sharecroppers' farms during 1930-59. Primary sources; 7 tables, ref., appendix.                    J. Powell

2799. Nall, Garry L. DRY-LAND FARMING ON THE HIGH PLAINS—A PERSPECTIVE. *Red River Valley Hist. R. 1974 1(2): 122-126.* Discusses the successes and failures of dry-farming methods and innovations in Texas since the 1890's.

2800. Nelson, Lawrence J. NEW DEAL AND FREE MARKET: THE MEMPHIS MEETING OF THE SOUTHERN COMMISSIONERS OF AGRICULTURE, 1937. *Tennessee Hist. Q. 1981 40(3): 225-238.* Following apparent recovery in 1936, cotton farmers in the South forgot about acreage reduction and expanded production in the following year. The result was predictable—prices fell. Southerners then looked to the Roosevelt administration for financial relief. In September, the Association of Southern Commissioners of Agriculture meeting in Memphis amidst considerable agitation found one of the leading cotton planters, Oscar G. Johnston of Mississippi, to be a persuasive advocate of federal policy based upon a combination of allotments and subsidies. The resulting controversy indicated that Southern opposition to New Deal farm policies was based more on a pragmatic approach to the economic programs than on opposition to the philosophy behind the New Deal. In a short time Southerners had begun to expect federal assistance. Mainly letters and newspapers; 54 notes.                    C. L. Grant

2801. Nelson, Lawrence J. OSCAR JOHNSTON, THE NEW DEAL, AND THE COTTON SUBSIDY PAYMENTS CONTROVERSY, 1936-1937. *J. of Southern Hist. 1974 40(3): 399-416.* Subsidies to corporate agribusiness enterprises have provoked controversy since the mid-1930's incidents involving Oscar Goodbar Johnston and the cotton industry. While retaining the presidency of the Delta & Pine Land Company, a large cotton producing corporation with majority British participation, Johnston also served the New Deal in the Agricultural Adjustment Administration, the Federal Cotton Producers' Pool, and the Commodity Credit Corporation. Republican Senator Arthur Vandenberg and the press raised the issues of conflict of interest and subsidies to foreign citizens by exposing the fact that while Johnston continued to administer cotton subsidies, one of the largest recipients of these funds was the Delta & Pine Land Company. Based on manuscripts and published primary and secondary sources; 75 notes.                    T. D. Schoonover

2802. Niemi, Albert W., Jr. INEQUALITY IN THE DISTRIBUTION OF SLAVE WEALTH: THE COTTON SOUTH AND OTHER SOUTHERN AGRICULTURAL REGIONS. *J. of Econ. Hist. 1977 37(3): 747-754.* Calculates "the degree of inequality in the distribution of slave wealth in five major agricultural regions (cotton, grain, tobacco, sugar, and rice) in the South in 1860." Findings support the traditional view of the antebellum South as a region characterized by highly unequal wealth distribution. Primary and secondary sources; 3 tables, 8 notes.                    D. J. Trickey

2803. Otto, J. S. and Anderson, N. E. SLASH-AND-BURN CULTIVATION IN THE HIGHLANDS SOUTH: A PROBLEM IN COMPARATIVE AGRICULTURAL HISTORY. *Comparative Studies in Soc. and Hist. [Great Britain] 1982 24(1): 131-147.* Slash-and-burn cultivation is analyzed in terms of its history, reasons for its development and subsequent decline, plus its positive and negative results. In the South highlands it has generally given way to intensive agriculture, livestock raising, and commercial forestry. The tradition of slash-and-burn cultivation can be traced to the Scotch-Irish settlers of Pennsylvania and is still practiced on the small farms of the Ozarks and the Appalachians. 58 notes, fig.

S. A. Farmerie

2804. Otto, John Solomon. SLAVEHOLDING GENERAL FARMERS IN A "COTTON COUNTY." *Agric. Hist. 1981 55(2): 167-178.* General farmers who used slaves in the antebellum South have been little studied, due to a scarcity of written records. Uses oral interviews with the descendants from one such farm in Yell County, Arkansas, to study the agricultural methods of small farmers. Farmers grew crops only on small patches where the forest was killed but not cleared. Livestock roamed the woods unfenced. These methods reduced labor needs but wasted fertility and increased the average farm size as patches were abandoned when they wore out. Based on oral interviews and secondary sources; map, table, 34 notes.

D. E. Bowers

2805. Otto, John Solomon and Burns, Augustus Marion, III. TRADITIONAL AGRICULTURAL PRACTICES IN THE ARKANSAS HIGHLANDS. *J. of Am. Folklore 1981 94(372): 166-187.* The agricultural practices of Ozarkia in the Arkansas Highlands were rooted in a variety of traditions. If open-range herding had British antecedents, slash-and-burn farming combined Native American with British techniques. Similarly, the practice of farming stream bottoms in the hollows was Native American and Scottish. Upland farming had Scottish, Irish, and English roots, while ox-drawn bull-tongue plows seem derived from northern Ireland. Based on oral traditions and letters from black and white informants relating to the history of the Hardy Banks farm; 2 illus., 2 maps, 66 notes.

W. D. Piersen

2806. Oubre, Claude F. "FORTY ACRES AND A MULE:" LOUISIANA AND THE SOUTHERN HOMESTEAD ACT. *Louisiana Hist. 1976 17(2): 143-157.* One of the tragedies of reconstruction was the failure to provide the ex-slaves with economic security, especially land. The chaotic conditions prevailing in the land offices were exemplified in Louisiana. "When homesteading interfered with economic and party interests, loyal whites chose to aid railroad companies rather than press the cause of Negro land ownership." 27 notes.

E. P. Stickney

2807. Owen, Blanton. THE FARM SLED OF THE SOUTHERN APPALACHIAN HIGHLANDS: ITS CONSTRUCTION, USE AND OPERATION. *Pioneer Am. Soc. Tr. 1980 3: 25-45.* Describes the different types of farm sleds used for hauling in western North Carolina.

2808. Pagan, John Ruston. GROWTH OF THE TOBACCO TRADE BETWEEN LONDON AND VIRGINIA, 1614-40. *Guildhall Studies in London Hist. [Great Britain] 1979 3(4): 248-262.* A superb network of waterways and an abundance of easily accessible virgin land were the two physical assets which enabled Virginia to become a great tobacco producer. London, which accounted for most of England's imports, dominated the Virginia tobacco trade, and by 1640 Virginia dominated the English tobacco market. 3 tables, 93 notes.

T. L. Underwood

2809. Paisley, Clifton. MADISON COUNTY'S SEA ISLAND COTTON INDUSTRY, 1870-1916. *Florida Hist. Q. 1976 54(3): 285-305.* Sea Island cotton, with its long fiber of great strength, commanded a premium price in the areas of northern Florida and southern Georgia where it was grown. It brought prosperity and ginning companies to Madison County, Florida, until boll weevils destroyed this variety of cotton. After 1916 more emphasis was placed on other crops such as peanuts and tobacco. 87 notes.

P. A. Beaber

2810. Parker, William N. LABOR PRODUCTIVITY IN COTTON FARMING: THE HISTORY OF A RESEARCH. *Agric. Hist. 1979 53(1): 228-244.* Attempts to estimate labor productivity re-

gionally in cotton farming in the postbellum South by statistical analysis, based on quantitative methods research carried on for 20 years by several people. 5 tables, 14 notes, biblio.

R. V. Ritter

2811. Parvis, Paul B. A REPORT ON THE PROGRESS OF THE DELAWARE AGRICULTURAL MUSEUM. *Working Papers from the Regional Econ. Hist. Res. Center 1981 4(3): 70-82.* Traces the history of the Delaware Agricultural Museum from 1973, when interest first began to develop for founding a state agricultural museum, through its opening in 1980, to its plans for the future; and provides an indication of the museum's holdings.

2812. Peters, Edmund A. JOSEPH DANNE: OKLAHOMA PLANT GENETICIST AND HIS TRIUMPH WHEAT. *Chronicles of Oklahoma 1981 59(1): 54-72.* Oklahoma's self-taught plant breeder Joseph Danne (1887-1959) developed several varieties of Triumph Wheat which today dominate southern plains wheat farming. The hybridization project was Danne's lifetime obsession and he worked constantly to improve the initial strain. An intensely private man, he rejected efforts to market the hybrid prematurely merely for the sake of fame and profits. He willingly wrote descriptive reports on this new wheat but closely guarded its secret until his death. Always a contributor to charities, he willed his property and seed stock to a foundation for orphans and other needy people. Based on Joseph Danne's correspondence; 5 photos, map, 48 notes.

M. L. Tate

2813. Pfeffer, Max J. SOCIAL ORIGINS OF THREE SYSTEMS OF FARM PRODUCTION IN THE UNITED STATES. *Rural Sociol. 1983 48(4): 540-562.* Examines the historical development of three different systems of labor organization for farming: the wage labor of corporate farming in California, sharecropping in the South, and family farming in the Midwest.

2814. Pier, Andrew V. SLOVAK COLLECTIVE FARMS IN FLORIDA. *Jednota Ann. Furdek 1978 17: 25-28.* Begun in 1912 by Lutherans of Slovak ancestry, the agricultural cooperative of A. Duda and Sons Corporation in Slavia, Florida, grew from 40 to more than 100,000 acres in Florida, as well as much acreage elsewhere in the United States and three million acres in Australia.

2815. Poliakoff, Phaye. "THOUGHT WE WERE JUST SOME POOR OLD COUNTRY PEOPLE": AN INTERVIEW WITH ALICE BALANCE. *Southern Exposure 1983 11(6): 30-32.* Alice Balance recalls her youth on a farm in Bertie County, North Carolina, her sharecropping days, and being forced off the land by mechanized farming.

2816. Porter, Jane M. EXPERIMENT STATIONS IN THE SOUTH, 1877-1940. *Agric. Hist. 1979 53(1): 84-101.* Surveys the development of agricultural experiment stations in the South from the establishment of the first one in North Carolina in 1877 up to World War II. Beginning with fertilizer testing, other helpful functions followed, including research and regulatory and extension functions, which were later more carefully separated. Beginning through the land-grant agricultural colleges, the stations gained the help of the Department of Agriculture through federal grants for experimentation and research in all fields of rural need, economic, social, and farm problems. "The research results produced by the stations provided a fund of agricultural knowledge which, if widely applied, could have produced a green revolution in the South." Table, 39 notes. Comment by Irvin May, pp. 102-104.

R. V. Ritter

2817. Ransom, Roger and Sutch, Richard. THE IMPACT OF THE CIVIL WAR AND OF EMANCIPATION ON SOUTHERN AGRICULTURE. *Explorations in Econ. Hist. 1975 12(1): 1-28.* Challenges the traditional view that the Civil War had a devastating impact on agricultural production in the years 1865-80. Most of the decline was the result of emancipation and of a sharp decline in per-capita output. The loss of capital, workstock, and transportation facilities was overcome fairly quickly, but the freedmen chose to work less than had been required of them as slaves. As a consequence, even as late as the end of the century, per-capita output barely exceeded three-quarters of the 1860 standard. Based on published records and secondary accounts.                                              P. J. Coleman

2818. Ransom, Roger and Sutch, Richard. THE "LOCK-IN" MECHANISM AND OVERPRODUCTION OF COTTON IN THE POSTBELLUM SOUTH. *Agric. Hist.* 1975 49(2): 405-425. Southern merchants who had a monopoly in their communities were able to capture farmers in a cycle of debt which most could not escape. The authors show how merchants required farmers to grow large amounts of cotton to pay their debts for corn, thus preventing farmers from growing enough corn to become self-sufficient. Merchants charged exorbitant rates for extending credit. 2 tables, 2 graphs, 45 notes.                                              D. E. Bowers

2819. Reid, Joseph D., Jr. ANTEBELLUM SOUTHERN RENTAL CONTRACTS. *Explorations in Econ. Hist.* 1976 13(1): 69-83. Leasing and sharecropping were carried on during the 40 years preceding the Civil War. Written contracts governed the arrangements and landlords continuously administered them. Tenancy was not inherently inefficient, though it is not known why one tenure was chosen over another. Based on manuscripts at the University of North Carolina Library, Chapel Hill, published documents, and secondary accounts; 18 notes, appendix, biblio.                 P. J. Coleman

2820. Reid, Joseph D., Jr. THE EVALUATION AND IMPLICATIONS OF SOUTHERN TENANCY. *Agric. Hist.* 1979 53(1): 153-169. Tenancy, sharecropping and renting, were rungs on an agricultural ladder "to coordinate owned with unowned inputs into agriculture." The data on post-bellum tenancy support the idea that the effect was more rapidly and efficiently to restore productivity to southern agriculture. "The legacy of ante-bellum slavery in agriculture was post-bellum tenancy." That this did not lead to prosperity was not the fault of tenancy. 58 notes.                             R. V. Ritter

2821. Reid, Joseph D., Jr. SHARECROPPING IN HISTORY AND THEORY. *Agric. Hist.* 1975 49(2): 426-440. Develops a market equilibrium model of sharecropping for the post-Civil War South and elsewhere. Sharecropping was successful because the system gave both landlord and tenant an interest in cooperating to produce a large crop. Sharecropping was preferred by new immigrants, the poor, and unskilled tenants because of managerial aid from the landlord. 34 notes, appendix.                       D. E. Bowers

2822. Reynolds, Bruce J.; Lowitt, Richard, (commentary). TELCOT: A CASE STUDY OF ELECTRONIC MARKETING. *Agric. Hist.* 1982 56(1): 83-98, 117-121. Traditionally cotton selling was handled at individual cotton gins where local buyers competed. As market news became more available, farmers looked for ways to achieve better prices through cooperative marketing. The Plains Cotton Cooperative Association of Lubbock, Texas, pioneered in the use of computer information networks to aid in selling cotton. TELCOT, which it established in 1975, permits merchants and farmers to join together via an on-line computer to auction cotton. It gives farmers local access to buyers, allows rapid interior assembly of cotton, and promotes efficiency in the complicated pricing of cotton through different quality levels. Comments, pp. 117-121. Based on interviews and other primary and secondary sources; 36 notes.                                              D. E. Bowers

2823. Rosengarten, Theodore. ALL GOD'S DANGERS. *Southern Exposure* 1974 2(2/3): 22-31. Discusses the life and experiences of Negro cotton sharecropper Nate Shaw in Alabama, 1880's-1960's.

2824. Rothrock, Thomas. THE ARKANSAS STATE HORTICULTURAL SOCIETY. *Arkansas Hist. Q.* 1975 34(3): 242-267. The Arkansas State Horticultural Society was established in 1879 in Little Rock and has held annual meetings ever since. Among its activities have been the presentation of papers at meetings on numerous agricultural subjects, the support of legislation favorable to the agricultural interests of members, the sponsorship of agricultural fairs, and the establishment of a state agricultural bureau. Based on pub-

lished proceedings of annual meetings, newspaper accounts, published state government documents, and secondary sources; 5 illus., 85 notes.                                              T. L. Savitt

2825. Rothrock, Thomas. A KING THAT WAS. *Arkansas Hist. Q.* 1974 33(4): 326-333. From the 1890's to the 1930's apple growing was a key industry in northwest Arkansas. Those orchard owners able to survive the Depression, droughts, freezes, and scarcity of farm help in the 1940's still had to contend with insects (particularly the codling moth) that had developed a resistance to insecticides. Also describes planting and marketing procedures of the past. 6 illus.                                              T. L. Savitt

2826. Saloutos, Theodore. AGRICULTURAL ORGANIZATIONS AND FARM POLICY IN THE SOUTH AFTER WORLD WAR II. *Agric. Hist.* 1979 53(1): 377-404. Discusses the reasons for the shifts in membership gains or declines in the major farm organizations in the South during 1946-76. The American Farm Bureau Federation (AFBF) outstripped the older National Farmers' Union (NFU) and the Grange, both of which went into a sharp decline. Essentially, although they were at odds with national leadership over farm price policy, the liberal stands of the NFU on a number of issues, including integration and cooperation with organized labor, were hardly inviting to southern farmers. The AFBF, being more sensitive to the needs of the changing South, attracted a hard core of support from farmers and nonfarmers alike. 107 notes.                                              R. V. Ritter

2827. Scarpaci, J. Vincenza. LABOR FOR LOUISIANA'S SUGAR CANE FIELDS: AN EXPERIMENT IN IMMIGRANT RECRUITMENT. *Italian Americana* 1981 7(1): 19-41. Discusses the labor recruitment of Italian immigrants in the sugar industry in Louisiana after the recruitment of Negro, Chinese, Scandinavian, Spanish, and Portuguese laborers proved unsuccessful in reducing labor shortages, focusing on government programs to encourage white immigration to the United States.

2828. Scarpaci, Jean Ann. IMMIGRANTS IN THE NEW SOUTH: ITALIANS IN LOUISIANA'S SUGAR PARISHES, 1880-1910. *Labor Hist.* 1975 16(2): 165-183. In the late 19th century the scarcity of labor during the sugar cane harvest in Louisiana attracted thousands of Italian immigrants to the sugar parishes. The immigrants were a temporary element in the state's population, yet the Italians were the largest immigrant group in Louisiana in 1900. Italians and Negroes apparently tolerated one another while on the same occupational level, but as Italians became more successful racial prejudice became more dominant. Based upon population censuses and government reports; 42 notes.                L. L. Athey

2829. Scarpaci, Jean Ann. IMMIGRANTS IN THE NEW SOUTH: ITALIANS IN LOUISIANA'S SUGAR PARISHES, 1880-1910. Cantor, Milton, ed. *American Workingclass Culture: Explorations in American Labor and Social History* (Westport, Conn.: Greenwood, 1979): 377-396. Reprint of an article originally published in *Labor History*.

2830. Schaefer, Donald and Schmitz, Mark. EFFICIENCY IN ANTEBELLUM SOUTHERN AGRICULTURE: A COVARIANCE APPROACH. *Southern Econ. J.* 1982 49(1): 88-98. Compares cotton production in the antebellum South on farms according to size, use of slave or free labor, and soil type during 1845-61.

2831. Schaefer, Donald F. PRODUCTIVITY IN THE ANTEBELLUM SOUTH: THE WESTERN TOBACCO REGION. *Res. in Econ. Hist.* 1978 3: 305-346. The relative agricultural productivity of slaveholders and nonslaveholders is estimated for the tobacco region of Kentucky and Tennessee in 1850 and 1860, using the index of total factor productivity as the basis for comparison. The results imply that slaveholders were approximately 18% more productive than nonslaveholders in 1860, whereas they were 9% less productive in 1850. This paper explores the sources of these differences. The slaveholders' advantage in 1860 is shown to be explainable by scale of operation, whereas their relative disadvantage in 1850 is seen to be ameliorated by that factor. The reasons that productivity varied with scale are not certain, but two possible explanations include labor specialization and differences in land quality.     J

2832.  Schaefer, Donald. YEOMEN FARMERS AND ECONOMIC DEMOCRACY: A STUDY OF WEALTH AND ECONOMIC MOBILITY IN THE WESTERN TOBACCO REGION, 1850-1860. *Explorations in Econ. Hist. 1978 15(4): 421-437.* Tentative results for Kentucky and Tennessee suggest that yeoman farmers were not being forced out, though the gap in wealth between them and planters widened. As a consequence, some yeoman farmers may have chosen to migrate to the developing cotton region to the south and west. Based on manuscript census records and published accounts; 9 tables, fig., 14 notes, appendix, 19 ref.

P. J. Coleman

2833.  Schmitz, Mark. THE TRANSFORMATION OF THE SOUTHERN CANE SUGAR SECTOR, 1860-1930. *Agric. Hist. 1979 53(1): 270-285.* Any description and analysis of the cane sugar sector must consider legal and economic developments elsewhere, particularly the whims of Congress. Following the Civil War there came a "new organizational hierarchy based on large manufacturing units and independent cane growers." There was also a shift in nonsouthern supply and demand while there were reduced subsidies to cane producers, diminishing their role in supplying US consumption. Most of the study centers in Louisiana. 5 tables, 42 notes.

R. V. Ritter

2834.  Schmitz, Mark D. ECONOMIES OF SCALE AND FARM SIZE IN THE ANTEBELLUM SUGAR SECTOR. *J. of Econ. Hist. 1977 37(4): 959-980.* This article explains the emergence of a plantation economy in the antebellum sugar sector (n Lousana, 1850's]. The hypothesis of ncreasng returns to scale was tested usng a Zellner-Revankar generalzed producton functon model. Economes of scale were found usng samples from the manuscrpt censuses, but these scale economes dmnshed wth sze. A second mportant factor n explanng the sze dstrbuton of farms was the dual technology n the manufacturng stage of sugar producton. Farms wth nferor horse-power mlls had poorer survval records and less flexblty n expanson than those usng steam power mlls.     J

2835.  Schmitz, Mark D. FARM INTERDEPENDENCE IN THE ANTEBELLUM SUGAR SECTOR. *Agric. Hist. 1978 52(1): 93-103.* Scholars of the antebellum South generally believe that southern cash crop plantation owners never grew enough subsistence commodities to feed themselves or their slave population. Owners of sugar plantations, in fact, raised a surplus of corn which they used to fatten hogs they purchased for subsistence use from smaller farms in the region. Primary and secondary sources; 7 tables, 27 notes.

R. T. Fulton

2836.  Schwartz, Michael H. AN ESTIMATE OF THE SIZE OF THE SOUTHERN FARMERS' ALLIANCE, 1884-1890. *Agric. Hist. 1977 51(4): 759-769.* At its height in 1890, the Southern Farmers' Alliance probably numbered about 857,000 members. This figure was reached by making estimates of state membership using average club size where actual membership was unknown and interpolating data so estimates would be for 1 January of each year. These membership figures are well below previous estimates of up to three million members, but still represent an impressive percentage of adult southern males. 2 tables, chart, 16 notes.

D. E. Bowers

2837.  Schweitzer, Mary McKinney. ECONOMIC REGULATION AND THE COLONIAL ECONOMY: THE MARYLAND TOBACCO INSPECTION ACT OF 1747. *J. of Econ. Hist. 1980 40(3): 551-569.* In 1747 the colony of Maryland enacted a law to improve the general quality of tobacco exports. Tobacco prices rose significantly after the law went into effect, while total tobacco exports continued to increase. The widespread use of tobacco as money, coupled with the exchange of inspection notes for tobacco at inspection sites, led to changes in the Maryland money supply due to

the law. Transaction costs fell as a result of marketing all Maryland tobacco through inspection warehouses. The law also appears to have accelerated the trend toward diversification of the economy.

J

2838.  Scruggs, C. G. and Moseley, Smith W. THE ROLE OF AGRICULTURAL JOURNALISM IN BUILDING THE RURAL SOUTH. *Agric. Hist. 1979 53(1): 22-29.* Traces the history and influence of several farm journals on southern agriculture. Several became casualties of the Civil War, but others replaced them. One of the most notable and influential was the *Progressive Farmer* founded in 1866 by Col. Leonidas L. Polk. Three types of copy predominated: editorial opinion and promotion, news of world or national affairs, and letters of farmers, an exchange of information on every phase of farm life and methods. These periodicals became powerful forces against the evils of farm tenantry, high interest rates, railroad exploitation, poor schools, and poor health. They, more positively, became "a university in a mailbox." Their influence reached also into the larger world of journalism which came to realize the importance of having farm editors and farm-oriented departments. 2 notes. Comment by William K. Scarborough, pp. 60-61.

R. V. Ritter

2839.  Shankman, Arnold. THE MENACING INFLUX: AFRO-AMERICANS ON ITALIAN IMMIGRATION TO THE SOUTH, 1880-1915. *Mississippi Q. 1977-78 31(1): 67-88.* Belief in Darwinism gave Southern planters and landowners the idea of importing cheap European agricultural labor to replace black labor during 1880-1915. This unleashed fear and invective from Southern black newspapers, which proved unfounded, since most Italian Americans remained in urban areas to begin small mercantile operations.

2840.  Sheftall, John McKay. OGEECHEE OLD TOWN: A GEORGIA PLANTATION, 1540-1860. *Richmond County Hist. 1982 14(2): 27-42.* Traces the history of Ogeechee Old Town, on the Ogeechee River, which like other plantations was the location of an Indian village; focuses on the ownership of Old Town and its status as a plantation until 1860.

2841.  Sheridan, Richard C. CHEMICAL FERTILIZERS IN SOUTHERN AGRICULTURE. *Agric. Hist. 1979 53(1): 308-318.* Discusses the development of chemical fertilizers and their use in southern agriculture. The primary plant nutrients are nitrogen, phosphorus, and potassium. The first such products were produced in Baltimore, Maryland, and production spread to other southeastern states. The 1933 creation of the Tennessee Valley Authority included responsibility for developing new and better fertilizers. Major changes in the industry in recent years will continue. 24 notes.

R. V. Ritter

2842.  Shlomowitz, Ralph. THE ORIGINS OF SOUTHERN SHARECROPPING. *Agric. Hist. 1979 53(3): 557-575.* The author examined the records of the Bureau of Refugees, Freedmen, and Abandoned Lands, usually referred to as the Freedmen's Bureau. The Bureau approved and enforce southern labor contracts between planters and freedmen. Notable for their wide variety of terms, the contracts offered as many as seven forms of compensation: standing wages, share of the crop, sharing of time, standing rent, wages in kind, money payment per task, and explicit incentive schemes. In most of these agreements the planter contracted his labor force as a group. In this study a 5% sample of labor contracts for South Carolina was taken. Primary and secondary sources; 2 tables, 32 notes.

R. T. Fulton

2843.  Siceloff, John. TOBACCO IN TRANSITION. *Southern Exposure 1976 3(4): 46-52.* Discusses new methods of cultivating, raising, and curing tobacco in the South, 1970's.

2844.  Silverman, Jason H. OF BLACK UTOPIAS. *Rev. in Am. Hist. 1982 10(1): 60-64.* Reviews Janet Sharp Hermann's *The Pursuit of a Dream* (1981), an account of the model slave plantation established by Joseph Davis, Jefferson Davis's elder brother, at Davis Bend, near Vicksburg, Mississippi, and its transformation following the Civil War; it was based on the utopian theories of Robert Owen, although Davis rejected Owen's paternalism and ran his plantation based on cooperation.

2845. Smallwood, James. PERPETUATION OF CASTE: BLACK AGRICULTURAL WORKERS IN RECONSTRUCTION TEXAS. *Mid-America 1979 61(1): 5-23.* At the end of the Civil War, Texas whites sought to maintain the pre-war caste status of the former slaves. In spite of work by the Freedmen's Bureau and the Army in enforcing Reconstruction laws, the former slaves were kept in a sharecropper status or as low-paid field hands. A partial reason was lack of black economic resources, but the evidence indicates that white racism was the major factor. Primary and secondary sources; 64 notes.                                                          J. M. Lee

2846. Smallwood, James. THE SOUTHERN PLAINS AND THE EXPANSION OF THE COTTON KINGDOM. *West Texas Hist. Assoc. Year Book 1980 56: 35-48.* Cotton was first cultivated in West Texas in 1889, began to be an important crop in World War I, and was firmly established in the 1920's.

2847. Smith, John David. "KEEP 'EM IN A FIRE-PROOF VAULT": PIONEER SOUTHERN HISTORIANS DISCOVER PLANTATION RECORDS. *South Atlantic Q. 1979 78(3): 376-391.* Writers of southern history through the 19th century lacked primary sources. Such sources were sometimes found even in corn cribs, where the weather and rodents had free access to them. It was Ulrich B. Phillips (1877-1934) who first overcame the paucity of sources and made an effort to utilize the plantation records in his writing as well as to collect sources. Phillips believed strongly in plantation records as a source for the writing of history because they were "unconscious sources" for the study of slavery. He urged that they be gathered and placed in fireproof vaults. Based on the Phillips Papers in the Southern Historical Collection, University of North Carolina, and the Herbert Anthony Kellar Papers, State Historical Society of Wisconsin, and secondary materials; 29 notes.
                                                          H. M. Parker, Jr.

2848. Smith, Peter C. and Raitz, Karl B. NEGRO HAMLETS AND AGRICULTURAL ESTATES IN KENTUCKY'S INNER BLUEGRASS. *Geographical R. 1974 64(2): 217-234.* "Two distinct forms of settlement are found in Kentucky's Inner Bluegrass region: the large agricultural estate and the Negro hamlet. The parklike estates were created by migrants from the Virginia and Maryland Tidewater country in the early nineteenth century. Interspersed with the estates are small Negro hamlets that were developed as labor villages for the estates following the Civil War. Even today a synergistic social and economic relationship continues between the hamlet Negro and the white estate owner. This settlement pattern has also developed in other areas which have similar land-tenure systems, scales of operation, aristocratic traditions, and labor-intensive estate farming."                                                          J

2849. Snyder, Robert E. HUEY LONG AND THE COTTON-HOLIDAY OF 1931. *Louisiana Hist. 1977 18(2): 135-160.* Overproduction of cotton had become a major problem by 1931, but proposals to destroy part of the crop were rejected by southerners. Louisiana's Huey P. Long took the lead in proposing the cotton-holiday plan which would have solved the problem by prohibiting all cotton production in 1932. Following heated debate all over the South, the New Orleans Cotton Conference, in August 1931, endorsed Long's plan and the Louisiana legislature quickly became the first to enact a law prohibiting cotton production in the state in 1932. Most of the other cotton producing states appeared willing to follow Louisiana's lead, but waited to see what Texas would do. Texas Governor Ross Sterling strongly opposed Long's plan, the Texas legislature refused to enact it, and the cotton-holiday plan collapsed. A major defeat for Huey Long, it nevertheless represented the first step toward "scarcity of production" as a cure for the depression. Primary sources; 79 notes.          R. L. Woodward, Jr.

2850. Stephens, Lester D. FARISH FURMAN'S FORMULA: SCIENTIFIC FARMING AND THE "NEW SOUTH." *Agric. Hist. 1976 50(2): 377-390.* Farish Furman began experimenting with fertilizers in 1878 on his Georgia cotton farm. By studying the cotton

plant he devised a formula for compost involving manure, acid phosphate, kainit, and cottonseed which restored his depleted lands to fertility. His fertilizer quickly became popular, and was probably a factor in raising cotton yields throughout the South. 28 notes.
                                                          D. E. Bowers

2851. Stephens, S. G. THE ORIGIN OF SEA ISLAND COTTON. *Agric. Hist. 1976 50(2): 391-399.* Details the 200-year history of the cultivation of Sea Island cotton in South Carolina and Georgia, and speculates on its origin. Historical records and experimental hybridization suggest that Sea Island cotton originated with a natural cross between native West Indian cotton and a primitive variety of *G. barbadense* also grown there. The cross probably occurred on Barbados or Jamaica. 27 notes.                         D. E. Bowers

2852. Tolany, Stewart E. FERTILITY OF SOUTHERN BLACK FARMERS IN 1900: EVIDENCE AND SPECULATION. *J. of Family Hist. 1983 8(4): 314-332.* A comparison of fertility among white and black farmers in the South shows very different predictors of fertility. Black fertility was higher in factory areas and did not vary with land shortages, while white fertility was lower in factory areas and where there were land shortages. 3 tables, 13 notes, biblio.                                                          T. W. Smith

2853. Townsend, Mary Ann. HOG KILLING ON QUEENFIELD FARM, MANQUIN, VIRGINIA. *North Carolina Folklore J. 1973 21(1): 32-34.* A North Carolina State University student relates her father's account of the raising and butchering of hogs on a Virginia farm.                                                          R. N. Lokken

2854. Trimble, Stanley W. COMMENTARY ON "LAND USE CHANGE IN A PIEDMONT COUNTY," BY JOHN FRASER HART. *Ann. of the Assoc. of Am. Geog. 1983 73(2): 285-288.* Response to Hart's article; discusses factors affecting the progressive abandonment of cropland in Carroll County, Georgia, since the late 19th century.

2855. Tullos, Allen. PLANS FOR A NEW SOUTH. *Southern Exposure 1974 2(2/3): 91-93.* Discusses the need for regional planning in rural settlements of the South in order to maintain the benefits of country life, 1970's.

2856. Turner, Charles Jackson. CHANGES IN AGE COMPOSITION OF THE RURAL BLACK POPULATION OF THE SOUTH 1950 TO 1970. *Phylon 1974 35(3): 268-275.* During 1950-70 the rural black population of the South declined by 1.5 million. The farm population declined by 86 percent, but the nonfarm rural population grew by 50 percent. The loss of farm population was greatest among those who were 20 or younger in 1950; they left for cities. Older farmers left for nonfarm but rural endeavors, thereby increasing nonfarm totals. As a result, the average age on the farms increased only slightly during this 20-year period, but the average age of rural nonfarm increased drastically. Based on primary and secondary sources; 2 tables, 13 notes.          B. A. Glasrud

2857. Wade, Judith Masce. MARGARET ELIZABETH DANIEL LEE: PINELLAS PIONEER. *Tampa Bay Hist. 1981 3(1): 82-86.* Brief introductory background of Margaret Elizabeth Daniel Lee (1887-1980) and her family's presence in Pinellas County, Florida, beginning around 1850, followed by an excerpt from her journal written in 1963 about her life in a farm family.

2858. Wadley, Janet K. and Lee, Everett S. THE DISAPPEARANCE OF THE BLACK FARMER. *Phylon 1974 35(3): 276-283.* The black farmer in the United States has nearly disappeared. As a result, the remaining black farms are small and concentrated in areas where cotton and tobacco are the chief crops. North Carolina is a critical state for determining the future of blacks in agriculture; many of the small black owners and tenants live in that state. Most farm operators in the South are old, and young farmers continue to leave. World War II and the social and technological changes that it precipitated sounded the knell for the small farmer, and Negroes were the first to be displaced. Based on the census and secondary sources; table, 9 notes.                         B. A. Glasrud

2859. Wechsler, Debby. HEALTHY FOOD IN A LIVING LANDSCAPE: ORGANIC FARMING IN THE SOUTH. *Southern Exposure 1983 11(6): 14-19.* Southern farmers are trying organic and biological farming with increasing sophistication and in increasing numbers.

2860. Wheeler, David L. THE ORIGIN AND DEVELOPMENT OF THE CATTLE FEEDING INDUSTRY IN THE SOUTHERN HIGH PLAINS. *Panhandle-Plains Hist. Rev. 1976 49(1): 81-90.* The Texas Panhandle has become a major beef producing region since the 1930's when irrigation was introduced to create a surplus of feed grains. Good profits and high demand encouraged major cattle raising programs by the 1950's and large feedyards were constructed to handle the increased population. However, substantial amounts of water must soon be discovered and new markets must be opened or the Panhandle's cattle industry will have to retrench by the 1980's. Based on secondary sources; 55 notes.

M. L. Tate

2861. Whisenhunt, Donald W. HUEY LONG AND THE TEXAS COTTON ACREAGE CONTROL LAW OF 1931. *Louisiana Studies 1974 13(2): 142-153.* Studies the reaction to Governor Huey P. Long's proposal that all cotton-producing states forbid the planting of cotton in 1932 as a means of bolstering the sagging price of cotton. Getting Texas' approval and cooperation was crucial to its success; hence great pressure, not only from Long but also from other states. Texas finally passed its own less stringent regulatory bill, but that law was declared unconstitutional. The debate, however, did have value for the future in preparing the thinking of southern agriculture for the later New Deal crop limitation measures. 69 notes.

R. V. Ritter

2862. Whiting, Cynthia L. A HISTORY OF THE PEACH INDUSTRY IN LINCOLN PARISH: SIXTY YEARS OF GROWTH AND SUCCESS (1921-1981). *North Louisiana Hist. Assoc. J. 1983 14(4): 175-190.* Two family orchards, each with over 200 acres in production, lead the peach industry in Lincoln Parish, northern Louisiana. The parish produced almost two-thirds of the peaches produced in Louisiana in 1981. The industry has grown from a small beginning in 1921, with most of the growth occurring after the 1940's. 57 notes.

J. F. Paul

2863. Whitten, David O. AMERICAN RICE CULTURE: 1680-1980: A TERCENTENARY CRITIQUE. *Southern Studies 1982 21(1): 5-26.* Rice has been an important agricultural product of the United States since colonial times. During 1680-1780 rice farming was introduced and implemented from upland culture to wet culture on the inland swamps of South Carolina. From 1780 to the Civil War the tidal rivers of South Carolina and Georgia were the heart of the growing area. Since the Civil War, and with the advent of mechanized farming, rice culture has flourished in Louisiana, Texas, and Arkansas. Discusses methods of cultivation and developments in machinery for working rice. Primary sources; 4 tables, 83 notes.

J. J. Buschen

2864. Wiener, Jonathan M. FEMALE PLANTERS AND PLANTERS' WIVES IN CIVIL WAR AND RECONSTRUCTION ALABAMA, 1850-1870. *Alabama Rev. 1977 30(2): 135-149.* Close examination of census reports on 236 plantations in five Alabama black-belt counties, 1850-70, shows that the Civil War did not radically alter the responsibilities and roles of women. Women married older planters, and birth rates dropped markedly during 1863-68. But women were not more likely to operate plantations than in earlier years, nor did a generation of women find themselves without men. Primary and secondary sources; 2 charts, 17 notes.

J. F. Vivian

2865. Wiener, Jonathan M. PLANTER PERSISTENCE AND SOCIAL CHANGE: ALABAMA, 1850-1870. *J. of Interdisciplinary Hist. 1976 7(2): 235-260.* A study of social mobility in Alabama before and after the Civil War to determine the accuracy of the traditional but untested view that there was a radical discontinuity created by the war. It has been thought that there was a relatively stable, persistent elite of slaveholding aristocrats before, and, through the destruction of this elite, the war brought about a sharp

increase in upward mobility among urban businessmen. This new study is based on data from the US census. "There was virtually no evidence that the war and Reconstruction led to a 'revolution of land titles,' or to the 'downfall of the old planter class.'" The Alabama elite was successful in preserving its social position and its land through war and Reconstruction, contrary to the commonly held opinion. 6 tables, 35 notes.

R. V. Ritter

2866. Wiener, Jonathan M. PLANTER-MERCHANT CONFLICT IN RECONSTRUCTION ALABAMA. *Past and Present [Great Britain] 1975 (68): 73-94.* Presents evidence, largely from US census schedules, indicating that the abolition of slavery did not result in the destruction of the planter class, but rather its persistence and metamorphosis. In Marengo County, Alabama, the crop lien was developed in the immediate postwar years as a new way of extracting the surplus from agricultural labor. Lien-holding merchants who formed a challenge to the planter elite were overcome by the use of political power. In Alabama the planter-dominated state legislature severely limited the activities of the merchants, confining their pursuit of wealth and power to the hills. Moreover, the challenge was limited for the merchants' fortunes depended on the maintenance of the status quo in the mode of production. Consequently, the planters became planter-merchants, in the hills the merchants became merchant-landlords, and the postwar South remained dominated by a reactionary agrarian elite. Primary and secondary sources; 39 notes.

R. G. Neville

2867. Winberry, John J. REPUTATION OF CAROLINA INDIGO. *South Carolina Hist. Mag. 1979 80(3): 242-250.* Gives the history of South Carolina's commercial crop, indigo, from the revival of its production in the 1740's until the 1790's.

2868. Woodman, Harold D. THE OLD SOUTH: GLOBAL AND LOCAL PERSPECTIVES ON POWER, POLITICS, AND IDEOLOGY. *Civil War Hist. 1979 25(4): 339-351.* Raimondo Luraghi's *The Rise and Fall of the Plantation South* traces southern ideology to a premodern "seigneurial" system flowing through Canada from the Italian Renaissance. From colonial beginnings, Puritan bourgeois northern ideology opposed it. Industrialism brought northern aggression, including ideological offensives, eventuating in war and a "sort of Southern state socialism," comparable to Russia's and China's. J. Miller Thornton III's *Politics and Power in a Slave Society: Alabama, 1800-1860* traces secession to small farmers' efforts to restore government to protect individual autonomy against Republicans and emerging Yankee-type planters. Planters promoted diversification, but never at their expense; costs ruined small farmers. Republican strength and border-state hesitancy frightened and disillusioned them. Secondary sources; 11 notes.

R. E. Stack

2869. Woodman, Harold D.; Fite, Gilbert C., (commentary). POSTBELLUM SOCIAL CHANGE AND ITS EFFECTS ON MARKETING THE SOUTH'S COTTON CROP. *Agric. Hist. 1982 56(1): 215-230, 244-248.* Class as well as race separated Southern black farmers from white farmers for generations after the Civil War. Many white landowners and tenants slipped in status as they became indebted to furnishing merchants and lost control of the marketing of their crop. Many black tenants by the 20th century were working on centralized plantations, like the Delta and Pine Land Company in Mississippi, which controlled every aspect of their work and left them little better off than laborers. These differences as well as racial differences made it impossible for the two groups to become closer allies. Comments, pp. 244-248; 24 notes.

D. E. Bowers

2870. Woodman, Harold D. POST-CIVIL WAR SOUTHERN AGRICULTURE AND THE LAW. *Agric. Hist. 1979 53(1): 319-337.* "Economic reconstruction may be seen as the building of a new social organization to replace the one destroyed by the war." Examines one facet of the transformation: the evolution of the law relating to agriculture. Traces "the ways in which the legislatures and the courts sought to deal with a wide range of new problems arising from emancipation and in so doing create the legal basis for a new dominant agricultural class based on a peculiarly southern free-labor system." In effect the formal laws in one generation's time were obviated by the informal laws which protected only landlords and local merchants, the guarantees for the workers becoming meaningless. 36 notes. Comment by John E. Lee, Jr., pp. 372-376.                                                              R. V. Ritter

2871. Wright, Gavin. COTTON COMPETITION AND THE POST-BELLUM RECOVERY OF THE AMERICAN SOUTH. *J. of Econ. Hist. 1974 34(3): 610-635.* Tests several hypotheses accounting for the slow growth of southern per capita income following the Civil War. Results indicate that neither war-induced increases in cotton production by foreign suppliers nor unfavorable postwar monetary exchange rates were the primary cause of the retardation in southern per capita income. Evidence shows that the slow growth of world cotton demand is associated with slow southern income growth. Based on contemporary statistical data and secondary sources; 7 tables, 39 notes.                     O. H. Reichardt

2872. Wright, Gavin and Kunreuther, Howard. COTTON, CORN AND RISK IN THE NINETEENTH CENTURY. *J. of Econ. Hist. 1975 35(3): 526-551.* Employs econometric models of decisionmaking in the presence of risk to explain the shift from self-sufficiency in foods in the South in 1860 to single-crop dependence on cotton by 1880. Suggests that cautious small tenant farmers in 1880 had little prospect of ever owning their own land and were driven to gamble in cotton. Based on primary and secondary sources; 6 tables, 62 notes.                                                     D. J. Trickey

2873. Wright, Gavin. ONE KIND OF FREEDOM. *Civil Liberties Rev. 1978 5(1): 47-50.* Roger L. Ransom and Richard Sutch's *One Kind of Freedom: The Economic Consequences of Emancipation* (Cambridge: Cambridge U. Pr., 1977) considers 19th-century southern agricultural institutions the cause of the slow economic progress of Negroes after emancipation.

2874. Wright, Gavin. SLAVERY AND THE COTTON BOOM. *Explorations in Econ. Hist. 1975 12(4): 439-451.* The pace of economic expansion in the South was principally determined by the rate of growth of world demand for cotton. Because demand was high between 1820 and 1860, slave labor was profitable; but because the demand for cotton collapsed and stagnated between 1860 and 1900, slave prices would have declined, the growth of southern income would have fallen sharply, and slave labor would have been regarded as less efficient and profitable. Based on published documents and secondary accounts; 26 notes.          P. J. Coleman

2875. Young, Thomas Daniel. A PRESCRIPTION TO LIVE BY: RANSOM AND THE AGRARIAN DEBATES. *Southern Rev. 1976 12(3): 608-621.* Account of the four debates participated in by John Crowe Ransom during 1930-31 in defense of the anti-industrial cultural ideal for the South that had been presented in the volume *I'll Take My Stand.*

2876. —. BLACK LAND LOSS: THE PLIGHT OF BLACK OWNERSHIP. *Southern Exposure 1974 2(2/3): 112-121.* Discusses the need for land tenure reform for Negroes and small farmers in rural settlements of the South in the 1970's.

2877. —. [COTTON, CORN, AND RISK: 19TH CENTURY]. *Explorations in Econ. Hist. 1977 14(2): 167-195.*
McGuire, Robert and Higgs, Robert. COTTON, CORN, AND RISK IN THE NINETEENTH CENTURY: ANOTHER VIEW, *pp. 167-182.*
Wright, Gavin and Kunreuther, Howard. A REPLY, *pp. 183-195.*
An exchange of views about farmers' choices between cotton and corn production in the South, prompted by Wright and Kunreuther's article in the *Journal of Economic History* 1975 35(3): 526-551. (See abstract in this chapter).
                                                              P. J. Coleman

2878. —. DID SOUTHERN FARMERS DISCRIMINATE? AN EXCHANGE. *Agric. Hist. 1975 49(2): 441-447.*
Roberts, Charles A. THE EVIDENCE REEXAMINED, pp. 441-445. Contends that Higgs' recent article in *Agricultural History* on comparative wage rates for southern white and black agri-

cultural workers in 1898-99 understates the difference between wage rates because it doesn't compare the value of board and rations given white and black workers, respectively.
Higgs, Robert. INTERPRETIVE PROBLEMS AND FURTHER EVIDENCE, pp. 445-447. Replies that many white workers did not receive board, whereas most blacks did receive rations, and offers further evidence that real wages were about the same regardless of race. Table, 16 notes.          D. E. Bowers

2879. —. [POSTBELLUM SOUTHERN AGRICULTURE]. *J. of Econ. Hist. 1973 33(1): 106-176.*
Reid, Joseph D., Jr. SHARECROPPING AS AN UNDERSTANDABLE MARKET RESPONSE: THE POST-BELLUM SOUTH, *pp. 106-130.* Examines reasons for the South's inefficient agricultural system, 1860-80. Table, fig., 53 notes, appendix.
Ransom, Roger L. and Sutch, Richard. THE EX-SLAVE IN THE POST-BELLUM SOUTH: A STUDY OF THE ECONOMIC IMPACT OF RACISM IN A MARKET ENVIRONMENT, *pp. 131-148.* Economic opportunity was denied the Negro freedman because of his race, yet there is no indication that southern productivity would have risen were racial discrimination eliminated. 5 tables, 14 notes, appendix.
Higgs, Robert. RACE, TENURE, AND RESOURCE ALLOCATION IN SOUTHERN AGRICULTURE, 1910, *pp. 149-169.* "Investigates the organization of southern agricultural enterprise in 1910, with special regard for the interrelations of race, land tenure conditions, and the allocation of resources." 3 tables, fig., 23 notes.
Wright, Gavin. COMMENTS ON PAPERS BY REID, RANSOM AND SUTCH, AND HIGGS, *pp. 170-176.*
                                                              C. W. Olson

2880. —. PRESERVING FOR THE FUTURE: AN INTERVIEW WITH THREE GENERATIONS OF THE STARKEY FAMILY. *Tampa Bay Hist. 1981 3(2): 58-75.* An interview with J. B. Starkey, Sr., J. B. Starkey, Jr., and his son, Frank Starkey, of the Umberton Ranch in Pasco and Pinellas counties, Florida.

2881. —. [WORLD DEMAND FOR COTTON DURING THE NINETEENTH CENTURY]. *J. of Econ. Hist. 1979 39(4): 1015-1024.*
Hanson, John R., II. WORLD DEMAND FOR COTTON DURING THE NINETEENTH CENTURY: WRIGHT'S ESTIMATES RE-EXAMINED, *pp. 1015-1021.* Questions Gavin Wright's interpretations and statistics (see abstract in this chapter) which treat the Anglo-American cotton trade as a proxy for world cotton trade, 1860's-1900. 3 tables, 17 notes.
Wright, Gavin. WORLD DEMAND FOR COTTON DURING THE NINETEENTH CENTURY: REPLY, *pp. 1023-1024.*

## Urbanization, Industrialization, and Modernization
### *(including mining, textile industry, lumbering, transportation, and communications)*

2882. Adams, Donald R., Jr. EARNINGS AND SAVINGS IN THE EARLY 19TH CENTURY. *Explorations in Econ. Hist. 1980 17(2): 118-134.* Records of E. I. Du Pont de Nemours in Delaware, Maryland, from 1813 to 1860 show that the firm did not exploit its workers, that real wages increased significantly over time, and that all employees, even those in the lowest wage categories, were able to save on a regular basis. The highest paid workers saved a larger percentage of their wages than did the lowest paid, but a substantial proportion of all workers succeeded in accumulating savings equal to or higher than their annual incomes. Based on manuscript records, published statistics, and secondary accounts; 9 tables, 19 notes, 13 ref.                                      P. J. Coleman

2883. Adams, Donald R., Jr. THE STANDARD OF LIVING DURING AMERICAN INDUSTRIALIZATION: EVIDENCE FROM THE BRANDYWINE REGION, 1800-1860. *J. of Econ. Hist. 1982 42(4): 903-917.* The question of whether tangible economic growth occurred during the American industrial revolution has been aggravated by the lack of reliable data. A rich source of evidence on worker earnings and savings in the Brandywine River Valley, a center of 19th-century industrial activity, is found in the records of the E. I. DuPont and Company. These indicate that these workers shared in the antebellum process of American economic growth. Based on records of the E. I. DuPont and Company; 8 tables, 14 notes, appendix.                    J. Powell

2884. Akin, Edward N. THE SLY FOXES: HENRY FLAGLER, GEORGE MILES, AND FLORIDA'S PUBLIC DOMAIN. *Florida Hist. Q. 1979 58(1): 22-36.* Henry Flagler gained control over Florida's east coast through "intrigue, manipulation, and political chicanery." The Florida Coast Line Canal and Transportation Company headed by George Miles was the vehicle of achievement. This operation gives insight into land speculation and promotion in late 19th-century Florida. Based on the Flagler correspondence and state records; 59 notes.                    N. A. Kuntz

2885. Andrews, Andrea R. THE BALTIMORE SCHOOL BUILDING PROGRAM, 1870 TO 1900: A STUDY OF URBAN REFORM. *Maryland Hist. Mag. 1975 70(3): 260-274.* The "one-sided Progressive picture of the ward-based machine as totally corrupt and evil" needs redressing, yet the rapidly growing late-19th-century city was developing serious needs which the locally oriented city government was not equipped to meet. Analyzes the problem of providing a growing school population with buildings and equipment, describing Baltimore city and the government politically dependent school board. School commissioners were primarily ward politicians appointed by council and bound to the dictates of the machine hierarchy. Inordinate stress on budgetary economy and property tax evasion resulted in chronic deficits and lack of funds. Lack of expertise and coordination produced a shortsighted, haphazard program, with overcrowded and hazardous makeshift buildings. The reformed City Charter of 1898 created the mechanism for "centralization, independence, objectivity, and expertise" with a new Board of Estimates and a mayor-appointed board for schools, but the reform system was no guarantee that partisanship and self-interest were dead. Moreover, the popular, local control of the ward system was removed while the potential for a machine still existed. Primary and secondary works; 2 tables, 55 notes.

G. J. Bobango

2886. Ansley, Fran and Bell, Brenda. DAVIDSON-WILDER 1932: STRIKES IN THE COAL CAMP. *Southern Exposure 1974 1(3/4): 113-136.* After World War I, the coal mining companies in eastern Tennessee whittled away the gains won by the United Mine Workers. When the miners struck the companies retaliated with yellow dog contracts, injunctions, National Guard troops, black lists, and deputized gunmen. Harrassment and violence were waged by both sides. The murder in 1933 of the local union president Barney Graham, along with the acquittal of his assailant, brought the turbulence to a climax. Leaderless, tired, and hungry, the miners went back to the mines without contracts. Based on oral interviews with participants and primary and secondary sources; 10 illus., 10 notes, biblio.                    G. A. Bolton

2887. Ansley, Fran and Bell, Brenda, eds. MINERS' INSURRECTIONS/CONVICT LABOR. *Southern Exposure 1974 1(3/4): 144-159.* Coal mining companies leased convicts from the state of Tennessee to replace miners and to break strikes. During 1891-93, miners waged strikes and armed resistance against the mining companies involved, especially Tennessee Coal Mining Company. Battles against the state militia, destruction of mining company equipment, and the freeing of convicts from the mines stemmed from the imposition of anti-union oaths required for employment. Eventually the state stopped leasing convicts to the highest bidder, purchasing its own mines and using convict labor. Based on oral interviews, primary and secondary sources; 11 illus., 10 notes, biblio.                    G. A. Bolton

2888. Armstrong, Dee A. and Coghill, W. W. THE OZARK-MAHONING COMPANY IN THE PERMIAN BASIN. *Permian Hist. Ann. 1980 20: 105-109.* Traces the history of the Ozark Chemical Company, predecessor of the Ozark-Mahoning Company,

during the period 1925-80, focusing on its search for sources of sodium sulfate and means of extracting it in the Permian Basin in Ward County, Texas.

2889. Arnold, Joseph L. THE NEIGHBORHOOD AND CITY HALL: THE ORIGIN OF NEIGHBORHOOD ASSOCIATIONS IN BALTIMORE, 1880-1911. *J. of Urban Hist. 1979 6(1): 3-30.* Baltimore has had a strong system of neighborhood association since the turn of the century. These organizations have persisted over time even in the face of changing neighborhoods and have played an important role in the organization of the city and policy formation and implementation. Baltimore's associations originally developed because of the distinctiveness and separateness of its neighborhoods. Having been long established these groups now show a notable ability to perpetuate themselves. 58 notes.

T. W. Smith

2890. Arnold, Joseph L. SUBURBAN GROWTH AND MUNICIPAL ANNEXATION IN BALTIMORE, 1745-1918. *Maryland Hist. Mag. 1978 73(2): 109-128.* Illustrates the rural-urban conflict as a central theme of American history by focusing on Baltimore City's annexations since the 18th century and the politics of intense belligerency which these generated in the surrounding counties for a century and a half. Baltimore County's political leaders were powerful in state politics and fought city fathers constantly seeking to expand the municipal tax base and political impact through population growth. Annexation proposals became central issues in statewide elections, and as late as 1968 during the debates on the new state constitution, Baltimore and Anne Arundel Counties helped defeat the new charter decisively by fighting its "regional government" features. Suburban sprawl today, however, has caused the "tool of annexation as a practical administrative device" to have been lost. Local archives, state legislative debates, secondary sources; 2 maps, 55 notes.                    G. J. Bobango

2891. Atack, Jeremy. RETURNS TO SCALE IN ANTEBELLUM UNITED STATES MANUFACTURING. *Explorations in Econ. Hist. 1977 14(4): 337-359.* Substantial scale economies existed in antebellum manufacturing. Larger plants in the South, West, and North secured advantages not open to smaller plants. There is no evidence that the South failed to take advantage of economies of scale or that the low demand in the South discouraged large-scale manufacturing. Based on published statistics and on secondary accounts; 3 fig., 4 tables, 11 notes, 32 ref.                    P. J. Coleman

2892. Bachtel, Douglas C. and Molnar, Joseph J. BLACK AND WHITE LEADER PERSPECTIVES ON RURAL INDUSTRIALIZATION. *Rural Sociol. 1980 45(4): 663-680.* Discusses different perspectives of black and white leaders toward the social and economic consequences of industrial growth in rural areas, based on a study in an eight-county area in Alabama of local, state, and federal officials and how they felt about the possible impact of the Tennessee-Tombigbee Waterway in particular and industrialization in general.

2893. Bahr, Betsy. THE ANTIETAM WOOLEN MANUFACTURING COMPANY: A CASE STUDY IN AMERICAN INDUSTRIAL BEGINNINGS. *Working Papers from the Regional Econ. Hist. Res. Center 1981 4(4): 27-46.* Traces the two year long operation of the Antietam Woolen Manufacturing Company in Funkstown, Maryland, from June 1814 to 1816 as an example of one of the numerous textile mills that formed to meet a higher demand for cloth during the Napoleonic Wars but was squeezed out of business shortly after because of English competition after the wars.

2894. Bailey, Kenneth R. A JUDICIOUS MIXTURE: NEGROES AND IMMIGRANTS IN THE WEST VIRGINIA MINES, 1880-1917. *West Virginia Hist. 1973 34(2): 141-161.* Ethnic and racial changes in West Virginia from the 1870's to the 1920's resulted from the expansion of the coal mining industry. Until 1890 few foreigners came to the mines, but by 1915 they constituted more than half of the work force. Recruitment by mining interests, with its accompanying abuses and efforts to check them, largely accounts for the influx. The introduction of Negroes, generally as an effort to check unionism, was only partly successful, as ties of common economic problems often overcame racial and ethnic differences. Based on newspapers; 81 notes.                                    C. A. Newton

2895. Bailey, Thomas E. STORM ON CUMBERLAND MOUNTAIN: THE STORY OF THE COWAN PUSHER DISTRICT. *Tennessee Hist. Q. 1975 34(3): 227-248.* In 1845 a group of Tennessee businessmen began planning a railroad between Nashville and Chattanooga over a bed surveyed by J. Edgar Thompson. Because the line faced the imposing obstacle of Cumberland Mountain between Cowan and Sherwood, a decision was made to drill through the mountain. Even so, the grade was so steep that it necessitated a pusher service for the long trains that negotiated the mountain, a practice which continues to this day. Primary and secondary sources; 4 illus., 2 maps, 12 notes.        M. B. Lucas

2896. Bails, Dale. TWO MUNICIPAL REVENUE SOURCES CONTRASTED. *Am. J. of Econ. and Sociol. 1974 33(2): 187-199.* Contrasts the land value tax and the property tax with respect to their effects on land use and urban sprawl and their administrative feasibility. Three case studies are reviewed: Pittsburgh, Pennsylvania; Fairhope, Alabama; and Southfield, Michigan. Secondary sources; 33 notes.                                  W. L. Marr

2897. Baldwin, John T., Jr. "THREE APPLES FOR A DIME," AND OTHER RECOLLECTIONS OF THE EARLY DAYS OF BERNICE. *North Louisiana Hist. Assoc. J. 1973 4(2): 65-68.* In 1899, C. C. Henderson, "in the process of building a railroad south from El Dorado, Arkansas," bought 300 acres of land from Allan Lowery and Dave Cole, and started the town of Bernice. The railroad operated as the Arkansas Southern and was finally sold to the Rock Island Railroad. Before the railroad, "there was nothing but forest, virgin timber," and the area was called the "big woods." Later, a sawmill and logging camps were established, branch lines constructed, and churches, a bank, a hotel, a school, and a post office were built. Photo, 5 notes.             A. N. Garland

2898. Banks, Alan J. LAND AND CAPITAL IN EASTERN KENTUCKY, 1890-1915. *Appalachian J. 1980 8(1): 8-18.* Discusses the investment of large amounts of capital by American business giants in the Southern states after the Civil War, focusing on the economic boom that occurred from 1890 to 1915 due to investments in coal, iron, timber, and fireclay industries in eastern Kentucky, which exploited the noncapitalistic small farmers and artisans and changed the class structure.

2899. Banks, William N. DANIEL PRATT, TRANSPLANTED YANKEE. *Hist. New Hampshire 1974 29(3): 133-150.* A native of Temple, New Hampshire, Daniel Pratt (1799-1873), spent most of his adult life in Alabama. After establishing himself as a builder and architect, Pratt began manufacturing cotton gins. The success of his diverse industrial endeavors in Alabama enabled him to patronize the arts, and led the *Dictionary of American Biography* to call him "the first great manufacturer of Alabama." 9 illus., 20 notes.                                            D. F. Chard

2900. Barr, Debbie. THE VILLAGE OF VERNON: TODAY AND YESTERDAY. *North Louisiana Hist. Assoc. J. 1978 9(2): 79-84.* Vernon, in Jackson Parish, Louisiana, was organized in 1846, with no corporate borders. Traces the history of its origins, rise, and decline. The town at one time was the county seat. Discusses developments in agriculture, religion, politics, education, recreation, and transportation. Secondary sources; 24 notes.
                                                   H. M. Parker, Jr.

2901. Bateman, Fred and Weiss, Thomas. MANUFACTURING IN THE ANTEBELLUM SOUTH. *Res. in Econ. Hist. 1976 1: 1-44.* The South was backward only in comparison with the northeastern states, not in comparison with the world as a whole. Lists and analyzes the prevailing theories which attempt to explain the lag, finding none of them adequate. The problem remains unsolved, but considerable evidence is offered to suggest that the attitudes of southern investors lie at the heart of the problem. 15 tables, 22 notes, ref.                               V. L. Human

2902. Bateman, Fred and Weiss, Thomas. MARKET STRUCTURE BEFORE THE AGE OF BIG BUSINESS: CONCENTRATION AND PROFIT IN EARLY SOUTHERN MANUFACTURING. *Business Hist. R. 1975 49(3): 312-336.* Concludes that pure competitive conditions did not exist in pre-Civil War America but that, instead, "imperfectly competitive markets, producer concentration, and the power to control price by individual sellers clearly were possible theoretically" prior to the rise of big business in the United States. Statistics indicate that the average degree of concentration in Southern industry was already high by 1860. Based primarily on US Census of Manufacturing records; 4 tables, 19 notes, 4 appendixes.                  C. J. Pusateri

2903. Bateman, Fred; Foust, James; and Weiss, Thomas. PROFITABILITY IN SOUTHERN MANUFACTURING: ESTIMATES FOR 1860. *Explorations in Econ. Hist. 1975 12(3): 211-231.* Summarizes the explanations previously offered for the low level of industrial investment and previous estimates of profitability. On the basis of a sample of about 200 firms in each of 10 states, shows that manufacturers generally earned a high rate of return, ranging from a mean low of 23 percent annually in South Carolina to a mean high of 45 percent annually in Tennessee. The regional annual mean was 31 percent, a much higher rate of return than was received from investments in slaves or slave-based operations. Analyzes the possible reasons for this disequilibrium. Based on manuscript census returns, published census reports, and secondary accounts.                                    P. J. Coleman

2904. Beirne, D. Randall. HAMPDEN-WOODBERRY: THE MILL VILLAGE IN AN URBAN SETTING. *Maryland Hist. Mag. 1982 77(1): 6-26.* Despite physical, economic, and social changes in other Baltimore communities over the last 100 years, Hampden-Woodberry, in the valley of the Jones Falls just north of the old city line, still exudes much of the atmosphere of the 19th-century mill village. Geographical and social isolation have preserved the homogeneity and identity of the area, which was once the dominant cotton duck sailcloth producer in America. Reviews the growth, paternalistic mill system, and major industrial leaders of this unique mill town, with its strong family and factory-town orientation. Its political influence has declined dramatically since the turn of the century when it exerted considerable control on Baltimore political life. US Census data, oral interviews, Maryland Annual Statistical Reports.                               G. J. Bobango

2905. Beirne, D. Randall. LATE NINETEENTH CENTURY INDUSTRIAL COMMUNITIES IN BALTIMORE. *Maryland Hist. 1980 11(1): 38-47.* Describes the process of eight Baltimore industrial villages becoming nuclei for present urban communities. These communities succeeded or failed in remaining stable portions of Baltimore depending upon the concomitant success or failure of the industries which bred these satellite industrial villages. Map, 46 notes.                                         G. O. Gagnon

2906. Beirne, D. Randall. RESIDENTIAL GROWTH AND STABILITY IN THE BALTIMORE INDUSTRIAL COMMUNITY OF CANTON DURING THE LATE NINETEENTH CENTURY. *Maryland Hist. Mag. 1979 74(1): 39-51.* Movement, not residential persistence, describes the United States at the end of the 19th century, but Baltimore's industrial settlement of Canton demonstrated extraordinarily high persistence during 1880-1930. Compared to a decennial population turnover of 40-60% for most of the country, Canton showed a 75% persistence rate. This is attributed to the protective umbrella of the Canton Company, which practiced old fashioned welfare work and paternalism among its largely immigrant workers, and heavily financed and built local company housing. Available evidence also suggests ethnic specialization of occupations, and "the merging of a number of ethnic neighborhoods into a solid social community" by the company's policies, which contrasts with the ethnic segregation of other industrial towns. Map, 2 tables, 59 notes.                     G. J. Bobango

2907. Bellamy, Jan. TWO UTILITIES ARE BETTER THAN ONE. *Reason 1981 13(6): 23-30.* Outlines benefits for consumers in Lubbock, Texas, from having two sources of electric power from which to choose—the city-owned Lubbock Power and Light Company and the investor-owned Southwestern Public Service Company compete for business on the basis of the service they are able to offer their customers with the result that prices are held down and quality of service is raised.

2908. Berry, Mrs. John. CLYDE'S YESTERDAYS. *West Texas Hist. Assoc. Year Book 1978 54: 82-91.* Discusses the informal history of Clyde, an agricultural-pastoral community in Callahan County, Texas, from its beginnings in 1880 to the present.

2909. Bixby, Arthur M., Sr. NORFOLK AND WESTERN'S RO-ANOKE SHOPS AND ITS LOCOMOTIVES. *Railroad Hist. 1977 (137): 20-37.* Discusses the Roanoke Machine Works during 1881-1976, in Roanoke, Virginia, which later became the Roanoke and Western's machine shop, a major center for the repair and production of railroad equipment.

2910. Bjornseth, Dick. HOUSTON DEFIES THE PLANNERS ... AND THRIVES. *Reason 1978 9(10): 16-22.* Economic stability, lower costs, aesthetics, individual incentives, and cost breaks for small businessmen all have resulted from Houston's lack of zoning ordinances, 1962-77.

2911. Blosser, Susan Sokol. CALVIN J. COWLES'S GAP CREEK MINE: A CASE STUDY OF MINE SPECULATION IN THE GILDED AGE. *North Carolina Hist. R. 1974 51(4): 379-400.* Studies the North Carolina mining operations of Calvin J. Cowles (1821-1907). Cowles owned property which assayed well for copper production, but lacked funds to develop it until he met William C. Brandreth of New York with whom he formed a mining company. Little mining was actually done. Brandreth was financially shaky and the regular stock market manipulations and company name changes infuriated Cowles, who never received a return from his mine. 2 maps, 7 photos, 110 notes.          V. L. Human

2912. Board, Prudy Taylor. EDISON PARK: LIVING AND LEARNING IN FORT MYERS. *Tampa Bay Hist. 1981 3(2): 30-39.* Edison Park officially opened as a subdivision in 1926 as a development of James D. Newton; the developer and his exclusive residential community are still very active in this Florida coastal community.

2913. Bolding, Gary. CHANGE, CONTINUITY AND COMMERCIAL IDENTITY OF A SOUTHERN CITY: NEW ORLEANS, 1850-1950. *Louisiana Studies 1975 14(2): 161-178.* Notes that people in New Orleans developed a strong veneration for the Mississippi River, and that in the antebellum period this sentiment was largely responsible for the city's failure to adapt to technological change. By the latter 19th century New Orleans had lost its favored trade position, and its citizens began to search for a new commercial identity. Businessmen emphasized technological change while also advertising the city as the focus of world trade. The 20th century witnessed a further effort to stress both commercial and industrial activities and in the process the residents lost contact with the river that earlier made them so prominent. By the 1950's, however, the Mississippi River once more played a prominent role in the rhetoric and commercial mind of the business community which promoted New Orleans as an international city, transport center, and industrial port. Primary and secondary sources; 51 notes.
B. A. Glasrud

2914. Brannan, Beverly W. DISCOVERING THEODOR HORY-DCZAK'S WASHINGTON. *Q. J. of the Lib. of Congress 1979 36(1): 38-67.* Little is known of Theodor Horydczak's private life, except that he was probably an Eastern European immigrant who served in the Signal Corps and was employed by the Army in Washington, D.C., before becoming a commercial photographer there. His photographs of technological developments, of mechanization and streamlining in consumer products, of the architecture of private, commercial, and federal buildings, and of suburban growth and everyday life in the nation's capital provide a record of changes during the 1920's, 1930's, and 1940's. His collection of prints and negatives, both black-and-white and color, was given to

the Library of Congress in 1973. Based on the Theodor Horydczak collection in the Prints and Photographs Division of the Library of Congress; 34 photos, 13 notes.          A. R. Souby

2915. Branscome, James. THE TVA: IT AIN'T WHAT IT USED TO BE. *Am. Heritage 1977 28(2): 68-78.* Sketches the history of the Tennessee Valley Authority (TVA) from 1824, when John Calhoun first proposed it, to the present. Development of nitrate production facilities at Muscle Shoals, Alabama began in 1917. Attempts to dispose of this facility led to efforts by Senator George Norris and others to create the TVA in order to conserve natural resources and provide electric power. Success came in 1933, but the agency has been beset by critics ever since. Major contributions to the war effort in World War II helped silence many of them. Now critics question the agency's atomic plans, coal usage, and other aspects while the agency continues to serve a seven-state area in the South. 10 illus.          J. F. Paul

2916. Brophy, William J. BLACK BUSINESS DEVELOPMENT IN TEXAS CITIES, 1900-1950. *Red River Valley Hist. Rev. 1981 6(2): 42-55.*

2917. Brown, A. E. THE LOUISIANA & ARKANSAS RAILWAY: STRUCTURE AND OPERATION IN THE AGE OF STEAM. *Railroad Hist. 1981 (144): 51-59.* Provides a history of the Louisiana & Arkansas Railway, one of the last major railroads formed in the United States, noting its chartering in 1898 near Springhill, Louisiana, and its assimiliation of the Louisiana Railway & Navigation Co. in 1929.

2918. Brown, D. Clayton. NORTH CAROLINA RURAL ELECTRIFICATION: PRECEDENT OF THE REA. *North Carolina Hist. Rev. 1982 59(2): 109-124.* During 1917-36, the North Carolina state government promoted rural electrification for agricultural residents. Among the leaders of this movement were Eugene C. Branson, professor of Rural Social Economics at the University of North Carolina, and Clarence H. Poe, editor of the popular journal, the *Progressive Farmer*. As the first state to attempt to initiate its own program, North Carolina set a precedent for, and effectively prodded the Roosevelt administration into, establishing the Rural Electrification Administration in 1935. Also, Branson's efforts publicized the necessity of electrification for modern farm life and politicized the issue. Based on REA documents, governors' and presidents' papers, and personal papers in the National and North Carolina State archives, newpapers and farm journal articles, and published government documents; 3 illus., 7 photos, 38 notes.
T. L. Savitt

2919. Brown, Martha Frances. [DALTON—CARPET CAPITAL OF THE WORLD—AND THE WOMAN WHO STARTED IT ALL]. *Georgia Life 1977 4(3): 11-15.*
DALTON: CARPET CAPITAL OF THE WORLD, *pp. 11-12.*
MEET THE LADY WHO STARTED DALTON'S CARPET INDUSTRY, *pp. 14-15.*
In 1895, Catherine Evans, young Dalton resident, designed an original bedspread using tufts; this method eventually spread into the carpet industry, and by 1974 90 percent of the world's carpets were tufted rather than woven, making industrial Dalton now a name synonymous with carpeting.

2920. Browne, Gary L. CULTURAL CONSERVATISM AND THE INDUSTRIAL REVOLUTION: THE CASE OF BALTIMORE, 1776-1860. *Continuity 1981 (2): 19-41.* Between 1776 and 1860, Baltimore changed from the relatively tranquil, clannish, and aristocratic social economy typical of the 18th century to a vibrant, open, democratic and mobile 19th-century social economy in which each citizen had a part in a structured social order. The cultural changes that took place over these four generations demonstrates the limitations and definitions of the economic changes that took place coterminously.          W. A. Wiegand

2921. Browne, Gary L. THE EVOLUTION OF BALTIMORE'S MARKETING CONTROLS OVER AGRICULTURE. *Maryland Hist. 1980 11(1): 1-11.* Analyzes the nexus created by Baltimore's growth as an entrepôt with the urban need for regulatory institutions over the agricultural sector in Baltimore's hinterlands. The city's increasing institutional rigidity created a "boom or bust" pattern, which endured throughout the 19th century, for the powerless agricultural sector. 21 notes. G. O. Gagnon

2922. Brownell, Blaine. URBAN THEMES IN THE AMERICAN SOUTH. *J. of Urban Hist. 1976 2(2): 139-145.* The journal's southern cities have been the orphans of American urban history. This neglect leads to an unbalanced view of the urban history and metropolitan growth of the United States by picturing the northeastern experience as typical of the nation. 7 notes. T. W. Smith

2923. Brownell, Blaine A. THE COMMERCIAL-CIVIC ELITE AND CITY PLANNING IN ATLANTA, MEMPHIS, AND NEW ORLEANS IN THE 1920'S. *J. of Southern Hist. 1975 41(3): 339-368.* An analysis of the origins and development of modern urban planning as exemplified by three southern cities. The general trend was everywhere similar; a nationwide passion for planning had developed. Business and commercial interests were the prime movers. They wanted to create cities which were firstly efficient and secondarily beautiful. The movement declined by 1930, primarily because of the great depression but also because of disillusionment. The problems were enormous; time, facilities, and financing were limited. 54 notes. V. L. Human

2924. Buker, George E. TAMPA'S MUNICIPAL WHARVES. *Tampa Bay Hist. 1983 5(2): 37-46.* The Army Corps of Engineers had dredged shipping channels to Tampa, Florida, since 1888, but these served only private wharves; new dredging and policies finally made public wharves possible in 1928.

2925. Burns, Anna C. FRANK B. WILLIAMS, CYPRESS LUMBER KING. *J. of Forest Hist. 1980 24(3): 127-133.* Frank B. Williams (1849-1929) entered the cypress lumber business in southern Louisiana in the 1870's. He obtained vast swamplands acreage, embraced modern logging and sawmilling technology, developed new markets for cypress lumber, and became the leading manufacturer. Within his own lifetime, however, the industrial cycle of cypress came nearly to an end as the swamp forests were practically exhausted. Based on company and family records and secondary sources; 6 illus., 27 notes. R. J. Fahl

2926. Burns, Anna C. THE GULF LUMBER COMPANY, FULLERTON: A VIEW OF LUMBERING DURING LOUISIANA'S GOLDEN ERA. *Louisiana Hist. 1979 20(2): 197-207.* Samuel Holmes Fullerton (1852-1939), an Irish immigrant and entrepreneur, developed the Gulf Lumber Co. on some 106,000 acres of exceptionally productive virgin timberland near Leesville, Louisiana. The company town of Fullerton grew to a population of about 5,000 during the huge mill's peak years, 1917-22. As in other mill towns, the company owned everything; unlike the others, however, Gulf Lumber demonstrated keen interest in its employees' welfare—offering numerous fringe benefits and fair prices at the company store. Once the timber was harvested, the town disappeared and the land was sold. Partially based on contemporary newspapers and journals; 51 notes. D. B. Touchstone

2927. Carlson, Paul. THE DISCOVERY OF SILVER IN WEST TEXAS. *West Texas Hist. Assoc. Year Book 1978 54: 55-64.* Discusses silver mining in West Texas from its discovery in 1880 by John W. Spencer, the subsequent control by large interests, and the end of production in 1942, concluding that the pattern of mining involved was typical in the West.

2928. Carlson, Paul. WILLIAM L. BLACK AND THE BEGINNING OF THE WEST TEXAS ANGORA GOAT INDUSTRY. *West Texas Hist. Assoc. Year Book 1980 56: 3-13.* Discusses William Leslie Black's contributions, beginning in the 1880's.

2929. Caudill, Harry M. THE STRANGE CAREER OF JOHN C. C. MAYO. *Filson Club Hist. Q. 1982 56(3): 258-289.* John Caldwell Calhoun Mayo was born and reared on a small country farm in Appalachia and died the richest man in Kentucky. He achieved this transformation by being the first person to recognize the commercial possibilities of the vast coal reserves of southeastern Ken-

tucky. Mayo developed the broadform deed that allowed him and his partners to purchase mineral rights to large tracts of poor mountain farm land at greatly reduced prices. Joining with West Virginia Senator Clarence Wayland Watson, Virginia Congressman Campbell Bascom Slemp, and industrialists John Davison Rockefeller and John Newlon Camden, Mayo became a political and financial power in three states. He was able to maintain his empire by convincing the Kentucky Supreme Court to uphold a law liquidating Virginia Revolutionary War land claims in the coal mining counties of Kentucky. Based on contemporary newspapers and unpublished studies. G. B. McKinney

2930. Cawley, Peter. FORT WORTH RIDES AGAIN. *Hist. Preservation 1980 32(1): 10-16.* From the 1870's through World War II, Fort Worth was a bustling cow town. Responding to its subsequent decline, those interested in revitalizing the inner city initiated the Fort Worth Stockyard Area Redevelopment Project. A commercial success, the Project has not ameliorated unemployment. Critics such as ethnic groups argue that public money would be better used for industrial development or job training, but others insist that preserving and promoting the community's historical character is a necessary first step toward long-range, all-encompassing urban renewal. 8 photos.

2931. Chatham, Howard G. THE ORIGIN AND DEVELOPMENT OF CHATHAM, JACKSON PARISH. *North Louisiana Hist. Assoc. J. 1983 14(2-3): 120-129.* Jackson Parish was formed in 1845, but the town of Chatham was not surveyed and staked out until 1905. Officially named Chatham in 1908, and incorporated as a village in 1909, Chatham lost a contested election in 1911 to determine the site of the parish government. It became a town in 1938 and has continued to grow to its present population of about 850. Illus., 26 notes. J. F. Paul

2932. Chesnutt, E. F. LITTLE ROCK GETS ELECTRIC LIGHTS. *Arkansas Hist. Q. 1983 42(3): 239-253.* Discusses companies that provided electric power to Little Rock, Arkansas. Based on newspapers, city directories, and other primary sources; map, 47 notes. G. R. Schroeder

2933. Chrysler, Elizabeth. ALLENDALE: ROOT OF THE NORTHWEST LOUISIANA DAIRY INDUSTRY. *North Louisiana Hist. Assoc. J. 1979 10(3): 98-102.* The dairy industry in northwest Louisiana began at the Allendale Plantation in De Soto Parish in 1886. The buildings are representative of early Louisiana plantations; the home was begun in the 1850's. Secondary sources; 4 illus., 2 notes. J. F. Paul

2934. Clark, Blue. THE BEGINNING OF OIL AND GAS CONSERVATION IN OKLAHOMA, 1907-1931. *Chronicles of Oklahoma 1977-78 55(4): 375-391.* Traces the gradual development of Oklahoma's oil and gas conservation policies which other petroleum states later copied. At first the enforcement was lax due to small investigatory staffs and laws filled with loopholes, but by the 1920's the Oklahoma Corporation Commission was able to enforce stricter regulations. A decreasing demand for petroleum during the Depression helped cut production and eliminate some waste. Based on government reports and newspapers; 3 photos, map, 45 notes. M. L. Tate

2935. Cochran, Thomas C. EARLY INDUSTRIALIZATION IN THE DELAWARE AND SUSQUEHANNA RIVER AREAS: A REGIONAL ANALYSIS. *Social Sci. Hist. 1977 1(3): 283-306.* Geography and demography are two basic elements in the industrialization of any region. A unique combination of events influenced by these two elements made the Delaware, Upper Chesapeake, Susquehanna River region "the principal American area of the coal and iron stage of industrialization." Banks, wheat production, water routes, topography, immigration, war, state corporation laws, and politics were some of the factors involved in the early industrialization of this region during 1700-1865. Based on secondary sources; 26 notes. T. L. Savitt

2936. Coerver, Don M. and Hall, Linda B. NEIMAN-MARCUS: INNOVATORS IN FASHION AND MERCHANDISING. *Am. Jewish Hist. Q. 1976 66(1): 123-136.* As innovative merchants and merchandizers Neiman-Marcus of Dallas, Texas, revolutionized the Southwestern approach to fashion. Relates the story of the store, its founders, and its progress until the present. 44 notes.
F. Rosenthal

2937. Coffin, Tom. BUSTED BY LAW: ORGANIZING IN THE CONSTRUCTION INDUSTRY. *Southern Exposure 1980 8(1): 26-34.* A first-person account of an engineering technician in the construction industry who attempted to organize for the International Union of Operating Engineers, Local 926, at a branch of the Law Engineering Testing Company, Inc., in Atlanta, Georgia. He did not enter the company to become a labor organizer, but after a year he saw the union shop as the only viable way to upgrade wages and the classification of laborers. He was fired in 1978 because of his attempts to form a union. His appeal to the National Labor Relations Board (NLRB) was denied, he claimed, on the basis of a false, backdated company memo. 9 photos.
H. M. Parker, Jr.

2938. Cohn, Raymond L. LOCAL MANUFACTURING IN THE ANTEBELLUM SOUTH AND MIDWEST. *Business Hist. Rev. 1980 54(1): 80-91.* Antebellum manufacturing firms in the Midwest and the South are classified as either consumer-oriented or export-oriented. The author finds that manufacturing in both sections was about evenly divided between the two classifications. The findings contradict the earlier arguments of Douglass North that Midwestern production tended to be located near the resources utilized and highly export-oriented, thus contributing to the overall economic development of the region, and that in the South consumer-oriented firms failed to develop. Utilizes principally the 1860 census data; 4 tables, 25 notes, appendix.
C. J. Pusateri

2939. Corbett, William P. RESOURCES FOR MODERN HIGHWAY DEVELOPMENT: OKLAHOMA AS A CASE STUDY. *Government Publ. Rev.: An Int. J. of Issues and Information Resources 1981 8A(6): 473-483.* Traces the creation of highways in Oklahoma from 1824 to 1981, particularly on the local and state levels in conjunction with federal policy; notes pertinent archival collections and government publications.

2940. Crocker, Les. AN EARLY IRON FOUNDRY IN NORTHERN MISSISSIPPI. *J. of Mississippi Hist. 1973 35(2): 113-126.* "From its probable beginning sometime before 1845 until its destruction in 1862, the Holly Springs Iron Works existed as a singularly unique industry in an agricultural area." It was the South's largest casting foundry and fourth largest iron works. The works manufactured household hardware, producing the ornaments for the architecture of the antebellum South, and repaired small arms during the Civil War. Based on primary sources; 44 notes.
J. W. Hillje

2941. Croker, Thomas C., Jr. THE LONGLEAF PINE STORY. *J. of Forest Hist. 1979 23(1): 32-43.* Longleaf pine forests stretching from Virginia to Texas have been an integral part of southern history. The magnificent virgin forest gave sustenance to Indians, to pioneer settlers, and later to commercial turpentiners and lumbermen. Logs were removed by river rafting, animal power, railroad, and finally by truck to serve lucrative domestic and foreign markets for lumber. Decades of overcutting, however, merged with the Great Depression to add economic hardship and misery to the longleaf region (principally the coastal plains). The Civilian Conservation Corps, working in concert with Forest Service managers and researchers, restored some hope through reforestation and curbing promiscuous woods burning. A body of silvicultural knowledge gradually arose to assist nature's regeneration of longleaf and to challenge the industrial pulpwood farmers who sought to grow "easier" species. Sensitivity to the historic and economic values of longleaf pine eventually will result in restoration of this noble forest tree. Based on secondary sources and a career of research; 12 illus., map, biblio., note.
R. J. Fahl

2942. Curry, Leonard P. URBANIZATION AND URBANISM IN THE OLD SOUTH: A COMPARATIVE VIEW. *J. of Southern Hist. 1974 40(1): 43-60.* Challenges "the myth of the plantation (or, at least, rural) Old South," seeking "a quantitative and qualitative comparison of southern and nonsouthern" urbanization during 1800-50 to determine whether the southern urban experience differed from that of the rest of the country. In addition to analyzing urban population data, compares the public services of northern and southern cities such as fire and police protection, garbage disposal, public health inspection, and consumer protection. Develops a Comparative Urban Rate of Increase index which suggests that "urban development in the Old South was neither massively different nor consistently inferior to that in the rest of the United States." Based on published primary and secondary sources; 2 figs., 26 notes.
T. D. Schoonover

2943. Curtis, Michael. EARLY DEVELOPMENT AND OPERATIONS OF THE GREAT SOUTHERN LUMBER COMPANY. *Louisiana Hist. 1973 14(4): 347-368.* Covers the Great Southern Lumber Company in Washington Parish out of Bogalusa, Louisiana, 1871-1955.

2944. Dayton, William. PASCO PIONEERS: CATHOLIC SETTLEMENTS IN SAN ANTONIO, ST. LEO AND VICINITY. *Tampa Bay Hist. 1979 1(2): 32-39.* Discusses the history, cultural diversity, and development of the towns of rural, isolated Pasco County, 1881-1960's.

2945. Derrick, W. Edwin and Smallwood, James. MILES OF TRACK: THE COMING OF RAILROADS TO OKLAHOMA. *Red River Valley Hist. Rev. 1981 6(3): 87-93.* Covers most of the important rail developments in the state and the hardships of building such roads; by the time of statehood in 1907, the network of railroads in Oklahoma was virtually complete.

2946. Dew, Lee A. THE TENNESSEE SUGAR RATE CASES. *Tennessee Hist. Q. 1982 41(2): 171-182.* The importation of sugar into Tennessee led to intense wholesale competition from region transportation centers for surrounding markets. In 1895 Nashville merchants filed suit to lower their railroad freight rate disadvantage to Louisville, Kentucky, competitors. This began a series of sugar rate cases before the Interstate Commerce Commission that ended with smaller cities with no river transport winning rough equality with their geographically more blessed neighbors. Rate discrimination affected the South not only regionally but also internally as small cities suffered at the expense of larger transportation centers and basing-point towns. Based on I.C.C. records and other sources; 34 notes.
W. D. Piersen

2947. Dobkin, J. B. TRAILS TO TAMPA BAY: A PHOTO ESSAY. *Tampa Bay Hist. 1979 1(1): 24-30.* Brief survey of tourism in Florida's Tampa Bay area; highlights steam transportation, overland travel, and railroad connections, 1876-1922, and includes 15 photos.

2948. Dobson, Jeffrey R. and Doyon, Roy. EXPANSION OF THE PINE OLEORESIN INDUSTRY IN GEORGIA: 1842 TO CA. 1900. *West Georgia Coll. Studies in the Social Sci. 1979 18: 43-57.* Discusses the pine oleoresin industry in Georgia, analyzing its economic and cultural significance, the extent of its exploitation, and the primary factors determining location.

2949. Doherty, Herbert J., Jr. JACKSONVILLE AS A NINETEENTH-CENTURY RAILROAD CENTER. *Florida Hist. Q. 1980 58(4): 373-386.* Jacksonville gained significance as business and commercial interests realized the importance of rail transportation. One crucial improvement was the standardization of track. The city built Jacksonville Terminal in 1919 only to witness a decline in railroads during the 1930's and after. Based on Florida newspapers and secondary sources; 5 illus., 34 notes.
N. A. Kuntz

2950. Doyle, Don H. THE URBANIZATION OF DIXIE. *J. of Urban Hist. 1980 7(1): 83-91.* This review essay covers Claudia Dale Goldin's *Urban Slavery in the American South,* Howard N. Rabinowitz's *Race Relations in the Urban South, 1865-1980,* Eugene J. Watts's *The Social Bases of City Politics*, Carl V. Harris's *Political Power in Birmingham, 1871-1921*, David R. Goldfield's *Urban Growth in the Age of Sectionalism*, and Blaine A. Brownell's *The Urban Ethos in the South, 1920-1930*. Urban research on the South is applauded not only as adding light to a neglected area of both southern and urban history but also because the central themes of southern history are more highly defined in the cities. 4 notes.                                                T. W. Smith

2951. Druzhinina, E. I. VOZNIKNOVENIE GORODOV NA IUGE UKRAINY I V SSHA: OBSHCHEE I OSOBENNOE [The emergence of towns in the south of the Ukraine and in the South of the United States: common and specific features]. *Novaia i Noveishaia Istoriia [USSR] 1976 (2): 69-76*. The emergence of towns in the south of the Ukraine had much in common with the rise of towns in the South, due to similar economic and social conditions. The author also notes substantial differences. The Russian government was interested in the speedy settlement and economic development of the strategic frontier area and encouraged the agricultural, commercial, and industrial development of southern provinces.                                                              J/S

2952. Earle, Carville and Hoffman, Ronald. URBAN DEVELOPMENT IN THE EIGHTEENTH CENTURY SOUTH. *Perspectives in Am. Hist. 1976 10: 7-78*. A close correlation exists between the development of major agricultural products and the development of urban systems in the South during the 18th century. Although the three major export crops, wheat, rice, and tobacco, had expanding markets throughout the century, they traveled through coastal cities via different routes. Each required a different system of handling and packaging. Each fostered the growth of related industries and brought about the elimination of nonrelated industries. The effects of the relationship between agriculture and industry are reflected in the scattered, nonuniform patterns of Southern urbanization. These patterns laid the foundations and "predisposed production regions to divergent trajectories of [the South's] long run economic development." Table, 111 notes, appendix with 21 notes.

W. A. Wiegand

2953. Edmonson, James. OF FRUIT AND FOREST: THE BASKET INDUSTRY IN DELAWARE, 1840-1960. *Delaware Hist. 1978 18(1): 93-123*. The basket industry was once integral to Delaware's economy, largely derived from the state's peach industry. The presence of forests for wood, the demands of shippers for standardized containers, and improvements in the technology of basket-making transformed the industry by the 1870's. Low capital costs allowed many individuals to enter the industry and the basic structure did not change until full mechanization occurred in the 1920's. The decline in the availability of raw materials for the baskets, changes in Delaware's agriculture, mechanization and increased capitalization, and changes in agricultural markets led to the collapse of the industry by 1960.                          R. M. Miller

2954. Edson, William D. THE CLINCHFIELD RAILROAD: A BRIEF OPERATING HISTORY. *Railroad Hist. 1983 (148): 82-86*. Recounts the early history of the Clinchfield Railroad, which runs between Kentucky and South Carolina, from its beginnings as the Charleston, Cincinnati & Chicago Railroad in 1886 to its 1924 reorganization under its modern name.

2955. Edson, William D., comp. LOCOMOTIVES OF THE LOUISIANA & ARKANSAS AND COMPONENT LINES. *Railroad Hist. 1981 (144): 60-75*. Provides a roster and photographic record of locomotives owned by the Louisiana & Arkansas Railway from 1896 to 1929, and of the component lines of the Louisiana Railway & Navigation Co., the Louisiana Railway & Navigation Co. of Texas, and the Louisiana, and Arkansas & Texas.

2956. Edson, William D. STEAM LOCOMOTIVES OF THE CLINCHFIELD. *Railroad Hist. 1983 (148): 87-100*. Lists and presents photographs of steam locomotives operated by the Clinchfield Railroad during 1887-1954.

2957. Edward, C. ELI WHITNEY: EMBATTLED INVENTOR. *Am. Hist. Illus. 1974 8(10): 4-9; 44-47*. Notes several inventions of Eli Whitney, his problems as an inventor, and the industrial and social changes made possible by this founding father of American industry.

2958. Eisterhold, John A. CHARLESTON: LUMBER AND TRADE IN A DECLINING SOUTHERN PORT. *South Carolina Hist. Mag. 1973 74(2): 61-72*. Traces the exploitation of the timber resources of South Carolina and its relationship to the development of Charleston as an important southern port during the colonial period. Charleston became preeminent among southern ports in the coastal and international exportation of lumber. After the peak in 1850 decline set in. A decade later Charleston was well below its rivals. 67 notes.                                          D. L. Smith

2959. Eisterhold, John A. MOBILE: LUMBER CENTER OF THE GULF COAST. *Alabama R. 1973 26(2): 83-104*. Discusses the antebellum lumber industry and export market at Mobile. Large tracts of pine, cypress, and hardwoods in Alabama gave Mobile major importance by the 1820's, when steam sawmills were introduced along nearby rivers and streams. Production and exports rose steadily in the 1830's and 1840's; peak production came in 1854-55. Economic preferences for cotton, increased local and regional demand for lumber, and the mounting cost of shipping space later caused the export market to decline. The West Indies, France, and Spain were chief markets. Problems included a chronic shortage of skilled workers, racial tensions, and early attempts at unionization. Based on primary and secondary sources; 128 notes.

J. F. Vivian

2960. Eller, Ronald D. THE COAL BARONS OF THE APPALACHIAN SOUTH, 1880-1930. *Appalachian J. 1977 4(3/4): 195-207*. The remarkably homogeneous social group of coal barons in the Appalachian South began as isolated mine operators employing a small number of miners, and then, as the industry matured and expanded, were forced to accept, at least to some degree, their social responsibilities and to manage their labor force.

M. T. Wilson

2961. Ernst, Joseph A. Merrens, H. Roy. "CAMDEN'S TURRETS PIERCE THE SKIES!": THE URBAN PROCESS IN THE SOUTHERN COLONIES DURING THE EIGHTEENTH CENTURY. *William and Mary Q. 1973 30(4): 549-574*. Disputes the traditional theory that southern urban centers were not important. The significance of urban places is measured by contemporary criteria of number of dwellings, population, and function. Small urban centers in the South performed urban functions of exchange, collection, storage, and distribution of commodities. A case study is made of origins and rise of Camden, South Carolina, which is related to a general discussion of the urban process in North Carolina, Virginia, and Maryland. Southern towns and cities formed a hierarchical arrangement and an urban system that fitted into a regional economy. Based on contemporary travel literature, original documents, and monographs; 55 notes.            H. M. Ward

2962. Fall, Ralph E. MR. J. WOOLFOLK'S STAGECOACH LINE, CAROLINE COUNTY, VIRGINIA. *Virginia Cavalcade 1977 27(1): 20-29*. Discusses the stagecoach line originated in Caroline County, Virginia, in 1742, by an Englishman, Head Lynch, and taken over by John George Woolfolk in 1787; the line operated until 1846 when it collapsed from inability to compete with railroads.

2963. Feller, Irwin. THE DIFFUSION AND LOCATION OF TECHNOLOGICAL CHANGE IN THE AMERICAN COTTON-TEXTILE INDUSTRY, 1890-1970. *Technology and Culture 1974 15(4): 569-593*. New England cotton-textile manufacturers lost the competitive struggle with new plants opening in the South, not because they failed to invest in innovations like the Draper automatic loom, but because of labor costs and other disadvantages. By contrast, the textile-machine industry remained in the North until the 1950's, when enough skilled labor became available in the South. Based on secondary sources; 56 notes.         C. O. Smith

2964. Fickle, James E. THE S.P.A. AND THE N.R.A.: A CASE STUDY OF THE BLUE EAGLE IN THE SOUTH. *Southwestern Hist. Q. 1976 79(3): 253-278.* The Southern Pine Association, organized in 1914 to deal with industry problems, became the logical group to help formulate and oversee the NRA's lumber code in the 1930's. Although most small lumber mills remained outside the SPA, it set up an elaborate field structure to attempt enforcement of the Code. There were constant quarrels over production allotments, complaints of discrimination by the small non-SPA mills, and difficulties in maintaining wage, hour, and price levels. By the end of 1934 the Code had collapsed from lack of effective policing. Based on primary and secondary sources; 54 notes.
J. H. Broussard

2965. Finger, Bill. TEXTILE MEN: LOOMS, LOANS AND LOCKOUTS. *Southern Exposure 1976 3(4): 54-65.* Presents biographies of southern textile industry figures, 1918-40: J. Spencer Love, a mill owner, Lacy Wright, a mill hand, and Joe Pedigo, a labor organizer.

2966. Floyd, Fred. THE STRUGGLE FOR RAILROADS IN THE OKLAHOMA PANHANDLE. *Chronicles of Oklahoma 1976/ 77 54(4): 489-518.* Examines difficulties of residents of the Oklahoma panhandle area in attaining adequate railroad systems due to confusing territorial status and poor economic conditions, 1880's-1930's.

2967. Fugate, Robert. THE BANCOKENTUCKY STORY. *Filson Club Hist. Q. 1976 50(1): 29-46.* Unravels the complicated financial developments that led to the closing of the National Bank of Kentucky and the BancoKentucky Company in 1930. Both businesses were dominated by speculator James B. Brown of Louisville. As early as 1925 Federal officials warned the directors of the National Bank of Brown's unsafe policies. In an effort to buttress the weakened bank, Brown formed BancoKentucky Company in 1929 and gained control of several banks in the region. By 1930 a combination of speculative loans, the onset of the depression, and a disastrous merger with Caldwell and Company of Nashville, Tennessee, destroyed both the holding company and the bank. Documented from legal records and newspapers. 46 notes.
G. B. McKinney.

2968. Gage, Patricia Anthony. WINN PARISH IN RETROSPECT: A BRISK ROMP THROUGH LOCAL HISTORY. *North Louisiana Hist. Assoc. J. 1981 12(2-3): 99-103.* A brief history of Winn Parish, Louisiana, from the earliest Indian inhabitants, focusing on 1650-1950. The parish was established in 1852. Named after Walter O. Winn, later the first judge to hold court in the parish, the parish thrived. Winn Parish voted against secession in the Civil War, and after the war continued its growth, particularly during the first decade of the 20th century. 2 notes.        J. F. Paul

2969. Galphin, Bruce. ATLANTA: CITY OF TRADITION AND PROGRESS. *Americas 1974 26(3): 50-55.* Brief history of the city of Atlanta, Georgia.        S

2970. Garner, John S. THE SAGA OF A RAILROAD TOWN: CALVERT, TEXAS (1868-1918). *Southwestern Hist. Q. 1981 85(2): 139-160.* About 1850, Robert Calvert, a wealthy and ambitious planter, took the initiative to lure the Houston and Texas Central Railway into his area of the Brazos Valley. In 1868, the railroad reached Calvert's plantation and a townsite was named in his honor. Based on a monocultural cotton economy, Calvert languished as cotton prices fell during the late 19th century, and the town never became a thriving commercial or railroad center. Instead, it provides an excellent example of late 19th-century architecture and town design. Based on local records, federal and state publications, newspapers, and secondary sources; 9 photos, map, 37 notes.        R. D. Hurt

2971. Garofalo, Charles. THE ATLANTA SPIRIT: A STUDY IN URBAN IDEOLOGY. *South Atlantic Q. 1975 74(1): 34-44.* The Chamber of Commerce's monthly *The City Builder* (1916-35) published attempts of local boosters to define Atlanta's unique characteristics and to apply them to daily city life. Money, morality, idealism, and sanctification of the city became known collectively as "the Atlanta Spirit," which, it was felt, united all citizens in a religious fervor of boosterism. Local businessmen hoped to attract new industries and populations by these zealous appeals to civic pride, which included the black community. No effort was ever made, however, to assess realistically the impact of these efforts on the local populace. Based on primary and secondary sources; 27 notes.
W. L. Olbrich

2972. Garofalo, Charles. THE SONS OF HENRY GRADY: ATLANTA BOOSTERS IN THE 1920S. *J. of Southern Hist. 1976 42(2): 187-204.* The Atlanta Chamber of Commerce was deeply interested in the urbanization and industrialization of both Atlanta and Georgia. Henry Grady (1851-89) was their model, "the spirit of Atlanta," whom all southern businessmen sought to emulate in elevating the South. In an effort to attract northern capital and further industrialization, the Atlanta Chamber of Commerce boosted and published information about the labor force, particularly its skill, cleanliness, and docility, observing that the Blacks knew their place. They also became interested in agricultural growth, improvement in productivity, in the cultural and economic value of the state education system, and the talent of its businessmen. Based on primary and secondary sources; 55 notes.        T. D. Schoonover

2973. Gibb, Hugh R. MENDES COHEN: ENGINEER, SCHOLAR AND RAILROAD EXECUTIVE. *Maryland Hist. Mag. 1979 74(1): 1-10.* A testimonial to the life and career of Mendes Cohen (1831-1915) of Baltimore, whose engineering innovations were instrumental in the expansion of the early Baltimore & Ohio. As president of the Pittsburgh & Connellsville Railroad, he unsuccessfully fought the Pennsylvania Railroad for control of the Pittsburgh traffic in the 1870's. One of Baltimore's leading citizens, he served on commissions for everything from streetcar fenders to a sanitary sewage system, and was closely involved with the Maryland Historical Society—as secretary during 1882-1904 and as president during 1904-13. His home at 825 North Charles Street was a center of civic activity, philanthropy, and American railroad history. Primary sources; 27 notes.        G. J. Bobango

2974. Goldfarb, Stephen J. A NOTE ON LIMITS TO THE GROWTH OF THE COTTON-TEXTILE INDUSTRY IN THE OLD SOUTH. *J. of Southern Hist. 1982 48(4): 545-558.* Growth in the Southern textile industry was impeded by the separation of locations with suitable power from effective transportation connections to regional or national markets. Before the Civil War, those areas which did combine adequate power with good transportation connections to wider markets, such as Columbus and Augusta, Georgia; Richmond, Virginia; Fayetteville, North Carolina; and Florence, Alabama, did develop flourishing textile industry. Based on *Historical Statistics of the United States,* printed census reports, and various printed primary sources; 43 notes, 2 tables.
T. D. Schoonover

2975. Goldfield, David Reed. THE URBAN SOUTH: A REGIONAL FRAMEWORK. *Am. Hist. Rev. 1981 86(5): 1009-1034.* A regional analysis is an appropriate method for the study of Southern urbanization, in contrast to the more traditional procedure of viewing the city as a distinctive environment, dominating and different from the countryside. Three persistent regional characteristics have affected Southern urbanization since the colonial era: ruralism (including staple crop agriculture and rural cultural and religious values), biracialism, and colonialism (the economic subservience of the South to Northern capital and business services). Together, these factors produced an urban system predominated by small cities and towns carrying on marketing or basic industrial processing functions, with a chronically low investment in human capital. Southern cities, therefore, reflected regional human, cultural, and economic debilities into the sunbelt era of the 1970's. Based on social science literature on regionalism, secondary historical works, and the work of Southern novelists and propagandists; 84 notes.
A

2976. Grable, Stephen W. APPLYING URBAN HISTORY TO CITY PLANNING: A CASE STUDY IN ATLANTA. *Public Hist. 1979 1(4): 45-59.* Discusses the refusal of architects and urban planners to use historical methods in their urban problem-solving, and presents the case of Atlanta's deteriorating neighborhood, Bedford-Pine, which benefited by applying urban history to its revitalization efforts in the mid-1960's, tracing Atlanta's history from 1880 to 1970.

2977. Grant, H. Roger. "INTERURBANS ARE THE WAVE OF THE FUTURE": ELECTRIC RAILWAY PROMOTION IN TEXAS. *Southwestern Hist. Q. 1980 84(1): 29-48.* During the 1890's, electric railway developers promised to bring affordable, clean, convenient transportation to Texas. Although the boom period lasted from 1909 until a little beyond World War I, the failure rate was high. Of the 22,500 miles of electric railway planned for Texas, only 500 miles of track were laid. Many lines failed because the companies had been founded by individuals or groups who had little money or railway experience. By the 1930's, automobiles and trucks provided cheap, efficient interurban transportation. The result was the demise of the electric railway system. Mainly secondary sources; 19 photos, map, 22 notes.                                  R. D. Hurt

2978. Griggs, Walter E., Jr. THE CHURCH HILL TUNNEL. *Railroad Hist. 1976 (135): 43-58.* Recounts the history of construction of Richmond, South Carolina's Church Hill Tunnel, 1872-1926, which was originally built to provide cross-town service for town inhabitants, but proved too dangerous and after a series of three severe cave-ins (the last in 1925 buried an entire train) was sealed up and permanently put out of use. 2 maps, diagram, 2 photos, 73 notes.

2979. Guerard, Albert J. A VIEW FROM THE PERSIMMON TREE: HOUSTON 1924-72. *Southern Rev. 1974 10(2): 286-306.*

2980. Hadsell, Richard M. and Coffey, William E. FROM LAW AND ORDER TO CLASS WARFARE: BALDWIN-FELTS DETECTIVES IN THE SOUTHERN WEST VIRGINIA COAL FIELDS. *West Virginia Hist. 1979 40(3): 268-286.* William G. Baldwin and Thomas L. Felts formed Baldwin-Felts Detectives in the 1890's and for 30 years provided a private police and guard service for West Virginia coal mines. Their agents infiltrated unions, evicted undesirables, guarded nonstrikers, and kept order on mine property. Their antiunion activities became paramount and many were killed in gun battles or ambushes. By the 1930's they were outmoded and even illegal. Based on Justus Collins papers and other primary sources; 72 notes.                             J. H. Broussard

2981. Haites, Erik F. and Mak, James. THE DECLINE OF STEAMBOATING ON THE ANTE-BELLUM WESTERN RIVERS: SOME NEW EVIDENCE AND AN ALTERNATIVE HYPOTHESIS. *Explorations in Econ. Hist. 1973 11(1): 25-36.* Compares former estimates of construction and operating tonnage of steamboats with newly derived estimates for 1811-60. Argues that the generally accepted view that railroad expansion led to an absolute decline in steamboating is erroneous. Cites movements in general economic activity as the most important influence on western steamboat activity. Based on statistics and secondary sources; 3 tables, 25 notes, appendix.                             P. J. Coleman

2982. Hale, Duane K. GOLD IN OKLAHOMA: THE LAST GREAT GOLD EXCITEMENT IN THE TRANS-MISSISSIPPI WEST, 1889-1918. *Chronicles of Oklahoma 1981 59(3): 304-319.* Since the mid-1700's, Spanish miners had extracted gold from the Wichita Mountains of southwestern Oklahoma, but operations had ceased by the time of US acquisition of the region. Gold fever was reborn in 1889 when isolated gold and silver specimens were found at diverse points in and near the Wichita Mountains. Within a decade, several thousand miners had begun tunneling operations, and government geologists confirmed the area's potential for wealth. Unfortunately, none of the operations proved profitable because of wide dispersal of mineral deposits. Based on "State Mineral Survey" and newspapers; 4 photos, map, 85 notes.   M. L. Tate

2983. Hall, Bob. JOURNEY TO THE WHITE HOUSE: THE STORY OF *COCA-COLA*. *Southern Exposure 1977 5(1): 32-42.* Asa Griggs Candler, the Atlanta entrepreneur who originally capitalized on the development of the soft drink formula, originally stressed the therapeutic values of his drink in advertising. By the early 1900's, Candler realized that emphasizing Coca-Cola's alleged medicinal aspects limited the potential clientele of the beverage. He therefore switched to the appeal that Coke and pleasure were synonymous. Many times a millionaire, Candler turned over his holdings to his sons when he reached age 64. They, in turn, sold the enterprise to a group of bank and trust companies. The southern-dominated concern achieved new heights through the direction of Ernest Woodruff.                                      N. Lederer

2984. Hancock, Harold B. DELAWARE FURNITUREMAKING, 1850-1870: TRANSITION TO THE MACHINE AGE. *Delaware Hist. 1977 17(4): 250-294.* Describes the lives and products of Delaware furnituremakers in the 19th century. Furniture craftsmen suffered from inflation, an increase in the number of immigrant craftsmen, strikes, and the transition to machine production which gradually eroded the craftsmen's prominence. Wilmington remained the center of production in the state. Many workers worked in small shops even to 1870. Change was gradual, and the quality of craftsmanship did not decline dramatically, despite the changes in tastes to heavier Victorian pieces. Lists almost 350 cabinetmakers and 70 apprentices in Delaware in the mid-19th century. 4 illus., 18 notes.                                           R. M. Miller

2985. Handley, Lawrence R. SETTLEMENT ACROSS NORTHERN ARKANSAS AS INFLUENCED BY THE MISSOURI AND NORTH ARKANSAS RAILROAD. *Arkansas Hist. Q. 1974 33(4): 273-292.* The railroad shaped the pattern of settlement and economic growth of northern Arkansas towns between 1880 and the 1920's. 33 new settlements arose, five disappeared and several small towns and industries grew rapidly as the railroad passed along a 303-mile route between Seligman, Missouri, and Helena, Arkansas. Maps illustrate the alteration of village residence, road, and commercial growth patterns to take advantage of the railroad. Based on newspaper accounts, interviews and secondary sources; 7 maps, 62 notes.                                       T. L. Savitt

2986. Harrington, Drew. WILLIAM L. BURTON: CYPRESS MILLIONAIRE AND PHILANTHROPIST. *Louisiana Hist. 1983 24(2): 155-164.* Career of the cypress lumberman, who, alone or with various partners, developed lumber interests in the area of Vicksburg, Mississippi, in Louisiana, and in Florida, and engaged in real estate developments on the North Shore of Long Island. His philanthropic interests included a home for orphan boys, the Young Men's Christian Association, and various churches. Based on city and company records, newspapers, interviews; 43 notes.

R. E. Noble

2987. Harvey, Katherine A. BUILDING A FRONTIER IRON WORKS: PROBLEMS OF TRANSPORT AND SUPPLY, 1837-1840. *Maryland Hist. Mag. 1975 70(2): 149-166.* Discusses "the major logistical problems and . . . solutions" of the George's Creek Coal and Iron Company in building a sizable complex of blast furnaces, foundry, and rolling mill on land southwest of Cumberland, Maryland, at today's Lonaconing. Distance from manufacturing centers and labor supplies required the fullest possible use of materials from company lands. Technical problems of hauling stone, brickmaking for lime-kilns, building quarry railroads and tramways, and lifting blocks into place on the stack are reported from journals kept by superintendents. The first run-out of iron came in May 1839, by which time workers and their families brought the population to 700 in what had been "almost a wilderness." Miners were recruited from Pennsylvania and the scarcity of finished lumber for houses led to erecting a company sawmill, while housing materials were purchased from far and wide. The entire venture was predicated on access to eastern markets via the Chesapeake and Ohio Canal, but by June 1839 the canal was still 50 miles from Cumberland. The problems of transporting heavy goods to and from the region otherwise were insuperable, so the big furnace was blown out and the staff reduced. Only years later did the business resume; but in coal, not iron. Primary sources; 3 illus., 89 notes.

G. J. Bobango

2988. Harvey, Katherine A. WILLIAM ALEXANDER: A COMMISSION MERCHANT IN A NEW ROLE, 1837-43. *Maryland Hist. Mag. 1976 71(1): 26-36.* Surveys the activities of William Alexander, Baltimore commission merchant for the George's Creek Coal and Iron Company at Lonaconing. From his shop at Pratt and Light streets Alexander supplied the company store with clothing and dry goods, groceries, wines, and tobaccos, and his low prices enabled the store to make money. Seldom asking his principals for advice or recommendations, Alexander zealously promoted the company's interests along with his own, and his conscientious attention to packing, selecting wagoners, and acquiring scarce supplies, along with his willingness to do small favors for company personnel, made him invaluable and unique. Some evidence suggests he was preparing to be the marketer for the company's iron products, had it not fallen into hard times. Moreover, the advancing railroads eventually deprived the eastern factor of his position, as did the increasing numbers of traveling salesmen. Still, the contribution of the commission merchant to America's industrial development was considerable. Based on the author's *The Best-Dressed Miners* (Ithaca, 1969), and primary and secondary sources; 74 notes.                                                                G. J. Bobango

2989. Hawkes, Roland K. SPATIAL PATTERNING OF URBAN POPULATION CHARACTERISTICS. *Am. J. of Sociol. 1973 78(5): 1216-1235.* This paper develops a mathematical expression of the classic zone and sector phenomena in the distribution of residential neighborhood characteristics in urban areas. Problems of evaluation are discussed, and the use of the model is illustrated with the 1960 census tract statistics for Baltimore, Maryland.
                                                                                                          J

2990. Henderson, William D. "A GREAT DEAL OF ENTERPRISE": THE PETERSBURG COTTON MILLS IN THE NINETEENTH CENTURY. *Virginia Cavalcade 1981 30(4): 176-185.* Discusses the establishment of several cotton mills in Petersburg, Virginia, during 1826-39 and their subsequent effect on child labor practices and on industrial development in the region from the late 1800's until the end of World War II, when Petersburg's predominance in the textile industry came to an end.

2991. Henderson, William D. RAPIDS AND POWER: THE APPOMATTOX RIVER AND ELECTRICAL POWER IN PETERSBURG, VIRGINIA. *Virginia Cavalcade 1978 27(4): 148-163.* Evolution in electric power generation through use of the Appomattox River has delivered electrical power to Petersburg, Virginia, 1884-1978.

2992. Herndon, G. Melvin. FOREST PRODUCTS OF COLONIAL GEORGIA. *J. of Forest Hist. 1979 23(3): 130-135.* The economy of colonial Georgia was based on forest products as well as the better known agricultural staples of rice and indigo. From the colony's beginnings in the 1730's, various entrepreneurs experimented with forest industries, notably lumbering. After slavery was introduced (1749) and Georgia became a royal colony (1752), production increased rapidly as an adjunct to plantation agriculture. A lively export trade developed with Great Britain, the West Indies, southern Europe, and the other mainland colonies of America. Timber and naval stores contributed measurably to a more diversified economy on the eve of Revolution. 3 illus., table, 34 notes.
                                                                                                          R. J. Fahl

2993. Herndon, G. Melvin. TIMBER PRODUCTS OF COLONIAL GEORGIA. *Georgia Hist. Q. 1973 57(1): 56-62.* The lumber industry was one of the principal economic staples of colonial Georgia. The long-leafed pine was used for house construction; the white oak and red oak became hogshead and barrel staves and headings; and the cypress was valued for shingles. Most of Georgia's timber products were exported to the West Indies. 30 notes.
                                                                                                          D. L. Smith

2994. Hill, Carol A. and DePaepe, Duane. SALTPETER MINING IN KENTUCKY CAVES. *Register of the Kentucky Hist. Soc. 1979 77(4): 247-262.* Saltpeter, needed for gunpowder, was mined extensively from Kentucky caves by 1800. Vital to the US war ef-

fort in 1812, the mines proved important to the economic development of the state. Discusses the history and processes of saltpeter mining in Kentucky. 4 illus., 52 notes.                    J. F. Paul

2995. Hodge, Jo Dent. THE LUMBER INDUSTRY IN LAUREL, MISSISSIPPI, AT THE TURN OF THE NINETEENTH CENTURY. *J. of Mississippi Hist. 1973 35(4): 361-379.* Traces the development of the lumber industry in and around Laurel 1882-1916, when the town "grew from a crude lumber camp into an enterprising community around which centered the yellow pine industry of the nation." Laurel became "the lumber manufacturing center of the South" and by 1916 "was shipping more yellow pine lumber than any city in the world." The Eastman-Gardiner Company, headed by George and Silas Gardiner, "two of America's foremost lumber barons," and their brother-in-law, Lauren Eastman, furnished exceptional business and civic leadership after entering the area in 1890. Based largely on newspapers; 93 notes.
                                                                                                          J. W. Hillje

2996. Hoffius, Steve. RAILROAD FEVER. *Southern Exposure 1977 5(1): 47-58.* Few subjects in southern history have generated as much mythology and nostalgia as the railroads. Railroads played an important role in southern popular music and literature as well as in the daily lives of southerners. Even though the railroads considered passenger service to be an inconvenience, they served as the primary southern mode of transportation from the 1830's until recent years. Southern railroad companies today, such as the Seaboard, Norfolk & Western and the Southern Railway, realize large profits from their freight service and investments.
                                                                                                          N. Lederer

2997. Hofsommer, Donovan L. THE ACME, RED RIVER & NORTHERN: AN EARLY TEXAS SHORT LINE RAILROAD. *Red River Valley Hist. Rev. 1980 5(4): 17-26.* Recounts the history of the Acme, Red River & Northern Railroad, chartered in 1902 and directed from then on by Samuel L. Lazarus (b. 1855) to serve the interest of the gypsum mills which were developed a short distance northwest of present-day Quanah, in Hardeman County, Texas.

2998. Hofsommer, Donovan L. BAWLING CATTLE AND BARKING BRAKEMEN: AN OKLAHOMA RAILROAD MEMORY. *Chronicles of Oklahoma 1976 54(3): 360-369.* Examines the role of the Missouri, Kansas, and Texas Railway in the Oklahoma cattle industry, 1865-1972.

2999. Hofsommer, Donovan L. THE CONSTRUCTION STRATEGIES OF RAILROADS IN THE OKLAHOMA PANHANDLE. *Chronicles of Oklahoma 1980 58(1): 77-91.* By the 1890's people began to settle the Oklahoma Panhandle in sufficient numbers to warrant the construction of railroads to transport their agricultural products. Various proposals for construction misfired until 1912 when the Wichita Falls and Northwestern Railway (WF&NW) extended its track westward to the townsite of Forgan. This compelled the leaders of Beaver City, 10 miles to the south, to build their own track to intercept the WF&NW line. Eventually this blossomed into the Beaver, Meade and Englewood railroad (BM&E) which by 1931 extended 105 miles westward to Keyes, Oklahoma, and served thousands of Panhandle citizens. Illus., 3 photos, map, 29 notes.                                                                M. L. Tate

3000. Hofsommer, Donovan L. OKLAHOMA RAILROAD MAINTENANCE AUTHORITY: AN EXAMPLE OF RURAL PRESSURE GROUP POLITICS. *J. of the West 1974 13(4): 108-116.* Describes the efforts of businessmen, farmers, shippers, and legislators to retain rail service in western Oklahoma when the Missouri-Kansas Texas Railroad (MKT) attempted to abandon branch lines. When the MKT, nearly bankrupt, decided to stop service and sell the trackage for salvage in western Oklahoma, concerned residents of the area organized to prevent it. The Oklahoma Railroad Maintenance Authority was created and attempted to find financial backing to buy the rail lines from MKT. It failed because of lack of full support, opposition from trucking and shipping interests, lack of funds, poor political timing, and opposition to government control of railroads. Based on contemporary newspaper reports, US and Oklahoma government documents, and secondary sources; 20 notes. N. J. Street

3001. Hofsommer, Donovan L. RAILROADS AND RICHES: THE BURKBURNETT BOOM. *Great Plains J. 1974 14(1): 72-86.* The oil boom at Burkburnett, Texas, began in 1918 and ended by 1923. Oil had been produced in the area since 1902 and production continued after 1923, but for a short time the needs of thousands of workers, and the shipment of oil and equipment for new wells transformed the community and converted the Wichita Falls and Northwestern Railway into "an important artery of commerce." M. G.M.'s 1940 movie, *Boom Town*, was based on the Burkburnett boom. Based on primary and secondary materials; 12 illus., 15 notes. O. H. Zabel

3002. Hofsommer, Donovan L. TOWN BUILDING ON A TEXAS SHORT LINE: THE QUANAH, ACME & PACIFIC RAILWAY, 1909-1929. *Arizona and the West 1979 21(4): 355-368.* As the Quanah, Acme & Pacific Railway (Quanah Route) thrust from northeast Texas diagonally across the state toward El Paso, 1909-29, townsite development progressed with mixed success. Urban development had long accompanied new railroads as they pushed westward. The Quanah experience is unusual because of the relative lateness of its construction. Town building along the route offers a useful case study. 5 illus., 2 maps, 27 notes.

D. L. Smith

3003. Hofsommer, Donovan L. TOWNSITE DEVELOPMENT ON THE WICHITA FALLS AND NORTHWESTERN RAILWAY. *Great Plains J. 1977 16(2): 107-122.* During 1900-20, businessmen Joseph A. Kemp and Frank Kell of Wichita Falls, Texas, built the Wichita Falls and Northwestern Railway some 305 miles into the panhandle of Oklahoma. The railroad and townsite developments "promoted the settlement of one of the country's last frontiers." 6 illus., map, 33 notes. O. H. Zabel

3004. Hofsommer, Donovan L. WORKING ON THE (BRANCH LINE) RAILROAD. *Railroad Hist. 1977 (137): 80-93.* Examines the employees who worked the branch lines of the Missouri-Kansas-Texas Railroad's Northwestern District in Texas and Oklahoma, 1906-75.

3005. Hooks, Michael Q. THE ROLE OF PROMOTERS IN URBAN RIVALRY: THE DALLAS-FORT WORTH EXPERIENCE, 1870-1910. *Red River Valley Hist. Rev. 1982 7(2): 4-16.* Discusses a variety of promoters including merchants, bankers, journalists, editors, lawyers, and insurance agents who were responsible for both Dallas and Fort Worth, Texas, becoming major urban centers.

3006. Horn, Stanley F. and Crawford, Charles W. PERSPECTIVES ON SOUTHERN FORESTRY: THE *SOUTHERN LUMBERMAN*, INDUSTRIAL FORESTRY, AND TRADE ASSOCIATIONS. *J. of Forest Hist. 1977 21(1): 18-30.* Stanley F. Horn recounts anecdotes about his career as an editor of *Southern Lumberman,* a lumber trade journal, 1908-33, and offers opinions on the development of Southern lumbering.

3007. Huertas, Thomas F. DAMNIFYING GROWTH IN THE ANTEBELLUM SOUTH. *J. of Econ. Hist. 1979 39(1): 87-100.* The South's failure to industrialize more rapidly in the antebellum period did not lead to its immiserization. The South's terms of trade improved over the antebellum period so that its consumption potential expanded more rapidly than did production. Specialization in cotton production promoted a favorable movement of relative prices facing Southern producers. A customs union analysis shows that the South might have industrialized to a greater extent and might have raised its consumption potential further had it been able to impose an independent tariff on imports from all areas, including the rest of the United States. J

3008. Hurst, Harold W. DECLINE AND RENEWAL: ALEXANDRIA BEFORE THE CIVIL WAR. *Virginia Cavalcade 1981 31(1): 32-37.* Traces the history of Alexandria from 1790 to 1860, focusing on the city's decline around the turn of the century and renewal beginning in the 1840's.

3009. Isern, Thomas D. and Wilson, Raymond. LONE STAR: THE THOMPSON TIMBER INTERESTS OF TEXAS. *Red River Valley Hist. Rev. 1981 6(4): 25-37.* Benjamin Franklin Thompson and his sons established a commercial sawmill near Kilgore in 1852, a venture which grew with the family into the Thompson & Tucker Lumber Company, the J. M. Thompson Lumber Company, Thompson Brothers Lumber Company, and the Thompson & Ford Lumber Company with total assets of over five million in 1907; covers 1852-1959.

3010. Jacoway, Elizabeth. MARCHING TOWARD THE PAST. *Rev. in Am. Hist. 1983 11(2): 177-180.* Reviews David R. Goldfield's *Cotton Fields and Skyscrapers: Southern City and Region, 1607-1980* (1982), which argues that "the predominance of staple crop agriculture, a biracial society, and subservience to the national economy," have directed the course of Southern regional development and urbanization.

3011. Johnston, Kenneth D. THE MERGER OF RITCHIETOWN. *Upper Ohio Valley Hist. Rev. 1983 13(1): 28-31.* Profiles the Ritchie district, or Ritchietown, incorporated in 1851 as South Wheeling, and as the eighth ward of Wheeling, West Virginia, in 1870.

3012. Jolley, Clyde W. THE GRANDEUR THAT WAS ROME. *Georgia Life 1977 3(4): 15-17.* Traces the history of Rome, Georgia, including establishment, economic growth, and social life, 1834-1976.

3013. Jones, J. Marshall, Jr. THE HISTORY OF THE ARK-LA-TEX OIL INDUSTRY. *North Louisiana Hist. Assoc. J. 1981 12(2-3): 67-77.* A brief history of the oil and gas industry of eastern Texas, northern Louisiana, and southern Arkansas. The first successful well was drilled at Spindletop in southeast Texas in 1901. Quickly, other finds followed. In 1905, the Caddo Field had its beginning in Caddo Parish, Louisiana. This area was later the site of a conflict between independent producers and major oil companies. Still more discoveries were made in the 1920's and 30's. Secondary sources. J. F. Paul

3014. Jones, William M. A BRITISH PERIOD SAWMILL. *Escribano 1981 18: 84-105.* Provides a history of the mill built by John Hewitt in the 1770's in present-day Flagler County, Florida, based on excavations begun in 1977.

3015. Jordan, Terry G. EARLY NORTHEAST TEXAS AND THE EVOLUTION OF WESTERN RANCHING. *Ann. of the Assoc. of Am. Geographers 1977 67(1): 66-87.* Chronicles the development of the western American cattle ranching complex which was derived from an offshoot transplanted from the Carolinas 1820-50 in northeast Texas and later carried westward to be blended with Spanish, Acadian, and lower southern Anglo traditions of cattle-herding, 1870.

3016. Kaufman, Ralph. GLASS BLOWING: AMERICA'S FIRST INDUSTRY. *Pennsylvania Folklife 1980 29(4): 25-27.* The first glass blowing factory was in Jamestown, Virginia, in 1608; Casper Wistar in Salem, New Jersey, in 1739, and William Stiegel in Manheim, Pennsylvania, in 1765 established glass factories.

3017. Keating, Larry. CAMELOT TO CONTAINMENT. *Southern Exposure 1980 8(1): 77-81, 84-85.* During the last two decades the work of John Portman has come to epitomize the political economy of Atlanta and the Southeast. In the process of altering Atlanta, Portman has also fundamentally changed the relationship of the architect to financial and political power. The apex of his achievement as both designer and developer is the $230 million Peachtree

Center Complex. Portman has literally rebuilt the central business district of Atlanta without city, state or federal funds. 5 photos, chart.
                                                    H. M. Parker, Jr.

3018. Kemp, Emory L. and Kemp, Janet. BUILDING THE WESTON AND GAULEY BRIDGE TURNPIKE. *West Virginia Hist. 1980 41(4): 299-332.* Describes the building of a north-south turnpike from Weston to Gauley Bridge in western Virginia when other turnpikes connected the Ohio River in the west with areas in the east. With difficulty the turnpike was completed just before the Civil War. Although used by both sides in that conflict, it never lived up to its potential; yet it did attempt to open up a rugged Appalachian area that today remains desolate. Based on materials in the Virginia Board of Public Works, Virginia State Library, and reports of the Weston and Gauley Bridge Turnpike Company; 13 illus., 2 maps, 54 notes.
                                                    J. D. Neville

3019. Kennedy, R. Evan. BALTIMORE DOWNTOWN REVIVED THROUGH PRIVATE/PUBLIC COOPERATION. *Natl. Civic Rev. 1976 65(10): 503-505.* Born in the 1950's out of a realization by a few individuals that something was going badly wrong, a reconstruction effort has been taking place in downtown Baltimore—the city everybody tried to avoid if possible. And, thanks to the Beltway, it was possible. Its success is in large measure due to the local government support it received every step of the way.
                                                    J

3020. King, G. Wayne. THE EMERGENCE OF FLORENCE, SOUTH CAROLINA, 1853-1890. *South Carolina Hist. Mag. 1981 82(3): 197-209.* In 1846 the Wilmington and Manchester Railroad Company obtained a charter from South Carolina to construct a railroad from Wilmington into South Carolina. By 1853 the company completed the line in Florence. Three companies eventually serviced the area in an effort to profit from trade with the "continental interior" in the mid-19th century. Even after defeat in the Civil War, Florence still viewed itself as the "Magic City" of the Pee Dee region and the "New South" of Henry Grady. Based on contemporary newspapers and Florence Town Council Minutes; 26 notes.
                                                    R. H. Tomlinson

3021. Kipp, Samuel M., III. OLD NOTABLES AND NEWCOMERS: THE ECONOMIC AND POLITICAL ELITE OF GREENSBORO, NORTH CAROLINA, 1880-1920. *J. of Southern Hist. 1977 43(3): 373-394.* Studies of late 19th-century urban elites see a dichotomy of power between an older elite of wealth, intellect and status, and a newer, local political elite made up of lawyers, small proprietors, and professional politicians. Study of Greensboro, North Carolina's elite at the turn of the 20th century reveals some need for refinement and modification of the model. Greensboro was a rapidly urbanizing small town. Its elite was a relatively unified local group that dominated business, civic, religious, and fraternal organizations as well as political offices. Based upon manuscripts, printed primary and secondary sources; 5 tables, 28 notes.
                                                    T. D. Schoonover

3022. Knapp, Richard F. GOLDEN PROMISE IN THE PIEDMONT: THE STORY OF JOHN REED'S MINE. *North Carolina Hist. R. 1975 52(1): 1-19.* Provides a study of the Reed Gold Mine in Cabarrus County as an example of the kind of research needed to revive interest in the history of North Carolina gold mining. This mine, site (in 1790) of the first authenticated discovery of gold in the United States, started a gold mining boom which reached its peak in the 1850's. Sporadic operations continued on through the 1930's. Based on newspaper accounts, family manuscripts, and official published government documents, and primary and secondary sources; 11 illus., 73 notes.
                                                    T. L. Savitt

3023. Kulik, Gary B. BIRMINGHAM. *Am. Preservation 1978 1(3): 20-23.* Discusses the Sloss Company, whose city furnaces produced pig iron until their close in 1970. The furnaces, rebuilt during 1927-28, are a central element of the Birmingham, Alabama skyline and will be converted into an industrial museum by the city. Comments on the company's failure to innovate in laborsaving

equipment. Rejects as inadequate, the explanations that the Sloss Company iron works were a marginal producer and that Southern iron industries were backward. Covers 1881-1978. Illus.
                                                    J. Tull

3024. Lahmeyer Lobo, Eulália María. O COMÉRCIO ATLÂNTICO E A COMMUNIDADE DE MERCADORES NO RIO DE JANEIRO E EM CHARLESTON NO SÉCULO XVIII [Merchants of Rio de Janeiro and Charleston and the Atlantic commerce in the 18th century]. *Rev. de Hist. [Brazil] 1975 51(101): 49-106.* In the 18th century, Rio de Janeiro and Charleston were two Atlantic ports with comparable economic structures and social development. Both had the same type of export economy based on African slave labor. Although both economies were subject to the fluctuations of the international market, cycles in South Carolina were of shorter duration than those in Rio de Janeiro. Both economies were at transitional stages between classic slave-plantation and capitalist economies. Based on archival and secondary sources; 64 notes.
                                                    C. A. Preece

3025. Lankford, Ben. THE *WILLIE L. BENNETT* AND NOTES ON OTHER CHESAPEAKE BAY SKIPJACKS. *Nautical Res. J. 1983 29(2): 61-83.* A detailed description of the design and construction of a Chesapeake Bay sloop, known as a skipjack, typical of those used for oyster dredging.

3026. Larouche, Alain. LES CADJINS DU CANAL YANKEE: PROBLÈMES D'IDENTITÉ CULTURELLE DANS LA PAROISSE LAFOURCHE [The Cajuns of Canal Yankee: problems of cultural identity in Lafourche Parish]. *Cahiers de Géographie du Québec [Canada] 1979 23(59): 239-262.* Discusses industrialization, assimilation, ethnicity, and economic growth in Canal Yankee, Louisiana, a Cajun fishing village until the 1930's, when oil and gas resources transformed the community.

3027. Legan, Marshall Scott. RAILROAD SENTIMENT IN NORTH LOUISIANA IN THE 1850'S. *Louisiana Hist. 1976 17(2): 125-142.* Examines the inception of the idea of a railroad across northern Louisiana with the vision of transcontinentalism and economic significance to the state, and the reasons for the failure of the project so favorably begun. The Civil War disrupted the eastern section of the Vicksburg, Shreveport, and Texas railroad. In 1884 the railroad was finally completed to Shreveport. In the 20th century it was integrated into the Illinois Central railway system. 69 notes.
                                                    E. P. Stickney

3028. Leich, Jean F. BUSINESS AND INDUSTRY IN LINCOLN PARISH: 1848-1914. *North Louisiana Hist. Assoc. J. 1973 5(1): 1-9.* "The spirit of commercial enterprise goes back a long way in Lincoln Parish; back before the beginnings of the parish itself to the founding, in the wilds of North Louisiana, of a little town that was called Vienna." Vienna was incorporated in 1848; it became the first parish seat in 1873, when Lincoln Parish was founded. Discusses Vienna's good location on the much-traveled "Wire Road" along the telegraph line between Monroe and Shreveport; commerce in Vienna in the late 1800's; the coming of the railroad and the decline of Vienna; and the development of Ruston as the commercial center of the parish. From the Centennial Edition of the Ruston *Daily Leader*, 26 September 1973. 54 notes.
                                                    A. N. Garland

3029. Lewis, W. Davis. TECHNOLOGY AND THE SOUTH: A BICENTENNIAL PERSPECTIVE. *Southern Humanities Rev. 1976 (Special Issue): 83-95.* Discusses social and psychological implications of increased economic growth, technological change, and industrialization in the South in the 1970's, emphasizing dangers to individuality.

3030. Logan, Frenise A. A BRITISH EAST INDIA COMPANY AGENT IN THE UNITED STATES, 1839-1840. *Agric. Hist. 1974 48(2): 267-276.* Thomas Bayles visited the United States in 1839-40 on behalf of the East India Company to learn the cotton cultivation of the South so that the British could grow it competitively in India. Despite opposition from Southern planters, Bayles recruited several overseers who spent much of the 1840's in different parts of India trying to grow cotton. The experiment failed. Based on primary and secondary sources; 42 notes. D. E. Bowers

3031. London, Bruce and Palmieri, Richard P. FREDERICKS-BURG: THE ECOLOGICAL FOUNDATIONS OF URBAN HISTORY. *Pioneer Am. Soc. Tr. 1980 3: 122-139.* Compares the "ecological patterns (structure and change in the spatial distribution of racial, ethnic, and socioeconomic status groups)" of Fredericksburg, Virginia, in 1888 with the patterns of 1976.

3032. Long, Ozella N. CHALK: HOWARD COUNTY'S FIRST OIL TOWN. *Permian Hist. Ann. 1982 22: 35-43.* History of Otis Chalk, Texas, focusing on the oil boom of 1925-30's.

3033. Luebke, Paul; McMahon, Bob; and Risberg, Jeff. SELECTIVE RECRUITMENT IN NORTH CAROLINA. *Working Papers for a New Soc. 1979 6(6): 17-20.* Describes the current growing practice in the South of discouraging companies from establishing new plants because of decent wage rates and/or unionization, and efforts to reach a single state economic development policy in each southern state.

3034. Malizia, Emil. ORGANIZING TO OVERCOME UNEVEN DEVELOPMENT: THE CASE OF THE U.S. SOUTH. *Rev. of Radical Pol. Econ. 1978 10(3): 87-94.* An account of the reasons for the comparatively uneven economic development between the North and South during 1950-70.

3035. Mancil, Ervin. PULLBOAT LOGGING. *J. of Forest Hist. 1980 24(3): 134-141.* Pullboat logging was a system used in the cypress swamps of the southeastern states from about 1890 to 1925, although small operators continued in some marginal areas until the 1960's. A steam-powered skidder was mounted on a scow floating on a bayou or a canal dredged into the swamp. Cables ran between drums on the pullboat and a sheave block fastened to a tree at the end of a cleared trail or run; logs were attached to the cables and skidded in to the pullboat and then were transported by water to a sawmill. Pullboat crews often lived on company quarterboats where food, shelter, and other necessities were provided. Based on personal observation, interviews, and secondary sources; 14 illus., 10 notes. R. J. Fahl

3036. Maness, Lonnie E. A COMMENT ON LOCAL HISTORY. *West Tennessee Hist. Soc. Papers 1975 29: 162-165.* Appeals for good local history, asserting that the history of cities has been largely ignored until comparatively recent times. Argues that the study of cities is important for a proper understanding of developments on the regional, sectional, and national levels. Discusses three histories of Memphis, with particular emphasis on Judge J. P. Young's *Standard History of Memphis, Tennessee*, first published in 1912, and recently (1974) reprinted. Note.
H. M. Parker, Jr.

3037. Maroney, James C. THE INTERNATIONAL LONG-SHOREMEN'S ASSOCIATION IN THE GULF STATES DURING THE PROGRESSIVE ERA. *Southern Studies 1977 16(2): 225-232.* The International Longshoremen's Association, Gulf Coast District, maintained a conservative attitude in the early 20th century. Despite its moderation, the union movement was strongly opposed by well organized management. A powerful drive by management to promote the open shop rule almost eradicated union power by 1920. In race relations, separate and segregated locals but equal work for blacks and whites became standard. Blacks thus received more work and more opportunities for union officeholding. The black workers' gains resulted from economic rather than humanitarian factors; strikes and violence hurt white workers. Based on union records, unpublished M.A. theses, secondary sources; 19 notes. J. Buschen

3038. Maroney, James C. THE UNIONIZATION OF THURBER, 1903. *Red River Valley Hist. Rev. 1979 4(2): 27-32.* An account of efforts to unionize the mine workers of Thurber, Texas, in 1903,

which remained a union stronghold until mining operations ended in the 1920's; also discusses the establishment of coal mining in Thurber since the 1880's.

3039. Matthews, Glenna. AN IMMIGRANT COMMUNITY IN INDIAN TERRITORY. *Labor Hist. 1982 23(3): 374-394.* Krebs, Oklahoma, was founded in the late 1870's by Italian immigrants recruited by coal mining companies to work in the southeastern part of the Indian Territory. Faced with both exploitation by the coal companies and by restricted civil rights while under the jurisdiction of the Choctaw Indians, the Italian immigrants relied on their own institutions for coping with a difficult existence. They found solace in a mutual benefit association, the Columbus Society, in the Catholic Church, and in the family. Overwhelmingly working class, Krebs's citizens were active members of both the United Mine Workers of America and the Socialist Party. Based on interviews with Krebs residents, the 1900 US Census manuscript schedules for the Choctaw Nation, records of St. Joseph's Catholic Church at Krebs, and other primary sources; 3 tables, 49 notes.
L. F. Velicer

3040. Maxwell, Robert S. THE FIRST BIG MILL: THE BEGINNINGS OF COMMERCIAL LUMBERING IN TEXAS. *Southwestern Hist. Q. 1982 86(1): 1-30.* Although Spanish priests and monks were the first loggers in east Texas, the lumbering industry did not begin to flourish until after the Civil War. Northerners, such as Henry J. Lutcher and G. Bedell Moore, provided the necessary capital and organizational ability for the development of large, commercial sawmills and for the expansion of the railroad network. In 1877, Lutcher and Moore built the first large-scale sawmill in East Texas at Orange. That mill provided the basis for a comprehensive lumbering industry, and it marked the beginning of a bonanza lumbering era that did not end until the Great Depression of the 1930's. Based on the Lutcher and Moore Diary, Stephen F. Austin University, and secondary sources; 10 photos, map, 47 notes. R. D. Hurt

3041. Maxwell, Robert S. THE IMPACT OF FORESTRY ON THE GULF SOUTH. *Forest Hist. 1973 17(1): 30-35.* "Not until the great white pine forests of the Lake States neared exhaustion did the [lumber] industry turn to the yellow pine stands of the South." Early conservationists instituted scientific forestry practices in the Gulf South, preventing despoliation and paving the way for today's southern forest products industry. Illus., 2 photos, 26 notes.
D. R. Verardo

3042. Maxwell, Robert S. ONE MAN'S LEGACY: W. GOODRICH JONES AND TEXAS CONSERVATION. *Southwestern Hist. Q. 1974 77(3): 355-380.* By 1930 the great virgin pine forests of east Texas were cut out. Traces the career of William Goodrich Jones (1860-1950), an enlightened layman and the tireless catalyst among the lumber industry, state officials, and professional foresters for solution of the problems of conservation. He figured prominently in the founding of the Texas Forestry Association and the establishment of the State Department of Forestry. Today east Texas is reforested and assured of continued growth and sustained yield. 14 illus., 40 notes. D. L. Smith

3043. McCorkle, James L., Jr. THE ILLINOIS CENTRAL RAILROAD AND THE MISSISSIPPi COMMERCIAL VEGETABLE INDUSTRY. *J. of Mississippi Hist. 1977 39(2): 155-172.* From the 1880's on, the Illinois Central Railroad led railroads operating in Mississippi in the promotion of an increasingly extensive commercial vegetable industry. The railroad conducted demonstration work, established a special agriculture department, cooperated with state agencies, and participated in meetings. Producers often charged that railroad freight rates were excessive. Based on newspapers and Illinois Central Railroad records; 69 notes. J. W. Hillje

3044. McGrain, John W. THE DEVELOPMENT AND DECLINE OF DORSEYS FORGE. *Maryland Hist. Mag. 1977 72(3): 346-352.* Narrates the history of Caleb Dorsey's ironworks on the Patapsco in Howard County, Maryland, from its founding in 1761 to the destruction of its descendant, the Avalon Nail and Iron Company, by the flood of 1868. Property inventories from the prolonged litigation between the Dorsey heirs and those of William Whetcroft, a musket manufacturer, reveal the size and production of this early industrial region. Contrary to wide belief, Dorsey did not produce cannon for the Revolutionary Army, but operated a slitting mill. Only under Benjamin and James Ellicott, in the 1830's, did large-scale mechanized production develop there and at Elkridge Furnace. Primary and secondary sources; map, 29 notes.

G. J. Bobango

3045. McGrain, John W. "GOOD BYE OLD BURR": THE ROLLER MILL REVOLUTION IN MARYLAND, 1882. *Maryland Hist. Mag. 1982 77(2): 154-171.* The country millers of Maryland and other eastern and southern states passed through one mechanical revolution in the 1870's and another in the 1880's. By the end of the century many a fortune had been sunk into buying an array of highly specialized apparatus that in numerous instances generated insufficient revenue to pay for itself. From the centuries-old use of the common millstone to the "middlings purifier" to the "roller mill" of chilled steel patented in 1880, American millers witnessed a veritable stampede to install each new and more elaborate system, as flour milling expanded immensely. Along with this came a great debate over the food value of the pure white versus stone-ground brown flour. Based on the *American Miller,* 1879-99, contemporary press; 70 notes.

G. J. Bobango

3046. McGrain, John W. HISTORICAL ASPECTS OF LAKE ROLAND. *Maryland Hist. Mag. 1979 74(3): 253-273.* Lake Roland, known briefly as Swann Lake, was created in 1858 by damming Roland Run to provide Baltimore, Maryland, with an adequate water supply. A 40-foot high stonework dam impounded a lake of 116 acres. Made obsolete by heavy siltation and growing water demands, it was taken out of service in 1915 and developed as Robert E. Lee Park in 1944. The dam, 1861 valve house, remnants of industries displaced by the lake, and portions of railroad lines and accommodations serving the area are extant. Based on Baltimore City Water Department Reports, Baltimore County records, newspapers; 6 photos, 65 notes.

C. B. Schulz

3047. McIntyre, Glen. THE PEAVINE RAILROAD. *Chronicles of Oklahoma 1980 58(3): 315-324.* The Rock Island Railroad opened a rail line between Kingfisher and Chandler, Oklahoma in 1903. Nicknamed the "Peavine Railroad," this line developed an eastern branch through Cashion, Reeding, and Merrick, but the eastern branch failed to make a profit because it traversed a poorer agricultural region. By 1924 railroad executives closed the eastern branch, and 13 years later ended all service on the Peavine. Rising truck and automobile traffic had made it obsolete. Based on Oklahoma newspapers and state documents; 3 photos, 41 notes.

M. L. Tate

3048. McKenzie, Robert H. HORACE WARE: ALABAMA IRON PIONEER. *Alabama Rev. 1973 26(3): 157-172.* Horace Ware, Massachusetts-born pioneer of Alabama iron making, built a series of blast furnaces starting in the 1840's and Alabama's first rolling mill in 1858-61. Recovering gradually from the Confederacy's collapse, Ware pursued new furnace ventures in Alabama, Georgia, and Texas, not always in harmony with his partners. He retired in 1888, having rejected opportunities to acquire property in the Birmingham industry. A pioneer brown ore and charcoal operator, Ware was unable to appreciate the technological possibilities of hematite and coke. Based on primary and secondary materials; 36 notes.

J. F. Vivian

3049. Mealor, W. Theodore, Jr. FUNCTIONAL AND SPATIAL PATTERNS OF GEORGIA SHORT LINE RAILROADS, 1915-1978. *West Georgia Coll. Studies in the Social Sci. 1979 18: 25-42.* Surveys the functional characteristics of the short line systems and relates them to the failure, survival, or incorporations of the short lines into statewide networks.

3050. Means, Gay Griffith. RAILROAD CONSOLIDATION AND THE SHORT LINE RAILROADS OF LOUISIANA. *North Louisiana Hist. Assoc. J. 1983 14(4): 157-168.* Railroad consolidation and mergers occurred with great frequency in the late 19th and early 20th centuries. Jay Gould's Texas and Pacific Railroad

purchased most of the short lines in northern Louisiana during those years. The short lines were unable to compete against the corporate giants. 33 notes.

J. F. Paul

3051. Meredith, Howard L. and Shirk, George H. OKLAHOMA CITY: GROWTH AND RECONSTRUCTION, 1889-1939. *Chronicles of Oklahoma 1977 55(3): 293-308.* Discusses population growth patterns and neighborhood development in Oklahoma City from its 1889 founding to 1939. Railroads provided Oklahoma City with its first boom period. This was sustained during the early 20th century by the oil boom and industrial-commercial expansion. This entrenched prosperity gained it the state capital and insulated it from the worst effects of the Depression. Primary and secondary sources; 7 photos, 50 notes.

M. L. Tate

3052. Merryman, Terry Ann. HENRY HARDTNER: THE SEVERANCE TAX AND STATE REFORESTATION CONTRACTS. *North Louisiana Hist. Assoc. J. 1978 9(2): 71-78.* After 1910 the name of Henry Hardtner became synonymous with forestry conservation legislation in Louisiana and all the South. In that year Hardtner, owner of a milling company, was responsible for getting two important bills through the Louisiana legislature. The first provided that 3/4 of a cent would be levied on each 1,000 board feet of yellow pine and hardwood harvested in Louisiana, the proceeds to go into a conservation fund for forest preservation. The other act allowed an owner of denuded forest lands to enter into a reforestation contract with the state. Most mill owners did not believe that cutover land could be made profitable again, but Hardtner did. He also felt that forests should remain under private ownership. Based on Hardtner's scrapbooks and on secondary sources; 40 notes.

H. M. Parker, Jr.

3053. Middleton, William D. "GEMS OF SYMMETRY AND CONVENIENCE." *Am. Heritage 1973 24(2): 22-37, 99.* The Richmond trolley system, whose electric cars were described as "gems of symmetry and convenience," was launched in 1888. It was the largest street railway in the world and the first to present a truly practical means of urban transportation. It set in motion a great electric railway construction boom. Frank Julian Sprague (1857?-1934) deserves the credit for this development of successful electric transportation. The industry peaked about 1917. Although it has since declined, there is now renewed interest in the form of modern rapid-transit systems. 22 illus.

D. L. Smith

3054. Miller, Zane L. DEFINING THE CITY—AND URBAN HISTORY. *Rev. in Am. Hist. 1976 4(3): 436-441.* Review article prompted by Blaine A. Brownell's *The Urban Ethos in the South, 1920-1930* (Baton Rouge: Louisiana State U. Pr., 1975); discusses the introduction of cultural considerations into urban history.

3055. Milne, Dann. MIGRATION AND INCOME OPPORTUNITIES FOR BLACKS IN THE SOUTH. *Southern Econ. J. 1980 46(3): 913-917.* Urban migration of southern blacks is beneficial to blacks relative to whites with respect to earnings, and most beneficial in larger cities, 1965-70.

3056. Mixon, Wayne. JOEL CHANDLER HARRIS, THE YEOMAN TRADITION, AND THE NEW SOUTH MOVEMENT. *Georgia Hist. Q. 1977 61(4): 308-317.* Although Joel Chandler Harris has often been classed with the plantation romancers of the New South movement, his views were quite different from theirs. Harris's stories focus on middle-class, yeoman farmers rather then the gentry, and his attitude toward the New South shows a dislike of industrialization and the resultant materialism, while advocating agricultural improvements. Primary and secondary sources; 20 notes.

G. R. Schroeder

3057. Mladenka, Kenneth R. and Hill, Kim Quaile. THE DISTRIBUTION OF BENEFITS IN AN URBAN ENVIRONMENT: PARKS AND LIBRARIES IN HOUSTON. *Urban Affairs Q. 1977 13(1): 73-94.* Upper income areas had no advantage in park quality, acreage, numbers, or spatial distribution. However, regarding library quality and resources, upper class areas were strongly favored. This distribution of library services is justified only if circulation rates are the sole test of equity. Inequalities in the distribution of these services based on wealth and race are dispersed rather than cumulative. Bureaucrats, not elected officials, determine who benefits from public policy. 11 notes, biblio. L. Beecher

3058. Moore, John H. APPOMATTOX: PROFILE OF A MID-NINETEENTH CENTURY COMMUNITY. *Virginia Mag. of Hist. and Biog. 1980 88(4): 478-491.* Recounts a brief social history of the 1865 Confederate surrender site, created a county in 1845. All county records were destroyed in 1892, hampering research. Appomattox County, with Appomattox Courthouse its seat, prospered in the 1850's, producing tobacco, corn, and hogs. County social preferences included the Baptist Church, and John Breckenridge in the 1860 election. The area was spared most of the Civil War combat, but not the curious after the war. The town itself declined during Reconstruction, as economic and social activity shifted to a nearby railroad right-of-way. 14 notes. P. J. Woehrmann

3059. Moore, John Hebron. THE CYPRESS LUMBER INDUSTRY OF THE OLD SOUTHWEST AND PUBLIC LAND LAW, 1803-1850. *J. of Southern Hist. 1983 49(2): 203-222.* When West Florida and Louisiana were acquired in 1803 and 1811, the large lumber industry confronted a major problem as the timber was now on federal land. Denied access to this land, the cypress loggermen were compelled to obtain their lumber clandestinely. Details efforts to enforce the law and official actions taken at the state and federal levels to dispose of the cypress swamplands. Based on court records, government documents, and other primary sources; 87 notes. T. Schoonover

3060. Morris, Margaret W. THE COMPLETION OF THE WESTERN NORTH CAROLINA RAILROAD: POLITICS OF CONCEALMENT. *North Carolina Hist. R. 1975 52(3): 256-282.* Governor Zebulon B. Vance and his successor, Thomas J. Jarvis, strongly wished completion of a trunk railroad line through North Carolina from Beaufort to the Tennessee line. Between 1879 and 1885 Vance and Jarvis, using various political and legal tactics, supported opposing groups in their efforts to have the line built. Ultimately the Richmond and Danville Railroad Company won control of and completed the road, overcoming competition from New York- and Boston-based businessmen. Based on manuscript and public records, newspaper accounts, and secondary sources; 12 illus., 2 maps, 104 notes. T. L. Savitt

3061. Muller, Edward K. and Groves, Paul A. THE CHANGING LOCATION OF THE CLOTHING INDUSTRY: A LINK TO THE SOCIAL GEOGRAPHY OF BALTIMORE IN THE NINETEENTH CENTURY. *Maryland Hist. Mag. 1976 71(3): 403-420.* Examines the nature, growth, location, ownership, and industrial organization of Baltimore's post-civil war clothing industry. Unskilled women predominated in the putting out (outside shop) system of the new ready-to-wear warehouses and factory enterprises. The wholesale manufacturer "became the central organizing force" in expanding the industry, and the contracting system not only met the expanding demands for ready-to-wear garments, but spawned the infamous "sweatshop" networks. The pedestrian nature of the employment linkage meant that residential patterning of workers as the industry expanded depended more on business organization and availability of intraurban transit networks allowing middlemen to move raw materials to the sweatshops than on ethnic groupings or the availability of housing. Urban historians need to consider the location of employment more than they have, even though essential sources of data such as census enumerations are problematic. 3 illus., 6 figs., 5 tables, 51 notes. G. J. Bobango

3062. Muller, Edward K. and Groves, Paul A. THE EMERGENCE OF INDUSTRIAL DISTRICTS IN MID-NINETEENTH CENTURY BALTIMORE. *Geographical Rev. 1979 69(2): 159-178.* The prevalent view of land use in large, mid-nineteenth century North American cities is one of high density and of a chaotic intermixture of activities. The evolution of large-scale and new organizational forms of industrial production created centrifugal and localization forces among some manufacturing activities and resulted in industrial districts distinguished by product type, production mode, and labor-force composition. In Baltimore by 1860, despite the persistence of some elements of manufactural location from the older mercantile city, the new locational tendencies formed six functionally differentiated and spatially separated industrial districts. In the context of population growth, peripheral urban expansion, and predominantly pedestrian journeys-to-work, industrial localization imparted a cellular structure to the organization of work and residence. Based on US manufacturing censuses, contemporary published reports, and secondary sources; 5 maps, 6 tables, graph, 59 notes. J

3063. Myers, J. Walter, Jr. FOREST FARMERS ASSOCIATION: A VOICE FOR SOUTHERN TIMBER RESOURCES. *J. of NAL Assoc. 1978 3(3-4): 89-91.* Discusses the interests and activities of the Forest Farmers Association, founded in 1940; its members in the 15 southern states represent 70% of the total commercial forest lands in the South, particularly motivating forest owners to grow trees and teaching them to do it better.

3064. Nelms, Willie. GEORGE LAFAYETTE CARTER: EMPIRE BUILDER. *Virginia Cavalcade 1980 30(1): 12-21.* Centered in southwestern Virginia, George Lafayette Carter amassed on empire consisting of ironfields, flour mills, coal mines, and railroads throughout Virginia, West Virginia, Tennessee, and Kentucky, 1877-1936.

3065. Newman, Dale. WORK AND COMMUNITY LIFE IN A SOUTHERN TEXTILE TOWN. *Labor Hist. 1978 19(2): 204-225.* Studies a rural-industrial county in Piedmont North Carolina. White cotton mill operatives experienced less control over their daily activities and work than did blacks. White mill workers felt degraded when forced into mill work; blacks did not. Union activity originated with blacks in the 1970's. Although the effort failed, it reflected the values and heritage brought to the mill by black operatives. Based on interviews; 77 notes. L. L. Athey

3066. Nichols, Ashton. THE FISH IS FRESH, THE HERITAGE IS ALIVE! *Hist. Preservation 1979 31(3): 14-20.* The Cross Street Market, located in south Baltimore, Maryland, since 1846, has been the object of recent revitalization projects to preserve its tradition.

3067. Nichols, Cheryl Griffith. PULASKI HEIGHTS: EARLY SUBURBAN DEVELOPMENT IN LITTLE ROCK, ARKANSAS. *Arkansas Hist. Q. 1982 41(2): 129-145.* Pulaski Heights was an exclusive residential suburb of Little Rock. Although land was purchased in 1891, real development did not begin until the arrival of a streetcar line in 1903. Pulaski Heights became a part of Little Rock in 1915 and development was virtually complete by the 1920's. Map, 67 notes. G. R. Schroeder

3068. Oden, Jack P. CHARLES HOLMES HERTY AND THE BIRTH OF THE SOUTHERN NEWSPRINT PAPER INDUSTRY, 1927-1940. *J. of Forest Hist. 1977 21(2): 76-89.* Early sources of newsprint for American newspapers were forests of northeastern United States and Canada. Paper mills in those regions could produce enough newsprint for both countries. Pine trees of southeastern United States were considered unsuitable for newsprint because they were presumed to have a high resin content. Charles Holmes Herty (d. 1938) was a prominent Georgia chemist who discovered that the presumption about the unsuitability of pines for newsprint was erroneous. He organized and ran a research laboratory that worked out a process for making newsprint from pines. Primary and secondary sources; 11 photos, 64 notes. F. N. Egerton

3069. Oden, Jack P. ORIGINS OF THE SOUTHERN KRAFT PAPER INDUSTRY, 1903-1930. *Mississippi Q. 1977 30(4): 565-584.* Examines the wood pulp and paper industry and the manufacture of kraft paper, throughout the South, 1903-30.

3070. Olien, Diana Davids. KEEPING HOUSE IN A TENT: WOMEN IN THE EARLY PERMIAN BASIN OIL FIELDS. *Permian Hist. Ann. 1982 22: 3-14.* Describes the social conditions and the difficulties faced by homemakers in the oil fields of the Permian Basin, Texas, 1920's-30's.

3071. Pantazes, William N. THE GREEKS OF TARPON SPRINGS: AN AMERICAN ODYSSEY. *Tampa Bay Hist. 1979 1(2): 24-31.* Discusses the sponge industry in Tarpon Springs, Florida (1891-1959) and the Greek Americans who worked it; includes a 1979 interview with George Georgeiou, a former sponge boat captain.

3072. Parker, Russell D. ALCOA, TENNESSEE: THE EARLY YEARS, 1919-1939. *East Tennessee Hist. Soc. Publ. 1976 48: 84-103.* During its first 20 years, Alcoa, Tennessee, was a typical company town relatively free of social tensions with few efforts at unionization run by paternalistic officials, Victor J. Hultquist and Arthur B. Smith, who retired before the economic boom and altered the community situation brought about by World War II. Based on the Alcoa Company archives and oral interviews; 108 notes.　　　　　　　　　　　　　　　　D. A. Yanchisin

3073. Parker, Russell D. ALCOA, TENNESSEE: THE YEARS OF CHANGE, 1940-1960. *East Tennessee Hist. Soc. Publ. 1977 49: 99-115.* The paternalism of the Aluminum Company of America (ALCOA) toward its town, Alcoa, Tennessee, relaxed and underwent a change after 1940 as the company attempted to rid itself of the negative company-overlord image for three reasons: the company became more concerned with gaining public acceptance; the realization brought about by the 1937 strike that labor could not be held in an indefinite state of vassalage; and the lessening of ALCOA's role as a peddler of hydroelectric power. 87 notes.

D. A. Yanchisin

3074. Parker, Russell D. THE BLACK COMMUNITY IN A COMPANY TOWN: ALCOA, TENNESSEE, 1919-1939. *Tennessee Hist. Q. 1978 37(2): 203-221.* Alcoa, Tennessee, was a company town, not conducive to community leadership, black or white. Unskilled blacks were recruited to work in the Aluminum Company of America (Alcoa) plant, and blacks moved in almost as fast as whites. Blacks were allowed to purchase their homes in the Negro section. John T. Arter, a black man, was brought in as principal of the black school, and became the leader of the Negro community. His closest associates were John Brice and T. P. Marsh, but neither managed to wield influence after Arter's death. Leadership within the black community eventually fell to Hendrika Tol, a white woman, who had attended nearby Maryville College. Tol started a library for blacks and attempted to create a health plan for blacks, but without success. "Unionization in the mid-1930's reduced the vulnerability of black workers." Primary and secondary sources; 91 notes.　　　　　　　　　　　　　　　　M. B. Lucas

3075. Parramore, Thomas C. THE BARTONS OF BARTONSVILLE. *North Carolina Hist. R. 1974 51(1): 22-40.* Stephen Barton, Jr. (1806-65), brother of Clara Barton (1821-1912), moved from his native Massachusetts in 1856 to establish a short-lived mill village in Hertford County, North Carolina, based on a lumber trade with Norfolk, Virginia, and northern ports. The community and its thriving business activity were jeopardized by the commercial uncertainty of 1860 and by Barton's strict neutrality in the Civil War. The site was destroyed by Union soldiers in 1865. Primary and secondary sources; illus., map, 77 notes.　　W. B. Bedford

3076. Pearson, Ralph L. THE NATIONAL URBAN LEAGUE COMES TO BALTIMORE. *Maryland Hist. Mag. 1977 72(4): 523-533.* The Reverend Peter Ainslie and John R. Carey, founders of Baltimore's Interracial Conference, asked the National Urban League to conduct an in-depth sociological study of working conditions among Baltimore's black citizens in 1922, which led to the formation of a Baltimore branch of the League by 1924. Focuses on the League's interracial community achievements in its first decade and on the insights of "the first systematic... analysis of employment patterns among Baltimore's black(s)." Maryland's border-state location determined many aspects of the city's racial mores, with northern-style industrial development and southern-style segregation. High death rates, discrimination, physical degradation, and social maladjustment characterized the black community, mostly from lack of economic opportunity due to white unions and com-

pany hiring policies, all based on an emotionalism which sociological study could not overcome. Primary and secondary sources; 34 notes.　　　　　　　　　G. J. Bobango

3077. Peeples, Vernon E. CHARLOTTE HARBOR DIVISION OF THE FLORIDA SOUTHERN RAILROAD. *Florida Hist. Q. 1980 58(3): 291-302.* An analysis of town concern over the location of a railroad in southwest Florida. The final location would determine the future of Punta Gorda and Port Tampa. Punta Gorda received its railroad to Fort Myers, but its success was short-lived. The railroad meant the end of small steamers operating in the Gulf. Port Tampa received far more money for development, thereby curtailing Punta Gorda. Covers 1884-1904. Based on newspaper accounts, railroad and state records; 2 illus., 48 notes.　　N. A. Kuntz

3078. Pelzman, Joseph. THE TEXTILE INDUSTRY. *Ann. of the Am. Acad. of Pol. and Social Sci. 1982 (460): 92-100.* The U.S. textile industry has, over the last 20 years, been transformed from a small-scale, unintegrated, predominantly family-owned industry producing standardized fabrics and yarns in the Northeast to a large-scale, more concentrated, capital-intensive, technologically advanced, and internationally competitive industry located primarily in the Southeast. Pressure for this transformation came from competition from foreign low-cost producers and internal competition by domestic producers intent on introducing structural reforms and technical change. The industry's response to these foreign and domestic pressures took the form of both political and economic measures which resulted in a healthier, more profitable, and more competitive textile industry.　　　　　　　　　　J/S

3079. Perez, Lisandro and Cheng, Maisy L. THE REVIVAL OF POPULATION GROWTH IN NONMETROPOLITAN AMERICA: THE EXCEPTION OF LOUISIANA. *Southern Studies 1980 19(2): 193-210.* US population in the 20th century has become concentrated in large metropolitan centers. During 1970-75, however, nonmetropolitan counties nationally grew faster than metropolitan counties. Louisiana does not follow the national trend. The metropolitan areas of Louisiana grew considerably faster than did nonmetropolitan areas during these five years, and medium-sized cities grew very rapidly. In Louisiana there is still a substantial movement from nonmetropolitan regions to metropolitan areas. Based on US Census reports and other primary sources; 10 tables, 11 notes.

J. J. Buschen

3080. Pillsbury, Richard. FARRAR LUMBER COMPANY, FARRAR-MADE HOUSES: A GEORGIA PRODUCT. *Pioneer Am. 1981 13(1): 49-61.* Traces the history of the Farrar Lumber Company of Dalton, Georgia, founded by James B. Farrar in 1871, focusing on the company's production of precut houses; reprints a number of pages from Farrar's 1918 catalog showing various models and prices of precut homes.

3081. Pitcaithley, Dwight. ZINC AND LEAD MINING ALONG THE BUFFALO RIVER. *Arkansas Hist. Q. 1978 37(4): 293-305.* Traces the history of the rise and decline of lead and zinc mining in the Buffalo River area of Arkansas from the first discovery of the minerals in the 1700's through the boom of 1916-17 and subsequent decline in production. Poor transportation was always the greatest obstacle to the productivity of the region. Primary and secondary sources; illus., 46 notes.　　G. R. Schroeder

3082. Pratt, Joseph A. GROWTH OR A CLEAN ENVIRONMENT? RESPONSES TO PETROLEUM-RELATED POLLUTION IN THE GULF COAST REFINING REGION. *Business Hist. Rev. 1978 52(1): 1-29.* Traces the environmental impact of the growth of petroleum refining along the Gulf Coast of Texas from the early 1900's-60's. Petroleum-related pollution was substantial throughout the period. Prior to World War I, no serious attempts were made to control pollution. Later the companies themselves and the American Petroleum Institute implemented unsuccessful voluntary efforts that were followed after 1940 by governmental action. Based on governmental and industry records and publications; 51 notes.

C. J. Pusateri

3083. Primeaux, Walter J. THE DECLINE IN ELECTRIC UTILITY COMPETITION. *Land Econ. 1975 51(2): 144-148.* Describes competition between electric utility companies in The Dalles, Oregon, and Hagerstown, Maryland. Notes the differing decisions by state utility commissions and how they affected the competitive situation. 27 notes, biblio.                                    E. S. Johnson

3084. Prindle, David F. OIL AND THE PERMANENT UNIVERSITY FUND: THE EARLY YEARS. *Southwestern Hist. Q. 1982 86(2): 277-298.* Much of the 2 million acres of public lands provided by the Texas legislature for the support of the University of Texas was widely scattered and appeared worthless. In 1923, however, oil was discovered on university land in the Permian Basin. Since that time the University of Texas has had a large endowment for capital improvements. An ambiguity in the state constitution allowed Texas A & M University to claim part of the oil revenue in 1930. Both universities continue to accrue oil revenue for development. Based on university records at the University of Texas and Texas A & M University; 2 photos, map, 63 notes.
                                    R. D. Hurt

3085. Prindle, David F. THE TEXAS RAILROAD COMMISSION AND THE ELIMINATION OF THE FLARING OF NATURAL GAS, 1930-1949. *Southwestern Hist. Q. 1981 84(3): 293-308.* During the 1930's and 1940's, Texas oil producers flared natural gas from their wells, because it had minimal market value. The Texas Railroad Commission, which controlled the state's oil and gas industry, held that flaring destroyed a precious natural resource and that the pressure from recycled gas would increase oil production. Although the state authorized the Railroad Commission to end strip-and-flaring operations in 1935, oil producers continued to burn casinghead gas. The Railroad Commission was unable to prevent that flaring until William J. Murray, a staunch advocate of natural gas conservation, was appointed to the Commission in 1947. Murray's leadership, together with rising natural gas prices and Federal Power Commission support, enabled the Commission to close oil fields until producers stopped the wasteful practice of flaring casinghead gas. By 1949, Texan natural gas was strictly regulated and conserved. Based on the records of the Texas Railroad Commission and oral interviews; 58 notes.          R. D. Hurt

3086. Quinney, Valerie. MILL VALLEY MEMORIES. *Southern Exposure 1980 8(3): 98-109.* Reminiscences of childhood by 30 men and women who grew up in the textile mill village of Carrboro, North Carolina, before World War I, recorded in 1974 as part of an oral history project sponsored by the Chapel Hill Historical Society; ca. 1890's-1917.

3087. Rae, John B. COLEMAN DU PONT AND HIS ROAD. *Delaware Hist. 1975 16(3): 171-183.* Thomas Coleman Du Pont (1863-1930) early recognized the need for new highway technology to handle the increasing automobile traffic. Du Pont proposed the establishment of a unified highway building program, and in 1911 convinced the Delaware assembly to incorporate a private company, the Coleman Du Pont Road, Inc., more commonly known as the Boulevard Corporation. The company would build a road connecting the state from north to south, acquiring a 200 foot right of way which would include a divided highway for automobiles, trolley tracks, roadways for horsedrawn vehicles, and separate roadways for heavy motor traffic. Political opposition and litigation over the company's right to condemn land retarded the roadbuilding progress, and by 1916 Du Pont, as a member of the newly created state highway department, turned over the company to the state which abandoned the multiple roadway system in favor of the conventional two-lane concrete highway. The highway was later incorporated into the national primary road network as segments of US Routes 13 and 113. 33 notes.          R. M. Miller

3088. Ramsey, Bill. NOT THE BOMBS, JUST THE PARTS. *Southern Exposure 1979 7(4): 41-43.* Surveys facilities currently being used for the manufacture and assembly of the components used in the construction of US nuclear arms. Four out of the seven operating facilities are now located in the South. More and more production, previously outside, is being transferred to the southern plants. A modernization program is in progress. In addition, nuclear wastes from naval nuclear vessels are handled in the South and components for such vessels are likewise manufactured there. Lists and describes each of the four southern plants and its activities. Map.                                    R. V. Ritter

3089. Ratliff, Ophelia Wood. THE TEXAS & PACIFIC IN WARD COUNTY, 1880-1910. *Permian Hist. Ann. 1981 21: 97-109.* Provides detailed information about the purpose and construction of section houses along the rail route and discusses the railroad's impact on the development of the region.

3090. Rauchle, Bob. REMINISCENCES FROM THE GERMANTOWN SETTLEMENT IN GIBSON COUNTY, TENNESSEE. *Tennessee Folklore Soc. Bull. 1979 45(2): 62-67.* Gives a brief history of Germantown in Gibson County, Tennessee, from 1880 to 1941, based on the oral reminiscences of Louise Theresa Rauchle Casey, born in 1888.

3091. Rea, John C. THE TENNESSEE MIDLAND RAILWAY. *West Tennessee Hist. Soc. Papers 1981 35: 118-121.* A succinct history of the organization and growth of the line of the Tennessee Midland Railway from Memphis to Perryville, Tennessee—its greatest length. Organized in 1886, the line reached Perryville in 1890. However, the hopes for a profitable venture failed, and in 1895 the railroad was sold to cover its debts. It became part of other railroad lines. Based on newspaper accounts and secondary materials; 2 illus., map, 14 notes.          H. M. Parker, Jr.

3092. Reid, June R. THE TEXAS AND PACIFIC RAILROAD, MARTIN COUNTY. *Permian Hist. Ann. 1981 21: 79-83.* Traces the impact of the Texas & Pacific Railroad on the social and economic development of Martin County in west Texas from 1881 to 1976, focusing on the area's early settlers and on the construction of section houses along the route by the railroad company.

3093. Reidy, Jeanne P. BOCA GRANDE: THE TOWN THE RAILROAD BUILT. *Tampa Bay Hist. 1982 4(1): 21-32.* Traces the history of Boca Grande, Florida, founded on Gasparilla Island as a railroad town along the Alafia, Manatee and Gulf Railway Company's line.

3094. Reynolds, Terry S. CISTERNS AND FIRES: SHREVEPORT, LOUISIANA, AS A CASE STUDY OF THE EMERGENCE OF PUBLIC WATER SUPPLY SYSTEMS IN THE SOUTH. *Louisiana Hist. 1981 22(4): 337-367.* After unsuccessful attempts in the 1840's and 1850's to secure a public water supply through artesian wells, and an unsatisfactory system of underground cisterns for fire fighting in the 1860's and 1870's, Shreveport finally turned in the 1880's to private waterworks companies. The city's poor financial condition, a reluctance to incur public debt or raise taxes, and a preference for investing in railroad development determined this solution. After a number of false starts an experienced company was awarded the contract to build both a water and a sewerage system and a 30-year operating franchise. The work was completed in 1887. Based on government documents, newspapers, secondary sources; table, photo, 142 notes.          R. E. Noble

3095. Rikard, Marlene Hunt. GEORGE GORDON CRAWFORD: MAN OF THE NEW SOUTH. *Alabama Rev. 1978 31(3): 163-181.* George G. Crawford (d. 1936), president of the Tennessee Coal Iron and Railroad Company in Birmingham, Alabama, 1907-30, was a "realistic" leader in the New South. He worked for improved housing and health conditions, partly to reduce worker absenteeism; argued for balance between industry and agriculture; and promoted the South without unduly exaggerating its potential for growth. Primary and secondary sources; 43 notes.
                                    J. F. Vivian

3096. Riley, Mark B. EDGEFIELD: A STUDY OF AN EARLY NASHVILLE SUBURB. *Tennessee Hist. Q. 1978 37(2): 133-154.* Edgefield began as a community on the east side of the Cumberland River opposite Nashville's business district. In the late 19th century, with the introduction of streetcars, it became the suburban home of many of Nashville's most prominent citizens. Edgefield was annexed to Nashville during the civil booster movement in

1880. Beginning about 1900, East Nashville lost its attraction and began to fall behind West Nashville. In 1916 Edgefield was almost wiped out by a disastrous fire. Not until the 1960's did Edgefield begin to recover. In 1978 Edgefield became the first district in Davidson County to be given historic district status. Primary and secondary sources; 4 illus., 41 notes.                    M. B. Lucas

3097. Ritter, Christine. LIFE IN EARLY AMERICA: SOUTHERN FURNITURE MAKERS. *Early Am. Life 1977 8(6): 32-35.* Sketches furniture makers who operated shops in the South in the 18th century; includes common items and popular styles manufactured.

3098. Robbins, Peggy. STEAMBOAT A-COMIN'. *Am. Hist. Illus. 1979 14(7): 16-22, 24-25.* Gives the history of steamboats in America, particularly along the Mississippi River, from 1787 until the late 19th century, when other forms of transportation became more popular and faster.

3099. Rocawich, Linda. COASTAL PROFILES OF NINE SOUTHERN STATES: SOUTH COAST FOLLIES. *Southern Exposure 1982 10(3): 90-120.* Discusses the histories of the coastal areas and notes current conditions, especially the development of the area, the need for conservation, and government regulation of the areas.

3100. Rosenberg, Leon J. and Davis, Grant M. DALLAS AND ITS FIRST RAILROAD. *Railroad Hist. 1976 (135): 34-42.* Offers a history of railroads in Dallas, Texas, the influence. which they had on the exact placement of the city, and the political and economic events which brought the location of railroad connections about, 1843-73. 40 notes.

3101. Rousey, Dennis C. "HIBERNIAN LEATHERHEADS": IRISH COPS IN NEW ORLEANS, 1830-1880. *J. of Urban Hist. 1983 10(1): 61-84.* Examines the popular ethnic image of Boston and New York policemen that extended into 19th-century cities in the South as well. Traces the increased Irish representation on the New Orleans police force and examines the reaction of the Know-Nothing Party to Irish immigrant police. 6 tables, 29 notes.
                                                            T. W. Smith

3102. Rowland, A. Ray. THE AUGUSTA CITY DIRECTORY. *Richmond County Hist. 1973 5(1): 5-28.* An overview of city directories published for Augusta since 1841. Lists facts of publication and locations of all extant Augusta directories. 3 illus., 7 notes.
                                                            H. R. Grant

3103. Rubin, Louis D., Jr. THE BOLL WEEVIL, THE IRON HORSE, AND THE END OF THE LINE: THOUGHTS ON THE SOUTH. *Virginia Q. Rev. 1979 55(2): 193-221.* The author discusses change in the South since the 1930's as he examines his attachment to the Boll Weevil, a little gas-electric locomotive coach, now long gone. His discussion of Walker Percy's *The Last Gentleman* as representative of current Southern literature recognizes the important point that the South has remained the South. Changes occur, as they always have, and it is false to assume that there is only one "static perfection" against which the South's characteristics and ideals can be measured. The racial and other changes must be accepted as part of the real South not "yet concluded."
                                                            O. H. Zabel

3104. Satterfield, Carolyn Green. J. R. MCWANE: PIPE AND PROGRESS. *Alabama Rev. 1982 35(1): 30-37.* A brief history of the McWane Cast Iron Pipe Company and the McWane family. The family began its industrial ventures in Virginia, one member of the family, James Ransom McWane, eventually moving to Birmingham, Alabama. An early venture in iron forging failed, and James went to work for another iron company, served as a civilian volunteer in World War I, relaunched the business after the war, guided it through the Great Depression, and made it into the thriving business that it is today. 18 notes.          V. L. Human

3105. Sauder, Robert A. THE ORIGIN AND SPREAD OF THE PUBLIC MARKET SYSTEM IN NEW ORLEANS. *Louisiana Hist. 1981 22(3): 281-297.* Owing to its Creole heritage, New Orleans operated more public markets than any other city in the United States. The French Market, chartered in 1784, provided low-cost space, eliminated middlemen, and increased competition, insuring low food prices. Eventually almost every neighborhood had its public market. By the 20th century, the emphasis had shifted from protecting the consumer to providing municipal revenue and political patronage; the city restricted private markets and resisted the invasion of chain stores and supermarkets. The newer merchandising techniques won out and in the 1930's the public markets disappeared. Based on public documents and secondary sources; illus., 7 photos, map, 37 notes.                    R. E. Noble

3106. Schene, Michael G. THE EARLY FLORIDA SALVAGE INDUSTRY. *Am. Neptune 1978 38(4): 262-271.* Discusses the maritime salvage industry in Florida from the 1760's to the 1830's, focusing on salvage law and practices. Cites examples of types of salvage operations. Primary and secondary sources; 25 notes.
                                                            G. H. Curtis

3107. Schulman, Steven A. RAFTING LOGS ON THE UPPER CUMBERLAND RIVER. *Pioneer Am. 1974 6(1): 14-24.* Presents evidence that the logging era in the Kentucky and Tennessee counties of the upper Cumberland River Valley lasted for a longer time than in other major lumber regions of the Eastern United States. Due to the isolation of the area and lack of railroad competition, log rafts were constructed and floated to sawmills in Nashville, Tennessee. The trips down the river were initiated during winter and early spring when there was sufficient water to float the logs free from river banks where they had been brought for transportation. When not employed as raft hands, some of the men spent time aboard steamboats or ferries. Based on secondary sources, and several informants who previously worked in the logging industry ca. 1870-1930; 4 illus., 1 map, fig., 6 notes.
                                                            C. R. Gunter, Jr.

3108. Scriven, George B. THE SUSQUEHANNA AND TIDEWATER CANAL. *Maryland Hist. Mag. 1976 71(4): 522-526.* Reports the contents of a recently uncovered company permit record book for 17 October 1892 to 7 June 1893, about one year before canal operations ceased. It may be "the only such record available for the period of the canal operation." Surveys the history of the Maryland section of the canal, its locks, boats, cargoes, traffic, and toll rates. Three lists show boat and tonnage charges, names of vessels, and captains. Primary source.          G. J. Bobango

3109. Seely, Bruce E. WILMINGTON AND ITS RAILROADS: A LASTING CONNECTION. *Delaware Hist. 1980 19(1): 1-19.* Examines the role of railroads in transforming the urban and economic landscape of Wilmington in the 19th and 20th centuries. The railroad connection opened new markets of a national scale to the city's industrialists, with the railroad industry being an important market in itself. The railroads determined the physical location of business activity, and they became primary employers in the city, and remain so. Focuses particularly on the Philadelphia, Wilmington, and Baltimore Railroad's influence. Map, table, 42 notes.
                                                            R. M. Miller

3110. Selby, Edward B., Jr. and Meadows, John C. GEORGIA RAILROAD AND BANKING COMPANY: THE TAX CASES AND THE PLAN FOR CAPITAL READJUSTMENT. *Georgia Hist. Q. 1981 65(3): 240-250.* When the Georgia Railroad and Banking Company was formed in 1833, its charter contained a tax exemption provision. Various court battles over taxation and conflicts over readjusting the company's capital in the 1950's are described. Based on company documents, court records and other sources; 36 notes.                    G. R. Schroeder

3111. Shand, Hope. BILLIONS OF CHICKENS: THE BUSINESS OF THE SOUTH. *Southern Exposure 1983 11(6): 76-82.* Surveys the Southern poultry industry, which produces most US poultry, and discusses its structure.

3112. Sharrer, G. Terry. FLOUR MILLING IN THE GROWTH OF BALTIMORE, 1750-1830. *Maryland Hist. Mag. 1976 71(3): 322-333.* Discusses the American flour and grain trade to Europe and the West Indies as affected by famines, crop failures, and the Napoleonic Wars abroad, and the Jeffersonian embargo at home. Waterloo and the British Corn Laws greatly diminished these markets and US consumption and the trade with South America replaced them. Baltimore dominated the flour trade in both periods due to the milling technology of Oliver Evans, the introduction of steam power in processing, and the merchant-millers' development of drying processes which greatly retarded spoilage. Still, by 1830 New York's competition was felt keenly, and Baltimoreans were hard-pressed to match the merchantability standards despite more rigorous inspection controls than earlier, nor could they match the greater financial resources of their northern rivals. Primary and secondary sources; 30 notes.                    G. J. Bobango

3113. Sharrer, G. Terry; Schmitz, Mark, (commentary). THE MERCHANT-MILLERS: BALTIMORE'S FLOUR MILLING INDUSTRY, 1783-1860. *Agric. Hist. 1982 56(1): 138-150, 167-171.* In the years before 1815 the export of flour to the West Indies and South America became a major business for Baltimore merchants. The introduction of automated machinery and steam power encouraged merchants to specialize in flour, including a number of millers who also traded in flour. The growth of these domestic markets advanced Baltimore's importance as a milling center. Comments, pp. 167-171; 35 notes.                    D. E. Bowers

3114. Sheridan, Richard C. PRODUCTION OF SALTPETRE FROM ALABAMA CAVES. *Alabama Rev. 1980 33(1): 25-34.* In colonial and antebellum times most of America's saltpeter came from India. By 1812 saltpeter was available in large amounts from Alabama caves. It is a main "ingredient in the production of black gunpowder." Describes the production process of saltpeter, especially during the Civil War. Primary sources; 29 notes.

J. Powell

3115. Shirley, Michael. THE "CONSCIENTIOUS CONSERVATISM" OF ASA GRIGGS CANDLER. *Georgia Hist. Q. 1983 67(3): 356-365.* Presents the views of Asa Griggs Candler, a Southern Progressive founder of the Coca-Cola Company and mayor of Atlanta, who felt that the urban commercial elite had a responsibility to improve the living conditions of the Southern urban lower classes. Based on the Candler Papers and secondary sources; 34 notes.                    G. R. Schroeder

3116. Shofner, Jerrell H. NEGRO LABORERS AND THE FOREST INDUSTRIES IN RECONSTRUCTION FLORIDA. *J. of Forest Hist. 1975 19(4): 180-191.* Florida's forests provided the most extensive employment for ex-slaves when cotton production declined in the late 19th century. A wage-labor system evolved to ease the accommodation of ex-slaves to free labor and to compensate for the short supply of fluid capital. Despite limited success in organizing for collective bargaining, Florida timber workers were as well off as average wage earners of their time. 5 illus., map, 38 notes.                    L. Johnson

3117. Shook, R. W. YEARS OF TRANSITION: VICTORIA, TEXAS, 1880-1920. *Southwestern Hist. Q. 1974 78(2): 155-182.* Contemporary Victoria is a product of late 19th- and early 20th-century technological, economic, and social forces, including agriculture, transportation, communications, road improvement, new commercial ventures, banking, and extended professional services. "The village which had begun as an empresario headquarters and cattle center prospered as a result of its distance from Gulf storms and direct connections with larger towns to the east and north." 23 photos, 34 notes.                    R. V. Ritter

3118. Silver, Christopher. THE ORDEAL OF CITY PLANNING IN POSTWAR RICHMOND, VIRGINIA: A QUEST FOR GREATNESS. *J. of Urban Hist. 1983 10(1): 33-60.* Traces changes in the goals of urban redevelopment in Richmond, Virginia, placing city planning in its context among general political struggles. The main goals of city planning did not change with the rise of black political power. Fig., 55 notes, appendix.                    T. W. Smith

3119. Simmons, James C. THE GREAT SPINDLETOP OIL RUSH. *Am. West 1980 17(1): 10-13, 61-62.* The single most important oil find in the United States was made 10 January 1901, on a knob of land near Spindletop Springs near Beaumont, Texas, thanks to the persistence of landowner Pattillo Higgins and mining engineer Anthony F. Lucas. It shifted the center for the American oil industry from the Ohio-West Virginia-Pennsylvania region, broke Standard Oil's longstanding production and distribution monopoly, and inspired the invention of a technology that brought the birth of the modern oil industry, including such giants as Gulf and Texaco. Production of Spindletop's oil continues, but the importance of the field as a producing pool lasted only into the 1930's. 2 illus., note, biblio.                    D. L. Smith

3120. Simon, Richard M. THE DEVELOPMENT OF WORKING-CLASS CULTURE: A REVIEW ESSAY. *Appalachian J. 1982 9(4): 311-315.* Review article of David Alan Corbin's *Life, Work and Rebellion in the Coal Fields: The Southern West Virginia Miners, 1880-1922.*

3121. Simon, Richard M. MILL VILLAGE AND COAL TOWN COMPARED: A REVIEW ESSAY. *Appalachian J. 1980 8(1): 67-70.* Review essay of Dwight Billings's *Planters and the Making of a "New South": Class, Politics, and Development in North Carolina, 1865-1900* (Chapel Hill: U. of North Carolina Pr., 1979) which "analyzes the dependent economic development of North Carolina," and compares *Planters* with John Williams's *West Virginia and the Captains of Industry* (Morgantown: West Virginia U. Lib., 1976) about how coal barons, lawyers, and landowners controlled the conservative modernization of West Virginia.

3122. Simon, Richard M. UNEVEN DEVELOPMENT AND THE CASE OF WEST VIRGINIA: GOING BEYOND THE COLONIALISM MODEL. *Appalachian J. 1981 8(3): 165-186.* The economic transformation in West Virginia between 1880 and 1930 was centered in the coal-producing counties; the coal-town economy led to the underdevelopment of West Virginia.

3123. Smith, E. A. WHEN STEAMBOATS LEFT TAMPA BAY. *Tampa Bay Hist. 1980 2(1): 30-33.* Briefly discusses the steamboats that sailed to and from Tampa Bay during the late 19th-early 20th century, focusing on the *Mandeville*, the *Favorite*, the *Pokanoket*, the *Manatee*, the *Narwahl*, the *Jeanette*, the *I. W. Riggs*, and the *Genevieve*.

3124. Smith, Elizabeth Simpson. VESUVIUS FURNACE PLANTATION. *Historic Preservation 1976 28(2): 24-27.* Discusses the industrial, social and economic life of Vesuvius Furnace, an ironworks plantation established in 1791 in Lincoln County, North Carolina. Initially using slave labor like most of the agrarian plantations, it operated until about 1876. Illus., photo.                    R. M. Frame III

3125. Smith, Ralph A. THE WEST TEXAS BONE BUSINESS. *West Texas Hist. Assoc. Y. 1979 55: 111-134.* Discusses the economic significance of the massive western Texas bone industry which periodically flourished, 1872-1937.

3126. Spier, William. A SOCIAL HISTORY OF MANGANESE MINING IN THE BATESVILLE DISTRICT OF INDEPENDENCE COUNTY. *Arkansas Hist. Q. 1977 36(2): 130-157.* Cushing, Arkansas, was a manganese mining center which was developed in the late 1840's and reached its peak production during the 1890's-1930's. Most workers were either local farmers wishing to earn extra money during slack seasons or migrants from nearby states. Pay was only $1.50 per day or $4.00 per ton of coal mined and delivered to Batesville, the nearest railroad terminus. Workers enjoyed simple, but often rowdy, lives. There was little food, clothing, or shelter for their families, and only the hope for a big strike tomorrow kept them going. Based on interviews with former miners; 4 illus., 94 notes.                    T. L. Savitt

3127. Sprague, Stuart Seely. KENTUCKY AND THE CINCINNATI-CHARLESTON RAILROAD, 1835-1839. *Register of the Kentucky Hist. Soc. 1975 73(2): 122-135.* Recounts the unsuccessful efforts of South Carolinians to link Charleston and Cincinnati by rail. A charter, granted by Kentucky in 1836, did not lead to the necessary financial support. Efforts to achieve a more favorable charter in 1837 failed. Primary and secondary sources; 51 notes.
J. F. Paul

3128. Stakem, Karen A. HANS FROELICHER, JR.: CIVIC EDUCATOR. *Maryland Hist. Mag. 1982 77(2): 193-201.* Hans Froelicher, Jr., was a native Baltimorean whose many years of civic service included positions on the Mayor's Advisory Council to the Housing Bureau, the Mount Royal Improvement Association, and the Baltimore City Health Department Advisory Committee on Sanitation. At the same time, his career as an educator marked him as a leader of the progressive school movement. As headmaster of the Park School for 24 years, his position led to his involvement in the Baltimore Citizen's Planning and Housing Association, which made large strides in addressing the problems of substandard housing, especially under Froelicher's presidency during 1944-56.
G. J. Bobango

3129. Steinmeyer, George. A HISTORY OF THE OKLAHOMA GAS AND ELECTRIC COMPANY TO 1904. *Chronicles of Oklahoma 1973 51(2): 195-210.*

3130. Stewart, Peter C. RAILROADS AND URBAN RIVALRIES IN ANTEBELLUM EASTERN VIRGINIA. *Virginia Mag. of Hist. and Biog. 1973 81(1): 3-22.* Railroad construction provided a focus for the acceleration of economic rivalry between Richmond, Petersburg, and Norfolk from the 1830's through the 1850's. Richmond's place as a political center provided legislative leverage and attracted able promoters and sufficient capital. Richmond outdistanced its rivals handily, with Petersburg gaining little more than Norfolk. The rivalry left an enduring legacy. Based on railroad archives, manuscripts, and newspapers; 60 notes.
C. A. Newton

3131. Stewart, Peter C. THE SHINGLE AND LUMBER INDUSTRIES IN THE GREAT DISMAL. *J. of Forest Hist. 1981 25(2): 98-107.* The Great Dismal Swamp, an ecologically unique swampland on the Virginia-North Carolina border near the Atlantic coast, has a long history of forest exploitation. Since colonial times, entrepreneurs have devised means to extract the timber and convert it to shingles, lumber, and other products at mills located on the swamp's periphery. The principal operations are described. Despite generations of use—including construction of canals and conversion to agricultural land—many of the swamp's natural qualities remained intact. Recent awareness of the swamp's ecological importance led the Union Camp Corporation and other timber companies to donate large tracts to the Nature Conservancy, which in turn passed them to the federal government for creation of a national wildlife refuge. 4 illus., map, 54 notes.
R. J. Fahl

3132. Stoesen, Alexander R. ROAD FROM RECEIVERSHIP: CLAUDE PEPPER, THE DU PONT TRUST, AND THE FLORIDA EAST COAST RAILWAY. *Florida Hist. Q. 1973 52(2): 132-156.* Describes the battle between Senator Claude Pepper and Ed Ball, senior trustee of the Du Pont estate, over the future organization of the Florida East Coast Railroad. The railroad had passed into receivership in 1931 and by 1945 had built a surplus of 20 million. Pepper attempted to bring about a merger with the Atlantic Coast Line railroad, while Ball fought for independent management under du Pont control. Although no settlement was reached until 1958, the climax of the acrimonious battle came with Pepper's failure to win renomination in 1950. Primary and secondary sources; map, 102 notes.
J. E. Findling

3133. Sullivan, Ken. COAL MEN OF THE SMOKELESS COALFIELDS. *West Virginia Hist. 1980 41(2): 143-165.* Discusses the operators who developed the coalfields in the Winding Gulf, New River, and Pocahontas areas of West Virginia. Notes their places of origin, education, religion, social class, and age. Many of the men came from Great Britain via Pennsylvania. Covers ca. 1870-1941. Based on newspaper accounts, personal interviews, W. P. Tams, Jr.'s *The Smokeless Coalfields,* and the author's dissertation; 61 notes.
J. D. Neville

3134. Summerville, James. THE CITY AND THE SLUM: "BLACK BOTTOM" AND THE DEVELOPMENT OF SOUTH NASHVILLE. *Tennessee Hist. Q. 1981 40(2): 182-192.* Black Bottom was the name given to the area in south Nashville that was low and identified by darker soil. Originally settled by Irish in the 1850's, it had a sordid reputation by the time Negroes began to move in later in the century. Thereafter the area became a subject of controversy between those who profited from its misery and those who wanted to clean it up. Meanwhile, the area became associated with disease, high mortality, and poverty. Not until the 1960's and the use of federal funds was there a real beginning in ridding the city of Black Bottom and its problems. Now there is interest in restoring the waterfront and turning some of the area into a park. Mainly newspapers and letters.
C. L. Grant

3135. Surratt, Jerry L. THE MORAVIAN AS BUSINESSMAN: GOTTLIEB SCHOBER OF SALEM. *North Carolina Hist. Rev. 1983 60(1): 1-23.* Gottlieb Schober combined a business career with a life of service to the Moravian community of Salem, North Carolina. Raised in Bethlehem, Pennsylvania, until age 12, Schober was then sent to Salem to learn a trade through apprenticeship, where he mastered the making of deerskin breeches. A restless man of drive and initiative, Schober learned store management, tinsmithing, and papermaking, and continually attempted to earn extra money by trading outside the community, a forbidden practice. Reprimanded numerous times, Schober eventually accepted the community's rules. He served Salem as lawyer, church organist, postmaster, and public official. Based on published Moravian records and materials in the Moravian Archives, Winston-Salem, North Carolina; 12 illus., 65 notes.
T. L. Savitt

3136. Sussman, Carl. MOVING THE CITY SLICKERS OUT. *Southern Exposure 1974 2(2/3): 99-107.* Discusses socioeconomic aspects of urbanization in the South in the 1960's and 70's, emphasizing implications for local government and property values.

3137. Tazewell, William L. NORFOLK: A REMARKABLE RESURGENCE. *Virginia Cavalcade 1982 32(2): 76-85.* Burned twice in 1776 and attacked by federal forces in 1861, Norfolk recovered to become a major port and shipyard during the two world wars, and since then has revitalized its central city area.

3138. Thomas, Jerry B. JEDEDIAH HOTCHKISS, GILDED-AGE PROPAGANDIST OF INDUSTRIALISM. *Virginia Mag. of Hist. and Biog. 1976 84(2): 189-202.* Jedediah Hotchkiss, one of Virginia's most persistent advocates of industrialism from the end of the Civil War until his death in 1899, contributed significantly to the rise of industry in southwest Virginia and southern West Virginia. Though the industrial development did not include the hoped-for iron and steel industries, Hotchkiss managed to persuade investors to develop the coal industry. Based on the Hotchkiss Papers, Alderman Library, U. of Virginia, newspapers, and secondary accounts; 69 notes.
R. F. Oaks

3139. Thomas, Ronald C. THE FOUNDING OF A HAPPY TOWN: MARTIN, TENNESSEE. *West Tennessee Hist. Soc. Papers 1973 (27): 5-17.* Martin, Tennessee, was founded as a result of the migration of William Martin to Weakley County in 1832, his diligent work in securing railroad connections, and the expansion of the Nashville and Northwestern Railway into the southeastern section of the country by 1873; in 1893 the population had reached 2000.

3140. Thorn, Cecelia Jean. THE BELL FACTORY: EARLY PRIDE OF HUNTSVILLE. *Alabama Rev. 1979 32(1): 28-37.* From its obscure beginnings about 1817 to its closing in 1885, the Bell Factory was a combination of gristmill, distillery, cotton gin, and textile mill built along the Flint River. Emphasizes changes of ownership, management, labor conditions, and the Civil War. Primary and secondary sources; 31 notes.          J. F. Vivian

3141. Timmons, W. H. AMERICAN EL PASO: THE FORMATIVE YEARS, 1848-1854. *Southwestern Hist. Q. 1983 87(1): 1-36.* On 2 February 1848, the Treaty of Guadalupe Hidalgo ended the Mexican War, and the Rio Grande River became part of the boundary between the United States and Mexico. By 1849, eight settlements had been established on the American side of the river at the Pass of the North, and the Texas legislature approved the organization of El Paso County later that year. In 1852, the federal government established a post office at one of the early settlements, known as the Benjamin Franklin Coons ranch, and called the site El Paso. This bilingual, bicultural, and binational settlement complex became the foundation for the modern city of El Paso. Based on the records of the Office of the Commissary General and Office of the Quarter Master General, State Records Center and Archives, Santa Fe; Records of the War Department, Special Collections University of Texas, El Paso; and the Bartlett Papers, Texas State Library, Austin; 66 notes, 7 maps.          R. D. Hurt

3142. Turner, Charles W. THE LOUISA RAILROAD COMPANY: GENESIS OF CHESSIE'S SYSTEM. *Virginia Cavalcade 1980 29(3): 130-135.* Traces the early years of the Louisa Railroad Company of Virginia, which was chartered in 1836 by the General Assembly, destroyed during the Civil War, and rebuilt in 1866; it became the Chesapeake and Ohio Railroad in 1867, and is now the Chessie System, which extends from Newport News and Norfolk, Virginia to St. Louis, Missouri.

3143. Vance, James E., Jr. THE CLASSICAL REVIVAL AND URBAN-RURAL CONFLICT IN NINETEENTH CENTURY AMERICA. *Can. R. of Am. Studies 1973 4(2): 149-168.* Surveys the development of conflicts during the early 19th century between the exponents of an idyllic rural America and those who found many virtues in urban centers, praised the merchants and considered the city the "real, productive world." Similar conflicts erupted earlier in Europe and were brought to America during New World colonization. Early in the 1800's, antiurban views were popular in the United States. Thomas Jefferson (1743-1826) was the most able upholder of the virtues of rural life. Ultimately, the South adopted Roman models for maintaining urban-rural distinctions. Urban-rural conflicts in the North devolved into social divisions between the "responsible, propertied class and the [urban] mob." The Classical Revival in the North thus evoked classical Greek solutions to town and country hostilities.          H. T. Lovin

3144. Vedder, Richard K.; Gallaway, Lowell E.; and Klingaman, David. DISCRIMINATION AND EXPLOITATION IN ANTEBELLUM AMERICAN COTTON TEXTILE MANUFACTURING. *Res. in Econ. Hist. 1978 3: 217-262.* A "pessimistic" school of historians has argued that antebellum American cotton textile workers were "exploited" and female workers discriminated against, while some "optimistic" scholars argue that workers shared in an expected fashion in productivity gains over time. By statistically estimating production functions from data from the McLane Report (1833) and 1860 Census manuscripts, marginal products of the factors of production are obtained and compared with their factor prices. Workers were paid roughly their marginal products and other productive factors were likewise rewarded. It is concluded that the "optimists" are more likely correct and that neoclassical theory is consistent with observed wage and profit levels. Some job entry discrimination against females probably existed, however.          J

3145. Wakeley, Philip C. THE ADOLESCENCE OF FORESTRY RESEARCH IN THE SOUTH: A REFLECTIVE VIEW. *J. of Forest Hist. 1978 22(3): 136-145.* Earl L. Stone interviews the author who began his forty-year career with the Forest Service in 1924. Established in 1921, the Southern Forest Experiment Station in New Orleans (and its various field stations throughout the Gulf South) operated for many years on a modest scale. Minimal funding, spartan working conditions, suspicious natives, and other hazards, however, did not deter a small band of Forest Service scientists whose research had far-reaching impact on the health of

southern forests and forest industries. The interaction of administrators, researchers, industrial cooperators, and events affected the design and implementation of this work, as seen here from the perspective of the author's 40-year career in southern pine research. Consists of excerpts from a 1965 interview and brief sections of the author's manuscript history of the station. Illus., 9 photos.          R. J. Fahl

3146. Wakeley, Philip C. F. O.(RED) BATEMAN, PIONEER SILVICULTURALIST. *J. of Forest Hist. 1976 20(2): 91-99.* F. O. Bateman (d. 1941), chief ranger of the Great Southern Lumber Company in Louisiana, was a pioneer in the South's forestry practice. His outstanding contributions were in prevention and suppression of fires and in techniques of forest planting. In 1924 he developed planting techniques still in general use for southern pines. 5 illus., 12 notes.          L. F. Johnson

3147. Wall, Bennett H. LEON GODCHAUX AND THE GODCHAUX BUSINESS ENTERPRISES. *Am. Jewish Hist. Q. 1976 66(1): 50-66.* Reconstructs the life and influence of Leon Godchaux (1824-99), New Orleans merchant, plantation owner, sugar refiner, real estate developer, and financier, who proved that hard work, canny business judgment and ingenuity made it possible for a poor immigrant boy to rise rapidly to wealth and importance. Based on papers and clippings of the Godchaux family. 29 notes.          F. Rosenthal

3148. Wall, Rita Turner. THE VANISHING TENANT HOUSES OF RURAL GEORGIA. *Georgia Hist. Q. 1981 65(3): 251-262.* Describes the construction of black and white sharecroppers' homes from Reconstruction to World War II. 3 illus., 12 notes.          G. R. Schroeder

3149. Ward, James A. MISSISSIPPI'S SOUTHERN RAILROAD: A STUDY IN PERILS AND PERSEVERANCE. *Railroad Hist. 1981 (144): 29-49.* History of Mississippi's Southern Railroad from its beginnings in the 1840's until 1889, especially the economic and technical difficulties in expanding the original 14 mile line into a 140 mile line.

3150. Ward, James A. A NEW LOOK AT ANTEBELLUM SOUTHERN RAILROAD DEVELOPMENT. *J. of Southern Hist. 1973 39(3): 409-420.* Analyzes explanations and discussions of southern rail development in the antebellum period. Two explanations for southern rail inferiority are usually cited: 1) the economic development of the South did not require a more complex system, and 2) the South lacked capital to improve its lines up to the Northern level. Shows that the South did not lack the capability and finances to improve its rail system and attributes the inferiority to the slow recovery from the depression of the late 1830's, a shortage of trained civil engineers, and the disruption of overseas markets due to the Crimean War. Based on contemporary journal reports, primary and secondary sources; 31 notes.          N. J. Street

3151. Warner, Lee H. FLORIDA'S CAPITOLS. *Florida Hist. Q. 1983 61(3): 245-259.* Continued growth and expansion of Tallahassee's old state capitol (completed 1845) ended with the construction of a new capitol in the late 1960's. The original building was restored to its configuration of 1902 at a cost of $7 million. Florida appears committed to building new structures rather than additions to existing buildings in order to preserve its tradition. Based on state records, personal papers, and other sources; 7 fig., 39 notes.          N. A. Kuntz

3152. Watson, Alan D. THE FERRY IN COLONIAL NORTH CAROLINA: A VITAL LINK IN TRANSPORTATION. *North Carolina Hist. R. 1974 51(3): 247-260.* With one ferry in 1700, the ferry service had been regularly established throughout the eastern coastal plain by the 1760's. Ferries facilitated travel for various purposes, such as, to reduce the difficulties of settlers in going to court, vestry, or muster. Ferries in North Carolina were created in a decentralized manner. Post riders were given preference to speed the mail. After 100 years North Carolina's transportation system "had barely progressed beyond the most rudimentary level." Illus., 70 notes.                                                 E. P. Stickney

3153. Weaver, David C. SPATIAL STRATEGIES IN RAILROAD PLANNING IN GEORGIA AND THE CAROLINAS, 1830-1860. *West Georgia Coll. Studies in the Social Sci. 1979 18: 9-23.* Explores the geographic and political-economic considerations, regional and parochial, which determined the creation and fragmented nature of the railroad systems of this area.

3154. Weiher, Kenneth. THE COTTON INDUSTRY AND SOUTHERN URBANIZATION, 1880-1930. *Explorations in Econ. Hist. 1977 14(2): 120-140.* Using central place theory, shows that the hierarchy of central services associated with the cultivation and marketing of cotton and cotton byproducts shaped the pace and pattern of urbanization and were fundamentally responsible for the location, size, and growth of most southern cities through the 1920's. Published documents and secondary accounts; 2 figs., 5 tables, 27 notes, 14 refs.                       P. J. Coleman

3155. Welsh, Carol Holderby. CATTLE MARKET FOR THE WORLD: THE OKLAHOMA NATIONAL STOCKYARDS. *Chronicles of Oklahoma 1982 60(1): 42-55.* When Edward Morris and Company opened a packing plant in October 1910, Oklahoma City began a remarkable economic growth through stockyards and slaughterhouses. City fathers offered tax incentives, land, and even cash bonuses to entice other meat-packing firms. By the 1940's feeder-yard operations were beginning to replace the original packinghouses as the main enterprise. A 1980 fire at the Livestock Exchange Building not only destroyed one of Oklahoma City's most historic buildings, it also symbolized the end of an era. Based on Oklahoma City newspapers and interviews; 5 photos, 40 notes.
                                                            M. L. Tate

3156. Wennersten, John R. THE ALMIGHTY OYSTER: A SAGA OF OLD SOMERSET AND THE EASTERN SHORE, 1850-1920. *Maryland Hist. Mag. 1979 74(1): 81-93.* Recreates the boom decades of the Chesapeake Bay oyster industry of the 1870's and 1880's, centering on Crisfield and the Somerset County watermen, both drudgers and tongers. Conflict between the two main types of oyster fishermen led to creation of an Oyster Navy in 1868 to keep peace on the Bay. This, and the competition of Virginia and Maryland captains for the riches to be made in the oyster beds, produced a rough-and-tumble, lawless, wide-open environment reminiscent of the western frontier. Describes the hardships of oystering, the changing technology of processing and shipping, and the federal arbitration leading to the Jenkins-Black Award of 1877 that demarked the water boundary between Virginia and Maryland. The decline of the Chesapeake oyster industry after 1890 due to overharvesting is a classic example of the abuse of natural resources. 32 notes.                                                G. J. Bobango

3157. White, Dana F. and Crimmins, Timothy J. URBAN STRUCTURE, ATLANTA. *J. of Urban Hist. 1976 2(2): 231-251.* Discusses the urban structure of Atlanta during the late 19th and 20th centuries and the changes in residences followed by black club women and Colonial Dames. Analyzes shifts in black residential patterns and the impact of transportation. 9 maps, 9 notes.
                                                            T. W. Smith

3158. White, John H. THE *MISSISSIPPI:* A SOUTHERN FOUNDLING. *Railroad Hist. 1979 (140): 114-118.* Gives the history of the *Mississippi,* the oldest locomotive surviving from a railroad line related to the Illinois Central Railroad since the building of the locomotive's engine in 1836.

3159. Wilkstrom, Debbie. THE HORSE-DRAWN STREET RAILWAY: THE BEGINNING OF PUBLIC TRANSPORTATION IN SHREVEPORT. *North Louisiana Hist. Assoc. J. 1976 7(3): 83-90.* During 1870-72, different groups of Shreveport's citizens "formed three companies to build street railway lines through the downtown district and to outlying areas." Two of those companies eventually succeeded in building and operating street railway lines, although only one proved to be a profitable enterprise. The

first line was built by the Shreveport City Railroad Company; the second by the Fairfield Streetcar Company; the third company, which "failed before it really began," was the Texas Avenue Railway Company. By 1876, the first-named line was the only survivor. "This small line, though perhaps insignificant in itself, began the public transportation system of Shreveport." 58 notes.
                                                            A. N. Garland

3160. Williams, Bobby Joe. LET THERE BE LIGHT: TENNESSEE VALLEY AUTHORITY COMES TO MEMPHIS. *West Tennessee Hist. Soc. Papers 1976 (30): 43-66.* Traces the history of electric utilities in Memphis and the internecine struggles to bring Tennessee Valley Authority power from Muscle Shoals into Memphis in the 1930's. Traces the intricacies of the power struggle between a corporation owned utility as it is confronted by the prospects of a municipally owned utility which has access to inexpensive power created by a Federal agency. Based on the Watkins Overton Collection, Memphis State University, and contemporary newspapers; 2 illus., 88 notes.                  H. M. Parker, Jr.

3161. Williams, Mike and Menzer, Mitch. SOUTHERN STEEL. *Southern Exposure 1981 9(3): 74-79.* Discusses the history of the steel industry in Birmingham, Alabama, 1880-1981.

3162. Williams, Robert L. IN DALLAS, AS IN MOST AMERICAN CITIES, THE CONTRAST OF GLITTER AND SQUALOR. *Smithsonian 1978 9(8): 60-69.* Outlines problems of modern US cities, including race, education, crime, and the balancing of budgets, and inquires into who pays for city services People tend to flee to the suburbs, and the majority consider that cities are good places to visit but not to live in. The author chooses Dallas as typical of most US cities, and discusses Erik Jonsson, mayor of Dallas since 1964, and his Goals for Dallas program. Some of the policies have succeeded, but some problems remain. 12 illus.
                                                            G. L. Neville

3163. Wilson, William H. ADAPTING TO GROWTH: DALLAS, TEXAS, AND THE KESSLER PLAN, 1908-1933. *Arizona and the West 1983 25(3): 245-260.* When the Trinity River overflowed in the spring of 1908, it served as a catalyst to city planning in Dallas, Texas. Landscape architect and city planner George E. Kessler drafted a plan for systematic public improvements in the mode of the Fading City Beautiful concept, which postulated that public buildings, boulevards, and parks should be harmoniously beautiful as well as utilitarian. The Kessler plan prevailed for two decades and major accomplishments were registered. Streets were widened and improved, city-center railroad tracks were relocated, park acreage was quadrupled, and 15 square miles were opened to commercial development. With the coming of rapid physical sprawl and the automobile, traditional planning was replaced by traffic control, utilities regulation, recreation management, and boosterism. 2 maps, 3 illus., 38 notes.                                  D. L. Smith

3164. Wolfe, Margaret Ripley. CHANGING THE FACE OF SOUTHERN APPALACHIA: URBAN PLANNING IN SOUTHWEST VIRGINIA AND EAST TENNESSEE, 1890-1929. *J. of the Am. Planning Assoc. 1981 47(3): 252-265.* Capitalistic development lifted preindustrial natives from a simple agrarian-based existence and set them down in industrial villages and towns. American and European investors exploited natural and human resources, but they also initiated urban planning and regional development which, in some instances, set the tone for subsequent growth that elevated the standard of living for the local people. Three separate planning ventures at Stonega, Virginia; Kingsport, Tennessee; and Happy Valley, Tennessee reveal striking contrasts in objectives as well as the long-term consequences.                                      J

3165. Wolfe, Margaret Ripley. J. FRED JOHNSON, HIS TOWN, AND HIS PEOPLE: A CASE STUDY OF CLASS VALUES, THE WORK ETHIC, AND TECHNOLOGY IN SOUTHERN APPALACHIA, 1916-1944. *Appalachian J. 1979-80 7(1-2): 70-83.* History of Kingsport, Tennessee, during its period of industrialization under the direction of town father J. Fred Johnson.

3166. Wright, Gavin. CHEAP LABOR AND SOUTHERN TEXTILES BEFORE 1880. *J. of Econ. Hist. 1979 39(3): 655-680.* Labor costs historically have been decisive in determining the location of cotton textile production. Despite an apparent advantage in wage rates, however, the southern industry did not achieve *sustained* relative progress before about 1875. This study argues that in most times and places the region did not have "cheap labor" before this date. What matters is not just the level of wages in any year, but the quality of labor attracted at this wage and the geographic scope of the labor market within which firms operate. The scope of the labor market depends in turn on property rights and incentives toward recruitment activity. 5 tables, 3 fig., 66 notes.                          J

3167. Wright, Gavin. CHEAP LABOR AND SOUTHERN TEXTILES, 1880-1930. *Q. J. of Econ. 1981 96(4): 605-629.* The delay in the South's capture of the American cotton textile market was due to the slow process of capital accumulation and the rapid increase in real wages that occurred in the South as well as in the North.

3168. Yale, Andrew. OUR PLACE WAS BEALE STREET. *Southern Exposure 1978 6(3): 26-38.* Excerpts from oral interviews, musicians, street people, and storekeepers reveal aspects of Beale Street's existence in Memphis, Tennessee during the 1930's-40's when this street was the center of black entertainment and commercial life in the Mid South. Blues singers Furry Lewis and Booker White, hardware store owner Art Hutkins, and Casey Banks, promotions man, musician, and pool player, reflect on Beale Street activities, with special emphasis on the live entertainment and high quality food establishments once featured in the area which exerted considerable appeal for the white as well as the black community.
                                                                      N. Lederer

3169. Yonekawa, Shin'ichi. SAIRON BŌSEKI KIGYŌ SEICHŌ NO KOKUSAI HIKAKU [The growth of cotton spinning firms: A comparative study]. *Shakaikeizaishigaku (Socio-Economic Hist.) [Japan] 1982 47(5): 1-32.* Compares the growth of cotton spinning firms in Great Britain, the United States, India, and Japan during 1870-1939.

3170. Ziglar, William Larry. SHIPBUILDING ON THE PASCAGOULA RIVER. *J. of Mississippi Hist. 1974 36(1): 1-15.* Describes the shipbuilding industry in the Pascagoula River basin, chiefly from the 1870's through the 1960's. The industry has continued to grow since World War II, when "the basin developed into one of the major shipbuilding areas of the world." 65 notes.
                                                                      J. W. Hillje

3171. —. ANNAPOLIS. *Am. Preservation 1977 1(1): 27-33.* Provides a brief synopsis of the history of Annapolis, Maryland and the efforts of Historic Annapolis, Inc., during 1952-69, to obtain an historic district zoning law. 12 photos.          S. C. Strom

3172. —. "A BIG, BIG, BUSINESS." *Southern Exposure 1980 8(3): 36-40.* Real estate developer Perry Mendel's day nurseries, Kinder-Care Learning Centers, Incorporated, started in Montgomery, Alabama, in 1969 and now have over 600 centers in 35 states and two Canadian provinces.

3173. —. CAPITAL'S FLIGHT: THE APPAREL INDUSTRY MOVES SOUTH. Mora, Magdalena and DelCastillo, Adelaida R., ed. *Mexican Women in the United States: Struggles Past and Present* (Los Angeles: U. of California Chicano Studies Res. Center, 1980): 95-104. The garment industry provides a clear illustration of capital's mobility and its effect on the working class. Since World War II, thousands of jobs in the apparel sector were exported. Domestic production has dramatically shifted its geographic locus, as the firms have abandoned their birthplaces in the large industrial cities of the Northeast and Midwest in favor of the rural South. The reasons for this exodus and its effects on the working class, particularly in the Northeast and the South, are discussed. Reprinted from *NACLA Report on the Americas* formerly *NACLA's Latin America and Empire Report* 1977, 11(3): 2-9; 2 tables, 32 notes.
                                                                      J. Powell

3174. —. [HISTORICAL AND GEOGRAPHICAL ASPECTS OF 19TH-CENTURY BALTIMORE]. *Working Papers from the Regional Econ. Hist. Res. Center 1981 4(1-2): 76-155.*
Arnold, Joseph L. BALTIMORE'S NEIGHBORHOODS, 1800-1980, *pp. 76-98.* Describes the different stages that Baltimore's neighborhoods have gone through, focusing on the social, economic, and cultural forces that have contributed to the changes.
Muller, Edward K. SPATIAL ORDER BEFORE INDUSTRIALIZATION: BALTIMORE'S CENTRAL DISTRICT, 1833-1869, *pp. 100-140.* Traces the central area of Baltimore before industrialization, mass transportation, and the rapid growth that resulted in the mid-19th-century beginnings of a downtown, and includes tables and graphs of the concentration of various businesses in different areas.
Hershberg, Theodore. NINETEENTH-CENTURY BALTIMORE: HISTORICAL AND GEOGRAPHICAL PERSPECTIVES: COMMENTARY, *pp. 141-155.* Comments on the two previous articles.

3175. —. [LABOR SUPPLY, THE ACQUISITION OF SKILLS, AND THE LOCATION OF SOUTHERN TEXTILE MILLS, 1880-1900]. *J. of Econ. Hist. 1981 41(1): 65-73.*
Carlson, Leonard A. LABOR SUPPLY, THE ACQUISITION OF SKILLS, AND THE LOCATION OF SOUTHERN TEXTILE MILLS, 1880-1900, *pp. 65-71.* The development of the textile industry in the South was shaped by the fact that by 1870 most experienced workers lived in the Piedmont. Thus, a firm which wished to hire experienced workers would have been led to choose the Piedmont Plateau, similarly, mills producing more difficult finer count cloth would have chosen the Piedmont in order to hire experienced workers. Finally, the persistence of a virtually all white work force may be explained by the fact that most experienced workers were white and would have resisted working in integrated mills.
Oates, Mary J. DISCUSSION, *pp. 72-73.*                          J

3176. —. [LOW-SKILLED LABOR FOR SOUTHERN TEXTILE INDUSTRY]. *J. of Econ. Hist. 1976 36(1): 84-101.*
Terrell, Thomas E., Jr. EAGER HANDS: LABOR FOR SOUTHERN TEXTILES, 1850-1860, *pp. 84-99.* Was there an ample supply of low-skilled, free labor in the antebellum Southeast to develop a textile industry producing coarser goods? Using county-level data from the 1850 and 1860 manuscript censuses and other historical sources, we found there was a surplus of low-skilled, free (mostly white) labor in Edgefield County, South Carolina, where the textile industry was firmly established before the Civil War. If Edgefield County was not a unique case, then potential investors in southern textiles were probably not restrained by an inadequate labor force. Moreover, our Edgefield study reinforces other analyses which indicate that many whites hovered on the margins of southern society even in its most prosperous decade before the Civil War.
Gitelman, H. M. DISCUSSION, *pp. 100-101.*                       J

3177. —. PRIVATE UTILITIES: THE CORE OF THE PROBLEM: TACTICAL INFORMATION ON YOUR LOCAL UTILITY. *Southern Exposure 1979 7(4): 67, 77-97.* A series of charts on each of the 16 major utilities operating in the South, who owns and runs it, where it spends its money, what influence it exercises on whom. Especially important are lines of influence showing relationships of directors to other corporations, boards, and executives, also the top stockholders of each. The introduction discusses the various public relations emphases, viz., educational programs in public schools, public lectures, general advertising, lobbying, industry development, and picking law firms with the "proper" connections. Illus., map.                                       R. V. Ritter

3178. —. [REGIONAL ECONOMIC DEVELOPMENT]. *J. of Econ. Hist. 1975 35(1): 160-215.*
Rockoff, Hugh T. VARIETIES OF BANKING AND REGIONAL ECONOMIC DEVELOPMENT IN THE UNITED STATES, 1840-1860, *pp. 160-181.* Demand factors, such as percapita wealth and urbanization, determined financial development.

Economic regulation—free banking, usury, and mutual savings bank laws—changed to fit economic realities. Based on secondary sources and published statistics; 10 tables, 32 notes, appendix.

Bateman, Fred and Weiss, Thomas. COMPARATIVE REGIONAL DEVELOPMENT IN ANTEBELLUM MANUFACTURING, pp. 182-208. Effects of scale have been exaggerated for all regions. West and South resembled each other more than either resembled the eastern or middle states in terms of capital, labor, and output per firm. The West's greater variety of industries based on middle-sized firms, and the fact that southern textile firms were more efficient but did not exploit market position to increase average profits, may support a business-culture explanation of differential industrialization. Based on samples from manuscript censuses and secondary sources; 9 tables, 21 notes.

Duggan, Edward P. COMMENT, pp. 209-211. Regional development studies must consider additional dimensions, notably, spatial organization and information flow.

Green, George D. COMMENT, pp. 212-215. Rockoff evaded the issue of policy's influence by assuming that the money supply was perfectly elastic, because that was the factor most subject to state banking regulation. Bateman and Weiss needed to recognize that the antebellum monopolist was unlike modern corporate giants, but did point to a reaggregation of state data according to degrees of urbanization, dominant industries, or factor endowments.                                    J. W. Williams

3179.  —. TEXAS BECAME TEXAS. Am. Heritage 1977 28(3): 48-55. Traces the development and impact of the Texas oil industry, with 13 captioned photographs. Most of the photographs are from Early Texas Oil: A Photographic History by Walter Rundell, Jr. (Texas A & M Pr., 1977). 13 illus.              B. J. Paul

3180.  —. TEXTILE RESOURCES. Southern Exposure 1976 3(4): 80-85. The Institute for Southern Studies here provides a bibliography of books on the Southern textile industry and two famous strikes, 1929 and 1934; includes three diagrams on corporate interconnections.

3181.  —. [TRAILERS: THE FACTORY, THE BUSINESS, THE OWNERS]. Southern Exposure 1980 8(1): 14-25.

Schlesinger, Tom. TRAILERS: THE FACTORY, pp. 14-19. Describes the mass production of trailers by Taylor Homes in North Carolina, and interviews factory employees critical of mechanization throughout the Southeast; 1972-79. 2 photos.

—. TRAILERS: THE BUSINESS, pp. 19-23. The financial profile of the trailer industry constantly shifts. Prices for mobile homes have increased since the general recession of 1974, while production has decreased. 2 charts.

Beaver, Pat and Putzel, Mary Jane. TRAILERS: THE OWNERS, pp. 23-25. Interviews mobile home owners in Watauga County, North Carolina. 2 photos.              H. M. Parker, Jr./S

3182.  —. [URBANIZATION IN THE COLONIAL SOUTH]. William and Mary Q. 1974 31(4): 653-671.

Wellenreuther, Hermann. URBANIZATION IN THE COLONIAL SOUTH: A CRITIQUE, pp. 653-668. Criticizes Joseph A. Ernst and H. Roy Merrens's earlier article in this journal, especially for its definition of "town" and for too much reliance on descriptive features. 55 notes.

Siegel, Fred. FRED SIEGEL'S LETTER, pp. 668-669.

Ernst, Joseph A. and Merrens, H. Roy. JOSEPH A. ERNST AND H. ROY MERRENS REPLY, pp. 669-671. Calls for critics to eschew theoretical assumptions and to go to the sources.

                                                        H. M. Ward

## Southern Geography

3183.  Adkins, Howard G. THE GEOGRAPHIC BASE OF URBAN RETARDATION IN MISSISSIPPI, 1800-1840. West Georgia Coll. Studies in the Social Sci. 1973 12: 35-49. One of seven articles in this issue on "Geographic Perspectives on Southern Development."

3184.  Adkins, Howard G. THE HISTORICAL GEOGRAPHY OF EXTINCT TOWNS IN MISSISSIPPI. Southern Q. 1979 17(3-4): 123-152. Identifies now-extinct towns in Mississippi that had a population of more than 100, and why they became extinct. Based on a paper presented at a symposium entitled "The Sense of Place: Mississippi" at the University of Mississippi, October 1978. 5 tables, 5 fig., 49 notes.              B. D. Ledbetter

3185.  Aiken, Charles S. FAULKNER'S YOKNAPATAWPHA COUNTY: GEOGRAPHICAL FACT INTO FICTION. Geographical Rev. 1977 67(1): 1-21. William Faulkner's process of converting geographical reality into fiction is examined with a beginning toward synthesis. Lafayette County, Mississippi, was the primary source for his apocryphal Yoknapatawpha County. The latter is a mutation created by combining the real, the modified, and the imaginary. Faulkner used four techniques to modify the geography of Lafayette County—names were altered, components were omitted, locations were shifted, and reality was blended with fabrication. Because of Faulkner's prominence, in time the historic Lafayette County and the fictional Yoknapatawpha will gradually blend and become one, a process which is the reverse of what the author performed.              J

3186.  Aiken, Charles S. A GEOGRAPHICAL APPROACH TO WILLIAM FAULKNER'S "THE BEAR." Geographical Rev. 1981 71(4): 446-459. William Faulkner created the fictional setting of "The Bear" by drawing on his hunting experiences on the Cain plantation in Lafayette County and at James Stone's hunting camp in the Yazoo Delta, Panola County, Mississippi. Railroads in the story were patterned after actual ones in the landscape. During his lifetime Faulkner witnessed the replacement of the wilderness of the delta by the sharecropper-cotton plantations. The theme of landscape change and the inability to prevent change were based on Faulkner's attempt to preserve the wilderness at Stone's camp. Faulkner expanded the theme of landscape change in "Delta Autumn," his epilogue to "The Bear."              J

3187.  Ainsley, W. Frank and Florin, John W. THE NORTH CAROLINA PIEDMONT: AN ISLAND OF RELIGIOUS DIVERSITY. West Georgia Coll. Studies in the Social Sci. 1973 12: 30-34. One of seven articles in this issue on "Geographic Perspectives on Southern Development."

3188.  Ainsley, W. Frank, Jr. VERNACULAR HOUSES IN BRUNSWICK COUNTY, NORTH CAROLINA. Pioneer Am. Soc. Tr. 1981 4: 25-41. "Analyzes the geographical distribution of vernacular house types in Brunswick County, North Carolina," and briefly traces attempts to settle Brunswick County during the 1660's, although most settlement occurred during 1725-1800.

3189.  Alford, John J. THE CHESAPEAKE OYSTER FISHERY. Ann. of the Assoc. of Am. Geographers 1975 65(2): 229-239. "The Chesapeake Bay oyster fishery is hampered by the Maryland-Virginia state line."

3190.  Anthony, Allen. KENTUCKY BEND: A STRUGGLE FOR POLITICAL IDENTITY. Filson Club Hist. Q. 1981 55(2): 179-193. Discusses the creation of a political and geographical anomaly. A shift in the Mississippi River, where the states of Missouri, Tennessee, and Kentucky meet, left land that technically belonged to Kentucky physically separate from the rest of the state. This unusual situation will continue. Based on government documents and interviews; 39 notes.              G. B. McKinney

3191.  Baker, Russell P. OLD MILLER COUNTY, ARKANSAS. Arkansas Hist. Q. 1983 42(4): 346-348. Describes the boundary changes of Miller County, which was part of Arkansas during 1820-

38. Most of the county became part of either Oklahoma in 1825 or Texas in 1838. Based on newspapers, court records, and secondary sources; 2 maps, 19 notes.          G. R. Schroeder

3192. Bayor, Ronald H. ETHNIC RESIDENTIAL PATTERNS IN ATLANTA, 1880-1940. *Georgia Hist. Q. 1979 64(4): 435-446.* Examines residential patterns of German Jews, Russian Jews, and other Russians who settled in Atlanta; members of these groups were mobile but tended to relocate in areas with others of their ethnic group. Based on church records, city directories, census records, and secondary sources; map, 26 notes.

G. R. Schroeder

3193. Benham, Evelyn. PEARL RIVER "TALCATCHA." *J. of Mississippi Hist. 1976 38(2): 213-219.* Describes miscellaneous historical events, 1699-1976, related to the Pearl River, the 490-mile river in Mississippi called "Talcatcha" by the Chickasaw and Choctaw Indians. Based on published sources; 32 notes.

J. W. Hillje

3194. Bingham, Edgar. A BIBLIOGRAPHY OF APPALACHIAN GEOGRAPHY. *Appalachian J. 1977 5(1): 65-73.* Presents an annotated bibliography on Appalachia, 1925-75; topics include human geography, history, agriculture, forestry, mining, manufacturing, recreation, and transportation.

3195. Bishir, Catherine W. THE "UNPAINTED ARISTOCRACY": THE BEACH COTTAGES OF OLD NAGS HEAD. *North Carolina Hist. Rev. 1977 54(4): 367-392.* Nags Head, on North Carolina's Outer Banks, has been a summer resort since the 1830's. Aristocratic planters frequented the area in antebellum days to escape the heat and malaria of the mainland. There were hotels and summer cottages on the Albemarle Sound and on the ocean side. Nine homes have survived despite encroachments on Nags Head. Based on interviews with residents, newspaper articles, and secondary sources; 15 illus., map, 62 notes.          T. L. Savitt

3196. Black, Patti Carr. PRESERVING THE SENSE OF PLACE: STATE POLICY. *Southern Q. 1979 17(3-4): 79-85.* The public must be made aware that continued active support of preservation is vital for Mississippi to retain its man-made environment. Covers 1900-78. Based on a paper presented at a symposium entitled "The Sense of Place: Mississippi" at the University of Mississippi, October 1978.          B. D. Ledbetter

3197. Bodenhamer, David J. IMAGES AND IMPRESSIONS OF MISSISSIPPI AND THE SENSE OF PLACE: NATIVE VIEW/OUTSIDE VIEW: FORUM I. *Southern Q. 1979 17(3-4): 58-61.* In this critique of a symposium forum, concludes that Mississippi is usually seen by outsiders as backward, racist, and poverty stricken, but insiders usually deny these charges. Based on a forum critique at a symposium entitled "The Sense of Place: Mississippi" at the University of Mississippi, October 1978.          B. D. Ledbetter

3198. Breton, Ronald J.-L. and Louder, Dean R. LE GÉOGRAPHIE LINGUISTIQUE DE L'ACADIANA [The linguistic geography of Acadiana, 1970]. *Cahiers de Géographie du Québec [Canada] 1979 23(59): 217-238.* Using data from the 1970 census, argues that the French cultural area of Louisiana known as Acadiana is composed of four linguistic zones: exclusive French, solid majority, balanced, and minority.

3199. Brown, Bahngrell W. THE FIRST HUNDRED YEARS OF GEOLOGY IN MISSISSIPPI. *Southern Q. 1975 13(4): 295-302.* Covers 1777-1870. Mentions Sir Charles Lyell, Benjamin L. C. Wailes, Ruth Nutt, T. A. Conrad, and Eugene Hilgard, and considers Lyell and Hilgard the two most important figures. Lyell's experiences in Mississippi served to reinforce the logic of his uniformitarianism theory. 16 notes.          R. W. Dubay

3200. Brown, Pat. DUGOUTS, DOORYARDS, DIRT TANKS AND DAFFODILS (CROSBY COUNTY 1877-1936). *West Texas Hist. Assoc. Year Book 1981 57: 71-83.* Traces the settlement of Crosby County on the Llano Estacado in Texas from the home-

stead of German immigrant Hank Smith in 1877 to a group of Indiana Quakers in 1879; describes the native flora and plants introduced by the settlers.

3201. Burt, Eleanor Bales. A NOTE ON JEFFERSON COUNTY. *Tennessee Hist. Q. 1974 33(2): 228-230.* Outlines the settlement and development of Jefferson County, located between the French Broad and Holston rivers near Knoxville. The area was first permanently settled by Americans in 1783, and is an area of scenic beauty and industrial potential.          M. B. Lucas

3202. Campbell, Will D. STAYING HOME OR LEAVING. *Southern Q. 1979 17(3-4): 14-23.* Mississippi has a number of things wrong with it, especially the lack of progress. This lack of progress can be seen by a review of country music about the state. Based on a paper presented at a symposium entitled "The Sense of Place: Mississippi" at the University of Mississippi October, 1978.          B. D. Ledbetter

3203. Cappon, Lester J. RETRACING AND MAPPING THE BARTRAMS' SOUTHERN TRAVELS. *Pro. of the Am. Phil. Soc. 1974 118(6): 507-513.* Discusses the joint project of the Newberry Library and the Institute of Early American History and Culture in producing a volume of maps of the American Revolutionary Era (1760-90), including the travels of John Bartram and his son, William. John Bartram travelled through the Carolinas, Georgia, and east Florida during 1765-66; William traveled through Georgia, Tennessee, Alabama, Mississippi, and Louisiana during 1773-76. Their steps were retraced during 1917-40 by Francis Harper, zoologist and naturalist. Harper has edited the Bartrams' journals and diaries which have a five-fold value: "historical, anthropological, botanical, zoological, and geographical." The cartographic project is designed to complement Harper's editing with the goal of stimulating further research in science. 32 notes.          C. W. Olson

3204. Case, Robert. LA FRONTERA TEXANA Y LOS MOVIMIENTOS DE INSURRECCION EN MEXICO—1850-1900 [The Texan border and rebellions in Mexico: 1850-1900]. *Hist. Mexicana [Mexico] 1981 30(3): 415-452.* After the Treaty of Guadalupe Hidalgo of 1848 established the Rio Grande as the border between Mexico and Texas the 400 kilometers between Eagle Pass and Brownsville became the base of operations for Mexican rebels. They recruited men; purchased arms, ammunitions, and supplies; published antigovernment propaganda; and harassed the northern region of Mexico. A study of their activities and the reaction of both governments gives an idea of the border problems of the two countries, which continued into the present century. Based on primary material in Mexican and US national archives; 108 notes, biblio.          J. V. Coutinho

3205. Cashin, Edward J. SUMMERVILLE, RETREAT OF THE OLD SOUTH. *Richmond County Hist. 1973 5(2): 44-59.* Founded in the early 1800's, this popular residential village near Augusta grew rapidly after the Civil War, largely because of its healthy location on "the Hill." Summerville lost its identity in 1911 when residents voted for annexation to Augusta. One of six articles in this issue on Augusta. Based on manuscript collections, including those of the Georgia Historical Society Collections, and on newspapers; 60 notes.          H. R. Grant

3206. Caudill, Harry M. ORAL TRADITIONS BEHIND SOME KENTUCKY MOUNTAIN PLACE NAMES. *Register of the Kentucky Hist. Soc. 1980 78(3): 197-207.* Recounts tales of early storytellers concerning the origins of some Kentucky mountain place names. Does not vouch for the accuracy of the tales, but urges others to determine the origins of these and other place names. 3 illus.          J. F. Paul

3207. Chardon, Roland. NOTES ON SOUTH FLORIDA PLACE NAMES: NORRIS CUT. *Tequesta 1977 (37): 51-61.* Until 1905 Norris Cut was the principal waterway into Biscayne Bay and Miami. The name probably was derived from a transformation by surveyors of a Bahamian oral rendition of "Narrows Cut."

H. S. Marks

3208. Cissna, Volney. ZONING: A MEANS OF ENCOURAGING AND PROTECTING THE SENSE OF PLACE. *Southern Q. 1979 17(3-4): 89-92.* Zoning is a tool that must be effectively utilized in the future development of Mississippi to retain the character and protect the state's sense of place. Based on a paper presented at a symposium entitled "The Sense of Place: Mississippi" at the University of Mississippi, October 1978.

B. D. Ledbetter

3209. DeVorsey, Louis, Jr. DATING THE EMERGENCE OF A SAVANNA RIVER ISLAND: AN HYPOTHESIS IN FORENSIC HISTORICAL GEOGRAPHY. *Environmental Rev. 1980 4(2): 6-19.* Presents the 18th century geographic history of the Savannah River, specifically the Barnwell Island area, during the 18th century, in light of a long dispute between Georgia and South Carolina over their common boundary in the lower Savannah River eventually accepted for adjudication by the Supreme Court in 1977.

3210. Dorais, Louis-Jacques. LES LANGUES [The languages]. *Vie Française [Canada] 1980 34(7-9): 13-15.* A geographic study of French dialects (standard French, Cajun, and Creole) in Louisiana, 18th-20th centuries.

3211. Dorais, Louis-Jacques. LES RÉGIONS: LES AVOYELLES [The regions: Avoyelles]. *Vie Française [Canada] 1980 34(7-9): 52-53.* A historical sketch of northern Louisiana's French-speaking Avoyelles Parish, centering on a comparison with linguistic and folkloristic traits of other Louisiana French-speaking areas; 1790-1980.

3212. Downey, James. MISSISSIPPI MUSIC: THAT GOSPEL SOUND. *Southern Q. 1979 17(3-4): 216-223.* In studying Mississippi's sense of place, gospel sounds, the sounds of the Bible Belt must be considered. The impact of gospel music is significant throughout the state as it reflects the values of Mississippians. Based on a paper presented at a symposium entitled "The Sense of Place: Mississippi" at the University of Mississippi, October 1978. 9 notes.

B. D. Ledbetter

3213. Edmonson, James H. DENMARK, TENNESSEE: THE FIRST 150 YEARS. *West Tennessee Hist. Soc. Papers 1980 (34): 88-95.* Never much more than a village, Denmark is now little more than a crossroads community. Denmark had promise, but the lack of rails into the community definitely affected its ability to develop. Discusses the churches and schools and the minor role of the Civil War in its history. A speech by the author in 1979 for the town's 150th anniversary. Secondary sources; 25 illus., map, 14 notes.

H. M. Parker, Jr.

3214. Elliott, Jack D., Jr. LEFTWICH'S "COTTON GIN PORT AND GAINES' TRACE" RECONSIDERED. *J. of Mississippi Hist. 1980 42(4): 348-361.* The 1903 *Publications of the Mississippi Historical Society* contained an article by George J. Leftwich on Cotton Gin Port and Gaines' Trace, "a collection of a few facts and a great number of misconceptions and poorly founded inferences concerning three geographically related sites: the extinct town of Cotton Gin Port, Bienville's fort, and the Gaines Trace." Leftwich's errors, repeated by later historians, have resulted in increased obfuscation. Corrects two of Leftwich's major errors: his location of Jean Baptiste LeMoyne, Sieur de Bienville's fort on the Tombigbee River and his confusion over two different roads in identifying Gaines' Trace. Based on *Mississippi Provincial Archives: 1729-1740,* periodical literature, and secondary sources; 23 notes.

M. S. Legan

3215. Engerrand, Steven W. BLACK AND MULATTO MOBILITY AND STABILITY IN DALLAS, TEXAS, 1880-1910. *Phylon 1978 39(3): 203-215.* Blacks and mulattoes made up a large percentage (21.3% in 1900) of the population of Dallas, Texas, in the years 1880-1910. They tended to find work in semiskilled, service, or unskilled occupations, though a few, especially mulattoes, were professionals or proprietors. Despite this, the black and mulatto population tended to stay in Dallas during 1880-1910 at a greater rate (32% and 31.4%) than did the native white (22.2%) or white immigrant (18.8%) populations. This was especially true of those Afro-Americans in Dallas who owned property. 6 tables, 20 notes.

J. C. Billigmeier

3216. Fenton, James I. CEDAR LAKE: MIRROR OF STAKED PLAINS HISTORY. *Permian Hist. Ann. 1981 21: 33-48.* Traces the ecological and economic history of the Staked Plains in northwest Texas since 1819, when the first white Americans surveyed the area, focusing on Cedar Lake, a major body of water; discusses the various waves of travelers and settlers who passed through the region and exploited its natural resources.

3217. Fewkes, Charles K. IN MEMORIAM: GEORGE S. SHIRK (1913-1977). *Names 1978 26(2): 192-195.* George Shirk wrote *Oklahoma Place Names* in 1965; it served as a guide for others interested in name tracing.

3218. Filby, Vera Ruth. FROM FOREST TO FRIENDSHIP. *Maryland Hist. Mag. 1976 71(1): 93-102.* A brief history of Baltimore's former Friendship Airport (now Baltimore-Washington International) and the Elkridge Landing Road region in which it sits, from John Smith's first sighting in 1608 to the present. Details the nomenclature of place names and geographic features through land grant records, with stress on the section of Anne Arundel County once called "Walker's Inheritance," and relates the changing nature of land use from logging to farming to mining. The airport name came from that of the Friendship Methodist Episcopal Church, South, which held services until Easter Sunday, 1948, and served the region of tobacco farms and market gardens. Many cemeteries had to be moved to build the airport, and "accelerating business and industrial development" has been the story since. The "surviving islands of field and forest are being lost today," and the rapid wasting of the natural environment continues. An abridged version of this article is in *Anne Arundel County History Notes* (1974). Illus.

G. J. Bobango

3219. Fischer, LeRoy H. and Isern, Thomas D. HORSETHIEF CANYON: LANDMARK ON THE CIMARRON RIVER. *Chronicles of Oklahoma 1978 56(1): 34-39.* Along the banks of the Cimarron River in Logan County, Oklahoma, rises Horsethief Canyon, legendary refuge of outlaws, source of timber, and recreation spot for pioneer families. Its violent past has been overdramatized, but Horsethief Canyon remains an important historical landmark. Based on newspapers; 3 photos, 8 notes.

M. L. Tate

3220. Fraas, Elizabeth. AN UNUSUAL MAP OF THE EARLY WEST. *Register of the Kentucky Hist. Soc. 1975 73(1): 62-69.* Notes on the possible origin of "A General Map of the New Settlement Called Transilvania," a 200 year old map now owned by the University of Kentucky. Authorship and other circumstances are unclear. The author hopes further research will follow. Based on primary and secondary sources; illus., 9 notes.

J. F. Paul

3221. Gaby, Donald C. MIAMI'S EARLIEST KNOWN GREAT HURRICANE. *Tequesta 1974 (34): 64-67.* Miami was battered by a hurricane on 13 September 1824. Evidence of its devastation was noticed over a century later, when damage by the 1926 hurricane revealed the effects of the earlier storm. Other sources state a hurricane passing through the Caribbean came ashore at Miami, traveled up the coast to Cape Canaveral, went to sea and landed again on the Georgia coast. This evidently was Miami's earliest known great hurricane. Based on primary and secondary sources; 9 notes.

H. S. Marks

3222. Gettys, Marshall. EURO-AMERICAN HISTORICAL ARCHAEOLOGY IN OKLAHOMA. *Chronicles of Oklahoma 1981-82 59(4): 448-464.* Oklahoma's Euro-American archeological sites have failed to attract a level of scholarly attention equal to American Indian sites. The value of some of these locations is assessed, along with the scientific reports compiled by archeologists. Among the sites are: Forts Towson, Washita, Sill and Cantonment; Kiowa and Comanche Indian Agency commissaries; Civil War battlefield at

Honey Springs; Fairchild Winery; Muskogee-Fort Gibson trolley car route; and the Cushing Oil Field. Based on archeological site studies; map, 4 photos, 79 notes.                                    M. L. Tate

3223. Gibson, Arrell Morgan. WATERWAYS OF OKLAHOMA. *Red River Valley Hist. Rev. 1981 6(3): 6-17.* Focusing on the 19th century, shows the significance of rivers, holding that they determine the region's economic orientation until after the Civil War and thereafter continue to be important; steamers influenced the coming of the urban frontier by accelerating the development of river towns.

3224. Gold, Gerald L. THE FRENCH FRONTIER OF SETTLEMENT IN LOUISIANA: SOME OBSERVATIONS ON CULTURE CHANGE IN MAMOU PRAIRIE. *Cahiers de Géographie du Québec [Canada] 1979 23(59): 263-279.* Studies the cultural change caused by removal of tenant farmers in the southwestern prairies region of Louisiana from the pre-1952 cotton sharecropping communities to service centers.

3225. Gordon, Martin K. CONGRESS AND THE DISTRICT OF COLUMBIA: THE MILITARY IMPACT ON FEDERAL CONTROL. *Capitol Studies 1978 6(2): 39-53.* Discusses the desire of Congress to retain control of the District of Columbia Militia for self-protection as one reason for its refusal since 1800 to grant the District full home rule.

3226. Greer, Fred. THERE WAS ONCE A CAMPBELL COUNTY. *Georgia Life 1978 5(2): 16-20.* Campbell County was established in 1823 and made part of Fulton County in 1931.

3227. Griessman, B. Eugene and Henson, Curtis T., Jr. THE HISTORY AND SOCIAL TOPOGRAPHY OF AN ETHNIC ISLAND IN ALABAMA. *Phylon 1975 36(2): 97-112.* An "ethnic island" has emerged during the past century-and-a-half along the west bank of the Tombigbee River, 35 miles north of Mobile, in present-day Washington County. The inhabitants, who are often referred to as Cajans or Cajuns, are a mixture of red, black, and white. Probably the first settlers in the area were Daniel Reed and his wife Rose, who moved there early in the 19th century. The authors trace the background of the settlement, and its growth, and discuss how demographic and social topographic characteristics such as the roads and transportation networks, the schools, the churches, the land tenure, and economic conditions helped keep the settlement isolated. Recently, the members of the community have been merging with the society that surrounds them. Primary and secondary sources; 5 tables, 28 notes.              B. A. Glasrud

3228. Griggs, William C. MAN AND THE PALO DURO CANYON: FROM CORONADO TO GOODNIGHT. *Panhandle-Plains Hist. Rev. 1978 51: 117-144.* Coronado's 1541 excursion through Palo Duro Canyon marked the first advance of Europeans into the Texas Panhandle. Though later Spanish explorers traversed the same region, white settlers did not reach the area until after the Comanches and Kiowas had been driven permanently from the Panhandle during the 1874-75 Red River War. Charles Goodnight introduced the first large ranching operations to the region in 1876 when he entered into partnership with financier John G. Adair and established the JA Ranch in Palo Duro Canyon. Conflicting land claims with newly arriving farmers prompted Goodnight to divide the ranch and sell its lands during the 1880's. Secondary sources; 2 photos, 104 notes.                                  M. L. Tate

3229. Habig, Marion A., ed.; Leutenegger, Benedict, transl.; and Puelles, José María de Jesús. PUELLES' REPORT OF 1827 ON THE TEXAS-LOUISIANA BOUNDARY. *Louisiana Hist. 1978 19(2): 133-181.* A translation of the "Report to the President of the Mexican Republic on the Boundaries between the Provinces of Texas and Louisiana," prepared by the Franciscan missionary Father José María de Jesús Puelles (1772-1840) in 1827. The original *Informe* was published in Zacatecas in 1828. This report supports Spanish and Mexican claims that the boundary between Texas and Louisiana was the Calcasieu River and Arroyo Hondo, rather than the Sabine River as the United States claimed. Puelles detailed the history of the border region chronologically from 1512 to 1813. He

had made a thorough investigation of the question in 1806-07, and prepared this report in response to a request by the Mexican government in 1827. Reproduces his map, which accompanied the report. 180 notes.                                R. L. Woodward, Jr.

3230. Hager, Jean. ON THE BANKS OF THE ARKANSAS: BLACKBURN, AN OKLAHOMA TOWN. *Chronicles of Oklahoma 1980-81 58(4): 420-431.* Indian trader John Skinner laid out the townsite of Blackburn during September, 1893 hoping that it would be in the path of the Kansas, Oklahoma, Central, and South Western Railroad. Merchants soon established stores and within three years the township population reached 2,272. Unfortunately, the anticipated railroad never materialized and a 1905 oil boom quickly fizzled. Successful farming continues in the area today, but Blackburn is only a tiny community. Based on newspapers; 3 photos, 24 notes.                                          M. L. Tate

3231. Hale, Duane Kendall. CYRUS N. RAY: THE ABILENE MAN. *West Texas Hist. Assoc. Year Book 1979 55: 17-36.* Cyrus N. Ray (1880-1966) was a physician and an amateur but pioneer Texas archeologist whose numerous discoveries in the Abilene area were never fully acknowledged by professional archeologists.

3232. Haley, Jack D. THE WICHITA MOUNTAINS: THE STRUGGLE TO PRESERVE A WILDERNESS. *Great Plains J. 1973 13(1): 70-99, (2): 149-186.* Part I. Summarizes the Federal acquisition of Indian land in the Wichita Mountains of southwestern Oklahoma and its reservation from entry. Local and national conservationists, including Theodore Roosevelt, succeeded in having the area designated a national forest in 1901 and a national game preserve in 1905, especially to preserve the rapidly vanishing buffalo. Based on secondary sources; 13 illus., map, 54 notes. Part II. Summarizes the establishment of the Wichita National Game Preserve in 1905 to preserve the buffalo. Describes the selection of a range, the acquisition of the buffalo and other animals, and the success of Franklin S. Rush as supervisor. The preserve has been a prototype. Based on primary and secondary sources; 22 illus., map, 62 notes.                                        O. H. Zabel

3233. Hall, John Whitling. GEOGRAPHICAL VIEWS OF RED RIVER VALLEY, 1873. *North Louisiana Hist. Assoc. J. 1982 13(4): 107-117.* Based on photographs in *Photographic Views of the Red River Raft,* a collection, made in 1873, which gives an insight into the landscape of the Red River Valley at that time. The photos were made to illustrate the work done by the Army Corps of Engineers in removing the last vestiges of the Great Raft of the river. Map, 7 photos, 17 notes.                           J. F. Paul

3234. Hart, John Fraser. MIGRATION TO THE BLACKTOP: POPULATION REDISTRIBUTION IN THE SOUTH. *Landscape 1981 25(3): 15-19.* Traces the evolution from agriculture to industry that has occurred in the South since World War II, focusing on the redistribution of the population from the backcountry to homes along paved highways, particularly in Carroll County, Georgia, from 1921 to 1979.

3235. Heard, Diane M. WINN PARISH SETTLEMENTS ALONG THE EL CAMINO REAL. *North Louisiana Hist. Assoc. J. 1976 7(2): 69-74.* One of the few well-established overland routes in the country, El Camino Real (the King's Highway) was made by migrating buffaloes and first used by the Indians. Leading from St. Augustine, Florida, and going through Tallahassee, Pensacola, and Mobile to Natchez, Mississippi, it then crossed Louisiana through what are today Concordia, Catahoula, LaSalle, and Winn parishes to Natchitoches, and proceeded to San Augustine, San Antonio, and Mexico City. When the Red River changed its course in 1832, the road moved northward to cross the river at St. Maurice in Winn Parish. Later called the Natchez Trace-Harrisonburg Road, it "continued to be of vital importance to western travel until the first decade of the 20th century. With the coming of the railroads and automobiles, the road began to decline in value as an overland route of transportation." Many settlements were established in Winn Parish along El Camino Real, but today "only traces of the historic road are noticeable." 22 notes.           A. N. Garland

3236. Hederman, Rea S. THE NEWSPAPER'S ROLE AND THE SENSE OF PLACE. *Southern Q. 1979 17(3-4): 118-122.* Local newspapers should seek out and report the realities of life in the state, even though would differ with the Mississippian's concept of those realities. Based on a paper presented at a symnposium entitled "The Sense of Place: Mississippi" at the University of Mississippi, October 1978.                B. D. Ledbetter

3237. Hertzberg, Steven. UNSETTLED JEWS: GEOGRAPHIC MOBILITY IN A NINETEENTH CENTURY CITY. *Am. Jewish Hist. Q. 1977 67(2): 125-139.* Analyzes Jewish mobility in Atlanta, Georgia, between 1870 and 1896. Using institutional records, census schedules, city directories, and tax lists, seven tabulations are presented. Variables such as economic and marital status, and urban or rural background, are considered. It appears that Jews remained in Atlanta to a high degree (88% of Jewish immigrants v. 79% of gentile immigrants, or 71% vs. 50% as to upward social improvement) because of economic success, urban background, and advantages of living in an established center of Jewish activities. 7 tables, 16 notes.                F. Rosenthal

3238. Hilliard, Sam B. AN INTRODUCTION TO LAND SURVEY SYSTEMS IN THE SOUTHEAST. *West Georgia Coll. Studies in the Social Sci. 1973 12: 1-15.* One of seven articles in this issue on "Geographic Perspectives on Southern Development."                S

3239. Hilliard, Sam Bowers. HEADRIGHT GRANTS AND SURVEYING IN NORTHEASTERN GEORGIA. *Geog. Rev. 1982 72(4): 416-429.* The system of headright grants was the principal means for the transfer of land in northeastern Georgia from state to private ownership. Plots of various sizes and shapes were surveyed by metes and bounds. Early settlers selected compactly shaped tracts usually of several hundred acres on land that was judged most valuable. Latecomers had to accept small plots with distorted shapes because there was little unclaimed land. Politics in Georgia during the late 1770s and early 1800s permitted the approval of thousands of fraudulent claims, although there is little evidence that they resulted in actual settlement.                J

3240. Holder, Gerald L. THE EIGHTEENTH CENTURY LANDSCAPE IN NORTHEAST GEORGIA. *Pioneer Am. 1981 13(1): 39-48.* Uses original survey plats to chart land boundaries since 1786 in what is now Wilkes County, Georgia; compares vegetation and hydrology patterns over time.

3241. House, Kurt. AN EARLY HISTORY OF LIVE OAK COUNTY, TEXAS. *West Texas Hist. Assoc. Year Book 1981 57: 84-98.* Traces the history of Live Oak County, southern Texas, from the first evidence of prehistoric human occupation in the area, to 1912, the period of large-scale settlement.

3242. Hudson, Roy. MISSISSIPPI: A NATIVE VIEW. *Southern Q. 1979 17(3-4): 62-63.* In race relations, progress has been made, but Mississippi still has a long way to go in this area. Based on a paper presented at a symposium entitled "The Sense of Place: Mississippi" at the University of Mississippi, October 1978.                B. D. Ledbetter

3243. Isern, Thomas D. JEFFERSON'S SALT MOUNTAIN: THE BIG SALT PLAIN OF THE CIMARRON RIVER. *Chronicles of Oklahoma 1980 58(2): 160-175.* Beginning with the expeditions of Zebulon Pike and Lewis and Clark, accounts of a western salt mountain filtered back to the East. George C. Sibley, post trader from Fort Osage, Missouri, traveled to this Big Salt Plain of the Cimarron River (west of present Freedom, Oklahoma) in 1811 and publicized its economic potential. Later explorers visited the site, but not until 1902 did anyone try to develop its commercial possibilities. All early efforts failed until 1935 when Ezra Blackmon established evaporation machinery on the salt flat. Despite some unprofitable years, the Blackmon Salt Company progressed and continues in business. Based on early travelers' accounts and secondary sources; 5 photos, 35 notes.                M. L. Tate

3244. Jackson, Sarah Evelyn. PLACE-NAMES IN ASHE COUNTY, NORTH CAROLINA. *Names 1978 26(1): 96-105.* Discusses the etymology of place-names of the northwest Ashe County, North Carolina, since the 1790's.

3245. Jones, Barclay Gibbs. APPLICATIONS OF CENTROGRAPHIC TECHNIQUES TO THE STUDY OF URBAN PHENOMENA: ATLANTA, GEORGIA, 1940-1975. *Econ. Geography 1980 56(3): 201-222.* Applies centrographic techniques to data on population and housing and finds that there was a notable expansion of moderate income rental and for-sale units at the periphery for migrants to the region.

3246. Jones, Barclay Gibbs and Manson, Donald M. THE GEOGRAPHY OF ENTERPRISE ZONES: A CRITICAL ANALYSIS. *Econ. Geog. 1982 58(4): 329-342.* Examines Wilkes-Barre, Pennsylvania, and Atlanta, Georgia; concludes that the enterprise zone concept is not workable on a large scale in the United States.

3247. Jordan, Terry G. ANTECEDENTS OF THE LONG-LOT IN TEXAS. *Ann. of the Assoc. of Am. Geographers 1974 64(1): 70-86.* The use of long-lots as a mode of land division in Texas during the 1730's-1880's diffused from central Europe through northern France, Quebec, and French colonies in Missouri and Louisiana.

3248. Kay, Carol M. and Kay, Donald. A PRELIMINARY SURVEY OF BRITISH-RECEIVED PLACE NAMES IN ALABAMA. *Alabama Rev. 1975 28(4): 282-285.* Place names of indigenous (Indian) derivation predominate in Alabama, but second most numerous are place names of suspected or deduced British origin, based on spelling and linguistic similarities. The preliminary checklist contains more than 70 names. Note.                J. F. Vivian

3249. Kay, Donald. BRITISH INFLUENCE ON KENTUCKY MUNICIPAL PLACE NAMES. *Kentucky Folklore Record 1974 20(1): 9-13.*

3250. Kay, Donald. BRITISH INFLUENCE ON MISSISSIPPI MUNICIPAL PLACE NAMES. *J. of Mississippi Hist. 1974 36(3): 269-272.* Municipal place names constitute "one of the most widespread influences of Britain on our language." Lists 78 Mississippi municipal place names and the British equivalents. Table, 3 notes.                J. W. Hillje

3251. Kay, Donald. MUNICIPAL BRITISH-RECEIVED PLACE NAMES IN TENNESSEE. *Appalachian J. 1974 2(1): 78-80.*

3252. Kellam, Amine. THE COBB'S ISLAND STORY. *Virginia Cavalcade 1974 23(4): 18-27.* Discusses the history of the hunting and fishing resort, Cobb's Island, on the Eastern Shore of Virginia, 1839-96.

3253. Kellogg, John. NEGRO URBAN CLUSTERS IN THE POSTBELLUM SOUTH. *Geographical Rev. 1977 67(3): 310-321.* Small Negro enclaves termed "urban clusters" formed on the periphery of southern cities immediately after the Civil War. This development was precipitated by the migration of Negroes to southern cities between 1865 and 1870. By the 1880's these newly formed enclaves had replaced the long-established antebellum urban Negro areas as the predominant Negro residential areas in the urban South. In the study cities of Lexington, Kentucky; Atlanta, Georgia; Richmond, Virginia; and Durham, North Carolina, urban clusters formed in poorly drained bottomlands, along railroads, and in other peripheral areas where residential land values were low. Subsequent to urban cluster formation a second stage of Negro community development began, characterized by the outward growth of a single, large Negro sector. Negro housing in urban clusters is substandard, but housing quality is higher in more recent additions to the Negro community, whether these additions were originally Negro or white.                J

3254. Kovacik, Charles F. THE DECLINING SOUTHERN SMALL TOWN. *West Georgia Coll. Studies in the Social Sci. 1977 16: 39-48.* Fort Motte, South Carolina, illustrates a pervasive trend of the 1960's South: the lack of employment opportunities is forcing rural blacks to migrate to larger towns.

3255. Kurokawa, Katsutoshi. YAZ MISHISHIPPI DERUTA NŌGYŌ NO TENKAI: SENSASU NO SEIRI NI MOTOZUKU GAIKAN [The development of the Yazoo-Mississippi Delta]. *Shakaikeizaishigaku (Socio-Economic Hist.) [Japan] 1977 42(4): 81-99.* Traces the development of the largest plantation area in the American South, the Yazoo-Mississippi Delta, ca. 1860-1930.

3256. Lamm, Joy. SO YOU WANT A LAND USE BILL? *Southern Exposure 1974 2(2/3): 52-62.* Discusses administrative implications of land use planning and the North Carolina Mountain Area Management Act (1974) for state government and local government, 1972-74.

3257. Lang, Marvel. POPULATION TRENDS IN JASPER COUNTY, MISSISSIPPI, 1833-1970: A HISTORICAL GEOGRAPHICAL PERSPECTIVE. *J. of Mississippi Hist. 1981 43(4): 294-308.* Describes population growth trends and how these have affected the numbers of Negroes and whites in Jasper County. Population growth was rapid from 1833 until 1910-20. After 1920, population growth slowed, peaking with 19,484 inhabitants in 1940. Since then the population has continuously declined. The racial mix of the county has remained relatively constant with 45-50% nonwhite. Census Records of Population; 12 tables, fig., 3 notes.
M. S. Legan

3258. Leach, Charles D. PLACING THE POST MARK'D WEST. *Pennsylvania Heritage 1982 8(4): 8-12.* Discusses the work of Charles Mason and Jeremiah Dixon of the Royal Observatory, hired to mark the boundary between Maryland and Pennsylvania beginning in 1763 after 80 years of arguments over the boundary; first called the Western Line, it is more commonly known as the Mason-Dixon Line.

3259. Lepionka, Larry. PURRYSBURG, AN ARCHAEOLOGICAL SURVEY. *Swiss Am. Hist. Soc. Newsletter 1980 16(2): 18-29.* Examines the methodology of archaeological research and the discoveries in 1979-80 at Purrysburg, Jasper County, South Carolina, which, as indicated by ceramics found in Purrysburg, show that it was probably inhabited during 1733-1820 by Swiss settlers, and after the early 19th century lost its distinct Swiss character and was assimilated in the culture of British Carolina.

3260. Lewis, Peirce. DEFINING A SENSE OF PLACE. *Southern Q. 1979 17(3-4): 24-46.* Mississippi is a much more progressive state than most people believe. A look at the relationship between blacks and whites in the state clearly indicates this. Based on a paper presented at a symposium entitled "The Sense of Place: Mississippi" at the University of Mississippi, October 1978.
B. D. Ledbetter

3261. Liggin, Edna. CORNIE CREEK, 1839-1976: FROM EARLY LEGENDS TO MODERN FESTIVAL. *North Louisiana Hist. Assoc. J. 1979 10(1): 27-30.* A description of Cornie Creek, Louisiana, along with some of the stories concerning the history of the creek.
J. F. Paul

3262. Louder, Dean. LA DIASPORA: DES CADJINS EN VILLE [The scattering of Cajuns in cities]. *Vie Française [Canada] 1980 34(7-9): 54-59.* A study of the economic and demographic evolution in the 20th century of the Cajun population in cities in Louisiana and Texas.

3263. Louder, Dean and Waddell, Eric. À LA RECHERCHE DE LA LOUISIANE [Research on Louisiana]. *Vie Française [Canada] 1980 34(7-9): 1-5.* An introduction to articles appearing in the issue on Louisiana's French-speaking areas, linguistic diversities, ethnic differences, and geographic or parish divisions.

3264. Louder, Dean R. and Breton, Roland J.-L. LES AIRES LINGUISTIQUES FRANÇAISES DE L'ACADIANA, 1970 [French linguistic areas in Acadian country, 1970]. *Vie Française [Canada] 1980 34(7-9): 6-12.* Provides a geographical and linguistic study of French-speaking areas of Louisiana on the basis of the 1970 census.

3265. Loughmiller, Campbell and Loughmiller, Lynn. THE BIG THICKET. *Am. Heritage 1977 28(4): 44-51.* Presents 17 photographs of the Big Thicket area of east Texas, accompanied by interviews with five residents. The authors have assembled the interviews in a book, *Big Thicket Legacy* (University of Texas Pr., 1977). 17 illus.
B. J. Paul

3266. Martin, Robert S. MAPS OF AN EMPRESARIO: AUSTIN'S CONTRIBUTION TO THE CARTOGRAPHY OF TEXAS. *Southwestern Hist. Q. 1982 85(4): 371-400.* In 1822, Stephen F. Austin produced the first detailed and generally accurate map of Texas. By so doing, he provided an important source of geographical information during a pivotal time in Texas history, and he founded the field of Texas cartography. Austin used his map to promote immigration and to convince the Mexican government that American settlers would help protect the Rio Grande frontier from hostile Indians. In 1829, Austin revised his map with the aid of personal observations, surveyors, reports, and information from settlers. This map was in common use until the late 1830's. Based on the Stephen F. Austin maps and papers at the University of Texas Library and secondary sources; 6 maps, 37 notes.
R. D. Hurt

3267. McBride, Robert M. LOST COUNTIES OF TENNESSEE. *East Tennessee Hist. Soc. Publ. 1979 51: 138-150.* Counties rapidly proliferated in Tennessee during the 19th century, until settling at the present 95 counties. Lists some counties that were abolished or reorganized. Reprinted from the *East Tennessee Historical Society's Publications,* Vol. 38; 29 notes, 3 maps.
D. A. Yanchisin

3268. McClendon, Sarah. MISSISSIPPI'S IMAGE: A VIEW FROM WASHINGTON. *Southern Q. 1979 17(3-4): 114-118.* To the outside media Mississippi "is characterized by poverty, disease, racism, sexism, corrupt government, and educational and economic backwardness." Based on a paper presented at a symposium entitled "The Sense of Place: Mississippi" at the University of Mississippi, October 1978.
B. D. Ledbetter

3269. McDavid, Raven I., Jr. and O'Cain, Raymond K. SOUTH CAROLINA COUNTY NAMES: UNRECONSTRUCTED INDIVIDUALISM. *Names 1978 26(1): 106-115.* Examine the common patterns evident in the naming of South Carolina counties since its first three counties were established in 1672.

3270. McDonald, Archie F. THE TEXAS ROAD. *Red River Valley Hist. Rev. 1981 6(3): 57-67.* Surveys the development of eastern Oklahoma's Texas Road, which developed out of the Osage Trace; the road followed a rough path from near Joplin, Missouri, through the modern Oklahoma towns of Vinita, Pryor, Salina, Muskogee, Checotah, and other points south.

3271. McKee, Jesse O. A GEOGRAPHICAL ANALYSIS OF THE ORIGIN, DIFFUSION, AND SPATIAL DISTRIBUTION OF THE BLACK AMERICAN IN THE UNITED STATES. *Southern Q. 1974 12(3): 203-216.* Historical analysis of Negro migration in the United States from 1619 to the present. Data relating to the growth, distribution, and diffusion of black population are supplied. Evidence suggests that blacks will continue to migrate from the South during the 1970's and will settle in large northern and far western cities. The pace of out-migration from the South will slow during the 1970's and the percentage of total black population residing in the South will drop below 50 percent by 1980. 3 tables, 37 notes.
R. W. Dubay

3272. Mercer, Theodore C. A NOTE ON RHEA COUNTY. *Tennessee Hist. Q. 1976 35(1): 92-94.* Outlines the development of Rhea County, Tennessee, since its establishment in 1807. Shifting growth patterns, influenced by railroad development, caused the county seat to be transferred from Washington to Dayton in 1890. Dayton's boom growth ended in 1913, when the British-financed Coal and Iron Company closed. The Scopes "evolution trial," whose issues are "still very much alive," was held in Dayton in 1925. Under the impetus of TVA programs, industrial and population growth has resumed during the past 40 years.

W. R. Hively

3273. Merrill, Boynton, Jr. WILL THE REAL SOUTH PLEASE STAND UP? *Rev. in Am. Hist. 1978 6(2): 214-218.* Review article prompted by Robert M. Ireland's *Little Kingdoms: The Counties of Kentucky, 1850-1891* (Lexington: U. Pr. of Kentucky, 1977).

3274. Miller, Mary R. PLACE-NAMES OF THE NORTHERN NECK OF VIRGINIA: A PROPOSAL FOR A THEORY OF PLACE-NAMING. *Names 1976 24(1): 9-23.* Since the 17th century, the toponymy of Virginia has passed through five distinct stages corresponding to political and social organization.

3275. Millet, Donald J. THE SAGA OF WATER TRANSPORTATION INTO SOUTHWEST LOUISIANA TO 1900. *Louisiana Hist. 1974 15(4): 339-347.* Discusses natural waterways in the Attakapas and Opelousas countries in the 19th century.

3276. Mintz, Leonora Ferguson. THE WORLD'S ONE AND ONLY ROCKMART. *Georgia Life 1978 4(4): 16-19.* In 1849, Joseph G. Blance discovered slate at Van Wert, Georgia, which was founded in 1832; the town was renamed Rockmart in 1872 under Mayor Charles Taylor Parker; slate is still the town's chief product.

3277. Montgomery, James R. THE NOMENCLATURE OF THE UPPER TENNESSEE RIVER. *East Tennessee Hist. Soc. Publ. 1979 51: 151-162.* The variations in naming and renaming of the Upper Tennessee River tributaries have led to some confusion and historical errors regarding the development and history of east Tennessee. Reprinted from the *East Tennessee Historical Society's Publications,* Vol. 28; 62 notes, 2 maps.          D. A. Yanchisin

3278. Moore, Joanne Cullom. THE DEVIL'S ELBOW. *West Tennessee Hist. Soc. Papers 1981 35: 5-24.* Three miles below Island 37, the Mississippi River makes a sudden turn to the left, the greatest bend between Cairo and New Orleans. This phenomenon is known as the Devil's Elbow. In 1876 the Mississippi cut across the neck of land, placing it on the Arkansas side of the river and severing it from Tennessee. The area today is known as Centennial Island. The vagaries of the Mississippi, of which this is an example, have led to all sorts of jurisdictional lawsuits. Discusses school, utility, and housing problems and numerous lawsuits, involving the Devil's Elbow. Based on federal, state, and local court decisions; 6 maps and surveys, 14 pictures, 61 notes.          H. M. Parker, Jr.

3279. Moore, John Hammond. THE RETROCESSION ACT OF 1846: ALEXANDRIA AND ARLINGTON RETURN TO THE FOLD. *Virginia Cavalcade 1976 25(3): 126-135.* Discusses Congress' passing of the Retrocession Act (1846) bringing the cities of Alexandria and Arlington back from the territorial boundaries of the District of Columbia to Virginia, emphasizing the role of Virginia Congressman R. M. T. Hunter.

3280. Moore, Tyrel G. ROLE OF FERRYBOAT LANDINGS IN EAST TENNESSEE'S ECONOMIC DEVELOPMENT, 1790-1870. *West Georgia Coll. Studies in the Social Sci. 1979 18: 1-18.* Argues that ferry landings were a significant factor in eastern Tennessee's economic development, functioning in this period as trading centers, outlets for local agricultural products, and important bridges between water and land transportation.

3281. Morgan, Buford. PLACE-NAMES IN THE WICHITAS. *Great Plains J. 1978 17: 49-103.* Few Indian place names remain in the Wichita Mountains in Oklahoma. The first English names were conferred in 1852 by an exploring party, but most were given after the area was opened to settlement in 1901. Indicates certain

names, the origin of which is not determined, and lists and describes 200 others in alphabetical order. Primary and secondary sources; photo, 126 notes.          O. H. Zabel

3282. Morris, Willie. A SENSE OF PLACE AND THE AMERICANIZATION OF MISSISSIPPI. *Southern Q. 1979 17(3-4): 3-13.* A native Mississippian discusses the 20th-century developments in the state. Mississippi has come a long way in the Americanization process but still has a long way to go. While adopting many more traditional American values, Mississippi is still unique. Based on a paper read at a symposium at the University of Mississippi, October 1978 entitled "The sense of Place: Mississippi."

B. D. Ledbetter

3283. Morrison, Charles. EARLY LAND GRANTS AND SETTLERS ALONG PATTERSON CREEK. *West Virginia Hist. 1979 40(2): 164-199.* Patterson Creek Manor was part of the huge Fairfax estate in the Virginia Northern Neck west of the Blue Ridge. Lots of several hundred acres were granted in 1748-62. Settlement was retarded by the terror of the French and Indian War, but by the 1770's the area was well populated. Some of this land was involved in the Virginia litigation of the 1780's and 1790's which led to the US Supreme Court case of *Martin v. Hunter's Lessee.* Primary and secondary sources; 51 notes, 2 maps.          J. H. Broussard

3284. Murphy, Marcus Lane. THE GENESIS OF A HOMETOWN. *North Louisiana Hist. Assoc. J. 1982 13(1): 27-33.* Begun in the middle 1840's, Arcadia was strategically located as a halfway point between Shreveport and Monroe, Louisiana. Officially named in 1851, Arcadia was incorporated in 1855. In 1893, it became the parish seat for Bienville Parish. 19 notes.          J. F. Paul

3285. O'Grady, Patricia D. THE OCCUPATION OF SAPELO ISLAND SINCE 1733. *West Georgia Coll. Studies in the Social Sci. 1980 19: 1-8.* Traces the ownership and occupation of Sapelo Island, one of Georgia's sea islands, from the establishment of an English colony there in 1733 until the beginning of archaeological studies there in 1974.

3286. Overbeck, Ruth Ann. COLBERT'S FERRY. *Chronicles of Oklahoma 1979 57(2): 212-223.* Benjamin Franklin Colbert, a Chickasaw Indian, built a ferry across the Red River just north of present-day Denison, Texas, sometime during the 1840's. By 1858 most competing ferries had been driven out of business and Colbert monopolized much of the California-bound wagon trade as well as contracting for the business of the Butterfield Overland Mail Company. The ferry continued to flourish during the Civil War, and by 1875 Colbert had constructed a bridge to carry most of the wagon traffic. Though the bridge was soon destroyed by floods, the ferry remained in service until 1915 when a more permanent bridge was built. Primary and secondary sources; 2 photos, map, 36 notes.

M. L. Tate

3287. Parker, Mary Ann. THE ELUSIVE MERIDIAN. *Chronicles of Oklahoma 1973 51(2): 150-158.* The problem of the location of the 100th meridian, part of boundary between Texas and Oklahoma, began with its creation in the 1819 Adams-Onís Treaty with Spain, and was only ended in 1930 by a Supreme Court decision.

3288. Peacock, Blanche G. A NOTE ON LAKE COUNTY. *Tennessee Hist. Q. 1977 36(4): 537-538.* Lake County, in the northwest corner of Tennessee, is the only county in Tennessee that is entirely Mississippi Delta land. Lake County is the third smallest in the state. Its major recreational area is Reelfoot Lake.

M. B. Lucas

3289. Pearson, Bruce L. ON THE INDIAN PLACE-NAMES OF SOUTH CAROLINA. *Names 1978 26(1): 58-67.* Discusses the difficulties encountered when attempting to find the origin of Indian place-names in South Carolina, and reviews the information published on the subject since 1894.

3290. Pederson, Lee. LEXICAL DATA FROM THE GULF STATES. *Am. Speech 1980 55(3): 195-203.* In the current *Linguistic Atlas of the Gulf States* (LAGS) project, word study is being pursued through regional word geography, urban word geography, and inventoried research. Total dependence on the tape recorder distinguishes the LAGS project from other regional projects. Interviewers have accumulated regional lexicons in depth. The urban lexicon has rapidly changed and enlarged.

D. A. Yanchisin

3291. Pederson, Lee. THE LINGUISTIC ATLAS OF THE GULF STATES: INTERIM REPORT THREE. *Am. Speech 1976 51(3-4): 201-207.* Work progresses on *The Linguistic Atlas of the Gulf States,* which is to be a dictionary-atlas with records now stored on 96,000 frames of microfiche. It will be accompanied by a published handbook, dictionary, and volumes of maps. Preparation of the urban information was completed during 1975-76, when the protocols and handbook were planned. The microfiche and handbook will be released on schedule in 1980. 8 notes.          D. A. Yanchisin

3292. Petersen, Ron. TWO EARLY BOUNDARY LINES WITH THE CHEROKEE NATION. *J. of Cherokee Studies 1981 6(1): 14-33.* The Hopewell Treaty (1785) created the Holston River Treaty concerning the first western Cherokee boundary. Governor William Blount, acting under orders from President Jefferson, attempted to survey a western border. Consequently, several lines were mapped. The Hawkins-Pickens Line was replaced by the 1st Knox Treaty (1794), which was amended by the Knox II (or Tellico) Treaty (1798). Return J. Meigs surveyed a new line in 1802, because of previous failures to map the area between the Tennessee and Little Tennessee rivers and conflicting points along several ridges. Added problems included cartographic accuracy and availability of previously drawn documents, which ultimately forced the Cherokees to cede territory once promised by President George Washington. 5 maps, engraving, 60 notes.          K. E. Gilmont

3293. Peterson, Peter L. A PARK FOR THE PANHANDLE: THE ACQUISITION AND DEVELOPMENT OF PALO DURO CANYON STATE PARK. *Panhandle-Plains Hist. Rev. 1978 51: 145-178.* Organized attempts to win Texas state park status for Palo Duro Canyon began in 1906, but not until 1934 did it formally open as a park. Numerous private land claims in the canyon made transfer of title difficult, but efforts by prominent citizens of Canyon and Amarillo, Texas, gradually helped solve the problem. Civilian Conservation Corps projects during the 1930's improved park facilities, and by the 1950's it had become an important tourist attraction and source of regional pride throughout the Texas Panhandle. Primary and secondary sources; 10 photos, 60 notes.
M. L. Tate

3294. Peterson, Susan. THE BUTTERFIELD OVERLAND MAIL IN INDIAN TERRITORY, 1858-1861. *Red River Valley Hist. Rev. 1981 6(3): 77-86.* Focuses on the establishment of the Butterfield Overland Trail; although Butterfield only operated his mail service through Oklahoma during 1858-61, his road stretched from Fort Smith, Arkansas, to Colbert's Ferry on the Red River, bisecting the Choctaw Nation; after the mail service ended, the road continued to be used, and State Highway 271 later closely followed the old route.

3295. Pettie, Sharon T. PRESERVING THE GREAT DISMAL SWAMP. *J. of Forest Hist. 1976 20(1): 28-33.* The Great Dismal Swamp, bordering the tidewater areas of Virginia and North Carolina, was surveyed in 1728 by William Byrd and in 1763 by George Washington, who built a canal for lumbering operations. The canal, possibly the oldest usable canal in the United States, was the first in a long series of schemes to exploit the swamp's rich natural resources. Transportation and lumbering prospered in the swamp until the Civil War, and were renovated in the 1870's. The federal government bought the Dismal Swamp Canal in 1929 as part of the Intracoastal Waterway. In the 1970's several lumbering and land companies have taken steps to preserve the swamp, part of which is now the Dismal Swamp National Wildlife Refuge. 6 illus., map, note.          L. F. Johnson

3296. Pierce, Rita S. and Moore, Gordon. FROM DUST TO DUST: GIBBON, AN OKLAHOMA TOWN. *Chronicles of Oklahoma 1983 61(2): 116-129.* William H. McGibbon established a townsite in Grant County, Oklahoma, during the 1893 land rush. Mistakenly misnamed "Gibbon" three years later, the town thrived amid the rich farm belt. A branch railroad attracted new businesses to the town, which by 1910 had a school, church, and bank for its population of 478. Collapse of national grain prices after World War I severely undermined the region's economy, and when the major highway construction of the 1920's bypassed Gibbon, the town gradually died. Based on newspapers and census materials; illus., 3 photos, 40 notes.          M. L. Tate

3297. Pilkey, Orrin H., Jr. and Neal, William J. THE FOLLY OF STABILIZING OREGON INLET. *Southern Exposure 1982 10(3): 10-12.* The criticisms of the US Army Corps of Engineers' plans for Oregon Inlet in North Carolina include the fact that the inlet is migratory and the jetty design accelerates erosion of the beaches; consequently the inlet cannot be stabililized.

3298. Pittman, Paul. CHANGES IN MISSISSIPPI AND THE MEDIA. *Southern Q. 1979 17(3-4): 108-114.* Mississippi is a place of uncertainty, as has been reflected by both national and state news media. Based on a paper presented at a symposium entitled "The Sense of Place: Mississippi" at the University of Mississippi, October 1978.          B. D. Ledbetter

3299. Posey, Darrell A. ORIGIN, DEVELOPMENT AND MAINTENANCE OF A LOUISIANA MIXED-BLOOD COMMUNITY: THE ETHNOHISTORY OF THE FREEJACKS OF THE [FIFTH] WARD SETTLEMENT. *Ethnohistory 1979 26(2): 177-192.* The Fifth Ward Settlement is composed of approximately 2,500 mixed-blood (Black, White and Indian) inhabitants called "Freejacks." The Settlement has developed as a result of various social, racial and legal distinctions that have altered the nature of the Settlement over its 150 year history. The origins and early development of the community are rooted in racial oppression, geographical isolation and cultural diversity. Today most of the restrictive racial barriers are removed, yet the Freejacks themselves seek to maintain boundaries to delineate the Settlement and preserve a distinctive identity.
J

3300. Powers, Mary C. W. D. SMITHERS: PHOTOGRAPHER-JOURNALIST OF THE SOUTHWEST. *Lib. Chronicle of the U. of Texas at Austin 1982 19: 124-147.* Reviews the career of W. D. Smithers, an untrained photojournalist who participated in and recorded much of the history of the Texas-Mexico border area after 1910.

3301. Pursell, Donald E. AGE AND EDUCATIONAL DIMENSIONS IN SOUTHERN MIGRATION PATTERNS, 1965-1970. *Southern Econ. J. 1977 44(1): 148-154.* Imparts internal migration information for 12 southern states concluding that 11 of the 12 were net importers of human capital and that of those males who moved the largest percentage were under 25 with more than 12 years of education.

3302. Rathjen, Frederick W. THE FEDERAL ROLE IN OPENING THE PANHANDLE. *Panhandle-Plains Hist. Rev. 1976 49(1): 1-24.* Traces the important role of the federal government in opening the Texas Panhandle to settlement by 1876. Beginning with Stephen Long's exploration of the Canadian River in 1820, a series of military expeditions under James W. Abert, Randolph B. Marcy, and Amiel W. Whipple explored the arid region and laid out trails for western migration. These expeditions also collected information about various Indian tribes which proved crucial to the army's victory in the Red River War of 1874-75. With the tribes confined to Indian Territory, settlers moved into the Panhandle and found protection from newly established Fort Elliott which provided medical, postal and telegraphic service for the infant communities. Army payrolls spurred economic growth while also preserving law and order. Based on primary and secondary sources; 59 notes.
M. L. Tate

3303. Redmond, Mary S. ATTEMPTED SECESSION IN OKLAHOMA: THE FOUR-MILE STRIP, 1935-1950. *Chronicles of Oklahoma 1982 60(2): 167-173.* Citizens living within the 96-square-mile strip of southern Grady County, Oklahoma, tried to break away and join neighboring Stephens County in 1935, 1940, and 1950. Each attempt failed to win a majority of votes, but the debate demonstrated the problems of people who live closer to the county seat (Duncan) of a neighboring county than to their own county seat (Chickasha). 2 maps, 2 photos.                M. L. Tate

3304. Reed, John Shelton. "THE CARDINAL TEST OF A SOUTHERNER": NOT RACE BUT GEOGRAPHY. *Public Opinion Q. 1973 37(2): 232-240.* Discusses the continuing high group identity among white southerners. The traditional explanation (anti-Negro hostility) is inadequate. Better reasons are shared historical experiences, socialization processes, and most significantly, a shared geography. A sense of geographical identity cuts across age, class, and sex distinctions. White southerners can be considered an ethnic minority group with considerable survival abilities. 4 tables, 26 notes.                                               V. L. Human

3305. Rehder, John B. SUGAR PLANTATIONS IN LOUISIANA: ORIGIN, DISPERSAL, AND RESPONSIBLE LOCATION FACTORS. *West Georgia Coll. Studies in the Social Sci. 1973 12: 78-93.* One of seven articles in this issue on "Geographic Perspectives on Southern Development."                              S

3306. Rindfuss, Ronald R. CHANGING PATTERNS OF FERTILITY IN THE SOUTH: A SOCIAL-DEMOGRAPHIC EXAMINATION. *Social Forces 1978 57(2): 621-635.* This paper examines the trend in the fertility difference between the South and the remainder of the United States—a differential which has existed since colonial times. The paper begins with a consideration of the reasons why there might be a regional fertility differential. The rest of the paper examines the trend in this differential. It is found that the long-standing higher fertility of the South, relative to the rest of the country, has ceased. But this does not mean that the differential has disappeared. The South currently has lower levels of fertility than the non-South, and this is because Southerners *prefer* fewer children than nonsoutherners.                            J

3307. Roberson, Jere W. EDWARD P. MC CABE AND THE LANGSTON EXPERIMENT. *Chronicles of Oklahoma 1973 51(3): 343-355.* Biographical sketch of Edward P. McCabe (1850-1920), promoter of Negro migration from Kansas to Langston, Oklahoma, which he founded; emphasizes the role of frontier newspapers in the migration.

3308. Rock, Maxine A. CUMBERLAND ISLAND: SANDY TREASURE OF THE GOLDEN ISLES. *Natl. Parks and Conservation Mag. 1973 47(8): 4-7.* Discovered by the Spanish in 1521, Georgia's Cumberland Island housed plantations in the 19th century and the "idle rich" in the early 20th century, and eventually was established as part of the National Park Service as Cumberland Island National Seashore in 1972.

3309. Roper, James E. FORT SAN FERNANDO DE LAS BARRANCAS: WHERE WAS IT, EXACTLY? *West Tennessee Hist. Soc. Papers 1980 (34): 5-27.* One of the problems in modern Memphis history deals with the exact location of the Spanish Fort San Fernando de las Barrancas (1795-97). Just where was it in relation to modern Memphis? One of the major difficulties in locating the position of the fort is the lack of any prominent topographical features. Another is the absence of any precise map of the fort's location which can be overlayed on a contemporary map of Memphis with any degree of accuracy. Based largely on *Archivo General de Indias, Papeles de Cuba* (Madrid) Abraham P. Nasatir, *Spanish War Vessels on the Mississippi, 1792-1796,* and other secondary studies; illus., 3 maps, 100 notes.            H. M. Parker, Jr.

3310. Ross, John R. CONSERVATION AND ECONOMY: THE NORTH CAROLINA GEOLOGICAL SURVEY, 1891-1920. *Forest Hist. 1973 16(4): 20-27.* The North Carolina General Assembly created the Geological Survey in 1891. Joseph Austin Holmes (1859-1915) of the University of North Carolina soon won national acclaim for his direction of the survey. It promoted conservation, identified industrial sites, reclaimed swampland, and sought to improve the fishing industry. By 1915 "the Fisheries Commission Bill, the Forest Fire Law, the creation of Mt. Mitchell State Park, a bill

to permit the state to acquire forest, and an act designating Arbor Day" were in effect. The survey modified indifference and localism that had blocked conservation in the South. Based on papers of the North Carolina Geological Survey, private papers, and secondary sources; 4 photos, 24 notes.                    D. R. Verardo

3311. Ruffin, Thomas F. THE ELUSIVE BORDER. *North Louisiana Hist. Assoc. J. 1977 8(3): 95-113.* After 1812 when Louisiana became a state, its exact boundary in the northwest corner presented a problem. The Republic of Texas and the state of Arkansas also were involved. Since the 1700's there never had been a well-defined boundary line separating Spanish Texas from French Louisiana, and no definite line was laid down at the time of the Louisiana Purchase. The problem was not settled until 1841 when a joint boundary survey laid out a definitive boundary line for all to recognize. As a result of the survey Arkansas ceded an entire county to Texas, and Louisiana gave Texas over 450 square miles of its Caddo Parish. Primary and secondary sources; 7 maps, 67 notes.
                                              A. N. Garland

3312. Sallis, Charles. IMAGES OF MISSISSIPPI. *Southern Q. 1979 17(3-4): 67-69.* The nation has lost its purpose while the South has maintained a sense of belonging. "Perhaps we can lead the nation in finding its lost purpose and restoring its confidence and sense of community." Based on a paper presented at a symposium entitled "The Sense of Place: Mississippi" at the University of Mississippi, October 1978.                          B. D. Ledbetter

3313. Sanchez-Saavedra, E. M. "SURVEYED AND EXACTLY DRAWNE": VIRGINIA'S CARTOGRAPHERS AND THEIR MAPS. *Virginia Cavalcade 1976 25(3): 100-109.* Discusses cartography, maps, and surveying of Virginia by Captain John Smith, Augustine Herman, William Barton Rogers, and others 1612-1880's, including the use of chronometers in navigation.

3314. Savage, Robert L. and Gallagher, Richard J. POLITICOCULTURAL REGIONS IN A SOUTHERN STATE: AN EMPIRICAL TYPOLOGY OF ARKANSAS COUNTIES. *Publius 1977 7(1): 91-105.* Tests the validity of Daniel Elazar's concept of moralistic, traditional, and individualistic immigration streams in American history. Socioeconomic analysis of Arkansas counties confirms folk wisdom that the state is divided into two regions, the moralistic Ozarks and the more traditional delta. Scattered urban counties constitute a third subset, if not a distinct region, and appear to have individualistic traits. The study is weakly indicative of Elazar's categories. Based on secondary sources; 2 tables, fig., 15 notes.                                            A. Clive

3315. Scarborough, William K. FROM PROSPERITY TO POVERTY: ECONOMIC GROWTH AND CHANGE TO 1900. *Southern Q. 1979 17(3-4): 153-178.* Surveys the economic forces that have shaped the past in Mississippi, with the hope that this information will lead to a better understanding of the state's "sense of place." Based on a paper presented at a symposium entitled "The Sense of Place: Mississippi" at the University of Mississippi, October 1978. 4 notes.                        B. D. Ledbetter

3316. Schwartz, Sally. CANTWELL'S BRIDGE, DELAWARE: A DEMOGRAPHIC AND COMMUNITY STUDY. *Delaware Hist. 1980 19(1): 20-38.* Describes the growth of Cantwell's Bridge (now Odessa) on Appoquinimink Creek in Delaware. Attributes the town's growth to the favorable location on a water route linking farmers with the Delaware River and Philadelphia. The town experienced a very fluid population history, with high mobility. Immigration accounted for the growth of the town, and the railroad signalled its demise. Although ethnically diverse by the 19th century, a few older families, who controlled most of the good land, dominated the town's economic and social life and through intermarriage secured their hold on its political life. The town was typical of small-town America with its diverse populations, fluid social structure from the late 17th century through the mid-19th century, and its rapid fall from prominence in the face of new technology. 70 notes.                                            R. M. Miller

3317. Shepard, E. Lee. "THE EASE AND CONVENIENCE OF THE PEOPLE": COURTHOUSE LOCATIONS IN SPOT-SYLVANIA COUNTY, 1720-1840. *Virginia Mag. of Hist. and Biog. 1979 87(3): 279-299.* Traces attempts to change the county seat, where on court days much of the community gathered for social and economic, as well as legal, activity. Political and economic self-interest underlay calls for changes in county courts made in the name of public convenience. The General Assembly had to deal with various pressures for change, often in the form of petitions. Creation of new courts and county divisions were considered as options to seat change, and were sometimes adopted. 59 notes.
P. J. Woehrmann

3318. Shirk, George H. CRAWFORD SEMINARY POST OFFICE. *Chronicles of Oklahoma 1976/77 54(4): 468-473.* A post office, Crawford Seminary, was located in Indian Territory, 1848-63.

3319. Simmons, Dennis E. CONSERVATION, COOPERATION, AND CONTROVERSY: THE ESTABLISHMENT OF SHENANDOAH NATIONAL PARK, 1924-1936. *Virginia Mag. of Hist. and Biog. 1981 89(4): 387-404.* Discusses the political, social, legal, and financial problems that were overcome to establish the park, including the Skyline Drive. Conservationists, National Park Service leaders, and individuals desiring to restore and preserve scenic areas united with local and state business and political figures seeking profit and prestige and overcame opposition—federal, state, and local rivalries, uncertainty as to what the park should be, and resistance to removal from lands bought for the park. A private campaign raised money to buy the land. The Great Depression in effect cut down on the amount of land purchased, but New Deal work projects helped with construction. The early opening of one section of the park generated support for the completion of the park. By 1939, three years after the park opened, the facility had more visitors than any other in the National Park System. Drawn mainly from the author's 1978 PhD dissertation; 41 notes.
P. J. Woehrmann

3320. Simon, Richard M. REGIONS AND SOCIAL RELATIONS: A RESEARCH NOTE. *Appalachian J. 1983-84 11(1-2): 23-31.* Discusses, from a Marxist perspective, Appalachia as a geographical region, rather than as a class or culture.

3321. Skjong, Ronald R. EDWARD AVERY MCILHENNY AND THE LOUISIANA GULF COAST CLUB. *Southern Studies 1982 21(1): 105-116.* Edward Avery McIlhenny was chiefly responsible for wildlife conservation areas in Louisiana. During 1910-20 he got private and governmental support for protecting large areas of coastal lands for bird refuges. He was widely acclaimed for his efforts until 1922 when he attempted to develop a private hunting club on the Gulf Coast between two wildlife refuges. He believed only the wealthy could purchase and donate large tracts of land. He felt businessmen would join the club and thus help to protect, at least partially, the wildlife of the area; he also wished to develop southern Louisiana for tourism and business. The club failed after much adverse publicity. 31 notes.
J. J. Buschen

3322. Smith, Frank E. A SENSE OF PLACE FOR TODAY AND TOMORROW. *Southern Q. 1979 17(3-4): 92-102.* In Mississippi, the sense of place has long been stronger than in other states in the country. Mississippians will continue to display this unique characteristic. Based on a paper presented at a symposium entitled "The Sense of Place: Mississippi" at the University of Mississippi, October 1978.
B. D. Ledbetter

3323. Spoden, Muriel C. A NOTE ON SULLIVAN COUNTY. *Tennessee Hist. Q. 1976 35(2): 220-221.* Sullivan County, situated in the northeastern corner of Tennessee, was not known to be part of North Carolina (the state from which Tennessee was carved) until 1779. Several important wilderness trails crossed the county, and river routes also carried a stream of early settlers. The county was the site of the first Revolutionary War battle west of the Appalachian Mountains. Sullivan County abounds in places of historical interest and is at present the location of some of the nation's largest industries.
V. L. Human

3324. Stephenson, Richard W. THE MAPPING OF THE NORTHWEST BOUNDARY OF TEXAS, 1859-1860. *Terrae Incognitae [Netherlands] 1974 6: 39-50.* John H. Clark, US Boundary Commissioner, surveyed 800 miles of the Texas boundary, July 1858-January 1862. His field map, recently discovered in the Library of Congress map files, shows the annotations of Clark and his surveyor. This work was largely unknown to cartographers until after the Civil War. Primary and secondary sources; maps, 32 notes.
C. B. Fitzgerald

3325. Stone, Kirk H. THE GEOGRAPHICAL INHERITANCE OF CURRENT RURAL HOUSE DENSITIES IN EASTERN GEORGIA. *Georgia Hist. Q. 1982 66(2): 196-216.* Analyzes the number of rural houses in a strip of 20 counties on the eastern Georgia border, relating current densities to historical settlement patterns, which had more to do with the settler's habits than with the physical characteristics of the landscape. Based on maps and secondary sources; 8 fig., 38 notes.
G. R. Schroeder

3326. Stringer, Gary A. MISSISSIPPI IN THE MEDIA: FORUM III. *Southern Q. 1979 17(3-4): 103-108.* A critique of a session on "Mississippi in the Media." Paul Pittman, publisher of the *Tylertown Times,* journalist Sarah McClendon, Rea S. Hederman of the *Clarion-Ledger,* and Bert Case, news director for WLBT-TV in Jackson, participated in the session. Based on a paper presented at a symposium entitled "The Sense of Place: Mississippi" at the University of Mississippi, October 1978.
B. D. Ledbetter

3327. Thorne, Robert. PRESERVING CULTURAL RESOURCES. *Southern Q. 1979 17(3-4): 86-88.* To conserve the cultural resources of Mississippi and enhance the sense of-place of the state, public education must be given top priority. Covers 1900-78. Based on a paper presented at a symposium entitled "The Sense of Place: Mississippi" at the University of Mississippi, October 1978.
B. D. Ledbetter

3328. Thurston, William N. THE APALACHICOLA-CHATTAHOOCHEE-FLINT RIVER TRANSPORTATION ROUTE IN THE NINETEENTH CENTURY. *Georgia Hist. Q. 1973 57(2): 200-212.* The Chattahoochee and Flint Rivers unite to form the Apalachicola River. This system flows through the Georgia-Alabama borderlands and across northern Florida. Until replaced by railroads it provided the essential transportation for the economic development of the region. 23 notes.
D. L. Smith

3329. Todd, Evalyn E. HISTORIC HALIFAX. *Daughters of the Am. Revolution Mag. 1976 110(2): 186-191.* Discusses the history of Halifax, North Carolina, since its founding in 1759 and notes some important historical sites and restorations there.

3330. Turner, Frederick. BARATARIA. *Am. Heritage 1980 31(5): 65-75.* The Barataria region of Louisiana spreads south from New Orleans into the Gulf of Mexico and still appears as isolated as it did many years ago when first smuggling and later illegal slave running provided the main sources of income for inhabitants of the area. From the island of Grand Terre, Jean Lafitte took control of the region in 1811 and ruled it until 1815. After an interlude of sugar producing, the islands became elegant watering holes for the wealthy. Starting in 1893, several hurricanes destroyed that business. Oil companies have worked the area since the 1930's and much of the population is now engaged in oil-related work. 7 illus.
J. F. Paul

3331. Tyler, Jack D. BIRDS OF THE WICHITA MOUNTAINS. *Great Plains J. 1977 16(2): 135-162.* Describes the Wichita Mountains Wildlife Refuge in Oklahoma and species of birds found in the area. Records 286 Wichita Mountains species. Map, biblio.
O. H. Zabel

3332. Vance, Linda D. MAY MANN JENNINGS AND ROYAL PALM STATE PARK. *Florida Hist. Q. 1976 55(1): 1-17.* Largely through the conservation efforts of Mrs. May Mann Jennings (1872-1963) and her work with the Florida Federation of Women's Clubs, a section of the Everglades near Homestead became in 1915 Royal Palm State Park, the first in the state. Ultimately the park became part of the Everglades National Park, dedicated in 1947. Mrs. Jennings' efforts helped preserve the exotic plant and animal life there as well as the large stand of royal palms. Based on MS. and newspaper sources; 6 photos, 42 notes.          P. A. Beaber

3333.  Vanderhill, Burke G. THE ALACHUA TRAIL: A RECONSTRUCTION. *Florida Hist. Q. 1977 55(4): 423-438.* Well known in colonial and precolonial times, the Alachua Trail stretched from the Altamaha River in Georgia to the Alachua country in northern Florida. Although it fell into disuse by the end of the 19th century, some features are still visible and some parts are used as modern highways. Reconstructs the route of the trail from early maps and landscape evidence and has recommended appropriate commemorative markers. 3 maps, 36 notes.          P. A. Beaber

3334.  Vanderhill, Burke G. and Unger, Frank A. GEORGIA-FLORIDA LAND BOUNDARY: PRODUCT OF CONTROVERSY AND COMPROMISE. *West Georgia Coll. Studies in the Social Sci. 1979 18: 59-73.* Discusses the Georgia-Florida land boundary—the so-called "Georgia Fractions"—from its initial drawing in 1763 through numerous subsequent surveys, ending with the Supreme Court decision of *Coffee* v. *Groover* (US, 1887).

3335.  Vanderhill, Burke G. THE HISTORIC SPAS OF FLORIDA. *West Georgia Coll. Studies in the Social Sci. 1973 12: 59-77.* One of seven articles in this issue on "Geographic Perspectives on Southern Development."          S

3336.  Waddell, Eric and Fournier, Louise. LES RÉGIONS: LE TÊCHE [The regions: the Têche]. *Vie Française [Canada] 1980 34(7-9): 35-39.* A brief sociological and ethnic history since 1765, of the Bayou Têche region of Louisiana, including the cities of Pont Breaux and Saint Martinville, which is composed of Acadians, black and colored Creoles.

3337.  Wade, Willie. A HISTORY OF SHEFFIELD, TEXAS. *West Texas Hist. Assoc. Year Book 1980 56: 103-110.* History of Sheffield, a small ranch and oil town in the Trans-Pecos region of Texas, 1590-1978.

3338.  Wainwright, Nicholas B. MASON AND DIXON'S MAP. *Princeton U. Lib. Chronicle 1983 45(1): 28-32.* Recounts the role of Benjamin Chew in the Pennsylvania-Maryland border dispute and the Mason-Dixon survey that resolved it; the Princeton University Library recently acquired some of the survey documents from the Chew family.

3339.  Wales, Robert W. ENVIRONMENT, A SENSE OF PLACE AND PUBLIC POLICY. *Southern Q. 1979 17(3-4): 71-79.* The environment needs to be studied to determine how it affects the sense of place of any area. This has been neglected in Mississippi in the past, but hopefully it will not be neglected in the future. Covers 1900-78. Based on a Paper presented at a symposium entitled "The Sense of Place: Mississippi" at the University of Mississippi, October 1978.          B. D. Ledbetter

3340.  Wallach, Bret. THE SLIGHTED MOUNTAINS OF UPPER EAST TENNESSEE. *Ann. of the Assoc. of Am. Geog. 1981 71(3): 359-373.* Traces the history of development of mountain land in northeastern Tennessee since the 18th century, focusing on the 150,000 hectares purchased by the federal government between 1915 and 1941 and efforts by the Forest Service to reforest this section of the Appalachian Mountains.

3341.  Watson, Bud. BORDER WARS: SHOWDOWN AT THE STATE LINE IN THE CHESAPEAKE BAY. *Southern Exposure 1982 10(3): 77.* With the arrival of Virginia Marine Resources Commission inspector Juney Crockett, a native of Tangier Island, Virginia, the old border feud over Chesapeake Bay fishing with Maryland continues.

3342.  Watts, Ann DeWitt. CITIES AND THEIR PLACE IN SOUTHERN APPALACHIA. *Appalachian J. 1981 8(2): 105-118.* Shows how important urban places are to generally rural Appalachia and suggests geographically influenced reasons for their loca-

tion; offers new insight into some statistical measures of the quality of Appalachian life; and suggests a development process for the region.

3343.  Wells, Ann Harwell. A CHECKLIST OF TENNESSEE MAPS, 1800-1819. *Tennessee Hist. Q. 1981 40(1): 13-45.* Information is given on 24 maps of Tennessee published between 1800 and 1819; 18 of the maps were published in Philadelphia by Matthew Carey in his atlases. The author provides size, scale, description, place of publication, and source of the maps. Primary sources; 6 illus., biblio.          C. L. Grant

3344.  Wells, Ann Harwell. EARLY MAPS OF TENNESSEE, 1794-1799. *Tennessee Hist. Q. 1976 35(2): 123-143.* Lists and reproduces, with a general description and history, eight maps of the state of Tennessee made during 1794-99. The first, made by General Daniel Smith, is one of the best. Three maps were published by Matthew Carey. Mapmaking procedures consisted of a survey, a cartographer's drawing, transference to a metal block, printing, and finally publication in a book or atlas. The eight reproduced maps include title, date, size, scale, where they were published, states, and other pertinent information. 8 maps, 49 notes.
                                                                     V. L. Human

3345.  Weslager, C. A. NEW CASTLE, DELAWARE—AND ITS FORMER NAMES. *Names 1976 24(2): 101-105.* Explores the toponymy of New Castle, 1638-1976.

3346.  Wilhelm, Gene, Jr. APPALACHIA: IN-MIGRATION IN THE TWENTIETH CENTURY. *Appalachian J. 1974 1(4): 301-306.*

3347.  Wilhelm, Gene, Jr. APPALACHIAN ISOLATION: FACT OR FICTION? *Appalachian J. 1977 4(4): 77-91.* Although Appalachian isolation is usually considered a result of geography, this study of mountain roads and socioeconomic contacts with outside areas demonstrates that attitudes, not mountains, isolated the Appalachian people since the end of the Civil War.

3348.  Woodbury, Mrs. Harry. A NOTE ON SHELBY COUNTY. *Tennessee Hist. Q. 1979 38(1): 79-82.* Shelby County, the "hub of the Mid-South," is located in the southwest corner of Tennessee. It is the largest county in the state in both territory and population, with Memphis as its principal city. The county is rich in history from Indian times, through the Civil War, to the present.
                                                                     M. B. Lucas

3349.  Woods, H. Ted. COLUMBIA ESTABLISHED AS A PORT IN EARLY 1800'S. *North Louisiana Hist. Assoc. J. 1974 5(2): 73-76.* Caldwell Parish was carved from the original parishes of Ouachita and Catahoula and was established by an act of the state legislature on 8 March 1838. The settlement at Columbia had a fragmented early history. Its site was first settled in 1827 by Daniel Humphries. Its importance was as a river port and trading center. Destroyed by fire in 1876, 1900, and again in 1909, the city was rebuilt each time. Today Columbia has a population of 4,500. Note.
                                                                     A. N. Garland

3350.  Worsham, John Gibson, Jr. "A PLACE SO LOFTY AND SECLUDED": YELLOW SULPHUR SPRINGS IN MONTGOMERY COUNTY. *Virginia Cavalcade 1977 27(1): 30-41.* Yellow Sulphur Springs, Virginia, was a spa and vacation spot, 1800-1923.

3351.  Young, T. D. MISSISSIPPI: A PERSONAL VIEW OF ITS PAST AND A HOPE FOR ITS FUTURE. *Southern Q. 1979 17(3-4): 47-57.* Mississippi has been wronged by negative statements about it. The state has produced its share of intellectuals and the standard of living is not as low as many of the inner-city slums of the United States. Based on a paper presented at a symposium entitled "The Sense of Place: Mississippi" at the University of Mississippi, October 1978.          B. D. Ledbetter

3352.  Young, T. D. MISSISSIPPI: TWO VIEWS FROM THE OUTSIDE. *Southern Q. 1979 17(3-4): 64-66.* From the 1930's until the mid-1960's Mississippi was viewed as backward and racist.

Now the state is changing that view for the better. Based on a paper presented at a symposium entitled "The Sense of Place: Mississippi" at the University of Mississippi, October 1978.

B. D. Ledbetter

3353. —. HISTORICAL MARKER DEDICATED AT RUSSELLVILLE. *North Louisiana Hist. Assoc. J. 1979 10(4): 129.* Tells of the dedication of a historical marker to commemorate Russellville's service as the second seat of government for Claiborne Parish. Founded in 1829, the town became a ghost town in 1836 when the parish seat was moved.    J. F. Paul

## Poverty in the South

3354. Bacon, Lloyd. MIGRATION, POVERTY, AND THE RURAL SOUTH. *Social Forces 1973 51(3): 348-355.* The 1967 *Survey of Economic Opportunity* data are employed to test hypotheses about differences in migration selectivity depending on the structural distance traversed in the migration process. Theoretically, the greater the structural distance crossed in the migration process, the more rigorous would be the selectivity. Conversely, where migration involves movement between similar places, little selectivity would be expected. Structural distance was defined as movement across both regional and rural-urban axes. Selectivity was defined by the relative incidence of poverty among the various residence and migration categories. Analysis of movement into and out of the rural South revealed empirical relationships between variables consistent with the theory employed, although important exceptions were found. These exceptions required a modification of the theory.

J

3355. Barber, Rims and Huttie, Joseph J., Jr. NIXONIAN ECONOMICS: ANOTHER VIEW. *New South 1973 28(2): 72-78.* The Nixon administration's dismantling of poverty programs is putting strains on Mississippi's poor.

3356. Bernhard, Virginia. POVERTY AND THE SOCIAL ORDER IN SEVENTEENTH-CENTURY VIRGINIA. *Virginia Mag. of Hist. and Biog. 1977 85(2): 141-155.* Although 17th-century Virginia has been portrayed as a society of profit-mad planters, Virginians developed a more humane attitude toward poverty than did the Puritans of New England. Because charity was considered an obligation for English gentlemen, their Virginia counterparts, who considered poverty natural in society rather than a sin, developed relatively generous means for coping with it. Primary and secondary sources; 51 notes.    R. F. Oaks

3357. Crenson, Matthew. ORGANIZATIONAL FACTORS IN CITIZEN PARTICIPATION. *J. of Pol. 1974 36(2): 356-378.* Examines seven citizen participatory groups in Baltimore 1969-70 to determine the effectiveness of political activity by the poor under public and private efforts to create "maximum feasible participation." While most of the difficulties that would afflict these programs were anticipated, their short life span was not. Mobilization of the poor by government for political action was "illogical." The government organized an assault on itself. This study also demonstrates that social isolation and political nonparticipation of the poor are not significant disabilities. The major organizational problems in Baltimore came from "intense organizational conflict" symptomatic of conditions existing prior to the effort to stimulate political activity among the poor. 4 tables, 17 notes.

A. R. Stoesen

3358. Dobelstein, Andrew. THE EFFECTS OF THE REFORM MOVEMENT ON RELIEF ADMINISTRATION IN NORTH CAROLINA: THE CONTRIBUTIONS OF ALEXANDER WORTH MC ALISTER. *South Atlantic Q. 1976 75(2): 245-257.* Examines the role of Alexander W. McAlister in North Carolina relief programs. Discusses the reasons for success and the Unit Plan of local administration. 35 notes.    R. W. Dubay

3359. Flynt, J. Wayne. SPINDLE, MINE, AND MULE: THE POOR WHITE EXPERIENCE IN POST-CIVIL WAR ALABAMA. *Alabama Rev. 1981 34(4): 243-286.* Four occupations—tenant farming, textiles, mining, and timbering—accounted for the overwhelming majority of the state's poor whites. The reality of their lives, the grinding poverty, the desire to better themselves, and, too often, the realization that they would not escape poverty are vividly portrayed in several case studies. Based on Federal Writers Project interviews in the Southern Historical Collection, University of North Carolina, and personal interviews located in the Samford University Archives; 78 notes.    C. R. Gunter, Jr.

3360. Hobson, Fred. THE POOR WHITE IN TRANSITION. *Southern Literary J. 1977 9(2): 166-174.* Discusses the image of poor whites in Southern literature of the 20th century.

3361. Jupiter, Clare. THE ASSEMBLIES: A NEW POWER STRUCTURE. *Southern Exposure 1979 7(1): 27-37.* Provides a brief biography of Virginia Community Development Organization founder and attorney Donald Anderson since his childhood in the 1930's, and describes the success of the VCDO's Assemblies (also known as the National Association for the Southern Poor) among blacks in the South, since its founding in 1968.

3362. Kolchin, Peter. RACE, CLASS, AND POVERTY IN THE POST-CIVIL WAR SOUTH. *Rev. in Am. Hist. 1979 7(4): 515-526.* Review essay of Jay R. Mandle's *The Roots of Black Poverty: The Southern Plantation Economy after the Civil War* (Durham, N.C.: Duke U. Pr., 1978), Roger L. Ransom and Richard Sutch's *One Kind of Freedom: The Economic Consequences of Emancipation* (Cambridge, Eng.: Cambridge U. Pr., 1977), and Jonathan M. Wiener's *Social Origins of the New South: Alabama, 1860-1885* (Baton Rouge: Louisiana State U. Pr., 1978).

3363. Moran, Robert E., Sr. PUBLIC RELIEF IN LOUISIANA FROM 1928 TO 1960. *Louisiana Hist. 1973 14(4): 369-385.*

3364. O'Malley, James R. BLACK POVERTY: A DIFFERENCE IN DEGREE IN THE SOUTH. *West Georgia Coll. Rev. 1974 (7): 25-36.* Analyzes impoverished areas in the south-central United States in 1970 and asserts that Negroes have greater economic advantages in areas where black population is low.

3365. Shloss, Carol. THE PRIVILEGE OF PERCEPTION. *Virginia Q. Rev. 1980 56(4): 596-611.* Deals with the contrasting ways in which photography was used in documenting southern poverty by Margaret Bourke-White who, with Erskine Caldwell, published *You Have Seen Their Faces* (1937) and Walker Evans and James Agee's *Let Us Now Praise Famous Men.* Agee saw Bourke-White and Evans "as symbols of antithetical approaches to the privilege of perception." He criticized Bourke-White for posing her subjects to present her conception of poverty, but he praised Evans for his "honest" use of the camera for documentation.

O. H. Zabel

3366. Watson, Alan D. PUBLIC POOR RELIEF IN COLONIAL NORTH CAROLINA. *North Carolina Hist. Rev. 1977 54(4): 347-366.* Colonial North Carolinians provided several types of relief to the poor at the parish, county, and provincial levels. Poverty was defined as need and so included the indigent, aged, widowed, orphaned, insane, sick, and disabled. Officials supported those in need by providing direct monetary aid, community households, food and clothing, medical supplies, doctoring and nursing, apprenticeships, and debt relief. Based on colonial parish and county records, and published provincial records; 3 illus., 3 tables, 83 notes.

T. L. Savitt

3367. Whisnant, David E. GROWING OLD BY BEING POOR: SOME CAUTIONARY NOTES ABOUT GENERALIZING FROM A CLASS PHENOMENA. *Soundings 1974 57(1): 101-112.* Premature aging in the population in Appalachia due to hardship, hazardous employment, and poverty has brought about reforms which emphasize improving working conditions and changing attitudes toward physical exercise and the exploitation of leisure time.

3368. Zelman, Donald L. ALAZAN-APACHE COURTS: A NEW DEAL RESPONSE TO MEXICAN AMERICAN HOUSING CONDITIONS IN SAN ANTONIO. *Southwestern Hist. Q. 1983 87(2): 123-150.* In July 1939, construction began on the first low-income public housing project in San Antonio, Texas. Opened in August 1940 and completed in late 1944, the project was known as the Alazan-Apache Courts. It represented a small but successful effort by the San Antonio Housing Authority, under the leadership of Father Carmelo Tranchese, and the US Housing Authority to provide jobs, promote better health, and improve the standard of living in San Antonio's poverty-stricken west side. Based on federal government records; the Carmelo Tranchese Papers at St. Mary's University, San Antonio; reports of the San Antonio Housing Authority; and local newspapers; 53 notes, 8 photos.

R. D. Hurt

## Southern Labor

3369. Abbott, Collamer M. THOMAS POLLARD: CORNISH MINER. *Rev. Int. d'Hist. de la Banque [Italy] 1973 6: 169-178.* Thomas Pollard (1815-1900), a miner and farmer in the Appalachian Mountains, was a typical example of many Cornish miners who migrated to the United States in the 19th century.

3370. Allen, John E. EUGENE TALMADGE AND THE GREAT TEXTILE STRIKE IN GEORGIA, SEPTEMBER 1934. Fink, Gary M. and Reed, Merl E., eds. *Essays in Southern Labor History: Selected Papers, Southern Labor History Conference, 1976.* (Westport, Conn.; London, England: Greenwood Pr., 1977): 224-243. Studies the history of the southern textile industry before and during the early years of the National Recovery Administration (NRA) as the setting for the strike of 1934, the course of the strike, and Governor Eugene Talmadge's role in getting the strike settled. That role was based philosophically in his staunchly conservative opposition to the whole NRA concept. The strike was an unmitigated disaster for Georgia's textile workers; no union men were rehired. Talmadge's duplicity regarding his intentions and "the brutality and flamboyance with which he suppressed the strike" was unprecedented. The workers were not fooled as to where his real loyalties lay, but the damage had been done. 74 notes.     R. V. Ritter

3371. Armstrong, Thomas F. FROM TASK LABOR TO FREE LABOR: THE TRANSITION ALONG GEORGIA'S RICE COAST, 1820-1880. *Georgia Hist. Q. 1980 64(4): 432-447.* Describes the antebellum task labor system of the slaves of the rice plantations in Chatham, Bryan, Liberty, McIntosh, Glynn, and Camden Counties, Georgia. Altered conditions after the Civil War are also discussed. Primary and secondary sources; 46 notes.

G. R. Schroeder

3372. Armstrong, Thomas F. GEORGIA LUMBER LABORERS, 1880-1917: THE SOCIAL IMPLICATIONS OF WORK. *Georgia Hist. Q. 1983 67(4): 435-450.* Focusing on patterns of work experience and their social and familial context, analyzes the families of lumber laborers in coastal Georgia. While family size was similar to that of other rural workers, lumberers were, due to the nature of their work, much more transient than other parts of the population. Based on census records and other primary and secondary sources; 44 notes.     G. R. Schroeder

3373. Banks, Alan. COAL MINERS AND FIREBRICK WORKERS: THE STRUCTURE OF WORK RELATIONS IN TWO EASTERN KENTUCKY COMMUNITIES. *Appalachian J. 1983-84 11(1-2): 85-102.* Describes the development of capitalism in a coal-mining district in southeastern Kentucky and in a firebrickmaking district in the northeastern part of the state.

3374. Bernard, Jacqueline. ORGANIZING HOSPITAL WORKERS. *Working Papers for a New Soc. 1976 4(3): 53-59.* Discusses the United Mine Workers of America's and the National Labor Relations Board's roles in the attempt to unionize hospital workers in Pikeville and Prestonsburg, Kentucky, 1973-76.

3375. Bethell, Tom and Hall, Bob. 1974: THE BROOKSIDE STRIKE. *Southern Exposure 1976 4(1-2): 114-123.* Coal miners who wished to join the United Mine Workers of America struck a Duke Power Company subsidiary's mine in Harlan County, Kentucky, in 1974.

3376. Bishop, Bill. 1931: THE BATTLE OF EVARTS. *Southern Exposure 1976 4(1-2): 92-103.* Coal miners attempting to organize for the United Mine Workers of America in Harlan County, Kentucky, went on strike and encountered evictions, hunger, violence, imprisonment, and abandonment by the union.

3377. Brown, Kenny L. PEACEFUL PROGRESS: AN ACCOUNT OF THE ITALIANS OF KREBS, OKLAHOMA. *Chronicles of Oklahoma 1975 53(3): 332-352.* During 1919, as the "Red Scare" gripped the nation, Governor J. B. A. Robertson of Oklahoma called for punitive action against a miner's strike. Because Italians represented the largest ethnic group in the strike, they received the bulk of criticism; yet throughout their 30 years of residence in the Krebs area, Italian miners had always demonstrated a moderate approach to reform, a revulsion toward violence, and a dedication to hard work. Even their association with the Socialist Party of Oklahoma and the United Mine Workers of America assumed a constructive and peaceful tone. Much maligned by xenophobic groups, their contributions to American society were positive and their assimilation into American society was rapid. Based on primary and secondary sources; 3 photos, 2 tables, 86 notes.     M. L. Tate

3378. Carpenter, Gerald. PUBLIC OPINION IN THE NEW ORLEANS STREET RAILWAY STRIKE OF 1929-1930. Fink, Gary M. and Reed, Merl E., eds. *Essays in Southern Labor History: Selected Papers, Southern Labor History Conference, 1976.* (Westport, Conn.; London, England, Greenwood Pr., 1977): 191-207. Studies the New Orleans Street Railway Strike of 1929-30 as an illustration of the incorrectness of the usual stereotype of southern public opinion as united against trade unionism. This is seen both in company (New Orleans Public Service, Inc.) appeals which reflected the public's acceptance of unionism and in union (Street and Electric Railway Employees of America) appeals for support resting on "positive concern for the principles of organized labor and negative objections to outside control." The usual generalizations therefore must be examined more critically. 65 notes.     R. V. Ritter

3379. Carr, Joe Daniel. LABOR CONFLICT IN THE EASTERN KENTUCKY COAL FIELDS. *Filson Club Hist. Q. 1973 47(2): 179-192.* Analyzes the industrial conflict in Harlan and Bell counties in eastern Kentucky during the 1930's, providing graphic examples of the exploitation of miners by the mining corporations. Violent confrontations at Evarts in 1931 and at Stanfill in 1939 are investigated in depth, and the roles of the United Mine Workers, the National Recovery Administration, and the National Labor Relations Board are also explored. Exposes the failure of the judicial system and the corruption of Harlan County sheriff Theodore Middleton. Based on the Louisville *Courier-Journal* and the New York *Times*; 58 notes.     G. B. McKinney

3380. Compton, Stephen C. EDGAR GARDNER MURPHY AND THE CHILD LABOR MOVEMENT. *Hist. Mag. of the Protestant Episcopal Church 1983 52(2): 181-194.* The strength of the child labor movement was greatly enhanced by Edgar Gardner Murphy (b. 1869), an Episcopal priest who has been credited with having done more than any other person to awaken the South to the wrongs of child labor. Murphy was greatly influenced by his mentor at the University of the South, William Porcher DuBose, who emphasized unity of persons to God, to themselves, and to each other as the key to life. Murphy was quite active in race and education in Alabama before he became involved in the child labor movement. Traces Murphy's role in getting the Child Labor Act enacted in Alabama in 1907, which ended the horrible conditions under which children worked in Southern cotton mills. Based largely on the published works of Murphy and the Edgar Gardner Murphy Papers in the Southern Historical Collection, University of North Carolina Library; photo, 60 notes.     H. M. Parker, Jr.

3381. Connette, Woody. WORKER OWNED: SOME SOUTHERN BEGINNINGS. *Southern Changes 1982 4(6): 11-15.* Discusses the problems and aspirations of modern worker-owned businesses, focusing on examples in the Deep South.

3382. Conway, Mimi. COTTON DUST KILLS, AND IT'S KILLING ME. *Southern Exposure 1978 6(2): 29-39.* Byssinosis, "brown lung disease," is a prevalent problem among long term employees of Southern cotton mills. The mill owners, including Burlington Industries, Inc. which enjoys an excellent reputation in the safety field, have strenuously endeavored to avoid payment of compensation for workers' claims of disability caused by byssinosis. The Carolina Brown Lung Association has been organized to forward workers' claims for compensation. Burlington's insurance agent, Liberty Mutual Insurance Co., has by and large to date successfully thwarted payments for byssinosis-caused illnesses through the workmen's compensation system. Liberty Mutual is probably liable to third party suits resulting from possible negligence in serving as safety inspectors for the mills. Based on personal interviews.

N. Lederer

3383. Cook, Bernard A. COVINGTON HALL AND RADICAL RURAL UNIONIZATION IN LOUISIANA. *Louisiana Hist. 1977 18(2): 227-238.* Covington Hall, a socialist organizer in the Louisiana lumber industry, promoted militant labor organizations and edited radical rural labor publications in Louisiana during 1907-16. His organization of the Forest and Farm Workers Union of the Industrial Workers of the World in 1916 was a failure, and socialism in Louisiana declined thereafter. The decline resulted from national causes, the exploitation of racial issues by lumber operators, the poverty and apathy of the workers, the earlier failure of the rural labor movement in Louisiana, the organized opposition of the companies and their political adjuncts, and the prosperity of World War I. Based on Hall's unpublished manuscript, "Labor Struggles in the Deep South," in the Tulane University Library, and on published primary and secondary sources; 49 notes.

R. L. Woodward, Jr.

3384. Cook, Bernard A. and Watson, James R. THE SAILORS AND MARINE TRANSPORT WORKERS' 1913 STRIKE IN NEW ORLEANS: THE AFL AND THE IWW. *Southern Studies 1979 18(1): 111-122.* Two major types of divisions among workers in New Orleans, Louisiana, traditionally have prevented them from working together and improving their lot: racial differences and antagonism between skilled and unskilled workers. Although several attempts were made to unite the workers, and brief periods of cooperation took place, antagonism has been the general attitude. The dock strike of June-July 1913 by the Sailors' Union (American Federation of Labor) and the Marine Transport Workers (Industrial Workers of the World) against the United Fruit Company in New Orleans failed because of these antagonisms, lack of cooperation, scabbing by members, and betrayals by leadership. 47 notes.

J. J. Buschen

3385. Cook, Bernard A. SECTION 15 OF THE I.W.A.: THE FIRST INTERNATIONAL IN NEW ORLEANS. *Louisiana Hist. 1973 14(3): 297-304.* Chronicles the establishment of Section 15 (the Louisiana chapter) of the International Workingmen's Association in New Orleans in 1871.

3386. Corbin, David A. "FRANK KEENEY IS OUR LEADER, AND WE SHALL NOT BE MOVED": RANK-AND-FILE LEADERSHIP IN THE WEST VIRGINIA COAL FIELDS. Fink, Gary M. and Reed, Merl E., eds. *Essays in Southern Labor History: Selected Papers, Southern Labor History Conference, 1976.* (Westport, Conn.; London, England: Greenwood Pr., 1977): 144-156. A study of the career of Frank Keeney as a labor leader in the West Virginia coal fields. His career in the United Mine Workers of America began in 1912. In 1916 he led a "rump" organization and was elected president. He forced investigation and correction of corruption among local union district leaders. He was convinced of the importance and value of indigenous leadership and acted accordingly. His independence alienated him from UMW leaders, including John L. Lewis. In 1931 his last important move, the organization of an independent union and the calling of a strike, was a failure and resulted in his ostracism by the UMW. 49 notes.

R. V. Ritter

3387. Cramer, M. Richard. RACE AND SOUTHERN WHITE WORKERS' SUPPORT FOR UNIONS. *Phylon 1978 39(4): 311-321.* Examines the connection of the racial attitudes of southern whites and their attitudes toward unionization, based on studies during the 1960's and 1970's, and concludes that prejudiced southern white workers are resistant to unionization efforts.

3388. Ellis, William E. LABOR-MANAGEMENT RELATIONS IN THE PROGRESSIVE ERA: A PROFIT SHARING EXPERIENCE IN LOUISVILLE. *Register of the Kentucky Hist. Soc. 1980 78(2): 140-156.* An account of the early profit sharing experience of the Louisville Varnish Company, headed by Patrick Henry Callahan. Callahan, a paternalist, viewed his plan as a viable alternative to labor-management conflict. The plan worked well during prosperity, but not during the Great Depression. Prosperity (and profit sharing) returned for the company in 1936, but with Callahan's death in 1940, no one in the company was as committed to the plan. Covers 1908-40. Based on personal manuscript collections and other sources; 2 illus., 32 notes.

J. F. Paul

3389. Falk, William W.; Grimes, Michael D.; and Lord, George F., III. PROFESSIONALISM AND CONFLICT IN A BUREAUCRATIC SETTING: THE CASE OF A TEACHERS' STRIKE. *Social Problems 1982 29(5): 551-560.* A survey of teachers' attitudes in a Southern city during a strike in 1979 reveals that strikers are more professionally oriented than nonstrikers, and they are unhappy in their jobs and want greater authority over them.

3390. Fickett, Laura J. WOODDALE: AN INDUSTRIAL COMMUNITY. *Delaware Hist. 1981 19(4): 229-242.* Describes the history of Wooddale on Red Clay Creek, Delaware, an industrial town that rose and fell with the fortunes of the Delaware Iron Works, the town's principal industry. Alan and James Wood built the company through good community relations and good marketing; they also invested in railroads and ancillary industries to develop the whole region. The life histories of several workers and a description of labor-management relations demonstrates the inclusive, humane character of the company and the Quaker beliefs of the Wood family. 50 notes.

R. M. Miller

3391. Fickle, James E. THE LOUISIANA-TEXAS LUMBER WAR OF 1911-1912. *Louisiana Hist. 1975 16(1): 59-85.* Ruthless exploitation of workers in the early 20th century in the lumber industry of western Louisiana and eastern Texas led to labor strife, culminating in the "Louisiana-Texas Lumber War of 1911-1912." During the lumber mill strikes of 1906-07 around Lake Charles, Louisiana, mill operators formed the Southern Lumber Operators Association, headed by Houston lumber magnate John Henry Kirby, to resist labor organization. Arthur Emerson and Jay Smith led the workers, but William ("Big Bill") Haywood also played an active role in the 1911-12 dispute, amid growing Socialist sympathies of the region's workers. Worker layoffs and a decline in economic conditions stimulated the dispute. Violence on both sides escalated, as the "War" attracted national attention. The operators, however, generally enjoyed greater support from government authorities; and in the end the strikes failed and labor organization declined. Primary sources, 90 notes.

R. L. Woodward, Jr.

3392. Fickle, James E. MANAGEMENT LOOKS AT THE LABOR PROBLEM: THE SOUTHERN PINE INDUSTRY DURING WORLD WAR I AND THE POSTWAR ERA. *J. of Southern Hist. 1974 40(1): 61-76.* Surveys management's view of labor conditions in the southern pine industry during 1910-20's. Troubled relations between labor and management in the pine industry before World War I continued during the war. Management would not admit the validity of labor's complaints regarding hours, wages, and working conditions, and used patriotic slogans to extract more production from the pine workers during the war. By the end of the war and afterwards, the lumber company operators sought to stem the migration of Negroes out of the South, and through the creation of an employment bureau in Chicago, actually attempted to reverse the flow of workers. Despite labor conditions, management continued to talk of the "contented workers." The views of the southern lumber operators, whether realistic or not, reflect the attitudes of influential and powerful figures toward social and economic issues during this period. Based on manuscript materials and published primary and secondary sources; 54 notes.     T. D. Schoonover

3393. Fickle, James E. RACE, CLASS, AND RADICALISM: THE WOBBLIES IN THE SOUTHERN LUMBER INDUSTRY, 1900-1916. Conlin, Joseph R., ed. *At the Point of Production: The Local History of the I.W.W.* (Westport, Conn.: Greenwood Pr., 1981): 97-113. Details the conflict between lumber workers and mill operators in eastern Texas and western Louisiana, especially from 1911 to 1912. Central to the conflict was Arthur L. Emerson, who formed his first local union at Carson in western Louisiana in 1910, leading to the founding of the Brotherhood of Timber Workers in 1911. The conflict with the mill operators reached violent proportions, as the BTW was backed by the Industrial Workers of the World and other organizations. On 7 July 1912, a gun battle erupted at an Emerson speech. Emerson and other unionists were jailed, and the operators were successful in breaking the financial and psychological strength of the union. By 1914 the BTW was practically destroyed. Mainly secondary sources; 70 notes. Portions of this chapter previously appeared in *Louisiana History* in 1975.
J. Powell

3394. Fink, Gary M. THE FOURTH SOUTHERN LABOR CONFERENCE. *Int. Labor and Working Class Hist. 1983 (23): 62-64.* Discusses recent trends in Southern labor relations historiography as revealed at the 1982 "Southern Labor Studies" conference in Atlanta, Georgia; institutional and social history covering the late 19th-20th centuries have achieved a recent synthesis and reconciliation.

3395. Foster, Jim. HEALTH AND SAFETY VERSUS PROFITS IN THE COAL INDUSTRY: THE *GATEWAY* CASE AND CLASS STRUGGLE. *Appalachian J. 1983-84 11(2): 122-141.* Reviews labor litigation, beginning with the 1935 Wagner Act, and examines how the ruling in *Gateway Coal Company* v. *United Mine Workers of America* (US, 1974) protected the interests of capitalism in the coal industry.

3396. Frederickson, Mary. FOUR DECADES OF CHANGE: BLACK WORKERS IN SOUTHERN TEXTILES, 1941-1981. *Radical Am. 1982 16(6): 27-44.* During and since the 1960's, blacks have doubled their proportion of the work force in Southern textile mills from one-tenth to one-fifth. This change laid the ground work in many communities for the local civil rights movement. Blacks, for a variety of reasons, were more likely to be involved in supporting unionization. They are now more involved in direct production activity and even in white-collar jobs than before. Still the textile workers of the South earn 60% of the national manufacturing average pay, and they face automation, threats to gains in wages and working conditions, and plant closings. Based in part on interviews with Georgia workers; 32 notes, 6 illus.
C. M. Hough

3397. García, Mario T. RACIAL DUALISM IN THE EL PASO LABOR MARKET, 1880-1920. *Aztlán 1976 6(2): 197-217.* Mexicans in El Paso suffered from structural discrimination. They received less pay for the same work as Anglos and did not have opportunities for advancement. Most Mexicans tolerated their subordinate economic position, believing they would soon return to Mexico. Some Mexican *obreros* engaged in strikes and labor organization. Based on US census documents, newspapers, and secondary sources; 61 notes.     R. Griswold del Castillo

3398. Goldberg, Stephen B. and Brett, Jeanne M. AN EXPERIMENT IN THE MEDIATION OF GRIEVANCES. *Monthly Labor Rev. 1983 106(3): 23-30.* Chronicles a mediation experiment with the coal industry in Virginia and Kentucky in 1980, demonstrating the advantages and effectiveness of grievance mediation over binding arbitration.

3399. Grant, Jim. THE ORGANIZED UNORGANIZED. *Southern Exposure 1976 4(1-2): 132-135.* Examines unionization movements in the South since the 1920's; mentions northern industries which moved south to avoid organization and members' and organizers' stepped-up efforts to maintain union organization, 1968-74.

3400. Green, Ben. "IF WE'D STUCK TOGETHER": ORGANIZING FISHERS IN FLORIDA. *Southern Exposure 1982 10(3): 69-76.* The attempts from 1930 to 1958 of Bob Knowlton and United Packinghouse Workers of America national organizer Ed Beltrame to organize Cortez mullet fishermen into a union failed because the fishermen and fish dealers were in the same families.

3401. Green, James R. THE BROTHERHOOD OF TIMBER WORKERS 1910-1913: A RADICAL RESPONSE TO INDUSTRIAL CAPITALISM IN THE SOUTHERN U.S.A. *Past and Present [Great Britain] 1973 (60): 161-200.* Analyzes factors behind the struggle of the Brotherhood of Timber Workers (BTW) and Industrial Workers of the World (IWW) with the lumber companies of Louisiana and Texas, 1910-13. Both black and white workers and farmers cooperated out of hatred for the northern syndicates, which was greater than any fear of the IWW agitators' revolutionary ideas. The BTW and IWW created a radical, collective response to industrial capitalism, remarkable in an era of racial segregation. US Labor Department documents, censuses, Kirby Papers, newspapers.
E. M. Sirriyeh

3402. Green, Jim. THE BROTHERHOOD. *Southern Exposure 1976 4(1-2): 21-29.* The Brotherhood of Timber Workers was founded 1911-13, in western Louisiana and eastern Texas by white and black workers who hoped to combat the repressive Southern Lumber Operators' Association.

3403. Hancock, Harold B. THE INDENTURE SYSTEM IN DELAWARE, 1681-1921. *Delaware Hist. 1974 16(1): 47-59.* Dutch, Swedish, and English colonists practiced indenture to repay transportation costs to America (or other debts), and later used it "to provide for poor children and to see that they learned a trade." Debtors found indenture "a convenient means by which to work off their obligations," and the British used it to dump "undesirables" in the colony. Terms of indenture became fixed and formalized and gave overwhelming supervisory and disciplinary powers to the master. Negroes found that apprenticeship laws discriminated against them, but in time indenture enabled beneficent masters to manumit their slaves. In the 19th century apprenticeship generally served to introduce youths to useful trades and especially to provide workers for industry. Indenture declined after the Civil War but was not formally abolished until 1921. Based largely on court records; 39 notes.     R. M. Miller

3404. Hellwig, David J. BLACK ATTITUDES TOWARD IMMIGRANT LABOR IN THE SOUTH, 1865-1910. *Filson Club Hist. Q. 1980 54(2): 151-168.* Maintains that black concern about immigrant labor competition was strongest during 1865 to 1875 and 1900 to 1907. Most blacks felt that white southerners would use the Chinese to force blacks to accept even more degraded working and social conditions. Notes that many blacks did not address themselves to this question—particularly after few immigrants settled in the south. Based on contemporary black newspapers and the published papers and memoirs of black leaders; 43 notes.
G. B. McKinney

3405. Hield, Melissa. "UNION-MINDED": WOMEN IN THE TEXAS ILGWU, 1933-1950. *Frontiers 1979 4(2): 59-70.* Details the prounion struggles of black, Mexican American, and Anglo women in the Texas garment industry during 1933-50, based on interviews with eight women then active in the International Ladies' Garment Workers' Union.

3406. Hughes, Chip. A NEW TWIST FOR TEXTILES. *Southern Exposure 1976 3(4): 73-79.* Labor organization and membership among employees of southern textile mills began to grow with the advent of civil rights legislation and the hiring of blacks; membership and pressure in the unions grew through the 1960's and promises to be a major point of contention for mill workers in the 1970's.

3407. Javersak, David T. RESPONSE OF THE O.V.T. & L.A. TO INDUSTRIALISM. *J. of the West Virginia Hist. Assoc. 1980 4(1): 35-45.* The Ohio Valley Trades and Labor Assembly, an independent, centralized labor assembly of Ohio County, West Virginia, responded to industrialism with humanitarian, social, and relief services, political activism, and aggressive advocacy for its member locals, 1882-1914.

3408. Judkins, Bennett M. OCCUPATIONAL HEALTH AND THE DEVELOPING CLASS CONSCIOUSNESS OF SOUTHERN TEXTILE WORKERS: THE CASE OF THE BROWN LUNG ASSOCIATION. *Maryland Hist. 1982 13(1): 55-71.* Traces the history of the Southern Brown Lung Association to test the validity of conflicting movement theories. Traditionalists stress that movement membership and leaders emerge from basic grievances and shared values, while modernists emphasize professional cadres leading self-interested members. The Brown Lung Association's experience supports the traditionalist theory, but cadres provided initial impetus. Based on participant observation, interviews, content analysis, and published sources; 27 notes.                      G. O. Gagnon

3409. Kann, Kenneth. THE KNIGHTS OF LABOR AND THE SOUTHERN BLACK WORKER. *Labor Hist. 1977 18(1): 49-70.* Surveys attempts 1880-87 by the Knights of Labor to organize southern blacks into unions. The racial issue was divisive, but the Knights demonstrated that southern workers of both races could be united on common interests and goals. Based on reports of the Knights of Labor and newspapers; 60 notes.        L. L. Athey

3410. Lawrence, Ken. THE ROOTS OF CLASS STRUGGLE IN THE SOUTH. *Radical Am. 1975 9(2): 15-36.* Discusses labor unions and organizations since 1810.

3411. Levine, Susan. HIDDEN HISTORIES: SOUTHERN LABOR AND THE WOMAN WORKER. *Rev. in Am. Hist. 1978 6(3): 288-292.* Review article prompted by *Class, Sex, and the Woman Worker* (Westport, Conn.: Greenwood Pr., 1977), edited by Milton Cantor and Bruce Laurie, and *Essays in Southern Labor History: Selected Papers, Southern Labor History Conference, 1976* (Westport, Conn.: Greenwood Pr., 1977), edited by Gary M. Fink and Merl E. Reed.

3412. Loveday, Amos J., Jr. ORIGINS OF THE 1885 STRIKE IN THE WHEELING IRON AND STEEL MILLS. *Upper Ohio Valley Hist. Rev. 1983 13(1): 10-20.* Examines the nailmaking industry in the Wheeling, West Virginia area, and the disputes between labor and management that led to a yearlong strike at the Laughlin Nail Works in Martins Ferry, Ohio.

3413. Lozier, John. AMBIVALENCE TOWARD PROMOTION AMONG APPALACHIAN COAL MINERS: THE LEGEND OF LARRY HARPER. *Appalachian J. 1975 2(2): 111-115.* Investigates the 1953 suicide of Larry Harper, an Appalachian coal miner whose promotion to foreman created distance between him and the labor unions.

3414. Luening, William. CIGAR CITY RISES FROM THE ASHES. *Hist. Preservation 1982 34(4): 46-51.* Describes and lists the nearly defunct mutual aid societies formed by individual ethnic groups of cigar factory workers in Tampa, Florida, around the turn of the century to provide social activities, health and welfare services, and educational needs.

3415. Maroney, James C. THE TEXAS-LOUISIANA OIL FIELD STRIKE. Fink, Gary M. and Reed, Merl E., eds. *Essays in Southern Labor History: Selected Papers, Southern Labor History Conference, 1976.* (Westport, Conn.; London, England: Greenwood Pr., 1977): 161-172. Studies of the 1917 strike of Texas and Louisiana oil field workers as an illustration of some employers' inexorable opposition to organized labor and great resentment of all concessions made to labor by the Wilson administration. Producers gained

a clear victory in opposition to the findings of the President's Mediation Commission. Union effectiveness was not to be regained before the 1930's. It all ended in employer unity, but continued division in the ranks of union members. 32 notes.
                                                                 R. V. Ritter

3416. Martin, Charles H. SOUTHERN LABOR RELATIONS IN TRANSITION: GADSDEN, ALABAMA, 1930-1943. *J. of Southern Hist. 1981 47(4): 545-568.* A review of labor organizing and the rise of unionism in Gadsden, Alabama. The town was dominated by three industries, which acted in concert to oppose all unionization efforts. Covers the early failures of organizers, the accompanying violence, and the influence of big wartime contracts in enabling the federal government to force the industries to comply. The Southern story was not very different from the Northern variety, except that Southern workers were mildly less enthusiastic about unionization, and the local "establishment" worked the "outsider" and "Northern carpetbagger" themes intensively, and to considerable effect. 47 notes.                        V. L. Human

3417. McConville, Ed. OLIVER HARVEY: "GOT TO TAKE SOME RISKS." *Southern Exposure 1978 6(2): 24-28.* Harvey was involved for many years in the effort to organize a union of health service workers at the Duke University Medical Center in Durham, North Carolina. Despite poor working conditions at Duke, unionization was an uphill battle given to the hostile attitude of the power establishment in Durham and the intransigent anti-union attitude of the Duke Hospital administration. Harvey also became involved in local civil rights agitation during the 1960's. The fight for union recognition at Duke, including the demand for a minimum wage of $1.60 per hour, culminated in a strike supported by students and faculty in 1968. The union finally came to Duke as a result of a NLRB election in 1972. Oliver Harvey, now retired, continues to work for the betterment of health service workers on an unofficial basis. Based on oral interviews.                      N. Lederer

3418. McConville, Ed. WILL HE OR WON'T HE. *Southern Exposure 1976 4(1-2): 128-131.* Examines factors influencing labor unions' ability to organize southern laborers, including the southern mind, individualism, and external working conditions, 1970's.

3419. McDonald, Joseph A. UNION ATTITUDES AND CLASS CONSCIOUSNESS: THE CASE OF THE TUFTED TEXTILE INDUSTRY. *Appalachian J. 1981 9(1): 37-49.* Analyzes the reasons why tufted textile workers in Dalton, Georgia, as in many areas in the South, have been slow to unionize.

3420. McLaurin, Melton A. THE RACIAL POLICIES OF THE KNIGHTS OF LABOR AND THE ORGANIZATION OF SOUTHERN BLACK WORKERS. *Labor Hist. 1976 17(4): 568-585.* The Knights of Labor developed a paradoxical strategy in race relations in organizing attempts in the South. The K. of L. tried both to circumvent the race issue by emphasizing economic grievances and to solve the issues by compromising its antebellum reform heritage with southern prejudices. Although the K. of L. was the first serious attempt to organize southern blacks, racial prejudice slowly forced it to become a black union—which sounded its death knell in the South. Based on the Powderly papers and newspapers; 65 notes.                        L. L. Athey

3421. Morgan, Philip D. WORK AND CULTURE: THE TASK SYSTEM AND THE WORLD OF LOWCOUNTRY BLACKS, 1700 TO 1880. *William and Mary Q. 1982 39(4): 563-599.* The task system originated in the colonial period, became routinized during the revolutionary era, and had completely matured by the time of the Civil War. Emphasis is placed on slaves working for themselves when tasks were completed. Problems of the system are discussed, including how to control slaves in the use of their free time, conflict over what was considered a fair day's work, and relationship between those in charge and the workers. Task labor continued after the Civil War in the form of hiring out, sharecropping, and the "two day" system of working part-time on the employer's crop. The task system was appealing to freedmen because it removed them from personal constraints by employers. The task system was a factor in ex-slaves adapting to freedom. Based on contemporary records, particularly depositions; table, 152 notes.

H. M. Ward

3422. Naison, Mark. ALL GOD'S DANGERS AND ORAL HISTORY. *J. of Ethnic Studies 1977 4(4): 105-110.* Review article prompted by Theodore Rosengarten's *All God's Dangers* (New York: Alfred Knopf, 1974), an oral memoir of a black tenant farmer, Nate Shaw, who participated in the Alabama Sharecropper's Union in 1931. The old man's reminiscences reveal how southern white racism functioned as an instrument of class power, the importance of the kinship group as the only legitimate instrument blacks had to negotiate with the states or conduct collective economic activity, and the division among blacks between those who internalized the work ethic and those who refused. The Sharecropper's Union, organized by the American Communist Party, was the first outside help to appear since Reconstruction. Shaw committed himself to it totally, and a few months after joining was captured in a shootout with deputy sheriffs and given 12 years in prison. The Union began to organize blacks but could not sustain a movement to transform southern rural society. New Deal programs led to massive dispossession of sharecroppers because modernization and crop reduction were under complete control of white planters. For Shaw, however, his brief militancy remained the focal point of his identity. 7 notes.

G. J. Bobango

3423. Nelson, Daniel. A CIO ORGANIZER IN ALABAMA: 1941. *Labor Hist. 1977 18(4): 570-584.* Presents 19 documents authored by John D. House, a member of the United Rubber Workers who led the third attempt to unionize the Goodyear Tire and Rubber Company plant in Gadsden, Alabama, in 1941. The effort failed. Based on the John D. House Papers, University of Akron; 16 notes.

L. L. Athey

3424. Nelson-Cisneros, Victor B. LA CLASE TRABAJADORA EN TEJAS, 1920-1940 [The working class in Texas, 1920-1940]. *Aztlán 1976 6(2): 239-265.* In Texas Mexican Americans were relegated to the lowest-paid jobs and worked in subhuman conditions. They were unable to organize stable agricultural or industrial unions due to the geographic mobility of membership, failures of leadership, poverty, and the AFL's racist policies. Some short-lived, successful Chicano unions engaged in strikes, among them the Asociación de journaleros, U.C.A.P.A.W.A., and the Pecan Shelling Workers of San Antonio. Based on interviews and secondary sources; 125 notes.

R. Griswold del Castillo

3425. Nelson-Cisneros, Victor B. UCAPAWA ORGANIZING ACTIVITIES IN TEXAS, 1935-50. *Aztlán 1978 9: 71-84.* A study of the activities of the United Cannery, Agricultural, Packing and Allied Workers of America, which changed its name in 1944 to Food, Tobacco, Agricultural and Allied Workers Union of America (FTA), to include the tobacco workers, as it sought to organize Mexican Americans in Texas, 1937-50. Agricultural and packing shed workers on the one hand, and grain and cotton process workers on the other, are considered. The unions lost influence and membership for reasons which included possible communist infiltration and the deportation of Mexican citizens. Based on primary sources, viz., the union newspaper, labor archives at the University of Texas, Arlington, and other sources. 52 notes.

R. V. Ritter

3426. Nolan, Dennis R. and Jonas, Donald E. TEXTILE UNIONISM IN THE PIEDMONT, 1901-1932. Fink, Gary M. and Reed, Merl E., eds. *Essays in Southern Labor History: Selected Papers, Southern Labor History Conference, 1976.* (Westport, Conn.; London, England: Greenwood Pr., 1977): 48-79. A study designed to round out the argument previously developed which attributes to outside forces the failure of the textile unions to form stable local organizations and negotiate improvements in wages and working conditions. The workers and unions also brought on problems themselves, by "rash and poorly planned strikes, internal feuds, poor leadership, and the failure of interested groups to provide financial aid." The textile industry in the Piedmont Plateau is the lo-

cale for the study. Whatever the strength of outside forces, the workers and their organizations often were their own worst enemies. 75 notes.

R. V. Ritter

3427. Olsen, Peter. BLACK AMERICANS AND THE SEA. *Negro Hist. Bull. 1974 37(2): 219-222.* Examines 19th-century maritime occupations, primarily in the antebellum South, which employed freedmen and slaves; water routes for escape used by fugitive slaves; and the sea experiences of Frederick Douglass, 1840's-70's.

3428. Parham, Groesbeck and Robinson, Gwen. "IF I COULD GO BACK..." *Southern Exposure 1976 4(1-2): 16-20.* Dobbie Sanders, a steel worker, tells about his life working in steel mills throughout the South, 1922-59.

3429. Parham, T. D., Jr. BLACK JOB EXPECTATION: A COMPARATIVE ANALYSIS. *J. of Black Studies 1978 8(3): 299-307.* Advantaged, socially differentiated black communities such as Tuskegee (Alabama), Groveton (Virginia) and Durham (North Carolina) best provide data for "a favorable report on occupational opportunities for the emerging work force." In these cities, black high school seniors based their job preferences primarily on the extent to which jobs were open to them, but white high school seniors' job preferences were more closely related to their attitudes and values. This pattern was more pronounced in job expectation than in job aspiration. Blacks scoring low (whites, high) in humanitarianism expected to enter helpful and military occupations. Whites scoring low in humanitarianism preferred intrinsic reward jobs, low scoring blacks did not. Based on responses from 229 white, 412 black, 13 "other" students; 3 tables, note.

R. G. Sherer

3430. Paulson, Darryl. MASTERS OF IT ALL: BLACK BUILDERS IN THIS CENTURY. *Southern Exposure 1980 8(1): 9-10.* Jim Crow kept black construction workers out of many white unions, denying them lucrative jobs in the white community, but black builders—in their own unions, in a few integrated unions, and outside unions—continued to ply their trades with superior skills based on years of antebellum experience. Today blacks comprise 8.8% of building trades union members. Further, integrated construction unions may be able to pursue a more aggressive organizing drive against New South open-shop employers, appealing to black workers as well as white. 3 photos.

H. M. Parker, Jr.

3431. Pellet, Gail. THE MAKING OF *HARLAN COUNTY, U.S.A.:* AN INTERVIEW WITH BARBARA KOPPLE. *Radical Am. 1977 11(2): 33-42.* The film was originally subsidized by the rank and file organization, Miners for Democracy, to be a history of this group. Instead it became documentary of the strike in 1973 by a newly formed local of the United Mine Workers of America in Kentucky against the Brookside Mine owners who refused to recognize the union. The makers of the film were able to win the trust of the striking miners. This resulted in graphic footage of various aspects of the strike, including courtroom scenes and violence. Miner's wives play an important role in the film as they did in the strike. The film's funding and distribution largely came from volunteer effort. Based on an oral interview with Barbara Kopple, producer and director of the film.

N. Lederer

3432. Pérez, Louis A., Jr. REMINISCENCES OF A *LECTOR*: CUBAN CIGAR WORKERS IN TAMPA. *Florida Hist. Q. 1975 53(4): 443-449.* Describes from personal experience the *lector's* (reader's) function and influence among the Cuban illiterate workers in a Tampa cigar factory. "A highly developed proletarian consciousness and a long tradition of trade union militancy accompanied the Cuban tobacco workers to the United States." They embraced a variety of radical ideologies. The *lector* often served as a disseminator of the proletarian tradition, as well as a broad variety of written materials. Conflicts arose between the workers and factory owners over the *lector's* pay and pro-labor materials. 13 notes.

R. V. Ritter

3433. Powell, Daniel A. PAC TO COPE: THIRTY-TWO YEARS OF SOUTHERN LABOR IN POLITICS. Fink, Gary M. and Reed, Merl E., eds. *Essays in Southern Labor History: Selected Papers,*

*Southern Labor History Conference, 1976.* (Westport, Conn.; London, England: Greenwood Pr., 1977): 244-255. A narrative of 1943-75 relative to southern labor's entry into politics, and an evaluation of its effect. With labor at an all-time low the CIO's organization of its Political Action Committee (PAC) in 1943 was of epochal significance; likewise AFL's organization of its Labor's League for Political Education (LLPE). With the merger of the parent organizations these also merged to form the Committee on Political Education (COPE) in 1955. The race issue's emergence to a major place in southern politics slowed up COPE's effectiveness, sidetracking interest from the authentic issues. The situation has been improved significantly in recent years, and it is anticipated that COPE will become increasingly effective.          R. V. Ritter

3434.  Pozzetta, George E. ¡ALERTA TABAQUEROS! TAMPA'S STRIKING CIGARWORKERS. *Tampa Bay Hist. 1981 3(2): 19-30.* The 1910 general strike in Tampa, Florida was led by thousands of Cuban, Italian, and Spanish immigrants who worked in the community's single major industry, the manufacture of cigars; 1901-11.

3435.  Pozzetta, George E. A PADRONE LOOKS AT FLORIDA: LABOR RECRUITING AND THE FLORIDA EAST COAST RAILWAY. *Florida Hist. Q. 1975 54(1): 74-84.* Discusses the Florida East Coast Railway's use of the padrone, or labor boss, as a means of securing immigrant labor for railroad construction. Padroni were responsible for the recruiting and transporting of men to the job site, for which they collected a fee from the worker himself. On the job site, padroni ran the commissary and handled other financial matters for the workers, often doing so in a larcenous manner. However, the padrone system, with its faults, did provide a way for immigrants to make a living around the turn of the century. Reprints a letter written by a padrone, an advertisement from a New York Italian-language paper. Based on newspaper and secondary sources; 25 notes.          J. E. Findling

3436.  Quinney, Valerie. TEXTILE WOMEN: THREE GENERATIONS IN THE MILL. *Southern Exposure 1976 3(4): 66-72.* Interviews three women of the same family on their experiences in the southern textile industry; discusses changes in working conditions, life-styles, textiles, and union organization, 1908-52.

3437.  Raper, Arthur F. THE SOUTHERN NEGRO AND THE NRA. *Georgia Hist. Q. 1980 64(2): 128-145.* Discusses the effect of the National Recovery Administration's wage regulations on Negro labor in the South in 1933-34, including wage differentials between North and South, benefits and disadvantages to Negroes, Negroes' fears, employers' evasion of the rules, and why employees went along with lower wages. This article was written in 1934. Based on fieldwork.          G. R. Schroeder

3438.  Raynor, Bruce. UNIONISM IN THE SOUTHERN TEXTILE INDUSTRY: AN OVERVIEW. Fink, Gary M. and Reed, Merl E., eds. *Essays in Southern Labor History: Selected Papers, Southern Labor History Conference, 1976.* (Westport, Conn.; London, England: Greenwood Pr., 1977): 80-99. Textile unionization in the South has come on hard times; total disorganization and discouragement after losing ground for 25 years, is the order of the day. Studies some of the sources of past frustration in textile organizing, assesses the current state of labor relations in the industry, and projects future trends in textile unionism. The failures may be attributed to: 1) the effective (if illegal) antiunion tactics employed by mill owners, 2) a hostile political climate, and 3) the nature of the southern labor force. There have been, however, a sufficient number of significant changes in the labor situation and personnel to justify some optimism for the future. 31 notes.          R. V. Ritter

3439.  Rhee, Jong Mo. THE REDISTRIBUTION OF THE BLACK WORK FORCE IN THE SOUTH BY INDUSTRY. *Phylon 1974 35(3): 293-300.* Explores the remarkable shift in the distribution of the black workers in the South. As a proportion of the total number of employees in the South, black workers have declined markedly in the years since 1940. By 1970 there were 1.5 million fewer blacks in agriculture and personal services. The

1960's were years of accelerated change when considerable gains were made in every industrial area except mining for black laborers. The black males had left agriculture, the black females had left personal services. However, black females managed to upgrade themselves more than black males. Based on primary and secondary sources; 3 tables, 7 notes.          B. A. Glasrud

3440.  Roberts, Higdon. REACHING NEW FIELDS. *Southern Exposure 1976 4(1/2): 156-159.* Discusses labor education in the South, 1965-75.

3441.  Russell, Michael B. GREENVILLE'S EXPERIMENT: THE NON-UNION CULTURE. *Southern Exposure 1979 7(1): 94-97, 100.* The business elite and the Chamber of Commerce in Greenville, South Carolina, prevent unionizing efforts and convince Greenville's citizens that nonorganization is best; 1970's.

3442.  Shofner, Jerrell H. FORCED LABOR IN THE FLORIDA FORESTS, 1880-1950. *J. of Forest Hist. 1981 25(1): 14-25.* Two institutions—convict leasing and debt peonage—developed in Florida after Reconstruction to replace slavery as labor systems. Both were commonly employed in the lumber and turpentine industries to keep labor costs low. Although sanctioned by state law and local custom, these labor practices were sporadically threatened by federal officials from about 1900 until finally eradicated in the late 1940's by changing technology and reduced employment levels in the forest industries. Convict leasing and debt peonage, involving both blacks and whites, are illustrated through examples of federal investigations and court cases. Based on federal archival records and other primary and secondary sources; 9 photos, 39 notes.          R. J. Fahl

3443.  Shofner, Jerrell H. THE LEGACY OF RACIAL SLAVERY: FREE ENTERPRISE AND FORCED LABOR IN FLORIDA IN THE 1940S. *J. of Southern Hist. 1981 47(3): 411-426.* Despite its modern image, Florida in the 1940's was still dominated by the Jim Crow system and its related labor policies. The contract-labor law, originating in the farm tenancy and crop-lien system that replaced slavery, enabled employers like the United States Sugar Corporation to practice debt peonage with impunity. Vagrancy legislation, on the books since the 19th century, allowed white law enforcement officers, despite the efforts of organizations such as the Workers' Defense League, to deprive blacks of their civil rights. In northern Florida where forced labor originated, decades of abuse culminated in the Payne lynching of 1945, the surrounding publicity helped convince Florida it needed to improve its race-relations image. Based on Governors' Correspondence (Florida State Archives, Tallahassee) and other primary sources; 43 notes.
          E. L. Keyser

3444.  Shofner, Jerrell H. MARY GRACE QUACKENBOS, A VISITOR FLORIDA DID NOT WANT. *Florida Hist. Q. 1980 58(3): 273-290.* Mary Grace Quackenbos was instrumental in bringing forth charges of peonage in Florida's turpentine industry. Her investigations of misleading labor recruitment in New York City forced US Attorney General Charles J. Bonaparte and the Justice Department to act. White Floridians avoided the issue by resorting to character assassination, thereby failing to realize that the state's labor practices were far out-of-step with those of the nation. Covers 1905-10. Based on papers in the National Archives, newspaper accounts and other primary sources; 39 notes.          N. A. Kuntz

3445.  Shofner, Jerrell H. POSTSCRIPT TO THE MARTIN TABERT CASE: PEONAGE AS USUAL IN THE FLORIDA TURPENTINE CAMPS. *Florida Hist. Q. 1981 60(2): 161-173.* Legislation resulting from the Martin Tabert case was thought to end peonage in the Turpentine camps in 1923. Analysis reveals that the statutes changed little, and brings into question the effectiveness of statute law versus custom. There were numerous cases of peonage in the camps after 1923. The burden of proof was shifted to the laborer to disprove any allegation of debt to an employer. Peonage remained in the camps as late as 1949. Based on records in the National Archives, Florida newspapers, court records and other sources; 28 notes.          N. A. Kuntz

3446. Sisson, William A. FROM FARM TO FACTORY: WORK VALUES AND DISCIPLINE IN TWO EARLY TEXTILE MILLS. *Working Papers from the Regional Econ. Hist. Res. Center 1981 4(4): 1-26.* Discusses numerous studies of the changes in work habits and attitudes of workers who experienced the transformation from preindustrial to industrial society in the 19th century, and presents a study of two textile mills operating in the 1810's, the Duplanty, McCall and Company in Delaware and the Antietam Woolen Manufacturing Company in Funkstown, Maryland, in which workers and owners retained their preindustrial working habits and attitudes even after their experiences in the industrial workplace; 1814-19.

3447. Sloan, Cliff and Hall, Bob. "IT'S GOOD TO BE HOME IN GREENVILLE"... BUT IT'S BETTER IF YOU HATE UNIONS. *Southern Exposure 1979 7(1): 82-93.* Describes the efforts of labor organizers in the antiunion city of Greenville, South Carolina, in the 1970's, home of Michelin Tire Corporation and J.P. Stevens & Company, among others, and gives a brief history of the area's industry since 1873.

3448. Stamas, George D. THE PUZZLING LAG IN SOUTHERN EARNINGS. *Monthly Labor Rev. 1981 104(6): 27-36.* Studies the 17% wage differential between the south, its rapid economic and population growth notwithstanding, and the rest of the nation, 1973-78, and finds that factors responsible for lower southern wages include interregional differences in urbanization, racial composition, training, and unionization.

3449. Stillman, Don. RUNAWAYS: A CALL TO ACTION. *Southern Exposure 1976 4(1-2): 50-59.* Examines a so-far unsuccessful campaign, 1964-76, to bring the United Auto Workers of America to the Monroe Auto Equipment Company, Hartwell, Georgia.

3450. Straw, Richard A. THE COLLAPSE OF BIRACIAL UNIONISM: THE ALABAMA COAL STRIKE OF 1908. *Alabama Hist. Q. 1975 37(2): 92-114.* The United Mine Workers of America was the only large biracial union during the period 1840-1920. This policy came out of the use of Negroes as strike-breakers. The failure of the UMW in the Alabama strike of 1908 was southern racial attitudes, not the operators' actions. Details the strike, including the violence and racial conflict caused by the union's racial attitude. 64 notes.     E. E. Eminhizer

3451. Straw, Richard A. THE UNITED MINE WORKERS OF AMERICA AND THE 1920 COAL STRIKE IN ALABAMA. *Alabama Rev. 1975 28(2): 104-128.* The United Mine Workers ordered a general strike in Alabama in September, 1920 for higher wages and collective bargaining rights. Coal operators refused to negotiate, persuaded Governor Thomas E. Kilby to call out troops, and won a court injunction against the union. Strike forces weakened by February, 1921, with public opinion and state officials taking an anti-union stand, although the Birmingham press was more moderate and tried to promote a compromise. As in 1904 and 1908, the union failed in its objectives; only one United Mine Workers local functioned in Alabama by 1929, allowing mine operators to maintain open shop. Based on primary and secondary sources; 59 notes.     J. F. Vivian

3452. Supina, Philip D. HERNDON J. EVANS AND THE HARLAN COUNTY COAL STRIKE. *Filson Club Hist. Q. 1982 56(3): 318-335.* Herndon J. Evans, editor of the Pineville *Sun*, tried to present a balanced account of the coal miners' strike in Harlan County, Kentucky, during 1931-32. Evans, a local booster, deeply resented the efforts of Theodore Dreiser, Waldo Frank, and John Dos Passos in portraying Harlan County as a violent area. His efforts won some national recognition, but they did little to alleviate the suffering of the local population or to restore civil rights to miners who tried to join labor unions. Based on the Evans collection at the University of Kentucky Library.     G. B. McKinney

3453. Synnott, Marcia G. "REPLACING 'SAMBO': COULD WHITE IMMIGRANTS SOLVE THE LABOR PROBLEM IN THE CAROLINAS?" *Pro. of the South Carolina Hist. Assoc. 1982:* 77-89. Between 1865 and 1925, immigrant labor was periodically recruited in an attempt to solve the labor shortage in the Carolinas. Recruitment of immigrants was especially attractive in South Carolina, where it was hoped that European immigrants would balance the growing Negro population. The recruitment policies failed due to partisan politics, growing national support for immigration restriction, and lack of money. 22 notes.     J. W. Thacker, Jr.

3454. Terrill, Tom E. A NEW DAY IN DIXIE? *Rev. in Am. Hist. 1980 8(1): 98-103.* Review essay of John W. Hevener's *Which Side Are You On? The Harlan County Coal Miner, 1931-39* (Urbana: U. of Illinois Pr., 1978), and Mimi Conway's *Rise Gonna Rise: A Portrait of Southern Textile Workers* (Garden City, N.Y.: Anchor Pr., 1979); 1931-76.

3455. Tsonc, Peter Z. W. CHANGING PATTERNS OF LABOR FORCE PARTICIPATION RATES OF NONWHITES IN THE SOUTH. *Phylon 1974 35(3): 301-312.* Many significant changes have taken place recently in the population of the labor force by age, sex, and color in the South. For example, the proportion of young people in the labor force in the South declined in various sex-color groups. Among males, the proportion of old people declined as well. Only the young were smaller proportions of the labor force among white and nonwhite females. Other age groups assumed larger proportions. By 1970 the South was less dependent than previously on nonwhite men, young and old white males, and young nonwhite females. Based on primary sources; 4 tables, 4 graphs.     B. A. Glasrud

3456. Tyler, Alicia. DUST TO DUST. *Washington Monthly 1975 6(11): 49-58.* History of the exploitation of the Hawks Nest Tunnel workers by their employer, Union Carbide and Carbon Corporation; they contracted fatal silicosis and their attempt at judicial redress was futile.

3457. Usselman, Steven W. SCIENTIFIC MANAGEMENT WITHOUT TAYLOR: MANAGEMENT INNOVATIONS AT BANCROFT. *Working Papers from the Regional Econ. Hist. Res. Center 1981 4(4): 47-77.* Briefly discusses the scientific management innovations set forth by Frederick Winslow Taylor for American businesses, focusing on the scientific management techniques of management consultants Miller, Franklin, and Stevenson, an industrial engineering company from New York, which was hired in 1911 by the cotton textile finishing company, Joseph Bancroft and Sons Company of Wilmington, Delaware, after a Taylor associate was unsuccessful in streamlining the work load in several departments; reorganization was completed in 1927.

3458. Wells, Dave and Stodder, Jim. A SHORT HISTORY OF NEW ORLEANS DOCKWORKERS. *Radical Am. 1976 10(1): 43-69.* Despite rigid segregation and racial antipathy, white and black longshoremen united at various periods since the 1850's to work together for mutual economic gain. Racial solidarity dissolved into hostility under outside pressures and the effort of each race to achieve gains for themselves. The recent history of the New Orleans longshoremen's unions has been characterized by extreme corruption which can only be eradicated through a socialist society.     N. Lederer

3459. Wyche, Billy H. SOUTHERN INDUSTRIALISTS VIEW ORGANIZED LABOR IN THE NEW DEAL YEARS, 1933-1941. *Southern Studies 1980 19(20): 151-171.* Although the NIRA, or National Industrial Recovery Act (US, 1933), was at first greeted with enthusiasm by southern industrialists, they soon came to attack Section 7(a), which provided for collective bargaining. The general textile strike of 1934 and the emergence of the CIO (Congress of Industrial Organizations) aroused great fear and anger among the industrialists, who opposed the NLRA, or National Labor Relations Act (US, 1935), from the beginning. Economic rather than ideological factors played the leading role in shaping these views. Textiles, the leading industry of the South, had overexpanded and overproduced for many years, and costs had to be reduced. Union and management journals and other primary sources; 88 notes.     J. J. Buschen

3460. Youngdahl, James E. EEOC: MANDATE FOR LABOR. *Southern Exposure 1976 4(1-2): 70-74.* Examines the Equal Employment Opportunity Commission's role in southern labor disputes specifically over discrimination, 1930's-70's.

3461. Zeigler, Robert E. THE LIMITS OF POWER: THE AMALGAMATED ASSOCIATION OF STREET RAILWAY EMPLOYEES IN HOUSTON, TEXAS, 1897-1905. *Labor Hist. 1977 18(1): 71-90.* Studies the Amalgamated Association of Street Railway Employees and supports the thesis that a community often supported local labor organizations in opposition to corporations. The union failed in a lengthy, violent strike because of employer recalcitrance, not public hostility. Based on newspapers and union records; 44 notes. L. L. Athey

3462. Zieger, Robert H. THE UNION COMES TO COVINGTON: VIRGINIA PAPERWORKERS ORGANIZE, 1933-1952. *Pro. of the Am. Phil. Soc. 1982 126(1): 51-89.* Discusses the events which led after a score of years to the unionization of the West Virginia Pulp and Paper Company, Covington, Virginia. Their long encounter with an employer that resisted organization reflected the difficulty with which unions gained acceptance even in this period of success. Involved was the issue of rivalry between the AFL and the CIO. The importance of noneconomic issues, the struggle of the workers to gain regular and predictable conditions of employment, and their willingness to resort to sitdown and wildcat strikes to gain their goals demonstrated the continuance of the shop floor activism of the 1930's and 40's into the allegedly placid 50's. The role of black workers proved that in Covington, as well as in Detroit, black workers were vital to the success of industrial unionism. The working out of these central themes in a small Southern city reflected the depth and scope of the upheaval of American workers in the two decades after the birth of the New Deal. Based on papers of the International Brotherhood of Pulp, Sulphite, and Paper Mill Workers, State Historical Society of Wisconsin; Westvaco Papers, Dept. of Manuscripts and University Archives, Cornell University; National Labor Board Records (Record Group 25), National Archives; files of *The Covington Virginian;* oral interviews; 104 notes, biblio. H. M. Parker, Jr.

3463. —. AN INTERVIEW WITH RAY ROGERS. *Working Papers Mag. 1982 9(1): 48-57.* Union organizer Ray Rogers describes his campaign to force the J. P. Stevens Company to sign a contract.

# Politics, Law, and Legal Proceedings
### (including Office-Holding, Court Cases, Partisan Politics, Civil Rights)

3464. Abramowitz, Alan I. IS THE REVOLT FADING? A NOTE ON PARTY LOYALTY AMONG SOUTHERN DEMOCRATIC CONGRESSMEN. *J. of Pol. 1980 42(2): 568-572.* Since the New Deal, and especially since the end of World War II, the Democratic Party's national commitment to civil rights and economic liberalism strained the loyalty of the South. During the 1960's, a congressional conservative coalition of southern Democrats and Republicans became a powerful obstacle to liberal social and economic legislation. From 1965 through 1978, there has been no increase in party loyalty among southern Democrats and a decline in party loyalty among nonsouthern Democratic representatives. Southern party loyalty reached a low point with the 1972 presidential election and rebounded to more normal levels with the Watergate investigation. Illus., 8 notes. A. W. Novitsky

3465. Aiesi, Margaret and Rosenbaum, Walter A. NOT QUITE LIKE YANKEES: THE DIFFUSION OF PARTISAN COMPETITION IN TWO SOUTHERN CITIES. Steed, Robert P.; Moreland, Laurence W.; and Baker, Tod A., ed. *Party Politics in the South* (New York: Praeger, 1980): 152-174. Examines partisan diffusion in Richmond, Virginia, and Greenville, South Carolina, from 1972

to 1974. The diffusion of Republican voting in the two cities from the presidential to state and local levels is determined, and the significance of this diffusion is evaluated in terms of three theories of party realignment: a New Deal realignment, ideological realignment, and transient confusion. Based on election data from Greenville County Elections Commission, and Chesterfield County election commissions; 7 tables, 21 notes. J. Powell

3466. Akin, Edward N. WHEN A MINORITY BECOMES THE MAJORITY: BLACKS IN JACKSONVILLE POLITICS, 1887-1907. *Florida Hist. Q. 1974 53(2): 123-145.* Develops the thesis that the dynamics of the urban setting allowed Negroes to exercise political power and rights on a broader scale than the state's rural black population, illustrated by a case study of Jacksonville politics during the late 1880's. "When given proper latitude, black leaders were just as effective in the political arena as whites." It must, however, be acknowledged that Jacksonville blacks' political success could be a unique situation. 2 illus., 2 tables, 104 notes. R. V. Ritter

3467. Albert, Harold E. HOME RULE AND A NEW CONSTITUTION: ARTICLE BY ARTICLE IN SOUTH CAROLINA. *Natl. Civic Rev. 1977 66(10): 491-495.* With the major exception of the legislative article, the South Carolina constitution of 1895 has been successfully revised through an article-by-article method. A great step has been taken toward adequate governing power for local governments, and desperately needed tax and court reforms have been achieved. J

3468. Alexander, Thomas B. STRANGE BEDFELLOWS: THE INTERLOCKING CAREERS OF T. A. R. NELSON, ANDREW JOHNSON, AND W. G. (PARSON) BROWNLOW. *East Tennessee Hist. Soc. Publ. 1979 51: 54-77.* Tennessee politics of the 19th century cannot be understood without acknowledging the influence of such strong personalities as Thomas A. R. Nelson, Andrew Johnson, and William G. "Parson" Brownlow. The political careers of all three were closely associated. During the antebellum period, the Whigs Nelson and Brownlow opposed the Jacksonian Democrat Johnson in state elections. But with the secession crisis, all three men found themselves in the Unionist camp. The Emancipation Proclamation temporarily brought Johnson and Brownlow in alliance against Nelson, but it was Nelson who defended Johnson during his impeachment proceedings. Reprinted from the *East Tennessee Historical Society's Publications,* Vol. 24; 108 notes. D. A. Yanchisin

3469. Alonzo, Frank O. THE HISTORY OF THE MISSISSIPPI YOUTH COURT SYSTEM. *J. of Mississippi Hist. 1977 39(2): 133-153.* Describes the development of the Mississippi juvenile justice system during 1916-75. Focuses on legislation and major court cases. Describes the Industrial and Training School Act (1916), the establishment of special juvenile courts in 1940, the Youth Court Act (1946), and the establishment of a separate family court in 1964. 89 notes. J. W. Hillje

3470. Alonzo, Frank O. THE MISSISSIPPI JUVENILE COURT: AN OPERATIONAL PERSPECTIVE. *Southern Q. 1974 12(4): 317-321.* Mississippi established separate juvenile courts in 1940. Examines weaknesses and inconsistencies in chancery, traffic, mayoral, county, and municipal courts, and justices of the peace. Concludes that juvenile courts should be an adjunct to chancery courts. 18 notes. R. W. Dubay

3471. Anders, Evan. BOSS RULE AND CONSTITUENT INTERESTS: SOUTH TEXAS POLITICS DURING THE PROGRESSIVE ERA. *Southwestern Hist. Q. 1981 84(3): 269-292.* From 1882 through 1920, Democratic machine politics prevailed in Cameron County, Texas, under boss James B. Wells. The Wells political machine was astutely sensitive to constituents' needs, particularly those of ranchers, businessmen, and Mexican Americans. After 1905, however, railroad transportation and the development of irrigation lured large numbers of Anglo Americans into the county. These newcomers did not have ties to the political machine and this new majority resented boss-rule, political manipulation, and Mexican American participation in the governmental process. As a result, insurgent influence in local politics, together with Mexican border raids in 1915 and 1916 and growing racial hatred, caused the collapse of the Wells political machine in 1920. Based on the James B. Wells papers and newspapers; 12 illus., 28 notes.

R. D. Hurt

3472. Arendale, Marirose. TENNESSEE AND WOMEN'S RIGHTS. *Tennessee Hist. Q. 1980 39(1): 62-78.* While the Tennessee legislature dragged its feet in adopting the proposed 19th Amendment to the Constitution, it was the 10th legislature to pass on the Equal Rights Amendment. But reaction set in, and two years later, in 1974, the legislature rescinded its action. The arguments in both campaigns suggest that Tennessee, a border state with ties to the deep South, retains the regional conviction that a woman is the fulcrum around which family life revolves. Buttressed by Biblical references, this concept has stubbornly resisted contemporary pressures for change. Based largely on contemporary newspaper accounts; 2 illus., 44 notes.

H. M. Parker, Jr.

3473. Argersinger, Peter H. THE SOUTHERN SEARCH FOR ORDER. *R. in Am. Hist. 1975 3(2): 236-241.* J. Morgan Kousser's *The Shaping of Southern Politics: Suffrage Restriction and the Establishment of the One-Party South, 1880-1910* (New Haven, Conn.: Yale U. Pr., 1974) "focuses upon the motivation, participants, and effects of [black] suffrage restriction in the conviction that procedural changes reshaped the political system" in the South.

3474. Arnold, Joseph L. THE LAST OF THE GOOD OLD DAYS: POLITICS IN BALTIMORE, 1920-1950. *Maryland Hist. Mag. 1976 71(3): 443-448.* While Progressive-era reforms in Maryland did end classic-style bossism as embodied in the famous Rasin-Gorman machine, still the heirs of this machine continued to monopolize Baltimore city and county politics for 35 years, since "individual leaders and their relationships, not the total organizational structure, determine the continuing strength of machine control." Democrats successfully identified the Republicans with the voters' fear of black control during the 1920's, and both European and rural white immigrants registered heavily Democratic. Personal conflicts between Democratic bosses John J. (Sonny) Mahon and Frank Kelly, heirs of the two major machine factions, weakened their party's control at the center, and 15 years of battling between the forces led by William Curran and perennial mayor Howard Jackson splintered the party further. Local ward bosses were thus able to develop independent neighborhood machines, and control of city council and the mayoralty depended on shifting and temporary alliances of such local groups. Republicans, however, were never able to take advantage of such Democratic in-fighting. Primary and secondary sources; 13 notes.

G. J. Bobango

3475. Arrington, Theodore S. and Kyle, Patricia A. EQUAL RIGHTS AMENDMENT ACTIVISTS IN NORTH CAROLINA. *Signs 1978 3(3): 666-680.* Within a sample of pro-ERA and anti-ERA activists in North Carolina in 1975, female anti-ERA participants were "single-issue" activists, while other women and men (pro- and anti-ERA) generally fit accepted behavior patterns of elites. Neither geography nor indexes of personality measuring dogmatism explained the difference. The Survey Research Center Political Action Index showed strong partisanship among respondents who were typically middle-aged and wealthier than average. Suggests the need for comparative studies of the suffrage movement and ERA activists. Secondary sources; 7 tables, 28 notes.

S. P. Conner

3476. Baas, Jacob C., Jr. JOHN JAY JACKSON, JR., AND THE JACKSONS OF PARKERSBURG: THEIR FIRST ONE HUNDRED YEARS. *West Virginia Hist. 1976 38(1): 23-34.* John Jay Jackson, Jr. (1824-1907), was born into a prominent Scotch-Irish family of western Virginia. His great-grandfather, George Jackson (b. 1757), was a congressman; his grandfather, John George Jackson (1777-1828), served eight terms in Congress, married Dolly Madison's sister, and was a strong Jeffersonian. His father, John Jay Jackson (b. 1800), was illegitimate but served in the Army and became a prosperous Whig businessman, lawyer and state legisla-

tor. John Jay Jackson, Jr., grew up in Parkersburg, was educated at Princeton, and entered law practice in the 1840's. Primary sources; 38 notes.

J. H. Broussard

3477. Baggett, James Alex. ORIGINS OF EARLY TEXAS REPUBLICAN PARTY LEADERSHIP. *J. of Southern Hist. 1974 40(3): 441-454.* Texas' three Republican governors all served during the Reconstruction years and symbolized the tie between prewar Unionism and the post-Civil War Republican party. Traces the changing allegiance of many Whigs in Texas from the Know-Nothing Party to Unionism and then to the Republican Party. The Texas Republican party had little carpetbag influence, and while the black membership was larger than the white, the blacks did not rise to leadership positions. The few carpetbaggers who rose in the party were usually Union Army officers stationed in Texas, while some ex-Rebel officers also joined the Republican leadership group. There is no evidence to show that the early Republican leaders were not sincere, aware, experienced men. Based on manuscripts and published primary and secondary sources; table, 48 notes.

T. D. Schoonover

3478. Baldwin, John T., Jr. CAMPAIGNING WITH EARL LONG. *North Louisiana Hist. Assoc. 1976 8(1): 27-30.* Although for nearly 30 years Earl Kemp Long was an active candidate for public office in Louisiana, he has been "overshadowed by his more famous brother, Huey" and "has been a neglected figure in Louisiana history." He was somewhat shy, but "had a strong inner drive and could not resist the temptation to get out on the stump . . . his real joy lay in politics for its own sake." He was "the complete political animal . . . who was liked rather than revered, the one who attracted the voters because they felt he was one of them." 19 notes.

A. N. Garland

3479. Banning, Lance. THE MODERATE AS REVOLUTIONARY: AN INTRODUCTION TO MADISON'S LIFE. *Q. J. of the Lib. of Congress 1980 37(2): 162-175.* Traces James Madison's (1751-1836) political career from 1774, when he served as a member of the Orange County, Virginia, committee of safety, through his terms in the Virginia council of state, the Virginia state assembly, the Confederation Congress, the Constitutional Convention, and the House of Representatives, through his terms as secretary of state under Thomas Jefferson from 1801 to 1808, and finally as president from 1809 to 1817. Notes his major contributions, including the Virginia Plan, the Constitution, *The Federalist,* the Bill of Rights, and the Virginia Resolutions. Examines his political ideas, including his early attempts to strengthen the central government and his later attempts to limit the federal government's authority and to define states' rights; his creation, with Thomas Jefferson, of the nation's first political party; his early criticism of and reaction against Hamiltonian policy and his later acceptance of some of its elements; and the problems he encountered with the War of 1812. 14 illus.

A. R. Souby

3480. Barham, Mack E. LA MÉTHODOLOGIE DU DROIT CIVIL DE L'ÉTAT DE LOUISIANE [The methodology of the civil law in the state of Louisiana]. *Rev. Int. de Droit Comparé [France] 1975 27(4): 797-816.* In 1803 Louisiana adopted a civil law code based on the Napoleonic code. The procedure of the Louisiana courts resembled that of the common law courts of the other states more than that of the French courts, partly because of the greater availability of legal literature written in English. A struggle developed between those jurists who favored assimilation with the common law and those who sought to preserve the civil law tradition. Today the Louisiana State Law Institute is following the latter trend. Although some of the methods of Louisiana judges are derived from the common law, the Louisiana supreme court adheres to the civil law tradition because it serves the best interests of the people of the state. Primary and secondary sources; 99 notes.

J. S. Gassner

3481. Barnard, William D. GEORGE HUDDLESTON, SR., AND THE POLITICAL TRADITION OF BIRMINGHAM. *Alabama Rev. 1983 36(4): 243-258.* Briefly discusses the social and cultural conservatism and the economic liberalism of George Huddleston,

Sr., congressman from Birmingham, Alabama, during 1915-37. Based on newspapers, the Congressional Record, and secondary sources; 30 notes.                    G. R. Schroeder

3482. Barnard, William D. THE OLD ORDER CHANGES: GRAVES, SPARKS, FOLSOM, AND THE GUBERNATORIAL ELECTION OF 1942. *Alabama Rev. 1975 28(3): 165-184.* Conservative Democrat Chauncey Sparks won the 1942 gubernatorial election by default upon the death of liberal Democratic candidate Bibb Graves, assuring the continuance of probusiness and antilabor leadership since 1938. However, the runner-up was first-time candidate James E. Folsom who inherited major blocs of the Graves organization and whose sectional success in northern Alabama foreshadowed the emergence of a new liberal force that would dominate the state after 1946. Primary and secondary sources, including a private interview with Folsom; 56 notes.

J. F. Vivian

3483. Barnidge, James L. THE LOUISIANA CONSTITUTIONAL CONVENTION OF 1973: THE ROAD TO REVISION. *Louisiana Hist. 1974 15(1): 35-48.* Describes attempts to revise the 1921 Louisiana State Constitution.

3484. Bartley, Numan V. THE SOUTH AND SECTIONALISM IN AMERICAN POLITICS. *J. of Pol. 1976 38(3): 239-257.* Studies the impact of southern sectionalism on American politics. History and southern blacks have molded the group identity of southern whites. The attempted second party system of the Whigs collapsed quickly in the 1850's. Despite many occasions since then, when divisive issues have temporarily cut deeply into the Democrat's solid South, there is no likelihood that "the Americanization of Dixie" implies the coming of a viable two-party politics in the South or a decline of political sectionalism. 33 notes.         R. V. Ritter

3485. Baulch, J. R. GARNER HELD THE COW WHILE JIM WELLS MILKED HER. *West Texas Hist. Assoc. Year Book 1980 56: 91-99.* Texas Democratic politician John Nance Garner (a congressman after 1902) was an instrument of Texas political boss Jim Wells, 1896-1923.

3486. Beck, Paul Allen. PARTISAN DEALIGNMENT IN THE POSTWAR SOUTH. *Am. Pol. Sci. Rev. 1977 71(2): 477-496.* This study attempts to explain post-World War II southern electoral politics by examining the party identifications of southerners between 1952 and 1972. Pronounced decreases in Democratic loyalties and increases in Independent leanings appear during this period and constitute a dealignment of the southern electorate. While interregional population exchanges have diluted Democratic strength, their effects are almost counterbalanced by the mobilization of blacks into politics. Instead, the principal source of dealignment is the generational replacement of the native white electorate. Its youngest members, who entered the electorate after World War II, have come to favor political independence increasingly in recent years. This behavior seems partially attributable to a tendency for young native whites in particular to bring their partisan loyalties into line with their attitudes and party images on racial issues. Even so, there are clear signs that the racial question is losing its place as the major determinant of the region's politics. For the future, one can expect a continuation of dealignment politics and little chance of a partisan realignment.                          J

3487. Becnel, Thomas. LOUISIANA SENATOR ALLEN J. ELLENDER AND IWW LEADER COVINGTON HALL: AN AGRARIAN DICHOTOMY. *Louisiana Hist. 1982 23(3): 259-275.* Ellender and Hall had like backgrounds: both grew up on sugar plantations on Bayou Terrebonne under similar family and peer influences. But in later life Ellender was a thorough conservative, critic of organized labor, and segregationist opponent of every civil rights bill, while Hall became an Industrial Workers of the World spokesman, a champion of blacks, a socialist opponent of World War I, and an active radical throughout his life. It is not clear why they developed so differently, but Hall's family's loss of their land when he was 20 contributed to his radicalization. Based on interviews, Ellender's papers, Hall's writings, parish records, and secondary sources; 31 notes.                      R. E. Noble

3488. Bell, Frank C. THE LIFE AND TIMES OF JOHN R. LYNCH: A CASE STUDY, 1847-1939. *J. of Mississippi Hist. 1976 38(1): 53-67.* Describes the unique political career of John R. Lynch, the first black to hold public office in Mississippi (1869), a member of the Mississippi House of Representatives (1869-73), and the first black to be elected from Mississippi to the US House of Representatives (1873-77, 1882-83). Lynch stressed social and political equality and was "the antithesis of Booker T. Washington." Based on published sources; 30 notes.          J. W. Hillje

3489. Bergeron, Paul H. THE NULLIFICATION CONTROVERSY REVISITED. *Tennessee Hist. Q. 1976 35(3): 263-275.* Uses the thesis of William W. Freehling in *Prelude to Civil War: The Nullification Controversy in South Carolina, 1816-1836* (New York, 1966), as the starting point for a reexamination of the relationship between nullification sentiment and slavery in South Carolina. Based on population and election statistics pertinent to the state's legislative elections of October 1832, finds that Freehling's interpretation is inadequate and needs to be reassessed and that more investigations must be made to show that, in the nullification controversy, South Carolinians were intensely concerned by other than the tariff issue. Based on primary and secondary materials; 2 tables, 16 notes.                     A. E. Wiederrecht

3490. Billings, Warren M. PLEADING, PROCEDURE, AND PRACTICE: THE MEANING OF DUE PROCESS OF LAW IN SEVENTEENTH-CENTURY VIRGINIA. *J. of Southern Hist. 1981 47(4): 569-584.* An analysis of the development of modern due process of law in 17th-century Virginia. The term, as well as the practice, arrived from England, where it referred merely to the processes of getting the accused through court procedures. Both term and practice lacked flexibility, but the colonists were not content to let matters stand there. Covers the development and origins of such modern ideas as the right to jury trial, defense for the accused, right of the defendant to subpoena witnesses, and the rapid clearing of court dockets. By century's end, Virginia had endorsed the processes of change in legal practice, thus opening the door for a tradition that has not yet come to an end. 39 notes.

V. L. Human

3491. Billington, Monroe. RECENT SOUTHERN POLITICAL HISTORY: A REVIEW ESSAY. *Red River Valley Hist. Rev. 1978 3(3): 89-99.* Discusses the political history of the South since the end of World War II.

3492. Black, Earl. IS IT TRUE WHAT THEY SAY ABOUT DIXIE? *Polity 1975 8(1): 123-130.* Reviews six books (1970's) on politics in the South, primarily from 1945 to the 1960's.

3493. Black, Earl. A THEORY OF SOUTHERN FACTIONALISM. *J. of Pol. 1983 45(3): 594-614.* During 1920-80, two-thirds of all gubernatorial primaries in the South involved multifactionalism rather than bifactional circumstances. During this period, only Virginia exhibited strong unifactionalism, due to the significance of the Byrd organization. Even during 1920-49, multifactionalism was considerably more prevalent than was estimated in *Southern Politics in State and Nation* (1949) by V. O. Key, Jr. During this period, bifactionalism was significant only in Tennessee. The modest decline in multifactionalism since 1950 can be attributed to an increase in unifactionalism in the Deep South. 6 tables, 12 notes, biblio.

A. W. Novitsky

3494. Black, Merle. RACIAL COMPOSITION OF CONGRESSIONAL DISTRICTS AND SUPPORT FOR FEDERAL VOTING RIGHTS LEGISLATION IN THE AMERICAN SOUTH. *Social Sci. Q. 1978 59(3): 435-450.* Such support is related to racial composition in three time periods: (1) prior to the emergence of massive participation by blacks (1957 and 1960), (2) during the rapid expansion of the black electorate (1965 and 1969-1970) and (3) a decade after passage of the original act (1975). The research shows how the relationship between approval of the principle of federal intervention and district racial composition has been altered over time.                                                                                    J

3495.  Black, Merle and Black, Earl. REPUBLICAN PARTY DEVELOPMENT IN THE SOUTH: THE RISE OF THE CONTESTED PRIMARY. *Social Sci. Q. 1976 57(3): 566-578.* Notes that the contested Republican primary commonly follows a demonstration of Republican competitiveness in general elections. The size of the minority party's primary electorate is associated with interparty and intraparty competition.                                                       J

3496.  Bland, David H. and Reese, Pat Ray. KENTUCKY'S EXECUTIVE MANAGEMENT COMMISSION: WHAT THE EXECUTIVES THOUGHT. *State Government 1981 54(2): 39-44.* Discusses the Executive Management Commission of Kentucky Governor John Y. Brown, Jr., established in 1979 to assess the executive branch of state government; though it is too early to judge the impact of the recommendations of the commission, its members from the private sector were in general favorably impressed with the success of the project.

3497.  Bland, Sidney R. FIGHTING THE ODDS: MILITANT SUFFRAGISTS IN SOUTH CAROLINA. *South Carolina Hist. Mag. 1981 82(1): 32-43.* Details the activism of the woman suffrage movement in South Carolina which begain in the 1890's, although some organizing occurred as early as 1869, and was revitalized during the 1910's when the State Equal Suffrage League was established in 1914 as an affiliate of the National American Woman Suffrage Association (NAWSA), and when Alice Paul, using the tactics of the militant British movement led by Emmeline Pankhurst, formed the Congressional Union (later the National Woman's Party); 1890's-1919.

3498.  Bobbitt, Charles A. HUEY P. LONG: THE MEMPHIS YEARS. *West Tennessee Hist. Soc. Papers 1978 (32): 133-139.* Huey P. Long was first in Memphis in 1911. Soon he was out of work, and took any job. He was in and out of Memphis through 1914. During this three-year period he met Ed Crump, political leader of Memphis, and married Miss Rose McConnel. After leaving Memphis he went to Louisiana. None of his next appearances in Memphis, in the early 1930's, lasted more than a few hours. Based on contemporary newspaper accounts; 2 illus., 33 notes.

H. M. Parker, Jr.

3499.  Bohmer, David A. STABILITY AND CHANGE IN EARLY NATIONAL POLITICS: THE MARYLAND VOTER AND THE ELECTION OF 1800. *William and Mary Q. 1979 36(1): 27-50.* Contends, from examination of electoral and population data from all of Maryland's counties for the presidential election of 1800, that there was no substantial realignment. Nor was there any significant increase in voter participation. Voting patterns were similar in elections during 1796-1816. Most persons, however, who switched their voting preference in 1800 from that of the off-year election in 1798 voted for Jefferson. Evaluates ethnic voting patterns. Federalist strength still remained in Maryland after the election of 1800. Consults poll lists and federal and local records; 39 notes.

H. M. Ward

3500.  Boles, Janet K. THE TEXAS WOMAN IN POLITICS: ROLE MODEL OR MIRAGE? *Social Sci. J. 1984 21(1): 79-89.* Despite the popular image of Texas women as unusually politically active, their actual political participation is below the national average, reflecting more of the Southern than the Western tradition.

3501.  Born, Kate. MEMPHIS NEGRO WORKINGMEN AND THE NAACP. *West Tennessee Hist. Soc. Papers 1974 (28): 90-107.* The Memphis chapter of the NAACP was a major influence in the attempt to raise the economic and social status of the Negro, and a consistent force in active legal protest against injustices to blacks. In 1900 almost half of Memphis' population was black. Negroes successfully operated businesses and were in all crafts and unions. The Jim Crow laws of 1905 changed this and caused the social and economic regression of the Memphis Negro until 1937. Only the

NAACP stood as an advocate for the black workingman. Based on primary sources, with emphasis on the Walter F. White papers; 88 notes.

H. M. Parker, Jr.

3502.  Bourke, Paul F. and DeBats, Donald A. IDENTIFIABLE VOTING IN NINETEENTH-CENTURY AMERICA: TOWARD A COMPARISON OF BRITAIN AND THE UNITED STATES BEFORE THE SECRET BALLOT. *Perspectives in Am. Hist. 1977-78 11: 257-288.* Poll books in Virginia during the 19th century were used to identify influential citizens who could be contacted to propagandize for politicians seeking or desiring to retain office. British historians have come to similar conclusions about the ballot system in Great Britain during the same period. Based on poll books from Cumberland and Prince George counties.

W. A. Wiegand

3503.  Braden, Waldo W. and Strickland, William, comps. SOUTHERN PUBLIC ADDRESS: A BIBLIOGRAPHY OF THESES AND DISSERTATIONS. *Southern Speech Communication J. 1976 41(4): 388-408.* A bibliography of political speeches from the South, covering 1935-75.

3504.  Breckinridge, John B. THE DISTRICT OF COLUMBIA HOME RULE ACT. *Judicature 1974 57(8): 360-363.*

3505.  Bromberg, Alan B. JOHN MERCER LANGSTON: BLACK CONGRESSMAN FROM THE OLD DOMINION. *Virginia Cavalcade 1980 30(2): 60-67.* Surveys the career of John Mercer Langston (1829-97), lawyer, Republican politician, educator, diplomat, orator, and crusader for civil rights—and still the only black to represent Virginia in Congress (in the House of Representatives for five months in 1890-91).

3506.  Bromberg, Alan B. AN UNCONVENTIONAL CONFEDERATE: EXTRA BILLY SMITH AND THE CIVIL WAR. *Virginia Cavalcade 1981 30(4): 148-155.* Traces William "Extra Billy" Smith's (1797-1887) rise during the Civil War from colonel of the 49th Virginia Infantry, to general and his later political career, culminating with his service as governor of Virginia, emphasizing his performance as a military leader and later as an opponent of the excesses of Reconstruction.

3507.  Broussard, James H. PARTY AND PARTISANSHIP IN AMERICAN LEGISLATURES: THE SOUTH ATLANTIC STATES, 1800-1812. *J. of Southern Hist. 1977 43(1): 39-58.* Very little work has been done to analyze or describe the workings of state legislatures during the era of the first party system, 1789-1820. Analysis of the legislatures of Virginia and both Carolinas reveals the lack of party affiliation, the lack of a party clash over the speakership, the casual allocation of committee seats, the moderate degree of party cohesion and the irregular use of the caucus. These factors indicate that party played a very modest role in legislative decisionmaking in the South Atlantic states. Based on archival and printed primary and secondary materials; 4 tables, appendix, 21 notes.

T. D. Schoonover

3508.  Brown, Stephen W. SATISFACTION AT BLADENSBURG: THE PEARSON-JACKSON DUEL OF 1809. *North Carolina Hist. Rev. 1981 58(1): 23-43.* Joseph Pearson, a staunch Federalist from North Carolina's Salisbury district, made a speech in the House of Representatives shortly after taking his seat in 1809, in which he revived the charge that President Jefferson and Secretary of State Madison had knowingly encouraged an 1805-06 American filibustering expedition attempting to free Venezuela from Spanish rule. The Venezuela incident, craftily engineered by the patriot Francisco de Miranda, failed abroad but succeeded in embarrassing the American government and in creating a political storm. Pearson's speech, made three years after the fact, released political tensions again when West Virginia's John George Jackson responded belligerently. Threats of a duel ensued. Six months later, after some newspaper, mail, and personal exchanges, and one postponement, the duel occurred in Bladensburg, Maryland. Jackson was maimed. The two remained personal and political enemies for life. Based on *Annals of Congress,* Jackson's, Madison's and others' papers, and contemporary newspaper reports; 11 illus., 75 notes.

T. L. Savitt

3509. Brown, Thomas. SOUTHERN WHIGS AND THE POLITICS OF STATESMANSHIP, 1833-1841. *J. of Southern Hist. 1980 46(3): 361-380.* The old two-party South has been neglected and isolated as an area not deemed worthy of serious attention. The nagging question remains: Why did Southerners divide their loyalty between Democrats and Whigs when under attack as a region in the 1830's and 1840's? Clay's program of economic nationalism and concern for the general welfare allowed Southern Whigs to appear in an alluring combination as disinterested men of principle, party regulars, and statesmen. Based on the *Congressional Globe* and other printed primary and secondary sources; 46 notes.

T. D. Schoonover

3510. Bullock, Charles S., III. CONGRESSIONAL VOTING AND THE MOBILIZATION OF A BLACK ELECTORATE IN THE SOUTH. *J. of Pol. 1981 43(3): 662-682.* Since 1956, Southern black voter registration has increased by over two million, and the percentages of Negroes registered to vote rose from 25% to 60%. Legislators from districts with large black populations have become notably more responsive to their concerns. Generational replacement is a major factor as freshmen Democrats in the last three congresses have been most responsive, while freshmen Republicans have been more conservative than their predecessors. Subregional differences have decreased. While legislators from the deep South have responded to black political activity, rim state representatives with fewer black constituents have remained more consistent. 8 tables, 44 notes.

A. W. Novitsky

3511. Bullock, Charles S., III. THE ELECTION OF BLACKS IN THE SOUTH: PRECONDITIONS AND CONSEQUENCES. *Am. J. of Pol. Sci. 1975 19(4): 727-739.* In this paper, hypotheses about the conditions under which black candidates are elected to public office in the South are tested. Data are presented for county and municipal officeholders. The hypothesis that blacks are more likely to be elected when elections are at-large rather than by districts is tested. The relationship between proportion of blacks in the constituency and the election of blacks is explored. Finally, the likelihood that black-governed counties will have the resources to significantly improve the conditions of their constituents is discussed.

J

3512. Burckel, Nicholas C. FROM BECKHAM TO MCCREARY: THE PROGRESSIVE RECORD OF KENTUCKY GOVERNORS. *Register of the Kentucky Hist. Soc. 1978 76(4): 285-306.* Examines the progressive attitudes and records of John C. W. Beckham (D.), Augustus E. Willson (R.), and James B. McCreary (D.), governors of Kentucky during 1899-1915. Few political reforms emerged from Beckham's administrations, while Willson's term was described as frustrating. McCreary's election in 1911, coupled with national trends toward progressivism, led to "the most progressive record of any chief executive in Kentucky up to that time." Primary and secondary sources; 56 notes.

J. F. Paul

3513. Burckel, Nicholas C. GOVERNOR AUSTIN LANE CROTHERS AND PROGRESSIVE REFORM IN MARYLAND 1908-1912. *Maryland Hist. Mag. 1981 76(2): 184-201.* More than any other governor of Maryland, Austin Lane Crothers succeeded in achieving progressive reforms for which individuals and groups had unsuccessfully agitated in the past, and his administration (1908-12) is even more impressive when seen "against the backdrop of volatile state politics and the racial issue which dominated the political scene" between 1896 and his election. Examines Crothers's career prior to the governorship, his legislative battles in enacting a corrupt practices act, a primary election bill, a public utilities law, and endorsement of the income tax amendment. Throughout his term, Crothers faced the opposition of powerful ex-governor John Walter Smith and leading organization Democrat Arthur P. Gorman, Jr. Crothers' death in 1912 greatly helped the decline of progressivism in Maryland. Based on the Maryland Manuals, contemporary press, and secondary works; 51 notes.

G. J. Bobango

3514. Burger, Warren E. STANLEY F. REED. *Supreme Court Hist. Soc. Y. 1981: 10-13.* Traces the legal career of Stanley F. Reed, during which he served as a Supreme Court justice and as solicitor general of the United States, and discusses his legal philosophy, family life, and love for his native state of Kentucky. Based in part on the author's personal memories; photo.

G. V. Wasson

3515. Burran, James A. THE WPA IN NASHVILLE, 1935-1943. *Tennessee Hist. Q. 1974 34(3): 293-306.* With the creation of the Works Progress Administration in Tennessee in 1935 Colonel Harry S. Berry was named administrator. First priority was given to construction, but service projects received considerable support. With the steady growth of projects, however, charges of misuse of money and power grew. Rumors of boondoggling led to a 1939 investigation which revealed numerous irregularities. Nevertheless, the WPA in Nashville no doubt did the best that might have been expected given the bureaucracy. Primary and secondary sources; 35 notes.

M. B. Lucas

3516. Campbell, Bruce A. CHANGE IN THE SOUTHERN ELECTORATE. *Am. J. of Pol. Sci. 1977 21(1): 37-64.* This paper presents an analysis which measures the extent to which each of five sources of change in the party loyalties of the Southern electorate has been active during the periods 1952-1960 and 1960-1972. The measure of party loyalty is Converse's normal vote, with a set of updated parameters for the 1960-1972 period provided by Arthur H. Miller. The basic data sources are the six SRC presidential election studies ranging from 1952 to 1972, supplemented by data from the Matthews-Prothro and CSEP studies. In addition, data from the U.S. Census are used when possible in place of the estimates provided by the SRC samples. In both time periods, we find that change in the partisanship of individual Southerners is the dominant mechanism of change in the normal vote. In- and out-migration are of moderate importance, while the impacts of death and the entrance of youth into the electorate are negligible. Using Key's terminology, we find that white conversion has resembled the process of secular realignment over the past twenty years. Black conversion, on the other hand, is best interpreted as critical change, with a sharp reversal of partisanship between 1960 and 1964.

J

3517. Campbell, David and Feagin, Joe R. BLACK POLITICS IN THE SOUTH: A DESCRIPTIVE ANALYSIS. *J. of Pol. 1975 37(1): 129-162.* Explores a series of critical questions about elected black representation in city, county, and state governments in the South, from the 1965 Voting Rights Act to the present. Traces the reasons for growing black political power, then examines the following issues: 1) How many black elected officials are there in the once-Confederate states? 2) What governmental offices do black southerners now hold, and what trends over time in officeholding can be discerned? 3) Where are black elected officials geographically located, and what are the demographic characteristics of their political jurisdictions? 4) To what extent have black elected officials been effective in meeting the needs of their constituencies? A concluding section examines the implications of these findings for 1) the future of black political power in the South and 2) ongoing arguments about the shape and significance of ethnic politics in the United States.

J

3518. Campbell, Randolph B. POLITICAL CONFLICT WITHIN THE SOUTHERN CONSENSUS: HARRISON COUNTY, TEXAS 1850-1880. *Civil War Hist. 1980 26(3): 218-239.* Discusses opposition political parties in Harrison County, Texas: Whigs, Know-Nothings, Constitutional Unionists, opponents of secession, critics of reconstruction by former Confederates, and supporters of congressional Reconstruction. While always the minority view and opposed to the Democratic Party, the opposition leadership was still remarkably similar to the Democratic leadership in background. The opposition did not oppose southern values and was simply a significant variant of opinion in a basically homogenous society. Based on newspapers, census schedules, and secondary sources; 3 tables, 47 notes.

G. R. Schroeder

3519. Canon, Bradley C. FACTIONALISM IN THE SOUTH: A TEST OF THEORY AND A REVISITATION OF V. O. KEY. *Am. J. of Pol. Sci. 1978 22(4): 833-848.* The nature of electoral divisiveness is often explained by one of two competing theories: Riker's size principle or as a function of election rules.... This paper tests these theories in the context of Democratic Party factionalism in the South... data from 1932-77 indicates that with only minor exceptions multifactionalism occurs in double primary states and bifactionalism in single primary states....          J

3520. Canon, Bradley C. ISOLATING CAUSES OF FACTIONALISM IN THE SOUTH: A REVISITATION OF V. O. KEY, JR. Steed, Robert P.; Moreland, Laurence W.; and Baker, Tod A., ed. *Party Politics in the South* (New York: Praeger, 1980): 33-57. Utilizes data from all southern states plus five border states for the period 1932-79, to test two hypotheses, summarized by V. O. Key, Jr., in 1950, purporting to explain patterns of party factionalism in the South. The author attempts to determine whether the nature of factionalism within the Democratic Party in the South is primarily a function of the structure of the primary system, or a function of the presence or absence of charismatic politicians, arguing that the former is the more dominant cause. Based on data from *Congressional Quarterly, Guide to U.S. Elections* (Washington, D.C.: Congressional Quarterly, 1975); 8 tables, 13 notes. A revised and updated version of an article in the *American Journal of Political Science* in 1978 (see entry 17A:1924).          J. Powell

3521. Capps, Randall. SOME HISTORIC KENTUCKY ORATORS. *Register of the Kentucky Hist. Soc. 1975 73(4): 356-389.* Studies five Kentucky orators who made contributions to the history of Kentucky and the nation: Ben Hardin (1784-1852), John J. Crittenden (1786-1863), Cassius M. Clay (1810-1903), Henry Watterson (1840-1921), and Laura Clay (1849-1941). Primary and secondary sources; 82 notes.          J. F. Paul

3522. Carlson, James M. and Hamilton, Howard. DEMOCRATIC ELECTORAL COALITIONS. *Polity 1978 11(2): 290-297.* Examines the composition of Democratic Party electoral coalitions in three states for levels of president, governor, and senators, and their implications. From data in the Comparative State Election Project (1968), Illinois, North Carolina, and South Dakota were selected as representative of major regions. Analyzes the contributions of the poor, blacks and nonwhites, Catholics, union members and their families, and people under 30. Union members account for 40% of the Democratic vote in Illinois, but they are not part of the Democratic coalition in North Carolina; in South Dakota they exhibit greater loyalty than in Illinois and the nation as a whole but the small size of the group reduces its impact. Catholics' attachment to the Democratic Party is not uniform across the nation. In North Carolina blacks are the only dependable base of the party. Table, 11 notes.          E. P. Stickney

3523. Cassel, Carol A. CHANGE IN ELECTORAL PARTICIPATION IN THE SOUTH. *J. of Pol. 1979 41(3): 907-917.* Regional differences in presidential voting narrowed from 1952 to 1976 as both black and white females were mobilized into the southern electorate while nonsouthern voting, especially among the younger and less educated, declined. White southern males paralleled nonsouthern whites of both sexes in declining participation, despite the tumultuous period when differences in parties became clear and issue salience was high. The younger noncollege generation was the major source of the decline. 4 illus., table, 16 notes.          A. W. Novitsky

3524. Cassel, Carol A. CLASS BASES OF SOUTHERN POLITICS AMONG WHITES: 1952-1972. *Social Sci. Q. 1978 58(4): 700-707.* Relationships between party identification, presidential vote, and socioeconomic status are examined to test the hypothesis that status polarization developed among white southerners during the period. Finds that the minimal polarization is attributable mainly to northern migrants.

3525. Cassel, Carol A. COHORT ANALYSIS OF PARTY IDENTIFICATION AMONG SOUTHERN WHITES, 1952-1972. *Public Opinion Q. 1977 41(1): 28-33.* Cohort studies generally find that different generations retain the same pattern of partisanship throughout their lifecycles. In contrast, this study finds that changes *within* generations contribute greatly to the decline in traditional Democratic affilation among southern whites.          J

3526. Childs, David W. CONGRESSMAN JOE D. WAGGONNER: A STUDY IN POLITICAL INFLUENCE. *North Louisiana Hist. Assoc. J. 1982 13(4): 118-130.* Joe D. Waggonner represented Louisiana's 4th Congressional District during 1962-80. He ran for office as an avowed segregationist and anti-Communist, and he showed his legislative skills most clearly in the battle over busing between 1969 and 1972. Although he failed ultimately in his anti-busing effort, he maintained a position of influence in the Congress. Photo, 35 notes.          J. F. Paul

3527. Clark, J. Stanley. CAREER OF JOHN R. THOMAS. *Chronicles of Oklahoma 1974 52(2): 152-179.* Gives a biographical account of John Robert Thomas (1846-1914), Republican politician and lawyer. As a congressman from Illinois he actively supported naval development. Later appointed a federal district judge in Indian Territory, he moved to Muskogee; he also served on the first Oklahoma Code Commission. While visiting McAlester, he was shot to death during a prison outbreak. Illus., 4 photos.

N. J. Street

3528. Cobb, James C. COLONEL EFFINGHAM CRUSHES THE CRACKERS: POLITICAL REFORM IN POSTWAR AUGUSTA. *South Atlantic Q. 1979 78(4): 507-519.* Colonel W. Seaborn Effingham, a fictional character created by novelist Berry Fleming in *Colonel Effingham's Raid,* was a defender of southern traditions and succeeded in routing a boss-led machine in "Fredericksville." The colonel could see no sense in watching his nephew go off to World War II to fight dictators abroad when people were submitting to one in their own home town. Postwar Augusta, Georgia, was led by a deeply entrenched machine; when the veterans began returning they decided to go after the Crackers who had held power for decades. Fleming's novel served as their inspiration—a novel which all Augustans read. Defeated in 1943, the Augusta Citizens Union, composed of both blacks and whites, in 1946 ran a skillful, hard-hitting campaign which defeated the heavy-handed arrogance which characterized the Crackers. Based on interviews with Fleming, the author's Ph.D. dissertation (U. of Georgia), contemporary newspaper accounts and other secondary sources; table, 33 notes.          H. M. Parker, Jr.

3529. Cobb, James C. NOT GONE, BUT FORGOTTEN: EUGENE TALMADGE AND THE 1938 PURGE CAMPAIGN. *Georgia Hist. Q. 1975 59(2): 197-209.* Discusses the political career of Georgia Democratic governor Eugene Talmadge, 1926-38, emphasizing President Franklin D. Roosevelt's 1938 intervention to remove him from power due to attacks on the New Deal.

3530. Coffey, William. MATTHEW S. HOLT: A WEST VIRGINIA INDIVIDUALIST. *West Virginia Hist. 1978 39(2-3): 200-209.* Matthew S. Holt (1850-1939) was an iconoclast of Lewis County, West Virginia, of Scotch-Irish background. He published the Weston *Republican,* 1882-93, but then supported William Jennings Bryan, and ran for Congress, governor, and senator as a Socialist after 1900. He supported atheism and pacifism, was a doctor, publisher, and horsebreeder, and served two terms as mayor of Weston. Primary and secondary sources; 39 notes.          J. H. Broussard

3531. Conley, John A. BEYOND LEGISLATIVE ACTS: PENAL REFORM, PUBLIC POLICY, AND SYMBOLIC JUSTICE. *Public Hist. 1981 3(1): 26-39.* Focuses on prison reform in Oklahoma from 1910, when it constructed its penitentiary, to 1967, when it created a statewide corrections department.

3532. Conti, Eugene A., Jr. THE CULTURAL ROLE OF LOCAL ELITES IN THE KENTUCKY MOUNTAINS: A RETROSPECTIVE ANALYSIS. *Appalachian J. 1979-80 7(1-2): 51-68.* History and analysis of the economic elite and political leaders in southern Appalachia, particularly Kentucky, and their role in the "social, economic, and political evolution of the region as it emerged from a preindustrial situation prior to the Civil War" and until industrialization in the late 19th century.

3533. Cook, Charles Orson. *BOOSTERISM AND BABBITTRY: CHARLES HILLMAN BROUGH AND THE "SELLING" OF ARKANSAS. Arkansas Hist. Q. 1978 37(1): 74-83.* Charles Hillman Brough (1876-1935), college professor, Arkansas governor (1917-21), and orator, was well known as a propagandist for Arkansas during the 1920's and early 1930's. Although he spouted "facts" which pictured Arkansas as a veritable Garden of Eden, few nonresidents were influenced by his boosting. Primary and secondary sources; 35 notes.                                    G. R. Schroeder

3534. Cotter, Patrick R. SOUTHERN REACTION TO THE SECOND RECONSTRUCTION: THE CASE OF SOUTH CAROLINA. *Western Pol. Q. 1981 34(4): 543-551.* Three models of the South's reaction to the "Second Reconstruction" have been proposed: convergence, realignment, and dealignment. The models differ with respect to whether the increasing level of party competition occurring in the South indicates a major change in the nature of the region's politics. The three models also differ with regard to the relative importance of race and class on political preferences in contemporary Southern politics. The convergence model best describes the political change experienced by South Carolina since the 1920s.    J

3535. Coulter, E. Merton. HANGING AS A SOCIO-PENAL INSTITUTION IN GEORGIA AND ELSEWHERE. *Georgia Hist. Q. 1973 57(1): 17-55.* Hanging was the only penal institution colonial Georgians brought with them from England. It remained the principal form of capital punishment until 1924. Capital offenses at various times included rape, horse-stealing, counterfeiting, perjury, dueling, and murder. Describes several executions. 3 illus., 81 notes.
                                                         D. L. Smith

3536. Coulter, E. Merton. THE MYTH OF DADE COUNTY'S SECEDING FROM GEORGIA IN 1860. *Georgia Hist. Q. 1957 41(4): 349-364.* Debunks the myth that Dade Cunty seceded from Georgia, became the State of Dade in 1860, and remained that way until 4 July 1945 when with much publicity it "returned" to Georgia and the Union.

3537. Crane, Sophie and Crane, Paul. HISTORIC JAILS OF TENNESSEE. *Tennessee Hist. Q. 1980 39(1): 3-10.* A description of the six of Tennessee's 95 county jails listed in the National Register of Historic Places. These are the jails of Bedford, Franklin, Grundy, Hancock, Lawrence, and Scott Counties. Three (Bedford, Hancock, and Scott) are still in use. They are "a grim reminder of the past and a witness to the yet unsolved problem of how to protect society without completely dehumanizing the criminal and those who guard him." 6 photos.                          H. M. Parker, Jr.

3538. Creel, Von Russell. COURT IN PERIL: THE LEGISLATIVE-JUDICIAL STRUGGLE OF 1927-1929. *Chronicles of Oklahoma 1974 52(2): 220-236.* Describes the political difficulties of the Oklahoma State Supreme Court during 1927-30, discussing cases which evoked public criticism: *Jarman* v. *Mason, Dabney* v. *Hooker,* and *Simpson* v. *Hill.* The court was in open conflict with the legislature, and in 1929 impeachment charges were brought against several supreme court justices. Justice J. W. Clark's acquittal ended such legislative challenges to the court. Based on contemporary newspaper reports, state documents, and secondary sources; 5 photos, 21 notes.                                    N. J. Street

3539. Crooks, James B. POLITICS AND REFORM: THE DIMENSIONS OF BALTIMORE PROGRESSIVISM. *Maryland Hist. Mag. 1976 71(3): 421-427.* Today's history is rightfully paying more attention to the local and urban side of the Progressive era reforms. Reviews the efforts of Baltimore reformers to weaken Isaac Freeman Rasin's political machine and its boss rule. From the election of Alcaeus Hooper in 1895 to the formation of the New Charter Union in 1899, progressives such as Charles J. Bonaparte and William Keyser led members of the Baltimore Reform League and the Civil Service Reform Association to pronounced victories for good government candidates. The Municipal Art Society achieved

urban renewal and beautification projects, and other reformers promoted bond issues for sewage systems, civic centers, parks, paved streets, and community centers. A Board of Awards began supervising city contracts and franchises. By 1910 a city-wide congress met to coordinate physical and social planning for Baltimore. Substantial improvements came in public health, but child labor laws were delayed by businessmen, and city funds for programs were always insufficient since politicians were reluctant to upset voters by raising taxes. Reform, then, was not just ousting a corrupt boss, but "a complex movement attempting to come to grips with the realities of a rapidly urbanizing and industrializing nation." Primary and secondary sources; 17 notes.                              G. J. Bobango

3540. Crump, J. Griffin. J. MANSIR TYDINGS, 1905-1974. *J. of Intergroup Relations 1975 4(1): 3-6.* Obituary of Kentucky's human rights reformer J. Mansir Tydings.                              S

3541. Davidson, Chandler and Korbel, George. AT-LARGE ELECTIONS AND MINORITY-GROUP REPRESENTATION: A RE-EXAMINATION OF HISTORICAL AND CONTEMPORARY EVIDENCE. *J. of Pol. 1981 43(4): 982-1005.* Galveston, Texas, adopted the at-large election system in 1895. During the Progressive era, municipal at-large elections to replace ward-based systems were supported by business leaders throughout the United States to wrest control from the laboring classes and ethnic minorities. Progressivism in the South coincided with racial reaction, leading to the adoption of such other discriminatory measures as the poll tax, literacy tests, the grandfather clause, white primaries, gerrymander, the place system, run-offs, and economic sanctions. At-large elections have been maintained as barriers to minority officeholding until the recent successful court challenges which began with *White* v. *Regester* (1973). Recent studies covering 1969 to 1981 confirm that at-large elections systematically lead to minority underrepresentation. 3 tables, 69 notes.                            A. W. Novitsky

3542. Davis, William C. TAKING THE STUMP: CAMPAIGNING IN OLD-TIME KENTUCKY. *Register of the Kentucky Hist. Soc. 1982 80(4): 367-391.* Old fashioned campaign oratory flourished in antebellum Kentucky. Stump-speaking brought out the best and the worst in some politicians, but it was expected of all. Humor, trickery, endurance, and the ability to react to the unexpected were all elements of a successful stump-speaker. 4 illus., 41 notes.
                                                         J. F. Paul

3543. Denhardt, Robert B. and Jakes, Jay E. THE IMPACT OF DEMOCRATIC PARTY REFORM ON THE SOUTH. *J. of Pol. Sci. 1976 4(1): 36-51.* Guidelines for delegate selection for the 1972 Democratic Party convention adopted the McGovern-Fraser reforms which were committed to nondiscrimination. Adherence to the guidelines was mandatory for seating at the convention. Louisiana's resistance to guidelines became an issue. Southern states complied; the representation was achieved by normative, utilitarian compliance, and by the dynamics of political bargaining and negotiations. Based on participant-observer method by authors working in the McGovern campaign, and on questionnaires; 5 tables, 24 notes.
                                                         T. P. Richardson

3544. Dethloff, Henry C. THE LONGS: REVOLUTION OR POPULIST RETRENCHMENT? *Louisiana Hist. 1978 19(4): 401-412.* Compares the politics of Huey P. Long (d. 1935) with Populism and Progressivism in Louisiana. "Longism" had roots in those earlier movements, but "Longism" was more radical than Populism or Progressivism. The Long mystique was especially revolutionary. Based prinicpally on secondary sources; 36 notes.
                                                         R. L. Woodward

3545. Dickson, James Galen, Jr. DECISION-MAKING IN A RESTRICTIVE CONSTITUTIONAL ENVIRONMENT: IMPACT ON THE TEXAS GOVERNOR OF HIGH COURT DECISIONS AND ATTORNEY GENERAL OPINIONS. *Rocky Mountain Social Sci. J. 1973 10(1): 51-60.*

3546. Dillard, Tom. TO THE BACK OF THE ELEPHANT: RACIAL CONFLICT IN THE ARKANSAS REPUBLICAN PARTY. *Arkansas Hist. Q. 1974 33(1): 3-15.* Chronicles the struggle of blacks for equal participation in the state's Republican activities, 1867-1928.　　　　　　　　　　　　　　　　　　　　　S

3547. Dillard, Tom W. "GOLDEN PROSPECTS AND FRATERNAL AMENITIES": MIFFLIN W. GIBBS'S ARKANSAS YEARS. *Arkansas Hist. Q. 1976 35(4): 307-333.* Mifflin W. Gibbs (1823-1915) was a prominent figure in the Little Rock black community after his arrival from Ohio at age 48 until his death. Following a law apprenticeship, he rose to political prominence in the local and state Republican Party organizations and received national recognition as ambassador to Madagascar. Gibbs was also a local civil servant, civil rights activist, businessman, banker, and humanitarian. Based on manuscripts, published primary records, newspaper accounts, and secondary sources; 3 illus., 113 notes.
　　　　　　　　　　　　　　　　　　　　　T. L. Savitt

3548. Dobbins, Charles G. ALABAMA GOVERNORS AND EDITORS, 1930-1955: A MEMOIR. *Alabama Rev. 1976 29(2): 135-154.* Presents personal reminiscences of Governors Benjamin M. Miller, Bibb Graves, Frank Dixon, James Folsom, and Gordon Persons. Race has ceased to be a dominant political issue, and politics has produced a fluid, diverse leadership since the Depression. Based on primary and secondary sources; 4 notes.
　　　　　　　　　　　　　　　　　　　　　J. F. Vivian

3549. Dollar, Clyde D. OF ONIONS AND RAZORBACKS: A BRIEF HISTORY OF ARKANSAS. *Am. West 1978 15(5): 4-9, 60.* Hernando de Soto opened Arkansas history in the 1540's. Spanish heritage is confined to an occasional artifact, wild pigs, and "rifely conflicting narratives" of their exploits. Arkansas came into the French orbit with the Marquette-Joliet exploration in the 1670's and the fur trade which followed. French place names abound on today's map of the state. A part of America's Louisiana Purchase, it was first organized as a county of Missouri Territory, then as a territory in its own right, and finally, in 1836, as a state. It joined the Civil War Confederacy. Despite too many "colorful demagogues," Arkansas is emerging into maturity. Government is regarded as an "expression of collective will" rather than as a vehicle to destroy resources. 3 illus.　　　　D. L. Smith

3550. Dougan, Michael B. THE DOCTRINE OF CREATIVE DESTRUCTION: FERRY AND BRIDGE LAW IN ARKANSAS. *Arkansas Hist. Q. 1980 39(2): 136-158.* Discusses ferry and bridge law cases in Arkansas ca. 1837-1940 as they related to the landmark Supreme Court decision in the Massachusetts case, *Charles River Bridge* v. *Warren Bridge* (US, 1837). The last Arkansas toll bridge was discontinued in 1940. Mainly primary sources; 106 notes.　　　　　　　　　　　　　　G. R. Schroeder

3551. Driscoll, Mark and Lane, Margaret Anne. DOWN AT THE COURT HOUSE: A PHOTOGRAPHIC ESSAY. *Tampa Bay Hist. 1980 2(1): 34-48.* Provides information about Florida county court houses, taken from "Down At The Court House: Photographs and Stories of Florida's County Court Houses," an exhibit sponsored by the Florida Department of State; 1885-1969.

3552. Dur, Philip F. JEFFERSON CAFFERY OF LOUISIANA: HIGHLIGHTS OF HIS CAREER. *Louisiana Hist. 1974 15(1): 5-34, 15(4): 367-402.* Part I. Describes Caffery's early diplomatic career, 1911-33, in many foreign nations. Part II. Examines the diplomatic career of Jefferson Caffery, highlighting his terms of office in Cuba (1933-37) and Brazil (1937-44).

3553. Edsall, Thomas B. MONEY AND MORALITY IN MARYLAND. *Society 1974 11(4): 74-81.* Campaign financing reform in Maryland must take into account commercial interests' financing of elected officials in return for favors. One of five articles on state politics and public interests.

3554. Edwards, Edwin W. THE ROLE OF THE GOVERNOR IN LOUISIANA POLITICS: AN HISTORICAL STUDY. *Louisiana Hist. 1974 15(2): 101-116.* Covers evolution of power which rests in the office of governor of Louisiana, 1699-1974.

3555. Edwards, John Carver. WAR'S PROUD TRADITIONS AND BITTER LEGACIES: THE UNRECONSTRUCTED VIEWS OF A GEORGIA REB. *Southern Studies 1978 17(1): 57-67.* Robert Leonidas Rogers (1847-1927) fought in the Civil War. Later he practiced law, served as a judge, and was a newspaper editor. He became a Republican supporter of President McKinley (1843-1901), and the national Republican ticket, but stayed a Democrat in state politics. Throughout his life he supported various conservative southern and national organizations. He wrote vigorously in defense of the South's activities during the Civil War and complained of biased treatment of the South in textbooks and histories of the war. He actively opposed American entry into the League of Nations and internationalism. Based on primary materials in the Georgia Dept. of Archives and History and on secondary sources; 17 notes.　　　　　　　　　　　　　　　J. Buschen

3556. Ellis, John and Galishoff, Stuart. ATLANTA'S WATER SUPPLY 1865-1918. *Maryland Hist. 1977 8(1): 5-22.* Summarizes the efforts of Atlanta, Georgia, to provide water for its expanding population and businesses. By 1918, public funds had been committed to maintaining an adequate water supply. Bond issues were passed by the public because of fear of contaminated water and fires. Primary materials; 49 notes.　　　G. O. Gagnon

3557. Engstrom, Richard L. THE HALE BOGGS GERRYMANDER: CONGRESSIONAL REDISTRICTING, 1969. *Louisiana Hist. 1980 21(1): 59-66.* In 1969 the US Supreme Court required congressional redistricting in many states to achieve "one man, one vote" representation. However, this quest for fairness actually made it easier for legislatures in one-party states to gerrymander districts for political purposes. This was the case in Louisiana, where Hale Boggs (1914-72), a high-ranking liberal Democrat in the House of Representatives, had barely won reelection in 1968. Amid complaints of intense lobbying by special interests, the state legislature removed a large conservative area of Jefferson Parish from Boggs's district and added to it a more liberal portion of Orleans Parish. Based on Louisiana legislative documents and newspapers; 3 tables, 18 notes.　　　　　　　　　　　　　　D. B. Touchstone

3558. Engstrom, Richard L. HOME RULE IN LOUISIANA—COULD THIS BE THE PROMISED LAND? *Louisiana Hist. 1976 17(4): 431-455.* Louisiana's 1974 constitution provides a model for local government in the United States. The author reviews the history of home rule legislation in the United States, describing the legal mechanisms employed in several states. Focuses on local governance under the Louisiana 1921 constitution, which provided for only limited home rule. The 1974 constitution provides the potential for a revitalized and strengthened system of local government, greatly expanding local government initiative in government structure and organization as well as taxation. Whether this potential is realized will depend on attitudes and behavior of local officials and state legislators and judges. Therefore, the full impact of the new constitution will not be known for several years. Based on primary and secondary sources; 100 notes.
　　　　　　　　　　　　　　　　　　　　　R. L. Woodward

3559. Engstrom, Richard L. and O'Connor, Patrick F. RESTRUCTURING THE REGIME: SUPPORT FOR CHANGE WITHIN THE LOUISIANA CONSTITUTIONAL CONVENTION. *Polity 1979 11(3): 440-451.* In 1973-74, a Louisiana State Constitutional Convention successfully revised the three-volume, 254,000-word Constitution of 1921, which had been amended more than 500 times. The author examines the records of the convention and the attitudes of its delegates and concludes that the delegates' involvement in the structural status quo was inversely related to their support for revisions in the mammoth document. 4 tables, 23 notes.
　　　　　　　　　　　　　　　　　　　　　J. C. Billigmeier

3560. Everett, Dianna. THE WETTEST DROUGHT IN THE HISTORY OF TEXAS: A SURVEY OF THE ENFORCEMENT OF THE EIGHTEENTH AMENDMENT AND THE DEAN ACT, 1920-1933. *Panhandle-Plains Hist. Rev. 1979 52: 39-61.* Efforts to end liquor production and consumption in Texas paralleled the development of a national prohibition movement during the early 20th century. Texas joined a growing list of states when in 1918 it enacted a prohibition law, but problems of constitutionality and enforcement undercut its effectiveness. In 1919, Texas legislators passed the Dean Act to supplement the national Volstead Act and insure greater enforcement of prohibition. Too few agents, too many bootleggers, and too much public demand for alcohol forced a repeal of the 18th Amendment in 1933. Based on newspapers and government reports; 101 notes.
M. L. Tate

3561. Faries, Clyde J. CARMACK VERSUS PATTERSON: THE GENESIS OF A POLITICAL FEUD. *Tennessee Hist. Q. 1979 38(3): 332-347.* Traces the fierce 1896 battle for Tennessee's 10th Congressional District to its tragic end. Incumbent Democrat Josiah Patterson's (1837-1904) support for the Gold Standard led to his defeat by Edward Ward Carmack, who was supported by "Private" John Mills Allen (1846-1917), the congressman from Tupelo, Mississippi. The result was contested, exacerbating the feud, which continued until 1908 when Carmack was shot to death in a gunfight with Duncan and Robin Cooper, supporters of Patterson's son Malcolm (1861-1935), then Governor of Tennessee. Primary sources; 59 notes.
W. D. Piersen

3562. Fernandez, José B. and Shofner, Jerrell H. MARTYRS ALL: THE HERO OF KEY WEST AND THE INOCENTES. *Tequesta 1973 33: 30-39.* November 1971 marked the centenary of the execution of eight innocent students in Cuba by Spanish authorities who were trying to stop revolutionaries from gaining popular support. Cuban exiles now living in Miami marked the anniversary by placing caskets at various places in the United States. Based on primary sources; 32 notes.
H. S. Marks

3563. Fifer, J. Valerie. WASHINGTON, D.C.: THE POLITICAL GEOGRAPHY OF A FEDERAL CAPITAL. *J. of Am. Studies [Great Britain] 1981 15(1): 5-26.* Created in the 1790's, the District of Columbia has a complex political geography of sectional tensions, social considerations, and political manipulations that for 180 years insured its status of unique city-state in America. Such considerations account for the reluctance of Congress and, more recently, the state legislatures to grant district residents full political equality by means of a constitutional amendment. But 20th-century changes in the national capital and sociopolitical upheavals in the nation have undermined traditional geopolitics that long perpetuated the district's subservient position. Secondary sources; 5 maps, 14 notes.
H. T. Lovin

3564. Files, W. Dan. OUACHITA-MOREHOUSE DISTRICT COURTS (1812-1972). *North Louisiana Hist. Assoc. J. 1976 7(4): 151-157.* As established by the State Constitution of 1812 and later legislative acts, the Seventh Judicial District was established in 1814 to include all of North Louisiana except Natchitoches Parish. The District's early years are difficult to reconstruct, but James Dunlap appears to have been the first judge; he served from November 1813 to November 1823. Later state constitutions rearranged the judicial districts. In more recent times, Morehouse and Ouachita parishes have been in the multiple-judge Fourth Judicial District. Primary and secondary sources. An appendix contains the names of the judges of the Ouachita-Morehouse district courts from 1868 to 1972. 14 notes.
A. N. Garland

3565. Finger, Bill. WHAT YOU CAN DO: INTERVIEW WITH JOE INGLE. *Southern Exposure 1978 6(4): 88-93.* Joe Ingle, director of the Southern Coalition on Jails and Prisons, emphasizes his role and that of his group in their work of supporting alternatives to imprisonment and on the abolition of the death penalty. The group encourages ordinary citizens to visit prisoners, establish friendships, and then create outside structures in which both parties

can work together for reform. One of the group's main goals is to work through the legislative process to bring about an end to prison construction.
N. Lederer

3566. Fingerhut, Eugene R. TOM WATSON, BLACKS, AND SOUTHERN REFORM. *Georgia Hist. Q. 1976 60(4): 324-343.* Traces the career of the Georgia Populist leader Thomas E. Watson from about 1880 to the early 1900's, focusing on his attitudes toward Negroes. Early in his career he supported limited rights for blacks, especially the opportunity to vote, but later on he reversed his position and became a supporter of Negro disfranchisement because that position was more useful for the reforms he was then advocating. 8 notes.
G. R. Schroeder

3567. Fischer, Le Roy H. OKLAHOMA TERRITORY, 1890-1907. *Chronicles of Oklahoma 1975 53(1): 3-8.* Following the 1889 land rush into the Unassigned Lands, Congress created Oklahoma Territory on 2 May 1890. George W. Steele was appointed the first territorial governor, and by August a general election was held for positions in the territorial legislature. A bitter contest erupted between several towns seeking the capital, and it was not settled until 1910 when Oklahoma City received that prize. Meanwhile, Stillwater secured the Agricultural and Mechanical College, Norman acquired the University, and Edmond accepted the Normal School. By 1895 additional lands taken from Indian reservations were opened to homesteaders, and in the following year Greer County was added. Throughout the territorial period from 1890 to 1907, the Republican Party dominated political office because many settlers were Union Army veterans who profited from the Republican Homestead Act of 1862. Map.
M. L. Tate

3568. Fleming, John E. SLAVERY, CIVIL WAR AND RECONSTRUCTION: A STUDY OF BLACK WOMEN IN MICROCOSM. *Negro Hist. Bull. 1975 38(6): 430-433.* Sketches the lives of three former slaves: Sojourner Truth, Susie King Taylor, and Octavia Rogers Albert. They were black women who struggled against second-class citizenship and expanded their vocation as teachers to work toward the advancement of black people. Notes.
M. J. Wentworth

3569. Florestano, Patricia S. AREAWIDE GOVERNMENT AND MULTIPLE JURISDICTIONS: AN EXAMINATION OF SELECTED COUNTIES IN MARYLAND. *Publius 1980 10(3): 77-99.* Discusses the merits of areawide versus noncentralized patterns of government in four jurisdictions within the state of Maryland: Prince George's, Montgomery, Baltimore, and Howard counties. The first two are examples of noncentralized government, while the second two are examples of areawide government. The question of which form of jurisdiction is more desireable is complex. If citizen participation is important, then centralized government is more desirable. If fiscal equity is important, the answer is relative to the amount of taxes paid. Multiple jurisdictions appear to offer more services. Primary sources; 8 tables, 16 notes.
J. Powell

3570. Flynt, Wayne. RELIGION IN THE URBAN SOUTH: THE DIVIDED RELIGIOUS MIND OF BIRMINGHAM, 1900-1930. *Alabama Rev. 1977 30(2): 108-134.* Social Gospel activism at the turn of the century brought a number of pastors, priests, and rabbis together in overcoming Birmingham's image of a violent, sin city. Considerable success attended their efforts by World War I. Social work and public welfare were advanced, crime reduced, and prostitution controlled. Latent and powerful anti-Catholic and anti-Semitic elements gained ascendancy in the 1920's. Having turned to secular morality, religious leaders opened the door to the politicization of religion and institutional affairs. Primary and secondary sources; 73 notes.
J. F. Vivian

3571. France, Mary Duncan. "A YEAR OF MONKEY WAR": THE ANTI-EVOLUTION CAMPAIGN AND THE FLORIDA LEGISLATURE. *Florida Hist. Q. 1975 54(2): 156-177.* Throughout the 1920's the Florida legislature considered several bills which prohibited the teaching of Darwin's evolutionary theories or any theories which conflicted with fundamentalist theology. William Jennings Bryan, Representative Leo Stalnaker, and Senator W. J. Singletary, and others led the anti-evolutionist forces while the press and educators generally opposed the bills. In 1927 the legislature adopted a resolution calling for investigations of texts used in state supported institutions of higher learning but failed to pass a law prohibiting the teaching of Darwinism in the public schools. The controversy abated by the end of the 1920's, when the political power of the movement disintegrated. Based on primary and secondary sources; 3 photos, 81 notes.                    P. A. Beaber

3572.    Franzoni, Janet Brenner. TROUBLED TIRADER: A PSYCHOBIOGRAPHICAL STUDY OF TOM WATSON. *Georgia Hist. Q. 1973 57(4): 493-510.* Thomas E. Watson (1856-1922), prominent Georgia politician, legislator, congressman, and vice-presidential candidate, was an enigmatic figure. His colorful tirades and efforts ranged in extremes from pro- to anti-black, Catholic, and Jew. Psychological analysis may well hold the key to an understanding of his career. 79 notes.                    D. L. Smith

3573.    Frederickson, Mary. MYRA PAGE: DAUGHTER OF THE SOUTH, WORKER FOR CHANGE. *Southern Changes 1983 5(1): 10-15.* Since the 1920's, author and journalist Myra Page has championed civil rights, labor reform, and antiwar activism, focusing on the human side of broad social issues.

3574.    Fry, Joseph A. SENIOR ADVISER TO THE DEMOCRATIC "ORGANIZATION": WILLIAM THOMAS REED AND VIRGINIA POLITICS, 1925-1935. *Virginia Mag. of Hist. and Biog. 1977 85(4): 445-469.* Historians studying the career of Harry F. Byrd, Sr. have not given enough attention to the role of his closest friend and adviser, William Thomas Reed. During and after Byrd's governorship, Reed's behind-the-scenes activity made him one of the most influential men in Virginia. Based on the Byrd Papers, U. of Virginia, and the Reed Family Papers, Virginia Hist. Soc.; photo, 95 notes.                    R. F. Oaks

3575.    Galant, Debbie. ALONG FOR THE RIDE. *Southern Exposure 1980 8(4): 84-86.* Story of Connie Lynn Kyles, 20, now serving the third year of her 40-50 year sentence for second-degree murder; 1977-80.

3576.    Garrison, Bruce M. WILLIAM HODDING CARTER JR: A DIFFERENT PERSPECTIVE OF THE CRUSADING EDITOR. *Journalism Hist. 1976 3(3): 90-93, 96.* Newspaperman Carter's campaign against political corruption and unfair government, and his work for racial justice from the 1930's to the 1950's, led to several clashes with the authorities in Mississippi.

3577.    Gatlin, Douglas S. PARTY IDENTIFICATION, STATUS, AND RACE IN THE SOUTH: 1952-1972. *Public Opinion Q. 1975 39(1): 39-51.* "This article describes the redistributions in political party identifications that have taken place in the South in the last 20 years and analyzes the changing relationships between status, race, and party in the South compared to the rest of the nation."                    J

3578.    George, Paul. THE EVOLUTION OF MIAMI AND DADE COUNTY'S JUDICIARY, 1896-1930. *Tequesta 1976 36: 28-42.* The development of Miami 1896-1930 was reflected in the development of city and county courts. From the original city court (Municipal Court) and the county court (Circuit Court), a number of courts were created to carry out special functions. Two of the more important and successful were the Criminal Court of Record (county) and the Juvenile Court. Based on primary sources, mainly newspapers and statutes; 80 notes.                    H. S. Marks

3579.    George, Paul S. BOOTLEGGERS, PROHIBITIONISTS AND POLICE: THE TEMPERANCE MOVEMENT IN MIAMI, 1896-1920. *Tequesta 1979 39: 34-41.* Surveys attempts to enforce local and state prohibition laws in Miami, Florida, before national prohibition. Based on contemporary local newspaper articles; 34 notes.                    H. S. Marks

3580.    George, Paul S. COLORED TOWN: MIAMI'S BLACK COMMUNITY, 1896-1930. *Florida Hist. Q. 1978 56(4): 432-447.* The early 20th century marked the nadir of race relations in Flori-

da and especially Colored Town, the northwest section of Miami. Blacks were subject to Jim Crow legislation, inadequate municipal services, cramped housing, a dual system of justice, and white terrorism. Nevertheless, black citizens formed church and fraternal organizations, established a business and professional community, and played a vital role in the economic growth of Miami. The black community's troubles worsened in later decades. Based mainly on newspapers, government records, and secondary sources; 3 illus., map, 58 notes.                    P. A. Beaber

3581.    George, Paul S. POLICING MIAMI'S BLACK COMMUNITY, 1896-1930. *Florida Hist. Q. 1979 57(4): 434-450.* A double standard of justice endured in Miami, Florida, caused by racism. The police department accepted and promoted the white standard by the strict enforcement of Negro codes and by semi-official toleration of white terrorism. Such activities were designed to keep blacks in their place: Colored Town. Primary and secondary sources; 68 notes.                    N. A. Kuntz

3582.    George, Paul S. TRAFFIC CONTROL IN EARLY MIAMI. *Tequesta 1977 (37): 3-18.* Traffic congestion in downtown Miami was not controlled until H. H. Arnold was chosen head of the Traffic Bureau in 1925. By the 1930's the Traffic Bureau, given a separate identity, compared favorably with those of other cities.                    H. S. Marks

3583.    Gershman, Carl. THE CIVIL RIGHTS MOVEMENT IN PERSPECTIVE. *Midstream 1975 21(6): 60-68.* Reviews Thomas R. Brooks' *Walls Come Tumbling Down: A History of the Civil Rights Movement-1940-1970* (New Jersey: Prentice Hall, 1974); August Meier and Elliot Rudwick's *CORE: A Study in the Civil Rights Movement, 1942-1968* (New York: Oxford U. Press, 1973); and Jervis Anderson's *A. Philip Randolph: A Biographical Portrait* (New York: Harcourt, Brace, Javanovich, 1973). Traces the career of A. Philip Randolph, an integrationist in the civil rights movement.

3584.    Gibson, Dirk Cameron. HALE BOGGS ON J. EDGAR HOOVER: RHETORICAL CHOICE AND POLITICAL DENUNCIATION. *Southern Speech Communication J. 1981 47(1): 54-66.* Thomas Hale Boggs's 1971 denunciation of J. Edgar Hoover was an unexpected and highly controversial rhetorical act; explains why only Boggs stood in Congress to complain about Federal Bureau of Investigation behavior by considering his public and private motives: Boggs's anger at discovering his home telephone tapped, his philosophy regarding responsible government, and his distrust of Hoover.

3585.    Gilbert, Dee. STREET JOURNALISM. *Southern Exposure 1982 10(2): 17-20.* Activists Elizabeth Cousins Rogers and her husband, Walter "Rog" Rogers, moved to New Orleans, Louisiana, in 1940, after the labor-oriented Commonwealth College in Mena, Arkansas, where Elizabeth taught labor journalism, closed; in an interview, 90-year-old Elizabeth described the Rogers's work as "street journalism" because the pamphlets and leaflets they printed on "unions and progress and good political ideas," were distributed on the streets.

3586.    Gillespie, Robert Gill. VIRGIL ALEXIS GRIFFITH, 1874-1953. *J. of Mississippi Hist. 1975 37(3): 267-278.* Sketches the life and notes the achievements of former Mississippi Chief Justice Virgil Alexis Griffith who served on the Mississippi Supreme Court during 1928-49. After practicing law ca. 1898-1920, he made extensive contributions to the jurisprudence of Mississippi through two books and his work in writing and codifying state laws, but his opinions were his "greatest achievement." Based upon newspapers and court cases; 11 notes.                    J. W. Hillje

3587.    Gilley, B. H. KATE GORDON AND LOUISIANA WOMAN SUFFRAGE. *Louisiana Hist. 1983 24(3): 289-306.* Kate Gordon spearheaded Louisiana's woman suffrage movement. She advocated achieving woman suffrage on a state-by-state basis and opposed a national constitutional amendment because it would undermine the states' control over their own electorates. Gordon argued that suffrage should be extended to white women only. She and her supporters were able to place a woman suffrage amendment on the Louisiana ballot in 1918, but it lost. Based on private papers, suffrage club minutes, and newspapers; 69 notes.

R. E. Noble

3588. Ginzl, David J. PATRONAGE, RACE AND POLITICS: GEORGIA REPUBLICANS DURING THE HOOVER ADMINISTRATION. *Georgia Hist. Q. 1980 64(3): 280-293.* Accusations of irregularities in the dispensing of Republican Party patronage and the collection of "contributions" in Georgia resulted in the rise of political factions that struggled for control of the state party throughout Hoover's presidency. Factions were also based on race. Based on correspondence, newspapers and secondary sources; 30 notes.

G. R. Schroeder

3589. Ginzl, David J. THE POLITICS OF PATRONAGE: FLORIDA REPUBLICANS DURING THE HOOVER ADMINISTRATION. *Florida Hist. Q. 1982 61(1): 1-19.* Herbert Hoover's presidential sweep in 1928 raised hopes of returning Republicans to state offices. The Depression retarded reorganization efforts. The Hoover administration failed to heal rifts within the state and demonstrated political ineptness in dispensing patronage. Florida state Republican leaders resented outside interference. The result was confusion and division with the loss of all hope for reestablishing the party within the state. Based on the Hoover Presidential Papers (Hoover Presidential Library, West Branch, Iowa), state newspapers, and other sources; 4 fig., 45 notes.

N. A. Kuntz

3590. Giroux, Vincent A., Jr. THE RISE OF THEODORE G. BILBO (1908-1932). *J. of Mississippi Hist. 1981 43(3): 180-209.* Traces the political awakening of the poorer whites of Mississippi and Bilbo's rise to power in state politics with their support. The author describes the state's four distinct topographical regions—the Delta, the prairie region, the Gulf coast, and the hill country—and discusses the political and racial attitudes, factional splits in the state democratic party, and economic aspirations in each region. Political reforms, like the open primary law passed in 1903, allowed Bilbo, a hill country spokesman from the piney woods section, to obtain political support from most rural whites in all sections. Bilbo's colorful and checkered machinations in the state's public offices are sketched. Bilbo became Mississippi's most loved and at the same time most hated leader in the early 20th century.

M. S. Legan

3591. Godoy, Gustavo J. JOSÉ ALEJANDRO HUAU: A CUBAN PATRIOT IN JACKSONVILLE POLITICS. *Florida Hist. Q. 1975 54(2): 196-206.* A naturalized American citizen, José Alejandro Huah (1836-1905) was a successful Jacksonville businessman who involved himself in city politics and became a spokesman for the city's Cuban community. In the 1890's he became increasingly involved in the Cuban freedom movement. He raised money, organized supplies and equipment for expeditions to Cuba, and sponsored Florida appearances of José Martí, a leader in the Cuban freedom movement. Huau spent most of his fortune in the cause of Cuban freedom from Spain and before his death saw the establishment of the Republic of Cuba in 1902. Based on primary and secondary sources; 35 notes.

P. A. Beaber

3592. Goldstein, Jonathan. PREFACE TO THE ISSUE, "GEORGIA'S EAST ASIAN CONNECTION, 1733-1983." *West Georgia Coll. Studies in the Social Sci. 1983 22: ix-xii.* In addition to the post-1865 migrations of Chinese to Georgia and travel by Southerners in the Orient, trade has been an important factor in relations between Georgia and East Asia.

3593. Goode, Thomas H. and Riggs, Agnew M. THE PRIVATE PAPERS OF WEST VIRGINIA'S "BOY SENATOR," RUSH DEW HOLT. *West Virginia Hist. 1974 35(4): 296-318.* The private papers of Rush Dew Holt (1905-1955) include over 400 boxes of correspondence and other chiefly political material. Holt was a Democratic state legislator and US Senator from West Virginia, 1935-41. An anti-New Dealer, Holt became a Republican in 1950 and ran unsuccessfully for several offices thereafter. The Senate papers are the bulk of the collection, dealing with the Works Progress

Administration, the "court-packing" plan of 1937, the neutrality issue, and the growth of presidential power. Based on the Holt papers; 73 notes.

J. H. Broussard

3594. Grafton, Carl. COMMUNITY POWER METHODOLOGY AND ALABAMA POLITICS. *Alabama Hist. Q. 1976 38(4): 271-290.* Examines the methodologies and data used by historians to support the view that Alabama has been politically controlled by an elite. Detailed description of decisionmaking argues for the existence of an elite group. 39 notes.

E. E. Eminhizer

3595. Grafton, Carl. JAMES E. FOLSOM'S FIRST FOUR ELECTION CAMPAIGNS: LEARNING TO WIN BY LOSING. *Alabama Rev. 1981 34(3): 163-183.* Focuses on James (Big Jim) Folsom's four electoral defeats from 1933 to 1942, which served as lessons in strategy and tactics for his two successful gubernatorial campaigns in 1946 and 1954. Losing as a candidate to the state convention of 1933 to determine the state's position on prohibition, he gained valuable publicity in south Alabama. Two races in 1936 and 1938 against New Deal Congressman Henry B. Steagall gained the attention of the state's major newspaper. A subsequent move to north Alabama, which was to have future significance when understood in linking north and south Alabama counties with similar economies, was followed by his first gubernatorial race in 1942. Based on personal interviews with James E. Folsom and others; 57 notes.

C. R. Gunter, Jr.

3596. Grafton, Carl. JAMES E. FOLSOM'S 1946 CAMPAIGN. *Alabama Rev. 1982 35(3): 172-199.* James E. Folsom's successful 1946 campaign for the Alabama governorship employed "down home" techniques that were unusual in Alabama politics, including country music, folksy illustrations, and direct appeals to the people not the politicians. Based on interviews and newspapers; 59 notes.

G. R. Schroeder

3597. Grant, Philip A., Jr. CONGRESSIONAL COMMITTEE CHAIRMEN FROM OKLAHOMA, 1907-1937. *Chronicles of Oklahoma 1979 57(1): 49-54.* Among those Oklahomans who constituted a relatively high percentage of the overall number of committee chairmen were Representatives Bird S. McGuire, William W. Hastings, James V. McClintic, Charles D. Carter, Scott Ferris, Will Rogers, and Wilburn Cartwright, and Senators John W. Herreld, Elmer Thomas, Robert L. Owen, and Thomas P. Gore. Based on government publications; 3 photos, 28 notes.

M. L. Tate

3598. Grant, Philip A., Jr. A TRADITION OF POLITICAL POWER: CONGRESSIONAL COMMITTEE CHAIRMEN FROM OKLAHOMA, 1945-1972. *Chronicles of Oklahoma 1982-83 60(4): 438-447.* From the 79th Congress through the adjournment of the 92d Congress, Oklahoma congressmen played key roles as chairmen of powerful Senate and House committees. Five who chaired major committees or subcommittees were Representatives Jed Johnson, Ed Edmondson, John Jarman, Tom Steed, and Senator Mike Monroney. More renowned were Senators Elmer Thomas and Robert S. Kerr, as well as Representative Carl Albert who became Speaker of the House in 1971. All were Democrats and all sponsored major legislation. Based on congressional documents; 8 photos, 42 notes.

M. L. Tate

3599. Grantham, Dewey. CONCEPTUALIZING THE HISTORY OF MODERN SOUTHERN POLITICS. *Hist. Teacher 1983 17(1): 9-32.* The political culture of the modern South has developed in three stages. Flux and instability marked the era after the Civil War. Blacks and rural whites made the Republican Party a significant factor. But in the aftermath of the Populist political upheaval of the 1890's, the classic Solid South, dominated by the Democratic Party, emerged. The Solid South began to break down in 1948, and its dissolution has continued to the present. Secondary sources; 55 notes.

L. K. Blaser

3600. Grantham, Dewey W. THE CONTOURS OF SOUTHERN PROGRESSIVISM. *Am. Hist. Rev. 1981 86(5): 1035-1059.* An interpretation of Southern Progressivism as a regional phenomenon. The essay examines the origins of the Progressive impulse in the South, the identity and motivation of the Southern Progressives, the pattern of the Progressive campaigns in the Southern states, the confluence of regional and national reforms during the presidency of Woodrow Wilson, and some of the after affects of Progressivism on Southern politics and social attitudes. The interpretation stresses 1) the instrumental role of interest-group politics in Southern Progressivism, 2) the influence of the new commercial and professional classes in the region's reform movements, 3) a classification of the Progressive campaigns in terms of organized efforts to impose social controls, to ameliorate social ills, and to promote social efficiency, and 4) the unifying function of a complex of social values and aspirations that included order, morality, humanitarianism, development, and efficiency. The author suggests that the Progressives were able to function both as agents of modernization and as guardians of Southern tradition. 80 notes.                                       A

3601.   Grasmick, Harold G. RURAL CULTURE AND THE WALLACE MOVEMENT IN THE SOUTH. *Rural Sociol. 1974 39(4): 454-470.* Analysis of the 1968 presidential election results in North Carolina.

3602.   Grayson, A. G. NORTH CAROLINA AND HARRY TRUMAN, 1944-1948. *J. of Am. Studies [Great Britain] 1975 9(3): 283-300.* Analyzes responses in North Carolina to domestic policies of Harry S. Truman, particularly his positions on civil rights, labor, and other controversial issues. The North Carolina electorate at first supported Truman, but he lost support increasingly and was vigorously criticized by some North Carolina Democratic factions. However, he continued to enjoy more support in North Carolina than his contemporaries believed. Based on manuscripts, newspapers, and secondary sources; 76 notes.                     H. T. Lovin

3603.   Greenberg, Kenneth S. REPRESENTATION AND THE ISOLATION OF SOUTH CAROLINA, 1776-1860. *J. of Am. Hist. 1977 64(3): 723-743.* South Carolina, unlike the other colonies, kept the British tradition of virtual, rather than actual, representation. Very few attempts were ever made to provide actual political representation. Instead, South Carolina allowed plural votes and nonresident representatives, and resisted the idea that representatives were obliged to specific constituencies. Virtual representation was possible because the community of interest in South Carolina was homogeneous and direct. Virtual representation in national politics made South Carolina suspicious of opponents, who were seen as self-interested bigots. By 1860 South Carolina's views had forced the state into a rigid posture incapable of dealing with new ideas. Primary and secondary sources; 47 notes.            W. J. W. Leedom

3604.   Greene, Suzanne Ellery. BLACK REPUBLICANS ON THE BALTIMORE CITY COUNCIL, 1890-1931. *Maryland Hist. Mag. 1979 74(3): 203-222.* Failure in Maryland of post-Reconstruction moves to disenfranchise blacks insured continued presence of at least one black Republican member on Baltimore's city council through 1931. Harry Sythe Cummings, John Marcus Cargill, and Hiram Watty before World War I, and William L. Fitzgerald, Warner T. McGuinn, and Walter S. Emerson afterward were regularly reelected from predominantly black wards. All fought for improved status, facilities, and faculty of segregated schools for Negroes, an improved share of patronage jobs for blacks, and against white Democratic attempts to disenfranchise blacks and institute legal residential segregation. Based on Baltimore *City Council Journals,* newspaper accounts, papers of the six councilmen, and interviews with their descendants; chart with 18 notes, 85 notes.
                                                           C. B. Schulz

3605.   Guethlein, Carol. WOMEN IN LOUISVILLE: MOVING TOWARD EQUAL RIGHTS. *Filson Club Hist. Q. 1981 55(2): 151-178.* Concentrates on the Woman Suffrage movement in Louisville and Kentucky. The author relates the role that outside speakers including Frances Wright, Lucy Stone, Elizabeth Cady Stanton, Victoria Woodhull, Susan B. Anthony, Carrie Chapman Catt, Emmaline Pankhurst, and Anna Howard Shaw played in encouraging local efforts. The Kentucky Equal Rights Association led by Laura Clay and the Louisville Woman Suffrage Association sought to improve the lot of women in the state. Their activities led to legislation in 1893 and 1894 that gave women control over their own property for the first time. The most vigorous opponent of the cru-

sade for equal rights was Henry Watterson, editor of the Louisville *Courier-Journal.* Watterson's surprise conversion to the cause in 1918 helped to secure bipartisan support for the federal suffrage amendment in the state legislature in 1920. Based on contemporary newspapers and interviews; 122 notes.                G. B. McKinney

3606.   Guillory, Ferrel. SOUTHERN REPUBLICANS: NOT THAT THEY HATE WATERGATE LESS BUT LOVE THE SOUTHERN STRATEGY MORE. *Southern Voices 1974 1(1): 13-17.* Documents the growth of the Republican Party in the southern states since the 1940's.

3607.   Haas, Edward F. DE LESSEPS S. MORRISON AND THE GOVERNORSHIP: A REASSESSMENT. *Louisiana Studies 1976 15(2): 179-196.* The Louisiana gubernatorial election of 1952 was the turning point in the political career of Mayor deLesseps Story Morrison (1912-64) of New Orleans. The mayor, who had ambitions for the governorship and then national office, made a serious political blunder in 1951 and never recovered from it. By not declaring his candidacy early, Morrison lost the potential support of newspapers and at least two of the important men who later declared their own candidacies for the governorship. By the time Morrison made his decision, he had lost his chance and even his influence. It was procrastination and inactivity, rather than a false move, which frustrated a potentially rich political career. Based on Louisiana newspapers, letters in the Tulane U. Library, and secondary sources; 5 tables, 57 notes.                     J. Buschen

3608.   Hadley, Charles D. and Howell, Susan E. THE SOUTHERN SPLIT TICKET VOTER 1952-76: REPUBLICAN CONVERSION OR DEMOCRATIC DECLINE? Steed, Robert P.; Moreland, Laurence W.; and Baker, Tod A., ed. *Party Politics in the South* (New York: Praeger, 1980): 127-151. Attempts to discover the long-term significance of split ticket voting in the South, especially the question whether split ticket voting for presidential and congressional candidates indicates a halfway house between former Democratic identification and future Republican affiliation, or whether split ticket voting is simply an index of party dealignment. Party identification and attachment tend to be stable, changing more slowly than voting behavior. Based on 1952-76 election data from the University of Michigan Survey Research Center/Center for Political Studies; 7 tables, 33 notes.                     J. Powell

3609.   Hadley, Charles D. SURVEY RESEARCH AND SOUTHERN POLITICS: THE IMPLICATIONS OF DATA MANAGEMENT. *Public Opinion Q. 1981 45(3): 393-401.* With an identical data base—the election studies conducted over the 1952-76 period—scholars arrive at conflicting conclusions about the future politics of the South. One problem is alternative regional definitions. Another problem is the choice to analyze native whites, whites, or all election participants. Based on data presented here, these choices are not neutral; rather, they influence the research findings.                                                   J/S

3610.   Hagy, James William. WITHOUT A PROPER THEATRE: THE MANY CAREERS OF EBENEZER BROOKS. *Register of the Kentucky Hist. Soc. 1982 80(3): 267-280.* Ebenezer Brooks, preacher, doctor, author, teacher, and politician, was in the center of controversy in each of his careers. He was involved in the movement for statehood for Kentucky, although not as significantly as has been claimed. In fact, at the 4th Kentucky statehood convention in 1786, he opposed separation from Virginia. He was no more successful in preventing statehood than he had been in obtaining it earlier. Primary sources; 3 illus., 45 notes.                     J. F. Paul

3611.   Hahn, Nicolas Fischer. FEMALE STATE PRISONERS IN TENNESSEE: 1831-1979. *Tennessee Hist. Q. 1980 39(4): 485-497.* In Tennessee, an independent prison for women was established only gradually, over nearly 100 years. During the Civil War, the sexes were mixed together in the state's penitentiary. Beginning ca. 1880, the separation process occurred in five steps. First, female prisoners were isolated in one part of the penitentiary. Second, in the 1890's, a separate wing was built for them. At the turn of the century women were removed to a separate building. Fourth, in 1930, a cell-house was constructed apart from the main penitentiary but still on the main grounds and administratively dependent. Finally, in 1965, female prisoners were provided with a new and entirely autonomous prison. Primary sources; 45 notes.

J. Powell

3612. Hall, Kermit L. THE CIVIL WAR ERA AS A CRUCIBLE FOR NATIONALIZING THE LOWER FEDERAL COURTS. *Prologue 1975 7(3): 177-186.* At least in their institutional structure, the federal courts proved resistant to the impact of the Civil War and the early years of Reconstruction. "The changes made in 1862 and 1869, and those proposed in 1866, were more cosmetic than substantial." Republicans burdened the federal courts with new jurisdictional obligations, but proved "surprisingly tradition-minded," unwilling to break from their notions of parsimonious government and judicial representation that emphasized regional diversity over central authority. They clung to local judicial representation and circuit riding even when confronted by overcrowded dockets and southern resistance to Reconstruction. Primary and secondary sources; 59 notes.

W. R. Hively

3613. Halliburton, R., Jr. MISSISSIPPI'S CONTRIBUTION TO THE ANTI-EVOLUTION CRUSADE. *J. of Mississippi Hist. 1973 35(2): 175-182.* A legislative battle in Mississippi in 1926 resulted in an anti-evolution law, ultimately invalidated by the Mississippi Supreme Court in 1970. Based on secondary sources; 17 notes.

J. W. Hillje

3614. Hamilton, Holman. KENTUCKY'S TRADITION OF LEADERSHIP: FOUR EXEMPLARS OF THE EARLY DAYS. *Register of the Kentucky Hist. Soc. 1977 75(4): 316-321.* In a Boone Day speech, the author discusses the contributions of four of Kentucky's leading citizens, Isaac Shelby, George Rogers Clark, Henry Clay, and Zachary Taylor.

J. F. Paul

3615. Hamm, Keith E.; Harmel, Robert; and Thompson, Robert J. IMPACTS OF DISTRICTING CHANGE ON VOTING COHESION AND REPRESENTATION. *J. of Pol. 1981 43(2): 544-555.* Texas and South Carolina were two of five Southern states that moved from multi- to single-member districts for their lower legislative houses during the 1970's. In South Carolina, the districting change resulted in a rise in black membership in the House from three in 1973 to 13 in 1975, with most of the increase coming from the formerly large, urban, multimember districts. Black and Mexican-American representation also increased in Texas, especially after Harris, Bexar, and Dallas counties moved to single-member districts in 1973. While the change did not significantly affect the success of the Republican Party in South Carolina, it did increase the propensity for bloc formation and significant outliers from the delegations in both states. Illus., table, 15 notes.

A. W. Novitsky

3616. Hammack, David C. ECONOMIC INTEREST GROUPS AND PATH ANALYSIS: TWO APPROACHES TO THE HISTORY OF POWER. *J. of Interdisciplinary Hist. 1981 11(4): 695-704.* Reviews Carl V. Harris's *Political Power in Birmingham, 1821-1921* (1977), which focuses on the distribution of economic and political power in the city.

C. R. Gunter, Jr.

3617. Hammond, John L. RACE AND ELECTORAL MOBILIZATION: WHITE SOUTHERNERS, 1952-1968. *Public Opinion Q. 1977 41(1): 13-27.* The voting turnout rate among whites in the South has long been lower than elsewhere, but in recent years the gap has diminished. Neither the earlier difference nor the recent southern increase is due to the socioeconomic composition of the regions; rather, the increase has been greatest among southerners who believe that the major parties take distinct stands on racial issues. The change in southern turnout is therefore explained by the increased salience of racial issues, and they can therefore be expected to remain important in southern politics.

J

3618. Hancock, Ruby Jane. JUDGE HENRY HUDSON HANCOCK, 1868-1951. *Tequesta 1974 (34): 21-36.* Judge Henry Hudson Hancock was born in Polk County, Florida, in 1868. He became a teacher, married, and in 1901 homesteaded on the north shore of Lake Okeechobee. Okeechobee County was created in

1915. Hancock served as county judge 1915-22, and was an important county figure in educational, civic, and economic affairs. Based on personal recollections.

H. S. Marks

3619. Hardaway, Roger D. HOWELL EDMUNDS JACKSON: TENNESSEE LEGISLATOR AND JURIST. *West Tennessee Hist. Soc. Papers 1976 (30): 104-119.* Tennessee has had six jurists serve on the bench of the US Supreme Court. One of these was Howell Edmunds Jackson (1832-95), who served a short time (4 March 1893-8 August 1895) before his death. Prior to his appointment to the Supreme Court bench Jackson had served as representative to the state legislature, US Senator, and US Circuit Court Judge, where he gained a reputation as a rigid constructionist and an expert in patent law. While he was not one of the great associate justices, no charge has ever been laid against his integrity. While tending to be biased toward corporations, at the same time he felt that railroads should pay their fair share of taxes. Because of the brevity of his term, plus his low seniority on the Court, he was not assigned important cases. His opinions reveal, however, that he thought the judicial branch of government should leave lawmaking to the legislative branch. He attained several positions of power on the state and federal levels, serving with distinction in each capacity. Thus he stands as an important figure in Tennessee political history. Based largely on US Supreme Court decisions and secondary sources; illus., 118 notes.

H. M Parker, Jr.

3620. Harper, Alan D. DEMOCRATIC DOMINOES. *Rev. in Am. Hist. 1976 4(2): 284-290.* Review article prompted by Robert A. Garson's *The Democratic Party and the Politics of Sectionalism, 1941-1948* (Baton Rouge: Louisiana State U., 1974); discusses the separation of the South from the mainstream of Democratic Party politics and the Dixiecrat revolt, 1941-48.

3621. Harris, Carl V. ANNEXATION STRUGGLES AND POLITICAL POWER IN BIRMINGHAM. ALABAMA, 1890-1910. *Alabama Rev. 1974 27(3): 163-184.* Examines the three-way struggle among city, suburban, and corporate interests over urban annexation and taxation. The city promoted "Greater Birmingham" between 1893 and 1908, when a modest majority of suburbanites were persuaded to the advantages of annexation. The steel industry successfully resisted annexation until 1910. A coalition of reform groups enacted state legislation in 1908 providing no local tax exemptions for businesses. Corporate annexation broadened the city tax base, but another decade passed before the disparity between tax receipts and public expenditures was equalized. Primary and secondary sources; 36 notes.

J. F. Vivian

3622. Harris, Carl V. RIGHT OR LEFT FORK? THE SECTION-PARTY ALIGNMENT OF SOUTHERN DEMOCRATS IN CONGRESS, 1873-1897. *J. of Southern Hist. 1976 42(4): 471-506.* The restored southern Democratic faction soon became one of the largest party-sectional blocs in Congress. It has usually been ascribed the role proposed by Professor C. Vann Woodward, namely, that the southern Democrats confronted a forked road in the 1870's. The right fork led to the economically conservative eastern faction of the Democratic party, and the left fork to the radical agrarian western faction. Choosing the right fork, the southern Democrats became a bulwark of, instead of a menace to, the new order. Using quantitative tests to measure cohesion within blocs and to test likeness between blocs, reveals that, in general as well as on specific issues, the southern Democrats shifted their ties to other factions depending upon the issue being tested. On the crucial economic issues, focal to Woodward's thesis, the southern Democrats maintained a consistent left-fork alliance with the western left fork rather than the eastern right fork.

T. Schoonover

3623. Harris, Ted C. JEANNETTE RANKIN IN GEORGIA. *Georgia Hist. Q. 1974 58(1): 55-78.* Jeannette Rankin (1880-1973) of Montana, the nation's first congresswoman, chose Georgia as a retreat and second home. It became her base of operations for peace and feminism activities. 3 illus., 93 notes.

D. L. Smith

3624. Hatcher, John Henry. THE EDUCATION OF THE THIRTEENTH UNITED STATES CHIEF JUSTICE: FREDERICK MOORE VINSON. *West Virginia Hist. 1978 39(4): 285-323.* Details Vinson's boyhood education, his two years at Kentucky Normal of Louisa, his distinguished senior year at Centre College of Kentucky, and his two years at the Centre Law School. He had a brief flirtation with professional football, but knew that his future lay with the law. Sources include many letters to the author. Based on the author's doctoral dissertation, "Fred Vinson, Congressman from Kentucky, A Political Biography, 1890-1938," volume one of a three-volume biography; 118 notes.                E. P. Stickney

3625. Hatcher, John Henry. FRED VINSON: BOYHOOD AND EDUCATION IN THE BIG SANDY VALLEY. *Register of the Kentucky Hist. Soc. 1974 72(3): 243-261.* Sketches the early life of Frederick Moore Vinson, mentioning his romantic and provincial heritage and education. His two early interests were reading and baseball. Involvement in local law and politics whetted his appetite for a later career in Congress, the Court of Appeals, war-time economic stabilization and mobilization programs, and to appointments as Secretary of the Treasury and Chief Justice of the Supreme Court. 33 notes.                J. F. Paul

3626. Hauser, Robert E. "THE GEORGIA EXPERIMENT": PRESIDENT WARREN G. HARDING'S ATTEMPT TO REORGANIZE THE REPUBLICAN PARTY IN GEORGIA. *Georgia Hist. Q. 1978 62(4): 288-303.* When Warren G. Harding won the presidential election of 1920, he began planning to extend the Republican Party in the South, beginning in Georgia. Many members of the two factions in the existing Georgia party refused to unite behind John Louis Philips, Harding's man. This opposition, plus scandal, led to Republican defeat in the congressional election of 1922. Eventually the experiment failed and the old leadership, particularly Henry Lincoln Johnson, returned to power. Primary sources; 56 notes.                G. R. Schroeder

3627. Havard, William C. INTRANSIGENCE TO TRANSITION: THIRTY YEARS OF SOUTHERN POLITICS. *Virginia Q. Rev. 1975 51(4): 497-521.* Argues that since World War II "political change of great magnitude" has occurred in the South as reflected in the "changing status of the black," "the demise of the one-party system," and the growth of "cosmopolitanism."                O. H. Zabel

3628. Hawks, Joanne V.; Ellis, M. Carolyn; and Morris, J. Byron. WOMEN IN THE MISSISSIPPI LEGISLATURE (1924-1981). *J. of Mississippi Hist. 1981 43(4): 266-293.* Discusses the 44 women who have served in the Mississippi legislature since the adoption of the 19th amendment in 1923. Women have served in every legislature since 1924; seven who served in the 1952-1956 term constituted the largest group to serve at one time. By the 1980 session only one female remained, although on 2 February 1981, a second woman joined the legislature as a result of a special election. The identities of these women, their motivations in running for political office, the problems they faced, their major interests, and their accomplishments are discussed in an attempt to determine how their feminism influenced their attitudes toward their legislative duties, how their male colleagues accepted them, and how the press treated them. Based on questionnaires, interviews, and the daily press; 137 notes.                M. S. Legan

3629. Hawks, Joanne Varner. LIKE MOTHER, LIKE DAUGHTER: NELLIE NUGENT SOMERVILLE AND LUCY SOMERVILLE HOWORTH. *J. of Mississippi Hist. 1983 45(2): 116-128.* An overview of the lives of two Mississippi women who served in the state legislature. Nellie Somerville, the first woman elected to the Mississippi legislature, entered public service in 1923 as representative from Washington County through her earlier interests in the temperance and suffrage movements. She worked continuously to involve women in civic improvement projects and other responsibilities of citizenship. Howorth, the daughter, was elected as a state representative from Hinds County in 1931, but her influence would spread beyond the state's boundaries. Appointed initially to the Board of Veterans' Appeals by President Franklin D. Roosevelt, she became an influential part of the network of women in the federal government who were appointed by Roosevelt in the early years of the New Deal. Returning to Mississippi in 1957, she re-

mains active in public life. Based on an interview with Lucy Somerville Howorth, periodicals, M.A. theses, and secondary sources; 14 notes.                M. S. Legan

3630. Henker, Fred O., III. THE EVOLUTION OF MENTAL HEALTH CARE IN ARKANSAS. *Arkansas Hist. Q. 1978 37(3): 223-239.* Describes the development of facilities and programs for the care of mental illness which began in the 1870's, focusing on the insane asylums, the medical school, and private psychiatric practice. Mentions many names and dates. Primary and secondary sources; illus., 50 notes.                G. R. Schroeder

3631. Herring, George C. and Hess, Gary R. REGIONALISM AND FOREIGN POLICY: THE DYING MYTH OF SOUTHERN INTERNATIONALISM. *Southern Studies 1981 20(3): 247-277.* Rejects the general idea that during most of the 20th century, Southerners have been in the forefront of Americans advocating US involvement in world affairs. Notes that the term "internationalism" has evolved in meaning through this century, and discusses major issues of American relations with other parts of the world. The attitude of Southerners, leaders and masses, has shifted on different issues, but the South has not been consistently internationalist, or even internationalist in a broader sense. 78 notes.                J. J. Buschen

3632. Hilliard, Elbert R. THE LEGISLATIVE CAREER OF FIELDING WRIGHT. *J. of Mississippi Hist. 1979 41(1): 5-23.* One of the most influential political leaders in the state legislature during 1927-38, Fielding Wright was initially elected as senator from Sharkey and Issaquena counties in 1927. In 1931, he moved to the House of Representatives, where he was destined to do his most outstanding work. Serving during the stormy period of Theodore G. Bilbo's second administration and subsequent governors Martin Sennett Conner and Hugh White, Wright played major roles in obtaining favorable highway legislation, enactment of a general sales tax to obtain revenue, the passage of a homestead exemption, and a Balance Agriculture with Industry Program. Retiring from the Mississippi Legislature in 1938, Wright returned to political life as governor in 1946.                M. S. Legan

3633. Hine, Darlene Clark. THE ELUSIVE BALLOT: THE BLACK STRUGGLE AGAINST THE TEXAS DEMOCRATIC WHITE PRIMARY, 1932-1945. *Southwestern Hist. Q. 1978 81(4): 371-392.* After the Texas white primary law was ruled unconstitutional in *Nixon v. Herndon* (1927), the Texas Democratic Party tried every conceivable way of avoiding black voting in primaries. The state NAACP fought a losing battle against exclusion, as the Supreme Court allowed the party, but not the state, to impose a white primary: *Grovey v. Townshend* (1935). Nine years later the Court finally did outlaw a white primary under any pretext, in *Smith v. Allwright* (1944). Through this entire controversy, the state and national NAACP had led the campaign for black participation in Democratic politics. Primary and secondary sources; 49 notes.                J. H. Broussard

3634. Hirsch, Eleanor G. GRANDMA FELTON AND THE U.S. SENATE. *Mankind 1974 4(6): 52-57.* The story of one of the most active women reformers of the 19th and early 20th centuries.                S

3635. Hoder-Salmon, Marilyn. MYRTLE ARCHER MCDOUGAL: LEADER OF OKLAHOMA'S "TIMID SISTERS." *Chronicles of Oklahoma 1982 60(3): 332-343.* Myrtle Archer McDougal joined her attorney husband in Sapulpa during 1904 and within a decade rose to prominence in Oklahoma suffrage, health reform, and women's club movements. Armed with a powerful oratorical style, she promoted reform in women's dress styles; pensions for widowed, abandoned, and divorced mothers; a rural library movement; and a national prohibition crusade. Oil wealth allowed McDougal to pursue these causes almost full time after 1908, and during the following 20 years she served on nationally prestigious committees for the Democratic Party. Based on the Mary McDougal Axelson Collection at the University of Miami; 2 photos, 29 notes.                M. L. Tate

3636. Hoffer, Thomas W. and Butterfield, Gerald A. THE RIGHT TO REPLY: A FLORIDA FIRST AMENDMENT ABERRATION. *Journalism Q. 1976 53(1): 111-116.* The US Supreme Court declared the Florida right to reply statute unconstitutional in 1974. Part of an overall reform attempt, it was passed in 1913. It required newspapers to print a candidate's reply without cost if the newspaper attacked him. It was judged to interfere with the editorial function of the press. Based on primary and secondary sources; 29 notes.                                     K. J. Puffer

3637. Hollman, Kenneth W. ALABAMA'S STATE DEBT, 1920-1965. *Mississippi Q. 1979 32(4): 627-640.* Analyzes the social and economic causes of Alabama's public debt and its major characteristic: a cyclical nature with a sharply upward trend.

3638. Holmes, William F. THE ROOTS OF SOUTHERN POPULISM. *Georgia Hist. Q. 1983 67(4): 489-502.* Reviews Steven Hahn's *The Roots of Southern Populism: Yeoman Farmers and the Transformation of the Georgia Upcountry, 1850-1890* (1983). Commends many of Hahn's findings but criticizes his interpretation of class struggle conflict and the supposed change from precapitalist to capitalist society. Based on Hahn's book and secondary sources; 21 notes.                                     G. R. Schroeder

3639. Hopkins, Anne H. and Lyons, William. TOWARD A CLASSIFICATION OF STATE ELECTORAL CHANGE: A NOTE ON TENNESSEE, 1837-1976. *J. of Pol. 1980 42(1): 209-226.* Analysis of electoral trends in Tennessee shows that the state's political history included four eras of gradual partisan realignment (1837-74; 1876-84; 1912-50; and 1950-present) and one era of no change (1886-1910). The 1886 election illustrates the agrument that statewide statistics mask significant realignments at the county level. At that level, there are five eras of political change that begin with 10 or more counties realigning (1837, 1870, 1886, 1916, and 1948). 3 tables, graph, 22 notes.

A. W. Novitsky

3640. Horgan, James J. HAIL THE PASSING, GUARD THE TOMB: HOW THE LITERACY TESTS BLOCKED BLACK VOTERS. *Southern Exposure 1982 10(4): 62-66.* Literacy tests in reading, writing, constitutional interpretation, and citizenship were racist means of disfranchising Negroes in the South.

3641. Huff, A. V., Jr. URBANE BOURBON: JOSEPH W. BARNWELL AND THE SEARCH FOR A NEW ARISTOCRACY. *Pro. of the South Carolina Hist. Assoc. 1981: 133-141.* Examines the life and career of Joseph W. Barnwell (1846-1930) in an effort to ascertain the role played by the Bourbon aristocracy in the postbellum South. A lawyer and a power in Charleston Democratic politics, Barnwell's greatest influence was as an officer in the St. Cecilia Society during 1874-1922. Based on Barnwell's papers which include a memoir; 12 notes.                     J. W. Thacker, Jr.

3642. Humphrey, David C. PROSTITUTION AND PUBLIC POLICY IN AUSTIN, TEXAS, 1870-1915. *Southwestern Hist. Q. 1983 86(4): 473-516.* In 1870, Austin city fathers unsuccessfully attempted to eliminate prostitution. Instead, they were able only to relegate it to a limited section of the city known as Guy Town. This accommodation lasted until the Progressive era of the early 20th century. In 1913, a new antiprostitution movement began under the direction of Mayor Wooldridge. By rigorously enforcing the state law that prohibited houses of prostitution, Wooldridge eliminated Austin's red-light district. The crusade to end prostitution boosted Austin's image as a progressive city and set an example for other towns to follow. It did not, however, end prostitution in the city. Based on the records of the Austin City Council and on local newspapes; 80 notes, 10 photos, 3 tables, map.     R. D. Hurt

3643. Jackson, Joy J. PROHIBITION IN NEW ORLEANS: THE UNLIKELIEST CRUSADE. *Louisiana Hist. 1978 19(3): 261-284.* Presidential address, 20th Annual Meeting of the Louisiana Historical Association, Alexandria, Louisiana, 10 March 1978. The Louisiana legislature ratified the 18th Amendment in August 1918 by a narrow margin, as north and central Louisiana "dry" interests defeated the "wet" votes of southern Louisiana and New Orleans.

New Orleans opposed prohibition and was a center for bootlegging to dry regions throughout the Gulf South. Many establishments in the city secretly and openly defied the ban on alcoholic beverages. Despite heavy enforcement efforts, wine, beer, and liquor remained widely available throughout the period, and prohibition violation contributed to the rise of organized crime, gangsterism and bribery of public officials in New Orleans as in other large cities. Details enforcement efforts as well as popular opposition and flaunting of prohibition. Primary sources; 86 notes.     R. L. Woodward, Jr.

3644. Jacobs, Jon. HARRIS NECK, GEORGIA: CONSERVATION VS. COMMUNITY. *Southern Exposure 1982 10(3): 42-43.* In 1941 the military took possession of Harris Neck, promising return of the land to the black owners after the military departed; the land instead became Harris Neck National Wildlife Refuge, and the People Organized for Equal Rights, founded in 1971, has lobbied to have the land restored to its rightful owners.

3645. Jarrard, Mary W. EMERGING ERA PATTERNS IN EDITORIALS IN SOUTHERN DAILY NEWSPAPERS. *Journalism Q. 1980 57(4): 606-611.* Reports on the methods and findings of a survey of southern editorials on the Equal Rights Amendment which classified 59.02% of the editorials as "conservative." 2 tables, 46 notes.                                     J. S. Coleman

3646. Jeansonne, Glen. LEANDER PEREZ: A SOUTHERN DEMAGOGUE AND REFORMER. *Louisiana Studies 1975 14(3): 315-323.* Leander Perez held absolute power in Plaquemines Parish, Louisiana, for the better portion of a half century. An ultraconservative demagogue, Perez nevertheless brought some kinds of social reform to his parish. He found jobs for virtually everyone in the parish, made the parish into a miniature welfare state, and completed a long list of public works projects, all without costing the residents of the parish any money. On the other hand, Perez was a single-minded racist who fought continually any efforts at black advancement and integration. Notes that "his was a great talent turned inward." Based on primary and secondary sources; 27 notes.

B. A. Glasrud

3647. Jeansonne, Glen. WHAT IS THE LEGACY OF THE LONGS? AN HISTORIOGRAPHICAL OVERVIEW. *Louisiana Rev. 1980 9(2): 141-149.* Reviews literature on the political career of Huey P. Long, governor of Louisiana, 1928-31.                     S

3648. Jennings, Edward T., Jr. SOME POLICY CONSEQUENCES OF THE LONG REVOLUTION AND BIFACTIONAL RIVALRY IN LOUISIANA. *Am. J. of Pol. Sci. 1977 21(2): 225-246.* Develops and tests propositions about the relationship between certain aspects of political competition and public policy in the American states. Although much of the previous state politics literature has produced mixed results in testing some hypotheses derived from the writings of V. O. Key, this article demonstrates that the cases of Louisiana and Virginia offer a qualified confirmation of much of Key's work. The findings presented in this paper suggest that research directed at the analysis of interstate variation in public policy should not be focused on the closeness of electoral competition per se; rather, it should seek to analyze if, and how, political competition is organized along lines of socio-economic cleavage.                                     J

3649. Jewell, Malcolm E. PARTICIPATION IN SOUTHERN PRIMARIES. Steed, Robert P.; Moreland, Laurence W.; and Baker, Tod A., ed. *Party Politics in the South* (New York: Praeger, 1980): 8-32. Focuses on the development of Republican primaries for statewide offices during 1960-77, a topic virtually ignored by past researchers. Using data from all southern states, seeks to determine such matters as which states have experienced the growth of contested Republican primaries, what the implications of such growth are for the Democratic Party's primary and for the general electoral system, and where the voters in these Republican primaries come from. Also, identifies some aspects of primary politics of both regional and national significance, especially the changing status of the Democratic Party primary in the face of significant levels of participation in the Republican Party primary and increased two-party competition in the region. Based on voting turnout data in state gubernatorial primaries; 7 tables, 10 notes.          J. Powell

3650. Jones, Allen W. THE BLACK PRESS IN THE "NEW SOUTH": JESSE C. DUKE'S STRUGGLE FOR JUSTICE AND EQUALITY. *J. of Negro Hist. 1979 64(3): 215-228.* One of the most politically active and outspoken black editors in Alabama during the 1880's was Jesse C. Duke, founder of the Montgomery *Herald* in 1886. Duke's interest in politics was continuous and his loyalty to the Republican Party never faltered. The courageous stance of his editorials led to his departure from Alabama in fear for his life; he never returned. Based on the Booker T. Washington Papers in the Library of Congress and on the black press of Alabama; 81 notes.          N. G. Sapper

3651. Jones, Lewis P. TWO ROADS TRIED—AND ONE DETOUR. *South Carolina Hist. Mag. 1978 79(3): 206-218.* Examines the influence of four men on the politics of South Carolina in 1875-80, Wade Hampton's moderation, Francis Dawson and Daniel H. Chamberlain's fusion or cooperation, and Martin Witherspoon Gary's "straightoutism."

3652. Jordan, Christine. LAST OF THE JACKSONIANS. *Supreme Court Hist. Soc. Y. 1980: 78-88.* John Archibald Campbell, a native of Georgia, was educated at the University of Georgia and at West Point before being admitted to the Georgia bar in 1829. He developed a very successful private law practice in Alabama and was appointed to the Supreme Court in 1853. He resigned his seat in 1861 and the following year became Assistant Secretary of War for the Confederacy. After the war Campbell returned to private practice with great success and at the time of his death was considered one of the nation's leading lawyers. Campbell was a Jacksonian Democrat whose juridical career on both sides of the bench was marked by strong adherence to state sovereignty, strict construction of federal power, opposition to the power of corporations, and judicial guardianship of individual rights. Based on court records and other primary and secondary sources; illus., 53 notes.          S

3653. Jordan, Daniel P. JOHN RANDOLPH OF ROANOKE AND THE ART OF WINNING ELECTIONS IN JEFFERSONIAN VIRGINIA. *Virginia Mag. of Hist. and Biography 1978 86(4): 389-407.* Analyzes why Randolph (1773-1833) won 14 Virginia congressional races, 1799-1833. Concludes that he was the available and desirable old Republican partisan. Emphasizes voter esteem of his family, character, and electioneering methods over his defense of limited government. Randolph appealed directly to freeholders, using entertaining and enlightening oratory, sociability, and community of interest, particularly in agriculture, that led to an enduring voter attachment to him, and that discounted serious personal deficiencies. 86 notes.          P. J. Woehrmann

3654. Jupiter, Clare. LOST LIVES? A PROFILE OF DEATH ROW. *Southern Exposure 1978 6(4): 76-79.* Most condemned prisoners at the present time are imprisoned on Southern death rows. The historical southern propensity toward lynching appears to be an important factor in the popularity in the South for the death penalty. Most condemned prisoners are black as were most victims of lynchings. Crimes committed by blacks against whites in the South are punished more harshly than crimes committed by whites against anybody. Racial discrimination plays a role in this fact as does the reality that most accused blacks are poor and cannot afford decent legal representation. Illustrated by charts.          N. Lederer

3655. Kagramanov, Iu. M. "BELYE BALAKHONY" [The white cloaks]. *Voprosy Istorii [USSR] 1971 (3): 210-214.* Examines the history of the Ku Klux Klan. Restricted initially to post-Civil War Georgia and Alabama, the secret society grew in the 1920's to envelop the entire country. In 1922 the organization's enormous finances were put in order. Klan members influenced elections, but their importance waned from 1926, although a new wave of Ku Klux Klan terror struck in the 1930's. They aligned themselves with Hitler in the 1940's and were again active in the racist and anti-

communist mood of the mid 1950's. With the growth of the civil rights movement, however, they split into a number of autonomous groups. Secondary sources; 13 notes.          E. R. Sicher

3656. Kambol, Stephen A. SOUTHERN CONGRESSMEN AND THE 1912 ARMY APPROPRIATIONS BILL. *Southern Studies 1980 19(1): 50-64.* Scholars have long debated whether the southern states have a special militaristic mentality. This view can be assessed in view of the Army Appropriations Bill (US, 1912) which included questions of economy and efficiency, the effectiveness of the army, the control and size of the army, enlistment periods, the militia system, and imperialism and militarism. Congressional voting in the House was sharply influenced by party dictates; southern senators were divided in their vote. Although patriotic and believers in a strong defense, the southerners appear to have been no more militaristic than other congressmen in 1912. Based on the Congressional Record for the 62d Congress, 2d Session; 48 notes.
          J. J. Buschen

3657. Kerber, Stephen. JOHN W. TRAMMELL: THE CAREER OF A POLK COUNTY POLITICIAN. *Tampa Bay Hist. 1981 3(1): 17-31.* Biography of John W. Trammell beginning in 1882 with his arrival in Polk County, Florida, from Alabama; his political career began with his election as mayor in 1885; he resigned soon after and in 1886 and 1887 was elected treasurer; in 1888 he was elected to the Florida House of Representatives, and other services followed until his death in 1904.

3658. King, Mrs. Martin Luther, Jr. WHERE DO WE GO FROM HERE. *J. of Intergroup Relations 1975 4(2): 68-74.* Contends at the Southern Policy Conference on the Voting Rights Act of 1965 that the act is still vital to the civil rights movement.

3659. King, David R. THE BRUTALIZATION EFFECT: EXECUTION PUBLICITY AND THE INCIDENCE OF HOMICIDE IN SOUTH CAROLINA. *Social Forces 1978 57(2): 683-687.* In this note we report the results of a study of the effects of execution publicity on the incidence of homicide in a single State, South Carolina. The basic purpose is to see whether the data are consistent with the brutalization hypothesis; the use of the death penalty as a punishment by the state deadens people's respect for life and thus increases the incidence of homicide.          J

3660. Klingman, Peter D. JOSIAH T. WALLS AND BLACK TACTICS OF RACE IN POST CIVIL WAR FLORIDA. *Negro Hist. Bull. 1974 37(3): 242-246.* Examines the political attitudes of the Republican Party and Josiah T. Walls, a black Florida member of the House of Representatives, during and after Reconstruction, 1867-85.

3661. Klingman, Peter D. and Geithman, David T. NEGRO DISSIDENCE AND THE REPUBLICAN PARTY, 1864-1872. *Phylon 1979 40(2): 172-182.* Negro leaders tried to work in a moderate way in and with the Republican Party during 1864-72, to make as many gains for their race as possible. Describes the Southern States Convention in Columbia, South Carolina, October 1871. 41 notes.
          G. R. Schroeder

3662. Klotter, James C. FEUDS IN APPALACHIA: AN OVERVIEW. *Filson Club Hist. Q. 1982 56(3): 290-317.* Presents a detailed overview and analysis of the 19th-century family wars in Kentucky and West Virginia. Prominent among these vendettas were the Hatfield-McCoy feud, the Hargis-Marcum-Cockrell-Callahan feud, and the Rowan County war. Examines a variety of explanations for this violence including those of Henry D. Shapiro, John A. Williams, and Gordon B. McKinney. Finds all previous explanations not comprehensive enough and suggests that the breakdown of the legal system was the primary cause of the family murders. Based on contemporary newspaper accounts.
          G. B. McKinney

3663. Koeniger, A. Cash. THE POLITICS OF INDEPENDENCE: CARTER GLASS AND THE ELECTION OF 1936. *South Atlantic Q. 1981 80(1): 95-106.* In the 1936 presidential election, Carter Glass of Virginia ran considerably behind Franklin D. Roosevelt in vote-gathering. He essentially sat out the campaign because he could not support the New Deal. His role in the election marked the beginning of a hallmark in Virginia politics for the next three decades. Unable to reconcile his conservative convictions with the presidential candidate and national platform of his party, yet wedded to Democratic traditions, Glass took the only course that would enable him to maintain his integrity and remain a Democrat. His conduct met the approval of the Virginia electorate. It would be emulated and refined in the famed "golden silence" of Harry F. Byrd. Based on the Carter Glass Papers and the Harry F. Byrd Papers (both in the University of Virginia), the R. Walton Moore Papers (Franklin D. Roosevelt Library), and contemporary newspaper accounts; 27 notes.                          H. M. Parker, Jr.

3664. Kousser, J. Morgan. POST-RECONSTRUCTION SUFFRAGE RESTRICTIONS IN TENNESSEE: A NEW LOOK AT THE V.O. KEY THESIS. *Pol. Sci. Q. 1973 88(4): 655-683.* Analyzes suffrage restrictions enacted in post-Reconstruction Tennessee. Although the leading authority on southern politics, the late V.O. Key, Jr., suggested that in many states legal restrictions came after suppression of the black vote had become a *fait accompli* through violence and social pressure, the Tennessee example shows that the Key thesis may require modification.                    J

3665. Krane, Dale and Allen, Tip H., Jr. FACTIONAL DURABILITY IN MISSISSIPPI'S GUBERNATORIAL ELECTIONS, 1927-75. Steed, Robert P.; Moreland, Laurence W.; and Baker, Tod A., ed. *Party Politics in the South* (New York: Praeger, 1980): 58-80. Discusses patterns of Democratic factionalism in Mississippi, analyzing how factions may endure over time even in an area where politics may appear discontinuous and chaotic. Studies how electoral support is transferred from one candidate to another over time and how the intense pressure of changing race relations has affected factional persistence in the South. In a narrower sense the focus is on the dynamics of Mississippi politics, but in a broader sense it seeks to enhance understanding of Southern factional politics. Based mainly on secondary sources; 54 notes.              J. Powell

3666. Ladner, Heber. FAREWELL ADDRESS OF THE HONORABLE HEBER LADNER, SECRETARY OF STATE, STATE OF MISSISSIPPI. *J. of Mississippi Hist. 1979 41(2): 121-131.* This speech was delivered to a joint assembly of the Mississippi Legislature on Heber Ladner Day, 27 March 1979, and the presentation is now a part of the oral history collection of the Mississippi Department of Archives and History. A long-time political figure in the state, Ladner entered politics in 1931, but failed in his first race. After seeking the advice of Theodore G. Bilbo, Ladner was elected to the house as representative from Pearl River County in 1936, and became secretary of state after Walker Wood retired. Much of the address is devoted to his observations and reminiscences. Mentions important contributions by the governors from Martin Sennett Conner through Cliff Finch.         M. S. Legan

3667. Land, Guy Paul. JOHN F. KENNEDY'S SOUTHERN STRATEGY, 1956-1960. *North Carolina Hist. Rev. 1979 56(1): 41-63.* The John F. Kennedy 1960 presidential campaign really received its start at the 1956 Democratic Party convention when southern delegates began to perceive the Massachusetts senator as less liberal and less harmful than rival Vice-Presidential nominee Estes Kefauver. Over the next four years Kennedy and his followers designed and followed a "southern strategy" to gain votes for the presidential convention of 1960. They played on the South's antiunionism, fear of labor racketeering, and pride in America's greatness, to win friends and delegates. But the civil rights crises of the late 1950's, the rise of Lyndon Johnson, and the cultivation of southern moderates lost Kennedy the South at the convention, though not the nomination. He recovered and won the majority of southern electoral votes in the election. Based on personal and public papers of Kennedy, Johnson, and Theodore Sorenson, interviews and oral history tapes, newspaper articles, and secondary sources; 12 illus., 90 notes.                    T. L. Savitt

3668. Laska, Lewis L. MR. JUSTICE SANFORD AND THE FOURTEENTH AMENDMENT. *Tennessee Hist. Q. 1974 33(2): 210-227.* Edward Terry Sanford (1865-1930) was one of Tennes-

see's most distinguished jurists. Born in Knoxville of Unionist parents, he graduated from the University of Tennessee and later Harvard Law School, was a strong supporter of higher education, and an outstanding public speaker. After a successful law practice, Sanford was appointed to the US Supreme Court where his most famous decision was his defense of civil liberties in *Gitlow* v. *New York* (US, 1925). Primary and secondary sources; 52 notes.
                                                M. B. Lucas

3669. Latimer, Margaret K. BLACK POLITICAL REPRESENTATION IN SOUTHERN CITIES: ELECTION SYSTEMS AND OTHER CAUSAL VARIABLES. *Urban Affairs Q. 1979 15(1): 65-86.* Notes that after consistently having large numbers of blacks and an equally consistent pattern of political discrimination, change since the Voting Rights Act (US, 1965) has been impressive. Seeks to identify and measure the variables that account for the unevenness of black representation in Alabama, Louisiana, and South Carolina city governments. Evaluates competing hypotheses and concludes that direct elections facilitates while at-large elections hamper, minority political participation; that larger governing bodies and higher percentages of black population also increase black electoral possibilities. Finally, socioeconomic variables are less important than the preceding systemic variables. 3 tables, 11 notes, biblio.                                      L. N. Beecher

3670. Ledbetter, Billy D. THE ELECTION OF LOUIS T. WIGFALL TO THE UNITED STATES SENATE, 1859: A REEVALUATION. *Southwestern Hist. Q. 1973 77(2): 241-254.* Unionist Democrats swept the state and congressional elections in Texas in August 1859. In December the state legislature elected Louis T. Wigfall, the most radical states' righter in Texas, to the U.S. Senate. Discounts the conventional explanation that the turnabout was a repercussion from John Brown's mid-October raid at Harpers Ferry. It was due to a regrouping of the ultra-states'-righters who had controlled the party and dominated state politics during the 1850's and to the careful preparation of the Wigfall supporters for his campaign. 3 tables, 31 notes.       D. L. Smith

3671. Ledbetter, Cal, Jr. THE ANTIEVOLUTION LAW: CHURCH AND STATE IN ARKANSAS. *Arkansas Hist. Q. 1979 38(4): 299-327.* Discusses the history of the Arkansas Antievolution Law (1928) from preliminary legislative attempts to pass such an act, through the 1927 popular campaign which initiated the act and voted it into effect. The court cases involving Mrs. Susan Epperson, a Little Rock biology teacher, which resulted in the Supreme Court declaring the Arkansas law unconstitutional in 1968, are also described. 148 notes.                          G. R. Schroeder

3672. Ledbetter, Cal, Jr. JEFF DAVIS AND THE POLITICS OF COMBAT. *Arkansas Hist. Q. 1974 33(1): 16-37.*

3673. Ledbetter, Cal, Jr. THE OFFICE OF GOVERNOR IN ARKANSAS HISTORY. *Arkansas Hist. Q. 1978 37(1): 44-73.* Traces the development of Arkansas gubernatorial powers and limitations from the organization of the territory in 1819, through the state constitutions of 1836, 1861, 1864, 1868, and 1874, as well as the proposed but defeated constitution of 1917-18. Concludes by comparing the legislative and administrative powers of the president of the United States and the governor of Arkansas. Primary and secondary sources; 128 notes.                    G. R. Schroeder

3674. Lee, David. RURAL DEMOCRATS, EASTERN REPUBLICANS, AND TRADE-OFFS IN TENNESSEE, 1922-1932. *East Tennessee Hist. Soc. Publ. 1976 48: 104-115.* In 1922 Governor Austin Peay and his close advisor Luke Lea divided the Democratic Party in Tennessee into urban and rural factions. Peay took an interest in Eastern Tennessee and his rural faction of the Democratic Party often was supported by eastern Tennessee Republicans. 22 notes.                                        D. A. Yanchisin

3675. Lee, David D. THE SOUTH AND THE AMERICAN MAINSTREAM: THE ELECTION OF JIMMY CARTER. *Georgia Hist. Q. 1977 61(1): 7-12.* Describes how Jimmy Carter's presidential campaign emphasizing human values and attacking strong central government was a product of his southern background. His election demonstrates the new attitude of respect toward the South felt by America as a whole in 1976. Primary and secondary sources; 7 notes.                                    G. R. Schroeder

3676. Lefurgy, William G. BALTIMORE'S WARDS, 1797-1978: A GUIDE. *Maryland Hist. Mag. 1980 75(2): 145-153.* As election districts, administrative units, and self-contained areas of political and social activity ranging from law enforcement to public schools and public health supervision, Baltimore's wards have traditionally served important functions. A brief discussion of the uses wards have served since their inception is followed by a chronology of ward boundary changes from incorporation to the last alteration in 1918. The final section presents a descriptive checklist of extant ward maps since 1822. *Laws of Maryland* and Baltimore *Ordinances;* 31 notes.                        G. J. Bobango

3677. Leslie, James W. FERD HAVIS: JEFFERSON COUNTY'S BLACK REPUBLICAN LEADER. *Arkansas Hist. Q. 1978 37(3): 240-251.* Details the career of Ferdinand Havis (1846-1918), who was born a slave but rose to become a successful barber and businessman as well as leader of the Republican Party in Jefferson County. He held numerous city and county offices and was also a member of the state legislature. Newspapers and other primary sources; 3 illus., 46 notes.                   G. R. Schroeder.

3678. Levine, Marc V. STANDING POLITICAL DECISIONS AND CRITICAL REALIGNMENT: THE PATTERN OF MARYLAND POLITICS, 1872-1948. *J. of Pol. 1976 38(2): 292-325.* Studies voting behavior in Maryland from Reconstruction to the mid-20th century. Seeks to identify stable and unstable periods in Maryland politics and to explain why such trends occurred. Finds that the community impulses of the 19th century which fostered stability were disintegrating. This led to "evanescence of loyalties, declining voter participation, and a realignment in the 1930's." 11 tables, 6 figs., 66 notes.                          R. V. Ritter

3679. Lewis, H. H. Walker. THE LAWYERS' ROUND TABLE OF BALTIMORE. *Maryland Hist. Mag. 1975 70(3): 279-285.* Baltimore lawyers' clubs date from 1852, when the Friday Club and later the Temple Club were organized to promote congeniality among mixed groups of lawyers and professionals, but they did not survive the strains of the Civil War. The modern "Lawyers' Round Table" began with Judge Alfred Salem Niles of the Supreme Bench of Baltimore City in 1911, when he gathered a group of colleagues for regular dinner meetings for the presentation of papers and legal discussion. The original membership was the core of the Baltimore Reform League, which fought to break the Gorman-Rasin political machine in the 1895 election. Niles's group was more diverse both in profession and age than earlier clubs, and its example spawned many similar groups within the Maryland bar, a progeny which often mixes gastronomic intensity with intellectuality as the age of the membership increases. Prohibition presented certain problems for the Round Table meetings, at which few members seem to have been devotees of the "great moral issue" being upheld. Based on minute books of the earlier clubs, correspondence, and secondary works; 1 photo, 13 notes.       G. J. Bobango

3680. Libby, Billy W. SENATOR HIRAM REVELS OF MISSISSIPPI TAKES HIS SEAT, JANUARY-FEBRUARY, 1870. *J. of Mississippi Hist. 1975 37(4): 381-394.* Describes the reactions of the press, some US Senators, and others in 1870 to the news that the Mississippi legislature had elected a Negro, Hiram Revels, to the US Senate. After a three-day debate the Senate agreed to seat him by a vote of 48 to 8. Based on newspapers and the *Congressional Globe;* 21 notes.                               J. W. Hillje

3681. Littlefield, Daniel F., Jr. and Underhill, Lonnie E. DIVORCE SEEKER'S PARADISE: OKLAHOMA TERRITORY, 1890-1897. *Arizona and the West 1975 17(1): 21-34.* Soon after Oklahoma gained territorial status in 1890, the "divorce mill" came into being. A short residency requirement, confusion as to which court had jurisdiction in matters of divorce, and the publicity furnished by lawyers and hotel and boarding house owners made Oklahoma the "divorce center" of the nation. Many lawyers became wealthy and Oklahoma towns prospered from the spending of

temporary, divorce-seeking residents. The campaign of a territorial judge, the veto of legislation by the governor, a federal law lengthening residency requirements for divorce in territories, and a 1906 US Supreme Court decision ended Oklahoma's notorious divorce business. 4 illus., 25 notes.                           D. L. Smith

3682. Lyons, Grant. LOUISIANA AND THE LIVINGSTON CRIMINAL CODES. *Louisiana Hist. 1974 15(3): 243-272.* Discusses the life and career of Edward Livingston, the man largely responsible for the writing and passage of a set of liberal laws, Louisiana's system of criminal law, 1822.

3683. Mackle, Elliott. CYRUS TEED AND THE LEE COUNTY ELECTIONS OF 1906. *Florida Hist. Q. 1978 57(1): 1-18.* Cyrus R. Teed (d. 1908) was founder and leader of the Koreshan Unity, a celibate religious community of socialists, numbering about 200. In 1894 he established a settlement at Estero near Fort Myers in Lee County. By 1904 Teed desired control of county politics as a part of his plan to unite the whole society under his leadership. Opportunity arose in 1906 when he opposed disfranchisement aimed at blacks and Koreshans in county elections by forming the Progressive Liberty Party (PLP). This consisted of Koreshans, socialists, Republicans, and dissatisfied Democrats who voiced political sentiment through their newly formed newspaper, the *American Eagle.* Although defeated politically, Teed still retained followers after the election and was seen as a prophet upon his death in 1908. Based mainly on newspaper sources; illus., 48 notes.

P. A. Beaber/G. Fox

3684. Main, Eleanor C.; Gryski, Gerard S.; and Schapiro, Beth S. DIFFERENT PERSPECTIVES: SOUTHERN STATE LEGISLATORS' ATTITUDES ABOUT WOMEN IN POLITICS. *Social Sci. J. 1984 21(1): 21-28.* Presents results of a 16-state survey polling male and female legislators' opinions on various aspects of women's political participation.

3685. Majors, William R. A RE-EXAMINATION OF V. O. KEY'S *SOUTHERN POLITICS IN STATE AND NATION:* THE CASE OF TENNESSEE. *East Tennessee Hist. Soc. Publ. 1977 49: 117-135.* V. O. Key clearly oversimplified the role of factional politics in Tennessee. He mistakenly attributed a state-wide organization to Edward H. Crump. Actually, Crump had a solid power base in the large Memphis and Shelby County urban area that often combined with the loose old-boy network of Kenneth D. McKellar. Neither Crump nor McKellar determined Tennessee politics. They claimed victories when they won and ignored their losses. Throughout the 20th century, Tennessee politics have been based on the appeal of strong personalities and not on factional or political alliances. 64 notes.                               D. A. Yanchisin

3686. Mallard, Bruce. EXECUTIVE-LEGISLATIVE RELATIONS IN TENNESSEE: A HISTORICAL PERSPECTIVE. *Tennessee Hist. Q. 1981 40(3): 286-298.* Relations between the governor and the legislature in Tennessee have gone through five stages. As was true in most states initially, the governor had little power. In fact, not until the second stage ushered in by the adoption of a new constitution in 1870, which gave him the veto, was the governor's authority increased appreciably. The third stage, which began with the assumption of authority by Democratic Governor Austin Peay, extended from 1922 to 1965 and resulted in executive domination. Stages four and five since then have witnessed a reassertion of legislative independence. Now each branch has a share of governmental responsibility. Mostly interviews and newspaper accounts; 25 notes.                                      C. L. Grant

3687. Mancini, Matthew J. RACE, ECONOMICS, AND THE ABANDONMENT OF CONVICT LEASING. *J. of Negro Hist. 1978 63(4): 339-352.* Analyzes the convict lease system in Georgia as a component of that larger web of law and custom which effectively insured the South's racial hierarchy. Only when the system lost its profitability to the lessees was it finally abandoned. Covers 1868-1909. Based upon records in the Georgia Department of Archives and History; table, 2 fig., 41 notes.          N. G. Sapper

3688. Mann, Kenneth Eugene. BLANCHE KELSO BRUCE: UNITED STATES SENATOR WITHOUT A CONSTITUENCY. *J. of Mississippi Hist. 1976 38(2): 183-198.* Describes the senatorial career of Blanche Kelso Bruce (1841-98), the first black to serve a full term in the US Senate, 1875-81. He did not offer Negroes aggressive leadership, but he did deal with various racial issues. He made his greatest contributions to blacks after he left the Senate. Based on published and unpublished primary sources; 49 notes.
J. W. Hillje

3689. Mann, Kenneth Eugene. JOHN ROY LYNCH: U.S. CONGRESSMAN FROM MISSISSIPPI. *Negro Hist. Bull. 1974 37(3): 238-240.* Examines the life, attitudes, and political speeches of a Mississippi black member of the House of Representatives, 1873-83, John Roy Lynch (1847-1939), an ex-slave who spoke in favor of the Civil Rights Act (1874) and other matters.

3690. Marable, Manning. PATTERNS OF BLACK POLITICAL PROTEST, 1877-1977. *J. of Ethnic Studies 1979 7(1): 57-64.* Review essay of Numan Bartley and Hugh D. Graham's *Southern Politics and the Second Reconstruction* (The Johns Hopkins U. Pr., 1975), Laurence Grossman's *The Democratic Party and the Negro: Northern and National Politics, 1868-1892* (U. of Illinois Pr., 1976), William E. Nelson, Jr., and Philip J. Meranto's *Electing Black Mayors: Political Action in the Black Community* (Ohio State U. Pr., 1977), and Howard N. Rabinowitz's *Race Relations in the Urban South, 1865-1890* (Oxford U. Pr., 1978).

3691. Marable, Manning. THE QUESTION OF GENOCIDE. *J. of Intergroup Relations 1982 10(3): 19-29.* Discusses genocide as evidenced by the continuing violence against Negroes in the South, especially of young men and children in Atlanta; surveys some of the literature dealing with the problem.

3692. Marable, Manning. REACTION: THOUGHTS ON THE POLITICAL ECONOMY OF THE NEW SOUTH SINCE THE CIVIL RIGHTS MOVEMENT. *Radical Am. 1978 12(5): 8-21.* A new conservatism has characterized politics in the South since the victories of the civil rights movement of the 1960's; focuses on the South's political economy.

3693. Martin, Robert F. A PROPHET'S PILGRIMAGE: THE RELIGIOUS RADICALISM OF HOWARD ANDERSON KESTER, 1921-1941. *J. of Southern Hist. 1982 48(4): 511-530.* Kester, a Southerner, wavered from a liberal model to socialism-Marxism in the late 1920's and then back to liberalism in the late 1930's. Kester became disillusioned with socialism's model of reality and its tactics. The subsequent 30 years saw him continue his social consciousness, but he lost most of his vitality and enthusiasm. Based on the Kester Papers and Fellowship of Southern Churchman Papers, University of North Carolina, other manuscript collections, and printed primary materials; 63 notes.
T. D. Schoonover

3694. Martin, William C. and Hopkins, Karin. ATLANTA: POLITICAL TRANSFER AND SUCCESSION IN A SOUTHERN METROPOLIS. *J. of Intergroup Relations 1975 4(3): 22-32.* Traces the growing influence of Negroes on politics in Atlanta, Georgia, during the 1940's-74, and discusses the problems facing the city's new mayor, Maynard Jackson.
S

3695. Massey, David. OVER A BARREL: SOUTHERN WATERWAYS AND THE ARMY CORPS OF ENGINEERS. *Southern Exposure 1980 8(1): 92-100.* The thesis that public works are good works, which has dominated federally-supported water programs in the past, is being rapidly and seriously challenged. Southerners are organizing against water project boondoggles in their communities. The effectiveness of these local efforts will determine the course of public works and federal water policies. The chief culprit has been the US Army Corps of Engineers, which often erroneously promised that flooding would stop when a particular project was completed. Singled out as the greatest boondoggle of the Corps is the $2 billion Tennessee-Tombigbee Waterway. 5 photos, map, 4 charts, 18 notes.
H. M. Parker, Jr.

3696. Mathias, Frank F. HENRY CLAY AND HIS KENTUCKY POWER BASE. *Register of the Kentucky Hist. Soc. 1980 78(2): 123-139.* Analyzes Henry Clay's efforts to build a political power base in Kentucky during the 1820's and 1830's. Each of his successes at home, paradoxically, contributed to his failure to win the presidency. The economic struggle between the relief and antirelief factions caught Clay in the middle, and his maneuverings in Washington served to polarize Kentucky politics. Whig support for the antirelief forces worked in Kentucky but hurt the party (and Clay) nationally. 3 illus., 35 notes.
J. F. Paul

3697. Matthews, Jean V. LAW AND SOCIETY—NORTH AND SOUTH. *Can. Rev. of Am. Studies [Canada] 1982 13(3): 333-339.* Reviews Michael Stephen Hindus's *Prison and Plantation: Crime, Justice, and Authority in Massachusetts and South Carolina, 1767-1878* (1980) and Paul Finkelman's *An Imperfect Union: Slavery, Federalism, and Comity* (1981). These volumes exemplify historians' growing preoccupation with integrating legal developments into their social and political histories.
H. T. Lovin

3698. Matthews, John M. JULIAN L. HARRIS: THE EVOLUTION OF A SOUTHERN LIBERAL. *South Atlantic Q. 1976 75(4): 483-498.* Eldest son of folklorist Joel Chandler Harris, Julian Harris followed his father into journalism. At various times editor of the Atlanta *Constitution*, the New York-Paris *Herald*, and the Columbus, Georgia *Enquirer-Sun*, Harris made his mark as a Southern Progressive and muckraker. Although no great friend of blacks, Harris won a Pulitzer Prize for his editorials against the Ku Klux Klan. A close friend of H. L. Mencken and an outspoken critic of what he termed the "Protestant Inquisition," Harris never was secure in any southern job despite his extreme proSouth sentiments. In 1957 he violently criticized Eisenhower's use of troops in Little Rock, but, by then, his real influence had vanished. Primary and secondary sources; 36 notes.
W. L. Olbrich

3699. McCash, William B. THOMAS COBB AND THE CODIFICATION OF GEORGIA LAW. *Georgia Hist. Q. 1978 62(1): 9-23.* Thomas R. R. Cobb (1823-62) was a noted Georgia lawyer. Discusses his importance as the compiler of the *Digest of the Laws of Georgia* (1851) and especially as one of the preparers of the *Code of the State of Georgia* (1862). Primary and secondary sources; 31 notes.
G. R. Schroeder

3700. McCleskey, Clifton and Merrill, Bruce. MEXICAN AMERICAN POLITICAL BEHAVIOR IN TEXAS. *Social Sci. Q. 1973 53(4): 785-798.* Compared with Anglos and blacks, Mexican American political behavior in Texas is characterized by low rates of participation. However, on such measures of electoral behavior as party identification, ideological orientation, and political efficacy and alienation, they generally occupy an intermediate position between the other two groups. [The authors] present several different types of data including results from a state-wide survey.
J

3701. McDonald, Laughlin. VOTING RIGHTS ON THE CHOPPING BLOCK. *Southern Exposure 1981 9(1): 89-94.* Chronicles the denial of voting rights to blacks in Edgefield from the 1860's until the Voting Rights Act (US, 1965), and court rulings since 1965 which have continued to limit black voting rights.

3702. McFadyen, Richard E. ESTES KEFAUVER AND THE TRADITION OF SOUTHERN PROGRESSIVISM. *Tennessee Hist. Q. 1978 37(4): 430-443.* Tennessee Senator Estes Kefauver's (1903-63) work on the Senate Subcommittee on Antitrust and Monopoly gives insight into his posture as a southern Progressive. As a true Progressive, Kefauver opposed monopolies and businesses which were overly-protected by government regulations at the expense of the taxpayer. His investigation of the pharmaceutical industry brought him to the forefront of the modern consumer movement. Details the intricacies of the struggle which ultimately led in 1962 to the Kefauver-Harris amendments to the Food, Drug and Cosmetic Act, largely over the opposition of President John F. Kennedy who was allied with the pharmaceutical giants. Based on

Federal documents, particularly the *Congressional Record*, the Kefauver Collection at the University of Tennessee Library and secondary sources; 48 notes.                     H. M. Parker, Jr.

3703. McGovern, James R. HELEN HUNT WEST: FLORIDA'S PIONEER FOR ERA. *Florida Hist. Q. 1978 57(1): 39-53.* Helen Hunt West (1892-1964) in association with the National Women's Party, lectured and wrote on the need for an Equal Rights Amendment. Her major contribution to Florida politics was as a sponsor and supporter of a 1935 election law requiring equal participation by women at all levels of state party organization. A powerful lobbyist for the ERA in the US Congress during 1935-39, she eventually saw the endorsement of ERA by Republican and Democratic national conventions. Based mainly on the Helen Hunt West papers, Schlesinger Library; photo, 72 notes.          P. A. Beaber

3704. McGregor, Robert C. BETWEEN THE TWO WARS: ALABAMA IN THE HOUSE OF REPRESENTATIVES 1849-1861. *Alabama Hist. Q. 1980 42(3-4): 167-200.* Of the 21 men from Alabama serving in the US House of Representatives during 1849-61, 12 were radical Southern rights men and nine were conservatives. Slavery was a crucial issue, and sectional unity was seen as beneficial for preserving this Southern practice. The radicals gained in popularity as tensions between North and South grew. Several situations occurred that made the radicals appear to be the defenders of Southern institutions. Primary sources; 59 notes.

A. Drysdale

3705. McMilen, Neil R. PERRY W. HOWARD, BOSS OF BLACK-AND-TAN REPUBLICANISM IN MISSISSIPPI, 1924-1960. *J. of Southern Hist. 1982 48(2): 205-224.* Long after most Southern "black-and-tan" party organizations were lost to "lily-white" Republican Party organizations and after Perry W. Howard had left Mississippi to reside in Washington, D.C., or elsewhere in the North, Howard wisely played the politics of race to survive politically. From the 1920's until just before his death in 1961, he remained the Republican national committeeman from Mississippi and a perennial black showpiece of the Republican Party. Based on the Warren Harding and Herbert Hoover Papers, NAACP records, materials stored at Federal Records centers, other manuscripts, periodicals, and printed primary sources; 80 notes.

T. Schoonover

3706. Miller, H. Crane. CASTLES IN THE SAND: BUILDING ON BARRIER ISLANDS. *Southern Exposure 1982 10(3): 44-48.* Federal policy such as a willingness to provide flood insurance, roads, and other improvements, has encouraged development of the Barrier Islands, particularly in the South, despite the dangers involved in building on them.

3707. Miller, Marc. THE NUMBERS GAME: A *SOUTHERN EXPOSURE* SPECIAL REPORT. *Southern Exposure 1978 6(4): 25-29.* Statistics indicate that Southern prisons incarcerate a greater proportion of their citizens than do states in other regions of the country. Prison systems in the South are racist; prisoners are unskilled and uneducated; prison conditions in the South are worse than elsewhere. Southern prison systems are engaging in massive construction programs designed to alleviate overcrowding in their prisons, while they neglect appropriations to provide adequate pay for correctional officials and rehabilitative programs for inmates. Illustrated by six charts. Based on data from State documents.

N. Lederer

3708. Miller, Michael V. CHICANO COMMUNITY CONTROL IN SOUTH TEXAS: PROBLEMS AND PROSPECTS. *J. of Ethnic Studies 1975 3(3): 70-89.* Attempts to assess the political prospects for Chicanismo in South Texas. Poverty, illiteracy, substandard housing, and general economic exploitation have prevented interest-oriented political activity until recent years. Anglo techniques of electoral manipulation and illicit use of poll taxes severely hampered attempts at ethnic power-bloc formation. Other debilitative factors have been strong psychosocial attachments to Mexico by Chicanos, and the cultural trait of *envidia* which weakened any emerging ethnic leadership. Analyzes Crystal City as a "case history of organizational success," with its "revolutions" in 1963 and 1970.

The Anglo establishment was ousted by an all Mexican American slate, which took control of city government and the school system. Reasons for this success centered on catching the Anglo city manager off guard through organized poll tax payments by Chicanos' groups, and the fact that, unlike other South Texas cities, Crystal City had a union organization independent of local economic constraints. Finally *La Raza Unida* under José Gutierrez provided solid leadership. Whether other towns will be as successful, however, is dubious at this time. Primary and secondary sources; 20 notes.

G. J. Bobango

3709. Miller, Robert D. SAMUEL FIELD PHILLIPS: THE ODYSSEY OF A SOUTHERN DISSENTER. *North Carolina Hist. Rev. 1981 58(3): 234-262.* Samuel Field Phillips (1824-1903) of Chapel Hill, North Carolina, represented the best in Southern postwar Republicanism. An antebellum Whig legislator and opponent of secession, Phillips became a strong supporter of the Southern war effort until it became clear that the war could not be won. His advocacy of a negotiated settlement demonstrated the start of Phillips's transformation, always based on principle, to Republicanism. As a political leader in 1865 and 1866 he helped draft and enact a strict Black Code and exclusionary political laws, but, following a four year retirement from politics, Phillips accepted congressional Reconstruction and, in time, Republican racial views. His former allies rejected him, but President Grant appointed him solicitor general of the United States. Phillips argued several important civil rights cases before the Supreme Court, including *Plessy v. Ferguson* (1896). Based on numerous papers of North Carolina political figures, newspapers, and published legislative papers; 10 illus., 57 notes.                                        T. L. Savitt

3710. Mittlebeeler, Emmet V. THE DECLINE OF IMPRISONMENT FOR DEBT IN KENTUCKY. *Filson Club Hist. Q. 1975 49(2): 169-189.* Discusses the Kentucky legislation that outlawed *capias ad satisfaciendum* writs in 1821, thereby ending most imprisonment for debt in the state. This law was the first in the United States, but the practice had been in decline for decades. Relates the Kentucky experience to the general movement to reform debt laws. Based on published government manuscripts; 85 notes.

G. B. McKinney

3711. Moltke-Hansen, David. A BEAUFORT PLANTER'S RHETORICAL WORLD: THE CONTEXTS AND CONTENTS OF WILLIAM HENRY TRESCOT'S ORATIONS. *Pro. of the South Carolina Hist. Assoc. 1981: 120-132.* Examines the career and speeches of William Henry Trescot, who was a scholar, diplomat, and planter during the antebellum period. His speeches, delivered between 1847 and 1889, provide an excellent example of the prevailing views of the ruling aristocracy. Trescot was also known for his studies of US foreign policy during the American Revolution and the administration of George Washington. Based on Trescot's writings and published sources; 23 notes.          J. W. Thacker, Jr.

3712. Montgomery, Sally. THE CASE OF HEROLD ET AL. V. PARISH BOARD OF SCHOOL DIRECTORS ET AL. *North Louisiana Hist. Assoc. J. 1983 14(4): 137-146.* In *Herold et al. v. Parish Board of School Directors et al.*, one of the few cases in which a court ruled against prayer in schools, the Louisiana Supreme Court held that a resolution passed by the Caddo Parish School Board, which directed teachers and principals to begin the school day with religious exercises, was discriminatory. The board had responded to a constituent petition by adopting the resolution in March 1913. 33 notes.                                                J. F. Paul

3713. Moon, John S. and Saunders, Nancy Bowen. THE IDEOLOGICAL CHARACTERISTICS OF PARTY LEADERS: A CASE OF TEXAS. *Western Pol. Q. 1979 32(2): 209-214.* Examines the ideological characteristics of the Democratic and Republican leaders of Texas in terms of ideological content and consensus. Further, their ideological characteristics are compared with those of their counterparts at the national level and in other states. Texas Democratic and Republican leaders are two distinct groups of co-believers, and the ideological concepts of these leaders are similar, with some variations, to those of the national party leaders and California groups. With regard to the ideological consensus, varied characteristics are discovered as the Texas, California, and national party leaders are compared. The variations found in the ideological characteristics of these party leader groups suggest impacts of regionalism on idelogical groupings and a need for further research.

J

3714. Morgan, Cecil. A NEW CONSTITUTION FOR LOUISIANA. *Natl. Civic R. 1974 63(7): 343-356.* "Louisiana has a new constitution effective at midnight, December 31. Even though in the writer's opinion it still has too much legislation in it, structurally the new document represents definitely advanced thinking and opens the door to further improvement."

J

3715. Morris, Allen. FLORIDA LEGISLATIVE COMMITTEES: THEIR GROWTH SINCE 1822. *Florida Hist. Q. 1982 61(2): 125-147.* The Florida legislature expanded its standing committee structure from a small number in 1822 to 75 in 1931. Governmental powers of the various committees have increased due to tradition and court decisions. The system, while offensive to some, remains the only way of adequately dealing with the legislative work load. Focuses on the period since 1931. Based on the Florida House Journal, personal interviews, and other sources; 72 notes, 8 fig., chart.                                   N. A. Kuntz

3716. Morris, Allen and Maguire, Amelia Rea. THE UNICAMERAL LEGISLATURE IN FLORIDA. *Florida Hist. Q. 1980 58(3): 303-314.* Florida had a unicameral legislature from 1822 to 1838. A bicameral legislature came into existence to curtail "rash and imprudent legislation." In 1967 a movement to reestablish the unicameral legislature began because of the power of joint House and Senate committees. Advocates stated that in a unicameral legislature "responsibility" could be placed on specific individuals. Based on newspaper accounts and personal interviews; 42 notes.

N. A. Kuntz

3717. Morse, W. Eugene. "JUDGE" WILLIAM HEMINGWAY, 1869-1937. *J. of Mississippi Hist. 1974 36(4): 338-351.* Sketches the legal and political career of Mississippian William Hemingway (1869-1937). Mayor (1901-05) and City Attorney (1904-10, 1912-21) of Jackson, Hemingway revised the city's municipal ordinances three times and edited the 1917 revised legal code for the state of Mississippi. Professor of law at the University of Mississippi beginning in 1921, he played a prominent role in developing football and other athletic programs there and in the Southeastern Conference athletics. Based on material in the Mississippi Department of Archives and History. Illus., 14 notes.        J. W. Hillje

3718. Moss, Warner. GOVERNOR ALEXANDER G. MCNUTT (1802-1848). *J. of Mississippi Hist. 1980 42(3): 244-251.* This antebellum Democratic governor of Mississippi has been most often studied by literary scholars as the anonymous author of stories on southwestern humor. Reprints excerpts from two biographical references on Alexander G. McNutt to balance critical references in memoirs left by Mississippi Whigs, especially Henry S. Foote. The first, possibly written by McNutt himself, appeared in the *Mississippi Free Trader and Natchez Weekly Gazette* on 27 October 1837, during his gubernatorial campaign. The other was written by his nephew and law partner, Andrew Jackson Paxton, in 1891 in response to a tribute to McNutt by Senator J. Z. George at the Mississippi Constitutional Convention in 1890 and the expressed interest of McNutt's kinsmen in Virginia. 47 notes.

M. S. Legan

3719. Moyers, David M. FROM QUACKERY TO QUALIFICATION: ARKANSAS MEDICAL AND DRUG LEGISLATION, 1881-1909. *Arkansas Hist. Q. 1976 35(1): 3-26.* Arkansas, like many other states in the late 19th and early 20th centuries, moved slowly to regulate medical and pharmaceutical practice. During 1881-1909 the State Legislature, with prodding from local professional organizations, established some control over health care practitioners and drug dispensers. The goal was the elimination of

outright quackery and control of the quality of physicians and pharmacists within the state. Based on medical journal and newspaper articles, legislative records, and secondary sources; 93 notes.

T. L. Savitt

3720. Mugleston, William F. AN ATTEMPT TO BREAK THE "SOLID SOUTH." *Alabama Hist. Q. 1976 38(2): 126-136.* Julian Harris, son of Joel Chandler Harris, strongly opposed the one-party system that developed in the South after 1877. Discusses his efforts during 1909-12 to break the "Solid South" through *Uncle Remus' Magazine* which he edited. 22 notes.        E. E. Eminhizer

3721. Mundt, Robert J. and Heilig, Peggy. DISTRICT REPRESENTATION: DEMANDS AND EFFECTS IN THE URBAN SOUTH. *J. of Pol. 1982 44(4): 1035-1048.* Movements supporting district elections occurred during the 1970's in the majority of southern cities governed by at-large councils. While cities in the 5th Circuit were more likely than others to pursue the reform through litigation, referenda have been more frequent and more successful throughout the region. Previous electoral success rather than the size of the black community encouraged support for district representation. Socioeconomic characteristics of neither the black nor the general community affected attempts to establish such representation. The presence of a black middle class was helpful but not essential to the increase of representational equity once districts replaced at-large councils. 4 tables, 14 notes, biblio.

A. W. Novitsky

3722. Murray, Richard and Vedlitz, Arnold. RACE, SOCIOECONOMIC STATUS, AND VOTING PARTICIPATION IN LARGE SOUTHERN CITIES. *J. of Pol. 1977 39(4): 1064-1072.* Comparison of the voting behavior of black and white populations in Atlanta, New Orleans, Memphis, Dallas, and Houston in 73 major elections during 1960-74 reveals that blacks have now achieved near parity with whites in participation. Voting participation is strongly related to socioeconomic status among whites, but for blacks there is only an extremely modest positive relationship between the two factors. The strong black participation appears to be related to organizing campaigns during the struggle for civil rights. Primary and secondary sources; 2 tables, 10 notes.

A. W. Novitsky

3723. Murray, Richard and Vedlitz, Arnold. RACIAL VOTING PATTERNS IN THE SOUTH: AN ANALYSIS OF MAJOR ELECTIONS FROM 1960 TO 1977 IN FIVE CITIES. *Ann. of the Am. Acad. of Pol. and Social Sci. 1978 (439): 29-39.* Conflicting views have been advanced about racial voting patterns in the South. One contention is that blacks can most easily align with affluent whites rather than with middle or low income whites. A second argument maintains the opposite—that southern blacks' natural allies are more likely to be working class and poor whites. A third view is that one should expect to find shifting electoral coalitions across racial lines. The authors test these hypotheses with data from 109 major electoral contests in five large southern cities. Findings indicate no consistent pattern of biracial voting exists because several factors influence voting alignments in given elections. These include the traditional patterns of racial politics in given localities; the type of election that is being contested; and the race of the candidates themselves. With regard to the latter two points: it is clear, for example, that in partisan contests black-backed candidates do best with low income whites, unless the candidates are black, in which case it is most difficult to get poor whites to vote for any black office seeker. In light of these findings, the simple models of racial voting are deficient because they fail to specify the factors that influence voting patterns in particular contexts.        J

3724. Musselman, Thomas H. A CRUSADE FOR LOCAL OPTION: SHREVEPORT, 1951-1952. *North Louisiana Hist. Assoc. J. 1975 6(2): 59-73.* During the early 1950's, an active political campaign was waged "for the purpose of 'drying up' Shreveport" by members and supporters of the Shreveport Ministerial Association. "Both supporters and opponents of prohibition resorted to unsavory campaign tactics," and the "local option campaign of 1951 and 1952 was bitterly fought and roughly contested." At the end, on election day, 16 July 1952, "voters turned out in near record numbers to defeat prohibition in Shreveport with a total of 28,806 going to the polls." 77 notes.                                    A. N. Garland

3725. Naison, Mark. CLAUDE AND JOYCE WILLIAMS: PILGRIMS OF JUSTICE. *Southern Exposure 1974 1(3/4): 38-50.* Examines the Williams' involvement in social, economic, and political reforms in the South since the 1930's, including the organizing of miners and sharecroppers in Arkansas, the integration of United Auto Workers in Detroit, and participation in voter registration and desegregation campaigns. Discusses their persecution resulting from attempts to combine the Bible with social change. Based on personal interviews; 6 illus.                                    G. A. Bolton

3726. Ness, Gary C. THE *SOUTHERN POLITICS* PROJECT AND THE WRITING OF RECENT SOUTHERN HISTORY. *South Atlantic Q. 1977 76(1): 58-72.* Roscoe C. Martin of the University of Alabama expanded a study of the poll tax in the South into a massive post-World War II evaluation of southern political attitudes. An interviewing team, led by V. O. Key, Jr., worked hard to overcome southern antipathies and secured responses to 240 topics from 11 southern states. The final report—*Southern Politics in State and Nation* (1949)—received immediate popular acclaim, but invited mixed academic criticism. In recent years, the work has proved a springboard for more sophisticated efforts and a standard by which to measure the revisions offered in these efforts. 40 notes.                                    W. L. Olbrich

3727. Niswonger, Richard Leverne. WILLIAM F. KIRBY: ARKANSAS'S MAVERICK SENATOR. *Arkansas Hist. Q. 1978 37(3): 252-263.* Chronicles the career of William Fosgate Kirby (1867-1934), agrarian progressive Arkansas Democratic politician, who, during his term in the US Senate (1916-21) actively opposed many of President Woodrow Wilson's policies. Primary and secondary sources; 2 illus., 26 notes.                                    G. R. Schroeder

3728. Nodyne, Kenneth R. OHIO COUNTY AND THE ELECTION OF 1860: A PRELIMINARY STUDY. *J. of the West Virginia Hist. Assoc. 1980 4(1): 15-23.* Provides a statistical analysis of voter behavior, by ward, for the county (then in Virginia) in the presidential election.

3729. O'Brien, Gail W. POWER AND INFLUENCE IN MECKLENBURG COUNTY, 1850-1880. *North Carolina Hist. Rev. 1977 54(2): 120-144.* Eugene D. Genovese's model of a prewar South dominated by agrarians and C. Vann Woodward's depiction of a postwar South influenced by industrial promoters are not entirely accurate for Mecklenburg County, North Carolina, during 1850-80. A statistical study of powerful and influential people there indicates that wealthy, urban, middle-aged professionals were in power both before and after the Civil War, with little political change. Based on decennial census returns, newspaper articles, and secondary sources; 9 illus., 5 tables, 20 notes.                                    T. L. Savitt

3730. O'Brien, John T. "THE PEOPLE'S FAVORITE": THE RISE AND FALL OF MARTIN MEREDITH LIPSCOMB. *Virginia Cavalcade 1982 31(4): 216-223.* Bricklayer and bachelor Martin Meredith Lipscomb entered local politics in Richmond, Virginia, in 1853 when he unsuccessfully ran for mayor; he was elected city sergeant in 1854, but he met his political demise in 1857, though he remained active on the periphery of politics until his death in 1903.

3731. O'Connor, Jo Ann. SIMON BOLIVAR BUCKNER: KENTUCKY'S MISUNDERSTOOD GENTLEMAN. *Filson Club Hist. Q. 1978 52(4): 363-367.* Simon Bolivar Buckner was a Confederate general and later governor of Kentucky who was also successful in business. Photo.                                    G. B. McKinney

3732. O'Loughlin, John. THE IDENTIFICATION AND EVALUATION OF RACIAL GERRYMANDERING. *Ann. of the Assoc. of Am. Geog. 1982 72(2): 165-184.* Studies gerrymandering in Manhattan, New Orleans, and Mississippi, which involved areas with large black populations.

3733. Painter, Nell and Hudson, Hosea. HOSEA HUDSON: A NEGRO COMMUNIST IN THE DEEP SOUTH. *Radical Am. 1977 11(4): 7-23.* A worker in basic industry in Birmingham, Alabama in the 1920's, Hosea Hudson remained apolitical until drawn into politics through the agitation over the Scottsboro Boys trial in the early 1930's. He became involved in clandestine Communist Party work and has remained an active member of the party until the present. As a political radical, Hudson was involved in Deep South campaigns to organize the unemployed through welfare marches and demonstrations at social welfare offices. His politically extremist activities caused him to lose a succession of factory jobs once his involvement became known. Based on extensive oral interviews with Hudson.                                    N. Lederer

3734. Paulson, Darryl. STAY OUT, THE WATER'S FINE: DESEGREGATING MUNICIPAL SWIMMING FACILITIES IN ST. PETERSBURG, FLORIDA. *Tampa Bay Hist. 1982 4(2): 6-19.* Presents the traditions surrounding the segration of swimming facilities in St. Petersburg and the problems encountered during the 1940's-50's in implementing changes; covers 1930's-59.

3735. Peirce, Neil. THE CHANGING SCENE IN THE SUNSHINE STATE. *New South 1973 28(4): 48-61.* Strengths, weaknesses, and reform efforts of Florida's Democratic and Republican Parties.

3736. Peoples, Morgan. "OLD HOGS AND HOMINY" CHARLES SCHULER: DE SOTO PARISH PLANTER AND STATE PUBLIC SERVANT. *North Louisiana Hist. Assoc. J. 1979 10(2): 18-28.* Charles Schuler (1840-1911) was a planter and political leader in De Soto Parish, Louisiana. Shuler's highest office was commissioner of the State Board of Agriculture, 1905-1911, in which post he attempted to get Louisiana's farmers to diversify. He also founded the Louisiana State Fair in 1906. 4 illus., 32 notes.                                    J. F. Paul

3737. Peoples, Morgan D. EARL KEMP LONG: THE MAN FROM PEA PATCH FARM. *Louisiana Hist. 1976 17(4): 365-392.* Presents a biographical account of Earl K. Long from 1929 to his death in 1960, with particular reference to the time spent on his Winfield Parish farm. Long loved "politicking" and was active in Louisiana politics throughout this period. Based on published sources and personal interviews; 3 photos, 142 notes.                                    R. L. Woodward

3738. Perry, B. G. THE HISTORIAN AS POLITICAL LEADER. *J. of Mississippi Hist. 1974 36(4): 325-336.* In this address delivered before the annual meeting of the Mississippi Historical Society in March 1974, Senator B. G. Perry, President Pro Tempore of the Mississippi State Senate, contends that good historians and good politicians share certain necessary qualities, including "credibility, objectivity, sensitivity, judgment and leadership." Urges historians to use their "trained sensitivity" and "temperate professional judgment" to aid political leaders. Based on secondary sources; 43 notes.                                    J. W. Hillje

3739. Perry, Lewis. UP FROM ANTISLAVERY. *Rev. in Am. Hist. 1976 4(3): 401-408.* Review article prompted by James M. McPherson's *The Abolitionist Legacy: From Reconstruction to the NAACP* (Princeton: Princeton U. Pr., 1976); discusses the abolition movement's influence on race relations in the South, 1870's-1960's.

3740. Peyton, Rupert. REMINISCENCES OF HUEY LONG. *North Louisiana Hist. Assoc. J. 1976 7(4): 161-164.* The author first met Huey P. Long in August 1917, and during the following years their paths crossed many times. The author was a newspaperman in Shreveport and covered Long during the latter's term as governor and his campaign for election to the United States Senate. In 1932, the author was elected as one of four state representatives from Caddo Parrish and fought against many of Long's attempts to have the state legislature "enact dictatorial laws, many of which were directed against the Roosevelt administration." He was still serving on 10 September 1935, when Long died. To the author, "Long was not without his good qualities, although he advocated a form of government that belonged to the Dark Ages."

A. H. Garland

3741.   Phillips, Harry. TENNESSEE AND THE U.S. COURT OF APPEALS: THE SIXTH CIRCUIT. *Tennessee Hist. Q. 1954 33(1): 22-33.* Tennessee has been well represented on the US Court of Appeals for the Sixth Circuit. One of the most famous meetings of the court was the unusual one-week session of the court held in Nashville in 1897. The judges were three of the court's most famous: John Marshall Harlan, known for his support of civil rights in the post-Civil War period; William Howard Taft, the only man to be both Chief Justice of the Supreme Court and President; and Horace H. Lurton, Tennessean and formerly a distinguished law professor at Vanderbilt University. 30 notes.          M. B. Lucas

3742.   Pleasant, John R., Jr. RUFFIN G. PLEASANT AND HUEY P. LONG ON THE PRISONER-STRIPE CONTROVERSY. *Louisiana Hist. 1974 15(4): 357-366.* Contrasts the more humanitarian feelings of Louisiana governor Ruffin G. Pleasant (1916-20) and Huey P. Long (1928-40) in regard to prisoners; examines the controversy erupting over the reinstatement by Long of striped prison uniforms (which Pleasant had abolished) and increased guard brutality during Long's tenure.

3743.   Press, Charles. PARTISAN REALIGNMENT IN THE SOUTH. *Am. Pol. Q. 1976 4(3): 379-382.* Review article prompted by Numan V. Bartley and Hugh D. Graham's *Southern Politics and the Second Reconstruction* (Baltimore: Johns Hopkins University Press, 1976), and Louis M. Seagull's *Southern Republicanism* (New York: Schenkman Publishing Co., 1975). Both works follow a V. O. Key tradition and share the unifying theme of the southern arena of partisan realignment and of the emergence of a new majority coalition. The spotlight focuses on the emergence of southern Republicanism and genuine two-party competition as early as the revolt of the Texas Regulars in 1944. Both books divide the South into deep and rim southern states. Seagull presents a state-by-state analysis, while Bartley and Graham present their data in terms of six stages of postwar historical development.          P. Travis

3744.   Pruitt, Paul M., Jr. DEFENDER OF THE VOTELESS: JOSEPH C. MANNING VIEWS THE DISFRANCHISEMENT ERA IN ALABAMA. *Alabama Hist. Q. 1981 43(3): 171-185.* Narrates the actions of Joseph C. Manning in the fight against disfranchisement of blacks and poor whites in Alabama. Mentions his activities in founding the National Association for the Advancement of Colored People. Based on Manning's letters and articles plus other printed articles; 22 notes.          E. E. Eminhizer

3745.   Prysby, Charles L. ELECTORAL BEHAVIOR IN THE U.S. SOUTH: RECENT AND EMERGING TRENDS. Steed, Robert P.; Moreland, Laurence W.; and Baker, Tod A., ed. *Party Politics in the South* (New York: Praeger, 1980): 101-126. Explores the social and psychological bases of Republican voting behavior. Uses data on presidential and congressional election contests in 1972 and 1976 to ascertain the social sources of Republican voting in terms of race, social class, and geography, and psychological bases. Based on data from the University of Michigan's Survey Research Center/Center for Political Studies; 11 tables, 25 notes.          J. Powell

3746.   Rankin, David C. THE ORIGINS OF BLACK LEADERSHIP IN NEW ORLEANS DURING RECONSTRUCTION. *J. of Southern Hist. 1974 40(3): 417-440.* While more famous black political leaders are recognized in studies of Reconstruction, the large number of secondary black politicians receive no notice. Even the major black political figures appear as people whose life begins during the Civil War. Using quantitative methodology, focuses upon the origins of 240 black leaders of New Orleans. Profiles this leadership around such characteristics as antebellum legal status, residence, birthplace, date of birth, color, occupation, wealth, and literacy. Concludes that the black politician during Reconstruction in New Orleans was already before "the Civil War a young man of unusual ancestry, uncommon wealth, and exceptional ability,"

and in close contact with the most sophisticated black community in mid-19th century America. Based on manuscripts and published primary and secondary sources; 9 tables, 41 notes, appendix.

T. D. Schoonover

3747.   Reuss, Martin. THE ARMY CORPS OF ENGINEERS AND FLOOD-CONTROL POLITICS ON THE LOWER MISSISSIPPI. *Louisiana Hist. 1982 23(2): 131-148.* Contrasts the response to problems of flood control in two parts of the lower Mississippi watershed. In the Atchafalaya basin in south-central Louisiana, reasonable and theoretically valid engineering plans were developed in response to public and Congressional demands following the 1927 Mississippi flood. In the Yazoo basin in northwest Mississippi, seven reservoirs were built, despite analyses demonstrating a negative cost-benefit ratio for the projects, because of the persistence of the congressman from that district and because they fit the depression-induced demand for public works to help the unemployed. Based primarily on Mississippi River Commission papers and other government doucments; 3 maps, 49 notes.          R. E. Noble

3748.   Rice, Bradley R. THE GALVESTON PLAN OF CITY GOVERNMENT BY COMMISSION: THE BIRTH OF A PROGRESSIVE IDEA. *Southwestern Hist. Q. 1975 78(4): 365-408.* Reviews the origins and development of the Commission form of city government in Galveston, Texas. Historians generally argue that governmental reform was necessitated by the great hurricane of 1900, but citizen dissatisfaction and reform efforts were rife before that time. Reform was brought about by the business dominated Deep Water Committee. The Commission plan called for election of at-large delegates, who acted colletively as aldermen and individually as heads of various city departments. The city was elevated and a seawall was built. The Commission system was a great success and was widely adopted across the nation. 37 photos, 52 notes.

V. L. Human

3749.   Ridgway, Whitman H. COMMUNITY LEADERSHIP: BALTIMORE DURING THE FIRST AND SECOND PARTY SYSTEMS. *Maryland Hist. Mag. 1976 71(3): 334-348.* Borrowing concepts of strategic elites (positional and traditional) versus decisional elites from modern community power studies, focuses on the changing power structure of Baltimore from the conservative merchant oligarchy of the postrevolutionary era down to 1806, to the younger professional-skilled artisan polyarchy of the Jacksonian era, 1827-36. Studies the decisionmakers in the salient local concerns of internal improvements and the creation of a water company in the first era, and internal improvements and political reform in the second. "The most important difference . . . was the opportunity for men without ties to the old elite to rise to power during the second party period." While still landed, the new elite was younger, held fewer slaves, and was increasingly drawn from nonmerchant ranks. Primary and secondary works; 4 tables, 36 notes.

G. J. Bobango

3750.   Robbins, Peggy. SAM BASS: THE TEXAS ROBIN HOOD. *Am. Hist. Illus. 1982 17(4): 37.* Brief biography of the short-lived cowboy and bandit, Sam Bass, who became known as "the Texas Robin Hood" because he paid poor folks for various services and friendly gestures with gold pieces he had stolen.

3751.   Robinson, George W. CONSERVATION IN KENTUCKY: THE FIGHT TO SAVE CUMBERLAND FALLS, 1926-1931. *Register of the Kentucky Hist. Soc. 1983 81(1): 25-58.* A long struggle between proponents of a power dam near the Cumberland Falls and those who wished to preserve the cataract in its natural state ended after six bitter years in 1931. Samuel Insull's utility empire was arrayed against the citizens of Corbin, Kentucky, and others who wished to keep the falls untouched. Aided by many who had motives in mind other than pure conservation, and helped by Insull's depression-bred financial problems, conservationists scored a major victory in this lengthy struggle. 6 photos, 92 notes.

J. F. Paul

3752.   Robinson, Lori and DeYoung, Bill. SOCIALISM IN THE SUNSHINE: THE ROOTS OF RUSKIN, FLORIDA. *Tampa Bay Hist. 1982 4(1): 5-20.* Ruskin was a utopian settlement named after

English socialist intellectual John Ruskin and based on the ideas of Dr. George McAnelly Miller, former president of Ruskin colleges in Trenton, Missouri, and Glen Ellyn, Illinois; focuses on the town's settlement by A. P. Dickman and his two brothers and their families, who arrived in central Florida in 1908 from Missouri, and growth until 1967, when the Commongood Society formed by the Dickmans and other early settlers disbanded.

3753. Rodabaugh, Karl. CONGRESSMAN HENRY D. CLAYTON, PATRIARCH IN POLITICS: A SOUTHERN CONGRESSMAN DURING THE PROGRESSIVE ERA. *Alabama Rev. 1978 31(2): 110-120.* As Democratic Congressman from Alabama during 1897-1914, Henry D. Clayton managed to retain his posture as "Patriarch of his people, not the Tribune of his constituents." His inherited sense of family leadership and noblesse oblige, his careful dispensation of patronage, and his selected culling of federal largesse successfully offset the extension of civil service regulations, broadening of the franchise, and heightened local competition. Primary and secondary sources; 14 notes.              J. F. Vivian

3754. Rodabaugh, Karl. "FARMER GENE" TALMADGE AND THE RURAL STYLE IN GEORGIA POLITICS. *Southern Studies 1982 21(1): 83-96.* During 1927-46 Gene Talmadge dominated Georgia politics, using a rural style to evoke intense loyalty from thousands of rural supporters. This style was based on a conglomeration of beliefs. They included emphasis on the value of the small farmer's lifestyle, fundamentalist religious beliefs, habits of macho individualism and personal violence, and localistic lifestyle. Talmadge played on all of these themes regularly in his speeches and campaigns. Based on newspaper accounts; 66 notes.
                                                J. J. Buschen

3755. Rogers, Evelyna Keadle. FAMOUS GEORGIA WOMEN: REBECCA LATIMER FELTON. *Georgia Life 1978 5(1): 34-35.* Rebecca Latimer Felton (1835-1930), a resident of Georgia, was appointed as the first woman senator in the US Senate in 1922; discusses her career in politics and her participation in the fight for woman suffrage, 1860's-1922.

3756. Romero, Sidney J. THE INAUGURAL ADDRESSES OF THE GOVERNORS OF THE STATE OF LOUISIANA: TWEEDLEDUM-AND-TWEEDLEDEE—OR CONTRARIWISE? *Louisiana Hist. 1973 14(3): 229-254.* Attempts to link the rhetorical abilities of the governors of Louisiana with their relative strength as legislative leaders, 1813-1973.

3757. Roper, John Herbert. CHARLES BRANTLEY AYCOCK: A STUDY IN LIMITATION AND POSSIBILITY. *Southern Studies 1977 16(3): 277-291.* Charles Brantley Aycock (1859-1912), the "Education Governor" of North Carolina 1901-05, was known for building schools, establishing libraries, and supporting summer teacher improvement. Yet he campaigned in 1898 and 1900 on a strongly racist platform, supported disenfranchisement of most blacks in the state, and spent less on education for blacks than the previous administration. Aycock claimed he was taking a moderate stance, preserving peace, and preparing blacks for future, fuller participation in the intellectual and political life of the country. Primary and secondary sources; 39 notes.         J. Buschen

3758. Ruffin, Thomas F. THE COMMON MAN FIGHTS BACK. *North Louisiana Hist. Assoc. J. 1976 7(3): 91-95.* The constitution of the State of Louisiana, written in 1812, allowed an individual to vote only if he paid a state tax, or proved he had purchased Federal lands within the state from Congress, for the latter was exempt from taxation for five years. Even though land was inexpensive, those two provisions effectively disenfranchised two-thirds of those men who would otherwise have been qualified to vote. Eventually, "someone discovered" that the state constitution "required only the purchase of lands from the United States, not the continued ownership." Thus, a number of individuals banded together to buy Federal lands, in order to gain the right to vote. Another method used by the common man to gain the vote was developed by John Slidell, who used a forgotten provision of the constitution—voting in

one's county, even though by the 1840's counties existed in name only. The new constitution of 1845, and another written in 1852, gave the common man a more active voice in political matters.
                                                A. N. Garland

3759. Russell, Marvin F. THE RISE OF A REPUBLICAN LEADER: HARMON L. REMMEL. *Arkansas Hist. Q. 1977 36(3): 234-257.* Harmon L. Remmel (1852-1927) was a follower of Arkansas Republican Powell Clayton and eventually succeeded him to the state party leadership in 1913. During his rise to power, Remmel ran for governor three times (1894, 1896, and 1900, all unsuccessfully), served in many party offices and appointive state positions, was involved with patronage, and dealt with state party factions and the Republican Party's relationship with Theodore Roosevelt. Primary and secondary sources; illus., 127 notes.
                                                G. R. Schroeder

3760. Rustin, Bayard, et al. VOTING RIGHTS ACT—AN HISTORICAL PERSPECTIVE. *J. of Intergroup Relations 1975 4(2): 5-37.* Members of the Southern Policy Conference on the Voting Rights Act of 1965 outline the bill's history from 1865 to 1975 and discuss the need to renew the act in order to protect Negro civil rights in the South.

3761. Ryant, Carl. KENTUCKY AND THE MOVEMENT TO REGULATE CHAIN STORES, 1925-1945. *Filson Club Hist. Q. 1983 57(3): 270-285.* Discusses the origins of the 1930, 1934, and 1940 state laws that sought to tax and regulate chain stores in Kentucky. Traces the reasons why each law was found to be unconstitutional. Based on court and legislative records; 29 notes.
                                                G. B. McKinney

3762. St. Hilaire, Joseph M. THE NEGRO DELEGATES IN THE ARKANSAS CONSTITUTIONAL CONVENTION OF 1868: A GROUP PROFILE. *Arkansas Hist. Q. 1974 33(1): 38-69.*

3763. Salamon, Lester M. LEADERSHIP AND MODERNIZATION: THE EMERGING BLACK POLITICAL ELITE IN THE AMERICAN SOUTH. *J. of Pol. 1973 35(3): 615-646.* Data from black political candidates in Mississippi 1965-70 suggests parallels between that state and developing nations. The pattern involves initial action by a "radical, cosmopolitan elite" which is replaced by a conservative, traditional elite when basic goals are achieved. In Mississippi the civil rights movement was led by outsiders whom traditional black leaders opposed. After reenfranchisement the latter gained control of most black leadership positions and limited the pace of change. Nevertheless the old elite's monopoly was challenged and partially diminished, forcing them to take a more progressive stance. The demand for change placed in an electoral context results in continued stability, protection of the traditional system, and a "blunting of the reform impetus." Mississippi illustrates how a new social force can be accommodated into an "orderly progression" of events. 7 tables, 47 notes.
                                                A. R. Stoesen

3764. Sale, Kirkpatrick. THE SUNSHINE SYNDICATE BEHIND WATERGATE. *Southern Exposure 1973 1(2): 2-8.* Discusses the relationship between the Nixon administration, the Watergate Scandal, and politics in the Southern states.

3765. Schapsmeier, Edward L. and Schapsmeier, Frederick H. FARM POLICY FROM FDR TO EISENHOWER: SOUTHERN DEMOCRATS AND THE POLITICS OF AGRICULTURE. *Agric. Hist. 1979 53(1): 352-371.* Analyzes political alignments and policies in the South since the New Deal. Regardless of historic Jeffersonian principles, Southern agriculture pragmatically supported federal intervention, and resisted major reform of the post-New Deal parity-price-support acreage allotment system, thereby giving tacit approval for enlarging other aspects of the welfare state. They also were able to defy Presidents Roosevelt, Truman, and Eisenhower on the substance of farm programs. Added to this, southern power in Congress was evidenced in the use of seniority, parliamentary skill, and adroitness at forming voting coalitions. By such means they played a vital role in the formulation of major farm programs of the period. 71 notes. Comment by John E. Lee, Jr., pp. 372-376.

R. V. Ritter

3766. Schell, John T. A NEW LOOK AT THE OLD DOMINION. *New South 1973 28(1): 18-25.* Virginia has dropped its conservative political views and joined the mainstream of moderate-progressive America.

3767. Schlup, Leonard. ADLAI E. STEVENSON AND THE SOUTHERN CAMPAIGN OF 1892. *Q. Rev. of Hist. Studies [India] 1977-78 17(1): 7-14.* Reviews vice-presidential candidate Adlai E. Stevenson's efforts to hold the solid south for the Democratic Party during the presidential election of 1892. Farm economics were unfavorable; southern states threatened to go for the Populist candidate. Stevenson campaigned in North Carolina and Virginia, and when he was finished, victory was assured. He was successful because: 1) his family was from the south, 2) Republicans and Populists refused to merge, 3) the Populists nominated a northerner repugnant to the south, and 4) he played heavily on the racial issue to overcome economic fears. Ref.                V. L. Human

3768. Schlup, Leonard. ADLAI E. STEVENSON AND THE 1900 CAMPAIGN IN DELAWARE. *Delaware Hist. 1977 17(3): 191-198.* As the vice-presidential candidate on the William Jennings Bryan ticket in 1900, Adlai Stevenson of Illinois played the role of party accommodator, trying to win over conservative Democrats to Bryan. In mid-October, 1900, he made several significant speeches in Delaware, focusing on foreign policy, and ignoring local issues such as the John Addicks controversy in Delaware. Argues that Stevenson was anti-expansionist and, in many ways, backward in his conception of American foreign policy. Although his speeches were well attended, the Democrats did not carry the state. 17 notes.

R. M. Miller

3769. Schott, Matthew J. PROGRESSIVES AGAINST DEMOCRACY: ELECTORAL REFORM IN LOUISIANA, 1894-1921. *Louisiana Hist. 1979 20(3): 247-260.* By advocating such electoral reforms as the secret ballot, stiff requirements for voter registration, and the omission of party labels and symbols, Louisiana Progressives hoped to restrict and discourage lower-class voting. These elitist, moralistic reformers did eventually elect their leader, John M. Parker (1863-1939) to the governorship. However, in the long run they failed either to achieve their brand of electoral reform or to destroy the corrupt Regular Democrats, much of whose strength came from the New Orleans Machine and its poor, illiterate, immigrant supporters. Based on the John M. Parker Papers, Southwestern Archives, University of Southwestern Louisiana, Lafayette, and contemporary New Orleans newspapers, 28 notes.

D. B. Touchstone

3770. Schwartz, Michael; Rosenthal, Naomi; and Schwartz, Laura. LEADER-MEMBER CONFLICT IN PROTEST ORGANIZATIONS: THE CASE OF THE SOUTHERN FARMERS' ALLIANCE. *Social Problems 1981 29(1): 22-36.* Assesses the leader-member conflict in the Southern Farmers' Alliance, "the largest and most active of the protest groups which formed the basis of the Populist Party in the 1890's," and challenges Robert Michels's oligarchy argument that has explained "both the dominance of leadership elites in modern protest movement organizations and the frequent displacement of movement goals within the organizational framework" for 60 years; the alliance leadership's own interests led to the alliance's demise.

3771. Schweninger, Loren. BLACK CITIZENSHIP AND THE REPUBLICAN PARTY IN RECONSTRUCTION ALABAMA. *Alabama Rev. 1976 29(2): 83-103.* Throughout the Reconsturction era the Republican Party in Alabama was badly divided on the question of enfranchising the freedmen. A moderate wing defended the federal government and the 14th and 15th Amendments, while a conservative wing, led in part by Judge J. Haralson, an ex-slave, opposed the Constitution, the Grant Administration, and several federal patronage appointees. Tension and conflict plagued the party, and "doomed Alabama Reconstruction to failure from the outset." Based on primary and secondary sources; 88 notes.

J. F. Vivian

3772. Shankman, Arnold. DOROTHY TILLY, CIVIL RIGHTS, AND THE METHODIST CHURCH. *Methodist Hist. 1980 18(2): 95-108.* Dorothy Tilly (1883-1970), an outstanding woman in the Methodist Church in Georgia, was active in civil rights movements during much of her life. Through organizations of the Methodist Church and other organizations, she worked for the abolition of lynchings, the development of better education for black children, the prevention of race riots, and other civil rights movements. 56 notes.

H. L. Calkin

3773. Shankman, Arnold. A JURY OF HER PEERS: THE SOUTH CAROLINA WOMAN AND HER CAMPAIGN FOR JURY SERVICE. *South Carolina Hist. Mag. 1980 81(2): 102-121.* History of the struggle to allow women to serve on juries in South Carolina from 1921, when the state legislature granted women the right to vote eight months after the 19th Amendment was ratified, but excluded them from serving on juries, until 1967, when a state amendment on jury service for women was ratified.

3774. Shannon, Jasper B. HOW TO STAY ELECTED: A STORY OF LOCAL POLITICAL SUCCESS. *Register of the Kentucky Hist. Soc. 1981 79(2): 162-174.* An essay written in 1949 about John F. Sugg, long-time county clerk of Nicholas County, Kentucky. Discusses how one can get into a local office and stay there for a long period of time. Sugg, first elected in 1909, "retired" in 1922, but returned in 1933 and remained in office until defeated in 1957. Illus., 4 notes.

J. F. Paul

3775. Shelden, Randall G. FROM SLAVE TO CASTE SOCIETY: PENAL CHANGES IN TENNESSEE, 1830-1915. *Tennessee Hist. Q. 1979 38(4): 462-478.* In 1831, Tennessee opened its first state prison with an inmate population predominantly white. With the end of slavery, prison became a kind of substitute for servitude. Blacks came to predominate as inmates, and concomitantly convicts began to be leased out as cheap labor. Similarly, urban working-class children were often placed in training schools to control them and to exploit their labor. Based on the author's unpublished PhD dissertation; 63 notes.

W. D. Piersen

3776. Sherman, Brian. DRAWING THE LINES: A REAPPORTIONMENT PRIMER. *Southern Changes 1983 5(5): 12-18.* Much discrimination remains in the South in jurisdictions where white elites persist in using reapportionment as a means to prevent blacks and other minorities from full political participation; analyzes four 1983 cases involving reapportionment maps submitted to the Department of Justice for preclearance and discusses common methods of reapportionment discrimination.

3777. Shofner, Jerrell H. CUSTOM, LAW, AND HISTORY: THE ENDURING INFLUENCE OF FLORIDA'S "BLACK CODE." *Florida Hist. Q. 1977 55(3): 277-298.* The black codes and Jim Crow laws of the late 19th century gave legal sanction to segregation and white supremacy attitudes which already existed in social custom. The legal justification of segregation eventually crumbled. Racial prejudice still exists but Floridians, for the most part, have rejected the violent repressive segregationist practices of the past. With time, racial equality may be not only the law, but the social custom. Based on government documents, newspapers, and secondary sources; 52 notes.

P. A. Beaber

3778. Simon, Anne L. INEQUALITY UNDER THE LAW: THE LOUISIANA STORY. *Southern Studies 1977 16(3): 293-308.* Discusses women's rights. Louisiana adopted a new constitution in 1974. Article 1, section 3, concerns equal protection before the laws and the prohibition of discriminatory laws. Louisiana Supreme Court decisions since then show that the new constitution is no more effective in equal protection and prevention of sex discrimination than the old constitution or the 14th Amendment of the US Constitution. The Court has ruled that sex discrimination is permissible for a legitimate, reasonable, or significant State purpose; e.g., husbands are regarded as supporters of families, heads of families, and directors of joint property. Based on Louisiana and federal court decisions and on secondary sources; 49 notes.

J. Buschen

3779. Simpson, John A. WELDON HEYBURN AND THE IMAGE OF THE BLOODY SHIRT. *Idaho Yesterdays 1981 24(4): 20-28.* In 1910 Weldon B. Heyburn, Republican senator from Idaho, opposed loaning US military equipment to a reunion of Confederate soldiers. The South accused him of "bloody shirt" sectionalism, a phenomenon popular in the decades after the Civil War. Heyburn's motives were unclear. The northern Republicans in the Senate generally did not support him, and the Senate voted to approve the loan. Based on newspapers; 3 photos, 62 notes.

B. J. Paul

3780. Simpson, William. THE BIRTH OF THE MISSISSIPPI "LOYALIST DEMOCRATS" (1965-1968). *J. of Mississippi Hist. 1982 44(1): 27-45.* Discusses the events leading to the establishment of a Loyalist Democratic faction in 1968 after a predominantly black group from Mississippi, the Freedom Democrats, challenged the seating of the state's regular delegation at the 1964 national convention. Describes the disputes between the state NAACP, led by Aaron Henry, and the Freedom Democratic faction. Moderate black leaders, including Charles Evers, white liberals, including Hodding Carter, III, and state labor leaders, including Claude Ramsey, sought to establish a biracial coalition to either capture or reform the state Democratic machinery. The Loyalist Democrats, composed of the Young Democrats, the Freedom Democrats, the NAACP, the state AFL-CIO, the Prince Hall Masons, and the Mississippi Teachers Association, were able to win recognition and be seated over the state regulars at both the 1968 and the 1972 Democratic national conventions. Based on personal interviews, newspaper accounts, monographs, and dissertations; 49 notes.

M. S. Legan

3781. Sizemore, Margaret Davidson. FREDERICK G. BROMBERG OF MOBILE: ILLUSTRIOUS CHARACTER, 1837-1928. *Alabama Rev. 1976 29(2): 104-112.* Biographical sketch of Frederick G. Bromberg (1837-1928) whose family emigrated to Mobile in 1848. Bromberg was alternately a founder of the state Republican Party, postmaster, lawyer, legislator, congressman, and editor. A champion of black political rights, although not civil rights, Bromberg is best remembered for his vigorously stated exceptions to the southern view of Reconstruction. Based on primary and secondary sources; 27 notes.

J. F. Vivian

3782. Slaunwhite, Jerry. TILLMAN'S LIEUTENANT: JOHN LAURENS MANNING IRBY. *Pro. of the South Carolina Hist. Assoc. 1975: 30-47.* Discusses the political career of John Laurens Manning Irby (1854-1900), focusing on his relationship to Benjamin Ryan Tillman. Despite Irby's apparent success in politics, the author concludes that he was primarily a follower of Tillman, and his career began to decline due to the severance of his relationship to Tillman and his increasing addiction to alcohol. Based on newspapers and secondary sources; 62 notes.          J. W. Thacker, Jr.

3783. Sledge, Broox, comp. THE POST OFFICE HISTORY OF NOXUBEE COUNTY (1834-1965). *J. of Mississippi Hist. 1983 45(2): 124-147.* Lists the 48 different post offices organized in Noxubee County, Mississippi. Provides dates of establishment and termination (only five still exist), the names and tenures of the postmasters, and interesting geographical, biographical, and historical information concerning the citizens and communities where the post offices were located. Based on U.S. Postal Records.

M. S. Legan

3784. Sledge, Broox. A POSTAL HISTORY OF KEMPER COUNTY, 1834-1964. *J. of Mississippi Hist. 1974 36(1): 69-75.* Lists 87 post offices established in Kemper County 1834-1964. Includes date of establishment, name of first postmaster, and date of discontinuance.          J. W. Hillje

3785. Smith, C. Calvin. FROM "SEPARATE BUT EQUAL TO DESEGREGATION": THE CHANGING PHILOSOPHY OF L. C. BATES. *Arkansas Hist. Q. 1983 42(3): 254-270.* Analyzes the career of black journalist Lucious Christopher Bates, focusing on his years as the crusading editor of the *Arkansas State Press* (1941-59), in which he argued for blacks' right to vote in primary elections and for desegregated public education. Based on newspapers and interviews; 56 notes.          G. R. Schroeder

3786. Smith, Dale C. and Voyles, James E. NEW COALITIONS IN ALABAMA VOTING PATTERNS. *Alabama Rev. 1974 27(3): 197-212.* Analyzes current validity of V. O. Key's *Southern Politics* (N.Y.: Alfred A. Knopf, 1949) in relation to voting patterns for state and local offices in the 1970 elections. The "friends and neighbors" phenomenon that once assured candidates home-region loyalty is fading under the impact of increased black participation. There is still no distinct urban vote, and purely local contests continue to reflect traditional behavior. Yet state-wide elections indicate a trend toward economic, social, and sectional issues. Based on official state election returns and secondary sources; 4 maps, 2 charts, 31 notes.          J. F. Vivian

3787. Smith, Hugh, Mrs. LA FAYETTE HOYT DE FRIESE: ALABAMIAN OF FACT AND FICTION. *Alabama Rev. 1974 27(4): 243-262.* From an obscure, impoverished birth in rural Alabama, LaFayette Hoyt DeFriese (1852-1924) rose to become a prominent international lawyer whose elusive career found him serving as counsel to Queen Victoria and Queen Marie of Romania. Concentrates on DeFriese's boyhood, education (he studied under James R. Lowell at Harvard), and early legal career in New York and London. Based on primary and secondary sources.

J. F. Vivian

3788. Smith, W. Elwood and Foley, Douglas E. MEXICANO RESISTANCE TO SCHOOLING IN A SOUTH TEXAS COLONY. *Educ. and Urban Soc. 1978 10(2): 145-176.* Traces the development of Mexican Americans' recognition of their power of resistance against the Anglo power structure in a city in Texas, from the 1930's to 1969, particularly Mexican American resistance in the 1950's and Chicano student activism in the late 1960's.

3789. Snyder, Charles M. HARRIET PREWETT OF YAZOO CITY AND EX-PRESIDENT MILLARD FILLMORE: SHE CARRIED A TORCH WITH A SENSE OF HUMOR. *J. of Mississippi Hist. 1977 39(3): 193-204.* Describes 12 letters written to Millard Fillmore, 1857-60 and 1873, by Mrs. Harriet Nelson Prewett, a widow, poet, editor of the Yazoo City *Whig*, and supporter of Millard Fillmore in the 1856 presidential election. The letters, now kept in the archives of the State University of New York at Oswego, discuss political issues and suggest that she was attracted to him romantically. 10 notes.          J. W. Hillje

3790. Snyder, Robert E. THE CONCEPT OF DEMAGOGUERY: HUEY LONG AND HIS LITERARY CRITICS. *Louisiana Studies 1976 15(1): 61-84.* Huey P. Long (1893-1935) of Louisiana, the most famous of southern demagogues, aroused great criticism from politicians, novelists, and his own family. Long saw himself as an enlightened populist reformer, but others found him self-seeking, deceptive, and a threat to society. Hamilton Basso's novel *Sun in Capricorn* (1942) is one of four major novels in the 1940's which used Long's life to show the evils of demagoguery. The chief character, Gilgo Slade, uses sham, deceit, and blackmail to achieve power. Based on primary and secondary sources; 76 notes.

J. Buschen

3791. Southern Regional Council. AN UPDATE ON VOTING CHANGES IN THE SOUTH. *Southern Changes 1982 (Apr): 5-11.* Summarizes recent reapportionment plans in the South, emphasizing political conflicts over the dilution of minority voting strength.

3792. Staub, Michael E. "WE'LL NEVER QUIT IT." *Southern Exposure 1983 11(1): 42-52.* Describes the efforts of the residents of Bell County, Kentucky, since 1980 to clean up Yellow Creek, which has grown progressively more polluted since the 1920's due to industrial waste.

3793. Stein, Judith. MOVEMENT HISTORY. *Rev. in Am. Hist. 1983 11(3): 460-466.* Reviews Doug McAdam's *Political Process and the Development of Black Insurgency, 1930-1970* (1982), which examines the black civil rights movement from the perspective of social movement theory.

3794. Stein, Judith. "OF MR. BOOKER T. WASHINGTON AND OTHERS": THE POLITICAL ECONOMY OF RACISM IN THE UNITED STATES. *Sci. and Soc. 1974-75 38(4): 422-463.* Examines politics and race relations in the South, 1877-1910, focusing on Populism, Booker T. Washington, and the disfranchisement of Negroes during the first decade of the 20th century.

3795. Stephens, Robert G., Jr. REMARKS. *Richmond County Hist. 1976 8(1): 15-17.* Discusses Georgian William Few's participation in the American Revolution and the Continental Congress, 1771-89, and his political life in New York, 1790-1813.

3796. Tanner, Ralph M. THE WONDERFUL WORLD OF TOM HEFLIN. *Alabama Rev. 1983 36(3): 163-174.* Biography of James Thomas "Cotton Tom" Heflin, US senator from Alabama. 33 notes. G. R. Schroeder

3797. Tarpey, John F. UNCLE CARL. *US Naval Inst. Pro. 1982 108(1): 38-45.* Carl Vinson (1883-1981) of Georgia served in the US House of Representatives from 1914 to 1964, a record for length of service in that body. He served as chairman of the House Armed Services committee for 32 years and became a very powerful voice in defense matters. He was instrumental in seeing that the National Security Act of 1947 was passed, in successfully steering the services and Congress through the difficulties posed by the "revolt of admirals" in 1949, and in successfully challenging the executive branch on numerous occasions, thereby upholding the rights of Congress in certain matters pertaining to the military. He has also been called the "father of the modern two-ocean navy." In return, the navy, in an unprecedented step, named the CVN-70, its newest aircraft carrier, for a living American, Carl Vinson. Secondary sources; 11 notes, 8 photos. A. N. Garland

3798. Tarter, Brent and Kukla, Jon. FRED O. SEIBEL. *Virginia Cavalcade 1977 26(4): 148-161.* Discusses the political cartoons of Frederick O. Seibel for the *Richmond Times-Dispatch,* 1926-68.

3799. Templer, Otis W. INSTITUTIONAL CONSTRAINTS AND WATER RESOURCES: WATER RIGHTS ADJUDICATION IN TEXAS. *Rocky Mountain Social Sci. J. 1973 10(3): 37-45.* Outdated water rights laws hinder effective water resource development and management.

3800. Theisen, Lee Scott. A "FAIR COUNT" IN FLORIDA: GENERAL LEW WALLACE AND THE CONTESTED PRESIDENTIAL ELECTION OF 1876. *Hayes Hist. J. 1978 2(1): 20-30.* General Lew Wallace, author of *Ben Hur,* and a member of the Republican committee to recount the Florida votes in the 1876 presidential election, played a significant role in the electoral outcome of this state, and in the victory of Rutherford B. Hayes. In exchange for his efforts, Wallace's appointment as governor of the New Mexico Territory took almost two years; in the meantime, he became embroiled in Indiana state politics. Offers insight into the contested 1876 presidential election, state politics of the era, and the complicated late 19th-century spoils system. Primary sources; 7 illus., 31 notes. J. N. Friedel

3801. Thomas, Lajeane Gentry. GENERAL PIERRE EVARISTE JEAN BAPTISTE BOSSIER. *North Louisiana Hist. Assoc. J. 1980 11(1): 22-26.* Pierre Bossier was a Creole aristocrat who served as a military leader, planter, member of the Louisiana legislature and the US Congress, but he is best remembered for a tragic duel in which he shot a Whig opponent, General Francois Gainnie, in 1839. Bossier died a few years later at age 47, perhaps a suicide. Based on primary sources including the *Congressional Globe, Niles Weekly Register* and secondary items; 29 notes. J. F. Paul

3802. Thompson, John L. Thompson, William N. CAREERS OF MISSISSIPPI ATTORNEYS GENERAL. *J. of Mississippi Hist. 1973 35(2): 183-191.* An analysis of the careers of the 20 attorneys general of Mississippi 1874-1969, including their birthplace, county of residence, party, family size, religion, age, length of term, and other public offices held. The position of attorney general was a "middle rung" of their careers in legal office at the state or local level. Based on published sources; 11 notes. J. W. Hillje

3803. Treadway, Sandra Gioia. SARAH LEE FAIN: NORFOLK'S FIRST WOMAN LEGISLATOR. *Virginia Cavalcade 1980 30(3): 124-133.* Brief biography of Sarah Lee Fain (1888-1962), focusing on her interest in the Democratic Party, and her election to the House of Delegates in 1923, when she and Democrat Helen T. Henderson became the first women elected in Virginia; she served three terms, later worked for the federal government under Franklin D. Roosevelt, and remained active in politics until her death.

3804. VanWingen, John R. and Parker, Joseph B. MEASURING FRIENDS-AND-NEIGHBORS VOTING. *Am. Pol. Q. 1979 7(3): 367-383.* Although the friends-and-neighbors factor helps explain the results of Democratic primaries in several Southern states, an adequate measure of the phenomenon is conspicuously missing. A procedure for measuring the hometown support, the concentration of that support, and the importance of friends-and-neighbors is developed herein. The 1947 special general election and the 1978 Democratic primaries for the Mississippi U.S. Senate seat are analyzed to show how the measure is better than a previous one, how the importance of friends-and-neighbors in determining election outcomes can be calculated, and how one can detect if the importance is spurious. The analysis demonstrates that friends-and-neighbors was as important in the 1978 first primary as it was in the 1947 special general election. The high importance in the 1978 runoff is partially explained, however, by the emerging North-South cleavage in Mississippi politics. 6 tables, fig., 15 notes, biblio. J

3805. Vaughn, Courtney. THE LEGACY OF HUEY LONG. *Louisiana Hist. 1979 20(1): 93-101.* Reviews the historiography on Huey P. Long to resolve whether he was a demagogue or a reformer. Particular attention is paid to the practical and psychological impact of Long's regime on the people of Louisiana. Concludes that Long was a demagogue, and that his charisma caused his followers to lose their identities "in a collective, mass movement." Secondary sources; 35 notes. L. N. Powell

3806. Vose, Clement E. WHEN DISTRICT OF COLUMBIA REPRESENTATION COLLIDES WITH THE CONSTITUTIONAL AMENDMENT INSTITUTION. *Publius 1979 9(1): 105-126.* A study of the constitutional amendment process by analyzing the procedures being followed to promote an amendment granting congressional representation to the District of Columbia. Another approach would be statehood, but this seems inappropriate. By comparison with the ratification of the 23d Amendment which provided electoral votes for the District of Columbia, determines some of the favorable methods which may be used as well as some of the obstacles faced by virtue of the amendment process itself. 9 notes. Covers 1930-78. R. V. Ritter

3807. Walker, Randolph Meade. THE ROLE OF THE BLACK CLERGY IN MEMPHIS DURING THE CRUMP ERA. *West Tennessee Hist. Soc. Papers 1979 33: 29-47.* Scrutinizes the black community of Memphis, Tennessee, to understand how "Boss" Edward Hull Crump maintained his power from 1927 to 1948 with the aid of black voters. Most blacks supported him because they wanted to, because he was good to them. However, the limited black political participation was greatly influenced by the clergy, which has always been the dominant agent for public opinion within the southern black community. Five ministers from that period were interviewed and gave their perspective. A paternalistic dependency did exist among the black clergy of Memphis and Crump. This subservient position helped to form an atmosphere of complacency among the black preachers in Memphis when it came to matters affecting Crump. Crump knew how to handle the black masses with a few handpicked ministers. While not condoning their actions

of the time, the author says that the clergy, largely uneducated, did provide a quality of leadership in a climate that was both oppressive and exploitative. Based largely on oral interviews with clergy, contemporary newspaper accounts, and secondary sources; 84 notes.
                                                          H. M. Parker, Jr.

3808. Walser, Richard. DAMN LONG TIME BETWEEN DRINKS. *North Carolina Hist. Rev. 1982 59(2): 160-171.* For over a hundred years North and South Carolinians have repeated various versions of a purported duologue exchanged at a meeting of their governors in which one remarks to the other, "It's a damn long time between drinks." Though historians have tried to track the incident back to its origins, none has succeeded. Stories include meetings between James L. Orr of South Carolina and Jonathan Worth of North Carolina in 1867, Zebulon B. Vance and Wade Hampton in the 1870's, and Edward B. Dudley of North Carolina and Pierce M. Butler of South Carolina in 1838. Based on newspapers, historical journals, governors' biographies, and other secondary sources; 15 illus., 21 notes.          T. L. Savitt

3809. Watts, Eugene J. THE POLICE IN ATLANTA, 1890-1905. *J. of Southern Hist. 1973 39(2): 165-182.* Reviews the structure and operation of the Atlanta police department during 1890-1905. Atlanta had a centralized system; substations were requested, but not granted. Policemen were generally selected from the lower middle class. The Board of Police Commissioners had power to reelect or reject each policeman every two years. This system heavily involved the police in politics. The effectiveness of the department in controlling crime cannot be ascertained. Reform efforts near the end of the period revealed considerable corruption. 37 notes.
                                                          V. L. Human

3810. Watts, Eugene J. PROPERTY AND POLITICS IN ATLANTA, 1865-1903. *J. of Urban Hist. 1977 3(3): 295-322.* Examines the property holdings of candidates for local office in Atlanta during 1865-1903. Political candidates had more wealth than the average citizen. Wealthier candidates enjoyed better electoral success than poorer candidates. Also favoring electoral success was long-term city residence, southern birth, and youth. 8 tables, 23 notes.          T. W. Smith

3811. Weisberger, Bernard A. THE CARPETBAGGER: A TALE OF RECONSTRUCTION. *Am. Heritage 1973 25(1): 70-76.* Career of Pinckney B. S. Pinchback, first black Governor of Louisiana.

3812. Welch, Susan and Brown, Buster J. CORRELATES OF SOUTHERN REPUBLICAN SUCCESS AT THE CONGRESSIONAL DISTRICT LEVEL. *Social Sci. Q. 1979 59(4): 732-742.* A study of the bases of support for the resurgence of Republicanism in the southern states on the congressional level. Despite Republican strength on the presidential level, successes have been much more moderate on the congressional. Republicans have failed to penetrate Democratic strongholds in urban areas, black counties, and rural areas. Republican strength, though slowly growing, remains confined to the middle classes, much as it does elsewhere in the nation. Thus speculation concerning pending Republican dominance in the southland seems premature. 3 tables, 8 notes, ref.
                                                          V. L. Human

3813. Wellborn, Charles. THE BIBLE AND SOUTHERN POLITICS. *Religion in Life 1975 44(4): 418-427.* Discusses civil religion in the South in the 1960's and 1970's; mentions political speeches.

3814. Widener, Ralph W., Jr. CHARLES HILLMAN BROUGH. *Arkansas Hist. Q. 1975 34(2): 99-121.* Charles Hillman Brough, governor of Arkansas 1917-21, was native of Mississippi and former resident of Utah. He adopted Arkansas as his home when he began teaching at the state university in 1903. Brough was a staunch Democrat and a former student and personal friend of Woodrow Wilson. Based on primary and secondary sources; illus., 115 notes.          T. L. Savitt

3815. Wiggins, Charles W. ARE SOUTHERN PARTY LEADERS REALLY DIFFERENT? *J. of Pol. 1973 35(2): 487-492.* Tests V. O. Key, Jr.'s argument that under the one-party system, southern

parties and party leaders did little other than handle routine matters. Power tended to reside in unofficial leaders, while elected officials immersed themselves in national affairs. Party organization frequently acted as a clearing house for intraparty differences. Today this pattern remains essentially the same, except that leaders are more concerned with promoting a favorable party image—an activity induced by the developing two-party system in the South. 3 tables, 6 notes.          A. R. Stoesen

3816. Wigginton, Eliot and Thrasher, Sue. TO MAKE THE WORLD WE WANT: AN INTERVIEW WITH DOROTHY COTTON. *Southern Exposure 1982 10(5): 25-31.* Dorothy Cotton discusses her role and work in the Southern Christian Leadership Conference and the situation of black politics in the United States.

3817. Wildgen, John K. THE DETECTION OF CRITICAL ELECTIONS IN THE ABSENCE OF TWO-PARTY COMPETITION. *J. of Pol. 1974 36(2): 465-479.* Applies V. O. Key's concept of critical elections to single-party politics. Uses "geographical shifts in voting patterns" to describe variations in Louisiana Democratic primaries, 1952-64. Demonstrates the possibility of bringing the South "into the mainstream of analysis." 3 tables, 14 notes.
                                                          A. R. Stoesen

3818. Williams, E. Russ, Jr. JOHN RAY: FORGOTTEN SCALAWAG. *Louisiana Studies 1974 13(3): 241-262.* Studies the political career of John Ray over five decades of Louisiana politics, in which he faithfully supported his Republican Party. His scalawaggery destroyed his reputation in Louisiana and marred his record of public involvement. "Ray's accomplishment . . . seem seem inconsequential when compared to his efforts to equalize the black minority with its white counterpart. His efforts for the blacks would have made him a lasting reputation in a later century, but in his lifetime it sealed his infamy." Having supported the party least attuned to the majority, he has been almost forgotten. 92 notes.
                                                          R. V. Ritter

3819. Williams, Marilyn Thornton. PHILANTHROPY IN THE PROGRESSIVE ERA: THE PUBLIC BATHS OF BALTIMORE. *Maryland Hist. Mag. 1977 72(1): 118-131.* In Baltimore the public bath system was not a clear-cut result of urban progressive reform or of simple private philanthropy. They had a semiprivate, semipublic character. Describes the long struggle of the city's Free Public Bath Commission, led by Rev. Thomas Beadenkopf and Eugene Levering, to evince support from the municipal government and the public for public baths. Only when railroad magnate Henry Walters agreed to build four baths at his own expense if the city would then maintain them, did the movement succeed. By 1912 there were five permanent baths, but the era of their greatest use was brief. Increasing numbers of urban families got their own facilities in their homes, and it was not evident that the poor had their morals significantly changed or converted to standards of middle-class cleanliness. As maintenance costs rose and patronage fell, Baltimore closed its baths in 1960. Primary sources; 50 notes.
                                                          G. J. Bobango

3820. Williams, Nudie E. BLACK MEN WHO WORE WHITE HATS: GRANT JOHNSON, UNITED STATES DEPUTY MARSHAL. *Red River Valley Hist. Rev. 1980 5(3): 4-13.* Tells the story of Grant Johnson's service as deputy marshal from 1895 to 1906 in the Northern District of the Indian Territory at Eufala, Creek Nation, and gives a vivid picture of law enforcement in frontier Oklahoma and Texas.

3821. Williams, T. Harry. HUEY, LYNDON, AND SOUTHERN RADICALISM. *J. of Am. Hist. 1973 60(2): 267-293.* The most radical mass movement and the two most radical politicians of recent history were products of an allegedly conservative, undissenting South. The black civil rights movement broke the "enveloping silence" surrounding race relations in the South and may see a greater acceptance of black equality in that region than in the North. Both Huey Long and Lyndon Johnson were products of non-affluent families in historically radical sections, both strove for economic equality for whites, and both would extend that equality to blacks. Johnson was more manipulative, working successfully within the system, while Long was authoritarian, feeling that the political system frustrated radical change. 61 notes.

K. B. West

3822. Wilson, C. J. VOICES FROM MISSISSIPPI. *New South* 1973 28(2): 62-71. How several prominent Mississippians view their state's actions toward integration.

3823. Wimsatt, Mary Ann. POLITICAL AND ECONOMIC REC-OMMENDATIONS OF *I'LL TAKE MY STAND. Mississippi Q. 1980 33(4): 433-443.* The southern Agrarians who wrote *I'll Take My Stand* (1930) were far-sighted in their recognition of the dangers of technological expansion but short-sighted in their idealization of a life lived close to the soil; their arguments are best understood in the context of religious humanism—intended philosophically even more than as political and economic theory.

3824. Wingard, Joel D. "FOLDED IN A SINGLE PARTY": AGRARIANS AND PROLETARIANS. *Southern Rev. 1980 16(4): 776-781.* Differences between the rightist southern Agrarians and the leftist Marxist Proletarians during the 1930's seem not so glaring after 50 years; they may be seen "not as political enemies promoting antagonist visions of the ideal society but as lettered allies united in the defense of a human-centered culture against the onslaught of a dehumanized modernism."

3825. Wohl, Michael. NOT YET SAINT NOR SINNER: A FURTHER NOTE ON DANIEL CLARK. *Louisiana Hist. 1983 24(2): 195-205.* Surveys conflicting opinions of Clark. Appointed consul at New Orleans by Thomas Jefferson in 1801, he aspired to the governorship of Louisiana Territory and became a political and personal enemy of William C. C. Claiborne, the man who obtained the post. He and General James Wilkinson, one-time business associates, became bitter enemies. He was accused of complicity in the Burr conspiracy, but the evidence indicates that he played no direct part. 49 notes.

R. E. Noble

3826. Wolfe, Margaret Ripley. THE AGRICULTURAL EXPERIMENT STATION AND FOOD AND DRUG CONTROL: ANOTHER LOOK AT KENTUCKY PROGRESSIVISM, 1898-1916. *Filson Club Hist. Q. 1975 49(4): 323-338.* Melville Amasa Scovell and Robert McDowell Allen were leaders in Kentucky's effort to control the production of unsafe foods and drugs. Both men were part of the new college-trained middle-class reform movement of the Progressive era. Using agricultural experiment stations as their base of operations, Scovell and Allen were almost uniformly successful in prosecuting businesses in Kentucky. Allen also joined in the national crusade for pure food led by Dr. Harvey W. Wiley, chief chemist of the US Department of Agriculture. Allen took part in the International Food Congress in 1904 and was a moving force behind the passage of the Heyburn Act of 1906. Based on newspapers, government reports, and the Scovell and Wiley Papers; 59 notes.

G. B. McKinney

3827. Wood, W. Kirk. HENRY HARFORD CUMMING: CIVIC VIRTUE IN THE OLD SOUTH. *Richmond County Hist. 1977 9(1): 5-9.* Henry Harford Cumming was a private citizen of Augusta, Georgia, dedicated to civic responsibility, 1812-66.

3828. Wright, Gerald C., Jr. CONTEXTUAL MODELS OF ELECTORAL BEHAVIOR: THE SOUTHERN WALLACE VOTE. *Am. Pol. Sci. Rev. 1977 71(2): 497-508.* Many studies have sought to investigate contextual influences on individual electoral behavior using aggregate data. The shortcomings of this approach are discussed, focusing on the relationship between black concentration and southern white support for George Wallace for president in 1968. Through combining aggregate and individual-level data and comparing a series of models, black concentration is found to increase white support for Wallace. Intraregional differences in the relationship between white support for Wallace and local black concentration are equalized when contextual influences at the state level are brought into the analysis. Black concentration contextual effects are independent of those of urbanization, education, or residence in Wallace's home state of Alabama. Relative primary group

support for Wallace and relative issue proximity to Wallace are then shown to be the intervening variables linking contextual characteristics and electoral choice.

J

3829. Wyatt-Brown, Bertram. JEFFERSON'S NEPHEWS AND OTHER MURDERERS: THOUGHTS ON SOUTHERN VIOLENCE. *Rev. in Am. Hist. 1977 5(2): 203-210.* Review article prompted by Boynton Merrill, Jr.'s *Jefferson's Nephews: A Frontier Tragedy* (Princeton: Princeton U. Pr., 1976).

3830. Young, James Harvey. THREE SOUTHERN FOOD AND DRUG CASES. *J. of Southern Hist. 1983 49(1): 3-36.* Examines three food and drug cases that originated in the South but had impact upon national drug enforcement legislation and practices. The cases were the trial of Atlanta-based Coca Cola in 1911 for adding caffeine to its soft drink formula, the S. E. Massengill Company's case in 1939 for selling Elixir Sulfanilimide from its plant in Bristol, Tennessee, without first testing this drug, which was linked to 107 deaths, and the Sullivan's Pharmacy case for over-the-counter sales of sulfathiazole without prescription in Memphis, Tennessee. Based upon the Chandler and Coca-Cola Papers, Emory University; Supreme Court Transcripts (RG 97 and 88), National Archives; Wiley Papers, Library of Congress; various other manuscript holdings, newspapers, memoirs, and other printed primary materials; 177 notes.

T. D. Schoonover

3831. Young, Thomas Daniel. FROM FUGITIVES TO AGRARIANS. *Mississippi Q. 1980 33(4): 420-424.* The Scopes trial of 1925 and the ensuing ridicule of the South prompted four Fugitives—John Crowe Ransom, Donald Davidson, Allen Tate, and Robert Penn Warren—to join with eight Agrarians to produce *I'll Take My Stand* (1930), a neglected, misinterpreted, but prophetic warning that their fellow Americans were emphasizing false values.

3832. Zamora, Emilio. SARA ESTELA RAMÍREZ: UNA ROSA ROJA EN EL MOVIMIENTO [Sara Estela Ramírez: a red rose in the movement]. Mora, Magdalena and DelCastillo, Adelaida R., ed. *Mexican Women in the United States: Struggles Past and Present* (Los Angeles: U. of California Chicano Studies Res. Center, 1980): 163-169. Sara Estela Ramírez (1881-1910), a journalist and literary figure in southern Texas, was one of the women leaders in the Partido Liberal Mexicano. Her group was responsible for assuming public roles which persecuted leaders of the party could not undertake. Her writing legitimized the Liberal Party of Mexico and other movements by justifying the application of given moral and ethical considerations. 15 notes, appendix.

J. Powell

3833. —. CARTOONING IN THE LONE STAR STATE: A BEN SARGENT ALBUM. *Civil Liberties Rev. 1978 5(1): 28-35.* Comments on and reproduces political cartoons of Ben Sargent and their depiction of civil liberties principles, published in the Austin (Texas) *American-Statesman*.

3834. —. DR. LILLIE M. JACKSON: LIFELONG FREEDOM FIGHTER. *Crisis 1975 82(8): 297-299.* Dr. Lillie M. Jackson died at her home in Baltimore, Maryland, on 5 July 1975, at the age of 86. She dedicated her life to civil rights and was on the national Board of Directors of the NAACP for 27 years. Under her leadership the Baltimore chapter grew to 20,000 members. She became president of the branch in 1935 and immediately began to attack Jim Crow, zoning regulations, and discrimination in employment.

A. G. Belles

3835. —. ETHNIC RAMBLINGS OF A SENATOR. *Ukrainian Q. 1981 37(3): 229-236.* Criticizes Senator Charles Mathias of Maryland for discouraging ethnic influence in US foreign policy and reiterates the importance of the Captive Nations Week Resolution. 11 notes.

K. N. T. Crowther

3836. —. INTRODUCTION TO PART I. Steed, Robert P.; Moreland, Laurence W.; and Baker, Tod A., ed. *Party Politics in the South* (New York: Praeger, 1980): 3-7. Introduces the papers in this collection's Part I, "Intraparty Politics: Participation and Competition Within Parties," noting the divergence among them with respect to the nature of their data and the scope and range of their focus. Yet all the papers provide useful information on the role of primaries in Southern party politics from 1927 to 1979. By identifying changes in the primaries and clarifying a series of questions regarding their use, the essays contribute to our knowledge of party politics in the South. Note.                                    J. Powell

3837. —. [OPPOSITION TO TOXIC DUMPING]. *Southern Exposure 1981 9(3): 26-47.*
—. "GET IN THERE AND FIGHT," *pp. 26-27.*
Thomas, Kenny. "OUR GOVERNMENT WOULDN'T DO THIS TO US," *pp. 28-34.*
Brink, Betty. "A SLOW CREEPING DEATH": TACKLING THE TODD NUCLEAR DUMP, *pp. 34-38.*
Thomas, Ginny and Brooks, Bill. HALTING THE HEARD COUNTY LANDFILL: "BUDDY WE'RE HOME," *pp. 38-41.*
Grantham, Nell. "TOGETHER WE CAN DO IT": FIGHTING TOXIC HAZARDS IN TENNESSEE, *pp. 42-47.*
Describes the struggle waged by communities in four Southern states against the dumping of unsafe toxic wastes.

3838. —. SOUTH CAROLINA PRESS AND U.S. FOREIGN POLICY. *Pro. of the South Carolina Hist. Assoc. 1980: 133-152.*
Leemhuis, Roger P. SOUTH CAROLINA NEWSPAPERS AND AMERICAN FOREIGN POLICY IN THE 1890's, *pp. 133-147.* "South Carolina newspapers generally stood against an expansionist and 'jingoist' foreign policy, yet they were sensitive about the country's honor and position among the world powers. Editorials frequently displayed a populist outlook and a Democratic Party affiliation, while racism was a clear component of the anti-imperialist sentiment. The most significant factors were a concern for national security and interests, a concern about liberty and national character, and a deep humanitarianism." Based on newspapers and published works; 41 notes.
Moore, Winfred B., Jr. COMMENTARY ON "SHAPING FORCES IN SOUTH CAROLINA," *pp. 148-152.* The main criticism of Leemhuis involved the need for precise definitions of the terms used.                                           J. W. Thacker, Jr.

3839. —. [SOUTHERN POLITICS]. *Public Opinion Q. 1982 46(3): 422-425.*
Prysby, Charles L. A NOTE ON REGIONAL SUBSAMPLES FROM NATIONAL SAMPLE SURVEYS, *pp. 422-424.* Comments on Charles D. Hadley's article on Southern politics (see entry 19A:9600). Analysts of regional social and political behavior are often interested in a region that differs from the "region" as defined by survey designers. Hadley states that research should show a congruence in the definition of a region with the region used in the survey. Actually the use of any regional subsample is valid if it is drawn from a probability sample that is sufficiently large.
Hadley, Charles D. HADLEY'S REPLY, *pp. 424-425.* Welcomes Prysby's criticism, concurring upon reanalysis of his article that "one can use regional subgroups with confidence only when the number of respondents and sampling points is large enough to bring sampling error into tolerable bounds." However, the reader should be informed of the probability of error involved. Secondary sources; 2 notes.        J. Powell

3840. —. UNITED STATES SENATORS FROM GEORGIA. *Richmond County Hist. 1976 8(1): 23-28.* Roster of US senators from Georgia 1789-1975.

3841. —. [THE WALLACE VOTE IN THE SOUTH, 1968].
Schoenberger, Robert A. and Segal, David R. THE ECOLOGY OF DISSENT: THE SOUTHERN WALLACE VOTE IN 1968. *Midwest J. of Pol. Sci. 1971 15(3): 583-586.* The Wallace vote in the South was highest in areas with young populations, low levels of education, and low income. There was a positive correlation between the Wallace vote and the percent of blacks in a congressional district. "The greater the concentration of blacks in a congressional district, the greater the propensity of

whites in that district to vote for Wallace." Based on data in the *Congressional District Data Book* (88th Congress); table, 10 notes.
Wasserman, Ira M. and Segal, David R. AGGREGATION EFFECTS IN THE ECOLOGICAL STUDY OF PRESIDENTIAL VOTING. *Am. J. of Pol. Sci. 1973 17(1): 177-181.* Disputes contentions about the George C. Wallace vote in the South in 1968 by Schoenberger and Segal, who found that much of Wallace's support came from rural nonwhite areas.                                    E. P. Stickney/S

# Southern Military Traditions and Institutions

3842. Agnew, Brad. MILITARY ROADS IN INDIAN TERRITORY. *Red River Valley Hist. Rev. 1981 6(3): 31-47.* Focuses on the development of military roads in the state, noting early explorations that led to the establishment of these roads, including activities of such explorer-builders as Colonel Matthew Arbuckle, Captain John Stuart and Captain Randolph B. Marcy; many of the state's modern roads follow the old military trails.

3843. Boney, F. N. THE MILITARY TRADITION IN THE SOUTH. *Midwest Q. 1980 21(2): 163-174.* The United States has had a legend of a unique southern military tradition since the American Revolution, but the American people—North and South—lack a strong, formal military tradition. A French version appeared as a chapter in *Le Système militaire des États-Unis: bilan et perspectives, ed. Lucien Mandeville (Toulouse, 1976) [The Military System of the United States: Balance-sheet and Perspectives].*
                                                M. E. Quinlivan

3844. Boydstun, Q. B. THE RESTORATION OF OLD FORT GIBSON. *Chronicles of Oklahoma 1980 58(2): 176-191.* Describes the efforts to restore Fort Gibson, which had been established in eastern Oklahoma during 1824, closed in 1857, and periodically reopened as a military post or supply depot until its final abandonment in 1901. Local attempts to win state legislative approval for restoration funds began in the 1920's, but not until 1935 would New Deal relief money provide the workers to do the actual construction. The stockade was completed during the summer of the following year and subsequent building projects expanded the site as a popular tourist attraction. The National Park Service designated Fort Gibson Military Park as a historical landmark in 1963. 7 photos.                                       M. L. Tate

3845. Burns, Robert Carter. GENERAL AND ADMIRAL TOO. *East Tennessee Hist. Soc. Publ. 1976 48: 29-33.* Samuel Powatan Carter of Carter County, Tennessee, held the ranks of both general and admiral in the armed forces of the United States. After serving five years in the US Navy, he became one of the 60 men who formed the first class at Annapolis in 1845. When the Civil War broke out Carter was ordered from service aboard the steam sloop *Seminole* to temporary duty with the US Army. He performed meritorious duty during the war achieving the rank of Major General. At the conclusion of the war, he returned to duty with the Navy. Among his duty stations was a stint as Commandant of the Naval Academy. Illus., 9 notes.                          D. A. Yanchisin

3846. Casey, Powell A. NORTH LOUISIANA GUARD UNITS IN THE SPANISH-AMERICAN WAR, 1898. *North Louisiana Hist. Assoc. J. 1983 14(2-3): 111-116.* During the Spanish-American War, Louisiana contributed as volunteer units two regiments of infantry, three battalions of field artillery, and a battalion of naval militia. None participated in combat though several died from disease and accidents. Lists of volunteers are appended.
                                                J. F. Paul

3847. Christian, Garna L. ADDING ON FORT BLISS TO BLACK MILITARY HISTORIOGRAPHY. *West Texas Hist. Assoc. Year Book 1978 54: 41-54.* Discusses the history, significance, and the historiographical implications of the black troops who were stationed at Fort Bliss during 1865-80's and from 1898 to 1907, and discusses the relationship between the soldiers and the nearby city of El Paso.

3848. Corbett, William P. RIFLES AND RUTS: ARMY ROAD BUILDERS IN INDIAN TERRITORY. *Chronicles of Oklahoma 1982 60(3): 294-309.* Road-building activities consumed a great deal of the US Army's time during the Indian Territory's frontier stage of development. Colonel Mathew Arbuckle's construction of a road linking Fort Smith, Arkansas, and Fort Gibson, Indian Territory, during 1826 marked the first systematic project. As the Five Civilized Tribes were moved into the area during the 1830's, the need increased for additional forts and military roads, including connectors to the posts in northwest Texas. The establishment of Fort Sill in 1869 initiated a road-building project for western Indian Territory that lasted through the 1880's. Based on *The Territorial Papers of the United States* and the *Congressional Serial Set;* 2 maps, 4 photos, 22 notes. M. L. Tate

3849. Cox, Richard J. TWO MARYLANDERS IN THE EARLY NAVY: THE HAMBLETON FAMILY PAPERS, MS. 2021. *Maryland Hist. Mag. 1974 69(3): 317-321.* Describes the contents of a recent manuscript collection chronicling the naval careers of Samuel Hambleton (1777-1851) and his brother John Needles Hambleton (1798-1870). Samuel entered the service in 1806 as a purser, or paymaster, served with Oliver H. Perry in the Battle of Lake Erie, and wrote his sister 28 letters in this collection covering 1813-32, which "show in detail the life of a naval officer...." John Hambleton's 38 letters to his sister during 1820-32 reflect life on shipboard, particularly his Latin American travels aboard the *John Adams, Nonsuch,* and *Warren.* Primary and secondary sources; 2 illus., 8 notes. G. J. Bobango

3850. Daugherty, Fred A. and Woods, Pendleton. OKLAHOMA'S MILITARY TRADITION. *Chronicles of Oklahoma 1979-80 57(4): 427-445.* Surveys Oklahoma's military contributions since 1890, when the Oklahoma Territorial Militia was created. The Oklahoma National Guard served in the Spanish American War and on Mexican border duty in 1916, and participated in suppression of the Crazy Snake Rebellion of 1909 and of various domestic problems of the 1920's. During World War I, the Oklahoma Guard joined units from Texas to form the 36th Infantry Division and fought with distinction in France. During World War II, Oklahomans joined with troops from neighboring states to form the 45th Infantry Division and won praise for meritorious service in Sicily, Italy, France, and Germany. The 45th Infantry Division fought again in the Korean War and was disbanded in 1968. 12 photos. M. L. Tate

3851. deTreville, Virginia E. THE TWO AUGUSTAS. *Richmond County Hist. 1982 14(2): 12-17.* Discusses the pride the citizens of Augusta, Georgia, had in the USS *Augusta* and how in 1931 they presented the vessel with a silver service; portions of the service are now in the Augusta Richmond County Museum.

3852. Ethridge, Harrison M. GOVERNOR PATRICK HENRY AND THE REORGANIZATION OF THE VIRGINIA MILITIA, 1784-1786. *Virginia Mag. of Hist. and Biog. 1977 85(4): 427-439.* When the Virginia General Assembly passed a Militia Act to replace the Revolutionary Continental Army, Governor Patrick Henry was obliged to appoint officers for each county. Though he attempted to solicit advice, his appointments frequently caused resentment from local aristocrats, whose prestige was eroded, and the masses, who resented new military requirements. The social stresses of post-Revolutionary Virginia made it almost impossible for Henry to carry out his obligation. Based largely on the Executive Papers in the Virginia State Library; 64 notes. R. F. Oaks

3853. Findlay, Stephen M. THE *ALLEGHANY:* A REVISIONIST NOTE ON A MEMPHIS MYTH. *West Tennessee Hist. Soc. Papers 1978 (32): 70-83.* As part of its defense strategy, the Navy Department in 1845 selected Memphis as the site for the construction of a steam fleet. The Memphis Navy Yard lasted but a decade, and serviced only one ship, the *Alleghany,* which was only the second iron warship built for the Navy. Earlier historians have suggested

that the reason for the continual flaws and ultimate failure of the vessel was its construction in Pittsburgh and Memphis; however, the breakdown—the vessel was finally sold in 1869—resulted from structural and engineering defects in both machinery and hull, and had nothing to do with inefficiency of the Memphis Navy Yard. Failures hounded the ship, not the least of which was the poorly conducted Navy Department, which was shackled with politics. Based on newspaper accounts and Federal sources; 55 notes. H. M. Parker, Jr.

3854. Hasdorff, James C. REFLECTIONS ON THE TUSKEGEE EXPERIMENT: AN INTERVIEW WITH BRIG. GEN. NOEL F. PARRISH, USAF (RET.). *Aerospace Hist. 1977 24(3): 173-180.* Based on an oral interview with Brigadier General Noel F. Parrish, discusses the development of his career and his relationship with the black flying program during World War II. As commander of Tuskegee Army Air Field, Parrish became a principal figure in the training of Negroes. His involvement began as an evolutionary process in which he gave some support to a civilian pilot training school for blacks in Chicago which gradually increased its activities during the war years. Includes Parrish's assessment of the Tuskegee program. Primary and secondary sources; 12 notes.
A. M. Osur

3855. Hickey, Donald R. ANDREW JACKSON AND THE ARMY HAIRCUT: INDIVIDUAL RIGHTS VS. MILITARY DISCIPLINE. *Tennessee Hist. Q. 1976 35(4): 365-375.* In 1801 Thomas Butler, a Federalist who wore his hair in a queue, was courtmartialed for refusing to cut his hair. Andrew Jackson and other friends from middle Tennessee came to his defense. A petition signed by seventy-five of the leading citizens of Nashville was sent to President Thomas Jefferson objecting to the persecution of Colonel Butler. Although the President promised the charge would be downplayed, Butler was convicted. Primary and secondary sources; 39 notes. M. B. Lucas

3856. Johnson, Charles, Jr. FRAZIER A. BOUTELLE: MILITARY CAREER OF A BLACK SOLDIER. *J. of the Afro-American Hist. and Geneal. Soc. 1982 3(3): 99-104.* Sketches the military career of Frazier A. Boutelle from 1861 to 1897; he fought in the Civil War, served on the western frontier, and was responsible for various duties from recruitment to command assignments.

3857. Joshi, Manoj K. and Reidy, Joseph P. "TO COME FORWARD AND AID IN PUTTING DOWN THIS UNHOLY REBELLION": THE OFFICERS OF LOUISIANA'S FREE BLACK NATIVE GUARD DURING THE CIVIL WAR ERA. *Southern Studies 1982 21(3): 326-342.* The Civil War threatened the privileged position of free blacks in Louisiana. They had fought in earlier wars as a means of showing their loyalty, but the Confererates did not seek their support. Federal attitudes varied; at first black offers of military service were welcome, but soon a systematic exclusion of black officers began. Most other black soldiers then disappeared. During Reconstruction, freed blacks fought for economic and political benefits, but free blacks pressed for civil equality. Their differences crippled any chance at effective political influence. Based on War Department records; 41 notes. J. J. Buschen

3858. Kelly, Vicki L. IN THE SHADOW OF FAME: THE SAN JACINTO ORDNANCE DEPOT, 1939-1964. *Military Hist. of Texas and the Southwest 1976 13(2): 39-46.* Short history of the San Jacinto Ordnance Depot which served as a munitions storage area, 1939-64.

3859. Lashley, Tommy G. OKLAHOMA'S CONFEDERATE VETERANS HOME. *Chronicles of Oklahoma 1977 55(1): 34-45.* Created in 1909 through the efforts of two powerful Confederate veteran organizations, a home at Ardmore, Oklahoma, ultimately served the needs of several hundred Confederate veterans and their wives and widows. The home and an accompanying pension program made Oklahoma a pacesetter in establishing aid for Civil War servicemen. Despite a few minor administrative problems, the atmosphere of the institution remained genial and inviting. In 1949, the Oklahoma Legislature opened the home to veterans of the Spanish

American War, World War I and World War II and changed the name to the Oklahoma Veterans Home. Based on primary sources; 4 photos, chart, 21 notes. M. L. Tate

3860. Maness, Lonnie E. A WEST TENNESSEE WORLD WAR II FIGHTER PILOT: HAROLD JEFFERSON HOFFMAN OF MARTIN. *West Tennessee Hist. Soc. Papers 1981 35: 83-94.* A biography of Colonel Harold Jefferson Hoffman (1915-68), with emphasis on his military life of 25 years, from entrance into the armed forces in World War II until retirement in 1967. Emphasis is placed on his dedication to his parents, his wife and children, and his country. His community service included Boy Scout work and layman activity in the Methodist Church. His actions as a soldier reflected the highest of credit, both in war and peace, on himself and the armed forces of the United States. Based on his correspondence, numerous citations, and contemporary newspaper accounts; 6 pictures, 51 notes. H. M. Parker, Jr.

3861. McGovern, James R. PENSACOLA, FLORIDA: A MILITARY CITY IN THE NEW SOUTH. *Florida Hist. Q. 1980 59(1): 24-41.* Pensacola underwent urbanization as the result of its Naval Air Station, not of industrialization. Immigrants from nearby rural areas diluted the military presence. The city's evolution suggests a model for other southern cities influenced by the presence of military bases. Covers 1900-45. Based on reports in the *Pensacola Journal,* census returns, and city and county statistical records; 75 notes. N. A. Kuntz

3862. Morris, Beau. THE POLITICAL ORIGINS OF BARKSDALE AIR FORCE BASE. *North Louisiana Hist. Assoc. J. 1977 8(3): 131-136.* During 1923-28 Shreveport citizens fought hard to convince the US War Department to locate the Third Air Attack Group at their city. The War Department finally approved the proposed Shreveport site, but a special session of the state legislature had to be called to clear certain property matters. Governor Huey Long was willing to accept the legislature's action only if Shreveport's civic leaders supported his free school textbook program, a program which they had publicly denounced. Eventually the governor and the city compromised. Barksdale Air Field was dedicated on 2 February 1933. Secondary sources; 37 notes.
A. N. Garland

3863. Napier, John Hawkins, III. THE MILITANT SOUTH REVISITED: MYTHS AND REALITIES. *Alabama Rev. 1980 33(4): 243-265.* There was a strong military tradition in the South before and after the Civil War. Quotes scholars and writers and cites evidence from popular culture—including music, radio, and television—to state the case for Southern nationalism and militarism. 77 notes. J. Powell

3864. Peake, Louis A. WEST VIRGINIA'S BEST KNOWN GENERAL SINCE "STONEWALL JACKSON": JOHN L. HINES. *West Virginia Hist. 1977 38(3): 226-235.* General John Leonard Hines (1868-1968), of Irish parentage, was born in West Virginia, graduated from West Point, and spent his career with the Army. He fought in Cuba (1898), in the Philippines (1900), with the punitive expedition to Mexico (1916), and in France (1918). He became Army Chief of Staff 1924-26 and served in the Philippines again in 1930-32, until retirement. Primary and secondary sources; 42 notes. J. H. Broussard

3865. Robinson, Robert L. THE U.S. NAVY VS. CATTLE RUSTLERS: THE U.S.S. RIO BRAVO ON THE RIO GRANDE, 1875-1879. *Military Hist. of Texas and the Southwest 1979 15(2): 43-52.* Conflict between Americans and Mexicans along the Texas-Mexico border began in the 1840's and reached a peak in 1875, over cattle rustling; the US Navy patrolled the Rio Grande in the USS *Rio Bravo* to prevent cattle rustling.

3866. Robinson, Willard B. MARITIME FRONTIER ENGINEERING: THE DEFENSE OF NEW ORLEANS. *Louisiana Hist. 1977 18(1): 5-62.* Discusses the objectives, planning, and construction of fortifications protecting New Orleans during 1680-1896. Beginning with Fort Crèvecoeur (1680), depicts a large number of 18th-century French and Spanish forts in the New Orleans area, including the fortifications of the city itself. The early federal period witnessed several new fortifications, notably Forts Jackson, Pike, Philip, Macomb, and Livingston, and the Battery Bienvenue. These were expanded in midcentury as part of a national system of forts. New forts were added during the Civil War at Proctor's Landing and Ship Island. Few fortifications were added until some improvements in coast artillery were made in the 1890's. The forts were abandoned in 1920 because they were obsolete. Some of the forts, examples of military architecture of the 18th and 19th centuries, have been made into state historical parks. Others are falling into ruin. Primary sources; 27 illus., 109 notes.
R. L. Woodward, Jr.

3867. Rubin, Norman N. FROM THE SEA WITH WINGS: MARYLAND AND THE FLYING BOAT. *Maryland Hist. Mag. 1977 72(2): 277-287.* Records the 40-year era, 1929-69, of the unique form of vessel called the flying boat, built at Hagerstown, Dundalk, and Middle River, Maryland, primarily by the Martin and Fokker companies. Some of the craft, such as the Model 162, Navy Mariner PBM, went through many versions and thousands of flights during and after World War II. They were used especially by the Coast Guard for rescue work, operating in 10-foot seas where operations previously were prohibited. Discusses the structures, technical capabilities, and varieties of military and civilian use of these flexible clippers. 11 illus., 2 tables. G. J. Bobango

3868. Rulon, Philip Reed. THE CAMPUS CADETS: A HISTORY OF COLLEGIATE MILITARY TRAINING, 1891-1951. *Chronicles of Oklahoma 1979 57(1): 67-90.* Oklahoma State University opened its doors in 1891 and during its first year the school created a corps of male and female cadets. Early university presidents stressed the value of discipline and exercise for the student cadets, as well as the potential value for military preparedness. During the First and Second World Wars, Oklahoma State University resembled a military installation as the Reserve Officers' Training Corps (ROTC) and Women Appointed for Volunteer Emergency Service (WAVES) expanded their activities on campus. Following World War II, the university organized a very effective program for returning war veterans who used their financial aid from the GI Bill of Rights to return to school. Primary and secondary sources; 4 photos, 43 notes. M. L. Tate

3869. Sears, Betty M. IRA C. EAKER: THE MILITARY CAREER OF OKLAHOMA'S GREATEST AVIATOR. *Red River Valley Hist. Rev. 1978 3(3): 66-77.* General Ira C. Eaker served the Army Air Corps from 1917 to 1947, testing aircraft, making record-breaking flights, formulating military strategy, preparing for World War II, and leading the US 8th Bomber Command's B-17's over Europe.

3870. Stafford, John W. EGMONT KEY: SENTINEL OF TAMPA BAY. *Tampa Bay Hist. 1980 2(1): 15-29.* Describes the geography of Egmont Key, now a government reserve, an island located between Key West and Pensacola, where a lighthouse was built in 1848 and which became militarily important in the 1890's as a site for guarding the entrance to Tampa Bay, focusing on the island's history from its first known survey in 1757 by Don Francisco Maria Celi.

3871. Wallace, Sandra. HENRY LEE OF VIRGINIA. *Missouri Hist. Rev. 1976 71(1): 76-79.* Biographical sketch of Henry ("Light-Horse Harry") Lee (1756-1818). Illus., 23 notes.
W. F. Zornow

3872. Whitt, Samuel S. FRANK LAHM: PIONEER MILITARY AVIATOR. *Aerospace Historian 1973 19(4): 172-177.* Surveys the military career of Frank Purdy Lahm, who organized, built, and ran Randolph Field, Texas (1897-1963).

3873. Williams, Emily J. "A HOME... FOR THE OLD BOYS": THE ROBERT E. LEE CAMP CONFEDERATE SOLDIERS' HOME. *Virginia Cavalcade 1979 29(1): 40-47.* The Robert E. Lee Camp Confederate Soldiers' Home in Richmond, Virginia, founded in 1884 to shelter Confederate veterans, existed as a home until 1941 when the last residents died; the buildings are now a museum.

3874. Wing, William G. ESCAPE FROM INTERNMENT ON THE YACHT *ECLIPSE:* 1915. *Am. Neptune 1983 43(4): 267-273.* In 1915, two German auxiliary cruisers, *Prinz Eital Friedrich* and *Kronprinz Wilhelm,* were interned in Norfolk, Virginia, as combatants in a neutral port. Six junior officers from the latter purchased the private yacht *Eclipse,* illegally sailed for home on 10 October,

and disappeared. The sale and the federal government's total inaction in preventing what amounted to suicide are described. Based on interviews, State Department records, and secondary sources; 2 illus., 8 notes.                                                      J. C. Bradford

3875. —. SOBRE EL CAÑON THEODORICO [The cannon Theodore]. *Rev. de Hist. Militar [Spain] 1980 24(48): 179-182.* Historical notes related to a 24-pound cannon unearthed in Florida in 1973.                                                                              K. W. Estes

# INDIANS IN SOUTHERN HISTORY

## General

3876. Anders, Gary. THE INTERNAL COLONIZATION OF CHEROKEE NATIVE AMERICANS. *Development and Change [Netherlands] 1979 10(1): 41-55.* Examines the Cherokee Indians' relationship to the federal government since the 18th century, indicating that their present underdevelopment results from their role as internal colonists in the American political economy.

3877. Ballenger, T. L. THE KEETOOWAHS AND THEIR DANCES. *Chronicles of Oklahoma 1983 61(2): 194-199.* The Cherokee Indians created the Keetoowah Society during the early period of white contact. This secret organization of full-blooded Cherokee men used its influence to preserve tribal traditions during the chaotic removals to Oklahoma during the 1820's-30's. Keetoowah members maintained these traditions in the 20th century, and broadened their appeal with public stickball games and stomp dances, which are described in detail. 3 photos. M. L. Tate

3878. Begaye, Russell. THE STORY OF INDIAN SOUTHERN BAPTISTS. *Baptist Hist. and Heritage 1983 18(3): 30-39.* Discusses the formation and activities of Baptist missions within Indian communities during 1830-1970's, describing missionary work among the Cherokee, Choctaw, Navajo, and other tribes.

3879. Blend, Benay. THE INDIAN RIGHTS ASSOCIATION, THE DAWES COMMISSION, AND THE FIVE CIVILIZED TRIBES. *Red River Valley Hist. Rev. 1981 6(4): 4-14.* Discusses the Indian reform movement of the late 19th century, attempts to force assimilation, and the effects of these actions and concurrent legislation on the Five Civilized Tribes; covers 1880's-1910.

3880. Blumer, Thomas J. HISTORY AS A TOOL IN A FOLK-LIFE STUDY OF THE CATAWBA INDIANS OF SOUTH CAROLINA. *New York Folklore 1983 9(1-2): 67-74.* Discusses the value of the historical method in reconstructing life histories for two Catawba Indians, John Brown (1867-1927) and Mary "Dovie" Harris, and in eliciting and interpreting related folklore.

3881. Campbell, Janet and Campbell, David G. CHEROKEE PARTICIPATION IN THE POLITICAL IMPACT OF THE NORTH AMERICAN INDIAN. *J. of Cherokee Studies 1981 6(2): 92-106.* Tribal social and political organization formed not only a constant image of how well Indians were established as political entities in the history of the United States but also a constant reminder of how much the Europeans had to do to achieve the stability seen in tribal unity. The Cherokees of North Carolina region and later Oklahoma maintained a unique judicial system which influenced colonial lawmakers. Cherokees had attempted to establish the state of Sequoyah in 1905, which was rejected by President Theodore Roosevelt. Despite a federal policy of land deprivation and rejection of tribal recognition, Indians, especially Cherokees and the other Five Civilized Tribes, have withstood vast pressures to eliminate a highly structured society. Map, 5 photos, 27 notes. K. E. Gilmont

3882. Conrad, David E. WHIPPLE'S PACIFIC RAILROAD SURVEY IN THE INDIAN TERRITORY. *Red River Valley Hist. Rev. 1974 1(4): 391-415.* Account of an expedition commanded by Amiel Weeks Whipple in 1853 through the Indian Territory to find a feasible route for a transcontinental railroad, describing his relations with the Choctaw, Cherokee, Shawnee, and Delaware Indians en route.

3883. Covington, James W. SEMINOLE LEADERSHIP: CHANGING SUBSTANCE, 1858-1958. *Tequesta 1980 40: 31-38.* To the Seminole Indians, the traditional leader was a spokesman who determined and represented the consensus of the group. Important tribal decisions were deliberated in councils and at the an-

nual Green Corn Dance. During 1920-40, many changes took place. Livestock was introduced and so were democratic ideas. Elected councils, a constitution, and bylaws were accompanied by white oriented leaders who would tell the others what to do. Almost all had been trained in the methods of the Christian church. Based on secondary sources and records of the Bureau of Indian Affairs; 22 notes. H. S. Marks

3884. Downs, Dorothy. PATCHWORK CLOTHING OF THE FLORIDA INDIANS. *Am. Indian Art Mag. 1979 4(3): 32-41.* Provides a brief history of the Seminole Indians since the early 18th century and discusses their patchwork clothing.

3885. Ethridge, Robbie F. TOBACCO AMONG THE CHEROKEES. *J. of Cherokee Studies 1978 3(2): 77-86.* Tobacco historically has had medicinal and spiritual uses among the Cherokee Indians. Describes these uses and the rituals applied to them, as well as how tobacco fell into the Cherokee universe of thinking. Secondary sources; 52 notes. J. M. Lee

3886. Fischer, LeRoy H. MURIEL H. WRIGHT, HISTORIAN OF OKLAHOMA. *Chronicles of Oklahoma 1974 52(1): 3-29.* A biographical account of Muriel Hazel Wright, Oklahoma teacher, historian, and editor, who is an active member of Choctaw tribal affairs. In her writings and lectures, she has emphasized the role of the Indian in Oklahoma and American history and culture. Wright also served as editor of *The Chronicles of Oklahoma,* 1955-73. Includes a bibliography of her works. Based on autobiographical notes and secondary sources; 6 photos, 27 notes.

N. J. Street

3887. Ford, Jeanette W. FEDERAL LAW COMES TO INDIAN TERRITORY. *Chronicles of Oklahoma 1980-81 58(4): 432-439.* Despite attempts during the 1870's and the 1880's to administer Indian Territory from Arkansas and Kansas federal courts, the area remained lawless until Congress specifically created a federal court for Indian Territory in 1889. Initially there were separate courts for Indian Territory and Oklahoma Territory, but these were merged upon the creation of the state of Oklahoma in 1907. Problems of jurisdiction frequently arose because misdemeanor cases by Indians were handled only in tribal courts. Court records; 2 photos, 21 notes. M. L. Tate

3888. French, Laurence and Hornbuckle, Jim. THE HISTORICAL INFLUENCE OF THE EASTERN INDIANS ON CONTEMPORARY PAN-INDIANISM. *Indian Hist. 1977 10(2): 23-27.* As the new Indian movement gets under way, with national conferences and organizations promoting the welfare of native Americans, it is noteworthy that eastern Indians have led the struggle for Indian rights for more than 200 years. Minor tribes disappeared in the wake of white settlement, but the Cherokees, Creeks, Choctaws, and Chickasaws have survived wars, disease, removal to Oklahoma, and other major problems, to lead the American movement today. Biblio. E. D. Johnson

3889. French, Laurence and Bertoluzzi, Renitia. THE DRUNKEN INDIAN STEREOTYPE AND THE EASTERN CHEROKEES. *Appalachian J. 1975 2(4): 332-344.*

3890. Greene, Candace. STOVALL MUSEUM OF SCIENCE AND HISTORY: UNIVERSITY OF OKLAHOMA. *Am. Indian Art Mag. 1981 6(4): 46-51.* Traces the development of the collections of 19th-century Indian artifacts housed in the Stovall Museum of Science and History at the University of Oklahoma since the museum's establishment in 1943.

3891. Hemperley, M. R. INDIAN PLACE NAMES IN GEORGIA. *Georgia Hist. Q. 1973 57(4): 562-579.* Lists Indian place names with location, meaning, and pronunciation. Creek account for 55 percent and Cherokee 36 percent. The remainder are Chehaw, Chickasaw, Choctaw, Hitchitee, Shawnee, Seminole, Timucua, Uchee, and Yemassee.                                          D. L. Smith

3892. Hudson, Charles. UKTENA: A CHEROKEE ANOMALOUS MONSTER. *J. of Cherokee Studies 1978 3(2): 62-75.* The uktena resembled a rattlesnake, with horns and a diamond crest on its forehead. Generally thought dangerous, it could also be a source of power. Explores reasons for believing in this creature and how it fell into Cherokee modes of thought. Compares belief in the uktena to Chinese images in the dragon and the Lele mythology of Africa. Secondary sources; 3 illus., 39 notes.            J. M. Lee

3893. Jahoda, Gloria. SEMINOLE. *Florida Hist. Q. 1976 55(2): 129-133.* Relates the history of the Seminole Indians through legend and tribal lore. Acknowledges the aid of Sakim, medicine maker and interpreter of oral tradition for the Oak Hill Community in Tallahassee. Note.                                          P. A. Beaber

3894. Kelly, Lawrence C. INDIAN RECORDS IN THE OKLAHOMA HISTORICAL SOCIETY ARCHIVES. *Chronicles of Oklahoma 1976 54(2): 227-244.* Examines the work of historians Grant Foreman and Robert Lee Williams and their influence in promoting the Oklahoma Historical Society as the repository for all federal papers relating to Oklahoma Indians, and for the custody of all noncurrent federal records through the National Archives and Records Service, 1934.

3895. Kersey, Harry A. and Pullease, Donald E. BISHOP WILLIAM CRANE GRAY'S MISSION TO THE SEMINOLE INDIANS IN FLORIDA, 1893-1914. *Hist. Mag. of the Protestant Episcopal Church 1973 42(3): 257-274.* Discusses the missionary work of Episcopalian Bishop William Crane Gray to the Seminole Indians during 1893-1914.                                          S

3896. King, Duane H. and King, Laura H. THE MYTHICO-RELIGIOUS ORIGIN OF THE CHEROKEES. *Appalachian J. 1975 2(4): 259-264.* Discusses various legends and "wonder stories" from Cherokee oral tradition and reproduces an original transcript with an English translation of one of the most important sacred myths—a creation story—still surviving among the Eastern Cherokee Indians in the Big Cove area of the Qualla Boundary.

3897. LaCourse, Richard. AN INDIAN PERSPECTIVE: NATIVE AMERICAN JOURNALISM: AN OVERVIEW. *Journalism Hist. 1979 6(2): 34-38.* Traces the history of Indians in the media since the 1820's; focuses on Native American journalism since 1828, when the first Indian newspaper appeared, *The Cherokee Phoenix.*

3898. Larouche, Alain. LES PEUPLES: LES AMÉRINDIENS, AUTOCHTONES, SABINES OU CADJINS? [People: Amerindians, Aborigines, Sabines, or Cajuns?]. *Vie Française [Canada] 1980 34(7-9): 25-30.* A brief ethnohistory of Louisiana Indians since the 16th century.

3899. Lepre, Jerome. THE INDIAN CONNECTION AMONG GULF COAST FAMILIES. *J. of Mississippi Hist. 1980 42(4): 362-376.* A genealogical study relative to the existence of Indian blood on the family trees of such Gulf Coast colonial families as the Morans, the Ladners, and the Lafontaines. Discusses two principal theories regarding the Indian ancestry. The first concerns the tradition of an Indian woman named Emashapa or Frances Emily Baudrau, who seems to have been related to and associated with the Ladner and Lafontaine families. The second tradition concerns an Indian woman, Noatima or Marguerite Laforce, who may have been an ancestor of the author through the Moran family of North Biloxi, Mississippi. Concludes, however, that adequate documentation is still lacking on these families' Indian connection. Based on records in St. Louis Cathedral, New Orleans, Louisiana, and the Cathedral of the Immaculate Conception, Mobile, Alabama; 45 notes.                                          M. S. Legan

3900. Littlejohn, Hawk. THE REAWAKENING OF THE CHEROKEES. *Appalachian J. 1975 2(4): 276-279.* Discusses various problems of the Eastern Cherokee Indians over the centuries, focusing on Indian-white relations, social organization, racism, and consciousness of cultural identity.

3901. Lokey, Margaret H. and Wyatt, Beverly J. CHICKASAW EDUCATION AND MURRAY STATE COLLEGE. *Chronicles of Oklahoma 1981 59(3): 335-344.* Since the early 19th century, Chickasaw Indians have placed emphasis upon the value of white man's education. This feeling intensified after the tribe was forcibly removed to Indian Territory, and by the 1860's they had established five academies and a series of one room schools. Both whites and Indians attended these schools, which eventually graduated several US congressmen and two governors of Oklahoma. In 1908 Murray School opened as a secondary school in Tishomingo and eventually grew into Murray State College. Today its Indian enrollment represents 13% of the student body, and it offers a major in Indian Studies and an active Native American Club. Based on interviews and historical files at Murray State College; 5 photos.
                                          M. L. Tate

3902. Makofsky, Abraham. TRADITION AND CHANGE IN THE LUMBEE INDIAN COMMUNITY OF BALTIMORE. *Maryland Hist. Mag. 1980 75(1): 55-71.* The Lumbee Indians migrated to East Baltimore during World War II from their home in Robeson County, rural southeast North Carolina. Supposedly the descendants of the lost tribe of the ill-famed Roanoke Island colony of the 1580's, they have maintained a sense of ethnic uniqueness in the face of numerous obstacles. Today they form a nonreservation subculture in a major urban industrial center. The organizations and adaptive strategies they have used as they interact with the institutions and pressures of the city are highly illustrative of the folk-urban continuum concept. Family and church, along with life amidst a triethnic population, were the main mechanisms for transmitting an Indian heritage despite certain necessary modifications in their sociocultural system. Original fieldwork, secondary literature; 30 notes.                                          G. J. Bobango

3903. Munroe, Mary Barr. THE SEMINOLE WOMEN OF FLORIDA. *Tequesta 1981 41: 23-32.* Part of an unpublished manuscript by Mary Barr Munroe (d. 1922), found in the Library of Congress, provides a personal view of Seminole life in the late 19th and early 20th centuries. A general introduction is provided by Arva Moore Parks, an associate editor of *Tequesta.*
                                          H. S. Marks

3904. Penman, John T. HISTORIC CHOCTAW TOWNS OF THE SOUTHERN DIVISION. *J. of Mississippi Hist. 1978 40(2): 133-141.* Presents recent archaeological findings of Choctaw villages in two watersheds in southeast Mississippi. Seeks to reconcile the new evidence with earlier extant materials. The author suggests criteria for analyzing Choctaw ceramics and speculates on the possible locations of unrecorded villages and evaluates their potential for excavation. Through such evidence historians and archaeologists may better comprehend the Choctaws' settlement patterns, economic development, and early contacts with European culture.
                                          M. S. Legan

3905. Perry, Samuel D. RELIGIOUS FESTIVALS IN CHEROKEE LIFE. *Indian Hist. 1979 12(1): 20-22, 28.* General overview of rites and ceremonies among the Cherokee Indians.

3906. Porter, Frank W., III. BEHIND THE FRONTIER: INDIAN SURVIVALS IN MARYLAND. *Maryland Hist. Mag. 1980 75(1): 42-54.* Assesses the forces operating to preserve the separate status and Indian identity of American Isolate communities of eastern seaboard Indians such as the Nanticoke and Piscataway. Size of the mixed-race populations, the maintenance of family unity, ability to make the transition from an aboriginal to a Euro-American concept of land tenure, the effects of racial discrimination that promoted ethnic group cohesion, and the adoption of American core institutions served to hold the groups of Indian survivals together. Concludes that "the place of Indians in American society may be seen as one aspect of the question of the integration of minority groups into the social system," and the key to understanding identity systems. 42 notes.

G. J. Bobango

3907. Porter, Frank W., III. MATERIAL ACCULTURATION AMONG INDIAN SURVIVALS IN THE MIDDLE ATLANTIC REGION. *Pioneer Am. Soc. Tr. 1983 6: 37-48.* Material objects—architectural structures, domestic items, agricultural tools, hunting and fishing tools—indicate the degree of acculturation by Indians in Maryland, Delaware, Pennsylvania, and Virginia; covers the 18th-20th centuries.

3908. Purrington, Bruce L. REASSESSING CHEROKEE STUDIES. *Appalachian J. 1975 2(4): 252-257.* Discusses the Cherokee Indians from pre-history to the present, focusing on the influence of white culture on Indian social organization, and criticizes the methods and objectives of cultural anthropology for perpetuating racism.

3909. Rountree, Helen C. CHANGE CAME SLOWLY: THE CASE OF THE POWHATAN INDIANS OF VIRGINIA. *J. of Ethnic Studies 1975 3(3): 1-19.* Describes the Powhatan Indians, especially the Pamunkey and the Mattaponi, from 1607 to the present and the process of "incorporation" whereby their culture lost its independence yet persists today as a subculture. "Culture change has resulted in neither complete assimilation or complete extinction for the Powhatan," contrary to the common assumption that Powhatan society was extinct by 1700, a view based on English people's "wishful thinking." At first only tools and weapons changed, and the change to English-style agricultural economy was put off as long as possible. Yet the Indian land base was eaten away so steadily that by 1700 only a few thousand acres in all of eastern Virginia remained to them. Even so the white's notion of land ownership was resisted, and tribal ownership with family usufruct is still the rule for today's reservation tribes. The aboriginal culture remained strong "until well into the 18th century." Such gradualism accounts for their more organized society today, compared to that of other Indian groups, and the political system is one of the few examples of true syncretism, whereby trial identity remains strong. Primary sources; 47 notes.

G. J. Bobango

3910. Schlenker, Jon A. AN HISTORICAL ANALYSIS OF THE FAMILY LIFE OF THE CHOCTAW INDIANS. *Southern Q. 1975 13(4): 323-334.* Divides Choctaw history into five categories: Primitive Period, European Contact Period, Treaty and Missionary Period, Removal and Reservation Period, and US Citizenship Period. Studies each period in terms of kinship systems and family cycles and examines such factors as birth rates, marriage customs, role assignments, and rituals. 48 notes.

R. W. Dubay

3911. Wahrhaftig, Albert L. MORE THAN MERE WORK: THE SUBSISTENCE SYSTEM OF OKLAHOMA'S CHEROKEE INDIANS. *Appalachian J. 1975 2(4): 327-331.* Discussing social organization and division of labor among the men in Cherokee Indian settlements, notes that the economy is sustained by men over the age of 40, the function of the younger men being the assimilation of the dominant white culture.

3912. Waldowski, Paula. ALICE BROWN DAVIS: A LEADER OF HER PEOPLE. *Chronicles of Oklahoma 1980-81 58(4): 455-463.* Alice Brown Davis (1852-1935) was born into an illustrious mixed-blood Seminole family which represented the pro-acculturation faction of the tribe. Educated by missionaries, she devoted her life to Indian education and served as superintendent of the Seminole girls' school called Emahaka Mission. Despite her emphasis upon teaching white ways to Indian children, she struggled to maintain total Indian control over the school but ultimately lost the battle. In 1922 she became the first woman to serve as principal chief of the Seminole Nation. 3 photos, 43 notes.

M. L. Tate

3913. Wetmore, Ruth Y. THE GREEN CORN CEREMONY OF THE EASTERN CHEROKEES. *J. of Cherokee Studies 1983 8(1): 45-56.* The Green Corn Ceremony, which dates back at least two centuries among Eastern Cherokee Indians, consists of the Prelimi-

nary Green Corn Feast and the Ripe Green Corn Feast, in which participants hold dances and conduct council meetings. The Green Corn Ceremony has been interpreted as a fertility rite and as a reaffirmation of Cherokee social harmony. Illus., 2 photos, 80 notes.

K. E. Gilmont

3914. Wetmore, Ruth Y. THE ROLE OF THE INDIAN IN NORTH CAROLINA HISTORY. *North Carolina Hist. Rev. 1979 56(2): 162-176.* Roles of Indians in North Carolina have included 1) independent nations, 2) defeated adversaries, 3) invisible men, and 4) emerging communities. Indian-white relations changed over time from friendship to disappointment, suspicion and war, and subjection, and culminated in a new search for cultural identity and responsibility. Primary sources; 5 photos, map, 69 notes.

R. V. Ritter

3915. Whatley, George Fields. CEDARTOWN'S BIG SPRING. *Georgia Life 1978 4(4): 20-21.* Describes the discovery of Big Spring in 1796, the Cherokee Indians of the region, the settlers who founded Cedartown in 1854, and the use of Big Spring as a recreational area and water source.

3916. Wilson, Terry P. OSAGE INDIAN WOMEN DURING A CENTURY OF CHANGE, 1870-1980. *Prologue 1982 14(4): 185-201.* The social status of Osage women in Oklahoma underwent major transformations during 1870-1980 as a result of changes in the tribe as a whole. Osage women were revered as marital partners. They were able to retain their importance during the period of change while gaining new independence as a result of sharing as equal partners in tribal revenues and waging a successful campaign to share in tribal governance. The current status of Osage women is reflected in their ability to participate in ceremonial Indian dances. This was not allowed prior to the 1940's. Based on interviews, correspondence, newspapers, and National Archives records; 7 photos, 64 notes.

M. A. Kascus

3917. —. A HISTORICAL PERSPECTIVE ABOUT THE INDIANS OF NORTH CAROLINA AND AN OVERVIEW OF THE COMMISSION OF INDIAN AFFAIRS. *North Carolina Hist. Rev. 1979 56(2): 177-187.* This survey of the early history of Indian-White relations in North Carolina reveals unrelieved repression, discrimination, and altogether reprehensible treatment of the Indians. In the late 19th and early 20th centuries, feeble attempts were made to provide education. As late as 1970, according to the census, educational barriers still existed. A major step forward was taken in 1971 when the General Assembly established the Commission of Indian Affairs to improve the quality of life for Indian people in housing, community services, and education. Some progress has been made. A paper presented by A. Bruce Jones, executive director, for the North Carolina Commission of Indian Affairs at a meeting of the North Carolina Literary and Historical Association.

R. V. Ritter

# From Prehistory to 1899

3918. Adams, David Wallace. EDUCATION IN HUES: RED AND BLACK AT HAMPTON INSTITUTE, 1878-1893. *South Atlantic Q. 1977 76(2): 159-176.* In April 1878, Richard Henry Pratt succeeded in admitting a group of Kiowa and Cheyenne Indians to the all-black Hampton Institute. Under the Institute's superintendent, Samuel C. Armstrong, the Indians acquired English, Christianity, civilized manners and morals, and the will to labor. The Indians were segregated from the blacks with only black student proctors—Booker T. Washington was one—for outside contact. This highly paternalistic system was designed to raise the Indians out of their historical circumstances and make them part of American society. 38 notes.

W. L. Olbrich

3919. Agnew, Brad. THE CHEROKEE STRUGGLE FOR LOVELY'S PURCHASE. *Am. Indian Q. 1975 2(4): 346-361.* In 1816, subagent William Lovely arranged for nearly seven million acres to be purchased for Cherokees who had been removed west to present-day Arkansas. After 10 years of protracted negotiations, a compromise settlement gave the Indians a somewhat different area of about the same size, which included several million acres of the original purchase. This is one instance of a genuine concern for Indian rights and a sincere effort to seek a mutually beneficial compromise. Primary sources; 65 notes.                                G. L. Olson

3920. Ahern, Wilbert H. "THE RETURNED INDIANS": HAMPTON INSTITUTE AND ITS INDIAN ALUMNI, 1879-1893. *J. of Ethnic Studies 1983 10(4): 101-124.* Hampton Institute in Virginia was created in 1868 and quickly "emerged as the leading example of the industrial model of education for the ex-slaves." In 1878 Hampton took on the work of Indian education and became the model for Indian schooling. Describes the Hampton experience and then studies the behavior of the school's alumni to provide insights into the meaning of the experience for them. By the turn of the century, the possibilities of students to make use of their education had begun to grow limited and by the second decade the promise of education "failed to prove effective protection, policies obstructed the influence of returned students and schools received less support." Primary and secondary works; 40 notes.

3921. Aldrich, Duncan M. GENERAL STORES, RETAIL MERCHANTS, AND ASSIMILATION: RETAIL TRADE IN THE CHEROKEE NATION, 1838-1890. *Chronicles of Oklahoma 1979 57(2): 119-136.* The trader in the Cherokee Nation was no footloose, half-civilized adventurer as the stereotype often implies, but rather was a sophisticated entrepreneur who played a major role in tribal politics. Most of the leading traders from 1838 to 1890 were mixed-bloods such as John Ridge and John Ross who found themselves leaders of opposing factions during the removal crisis. Once they were relocated in Indian Territory by the end of the 1830's, these traders continued to hold economic and political power, and they served as primary agents of the acculturation process. Primary and secondary sources; map, 6 photos.                    M. L. Tate

3922. Alexander, Mary and Childress, Marilyn, ed. CENSUS OF CHEROKEES IN THE LIMITS OF GEORGIA IN 1835. *Social Educ. 1981 45(7): 564-566.* Includes statistics from page 49 of the Office of Indian Affairs' 1835 Census of Cherokees in Georgia and presents sample questions for social studies class discussion.

3923. Benton, Lee David. AN ODYSSEY INTO TEXAS: WILLIAM QUESENBURY WITH THE CHEROKEES. *Chronicles of Oklahoma 1982 60(2): 116-135.* A small group of Cherokees traveled from eastern Indian Territory into Texas where they sought lands for their people to settle. Accompanying them on this 1845 journey was William Minor Quesenbury, a white man from Van Buren, Arkansas, who recorded the trip in his personal journal, parts of which are reprinted here. In addition to describing the geography, Quesenbury told about a council, near present-day Waco, with a group of Chief Bowles's Cherokees and a council with Comanches further west. Cherokee efforts to gain part of the Texas land failed to pass Congress. 2 maps, 2 sketches, 30 notes.
                                                              M. L. Tate

3924. Bilotta, James D. MANIFEST DESTINY AND THE FIVE CIVILIZED TRIBES. *Indian Hist. 1977 10(3): 23-33.* In pursuance of the Indian Removal Act of 1830, the majority of the Five Civilized Tribes—the Cherokees, Choctaws, Chickasaws, Creeks and Seminoles—were forcibly moved by the US government from the Gulf states to Oklahoma. Briefly accounts this removal together with a historiographical glance at the treatment given that event in major history books of the 19th and 20th centuries. Most saw it as a part of the Manifest Destiny of the United States to span the continent. A few took the Indian point of view and saw it as a matter of military conquest. 53 notes.            E. D. Johnson

3925. Bonnifield, Paul. THE CHOCTAW NATION ON THE EVE OF THE CIVIL WAR. *J. of the West 1973 12(3): 386-402.* By 1860 the Choctaw Indians had become almost completely acculturated. English was widely spoken, public schools established, and farming and business activities flourished. The question of statehood within the Confederacy arose and two constitutions were drafted.

However, the Choctaw attitudes toward slavery and private ownership of land were points of conflict, and the matter was still unresolved when the Civil War began. 67 notes.          V. L. Human

3926. Boyce, Douglas W. DID A TUSCARORA CONFEDERACY EXIST? *Indian Historian 1973 6(3): 34-40.* There is little or no historical evidence that a confederacy existed before 1711.

3927. Brown, Gayle Ann. CONFEDERATE SURRENDERS IN INDIAN TERRITORY. *J. of the West 1973 12(3): 455-461.* Considers the processes of Confederate surrender during the Civil War in Indian Territory. The surrender of General Robert E. Lee left western commanders without a leader. General Kirby-Smith claimed that the western Confederacy could defend itself, but several governors disagreed. General Cooper in Indian Territory waited for precise official word. Indian General Stand Watie was the last Confederate general to surrender. 31 notes.         V. L. Human

3928. Brown, M. L. NOTES ON U.S. ARSENALS, DEPOTS, AND MARTIAL FIREARMS OF THE SECOND SEMINOLE WAR. *Florida Hist. Q. 1983 61(4): 445-458.* The 2d Seminole War was a proving ground for innovative military technology. Some new "hardware" included Joshua Shaw's percussion cap ignition system, breech-loading firearms, and the Colt revolving rifle. The war was the first to be supported by an "infant American military complex." The Ordnance Department was three years old and overcame major logistical problems to supply the army with all of its needs. Based on *Ordnance Reports,* 1835-42, and other sources; 5 charts, 33 notes.                                 N. A. Kuntz

3929. Brown, Philip M. EARLY INDIAN TRADE IN THE DEVELOPMENT OF SOUTH CAROLINA: POLITICS, ECONOMICS, AND SOCIAL MOBILITY DURING THE PROPRIETARY PERIOD, 1670-1719. *South Carolina Hist. Mag. 1975 76(3): 118-128.* In the late 17th century, traders of skins and Indian slaves made fortunes and by 1715 had political and economic control of South Carolina; however, their actions produced bloody Indian wars, such as the Yamasee War of 1715. From the tradesmen came the antebellum plantocracy later in the 18th century. Based on primary sources; 43 notes.                        R. H. Tomlinson

3930. Buice, David. LINCOLN'S UNISSUED PROCLAMATION. *Prologue 1978 10(3): 153-169.* Abraham Lincoln's failure to make a public commitment on behalf of the Five Civilized Tribes resident in the Indian Territory during the Civil War caused them great hardships. Many of these Indians supported the Confederacy owing to geographical proximity and to the lack of tangible aid and counsel from the Union. William P. Dole, commissioner of Indian affairs for the Union, failed to obtain Union troops to hold the Indians in line, while pro-Union Indian refugees in Kansas were compelled to exist without Union aid or support. After meeting with Cherokee Indian leader John Ross in 1862, Lincoln drafted a letter to Ross and a proclamation to the Five Civilized Tribes which would have established a promising new approach to relations between the government and the Indians. The documents were never issued. Based on archival research.        N. Lederer

3931. Buice, David. PRELUDE TO FORT SMITH: CONGRESS AND THE FIVE CIVILIZED TRIBES. *Red River Valley Hist. Rev. 1982 7(3): 4-17.* Describes the relationship between the federal government and the Five Civilized Tribes of the Indian Territory from the beginning of the Civil War in 1861 to the 1866 signing of the Fort Smith treaties; the relationship was tried by the defection of some Indians to the Confederate side and the inability of federal troops to provide protection for Union sympathizers.

3932. Burnett, John G. THE CHEROKEE REMOVAL THROUGH THE EYES OF A PRIVATE SOLDIER. *J. of Cherokee Studies 1978 3(3): 180-185.* Personal narrative relating the sufferings endured by the Cherokee Indians during the forced removal.

3933. Bushnell, Amy. "THAT DEMONIC GAME": THE CAMPAIGN TO STOP INDIAN PELOTA PLAYING IN SPANISH FLORIDA, 1675-1684. *Americas (Acad. of Am. Franciscan Hist.) 1978 35(1): 1-19.* Convinced that pelota, a traditional ball game played by Florida Indians, was harmful to social and political order and above all to the Indians' souls because of its violence and the sorcery, sexual license, and neglect of crops and defense it engendered, Spanish civil and religious authorities launched a campaign to eradicate it. The immediate results of the campaign are hard to assess, but the game did disappear, if only because the Indians were fast nearing extinction. Primary sources; 45 notes.

D. Bushnell

3934. Camp, Paul Eugen. THE ATTACK ON BRADEN CASTLE: ROBERT GAMBLE'S ACCOUNT. *Tampa Bay Hist. 1979 1(1): 55-60.* Reprints an undated manuscript written by Robert Gamble in which he describes the events of a Seminole Indian raid on the home of Joseph Addison Braden, Braden's Castle (so named because of its fortress-like appearance), in Bradenton, Florida, 1856, in the collection of the Richard Keith Call Papers of the Florida Historical Society.

3935. Campbell, Janet. THE FIRST AMERICANS' TRIBUTE TO THE FIRST PRESIDENT. *Chronicles of Oklahoma 1979 57(2): 190-195.* Attending the 4 July 1848 cornerstone laying for the Washington Monument were delegates from the Cherokee, Chickasaw, Stockbridge, Creek, and Choctaw nations. Several of these groups contributed money for the monument and others promised to contribute part of the stone. When the monument finally was completed in 1884, it bore a memorial stone only from the Cherokee. Secondary sources; 2 photos, 9 notes.

M. L. Tate

3936. Campbell, Janet and Sam, Archie. THE PRIMAL FIRE LINGERS. *Chronicles of Oklahoma 1975-76 53(4): 463-475.* Traces the history and culture of the Cherokee Indians prior to removal during the 1830's. Describes the seven great tribal ceremonies and accompanying dances, some of which are preserved in Oklahoma. The town of Nv-wo-ti, or Medicine Spring, in Muskogee County represents a direct contact with the past because its Natchez-Cherokee population honors and sustains the old traditions. 3 photos, 19 notes.

M. L. Tate

3937. Carlson, Paul H. WILLIAM R. SHAFTER, BLACK TROOPS, AND THE FINALE TO THE RED RIVER WAR. *Red River Valley Hist. Rev. 1978 3(2): 247-258.* Lieutenant Colonel William R. Shafter and his Seminole-Negro scouts hunted for Indians and explored, mapped, and recorded the flora and fauna of the uncharted Llano Estacado in 1875.

3938. Carter, L. Edward. THE SEMINOLE NATION AFTER LEAVING FLORIDA, 1855-1860. *Chronicles of Oklahoma 1977-78 55(4): 433-453.* Since removal from Florida to Indian Territory during the 1930's-40's, the Seminole Indians had been settled among the Creeks and forced to abide by their laws. A new treaty in 1856 guaranteed them lands and autonomy in western Indian Territory, but pressures from Comanches and Kiowas kept the Seminoles from fully settling there. The Civil War drove a wedge between Seminole factions and undermined postwar recovery. Primary and secondary sources; 3 photos, 2 maps, 62 notes.

M. L. Tate

3939. Chapman, B. B. CHEROKEE ALLOTMENTS IN THE OUTLET. *Chronicles of Oklahoma 1981-82 59(4): 401-421.* During 1893, 62 Cherokee Indians received land allotments in the Cherokee Outlet, since they had settled in the area before it was opened to white settlement. Robert L. Owen, agent to the Cherokees and land speculator in the Outlet, played a major role in establishing the allotments and James William Duncan served as the government's representative. Under the guidelines, the Cherokees were able to take first choice on land allotments, and their claims subsequently withstood all legal tests. Based on government documents and National Archives material from "Office of Indian Affairs, Letters Sent"; 3 photos, 46 notes.

M. L. Tate

3940. Clark, Blue. CHICKASAW COLONIZATION IN OKLAHOMA. *Chronicles of Oklahoma 1976 54(1): 44-59.* Explores the erosion of Chickasaw sovereignty and the tribe's removal to Indian Territory by the 1830's. Liquor, indebtedness, white land hunger,

and cultural conflict with white values led to intratribal tensions and disunity of purpose. Full-bloods, refusing eviction from their lands, conflicted with the mixed-blood aristocracy. A series of negotiations culminated in the 1832 Treaty of Pontotoc and provided for the final cession of all tribal lands east of the Mississippi River. Because they were the last of the Five Civilized Tribes to accept a home in the west, the Chickasaw Indians experienced a better-planned removal process and their migration was less severe. Secondary sources; 2 photos, map.

M. L. Tate

3941. Clark, Thomas D. THE JACKSON PURCHASE: A DRAMATIC CHAPTER IN SOUTHERN INDIAN POLICY AND RELATIONS. *Filson Club Hist. Q. 1976 50(3): 302-320.* Explains the diplomatic efforts of Andrew Jackson and Isaac Shelby to purchase the Chickasaw reservation located between the Tennessee and Mississippi Rivers in western Tennessee and Kentucky in 1818. The Chickasaws proved extremely reluctant to give up their treaty rights, and only by using bribery and verbal threats were Jackson and Shelby able to carry out their mission. Based on published government documents and the published correspondence of Jackson and John C. Calhoun; 84 notes.

G. B. McKinney

3942. Coe, Joffre L. THE INDIAN IN NORTH CAROLINA. *North Carolina Hist. Rev. 1979 56(2): 158-161.* An anthropological and cultural appraisal of the Indians whom John Lawson observed when he traveled through North Carolina in 1700. A brief review of prehistoric cultural development in the area shows that the tribes represented three racial varieties and spoke 30 dialects belonging to the Algonquian, Iroquois, or Siouan linguistic families. They represented vestiges of all periods from the Archaic through the Mississippian. The simplest societies developed in coastal areas, and the most complex in the mountains. Photo.

3943. Conard, A. Mark. THE CHEROKEE MISSION OF VIRGINIA PRESBYTERIANS. *J. of Presbyterian Hist. 1980 58(1): 35-58.* In the latter 1750's Virginia Presbyterians launched the first Christian mission among the Overhill Cherokee Indians in what is now Tennessee. Discusses the founding, operation, and decline of the labors of John Martin and William Richardson. Based on Richardson's diary (Wilberforce Eames Collection, Manuscript Division, New York Public Library), Eleazar Wheelock MSS (Dartmouth College), Letter Book of the Society for the Propagation of the Gospel in New England (Alderman Library, University of Virginia), ecclesiastical court records and secondary studies; 93 notes.

H. M. Parker, Jr.

3944. Conser, Walter H., Jr. JOHN ROSS AND THE CHEROKEE RESISTANCE CAMPAIGN, 1833-1838. *J. of Southern Hist. 1978 44(2): 191-212.* Studies the strategies and techniques of the Cherokee Indians' campaign of nonviolent resistance to removal to the West. Examines the intratribal conflicts between the National party, the largest group against removal, led by Chief John Ross, and the Treaty party, which favored removal, led by Major Ridge, John Ridge, and Elias Boudinot. The failure of Ross's campaign of nonviolence may be attributed, in part, to the changed perspectives of the Jacksonians toward the Indians.

M. S. Legan

3945. Corn, James F. CONSCIENCE OR DUTY: GENERAL JOHN E. WOOL'S DILEMMA WITH CHEROKEE REMOVAL. *J. of Cherokee Studies 1978 3(1): 35-39.* In June 1836 General John E. Wool was ordered to the Cherokee country of Tennessee, North Carolina, and Alabama to ascertain conditions there prior to possible Cherokee removal to the West. His orders indicated that he was to act against the Indians in case of hostilities, but the only hostilities were by local whites against the Cherokee. Complaints by white settlers led to a board of inquiry in September 1837 when Wool was exonerated for his temperate attitude toward the Cherokees. 2 illus., 19 notes.

J. M. Lee

3946. Corn Tassel and Tatum, William, transl. CHEROKEE REPLY TO THE COMMISSIONERS OF NORTH CAROLINA AND VIRGINIA, 1777. *J. of Cherokee Studies 1976 1(2): 128-129.* In July 1777 the Cherokee Indians ceded a large amount of land in what is now Tennessee to the whites in the Treaty of Long Island. Corn Tassel, a noted Cherokee chief and orator, delivered a reply to the white demand for a larger cession. He opposed giving the whites more land and considered them intruders and invaders with no rights to Indian land. Corn Tassel's reply was translated by William Tatum, a witness to the proceedings and is reprinted from the *Tennessee Historical Magazine* (1921 7:2). Note.                J. M. Lee

3947. Covington, James W. AGRICULTURE AS PRACTICED BY THE EASTERN TIMUCUANS OF FLORIDA: 1564-1590. *J. of NAL Assoc. 1978 3(1-2): 9-12.* Describes the agriculture of the Eastern Timucuan Indians of Florida, based on paintings by French artist Jacques LeMoyne in 1564, published along with LeMoyne's narrative in a book in 1591 in Germany by Flemish artist Theodore DeBry, and from Spanish accounts written in 1613, and a recent article on excavations in Alachua County, Florida.

3948. Dickinson, S. D. HISTORIC TRIBES OF THE OUACHITA DRAINAGE SYSTEM IN ARKANSAS. *Arkansas Archeologist 1980 21: 1-11.* A review of De Soto's chronicles, seventeenth and eighteenth century maps, and other French and Spanish documents reveals information on tribes and villages in many parts of southern Arkansas and northern Louisiana. Exact identification and exact location are sometimes difficult because of conflicting spelling and inaccurate maps. Knowledge of the sources and the potential for sites associated with these earliest European contacts should be kept in mind by archeological and historic researchers.                J

3949. Dobyns, Henry F. THREE APPROACHES, THREE INDIANS—NONE REALISTIC. *J. of Am. Ethnic Hist. 1982 2(1): 71-76.* Reviews *The European and the Indian: Essays in the Ethnohistory of Colonial North America* (1981), by James Axtell; *Settling with the Indians: The Meeting of English and Indian Cultures in America, 1580-1640* (1980), by Karen Kupperman; and *Savagism and Civility: Indians and Englishmen in Colonial Virginia* (1980), by Bernard Sheehan. 7 notes.                N. C. Burckel

3950. Drechsel, Emanuel J. TOWARDS AN ETHNOHISTORY OF SPEAKING: THE CASE OF MOBILIAN JARGON, AN AMERICAN INDIAN PIDGIN OF THE LOWER MISSISSIPPI VALLEY. *Ethnohistory 1983 30(1-4): 165-176.* Examines Antoine Simon Le Page du Pratz's *Histoire de la Louisiane* (1758) for sociolinguistic information on the Mobilian Jargon, the Chickasaw-Choctaw trade language of greater Louisiana. The information was confirmed through other sources, which supports the concept of extracting an ethnohistory of language from historical documents.

3951. Du Chateau, Andre Paul. THE CREEK NATION ON THE EVE OF THE CIVIL WAR. *Chronicles of Oklahoma 1974 52(3): 290-315.* Outlines the history of the Creek Nation before the Civil War. Delineates the boundaries of Creek lands in Indian Territory and describes the financial and legal structure, social and economic organization, and important religious activities of the tribe. In the 1850's Christian missionaries greatly influenced the Creeks, and the Nation was in the process of acculturation and change on the eve of the Civil War. The Civil War brought dissension within the Creek community. Based on US government documents, primary and secondary sources; 2 illus., 6 photos, map, 51 notes.                N. J. Street

3952. Dysart, Jane E. ANOTHER ROAD TO DISAPPEARANCE: ASSIMILATION OF CREEK INDIANS IN PENSACOLA, FLORIDA, DURING THE NINETEENTH CENTURY. *Florida Hist. Q. 1982 61(1): 37-48.* Prior to Indian removal from west Florida numerous individuals lost their Indian identity due to assimilation. An analysis of the records from churches and the Bureau of Indian Affairs indicates that pressure to conform to a biracial society was too great to resist. Becoming white was a method of avoiding the label "primitive savage." Little is known about Indians who married blacks. Based on 1832 census figures, Alabama census returns, records of the Bureau of Indian Affairs, and other sources; 41 notes.                N. A. Kuntz

3953. Ellsworth, Lucius F. and Dysart, Jane E. WEST FLORIDA'S FORGOTTEN PEOPLE: THE CREEK INDIANS FROM 1830 UNTIL 1970. *Florida Hist. Q. 1981 59(4): 422-439.* The civil rights movement of the 1960's brought many Indians to realize their heritage, the Creeks in Western Florida being an example. Dispersement beginning in the 1830's removed many from their tribe. Interracial marriage furthered the cultural breakdown. By the late 1960's the restoration of the Creeks of western Florida had started. Based on family records, newspapers, and other sources; 8 fig., 50 notes.                N. A. Kuntz

3954. Englund, Donald R. INDIANS, INTRUDERS, AND THE FEDERAL GOVERNMENT. *J. of the West 1974 13(2): 97-105.* The federal government had pledged to protect the Cherokee Indians from intruders in the Treaties of 1835 and 1866 but "there were numerous and prominent signs that the government actually wanted to expedite white intrusion into the Cherokee Nation. Several provisions of the Treaty of 1866 ... made the area attractive to whites." More detrimental were a series of administrative actions instituted by the Department of the Interior dealing with the right of the Cherokee government to determine the identity and legal status of intruders. This indicated "that the government was not sincere in its avowed policy of actively removing intruders." 26 notes.                D. D. Cameron

3955. Evans, E. Raymond. FORT MARR BLOCKHOUSE: THE LAST EVIDENCE OF AMERICA'S FIRST CONCENTRATION CAMPS. *J. of Cherokee Studies 1977 2(2): 256-262.* Fort Marr was erected in 1814 and probably named after George Washington Lent Marr. During the War of 1812 it was used as a supply depot and thereafter abandoned. During the Cherokee Removal of the 1830's it was used as a holding camp by General Scott. Conditions at Fort Marr for the Indians was generally wretched. After removal Fort Marr was demolished with the exception of one blockhouse. In 1922 it was removed to its present location in Benton, Tennessee, 15 miles from its original site. 2 illus., 23 notes.
                                    J. M. Lee

3956. Evans, E. Raymond. HIGHWAYS TO PROGRESS: NINETEENTH CENTURY ROADS IN THE CHEROKEE NATION. *J. of Cherokee Studies 1977 2(4): 394-400.* Notes the highways built through Cherokee territory in Tennessee and Georgia, paying particular attention to the taverns which sprang up to meet travelers' needs.

3957. Evans, E. Raymond, ed. JEDIDIAH MORSE'S REPORT TO THE SECRETARY OF WAR ON CHEROKEE INDIAN AFFAIRS IN 1822. *J. of Cherokee Studies 1981 6(2): 60-78.* Secretary of War John C. Calhoun commissioned the Reverend Jedidiah Morse to survey Indians in the Mississippi Valley. His travels encompassed most of the Tennessee Valley, where he surveyed life among Cherokee Indians. Including a letter by John Gambold on Cherokee school-church activities, the balance of the report describes Cherokee society, Presbyterian Church activities, and the work of the American Board of Commissioners for Foreign Missions among the Cherokees. Describing Cherokee society as highly organized and well educated, the report was the first federal study of an Indian tribe. 6 notes.                K. E. Gilmont

3958. Evans, E. Raymond. NOTABLE PERSONS IN CHEROKEE HISTORY: BOB BENGE. *J. of Cherokee Studies 1976 1(2): 98-106.* Bob Benge, a mixed-blood Cherokee leader, was born about 1760. He was extremely anti-American and led many forays against the Americans after the Revolution. He gained a considerable reputation among both Indians and whites for his exploits. Most of his career was military, and in Tennessee and Virginia. Benge, a relative of Sequoyah, was killed in ambush by a Virginia militia officer named Hobbs on 9 April 1794. Primary and secondary sources; map, 33 notes.                J. M. Lee

3959. Evans, E. Raymond. NOTABLE PERSONS IN CHEROKEE HISTORY: DRAGGING CANOE. *J. of Cherokee Studies 1977 2(1): 176-189.* Dragging Canoe was born about 1740 in an Overhill town on the Little Tennessee River and became a military leader in maturity. He opposed any land cessions to the whites, sided with the British during the American Revolution, and personally led many attacks. Following the Revolution he was involved in attempts to form an Indian alliance against the Americans. The defeat of St. Clair in November 1791 was a highlight of his career. He died 1 March 1792 at Lookout Mountain, Tennessee. Primary and secondary sources; 81 notes.    J. M. Lee

3960. Evans, E. Raymond. NOTABLE PERSONS IN CHEROKEE HISTORY: STEPHEN FOREMAN. *J. of Cherokee Studies 1977 2(2): 230-239.* Stephen Foreman was born on 22 October 1807 in north Georgia, the son of Anthony Foreman, a Scottish soldier, and Elizabeth Foreman. He was educated for the ministry at Candy's Creek and New Echota, Georgia, and at Union and Princeton Theological Seminaries. In 1833 he was licensed to preach by the Presbyterian Church. He led one group of Cherokee Indians west during the removal of the 1830's. After settling in Park Hill, Oklahoma, he was active in Cherokee government and established a school system. During this time he also translated parts of the Bible from Greek to Cherokee. He died in Oklahoma on 8 December 1881. Illus., 39 notes.    J. M. Lee

3961. Evans, E. Raymond. NOTABLE PERSONS IN CHEROKEE HISTORY: OSTENACO. *J. of Cherokee Studies 1976 1(1): 41-54.* Ostenaco was a noted leader of the 18th-century Cherokee Indians. Born in the early 1700's in Tennessee, Ostenaco gained fame in diplomacy and military feats. Generally pro-British and anti-French, he did have several quarrels with the English and was a party in the events leading to the 1761 Grant expedition. A highlight of his career was a trip in 1762 to London, where he had an audience with George III on 8 July. He was not active during the American Revolution and died around 1780. Primary and secondary sources; 4 figs., 66 notes.    J. M. Lee

3962. Ewan, Joseph W. A SEMINOLE REMINISCENCE. *Tequesta 1980 40: 43-46.* Recollections of a series of discussions with the Seminole leader Tiger Tail in 1875. Reprinted from the Miami *Metropolis*, 7 March 1903.    H. S. Marks

3963. Ewan, Joseph W. THE SEMINOLE'S CHRISTMAS. *Tequesta 1980 40: 39-42.* Recollections of Christmas Eve, 1874, when about 30 Seminole Indians celebrated Christmas with much gaity and liquor. Reprinted from the Miami *Metropolis*, 15 March 1901.    H. S. Marks

3964. Ewers, John C. THE INFLUENCE OF EPIDEMICS ON THE INDIAN POPULATIONS AND CULTURES OF TEXAS. *Plains Anthropologist 1973 18(60): 104-115.* Historic records indicate that Indian tribes residing in Texas prior to 1820 suffered no fewer than 30 epidemics during the period of white contact prior to 1890. The cumulative effect of successive epidemics was a major factor in the extinction of some of these tribes, and in continued population decreases among the others. Most probably these epidemics also caused significant cultural changes among the Indians who survived them in such varied aspects of life as warfare, political and social organization, and religious beliefs and practices.
J

3965. Fairbanks, Charles H. FROM MISSIONARY TO MESTIZO: CHANGING CULTURE OF EIGHTEENTH-CENTURY ST. AUGUSTINE. *Eighteenth-Century Florida and the Caribbean 1976: 88-99.* Two St. Augustine houses recently were excavated. The abundance of Indian ceramics and the study of food remains indicate the gradual absorption of Indians into Spanish society as food providers, craftsmen, or soldiers' wives. The chronic shortage of all supplies also must have stimulated the use of Indian pottery. The increased amount of British ceramics supports this view and indicates the penetrating power of British trade. Seminole artifacts and military equipment were conspicuously lacking. Biblio.
W. R. Hively

3966. Faulkner, Charles H. ORIGIN AND EVOLUTION OF THE CHEROKEE WINTER HOUSE. *J. of Cherokee Studies 1978 3(2): 87-93.* A discussion of the Cherokee Indians' winter, or "double oven" house. The archaeological evidence strongly suggests that it developed in the Middle Woodland period of the southeastern

Indians. Its architecture and construction are discussed on the evidence of several sites in Tennessee. Based on secondary sources; 4 illus., 26 notes.    J. M. Lee

3967. Feder, Bernard. THE RIDGE FAMILY AND THE DEATH OF A NATION. *Am. West 1978 15(5): 28-31, 61-63.* A brief history of the Cherokee Indians after 1785. Discusses friction with whites who coveted their lands in the southern Appalachians, fighting on the American side in the War of 1812, adoption of agriculture and white culture and establishment of the Cherokee Nation, the Cherokee-Georgia confrontation, the "Trail of Tears" removal to Oklahoma, and dissolution of the Cherokee Nation in 1893. A few hundred escaped removal and now live on a reservation in western North Carolina. Major Ridge, a Cherokee warrior who earned his rank by leading volunteers in service with Andrew Jackson in the War of 1812, became a wealthy planter and government leader, and helped to convince his people to adopt white ways as the only alternative to extinction. His son John Ridge, educated in a missionary school, was an eloquent spokesman for the Cherokee cause before eastern white audiences. 4 illus.
D. L. Smith

3968. Feest, Christian, ed. ANOTHER FRENCH ACCOUNT OF VIRGINIA INDIANS BY JOHN LEDERER. *Virginia Mag. of Hist. and Biog. 1975 83(2): 150-159.* A short piece entitled "La Medicine des Ameriquains de la Virginie," originally published in 1681, was probably written by the German explorer John Lederer. Published anonymously in the *Journal des Sçavans*, it describes medical practices of Virginia Indians. 38 notes.    R. F. Oaks

3969. Feest, Christian F. ZUR DOMESTIKATIONSGESCHICHTE DER NORDAMERIKANISCHEN INDIANER [Domestication of the North American Indian]. *Wiener Beiträge zur Gesch. der Neuzeit [Austria] 1980 7: 95-119.* Refutes the general implications of deficiency theory, which holds that European culture could, in the case of American Indians, be successfully substituted for voids in autochthonous Indian culture. Examines attempts by British colonists to domesticate Virginia Algonquians in the 17th century. Adoption of elements of European material culture, such as metals, alcohol, and script, by various Indian tribes illustrates the phenomenon of selectivity in acculturation and proves that the policy of civilizing the Indians was geared to the needs and expectations of the colonists, rather than to the natives' lifestyle. 73 notes.
S. Beer

3970. Fenton, William N. CHEROKEE AND IROQUOIS CONNECTIONS REVISITED. *J. of Cherokee Studies 1978 3(4): 239-249.* Analyzes John Morton's account of a visit among the Cherokee Indians in 1809; his knowledge of the Iroquois Indians allowed him to compare the customs of the groups, and his descriptions strengthen the view that similarities between the tribes resulted from the transfer of people between the groups rather than the view that the Iroquois originated in the South.

3971. Ferguson, Clyde R. CONFRONTATION AT COLERAINE: CREEKS, GEORGIANS, AND FEDERALIST INDIAN POLICY. *South Atlantic Q. 1979 78(2): 224-243.* Details a meeting at Coleraine on St. Mary's River, which was an American outpost just across from Spanish Florida and on the Creek Indians' side of the temporary boundary in the State of Georgia. Numerous factors contributed to making the meeting difficult—state's rights, the Federalist centralizing of Indian policy, the role of the federal government in affairs that appeared to abridge the claims of a state. In the end, the Treaty of Coleraine, signed 29 June 1796, reflected the success of the federal commissioners in attaining the goals of the Washington administration, a setback to Georgia's claims. Much of the work was later undone by the Jeffersonians who emphasized the role of the State at the expense of Indians. Based largely on American State Papers, Indian Affairs, other primary sources, and secondary monographs; 48 notes.    H. M. Parker, Jr.

3972. Finger, John R. THE ABORTIVE SECOND CHEROKEE REMOVAL, 1841-1844. *J. of Southern Hist. 1981 47(2): 207-226.* After the initial Cherokee removal in 1838, about 1,400 Cherokee Indians remained in western North Carolina or in nearby Tennessee, Georgia, or Alabama. Between 1841 and 1844 a further attempt was made to remove them. This misguided attempt failed because the Indians did not wish to go, the North Carolinians were not pushing to have them removed, and several prominent whites opposed the move. Finally, unlike 1838 no one was willing to enforce the removal. Based on the William Holland Thomas Papers (Western Carolina University), Bureau of Indian Affairs records, and other sources; 56 notes.                     T. D. Schoonover

3973.  Finger, John R. THE NORTH CAROLINA CHEROKEES, 1838-1866: TRADITIONALISM, PROGRESSIVISM AND THE AFFIRMATION OF STATE CITIZENSHIP. *J. of Cherokee Studies 1980 5(1): 17-29.* Under the leadership of William Holland Thomas, Cherokee Indians living in North Carolina struggled with the state of North Carolina and the federal government for recognition as citizens and for payment of claims under the Treaty of Echota. Thomas's efforts, including his organization of some Cherokees into a Confederate unit, finally won recognition by the state and national governments for Cherokee rights and, at the same time, an allowance for tribal customs. From Penrose Foundation and American Philosophical Society research grant; illus., 3 photos, 35 notes.                     K. E. Gilmont

3974.  Finger, John R. THE SAGA OF TSALI: LEGEND VERSUS REALITY. *North Carolina Hist. Rev. 1979 56(1): 1-18.* Historians have accepted uncritically the legend of Tsali, a Cherokee hero of the forced Indian removal westward in 1838. Myth has it that Tsali killed a federal soldier and was in turn tortured and executed by these soldiers, after having surrendered in order that his small band be allowed to remain in North Carolina. These legends are untrue: Tsali was probably not mistreated, nor did he play a major role in the murder of two soldiers. But he was captured (he did not surrender) and executed by a small tribe of Indians which did bargain to remain in North Carolina despite orders to other Cherokee tribes to leave. Based on an unpublished doctoral dissertation, manuscript letters, published official records, and secondary sources; 5 illus., map, 47 notes.                     T. L. Savitt

3975.  Fiorato, Jacqueline. THE CHEROKEE MEDIATION IN FLORIDA. *J. of Cherokee Studies 1978 3(2): 111-119.* In 1837, John Ross accepted the invitation of the United States to mediate the US-Seminole disputes. The reasons for this mission, while Cherokee-American controversies were so bitter, are explored. Argues that Ross hoped the successful conclusion of the Seminole War would result in a new Cherokee agreement with the government as an alternative to removal. 4 illus., 45 notes.                     J. M. Lee

3976.  Fischer, LeRoy H. THE CIVIL WAR ERA IN INDIAN TERRITORY. *J. of the West 1973 12(3): 345-355.* Introduces ten articles on aspects of the Civil War era in Indian Territory. 7 photos, map.                     V. L. Human

3977.  Flores, Dan L. THE RED RIVER BRANCH OF THE ALABAMA-COUSHATTA INDIANS, AN ETHNOHISTORY. *Southern Studies 1977 16(1): 55-72.* During 1800-31, a sizable band of Alabama and Coushatta Indians lived on the banks of the Red River in northwestern Louisiana. The site was propitious. The Indians practiced hunting and fishing, raised corn, and traded with white officials. Although there was some fighting with neighboring tribes, they were generally peaceful. During 1800-20 increasing numbers of white settlers appeared. They drove off the buffalo, sold whiskey, and squatted illegally. During the war with England in 1815, the Indians remained loyal to the Americans. Other Indians arrived in the area after being driven from their own homes by white settlers. Because of these pressures, almost all trace of the two tribes was gone by 1831. Most moved to eastern Texas. Primary and secondary sources; 80 notes.                     J. Buschen

3978.  Flores, Dan L. THE SAGA OF THE TEXAS IRON. *Red River Valley Hist. Rev. 1981 6(1): 58-70.* Describes the numerous expeditions into the Louisiana-Texas border country during the first decades of the 19th century by men who were searching for the "Texas Iron," a meteorite originally in the possession of the Wichita Indians, and whose existence became legend as white men tried to get pieces of it.

3979.  Fogelson, Raymond D. MAJOR JOHN NORTON AS ETHNO-ETHNOLOGIST. *J. of Cherokee Studies 1978 3(4): 250-255.* John Norton's journal of 1816, recording a visit to the Cherokee Indians in 1809, displays Norton's keen eye for detail and capacity to generalize; one example of his ethnological acumen is his "employment of his knowledge about language relationships as clues to cultural origins."

3980.  Foret, Michael J. THE FAILURE OF ADMINISTRATION: THE CHICKASAW CAMPIAGN OF 1739-1740. *Louisiana Rev. 1982 11(1): 49-60.* The Anglo-Chickasaw threat to Louisiana's security prompted France's unsuccessful military campaign, one which intense factionalism, bureaucratic in-fighting and paranoid indecisiveness reveals the inherent weakness in the provincial bipolar administration and the centralized home government; focuses on the efforts of French colonial leaders to justify their actions to Jérôme Phélypeaux, chief administrator of the French colonial empire.

3981.  Franklin, W. Neil, ed. OCONOSTOTA, CHEROKEE CHIEFTAIN, RECEIVES A MILITARY COMMISSION FROM KERLEREC, LOUISIANA GOVERNOR, 1761: FRENCH TEXT AND ENGLISH TRANSLATION. *East Tennessee Hist. Soc. Publ. 1977 49: 3-7.* Reproduces a military commission to Oconostota, a Cherokee chieftain, issued by the French governor of Louisiana, Louis Billouart de Kerlerec. The original document is in the National Archives; 16 notes, photo.                     D. A. Yanchisin

3982.  Franks, Kenny A. THE CONFEDERATE STATES AND THE FIVE CIVILIZED TRIBES: A BREAKDOWN OF RELATIONS. *J. of the West 1973 12(3): 439-454.* Reviews relations between the Confederacy and the Five Civilized Tribes of Indian Territory. Confederate promises made at the beginning of the war were not kept, and Union victories in 1863 ruined Indian morale. Indian troops resented fighting in Arkansas while their homelands were being ravaged. The estrangement turned into open hostility by the war's end. 54 notes.                     V. L. Human

3983.  Franks, Kenny A. POLITICAL INTRIGUE IN THE CHEROKEE NATION, 1839. *J. of the West 1974 13(4): 17-25.* Discusses the internal politics of the Cherokee Nation. Dissension and violence occurred over the Treaty of New Echota (1839) and control of the tribal government. The nation was divided into three factions: the Old Settlers, led by John Brown and John Rogers; the pro-treaty group, led by Stand Watie; and the anti-treaty group, led by John Ross. Anti-treaty partisans murdered three pro-treaty leaders, an incident which ignited a great division and near civil war. The Nation finally had to turn to the US government for help in solving its internal difficulties. The government took action because of fear of an uncontrollable uprising on its western borders. Based on US government documents and secondary sources; 32 notes.
                     N. J. Street

3984.  Galloway, Patricia. CHOCTAW FACTIONALISM AND CIVIL WAR, 1746-1750. *J. of Mississippi Hist. 1982 44(4): 289-327.* The Choctaw intratribal war of 1747-50, a response to the French view of the law of retaliation, demonstrates Choctaw resistance to acculturation in the area of crime and punishment. The Choctaws persistently believed that even an ally had to obtain justice through limited war. Describes tribal factions, intratribal conflicts, and the evolving leadership in each group. Attacks by English, French, or other Indian forces on the rebellious Choctaw factions and the tribal leaders' retaliatory responses are fully documented. Based on the Archives des Colonies, sèrie C13A, Correspondence générale Louisiane, *Mississippi Provincial Archives: French Dominion*, 1-3, other primary materials, and secondary sources; 99 notes.                     M. S. Legan

3985.  Gammon, Tim. BLACK FREEDMEN AND THE CHEROKEE NATION. *J. of Am. Studies [Great Britain] 1977 11(3): 357-364.* From the inception of the Cherokee Nation in 1839, the Cherokees and other Indians practiced racism against Negroes. Blacks were enslaved and, after 1866, discriminations against the Negro freedmen were practiced despite constitutional and treaty provisions to the contrary. James Milton Turner (1840-1915), a Negro lawyer from Missouri and sometime American Consul General in Liberia, challenged the restrictions successfully. In 1888, the US Congress indemnified the victims of racism. Government documents and secondary sources; 28 notes.　　　　　H. T. Lovin

3986. Gammon, Tim. THE BLACK FREEDMEN OF THE CHEROKEE NATION. *Negro Hist. Bull. 1977 40(4): 732-735.* Although the 1866 treaty between the United States and the Cherokee Indians prohibited discrimination against freedmen, the Cherokee legislature subsequently excluded them from any share of $300,000 distributed from land sale proceeds. An appeal to the Cleveland administration led Congress to remedy the injustice in 1888. The incident demonstrated that enforcement of any caste system comes in part from "middle or low caste members" (the Cherokee) whose security is based on having at least one caste below them. Based on primary sources; illus., photo, 18 notes.
　　　　　　　　　　　　　　　　　　　R. E. Noble

3987. Gardner, Robert G. EBENEZER LEE COMPERE, CHEROKEE GEORGIA BAPTIST MISSIONARY. *Viewpoints: Georgia Baptist Hist. 1976 5: 91-102.* Ebenezer Lee Compere, a missionary from the Baptist Church, ministered to the Cherokee Indians in northeast Oklahoma 1854-65.

3988. Geist, Christopher D. SLAVERY AMONG THE INDIANS: AN OVERVIEW. *Negro Hist. Bull. 1975 38(7): 465-467.* Chronicles slaveholding among the Five Civilized Tribes (Creeks, Choctaws, Chickasaws, Cherokees, and Seminoles), 1721-1835.

3989. Graebner, Laura Baum. AGRICULTURE AMONG THE FIVE CIVILIZED TRIBES, 1840-1906. *Red River Valley Hist. Rev. 1978 3(1): 45-61.* Discusses agriculture, farming techniques, landholding practices, and crop yield, 1840-1906, among the Five Civilized Tribes (Choctaws, Chickasaws, Cherokees, Creeks, and Seminoles) who were removed to the Indian Territory.

3990. Grant, C. L. and Davis, Gerald H. THE WEDDING OF COL. BENJAMIN HAWKINS. *North Carolina Hist. Rev. 1977 54(3): 308-316.* Benjamin Hawkins (1754-1816) was principal agent to the Indians south of Ohio during 1796-1816. During this time Hawkins lived in Georgia with Lavinia Downs, an illiterate woman. Hawkins, nearly dying in 1812, asked Moravian missionary Karsten Petersen to marry them and so legitimize their children's inheritance claims. A letter (reproduced here) from Petersen to his superior reveals that he was a humane man well suited for his job. Based on the letter, local court records, and published primary sources; 2 illus., 20 notes.　　　　T. L. Savitt

3991. Grinde, Donald. CHEROKEE REMOVAL AND AMERICAN POLITICS. *Indian Historian 1975 8(3): 33-42, 56.* The removal of the Cherokee Indians from the southern Appalachians to Oklahoma in the 1830's is one of the most tragic events in the history of the American Indian. Relates the story, political and military, from the inception of the idea in the 1780's through the "Trail of Tears" in 1838. Emphasizes the role of the President and Congress, and the interactions of American political forces, particularly during Andrew Jackson's administration. 47 notes.
　　　　　　　　　　　　　　　　　　　E. D. Johnson

3992. Haan, Richard L. THE "TRADE DO'S NOT FLOURISH AS FORMERLY": THE ECOLOGICAL ORIGINS OF THE YAMASSEE WAR OF 1715. *Ethnohistory 1982 28(4): 341-358.* The Yamassees and Lower Creeks ignited an Indian war that almost engulfed South Carolina because of complex shifts in South Carolina's environment. Between 1700 and 1710 the overhunting of coastal deer herds, the expansion of cattle and pig raising, the rapid development of rice cultivation, and the elimination of the Spanish mission Indians in northwestern Florida combined to exhaust the Yamassees' trade resources in deerskins and Indian slaves. This depletion forced the Yamassees deeper into debt and eventually into war.　　　　　　　　　　　　　　　　J/S

3993. Hammond, Sue. SOCIOECONOMIC RECONSTRUCTION IN THE CHEROKEE NATION, 1865-1870. *Chronicles of Oklahoma 1978 56(2): 158-170.* The Civil War proved disastrous for the Cherokee Indians of Indian Territory: their population was cut in

half and their lands were devastated. Despite the inadequacy of federal Reconstruction funds, the Cherokees dedicated themselves to hard work and began the painful road to recovery. They expanded educational facilities, increased agricultural production, and maintained themselves as a self-governing nation. Based on government reports; 3 photos, 44 notes.　　　　M. L. Tate

3994. Hampton, Carol. INDIAN COLONIZATION IN THE CHEROKEE OUTLET AND WESTERN INDIAN TERRITORY. *Chronicles of Oklahoma 1976 54(1): 130-148.* During 1855-94 26 tribes were forcibly settled in the Cherokee Outlet and the southwestern quadrant of present-day Oklahoma. Among the first colonizers were the Wichitas, Keechies, Tonkawas, Ionies, and Penateka Comanches who were moved from Texas to the Leased District. Following the Civil War the federal government established an agency for the Cheyennes and Arapahos near Fort Supply and a Comanche-Kiowa reservation immediately to the south. By 1875 the Army had broken the military power of these tribes and generally limited their movements to the reservations. At the same time Otoes, Missouris, Osages, Kansas, Pawnees, and Sac and Fox bands signed away lands in Kansas and assumed small tracts between the Five Civilized Tribes and the Southern Plains Tribes. Relocation of Apache prisoners of war at Fort Sill in 1894 represented the last phase of the removal process. Secondary sources; 3 photos, 2 maps.
　　　　　　　　　　　　　　　　　　　M. L. Tate

3995. Harriman, Helga H. ECONOMIC CONDITIONS IN THE CREEK NATION, 1865-1871. *Chronicles of Oklahoma 1973 51(3): 325-334.* With the cooperation of government Indian agents, the Creek Nation made progress in crop production, animal husbandry, and housing in post-Civil War Oklahoma.　　　S

3996. Hendrix, Janey B. REDBIRD SMITH AND THE NIGHTHAWK KEETOOWAHS. *J. of Cherokee Studies 1983 8(1): 22-39.* Redbird Smith and Ned Christie, leaders of the Conservative Oklahoma Cherokees, formed the Keetoowah Society in opposition to acculturation into white society. While drunk, Ned Christie killed Sheriff Dan Maples, for which a posse led by Sam Maples, son of the sheriff, encircled Christie and his followers and killed Christie. 2 photos, map, 32 notes.　　　　　　K. E. Gilmont

3997. Henegar, H. B. RECOLLECTIONS OF CHEROKEE REMOVAL. *J. of Cherokee Studies 1978 3(3): 177-179.* Personal narrative of the conveyance of Cherokee Indians from Tennessee; focuses on John Ross and Cherokee factionalism.

3998. Hester, Thomas R. TRADITION AND DIVERSITY AMONG THE PREHISTORIC HUNTERS AND GATHERERS OF SOUTHERN TEXAS. *Plains Anthropologist 1981 26(92): 119-128.* Archaeological and ethnohistorical research has been greatly accelerated in southern Texas in the past five years, making possible a more detailed view of the area's 11,000-year record to replace the model of a homogenous prehistoric cultural pattern. While a hunting and gathering subsistence tradition dominated, there is now substantial evidence of intraregional cultural diversity, which was the result of both spatially and temporally localized resources and, perhaps, of shifting spheres of extra-areal cultural influences. New geomorphological, climatic, and chronometric data also permit us to examine culture within a chronological framework.
　　　　　　　　　　　　　　　　　　　J/S

3999. Heth, Charlotte. STYLISTIC SIMILARITIES IN CHEROKEE AND IROQUOIS MUSIC. *J. of Cherokee Studies 1979 4(3): 128-162.* Examines dance and song forms common to the Cherokee and Seneca Indians, suggests musical reasons for these forms, "and discusses the interrelationships of the performing media."

4000. Higginbotham, Jay. ORIGINS OF THE FRENCH-ALABAMA CONFLICT, 1703-1704. *Alabama Rev. 1978 31(2): 121-136.* French interests at Fort Louis under Commandant Jean-Baptiste de Bienville tried to lure the small but strategically-located Alabama tribe away from British influence starting in 1703. Hostilities resulted and continued sporadically until 1715, when both sides effected an alliance that secured the central region against Indian and British rivals. Primary sources from French, English, and Spanish archives; 34 notes.                                    J. F. Vivian

4001. Higginbotham, Mary Alves. THE CREEK PATH MISSION. *J. of Cherokee Studies 1976 1(2): 72-86.* During 1820-37 a school and mission were operated at Creek Path, Alabama, under the auspices of the American Board of Commissioners for Foreign Missions. Its purposes were the education of Cherokee Indians and conversion to Christianity. The major impetus for the mission came from John Brown and his children David and Catherine, all mixed-blood Cherokees. Although the work of the mission was successful, Cherokee removal to the West forced its abandonment in 1837. Primary and secondary sources; map, 3 figs., 83 notes.
                                                                J. M. Lee

4002. Hoebel, E. Adamson. ON CHEYENNE SOCIOPOLITICAL ORGANIZATION. *Plains Anthropologist 1980 25(88 part 1): 161-169.* In a recent (1974) article John H. Moore has challenged the validity of earlier ethnologies of the Cheyenne Indians, with respect to their presentation of Cheyenne sociopolitical organization. Moore advances a dialectic model, positing matrilineal, matrilocal uterine bands from which were drawn the Peace Chiefs, who constituted a uterine tribal council. In frequent opposition, were the military societies, which Moore identifies as agnatic units of organization. Viewed historically, power shifted from the "uterine" bands and tribal council to the "agnatic" military societies. This article evaluates the validity of Moore's reading of the Cheyenne data and the heuristic value of the model he presents. It also presents new materials on the transformation of the Cheyenne Dog Soldier society into a virilocal, endogamous residential band. 3 notes, biblio.
                                                                      J

4003. Hogue, S. Homes and Trinkley, Michael. PROBABLE PEE DEE PHASE BURIALS FROM SOCV8, MARLBORO COUNTY, SOUTH CAROLINA. *Southern Indian Studies 1978 30: 3-16.* Two skeletons, female and child, believed to be Pee Dee Indians, plus some pottery were found near the Great Pee Dee River in Chesterfield and Marlboro counties, South Carolina. Dating of the site is approximately the early 18th century. There is some evidence of Siouan influence. Map, table, 8 photos.            K. E. Gilmont

4004. Holm, Tom. CHEROKEE COLONIZATION IN OKLAHOMA. *Chronicles of Oklahoma 1976 54(1): 60-76.* In 1785 a small group of Cherokees migrated to Arkansas where they formed the nucleus of the Cherokee Nation West. During the following 40 years other small groups moved west to join them; but the majority of Cherokees struggled to preserve their ancestral lands in Georgia. Conformity to white ways did not lessen the pressures against them which culminated in the Indian Removal Act (1830). President Andrew Jackson's refusal to honor federal treaty obligations left the Cherokees at the mercy of Georgia law, and by 1835 the faction led by Elias Boudinot, Major Ridge, and John Ridge accepted removal. The followers of John Ross held out three more years until they too were evicted. The resulting "Trail of Tears" furthered intratribal tensions and left the Cherokees divided until after the Civil War. Secondary sources; 5 photos, 3 maps.            M. L. Tate

4005. Holm, Tom. INDIAN LOBBYISTS: CHEROKEE OPPOSITION TO THE ALLOTMENT OF TRIBAL LANDS. *Am. Indian Q. 1979 5(2): 115-134.* Beginning in the late 1870's and continuing through to the 1890's the Cherokee Nation of Indian Territory sent delegations to Washington to battle a steady stream of congressional bills aimed at ending tribal sovereignty, which were backed by railroad interests, land speculators, white reformers, and government officials. They were also fought, though less tenaciously, by Choctaw, Creek, Chickasaw, and Seminole delegations. White reformers argued that these Native Americans should be assimilated into American society. An allotment plan, under which individual parcels would be awarded each Indian, was devised. The Dawes Commission was established in order to gather support for the measure. In 1898 the Curtis Act was passed, dividing the tribal estate despite continuing Cherokee protests. Primary sources; 81 notes.                                                    J. Powell

4006. Holman, Tom. WILLIAM G. COFFIN, LINCOLN'S SUPERINTENDENT OF INDIAN AFFAIRS FOR THE SOUTHERN SUPERINTENDENCY. *Kansas Hist. Q. 1973 39(4): 491-514.* Coffin was caught in the struggle between the North and South for control of Indian Territory. He insisted that every effort should be made to provide for the protection and well-being of the Indians in the territory during the times the Confederates drove them into Kansas and while they were returned to the territory under military protection. Coffin's dealings with the Indians, certain military commanders, his subordinates, the War Department, the Interior Department, and the Bureau of Indian Affairs reveals a story of wartime uncertainty. Agrees that the Indians suffered greatly and were used in ways that made their anguish greater, but concludes that their plight would have been infinitely worse had it not been for Coffin's constructive work. Based on books, articles and manuscripts in the Indiana Historical Society and National Archives; 55 notes.                                           W. F. Zornow

4007. Howard, R. Palmer and Allen, Virginia E. STRESS AND DEATH IN THE SETTLEMENT OF INDIAN TERRITORY. *Chronicles of Oklahoma 1976 54(3): 352-359.* Discusses diseases and medical problems encountered by the Indians removed to Indian Territory, 1830's-70's, and the stress which occurred between Indian and white medicine.

4008. Howell, Elmo. WILLIAM GILMORE SIMMS AND THE AMERICAN INDIAN. *South Carolina R. 1973 5(2): 57-64.* The novels of Simms reveal that that antebellum southern novelist characterized the Indian by a moderation unusual for the time. Like James Fenimore Cooper, Simms treated the brutality of Indians realistically, but he did not portray the good Indian as a "noble savage." In *The Yemassee* Simms treated Indian "inferiority" not as racial, but as cultural. In a later novel, *The Cassique of Kiawah*, he tried to be fair to both whites and Indians, but saw the white man as superior because a civilized man was superior to a savage. The burden of the white man was to prepare the Indian for civilized life. Based on the writings of Simms and on critical studies; 21 notes.                                             A. V. Huff, Jr.

4009. Hranisky, W. Jack. THE VIRGINIA ALGONQUIAN LANGUAGE. *Chesopiean 1982 20(3-4): 19-29.* Describes the sources for the vocabulary of the Algonquian Powhatan language of Virginia collected by Captain John Smith and William Strachey, who was the first secretary of the Virginia colony; discusses the classification of Powhatan within the Algonquian linguistic family and includes a list of current Powhatan words.

4010. Isern, Thomas D. CHICKASAW ACADEMY. *Methodist Hist. 1981 19(3): 131-145.* The Missionary Society of the Methodist Episcopal Church (South) became interested in providing schools for the Chickasaw Indians in 1844. Wesley Browning began preliminary work on the Chickasaw Academy but was withdrawn in 1851. John C. Robinson, his successor, developed a very successful school in the Indian Territory, which trained the students in the manual arts, agricultural subjects, and basic elementary education. The school operated successfully from 1852 to 1867. Based on records of the Office of Indian Affairs, National Archives, Washington, D.C., reports of the Office of the Commissioner of Indian Affairs, and reports of the Missionary Society of the Methodist Episcopal Church (South); 37 notes.                          H. L. Calkin

4011. Johnson, Charles, Jr. BLACK SEMINOLES: THEIR HISTORY AND THEIR QUEST FOR LAND. *J. of the Afro-American Hist. and Geneal. Soc. 1980 1(2): 47-58.* Traces the individual histories of members of the Seminole-Negro Indian Scout Detachment, which was composed of black Seminoles, from 1866 to 1922 in Texas, focusing upon their unsuccessful attempts to obtain land from the federal government and the lack of recognition accorded them for their role in putting down Indian unrest north of the Rio Grande after 1866.

4012. Jordan, H. Glenn. CHOCTAW COLONIZATION IN OKLAHOMA. *Chronicles of Oklahoma 1976 54(1): 16-33.* Demands for Indian removal from the eastern United States began with Thomas Jefferson's efforts to set aside a permanent Indian

Territory west of the Mississippi River. The Choctaw Indians, led by Pushmataha, negotiated a compromise settlement in the Treaty of 1825, but it was offset by the 1828 presidential election of Andrew Jackson who favored immediate eviction. This replaced the gradualist policy implemented by Secretary of War John C. Calhoun who had resigned in 1825. The Treaty of Dancing Rabbit Creek, signed on 27 December 1830, signaled the final stage of removal which was not totally completed until 17 years later. Some of the groups reached Indian Territory with relatively few problems, but others suffered numerous deaths from epidemics and starvation. Secondary sources; 2 photos, 2 maps.            M. L. Tate

4013. Kalashnikov, Viktor Mikhailovich. BOR'BA INDEISKOGO PLEMENI SEMINOLOV PROTIV EKSPANSII SSHA [The struggle of the Seminole Indian tribe against US expansionism]. *Novaia i Noveishaia Istoriia [USSR] 1983 (3): 114-130.* Critical review of white and American Indian historiography on the Seminole wars (1812-58), the longest and costliest Indian conflict. Bourgeois historiography continues to be tinged by racial bias and defends colonialism, while Indian writers deal mainly with the personal bravery of individual Seminole freedom fighters and disregard socioeconomic factors underlying American predatory expansionist policy. Only Marxist-Leninist studies give a truly scientific analysis of all aspects of the Seminole conflict. 49 notes.            N. Frenkley

4014. Kelly, James C. NOTABLE PERSONS IN CHEROKEE HISTORY: ATTAKULLAKULLA. *J. of Cherokee Studies 1978 3(1): 2-34.* Attakullakulla, also known as Little Carpenter, was born between 1700 and 1712. From 1730 to his death ca. 1780 he was an influential Cherokee diplomat. He was pro-British, except for an interlude in the 1750's when he sided with the French. During the American Revolution he remained loyal to the British, but accommodated himself to the Americans when no other alternative was available. An early highlight of his career was a trip to England in 1730. 7 illus., 190 notes.            J. M. Lee

4015. Kelly, James C. OCONOSTOTA. *J. of Cherokee Studies 1978 3(4): 221-238.* During 1760-82, Oconostota was the most powerful chief of the Cherokee Indians; observes his relations with the British.

4016. Kersey, Harry A., Jr. FLORIDA SEMINOLES AND THE CENSUS OF 1900. *Florida Hist. Q. 1981 60(2): 145-160.* Accurate census data for the Seminole Indians residing in Florida did not exist until the work of J. Otto Fries in 1900. Fries's correspondence with his superior, John M. Cheney, provides insight into Seminole cultural life and the location of specific groups. Based on Fries-Cheney correspondence, privately owned, and other sources; map, fig., 40 notes.            N. A. Kuntz

4017. King, Duane H. BENGE'S AXE. *J. of Cherokee Studies 1976 1(2): 107-109.* Bob Benge was a mixed-blood Cherokee military leader killed in 1794. A small axe supposedly belonging to him eventually was purchased by Dr. William M. Grigsby of Kingsport, Tennessee, in 1971. It is now on indefinite loan to the Museum of the Cherokee Indian in Cherokee, North Carolina. Photo.            J. M. Lee

4018. King, Duane H. CHEROKEE BOWS. *J. of Cherokee Studies 1976 1(2): 92-97.* Describes the typical Cherokee bow and methods of bowmaking. The bow and arrow was the principal weapon of the American Indian prior to the advent of Europeans. Traditional Cherokee methods of bowmaking and use differed from modern-day practices of archery and the materials used. Several historic Cherokee bows are now on exhibit at the Museum of the Cherokee Indian at Cherokee, North Carolina. Secondary sources and one personal communication; 8 figs., 5 notes.            J. M. Lee

4019. King, Duane H. and Evans, E. Raymond. THE DEATH OF JOHN WALKER, JR: POLITICAL ASSASSINATION OR PERSONAL VENGEANCE? *J. of Cherokee Studies 1976 1(1): 4-16.* Concludes that John Walker, Jr., was assassinated by James Foreman for political rather than private motivations. Walker was a proremoval Cherokee leader during the 1820's-30's. Although there were personal animosities between Walker and Foreman because of

Foreman's bootlegging of whiskey into Cherokee lands, Foreman had never acted on them. Foreman also was implicated in other politically motivated killings. John Ross may have been involved. Primary and secondary sources; 2 photos, map, 66 notes.            J. M. Lee

4020. King, Duane H. LONG ISLAND OF THE HOLSTON: SACRED CHEROKEE GROUND. *J. of Cherokee Studies 1976 1(2): 113-127.* Narrates the events relating to the Long Island of the Holston, a prized possession of the Cherkoee Indians for many years. The Long Island was traditionally a Cherokee meeting ground and was of strategic importance during the early national period on the frontier. Land surrounding the island was relinquished to whites in July 1777, but the island itself was retained. It was used as a meeting place by the Cherokees for the next 30 years but was ceded to the US government in 1806. In 1976, the city of Kingsport, Tennessee returned the land to the Eastern Band of Cherokees. Primary and secondary sources; map, 5 figs., 39 notes.            J. M. Lee

4021. King, Duane H. A POWDER HORN COMMEMORATING THE GRANT EXPEDITION AGAINST THE CHEROKEES. *J. of Cherokee Studies 1976 1(1): 23-40.* The Grant campaign against the Cherokee Indians in 1761 is shown on an 18th-century powder horn. After a series of clashes with the Cherokees, Lieutenant Colonel James Grant led 2,828 officers and men into Indian territory on the Carolina frontier. Someone, apparently an officer, carved a map of the campaign and its highlights on a powder horn scrimshaw style. Heirloom of an Irish family, it was presented in 1976 to the Museum of the Cherokee Indian. Primary and secondary sources; map, 20 figs., 31 notes.            J. M. Lee

4022. King, Duane H. WHO REALLY DISCOVERED THE CHEROKEE-IROQUOIS LINGUISTIC RELATIONSHIP. *J. of Cherokee Studies 1977 2(4): 401-404.* As early as 1769, Moravian missionary David Zeisberger speculated on the linguistic connections.

4023. Knight, Vernon J., Jr. and Adams, Sherée L. A VOYAGE TO THE MOBILE AND TOMEH IN 1700, WITH NOTES ON THE INTERIOR OF ALABAMA. *Ethnohistory 1981 28(2): 179-194.* Presents in translation a French document of 1700 by Charles Levasseur pertaining to the Mobile and Tomeh Indians of the northern Gulf Coast of southeastern North America. Ethnographic data from the document receive comment, with emphasis on settlement and subsistence in the Mobile Bay-delta region. In addition, the earliest known French town list of the interior of Alabama is included, with notes on the probable identifications and affiliations of the Indian towns.            J/S

4024. Leacock, Eleanor. THE CHANGING FAMILY AND LÉVI-STRAUSS, OR WHATEVER HAPPENED TO FATHERS? *Social Res. 1977 44(2): 235-259.* Based on evidence from the North American Montagnais, Cherokee, and Iroquois, during the 17th-19th centuries, disputes Claude Lévi-Strauss's formulations of woman-exchange and incest prohibitions as "unwarranted teleology reminiscent of eighteenth-century social-contract theorizing."

4025. Lees, William B. and Kimery-Lees, Kathryn M. THE FUNCTION OF COLONO-INDIAN CERAMICS: INSIGHTS FROM LIMERICK PLANTATION, SOUTH CAROLINA. *Hist. Archaeol. 1979 13: 1-13.* Indian ceramics in colonial sites from Virginia to Florida have traditionally been viewed as having been manufactured by local Indian groups for trade with European settlers. This paper focuses largely on the general function of this pottery, using material from an 18th- and 19th-century rice plantation in coastal South Carolina. This ware functioned as an integral part of the kitchen. Analysis of the occurrence of these ceramics at Limerick through time suggests that they are significantly more frequent during the colonial period than during the antebellum period. This temporal distribution has been suggested to be a result of economic stress during the colonial period, which resulted in the selection of inexpensive Indian wares over the more expensive European wares.            J/S

4026. LeFave, Don. TIME OF THE WHITETAIL: THE CHARLES TOWN INDIAN TRADE, 1690-1715. *Studies in Hist. and Soc. 1973 5(1): 5-15.* Studies the Indian trade in whitetail deer hides for local trade and shipment to England which centered in the Carolinas, the base camp being at Savannah Town (modern Augusta) for transport to Charles Town. For a time, trade in Indian slaves supplemented the take on the staple deer hides. The trade area was broad, extending from Pennsylvania south, concentrating in what is now North and South Carolina, Virginia, Georgia, and parts of Florida, Tennessee, Alabama, Mississippi, and Louisiana, involving several Indian tribes. The latter were often incited to war against each other to increase the quantities of hides and slaves. 43 notes.                                                 R. V. Ritter

4027. Littlefield, Daniel F., Jr. and Underhill, Lonnie E. THE GRANGER MOVEMENT IN THE CHEROKEE NATION. *Red River Valley Hist. Rev. 1979 4(1): 14-25.* Discusses the granger movement in the United States during the 1870's and its effects on the Cherokee Indians in Indian Territory who shared similar interests and concerns with Anglo farmers.

4028. Littlefield, Daniel F., Jr. and Underhill, Lonnie E. THE JUDICIARY OF THE WESTERN CHEROKEE NATION, 1839-1876. *Pacific Hist. 1978 22(1): 38-54.* The constitution of 1839 governed the Western Cherokee nation until the passage of the Curtis Act in 1898. The judiciary portion of the Constitution generally failed until reformed by the New Code of Cherokee Laws in 1879. Failure had wide-reaching significance—advocates of extinguishing tribal states pointed to the weak judiciary. Analysis shows the judicial system failed because a lack of rules governing court procedure and outdated criminal code. Based on published reports, laws, the *The Cherokee Advocate,* 39 notes.            G. L. Olson

4029. Littlefield, Daniel F., Jr. and Underhill, Lonnie E. TIMBER DEPREDATIONS AND CHEROKEE LEGISLATION, 1869-1881. *J. of Forest Hist. 1974 18(1/2): 4-13.* "Between the end of the Civil War and the beginning of the twentieth century, the timber industry boomed in the Indian Territory. Most of the walnut, pine, and cedar—in short, any timber of value—fell under the axes of lumbermen who either legally or illegally cut the timber for profit." Due to their governmental structure, the Cherokee were the most successful of the Five Civilized Tribes in regulating the traffic in timber. During 1869-81 the Cherokee established policies and wrote legislation which provided controlled timber cutting and guaranteed prosecution of offenders. Based on documents in the Indian Archives Division of the Oklahoma Historical Society and on personal letters; 4 photos, map, 48 notes.            D. R. Verardo

4030. Logsdon, Guy. INDIAN STUDIES RESOURCES AT THE UNIVERSITY OF TULSA. *Chronicles of Oklahoma 1977 55(1): 64-77.* Surveys the extensive holdings of Indian resource material in the McFarlin Library of the University of Tulsa. The Worcester-Robertson Family Papers, consisting of 2,713 calendared letters and approximately 2,500 additional items, form the cornerstone of the collection and include the correspondence and journals of Samuel Worcester and his descendants who worked closely with the Cherokees and Creeks from the 1820's to the end of the 19th century. In 1975, the John W. Shleppey Collection of approximately 6,000 items was granted to the McFarlin Library. In addition to housing many rare periodicals and broadsides printed by the Five Civilized Tribes, this collection also includes treaties, tribal minutes, court records, and agency reports. Smaller holdings within the McFarlin Library are also discussed. 5 photos.            M. L. Tate

4031. Logsdon, Guy. OKLAHOMA'S FIRST BOOK: *ISTUTSI IN NAKTSOKU*, BY JOHN FLEMING. *Chronicles of Oklahoma 1976 54(2): 179-191.* Discusses the printing of the first book in Indian Territory, 1835, *Istutsi in Naktsoku,* an elementary education primer for Cherokee Indians' children; reviews missionary education in the Territory, and church and governmental feelings about the same, 1819-36; and discusses the work of John Fleming in this regard. Reviews the attitudes of the American Board of Commissioners for Foreign Missions and their work among the Creek Indians and Osage Indians.

4032. Lowery, George; Payne, John Howard, introd. NOTABLE PERSONS IN CHEROKEE HISTORY: SEQUOYAH OR GEORGE GIST. *J. of Cherokee Studies 1977 2(4): 385-393.* Biography of Sequoyah transcribed from an 1835 council of the Cherokee Indians.

4033. Luebke, Barbara F. ELIAS BOUDINOTT, INDIAN EDITOR: EDITORIAL COLUMNS FROM THE *CHEROKEE PHOENIX. Journalism Hist. 1979 6(2): 48-53.* Provides examples of the editorial comments of Elias Boudinot (ca. 1803-39), editor of the first Native American newspaper, *The Cherokee Phoenix,* published 1828-34.

4034. Magnaghi, Russell M. CHANGING MATERIAL CULTURE AND THE HASINAI OF EAST TEXAS. *Southern Studies 1981 20(4): 412-426.* Examines the lifestyle and practices of Hasinai Indians of east Texas, who resisted assimilation into white civilization but still accepted material changes for two centuries. The Hasinai learned to raise and train horses, then sell them, as well as hides and slaves, to the Spanish and the French in return for arms, ammunition, alcohol, knives, axes, and cloth. They continued to live in traditional pole houses and follow old life patterns. In the late 19th century, forcible resettlement brought about their disappearance as an identifiable tribe. Primary sources; 88 notes.
                                                        J. J. Buschen

4035. Mathes, Valerie L. CHIEF JOHN ROSS. *Masterkey 1980 54(2): 67-71.* Cherokee Indian Chief John Ross (1790-1866), born of a Scottish emigrant father and a one-quarter Cherokee mother, was a member of the Cherokee legislature during 1817-19, President of the National Committee during 1819-26, Principal Chief of the Eastern Cherokee during 1828-39, and Principal Chief of the Nation during 1839-66.

4036. Mathes, Valerie L. PRINTER FOR THE CHEROKEE. *Masterkey 1981 55(4): 152-155.* Reports on the career of Congregationalist minister Samuel Austin Worcester (1798-1859), who first published newspapers, textbooks, and Bibles in the language of the Cherokee Indians, 1828-59.

4037. McCullar, Marion Ray. THE CHOCTAW-CHICKASAW RECONSTRUCTION TREATY OF 1866. *J. of the West 1973 12(3): 462-470.* The end of the Civil War left Indian treaties with the federal government unresolved. No Indian tribes had fought as fiercely or as long against the Union as the Choctaws and Chickasaws, yet these tribes were granted favorable postwar treaties from the Union due to their quick decisionmaking and aggressive determination to see that their demands were met. 29 notes.
                                                        V. L. Human and S

4038. McFadden, Marguerite. COLONEL JOHN THOMPSON DREW: CHEROKEE CAVALIER. *Chronicles of Oklahoma 1981 59(1): 30-53.* John Thompson Drew, mixed-blood Cherokee, played a key role in tribal history because of his ability to speak English, his businessman's acumen, and his powerful relatives. Despite a lack of formal education, Drew was licensed to practice law in 1851 and within two years was made Judge of the Canadian District of Indian Territory. During the Civil War he actively supported the Confederacy by raising a regiment of Cherokee soldiers, but the war destroyed his wealth. Based on John Drew Papers at Gilcrease Institute; 5 photos, 55 notes.            M. L. Tate

4039. McFadden, Marguerite. THE SAGA OF "RICH JOE" VANN. *Chronicles of Oklahoma 1983 61(1): 68-79.* Born to a mixed-blood Scottish-Cherokee trading family in 1798, Joseph Vann utilized lucrative family connections to become one of the richest Cherokees. An owner of vast tracts of land, a plantation home, and 110 slaves, he received almost $20,000 from the government for loss of his property during the Cherokee removals. By the late 1830's he had reestablished himself as a wealthy planter near Webbers Falls, Indian Territory, but died in a boating accident in 1844. The Civil War subsequently destroyed most of what Vann bequeathed to his family. 4 photos, 10 notes.            M. L. Tate

4040. McLoughlin, William G. CHEROKEE ANTI-MISSION SENTIMENT, 1824-1828. *Ethnohistory 1974 21(4): 361-370.* Recently discovered letters written by some Cherokee chiefs in 1824 throw new light on White Path's Rebellion of 1827. They indicate that what appears on the surface to be anti-mission factionalism may, in the case of large, advanced tribes scattered over wide regions, be better understood as conflict over the speed and degree of acculturation, particularly when a prominent group of well-to-do or nominally Christian mixed blood asserts undue influence over political centralization.          J

4041. McLoughlin, William G. CHEROKEE NATIONALISM AND THE RIGHT OF INTERNAL TAXATION. *Prologue 1982 14(2): 68-80.* Discusses the strong sense of nationalism that developed among the Cherokee Indians during 1817-20 with the election of a bicameral legislation, central judicial system, and police system. While the Cherokee were willing to recognize the jurisdiction of the federal government in foreign policy matters, they demanded recognition of their internal autonomy and insisted on home rule and control of internal trade. Focuses on their efforts during the 1820's to regulate internal trade and develop a system of taxation that would generate revenue to support their government. The end result of the effort was a confrontation with the federal government that had legal and constitutional ramifications. Based on letters received by the Office of Indian Affairs and received by the Office of the Secretary of War relating to Indian Affairs; 8 photos, 37 notes.

         M. A. Kascus

4042. McLoughlin, William G. CHEROKEES AND METHODISTS 1824-1834. *Church Hist. 1981 50(1): 44-63.* The Methodists began missionary activities among the Cherokee Indians in 1822. Prior to the removal of the tribe from the South to the West, Methodist missionaries, like the Reverend James Jenkins Trott, were involved in the political questions concerning state sovereignty and tribal loyalty. The denomination sought to sustain missionary activities by giving no political offense. Andrew Jackson's Indian policy caused Methodist leaders in the South to desesrt stands taken by their missionaries. The church came to support the president's removal policy and consequently lost support among the Cherokees. 53 notes.          M. D. Dibert

4043. McLoughlin, William G. and Conser, Walter H., Jr. THE CHEROKEES IN TRANSITION: A STATISTICAL ANALYSIS OF THE FEDERAL CHEROKEE CENSUS OF 1835. *J. of Am. Hist. 1977 64(3): 678-703.* The 1835 census of the Cherokee nation reinforces the opinion that the Cherokee Indians were rapidly acquiring wealth and skills that advanced them beyond other Indian tribes. Full-blooded Cherokees resisted white techniques and consequently were poorer than mixed white-Cherokee families. Of the 50 wealthiest families, almost all had intermarried with whites. But the census also shows that full- and mixed-blood Indians were not segregated, and that both groups had steadily increasing populations. Most Cherokees retained tribal loyalties and used European methods to enrich rather than transform their traditional life. Primary and secondary sources; 16 tables, 18 notes.      J. W. Leedom

4044. McLoughlin, William G. THE CHOCTAW SLAVE BURNING: A CRISIS IN MISSION WORK AMONG THE INDIANS. *J. of the West 1974 13(1): 113-127.* On 28 December 1858 a black slave killed his Choctaw master, Richard Harkins. He claimed he had been instigated by another slave, a woman. After he escaped and killed himself the woman, despite protestations of innocence, was burned at the stake by the widow of the murdered man. The victim was a member, along with the Harkinses, of the Congregational mission church of the Reverend Cyrus Byington. When the incident was revealed a year later it precipitated a crisis over slavery and the relation of the church to slavery among a slave-holding people like the Choctaw Indians. 34 notes.      R. V. Ritter

4045. McLoughlin, William G. CIVIL DISOBEDIENCE AND EVANGELISM AMONG THE MISSIONARIES TO THE CHEROKEES, 1829-1839. *J. of Presbyterian Hist. 1973 51(2): 116-140.*

4046. McLoughlin, William G. EXPERIMENT IN CHEROKEE CITIZENSHIP, 1817-1829. *Am. Q. 1981 33(1): 3-25.* By the terms of an 1817 treaty, 342 Cherokee heads of families in Georgia, North Carolina, Tennessee, and Alabama accepted an American offer of citizenship and 640 acres each in exchange for leaving the reservation. Frontier whites, however, forcibly ejected many of these new citizens from their land and threatened many others with violence. While the federal government can be blamed for not preparing these Cherokee for citizenship, the major reason the plan failed was opposition from within the tribe to the plan and pressure from the tribal council to stay on tribal land. The strong desire to stay in the Cherokee homeland is shown by the 1819 exchange of 3.8 million acres for a nonremoval guarantee, an exchange that was made in vain. Based on primary sources on National Archives microfilm and a register of life estates in the Georgia State Archives; 59 notes.      D. K. Lambert

4047. McLoughlin, William G. NEW ANGLES OF VISION ON THE CHEROKEE GHOST DANCE MOVEMENT OF 1811-1812. *Am. Indian Q. 1979 5(4): 317-345.* Historians have mistakenly attributed coherence and consistency to the Cherokee Ghost Dance and attributed its demise to failure of its predictions. Based on factionalism and cultural stress, it had many prophets. It failed because there were other viable political and religious options and because the period of anomie for the Cherokee had passed. Primary accounts; 30 notes.      G. L. Olson

4048. McLoughlin, William G. THOMAS JEFFERSON AND THE BEGINNING OF CHEROKEE NATIONALISM, 1806 TO 1809. *William and Mary Q. 1975 32(4): 547-580.* Traces origins and growth of Cherokee nationalism. The treaties of Willstown in 1806 ceded vast Cherokee territory in Tennessee, which led to a crisis among the Cherokees over the validity of the treaties. Discusses the role of Thomas Jefferson, Col. Return J. Meigs, and others in attempting to force Indian removal. In 1809 the Cherokees were reunited and took a stand against boundary arrangements and Jefferson's proposals for the Indians to be removed and become free simple farmers. Based on War Department and Indian Agency archives and secondary sources; 87 notes.      H. M. Ward

4049. Mellon, Knox, Jr. CHRISTIAN PRIBER'S CHEROKEE "KINGDOM OF PARADISE." *Georgia Hist. Q. 1973 57(3): 319-331.* Christian Gottlieb Priber (1697-ca. 1744), a German lawyer, came to the American colonies in the early 1730's to establish a utopian colony, the "Kingdom of Paradise." His dream embodied elements of Cherokee tribal life, radical European political and social philosophy, and a general mixture of primitivism and fairly sophisticated ideas of government. The English were concerned about the effect of Priber's influence with the Cherokee with whom they had a trade monopoly. Priber was arrested and spent the rest of his days in prison. 50 notes.      D. L. Smith

4050. Meredith, Howard L. and Milam, Virginia E. A CHEROKEE OF ELOH. *Indian Hist. 1975 8(4): 19-23.* The Cherokee *eloh* is the tribal heritage of history and religion. It exists in several versions. Gives the text of and discusses a version in the Cherokee newspaper *Indian Chieftain* in 1896. It relates an allegorical story of Cherokee origins, early relations with whites, and final removal to Oklahoma. 14 notes.      E. D. Johnson

4051. Meredith, Howard L. EMMET STARR'S MANUSCRIPT ESSAY ON THE TEXAS CHEROKEES. *Indian Historian 1977 10(1): 14-16.* Emmet Starr, a Cherokee historian of the late 19th century, left several published works on Cherokee history. This hitherto unpublished manuscript summarizes the attempt of the Cherokee Indians to obtain land grants in what is now Texas from Mexico in the 1820's. The later Republic of Texas promised the Cherokees security in their lands, but the promise was not kept. 4 notes.      E. D. Johnson

4052. Meredith, Howard L. WILL ROGERS' ROOTS. *Chronicles of Oklahoma 1979 57(3): 259-268.* Oklahoma humorist and social critic Will Rogers was born into a Cherokee family which had come to Indian Territory during the removals of the 1830's. His father, Clement V. Rogers, attained an important standing within

Cherokee society and served several terms on the Cherokee Senate. Clement Rogers also achieved financial success as a rancher and used his influence to help soften the negative aspects of white acculturation on the tribe. Will would later epitomize the best qualities of this bicultural lifestyle which his father had cultivated. Based on archival materials and secondary sources; 4 photos, 33 notes.

M. L. Tate

4053. Merrell, James H. CULTURAL CONTINUITY AMONG THE PISCATAWAY INDIANS OF COLONIAL MARYLAND. *William and Mary Q. 1979 36(4): 548-570.* The Piscataway Indians of Maryland, largely because of their distance from English settlements and engaging in trade with the English, were able to preserve their way of life. Describes cultural patterns and economic factors. Observes contacts and skirmishes with English explorers and settlers and other Indian tribes. Killamaquund, who usurped powers as chief, had to depend on the English for his rule, which contributed to the initial nonviolent intrusion on the Piscataway culture. With royal government in Maryland at the end of the century, Indian relations suffered, and the Piscataways moved to northern Virginia, and then in 1701 most of them moved to Pennsylvania. Based on early writings and archaeological evidence; map—Indian Villages of the Western Shore of Maryland, 106 notes.

H. M. Ward

4054. Miner, H. Craig. DENNIS BUSHYHEAD. Edmunds, R. David, ed. *American Indian Leaders: Studies in Diversity* (Lincoln: U. of Nebraska Pr., 1980): 192-205. Dennis Bushyhead (1826-1898), an acculturated, mixed-blood leader who attempted to unify the Cherokee Indians, was determined to defend the sovereignty of his tribe from state and federal encroachment. He appreciated the great political influence held by large corporations during the 1880's and decided that the Cherokees' only chance for survival lay in developing a partnership with the business community. If major railroad or mining companies were granted special privileges by the Cherokee Nation, perhaps they would use their political influence to help the tribe defend its status against the US government. This was the line of diplomacy he used during his years of tenure, 1879-87, as principal chief of the Cherokees. Map, 18 notes.

J. Powell

4055. Monk, J. Floyd. CHRISTMAS DAY IN FLORIDA, 1837. *Tequesta 1978 38: 5-38.* A step-by-step recapitulation of the Battle of Okeechobee, fought on Christmas Day, 1837, during the 2d Seminole War. Rejects the contention made shortly after the battle by Colonel Zachary Taylor that the 1st Missouri Volunteers broke ranks during the battle. Primary and secondary sources; illus., map, biblio.

H. S. Marks

4056. Mooney, James. THE CHEROKEE BALL PLAY. *J. of Cherokee Studies 1982 7(1): 10-24.* Cherokee ball play, occurring during the summer and early fall, is very similar to lacrosse. Preparation involves about nine to 12 men, who undertake strict diet, physical training, loss of sleep, and ritualistic dance near a holy place adjacent to a river. Each participant is specially prepared and is accompanied by a shaman, who repeats prayers and songs for success. The dance before the contest lasts the entire night. To inject protection against evil powers and provide success for the event, all players and accompanying spectators must observe strict ritualistic rules. When the two teams meet on a nearby field, the winner is the team that uses sticks with an attached net to carry the ball across the opponent's goal. A purification ceremony follows.

K. E. Gilmont

4057. Mooney, James. CHEROKEE PLANT LORE. *J. of Cherokee Studies 1982 7(1): 37.* Cherokee folklore on the whole range of plants, trees, shrubbery, and berries tells how corn originated, medicine began, cedar trees became red, some trees retain and shed winter foliage, explains poison ivy's effects on boys, and tells of the relationship of woman to man.

K. E. Gilmont

4058. Mooney, James. THE CHEROKEE RIVER CULT. *J. of Cherokee Studies 1982 7(1): 30-36.* To the Cherokee, the river is of paramount importance. Under a shaman's direction, an infant is blessed by the river, similar to a baptism but not immersion. To re-

ceive a blessing through the seven holy steps for life protection, an individual undergoes various stages of immersion regardless of temperature and season. With black and white beads in his hand, the shaman guides an individual toward healing and positive life attitudes, sometimes repeating the process many times until the white (goodness) dominates the black (death), in a finger-shuffling motion. Repetitious prayers are uttered while an individual is in or near the river to dispel evil spirits and to strengthen the will to live peacefully and fruitfully.

K. E. Gilmont

4059. Mooney, James. CHEROKEE THEORY AND PRACTICE OF MEDICINE. *J. of Cherokee Studies 1982 7(1): 25-29.* The Cherokee "doctor" utilizes selective known herbs and taboos to cure the patient not only of the illness but also of the possibility of spiritual contamination to others. Among Cherokees, the presence of and treatment with water is most important. Ceremonies have sanitary and religious effects. Diseases are classified according to an animal-association category.

K. E. Gilmont

4060. Moulton, Gary E. CHEROKEES AND THE SECOND SEMINOLE WAR. *Florida Hist. Q. 1975 53(3): 296-305.* Examines the ways in which Chief John Ross of the Cherokees was used by the federal government to encourage the Seminoles to cease hostilities. Colonel John H. Sherburne was sent from the War Department to negotiate with Chief Ross. There was, however, mutual misgiving as to the arrangement. Nevertheless Ross and his comrades attempted to carry out the mission to the Seminoles, only to have Seminole delegates who came for negotiation under a flag of truce taken captive. 30 notes.

R. V. Ritter

4061. Moulton, Gary E. CHIEF JOHN ROSS: THE PERSONAL DIMENSION. *Red River Valley Hist. R. 1975 2(2): 221-239.* Biography of John Ross, chief of the Cherokee Indians, from the removal to Indian Territory in 1838 until his death in 1867, focusing on his marriage to Mary Stapler Ross.

S

4062. Moulton, Gary E. CHIEF JOHN ROSS AND CHEROKEE REMOVAL FINANCES. *Chronicles of Oklahoma 1974 52(3): 342-359.* Describes the efforts of Principal Chief John Ross of the Cherokee Nation to get a fair removal treaty negotiated with the US government. He disapproved of the financial terms of the Treaty of New Echota (1835) and worked vainly against its ratification. Ross next supervised the Cherokee removal process and his brother Lewis took charge of finances. Actual emigration was difficult due to delays and harsh conditions. The US government did not accept John Ross' claims for removal expenses because of Lewis' questionable financial dealings. After reexamination and a change in presidential administrations, some of the claims were paid. The Cherokee Nation feuded over the removal expenses being charged to their "five million fund" guaranteed by the New Echota treaty. Cherokee claims to federal funds were not completely settled until 1906. Based on US government documents, primary and secondary sources; 2 illus., map, 32 notes.

N. J. Street

4063. Moulton, Gary E. JOHN ROSS. Edmunds, R. David, ed. *American Indian Leaders: Studies in Diversity* (Lincoln: U. of Nebraska Pr., 1980): 88-106. Although only one-eighth Cherokee by blood, John Ross fought to keep the Cherokee Indians from being removed from their homes in Georgia and Tennessee to present-day Oklahoma. Although Ross's efforts failed, he continued to serve the tribe as "principal chief" during the post-removal and Civil War period. His diplomatic efforts were severely impeded by the factionalism which existed in many of the tribes, and the inability of tribal leaders to unify their people. Mainly secondary sources; map, 32 notes.

J. Powell

4064. Moulton, Gary E. "VOYAGE TO ARKANSAS," NEW LETTERS OF JOHN ROSS. *Tennessee Hist. Q. 1976 35(1): 46-50.* Prints three never-before published letters from Cherokee Chief John Ross. The letters describe the first portion of Ross' journey, begun in December 1812, from his home in present-day Chattanooga to Dardanelle in Arkansas, where a western band of Cherokees had settled. After many adventures and hardships, Ross deposited more than $2,200 worth of goods with the western Cherokees in March 1813. He returned in April with favorable reports of the

western country. Most accounts had erroneously dated this trip in 1809. Based on John Ross' letters and on secondary sources; 4 notes.
W. R. Hively

4065. Nackman, Mark E. THE INDIANS OF TEXAS IN THE NINETEENTH CENTURY: A CROSS-SECTION OF AMERICAN INDIAN CULTURES. *Texas Q. 1975 18(2): 56-75.* Both the prairie Indians of Texas and the woodlands Indians of East Texas led sedentary lives. These tribes grew and hunted their food. During the first half of the 19th century Indians in the Texas plains, especially the Comanches, grew dependent on horses. Social ranking depended on military skills; selection of a wife depended on bravery in battle; indeed, all social activities related to warfare. But the failure of the various tribes to unite against the whites doomed their heroic but piecemeal resistance to failure. Secondary sources.
R. H. Tomlinson

4066. Nash, Gary B. WHITHER INDIAN HISTORY: REVIEW ESSAY. *J. of Ethnic Studies 1976 4(3): 69-76.* Reviews six recent works of Indian history, including Charles M. Hudson's *The Catawba Nation* and C. A. Weslager's *The Delaware Indians: A History*, plus two collections of conference papers edited by Hudson: *Red, White and Black: Symposium on Indians in the Old South* and *Four Centuries of Southern Indians*. Analyzes Indian-white relations and ethnohistory, and concludes that more examinations of internal change within Indian communities during 300 years of contact with Europeans, more local studies and a borrowing of conceptual models from African historians to study native responses to white conquest, are needed. Concludes with Francis Jennings' *The Invasion of America* and calls it "the most important book to appear in many years" in Indian history.
G. J. Bobango

4067. Neely, Sharlotte. THE QUAKER ERA OF CHEROKEE INDIAN EDUCATION, 1880-1892. *Appalachian J. 1975 2(4): 314-322.*

4068. Nolen, Curtis L. THE OKMULGEE CONSTITUTION: A STEP TOWARDS INDIAN SELF-DETERMINATION. *Chronicles of Oklahoma 1980 58(3): 264-281.* Twelve tribes from Indian Territory met in September 1870 to develop a plan for intertribal government, a concept that had been articulated since the days of Thomas Jefferson. At a second meeting three months later, the delegates drafted the Okmulgee Constitution which in many ways resembled the US Constitution. Objections came from several groups, including small tribes which felt that larger tribes would dominate the government, and from whites who believed that the concept gave Indians too much independence. Efforts for ratification continued until 1876, but white pressure against Indian self-determination ended any chances of success. Based on Journals of the General Council of the Indian Territory and secondary sources; 4 photos, 60 notes.
M. L. Tate

4069. Owsley, Douglas W. and Guevin, Bryan L. CRANIAL DEFORMATION—A CULTURAL PRACTICE OF THE EIGHTEENTH CENTURY OVERHILL CHEROKEES. *J. of Cherokee Studies 1982 7(2): 79-81.* Intentional deformation evidence from Tellico Reservoir excavations in North Carolina of infant skulls of Overhill Cherokee Indians is inconclusive. There is not enough evidence to prove that such a practice existed. 2 fig., 12 notes.
K. E. Gilmont

4070. Owsley, Douglas W. and O'Brien, Helen L. STATURE OF ADULT CHEROKEE INDIANS DURING THE EIGHTEENTH CENTURY. *J. of Cherokee Studies 1982 7(2): 74-78.* Analysis of adult bones excavated from the North Carolinian archaeological sites, Chota (40MR2), Citco (40MR7), Tanasee (40MR62), Tomotley (40MR5), and Toqua (40MR6), of Overhill Cherokees indicate an average height for males of 5 feet 6 inches and for females of 5 feet 3.5 inches by use of an osteometric board. Analysis was based upon measurement of the humerus, radius, ulna, femur, tibia, and fibula bones. 2 tables, photo, 22 notes.
K. E. Gilmont

4071. Painter, Floyd. FLUTED PROJECTILE POINTS OF BONE AND ANTLER FROM THE GREAT NECK SITE. *Chesopiean 1980 18(1-2): 35-37.* Describes projectile points from the Great Neck site in Virginia Beach, Virginia, with special attention to the cultural affiliations of the points.

4072. Painter, Floyd. ONE MAN'S TRASH IS ANOTHER MAN'S TREASURE: A STUDY IN DISCARDED TOOLS AND WEAPONS. *Chesopiean 1982 20(5-6): 17-37.* Examines projectile points found in the Middle Atlantic Region, mainly in Virginia, North Carolina, and South Carolina, ca. 10,000-5,000 BC; it was earlier believed that Indians lost these points, but now it seems that they, after various resharpening attempts, discarded these inadequate, dull points; therefore the majority of discovered points were not lost, but discarded.

4073. Parramore, Thomas C. THE TUSCARORA ASCENDANCY. *North Carolina Hist. Rev. 1982 59(4): 307-326.* Historians have viewed the Tuscarora Indians as significant in North Carolina only during the Tuscarora War of 1711-13. Actually they dominated the colony for over a century, first among Indian groups and then in dealings with English colonists. The Tuscarora sought to maintain territorial and trading sovereignty over much of eastern North Carolina from the late 1500's to their defeat in 1713. They defined the limits of English settlement in North Carolina during 1654-1712 and may have influenced the character of internal conflicts among the colonists, including the Culpeper Rebellion of 1677 and the Cary Rebellion of 1711. Based on contemporary political and travel accounts of colonial North Carolina and Virginia and colonial government records; 5 illus., 3 maps, 98 notes.
T. L. Savitt

4074. Payne, John Howard. THE CHEROKEE CAUSE. *J. of Cherokee Studies 1976 1(1): 17-22.* Reprints a letter, dated 11 October 1835, in defense of the Cherokee Indians. In the late 1820's and early 1830's the Cherokees were pressured by the US federal government and the state of Georgia to cede their eastern lands and migrate west. John Howard Payne, after meeting the antiremoval leader John Ross, attacked both the United States and Georgia for forcing the Cherokees out. He defended the Cherokees as a civilized group who should be allowed to remain on their native land. The letter was read into the Congressional records of the time but otherwise has never been published before. Editorial comment; illus.
J. M. Lee

4075. Perdue, Theda. REMEMBERING REMOVAL, 1867. *J. of Cherokee Studies 1982 7(2): 69-73.* Cornelia C. Chandler, in 1937, recounted how she, her family, and about 72 North Carolina Cherokee Indians immigrated to Arkansas in 1867 to the Goingsnake District, where economic and social conditions were poor. Her account includes food gathering, a meeting with Stand Watie, primitive schools, marriage to John A. Chandler, and birth of her children. In later years, she lived in Prairie City, now Ogechee, and Fairland, Arkansas. 26 notes.
K. E. Gilmont

4076. Perdue, Theda. RISING FROM THE ASHES: THE *CHEROKEE PHOENIX* AS AN ETHNOHISTORICAL SOURCE. *Ethnohistory 1977 24(3): 207-218.* The *Cherokee Phoenix* is a widely used source for early 19th century Cherokee ethnohistory. An analysis of the newspaper and its content, contributors, and circulation reveals, however, that scholars should be cautious in their use of the publication for ethnological information because it does not give an accurate picture of Cherokee society nor did the contents reach and affect most Cherokee people.
J

4077. Perdue, Theda. TRADITIONALISM IN THE CHEROKEE NATION: RESISTANCE TO THE CONSTITUTION OF 1827. *Georgia Hist. Q. 1982 66(2): 159-170.* Describes Cherokee Indian law and leadership customs and the various adaptations of them that led up to the traditionalists' resistance to the Constitution of 1827. 26 notes.
G. R. Schroeder

4078. Perttula, Timothy K. and Bruseth, James E. EARLY CADDOAN SUBSISTENCE STRATEGIES, SABINE RIVER BASIN, EAST TEXAS. *Plains Anthrop. 1983 28(99): 9-21.* Well preserved faunal and floral materials recovered from the Taddlock and Spoonbill sites in the Sabine River Basin of East Texas provide one of the first opportunities to document the subsistence strategies of sedentary hamlet occupations during the early Caddoan period. The Taddlock site, dated ca. 940-1000, has a large faunal assemblage indicating a generalized and balanced exploitation of small and large mammals, reptiles, and fish. The two components at Spoonbill, dated ca. 970-1260, are characterized by an extensive floral sample of wild plant foods, seeds, and maize. At both sites, maize constitutes less than 10% by weight of the total plant food remains. The early Caddoan inhabitants exploited a wide variety of animal and plant food, but at this time maize was likely one of several main sources of food energy rather than the focus of a specialized economy.                                                               J/S

4079. Porter, Frank W., III. A CENTURY OF ACCOMMODATION: THE NANTICOKE INDIANS IN COLONIAL MARYLAND. *Maryland Hist. Mag. 1979 74(2): 175-192.* European settlers who came to Maryland in 1634 hoped to civilize and convert to Christianity the aboriginal populations, obtain lands from them for European use, and carry on with them an exchange of furs and foodstuffs. The migratory seasonal subsistence patterns of the Nanticoke Indians of Maryland's eastern shore were severely disrupted by Indian attempts to accommodate their cultural patterns to white encroachment. Appeals to the Maryland Assembly and the Proprietor for protection against treaty-breaking whites, warmaking, and relegating themselves to clearly-defined plantations all failed to preserve Indian lands and culture from white expansion. Beginning in 1740, Nanticoke and Choptank tribes moved to Pennsylvania, then New York, and ultimately to Canada, living among and finally being absorbed by former enemies, the Iroquois. Based on Browne, *Archives of Maryland,* and other primary sources; 2 maps, 60 notes.                                                      C. B. Schulz

4080. Prucha, Francis Paul. THE BOARD OF INDIAN COMMISSIONERS AND THE DELEGATES OF THE FIVE TRIBES. *Chronicles of Oklahoma 1978 56(3): 247-264.* Created by Congress in 1869, the Board of Indian Commissioners was an unpaid advisory body on Native American affairs. The initial members worked with Indian leaders to resist the inroads of forced acculturation, but by 1874 the new delegates advocated a strong "civilizing" policy which was opposed by the great majority of Indian leaders. Resistance to these pressures proved futile and by 1898 even the Five Civilized Tribes of Indian Territory lost their tribal governments and special treaty status. Based on Reports of the Board of Indian Commissioners; 6 photos, 39 notes.                M. L. Tate

4081. Ramsey, David. ABNER DOUBLEDAY AND THE THIRD SEMINOLE WAR. *Florida Hist. Q. 1981 59(3): 318-334.* Abner Doubleday served as captain of Company E of the US First Artillery in Florida during the Third Seminole War, 1855-58. An autobiographical manuscript from 1869 contains 18 pages pertaining to his activities in and around Fort Dallas during the Seminole War. Based on primary sources in the New York Historical Society and on other sources; photo, 36 notes.            N. A. Kuntz

4082. Reed, Gerald A. FINANCIAL CONTROVERSY IN THE CHEROKEE NATION, 1839-1846. *Chronicles of Oklahoma 1974 52(1): 82-98.* Describes the financial controversies of the Cherokee Nation after the removal Treaty of New Echota (1835). Discusses mismanagement and graft involved with removal expense funds, and examines the questionable dealings of Cherokee Principal Chief John Ross and the Anti-Ross campaign. Primary and secondary sources; 3 illus., 2 photos, 83 notes.            N. J. Street

4083. Reid, John Phillip. THE EUROPEAN PERSPECTIVE AND CHEROKEE LAW. *Appalachian J. 1975 2(4): 286-293.* South Carolina British settlers' records, not Cherokee records, reveal all that is known of the 18th-century Cherokee legal mind, and these records are inaccurate because for the Cherokee Indians law was custom enforced largely through internal sanctions.

4084. Riley, Sam G. A NOTE OF CAUTION: THE INDIAN'S OWN PREJUDICE, AS MIRRORED IN THE FIRST NATIVE AMERICAN NEWSPAPER. *Journalism Hist. 1979 6(2): 44-47.*

Focuses on the discrimination of Indians against blacks, women, Germans, and Irish, as evidenced in the first Indian newspaper, *The Cherokee Phoenix,* published 1828-34.

4085. Romine, Dannye. ALEXANDER MC GILLIVRAY: SHREWD SCOT, CUNNING INDIAN. *Southern Humanities Rev. 1975 9(4): 409-421.* Discusses the life of Alexander McGillivray, a half Scot-half Creek Indian leader of the Creek Nation, and his efforts to maintain Indian lands and peace with the white man following the Revolutionary War.                              S

4086. Rothrock, Mary U. CAROLINA TRADERS AMONG THE OVERHILL CHEROKEES, 1690-1760. *East Tennessee Hist. Soc. Publ. 1979 51: 14-29.* For the most part, traders such as James Adair and Ludovick Grant, who dealt with the Overhill Cherokees located in present-day Monroe County, Tennessee, were a hardy lot, but if the risks were great so were the profits. Spaniards and Frenchmen also traded with the Overhill Cherokees, and the French seemed particularly well-suited to life with the Indians. In addition to their commercial and social transactions with the Indians, the Overhill traders were often thrust into the roles of interpreters and even diplomats. Reprinted from the *East Tennessee Historical Society's Publications,* Vol. 1; 39 notes, 2 illus.
D. A. Yanchisin

4087. Russell, Mattie U. DEVIL IN THE SMOKIES: THE WHITE MAN'S NATURE AND THE INDIAN'S FATE. *South Atlantic Q. 1974 73(1): 53-69.* The chief of the Cherokee Indians in North Carolina, Yonaguska, before his death in 1839 chose as his successor a 34-year-old white man, William Holland Thomas. Previously the chief had persuaded the clan to adopt Holland, who was then a fatherless boy. In 1848 Thomas was elected to the North Carolina Senate, and in 1861 he became a member of the secession convention. He had a distinguished career in the Confederate Army. In 1866 President Andrew Johnson pardoned him. He remained chief of the North Carolina Cherokee, Eastern Band, who owed their existence as a people to him. 44 notes.
E. P. Stickney

4088. Savage, William W., Jr. CREEK COLONIZATION IN OKLAHOMA. *Chronicles of Oklahoma 1976 54(1): 34-43.* The Creek Nation suffered from factionalism which extended back into the colonial era. Conservatives, or Red Sticks, allied themselves with the British during the War of 1812 and found themselves fighting both American militia and White Stick Creeks under Chief William McIntosh. The 1825 Treaty of Indian Springs called for the removal of both factions to Indian Territory, but most Conservatives adamantly refused. Further pressure produced a war 11 years later. At its conclusion, many Conservatives were marched overland to Indian Territory. There the separate groups continued their struggle for control of tribal politics through the 1860's, when the wounds slowly began to heal. Secondary sources; 3 photos, 2 maps.                                                          M. L. Tate

4089. Schene, Michael G. NOT A SHOT FIRED: FORT CHOKONIKLA AND THE "INDIAN WAR" OF 1849-1850. *Tequesta 1977 (37): 19-37.* Fort Chokonikla was erected near the mouth of the Caloosahatchee River on the southwest coast of Florida on the site of a trading post that was destroyed by Seminole Indians. Sickness forced the evacuation of the post in 1850. It was never used again.                                         H. S. Marks

4090. Schroedl, Gerald F. LOUIS-PHILIPPE'S JOURNAL AND ARCHAEOLOGICAL INVESTIGATIONS AT THE OVERHILL CHEROKEE TOWN OF TOQUA. *J. of Cherokee Studies 1978 3(4): 206-220.* Analyzes Louis Philippe's description of Toqua, in what is now Tennessee, in light of archaeological excavations.

4091. Scott, Winfield. IF NOT REJOICING, AT LEAST IN COMFORT: GENERAL SCOTT'S VERSION OF REMOVAL. *J. of Cherokee Studies 1978 3(3): 138-142.* Reprints Winfield Scott's account of the forced removal of Cherokee Indians carried out under his direction.

4092. Shafer, Harry J. THE ADAPTIVE TECHNOLOGY OF THE PREHISTORIC INHABITANTS OF SOUTHWEST TEXAS. *Plains Anthropologist 1981 26(92): 129-138.* Presents a model of the middle Archaic adaptations in the lower Pecos River area of southwest Texas. A basically unchanged adaptive continuum prevailed in the area for approximately 8,000 years. The conservatism and longevity seen in the adaptation centered significantly on the early and continued exploitation of perennial desert succulents such as sotol, lechuguilla and yucca both as food and raw material sources.                                                                              J/S

4093. Shammas, Carole. NATIVE AMERICANA. *Rev. in Am. Hist. 1981 9(1): 43-45.* Review essay of Karen Ordahl Kupperman's *Settling with the Indians: The Meeting of English and Indian Cultures in America, 1580-1640* (1980), and Bernard W. Sheehan's *Savagism and Civility: Indians and Englishmen in Colonial Virginia* (1980).

4094. Skinner, S. Alan. ABORIGINAL DEMOGRAPHIC CHANGES IN CENTRAL TEXAS. *Plains Anthropologist 1981 26(92): 111-118.* Over the past decade a wealth of information about the types, location and density of aboriginal campsites in Central Texas has been gathered. During the same period, chronological ordering has been refined and studies have begun to focus upon changes in man to land relations in time and space. Using the available paleoenvironmental data, an explanatory model reconstructs the shifting settlement patterns and population densities which preceded the widely dispersed historic Anglo American settlement of Central Texas in the 1800's.                                                    J

4095. Snell, William R. CANDY'S CREEK MISSION STATION, 1824-1837. *J. of Cherokee Studies 1979 4(3): 163-184.* Recounts William Holland's labors among the Cherokee Indians for the American Board of Commissioners for Foreign Missions in what is now Bradley County, Tennessee.

4096. Snell, William R. THE COUNCILS AT RED CLAY COUNCIL GROUND, BRADLEY COUNTY, TENNESSEE, 1832-1837. *J. of Cherokee Studies 1977 2(4): 344-355.* Summarizes the actions of the Cherokee government, which met at Red Clay.

4097. Stokeley, Jim. THE COUNSEL OF CALEB STARR. *J. of Cherokee Studies 1978 3(1): 54-66.* Caleb Starr was a trader living with the Cherokee Indians during the American Revolution. In 1776, when Americans were preparing to attack the Cherokees, Starr advised them to retreat into the mountains. This counsel had a temporary effect on the Cherokees, in that the American attack of that year found Cherokee towns deserted.                    J. M. Lee

4098. Strickland, William M. CHEROKEE RHETORIC: A FORCEFUL WEAPON. *J. of Cherokee Studies 1977 2(4): 375-384.* The Cherokee Indians' traditional reliance on public speaking was eloquently but ineffectually employed against the federal government's removal policy.

4099. Strickland, William M. THE RHETORIC OF REMOVAL AND THE TRAIL OF TEARS: CHEROKEE SPEAKING AGAINST JACKSON'S INDIAN REMOVAL POLICY. *Southern Speech Communication J. 1982 47(3): 292-309.* Analyzes rhetorical strategies used by Cherokee Indians to prevent removal from their native lands east of the Mississippi following President Andrew Jackson's Indian removal policy.

4100. Stumpf, Stuart. JAMES GLEN, CHEROKEE DIPLOMACY, AND THE CONSTRUCTION OF AN OVERHILL FORT. *East Tennessee Hist. Soc. Publ. 1978 50: 21-30.* During his long term as governor of South Carolina, James Glen held an imperialist vision. But his efforts to establish a British stronghold to control the trans-Appalachian region by constructing a fort among the principal overhill Cherokee towns in the Little Tennessee valley met with a series of unexpected setbacks. Finally constructed after Glen's recall, Fort Loudoun did not prevent war or restrain the Cherokee Indians as he had expected. 37 notes.            D. A. Yanchisin

4101. Sturtevant, William C., ed. JOHN RIDGE ON CHEROKEE CIVILIZATION IN 1826. *J. of Cherokee Studies 1981 6(2): 79-91.* Albert Gallatin asked Bureau of Indian Affairs Director Thomas L. McKenney to have John Ridge, graduate of the Cornwell, Connecticut, Foreign Mission School submit an overall description of Cherokee society. The report included the tribe's geographic boundaries, description of farming and occupational pursuits, laws and extent of tribal legislature, role of religion, and educational curricula. The report concludes with the participation of colonial missions, with a mention of the Moravian school, John Gambold, and a view of the former glory of the tribe. Photo, 12 notes.          K. E. Gilmont

4102. Sudgen, John. THE SOUTHERN INDIANS IN THE WAR OF 1812: THE CLOSING PHASE. *Florida Hist. Q. 1982 60(3): 273-312.* Examines the Creek War (1813-14) in Florida from the Indian point of view. The Indians believed that if the British were successful in the War of 1812 their lands would be returned. Notes, in particular, negotiations with Great Britain. At best, the Indians could only prolong the inevitable. British and American societies together believed in policies of expansion; even international rivalries would not maintain Indian land. Based on records in the War Office, London, papers in the Library of Scotland, Edinburgh, and other sources; 98 notes.                    N. A. Kuntz

4103. Symonds, Craig. THE FAILURE OF AMERICA'S INDIAN POLICY ON THE SOUTHWESTERN FRONTIER, 1785-1793. *Tennessee Hist. Q. 1976 35(1): 29-45.* Secretary of War Henry Knox intended to maintain peace on the southwestern frontier by honoring the Treaty of Hopewell (1785), but settlers there considered this policy irresponsible. Governor Blount, caught between his constituents' desires and a federal government incapable of fulfilling its promises to the Indians, negotiated with friendly Indian leaders, while hostile Indians went on the warpath. In 1793, Tennessee frontiersmen, led by General John Sevier, destroyed the Cherokee town of Etowah. This raid, rather than Knox's promises, restored an uneasy peace on the frontier. Based on primary and secondary sources; 51 notes.                    W. R. Hively

4104. Syndergaard, Rex. THE FINAL MOVE OF THE CHOCTAWS 1825-1830. *Chronicles of Oklahoma 1974 52(2): 207-219.* Points out injustices and problems of US Indian policy during 1825-30 with reference to the final removal of the Choctaw Nation from its tribal lands. Negotiations were difficult because the Choctaws were themselves divided over cessions and removal. The election of Andrew Jackson and the 1830 Indian Removal Bill altered the situation. Greenwood LeFlore led the tribe in negotiations, and the Treaty of Dancing Rabbit Creek (1830) was signed. Primary and secondary sources; 3 illus., map, 32 notes.      N. J. Street

4105. Tanner, Helen Hornbeck. CHEROKEES IN THE OHIO COUNTRY. *J. of Cherokee Studies 1978 3(2): 94-102.* Although the Cherokee Indians are thought of as southern, after 1750, there were long episodes of Cherokees living with the Delaware and Shawnee Indians of the Ohio Valley. The impact of the French and Indian War and the American Revolution led to considerable cooperation among these tribes. Cherokees fought General Anthony Wayne in his campaign leading to the Battle of Fallen Timbers, and the Cherokee and Shawnee appeared jointly before the Spanish governor at St. Louis in 1782. There is also evidence that Shawnees lived in Cherokee territory. 29 notes.          J. M. Lee

4106. Thomas, James. THE OSAGE REMOVAL TO OKLAHOMA. *Chronicles of Oklahoma 1977 55(1): 46-55.* During the late 1850's, the Osage Indians petitioned the federal government for the right to sell their lands in southeastern Kansas and take a new reservation in Indian Territory where they would be safe from white interlopers. While the government delayed action on the matter, the Osage suffered from starvation and periodic white raids against their property. The problem was compounded during the Civil War when both Union and Confederate forces stole from them. Finally, in 1870, a treaty was signed which granted the Osage one million acres in north central Indian Territory. Based on primary sources; map, photo, 24 notes.          M. L. Tate

4107. Thurman, Melburn D. NELSON LEE AND THE GREEN CORN DANCE: DATA SELECTION PROBLEMS WITH WALLACE AND HOEBEL'S STUDY OF THE COMANCHES. *Plains Anthrop. 1982 27(97): 239-243.* Shows that Ernest Wallace and E. Adamson Hoebel's erroneous report of a Comanche Green Corn Dance in *The Comanches: Lords of the South Plains* (1952) resulted from misuse of source material. Consideration of their methodology suggests that critical reanalysis of the corpus of Comanche ethnohistoric sources might be fruitful.                          J/S

4108. Trees, May. SOCIOECONOMIC RECONSTRUCTION IN THE SEMINOLE NATION, 1865-1870. *J. of the West 1973 12(3): 490-498.* The Civil War left the lands of the Seminole Indians in ruins. However, a new treaty was soon signed and new lands acquired. The Seminoles began farming and made great economic improvements. Social advances were slower, but steady, and by 1870 Seminole Indians were prosperous and well-governed. 27 notes.
V. L. Human

4109. Trinkley, Michael and Hogue, S. Homes. THE WACHESAW LANDING SITE: THE LAST GASP OF THE COASTAL WACCAMAW INDIANS. *Southern Indian Studies 1979 31: 3-17.* Excavations of Waccamaw and Winyah Indian burial sites adjacent to the Waccamaw River, referred to as Wachesaw Landing, Georgetown County, South Carolina, have yielded potsherd with various decorations and skeletons that indicate Siouxan influence and Pee Dee culture. 2 maps, chart, 3 photos.
K. E. Gilmont

4110. Turner, Alvin O. FINANCIAL RELATIONS BETWEEN THE UNITED STATES AND THE CHEROKEE NATION, 1830-1870. *J. of the West 1973 12(3): 372-385.* The Cherokee Indians in Georgia were beset by depredations on their territory and questionable financial relations with the federal government. They were removed to Indian Territory in 1835, and by 1860 they were the wealthiest of the Five Civilized Tribes. Federal troops abandoned tribal lands at the outbreak of the Civil War. The Cherokees sided with the Confederacy and their properties were destroyed in subsequent fighting. By 1870, the tribe was destitute. 34 notes.
V. L. Human

4111. Usner, Daniel H., Jr. FOOD FROM NATURE: LEARNING FROM THE CHOCTAW OF THE 18TH-CENTURY SOUTH. *Southern Exposure 1983 11(6): 66-69.* Surveys the foodways of the Choctaw Indians of the colonial Deep South, including Choctaw agricultural methods, crops, food preparation, hunting practices, and marketing practices; the Choctaw were efficient users of resources, and greatly influenced colonial Louisianans.

4112. Valliere, Kenneth L. BENJAMIN CURREY, TENNESSEAN AMONG THE CHEROKEES: A STUDY OF THE REMOVAL POLICY OF ANDREW JACKSON. *Tennessee Hist. Q. 1982 41(2): 140-158, (3): 239-256.* Part 1. Benjamin Currey, a loyal Jacksonian from Tennessee, was appointed superintendent of Cherokee removal in 1831. Though detested by a majority of the Cherokees, Currey for most of his five years in office advocated a policy of voluntary emigration. He was frustrated by the ambivalent feelings that President Jackson and Secretary of War Lewis Cass held toward such moderation, by the greed and duplicity of Georgia's whites, and by the resistance of the majority faction of the Cherokee under the leadership of Chief John Ross. Part 2. Currey's career as superintendent illustrates that before the Jackson administration disingenuously removed the Cherokees from Georgia under the so-called Treaty of New Echota, it first tried a moderate policy of voluntary emigration. Had Chief John Ross's majority faction of Cherokee Indians agreed to leave, there would have been no shameful Trail of Tears. Based on documents in the Georgia State Department of Archives and History, Atlanta, Georgia, and other sources; 8 illus., 78 notes.
W. D. Piersen

4113. Valliere, Kenneth L. THE CREEK WAR OF 1836, A MILITARY HISTORY. *Chronicles of Oklahoma 1979-80 57(4): 463-485.* The pressure of white settlement on the lands of the Lower Creeks in southern Alabama caused the brief but important Creek War of 1836. The Indian leaders Neamathla and Jim Henry

posed considerable threat to the southern frontier because they could have joined the Seminoles, whose concurrent war was exacting a heavy price on the US Army. Despite friction between military commanders General Winfield Scott and General Thomas S. Jesup, regular soldiers and state militia quelled the uprising and oversaw the removal of the Creeks to Indian Territory. Primary sources; map, 2 photos, 72 notes.
M. L. Tate

4114. Vaughan, Alden T. "EXPULSION OF THE SALVAGES": ENGLISH POLICY AND THE VIRGINIA MASSACRE OF 1622. *William and Mary Q. 1978 35(1): 57-84.* The Virginia Massacre (1622) shifted British Indian policy from integration to confrontation. Discusses reasons for Indian resistance and the duplicity of Jamestown's leaders. Emphasizes the role of John Smith for the early period. During 1614-22 there were again attempts at integration, largely under the guidance of George Thorpe. However, underlying tensions continued. By the early 1620's territorial pressure and contempt for Indian culture increased, leaving the Indians no choice but to resist. The massacre led to total war against the Indians and influenced Indian relations throughout the colonies. It also adversely affected English public confidence in the Virginia Company. Contemporary sources; 91 notes.
H. M. Ward

4115. Vaughn, Courtney Ann. JOB'S LEGACY: CYRUS BYINGTON, MISSIONARY TO THE CHOCTAWS IN INDIAN TERRITORY. *Red River Valley Hist. Rev. 1978 3(4): 5-18.* Cyrus Byington (1793-1868) served the Choctaw Indians in Mississippi, 1820-68.

4116. Vernon, Walter N. BEGINNINGS OF INDIAN METHODISM IN OKLAHOMA. *Methodist Hist. 1979 17(3): 127-154.* Methodist preaching to Indians in the Oklahoma-Arkansas area started by 1820 and expanded with the arrival of Creeks, Cherokees, Choctaws, and Chickasaws who were removed from the southeast in the 1830's. Methodists along the route showed compassion and helpfulness toward the Indians as they moved through or settled in a given state. More than 40 schools in Indian territory were started by 1845. Although generally successful, the Methodist itinerant system did not fit a ministry to Indians where longer tenures were needed to understand Indian culture and language. 3 illus., 69 notes.
H. L. Calkin

4117. Vernon, Walter N. METHODIST BEGINNINGS AMONG SOUTHWEST OKLAHOMA INDIANS. *Chronicles of Oklahoma 1980-81 58(4): 392-411.* Methodist minister William Stevenson initiated the first Protestant activities in Oklahoma in 1815, but no significant work began until the Five Civilized Tribes brought missionaries during the removals of the 1830's. Western Oklahoma missionizing began during the early 1890's when the Reverend John Jasper Methvin was assigned to the Comanches, Kiowas and Apaches near Fort Sill. Despite language barriers, lack of supplies, rivalry with a Catholic mission, and Methvin's personal opposition to Indian traditions and the spread of peyote religion, he was able to gain converts to the church and the attendant school. 7 photos, 43 notes.
M. L. Tate

4118. Vickers, Ovid. MISSISSIPPI CHOCTAW NAMES AND NAMING: A DIACHRONIC VIEW. *Names 1983 31(2): 117-122.* Prior to 1830, despite many contacts with other cultures, the Mississippi Choctaw naming traditions did not show change; Choctaw names are usually connotative, reflecting a characteristic or an attribute of an animal.

4119. Vipperman, Carl J. "FORCIBLY IF WE MUST": THE GEORGIA CASE FOR CHEROKEE REMOVAL, 1802-1832. *J. of Cherokee Studies 1978 3(2): 103-110.* Georgia based its claims for the Cherokee Indians' removal on the Compact of 1802, and agreement with the US government settling the Yazoo land frauds. In this agreement, the United States assumed the responsibility of extinguishing Indian land claims in Georgia. Georgia thus had a strong legal claim for evicting the Cherokee. The history of this claim is traced in reference to Cherokee political and cultural development. 37 notes.
J. M. Lee

4120. Vipperman, Carl J. THE "PARTICULAR MISSION" OF WILSON LUMPKIN. *Georgia Hist. Q. 1982 66(3): 295-316.* Describes the political career of Wilson Lumpkin, Georgia governor and senator, whose "particular mission" was the Cherokee removal from Georgia. Also discussed are the various violations of the Indian treaties resulting in eviction of the Cherokees. Based on documents, Lumpkin's account and other primary and secondary sources; 69 notes.                                G. R. Schroeder

4121. Ware, James W. INDIAN TERRITORY. *J. of the West 1977 16(2): 101-113.* At the outbreak of the Civil War, the major Indian tribes (Creek, Seminole, Chickasaw, Choctaw, and Cherokee) allied with the Confederacy. A splinter group of Upper Creeks, led by Opothleyahola, remained loyal to the United States. Confederate Indian military units, commanded by white and Indian officers, fought the Upper Creeks and Union forces in Indian Territory and in Arkansas. A continued shortage of arms, mounts, and equipment caused low morale and the gradual disintegration of military organization, leading to a decisive Union victory at the Battle of Honey Springs in 1863. From then on hostilities were limited to guerrilla fighting led by the capable Cherokee General Stand Watie. Noncombatant Indian refugees on both sides received little help from their respective governments. The destruction of their agricultural economic base and their social and political structures left the Indians easy victims of future white expansion. Based on government documents and on other primary and secondary sources; map, 6 photos, 55 notes.                                B. S. Porter

4122. Webb, Bernard L. THE HOMES OF FOUR INDIAN CHIEFS. *Georgia Life 1980 6(4): 30-32.* Describes four Georgia homes that once belonged to Indian chiefs of the Cherokee and Lower Creek Indian tribes dating from 1794 to 1823 and which still exist as museums.

4123. Webster, L. B. LETTERS FROM A LONELY SOLDIER. *J. of Cherokee Studies 1978 3(3): 153-157.* Reprints four letters written mainly from Tennessee by Captain L. B. Webster to his wife, Frances, on domestic matters and on his role in the forced removal of Cherokee Indians.

4124. Welsh, Louise. SEMINOLE COLONIZATION IN OKLAHOMA. *Chronicles of Oklahoma 1976 54(1): 77-103.* Once part of the Creek confederacy, the Seminole Indians began to break away during the 18th century and gradually moved further south into Florida. During 1817-49, three wars broke out between the Seminoles and the United States. The most severe began in 1835 when the leader Osceola and others resisted removal. Before the war ended seven years later, deaths reached several thousand and the government expended $30,000 to $40,000 for military activities. Osceola was captured under a white flag and died in prison. Most other chiefs bowed to removal to Indian Territory, where they suffered under Creek control until granted their own domain in 1856. Secondary sources; 6 photos, map.                                M. L. Tate

4125. Welsh, Michael. THE MISSIONARY SPIRIT: PROTESTANTISM AMONG THE OKLAHOMA SEMINOLES, 1842-1885. *Chronicles of Oklahoma 1983 61(1): 28-47.* During 1848 John and Mary Anne Lilley arrived at Oak Ridge, Indian Territory, and opened a Presbyterian mission and school for the Seminole Indians. Their success prompted the Baptists to send Joseph Samuel Murrow to establish a similar mission. Murrow soon converted Seminole principal chief John Jumper who became the most effective preacher among his people. The two religious groups drove a wedge within the tribe during the Civil War when the Presbyterians sided with the North and the Baptists with the South. In 1873, Presbyterians David and Antoinette Constant revitalized the school which was opened to Indians, blacks, and whites alike. Based on Oklahoma newspapers and manuscripts in the Oklahoma Indian Archives; 7 photos, 23 notes.                                M. L. Tate

4126. Welsh, Michael E. LEGISLATING A HOMESTEAD BILL: THOMAS HART BENTON AND THE SECOND SEMINOLE WAR. *Florida Hist. Q. 1978 57(2): 157-172.* Largely through the perseverance of Thomas Hart Benton (1782-1858), the Armed Occupation Act (US, 1842) passed, after President Tyler had declared

an end to hostilities of the Second Seminole War. The Act made lands in Florida available for homesteading. As a result, Florida's population increased, the area was explored, and the federal government became involved in the recurrent Indian problems. Based on government documents and secondary sources; 68 notes.

                                P. A. Beaber

4127. Wert, Jeffry. OLD HICKORY AND THE SEMINOLES. *Am. Hist. Illus. 1980 15(6): 28-35.* Without official US approval, Andrew Jackson invaded and captured Spanish Florida in 1818, defeating the Seminole Indians and angering Great Britain and Spain.

4128. Wiget, Andrew. ELIAS BOUDINOT, ELISHA BATES, AND *POOR SARAH:* FRONTIER PROTESTANTISM AND THE EMERGENCE OF THE FIRST NATIVE AMERICAN FICTION. *J. of Cherokee Studies 1983 8(1): 4-21.* Elias Boudinot, an Eastern Cherokee educated in Cornwall, Connecticut, and at Harvard Indian College, wrote *Poor Sarah, or Religion Exemplified in the Life and Death of an Indian Woman.* It is a tract of a dozen pages about two women, articulate and plain, who reflect upon life as influenced by Calvinistic-Moravian doctrines. *Poor Sarah* was sent to Elisha Bates, an Ohio Quaker with a long history of pro-Indian sentiments. Boudinot later became editor of *The Cherokee Phoenix,* signed the Treaty of New Echota (1835), and was assassinated for his participation in the removal treaty that led to the Trail of Tears. Illus., 2 photos, 93 notes, biblio.                                K. E. Gilmont

4129. Williams, Walter L. THE MERGER OF APACHES WITH EASTERN CHEROKEES: QUALLA IN 1893. *J. of Cherokee Studies 1977 2(2): 240-245.* After the defeat of the Apache Indians in the 1880's more than 500 of them were transferred to Florida and then Alabama and Oklahoma. In 1893 it was proposed to merge them with the Eastern Cherokee Indians, due to their high death rate in Florida. Captain William W. Wotherspoon investigated the Qualla Reservation in North Carolina in 1893 and advised against the project. He reported that the land was not sufficient for the two groups and that impoverishment and a lower standard of living would result. The Apaches were then transferred to Oklahoma, and in 1913 to New Mexico. 6 illus., 18 notes.

                                J. M. Lee

4130. Wilms, Douglas C. AGRARIAN PROGRESS IN THE CHEROKEE NATION PRIOR TO REMOVAL. *West Georgia Coll. Studies in the Social Sci. 1977 16: 1-15.* At the time of first European contact in the early 1700's, the Cherokee Indians in the Southeast were primarily hunter-gatherers who supplemented their diet with slash-and-burn agriculture; but by their final removal in 1838, through acculturation, they had become commercial farmers.

4131. Wilms, Douglas C. CHEROKEE ACCULTURATION AND CHANGING LAND USE PRACTICES. *Chronicles of Oklahoma 1978 56(3): 331-343.* During the 1790's American traders began to modify the culture of the Cherokee Indians who moved from their predominately agricultural existence to a dependence on manufactured goods. Subsequent "civilizing" programs by the US government and various missionary groups increased the dependency and turned the tribe away from a communal orientation toward private ownership. Increased power of mixed-blood factions in the tribe furthered the acculturation process. Primary and secondary sources; 4 photos, map, 35 notes.                                M. L. Tate

4132. Wilms, Douglas C. GEORGIA LAND LOTTERY OF 1832. *Chronicles of Oklahoma 1974 52(1): 52-60.* Describes Georgia's use of a land lottery system in 1832 as a means to expel the Cherokee Nation from its lands. Reviews Georgian claims to the land and outlines the basic lottery system procedure and Cherokee land use. Primary and secondary sources; 5 maps, 20 notes.

                                N. J. Street

4133. Wilms, Douglas C. A NOTE ON THE DISTRICT BOUNDARIES OF THE CHEROKEE NATION, 1820. *Appalachian J. 1975 2(4): 284-285.*

4134. Winsor, Henry M. CHICKASAW-CHOCTAW FINANCIAL RELATIONS WITH THE UNITED STATES, 1830-1880. *J. of the West 1973 12(3): 356-371*. Financial relations between the Chickasaw and Choctaw Indians and the United States were based on public sentiment and public need. In 1830, public sympathy for Indians was low and public need for land was high. The Chickasaws and Choctaws were moved from Alabama and Mississippi to Indian Territory, in present-day Oklahoma. Financial relations tended to favor the federal government. Following the Civil War, financial settlements became more liberal and by 1880 were definitely favoring the Indians. 66 notes.                          V. L. Human

4135. Woods, H. Ted. THE MEREDITH FAMILY AND THE CREEK INDIAN WAR. *North Louisiana Hist. Assoc. J. 1974 6(1): 27-29*. In early 1812, Arthur Lott from Georgia and Thomas Meredith from South Carolina were killed in separate incidents by Indians in Alabama while moving their families to Mississippi. It has been suggested that the murders of these two men were the events which "actually caused the Creek Indian War of 1813-1814." Members of the Meredith family later moved to Louisiana and today their descendants "constitute one of the largest families in several north and central parishes of the state." There are also a number of Lott descendants living in Louisiana. 4 notes.
                                                         A. N. Garland

4136. Wunder, John R. "DOESN'T ANYONE SPEAK INJUN IN THIS COURTROOM?": NEW PERSPECTIVES IN NATIVE AMERICAN LEGAL HISTORY. *Rev. in Am. Hist. 1977 5(4): 467-476*. Review article prompted by John Phillip Reid's *A Better Kind of Hatchet: Law, Trade, and Diplomacy in the Cherokee Nation during the Early Years of European Contact* (University Park: The Pennsylvania State U. Pr., 1976) and Rennard Strickland's *Fire and the Spirits: Cherokee Law from Clan to Court* (Norman: U. of Oklahoma Pr., 1975).

4137. Yerkes, Richard W. MICROWEAR, MICRODRILLS, AND MISSISSIPPIAN CRAFT SPECIALIZATION. *Am. Antiquity 1983 48(3): 499-518*. Analyzes microdrills, microcores, and microblades of the Mississippian period from the Powell mound and the Dunham tract of the Cahokia site near St. Louis, Missouri, and Jaketown perforators from the Poverty Point site, Louisiana, for microwear traces using H. L. Keeley's methods to learn about the use of the tools discovered in 1931.

4138. Young, Mary. THE CHEROKEE NATION: MIRROR OF THE REPUBLIC. *Am. Q. 1981 33(5): 502-524*. In the 30 years before the general removal of 1838-39, the Cherokee evolved culturally into a society that mirrored the larger white society surrounding it. That mirroring included the images of internal conflict; though the Cherokee were divided over a number of issues, they did not suffer any substantial internal divisions before their removal. Once they were in the West, however, with the constant threat to their lands removed, factional disputes over cultural alternatives increased substantially. Based on National Archives Microfilm, the Ross Papers, and other primary sources; 97 notes.
                                                       D. K. Lambert

4139. Young, Mary E. WOMEN, CIVILIZATION, AND THE INDIAN QUESTION. Deutrich, Mabel E. and Purdy, Virginia C., ed. *Clio Was a Woman: Studies in the History of American Women* (Washington, D.C.: Howard U. Pr., 1980): 98-110. Nineteenth-century US citizens labored to convert Indians to an idealized model of Christian civilization. They accomplished this by changing the Indians' relationship to property, work, and law. If Indian families could be confined to small farms and induced by private possession to work the land, they would convert millions of acres of hunting ground to land for use by white farmers. But with this sense of property, comes a sense of home, and it was felt that the female Indians, especially, should be educated according to the ideal of domestic femininity. An outstanding illustration of the US Indian Office's concern for modifying sex role definitions can be found in the work of agents and Presbyterian-Congregationalist missionaries among the Cherokee Indians: intermarriage, the rise to social prominence and political power of a mixed-blood elite of

planters, merchants, millers, and ferry-keepers, and the shift to male agriculture changed the status as well as the work of the Cherokee women. A discussion summary follows. 36 notes.
                                                         J. Powell

4140. Zellner, Richard. STAND WATIE AND THE KILLING OF JAMES FOREMAN. *Chronicles of Oklahoma 1981 59(2): 167-178*. The Cherokee Indians had been badly factionalized since the Removal Era of the 1830's. The factions of "Cherokee West," which had agreed to early removal from Georgia, and "Cherokee East," which had fought removal to the end, continued their rivalries in Indian Territory. Stand Watie represented the former group and his May 1842 murder of James Foreman from the latter faction created the possibility of bloody reprisals. An Arkansas court found Watie innocent by reason of self-defense. Fortunately, Cherokee Agent Pierce M. Butler cooled tempers and prevented further bloodshed. Based on the John Ross Papers and *Letters Received by the Office of Indian Affairs;* 47 notes.       M. L. Tate

4141. —. ANDREW JACKSON'S ADVICE TO THE CHEROKEES. *J. of Cherokee Studies 1979 4(2): 96-97*. Cherokee removal was consistently pursued as a major policy by Andrew Jackson throughout his career. In 1835, in advice to the Cherokee Indians, he forcibly reiterated this policy. He was convinced that the Cherokees had no choice but to remove west of the Mississippi or face extinction. Reproduced from *The Alleghany Democrat* (Alleghany, New York), 7 April 1835.                          J. M. Lee

4142. —. CHEROKEE TREATY RIGHTS. *J. of Cherokee Studies 1979 4(2): 71-74*. In the Treaty of 1791 the federal government guaranteed to the Cherokee Indians all lands not ceded by them to the government. The Cherokees were of the opinion that these rights to their land, among others, were secure, an opinion shared by others. Reproduced from *The New York American*, 15 September 1829.                                 J. M. Lee

4143. —. CONTINUED PRESSURE IN GEORGIA. *J. of Cherokee Studies 1979 4(2): 79-81*. From the early 1790's to the late 1830's, the state of Georgia demanded that the US government extinguish Cherokee land titles within state boundaries. Public opinion in other states often favored the Cherokees in opposition to Georgia. Reproduced from *The Republican* (Harrisburg, Pennsylvania), 26 March 1831.                                J. M. Lee

4144. —. THE DEATH OF HARRIET GOLD BOUDINOT. *J. of Cherokee Studies 1979 4(2): 102-107*. Harriet Gold Boudinot was a native of Cornwall, Connecticut, who became the wife of Elias Boudinot, a leader of the Treaty Party of Cherokees. Almost all of her married life, apparently about 10 years, was spent with the Cherokee Indians of northern Georgia. Her last days, and her death on 15 August 1836, were described in a letter to her parents from her husband. Reproduced from *The New York Observer*, 26 November 1836. Fig.                              J. M. Lee

4145. —. DEATH ON THE FRONTIER. *J. of Cherokee Studies 1979 4(2): 60-62*. During the 1790's, both Cherokee Indians and whites attacked each other, often with tragic results. Sometimes the Cherokee received aid from the Spanish in Florida, but this aid was withdrawn in 1794. Several episodes are described, and a letter from the Baron de Carondelet is included. Reproduced from the *Gazette of the United States*, 20 December 1794.    J. M. Lee

4146. —. DIARY OF ALEXANDER MONYPENNY: MARCH 20-MAY 31, 1761. *J. of Cherokee Studies 1977 2(3): 320-331*. Record of the James Grant military expedition against the Cherokee Indians in South Carolina.

4147. —. GEORGIA ACTIONS VIEWED AS DANGEROUS TO THE NATIONAL UNION. *J. of Cherokee Studies 1979 4(2): 93-95*. Pro-Cherokee opinion in the 1830's was found in Georgia as well as out. The state's anti-Indian policy was viewed with disgust there as well. In one contemporary article Georgians were compared unfavorably with the Spanish, regarding inhumanity toward Indians. Reproduced from *The New York American,* 13 January 1832.        J. M. Lee

4148. —. GEORGIA'S ATTACK ON THE MISSIONARIES. *J. of Cherokee Studies 1979 4(2): 82-92.* The American Board of Commissioners for Foreign Missions founded and maintained missions for the Cherokee Indians in order to improve Cherokee standards of living and education. To coerce the Cherokees the state of Georgia often harrassed the missionaries, even to the point of jailing Samuel A. Worcester and others. This aroused a great deal of unfavorable publicity for Georgia in other parts of the country. Reproduced from *The New York Spectator,* 23 August 1831.
J. M. Lee

4149. —. MILITARY ORDERS AND CORRESPONDENCE ON THE CHEROKEE REMOVAL. *J. of Cherokee Studies 1978 3(3): 143-152.* Reprints mainly military documents on the forced removals of Cherokee Indians.

4150. —. THOMAS JEFFERSON'S ADVICE TO THE CHEROKEES. *J. of Cherokee Studies 1979 4(2): 64-66.* Shortly before his retirement in 1809, Thomas Jefferson delivered two speeches to a Cherokee delegation. In the first, he advised the adoption of laws and industrious pursuits; in the second, he indicated a preference for Cherokee removal to the west of the Mississippi. Reproduced from *The National Intelligencer and Washington Advertiser,* 10 March 1809.        J. M. Lee

4151. —. A TRIBUTE TO JOHN RIDGE. *J. of Cherokee Studies 1979 4(2): 111-117.* John Ridge was a leader of the Treaty Party of Cherokees and a negotiator of the Treaty of New Echota. After Ridge's assassination in the summer of 1839, John F. Schermerhorn wrote a tribute to his character which traced and evaluated his career. Appended is a letter from Ridge which explained his position regarding Cherokee removal to the west. Reproduced from *The Daily Albany Argus* (Albany, New York), 9 August 1839.
J. M. Lee

4152. —. [UNITED STATES INDIAN AGENTS TO THE FIVE CIVILIZED TRIBES]. *Chronicles of Oklahoma 1973 51(1): 34-83.* Fischer, LeRoy H. INTRODUCTION, *pp. 34-36.* Background of the Indian agents of the Five Civilized Tribes in the Indian Territory during 1834-74, including a list of agents to the Creek and Seminole tribes.
Boyd, Joel D. CREEK INDIAN AGENTS, 1834-1874, *pp. 37-58.*
Brown, Elton Thomas. SEMINOLE INDIAN AGENTS, 1842-1874, *pp. 59-83.*        S

# The Twentieth Century

4153. Blumer, Thomas J. REBECCA YOUNGBIRD: AN INDEPENDENT CHEROKEE POTTER. *J. of Cherokee Studies 1980 5(1): 41-49.* Rebecca Youngbird, self-taught among the Eastern North Carolina Cherokee and Catawba Indians, developed her own style of pottery making. Utilizing clay mixtures, special knives and a "rubbing rock," she made black vases. Influenced by instruction from the Pueblo potter Maria Martinez, Youngbird incorporated southwestern tribal designs near the necks of vessels. Later pottery showed a blend of Cherokee and Pueblo traces with no motifs used by Catawbas. Now retired, her work can be seen at the Qualla Arts and Crafts Mutual on the Cherokee Reservation in North Carolina. From interviews with Cherokee potters and secondary sources; illus., 5 photos, 2 notes.        K. E. Gilmont

4154. Covington, James W. BRIGHTON RESERVATION, FLORIDA 1935-1938. *Tequesta 1976 36: 54-65.* The Brighton Reservation is one of the three Seminole Indian reservations in Florida. The Muskogee Seminoles living north of Lake Okeechobee were faced with economic adversity. In response the federal government purchased the 2,500-acre tract of land known as Indian Prairie which was northwest of Lake Okeechobee. It became known as Brighton Reservation. Additional purchases by 1938 enlarged the

reservation to 35,000 acres. Cattle production was the main economic base, but by 1943 the families on the reservation were yet to attain an annual average of $500 per family. Based on primary and secondary sources; 38 notes.        H. S. Marks

4155. Covington, James W. FLORIDA SEMINOLES: 1900-1920. *Florida Hist. Q. 1974 53(2): 181-197.* Surveys Seminole Indian lifestyle in the Everglades. The Seminoles maintained considerable independence from the whites, making contact chiefly at the trading posts where they exchanged the fruits of their hunting for basic necessities. They successfully resisted attempts to place them on a reservation, efforts to educate them, and attempts by various Christian sects to convert them. But this independence was ending by 1920 with the depletion of wildlife and the encroachment of the white man's world. 58 notes.        R. V. Ritter

4156. Covington, James W. TRAIL INDIANS OF FLORIDA. *Florida Hist. Q. 1979 58(1): 37-57.* The Miccosukee Indians separated from the main body of Seminole Indians and have achieved reservation land grants and recognition as a separate entity. These Trail Indians manage their own affairs. Based on Congressional and Interior Department records and other primary sources; 73 notes.
N. A. Kuntz

4157. Fogelson, Raymond D. CHEROKEE LITTLE PEOPLE RECONSIDERED. *J. of Cherokee Studies 1982 7(2): 92-98.* In Cherokee lore and society, the Little People exist everywhere. Little People may have different names, origins, and functions and may be invisible, but they constitute a force in the conduct of one's ways. Biblio.        K. E. Gilmont

4158. Fogelson, Raymond D. THE CONJUROR IN EASTERN CHEROKEE SOCIETY. *J. of Cherokee Studies 1980 5(2): 60-87.* Modern eastern Cherokee conjurers living in the Big Cove section have acted as advisors, counselors, divinators, doctors, and consultants in love. From interviews with Da 'si, Awani 'ski, and Na 'tsi and research from previous writings of Mooney and Olbrechts, it is evident that modern conjurers still retain some influence among conservative Cherokee Indians. Photo, 56 notes.
K. E. Gilmont

4159. Fogelson, Raymond D. and Walker, Amelia B. SELF AND OTHER IN CHEROKEE BOOGER MASKS. *J. of Cherokee Studies 1980 5(2): 88-101.* The Eastern Cherokee Booger Dance, comprised of men wearing buckeye or basswood masks, ornamented with colors and hair, resembling the male organ, is considered by some anthropologists a negative reaction to foreign, especially European, influences. The dancers first approach the spectators, jostle the women, perform either the Eagle or Bear Dance, and then depart. There is some relationship to Iroquoian False Face, and possibly Husk Face, dances. 4 photos, 14 notes.
K. E. Gilmont

4160. French, Laurence and Hornbuckle, Jim. AN ANALYSIS OF INDIAN VIOLENCE: THE CHEROKEE EXAMPLE. *Am. Indian Q.: A J. of Anthrop., Hist., and Literature 1977-78 3(4): 335-356.* Cultural frustration in the form of anomie and internal conflict, and a no longer viable "informal subculture control structure," provides reasons for seemingly excessive violence among Eastern Cherokee Indians in Appalachia. Some members of the group adhere to traditional culture, and some have joined "majority society," but most are "marginal Indians" without benefit of membership in either group. Deterioration of traditional mechanisms of aggression release and the imposition of oppressive formal controls of the reservation system result in sporadic eruptions of violence. Based on crime records of the Eastern Cherokee Tribe, secondary sources, and includes 12 case histories.        G. L. Olson

4161. French, Laurence and Hornbuckle, Jim. AN ANALYSIS OF INDIAN VIOLENCE: THE CHEROKEE EXAMPLE. *Am. Indian Q. 1977-78 3(4): 335-356.* Analyzes reported, violent crimes committed by Cherokee Indians during 1974-76, particularly as related to alcohol.

4162. French, Laurence. TOURISM AND INDIAN EXPLOITATION: A SOCIAL INDICTMENT. *Indian Hist. 1977 10(4): 19-24.* The Eastern Band of Cherokee Indians, in western North Carolina, exist in the midst of a tourist industry surrounding the historical drama "Unto These Hills." Unfortunately, the tribe benefits little from the millions of dollars resulting from the tourism, which is a white-dominated industry that employs few Indians. Even the nearby Western Carolina University at Cullowhee, North Carolina, benefits from the proximity of the Cherokees, and is only gradually becoming concerned with their welfare. Biblio.
E. D. Johnson

4163. Henry, Delaura. TRADITIONS IN THE CHOCTAW HOMELAND. *Historic Preservation 1974 26(1): 28-31.* The Mississippi band of Choctaw Indians, living near Philadelphia, Mississippi, is preserving tribal customs, values, and crafts through their annual Choctaw Indian Fair and a state-funded Arts and Crafts Program. 5 photos.
R. M. Frame III

4164. Hutchinson, James. A FLORIDA ARTIST VIEWS THE SEMINOLES. *Florida Hist. Q. 1976 55(2): 134-137.* Provides the name, size, and explanation of 12 paintings of the Seminole Indians' daily life and history by the contemporary artist James Hutchinson. The location of the paintings is not given, nor are they all dated. 12 illus.
P. A. Beaber

4165. Jackson, Gilliam. CULTURAL IDENTITY FOR THE MODERN CHEROKEES. *Appalachian J. 1975 2(4): 280-283.* Criticizes the decline in traditional Indian community activities because of assimilation into white society, and argues that one of the best ways to ensure continuance of Cherokee culture is to encourage use of the Cherokee language and "to return to the Indian day schools of the past."
S

4166. Jake, Lucille; James, Evelyn; and Bunte, Pamela. THE SOUTHERN PAIUTE WOMAN IN A CHANGING SOCIETY. *Frontiers 1983 7(1): 44-49.* Two elderly Paiute women reflect on the value of their traditional culture.

4167. Kersey, Harry A., Jr. FEDERAL SCHOOLS AND ACCULTURATION AMONG THE FLORIDA SEMINOLES, 1927-1954. *Florida Hist. Q. 1980 59(2): 165-181.* The desire to acculturate the Seminole Indians was the motive for having their children schooled in North Carolina. Commissioner of Indian Affairs John Collier played a large role in this educational campaign. By 1950 it became apparent that the children could not be expected to return to the reservation unchanged after experiencing the white man's education. Recent legislation recognizes the needs and values of the Seminole people. Based on the writings of John Collier, congressional hearings and other sources; 39 notes.
N. A. Kuntz

4168. Kersey, Harry A., Jr. THE "FRIENDS OF THE FLORIDA SEMINOLES" SOCIETY: 1899-1926. *Tequesta 1974 (34): 3-20.* In 1891 an Indian mission was established on land purchased at Immokalee, in Collier County. In 1899 the Friends of the Florida Seminoles was organized in Kissimmee. Jim Willson was secretary of the charitable organization from its founding until it became defunct in 1926. His wife, Minnie Moore Willson, is known in Florida history as the "mother of the Seminole Land Bill," enacted into law in 1915. This organization helped to protect Seminoles until the Bureau of Indian Affairs assumed the burden. Based on primary and secondary sources; 55 notes.
H. S. Marks

4169. Kersey, Harry A., Jr. PRIVATE SOCIETIES AND THE MAINTENANCE OF SEMINOLE TRIBAL INTEGRITY, 1899-1957. *Florida Hist. Q. 1978 56(3): 297-316.* Early in the 20th century the Seminole Indians lost their lands to rapid settlement of southern Florida and suffered the decline of their cash economy based on hunting and fishing. Three major private societies which eventually enabled the Seminoles to become reservation dwellers with a sound agricultural-herding economic base were the Friends of the Florida Seminoles (founded 1899), the Friends of the Seminoles (founded 1934), and the Seminole Indian Association (founded 1913). These societies aided in the transition by securing

reservations, by providing legal, educational, and social services, and by advocating Indian rights. Primary and secondary sources; 61 notes.
P. A. Beaber

4170. King, Duane H. HISTORY OF THE MUSEUM OF THE CHEROKEE INDIAN. *J. of Cherokee Studies 1976 1(1): 60-64.* Reviews antecedents of the Museum of the Cherokee Indian at Cherokee, North Carolina. The original collection was started by Burnham S. Colburn around 1915. The first building opened 9 May 1948 after the collection was acquired by the Cherokee Historical Association. The first museum burned in 1952. In the early 1970's several grants from a variety of sources, amounting to almost $1.5 million, allowed for the construction of a new museum which opened 15 June 1976. 3 photos, map.
J. M. Lee

4171. King, R. T. CLAN AFFILIATION AND LEADERSHIP AMONG THE TWENTIETH CENTURY FLORIDA INDIANS. *Florida Hist. Q. 1976 55(4): 130-152.* Clan membership is a major determining factor in tribal leadership of the Seminole Indians of Florida. Since the formation of the Seminole Tribe in 1957, the Bird clan, the most populous of the White moiety, has supplied most of the tribe's officers. Traditionally, military leaders and medicine men have come from the Red moiety. Based mainly on interviews and secondary sources; 30 notes.
P. A. Beaber

4172. Loftin, John D. THE "HARMONY ETHIC" OF THE CONSERVATIVE EASTERN CHEROKEES: A RELIGIOUS INTERPRETATION. *J. of Cherokee Studies 1983 8(1): 40-43.* Cherokee Indians typically are nonaggressive, generous, submissive to hierarchies, fearful of witchcraft, pragmatic more than idealistic, and can endure hardships without showing emotions. Moreover, they believe that the individual is important regardless of socioeconomic status, and bravery is highly valued. Cherokee philosophy is similar to that of many other Indian tribes. This attitude indicates a modern religious outlook. Biblio., 55 notes.
K. E. Gilmont

4173. Matthiessen, Peter. LA PETITE PERCHE ET LE TOMBEAU DU PEUPLE CHEROKEE [The snail darter and the fall of the Cherokees]. *Ann. de la Recherche Urbaine [France] 1980 (7): 77-96.* Discusses the effects the Tellico dam, the 25th and last hydraulic equipment program sponsored by the Tennessee Valley Authority, has had on the extinction of the snail darter and the ruin of the Cherokee Indians' cultural heritage due to flooding, and the 15-year fight by the Cherokee, environmentalists, and local and federal authorities against the TVA, which the TVA won; and the admission by officials that the dam may have doubtful economic benefits for the area in addition to damage already done; 1954-79.

4174. Meredith, Howard L. THE BACONE SCHOOL OF ART. *Chronicles of Oklahoma 1980 58(1): 92-98.* Acee Blue Eagle became head of the Art Department at Bacone College in 1935 and quickly established a national reputation for this Oklahoma school. Blue Eagle and his successors, Woody Crumbo, Dick West, C. Terry Saul, Charles Colbert, and Ruthe Blalock Jones, helped nourish several styles of American Indian art and produced dozens of students whose works have been displayed in leading galleries. These Bacone graduates have forged an important bridge of understanding between traditional Indian cultures and modern society. Secondary sources; 6 photos, 9 notes.
M. L. Tate

4175. Petter, Rodolphe. CHEYENNE INDIANS: A PHOTO ESSAY. *Mennonite Life 1982 37(2): 8-13.* Photographs of persons and scenes in Cheyenne areas of Oklahoma and Montana, taken by Mennonite missionary Rodolphe Petter. Taken from a collection in the Mennonite Library and Archives; 18 photos.
J. H. Sweetland

4176. Philp, Kenneth R. TURMOIL AT BIG CYPRESS: SEMINOLE DEER AND THE FLORIDA CATTLE TICK CONTROVERSY. *Florida Hist. Q. 1977 56(1): 28-44.* A long controversy at the Big Cypress Reservation in Hendry County arose when the US Department of Agriculture announced that the Seminole Indians' deer would have to be destroyed. The deer were thought to be infested with a cattle tick, which threatened the Florida cattle industry. Indian Commissioner John Collier and Secretary of the Interior

Harold L. Ickes sided with the Seminoles' cause and helped preserve their wilderness area from the Agriculture Department's intervention. Despite their eventual success in stopping the deer eradication program, the bureaucratic infighting and meddling in Indian affairs only increased the Indians' distrust of the US government. Covers 1935-43. Based mainly on government reports; 49 notes.
P. A. Beaber

4177. Reed, Mark. REFLECTIONS ON CHEROKEE STICK-BALL. *J. of Cherokee Studies 1977 2(1): 195-200.* Stickball is an ancient Cherokee game combining elements of a variety of sports and is still played in the 20th century on a field similar to a football field. Equipment includes a lightweight ball and two sticks per man similar to tennis rackets. Written in Cherokee with an English translation, 3 photos.
J. M. Lee

4178. Savage, William W. MONOLOGUES IN RED AND WHITE: CONTEMPORARY RACIAL ATTITUDES IN TWO SOUTHERN PLAINS COMMUNITIES. *J. of Ethnic Studies 1974 2(3): 24-31.* Examines attitudes of whites and Indians toward each other in two western Oklahoma towns of about 1500 population each. Cultural and racial stereotypes abound as whites comment on Indians' clannishness, immorality, laziness, and shrewdness, believing that Indians receive "vast amounts of money from the federal government." Linking of the Indian with the Negro as a potential "problem" is common. White attitudes are most rigid among those having little contact with Indians. Indian responses to interviews did not center on counterattacks against white culture and life-styles, but responded to particular charges against their people. Injustice against Indians, dual standards of law, and a true picture of federal aid form the Indian side of the story. "There is distinct and definable racial prejudice" in these communities, and the booster journalism and glosses of civic-minded regional historians retard any real solutions. Based on materials of the Doris Duke Oral History Project; 13 notes.
G. J. Bobango

4179. Sneed, Roseanna. TWO CHEROKEE WOMEN. *Frontiers 1981 6(3): 35-38.* Discusses Lucyann Davis Wolf and her daughter, Mary, respectively grandmother and mother of the author, and describes their family life in the Tennessee hills, 1900-35.

4180. Walkingstick, Dawnena. A PRE-CITIZENSHIP CERTIFICATE OF EDUCATIONAL COMPETENCY. *J. of Cherokee Studies 1976 1(2): 87-91.* Until 1924 American Indians were not generally considered US citizens. In 1920 Frell Owl, a Cherokee, was given a Certificate of Educational Competency when he graduated from Hampton Institute. This qualified him for citizenship. From 1924 to 1927 Mr. Owl attended Dartmouth College. Later he served in the Bureau of Indian Affairs. Although he never had oc-

casion to use the Certificate to prove his citizenship, the granting of it to him was the typical method of gaining citizenship for Indians before 1924 when Indians were made citizens by Congress. Based on personal communications and secondary source; 9 notes.
J. M. Lee

4181. Weeks, Charles J. THE EASTERN CHEROKEE AND THE NEW DEAL. *North Carolina Hist. Rev. 1976 53(3): 303-319.* Though the Indian New Deal offered a program designed to reverse misguided policies of the previous 50 years, it failed to have a significant impact on the social and economic condition of the Cherokees of western North Carolina. The influx of public money discouraged farming and handicraft work, thereby weakening the tribe's economic base. For personal, political, and economic reasons "white" Cherokees (mixed bloods who had adopted local white culture) resisted reforms offered by the New Deal. Based on manuscript archival records, published government documents, and secondary sources; 12 illus., 60 notes.
T. L. Savitt

4182. Wheat, Helen and Agnew, Brad. SPECIAL COLLECTIONS DEPARTMENT AT NORTHEASTERN OKLAHOMA STATE UNIVERSITY. *Chronicles of Oklahoma 1978 56(1): 73-84.* Emmet Starr, librarian at Northeastern Oklahoma State University in Tahlequah, began collecting documents of Cherokee history in 1913. A dual collecting effort by university librarians and historians expanded the holdings during the 1920's. In 1973 the Cherokee Collection received its first full-time curator and two years later moved into spacious quarters. Contents of the various manuscript holdings are discussed. Based on interviews and other primary sources; 5 photos, 20 notes.
M. L. Tate

4183. White, Max E. CONTEMPORARY USAGE OF NATIVE PLANT FOODS BY THE EASTERN CHEROKEES. *Appalachian J. 1975 2(4): 323-326.*

4184. —. AMERICAN INDIAN GENEALOGY: SELECTED SOURCES ON THE EASTERN CHEROKEE. *Prologue 1982 14(4): 227-236.* Discusses American Indian genealogy, focusing on selected sources on the eastern Cherokee Indians. Records documenting relations between the federal government and the Indians are a rich source of genealogical information. Two series of such Cherokee records are outlined: "Records Relating to the Enrollment of Eastern Cherokee by Guion Miller, 1908-1910" and "Eastern Cherokee Applications of the U.S. Court of Claims, 1906-1909." A wealth of other such records available at the National Archives are listed in the "Select Catalog of Microfilm Publications Relating to American Indians." Based on National Archives records; illus., photos, 5 notes.
M. A. Kascus

# SUBJECT INDEX

Subject Profile Index (ABC-SPIndex) carries both generic and specific index terms. Begin a search at the general term but also look under more specific or related terms. This index includes selective cross-references.

Each string of index descriptors is intended to present a profile of a given article; however, no particular relationship between any two terms in the profile is implied. Terms within the profile are listed alphabetically after the leading term. The variety of punctuation and capitalization reflects production methods and has no intrinsic meaning; e.g., there is no difference in meaning between "History, study of" and "History (study of)."

Cities, towns, and counties are listed following their respective states or provinces; e.g., "Ohio (Columbus)." Terms beginning with an arabic numeral are listed after the letter Z. The chronology of the bibliographic entry follows the subject index descriptors. In the chronology, "c" stands for "century"; e.g., "19c" means "19th century."

Note that "United States" is not used as a leading index term; if no country is mentioned, the index entry refers to the United States alone. When an entry refers to both Canada and the United States, both "Canada" and "USA" appear in the string of index descriptors, but "USA" is not a leading term. When an entry refers to any other country and the United States, only the other country is indexed.

The last number in the index string, in italics, refers to the bibliographic entry number.

## A

Abbot, John. Georgia (Savannah Valley). Illustrations. Natural history. 1776-1840. *1022*

Abel, John Jacob. Colleges and Universities. Johns Hopkins University Medical School. Maryland (Baltimore). Pharmacy. 1880-1933. *2156*

Abolition Movement. *See also* Antislavery Sentiments; Emancipation.

—. American Free Baptist Mission Society. Baptists. Missions and Missionaries. Schisms. 1830-69. *2374*

—. Anderson, Isaac. Presbyterian Church. Southern and Western Theological Seminary. Tennessee (Maryville). 1819-50's. *2406*

—. Berea College. Fee, John Gregg. Kentucky. Presbyterian Church. 1855-1904. *1874*

—. Blacks. Constitutional Amendments (15th). Douglass, Frederick. Theology. 1825-86. *2497*

—. Freedmen. Labor. Race relations. Slavery. 1830-63. *359*

—. McPherson, James M. (review article). Race relations. 1870's-1960's. 1976. *3739*

Academic freedom. Civil Rights. Educational Reform. Southern Political Science Association. 1928-79. *144*

—. Georgia, University of. Hill, Walter B. 1899-1905. *1837*

—. Texas. 1929-79. *1831*

Academies. Alabama. Girls. Livingston Female Academy. 1835-1910. *1836*

—. Louisiana (Claiborne Parish). ca 1830-1920. *1947*

Academy of Richmond County. Education. Georgia. 1783-1863. *1807*

Acadians. *See also* Creoles.

—. Cajuns. Conrad, Glenn. DelSesto, Steven. Gibson, Jon L. Louisiana. 18c-1978. *650*

—. Environment. Louisiana. 18c-19c. *2694*

—. Folklore. Louisiana. Social customs. 18c-1978. *1628*

—. French language. Louisiana. 1970. *3264*

Accidents. Folklore. Ghosts. North Carolina (Maco). Railroads. 19c-1973. *1650*

Acculturation. *See also* Assimilation.

—. Agriculture. Cherokee Indians. 1730's-1838. *4130*

—. Architecture. German Americans. German language. Swiss Americans. Virginia (Shenandoah Valley). 1720-1800. *1190*

—. Artifacts. Delaware. Indians. Maryland. Pennsylvania. Virginia. 18c-20c. *3907*

—. Attitudes. Cherokee Indians. Missions and Missionaries. White Path's Rebellion. 1824-28. *4040*

—. Blacks. Dialects. Georgia. Gullah (dialect). Sea Islands. South Carolina. 1940-80. *785*

—. Board of Indian Commissioners. Five Civilized Tribes. Indian Territory. 1869-98. *4080*

—. Caddo Indians (Hasinai). Social Customs. Texas, east. 1650-1856. *4034*

—. Census. Cherokee Indians. Economic Conditions. Population. 1809-35. *4043*

—. Cherokee Indians. 1810-40. *4138*

—. Cherokee Indians. Indian-White Relations. Social Organization. 1790's-1820's. *4131*

—. Chinese Americans. Discrimination. Georgia (Augusta). 1865-1980. *513*

—. Choctaw Indians. Confederate States of America. Indian-White Relations. 1855-61. *3925*

—. Choctaw Indians. Crime and Criminals. Factionalism. War. 1746-50. *3984*

—. Civil War. Creek Indians. Indian-White Relations. 1830's-61. *3951*

—. Collier, John. Florida. Indians. North Carolina. Schools. Seminole Indians. 1927-54. *4167*

—. Davis, Alice Brown. Educators. Indian-White Relations. Oklahoma. Seminole Indians. 1870-1935. *3912*

—. Ethnicity. German Americans. Religion. Social Organization. Texas (Hill Country). 1844-1910. *2334*

—. Georgia (Atlanta). Jews. Leadership. 1890-1940. *505*

—. Georgia, southeastern. Immigration. Scottish Americans. 1746-1860. *534*

—. Indian-White Relations. Virginia. 1607-1853. *3969*

—. Jews (Russian). May brothers. Oklahoma (Tulsa). Textile Industry. 1889-1970. *2646*

Ackland, Adelicia Hayes Franklin. Architecture. Belmont (estate). Interior decoration. Stereographs. Tennessee (Nashville). 1850-1970. *1198*

Ackland, William Hayes. Belmont (estate). Elites. Memoirs. Tennessee (Nashville). 1871-78. *600*

—. Belmont (estate). Memoirs. Tennessee (Nashville). 1855-67. *599*

Acme, Red River and Northern Railroad. Gypsum mills. Lazarus, Samuel L. Railroads. Texas (Hardeman County). 1890-1909. *2997*

Acree, Howard. Fireplaces. Kentucky, eastern. 1935-46. *1279*

Actors and Actresses. Bernhardt, Sarah. Georgia (Savannah). Theater. 1892. 1906. *991*

—. Films. Women. 1939-71. *463*

Adair family. Beatty, Ellen Adair White. Florida. Genealogy. Social Status. 1801-84. *681*

Adamic, Louis. Baraga, Frederick. Ethnic studies. Prisland, Marie. Slovenian Americans. 1687-1975. *579*

Adams, Charles P. Blacks. Colleges and Universities. Grambling State University. Louisiana. 1896-1928. *1977*

Adams, Henry Brooks. District of Columbia. Religion. Rock Creek Cemetery. Sculpture. Values. 1886-91. *821*

—. Heroes. James, Henry. Literature. National Characteristics. 1865-1930. *452*

Adams-Onís Treaty (1819). Boundaries. Oklahoma. Spain. Texas. 1819-1930. *3287*

Addresses. Baptists, Southern. Fraternal Address. Mullins, Edgar Young. 1919-20. *2229*

Adger, John B. Dabney, Robert Lewis. Hodge, Charles. Nevin, John W. Presbyterian Church. 1845-75. *2314*

Adolescence. *See also* Youth.

—. Blacks. Church attendance. Religiosity. Whites. 1964-74. *2258*

Adolescents' Literature. Fiction. 1907-17. *1079*

Adventists. Missions and Missionaries. Mountaineers. North Carolina (western). 1870-99. *2263*

Advertising. *See also* Marketing; Propaganda; Public Relations; Publicity.

—. Candler, Asa Griggs. Coca-Cola Company. 1880's-1970's. *2983*

—. Coca-Cola Company. 1886-1967. *2541*

A.E.O.C. (club). Harvard University. Rutledge, Thomas P. Social Organizations. 1832-35. *699*

Aeronautics, Military. Army Air Corps. Eaker, Ira C. World War I. World War II. 8th Bomber Command, US. 1917-47. *3869*

—. Blacks. Military General Staff. Parrish, Noel F. (interview). Tuskegee Army Air Field. World War II. 1941-45. *3854*

Aesthetics. Appalachia. Chairmakers. Folk art. 1950's-60's. *1548*

—. Lectures. Travel. Wilde, Oscar. 1882. *738*

AFL-CIO (Committee on Political Education). Politics. 1943-75. *3433*

Africa. *See also* Pan-Africanism.

—. Art. Blacks. Cemeteries. Death and Dying. 1880's-1977. *1777*

—. Arts and crafts. Blacks. Slavery. Social Customs. 1800-1975. *1772*

—. Blacks. Carpentry. Construction. 1625-1800. *1782*

—. Blacks. Folklore. Georgia. Sea Islands. South Carolina. 1970-80. *1774*

—. Blacks. Georgia. Moore, Janie Gilliard. Personal Narratives. Sea Islands. South Carolina. 1970-80. *1754*

—. Blacks. Georgia. Sea Islands. Social Customs. South Carolina. 1970-80. *1775*

—. Bowen, Thomas Jefferson. Chatelain, Heli. Folklore. Grout, Lewis. Missions and Missionaries. 1849-94. *1752*

—. Industrial arts education. Pan-Africanism. Racism. 1879-1940. *2078*

Africa, West. Blacks. Jazz. Louisiana (New Orleans; Congo Square). Music. Religion. Rites and Ceremonies. 18c-19c. *960*

Age. Blacks. Population. Rural Settlements. 1950-70. *2856*

—. Education. Migration, internal. 1965-70. *3301*

Agecroft Hall (manor). England (Lancashire). Furniture and Furnishings. Restorations. Virginia (Richmond). 16c-17c. 1926. *1328*

Aged. *See also* Pensions; Public Welfare.

—. Folklore. Poor. West Virginia. Witchcraft. Women. 1975. *1583*

*Agee* (film). Agee, James. Authors. Documentaries. 1910-55. *952*

Agee, James. *Agee* (film). Authors. Documentaries. 1910-55. *952*

—. Alabama. Depressions. Evans, Walker. McCloud, Emma Gudger. Sharecroppers. Whites. 1934. *786*

—. Bourke-White, Margaret. Evans, Walker. Photography. Poverty. ca 1930-39. *3365*

—. Friendship. McDowell, David. 1936-55. *985*

—. Journalism. Literature. Steinbeck, John. 1935-39. *1001*

—. Literature. Neighborhoods. Social Change. Tennessee (Knoxville). 1915-82. *788*

Agee, James *(Let Us Now Praise Famous Men)*. Language. Literary criticism. Richards, Ivor Armstrong. 1930-40. *915*

Aging. Appalachia. Attitudes. Leisure. Physical fitness. Poverty. Working conditions. 1950's-70. *3367*

Agrarianism. Authors. Government. Science and Society. 1930-80. *2768*

—. Bibliographies. Jones, Madison. Novels. 1952-82. *888*

—. Biography. Jackson, Thomas J. (Stonewall). Tate, Allen. 1927-28. *304*

—. Davidson, Donald. Literature. Mims, Edwin. 1923-58. *777*

—. Debates. Ransom, John Crowe. 1930-31. *2875*

—. Intellectuals. 1920-40. *2760*

—. Killebrew, Joseph Buckner. ca 1870-1910. *2741*

Agrarians. Counter culture. 1865-1973. *444*

—. Alabama. Haralson, J. Reconstruction. Republican Party. Suffrage. 1867-82. *3771*

—. Alabama. Industrial Arts Education. Tuskegee Institute. Washington, Booker T. 1870's-90's. *2023*

—. Alabama. Lutheran Church. Missions and Missionaries. 1916-78. *2398*

—. Alabama (Birmingham). Communist Party. Hudson, Hosea. 1920's-70's. *3733*

—. Alabama (Mobile). Bromberg, Frederick G. Political conditions. 1836-1908. *3781*

—. Alabama Sharecropper's Union. Communist Party. Personal Narratives. Racism. Rosengarten, Theodore (review article). Shaw, Nate. 1890-1945. *3422*

—. Alabama State College. Education. Paterson, William Burns. 1878-1915. *2069*

—. Alice Freeman Palmer Memorial Institute. Brown, Charlotte Hawkins. Education. North Carolina (Sedalia). 1902-71. *2016*

—. Alienation. Arkansas. Colleges and Universities. Political participation. Tennessee. 1968-69. *2019*

—. Allen, Macon B. Lawyers. 1844-94. *544*

—. Alleys. District of Columbia. Housing. Photographs. 1935-41. *2548*

—. Alleys. District of Columbia. Housing. Whites. 1850's-1970. *2547*

—. Alston, Mary Niven. Cooper, Anna Haywood. Episcopal Church, Protestant. Higher education. Robertson, Isabella Gibson. Women. 1875-1981. *1803*

—. Aluminum Company of America. Labor. Tennessee (Alcoa). 1919-39. *3074*

—. American Baptist Home Mission Society. Baptists. Colleges and Universities. 1865-1920. *2037*

—. American Missionary Association. Civil War. Education. Missouri. 1862-65. *2428*

—. American Missionary Association. Congregationalism. 1846-80. *2429*

—. Anderson, Donald. National Association for the Southern Poor. Poor. Virginia Community Development Organization. 1968-78. *3361*

—. Appalachia. Banjos. Minstrelsy. Music. 19c. *1697*

—. Appalachia. English Americans. Social Reform. Stereotypes. Whites. 1880-1915. *451*

—. Appalachia. Japanese Americans. Migration, Internal. 1860-1973. *403*

—. Apportionment. Discrimination. Whites. 1965-83. *3776*

—. Apportionment. Louisiana (New Orleans). Mississippi. New York City (Manhattan). 1962-76. *3732*

—. Archival Catalogs and Inventories. Baptists. Southwestern Baptist Theological Seminary (Fleming Library). Texas. 1875-1941. *2432*

—. Archival catalogs and inventories. Hampton Institute Archives. Indians. 1967-82. *384*

—. Arkansas. Bates, Lucious Christopher. Desegregation. Editors and Editing. 1941-59. *3785*

—. Arkansas. Constitutional conventions (state). Delegates. Politics. Reconstruction. 1868. *3762*

—. Arkansas. Race Relations. Republican Party. 1867-1928. *3546*

—. Arkansas (Helena). Colleges and Universities. Friends, Society of. Southland College. 1866-1925. *2024*

—. Arkansas (Independence County; Batesville, Ruddell Hill). Ozark Mountains. 1800-1973. *1755*

—. Arkansas (Jefferson County). Havis, Ferdinand. Political Leadership. Republican Party. 1846-1918. *3677*

—. Arkansas (Little Rock). Attitudes. Eckford, Elizabeth. Personal Narratives. Public schools. School Integration. 1957-79. *2100*

—. Arkansas (Little Rock). Desegregation. Trinidad and Tobago. 1955-59. *1973*

—. Arkansas (Little Rock). Gibbs, Mifflin W. Politics. Republican Party. 1878-1915. *3547*

—. Arkansas, University of. Colleges and Universities. Fisher, Isaac. 1902-11. *2092*

—. Armies. Freedmen's Bureau. Mississippi (Natchez district). Sharecropping. 1860's. *2704*

—. Arp, Bill (pseud. for Charles Henry Smith). Atlanta *Constitution*. Attitudes. Georgia. Newspapers. 1878-1903. *1609*

—. Art and Society. Faulkner, William. School integration. 1950's-60's. *996*

—. Artists. 1951-79. *1763*

—. Arts and crafts. Musical instruments. 1619-1938. *1760*

—. Attitudes. Authors. Faulkner, William. Race Relations. 1930's-79. *1116*

—. Attitudes. Birth control. Clergy. Population. Tennessee (Nashville). 20c. *2262*

—. Attitudes. Breckenridge family. Elites. Kentucky. Race. 1760-1935. *601*

—. Attitudes. Higher education. Segregation. Virginia. 1980. *2066*

—. Attitudes. Immigrants. Labor. 1865-1910. *3404*

—. Attitudes. Jazz. Musicians. Whites. 1920's-70's. *1740*

—. Attitudes. Political change. Social Change. Whites. 1964-76. *700*

—. Authors. 18c-20c. *1750*

—. Authors. Hurston, Zora Neale. Migration, Internal. Toomer, Jean. 1860-1960. *374*

—. Authors. Walker, Alice. Women. 1960's-83. *1728*

—. Badger, Robert. Badger, Roderick. Dentistry. Georgia. 1829-1958. *2165*

—. Baltimore Almshouse. Immigrants. Maryland. Medicine (practice of). Poor. 1828-50. *2133*

—. Baltimore Normal School for the Education of Colored Teachers. Bowie State College. Education. Maryland. Wells, Nelson. 1843-72. *1931*

—. Baltimore Normal School for the Education of Colored Teachers. Industrial Arts Education. Maryland Normal and Industrial School. Public Schools. 1908-14. *1933*

—. Bands. Colleges and Universities. Jazz. Morris, Kelso B. Music. Personal narratives. Texas (Marshall). Wiley College. 1925-35. *1756*

—. Banjos. Blues. Music. North Carolina (Alamance County). Roberts, James Phillips "Dink" (interview). 1974. *837*

—. Baptists. Education. Missions and Missionaries. 1862-81. *2427*

—. Baptists. Georgia. 1750's-1830's. *2458*

—. Baptists. Georgia (Richmond County). Kiokee Church. Marshall, Daniel. Settlement. 1784-1819. *2304*

—. Baptists. Jasper, John. Sermons. Virginia (Richmond). 1812-1901. *2213*

—. Baptists (Southern). 1845-1980. *2519*

—. Baptists (Southern). 1951-81. *2211*

—. Baptists, Southern. Education. Paternalism. 1880's-90's. *2473*

—. Baptists (Southern). Emancipation. Race Relations. 1863-67. *2385*

—. Baptists (Southern). Home Mission Board. Race Relations. 1845-1981. *2370*

—. Baptists, Southern. Metropolitan Areas. Models. 1951-81. *2459*

—. Bartley, Buddy. Bolden, Buddy. Historiography. Jazz. Louisiana (New Orleans). Musicians. ca 1895. *1041*

—. Bennett College. Georgia (Atlanta). Higher education. North Carolina (Greensboro). Spelman College. Women. 1970's. *2005*

—. Berea College. Day, Carl. Discrimination, Educational. Kentucky. Lincoln Institute. 1904-12. *2097*

—. Berea College. Higher Education. Integration. Kentucky. 1858-1908. *2045*

—. Bethune, Mary McLeod. Bethune-Cookman College. Florida (Daytona Beach). 1875-1955. *2029*

—. Bibliographies. 1970-72. *365*

—. Bibliographies. Folk Art. 1842-1976. *1747*

—. Bibliographies. Folklore. Tennessee. 19c-20c. 1940's-70's. *393*

—. Bibliographies. Oklahoma. 1880-1980. *392*

—. Black magic. Jazz. Louisiana (New Orleans). Voodoo. Women. ca 19c. *1719*

—. Bluefield State College. Colleges and Universities. West Virginia State College. 1890-1965. *2018*

—. Blues. Daily Life. Music. 1924-82. *1759*

—. Blues. Folk Songs. Methodology. Music. 1960's-70's. *1732*

—. Boll weevils. Cotton. 1929-77. *2728*

—. Boll weevils. Cotton. Employment. Migration, Internal. 1910-30. *2736*

—. Boritt, Gabor S. Economic conditions. Economic conditions (review article). James, John A. Mandle, Jay R. Oubre, Claude F. Social Change. 1860-1900. *2597*

—. Bossism. City Politics. Clergy. Crump, Edward Hull. Tennessee (Memphis). 1927-48. *3807*

—. Boutelle, Frazier A. Military. 1861-95. *3856*

—. Bowie State College. Education, Finance. Maryland (Baltimore). Teacher training. 1866-1908. *1932*

—. Brown, Ed. Georgia. Sharecroppers. ca 1920-40. *2771*

—. *Brown v. Board of Education* (US, 1954). Discrimination, Educational. NAACP. Public schools. South Carolina (Clarendon County). Supreme Court. 1948-54. *2026*

—. Bruce, Blanche Kelso. Mississippi. Reconstruction. Senate. 1875-81. *3688*

—. Bureaucracies. Education. Employment. 1970's. *2072*

—. Business. Cuban Americans. Economic structure. Florida (Miami). 1920's-80. *2653*

—. Business. Entertainment. Tennessee (Memphis; Beale Street). 1930's-78. *3168*

—. Business. Tennessee (Memphis; Beale Street). Urban Renewal. 1963-70's. *1164*

—. Cajuns. Louisiana (Houma). Population. Texans. 1945-73. *1683*

—. Cakewalks. Dance. Race Relations. Satire. 1860-1910. *1714*

—. Caldwell County Tri-Cultural Oral History Project. Mexican Americans. Oral History. Texas. Whites. 1976-79. *271*

—. Capital. Land Tenure. 1861-1980. *361*

—. Capital. Poverty. 1968-80. *2621*

—. Careers. Stereotypes. Women. 1966-80. *2074*

—. Carnegie, Mary Elizabeth Lancaster. Colleges and Universities. Miller, Rita E. Nurses and Nursing. Women. 1942-51. *2009*

—. Carpentry. Texas. Textiles. 1830-70. *1778*

—. Carpetbaggers. Governors. Louisiana. Pinchback, Pinckney B. S. 1862-90. *3811*

—. Carter, Fannie Cobb. Education. West Virginia. Youth. 1891-1977. *1995*

—. Carver, George Washington. Scientists. 1900-75. *2769*

—. Catholic Church. Education. Georgia (Savannah). Louisiana (New Orleans). Maryland (Baltimore). Religious Orders. Women. 1829-1982. *2058*

—. Catholic University of America. Colleges and Universities. Discrimination. District of Columbia. Wesley, Charles H. 1914-48. *1988*

—. Chautauqua Society. Louisiana (Grambling, Ruston). Teacher Training. 1890-1906. *1942*

—. Cheshire, Joseph Blount, Jr. Episcopal Church, Protestant. North Carolina. Paternalism. Race Relations. 1870-1932. *2275*

—. Chesnutt, Charles W. Fiction. Literary Criticism. North Carolina. 1887-1900. *1709*

—. Cheyenne Indians. Hampton Institute. Indians. Kiowa Indians. Pratt, Richard Henry. Virginia. 1878-93. *3918*

—. Children. Folklore. Louisiana (Bienville Parish). 20c. *1766*

—. Children. Geophagy. Mississippi (Holmes County). Poverty. Women. 1975. *2174*

—. Christian, Marcus B. Dillard University. Federal Writers' Project. Historiography. Work Progress Administration. 1930's-79. *380*

—. Church, Robert Reed, Sr. Tennessee (Memphis). Wealth. Wills. 1912. *630*

—. Church Schools. Colleges and universities. Tennessee. 1865-1920. *1994*

—. Cities. City councils. Representation. 1970's. *3721*

—. Cities. Culture. Harlem Renaissance. Texas. 1930-54. *1768*

—. Cities. Florida (Jacksonville). Political Participation. 1887-1907. *3466*

—. Cities. Housing. Settlement. 1850-1930. *3253*

—. Cities. Income. Migration, Internal. 1965-70. *3055*

—. Cities. Lemon, Lester. Tennessee. 1900-30. 1978. *402*

—. Cities. Voting and Voting Behavior. 1960-77. *3723*

—. Citizenship Education Program. Georgia (McIntosh). Southern Christian Leadership Conference. 1960-80. *1978*

—. City Government. Maryland (Baltimore). Political protest. Public schools. 1865-1900. *2084*

—. City Government. Maryland (Baltimore). Republican Party. 1890-1931. *3604*

—. City planning. Political Change. Virginia (Richmond). 1945-75. *3118*

—. Civics. Curricula. Political participation. 1970's. *2060*

—. Civil Rights. Clark, Septima. NAACP. South Carolina. Southern Christian Leadership Conference. Suffrage. Teaching. 1916-79. *2012*

—. Civil rights. Hancock, George B. Jackson, Luther P. Virginia. Young, Plummer B. 1930-45. *373*

—. Civil rights. Henry, Aaron. Mississippi. Personal Narratives. 1922-63. *378*

—. Civil Rights. Labor Unions and Organizations. Textile Industry. 1950's-70's. *3406*

—. Civil rights. Lincoln, Abraham. 1854-65. *358*

—. Civil Rights. Sociology. Work, Monroe Nathan. 1900-45. *387*

—. Civil rights. Voting Rights Act (US, 1965). 1865-1975. *3760*

—. Civil Rights. Women. 19c-20c. *385*

—. Civil rights movement. Suffrage. Voting Rights Act (US, 1965). 1965-75. *3658*

—. Folk Medicine. Rural Settlements. 1970-73. *2136*

—. Folk Songs. Ledbetter, Huddie "Leadbelly". Louisiana. Love, Blanche. 1880's-1949. 1976. *1129*

—. Folk Songs. Political Protest. Shack bully (character). 1920's. *1724*

—. Folklore. Laundry. Women. 17c-20c. *1716*

—. Folklore. Mississippi (Homochitto River Valley). Social customs. 1973. *1708*

—. Folklore. Research. Sea Islands. 1975. *1776*

—. Food. Social Customs. Tennessee (Memphis). Whites. 20c. *1575*

—. Football. High Schools. Race Relations. 1972-76. *2042*

—. Fort Bliss. Military History. Texas (El Paso). 1865-1907. *3847*

—. Free Southern Theatre. Louisiana (New Orleans). Theater. 1963-77. *1734*

—. *Free Speech.* Lynching. Newspapers. Tennessee (Memphis). Wells, Ida B. 1892. *1711*

—. Gaines, Ernest *(Autobiography of Miss Jane Pittman)*. Haley, Alex *(Roots)*. Novels. Walker, Margaret *(Jubilee)*. 18c-1979. *1761*

—. Genealogy. Howard University (Moorland-Spingarn Research Center). 1867-1981. *368*

—. Genocide. Georgia (Atlanta). Racism. 20c. *3691*

—. Geographic Mobility. Occupations. Texas (Dallas). 1880-1910. *3215*

—. George Washington Carver Comprehensive High School. Georgia (Atlanta). High Schools. 1970's. *2032*

—. Georgia. Populism. Reform. Suffrage. Watson, Thomas E. 1880-1922. *3566*

—. Georgia. Sea Islands. Social Change. South Carolina. ca 1930-80. *474*

—. Georgia (Atlanta). Haven, Gilbert. Protestant Churches. Segregation. 1865-1906. *2397*

—. Georgia (Atlanta). Jackson, Maynard. Politics. 1940's-74. *3694*

—. Georgia (Atlanta). Migration, Internal. Urban renewal. 1960's. *597*

—. Georgia (Atlanta). Residential patterns. Transportation. Women. 1910-40. *3157*

—. Georgia (Augusta, The Terri). 1865-1973. *583*

—. Georgia (Cuthbert). Henderson, Fletcher. Howard Normal School. 1857-1943. *1986*

—. Ghettos. Tennessee (Nashville; Black Bottom). 1850-1980. *3134*

—. *Gone with the Wind* (film). NAACP. Slaves. Stereotypes. 1939-40. *479*

—. Gullah (dialect). Research. Sea Islands. 16c-1974. *379*

—. Haley, Alex *(Roots)*. History Teaching. *Roots* (program). 1977. *391*

—. Harlem Renaissance. Howard University. Literature. Locke, Alain. Philosophy. 1920's-30's. *1738*

—. Harper, Frances W. (Aunt Chloe poems). Poetry. Women. 19c. *1742*

—. Harris, Cicero. Harris, Robert. Harris, William. Reconstruction. Teaching. 1864-70. *2091*

—. Harris, Julian. Journalism. Liberalism. 1900-60. *3698*

—. High Schools. Occupations. Whites. 1970's. *3429*

—. Higher education. Mississippi. 1865-1920. *2020*

—. Historiography. Louisiana (New Orleans). Political Leadership. Reconstruction. ca 1800-75. *3746*

—. Historiography. Quarles, Benjamin. 18c-19c. 1948-79. *388*

—. Holloway, Lou. Mississippi. Music. Personal narratives. Piney Woods School. Rays of Rhythm. 1940-49. *911*

—. House of Representatives. Langston, John Mercer. State Politics. Virginia. 1849-97. *3505*

—. House of Representatives. Lynch, John Roy. Mississippi. 1847-1939. *3689*

—. House of Representatives. Lynch, John Roy. Mississippi. Reconstruction. 1869-1939. *3488*

—. Houses, strip. Poor. Tennessee. 1900-30. *1217*

—. Howard, Perry W. Mississippi. Politics. Republican Party. 1924-60. *3705*

—. Hurston, Zora Neale. Literature. Wright, Richard. 1921-70's. *1746*

—. Immigrants. Italians. Louisiana. Race Relations. Sugarcane. 1880-1910. *2828*

—. Immigration. Latin Americans. Louisiana. Race Relations. Sugarcane. 1880-1910. *2829*

—. Indian Wars. Llano Estacado. Red River War. Schafter, William R. 1875. *3937*

—. Indians. Land. Scouts and guides. Seminole-Negro Indian Scout Detachment. Texas. 1866-1922. *4011*

—. Industrial Relations. Lumber and Lumbering. Migration, Internal. Pine trees. ca 1912-26. *3392*

—. Industry. Labor. 1940-70. *3439*

—. Jazz. Louisiana (New Orleans). Music. Personal Narratives. Robinson, Nathan (Jim). Trombones. Turner, Frederick. 1892-1972. *1099*

—. Jazz. Lyrics. Music. Race. 20c. *1720*

—. Jazz. Music. 17c-1920's. *1751*

—. Jazz. Music. 1920's-70's. *1712*

—. Jazz. Musicians. Perryman, Gus (interview). Riverboats. 1910's-30's. *1723*

—. Johnson, Charles S. Public schools. School Integration. Southern Educational Reporting Service. Whites. 1954-60's. *2002*

—. Kentucky. Lincoln Institute. Tydings, J. Mansir. Young, Whitney M. 1935-37. *2096*

—. Kentucky. Oral history. 1972-79. *407*

—. Kentucky (Gallatin County). Marriage. Public Records. 1866-1913. *508*

—. Kentucky (Louisville). School Integration. 1954-77. *1967*

—. Kentucky (Stoney Point). Land Tenure. Social Conditions. 1848-1969. *2695*

—. Key, V. O., Jr. Suffrage. Suffrage. Tennessee. 19c. *3664*

—. Knight, Etheridge. Poetry. 1968-80. *1741*

—. Knights of Labor. Labor Unions and Organizations. 1880-87. *3409*

—. Kousser, J. Morgan (review article). Political systems. Suffrage. 1880-1910. 1974. *3473*

—. Labor. 1700-1800. *3421*

—. Labor. 1940-70. *3455*

—. Labor. Prisons. Tennessee. 1830-1915. *3775*

—. Labor. Textile Industry. 1941-81. *3396*

—. Labor Unions and Organizations. Maryland. NAACP. Teachers. 1930's. *2089*

—. Lafon, Thomy. Louisiana (New Orleans). Philanthropy. ca 1830-93. *408*

—. Land tenure. Migration, Internal. 1910-74. *2787*

—. Lee, Molly Huston. Librarians. North Carolina (Raleigh). Richard B. Harrison Library. 1930-75. *228*

—. Lee, Molly Huston. Libraries. North Carolina (Raleigh). Richard B. Harrison Library. 1935-68. *229*

—. Letters. Lynch, James. Methodist Episcopal Church. Mississippi. Reconstruction. 1868-69. *2291*

—. Lilly, Octave, Jr. (obituary). Poetry. 1930-60. *1730*

—. Literary Criticism. Wright, Richard (*Uncle Tom's Children*). 1938-73. *1735*

—. Literature. Miscegenation. 1855-1974. *831*

—. Literature. Oral history. Women. 1976. *962*

—. Louisiana. Ray, John. Republican Party. Scalawags. ca 1836-88. *3818*

—. Louisiana (New Orleans). Provost, Tessie. Public schools. School Integration. 1960-79. *2101*

—. Louisiana, northern. Politics. Religion. 1865-77. *2284*

—. Lynching. Population. 1889-1931. *366*

—. Maryland (Baltimore). Private Schools. 1794-1860. *1997*

—. McCabe, Edward Preston. Migration, Internal. Newspapers. Oklahoma (Langston). 1850-1920. *3307*

—. McCabe, Edward Preston. Migration, Internal. Oklahoma (Langston). 1863-1960. *377*

—. Medical education. Meharry Medical College. Tennessee (Nashville). 1860's-1970's. *2126*

—. Men. Migration, Internal. Occupations. 1967. *2619*

—. Methodist Church. 1769-1968. *2253*

—. Migration, Internal. Population. Rural areas. South Carolina (Fort Motte). Unemployment. 1960-70. *3254*

—. Migration, Internal. Rural-Urban Studies. 1889-1974. *364*

—. Minorities. Politics. Voting Rights Act, 1965. 1965-75. *3517*

—. Minstrelsy. Racism. Social Status. 1854-75. *1640*

—. Mississippi. Public Opinion. Revels, Hiram. Senate. 1870. *3680*

—. Mississippi (Jackson). Tougaloo College. 1869-1975. *1929*

—. Mississippi (Jasper County). Population. Whites. 1833-1970. *3257*

—. Moore, Aaron McDuffie. North Carolina (Durham). Philanthropy. Social reform. 1863-1923. *633*

—. Mortality. 1850-1910. *628*

—. Moving Star Hall. Sects, Religious. South Carolina (Johns Island). 18c-1970. *2226*

—. Musicians. Plantations. Social status. 1820's-50's. *1721*

—. North Carolina. Poets. Women. 1975-80. *1122*

—. North Carolina. School Integration. 1967-73. *1979*

—. Oral history. Public history. Texas (Caldwell County). 1976-78. *397*

—. Page, Thomas Nelson (*In Ole Virginia*). Plantations. 1829-60. *2767*

—. Physicians. Racism. Social Reform. 1900-40. *2109*

—. Political change. 1945-75. *3627*

—. Political Parties. Sectionalism. 1830-1976. *3484*

—. Political Protest (review article). 1877-1978. *3690*

—. Population. Poverty. 1970. *3364*

—. Public schools. School Integration. Virginia (Prince Edward County). 1954-64. *2102*

—. Racism (review article). 1780-1914. *576*

—. Reconstruction. Republican Party. Southern States Convention. 1864-72. *3661*

—. Religion. Spiritualism. 1918-81. *2188*

—. Self-image. 17c-1970's. *399*

—. Slave Revolts. Styron, William. Turner, Nat. 19c. 1960's-70's. *1121*

—. Slavery. 1865-1940. *540*

—. Slavery. Social Customs. 1800-1900. *401*

—. Speech. Whites. 1970-79. *763*

—. Suffrage. 1890-20c. *3640*

—. Texas (Lubbock). 1910-70's. *566*

Blacks, free. Civil Rights. Civil War. Louisiana. Military Service. Reconstruction. 1850-90. *3857*

—. Louisiana (New Orleans). Poetry. 1845. *1737*

Blacksmiths. Simmons, Philip. South Carolina (Charleston). 1855-1979. *683*

Blackwood, James. Cash, Johnny. Lewis, Jerry Lee. Music. Pentecostals. Wynette, Tammy. 1950's-70's. *1672*

Blaettermann, George W. College teachers. Language. Virginia, University of. 1782-1850. *1820*

Blair, James. Church of England. Church of Scotland. Virginia. William and Mary, College of. 1679-1720. *2448*

—. Church of England. Clergy. Vestries. Virginia. 1700-75. *2296*

Blalock, Alice Grundy. College teachers. Grambling State University. Louisiana. ca 1920-70. *1976*

Blance, Joseph G. Georgia (Rockmart). Parker, Charles Taylor. Slate. 1832-1978. *3276*

Bleser, Carol. Hammond family (review article). Letters. Social change. South Carolina. 19c-1950's. *693*

Blockade running trade. Civil War. Importing and Exporting Company of South Carolina. South Carolina. 1862-76. *2637*

Blood transfusions. France. Louisiana (New Orleans). Medicine. 1853-58. *2153*

Blotner, Joseph (review article). Biography. Faulkner, William. 1924-62. *1097*

—. Biography. Faulkner, William. Novels. 1920's-74. *973*

Blue Eagle, Acee. Art. Bacone College (Art Department). Indians. Oklahoma. 1935-80. *4174*

Blue Ridge Mountains. Appalachia. Folk culture. 1730-1800. *1690*

—. Appalachia. North Carolina. Quilts. Virginia. 1982. *1543*

—. Artisans. Dulcimers. North Carolina, western. 1960's-70's. *1551*

—. Coffey, Ann. Folklore. Frank C. Brown Collection of North Carolina Folklore. North Carolina, western. Sutton, Maude Minish. 1920's-30's. *1611*

—. Settlement. Virginia. 1740's-1970's. *1691*

Blue Ridge Parkway Folklife Project. Daily Life. Library of Congress (American Folklife Center). National Parks and Reserves. North Carolina. Photographs. Virginia. 1978. *1488*

Bluefield State College. Blacks. Colleges and Universities. West Virginia State College. 1890-1965. *2018*

Bluegrass. Clay, Henry. Kentucky. Letters. 1838. *1482*

—. Concert halls. Lucy Opry. Music. Tennessee (Memphis). 1966-82. *1515*

—. Folklore. Music. Religion. 1770-1970. *1570*

—. Lucy Opry. Music. Tennessee (Memphis). 1966-83. *1514*

Blues. Armstrong, Louis. Jazz. Music. 1925-29. *1718*

—. Autobiography. Lipscomb, Mance. Migration, Internal. Music. Texas (Houston). 1956. *943*

—. Banjos. Blacks. Music. North Carolina (Alamance County). Roberts, James Phillips "Dink" (interview). 1974. *837*

—. Bibliographies. Music. 19c-1970's. *1771*

—. Blacks. Daily Life. Music. 1924-82. *1759*

—. Blacks. Folk Songs. Methodology. Music. 1960's-70's. *1732*

—. Davis, Gary. Fuller, Blind Boy (pseud. of Fulton Allen). Music. North Carolina (Durham). Piedmont Plateau. 1930's-70's. *997*

—. Music. 16c-1976. *1753*

Broaddus, Andrew, I. Kentucky. Travel accounts. 1817. *2203*

Brobson, William P. Delaware. Diaries. 1825-28. *764*

Bromberg, Frederick G. Alabama (Mobile). Blacks. Political conditions. 1836-1908. *3781*

Brooke, Francis Key. Carden, Joseph. Clergy. Episcopal Church, Protestant. Oklahoma (Ardmore; St. Philip's Church). 1893-1927. *2293*

Brooks, Cleanth. Literary Criticism. Percy, Walker. ca 1940-79. *1136*

—. Literature. Louisiana State University. Periodicals. *Southern Review.* Warren, Robert Penn. 1925-42. *1090*

Brooks, Ebenezer. Kentucky. Statehood. 1775-1800. *3610*

Brophy, Lawrence William. Arkansas. Missouri. Movie theaters. Oklahoma. 1907-26. *1500*

Brotherhood of Timber Workers. Emerson, Arthur L. Industrial Workers of the World. Labor Disputes. Louisiana, western. Lumber and Lumbering. Texas, east. 1900-16. *3393*

—. Industrial Workers of the World. Louisiana. Lumber and Lumbering. Race Relations. Texas. 1910-13. *3401*

—. Louisiana, western. Lumber and Lumbering. Race Relations. Southern Lumber Operators' Association. Texas, east. 1911-13. *3402*

Brough, Charles Hillman. Arkansas. Democratic Party. State Politics. Wilson, Woodrow. 1903-35. *3814*

—. Arkansas. Historians. 1890-1915. *198*

—. Arkansas. Public Relations. 1920's-35. *3533*

Brown, Alexander. Banking. Business History. Maryland (Baltimore). Social change. Trade. ca 1800-34. *2553*

Brown and Root, Inc. Construction. Corporations. Housing. Rural areas. ca 1977-79. *2661*

Brown, Bubberson. Daily life. Gadsden, Sam. Personal narratives. Sea Islands. South Carolina (Edisto Island). 1893-1917. *569*

Brown, Charlotte Hawkins. Alice Freeman Palmer Memorial Institute. Blacks. Education. North Carolina (Sedalia). 1902-71. *2016*

Brown, Ed. Blacks. Georgia. Sharecroppers. ca 1920-40. *2771*

Brown, J. Newton. Baptists, Southern. New Hampshire Covenant. 1833-1972. *2255*

Brown, James B. BancoKentucky Company. Banking. Kentucky (Louisville). National Bank of Kentucky. 1925-30. *2967*

Brown, John (1867-1927). Catawba Indians. Folklore. Harris, Mary "Dovie". Methodology. South Carolina. 1885-1962. *3880*

Brown Lung Association. Class consciousness. Industrial safety. Textile Industry. 1970-80. *3408*

Brown lung disease. Burlington Industries, Inc. Carolina Brown Lung Association. Cotton. Liberty Mutual Insurance. 1970's. *3382*

—. Carolina Brown Lung Association. Textile industry. Workers' Compensation. 1970's. *2795*

*Brown v. Board of Education* (US, 1954). Blacks. Discrimination, Educational. NAACP. Public schools. South Carolina (Clarendon County). Supreme Court. 1948-54. *2026*

Browne, Gary Lawson. Brownell, Blaine A. Cities (review article). Goldfield, David R. Ridgeway, Whitman H. 1789-1861. *193*

Brownell, Blaine A. Browne, Gary Lawson. Cities (review article). Goldfield, David R. Ridgeway, Whitman H. 1789-1861. *193*

—. Goldfield, David R. Goldin, Claudia Dale. Harris, Carl V. Rabinowitz, Howard N. Urbanization (review article). Watts, Eugene J. 1820-1980. *2950*

Brownell, Blaine A. (review article). Cities. Social Conditions. 1920-30. 1970's. *3054*

Brownlow, William G. "Parson". Johnson, Andrew. Nelson, Thomas A. R. State Politics. Tennessee. 1840-77. *3468*

Bruce, Blanche Kelso. Blacks. Mississippi. Reconstruction. Senate. 1875-81. *3688*

Bruce, Edward Caledon. Artists. Reporters and Reporting. Virginia. 1847-1901. *1060*

Bruce, Philip Alexander. Literary criticism. Newspapers. Richmond *Times.* 1889. *1065*

Bryan, William Jennings. Americans. Foreign Policy. Political Campaigns (presidential). Stevenson, Adlai E. (1835-1914). 1900. *3768*

Bryson, Henry. Diaries. Evangelism. Presbyterian Church, Associate Reformed. 1826-27. *2523*

Buckner, Lewis S. Carpentry. Tennessee (Sevierville). ca 1856-1924. *1762*

Buckner, Simon Bolivar. Business. Confederate Army. Kentucky. State Government. 1823-1914. *3731*

Buffalo. Game preserves. Oklahoma (Wichita Mountains). Rush, Franklin S. Wichita National Game Preserve. 18c-1923. *3232*

Buffalo Bill. *See* Cody, William F. (Buffalo Bill).

Buffalo Bill's Wild West. Cody, William F. (Buffalo Bill). Drama company. Louisiana (New Orleans). 1884-85. *1473*

Building permits. Archives, National. District of Columbia. 1877-1949. *1209*

Buildings. *See also* Architecture.

—. Alabama, University of (Tuscaloosa). 1831-65. *1869*

—. Allendale Plantation. Dairying. Louisiana (De Soto Parish). 1850's-1930. *2933*

—. Architects. Long, Robert Cary, Sr. Maryland (Baltimore). Rogers, Nicholas. 1774-1822. *1151*

—. Archives. Drawings. Louisiana (New Orleans). Watercolors. 1802-1918. *1181*

—. Archives. Public Records Office. Virginia (Williamsburg). 1747. *201*

—. Armory, 104th Medical Regiment. Maryland (Baltimore). National Guard. 1858-1962. *1350*

—. Art Deco. Florida (Miami Beach). Miami Design Preservation League. Preservation. 1920-35. 1978. *1186*

—. Art Deco. Florida (Miami Beach). Preservation. 1930's. *1252*

—. Colleges and universities. Texas. 1830's-1930's. *1338*

—. Courthouses. Virginia (Rockingham County, Harrisonburg). 1777-1897. *1367*

—. Courthouses. Virginia (Russell County). 1787-1874. *1233*

—. Elks Lodge. Louisiana Purchase Exposition (St. Louis, 1904). Missouri. Oklahoma (El Reno). Preservation. 1904-79. *1395*

—. Environment. Quilts. 1839-1970's. *1523*

—. Florida (Manatee Village). Heritage of Manatee's Environment. Preservation. 1859-89. 1974-76. *1283*

—. Florida (New Smyrna). Pellicer, Francisco. Peso de Burgo, José "Pepino". 1780-1831. *1226*

—. Georgia. Historic Columbus Foundation. Restorations. 1966-78. *1270*

—. Georgia (Columbus). Preservation. Springer Opera House. 1820-1980. *1356*

—. Georgia (Columbus). Restorations. 1970's. *1271*

—. Georgia (Savannah). Preservation. 1961-77. *1218*

—. Historical Sites and Parks. Log construction. Tennessee (Bledsoe's Lick, Castalian Springs). Wynnewood (estate). 1828-1973. *1216*

—. Jones, Jesse Holman. Rice Hotel. Texas (Houston). 1837-1974. *1354*

—. Kentucky (Head of Hollybush). Oral history. 1880's-1960. *1278*

—. Oklahoma Historical Society. Oklahoma (Kingfisher, Norman, Oklahoma City). 1893-1930. *177*

—. Preservation. Virginia (Waterford). 1733-1983. *1224*

Bulger, Peggy A. Folk Art. Personal narratives. 1976-79. *1446*

Bungalows. Architecture. Florida (Tampa Bay). 1840's-1930. *1334*

Bureaucracies. Blacks. Education. Employment. 1970's. *2072*

—. City Government. Libraries. Parks. Social Classes. Texas (Houston). 1970's. *3057*

Burials. Indians. Pee Dee Indians. South Carolina (Marlboro County). ca 1716. *4003*

Burlington Industries, Inc. Brown lung disease. Carolina Brown Lung Association. Cotton. Liberty Mutual Insurance. 1970's. *3382*

Burnett, John G. Cherokee Indians. Indian-White Relations. Personal narratives. Removals, forced. 1838-39. *3932*

Burns, Bertha Porter. Baptists. Burns, Marion Van. Clergy. Louisiana (Shiloh). Teachers. 1884-1975. *616*

Burns, Marion Van. Baptists. Burns, Bertha Porter. Clergy. Louisiana (Shiloh). Teachers. 1884-1975. *616*

Burton, Robert Wilton. Alabama. Authors. Hooper, George W. Towles, Catharine. ca 1850-1900. *908*

Burton, William L. Cypress. Florida. Louisiana. Lumber and Lumbering. Philanthropy. 1870-1927. *2986*

Bush Hill Cemetery. Epitaphs. South Carolina (Williston). 1835-1905. *1486*

Bush River Quaker Meeting. Friends, Society of. Maryland. 1706-1826. *2478*

Bushyhead, Dennis. Cherokee Indians. Corporations. Indian-White Relations. Political Leadership. 1879-98. *4054*

Bushyhead, Jesse. Baptists. Cherokee Indians. Indians. Schisms. Slavery. 1830-45. *2375*

Business. *See also* Advertising; Banking; Competition; Consumers; Corporations; Management; Manufactures; Marketing; Real Estate Business.

—. Alabama. Civil War. Elites. Plantations. Social mobility. 1850-70. *2865*

—. Alabama. Leadership. 1800-1977. *2609*

—. Bass, Henry B. Historians. Oklahoma (Enid). Public services. 20c. *668*

—. Blacks. Cuban Americans. Economic structure. Florida (Miami). 1920's-80. *2653*

—. Blacks. Entertainment. Tennessee (Memphis; Beale Street). 1930's-78. *3168*

—. Blacks. Tennessee (Memphis; Beale Street). Urban Renewal. 1963-70's. *1164*

—. Buckner, Simon Bolivar. Confederate Army. Kentucky. State Government. 1823-1914. *3731*

—. Chambers of Commerce. Nonunionization. South Carolina (Greenville). 1970's. *3441*

—. Child Care. Kinder-Care Learning Centers. Mendel, Perry. 1969-80. *3172*

—. Chinese Americans. Immigration. Texas. 1870-1970. *657*

—. City Government. Georgia (Atlanta). Public Schools. Sutton, Willis. 1921-43. *1854*

—. City Planning. Development. Indiana (Kingsport). North. Towns. 1880-1950. *1156*

—. City Planning. Public lands. Tennessee (Memphis). 1971-76. *1165*

—. Downtown areas. Economic Conditions. Maryland (Baltimore). Neighborhoods. Social Conditions. 1800-1980. *3174*

—. Economic Conditions. Epidemics. Lasker, Morris. Letters. Personal narratives. Texas (Milliken). 1860-66. *608*

—. Economic Conditions. Farms, small. 1970's. *2675*

—. Florida (Jacksonville). Railroads. 1865-1930. *2949*

—. Godchaux, Leon. Louisiana (New Orleans). 19c. *3147*

—. Housing. Labor. Mechanization. Mobile homes. Taylor Homes. 1972-79. *3181*

—. Jews. Retail Trade. 1790-1960. *2649*

—. Labor. Ownership. 1979-82. *3381*

—. Local Government. Virginia (Richmond). Wynne, Thomas Hicks. 1840's-75. *562*

—. Management. Plantations. Profit. ca 1830-60. *2794*

—. Moravians. North Carolina (Salem). Schober, Gottlieb. 1769-1830. *3135*

—. Physicians. Radford, John Blair. Virginia. 1823-72. *2171*

—. Tennessee (Jackson). 1865-1950. *2613*

Business history. Alabama. 1920-73. *210*

—. Archives. West Virginia University (West Virginia Collection). 1760-1972. *320*

—. Banking. Brown, Alexander. Maryland (Baltimore). Social change. Trade. ca 1800-34. *2553*

—. Rutherfoord, Thomas. Virginia (Richmond). 1784-1852. *2638*

Busing. Integration. Mass Media. Tennessee (Nashville). 1970-73. *2081*

Butchart, Ronald E. Freedmen. Jones, Jacqueline. Reconstruction. Teachers (review article). 1862-75. 1980. *2071*

Butler, Pierce M. Cherokee Indians. Foreman, James. Indian Territory. Murder. Political factions. Watie, Stand. 1830-42. *4140*

Butler, Thomas. Courts Martial and Courts of Inquiry. Haircuts. Military discipline. Tennessee. 1801. *3855*

Butler, Thomas (family). Documents. Landscaping. Louisiana State University, Department of Archives. Plantations. 1768-1900. *1375*

Butterfield Overland Trail. Indian Territory. 1858-61. *3294*

Buttermaking. Churns. Cottage industries. Dairying. Delaware. Pennsylvania. Women. 1750-1850. *2744*

Byington, Cyrus. Choctaw Indians. Indians. Missions and Missionaries. Mississippi. Protestantism. 1820-68. *4115*

Byrd, Charles Willing. Converts. Shakers. 1770-1828. *2469*

Byrd, Harry F., Sr. Democratic Party. Reed, William Thomas. State Politics. Virginia. 1925-35. *3574*

Byrd, William. Diaries. 1709-41. *780*

Byrd, William, III. Bibliographies. Libraries. Virginia. 1778-1803. 1978. *311*

# C

—. Business. Public lands. Tennessee (Memphis). 1971-76. *1165*
—. Construction. Texas (Houston area). 1975-82. *1163*
—. District of Columbia. Ellicott, Andrew. France (Paris). L'Enfant, Pierre Charles. 1754-1825. *1251*
—. District of Columbia. L'Enfant, Pierre Charles. 1796-1825. *1344*
—. District of Columbia. L'Enfant, Pierre Charles. Washington, George. 1789-91. *1361*
—. Economic conditions. Texas (Houston). Zoning. 1962-77. *2910*
—. Elites. Georgia (Atlanta). Louisiana (New Orleans). Tennessee (Memphis). 1907-30. *2923*
—. Kessler, George E. Texas (Dallas). 1908-33. *3163*
—. Land use. Texas (Houston). 1940-82. *1241*
City Politics. *See also* City Government.
—. Alabama (Birmingham). Anti-Catholicism. Anti-Semitism. Reform. Social Gospel. 1900-30. *3570*
—. Automobile Industry and Trade. Davis, Elmer Ellsworth. Stables. Texas (Denison). 1894-1939. *604*
—. Baseball teams. Ownership. Progressive era. ca 1877-1916. *1630*
—. Blacks. Bossism. Clergy. Crump, Edward Hull. Tennessee (Memphis). 1927-48. *3807*
—. Bossism. Democratic Party. Maryland (Baltimore). 1919-47. *3474*
—. Cuba. Florida (Jacksonville). Huah, José Alejandro. Independence Movements. Martí, José. 1836-1905. *3591*
—. Elections. Georgia (Atlanta). Political candidates. Property. 1865-1903. *3810*
—. Lipscomb, Martin Meredith. Virginia (Richmond). 1853-57. *3730*
—. Maryland (Baltimore). Progressivism. 1895-1911. *3539*
Civic pride. Architecture. Economic Conditions. Railroad stations. Urbanization. 1890-1920. *1172*
Civic responsibility. Cumming, Henry Harford. Georgia (Augusta). 1812-66. *3827*
Civics. Blacks. Curricula. Political participation. 1970's. *2060*
Civil disobedience. Cherokee Indians. Evangelism. Missions and Missionaries. 1829-39. *4045*
Civil law. Common law. Courts. Louisiana. 19c-20c. *3480*
Civil religion. Christianity. Political Speeches. 1960's-70's. *3813*
—. Culture. Lost Cause (theme). 1865-1920. *2525*
Civil Rights. *See also* Academic Freedom; Equal Rights Amendment; Freedom of the Press; Human Rights; Religious Liberty.
—. Academic freedom. Educational Reform. Southern Political Science Association. 1928-79. *144*
—. Allin, John M. Clergy. Episcopal Church, Protestant. Mississippi. Political Attitudes. 1964-73. *2183*
—. American Missionary Association. Education. Florida. Freedmen. 1864-74. *2430*
—. Antiwar Sentiment. Labor. Page, Myra. 1920's-82. *3573*
—. Arkansas. Cherokee Indians. Indians. Land. Lovely, William. 1816-28. *3919*
—. Austin *American-Statesman*. Cartoons and Caricatures. Newspapers. Political Commentary. Sargent, Ben. Texas. 1977-78. *3833*
—. Blacks. Clark, Septima. NAACP. South Carolina. Southern Christian Leadership Conference. Suffrage. Teaching. 1916-79. *2012*
—. Blacks. Hancock, George B. Jackson, Luther P. Virginia. Young, Plummer B. 1930-45. *373*
—. Blacks. Henry, Aaron. Mississippi. Personal Narratives. 1922-63. *378*
—. Blacks. Labor Unions and Organizations. Textile Industry. 1950's-70's. *3406*
—. Blacks. Lincoln, Abraham. 1854-65. *358*
—. Blacks. Sociology. Work, Monroe Nathan. 1900-45. *387*
—. Blacks. Voting Rights Act (US, 1965). 1865-1975. *3760*
—. Blacks. Women. 19c-20c. *385*
—. Blacks, free. Civil War. Louisiana. Military Service. Reconstruction. 1850-90. *3857*
—. Cable, George Washington. Essays. Novels. ca 1875-1925. *1018*
—. Constitutional Amendments (14th). *Gitlow v. New York* (US, 1925). Sanford, Edward Terry. Supreme Court. ca 1890-1930. *3668*
—. Duke University Medical Center. Harvey, Oliver. Labor Unions and Organizations. North Carolina (Durham). 1930's-70's. *3417*
—. Five Civilized Tribes. Indian-White Relations. 18c-20c. *3888*

—. Georgia. Methodist Church. Tilly, Dorothy. 1900's-70. *3772*
—. Highlander Research and Education Center. Labor Reform. Schools. Tennessee. 1932-82. *1952*
—. Jackson, Lillie M. Maryland (Baltimore). NAACP. 1935-75. *3834*
—. Jews. Social Organizations. 1776-1982. *2443*
Civil rights movement. Alabama (Tuscaloosa). Clergy. Integration. Whites. 1976-77. *2184*
—. Blacks. Suffrage. Voting Rights Act (US, 1965). 1965-75. *3658*
—. Creek Indians. Florida, western. 1830-1970. *3953*
—. Jews. 1954-70. *1987*
—. Johnson, Lyndon B. Long, Huey P. Radicals and Radicalism. 1920-70. *3821*
Civil Rights Movement (review article). Blacks. McAdam, Doug. 1930-70. *3793*
Civil Rights (review article). Randolph, A. Philip. 1910-70. *3583*
Civil War. *See also* battles and campaigns by name; Reconstruction; Secession; Slavery.
—. Acculturation. Creek Indians. Indian-White Relations. 1830's-61. *3951*
—. Agricultural production. Emancipation. 1865-80. *2817*
—. Alabama. Business. Elites. Plantations. Social mobility. 1850-70. *2865*
—. Alabama. Family. Slavery. Social Change. Whites. 1850-70. *504*
—. Alabama. Gunpowder. Industry. Saltpeter. 1812-76. *3114*
—. Alabama. Livestock. Reconstruction. 1850-1900. *2789*
—. Alabama. Plantations. Reconstruction. Women. 1850-70. *2864*
—. American Missionary Association. Blacks. Education. Missouri. 1862-65. *2428*
—. Appalachia. Highway Engineering. West Virginia. Weston and Gauley Bridge Turnpike. 1811-1922. *3018*
—. Appalachia. Mountaineers. Politics. Regionalism. 1860-99. *715*
—. Armies. Banks, Nathaniel Prentiss. Education. Louisiana. 1863-65. *2040*
—. Armies. Carter, Samuel Powatan. Military General Staff. Navies. *Seminole* (vessel). 1819-91. *3845*
—. Baptists. Louisiana. Mount Lebanon University. 1835-90's. *1806*
—. Baptists, Southern (Foreign Mission Board). Missions and Missionaries. 1861-66. *2272*
—. Bibliographies. Reconstruction. Slavery. 1830-80. 1974. *196*
—. *Birth of a Nation* (film). Films. Griffith, D. W. 1915. *413*
—. Blacks. Reconstruction. Slavery. Women. 19c. *3568*
—. Blacks, free. Civil Rights. Louisiana. Military Service. Reconstruction. 1850-90. *3857*
—. Blockade running trade. Importing and Exporting Company of South Carolina. South Carolina. 1862-76. *2637*
—. Catton, Bruce. Editors and Editing. Historiography. 1954-78. *163*
—. Cherokee Indians. Confederate States of America. Georgia. Indians. Removals, forced. 1830-70. *4110*
—. Cherokee Indians. Drew, John Thompson. Indian Territory. Indians. Law. Leadership. 1850-65. *4038*
—. Coffin, William G. Federal Government. Indian Territory. Indians. 1861-65. *4006*
—. Confederate Army. Five Civilized Tribes. Indians. 1860-65. *3982*
—. Confederate States of America. Indian Territory. Surrender. Watie, Stand. 1865. *3927*
—. Cook, Robert C. Mississippi (Columbus; Magowah Place). Personal Narratives. Veterans. 1861-65. 1915-29. *428*
—. Cooke, Alistair. Historiography. Northerners. Reconstruction. 1860-76. 20c. *275*
—. Corona Female College. Gaston, L. B. Gaston, Susan P. Hospitals. Mississippi (Corinth). 1857-64. *1907*
—. Coups d'Etat. Ellet, Charles. Letters. Methodology. Military Organization. Primary sources. 1863. 1979. *221*
—. Courts. Reconstruction. ca 1861-69. *3612*
—. Daily Life. Economic Conditions. Social Conditions. Virginia (Appomattox Courthouse). 1845-65. *3058*
—. District of Columbia. Navies. Remey, "Molly" Mason. Women. 1845-1938. *694*
—. Episcopal Church, Protestant. Kentucky (Bowling Green). Ringgold, Samuel. Tennessee (Knoxville). 1860-1911. *2187*

—. Faulkner, William. Literature. Mississippi (Lafayette County, Oxford). 1860-65. 1925-62. *987*
—. Federal government. Five Civilized Tribes. Indian Territory. 1861-66. *3931*
—. Five Civilized Tribes. Indian Territory. Lincoln, Abraham. Ross, John. 1860's. *3930*
—. Foote, Shelby. Novels. 1861-65. 20c. *308*
—. Governors. Military General Staff. Reconstruction. Smith, William "Extra Billy". Virginia Infantry, 49th. 1797-1887. *3506*
—. Harrison, Constance Cary. Novels. Plantations. 1863-1911. *1045*
—. Historians. Mississippi, University of. Wiley, Bell Irvin (obituary). ca 1926-80. *274*
—. Historians. Wiley, Bell Irvin (obituary). ca 1930-80. *111*
—. Indian Territory. Indians. 1860-65. *3976*
—. Kentucky. Shakers. 1861-65. *2408*
—. Kentucky (South Union, Logan County). Post offices. Shakers. 1800-1971. *2648*
—. Literary Criticism. Mitchell, Margaret (*Gone with the Wind*). Social Conditions. Tolstoy, Leo (*War and Peace*). 1863-1936. *2447*
—. Louisiana (New Orleans). Nationalism. Palmer, Benjamin Morgan. Racism. Secession. 1860-1902. *2419*
—. Medicine (practice of). 1861-65. *2159*
—. Protestantism. 1861-65. *2249*
—. Region. Slavery. World view. 1850's-70's. *707*
Civilian Conservation Corps. Land Tenure. Texas (Palo Duro Canyon State Park). Tourism. 1906-66. *3293*
Claiborne, William Charles Cole. Bosque y Fanqui, Cayetana Susana. Grymes, John R. Louisiana. 1790-1890. *551*
Clapp, Theodore. Louisiana (New Orleans). Slavery. Theology. Unitarianism. 1822-56. *2421*
Clark, George Rogers. Clay, Henry. Kentucky. Shelby, Isaac. Taylor, Zachary. 1775-1850. *3614*
Clark, John H. Boundaries. Maps. Surveying. Texas (northwestern). 1858-62. *3324*
Clark, Septima. Blacks. Civil Rights. NAACP. South Carolina. Southern Christian Leadership Conference. Suffrage. Teaching. 1916-79. *2012*
Clarke, Asia Booth. Booth, Rosalie. 1823-89. *584*
Class consciousness. Brown Lung Association. Industrial safety. Textile Industry. 1970-80. *3408*
Class struggle. Georgia. Hahn, Steven. Populism. Social Change (review article). 1850-90. *3638*
—. Historiography. Louisiana. Shugg, Roger (review article). 1800-60. 1939-76. *296*
—. Labor unions and organizations. 1810-1975. *3410*
Classes. *See* Social Classes.
Classical Music. Jazz. Music. 1897-1970's. *1717*
Classical Revival. Cities. Jefferson, Thomas. Rural areas. ca 1800-40. *3143*
Classical Studies. Cumberland College. Educators. Priestley, James. Scholarship. 1774-1821. *290*
—. Fay, Edwin Whitfield. Scholars. Texas, University of (Austin). 1890-1920. *1923*
Classical traditions. 19c-20c. *1126*
—. Architecture. Aristocracy. Greek Revival Style. 1820's-50's. *1225*
—. Humphreys, Milton W. 1860-1919. *14*
—. Literature. Regions. Rome. 19c-20c. *812*
Classics. Agriculture. Educational Policy. Temple, Oliver Perry. Tennessee, University of. 1869-1900. *1885*
—. Congregationalism. House, J. T. Kingfisher College. Oklahoma. 1890-1922. *1893*
—. Elites. Europe. Plantations. Virginia. 19c. *765*
—. Higher education. Students. 1693-1924. *1790*
Clay, Henry. Bluegrass. Kentucky. Letters. 1838. *1482*
—. Clark, George Rogers. Kentucky. Shelby, Isaac. Taylor, Zachary. 1775-1850. *3614*
—. Kentucky. Political Factions. State Politics. 1820-44. *3696*
Clay, Margaret Muse. Baptists. Crawford Manuscript. Folk Medicine. Lea, Maggie Tate. Mississippi (Amite County). Virginia (Chesterfield). ca 1773. ca 1890. *1083*
Clayton, Henry D. Alabama. Democratic Party. House of Representatives. 1897-1914. *3753*
Clemens, Samuel Langhorne. *See* Twain, Mark.
Clergy. *See also* specific denominations by name.
—. Alabama (Tuscaloosa). Civil rights movement. Integration. Whites. 1976-77. *2184*
—. Allen, Carey H. Kentucky. Presbyterian Church. Virginia. 1767-95. *2248*
—. Allin, John M. Civil rights. Episcopal Church, Protestant. Mississippi. Political Attitudes. 1964-73. *2183*
—. American Revolution. Baptists. Georgia. Marshall, Daniel. 1747-1823. *2303*

—. Attitudes. Birth control. Blacks. Population. Tennessee (Nashville). 20c. *2262*

—. Autobiography. Daily Life. Delaware (Sussex County). Methodist Protestant Church. Morgan, William. 1780-1857. *2301*

—. Bacon, Thomas. Church of England. Maryland. ca 1745-68. *2252*

—. Baptists. Burns, Bertha Porter. Burns, Marion Van. Louisiana (Shiloh). Teachers. 1884-1975. *616*

—. Baptists. Cartledge, Samuel. Georgia. South Carolina. 1790-1843. *2230*

—. Baptists. Georgia. Historians. King, Spencer B., Jr. King, Spencer B., Sr. Mercer University. 1880-1973. *2341*

—. Baptists. Hartsfield, Green W. Louisiana (northern). Social Conditions. 1860-96. *645*

—. Baptists. Professionalization. Theology. Virginia. 1760-90. *2423*

—. Baptists, Southern. Campbell, Will. Garner, Thad. Personal Narratives. 20c. *2223*

—. Baptists (Southern). Loveland, Anne C. (review article). Methodist Church. Presbyterian Church. Slavery. 1800-60. *2246*

—. Bayless, John Clark. Kentucky. Presbyterian Church. 1841-75. *2329*

—. Blacks. Bossism. City Politics. Crump, Edward Hull. Tennessee (Memphis). 1927-48. *3807*

—. Blacks. Colleges and Universities. Phillips, Daniel W. Race Relations. Roger Williams University. Tennessee (Nashville). 1867-1910. *1948*

—. Blacks. Lutheran Church (North Carolina Synod). 1865-89. *2399*

—. Blacks. Methodist Episcopal Church. 1784-1864. *2310*

—. Blacks. Protestant churches. ca 1800-65. *2190*

—. Blair, James. Church of England. Vestries. Virginia. 1700-75. *2296*

—. Brooke, Francis Key. Carden, Joseph. Episcopal Church, Protestant. Oklahoma (Ardmore; St. Philip's Church). 1893-1927. *2293*

—. Church of England. Georgia. Herbert, Henry. 1732-33. *2359*

—. Church of England. Gordon, John. Maryland (Talbot County). St. Michael's Parish. 1749-90. *2466*

—. Church of England. Tobacco. Virginia. Wages. 1750-70. *2311*

—. Church of England. Virginia. 1726-76. *2295*

—. Denominationalism. Southern Baptist Theological Seminary. Theology. 18c-1980. *2454*

—. Drummond, Miriam F. Foster, Corneilius Emmett. Louisiana. Personal Narratives. 19c. *555*

—. Episcopal Church, Protestant. Jarratt, Devereux. Letters. Virginia. 1770-1800. *2316*

—. Episcopal Church, Protestant. Kentucky (Versailles). St. John's Church. 1829-1976. *2426*

—. Folklore. Georgia, west-central. Humor. 19c-20c. *1463*

—. Georgia. Methodist Episcopal Church, South. Pierce, George Foster. Pierce, Lovick. 1785-1884. *2225*

—. Kentucky. Presbyterian Church. Templin, Terah. 1780-1818. *2515*

Cleveland, Grover. Cherokee Indians. Discrimination. Freedmen. Indians. Treaties. 1866-88. *3986*

Climate. *See also* Weather.

—. Agricultural Production. Land. Louisiana. Sugarcane. 19c. *2738*

Clinch Valley College. Appalachian studies. Industrial technology. 1960's-81. *197*

Clinchfield Railroad. Locomotives. Photographs. Railroads. Steam power. 1887-1954. *2956*

—. Railroads. 1886-1924. *2954*

Clinton Foundation. Georgia. Old Clinton Historical Society. Preservation. 1973-79. *38*

Clothing. *See also* Costume.

—. Florida. Indians. Patchwork. Seminole Indians. 18c-1979. *3884*

Cluskey, Charles B. Architecture. Georgia (Augusta). Governor's Mansion. Greek Revival Style. Medical College of Georgia. 1820's-30's. *1201*

Coal. Alabama. Kilby, Thomas E. Strikes. United Mine Workers of America. 1890-1929. *3451*

—. Economic Conditions. Models. West Virginia. 1880-1930. *3122*

Coal Mines and Mining. Appalachia. Daily Life. Novels. Settle, Mary Lee. 1649-1980. *1040*

—. Appalachia. *Gateway Coal Company* v. *United Mine Workers of America* (US, 1974). Health. Labor Law. Safety. 1935-74. *3395*

—. Appalachia. Labor. 1880-1930. *2960*

—. Appalachia. Poverty. 1890-1972. *2582*

—. Baldwin-Felts Detectives. Law Enforcement. West Virginia (southern). 1890's-1935. *2980*

—. Blacks. Immigrants. West Virginia. 1880-1917. *2894*

—. Boggs, Dock. Folk music. Musicians. Virginia (West Norton). 1920's-60's. *1599*

—. Brickmaking. Capitalism. Economic Development. Industrial Relations. Kentucky, eastern. Social Change. 1870-1930. *3373*

—. Carter, George Lafayette. Iron Industry. Railroads. 1877-1936. *3064*

—. Choctaw Indians. Indians. Italian Americans. Oklahoma (Krebs). Sierra Leone. 1875-1907. *3039*

—. Convict labor. State Government. Strikes. Tennessee. 1891-93. *2887*

—. Conway, Mimi. Hevener, John W. Labor (review article). Textile Industry. 1931-79. *3454*

—. Davidson-Wilder (firm). Folk songs. Lowry, Tom (interview). Strikes. Tennessee. 1932. *1419*

—. Davidson-Wilder Strike of 1932. Graham, Barney. Strikes. Tennessee, east. United Mine Workers of America. 1932-33. *2886*

—. Editors and Editing. Evans, Herndon J. Kentucky (Harlan County). Pineville *Sun*. Strikes. 1929-32. *3452*

—. Entrepreneurs. West Virginia. 1870-1941. *3133*

—. *Harlan County, U.S.A.* (film). Kentucky. Kopple, Barbara (interview). Strikes. United Mine Workers of America. 1973-76. *3431*

—. Harper, Larry. Labor Unions and Organizations. Suicide. West Virginia (Stony Creek). 1940's-54. *3413*

—. Hotchkiss, Jedediah. Industrialization. Virginia, southwestern. West Virginia, southern. 1828-99. *3138*

—. Keeney, Frank. United Mine Workers of America. West Virginia. 1916-31. *3386*

—. Kentucky. Labor Disputes. Mediation. Virginia. 1980. *3398*

—. Kentucky. Mayo, John Caldwell Calhoun. 1864-1914. *2929*

—. Kentucky (Harlan, Bell counties). Labor Disputes. Political Corruption. 1920-39. *3379*

—. Kentucky (Harlan County; Evarts). Strikes. United Mine Workers of America. 1931. *3376*

—. Labor Unions and Organizations. Racism. Strikes. United Mine Workers of America. 1894-1920. *3450*

—. Labor Unions and Organizations. Texas (Thurber). 1880's-1920's. *3038*

Coal Mines and Mining (review article). Corbin, David Alan (*Life, Work and Rebellion in the Coal Fields*). West Virginia (southern). 1880-1922. *3120*

Coast Guard. Maryland. Seaplanes. World War II. 1929-69. *3867*

Coasts. Appalachia, southern. Dialects. Georgia. Kurath, Hans. South Carolina, 1977. *779*

—. Cajuns. Creoles. Louisiana. 1765-1982. *673*

—. Development. 1776-1982. *3099*

Coats of arms. Seals, official. Virginia. William and Mary, College of. 1690-1930. *1945*

Cobb, Thomas R. R. Georgia. Law. 1847-62. *3699*

Cobb-Hill Street Community Association. Georgia (Athens). Historic Cobbham Foundation. Neighborhoods. Preservation. 1834-19. *1358*

Coca-Cola Company. Advertising. 1886-1967. *2541*

—. Advertising. Candler, Asa Griggs. 1880's-1970's. *2983*

—. Courts. Federal Regulation. Food and Drug Administration. Georgia. Massengill, S. E. Company. Sullivan, Jordan James. Tennessee. 1906-40. *3830*

—. Methodist Church. Religious education. 1840's-1970's. *2299*

Cocaine. Drug abuse. Opium. 1860-1920. *2118*

Cockfighting. Gambling. 1979. *1527*

—. Louisiana. Social Customs. Sports. 20c. *1475*

Cocking, Walter D. Blacks. Georgia. Higher education. Talmadge, Eugene. 1937-43. *1981*

—. Georgia, University of. Holley, Joseph Winthrop. Racism. Talmadge, Eugene. 1941. *2057*

Cockrell, Sarah Horton. Frontier and Pioneer Life. Texas (Dallas). 1819-92. *561*

Cody, William F. (Buffalo Bill). Buffalo Bill's Wild West. Drama company. Louisiana (New Orleans). 1884-85. *1473*

Coffey, Ann. Blue Ridge Mountains. Folklore. Frank C. Brown Collection of North Carolina Folklore. North Carolina, western. Sutton, Maude Minish. 1920's-30's. *1611*

Coffin, Tom. Construction. Georgia (Atlanta). International Union of Operating Engineers, Local 926. Labor Unions and Organizations. Law Engineering Testing Company. National Labor Relations Board. Personal Narratives. 1973-78. *2937*

Coffin, William G. Civil War. Federal Government. Indian Territory. Indians. 1861-65. *4006*

Cohen, Mendes. Engineering. Maryland (Baltimore). Railroads. 1847-1915. *2973*

Cohen, Octavus Roy. Alabama (Birmingham). Fiction. Journalism. Loafers (literary group). 1920's. *803*

Coin Collecting. *See* Numismatics.

Coincoin. Blacks. Family. Louisiana (Metoyer). Slavery. 1742-1850. *631*

—. Creoles. Family. Louisiana (Cane River, Natchitoches). Race relations. Social status. 1767-20c. *632*

Colbert, Benjamin Franklin. Ferries. Red River. Texas. 1840-1915. *3286*

Colbert, William Williams. Louisiana (Bienville Parish). Plantations. 1849-90. *2692*

Cole family. North Carolina. Pottery. 1700's-1977. *1423*

Coleman, Kenneth. Bibliographies. Georgia, University of. Historians. 1941-76. *207*

Coleraine, Treaty of. Creek Indians. Federal Policy. Georgia. Indian-White Relations. 1796. *3971*

Coliseum Square Association. Louisiana. New Orleans Historic District Landmarks Committee. Preservation. 1807-1978. *1403*

Collages. Art. Bearden, Romare. 1920-81. *1749*

Collections. Cook, Morris. Dobie, J. Frank. Texas, University of (San Antonio). 1933-74. *352*

—. Delaware. Economic History. Historical Society of Pennsylvania. 1727-1897. 1974. *2642*

—. Documents. Indian studies. Shleppey, John W. Tulsa, University of (McFarlin Library). Worcester, Samuel Austin. 1820-1900. 1975-77. *4030*

—. Folklore. Western Kentucky University (Allan M. Trout Collection). 1969. *1596*

—. Gimbel, Richard. Poe, Edgar Allan. Raven (manuscript). 1959-73. *905*

College Building. Architecture. Heiman, Adolphus. Tennessee (Nashville). 1836-1974. *1299*

College teachers. Blaettermann, George W. Language. Virginia, University of. 1782-1850. *1820*

—. Blalock, Alice Grundy. Grambling State University. Louisiana. ca 1920-70. *1976*

—. Dismissals. Oklahoma, University of. Parrington, Vernon L. 1897-1908. *1911*

Colleges and Universities. *See also* names of individual institutions; Dissertations; Graduate Schools; Higher Education; Students.

—. Abel, John Jacob. Johns Hopkins University Medical School. Maryland (Baltimore). Pharmacy. 1880-1933. *2156*

—. Adams, Charles P. Blacks. Grambling State University. Louisiana. 1896-1928. *1977*

—. Agricultural experiment stations. Federal Government. 1877-1940. *2816*

—. Agriculture. Blacks. 1977-79. *2766*

—. Agriculture. Blacks. Whites. 1862-1977. *2043*

—. Alabama. Blacks. Ethnicity. Talladega College. 1875-1980. *1972*

—. Alabama. Blacks. Tuskegee Institute. 1875-1981. *2008*

—. Alabama (Birmingham, Mobile). Competition. Medical education. 1912-20. *1784*

—. Alabama (Florence). Florence University for Women. Women. 1890-1911. *1827*

—. Alienation. Arkansas. Blacks. Political participation. Tennessee. 1968-69. *2019*

—. American Baptist Home Mission Society. Baptists. Blacks. 1865-1920. *2037*

—. Anecdotes. Mississippi. Students. ca 1950's-70's. *1439*

—. Appalachian studies. Interest Groups. Politics. 1978. *119*

—. Architecture. Episcopal Church, Protestant. South, University of the. Tennessee (Sewanee). 1857-1979. *1892*

—. Architecture. Tennessee, University of (Knoxville). 1794-1980. *1925*

—. Archival Catalogs and Inventories. Marshall University (James E. Morrow Library; Special Collections Department). West Virginia. 1804-1982. *289*

—. Arkansas. Commonwealth College. Education, Experimental Methods. Labor. Radicals and Radicalism. Student activism. 1925-35. *1805*

—. Arkansas (Helena). Blacks. Friends, Society of. Southland College. 1866-1925. *2024*

—. Arkansas, University of. Blacks. Fisher, Isaac. 1902-11. *2092*

—. Bands. Blacks. Jazz. Morris, Kelso B. Music. Personal narratives. Texas (Marshall). Wiley College. 1925-35. *1756*

—. Baptists. Dodd College. Louisiana (Shreveport). 1937. *1960*

—. Baptists. Dodd College. Louisiana (Shreveport). Women. 1927-42. *1959*

—. Baptists. Education. Everett Institute. Louisiana (Spearsville). 1893-1908. *1796*

—. Berea College. Egalitarianism. Kentucky. 20c. *1823*

—. Bible, Dana X. Football. Sports. Texas, University of. 1937-46. *1927*

—. Black Mountain College. Duberman, Martin. North Carolina. 1933-57. *1919*

—. Black Nationalism. Student activism. 1890-1972. *2061*

—. Blacks. Bluefield State College. West Virginia State College. 1890-1965. *2018*

—. Blacks. Carnegie, Mary Elizabeth Lancaster. Miller, Rita E. Nurses and Nursing. Women. 1942-51. *2009*

—. Blacks. Catholic University of America. Discrimination. District of Columbia. Wesley, Charles H. 1914-48. *1988*

—. Blacks. Church Schools. Tennessee. 1865-1920. *1994*

—. Blacks. Clergy. Phillips, Daniel W. Race Relations. Roger Williams University. Tennessee (Nashville). 1867-1910. *1948*

—. Blacks. Courts. North Carolina, University of. School Integration. 1981-82. *1971*

—. Blacks. Desegregation. Oklahoma, University of. 1946-50. *2015*

—. Blacks. Economic conditions. Langston University. McCabe, Edward Preston. Oklahoma. Social Change. 1896-1982. *2079*

—. Blacks. Equal opportunity. Maryland. 1908-75. *2055*

—. Blacks. Florida. 1852-1971. *2053*

—. Blacks. Fort Valley State College. Georgia (Peach County). *Hunnicutt et al. v. Burge et al.* (Georgia, 1972). Racism. School Integration. 1972-78. *1970*

—. Blacks. Gaines, Wesley John. Georgia (Atlanta). Morris Brown College. 1881-1932. *2068*

—. Blacks. Johnson, Charles S. 1928-56. *2052*

—. Blacks. Louisiana (New Orleans). Southern University. 1879-87. *1955*

—. Blacks. Maryland (Somerset). Princess Anne Academy. 1890-1930. *2090*

—. Blacks. Politics. Segregation. Tennessee State University. Tennessee, University of. Whites. 1869-1977. *1862*

—. Buildings. Texas. 1830's-1930's. *1338*

—. Castañeda, Carlos Eduardo. Librarians. Texas, University of, Austin (Benson Latin American Collection). 1920-27. *5*

—. Chicago, University of (School of Library Science). Librarians. North Carolina, University of, Chapel Hill. Wilson, Louis Round. 1901-76. *267*

—. Church of England. King's College. Maryland (Chestertown). Scotland (Aberdeen). Washington College. 1743-82. *1846*

—. Coulter, Ellis Merton (obituary). Georgia, University of. Historians. ca 1930's-81. *262*

—. Courts. Hocutt, Thomas R. McCoy, Cecil A. North Carolina, University of (School of Pharmacy). Pearson, Conrad O. School Integration. 1933. *2088*

—. Dance. Folk arts. Methodology. Social Customs. 1980. *263*

—. Dawson, William. Leadership. William and Mary, College of. 1725-52. *1913*

—. Desegregation. Education, Finance. Lawsuits. Tennessee. 1968-81. *2017*

—. Desegregation. Texas, University of. 1938-60. *2001*

—. Development. Texas, University of, Austin. 1923-83. *1957*

—. Dickey, Dallas C. Rhetoric. 1938-57. *20*

—. Dugger, Ronnie (review article). Educational Administration. Texas, University of. 1974. *1909*

—. Duke University. North Carolina (Durham). Sanford, Terry. 1973-74. *1900*

—. Education, Experimental Methods. Florida (Sarasota). New College. State Aid to Education. 1950's-75. *1855*

—. Educational Administration. Personal Narratives. Spurr, Stephen H. Texas, University of. 1971-74. *1943*

—. Educational Policy. Texas, University of. 1883-1970. *1897*

—. Educational Reform. Industrialization. North Carolina, University of. Social Change. 1850-75. *1890*

—. Endowments. Oil and Petroleum Products. Public lands. Texas A. & M. University. Texas, University of. 1923-40. *3084*

—. Freeman, Ellis. Kentucky. Louisville, University of (Psychology Department). Psychology. 1907-53. *1792*

—. French studies. Maison Française. Spurlin, Paul Merrill. 1936-80. *1868*

—. Geography. 1940's-50's. *249*

—. Georgia Institute of Technology. Technical Education. 1880-1910. *1795*

—. Gilman, Daniel Coit. Johns Hopkins University. Letters. Maryland (Baltimore). Sylvester, James Joseph. Teaching. 1825-84. *1841*

—. Historiography. Oklahoma State University (History Department). 1894-1983. *1904*

—. Jefferson College. Mississippi (Natchez). 1802-1975. *1940*

—. Jefferson, Thomas. Virginia, University of. 1779-1826. *1887*

—. Kentucky. Louisville, University of. 1798-1982. *1809*

—. Kentucky (Lexington). Science. Transylvania University. 1799-1857. *1804*

—. Legislation. Runnels, Hardin R. Texas, University of. 1853-83. *1908*

—. Libraries. Manuscripts. Mississippi. 1976. *71*

—. Libraries. Manuscripts. Mississippi. 1978-79. *81*

—. Libraries. Manuscripts. Mississippi. 1979-80. *80*

—. Libraries. South Carolina College Library. 1802-1900. *1902*

—. Library Science. North Carolina, University of (Chapel Hill). 1929-81. *1919*

—. Louisiana (Mansfield). Mansfield Female College. Reunions. Women. 1844-1930. 1974. *1920*

—. Maryland (Annapolis). St. John's College. 1929-74. *1962*

—. Mississippi (Rodney). Oakland College. Presbyterian Church. 1830-71. *1936*

—. Publishers and Publishing. 1970's-82. *97*

—. Richmond College. Virginia (Richmond). 1843-60. *1895*

—. Segregation. State Government. Texas. 1876-1947. *2013*

—. Southwestern at Memphis College. Tennessee (Memphis). 1848-1981. *1937*

—. Tennessee (Jackson). Union University. 1825-1975. *1886*

—. Tennessee (Jackson). Union University. 1825-1975. *1956*

—. Texas, University of. 1880-1982. *1901*

Collier, John. Acculturation. Florida. Indians. North Carolina. Schools. Seminole Indians. 1927-54. *4167*

Collier, Ruby Eddins. Folklore. Personal Narratives. Texas (Monterey). ca 1850's. 1971. *1604*

Collins, Curley. Country music. Forman, Tex. Georgia (Atlanta). Musicians. Personal narratives. Pop Eckler and His Young'uns. Radio. 1936-42. *1470*

Collins, Jimmy *(Test Pilot)*. Faulkner, William. Literary Criticism. 1935. *863*

Collins, Richard H. Caudill, Harry M. Historiography. Kentucky (review article). 19c-20c. *141*

Colonel Effingham (fictional character). Bossism. Crackers (faction). Democratic Party. Fleming, Berry *(Colonel Effingham's Raid)*. Georgia (Augusta). Political reform. 1943-50. *3528*

Colonial Government. *See also* Imperialism.

—. Cherokee Indians. Georgia. Lumber and Lumbering. Priber, Christian Gottlieb. Utopians. 1730's-ca 1744. *4049*

Colonial Society of French Emigrants. Alabama (Demopolis). French Americans. Immigration. Lee, William. Pennsylvania (Philadelphia). 1816-17. *2718*

Colonization. *See also* Settlement.

—. Archaeology. Georgia (Sapelo Island). 1733-1974. *3285*

—. Georgia. Liberia. Tubman, Emily. 1818-85. *1725*

Colorado Opera House. Frenkel Opera House. Texas (Colorado City). Theater. 1884-1971. *1081*

Colored Farmers' Alliance. Blacks. Humphrey, R. M. Labor Unions and Organizations. Strikes. 1876-91. *2703*

Colored Methodist Episcopal Church. Freedmen. Methodist Episcopal Church, South. Religious liberty. Segregation. 1865-70. *2292*

Columbia Records Company. Deal family. Gospel music. Music. North Carolina. 1927-29. *885*

Columbia Restaurant. Louisiana (Shreveport). ca 1900-69. *1208*

Comanche Indians. Gentilz, Theodore. Mexican Americans. Painting. Social Customs. Texas (San Antonio). 1843-79. *1148*

—. Green corn dance. Hoebel, E. Adamson. Indians. Methodology. Rites and Ceremonies. Texas. Wallace, Ernest. 1830-95. 1952-81. *4107*

Comedy. Cerou, Pierre *(Amant auteur et valet)*. Louisiana (New Orleans). Theater. 1764. *895*

Commerce. *See also* Banking; Business; Chambers of Commerce; International Trade; Monopolies; Prices; Retail Trade; Statistics; Tariff; Trade; Transportation.

—. Agricultural Labor. Landlords and Tenants. Law. Social organization. 1865-1900's. *2870*

—. American Revolution. Georgia (Savannah). Jews. Memoirs. Sheftall, Levi. 1739-1809. *2470*

—. Brazil (Rio de Janeiro). Ports. South Carolina (Charleston). 18c. *3024*

—. Galt, James. Galt, William, Jr. Plantations. Slavery. Virginia. 1800-76. *2734*

Committee on Baptist History. Baptists. Georgia. 1948-78. *2501*

Common law. Civil law. Courts. Louisiana. 19c-20c. *3480*

Commonwealth College. Arkansas. Colleges and Universities. Education, Experimental Methods. Labor. Radicals and Radicalism. Student activism. 1925-35. *1805*

Communes. *See also* names of individual communes; Counter Culture; Utopias.

—. Christianity. Georgia. Jordan, Clarence. Koinonia Farm. 1942-60's. *2288*

—. Llano del Rio Cooperative Colony. Louisiana (Vernon Parish). Socialism. 1917-38. *638*

Communications. *See also* Language; Mass Media; Newspapers; Postal Service; Telecommunication.

—. Bibliographies. 19c-20c. *293*

—. Newspapers. North Carolina. Public Opinion. Raleigh *Star*. 1810. *1442*

Communications Technology. Louisiana (New Orleans). Radio. Television. WWL (station). 1940-50. *1623*

Communist Party. Alabama (Birmingham). Blacks. Hudson, Hosea. 1920's-70's. *3733*

—. Alabama Sharecropper's Union. Blacks. Personal Narratives. Racism. Rosengarten, Theodore (review article). Shaw, Nate. 1890-1945. *3422*

Community colleges. Louisiana (Caddo Parish). 1930's. *1958*

Community (concept). Kentucky, south-central. Social Organizations. Square dancing. 1880-1940. *1490*

Community Design Centers. Construction. Design. 1980. *1154*

Community participation. Archives. Houston Metropolitan Research Center. Texas. 1974-82. *31*

—. Harte, Houston. Newspapers. Texas (San Angelo). 1900's-72. *1458*

Community services. Education. Housing. Indian-White relations. North Carolina Commission of Indian Affairs. ca 1700-1978. *3917*

Company towns. Aluminum Company of America. Tennessee (Alcoa). 1919-60. *3073*

Comparative Studies. Fredrickson, George M. (review article). Race relations. South Africa. 18c-20c. *473*

—. Racism. South Africa. 19c-20c. *404*

Compere, Ebenezer Lee. Baptists. Cherokee Indians. Missions and Missionaries. Oklahoma, northeastern. 1854-65. *3987*

Competition. Alabama (Birmingham, Mobile). Colleges and Universities. Medical education. 1912-20. *1784*

—. Dance. Individualism. Louisiana (New Orleans). Minstrelsy. 1840's-50's. *1476*

—. Economic conditions. Manufacturing. Market structure. 1850-60. *2902*

—. Electric power. Prices. Private sector. Public Utilities. Texas (Lubbock). 1916-81. *2907*

Composers. Blacks. Joplin, Scott. Music. 20c. *1767*

—. Blacks. Joplin, Scott. Ragtime. 1900-17. 1970's. *1727*

Computers. *See also* names of specific computers, e.g. IBM 370 (computer).

—. Agricultural Cooperatives. Cotton. Marketing. Plains Cotton Cooperative Association. Telecommunication. Texas (Lubbock). 1920's-70's. *2822*

Concentration Camps. *See also* Internment.

—. Cherokee Indians. Fort Marr. Indians. Removals, forced. Tennessee. 1830's. *3955*

Concert halls. Bluegrass. Lucy Opry. Music. Tennessee (Memphis). 1966-82. *1515*

Concerts. Barnum, P. T. Lind, Jenny. Louisiana. Music. 1851. *896*

Concord Baptist Association. Baptists, Southern. Louisiana (Webster Parish). 1832-1972. *2349*

Conductors. Klasmer, Benjamin. Maryland (Baltimore). Music. 1909-49. *834*

Cone, Claribel. Art collectors. Cone, Etta. Maryland (Baltimore). Matisse, Henri. Stein, Gertrude. 1900-51. *836*

Cone, Etta. Art collectors. Cone, Claribel. Maryland (Baltimore). Matisse, Henri. Stein, Gertrude. 1900-51. *836*

Confederate Army. *See also* Confederate States of America.

Corbin, David Alan (*Life, Work and Rebellion in the Coal Fields*). Coal Mines and Mining (review article). West Virginia (southern). 1880-1922. *3120*

Corn. Cotton. Crops. Farmers. 19c. *2877*
—. Cotton. Farmers. 1850-1909. 1973-77. *2788*

Corn Tassel (chief). Cherokee Indians. Indian-White Relations. Land. Long Island, Treaty of. 1777. *3946*

Corner-notching. Architecture. Log construction. Texas. 1815-1940. *1255*

Cornices. Architecture. Bricks. Virginia (Rockbridge County). 1790-1870. *1351*

Cornish Americans. Agriculture. Appalachia. Immigration. Mining. Pollard, Thomas. 19c. *3369*
—. Appalachia. Copper Mines and Mining. 1830-90. *2533*

Corona Female College. Civil War. Gaston, L. B. Gaston, Susan P. Hospitals. Mississippi (Corinth). 1857-64. *1907*

Corporations. *See also* Public Utilities.
—. Agriculture. Dart and Kraft Company. Exhibits and Expositions. Florida (Orlando). Walt Disney World (Experimental Prototype Community of Tomorrow). 1983. *2732*
—. Appalachia. Economic Conditions. Gaventa, John (review article). 1890-1980. *2577*
—. Brown and Root, Inc. Construction. Housing. Rural areas. ca 1977-79. *2661*
—. Bushyhead, Dennis. Cherokee Indians. Indian-White Relations. Political Leadership. 1879-98. *4054*
—. Economic development. Location. Public Policy. 1979. *3033*

"Corrido de Gregorio Cortez" (ballad). Ballads. "Discriminación a un Martir". Mexican Americans. Political Protest. Social change. Texas (Three River). 20c. *717*

Costume. Social Status. South Carolina (Charleston). 1769-82. *574*

Cottage industries. Buttermaking. Churns. Dairying. Delaware. Pennsylvania. Women. 1750-1850. *2744*

Cottages. North Carolina (Outer Banks; Nags Head). Resorts. 1830-1977. *3195*

Cotten, Fred Rider (obituary). History. Texas State Historical Association. 1894-1974. *568*

Cotton. Agricultural Cooperatives. Computers. Marketing. Plains Cotton Cooperative Association. Texas. Telecommunication. 1920's-70's. *2822*
—. Agricultural Labor. Productivity. Quantitative methods. 1850's-1900's. 1958-78. *2810*
—. Agricultural Policy. Association of Southern Commissioners of Agriculture. New Deal. Tennessee (Memphis). 1936-37. *2800*
—. Agricultural Production. Arkansas (Yell County). Farmers. Slaves. ca 1850-59. *2804*
—. Agricultural Production. Economic Conditions. Soybeans. 1920's-75. *2714*
—. Agricultural Production. Economic Development. Land. Legislation. 1820-60. *2759*
—. Agricultural Technology and Research. Sharecroppers. Tractors. 1915-60. *2798*
—. Agriculture. Economic Conditions. Periodicals. 1850's-1900. *2697*
—. Agriculture. Efficiency. Technology. 1845-61. *2830*
—. Agriculture. Oklahoma, eastern. Sharecroppers. 1920-40. *2726*
—. Agriculture Department. Boll weevils. Mechanization. Pesticides. 1890's-1960's. *2731*
—. Alabama. Blacks. Sharecroppers. Shaw, Nate. 1880's-1960's. *2823*
—. Alabama. Manufacturers. Pratt, Daniel. 1799-1873. *2899*
—. Alexander Brown and Sons. Banking. England (Liverpool). Foreign exchange. USA. 1820-80. *2602*
—. Alexander Brown and Sons. Great Britain. International Trade. 1820-60. *2749*
—. Bayles, Thomas. British East India Company. India. 1839. *3030*
—. Beard, Charles. Economic conditions. Exchange rates. 1866-79. *2665*
—. Blacks. Boll weevils. 1929-77. *2728*
—. Blacks. Boll weevils. Employment. Migration, Internal. 1910-30. *2736*
—. Blacks. Farmers. Marketing. Social change. Social Classes. Whites. 1865-1940. *2869*
—. Blacks. Labor Unions and Organizations. North Carolina. Textile Industry. Whites. 1908-74. *3065*
—. Boll weevils. Florida (Madison County). 1870-1916. *2809*
—. Brown lung disease. Burlington Industries, Inc. Carolina Brown Lung Association. Liberty Mutual Insurance. 1970's. *3382*

—. Capital. Labor. Textile Industry. Wages. 1880-1930. *3167*
—. Child labor. Economic Growth. Virginia (Petersburg). 1826-1945. *2990*
—. Corn. Crops. Farmers. 19c. *2877*
—. Corn. Farmers. 1850-1909. 1973-77. *2788*
—. Crops. Tenancy. 1860-80. *2872*
—. Debt. Economic Conditions. Farmers. 1865-90. *2818*
—. Debt. Farmers. Merchants. ca 1865-90. *2680*
—. Delta and Pine Land Company. Economic Regulations. Federal Government. Johnston, Oscar Goodbar. Subsidies. 1933-37. *2801*
—. Depressions. Long, Huey P. Louisiana. Texas. 1931. *2849*
—. Discrimination, Employment. Productivity. Textile Industry. 1830's-60's. *3144*
—. Economic conditions. Income. Monetary exchange rates. ca 1820-85. *2871*
—. Economic Conditions. Johnson, Lyndon B. Price controls. 1965-66. *2558*
—. Economic Development. Louisiana (New Orleans). 1870-81. *2572*
—. Exports. North Carolina (Wilmington). Sprunt, Alexander and Son. 1866-1956. *2748*
—. Farmers. ca 1880-1915. *2705*
—. Farmers. Income. Productivity. ca 1880-1910. *2706*
—. Farming. Fertilizers. Furman, Farish. 1878-83. *2850*
—. Georgia. Sea Islands. South Carolina. 1756-1956. *2851*
—. Great Britain. India. Japan. 1870-1939. *3169*
—. Great Britain. International Trade. 1860's-1900. *2881*
—. Great Britain. Plantations. Slavery. 17c-19c. *2753*
—. Investments. Prices. Quantitative Methods. Tariff. 1840-60. *2742*
—. Louisiana (Mamou Prairie). Migration, Internal. Sharecroppers. Social Change. 1910-79. *3224*
—. Louisiana (Tensas Parish). Mississippi River. Steamboats. 1843-1904. *2578*
—. Marketing. Urbanization. 1880-1930. *3154*
—. Mississippi. Reconstruction. Small farms. Tenancy. Whites. ca 1865-80. *2756*
—. Mississippi (Delta). Mules. 1820-1950. *2684*
—. New England. Technology. Textile Industry. 1890-1970. *2963*
—. Slavery. 1820-1900. *2874*
—. Technology. 18c-1973. *2664*
—. Texas, West. 1889-1979. *2846*
—. Textile industry. ca 1830-60. *2974*

Cotton Acreage Control Law (Texas, 1931). Crops. Long, Huey P. New Deal. 1931-33. *2861*

Cotton, Dorothy. Blacks. Personal narratives. Politics. Southern Christian Leadership Conference. 1960-82. *3816*

Coulon, George David. Louisiana (New Orleans). Painting. ca 1850-1904. *806*

Coulter, Ellis Merton. Bibliographies. Georgia. Historiography. 1912-77. *317*
—. Biography. 1940-76. *316*
—. Racism. 1890-1979. *494*

Coulter, Ellis Merton (obituary). Colleges and Universities. Georgia, University of. Historians. ca 1930's-81. *262*

—. *Georgia Historical Quarterly*. Historians. Periodicals. 1890-1981. *281*

Council of Southern Mountain Workers. Rural Development. Standard of Living. 1913-72. *2647*

Councils and Synods. Delegates. Episcopal Church, Protestant. Kinsolving, George Herbert. Texas. Veto. Women. 1921-70. *2218*

Counseling. *See also* Social Work.
—. Crane, William E. Presbyterian Church. Social Change. 1925-75. *2378*

Counter Culture. *See also* Communes.
—. Agrarians. 1865-1973. *444*

Counties. Mississippi (Wayne County, Chickasawhay River). Petitions. 1808-09. *194*
—. South Carolina. Toponymy. 1672-1977. *3269*
—. Tennessee. 1777-1919. *3267*

Country blues style. Music. Recordings. Tennessee. 1928. *945*

Country Life. *See also* Agricultural Organizations; Rural Settlements.
—. Agricultural Production. Industry. Mechanization. North Carolina, eastern. Tobacco. 1880's-1976. *2730*
—. Alabama (Fairfield). General stores. Jones, John C. H. Ledgers. 1873. *688*
—. Anderson, James Wallace. Anderson, Mary. City Life. District of Columbia. Farms. Letters. Maryland (Rockville area). 1854-1960. *500*
—. Art. North Carolina. Thomason, Eugene Healan. 1930's-72. *924*

—. Blacks. Jackson, Gussie (interview). Midwives. 20c. *2175*
—. Blacks. Murder. Religion. Whites. 1916-20. *2508*
—. Brice, James Moffatt. Editors and Editing. *News-Banner*. Newspapers. Personal narratives. Tennessee (Troy). 1879-1925. *1497*
—. Caldwell, Erskine. Georgia. Novels. Poor. 1930's. 1970's. *445*
—. Cheshire, Johnathan Singleton. Diaries. Louisiana (Webster Parish). Medicine (practice of). 1882-88. *2158*
—. Farms, Tenant. Maryland. Tabb's Purchase (estate). Tableware. 19c. *1581*
—. Films. Mountaineers. 1935-55. *414*
—. Georgia. Politics. Talmadge, Eugene. 1927-46. *3754*
—. Georgia, eastern. Houses. 1733-1980. *3325*
—. Hogs and Hog Raising. Virginia (Manquin, Queenfield Farm). 20c. *2853*
—. Ice cream suppers. Kentucky (Hopkins, McLean Counties). 1930's-40's. *1661*
—. Iddings, Fanny Pierce. Maryland (Montgomery County). Personal Narratives. Pierce, Edward. 1728-1968. *1305*
—. Kentucky (Owens County). Livers, Bill. Personal Narratives. 1900's-78. *1418*
—. Louisiana. Murder. Social Customs. Weapons. 19c-1979. *503*
—. Novels. 1950's. *841*
—. Periodicals. *Progressive Farmer*. Values. Women. 1930-40. *483*
—. Regional Planning. Rural settlements. 1970's. *2855*

Country music. Collins, Curley. Forman, Tex. Georgia (Atlanta). Musicians. Personal narratives. Pop Eckler and His Young'uns. Radio. 1936-42. *1470*
—. Fiddles. Georgia Old-Time Fiddlers' Convention. Music. 1920. *1469*
—. *Louisiana Hayride* (program). Music. Radio. 1948-54. *1673*
—. Maryland. Music. Pennsylvania. 1930's-77. *1453*
—. Mississippi. Music. Progress. 1930. *3202*
—. Music. Old Time Country Radio Reunion. Radio. Tennessee (Jonesboro). 1979. *1434*
—. Music. Texas Playboys. Wills, Bob. 1920-80. *1654*

Country-Western Music. Appalachia. Kincaid, Bradley. Music. 1925-82. *1667*
—. Attitudes. Music. Social Change. 1970's. *1460*
—. *Midday Merry Go-Round* (program). Music. Radio. Tennessee (Knoxville). 1921-41. *1647*
—. Music. Texas (Houston). 1920's-50's. *830*

County Government. *See also* Local Government; State Government.
—. Archives. Court records. Virginia State Library. ca 1650-1952. *109*
—. Arkansas (Washington). Postal Service. Sanders, Simon T. 1797-1882. *2616*
—. Boundaries. Oklahoma (Grady, Stephens counties). 1935-50. *3303*
—. Courthouses. Location. Virginia (Spotsylvania County). 1720-1840. *3317*
—. Ireland, Robert M. (review article). Kentucky. 1850-91. 1977. *3273*
—. Kentucky (Nicholas County). Local Politics. Officeholding. Sugg, John F. 1909-49. *3774*

County Governments. Historical Markers. Louisiana (Claiborne Parish; Russellville). Sesquicentennial Celebrations. 1829-36. 1979. *3353*

County Records (company). Music. Recordings. Virginia (Floyd County). 1920's-80. *1701*

County Records. Archives. County Government. Virginia State Library. ca 1650-1952. *109*
—. City Life. Maryland (Baltimore). 1682-19c. *297*

Courthouses. Architecture. Construction. State government. Virginia (Grayson County). 1792-1909. *1309*
—. Architecture. Construction. Virginia (Rockbridge County). 1778-1897. *1272*
—. Architecture. Construction. Virginia (Washington County). 1777-1868. *1234*
—. Architecture. Virginia (Smyth County). 1832-1905. *1239*
—. Buildings. Virginia (Rockingham County, Harrisonburg). 1777-1897. *1367*
—. Buildings. Virginia (Russell County). 1787-1874. *1233*
—. County Government. Location. Virginia (Spotsylvania County). 1720-1840. *3317*
—. Exhibits and Expositions. Florida. Photographs. 1885-1969. *3551*

Dumb-bell (device). Folklore. Georgia (Grady County). Practical jokes. Prehistory-1900's. *1522*

Dunbar High School. Blacks. District of Columbia. High Schools. 1870-1955. *2077*

Dunbar-Nelson, Alice. Blacks. Delaware (Wilmington). Literature. Women. 1875-1935. *1744*

Duplanty, McCall and Company. Antietam Woolen Manufacturing Company. Attitudes. Delaware. Maryland (Funkstown). Textile Industry. Working Conditions. 1814-19. *3446*

DuPont Cemetery. Inscriptions. South Carolina (Purrysburg). Strobhar Cemetery. Tombstones. 1736-1872. *1542*

Dupont, E. I. and Company. Brandywine River Valley. Delaware. Documents. Economic growth. Industrialization. Pennsylvania. Standard of living. 1800-60. *2883*

—. Maryland (Delaware). Savings. Wages. 1813-60. *2882*

DuPont estate. Ball, Ed. Florida East Coast Railway. Pepper, Claude. Railroads. 1926-58. *3132*

DuPont, Pierre S. Blacks. Delaware. Philanthropy. Public Schools. 1918-30. *2082*

—. Delaware. Modernization. Public Schools. State Government. Taxation. 1920-40. *1865*

DuPont, Thomas Coleman. Delaware. Highway Engineering. 1900-35. *3087*

duPratz, Antoine Simon Le Page (*Histoire de la Louisiane*). Chickasaw Indians. Choctaw Indians. Dialects. Indians. Language. Methodology. Mississippi River Valley (lower). ca 1720-58. *3950*

Durham, James. Blacks. Letters. Louisiana (New Orleans). Medicine (practice of). Rush, Benjamin. 1783-1802. *2161*

—. Blacks. Louisiana (New Orleans). Medicine (practice of). Rush, Benjamin. 1760's-1802. *2180*

Durham, William J. Craft, Juanita. NAACP. Smith, Antonio Maceo. Texas. White, Lulu B. 1933-50. *375*

Durrett, Reuben Thomas. Archives. Historians. Kentucky. 1880-1913. *41*

Dust Bowl. Erosion. Farmers. Migration, Internal. Oklahoma. 1921-30's. *2784*

Dykeman, Wilma (review article). Historians. Tennessee. 18c-1976. *721*

# E

Eaker, Ira C. Aeronautics, Military. Army Air Corps. World War I. World War II. 8th Bomber Command, US. 1917-47. *3869*

East End Historical District. Architecture. Neighborhoods. Preservation. Texas (Galveston). Victorian style. 1972-77. *1327*

East Louisiana State Hospital. Hospitals. Louisiana (Jackson). Mental health care. 1960-72. *2160*

East, P. D. Carter, William Hodding, Jr. Cash, Wilbur J. (*Mind of the South*). Journalism. Kilpatrick, James J. 1940's-60's. *900*

*East Tennessee Historical Society's Publications*. Bibliographies. Periodicals. Tennessee. 18c-20c. *10*

—. Periodicals. 1929-79. *127*

East Tennessee State University. Furthering the Folk Arts in Tennessee (symposium). Tennessee. 1978. *1432*

Eaton, Clement. Historians. Travel accounts. 1935-53. *277*

Ebenezer Lutheran Church. Inscriptions. Mount Bethel Baptist Church. South Carolina (Anderson County). Tombstones. 1856-1978. *1487*

Ebey, George. Anti-Communist Movements. Educational administrators. Liberalism. Schools. Texas (Houston). 1937-53. *1798*

Ecclesiastical questions. Kentucky. New School Synod. Presbyterian Church. 1837-58. *2403*

Eckford, Elizabeth. Arkansas (Little Rock). Attitudes. Blacks. Personal Narratives. Public schools. School Integration. 1957-79. *2100*

*Eclipse* (vessel). Escapes. Germany. Internment. *Kronprinz Wilhelm* (vessel). Navies. *Prinz Eital Friedrich* (vessel). Virginia (Norfolk). 1915. *3874*

Ecology. *See also* Conservation of Natural Resources; Environment; Nature Conservation; Pollution; Wilderness.

—. Metropolitan areas. Migration, Internal. Population. 1940-60. 1970-75. *2627*

Economic Aid. Agricultural Policy. Congress. 1921-32. *2725*

Economic Conditions. *See also* terms beginning with Economic; Natural Resources; Statistics.

—. 1860-1973. *2625*

—. Acculturation. Census. Cherokee Indians. Population. 1809-35. *4043*

—. Agricultural labor. Plantations. Social Change. 1920-60. *2752*

—. Agricultural Production. Congress. Louisiana. Subsidies. Sugar. 1860-1930. *2833*

—. Agricultural Production. Cotton. Soybeans. 1920's-75. *2714*

—. Agricultural Production. Farmers. Standard of living. Tennessee Valley Authority. 1933-79. *2708*

—. Agriculture. Cotton. Periodicals. 1850's-1900. *2697*

—. Agriculture. Farms (tenant). Productivity. 1850's-90's. *2820*

—. Agriculture. Goldfield, David R. Social Conditions. Urbanization. 1607-1980. *3010*

—. Agriculture. Kentucky (Kentucky Bend). Mississippi River. 1810's-90's. *2536*

—. Alabama. Debt. State Government. 1920-65. *3637*

—. Appalachia. Corporations. Gaventa, John (review article). 1890-1980. *2577*

—. Appalachia. Day, John (*Bloody Ground*). Social Conditions. 1941. *1049*

—. Appalachia. Political science. 1960's-70's. *44*

—. Appalachian studies. Social change. 1970's. *118*

—. Architecture. Civic pride. Railroad stations. Urbanization. 1890-1920. *1172*

—. Architecture. Mississippi. Natchez Pilgrimage of Homes. Preservation. Towns, small. 1900-80. *1219*

—. Arkansas. Discovery and Exploration. State Government. 1540's-1978. *3549*

—. Attitudes. Investments. Manufactures. 1850-60. *2901*

—. Baptists, Southern. 1900-80. *2445*

—. Beard, Charles. Cotton. Exchange rates. 1866-79. *2665*

—. Blacks. Boritt, Gabor S. Economic conditions (review article). James, John A. Mandle, Jay R. Oubre, Claude F. Social Change. 1860-1900. *2597*

—. Blacks. Colleges and Universities. Langston University. McCabe, Edward Preston. Oklahoma. Social Change. 1896-1982. *2079*

—. Blacks. Cooperatives. Discrimination. Federation of Southern Cooperatives. Prejean, Charles. 1967-82. *2542*

—. Business. Downtown areas. Maryland (Baltimore). Neighborhoods. Social Conditions. 1800-1980. *3174*

—. Business. Epidemics. Lasker, Morris. Letters. Personal narratives. Texas (Milliken). 1860-66. *608*

—. Business. Farms, small. 1970's. *2675*

—. Calvert, Robert. Houston and Texas Central Railway. Railroads. Texas (Calvert). 1868-1918. *2970*

—. Churches. Location. Maryland (Baltimore). Protestantism. 1840-70. *2276*

—. City Life. Social Conditions. Virginia (Alexandria). 1790-1860. *3008*

—. City Planning. Texas (Houston). Zoning. 1962-77. *2910*

—. Civil War. Daily Life. Social Conditions. Virginia (Appomattox Courthouse). 1845-65. *3058*

—. Coal. Models. West Virginia. 1880-1930. *3122*

—. Competition. Manufacturing. Market structure. 1850-60. *2902*

—. Conservatism. Politics. 1968-78. *3692*

—. Convict labor. Georgia. Racism. 1868-1909. *3687*

—. Cotton. Debt. Farmers. 1865-90. *2818*

—. Cotton. Income. Monetary exchange rates. ca 1820-85. *2871*

—. Cotton. Johnson, Lyndon B. Price controls. 1965-66. *2558*

—. Creek Indians. Indian Territory. Indian-White Relations. 1865-71. *3995*

—. Creek Indians. Indian Wars. South Carolina. Trade. Yamassee War. 1710-15. *3992*

—. Cuban Americans. Florida (Miami). Social Conditions. 1940-80. *2615*

—. Daily Life. Georgia (Polk County). 19c-1977. *2598*

—. Daily Life. Social Conditions. Tennessee (Denmark). 1829-1979. *3213*

—. Daily Life. Social Customs. Texas (Sheffield). 1590-1978. *3337*

—. Delaware (Odessa). Population. Social Classes. 1660-1870. *3316*

—. Delaware (Wilmington). Philadelphia, Wilmington, and Baltimore Railroad. Railroads. 19c-20c. *3109*

—. Elites. Kentucky. Mountaineers. Political Leadership. Social Organization. 1790-19c. *3532*

—. Europeans. Travel (accounts). West Virginia (Wheeling). 1802-42. *733*

—. Foreman, Clark Howell. National Emergency Council (report). Politics. Roosevelt, Franklin D. 1938. *2565*

—. Georgia (Atlanta). Jews. Social Mobility. 1870-1911. *2594*

—. Georgia (Carroll County). Migration, Internal. 1921-79. *3234*

—. Historiography. Political Leadership. ca 1865-1979. *2672*

—. Income. Political power. Social Classes. 1970's. *2587*

—. Law. Maryland. Transportation. 1820-40. *2540*

—. Local government. Property. Urbanization. 1960's-70's. *3136*

—. Mandle, Jay R. Plantations. Regionalism (review article). Thompson, Edgar T. Wright, Gavin. 1865-1978. *2580*

—. Marxism. Slavery. Social Organization. 17c-1860. *2573*

—. Oklahoma panhandle. Railroads. Territorial status. 1880's-1930's. *2966*

—. Prices. Rice. South Carolina. 1720's. *2559*

—. Railroads. 1830-60. *3150*

—. South Carolina (Charleston). Trade. 1865-1979. *2617*

—. Tobacco. Virginia. 1613-1732. *2663*

Economic conditions (review article). Blacks. Boritt, Gabor S. Economic conditions. James, John A. Mandle, Jay R. Oubre, Claude F. Social Change. 1860-1900. *2597*

—. Mandle, Jay R. Ransom, Roger L. Sutch, Richard. Wiener, Jonathan M. 1850-1910. 1977-78. *3362*

Economic Development. 1865-1970. *2624*

—. Agricultural Production. Cotton. Land. Legislation. 1820-60. *2759*

—. Agriculture. 1770-1900. *2662*

—. Agriculture. Mitchell, Robert D. (review article). Settlement. Virginia (Shenandoah Valley). 18c. 1977. *2754*

—. Appalachia. Capitalism. Novels. Skidmore, Hubert. Social Change. 1936-38. *2571*

—. Appalachia. Gold Rushes. 1828. *2659*

—. Banking. Manufacturing. Urbanization. 1840-60. *3178*

—. Banking. Regionalism. 1960's-74. *2568*

—. Blacks. Historiography. 1850's-20c. *2657*

—. Blacks. Southern Consumers Cooperative. 1963-83. *2560*

—. Brickmaking. Capitalism. Coal Mines and Mining. Industrial Relations. Kentucky, eastern. Social Change. 1870-1930. *3373*

—. Charlotte Harbor Railroad. Florida (Newnansville). Rural Settlements. ca 1825-87. *2658*

—. Cherokee Indians. Federal government. Indians. 18c-1978. *3876*

—. Chesapeake Bay. Population. Social Conditions. ca 1607-1790's. *769*

—. Corporations. Location. Public Policy. 1979. *3033*

—. Cotton. Louisiana (New Orleans). 1870-81. *2572*

—. Emancipation. 1859-1900. *2655*

—. Enterprise zones. Geography. Georgia (Atlanta). Pennsylvania (Wilkes-Barre). 1919-70. *3246*

—. Ferry landings. Tennessee, east. 1790-1870. *3280*

—. Florida (Indian Key). 1829-1976. *2634*

—. Florida Southern Railroad (Charlotte Harbor Division). Railroads. 1884-1904. *3077*

—. Health. Regionalism. 1975. *2550*

—. Identity. Louisiana (New Orleans). Mississippi River. Technology. Trade. 1850-1950. *2913*

—. Income. Productivity. 1865-70's. *2607*

—. Industrialization. Johnson, J. Fred. Technology. Tennessee (Kingsport). Values. Work ethic. 1916-44. *3165*

—. Industry. Political Change. Regionalism. 1970-80. *2574*

—. Industry. Population. Recessions. 1970-77. *2562*

—. Irish Americans. Tennessee (Memphis). 1850-80. *640*

—. Louisiana (Kenner). Settlement. 1717-1982. *2538*

—. Maryland. Tobacco. Virginia. 1617-1730. *2792*

—. Mississippi. ca 1815-1973. *2570*

—. Mississippi River. Packet boats. 19c. *2585*

—. Oklahoma (Gibbon). 1890's-1945. *3296*

—. Politics. Textile industry. 1960's-82. *3078*

—. Railroads. Steamboats. Transportation, Commercial. Western States. 1811-60. *2981*

—. Social Classes. 1865-1955. *2650*

—. Tennessee (Rhea County). 1807-1975. *3272*

—. Values. 1865-1980. *2610*

—. Baptists, Southern. Church membership. Urbanization. 1920's. *2488*

—. Blacks. Farmers. Religion. Social Conditions. 1800-60. *2259*

—. Boles, John B. (review article). Racism. Religion. Smith, H. Shelton (review article). 1972. *2302*

—. Jones, Charles Colcock. Race Relations. Utopias. 1804-63. *2364*

—. Twain, Mark. 1870-1910. *2322*

Evangelism. Baptists. Florida. Graham, Billy. 1936-79. *2269*

—. Baptists, Southern. Big Hatchie Baptist Association. Missions and Missionaries. 1828-1903. *2267*

—. Bryson, Henry. Diaries. Presbyterian Church, Associate Reformed. 1826-27. *2523*

—. Cherokee Indians. Civil disobedience. Missions and Missionaries. 1829-39. *4045*

—. Converts. Louisiana (New Orleans). Protestant Churches. Slavery. 1800-61. *2418*

—. Death and Dying. Literature. 1800-65. *421*

—. Diaries. Georgia (Augusta). Methodist Episcopal Church. Norman, Jeremiah. 1798-1801. *2472*

—. Holston River Valley. Methodist Church. Russell, Elizabeth H. C. Virginia. 1770-1825. *2217*

—. Protestantism. Slavery. 18-19c. *2365*

Evangelization. Christianity. Freedmen. Presbyterian Church. 1872-1900. *2484*

Evans, Catherine. Carpet industry. Georgia (Dalton). 1895-1970's. *2919*

Evans, George W. Frontier and Pioneer Life. Texas rangers. 1849-1907. *672*

Evans, Herndon J. Coal Mines and Mining. Editors and Editing. Kentucky (Harlan County). Pineville *Sun*. Strikes. 1929-32. *3452*

Evans, Lawton B. Georgia (Augusta, Evans County). Public schools. 1882-1934. *1851*

Evans, Walker. Agee, James. Alabama. Depressions. McCloud, Emma Gudger. Sharecroppers. Whites. 1934. *786*

—. Agee, James. Bourke-White, Margaret. Photography. Poverty. ca 1930-39. *3365*

Evening and Continuation Schools. Blacks. Cooks. Georgia (Athens). 1910. *2051*

Everett Institute. Baptists. Colleges and Universities. Education. Louisiana (Spearsville). 1893-1908. *1796*

Evergreen Place (farm). Portraits. Tennessee (Nashville). Weakley family. 1764-1892. *1037*

Evil. Folklore. Kentucky. Oil and Petroleum Products. Prehistory-1829. *1413*

Evolution. Creationism. Georgia. Teaching. 20c. *1858*

Ewan, J. W. Christmas. Indians. Personal narratives. Seminole Indians. 1874. *3963*

—. Indians. Personal narratives. Seminole Indians. Tiger Tail (man). 1875. *3962*

Ewell, Benjamin Stoddert. Virginia (Williamsburg). William and Mary, College of. 1854-88. *1912*

Excavations. *See also* Artifacts.

—. Alabama, University of. 1818-1976. *1848*

—. Archaeology. Oklahoma. 1830's-1915. *3222*

—. Ballast. England (London). Florida (Fernandina Beach). 16c-19c. 1972-76. *176*

—. Cherokee Indians. Diaries. Indians. Louis Philippe. Tennessee (Toqua). 1797. *4090*

—. Florida (Pensacola). Houses. Panton, William. 1796-1848. *1381*

Exchange rates. Beard, Charles. Cotton. Economic conditions. 1866-79. *2665*

Executive Management Commission. Kentucky. 1979. *3496*

Executive Power. Arkansas. Constitutions, state. Governors. 1819-1970's. *3673*

Exhibits and Expositions. *See also* Art.

—. Agriculture. Corporations. Dart and Kraft Company. Florida (Orlando). Walt Disney World (Experimental Prototype Community of Tomorrow). 1983. *2732*

—. Agriculture. Lafayette, Marquis de (visit). Maryland Agricultural Society. 1824-32. *2676*

—. Blacks. Labor. Photographs. 1880's-1976. *357*

—. Courthouses. Florida. Photographs. 1885-1969. *3551*

—. Daily Life. Maryland (Baltimore). Museums. Peale Museum. 1800-1955. *1388*

—. Painting. 1564-1980. *1146*

—. Painting. Self-perception. Social Change. 1564-1980. *711*

Exiles. Liberal Party. Mexican Americans. Mexico. Propaganda. Texas. Women. 1898-1910. *3832*

Explorers. *See also* Discovery and Exploration; Mountain Men.

—. Goodnight, Charles. Indians. Ranches. Settlement. Texas (Palo Duro Canyon). 1541-1900. *3228*

—. Indians. Lederer, John. Medicine, practice of. Travel accounts. Virginia. 1681. *3968*

Exports. Alabama (Mobile). Lumber and Lumbering. 1760-1860. *2959*

—. Consumers. Manufactures. North Central States. 1860. *2938*

—. Cotton. North Carolina (Wilmington). Sprunt, Alexander and Son. 1866-1956. *2748*

—. Economic Regulations. Maryland. Money. Prices. Tobacco Inspection Act (1747). 1747. *2837*

—. Georgia. Lumber and Lumbering. 1732-75. *2992*

—. Lumber and Lumbering. Ports. South Carolina (Charleston). 18c-1860. *2958*

# F

Factionalism. Acculturation. Choctaw Indians. Crime and Criminals. War. 1746-50. *3984*

Factories. Blacks. Farmers. Fertility. Land Tenure. Whites. 1900. *2852*

Fain, Sarah Lee. Democratic Party. Elections. State Politics. Virginia (Norfolk). Women. 1888-1962. *3803*

Fairchild Wine Vault. Oklahoma (Oklahoma City). Winemaking. 1890-1925. *1221*

Fairfield Glade. Cumberland Homesteads. Housing. New Deal. Resettlement. Tennessee. 1934-80. *1353*

Faith healing. Arkansas, northeastern. Pentecostals. Sects, Religious. 1937-73. *2238*

Falconhurst series. Horner, Lance. Novels. Onstott, Kyle. 1957-73. *416*

Family. *See also* Divorce; Marriage.

—. Alabama. Civil War. Slavery. Social Change. Whites. 1850-70. *504*

—. Appalachia. Folk songs. 1972-73. *1589*

—. Appalachia. Ritchie, Jean (review essay). Singing. 1955-80. *1547*

—. Archival Catalogs and Inventories. Louisiana, northwestern. 19c. *214*

—. Baptists. Values. 17c-1970's. *2491*

—. Baptists, Southern. 1845-1981. *2441*

—. Baptists (Southern). 1863-1980. *2308*

—. Blacks. Coincoin. Louisiana (Metoyer). Slavery. 1742-1850. *631*

—. Blacks. Homecomings. Kinship. North Carolina (Montgomery County). Reunions. Rites and Ceremonies. 19c-1970's. *381*

—. Catholic Church. Georgia. O'Connor, Flannery (ancestry). ca 1733-1949. *868*

—. Cemeteries. Social Customs. Tennessee (Coffee County). 1908-74. *1425*

—. Choctaw Indians. 1700-1975. *3910*

—. Cigar industry. Florida (Tampa). Italian Americans. Women. 1890-1930. *636*

—. Coincoin. Creoles. Louisiana (Cane River, Natchitoches). Race relations. Social status. 1767-20c. *632*

—. Czech Americans. Labor. Land. Mexican Americans. Social Organization. Texas (Nueces County). 1880-1930. *2673*

—. Drama. Williams, Tennessee (*Memoirs*). ca 1919-75. *814*

—. Farms. Literature. Sex roles. Social Status. Women. 1800-60. *516*

—. Faulkner, William. Hemingway, Ernest. Middle Classes. World view. 1900-50. *1024*

—. Genealogy. Mexico, Gulf of. Mississippi. 18-19c. *612*

—. Georgia. Piedmont Plateau. Pottery. 19c-1970's. *1451*

—. Indians. Lévi-Strauss, Claude. Social Customs. 17c-19c. *4024*

—. Interpersonal Relations. Oklahoma. Rogers, Clement V. Rogers, Will. 1879-1911. *1633*

—. Morality. North Carolina, University of. Students. 1968-73. *1864*

—. Tucker, Beverley. Virginia. Youth. 1784-90's. *515*

Family History. *See* Genealogy.

Fandangle (celebration). Texas (Fort Griffin). 1938-78. *1479*

Far Western States. *See also* individual states (including Alaska and Hawaii).

—. Baptists (Southern). Illinois. New Mexico. 1942-78. *2298*

Farm implements. Appalachia. Architecture. Carson, Marguerite Estep. Folk art. Furniture and Furnishings. 17c-20c. *33*

Farmers. Agricultural Extension Service Agents. Blacks. 1920's-30's. *2701*

—. Agricultural Production. Arkansas (Yell County). Cotton. Slaves. ca 1850-59. *2804*

—. Agricultural Production. Economic Conditions. Standard of living. Tennessee Valley Authority. 1933-79. *2708*

—. Agricultural reform. Editors and Editing. Periodicals. Poe, Clarence Hamilton. *Progressive Farmer*. 1899-1964. *2698*

—. Attitudes. Crops. Kentucky. Livestock. Location. 1973-74. *2699*

—. Bennitt, James. North Carolina. 1830-70. *2793*

—. Blacks. Cotton. Marketing. Social change. Social Classes. Whites. 1865-1940. *2869*

—. Blacks. Education. Tuskegee Institute. Washington, Booker T. 1881-1915. *2021*

—. Blacks. Evangelicalism. Religion. Social Conditions. 1800-60. *2259*

—. Blacks. Factories. Fertility. Land Tenure. Whites. 1900. *2852*

—. Blacks. North Carolina. Social Change. 1950-70. *2858*

—. Cherokee Indians. Grange. Indian Territory. 1870's. *4027*

—. Corn. Cotton. 1850-1909. 1973-77. *2788*

—. Corn. Cotton. Crops. 19c. *2877*

—. Cotton. ca 1880-1915. *2705*

—. Cotton. Debt. Economic Conditions. 1865-90. *2818*

—. Cotton. Debt. Merchants. ca 1865-90. *2680*

—. Cotton. Income. Productivity. ca 1880-1910. *2706*

—. Daily, Charles Henry. Kentucky. Memoirs. Teachers. 1850-1930. *1819*

—. Daily Life. Story, Elliott L. Virginia (Southampton County). 1838-80. *2733*

—. Dust Bowl. Erosion. Migration, Internal. Oklahoma. 1921-30's. *2784*

—. Harris, Joel Chandler. Industrialization. ca 1880-1900. *3056*

—. Kentucky. Lumber and Lumbering. 1860's-1920's. *2557*

—. Kovac, George. Personal narratives. Refugees. Yugoslavs. 1913-65. *2603*

—. Louisiana State Fair. Political Leadership. Schuler, Charles. State Board of Agriculture. 1840-1911. *3736*

—. Methodology. Southern Farmers' Alliance. 1884-90. *2836*

—. Social Customs. Travel accounts. 1850-70. *749*

Farmers, yeoman. Income. Kentucky. Migration, Internal. Tennessee. Tobacco. 1850-60. *2832*

Farmhouses. Architecture. North Carolina (Gates, Pasquotank, Perquimans counties). Social Classes. 1660-1860. *1269*

Farming. Agricultural Technology and Research. Texas. 1890-1975. *2799*

—. Cotton. Fertilizers. Furman, Farish. 1878-83. *2850*

—. Economic Growth. Federal Government. Indians. Reconstruction. Seminole Indians. Social conditions. 1865-70. *4108*

—. Economic Structure. Plantations. Statistics. ca 1865-1910. *2773*

Farms. Alabama. Blacks. Kentucky. Population. Statistics. 1900-70. *2693*

—. Anderson, James Wallace. Anderson, Mary. City Life. Country Life. District of Columbia. Letters. Maryland (Rockville area). 1854-1960. *500*

—. Balance, Alice. Daily Life. North Carolina (Bertie County). Personal Narratives. 1920-83. *2815*

—. Blacks. Ownership. 1865-1973. *2711*

—. Children. Diseases. Health. Mortality. 1900-50. *2112*

—. Education. Whatley, Booker T. 1974-83. *2679*

—. Family. Literature. Sex roles. Social Status. Women. 1800-60. *516*

—. Folklore. Kentucky (Butler, Warren Counties). Language. Stewart family. Toponymy. 1850-1978. *1595*

—. Homeplace-1850 (farm). Kentucky. Museums. Tennessee Valley Authority. 1850. 1979. *143*

—. Land tenure. Political power. Racism. 1877-1915. *2774*

—. Louisiana (Bienville Parish). Restorations. Sylvan Retreat (house). 1848-1978. *1281*

—. Plantations. Sugar. 1850's. *2835*

Farms (small). Agriculture. Florida Marketing Bureau. Marketing. Mayo, Nathan. State government. ca 1917-60. *2757*

—. Blacks. Federal aid. Federation of Southern Cooperatives. Rural settlements. 1967-74. *2775*

—. Blacks. Land tenure. Rural settlements. 1970's. *2876*

—. Business. Economic Conditions. 1970's. *2675*

Farms (tenant). Agriculture. Economic Conditions. Productivity. 1850's-90's. *2820*

—. Alabama. Blacks. Social Reform. Southern Improvement Company. Virginia. 1900-20. *2668*

—. Country Life. Maryland. Tabb's Purchase (estate). Tableware. 19c. *1581*

Farrar Lumber Company. Georgia (Dalton). Housing. 1871-1918. *3080*

Farrelly, John P. Catholic Church. Irish Americans. Morris, John. Nisth, Stritch, Samuel A. Tennessee. 19c-1958. *2475*

Fashion. Department stores. Merchandising. Neiman-Marcus. Texas (Dallas). 1880-1970. *2936*

Fast food industry. Architecture. Franchises. Regions. 1925-80. *1398*

Faubus, Orval. Graves. Hamer, Fanny Lou. Horton, James Edwin. Kennedy, John F. Personal Narratives. Scottsboro Boys. 1930's-70's. *410*

Faulkner, William. 1900-27. *953*
—. Art. Individualism. 1951-58. *845*
—. Art and Society. Blacks. School integration. 1950's-60's. *996*
—. Attitudes. Authors. Blacks. Race Relations. 1930's-79. *1116*
—. Attitudes. Fiction. World War I. 1920's. *811*
—. Attitudes. Films. 1910-40. *873*
—. Bibliographies. 20c. *965*
—. Bibliographies. 20c. *1143*
—. Biography. Blotner, Joseph (review article). 1924-62. *1097*
—. Biography. Blotner, Joseph (review article). Novels. 1920's-74. *973*
—. Calvinism. Literature. 1920's-75. *927*
—. Carter, Katrina. Stone, Phil. 1914-60. *1077*
—. Civil War. Literature. Mississippi (Lafayette County, Oxford). 1860-65. 1925-62. *987*
—. Collins, Jimmy (*Test Pilot*). Literary Criticism. 1935. *863*
—. Copyright. Novels. 1921-75. *966*
—. Cowley, Malcolm. Literary Criticism. 1940's. *1043*
—. Crane, Stephen. Literature. Religion. 19c-20c. *890*
—. Editors and Editing. Literary Criticism. Short stories. 1919-32. *1005*
—. Eisenhower, Dwight D. Foreign Relations. People-to-People Program (Writers' Group). Rabb, Maxwell M. State Department. UNESCO (National Commission). 1954-61. *809*
—. Family. Hemingway, Ernest. Middle Classes. World view. 1900-50. *1024*
—. Fiction. History. 1929-42. *819*
—. Fiction. Mississippi (Lafayette County). Yoknapatawpha County (fictional place). 1897-1962. *3185*
—. Fiction. Yoknapatawpha County (fictional place). 1920's-62. *787*
—. Fictional characters. 1920's-62. *804*
—. Fictional Characters. Jazz. Names. 1920-62. *961*
—. Hemingway, Ernest. Language. Literature. Twain, Mark. 19c-1950's. *1026*
—. History. 20c. *1057*
—. Indians. Literature. 1930-57. *876*
—. Japan. Personal Narratives. Shellenberger, Jack H. Travel. US Information Service. 1955. *1051*
—. Knowledge. Literary characters. Physics. Quantum mechanics. 1920's-30's. *1033*
—. Literary Criticism. 1920's-62. 1974-80. *1142*
—. Literary Criticism. Mississippi. Yoknapatawpha County (fictional place). 1974. *1014*
—. Literary Criticism. Modernism. 1915-60. *1112*
—. Literary themes. Novels. Warren, Robert Penn. 1850's-20c. *914*
—. Literature. 1926-62. *805*
—. Literature. Nobel Prizes. Speeches. 1950. *907*
—. Literature. Page, Thomas Nelson. Welty, Eudora. 19c-20c. *1050*
—. Literature. Southern gentlemen (concept). 1924-42. *972*
—. Literature. Southern Literary Renaissance. ca 1929-60's. *1132*
—. Manuscripts. 1920-29. *999*
—. Novels. 1929-62. *919*
—. O'Neill, Eugene. 1921-31. *1130*
—. Poetry. 1921-24. *818*
—. Wolfe, Thomas. 1920's-70. *1107*
—. World War I. 1917-30. *853*

Faulkner, William (*Big Woods*). Attitudes. Environment. 1930-55. *1009*
—. Literary themes. Wilderness. 1934-55. *926*

Faulkner, William (*Flags in the Dust*). Books (editions). Manuscripts. ca 1925-77. *862*
—. Day, Douglas (review article). Novels. Publishers and Publishing. 1973-74. *904*

Faulkner, William (*Go Down, Moses*). Roth Edmonds (fictional character). 1940-49. *1138*

Faulkner, William (review article). Bezzerides, A. L. Literature. Minter, David. Stonum, Gary Lee. Wittenberg, Judith Bryant. 20c. *880*

Faulkner, William ("The Bear"). Fiction. Mississippi (Lafayette County, Panola County, Yazoo Delta). Plantations. Railroads. Wilderness. 19c-20c. *3186*

Faulkner, William (*The Sound and the Fury*). Jason Compson (fictional character). Literary characters. Values. 1929. *848*

Faust, Drew Gilpin (review article). Intellectuals. Proslavery Sentiments. Psychology. 1840-60. 1978. *944*

Fay, Edwin Whitfield. Classical studies. Scholars. Texas, University of (Austin). 1890-1920. *1923*

Federal aid. Blacks. Farms, small. Federation of Southern Cooperatives. Rural settlements. 1967-74. *2775*
—. Flood control. Mississippi (Yazoo Valley). Navigation, Inland. Whittington, Will M. 1873-1977. *2614*
—. Ports. Texas (Galveston). 1851-90. *1320*

Federal Bureau of Investigation. Boggs, Thomas Hale. Hoover, J. Edgar. Speeches. 1971. *3584*

Federal Government. *See also* names of individual agencies, bureaus, and departments, e.g. Bureau of Indian Affairs, Office of Education, but State Department, Defense Department, etc.; Congress; Constitutions; Government; Legislation; Supreme Court.
—. Agricultural experiment stations. Colleges and Universities. 1877-1940. *2816*
—. Agricultural Industry. Economic Regulations. Mississippi. Prices. Texas. Voluntarism. 1925-40. *2783*
—. Archives, National. Foreman, Grant. Indians. Oklahoma Historical Society. Williams, Robert Lee. 1934. *3894*
—. Blacks. Conservation of Natural Resources. Georgia (Harris Neck). Land Tenure. Lobbying. People Organized for Equal Rights. 1941-82. *3644*
—. Blacks. House of Representatives. Intervention. Population. Voting Rights Act (US, 1965). 1940-75. *3494*
—. Blacks. Public Schools (review article). Reconstruction. Vaughn, William Preston. Warren, Donald R. 1865-76. 1974. *2086*
—. Cherokee Indians. Economic Development. Indians. 18c-1978. *3876*
—. Cherokee Indians. Georgia. Land. Letters. Payne, John Howard. Ross, John. 1820's-30's. *4074*
—. Cherokee Indians. Indians. New Echota, Treaty of. Ross, John. Watie, Stand. 1839. *3983*
—. Cherokee Indians. Indian-White Relations. Taxation. Tribal government. 1820's. *4041*
—. Civil War. Coffin, William G. Indian Territory. Indians. 1861-65. *4006*
—. Civil War. Five Civilized Tribes. Indian Territory. 1861-66. *3931*
—. Cotton. Delta and Pine Land Company. Economic Regulations. Johnston, Oscar Goodbar. Subsidies. 1933-37. *2801*
—. Custom House. Restorations. Tennessee (Nashville). 1877-1977. *1330*
—. Economic Growth. Farming. Indians. Reconstruction. Seminole Indians. Social conditions. 1865-70. *4108*
—. Five Civilized Tribes. Indian agents. Indian Territory. Indians. 1834-74. *4152*
—. Fort Elliott. Migration, Internal. Military expeditions. Settlement. Texas Panhandle. 1820-90. *3302*
—. Howorth, Lucy Somerville. Mississippi. New Deal. Somerville, Nellie Nugent. State Legislatures. 1923-57. *3629*
—. Indian Territory. Kansas. Land transfers. Osage Indians. 1855-72. *4106*
—. Indians. Ross, John. Seminole War, 2d. Sherburne, John H. 1832-38. *4060*

Federal Policy. *See also* Domestic Policy.
—. Barrier Islands. Development. 1979-82. *3706*
—. Cherokee Indians. Indian Territory. Land Tenure. Lobbying. 1878-98. *4005*
—. Cherokee Indians. Indians. New Deal. North Carolina, western. 1930's. *4181*
—. Cherokee Indians. Indian-White Relations. Treaties. Whites. 1835-1900. *3954*
—. Choctaw Indians. Indian Territory. Oklahoma. Removals, forced. 1803-47. *4012*
—. Coleraine, Treaty of. Creek Indians. Georgia. Indian-White Relations. 1796. *3971*
—. Frontier. Indian Wars. Knox, Henry. 1785-93. *4103*
—. Historiography. Public lands. 1810's-70's. *2719*

Federal Programs. Agricultural Policy. Congress. Democratic Party. Presidents. 1933-61. *3765*
—. Blacks. Mississippi. Nixon, Richard M. Poverty. 1967-73. *3355*

Federal Regulation. *See also* Economic Regulations.
—. Coca-Cola Company. Courts. Food and Drug Administration. Georgia. Massengill, S. E. Company. Sullivan, Jordan James. Tennessee. 1906-40. *3830*
—. Henderson, William K. Louisiana (Shreveport). Radio. 1925-35. *1624*

Federal Writers' Project. Blacks. Christian, Marcus B. Dillard University. Historiography. Louisiana. Work Progress Administration. 1930's-79. *380*
—. Blacks. Dillard University. Folklore. *Gumbo Ya-Ya* (publication). Louisiana. Saxon, Lyle. 1930's. *1722*
—. Blacks. Florida. Folklore. Hurston, Zora Neale. 1901-60. *1739*
—. Musical instruments. Personal Narratives. Slaves. 1829-60. 1935-39. *1748*
—. Tobacco. 1933-39. *2671*

Federation of Southern Cooperatives. Blacks. Cooperatives. Discrimination. Economic Conditions. Prejean, Charles. 1967-82. *2542*
—. Blacks. Farms, small. Federal aid. Rural settlements. 1967-74. *2775*

Fee, John Gregg. Abolition Movement. Berea College. Kentucky. Presbyterian Church. 1855-1904. *1874*
—. Berea College. Hanson, John G. Kentucky (Madison County). Morality. Religious Education. Rogers, John A. R. 1858-1979. *1818*

Fellowship of Southern Churchmen. Christianity. Radicals and Radicalism. Social Reform. 1934-57. *2360*

Felton, Rebecca Latimer. Georgia. Politics. Senate. Suffrage. Women. 1860's-1922. *3755*
—. Georgia. Senate. Women. 1871-1922. *3634*

Feminism. China. Haygood, Laura A. Methodist Episcopal Church (South). Missions and Missionaries. 1884-1900. *2402*
—. Diaries. Thomas, Ella Gertrude Clanton. 1848-89. *623*
—. Georgia. Peace Movements. Rankin, Jeannette. 1924-73. *3623*
—. Harrison, Henry Sydnor. Novels. 1911-31. *951*
—. Literary characters. Novels. Rives, Amélie. 1863-1945. *714*
—. Protestant Churches. Women. 1920's. *2181*

Ferguson, Anne Williams. Boarding Schools. Chatham Hall. Episcopal Church, Protestant. Personal Narratives. Virginia. 1940's. *1903*

Ferguson-Caldarera House. Arkansas. Bozeman House. Frederick Hanger House. Housing. National Register of Historic Places. 19c-1980. *93*

Ferrell, Sarah Coleman. Georgia (La Grange). Landscaping. Terraces (home). 1841-1903. *1246*

Ferries. Arkansas. Bridges. *Charles River Bridge* v. *Warren Bridge* (US, 1837). Supreme Court. ca 1837-1940. *3550*
—. Colbert, Benjamin Franklin. Red River. Texas. 1840-1915. *3286*
—. North Carolina. Transportation. 1700-1900. *3152*

Ferry landings. Economic development. Tennessee, east. 1790-1870. *3280*

Fertility. Blacks. Factories. Farmers. Land Tenure. Whites. 1900. *2852*
—. Demography. 1800-1978. *3306*

Fertilizers. Agricultural Technology and Research. Chemical Industry. Tennessee Valley Authority. 1840's-1979. *2841*
—. Cotton. Farming. Furman, Farish. 1878-83. *2850*

Festivals. Blacks. Delaware (Wilmington). Spencer, Peter. 1814-1981. *1715*
—. Music. Singing. Societies. West Virginia (Wheeling). 1855-1906. *1699*

Feuds. Jones family. Liddell family. Louisiana (Catahoula Parish). 1848-70. *606*
—. Kentucky. Law. Violence. West Virginia. 1820-1903. *3662*

Few, William. American Revolution. Congress. Georgia. New York. 1771-1828. *3795*

Fiction. *See also* Novels.
—. Adolescents' Literature. 1907-17. *1079*
—. Alabama (Birmingham). Cohen, Octavus Roy. Journalism. Loafers (literary group). 1920's. *803*
—. Attitudes. Faulkner, William. World War I. 1920's. *811*
—. Bibliographies. Simms, William Gilmore. 1825-70. *1082*
—. Bibliographies. Wade, John Donald. 1910-55. *1074*
—. Blacks. Chesnutt, Charles W. Literary Criticism. North Carolina. 1887-1900. *1709*
—. Blacks. Dixon, Thomas (*Leopard's Spots*). Reconstruction. Stowe, Harriet Beecher (*Uncle Tom's Cabin*). 1850-1900. *1019*
—. Blacks. Styron, William (interview). 1951-76. *993*
—. Cable, George Washington. Louisiana (New Orleans). Presbyterian Church. ca 1870-1925. *436*
—. Cable, George Washington (*Grandissimes*). 1880. *797*

—. Centennial Celebrations. Cuba. Political executions. 1871. 1971. *3562*

—. Cherokee Indians. Diplomacy. Indian-White Relations. Ross, John. Seminole War, 2d. 1837. *3975*

—. Clothing. Indians. Patchwork. Seminole Indians. 18c-1979. *3884*

—. Conservation of Natural Resources. Jennings, May Mann. Royal Palm State Park. 1910's-63. *3332*

—. Courthouses. Exhibits and Expositions. Photographs. 1885-1969. *3551*

—. Courts. Discrimination. Hawkins, Virgil Darnell. Legal education. 1949-76. *1982*

—. Creek Indians. Great Britain. Indian Wars. War of 1812. 1811-16. *4102*

—. Cuban Americans. Immigrants. Medical care. Voluntary Associations. 19c-20c. *689*

—. Daily Life. Indians. Manuscripts. Seminole Indians. 1886-1922. *3903*

—. Daily Life. Photographs. 1940-49. *697*

—. Doubleday, Abner. First Artillery, US. Indian Wars. Military Campaigns. Personal Narratives. Seminole War, 3d. 1855-58. *4081*

—. Editors and Editing. Leadership. Panama City *Pilot.* West, Lillian Carlisle. Women. 1916-37. *1561*

—. Elections (presidential). Hayes, Rutherford B. Spoils system. State politics. Wallace, Lew. 1876-78. *3800*

—. Elementary education. Peabody Fund. Reconstruction. Segregation. 1869-76. *1856*

—. Episcopal Church, Protestant. Gray, William Crane. Indian-White Relations. Missions and Missionaries. Seminole Indians. 1893-1914. *3895*

—. Equal Rights Amendment. National Women's Party. Politics. West, Helen Hunt. Women. 1917-52. *3703*

—. Europeans, southern. Immigration. Social Change. 1865-1910. *647*

—. Flagler, Henry Morrison. Land. Miles, George. Speculation. 1845-1910. *2884*

—. Forests and Forestry. Labor. Peonage. 1870's-1950. *3442*

—. Fort Chokonikla. Indians. Seminole Indians. 1849-50. *4089*

—. Freedom of the Press. Newspapers. Supreme Court. 1901-74. *3636*

—. Friends of the Florida Seminoles. Friends of the Seminoles. Indians. Seminole Indian Association. 1899-1957. *4169*

—. Friends of the Florida Seminoles. Seminole Indians. Willson, Jim. Willson, Minnie Moore. 1890-1930. *4168*

—. Funeral homes. Genealogy. Methodology. ca 1880-1982. *179*

—. Germans. Travel accounts. 1784-1982. *506*

—. Heade, Martin Johnson. Landscape Painting. 1883-1904. *827*

—. Hoover, Herbert C. Patronage. Republican Party. State Politics. 1928-33. *3589*

—. Hotels. Photographs. 1880's-1983. *1223*

—. Indian Territory. Indian Wars. Osceola. Removals, forced. Seminole Indians. 1800-60. *4124*

—. Indian-White Relations. Miccosukee Indians. 1950-79. *4156*

—. Indian-White Relations. Pelota (game). Spain. 1675-84. *3933*

—. Jackson, Andrew. Seminole War, 1st. 1818. *4127*

—. Justice Department. Labor recruitment. New York City. Peonage. Quackenbos, Mary Grace. Turpentine industry. 1905-10. *3444*

—. Law. Peonage. Tabert, Martin. Turpentine camps. 1923-50. *3445*

—. Leadership. Seminole Indians. Social Organization. 20c. *4171*

—. Local history. Periodicals. Public history. South Florida, University of. *Tampa Bay History.* ca 1978-81. *195*

—. Local History. Research. St. Augustine Historical Society Library. 1972-77. *248*

—. Louisiana (New Orleans). Painting. Sully, George Washington. 1829-39. *856*

—. Maritime law. Salvage. 1760's-1830's. *3106*

—. Miami, University of. Naval Air Forces. Richmond Air Force Base. 1942-70. *2604*

—. Missouri Volunteers, 1st. Okeechobee (battle). Seminole War, 2d. Taylor, Zachary. 1837. *4055*

—. O'Brien, Lucy Fulghum. Personal narratives. Reporters and Reporting. Tampa *Tribune.* 1935-50's. *1598*

—. Oral tradition. Seminole Indians. Prehistory-1970's. *3893*

—. Painting. Smith, James Calvert. Spain. 1821. 1879-1962. *826*

—. Political Parties. 1936-71. *3735*

—. Preservation. St. Augustine Restoration Foundation. 1277

—. Spas. 1840-1973. *3335*

—. State Legislatures. 1822-1970. *3715*

—. State Legislatures. Unicameralism. 1822-1977. *3716*

—. Water hyacinths. 1890-1982. *2681*

—. Women. 1890-1978. *520*

Florida (Boca Grande). Daily Life. Railroads. 1885-1981. *3093*

Florida (Boca Raton). Agriculture. Japanese Americans. Yamato colony. 1904-75. *649*

Florida (Bradenton). Braden, Joseph Addison. Gamble, Robert. Indian Wars. Personal Narratives. Seminole Indians. 1856. *3934*

Florida (Cedar Key). Folklore. Mormons. 1880's-1975. *2490*

Florida (Coral Gables). Architecture. City Planning. Preservation. 1920's. 1960-70's. *692*

Florida (Cortez). Beltrame, Ed. Fishing. Knowlton, Bob. Labor Unions and Organizations. United Packinghouse Workers of America. 1930-58. *3400*

Florida (Dade County; Miami). Courts. 1896-1930. *3578*

Florida (Daytona Beach). Bethune, Mary McLeod. Bethune-Cookman College. Blacks. 1875-1955. *2029*

Florida (DeFuniak Springs). Chautauquas. Cultural events. Education. 1899-1935. *1870*

Florida (Duval County). Economic structure. Reconstruction. Upper classes. 1850-70. *2591*

Florida East Coast Railway. Ball, Ed. DuPont estate. Pepper, Claude. Railroads. 1926-58. *3132*

—. Flagler, Henry Morrison. Immigration. Settlement. 1865-1910. *646*

—. Immigrants. Italian Americans. Labor recruitment. Padrone system. Railroads. ca 1890-1901. *3435*

Florida (Egmont Key). Lighthouses. Military. 1757-1980. *3870*

Florida (Everglades). Indian-White Relations. Seminole Indians. Trading posts. 1900-20. *4155*

Florida (Fernandina Beach). Ballast. England (London). Excavations. 16c-19c. 1972-76. *176*

Florida (Flagler County). Hewitt, John. Sawmills. 17c-20c. *3014*

Florida (Fort Myers; Edison Park). Development. Newton, James D. 1926-80. *2912*

Florida (Glades County; Palmdale). Homesteading and Homesteaders. Personal narratives. Wadlow, Ralph. 1932-69. *2644*

Florida (Indian Key). Economic Development. 1829-1976. *2634*

Florida (Jacksonville). Architecture. Klutho, Henry John. Prairie School. 1901-17. *1167*

—. Blacks. Cities. Political Participation. 1887-1907. *3466*

—. Business. Railroads. 1865-1930. *2949*

—. Child care. Children. Georgia (Swainsboro). North Carolina (Durham). 1960-80. *1839*

—. City politics. Cuba. Huah, José Alejandro. Independence Movements. Martí, José. 1836-1905. *3591*

—. Desegregation. Public schools. Students. 1960's-70's. *1999*

Florida (Jasper). Authors. Personal narratives. Smith, Lillian. ca 1915-32. *1075*

Florida (Jupiter). DuBois family. Houses. 1880-1981. *598*

Florida (Key West). Architecture. Preservation. 19c-20c. *1284*

Florida (Lake Okeechobee). Brighton Reservation. Indians (reservations). Seminole Indians. 1935-43. *4154*

Florida (Lee County). *American Eagle.* Elections. Koreshan Unity (community). Newspapers. Progressive Liberty Party. Teed, Cyrus Reed. 1894-1908. *3683*

—. Koreshan Unity. Politics. Sects, Religious. Teed, Cyrus Reed. Utopias. 1880-1909. *2416*

Florida (Madison County). Boll weevils. Cotton. 1870-1916. *2809*

Florida (Manatee County; Bradenton). Allin, Jean. Preservation. Public Records. 1977-79. *4*

Florida (Manatee Village). Buildings. Heritage of Manatee's Environment. Preservation. 1859-89. 1974-76. *1283*

Florida Marketing Bureau. Agriculture. Farms (small). Marketing. Mayo, Nathan. State government. ca 1917-60. *2757*

Florida (Miami). Arnold, H. H. Automobiles. Traffic control. 1896-1935. *3582*

—. Blacks. Business. Cuban Americans. Economic structure. 1920's-80. *2653*

—. Cuban Americans. Economic Conditions. Social Conditions. 1940-80. *2615*

—. Flagler, Henry Morrison. Sewell, Everest G. Tourism. 1895-1940. *2583*

—. Hurricanes. 1824. 1926. *3221*

—. Jackson, James M., Jr. Physicians. 1896-1924. *2170*

—. Law Enforcement. Prohibition. Smuggling. 1896-1920. *3579*

—. Law Enforcement. Racism. Terrorism. 1896-1930. *3581*

—. Letters. Rockefeller, John D. Tuttle, Julia. 1886-90. *497*

Florida (Miami Beach). Architecture. Art Deco. New Yorker Hotel. 1981. *1207*

—. Art Deco. Buildings. Miami Design Preservation League. Preservation. 1920-35. 1978. *1186*

—. Art Deco. Buildings. Preservation. 1930's. *1252*

—. Art Deco. Historic Districts. Restorations. ca 1925-81. *1160*

—. Fisher, Carl Graham. Indianapolis Speedway. Land. ca 1880-1939. *2608*

Florida (Miami; Colored Town). Racism. 1896-1930. *3580*

Florida (Miami; Lemon City). Libraries. 1889-1905. *1794*

Florida (Miami; Little Havana). Cuban Americans. Social customs. 1959-80's. *1447*

Florida (New Smyrna). Buildings. Pellicer, Francisco. Peso de Burgo, José "Pepino". 1780-1831. *1226*

Florida (Newnansville). Charlotte Harbor Railroad. Economic Development. Rural Settlements. ca 1825-87. *2658*

Florida (Norris Cut). Toponymy. Waterways. 1822-1905. *3207*

Florida, northern. Alachua Trail. Georgia. 17c-20c. *3333*

Florida (Okeechobee County). Hancock, Henry Hudson. Judges. 1901-51. *3618*

Florida (Orlando). Agriculture. Corporations. Dart and Kraft Company. Exhibits and Expositions. Walt Disney World (Experimental Prototype Community of Tomorrow). 1983. *2732*

Florida (Palm Beach). Architecture. Mizner, Addison. 1918-31. *1183*

—. Architecture. Mizner, Addison. Singer, Paris. 20c. *1256*

—. Elites. Law. Preservation. 1920's. 1960's-70's. *1314*

Florida (Palm Beach; Breakers Pier). Ports. 1885-1930. *1176*

Florida (Pasco County). Catholic Church. Settlement. 1881-1960's. *2944*

Florida (Pasco, Pinellas counties). Agriculture. Personal narratives. Starkey, J. B., Sr. (family). Umberton Ranch. 1980. *2880*

Florida (Pensacola). Assimilation. Creek Indians. Indians. 1832-70. *3952*

—. Blacks. 1896-1920's. *2552*

—. City Government. Progressive era. Prostitution. Social Change. 1900-40. *626*

—. Excavations. Houses. Panton, William. 1796-1848. *1381*

—. Manuscripts. West Florida, University of (library). 1967-73. *298*

—. Naval Air Forces. Urbanization. 1900-45. *3861*

—. Yellow fever. 19c. *2157*

Florida (Pinellas County). Agriculture. Lee, Margaret Elizabeth Daniel. Personal Narratives. 1850-1963. *2857*

Florida (Polk County). Political Leadership. Trammell, John W. 1882-1904. *3657*

Florida (Ruskin). Dickman, A. P. (family). Miller, George McAnelly. Socialism. Utopias. 1900-67. *3752*

Florida (St. Augustine). Architecture. Cathedrals. Catholic Church. 1784-1966. *1197*

—. Architecture. Neoclassicism. 1775-99. *1275*

—. Architecture. Urbanization. 1565-1821. *1297*

—. Decorative arts. Frontier and Pioneer Life. Ximenez-Fatio house. 1798-1970's. *1238*

—. Fiction, historical. 16c-20c. *956*

—. Flagler, Henry Morrison. Hotel Ponce de Leon. Maybeck, Bernard. Tiffany, Louis. 1885-1974. *1228*

—. Flagler, Henry Morrison. Model Land Company. Real Estate Business. 1885-1920's. *2641*

—. Fort Matanzas National Monument. Monuments. 1820-1965. *8*

—. Great Britain. Indians. Spanish. Trade. 1700-83. *3965*

—. Souvenirs. 1840-1920. *1520*

—. Tolomato Cemetery. 1704-1876. *545*

Florida (St. Augustine; City Gate). Historical Sites and Parks. 1704-1966. *1349*

—. Historical Sites and Parks. 1903-07. 1963-72. *1355*

Florida (St. Petersburg). Desegregation. Swimming. 1930's-59. *3734*

—. Cabell, James Branch. Literature. Virginia (Richmond). 1898-1912. *949*

—. Literary characters. Novels. Women. 1898-1913. *1046*

Glasgow, Ellen *(Barren Ground)*. Middle classes. Novels. Social history. Virginia. 1894-1925. *588*

Glass and Glassmaking. New Jersey (Salem). Pennsylvania (Manheim). Stiegel, William. Virginia (Jamestown). Wistar, Casper. 18c. *3016*

Glass, Carter. Cannon, James, Jr. Methodist Church. Political Corruption. Virginia. 1909-34. *2409*

—. Political Campaigns (presidential, senatorial). Virginia. 1936. *3663*

Glen, James. Cherokee Indians. Fort Loudoun. Indians. Tennessee. 1743-56. *4100*

Godchaux, Leon. Business. Louisiana (New Orleans). 19c. *3147*

Godwin, Gail. Authors. Women. 1950's-83. *1017*

Gold. *See also* Money.

—. Black Friday. Gould, Jay. Monetary Systems. New York. 1869-70. *2654*

Gold mines and mining. North Carolina (Cabarrus County). Reed Gold Mine. 1790-1930's. *3022*

Gold Rushes. Appalachia. Economic Development. 1828. *2659*

—. Oklahoma (Wichita Mountains). 1889-1918. *2982*

Goldfield, David R. Agriculture. Economic Conditions. Social Conditions. Urbanization. 1607-1980. *3010*

—. Browne, Gary Lawson. Brownell, Blaine A. Cities (review article). Ridgeway, Whitman H. 1789-1861. *193*

—. Brownell, Blaine A. Goldin, Claudia Dale. Harris, Carl V. Rabinowitz, Howard N. Urbanization (review article). Watts, Eugene J. 1820-1980. *2950*

Goldin, Claudia Dale. Brownell, Blaine A. Goldfield, David R. Harris, Carl V. Rabinowitz, Howard N. Urbanization (review article). Watts, Eugene J. 1820-1980. *2950*

Goldsmith's (department store). Ottenheimer, Ike. Retail Trade. Tennessee (Memphis). 1900-63. *2643*

*Gone with the Wind* (film). Blacks. NAACP. Slaves. Stereotypes. 1939-40. *479*

—. Films. Lambert, Gavin (review article). 1939. 1973. *493*

—. Films. Public Opinion. 1939-80. *431*

Gonzales, John Edmond. Editors and Editing. *Journal of Mississippi History*. McCain, William D. Mississippi. 1939-79. *1531*

Goodnight, Charles. Explorers. Indians. Ranches. Settlement. Texas (Palo Duro Canyon). 1541-1900. *3228*

Goodwin, William A. R. Historical Sites and Parks. Rockefeller, John D., Jr. Virginia (Williamsburg). 1926-80. *178*

Goodyear Tire and Rubber Company. Alabama (Gadsden). House, John D. Rubber. United Rubber Workers. 1941. *3423*

Gordon, Caroline. Letters. Literary Criticism. O'Connor, Flannery *(Wise Blood)*. 1951-64. *867*

Gordon, David. Arts and Crafts. Furniture and Furnishings. Gordon, James. South Carolina (Black Mingo). 1815-75. *1428*

Gordon, James. Arts and Crafts. Furniture and Furnishings. Gordon, David. South Carolina (Black Mingo). 1815-75. *1428*

Gordon, John. Church of England. Clergy. Maryland (Talbot County). St. Michael's Parish. 1749-90. *2466*

Gordon, Kate. Louisiana. Suffrage. Women. 1896-1918. *3587*

Gospel music. Columbia Records Company. Deal family. Music. North Carolina. 1927-29. *885*

—. Fundamentalism. Music. Texas. Whites. 1930's. *2401*

—. Georgia, southern. Protestant churches. Singing. 1873-1978. *1649*

—. Mississippi. Music. Values. 1890-1978. *3212*

—. Music. Peck, Emory Speer. 1893-1975. *1781*

Gothic Revival Style. Architecture. Churches. Holy Trinity Episcopal Church. Restorations. Tennessee (Nashville). 1840's-1970's. *1300*

—. Architecture. Davis, Alexander Jackson. Drawings. Virginia (Lexington). Virginia Military Institute. 1848-1940's. *1273*

—. Architecture. Episcopal Church, Protestant. Upjohn, Richard. Wills, Frank. 1835-60. *1319*

—. Architecture. Jacob, Thomas Prather. Kentucky (Louisville). Wight, Peter Bonnett. 1866-92. *1253*

—. Churches. Delaware (Wilmington). Episcopal Church, Protestant. Methodist Church. 1850-90. *766*

Gottschalk, Louis M. Gálvez, Bernardo de. Historic New Orleans Collection. Louisiana (New Orleans). Manuscripts. 18c-20c. *28*

Goucher College. Careers. Education. Goucher, John F. Maryland (Baltimore). Social work. Women. 1892-1910. *1934*

Goucher, John F. Careers. Education. Goucher College. Maryland (Baltimore). Social work. Women. 1892-1910. *1934*

Gould, Jay. Black Friday. Gold. Monetary Systems. New York. 1869-70. *2654*

—. Louisiana, northern. Mergers. Railroads. Texas and Pacific Railroad. 1870-1914. *3050*

Government. *See also* City Government; Colonial Government; Constitutions; County Government; Federal Government; Local Government; Political Science; Politics; Provincial Government; Public Employees; State Government.

—. Agrarianism. Authors. Science and Society. 1930-80. *2768*

—. Agriculture. Blacks. Education. Productivity. 1945-64. *2739*

—. Archives. Bibliographies. Mississippi Department of Archives and History. 1975. *292*

—. Cherokee Indians. 1730-1906. *3881*

—. Indian Territory. Indians. Okmulgee Constitution. Self-determination. 1870-76. *4068*

—. Long, Huey P. Louisiana. Personal Narratives. Peyton, Rupert. 1917-35. *3740*

—. Madison, James. Political Theory. Virginia. 1774-1817. *3479*

—. Maryland (Baltimore). Political Participation. Poor. 1969-70. *3357*

Government Employees. *See* Public Employees.

Government Enterprise. Chesapeake Bay. Maryland. Oyster industry. Virginia. -1973. *2535*

Government regulation. Agriculture. Chemical Industry. Food Adulteration and Inspection. Mississippi State Chemical Laboratory. 1882-1979. *2626*

—. Agriculture. Maryland (Baltimore). 1750-1820. *2921*

—. Chain stores. Kentucky. Taxation. 1925-45. *3761*

Governors. Alabama. Memoirs. Race Relations. 1923-55. *3548*

—. Arkansas. Constitutions, state. Executive Power. 1819-1970's. *3673*

—. Aycock, Charles Brantley. Education. North Carolina. Racism. 1895-1912. *3757*

—. Blacks. Carpetbaggers. Louisiana. Pinchback, Pinckney B. S. 1862-90. *3811*

—. Civil War. Military General Staff. Reconstruction. Smith, William "Extra Billy". Virginia Infantry, 49th. 1797-1887. *3506*

—. Crothers, Austin Lane. Maryland. Progressivism. 1904-12. *3513*

—. Floyd, John. Medicine (practice of). Virginia. 1802-36. *2115*

—. Folklore. North Carolina. South Carolina. 1838-1982. *3808*

—. Inaugural addresses. Louisiana. Rhetoric. State Legislatures. 1813-1973. *3756*

—. Intergovernmental relations. State Legislatures. Tennessee. 1796-1980. *3686*

—. Louisiana. Political power. State Government. 1699-1974. *3554*

—. Mississippi. Political Leadership. State Legislatures. Wright, Fielding. 1927-38. *3632*

—. State Government. Texas. 1876-1965. *3545*

Governor's Mansion. Architecture. Cluskey, Charles B. Georgia (Augusta). Greek Revival Style. Medical College of Georgia. 1820's-30's. *1201*

Governor's Palace. Architecture. Virginia (Williamsburg). 1705-1934. *1385*

Graduate schools. Blacks. Desegregation. Discrimination, Educational. Lawsuits. North Carolina. Professional education. 1930-51. *1974*

Grady, Henry. Atlanta Chamber of Commerce. Georgia. Industrialization. Urbanization. 1920's. *2972*

Graham, Barney. Coal Mines and Mining. Davidson-Wilder Strike of 1932. Strikes. Tennessee, east. United Mine Workers of America. 1932-33. *2886*

Graham, Billy. Baptists. Evangelism. Florida. 1936-79. *2269*

Graham, Hugh D. Bartley, Numan V. Political Parties (review article). Seagull, Louis M. 1944-70's. *3743*

Grambling State University. Adams, Charles P. Blacks. Colleges and Universities. Louisiana. 1896-1928. *1977*

—. Blalock, Alice Grundy. College teachers. Louisiana. ca 1920-70. *1976*

Gramsci, Antonio. Behavior. Genovese, Eugene D. Hegemony (concept). Slavery. 1812-65. *405*

Granade, John Adam. Appalachia. Hymns. Methodist Church. Revivals. 1800-07. *2320*

Grand Ole Opry. Bandy, Henry L. Kentucky (Allen County). Musicians. 1890's-1940's. *1507*

Grange. Agricultural Policy. American Farm Bureau Federation. National Farmers' Union. 1946-76. *2826*

—. Cherokee Indians. Farmers. Indian Territory. 1870's. *4027*

Grant, James. Cherokee Indians. Diaries. Indian Wars. Monypenny, Alexander. South Carolina. 1761. *4146*

—. Cherokee Indians. Indian Wars. Powder horns. Scrimshaw. 1761. 1976. *4021*

Grantham, Dewey W. (review article). O'Brien, Michael. 1870-1979. *278*

Grave robbers. Anatomy. Davis, John A. G. Medical education. Virginia. ca 1845-65. *2110*

Graves. *See also* Burials; Tombstones.

—. Faubus, Orval. Hamer, Fanny Lou. Horton, James Edwin. Kennedy, John F. Personal Narratives. Scottsboro Boys. 1930's-70's. *410*

Graves, Bibb. Alabama. Democratic Party. Elections, gubernatorial. Folsom, James E. Sparks, Chauncey. 1926-50. *3482*

Graves, James Robinson. Baptists. Landmarks. Whitsitt Controversy. 1850-1950. *2411*

—. Baptists. Newspapers. *Tennessee Baptist*. 1820-93. *2457*

—. Baptists, Southern. Mullins, Edgar Young. Theology. 1840-1928. *2412*

Graves, James Robinson *(Little Seraph)*. Baptists (Southern). Hymnals. 1850-75. *2392*

Gray, Clarence. Folk Medicine. West Virginia. 1978. *2131*

Gray, Richard (review article). Literature. 20c. *930*

Gray, William Crane. Episcopal Church, Protestant. Florida. Indian-White Relations. Missions and Missionaries. Seminole Indians. 1893-1914. *3895*

Grazing. Agricultural Reform. Alabama. 19c. *2751*

Great Awakening. Bordley, Stephen. Church of England. Letters. Maryland. Whitefield, George. 1730-40. *2245*

—. Education. Georgia (Savannah). Orphans. Whitefield, George. 1738-71. *1928*

Great Britain. *See also* Ireland; Scotland.

—. Agriculture. American Revolution. Strickland, William. 1794-95. *2735*

—. Aitken, George Atherton. Libraries. Literature. Texas, University of (Austin). 18c. 20c. *291*

—. Alabama Indians. Bienville, Jean-Baptiste de. Fort Louis. France. Indian-White Relations. 1703-15. *4000*

—. Alexander Brown and Sons. Cotton. International Trade. 1820-60. *2749*

—. American Revolution. Cherokee Indians. Dragging Canoe (man). 1740-92. *3959*

—. Anticlericalism. Church of England. Virginia. ca 1635-1783. *2505*

—. Appalachia. Somervell, D. C. Toynbee, Arnold J. *(Study of History)*. 20c. *24*

—. Astor, Nancy Langhorne. House of Commons. Virginia. Women. 1897-1964. *605*

—. Attakullakulla. Cherokee Indians. Diplomacy. Indians. 1730-80. *4014*

—. Attitudes. Race relations. Travelers. ca 1865-1914. *752*

—. Baptists. USA. 1633-1900. *2415*

—. Cherokee Indians. Diplomacy. France. Ostenaco. 1700-80. *3961*

—. Cities. Kentucky. Toponymy. 18c-1974. *3249*

—. Cotton. India. Japan. 1870-1939. *3169*

—. Cotton. International Trade. 1860's-1900. *2881*

—. Cotton. Plantations. Slavery. 17c-19c. *2753*

—. Creek Indians. Florida. Indian Wars. War of 1812. 1811-16. *4102*

—. Dodson, John George. Slavery. Travel (accounts). 1853-54. *750*

—. Florida (St. Augustine). Indians. Spanish. Trade. 1700-83. *3965*

—. France. International Trade. Monopolies. North America. Price, Jacob (review article). Tobacco. 17c-18c. *2716*

—. Indian Wars. Smith, John. Thorpe, George. Virginia Massacre (1622). 1607-37. *4114*

—. International trade. Maryland. Statistics. Virginia. 1740-91. *2628*

—. Kentucky. Travel (accounts). 1780's. *736*

—. Letters. Politics. South Carolina. Travel. Trelawny, Edward John. 1833-35. *732*

—. Minstrelsy. Theater. USA. 18c-19c. *781*

—. Poll books. Virginia (Cumberland, Prince George counties). Voting and Voting Behavior. 19c. *3502*

Great Plains. *See also* Midwest; North Central States.

—. Power Resources. 1859-1940. *2546*

# H

Harwell, Richard (review article). Films. Letters. Mitchell, Margaret *(Gone with the Wind)*. Novels. 1936-49. *1023*

Hast, Louis H. German Americans. Kentucky (Louisville). Music. 1848-90. *798*

Haven, Gilbert. Blacks. Georgia (Atlanta). Protestant Churches. Segregation. 1865-1906. *2397*

Havis, Ferdinand. Arkansas (Jefferson County). Blacks. Political Leadership. Republican Party. 1846-1918. *3677*

Hawkins, Benjamin. Downs, Lavinia. Georgia. Indians.. Marriage. Petersen, Karsten. 1796-1816. *3990*

Hawkins, Virgil Darnell. Courts. Discrimination. Florida. Legal education. 1949-76. *1982*

Haycraft, Jesse Robert. Kentucky (Grayson County). Music. 1935-76. *1459*

Hayes, Rutherford B. Elections (presidential). Florida. Spoils system. State politics. Wallace, Lew. 1876-78. *3800*

Haygood, Laura A. China. Feminism. Methodist Episcopal Church (South). Missions and Missionaries. 1884-1900. *2402*

Hayne, Paul Hamilton. *Atlantic Monthly.* Howells, William Dean. Literary Criticism. 1871-81. *978*

—. *Critic.* Periodicals. Thompson, James Maurice. 19c. *1063*

Hayne, Paul Hamilton (obituary). Georgia. Poetry. 1886. *937*

Heade, Martin Johnson. Florida. Landscape Painting. 1883-1904. *827*

Health. Appalachia. Coal Mines and Mining. *Gateway Coal Company v. United Mine Workers of America* (US, 1974). Labor Law. Safety. 1935-74. *3395*

—. Appalachia, southern. Attitudes. Haiti. 1978-79. *2117*

—. Children. Diseases. Farms. Mortality. 1900-50. *2112*

—. Economic development. Regionalism. 1975. *2550*

Health, Education, and Welfare Department. Education. Equal opportunity. Justice Department. 1968-74. *2080*

Health Insurance. *See also* Insurance.

—. Arkansas (Little Rock). Medical Care. Trinity Hospital. 1923-54. *2645*

Health services. Education. Minorities. Radicals and Radicalism. Southern Conference Education Fund. 1946-76. *1832*

Hearon, Cleo. Chicago, University of. Dodd, William E. Letters. Mississippi. 1910. *1867*

Heflin, James Thomas. Alabama. Senate. ca 1890's-1930. *3796*

Hegel, Georg. Cash, Wilbur J. *(Mind of the South).* Historiography. 19c-20c. *240*

Hegemony (concept). Behavior. Genovese, Eugene D. Gramsci, Antonio. Slavery. 1812-65. *405*

Heiman, Adolphus. Architecture. College Building. Tennessee (Nashville). 1836-1974. *1299*

—. Architecture. Tennessee (Nashville). 1837-62. *1318*

Hemings, Sally. Illegitimacy. Jefferson, Thomas. 1770's-1979. *548*

—. Jefferson, Thomas (descendants). Miscegenation. Virginia. ca 1780-1976. *512*

Hemingway, Ernest. Death and Dying. Novels. Percy, Walker. 20c. *789*

—. Family. Faulkner, William. Middle Classes. World view. 1900-50. *1024*

—. Faulkner, William. Language. Literature. Twain, Mark. 19c-1950's. *1026*

Hemingway, William. Local Government. Mississippi, University of. 1901-37. *3717*

Henderson, C. C. Louisiana (Bernice). Railroads. 1899-1910. *2897*

Henderson, Elbert Calvin (Bert). Alabama. Poets. 1920's-74. *843*

Henderson, Fletcher. Blacks. Georgia (Cuthbert). Howard Normal School. 1857-1943. *1986*

—. Georgia. Jazz. Music. Orchestras. 1897-1952. *1731*

Henderson, William K. Federal Regulation. Louisiana (Shreveport). Radio. 1925-35. *1624*

Henkel Square. German Americans. Letters. Log cabins. Restorations. Texas (Round Top). 1840's-83. *1405*

Hennessey affair. Italian Americans. Louisiana (New Orleans). Lynching. 1880-1920. *577*

Henry, Aaron. Blacks. Civil rights. Mississippi. Personal Narratives. 1922-63. *378*

Henry, Bill. Daily Life. Personal Narratives. Stewart, Alex. Tennessee (East; Hancock County). 1891-1981. *586*

Henry, Patrick. Militia (officers). Social Classes. State Government. Virginia. 1784-86. *3852*

Hensley, George Went. Appalachia, southern. Pentecostal Holiness Church. Snake handlers. 1909-73. *2337*

Henson, Mike *(Ransack)*. Appalachia. Novels (review article). Welch, Jack *(Life at an Early Age)*. 1981. *1039*

Heraldry. Cabildo (building). Cardelli, Pietro. Louisiana (New Orleans). Sculpture. 1821. *1391*

—. Maryhelp Abbey. North Carolina. 1876-1983. *1161*

Herbert, Henry. Church of England. Clergy. Georgia. 1732-33. *2359*

Herbs. Folk medicine. Tennessee. 19c. *2116*

—. Medicine (practice of). Rogers, Sod. Tennessee (Tipton County). 1931-82. *1562*

Herdsmen. Livestock. ca 1830-80. *2785*

Heritage of Manatee's Environment. Buildings. Florida (Manatee Village). Preservation. 1859-89. 1974-76. *1283*

Heritage Plaza. Georgia (Albany). Restorations. Thronateeska Heritage Foundation. 1974-79. *1266*

Hermann, Janet Sharp (review article). Blacks. Davis Bend (plantation). Mississippi. Utopias. ca 1850-81. *2844*

Hermitage. Jackson, Andrew. Jackson, Rachel. Tennessee (Nashville). Tombstones. 1828-1976. *1166*

Hermits. Virginia (White Top Mountain). Waters, Wilburn. 1832-75. *514*

Heroes. Adams, Henry Brooks. James, Henry. Literature. National Characteristics. 1865-1930. *452*

—. American Revolution. Humor. Porgy (character). Simms, William Gilmore. 1775-83. 1835-55. *846*

—. Appalachia. Jefferson, Thomas. Literature. Thoreau, Henry David. 1977. *710*

—. Music. Popular Culture. Presley, Elvis. Rock music. 1955-77. *1566*

*Herold et al. v. Parish Board of School Directors et al.* (Louisiana, 1914). Louisiana. Religion in the Public Schools. Supreme courts (state). 1913-15. *3712*

Herty, Charles Holmes. Georgia. Newsprint. Pine trees. Scientific Experiments and Research. Turpentine. 1901-04. 1930-39. *2561*

—. Newsprint. Paper mills. Pine trees. Scientific Experiments and Research. 1927-40. *3068*

Hertzog, Carl. Cisneros, Jose. Culture. Lea, Tom. Sonnichsen, C. L. Sullivan, Maud. Texas (El Paso). 1920's-75. *1000*

Hevener, John W. Coal Mines and Mining. Conway, Mimi. Labor (review article). Textile Industry. 1931-79. *3454*

Hewitt, John. Florida (Flagler County). Sawmills. 17c-20c. *3014*

Heyburn, Weldon B. Political Attitudes. Sectionalism. Senate. 1910. *3779*

Higgins, Pattillo. Lucas, Anthony F. Oil Industry and Trade. Spindletop Oil Rush. Texas (Beaumont). 1901-30's. *3119*

High, Mrs. Joseph M. Art Galleries and Museums. Georgia (Atlanta). High Museum of Art. Woodruff, Robert W. 1926-83. *1117*

High Museum of Art. Art Galleries and Museums. Georgia (Atlanta). High, Mrs. Joseph M. Woodruff, Robert W. 1926-83. *1117*

High Schools. *See also* Evening and Continuation Schools; Junior High Schools; Secondary Education

—. Arkansas (Searcy). Galloway College. Methodist Church (Southern). 1889-1907. *1842*

—. Attitudes. Georgia. Integration. Students. 1965. 1980. *2065*

—. Blacks. District of Columbia. Dunbar High School. 1870-1955. *2077*

—. Blacks. Football. Race Relations. 1972-76. *2042*

—. Blacks. George Washington Carver Comprehensive High School. Georgia (Atlanta). 1970's. *2032*

—. Blacks. Occupations. Whites. 1970's. *3429*

—. Religiosity. Students. Texas, northeastern. 1964-79. *2257*

Higher Education. *See also* Colleges and Universities; Professional Education; Technical Education.

—. Alabama. Florence University for Women. Women. 1890-1910. *1826*

—. Alabama (Florence). Boosterism. Southern Female University. 1886-1909. *1829*

—. Alston, Mary Niven. Blacks. Cooper, Anna Haywood. Episcopal Church, Protestant. Robertson, Isabella Gibson. Women. 1875-1981. *1803*

—. Appalachia. Educational reform. 1970's. *1843*

—. Attitudes. Blacks. Segregation. Virginia. 1980. *2066*

—. Baptists, Southern. Carey, William. Missions and Missionaries. 1826-1976. *2511*

—. Bennett College. Blacks. Georgia (Atlanta). North Carolina (Greensboro). Spelman College. Women. 1970's. *2005*

—. Berea College. Blacks. Integration. Kentucky. 1858-1908. *2045*

—. Blacks. Cocking, Walter D. Georgia. Talmadge, Eugene. 1937-43. *1981*

—. Blacks. Mississippi. 1865-1920. *2020*

—. Brewer, Fisk Parsons. Integration. South Carolina, University of. 1873-76. *1954*

—. Classics. Students. 1693-1924. *1790*

—. Curricula. History teaching. West Virginia. 1969-77. *126*

—. Dabney, Virginius. Virginia, University of (review article). 1819-1981. *1879*

—. Educational policy. State Politics. West Virginia. 1863-1969. *1825*

—. Liberal arts. Reform. 1850-60. *1878*

—. Louisiana (Caldwell Parish). 1838-79. *1884*

—. Tennessee (Brownsville). West Tennessee Baptist Female College. Women. 1850-1910. *1917*

Higher Education (review article). Nall, Kline A. Rushing, Jane G. Southern Methodist University. Texas Tech University. Thomas, Mary. 1920-75. *1949*

Highlander Folk School. Education. Horton, Myles. Political activism. Tennessee. 1930-80. *1830*

Highlander Research and Education Center. Civil rights. Labor Reform. Schools. Tennessee. 1932-82. *1952*

Highway Engineering. *See also* Roads.

—. Appalachia. Civil War. West Virginia. Weston and Gauley Bridge Turnpike. 1811-1922. *3018*

—. Armies. Indian Territory. 1826-80. *3848*

—. Delaware. DuPont, Thomas Coleman. 1900-35. *3087*

Highways. Alabama. Historical markers. 1765-1978. *162*

—. Alabama. Historical markers. 1820-1978. *161*

—. Bibliographies. Oklahoma. Public Records. 1824-1981. *2939*

—. Cherokee Indians. Georgia. Indian-White Relations. Taverns. Tennessee. 1800-25. *3956*

Hilgard, Eugene. Geology. Lyell, Charles. Mississippi. 1699-1876. *3199*

Hill, Samuel S., Jr. Historiography. Loveland, Anne C. Religion (review article). Wilson, Charles Reagan. 1941-81. *2206*

Hill, Walter B. Academic Freedom. Georgia, University of. 1899-1905. *1837*

—. Educational Administration. Georgia, University of. 1897-1901. *1838*

Hindus, Michael Stephen. Finkelman, Paul. Law (review article). Slavery. 1767-1878. *3697*

Hines, John Leonard. Armies. Military General Staff. West Virginia. 1891-1932. *3864*

Hispanic Americans. Architecture. Ranching. Texas, south. 1750-1900. *1336*

Historians. Alabama. Beverly, John William. Blacks. 1901-24. *396*

—. Alabama. Howard, Milo Barrett, Jr. (obituary). 1933-81. *2*

—. Alabama Historical Association (28th annual meeting). 1975. *110*

—. *Alabama Review.* Bibliographies. Periodicals. 1840's-1975. *209*

—. Alabama (Tuscaloosa). Bibliographies. 1816-1973. *91*

—. Archives. Durrett, Reuben Thomas. Kentucky. 1880-1913. *41*

—. Arkansas. Brough, Charles Hillman. 1890-1915. *198*

—. Authors. North Carolina. Obituaries. Reporters and Reporting. 1980-81. *1010*

—. Ballenger, Tom Lee. Cherokee Indians. Indians. Oklahoma. 1905-82. *3*

—. Baptists. Clergy. Georgia. King, Spencer B., Jr. King, Spencer B., Sr. Mercer University. 1880-1973. *2341*

—. Baptists. Georgia. King, Spencer Bidwell, Jr. (obituary). 1930's-77. *2283*

—. Bass, Henry B. Business. Oklahoma (Enid). Public services. 20c. *668*

—. Bibliographies. Bridwell, Margaret Morris. Kentucky. 1940's-73. *121*

—. Bibliographies. Coleman, Kenneth. Georgia, University of. 1941-76. *207*

—. Bolton, Herbert Eugene. Castañeda, Carlos Eduardo. Texas. 1921-36. *7*

—. Castañeda, Carlos Eduardo. Mexican Americans. Texas. 1896-1927. *6*

—. Choctaw Indians. Oklahoma. Wright, Muriel Hazel. 1889-1974. *3886*

—. Civil War. Mississippi, University of. Wiley, Bell Irvin (obituary). ca 1926-80. *274*

—. Civil War. Wiley, Bell Irvin (obituary). ca 1930-80. *111*

—. Colleges and Universities. Coulter, Ellis Merton (obituary). Georgia, University of. ca 1930's-81. *262*

—. Coulter, Ellis Merton (obituary). *Georgia Historical Quarterly*. Periodicals. 1890-1981. *281*

—. Dabbs, James McBride. Protestantism. Race Relations. 1896-1970. *446*

—. Davis, Edwin Adams. Editors and Editing. *Louisiana History*. 1958-73. *326*

—. Dykeman, Wilma (review article). Tennessee. 18c-1976. *721*

—. Eaton, Clement. Travel accounts. 1935-53. *277*

—. Editors and Editing. Rachal, William Munford Ellis (obituary). Virginia Historical Society. 1910-80. *355*

—. Foreman, Carolyn Thomas. Foreman, Grant. Oklahoma. 1897-1967. *68*

—. Frontier and Pioneer Life. Red, William Stuart. Religion. Texas. 1875-1933. *2319*

—. Garrison, George Pierce. Texas, University of (Austin). 1884-1910. *113*

—. Intellectuals. Phillips, Ulrich B. 1877-1934. *2636*

—. Johnson, Guion Griffis. Johnson, Guy B. Personal Narratives. Social conditions. 1920-81. *165*

—. Methodology. Phillips, Ulrich B. (*History of. 1830-60. 1908.* 313

—. Mississippi Historical Society. Perry, B. G. Politicians. 1789-1974. *3738*

—. Oklahoma. Shirk, George. 1913-77. *691*

—. Personal Narratives. Richardson, Rupert N. Texas. 1920's-81. *13*

—. South Carolina Historical Society. Waring, Joseph Ioor (obituary). 1897-1977. *620*

—. Summers, Lewis Preston. Virginia (Washington County). 1890-1943. *23*

—. Texas State Historical Association. 1938-46. *260*

Historic American Building Survey. Georgia (Savannah River area). O'Kain, Dennis. Photographs. Richard B. Russell Dam. 1793-1927. *1400*

Historic Annapolis, Inc. Historical Sites and Parks. Law. Maryland (Annapolis). Zoning. 1649-1845. 1952-1969. *3171*

Historic Cobbham Foundation. Cobb-Hill Street Community Association. Georgia (Athens). Neighborhoods. Preservation. 1834-19. *1358*

Historic Columbus Foundation. Buildings. Georgia. Restorations. 1966-78. *1270*

Historic Districts. Art Deco. Florida (Miami Beach). Restorations. ca 1925-81. *1160*

Historic New Orleans Collection. Gálvez, Bernardo de. Gottschalk, Louis M. Louisiana (New Orleans). Manuscripts. 18c-20c. *28*

Historic Oakland Cemetery, Inc. Architecture. Georgia (Atlanta). Oakland Cemetery. Preservation. 1850-1979. *1366*

Historic Preservation of Shreveport Committee. Louisiana. Preservation. 1972-78. *1364*

Historic Preservation Office. Georgia. 1969-79. *200*

Historic Savannah Foundation. Architecture. Education. Georgia (Savannah). Preservation. 1955-79. *1332*

—. Georgia (Savannah). Historical Sites and Parks. Preservation. 18c-19c. 1954-79. *1282*

Historical Association of Alabama (27th annual meeting). Alabama. 1974. *43*

Historical markers. Alabama. Highways. 1765-1978. *162*

—. Alabama. Highways. 1820-1978. *161*

—. County Governments. Louisiana (Claiborne Parish; Russellville). Sesquicentennial Celebrations. 1829-36. 1979. *3353*

Historical Sites and Parks. *See also* Restorations.

—. Architecture. Georgia. Macon Heritage Foundation. Preservation. 1975-79. *1394*

—. Architecture. Georgia. Preservation. Thomasville Landmarks, Inc. 1964-79. *106*

—. Architecture. Georgia (Macon). Middle Georgia Historical Society, Inc. Preservation. 1964-79. *208*

—. Buildings. Log construction. Tennessee (Bledsoe's Lick, Castalian Springs). Wynnewood (estate). 1828-1973. *1216*

—. Coordinating and Development Council of Northwest Louisiana. Louisiana. Preservation. 1975-78. *149*

—. Cunningham, Ann Pamela. Mount Vernon Ladies' Association. Virginia. 1816-75. *1174*

—. Dams. Maryland (Lake Roland). Robert E. Lee Park. Water supply. 1858-1978. *3046*

—. Davis, John. Devon Farm. Tennessee (Davidson, Williamson counties). 1795-1975. *1202*

—. Deery, William. Irish Americans. Tennessee (Blountville). Trading Posts. 1795-1970's. *1192*

—. Delaware (New Castle). 1790. *776*

—. Education. Georgia Historical Commission. Preservation. 1951-73. *122*

—. Florida (St. Augustine; City Gate). 1704-1966. *1276*

—. Florida (St. Augustine; City Gate). 1903-07. 1963-72. *1355*

—. Georgia. Legislation. Preservation. 1889-1979. *251*

—. Georgia (Savannah). Historic Savannah Foundation. Preservation. 18c-19c. 1954-79. *1282*

—. Goodwin, William A. R. Rockefeller, John D., Jr. Virginia (Williamsburg). 1926-80. *178*

—. Historic Annapolis, Inc. Law. Maryland (Annapolis). Zoning. 1649-1845. 1952-1969. *3171*

—. Houses. Texas (Odessa). White-Pool House. 1887-1978. *1260*

—. James Monroe Museum and Memorial Library. Law. Monroe, James. Virginia (Fredericksburg). 1786-1973. *312*

—. Kentucky (Elizabethtown). Lincoln, Thomas. Log cabins. Restorations. Thomas, Hardin. 1790. 1974. *1292*

—. Louisiana. National Trust for Historic Preservation. Preservation. 1978. *216*

—. Louisiana Historic Preservation Office. Preservation. 1971-78. *142*

—. North Carolina (Halifax). Restorations. 1759-1976. *3329*

—. North Carolina (New Bern). Restorations. Tryon Palace. 1767-70. 1975. *1236*

Historical Societies. Arkansas. Genealogy. 1977-78. *325*

—. Arkansas Historical Association (34th annual meeting). 1975. *27*

—. Baptists. Periodicals. 1950's-70's. *2256*

—. Maryland Historical Society. Oral history. 1938-75. *183*

—. Mississippi Historical Society (annual meeting). 1975. *79*

—. North Carolina Literary and Historical Association. 1900-75. *166*

—. Public Opinion. Tennesseans. Values. 1931. 1976. *719*

Historical Society of Pennsylvania. Collections. Delaware. Economic History. 1727-1897. 1974. *2642*

Historicism. Fiction. Welty, Eudora. 1800-30. 20c. *851*

Historiography. *See also* Historians; Quantitative Methods.

—. 17c-20c. *315*

—. 1865-1979. *70*

—. 19c. 1970's. *268*

—. Agriculture. Plantations. Urbanization. 20c. *2584*

—. Appalachia. 1930's-70's. *100*

—. Archaeology. Holden, William Curry (obituary). Texas Tech University. 1920's-78. *234*

—. Bartley, Buddy. Blacks. Bolden, Buddy. Jazz. Louisiana (New Orleans). Musicians. ca 1895. *1041*

—. Bibliographies. Coulter, Ellis Merton. Georgia. 1912-77. *317*

—. Bibliographies. Delaware. 17c-1978. *137*

—. Bibliographies. Delaware. 1971-72. *233*

—. Bibliographies. Modernization. 19c. *239*

—. Bicentennial Celebrations. Frantz, Joe B. (*Texas: A Bicentennial History*). Texas. 1974-76. *112*

—. Bienville, Sieur de. Leftwich, George J. Mississippi (Tombigbee River area: Cotton Gin Port, Gaines' Trace). 1729-40. 1903-80. *3214*

—. Blacks. Christian, Marcus B. Dillard University. Federal Writers' Project. Louisiana. Work Progress Administration. 1930's-79. *380*

—. Blacks. Documents. Editors and Editing. Washington, Booker T. 1967. *139*

—. Blacks. Economic development. 1850's-20c. *2657*

—. Blacks. Louisiana (New Orleans). Political Leadership. Reconstruction. ca 1800-75. *3746*

—. Blacks. Quarles, Benjamin. 18c-19c. 1948-79. *388*

—. Cash, Wilbur J. Social change. 1830-1940. *459*

—. Cash, Wilbur J. (*Mind of the South*). Hegel, Georg. 19c-20c. *240*

—. Catton, Bruce. Civil War. Editors and Editing. 1954-78. *163*

—. Caudill, Harry M. Collins, Richard H. Kentucky (review article). 19c-20c. *141*

—. Cities. Local history. Tennessee (Memphis). 1912. 1975. *3036*

—. Civil War. Cooke, Alistair. Northerners. Reconstruction. 1860-76. 20c. *275*

—. Class Struggle. Louisiana. Shugg, Roger (review article). 1800-60. 1939-76. *296*

—. Colleges and Universities. Oklahoma State University (History Department). 1894-1983. *1904*

—. Conservatives. Race Relations. 1865-1973. *362*

—. Demagoguery. Long, Huey P. Louisiana. State Government. 1928-73. *3805*

—. deSoto expedition. Novels. Pickett, Albert J. Simms, William Gilmore. 1539-42. 1842-60. *303*

—. Duality. 1970's. *202*

—. DuBois, W. E. B. Phillips, Ulrich B. Slavery. ca 1620-1865. 1896-1940. *398*

—. DuBois, W. E. B. (*Black Reconstruction in America*). Plagiarism. Reconstruction. Wesley, Charles H. (*Negro Labor in the United States*). 1927-35. *386*

—. Economic Conditions. Political Leadership. ca 1865-1979. *2672*

—. Elites. Genovese, Eugene D. North Carolina (Mecklenburg County). Political Leadership. Woodward, C. Vann. 1850-80. *3729*

—. Elliott, Stephen. Episcopal Church, Protestant. 1840-66. *2390*

—. Federal Policy. Public lands. 1810's-70's. *2719*

—. Five Civilized Tribes. Manifest Destiny. Oklahoma. Removals, forced. 19c-20c. *3924*

—. Genovese, Eugene D. Marxism. 1965-72. *400*

—. Genovese, Eugene D. Slavery. 1800-65. 1963-79. *394*

—. Hill, Samuel S., Jr. Loveland, Anne C. Religion (review article). Wilson, Charles Reagan. 1941-81. *2206*

—. Identity. Liberalism. Woodward, C. Vann. 1930-60. *462*

—. Indians (review article). Social Change. 1670-1775. 1970's. *4066*

—. Indian-White Relations. Seminole wars. 1812-58. *4013*

—. Kentucky. ca 1775-1980. *188*

—. Kentucky. ca 1790-1979. *37*

—. Key, V. O., Jr. Martin, Roscoe C. Political attitudes. *Southern Politics* project. 1944-70. *3726*

—. Labor. 19c-20c. *3394*

—. Lee, Robert E. 1865-1940. *427*

—. Liberalism. Populism. Realism. Woodward, C. Vann. 1950-78. *306*

—. Methodology. Oklahoma. 1890-1930's. *254*

—. Militancy. Violence. 1829-1978. *455*

—. Mississippi. 1963-79. *124*

—. Oral history. Tennessee. 1975. *61*

—. Phillips, Ulrich B. Slavery. 1908-34. 1976. *62*

—. Phillips, Ulrich B. (thesis). Pollard, Edward A. (*Lost Cause Regained*). Reconstruction. 1859-72. *454*

—. Phillips, Ulrich B. Woodward, C. Vann. 20c. *255*

—. Politics. 1850's-20c. *11*

—. Politics. Social Conditions. Virginia. 1740-90. *273*

—. Politics (review article). 1945-78. *3491*

—. Race Relations. Washington, Booker T. 1898-1972. *372*

—. Racism. Woodward, C. Vann (*Tom Watson: Agrarian Rebel*). ca 1920-38. *257*

—. Reconstruction. 1865-83. 1973-76. *64*

—. Rhodes, James Ford (*History of the United States from the Compromise of 1850*). Slavery. Wilson, Woodrow. ca 1890-1920. *276*

—. Scholarship. 1920's-30's. *145*

—. Settlement. Texas. 1870's-1970's. *389*

—. Slavery. 1956-74. *66*

—. Texas. 1836-1936. *283*

Historiography (review article). Black Studies. Phillips, Ulrich B. Racism. 1964-74. *367*

History. *See also* particular branches of history, e.g. business history, oral history, psychohistory, science, history of; Ideas, History of.

—. Alabama Historical Association (26th annual meeting). Societies. 1973. *155*

—. Alabama Historical Association (29th annual meeting). 1975-76. *287*

—. American Revolution. Novels. Simms, William Gilmore. 1775-83. 1834-69. *891*

—. Archives. Atlanta Historical Society Archives. Georgia. 1774-1974. *2530*

—. Arkansas Historical Association (35th annual meeting). 1976. *26*

—. Arkansas History Commission. 1906-13. *269*

—. Bibliographies. Dissertations. Literature. Mississippi. 1974. *72*

—. Bibliographies. Dissertations. Literature. Mississippi. Theses. 1976. *78*

—. Bibliographies. Maryland. 17c-1974. *22*

—. Bibliographies. Periodicals. 1600-1982. *350*

—. Bibliographies. Periodicals. 17c-1970's. *343*

—. Bibliographies. Periodicals. 17c-20c. 1980-81. *348*

—. Bibliographies. Periodicals. 18c-20c. 1977-78. *347*

—. Bibliographies. Periodicals. 1972. *351*

—. Bibliographies. Periodicals. 1974. *342*

—. Bibliographies. Periodicals. 1975. *341*

—. Bibliographies. Periodicals. 1977. *344*

—. Bibliographies. Periodicals. 1979. *349*

—. Bibliographies. Periodicals. 1980. *345*

—. Cash, Wilbur J. (*Mind of the South*). 1941. *67*

—. Cather, Willa (*Death Comes for the Archbishop*). Fiction, historical. 1927-47. *1131*

—. Cotten, Fred Rider (obituary). Texas State Historical Association. 1894-1974. *568*

—. Culture. Davenport, F. Garvin, Jr. Literature. Loewenberg, Bert James. Regionalism. 1970-73. *971*

—. Faulkner, William. 20c. *1057*

—. Faulkner, William. Fiction. 1929-42. *819*

—. Georgia. Public Opinion. 1980. *36*

—. Literature. Myths and Symbols. Tate, Allen. 1922-41. *128*

—. Louisiana Historical Association (15th annual meeting). 1973. *236*

—. Louisiana Historical Association (16th annual meeting). 1974. *12*

—. Louisiana Historical Association (17th annual meeting). 1975. *42*

—. Mississippi Historical Society (annual meeting). 1976. *272*

—. *North Carolina Historical Review*. Periodicals. 1924-74. *1610*

—. Southern Historical Association. 1934-35. *246*

History Teaching. Blacks. Haley, Alex (*Roots*). *Roots* (program). 1977. *391*

—. Curricula. Higher education. West Virginia. 1969-77. *126*

—. Freedmen's Bureau. Reconstruction. Secondary Education. Textbooks. 1971-80. *376*

—. Mississippi, University of. Riley, Franklin L. Scholarship. 1897-1914. *1866*

—. North Carolina. State government. 1960's-70's. *174*

Hoaxes. Cable, George Washington (*Strange True Stories of Louisiana*). Houssaye, Sidonie de la. Louisiana. 1889. *1615*

Hocutt, Thomas R. Colleges and Universities. Courts. McCoy, Cecil A. North Carolina, University of (School of Pharmacy). Pearson, Conrad O. School Integration. 1933. *2088*

Hodge, Charles. Adger, John B. Dabney, Robert Lewis. Nevin, John W. Presbyterian Church. 1845-75. *2314*

Hoebel, E. Adamson. Comanche Indians. Green corn dance. Indians. Methodology. Rites and Ceremonies. Texas. Wallace, Ernest. 1830-95. 1952-81. *4107*

Hoffman, Harold Jefferson. Air Forces. Tennessee (Martin). 1933-68. *3860*

Hogs and Hog Raising. Country Life. Virginia (Manquin, Queenfield Farm). 20c. *2853*

—. Cumberland River Valley. Folklore. Kentucky. 1900-50's. *1508*

Holden, William Curry (obituary). Archaeology. Historiography. Texas Tech University. 1920's-78. *234*

Holiday, Billie. Films. Furie, Sidney. Jazz. *Lady Sings the Blues* (film). Music. 1930's. 1972. *1779*

Holifield, E. Brooks. Christianity (review article). Raboteau, Albert J. Slavery. 1795-1860. *2204*

Holland, William. American Board of Commissioners for Foreign Missions. Cherokee Indians. Tennessee (Bradley County). 1824-37. *4095*

Holley, Joseph Winthrop. Cocking, Walter D. Georgia, University of. Racism. Talmadge, Eugene. 1941. *2057*

Holloway, Lou. Blacks. Mississippi. Music. Personal narratives. Piney Woods School. Rays of Rhythm. 1940-49. *911*

Holly Grove Methodist Church. Louisiana. Methodist Church. ca 1825-1980. *2463*

Holly Hill House. Architecture. Maryland (Anne Arundel, Charles counties). Sarum House. 1680-1720. *1188*

Holly Springs Iron Works. Iron industry. Mississippi. 1845-62. *2940*

Holmes, Joseph Austin. Conservation of Natural Resources. Geological Survey. North Carolina. 1891-1920. *3310*

Holston River Valley. Evangelism. Methodist Church. Russell, Elizabeth H. C. Virginia. 1770-1825. *2217*

Holt, Jacob W. Architecture. North Carolina (central). Virginia (southern). 1840-80. *1162*

Holt, Matthew S. Individualism. Politics. West Virginia (Lewis County). 1870-1939. *3530*

Holt, Rush Dew. Documents. New Deal. Senate. West Virginia. 1920-55. *3593*

Holtville School. Alabama. Progressive education. 1920's-78. *1833*

Holy Cross Abbey. Trappists. Virginia (Shenandoah Valley). Wormeley Manor. 1744-1980. *2506*

Holy Trinity Episcopal Church. Architecture. Churches. Gothic Revival Style. Restorations. Tennessee (Nashville). 1861-65. *1300*

Home Economics. *See also* Arts and Crafts; Consumers; Folk Art; Food Consumption; Fuel; Furniture and Furnishings.

—. Appalachia. Manufactures. Social customs. 1840-70. *759*

Home Mission Board. Baptists (Southern). Blacks. Race Relations. 1845-1981. *2370*

Home rule. Constitutions, State. Local government. Louisiana. 1851-1974. *3558*

Home Rule Act (1973). City Government. District of Columbia. 1780's-1973. *3504*

Homecomings. Blacks. Family. Kinship. North Carolina (Montgomery County). Reunions. Rites and Ceremonies. 19c-1970's. *381*

Homeplace-1850 (farm). Farms. Kentucky. Museums. Tennessee Valley Authority. 1850. 1979. *143*

Homestead Strike. Bond issues. Carnegie, Andrew. Libraries. Ohio Valley Trades and Labor Assembly. West Virginia (Wheeling). 1892-1911. *160*

Homesteading and Homesteaders. Armed Occupation Act (US, 1842). Benton, Thomas Hart. Florida. Indians. Seminole War, 2d. 1842. *4126*

—. DeMoss, Nettie. Oklahoma (Peggs, Sand Springs, Tahlequah). Personal Narratives. 1895-1937. *2567*

—. Florida (Glades County; Palmdale). Personal narratives. Wadlow, Ralph. 1932-69. *2644*

—. Freedmen. Louisiana. Reconstruction. 1865-83. *2806*

—. Frontier and Pioneer Life. Indian Territory. 1889-1903. *2764*

Homicide. *See* Murder.

Homosexuality. Grimké, Angelina Weld. Literature. McCullers, Carson. Smith, Lillian. Women. 1926-80. *1047*

Honor. Social status. Values. 1820-61. *433*

Hooper, George W. Alabama. Authors. Burton, Robert Wilton. Towles, Catharine. ca 1850-1900. *908*

Hoover, Edward (family). Archaeology. Daily Life. Kentucky (Louisville). Middle Classes. 1880's-1930's. *242*

Hoover, Herbert C. Florida. Patronage. Republican Party. State Politics. 1928-33. *3589*

—. Georgia. Patronage. Political factions. Race Relations. Republican Party. 1928-32. *3588*

Hoover, J. Edgar. Boggs, Thomas Hale. Federal Bureau of Investigation. Speeches. 1971. *3584*

Hope, Lugenia. Blacks. Cummings, Ida A. Jenkins, Lizzie A. Self-help programs. Washington, Margaret M. Women. 1895-1925. *2046*

Hopeton (plantation). Crops. Georgia (Glynn County). Plantations. 1818-52. *2689*

Hopley, Catherine. Brazil. Darwin, Charles. Plantations. Slavery. Stereotypes. 1831-63. *729*

Horn, Stanley F. Bibliographies. Tennessee. 1935-78. *180*

—. Industry. Lumber and Lumbering. Periodicals. Personal Narratives. *Southern Lumberman*. Trade associations. 1908-33. *3006*

Horner, Lance. Falconhurst series. Novels. Onstott, Kyle. 1957-73. *416*

Horse breeding. North Carolina (Northampton county). 1762-1900. *713*

Horse racing. *American Farmer*. Animal husbandry. Maryland. Periodicals. Skinner, John Stuart. 1819-29. *1429*

—. Daily Life. Kentucky (Louisville). Noland, Charles Fenton Mercer. Periodicals. *Spirit of the Times*. 1839-42. *751*

—. Downs, Sawyer. Louisiana (Bossier Parish). Sawyer, Earl. 1965-72. *1671*

—. Mint julep (drink). 1660-1949. *1576*

—. Regionalism. 1823-50. *1656*

Horses. Mizell, Terrence A. Personal Narratives. Tennessee. Trade. 1940's-70's. *1584*

Horticulture. *See also* Landscaping.

—. Agriculture. Arkansas State Horticultural Society. 1879-1975. *2824*

Horton, George Moses. North Carolina (Chapel Hill). Poetry. Slaves. 1797-1884. *1745*

Horton, James Edwin. Faubus, Orval. Graves. Hamer, Fanny Lou. Kennedy, John F. Personal Narratives. Scottsboro Boys. 1930's-70's. *410*

Horton, Myles. Education. Highlander Folk School. Political activism. Tennessee. 1930-80. *1830*

—. Moyers, Bill. Personal Narratives. Radicals and Radicalism. Tennessee (Chattanooga area). 1932-81. *1591*

Horydczak, Theodor. District of Columbia. Photographs. Social Change. 1920's-40's. *2914*

Hospitals. Baltimore City Hospital. Maryland. 1772-1964. *2142*

—. Chimborazo Hospital. Confederate Army. McCaw, James Brown. Military Medicine. Virginia (Richmond). 1861-65. *2120*

—. Civil War. Corona Female College. Gaston, L. B. Gaston, Susan P. Mississippi (Corinth). 1857-64. *1907*

—. East Louisiana State Hospital. Louisiana (Jackson). Mental health care. 1960-72. *2160*

—. Kentucky (Pikeville, Prestonsburg). Labor Unions and Organizations. National Labor Relations Board. United Mine Workers of America. 1973-76. *3374*

—. Mississippi (Biloxi, Gulfport). 1907-63. *2108*

Hotchkiss, Jedediah. Coal Mines and Mining. Industrialization. Virginia, southwestern. West Virginia, southern. 1828-99. *3138*

Hotel Ponce de Leon. Flagler, Henry Morrison. Florida (St. Augustine). Maybeck, Bernard. Tiffany, Louis. 1885-1974. *1228*

Hotels. Florida. Photographs. 1880's-1983. *1223*

House, J. T. Classics. Congregationalism. Kingfisher College. Oklahoma. 1890-1922. *1893*

House, John D. Alabama (Gadsden). Goodyear Tire and Rubber Company. Rubber. United Rubber Workers. 1941. *3423*

House of Burgesses. Church of England. Petitions. Public policy. Virginia. 1700-75. *2191*

House of Commons. Astor, Nancy Langhorne. Great Britain. Virginia. Women. 1897-1964. *605*

House of Representatives. *See also* Legislation; Senate.

—. Alabama. Clayton, Henry D. Democratic Party. 1897-1914. *3753*

—. Alabama. Political Attitudes. 1849-61. *3704*

—. Blacks. Federal Government. Intervention. Population. Voting Rights Act (US, 1965). 1940-75. *3494*

—. Blacks. Langston, John Mercer. State Politics. Virginia. 1849-97. *3505*

—. Blacks. Lynch, John Roy. Mississippi. 1847-1939. *3689*

—. Blacks. Lynch, John Roy. Mississippi. Reconstruction. 1869-1939. *3488*

—. Boggs, Hale. Gerrymandering. Lobbying. Louisiana. State Legislatures. 1968-69. *3557*

—. Duels. Jackson, John George. Maryland (Bladensburg). Pearson, Joseph. Politics. 1805-12. *3508*

—. Illinois. Judges. Navies. Oklahoma (Muskogee). Thomas, John Robert. 1870's-1924. *3527*

—. Louisiana. Waggonner, Joe D. 1962-80. *3526*

—. Military. Vinson, Carl. 1914-81. *3797*

Households. Economic Structure. Plantations. Social Organization. 1783-1865. *567*

Houses. *See also* Estates; Mansions; Plantations.

—. Alabama, University of. Architecture. Greek Revival style. 1837-1908. *1294*

—. Anglo Irish. Mexico. Rio Grande. Texas. 19c. *1307*

—. Appalachia. Wallpaper. 1860-1940. *1572*

—. Architecture. Arkansas (Independence County). Social Customs. 1820-1978. *1202*

—. Architecture. French, John Jay (residence). Texas (Beaumont). 1845. *1203*

—. Architecture. Rural settlements. Virginia. 17c-19c. *1243*

—. Architecture. Virginia. 1710-1800. *1378*

—. Architecture. Virginia (eastern shore). 1638-1843. *1376*

—. Chaumiere des Prairies (residence). Kentucky (Lexington area). Meade, David. 1744-1832. *1313*

—. Cherokee Indians. Creek Indians. Georgia. Indians. 1794-1823. *4122*

—. Confiscations. Debt. Moratoriums. Property. Texas. 1829-1921. *2611*

—. Construction. Georgia. Rural areas. Sharecroppers. 1865-1941. *3148*

—. Country Life. Georgia, eastern. 1733-1980. *3325*

—. Cownes (estate). Personal narratives. Virginia (King William County). 1920's-30's. *1158*

—. Creoles. Louisiana (New Orleans). 19c. *1191*

—. DuBois family. Florida (Jupiter). 1880-1981. *598*

—. Excavations. Florida (Pensacola). Panton, William. 1796-1848. *1381*

—. Fulton, Weston M. (residence). Tennessee (Knoxville). 1929. *1293*

—. Historical Sites and Parks. Texas (Odessa). White-Pool House. 1887-1978. *1260*

—. Leigh, Gilbert (residence). North Carolina (Edenton). Restorations. 1759-1969. *1304*

—. Log construction. Louisiana. 19c-20c. *1308*

—. Mississippi (Natchez). Preservation. 1700-1979. *1177*

—. Congress of Peninsula Organizations. Ethnic Groups. Maryland (Baltimore; South Baltimore). Social Change. 1880-1980. *558*

—. Economic development. Political Change. Regionalism. 1970-80. *2574*

—. Economic Development. Population. Recessions. 1970-77. *2562*

—. Horn, Stanley F. Lumber and Lumbering. Periodicals. Personal Narratives. *Southern Lumberman.* Trade associations. 1908-33. *3006*

—. Investments. Profitability. 1830-70. *2903*

—. Labor Unions and Organizations. Nonunionization. South Carolina (Greenville). 1873-1979. *3447*

—. Location. Textile Industry. Working class. 1950-74. *3173*

—. Maryland (Baltimore). 1830's-60's. *3062*

—. Maryland (Baltimore). Residential patterns. Urbanization. Villages. 1880-1925. *2905*

Infants. Folk medicine. Tennessee. 1974. *1530*

Influenza. Death and Dying. Epidemics. Kentucky. 1918-19. *2107*

Ingle, Joe (interview). Capital Punishment. Construction. Legislation. Prisons. Reform. Southern Coalition on Jails and Prisons. 1978. *3565*

Initiatives. Anti-evolution Law (1928). Arkansas. Church and state. Courts. Epperson, Susan. 1900's-68. *3671*

Inman Park Restoration, Inc. Georgia (Atlanta). Neighborhoods. Preservation. 1880's. 1970-79. *1348*

Insanity. *See* Mental Illness.

Inscriptions. Baptists. Louisiana (Bienville Parish). Mount Lebanon University. Tombstones. 1848-1976. *524*

—. Bibliographies. Cemeteries. Georgia Genealogical Society. Tombstones. 1817-1946. *82*

—. Cemeteries. Louisiana (Jackson Parish). Rural Settlements. Tombstones. 1845-1930's. *528*

—. DuPont Cemetery. South Carolina (Purrysburg). Strobhar Cemetery. Tombstones. 1736-1872. *1542*

—. Ebenezer Lutheran Church. Mount Bethel Baptist Church. South Carolina (Anderson County). Tombstones. 1856-1978. *1487*

—. Kentucky (Henry County). Tombstones. 1770-1970. *1545*

—. Louisiana (Claiborne Parish). Tombstones. 1828-73. *525*

—. Louisiana (De Soto Parish). Tombstones. 1843-1978. *530*

—. Louisiana (Lincoln Parish). Pioneers. Tombstones. 19c-1973. *529*

—. Louisiana (Morehouse Parish). Pioneers. Tombstones. 1844-1957. *527*

—. Louisiana (Ouachita Parish). Tombstones. ca 1830-1920. *531*

—. Louisiana (Union Parish). Tombstones. 1839-1970's. *526*

—. Louisiana (Winn Parish). Populism. Socialism. Tombstones. 1852-1975. *523*

—. Tombstones. West Virginia (West Liberty). 1786-1946. *635*

Insects. Diseases. Indians. Population. Prehistory-19c. *2162*

Institute for Southern Studies (report). Periodicals. Social Conditions. *Southern Exposure.* 1979. *334*

Insurance. *See also* types of insurance, e.g. Automobile Insurance, Industrial Insurance, Unemployment Insurance, etc.

—. North. 1874-1900. *2629*

Insurrections. *See* Rebellions.

Integration. *See also* Assimilation.

—. Alabama (Tuscaloosa). Civil rights movement. Clergy. Whites. 1976-77. *2184*

—. Attitudes. Georgia. High Schools. Students. 1965. 1980. *2065*

—. Berea College. Blacks. Higher Education. Kentucky. 1858-1908. *2045*

—. Blacks. Delaware. Public Schools. Steward, Theophilus Gould. 1867-82. *2031*

—. Blacks. Enoch Pratt Free Library. Libraries. Maryland (Baltimore). 1882-1915. *1031*

—. Brewer, Fisk Parsons. Higher education. South Carolina, University of. 1873-76. *1954*

—. Busing. Mass Media. Tennessee (Nashville). 1970-73. *2081*

—. Mississippi. Political Commentary. State Politics. 1970-72. *3822*

Intellectual history. 19c-20c. 1960-75. *954*

—. Black Mountain College. Duberman, Martin (review article). North Carolina. 1933-56. *1910*

Intellectuals. Agrarianism. 1920-40. *2760*

—. Faust, Drew Gilpin (review article). Proslavery Sentiments. Psychology. 1840-60. 1978. *944*

—. Historians. Phillips, Ulrich B. 1877-1934. *2636*

—. King, Grace. Literature. Women. 1885-1932. *823*

—. Mississippi. Standard of living. 1900-78. *3351*

—. Presbyterian Church. Revivals. Virginia. 1787-1837. *2482*

—. Proslavery Sentiments. 1800-65. *864*

—. Virginia. 17c-19c. *1068*

Interest Groups. *See also* Pressure Groups.

—. Appalachian studies. Colleges and Universities. Politics. 1978. *119*

Intergovernmental relations. Governors. State Legislatures. Tennessee. 1796-1980. *3686*

Interior decoration. Ackland, Adelicia Hayes Franklin. Architecture. Belmont (estate). Stereographs. Tennessee (Nashville). 1850-1970. *1198*

—. Architecture. Camden (house). Pratt, William C. Starkwether, Norris G. Virginia (Port Royal area). 1859-1970. *1247*

Intermarriage. Ethnicity. French Americans. Louisiana (New Orleans). 1790-1840. *603*

Internal Migration. *See* Migration, Internal.

International Brotherhood of Pulp, Sulphite, and Paper Mill Workers. Labor Unions and Organizations. Paper Industry. Virginia (Covington). West Virginia Pulp and Paper Company. 1933-52. *3462*

International Ladies' Garment Workers' Union. Texas. Textile Industry. Women. 1933-50. *3405*

International Longshoremen's Association. Race relations. 1866-1920. *3037*

International Trade. Alexander Brown and Sons. Cotton. Great Britain. 1820-60. *2749*

—. Cotton. Great Britain. 1860's-1900. *2881*

—. France. Great Britain. Monopolies. North America. Price, Jacob (review article). Tobacco. 17c-18c. *2716*

—. Great Britain. Maryland. Statistics. Virginia. 1740-91. *2628*

—. Japan. Louisiana (New Orleans). 1900-75. *2656*

International Union of Operating Engineers, Local 926. Coffin, Tom. Construction. Georgia (Atlanta). Labor Unions and Organizations. Law Engineering Testing Company. National Labor Relations Board. Personal Narratives. 1973-78. *2937*

International Workingmen's Association (Section 15). Louisiana (New Orleans). 1871. *3385*

Internationalism. 1900-80. *3631*

Internment. Debt. Kentucky. Law Reform. 1790-1839. *3710*

—. *Eclipse* (vessel). Escapes. Germany. *Kronprinz Wilhelm* (vessel). Navies. *Prinz Eital Friedrich* (vessel). Virginia (Norfolk). 1915. *3874*

Interpersonal Relations. *See also* Friendship; Human Relations.

—. Ethnic Groups. Georgia (Atlanta). Jews. Marx, David. 1890-1930. *2198*

—. Family. Oklahoma. Rogers, Clement V. Rogers, Will. 1879-1911. *1633*

Interstate Commerce Commission. Sugar. Tennessee. Transportation. 1895-1925. *2946*

Intervention. Blacks. Federal Government. House of Representatives. Population. Voting Rights Act (US, 1965). 1940-75. *3494*

Inventories. Wealth. 1744. *2589*

Inventors. Industrial Technology. Social change. Whitney, Eli. 1792-1825. *2957*

Investments. Attitudes. Economic Conditions. Manufactures. 1850-60. *2901*

—. Cotton. Prices. Quantitative Methods. Tariff. 1840-60. *2742*

—. Economic growth. Maryland (Baltimore). Social Problems. 1745-1950's. *2623*

—. Industry. Profitability. 1830-70. *2903*

—. Kentucky, eastern. Social Change. 1890-1915. *2898*

Irby, John Laurens Manning. South Carolina. State Politics. Tillman, Benjamin Ryan. 1854-1900. *3782*

Ireland. *See also* Great Britain.

—. Appalachia. Ballads. *Rose Connoley.* 1800-1979. *1689*

Ireland, Robert M. (review article). County Government. Kentucky. 1850-91. 1977. *3273*

Irish Americans. Alabama (Leesburg). Bass, Tommie. Humor. 16c-1973. *1674*

—. Attitudes. Immigrants. Know-Nothing Party. Louisiana (New Orleans). Police. 1830-80. *3101*

—. Canada. Kentucky (Louisville). Leadership. Presbyterian Church. Robinson, Stuart. 1858-81. *2514*

—. Catholic Church. Democratic Party. *Kentucky Irish American.* Newspapers. 1898-1968. *1605*

—. Catholic Church. Farrelly, John P. Morris, John. Stritch, Samuel A. Tennessee. 19c-1958. *2475*

—. Deery, William. Historical Sites and Parks. Tennessee (Blountville). Trading Posts. 1795-1970's. *1192*

—. Economic development. Tennessee (Memphis). 1850-80. *640*

—. Georgia (Augusta). Immigration. 1830-1970. *518*

Irish traveler cant. Folklore. 1840-1955. *1519*

Iron. Alabama. Ware, Horace. 1840-90. *3048*

—. Bridges. Engineers. West Virginia. Wheeling Suspension Bridge. 1709-1849. *1257*

Iron Industry. *See also* Steel Industry.

—. Alabama (Birmingham). Furnaces. Museums. Preservation. Sloss Company. 1881-1978. *3023*

—. Alabama (Birmingham). McWane Cast Iron Pipe Company. 1896-1980. *3104*

—. Carter, George Lafayette. Coal Mines and Mining. Railroads. 1877-1936. *3084*

—. Delaware (Red Clay Creek; Wooddale). Friends, Society of. Industrial Relations. Wood, Alan. Wood, James. 1814-73. *3390*

—. Holly Springs Iron Works. Mississippi. 1845-62. *2940*

—. Laughlin Nail Works. Ohio (Martins Ferry). Strikes. West Virginia (Wheeling). 1833-86. *3412*

Iron Mining. Chesapeake and Ohio Canal. George's Creek Coal and Iron Company. Maryland (Lonaconing area). 1837-40. *2987*

Ironworks. Dorsey, Caleb. Maryland (Howard County). 1761-1868. *3044*

—. North Carolina (Lincoln County). Plantations. Slavery. Vesuvius Furnace. 1791-1876. *3124*

Iroquois Indians. Cherokee Indians. Indians. Linguistics. Zeisberger, David. 1769. *4022*

—. Cherokee Indians. Indians. Morton, John. Social Customs. Travel accounts. 1809. *3970*

Iroquois Indians (Seneca). Cherokee Indians. Indians. Music. 1970's. *3999*

Iroquois Indians (Tuscarora). Indians. North Carolina. 1586-1713. *4073*

Irrigation. *See also* Dams.

—. Agricultural Technology and Research. Texas. 1930-75. *2723*

Irwin, Harriet Morrison. Houses (hexagonal). Patents. 1860-1900. *1242*

Isolation. Appalachia. Attitudes. Geography. 1730's-1930's. *3347*

Israel. Louisiana (New Orleans). New Orleans *Times-Picayune.* News, foreign. Newspapers. 1973. *1528*

Italian Americans. Agricultural labor. Blacks. Immigration. Newspapers. 1880-1915. *2839*

—. Anarchism and Anarchists. Florida (Tampa). Social Customs. Socialism. 1890-1902. *648*

—. Assimilation. Immigrants. 19c. *521*

—. Blacks. Immigration. Louisiana. Race Relations. Sugarcane. 1880-1910. *2829*

—. Choctaw Indians. Coal Mines and Mining. Indians. Oklahoma (Krebs). Sierra Leone. 1875-1907. *3039*

—. Cigar industry. Family. Florida (Tampa). Women. 1890-1930. *636*

—. D'Aritano, Reginia. D'Aritano, Roy. Folk songs. Immigrants. West Virginia. 1860's-1942. *1677*

—. Discrimination. Immigrants. Louisiana. 1871-1905. *663*

—. Employment. Florida (Tampa; Ybor City). Social Customs. 1880-1920. *637*

—. Florida East Coast Railway. Immigrants. Labor recruitment. Padrone system. Railroads. ca 1890-1901. *3435*

—. Hennessy affair. Louisiana (New Orleans). Lynching. 1880-1920. *577*

—. Immigration. Labor recruitment. Sugar industry. 1880-1910. *2827*

—. Louisiana (New Orleans). Press. Stereotypes. 1880-1920. *1568*

—. Mining. Oklahoma (Krebs). Robertson, J. B. A. Strikes. 1890-1920. *3377*

Italians. Blacks. Immigrants. Louisiana. Race Relations. Sugarcane. 1880-1910. *2828*

—. Cities. Louisiana (New Orleans). Residential segregation. 20c. *622*

Italy. Bertinatti, Eugenia Bate Bass. Estates. Property. Tennessee. Travel. 1826-1906. *557*

*It's Grits* (film). Daily Life. Documentaries. Grits. *Kudzu* (film). Soil conservation. 1930-78. *2750*

# J

Jackson, Andrew. Cherokee Indians. Congress. Politics. Removals, forced. 1780-1838. *3991*

—. Cherokee Indians. Currey, Benjamin. Indians. Removals, forced. 1831-36. *4112*

—. Cherokee Indians. Indians. Removals, forced. Rhetoric. 1829-39. *4099*

—. Cherokee Indians. Indian-White Relations. Removals, forced. 1835. *4141*

Lawsuits. Blacks. Desegregation. Discrimination, Educational. Graduate schools. North Carolina. Professional education. 1930-51. *1974*
—. Colleges and universities. Desegregation. Education, Finance. Tennessee. 1968-81. *2017*
Lawyers. *See also* Judges.
—. Alabama. DeFriese, LaFayette Hoyt. 1850-1924. *3787*
—. Allen, Macon B. Blacks. 1844-94. *544*
—. Attorneys general. Mississippi. State Government. 1874-1969. *3802*
—. Campbell, John Archibald. Jacksonianism. Supreme Court. 1829-89. *3652*
—. Divorce. Oklahoma Territory. 1890-1906. *3681*
—. Marshall, Thurgood. Maryland. University of, School of Law. Murray, Donald G. NAACP. School Integration. 1930-54. *2025*
Lawyers' Round Table. Baltimore Reform League. Maryland. Niles, Alfred Salem. Voluntary Associations. 1852-1972. *3679*
Lazarus, Samuel L. Acme, Red River and Northern Railroad. Gypsum mills. Railroads. Texas (Hardeman County). 1890-1909. *2997*
Lea, Luke. Democratic Party. Peay, Austin. Political Factions. Republican Party. State Government. Tennessee, East. 1922-32. *3674*
Lea, Maggie Tate. Baptists. Clay, Margaret Muse. Crawford Manuscript. Folk Medicine. Mississippi (Amite County). Virginia (Chesterfield). ca 1773. ca 1890. *1083*
Lea, Tom. Cisneros, Jose. Culture. Hertzog, Carl. Sonnichsen, C. L. Sullivan, Maud. Texas (El Paso). 1920's-75. *1000*
Lead mining. Arkansas (Buffalo Valley). Transportation. Zinc mining. ca 1720-1930's. *3081*
Leadership. *See also* Political Leadership.
—. Acculturation. Georgia (Atlanta). Jews. 1890-1940. *505*
—. Alabama. Business. 1800-1977. *2609*
—. Baptists (Southern). Social Conditions. South Carolina. 17c-20c. *2235*
—. Canada. Irish Americans. Kentucky (Louisville). Presbyterian Church. Robinson, Stuart. 1858-81. *2514*
—. Cherokee Indians. Civil War. Drew, John Thompson. Indian Territory. Indians. Law. 1850-65. *4038*
—. Cherokee Indians. Georgia. Indians. Oklahoma. Removals, forced. Ross, John. Tennessee. 1815-66. *4063*
—. Chickasaw Indians. France. Indian-White Relations. Louisiana. Military Campaigns. 1739-40. *3980*
—. Colleges and Universities. Dawson, William. William and Mary, College of. 1725-52. *1913*
—. Congress. Democratic Party. Oklahoma. Political power. 1945-72. *3598*
—. Editors and Editing. Florida. Panama City *Pilot*. West, Lillian Carlisle. Women. 1916-37. *1561*
—. Elites. Maryland (Baltimore). 1781-1806. 1827-36. *3749*
—. Florida. Seminole Indians. Social Organization. 20c. *4171*
—. Jews. Levi, Abraham. Texas (Victoria). 1850-1902. *2451*
—. Labor Unions and Organizations. People's Institute of Applied Religion. Williams, Claude. Williams, Joyce. 1940-75. *2494*
—. Political Parties. 1865-1973. *3815*
—. Populism. Southern Farmers' Alliance. 1890's. *3770*
*Lector* (reader). Cubans. Florida (Tampa). Labor Disputes. Perez, Louis A., Jr. Personal Narratives. Tobacco. ca 1925-35. *3432*
Lectures. Aesthetics. Travel. Wilde, Oscar. 1882. *738*
—. Decorative Arts. Georgia. Wilde, Oscar. 1882. *939*
—. Edwards, Harry Stillwell. Georgia. Lyceum movement. Nye, Edgar Wilson "Bill". Riley, James Whitcomb. 1888. *938*
—. Edwards, Harry Stillwell. Humorists. Nye, Edgar Wilson "Bill". Redpath Lyceum Bureau. Riley, James Whitcomb. 1888. *1556*
Ledbetter, Huddie "Leadbelly". Blacks. Folk Songs. Louisiana. Love, Blanche. 1880's-1949. 1976. *1129*
Lederer, John. Explorers. Indians. Medicine, practice of. Travel accounts. Virginia. 1681. *3968*
Ledgers. Alabama (Fairfield). Country Life. General stores. Jones, John C. H. 1873. *688*
Lee, Henry ("Light-Horse Harry"). Virginia. 1756-1818. *3871*
Lee, Margaret Elizabeth Daniel. Agriculture. Florida (Pinellas County). Personal Narratives. 1850-1963. *2857*

Lee, Mary Edmunds Tabor. Louisiana (Shiloh). 1840's-1926. *619*
Lee, Molly Huston. Blacks. Librarians. North Carolina (Raleigh). Richard B. Harrison Library. 1930-75. *228*
—. Blacks. Libraries. North Carolina (Raleigh). Richard B. Harrison Library. 1935-68. *229*
Lee, Robert E. Historiography. 1865-1940. *427*
—. Miley, Michael. Photography. Virginia (Lexington). 1865-1918. *1035*
Lee, William. Alabama (Demopolis). Colonial Society of French Emigrants. French Americans. Immigration. Pennsylvania (Philadelphia). 1816-17. *2718*
LeFlore, Greenwood. Choctaw Indians. Indian Removal Bill. Treaty of Dancing Rabbit Creek (1830). 1825-30. *4104*
Leftwich, George J. Bienville, Sieur de. Historiography. Mississippi (Tombigbee River area: Cotton Gin Port, Gaines' Trace). 1729-40. 1903-80. *3214*
Legal education. Courts. Discrimination. Florida. Hawkins, Virgil Darnell. 1949-76. *1982*
—. District of Columbia. Gillett, Emma M. Mussey, Ellen Spencer. Washington College of Law. Women. 1869-1949. *1857*
—. Neal, John R. Tennessee, University of. 1893-1959. *1844*
Legends. Caldwell, Erskine. Folklore. Literature. 1929-70's. *1695*
—. Eleven Jones' Cave. Kentucky (Jefferson County). Spelunking (survey trips). 1831-1967. *1501*
—. Treasure. 16c-1978. *1593*
Legislation. *See also* Congress; Law.
—. Agricultural Production. Cotton. Economic Development. Land. 1820-60. *2759*
—. Capital Punishment. Construction. Ingle, Joe (interview). Prisons. Reform. Southern Coalition on Jails and Prisons. 1978. *3565*
—. Colleges and Universities. Runnels, Hardin R. Texas, University of. 1853-83. *1908*
—. Georgia. Historical Sites and Parks. Preservation. 1889-1979. *251*
—. Metropolitan Areas. Public Schools. State Aid to Education. Texas Education Agency. 1970-80. *1787*
Lehman, George. Audubon, John James (*Birds of America*). Maryland (Baltimore). 1831-36. *881*
Leigh, Gilbert (residence). Houses. North Carolina (Edenton). Restorations. 1759-1969. *1304*
Leisure. *See also* Recreation.
—. Aging. Appalachia. Attitudes. Physical fitness. Poverty. Working conditions. 1950's-70. *3367*
—. Cajuns. Daily life. Louisiana. Modernization. Social Customs. 1900-79. *499*
—. Cajuns. Louisiana. Social Customs. 19c-20c. *660*
—. Ethics. Social organization. 18c-20c. *760*
—. Lifestyles. 1977. *770*
Lemee House. Law. Louisiana. Natchitoches Historic District. Preservation. 18c-1980. *1341*
Lemon, Lester. Blacks. Cities. Tennessee. 1900-30. 1978. *402*
LeMoyne, Jacques. Agriculture. Florida. Painting. Timucuan Indians, Eastern. ca 1564-1620. *3947*
L'Enfant, Pierre Charles. Architecture. City Planning. District of Columbia. 1791. *1214*
—. Architecture. City Planning. District of Columbia. Politics. Republicanism. 1783-1800. *1380*
—. City Planning. District of Columbia. 1796-1825. *1344*
—. City Planning. District of Columbia. Ellicott, Andrew. France (Paris). 1754-1825. *1251*
—. City Planning. District of Columbia. Washington, George. 1789-91. *1361*
Leopold, Nathan. Candler, Warren A. Conservatism. Loeb, Richard. Methodist Episcopal Church, South. Scopes, John Thomas. Trials. 1921-41. *2197*
Leshe, Mary Jane Conly. Louisiana (Bienville Parish). 1849-1932. *625*
Letterbooks. Plantations. Raper, Robert. South Carolina. Trade. 1759-65. *2779*
Letters. Anderson, James Wallace. Anderson, Mary. City Life. Country Life. District of Columbia. Farms. Maryland (Rockville area). 1854-1960. *500*
—. Arkansas. Cherokee Indians. Ross, John. Tennessee. 1812-13. *4064*
—. Authors. Boozer, William. Stuart, Jesse. 1968-78. *808*
—. Bishop, John Peale. Friendship. Tate, Allen. 1931. *1135*
—. Blacks. Durham, James. Louisiana (New Orleans). Medicine (practice of). Rush, Benjamin. 1783-1802. *2161*

—. Blacks. Lynch, James. Methodist Episcopal Church. Mississippi. Reconstruction. 1868-69. *2291*
—. Bleser, Carol. Hammond family (review article). Social change. South Carolina. 19c-1950's. *693*
—. Bluegrass. Clay, Henry. Kentucky. 1838. *1482*
—. Bordley, Stephen. Church of England. Great Awakening. Maryland. Whitefield, George. 1730-40. *2245*
—. Bremer, Fredrika. Sweden. Travel (accounts). 1851. *747*
—. Business. Economic Conditions. Epidemics. Lasker, Morris. Personal narratives. Texas (Milliken). 1860-66. *608*
—. Capitols (dome). Construction. District of Columbia. Jones, J. Glancy. Meigs, Montgomery Cunningham. 1853-58. *1402*
—. Census. Cheney, John M. Florida. Fries, J. Otto. Indians. Seminole Indians. 1860-1900. *4016*
—. Cherokee Indians. Federal government. Georgia. Land. Payne, John Howard. Ross, John. 1820's-30's. *4074*
—. Cherokee Indians. Frontier and Pioneer Life. Indian-White Relations. Removals, forced. Tennessee. Webster, L. B. 1838. *4123*
—. Chicago, University of. Dodd, William E. Hearon, Cleo. Mississippi. 1910. *1867*
—. Civil War. Coups d'Etat. Ellet, Charles. Methodology. Military Organization. Primary sources. 1863. 1979. *221*
—. Clergy. Episcopal Church, Protestant. Jarratt, Devereux. Virginia. 1770-1800. *2316*
—. Colleges and Universities. Gilman, Daniel Coit. Johns Hopkins University. Maryland (Baltimore). Sylvester, James Joseph. Teaching. 1825-84. *1841*
—. Cooke, Philip Pendleton. Poe, Edgar Allan. *Southern Literary Messenger*. 1847-49. *1095*
—. Daily Life. Maryland (Baltimore). Preston, Madge. Preston, William P. 1855-67. *796*
—. Fillmore, Millard. Mississippi (Yazoo City). Prewett, Harriet Nelson. 1857-73. *3789*
—. Films. Harwell, Richard (review article). Mitchell, Margaret (*Gone with the Wind*). Novels. 1936-49. *1023*
—. Fitzgerald, Sally. O'Connor, Flannery (review article). 1955-64. *903*
—. Florida (Miami). Rockefeller, John D. Tuttle, Julia. 1886-90. *497*
—. Georgia. Jones, Charles C. (family). Novels. 1854-68. *902*
—. Georgia. Manigault, Charles. Milling. Rice. 1852. *2688*
—. German Americans. Henkel Square. Log cabins. Restorations. Texas (Round Top). 1840's-83. *1405*
—. Gordon, Caroline. Literary Criticism. O'Connor, Flannery (*Wise Blood*). 1951-64. *867*
—. Great Britain. Politics. South Carolina. Travel. Trelawny, Edward John. 1833-35. *732*
—. Hambleton, John Needles. Hambleton, Samuel. Maryland. Navies. 1813-32. *3849*
—. Johnston, John. Medicine (practice of). Virginia (Rockbridge). 1790-1800. *2173*
—. Literature. Tate, Allen. Tate, Caroline Gordon. 1925-37. *916*
—. Madison, James. Scott, Susan Randolph Madison. Sex roles. 1811. *423*
Letters-to-the-editor. Capers, William. *Christian Advocate*. Methodism. Newspapers. Slavery. 1854. 1875. *2422*
—. Daily Life. Georgia (Decatur). Ohio. Springfield *Weekly News*. Willard, Levi. 1826-64. 1876. *538*
Levasseur, Charles. Alabama. French. Indians. Tomeh Indians. Travel accounts. 1700. *4023*
Levi, Abraham. Jews. Leadership. Texas (Victoria). 1850-1902. *2451*
Levin, Louis H. Maryland. Pluralism. 1889-1923. *1860*
Lévi-Strauss, Claude. Family. Indians. Social Customs. 17c-19c. *4024*
Levy, Uriah Phillips. Jefferson, Thomas. Monticello. Virginia. 1809-1980. *1220*
Lewis, Janet. Personal Narratives. Poets. 1899-1982. *2300*
Lewis, Jerry Lee. Blackwood, James. Cash, Johnny. Music. Pentecostals. Wynette, Tammy. 1950's-70's. *1672*
Lewis, Robert Donald. Agricultural Technology and Research. Crops. Personal Narratives. Texas Agricultural Experiment Station. 1946-62. *2762*
Lexicology. *See also* Linguistics; Names.
—. *Linguistic Atlas of the Gulf States*. Regionalism. Research. 1970's. *3290*
Liberal arts. Higher education. Reform. 1850-60. *1878*

Liberal Party. Andrade, Flores de. Immigration. Mexico. Personal narratives. Revolutionary Movements. Texas (El Paso). 1890-1911. *570*
—. Exiles. Mexican Americans. Mexico. Propaganda. Texas. Women. 1898-1910. *3832*
Liberalism. Anti-Communist Movements. Ebey, George. Educational administrators. Schools. Texas (Houston). 1937-53. *1798*
—. Blacks. Harris, Julian. Journalism. 1900-60. *3698*
—. Historiography. Identity. Woodward, C. Vann. 1930-60. *462*
—. Historiography. Populism. Realism. Woodward, C. Vann. 1950-78. *306*
Liberalism (review article). Chandler, Daniel Leon. Politics. Race. Sosna, Morton. 1977. *117*
Liberals. Myrdal, Gunnar *(An American Dilemma)*. Race Relations. Whites. 1944-75. *279*
Liberia. *See also* Africa, West.
—. Colonization. Georgia. Tubman, Emily. 1818-85. *1725*
Liberty Hall Academy Library. Books. Virginia (Lexington). Washington and Lee University. 1776-1829. *190*
Liberty Mutual Insurance. Brown lung disease. Burlington Industries, Inc. Carolina Brown Lung Association. Cotton. 1970's. *3382*
Librarians. Blacks. Lee, Molly Huston. North Carolina (Raleigh). Richard B. Harrison Library. 1930-75. *228*
—. Castañeda, Carlos Eduardo. Colleges and Universities. Texas, University of, Austin (Benson Latin American Collection). 1920-27. *5*
—. Chicago, University of (School of Library Science). Colleges and Universities. North Carolina, University of, Chapel Hill. Wilson, Louis Round. 1901-76. *267*
Libraries. *See also* names of individual libraries; Archives; Museums.
—. Aitken, George Atherton. Great Britain. Literature. Texas, University of (Austin). 18c. 20c. *291*
—. Alabama. Georgia. Louisiana. Mississippi. 1908-73. *245*
—. Archives. Louisiana (Jefferson City, New Orleans). 1850-1972. *136*
—. Archives. Texas, University of (Eugene C. Barker Texas History Center). 1883-1950. *32*
—. Bibliographies. Byrd, William, III. Virginia. 1778-1803. 1978. *311*
—. Blacks. Enoch Pratt Free Library. Integration. Maryland (Baltimore). 1882-1915. *1031*
—. Blacks. Lee, Molly Huston. North Carolina (Raleigh). Richard B. Harrison Library. 1935-68. *229*
—. Bond issues. Carnegie, Andrew. Homestead Strike. Ohio Valley Trades and Labor Assembly. West Virginia (Wheeling). 1892-1911. *160*
—. Bureaucracies. City Government. Parks. Social Classes. Texas (Houston). 1970's. *3057*
—. Centennial Celebrations. Maryland (Baltimore). Peabody Library. 1978. *206*
—. Charleston, College of (Library; Special Collections). South Carolina. 1667-1979. *217*
—. Colleges and Universities. Manuscripts. Mississippi. 1976. *71*
—. Colleges and Universities. Manuscripts. Mississippi. 1978-79. *81*
—. Colleges and Universities. Manuscripts. Mississippi. 1979-80. *80*
—. Colleges and Universities. South Carolina College Library. 1802-1900. *1902*
—. Dialectic Society. North Carolina, University of (Library). Philanthropic Society. 1886-1906. *318*
—. Florida (Miami; Lemon City). 1889-1905. *1794*
—. LaRue, Edgar (family). Louisiana. 1799-1975. *581*
—. Texas State Library. 1909-73. *309*
—. Virginia. 1754-89. *270*
Library of Congress (American Folklife Center). Blue Ridge Parkway Folklife Project. Daily Life. National Parks and Reserves. North Carolina. Photographs. Virginia. 1978. *1488*
*Library of Southern Literature*. Literature. 1900-. *875*
Library Science. Colleges and Universities. North Carolina, University of (Chapel Hill). 1929-81. *1915*
Lich, Balthasar. Lich, Elisabeth Scholl. Ranching. Texas (Cypress Creek). 1857-1921. *615*
Lich, Elisabeth Scholl. Lich, Balthasar. Ranching. Texas (Cypress Creek). 1857-1921. *615*
Liddell family. Feuds. Jones family. Louisiana (Catahoula Parish). 1848-70. *606*
Liederkranz (society). German Americans. Immigration. Kentucky (Louisville). Know-Nothing movement. Music. 1848-77. *1510*

—. German Americans. Kentucky (Louisville). Music. 1877-1959. *1511*
Life Insurance Company of Georgia. Entrepreneurs. Friendship. Georgia. Kinship. 1891-1950. *2545*
Lifestyles. Altman, Robert. Conservatism. Films. 1969-75. *466*
—. Leisure. 1977. *770*
Liggin, John Lewis. Educators. Louisiana, northern. 1887-1950. *1835*
Lighthouse keepers. Mississippi (Biloxi). Women. 1854-61. 1867-1929. *676*
Lighthouses. Florida (Egmont Key). Military. 1757-1980. *3870*
—. Texas. 1850-1900. *1210*
—. Virginia. 1718-1963. *1193*
Lightning. Folklore. Kentucky. 1864-1939. *1663*
Lightship (vessel). Territorial Waters. Virginia. 1819-1965. *1387*
Lilly, Octave, Jr. (obituary). Blacks. Poetry. 1930-60. *1730*
Limerick Plantation. Indians. Pottery. South Carolina. 1709-1865. *4025*
Limestone. Architecture. Environment. Maryland (Washington County). Wood. 1736-1840. *1363*
Lincoln, Abraham. Assassination. Baptists. Florida (Umatilla). Southern Baptist winter assembly grounds. 1865. 1925-29. *2186*
—. Blacks. Civil rights. 1854-65. *358*
—. Civil War. Five Civilized Tribes. Indian Territory. Ross, John. 1860's. *3930*
Lincoln Institute. Berea College. Blacks. Day, Carl. Discrimination, Educational. Kentucky. 1904-12. *2097*
—. Blacks. Kentucky. Tydings, J. Mansir. Young, Whitney M. 1935-37. *2096*
Lincoln School. Blacks. Education. Reed, Phillip Nathanial. West Virginia (Wheeling). 1866-1975. *2022*
Lincoln, Thomas. Historical Sites and Parks. Kentucky (Elizabethtown). Log cabins. Restorations. Thomas, Hardin. 1790. 1974. *1292*
Lind, Jenny. Barnum, P. T. Concerts. Louisiana. Music. 1851. *896*
*Linguistic Atlas of the Gulf States*. Lexicology. Regionalism. Research. 1970's. *3290*
—. Microfiche. Publishers and Publishing. 1975-76. *3291*
Linguistics. *See also* Dialects; Language; Speech.
—. Archives. Folklore. Kentucky (Edmonson County). Wilson, Gordon. 1959-67. *1703*
—. Cherokee Indians. Indians. Iroquois Indians. Zeisberger, David. 1769. *4022*
—. Kentucky (Mammoth Cave region). Surnames. 1775-1971. *784*
Lipscomb, Mance. Autobiography. Blues. Migration, Internal. Music. Texas (Houston). 1956. *943*
Lipscomb, Martin Meredith. City Politics. Virginia (Richmond). 1853-57. *3730*
Liquor industry. Distillers. Kentucky. 1802-62. *2555*
Literary characters. Faulkner, William. Knowledge. Physics. Quantum mechanics. 1920's-30's. *1033*
—. Faulkner, William *(The Sound and the Fury)*. Jason Compson (fictional character). Values. 1929. *848*
—. Feminism. Novels. Rives, Amèlie. 1863-1945. *714*
—. Glasgow, Ellen. Novels. Women. 1898-1913. *1046*
Literary criticism. 1890-1982. *1027*
—. Agee, James *(Let Us Now Praise Famous Men)*. Language. Richards, Ivor Armstrong. 1930-40. *915*
—. Appalachia. Folk culture. Regionalism. 1812-1979. *774*
—. *Atlantic Monthly*. Hayne, Paul Hamilton. Howells, William Dean. 1871-81. *978*
—. Authors. Harris, Corra. Trent, William Peterfield. 17c-1905. *1059*
—. Blacks. Chesnutt, Charles W. Fiction. North Carolina. 1887-1900. *1709*
—. Blacks. Wright, Richard *(Uncle Tom's Children)*. 1938-73. *1735*
—. Brooks, Cleanth. Percy, Walker. ca 1940-79. *1136*
—. Bruce, Philip Alexander. Newspapers. Richmond *Times*. 1889. *1065*
—. Civil War. Mitchell, Margaret *(Gone with the Wind)*. Social Conditions. Tolstoy, Leo *(War and Peace)*. 1863-1936. *2447*
—. Collins, Jimmy *(Test Pilot)*. Faulkner, William. 1935. *863*
—. Cowley, Malcolm. Faulkner, William. 1940's. *1043*
—. Editors and Editing. Faulkner, William. Short stories. 1919-32. *1005*
—. Faulkner, William. 1920's-62. 1974-80. *1142*
—. Faulkner, William. Mississippi. Yoknapatawpha County (fictional place). 1974. *1014*
—. Faulkner, William. Modernism. 1915-60. *1112*

—. Gordon, Caroline. Letters. O'Connor, Flannery *(Wise Blood)*. 1951-64. *867*
—. Poe, Edgar Allan. Symbolism in Literature. Wilbur, Richard. 1820's-49. 1959. *970*
Literary Symbolism. *See* Symbolism in Literature.
Literary techniques. Fiction. 19c-20c. *1069*
Literary themes. Faulkner, William. Novels. Warren, Robert Penn. 1850's-20c. *914*
—. Faulkner, William *(Big Woods)*. Wilderness. 1934-55. *926*
—. Mencken, H. L. Savage South (motif). 1917-56. *857*
—. Pastoral ideal. Simpson, Lewis P. (review article). Social Customs. 19c-20c. *1028*
Literature. *See also* Adolescents' Literature; Authors; Autobiography; Biography; Books; Drama; Fiction; Humor; Journalism; Language; Memoirs; Novels; Poetry; Satire; Symbolism in Literature; Travel Accounts.
—. 1877-1974. *929*
—. Adams, Henry Brooks. Heroes. James, Henry. National Characteristics. 1865-1930. *452*
—. Agee, James. Journalism. Steinbeck, John. 1935-39. *1001*
—. Agee, James. Neighborhoods. Social Change. Tennessee (Knoxville). 1915-82. *788*
—. Agrarianism. Davidson, Donald. Mims, Edwin. 1923-58. *777*
—. Agrarians. *I'll Take My Stand*. Politics. 1930-80. *901*
—. Agrarians. Politics. Proletarians. 1930-39. *3824*
—. Aitken, George Atherton. Great Britain. Libraries. Texas, University of (Austin). 18c. 20c. *291*
—. American Revolution. Romanticism. Simms, William Gilmore. 1830's-70's. *815*
—. Appalachia. 1962-77. *773*
—. Appalachia. Attitudes. Griffin, Susan. Kolodny, Annette. Land. Women. 19c-20c. *1025*
—. Appalachia. Culture. 1970's. *1078*
—. Appalachia. Frontier. Romanticism. 1870-1977. *1048*
—. Appalachia. Heroes. Jefferson, Thomas. Thoreau, Henry David. 1977. *710*
—. Appalachia. Myths and Symbols. Simms, William Gilmore. 1847-50. *1055*
—. Appalachia. Values. 1976. *1114*
—. Appalachia. Wolfe, Thomas. 1900-38. *884*
—. Attitudes. Fitzgerald, F. Scott. 1917-45. *728*
—. Baptists. Newspapers. *South Western Baptist*. Taliaferro, Hardin Edwards. 1810-75. *1106*
—. Berry, William T. Bookselling. Tennessee (Nashville). 1835-76. *1652*
—. Bezzerides, A. L. Faulkner, William (review article). Minter, David. Stonum, Gary Lee. Wittenberg, Judith Bryant. 20c. *880*
—. Bibliographies. 1607-1979. *824*
—. Bibliographies. 1607-1980. *65*
—. Bibliographies. Crews, Harry. 1963-81. *2280*
—. Bibliographies. Dissertations. 1969-75. *1104*
—. Bibliographies. Dissertations. History. Mississippi. 1974. *72*
—. Bibliographies. Dissertations. History. Mississippi. Theses. 1976. *78*
—. Bibliographies. Scholarship. 1974. *1140*
—. Bibliographies. *Southern Literary Culture*. 1948-79. *969*
—. Blacks. Delaware (Wilmington). Dunbar-Nelson, Alice. Women. 1875-1935. *1744*
—. Blacks. Harlem Renaissance. Howard University. Locke, Alain. Philosophy. 1920's-30's. *1738*
—. Blacks. Hurston, Zora Neale. Wright, Richard. 1921-70's. *1746*
—. Blacks. Miscegenation. 1855-1974. *831*
—. Blacks. Oral history. Women. 1976. *962*
—. Brooks, Cleanth. Louisiana State University. Periodicals. *Southern Review*. Warren, Robert Penn. 1925-42. *1090*
—. Cabell, James Branch. Glasgow, Ellen. Virginia (Richmond). 1898-1912. *949*
—. Cabell, James Branch. Wagenknecht, Edward (review article). 20c. *950*
—. Cable, George Washington *(Old Creole Days)*. Louisiana. 1879-1925. *1094*
—. Cajuns. Folk Songs. French language. Louisiana. Music. 1948-80. *1412*
—. Caldwell, Erskine. Folklore. Legends. 1929-70's. *1695*
—. Calvinism. Faulkner, William. 1920's-75. *927*
—. Carver, Ada Jack. Louisiana (Natchitoches area). 1920's. *439*
—. Cather, Willa. Nostalgia. 1890-1930. *792*
—. Christianity. O'Connor, Flannery. Solzhenitsyn, Alexander. Western nations. 1940's-75. *975*
—. Civil War. Faulkner, William. Mississippi (Lafayette County, Oxford). 1860-65. 1925-62. *987*

Lott, Arthur. Alabama. Creek Indians. Indian Wars. Louisiana. Meredith, Thomas. Murder. 1812-14. *4135*

Louis, Joe. Attitudes. Boxing. 1934-51. *1638*

Louis Philippe. Beaujolais, Count of. France. Montpensier, Duc de (Antoine). Travel. West Virginia (Charles Town, Harper's Ferry, Wheeling). 1797. *740*

—. Cherokee Indians. Diaries. Excavations. Indians. Tennessee (Toqua). 1797. *4090*

Louisa Railroad Company. Railroads. Virginia. 1836-1980. *3142*

Louisiana. Acadians. Cajuns. Conrad, Glenn. DelSesto, Steven. Gibson, Jon L. 18c-1978. *650*

—. Acadians. Environment. 18c-19c. *2694*

—. Acadians. Folklore. Social customs. 18c-1978. *1628*

—. Acadians. French language. 1970. *3264*

—. Adams, Charles P. Blacks. Colleges and Universities. Grambling State University. 1896-1928. *1977*

—. Agricultural Production. Climate. Land. Sugarcane. 19c. *2738*

—. Agricultural Production. Congress. Economic Conditions. Subsidies. Sugar. 1860-1930. *2833*

—. Agricultural Production. Georgia. North Carolina. Rice. South Carolina. 1860's-1911. *2691*

—. Agricultural Technology and Research. Economies of scale. Plantations. Sugar. 1850's. *2834*

—. Agriculture. Blacks. Mechanization. Sugar industry. 1865-1914. *2710*

—. Alabama. Creek Indians. Indian Wars. Lott, Arthur. Meredith, Thomas. Murder. 1812-14. *4135*

—. Alabama. Georgia. Libraries. Mississippi. 1908-73. *245*

—. Amalgamated Association of Street and Electric Railway Employees of America. Labor Unions and Organizations. Local Government. New Orleans Public Service Inc. Public utilities. 1894-1929. *2575*

—. American Federation of Labor. Industrial Workers of the World. Marine Transport Workers. Sailors' Union. Strikes. United Fruit Company. 1913. *3384*

—. Architecture. Archival Catalogs and Inventories. Tulane University Library. 1830-1978. *1206*

—. Architecture. Churches. French. 1685-1830. *1392*

—. Architecture. Koch, Richard. Mississippi. Photographs. Tulane University Library. 1930-65. *844*

—. Armies. Banks, Nathaniel Prentiss. Civil War. Education. 1863-65. *2040*

—. Arts. Shreveport Art Club. 1922-81. *995*

—. Assimilation. Cajuns. 1755-1860. *501*

—. Aswell, James B. Educators. Politics. 1869-1931. *1861*

—. Authors. Slaughter, Marianne Marbury. 1860's-1928. *1013*

—. Baptist Historical Society. Hartsfield, Green W. Paxton, W. E. Publishers and Publishing. 1850-1900. *2414*

—. Baptists. Civil War. Mount Lebanon University. 1835-90's. *1806*

—. Barnum, P. T. Concerts. Lind, Jenny. Music. 1851. *896*

—. Basso, Hamilton. Demagoguery. Long, Huey P. Novels. 1920-76. *3790*

—. Bateman, F. O. "Red". Forests and Forestry. Great Southern Lumber Company. 20c. *3146*

—. Bibliographies. Drama. Nolan, Paul T. 1970's. *977*

—. Bibliographies. Long, Huey P. State Politics. 1930-69. *3647*

—. Blacks. Carpetbaggers. Governors. Pinchback, Pinckney B. S. 1862-90. *3811*

—. Blacks. Christian, Marcus B. Dillard University. Federal Writers' Project. Historiography. Work Progress Administration. 1930's-79. *380*

—. Blacks. Dillard University. Federal Writers' Project. Folklore. *Gumbo Ya-Ya* (publication). Saxon, Lyle. 1930's. *1722*

—. Blacks. Educators. 1964-72. *1975*

—. Blacks. Folk Songs. Ledbetter, Huddie "Leadbelly". Love, Blanche. 1880's-1949. 1976. *1129*

—. Blacks. Immigrants. Italians. Race Relations. Sugarcane. 1880-1910. *2828*

—. Blacks. Immigration. Italian Americans. Race Relations. Sugarcane. 1880-1910. *2829*

—. Blacks. Ray, John. Republican Party. Scalawags. ca 1836-88. *3818*

—. Blacks, free. Civil Rights. Civil War. Military Service. Reconstruction. 1850-90. *3857*

—. Blalock, Alice Grundy. College teachers. Grambling State University. ca 1920-70. *1976*

—. Boggs, Hale. Gerrymandering. House of Representatives. Lobbying. State Legislatures. 1968-69. *3557*

—. Bosque y Fanqui, Cayetana Susana. Claiborne, William Charles Cole. Grymes, John R. 1790-1890. *551*

—. Bossier, Pierre. Political Leadership. 1838-45. *3801*

—. Botany. Hale, Josiah. ca 1791-1856. *858*

—. Boundaries. Mexico. Puelles, José María de Jesús. Texas. 1512-1813. 1827-28. *3229*

—. Brotherhood of Timber Workers. Industrial Workers of the World. Lumber and Lumbering. Race Relations. Texas. 1910-13. *3401*

—. Burton, William L. Cypress. Florida. Lumber and Lumbering. Philanthropy. 1870-1927. *2986*

—. Cable, George Washington (*Old Creole Days*). Literature. 1879-1925. *1094*

—. Cable, George Washington (*Strange True Stories of Louisiana*). Hoaxes. Houssaye, Sidonie de la. 1889. *1615*

—. Cajuns. 18c-20c. *684*

—. Cajuns. Cities. Geographic Mobility. Texas. ca 1920-80. *3262*

—. Cajuns. Coasts. Creoles. 1765-1982. *673*

—. Cajuns. Daily life. Leisure. Modernization. Social Customs. 1900-79. *499*

—. Cajuns. Folk Songs. French language. Literature. Music. 1948-80. *1412*

—. Cajuns. Leisure. Social Customs. 19c-20c. *660*

—. Camp Fire Girls. Cheers. Folklore. Girls. 1975-76. *1648*

—. Catholic Church. Chopin, Kate. Christianity. Fiction. 1870-1910. *807*

—. Catholic Church. Daughters of the Cross. McCants, Dorothea Olga. Missions and Missionaries. Publishers and Publishing. ca 1855-1900. 1970's. *2233*

—. Catholic Church. Indians. Missions and Missionaries. 18c-20c. *2444*

—. Centenary College. Dance. Educational Policy. Methodist Church. 1941. *1922*

—. Chickasaw Indians. France. Indian-White Relations. Leadership. Military Campaigns. 1739-40. *3980*

—. Chiropractic. Law. 1921-74. *2129*

—. Chopin, Kate. Novels. 1870-99. *918*

—. Civil law. Common law. Courts. 19c-20c. *3480*

—. Class Struggle. Historiography. Shugg, Roger (review article). 1800-60. 1939-76. *296*

—. Clergy. Drummond, Miriam F. Foster, Cornelius Emmett. Personal Narratives. 19c. *555*

—. Cockfighting. Social Customs. Sports. 20c. *1475*

—. Coliseum Square Association. New Orleans Historic District Landmarks Committee. Preservation. 1807-1978. *1403*

—. Conservation of Natural Resources. Forests and Forestry. Hardtner, Henry Ernest. 1892-1935. *2554*

—. Conservatism. Ellender, Allen J. Hall, Covington. Radicals and Radicalism. 1871-1972. *3487*

—. Constitutional conventions, state. 1973-74. *3559*

—. Constitutions. 1974. *3714*

—. Constitutions, state. 1921. 1973. *3483*

—. Constitutions, State. Courts. Sex discrimination. 1970-77. *3778*

—. Constitutions, State. Home rule. Local government. 1851-1974. *3558*

—. Constitutions, State. Slidell, John. Suffrage. 1812-52. *3758*

—. Contracts. Forests and Forestry. Hardtner, Henry Ernest. Lumber and Lumbering. Severance tax. State Government. 1910-35. *3052*

—. Coordinating and Development Council of Northwest Louisiana. Historical Sites and Parks. Preservation. 1975-78. *149*

—. Cotton. Depressions. Long, Huey P. Texas. 1931. *2849*

—. Country Life. Murder. Social Customs. Weapons. 19c-1979. *503*

—. Creoles. 1860-1980. *685*

—. Creoles. Discrimination. Fifth Ward Settlement. Identity. 1785-1979. *3299*

—. Creoles. Jamaica. Journalism. Novels. Roberts, W. Adolphe. 1929-49. *418*

—. Criminal Law. Livingston, Edward. 1822. *3682*

—. Cypress. Lumber and Lumbering. Public Lands. West Florida. 1803-52. *3059*

—. Demagoguery. Historiography. Long, Huey P. State Government. 1928-73. *3805*

—. Democratic Party. Elections. Political Parties. Primaries. 1952-64. *3817*

—. Dialects. French language. 18c-20c. *3210*

—. Discrimination. Immigrants. Italian Americans. 1871-1905. *663*

—. Education. Long, Huey P. Working Class. 1928-35. *1816*

—. Education, Finance. Public Schools. Race. 1890-1910. *2036*

—. Elections. Elites. Political Reform. Poor. Progressive Party. 1894-1921. *3769*

—. Elections (gubernatorial). Morrison, deLesseps S. Political Campaigns. 1951-52. *3607*

—. Ethnic Groups. French language. 1970-79. *3263*

—. Fiction. Frontier and Pioneer Life. Humor. Owen, Tom. Thorpe, Thomas Bangs. 1839-59. *450*

—. Forest and Farm Workers Union. Hall, Covington. Labor Unions and Organizations. Lumber and lumbering. Socialism. 1907-16. *3383*

—. France. Medicine (practice of). Pharmacy. Spain. 1717-1852. *2122*

—. Francophones. Population. 20c. *1603*

—. Freedmen. Homesteading and Homesteaders. Reconstruction. 1865-83. *2806*

—. French Americans. 18c-20c. *543*

—. French language. Newspapers. 1794-1860. *1430*

—. Fullerton, Samuel Holmes. Gulf Lumber. Lumber and Lumbering. 1906-27. *2926*

—. Gordon, Kate. Suffrage. Women. 1896-1918. *3587*

—. Government. Long, Huey P. Personal Narratives. Peyton, Rupert. 1917-35. *3740*

—. Governors. Inaugural addresses. Rhetoric. State Legislatures. 1813-1973. *3756*

—. Governors. Political power. State Government. 1699-1974. *3554*

—. *Herold et al. v. Parish Board of School Directors et al.* (Louisiana, 1914). Religion in the Public Schools. Supreme courts (state). 1913-15. *3712*

—. Historic Preservation of Shreveport Committee. Preservation. 1972-78. *1364*

—. Historical Sites and Parks. National Trust for Historic Preservation. Preservation. 1978. *216*

—. Holly Grove Methodist Church. Methodist Church. ca 1825-1980. *2463*

—. House of Representatives. Waggonner, Joe D. 1962-80. *3526*

—. Houses. Log construction. 19c-20c. *1308*

—. Indians. 1500-1980. *3898*

—. Indians. Meteorites. Texas. Wichita Indians. 1808-26. *3978*

—. Key, V. O., Jr. Methodology. Public policy. State Politics. Virginia. 1929-70's. *3648*

—. Lake, Hattie. Teachers. 1847-78. *1877*

—. LaRue, Edgar (family). Libraries. 1799-1975. *581*

—. Law. Lemee House. Natchitoches Historic District. Preservation. 18c-1980. *1341*

—. Location. Plantations. Sugar. 1742-1870. *3305*

—. Long, Earl K. State Politics. *3284*

—. Long, Huey P. Pleasant, Ruffin G. Prisons. Uniforms. 1916-40. *3742*

—. Long, Huey P. Populism. Progressivism. State Government. 1891-1935. *3544*

—. Manufactures. Natural resources. Spanish moss. 19c-1980. *2563*

—. Metropolitan areas. Population. 1970-75. *3079*

—. New Orleans *Daily Picayune*. Newspapers. Nicholson, Eliza Jane. Poets. 1849-96. *1532*

—. Nicholls State University. 1944-73. *1953*

—. Novels. Plantations. Regionalism. Saxon, Lyle (*Children of Strangers*). 1920's-40's. *1092*

—. Oil Industry and Trade. Strikes. Texas. 1917-18. *3415*

—. Oral history. Research. 1936-79. *158*

—. Photographs. Red River Valley. 1873. *3233*

—. Physicians. 1886. *2114*

—. Politics. 1785-1810. *3825*

—. Prévost, Abbé (*Manon Lescaut*). 1719-31. *726*

—. Public transportation. Shreveport City Railroad Company. Street railways. 1870-76. *3159*

—. Public Welfare. 1928-60. *3363*

—. Red River. Steamboats. ca 1840-1910. *2592*

—. Spanish-American War. Volunteer Armies. 1898. *3846*

Louisiana (Acadia Parish). Germans. Immigration. 1870's-1917. *602*

Louisiana (Acadiana). French language. 1970's. *1539*

—. Language. 1931-80. *3198*

Louisiana (Algiers, Gretna). Mules. Railroads. Zagel, Hermann. 1883-84. *753*

Louisiana and Arkansas Railway. Arkansas. Railroads. 1898-1949. *2917*

—. Locomotives. Railroads. 1896-1929. *2955*

Louisiana (Arcadia). 1840-93. *3284*

Louisiana (Attakapas, Opelousas areas). Transportation. Waterways. 19c. *3275*

Louisiana (Avoyelles Parish). Folklore. French language. 1790-1980. *3211*

Louisiana, northern. Arkansas, southern. Oil Industry and Trade. Texas, east. 1900-35. *3013*
—. Baptists. Brinson, James. Methodist Church. Missions and Missionaries. Pine Hills Baptist Church. Stevenson, William. ca 1800-40. *2243*
—. Baptists. Clergy. Hartsfield, Green W. Social Conditions. 1860-96. *645*
—. Blacks. Politics. Religion. 1865-77. *2284*
—. Camp meetings. Foster, Elizabeth Pyburn. Old Siloam Camp Ground. Personal Narratives. Protestantism. 19c. *1498*
—. Catholic Church. Church records. Preservation. 1716-1840's. 1930's-74. *2250*
—. Documents. Longino, Luther. Medicine (practice of). 1857-1948. *2149*
—. Doyle family. 1843-1981. *533*
—. Educators. Liggin, John Lewis. 1887-1950. *1835*
—. Gould, Jay. Mergers. Railroads. Texas and Pacific Railroad. 1870-1914. *3050*
—. Music. 1812-1977. *1457*
—. Natural Gas. Natural Resources. Oil Industry and Trade. 20c. *2586*
—. Phillips, Ambrose Augustus. Spring Lake Plantation. 1860-1976. *1371*
—. Railroads. 1851-84. *3027*
Louisiana, northwestern. Alabama Indians. Coushatta Indians. Indian-White Relations. Red River. 1800-31. *3977*
—. Archival Catalogs and Inventories. 19c-20c. *215*
—. Archival Catalogs and Inventories. Family. 19c. *214*
—. Arkansas. Boundaries. Texas. 18c-1841. *3311*
Louisiana (Ouachita Parish). Boscobel Cottage. Plantations. Restorations. 1820-1978. *1227*
—. Inscriptions. Tombstones. ca 1830-1920. *531*
Louisiana (Plaquemines Parish). Perez, Leander. Public Welfare. Racism. Social reform. 1919-69. *3646*
Louisiana (Poverty Point site). Artifacts. Indians. Missouri (Cahokia site). Prehistory. *4137*
Louisiana Purchase Exposition (St. Louis, 1904). Buildings. Elks Lodge. Missouri. Oklahoma (El Reno). Preservation. 1904-79. *1395*
Louisiana (Red River). Bridges. ca 1884-1968. *1342*
Louisiana (Ruston). Kidd-Davis House. Preservation. 1975-78. *1196*
Louisiana (St. Joseph). Newspapers. *Tensas Gazette*. 1852-1974. *1452*
Louisiana (St. Martin Parish). Creoles. French language. 1809-1978. *1565*
Louisiana (Shiloh). Baptists. Burns, Bertha Porter. Burns, Marion Van. Clergy. Teachers. 1884-1975. *616*
—. Lee, Mary Edmunds Tabor. 1840's-1926. *619*
Louisiana (Shreveport). Baptists. Colleges and Universities. Dodd College. 1937. *1960*
—. Baptists. Colleges and Universities. Dodd College. Women. 1927-42. *1959*
—. Barksdale Air Force Base. Long, Huey P. Politics. State legislatures. 1923-33. *3862*
—. Bishops. Episcopal Church, Protestant. Polk, Leonidas. 1830-1916. *2285*
—. Caspiana Plantation ("Big House"). Hutchinson family. Restorations. 1850-1978. *1370*
—. Cemeteries. 1839-1975. *532*
—. Columbia Restaurant. ca 1900-69. *1208*
—. Epidemics. Yellow fever. 1873. *2139*
—. Federal Regulation. Henderson, William K. Radio. 1925-35. *1624*
—. Political campaigns. Prohibition. 1950-52. *3724*
—. St. Vincent Academy. -1973. *1287*
—. Water supply. 1840-87. *3094*
Louisiana (southeastern). Ethnic Groups. French language. 1911-80. *580*
Louisiana, southern. Cypress. Lumber and Lumbering. Swamps. Williams, Frank B. 1869-1929. *2925*
—. Diaries. Plantations. 1839-59. *554*
Louisiana (Spearsville). Baptists. Colleges and Universities. Education. Everett Institute. 1893-1908. *1796*
Louisiana State Fair. Farmers. Political Leadership. Schuler, Charles. State Board of Agriculture. 1840-1911. *3736*
Louisiana State University. Brooks, Cleanth. Literature. Periodicals. *Southern Review*. Warren, Robert Penn. 1925-42. *1090*
—. Mathematics. Nicholson, James W. 1860's-1917. *933*
Louisiana State University, Department of Archives. Butler, Thomas (family). Documents. Landscaping. Plantations. 1768-1900. *1375*
Louisiana State University, Department of Archives and Manuscripts. Manuscripts. Spain. West Florida. 1763-1800. *45*
Louisiana State University (Department of Speech). Debates. LSU Forum. 1960's-80's. *1926*
Louisiana Technical University. Football. 1901-79. *1444*

Louisiana (Tensas Parish). Cotton. Mississippi River. Steamboats. 1843-1904. *2578*
Louisiana (Union Parish). Inscriptions. Tombstones. 1839-1970's. *526*
Louisiana (Vernon). 1846-1978. *2900*
—. Elementary Education. Smith, Anna Calhoun. 1885-1901. *1924*
Louisiana (Vernon Parish). Communes. Llano del Rio Cooperative Colony. Socialism. 1917-38. *638*
Louisiana (Webster Parish). Baptists, Southern. Concord Baptist Association. 1832-1972. *2349*
—. Cheshire, Johnathan Singleton. Country Life. Diaries. Medicine (practice of). 1882-88. *2158*
—. Doyline School. Schools. Students. Teachers. 1905. *1802*
Louisiana, western. Brotherhood of Timber Workers. Emerson, Arthur L. Industrial Workers of the World. Labor Disputes. Lumber and Lumbering. Texas, east. 1900-16. *3393*
—. Brotherhood of Timber Workers. Lumber and Lumbering. Race Relations. Southern Lumber Operators' Association. Texas, east. 1911-13. *3402*
Louisiana (Winfield Parish). Long, Earl K. Politics. 1929-60. *3737*
Louisiana (Winn Parish). ca 1650-1950. *2968*
—. Caminos Reales. Roads. Prehistory-1910. *3235*
—. Camp meetings. Hudson Holiness Interdenominational Camp. 1899-1977. *2279*
—. Inscriptions. Populism. Socialism. Tombstones. 1852-1975. *523*
Louisiana (7th Judicial District). Constitutions, State. Judges. 1812-1972. *3564*
Louisiana-Texas Lumber War of 1911-1912. Labor disputes. Lumber and lumbering. Texas, east. 1906-16. *3391*
Louisville, University of. Colleges and Universities. Kentucky. 1798-1982. *1809*
Louisville, University of (Psychology Department). Colleges and Universities. Freeman, Ellis. Kentucky. Psychology. 1907-53. *1792*
Louisville Varnish Company. Callahan, Patrick Henry. Industrial Relations. Kentucky. Profit sharing. 1908-40. *3388*
Love, Blanche. Blacks. Folk Songs. Ledbetter, Huddie "Leadbelly". Louisiana. 1880's-1949. 1976. *1129*
Loveland, Anne C. Hill, Samuel S., Jr. Historiography. Religion (review article). Wilson, Charles Reagan. 1941-81. *2206*
Loveland, Anne C. (review article). Baptists (Southern). Clergy. Methodist Church. Presbyterian Church. Slavery. 1800-60. *2246*
Lovely, William. Arkansas. Cherokee Indians. Civil Rights. Indians. Land. 1816-28. *3919*
Lovingood, Sut (fictional character). Eroticism. Harris, George Washington. 1900. *1619*
Lowe, Richard G. Campbell, Randolph B. Politics. Social Organization. Texas (review article). Wealth. 1830's-60. 1977. *642*
Lowry, Tom (interview). Coal Mines and Mining. Davidson-Wilder (firm). Folk songs. Strikes. Tennessee. 1932. *1419*
Loyalists. American Revolution. Novels. Simms, William Gilmore. South Carolina. 1780-83. 19c. *913*
Loyless, Thomas W. *Augusta Chronicle*. Editors and Editing. Georgia. Newspapers. 1903-26. *1456*
Lozano, José C. Folk healer. Jaramillo, Pedrito. Texas (south). 19c. *2104*
LSU Forum. Debates. Louisiana State University (Department of Speech). 1960's-80's. *1926*
Lucas, Anthony F. Higgins, Pattillo. Oil Industry and Trade. Spindletop Oil Rush. Texas (Beaumont). 1901-30's. *3119*
Lucy Opry. Bluegrass. Concert halls. Music. Tennessee (Memphis). 1966-82. *1515*
—. Bluegrass. Music. Tennessee (Memphis). 1966-83. *1514*
Ludvigh, Samuel. Maryland. Travel accounts. 1846-47. *746*
Lumbee Indians. Indian-White Relations. Maryland (Baltimore). Social Customs. ca 1586-1979. *3902*
Lumber and Lumbering. Alabama (Mobile). Exports. 1760-1860. *2959*
—. Barton, Stephen, Jr. North Carolina (Hertford County; Bartonsville). Rural Settlements. 1856-65. *3075*
—. Blacks. Industrial Relations. Migration, Internal. Pine trees. 1912-26. *3392*
—. Brotherhood of Timber Workers. Emerson, Arthur L. Industrial Workers of the World. Labor Disputes. Louisiana, western. Texas, east. 1900-16. *3393*
—. Brotherhood of Timber Workers. Industrial Workers of the World. Louisiana. Race Relations. Texas. 1910-13. *3401*

—. Brotherhood of Timber Workers. Louisiana, western. Race Relations. Southern Lumber Operators' Association. Texas, east. 1911-13. *3402*
—. Burton, William L. Cypress. Florida. Louisiana. Philanthropy. 1870-1927. *2986*
—. Canals. Dismal Swamp. Nature Conservation. North Carolina. Virginia. 1700-1976. *3295*
—. Cherokee Indians. Colonial Government. Georgia. Priber, Christian Gottlieb. Utopians. 1730's-ca 1744. *4049*
—. Contracts. Forests and Forestry. Hardtner, Henry Ernest. Louisiana. Severance tax. State Government. 1910-35. *3052*
—. Cypress. Louisiana. Public Lands. West Florida. 1803-52. *3059*
—. Cypress. Louisiana, southern. Swamps. Williams, Frank B. 1869-1929. *2925*
—. Cypress. Pullboat logging. Swamps. 1889-1961. *3035*
—. Dismal Swamp. North Carolina. Virginia. 1760's-1970's. *3131*
—. Exports. Georgia. 1732-75. *2992*
—. Exports. Ports. South Carolina (Charleston). 18c-1860. *2958*
—. Farmers. Kentucky. 1860's-1920's. *2557*
—. Forest and Farm Workers Union. Hall, Covington. Labor Unions and Organizations. Louisiana. Socialism. 1907-16. *3383*
—. Fullerton, Samuel Holmes. Gulf Lumber. Louisiana. 1906-27. *2926*
—. Georgia. 18c. *2993*
—. Georgia. Labor. Social Organization. 1880-1917. *3372*
—. Great Southern Lumber Company. Louisiana (Bogalusa). 1871-1955. *2943*
—. Horn, Stanley F. Industry. Periodicals. Personal Narratives. *Southern Lumberman*. Trade associations. 1908-33. *3006*
—. Labor disputes. Louisiana-Texas Lumber War of 1911-1912. Texas, east. 1906-16. *3391*
—. Lutcher, Henry J. Moore, G. Bedell. Sawmills. Texas, East. 1870-1930. *3040*
—. Mississippi (Laurel). 1882-1916. *2995*
—. National Recovery Administration. Southern Pine Association. 1933-35. *2964*
—. Texas (Kilgore area). Thompson, Benjamin Franklin (family). 1852-1959. *3009*
Lumpkin, Wilson. Cherokee Indians. Georgia. Indian-White Relations. Removals, forced. ca 1820-38. *4120*
Lungkwitz, Hermann. Art. Frontier and Pioneer Life. German Americans. Petri, Richard. Texas (Pedernales River). 1852-57. *984*
Lunsford, Bascom Lamar. Appalachia. Folk songs. North Carolina. Social conditions. 1882-1973. *1494*
—. Culture. Mountain Dance and Folk Festival. North Carolina (Asheville). Social Change. 1928-78. *1685*
Luraghi, Raimondo. Ideology (review article). Plantations. Politics. Thornton, J. Miller, III. 1607-1860. 1970's. *2868*
Lurton, Horace H. Court of Appeals. Harlan, John Marshall. Taft, William Howard. Tennessee. 1897. *3741*
Lutcher, Henry J. Lumber and Lumbering. Moore, G. Bedell. Sawmills. Texas, East. 1870-1930. *3040*
Lutheran Church. Alabama. Bakke, Niles J. Young, Rosa J. 1839-1965. *2266*
—. Alabama. Blacks. Missions and Missionaries. 1916-78. *2398*
—. Alabama. Photographs. 1971-74. *2517*
—. Boltzius, John Martin. Diaries. Georgia (Ebenezer). Mühlenberg, Henry Melchoir. South Carolina (Charleston). Travel. 1742. *2330*
—. Slavery. 1790-1865. *2400*
Lutheran Church (Missouri Synod). Circuit riders. Frontier and Pioneer Life. German Americans. Oklahoma. Texas. Wacker, Hermann Dietrich. 1847-1938. *2461*
—. St. Paul's Church. Texas (Serbin). Wends. 1850's. *2362*
Lutheran Church (North Carolina Synod). Blacks. Clergy. 1865-89. *2399*
Lyceum movement. Edwards, Harry Stillwell. Georgia. Lectures. Nye, Edgar Wilson "Bill". Riley, James Whitcomb. 1888. *938*
Lyell, Charles. Geology. Hilgard, Eugene. Mississippi. 1699-1876. *3199*
Lying contest. Folklore. North Carolina (Cape Fear County). 1974. *1606*
Lynch, James. Blacks. Letters. Methodist Episcopal Church. Mississippi. Reconstruction. 1868-69. *2291*
Lynch, John Roy. Blacks. House of Representatives. Mississippi. 1847-1939. *3689*

—. Blacks. House of Representatives. Mississippi. Reconstruction. 1869-1939. *3488*

Lynchburg College. Methodist Protestant Church. Virginia (Lynchburg). 1855-69. *1896*

Lynching. Blacks. *Free Speech.* Newspapers. Tennessee (Memphis). Wells, Ida B. 1892. *1711*

—. Blacks. Population. 1889-1931. *366*

—. Capital Punishment. Crime and Criminals. Discrimination. Judicial Process. 1978. *3654*

—. Hennessey affair. Italian Americans. Louisiana (New Orleans). 1880-1920. *577*

Lyon, James A. Mississippi (Columbus). Presbyterian Church (Southern). 1860-75. *2529*

Lyrics. Blacks. Jazz. Music. Race. 20c. *1720*

# M

Mabry, Catherine Cook. Louisiana (Bernice). Women. 1885-1913. *617*

Mabry, Joseph A. Forrest, Nathan Bedford. Houston, Sam. State Politics. Tennessee. Upper Classes. Violence. 1800-80. *679*

MacDowell, Katherine Sherwood Bonner. Frank, William L. (review article). Literature. 1864-83. 1976. *1070*

Macon Heritage Foundation. Architecture. Georgia. Historical Sites and Parks. Preservation. 1975-79. *1394*

Madison, James. Government. Political Theory. Virginia. 1774-1817. *3479*

—. Letters. Scott, Susan Randolph Madison. Sex roles. 1811. *423*

Madstones. Animal bites. Folk Medicine. Virginia. 19c. *2137*

—. Barlow, Vivian J. Folk Medicine. Kentucky (Barlow). ca 1695-1901. *2146*

Magazines. *See* Periodicals.

Magnolia Mound Plantation House. Architecture. Furniture and Furnishings. Louisiana (Baton Rouge). Plantations. 1791-1982. *1157*

Maison Française. Colleges and Universities. French studies. Spurlin, Paul Merrill. 1936-80. *1868*

Management. *See also* Industrial Relations.

—. Business. Plantations. Profit. ca 1830-60. *2794*

—. Congress of Industrial Organizations. Labor Unions and Organizations. National Industrial Recovery Act (US, 1933). National Labor Relations Act (US, 1935). Textile Industry. 1933-41. *3459*

Mandle, Jay R. Blacks. Boritt, Gabor S. Economic conditions. Economic conditions (review article). James, John A. Oubre, Claude F. Social Change. 1860-1900. *2597*

—. Economic Conditions. Plantations. Regionalism (review article). Thompson, Edgar T. Wright, Gavin. 1865-1978. *2580*

—. Economic Conditions (review article). Ransom, Roger L. Sutch, Richard. Wiener, Jonathan M. 1850-1910. 1977-78. *3362*

Manganese mining. Arkansas (Cushing). Mining. Social Conditions. 1849-1959. *3126*

Manifest Destiny. Five Civilized Tribes. Historiography. Oklahoma. Removals, forced. 19c-20c. *3924*

Manigault, Charles. Georgia. Letters. Milling. Rice. 1852. *2688*

Manning, Joseph C. Alabama. Blacks. Discrimination. NAACP. Suffrage. Whites. 1895-1930. *3744*

Mansfield Female College. Colleges and Universities. Louisiana (Mansfield). Reunions. Women. 1844-1930. 1974. *1920*

Mansions. Marland, Ernest W. Oil industry and trade. Oklahoma (Ponca City). 1920's-75. *1170*

Manufacturers. Alabama. Cotton. Pratt, Daniel. 1799-1873. *2899*

Manufactures. *See also* names of articles manufactured, e.g. Furniture and Furnishings, etc.; names of industries, e.g. Steel Industry, etc.; Corporations; Patents; Prices.

—. Appalachia. Home Economics. Social customs. 1840-70. *759*

—. Attitudes. Economic Conditions. Investments. 1850-60. *2901*

—. Consumers. Exports. North Central States. 1860. *2938*

—. Louisiana. Natural resources. Spanish moss. 19c-1980. *2563*

—. Nuclear Arms. ca 1942-79. *3088*

Manufacturing. Banking. Economic development. Urbanization. 1840-60. *3178*

—. Competition. Economic conditions. Market structure. 1850-60. *2902*

—. Economies of scale. 1850-60. *2891*

Manuscripts. *See also* Documents.

—. Archives. Bibliographies. Mississippi Department of Archives and History. 1975. *140*

—. Archives. Mississippi Department of Archives and History. 1973. *191*

—. Asplund, John. Backus, Isaac. Baptists. Edwards, Morgan. Georgia. Smith, Hezekiah. 18c. *2282*

—. Books (editions). Faulkner, William (*Flags in the Dust*). ca 1925-77. *862*

—. Cherokee Indians. Land grants. Mexico. Starr, Emmet. Texas. 1820's-30's. *4051*

—. Colleges and Universities. Libraries. Mississippi. 1976. *71*

—. Colleges and Universities. Libraries. Mississippi. 1978-79. *81*

—. Colleges and Universities. Libraries. Mississippi. 1979-80. *80*

—. Daily Life. Florida. Indians. Seminole Indians. 1886-1922. *3903*

—. Faulkner, William. 1920-29. *999*

—. Florida (Pensacola). West Florida, University of (library). 1967-73. *298*

—. Gálvez, Bernardo de. Gottschalk, Louis M. Historic New Orleans Collection. Louisiana (New Orleans). 18c-20c. *28*

—. Louisiana State University, Department of Archives and Manuscripts. Spain. West Florida. 1763-1800. *45*

Map Drawing. Boundaries. Cherokee Indians. Indians. 1785-1802. *3292*

—. Navigation. Surveying. Virginia. 1612-1880's. *3313*

Maps. Austin, Stephen F. Texas. 1821-39. *3266*

—. Bartram, John. Bartram, William. Diaries. Harper, Francis. Travel. 1765-76. 1917-40. *3203*

—. Boundaries. Clark, John H. Surveying. Texas (northwestern). 1858-62. *3324*

—. Boundaries (disputes). Chew, Benjamin. Documents. Maryland. Mason-Dixon Line. Pennsylvania. Princeton University Library. 1731-68. *3338*

—. Fort San Fernando de las Barrancas. Spain. Tennessee (Memphis area). 1795-97. *3309*

—. Kentucky. 1775. *3220*

—. Tennessee. 1794-99. *3344*

—. Tennessee. 1800-19. *3343*

Mardi Gras. Harper, William Poynot. Louisiana (New Orleans). 1866-72. *1496*

—. Louisiana (New Orleans). 1718-1978. *1634*

Marie Madeleine of St. Stanislaus. Catholic Church. France. Louisiana (New Orleans). Ursulines. Women. 1727-60. *2431*

Marine Engineering. Louisiana (New Orleans). Military Camps and Forts. 1680-1970's. *3866*

Marine Transport Workers. American Federation of Labor. Industrial Workers of the World. Louisiana. Sailors' Union. Strikes. United Fruit Company. 1913. *3384*

Maritime archaeology. Methodology. Shipwrecks. Virginia (Portsmouth; Scott Creek). 1893-1982. *205*

Maritime Law. *See also* Fishing Rights; Territorial Waters.

—. Florida. Salvage. 1760's-1830's. *3106*

Market structure. Competition. Economic conditions. Manufacturing. 1850-60. *2902*

Marketing. Agricultural Cooperatives. Bingham, Robert Worth. Sapiro, Aaron. Tobacco. 1920's. *2709*

—. Agricultural Cooperatives. Computers. Cotton. Plains Cotton Cooperative Association. Telecommunication. Texas (Lubbock). 1920's-70's. *2822*

—. Agriculture. Farms (small). Florida Marketing Bureau. Mayo, Nathan. State government. ca 1917-60. *2757*

—. Blacks. Cotton. Farmers. Social change. Social Classes. Whites. 1865-1940. *2869*

—. Cotton. Urbanization. 1880-1930. *3154*

Markets. Louisiana (New Orleans). 1780-1940. *3105*

Marland, Ernest W. Mansions. Oil industry and trade. Oklahoma (Ponca City). 1920's-75. *1170*

Marriage. *See also* Divorce; Family; Sex.

—. Blacks. Kentucky (Gallatin County). Public Records. 1866-1913. *508*

—. Childbirth. Death and Dying. Rites and Ceremonies. Social Customs. Tennessee, east. 20c. *1555*

—. Downs, Lavinia. Georgia. Hawkins, Benjamin. Indians.. Petersen, Karsten. 1796-1816. *3990*

—. Property. South Carolina. Women. 1730-1830. *659*

Marriage records. Baptists. Maryland (Baltimore). Richards, Lewis. 1784-89. *218*

Marriage registers. Davis, William Hervey. Presbyterian Church. South Carolina. 1837-80. *2260*

Marshall, Daniel. American Revolution. Baptists. Clergy. Georgia. 1747-1823. *2303*

—. Baptists. Blacks. Georgia (Richmond County). Kiokee Church. Settlement. 1784-1819. *2304*

Marshall, George C. Virginia Historical Society. 1973. *338*

Marshall, Thurgood. Lawyers. Maryland, University of, School of Law. Murray, Donald G. NAACP. School Integration. 1930-54. *2025*

Marshall University (James E. Morrow Library; Special Collections Department). Archival Catalogs and Inventories. Colleges and Universities. West Virginia. 1804-1982. *289*

Marshals, deputy. Creek Indians. Indians. Johnson, Grant. Law enforcement. Oklahoma. Texas. 1895-1906. *3820*

Martí, José. City politics. Cuba. Florida (Jacksonville). Huah, José Alejandro. Independence Movements. 1836-1905. *3591*

Martin, Absalom. Frontier and Pioneer Life. Military Service. Surveying. West Virginia (Wheeling area). 1758-1802. *678*

Martin, John. Cherokee Indians. Indians. Missions and Missionaries. Presbyterian Church. Richardson, William. Tennessee. Virginia. 1755-63. *3943*

*Martin Luther King, Jr. Elementary School Children v. Ann Arbor School District Board* (Michigan, 1979). Blacks. Education. English language. Racism. Social Classes. 1979. *2075*

Martin, Roscoe C. Historiography. Key, V. O., Jr. Political attitudes. *Southern Politics* project. 1944-70. *3726*

Martin, William. Nashville and Northwestern Railway. Tennessee (Martin). 1832-93. *3139*

Marx, David. Ethnic Groups. Georgia (Atlanta). Interpersonal Relations. Jews. 1890-1930. *2198*

Marxism. *See also* Anarchism and Anarchists; Class Struggle; Socialism.

—. Economic Conditions. Slavery. Social Organization. 17c-1860. *2573*

—. Genovese, Eugene D. Historiography. 1965-72. *400*

Maryhelp Abbey. Heraldry. North Carolina. 1876-1983. *1161*

Maryland. Acculturation. Artifacts. Delaware. Indians. Pennsylvania. Virginia. 18c-20c. *3907*

—. Agriculture. Bibliographies. 17c-1976. *310*

—. *American Farmer.* Animal husbandry. Horse racing. Periodicals. Skinner, John Stuart. 1819-29. *1429*

—. Anti-Catholicism. France. Politicians. Protestants. 1750's. *2210*

—. Architects. Calverton (estate). Long, Robert Cary, Sr. Ramée, Joseph Jacques. 1815-72. *1310*

—. Architecture. Virginia. 1607-1715. *1187*

—. Archives. Baltimore Region Institutional Studies Center. 1821-1980. *130*

—. Bacon, Thomas. Church of England. Clergy. ca 1745-68. *2252*

—. Baltimore Almshouse. Blacks. Immigrants. Medicine (practice of). Poor. 1828-50. *2133*

—. Baltimore City Hospital. Hospitals. 1772-1964. *2142*

—. Baltimore Normal School for the Education of Colored Teachers. Blacks. Bowie State College. Education. Wells, Nelson. 1843-72. *1931*

—. Baltimore Reform League. Lawyers' Round Table. Niles, Alfred Salem. Voluntary Associations. 1852-1972. *3679*

—. Beekeeping. 1634-1976. *2682*

—. Beekeeping. 1634-1976. *2683*

—. Bibliographies. 1634-1980. *51*

—. Bibliographies. 1634-1981. *50*

—. Bibliographies. 1788-1978. *49*

—. Bibliographies. 1974-75. *53*

—. Bibliographies. 1974. *54*

—. Bibliographies. 1976. *47*

—. Bibliographies. 1977. *48*

—. Bibliographies. 1979. *52*

—. Bibliographies. History. 17c-1974. *22*

—. Bibliographies. Pamphlets. 1819-32. *146*

—. Blacks. Colleges and Universities. Equal opportunity. 1908-75. *2055*

—. Blacks. Labor Unions and Organizations. NAACP. Teachers. 1930's. *2089*

—. Bordley, Stephen. Church of England. Great Awakening. Letters. Whitefield, George. 1730-40. *2245*

—. Boucher, Jonathan. Catholic Church. Church of England. Religious Liberty. 1774-97. *2234*

—. Boundaries. Chesapeake Bay. Fishing. Virginia. 1820-1982. *3341*

—. Boundaries. Mason-Dixon Line. Pennsylvania. 1732-64. *3258*

—. Boundaries (disputes). Chew, Benjamin. Documents. Maps. Mason-Dixon Line. Pennsylvania. Princeton University Library. 1731-68. *3338*

—. Bush River Quaker Meeting. Friends, Society of. 1706-1826. *2478*

—. American Revolution. Commerce. Georgia (Savannah). Jews. Sheftall, Levi. 1739-1809. *2470*

—. Daily, Charles Henry. Farmers. Kentucky. Teachers. 1850-1930. *1819*

—. Georgia (Milledgeville). Hansell, Augustin H. 1817-61. *496*

—. Guerard, Albert J. Texas (Houston). 1924-72. *2979*

Memphis Medical College. Medicine (practice of). Tennessee. Yandell, Lunsford Pitts. 1858-65. *2106*

Memphis Navy Yard. *Alleghany* (vessel). Navies. Tennessee. 1845-69. *3853*

Men. Blacks. Migration, Internal. Occupations. 1967. *2619*

—. Folklore. Georgia (Okefenokee Swamp Rim). Social Customs. "Talking Trash". 1966-72. *1468*

—. Social Customs. Toasts. Whites. 1966-78. *1544*

Mencken, H. L. Authors. Maryland (Baltimore). Reese, Lizette Woodworth. 1850-1945. *893*

—. Literary themes. Savage South (motif). 1917-56. *857*

Mendel, Perry. Business. Child Care. Kinder-Care Learning Centers. 1969-80. *3172*

Mennonites. Rhodes families. Virginia. 1770's-1900. *669*

Mental health care. East Louisiana State Hospital. Hospitals. Louisiana (Jackson). 1960-72. *2160*

Mental Illness. *See also* Handicapped; Psychiatry.

—. Arkansas. Medical care. 1870's-1970's. *3630*

Mercer, Jesse *(Cluster of Spiritual Songs)*. Georgia. Hymnals. 1813. *2215*

Mercer University. Baptists. Clergy. Georgia. Historians. King, Spencer B., Jr. King, Spencer B., Sr. 1880-1973. *2341*

Merchandising. Department stores. Fashion. Neiman-Marcus. Texas (Dallas). 1880-1970. *2936*

Merchants. Alabama. Planter class. Reconstruction. State Government. 1865-70's. *2866*

—. Barnard, George. Indians. Pioneers. Texas (Waco). Trade. 1830-83. *2651*

—. Cotton. Debt. Farmers. ca 1865-90. *2680*

Mercier, Alfred. Louisiana (New Orleans). Novels. 1820-90. *1016*

Mercury. Georgia. Harden, John M. B. Medicine (practice of). 1810-48. *2169*

Meredith, Thomas. Alabama. Creek Indians. Indian Wars. Lott, Arthur. Louisiana. Murder. 1812-14. *4135*

Mergers. Gould, Jay. Louisiana, northern. Railroads. Texas and Pacific Railroad. 1870-1914. *3050*

Merle, David (interview). Folklore. North Carolina (Carteret County; Salter Path). -1973. *1660*

Merrick, John Austin. Episcopal Church, Protestant. Tennessee (Sewanee). Theology. University of the South. 1850-77. *2185*

Merrill, Boynton, Jr. (review article). Jefferson, Thomas (family). Violence. 19c. 1976. *3829*

Merry, Nelson. Baptists. First Baptist Church. Race Relations. Tennessee (Nashville). 1810-65. *2462*

Messer, Irvin. Appalachia. Artisans. Baskets. Chairs. 1981. *1573*

Meteorites. Indians. Louisiana. Texas. Wichita Indians. 1808-26. *3978*

Methodism. Capers, William. *Christian Advocate*. Letters-to-the-editor. Newspapers. Slavery. 1854. 1875. *2422*

—. Circuit riders. Jones, John Griffing. Mississippi. Slavery. 1821-88. *2381*

—. Indians. Oklahoma. 1820-45. *4116*

Methodist Church. Appalachia. Granade, John Adam. Hymns. Revivals. 1800-07. *2320*

—. Asbury, Francis. Circuit riders. Missions and Missionaries. Pioneers. Red River Valley. 1784-1839. *2498*

—. Autobiographies. North Carolina. Young, John. 1747-1837. *2467*

—. Baptists. Bode, Frederick A. (review article). Capitalism. North Carolina. Populism. 1894-1903. 1975. *2380*

—. Baptists. Brinson, James. Louisiana, northern. Missions and Missionaries. Pine Hills Baptist Church. Stevenson, William. ca 1800-40. *2243*

—. Baptists (Southern). Clergy. Loveland, Anne C. (review article). Presbyterian Church. Slavery. 1800-60. *2246*

—. Blacks. 1769-1968. *2253*

—. Camp meetings. Church of the Nazarene. Louisiana (Mineral Springs). 1860's-1926. *2350*

—. Cannon, James, Jr. Glass, Carter. Political Corruption. Virginia. 1909-34. *2409*

—. Centenary College. Dance. Educational Policy. Louisiana. 1941. *1922*

—. Centenary College. Mississippi Conference. Religious Education. 1838-44. *1914*

—. Cherokee Indians. Indians. Missions and Missionaries. Sovereignty. 1824-34. *4042*

—. Churches. Delaware (Wilmington). Episcopal Church, Protestant. Gothic revival style. 1850-90. *766*

—. Circuit riders. Kitchens, Rufus. Texas, West. 1932-58. *2520*

—. Civil rights. Georgia. Tilly, Dorothy. 1900's-70. *3772*

—. Coca-Cola Company. Religious education. 1840's-1970's. *2299*

—. Davis, Joseph H. (family). North Carolina (Murfreesboro area). Southall, John Wesley (family). Wesleyan Female College. 1854-59. *1944*

—. Evangelism. Holston River Valley. Russell, Elizabeth H. C. Virginia. 1770-1825. *2217*

—. Freedmen. Hartzell, Joseph C. Missions and Missionaries. Republican Party. 1870-73. *2352*

—. Georgia. McEachern, David Newton. 1831-1951. *2372*

—. Holly Grove Methodist Church. Louisiana. ca 1825-1980. *2463*

—. Louisiana (New Orleans). Winans, William. 1813-14. *2313*

—. Missions and Missionaries. Texas. Women. 1930's-80. *2509*

Methodist Church (Southern). Arkansas (Searcy). Galloway College. High Schools. 1889-1907. *1842*

Methodist Episcopal Church. Blacks. Clergy. 1784-1864. *2310*

—. Blacks. Letters. Lynch, James. Mississippi. Reconstruction. 1868-69. *2291*

—. Church records. Grimes, Addison McLaughlin. West Virginia (Webster County). 1880's-1963. *2232*

—. Debates. Race. Unification. Virginia. 1924-25. *2357*

—. Diaries. Evangelism. Georgia (Augusta). Norman, Jeremiah. 1798-1801. *2472*

—. Doub, Peter. Education. North Carolina. Slavery. Women. 1796-1869. *2312*

—. Newspapers. 1861-65. *2383*

Methodist Episcopal Church, South. Candler, Warren A. Conservatism. Leopold, Nathan. Loeb, Richard. Scopes, John Thomas. Trials. 1921-41. *2197*

—. Chickasaw Academy. Education. Indian Territory. 1844-67. *4010*

—. China. Feminism. Haygood, Laura A. Missions and Missionaries. 1884-1900. *2402*

—. Clergy. Georgia. Pierce, George Foster. Pierce, Lovick. 1785-1884. *2225*

—. Colored Methodist Episcopal Church. Freedmen. Religious liberty. Segregation. 1865-70. *2292*

—. Mississippi. Religious Education. Thornton, Thomas C. 1841-60. *2433*

Methodist Protestant Church. Autobiography. Clergy. Daily Life. Delaware (Sussex County). Morgan, William. 1780-1857. *2301*

—. Lynchburg College. Virginia (Lynchburg). 1855-69. *1896*

Methodology. *See also* Models; Quantitative Methods; Research.

—. Alabama. Decisionmaking. Elites. State Politics. 20c. *3594*

—. Anthropology, cultural. Cherokee Indians. Indian-White Relations. Racism. Social organization. Prehistory-1975. *3908*

—. Archaeology. Georgia. Metropolitan Atlanta Rapid Transit Authority Project. 1962-79. *83*

—. Biography. Cather, Willa. Novels. ca 1873-1920's. *314*

—. Blacks. Blues. Folk Songs. Music. 1960's-70's. *1732*

—. Brown, John (1867-1927). Catawba Indians. Folklore. Harris, Mary "Dovie". South Carolina. 1885-1962. *3880*

—. Chickasaw Indians. Choctaw Indians. Dialects. duPratz, Antoine Simon Le Page *(Histoire de la Louisiane)*. Indians. Language. Mississippi River Valley (lower). ca 1720-58. *3950*

—. Civil War. Coups d'Etat. Ellet, Charles. Letters. Military Organization. Primary sources. 1863. 1979. *221*

—. Colleges and Universities. Dance. Folk arts. Social Customs. 1980. *263*

—. Comanche Indians. Green corn dance. Hoebel, E. Adamson. Indians. Rites and Ceremonies. Texas. Wallace, Ernest. 1830-95. 1952-81. *4107*

—. Economic History. Income. 1840's. 1973-75. *2660*

—. Farmers. Southern Farmers' Alliance. 1884-90. *2836*

—. Florida. Funeral homes. Genealogy. ca 1880-1982. *179*

—. Historians. Phillips, Ulrich B. *(History of. 1830-60. 1908.* 313

—. Historiography. Oklahoma. 1890-1930's. *254*

—. Key, V. O., Jr. Louisiana. Public policy. State Politics. Virginia. 1929-70's. *3648*

—. Maritime archaeology. Shipwrecks. Virginia (Portsmouth; Scott Creek). 1893-1982. *205*

—. Maryland (Charles County). Population. 1700-10. *301*

—. Photography. Research. 19c-20c. *360*

—. Politics. 1952-76. *3609*

—. Politics. 1982. *3839*

Methvin, John Jasper. Five Civilized Tribes. Indian-White Relations. Missions and Missionaries. Oklahoma, Western. 1890-94. *4117*

Metropolitan Areas. *See also* terms beginning with the word urban; Cites.

—. Baptists, Southern. Blacks. Models. 1951-81. *2459*

—. Ecology. Migration, Internal. Population. 1940-60. 1970-75. *2627*

—. Legislation. Public Schools. State Aid to Education. Texas Education Agency. 1970-80. *1787*

—. Louisiana. Population. 1970-75. *3079*

Metropolitan Atlanta Rapid Transit Authority Project. Archaeology. Georgia. Methodology. 1962-79. *83*

Mexican Americans. Alazan-Apache Courts. Housing. Texas (San Antonio). 1930-44. *3368*

—. Assimilation. Jews. Mexico (Nuevo Reyno de León). Texas. 16c-20c. *661*

—. Ballads. "Corrido de Gregorio Cortez" (ballad). "Discriminación a un Martir". Political Protest. Social change. Texas (Three River). 20c. *717*

—. Blacks. Caldwell County Tri-Cultural Oral History Project. Oral History. Texas. Whites. 1976-79. *271*

—. Castañeda, Carlos Eduardo. Historians. Texas. 1896-1927. *6*

—. Catholic Church. Texas, south. 1836-1911. *2335*

—. Comanche Indians. Gentilz, Theodore. Painting. Social Customs. Texas (San Antonio). 1843-79. *1148*

—. Czech Americans. Family. Labor. Land. Social Organization. Texas (Nueces County). 1880-1930. *2673*

—. Daily Life. Photography, Journalistic. Smithers, W. D. Texas. 1910-60's. *653*

—. Elections. Texas (Crystal City). 1910-75. *3708*

—. English language. Names (personal). Spanish language. Texas (El Paso). 1981. *703*

—. Ethnicity. Texas. -1973. *627*

—. Exiles. Liberal Party. Mexico. Propaganda. Texas. Women. 1898-1910. *3832*

—. Folk Medicine. Jaramillo, Pedrito. Texas (Los Almos). 1881-1907. *2103*

—. Folk songs. Rio Grande. Texas. 1860-1982. *1608*

—. Labor Unions and Organizations. Strikes. Texas. 1920-40. *3424*

—. Labor Unions and Organizations. Texas. United Cannery, Agricultural, Packing and Allied Workers of America. 1935-50. *3425*

—. Middle Classes. Public schools. School Integration. Texas. 1929-57. *2064*

—. Migration. Social Conditions. Texas, south. Whites. 1850-1900. *2566*

—. Minorities. Politics. Public Schools. Self-perception. Texas (south). 1930's-69. *3788*

—. Music. Norteña (music). Photographs. Texas (San Antonio). 1930's-82. *1675*

—. Music. Texas. 1860's-1980. *1626*

—. Political participation. Race Relations. Social Change. Texas (Cameron County). Wells, James B. 1882-1920. *3471*

—. Political participation. State Politics. Texas. -1973. *3700*

—. Race Relations. Texas. 19c. *611*

Mexicans. Discrimination. Labor Unions and Organizations. Texas (El Paso). 1880-1920. *3397*

Mexico. Andrade, Flores de. Immigration. Liberal Party. Personal narratives. Revolutionary Movements. Texas (El Paso). 1890-1911. *570*

—. Anglo Irish. Houses. Rio Grande. Texas. 19c. *1307*

—. Borderlands. Diplomacy. Trade. 1858-1905. *2539*

—. Boundaries. Louisiana. Puelles, José María de Jesús. Texas. 1512-1813. 1827-28. *3229*

—. Boundaries. Rebellions. Texas (Brownsville, Eagle Pass area). 1850-1900. *3204*

—. Cattle rustling. Navies. *Rio Bravo* (vessel). Rio Grande. Texas. 1840's-79. *3865*

—. Cherokee Indians. Land grants. Manuscripts. Starr, Emmet. Texas. 1820's-30's. *4051*

—. Cowboys. Texas. -1972. *1698*

—. Alabama (Creek Path). American Board of Commissioners for Foreign Missions. Cherokee Indians. 1820-37. *4001*

—. Alabama (Mobile). China. Presbyterian Church. Stuart, Mary Horton. 1840's-1926. *2305*

—. Architecture. Artisans. Churches. Texas (San Antonio). 18c. *1345*

—. Arkansas (Jonesboro). Catholic Church. Olivetan Benedictine Sisters. Renggli, Rose (Mother Mary Beatrice). 1847-1942. *2499*

—. Asbury, Francis. Circuit riders. Methodist Church. Pioneers. Red River Valley. 1784-1839. *2498*

—. Baptists. Blacks. Education. 1862-81. *2427*

—. Baptists. Brinson, James. Louisiana, northern. Methodist Church. Pine Hills Baptist Church. Stevenson, William. ca 1800-40. *2243*

—. Baptists. Cherokee Indians. Compere, Ebenezer Lee. Oklahoma, northeastern. 1854-65. *3987*

—. Baptists. China. Shuck, Eliza G. Sexton. 1844-51. *2326*

—. Baptists. Daniell, David Gonto. Georgia. McCall, Moses N., Jr. Monroe Female College. Teachers. 1808-85. *2228*

—. Baptists. Indians. Oklahoma. Presbyterian Church. Seminole Indians. 1842-85. *4125*

—. Baptists, Southern. 1845-1973. *2446*

—. Baptists, Southern. Big Hatchie Baptist Association. Evangelism. 1828-1903. *2267*

—. Baptists, Southern. Carey, William. Higher education. 1826-1976. *2511*

—. Baptists (Southern). China. Roberts, Issachar Jacob. 1837-47. *2531*

—. Baptists, Southern. Church Finance. 1792-1976. *2393*

—. Baptists (Southern). Indians. 1830-1970's. *3878*

—. Baptists, Southern. Laity. 1715-1975. *2442*

—. Baptists, Southern. Voluntarism. 1940's-78. *2240*

—. Baptists, Southern (Foreign Mission Board). Civil War. 1861-66. *2272*

—. Blacks. Education (review article). Engs, Robert Francis. Philanthropy. Prather, H. Leon, Sr. Williams, Mildred M. 1861-1968. *1965*

—. Byington, Cyrus. Choctaw Indians. Indians. Mississippi. Protestantism. 1820-68. *4115*

—. Catholic Church. Daughters of the Cross. Louisiana. McCants, Dorothea Olga. Publishers and Publishing. ca 1855-1900. 1970's. *2233*

—. Catholic Church. Education. Florida (Ybor City). Poor. Sisters of St. Joseph. 1891-1943. *654*

—. Catholic Church. Indians. Louisiana. 18c-20c. *2444*

—. Cherokee Indians. Christianity. Indian-White Relations. Property. Social Change. Women. 19c. *4139*

—. Cherokee Indians. Civil disobedience. Evangelism. 1829-39. *4045*

—. Cherokee Indians. Elementary Education. Fleming, John. Indian Territory. Primers. 1819-36. *4031*

—. Cherokee Indians. Georgia. Indian-White Relations. Law Enforcement. Removals, forced. Worcester, Samuel Austin. 1831. *4148*

—. Cherokee Indians. Indians. Martin, John. Presbyterian Church. Richardson, William. Tennessee. Virginia. 1755-63. *3943*

—. Cherokee Indians. Indians. Methodist Church. Sovereignty. 1824-34. *4042*

—. Cherokee Indians. Indians. Printing. Worcester, Samuel Austin. 1828-59. *4036*

—. China. Feminism. Haygood, Laura A. Methodist Episcopal Church (South). 1884-1900. *2402*

—. Choctaw Indians. Congregationalism. Harkins, Richard. Murder. Slavery. 1858-59. *4044*

—. Episcopal Church, Protestant. Florida. Gray, William Crane. Indian-White Relations. Seminole Indians. 1893-1914. *3895*

—. Five Civilized Tribes. Indian-White Relations. Methvin, John Jasper. Oklahoma, Western. 1890-94. *4117*

—. Freedmen. Hartzell, Joseph C. Methodist Church. Republican Party. 1870-73. *2352*

—. Georgia. Wesley, John. 1736-38. *2388*

—. Indian-White Relations. Land. Maryland. Nanticoke Indians. 1634-1750. *4079*

—. Methodist Church. Texas. Women. 1930's-80. *2509*

Mississippi. 1900-78. *3322*

—. Agricultural cooperatives. Blacks. Republic of New Afrika. 1866-1974. *390*

—. Agricultural Industry. Economic Regulations. Federal government. Prices. Texas. Voluntarism. 1925-40. *2783*

—. Alabama. Georgia. Libraries. Louisiana. 1908-73. *245*

—. Allin, John M. Civil rights. Clergy. Episcopal Church, Protestant. Political Attitudes. 1964-73. *2183*

—. Americanization. Values. 1900-78. *3282*

—. Anecdotes. Colleges and Universities. Students. ca 1950's-70's. *1439*

—. Anti-evolution controversy. 1926-70. *3613*

—. Apportionment. Blacks. Louisiana (New Orleans). New York City (Manhattan). 1962-76. *3732*

—. Architecture. Benjamin, Asher. Handbooks. 1817-60. *1204*

—. Architecture. Economic Conditions. Natchez Pilgrimage of Homes. Preservation. Towns, small. 1900-80. *1219*

—. Architecture. Jefferson College. 1802-95. *1274*

—. Architecture. Koch, Richard. Louisiana. Photographs. Tulane University Library. 1930-65. *844*

—. Archives and History, Department of. Oral history. 1976. *151*

—. Attorneys general. Lawyers. State Government. 1874-1969. *3802*

—. Bibliographies. Dissertations. 18c-20c. *74*

—. Bibliographies. Dissertations. 1972. *135*

—. Bibliographies. Dissertations. 1973. *134*

—. Bibliographies. Dissertations. History. Literature. 1974. *72*

—. Bibliographies. Dissertations. History. Literature. Theses. 1976. *78*

—. Bibliographies. Dissertations. Theses. 1975. *73*

—. Bibliographies. Dissertations. Theses. 1977. *77*

—. Bibliographies. Dissertations. Theses. 1978. *76*

—. Bibliographies. Dissertations. Theses. 1981. *75*

—. Bilbo, Theodore G. Political Leadership. State Government. Whites. 1908-32. *3590*

—. Biography. McNutt, Alexander G. Paxton, Andrew Jackson. Political Campaigns (gubernatorial). ca 1837-48. 1891. *3718*

—. Blacks. Bruce, Blanche Kelso. Reconstruction. Senate. 1875-81. *3688*

—. Blacks. Civil rights. Henry, Aaron. Personal Narratives. 1922-63. *378*

—. Blacks. Davis Bend (plantation). Hermann, Janet Sharp (review article). Utopias. ca 1850-81. *2844*

—. Blacks. Developing nations. Elites. Political Leadership. 1965-70. *3763*

—. Blacks. Education. Freedom Schools. Social change. 1964-65. *2063*

—. Blacks. Education. Jones, Laurence. Piney Woods School. 1954. *2095*

—. Blacks. Federal Programs. Nixon, Richard M. Poverty. 1967-73. *3355*

—. Blacks. Folk art. Photographs. 20c. *1733*

—. Blacks. Higher education. 1865-1920. *2020*

—. Blacks. Holloway, Lou. Music. Personal narratives. Piney Woods School. Rays of Rhythm. 1940-49. *911*

—. Blacks. House of Representatives. Lynch, John Roy. 1847-1939. *3689*

—. Blacks. House of Representatives. Lynch, John Roy. Reconstruction. 1869-1939. *3488*

—. Blacks. Howard, Perry W. Politics. Republican Party. 1924-60. *3705*

—. Blacks. Letters. Lynch, James. Methodist Episcopal Church. Reconstruction. 1868-69. *2291*

—. Blacks. Public Opinion. Revels, Hiram. Senate. 1870. *3680*

—. Bratton, Theodore DuBose. Conference for Education in the South. Episcopal Church, Protestant. Race Relations. 1908. *2456*

—. Byington, Cyrus. Choctaw Indians. Indians. Missions and Missionaries. Protestantism. 1820-68. *4115*

—. Carter, William Hodding, Jr. Editors and Editing. Political Reform. Race Relations. ca 1930-60. *3576*

—. Chicago, University of. Dodd, William E. Hearon, Cleo. Letters. 1910. *1867*

—. Choctaw Indians. Indians. Names (personal). 17c-19c. *4118*

—. Circuit riders. Jones, John Griffing. Methodism. Slavery. 1821-88. *2381*

—. Cities. Toponymy. 18c-19c. *3250*

—. Colleges and Universities. Libraries. Manuscripts. 1976. *71*

—. Colleges and Universities. Libraries. Manuscripts. 1978-79. *81*

—. Colleges and Universities. Libraries. Manuscripts. 1979-80. *80*

—. Cotton. Reconstruction. Small farms. Tenancy. Whites. ca 1865-80. *2756*

—. Country Music. Music. Progress. 1930-78. *3202*

—. Culture. Education. Public Schools. 1900-78. *3327*

—. Democratic Party. Political Factions. 1965-68. *3780*

—. Democratic Party. Political Factions. Primaries (gubernatorial). 1927-75. *3665*

—. Democratic Party. Primaries. State Government. 1947-78. *3804*

—. Economic development. ca 1815-1973. *2570*

—. Economic growth. 1770-1900. *3315*

—. Economic History. 1699-1840. *3183*

—. Editors and Editing. Gonzales, John Edmond. *Journal of Mississippi History.* McCain, William D. 1939-79. *1531*

—. Environment. Public policy. 1900-78. *3339*

—. Family. Genealogy. Mexico, Gulf of. 18-19c. *612*

—. Faulkner, William. Literary Criticism. Yoknapatawpha County (fictional place). 1974. *1014*

—. Federal government. Howorth, Lucy Somerville. New Deal. Somerville, Nellie Nugent. State Legislatures. 1923-57. *3629*

—. Gant, Harris A. Public Health. Reed Commission. Yellow fever. 1898-1905. *2144*

—. Geology. Hilgard, Eugene. Lyell, Charles. 1699-1876. *3199*

—. Gospel Music. Music. Values. 1890-1978. *3212*

—. Governors. Political Leadership. State Legislatures. Wright, Fielding. 1927-38. *3632*

—. Historiography. 1963-79. *124*

—. Holly Springs Iron Works. Iron industry. 1845-62. *2940*

—. Illinois Central Railroad. Produce. Railroads. 1880's-1940. *3043*

—. Integration. Political Commentary. State Politics. 1970-72. *3822*

—. Intellectuals. Standard of living. 1900-78. *3351*

—. Judicial Administration. Juvenile courts. 1940-74. *3470*

—. Juvenile courts. 1916-75. *3469*

—. Ladner, Heber. Speeches. State Government. 1931-79. *3666*

—. Mass Media. Press. Social Change. 1900-78. *3298*

—. Mass Media. Public Opinion. 1970-78. *3268*

—. Methodist Episcopal Church (South). Religious Education. Thornton, Thomas C. 1841-60. *2433*

—. Names. Plants. 1930's-70's. *1437*

—. Newspapers. Public Opinion. Reporters and Reporting. 1978. *3236*

—. Poets. 19c-20c. *979*

—. Poverty. Public Opinion. Race Relations. 1900-78. *3197*

—. Preservation. Public awareness. 1900-78. *3196*

—. Private schools. Public Schools. Residential segregation. -1973. *2035*

—. Public Opinion. Race Relations. Social Change. 1930-78. *3352*

—. Race relations. 1900-78. *3242*

—. Race Relations. 1900-78. *3260*

—. Railroads. Southern Railroad. 1840-89. *3149*

—. State Legislatures. Women. 1924-81. *3628*

—. Towns. 1770-1978. *3184*

—. Values. 1900-78. *3312*

—. Zoning. 1978. *3208*

Mississippi (Amite County). Baptists. Clay, Margaret Muse. Crawford Manuscript. Folk Medicine. Lea, Maggie Tate. Virginia (Chesterfield). ca 1773. ca 1890. *1083*

Mississippi (Biloxi). Lighthouse keepers. Women. 1854-61. 1867-1929. *676*

Mississippi (Biloxi, Gulfport). Hospitals. 1907-63. *2108*

Mississippi (Clinton). Daily Life. 18c-1861. *437*

Mississippi (Columbus). Lyon, James A. Presbyterian Church (Southern). 1860-75. *2529*

Mississippi (Columbus; Magowah Place). Civil War. Cook, Robert C. Personal Narratives. Veterans. 1861-65. 1915-29. *428*

Mississippi Conference. Centenary College. Methodist Church. Religious Education. 1838-44. *1914*

Mississippi (Copiah County). Agricultural Industry. Produce. 1870's-1940's. *2782*

Mississippi (Corinth). Civil War. Corona Female College. Gaston, L. B. Gaston, Susan P. Hospitals. 1857-64. *1907*

Mississippi (Delta). Cotton. Mules. 1820-1950. *2684*

Mississippi Department of Archives and History. Archives. Bibliographies. Government. 1975. *292*

—. Archives. Bibliographies. Manuscripts. 1975. *140*

—. Archives. Manuscripts. 1973. *191*

—. Archives. Oral history. 1958-75. *150*

—. McLemore, Richard Aubrey. 1950-76. *30*

Mississippi Historical Society. Historians. Perry, B. G. Politicians. 1789-1974. *2388*

—. Mississippi River Valley (Lower; conference). 17c-20c. 1982. *211*

Mississippi Historical Society (annual meeting). Historical societies. 1975. *79*

—. History. 1976. *272*

—. Local history. 1978. *35*

Mississippi (Holmes County). Blacks. Children. Geophagy. Poverty. Women. 1975. *2174*

Mississippi (Homochitto River Valley). Blacks. Folklore. Social customs. 1973. *1708*

Mississippi (Jackson). Blacks. Tougaloo College. 1869-1975. *1929*

—. Daily Life. Fiction. Welty, Eudora ("Death of a Traveling Salesman"). 1936-79. *1115*

—. Fiction. Welty, Eudora. 1909-82. *850*

Mississippi (Jasper County). Blacks. Population. Whites. 1833-1970. *3257*

Mississippi (Kemper County). Post offices. 1834-1964. *3784*

Mississippi (Lafayette County). Faulkner, William. Fiction. Yoknapatawpha County (fictional place). 1897-1962. *3185*

Mississippi (Lafayette County, Oxford). Civil War. Faulkner, William. Literature. 1860-65. 1925-62. *987*

Mississippi (Lafayette County, Panola County, Yazoo Delta). Faulkner, William ("The Bear"). Fiction. Plantations. Railroads. Wilderness. 19c-20c. *3186*

Mississippi (Laurel). Lumber and lumbering. 1882-1916. *2995*

*Mississippi* (locomotive). Illinois Central Railroad. Railroads. 1836-1979. *3158*

Mississippi (Lucedale). Arts and Crafts. Bear grass rope. Simmons, Robert (interview). 1971. *1462*

Mississippi (Natchez). Colleges and Universities. Jefferson College. 1802-1975. *1940*

—. Houses. Preservation. 1700-1979. *1177*

Mississippi (Natchez district). Armies. Blacks. Freedmen's Bureau. Sharecropping. 1860's. *2704*

Mississippi (Noxubee County). Post offices. 1834-1965. *3783*

Mississippi (Pascagoula River). Shipbuilding. 1870's-1974. *3170*

Mississippi (Pearl River). 1699-1976. *3193*

Mississippi (Philadelphia). Arts and Crafts. Choctaw Indian Fair. 1974. *4163*

Mississippi River. Agriculture. Economic Conditions. Kentucky (Kentucky Bend). 1810's-90's. *2536*

—. Banvard, John. Paintings. 1815-91. *1144*

—. Boats. Fishing. 1800-1978. *1464*

—. Boundaries. Jurisdiction. Tennessee (Centennial Island). 19c. *3278*

—. Boundaries. Kentucky. 1765-1981. *3190*

—. Cotton. Louisiana (Tensas Parish). Steamboats. 1843-1904. *2578*

—. Economic Development. Identity. Louisiana (New Orleans). Technology. Trade. 1850-1950. *2913*

—. Economic development. Packet boats. 19c. *2585*

—. Land. Recreation. Tennessee (Lake County). 19c-1977. *3288*

—. Steamboats. 1787-19c. *3098*

Mississippi River (lower). Army Corps of Engineers. Flood control. Politics. 1927-41. *3747*

Mississippi River Valley (lower). Chickasaw Indians. Choctaw Indians. Dialects. duPratz, Antoine Simon Le Page (*Histoire de la Louisiane*). Indians. Language. Methodology. ca 1720-58. *3950*

Mississippi River Valley (Lower; conference). Mississippi Historical Society. 17c-20c. 1982. *211*

Mississippi (Rodney). Colleges and Universities. Oakland College. Presbyterian Church. 1830-71. *1936*

Mississippi, southeastern. Choctaw Indians. Indians. Villages. 18c. 1975. *3904*

Mississippi, southwestern. Louisiana (New Orleans). Painting. Portraits. West, William E. 1817-19. *869*

Mississippi State Chemical Laboratory. Agriculture. Chemical Industry. Food Adulteration and Inspection. Government regulation. 1882-1979. *2626*

Mississippi State University. Agriculture. Curricula. Educators. 1878-1978. *1888*

—. Centennial Celebrations. Curricula. Educational Administration. State Politics. Students. 1878-1978. *1889*

Mississippi Supreme Court. Griffith, Virgil Alexis. Jurisprudence. 1874-1953. *3586*

Mississippi (Taylorsville). Ransom, John Crowe. 1904-07. *1137*

Mississippi (Tombigbee River area: Cotton Gin Port, Gaines' Trace). Bienville, Sieur de. Historiography. Leftwich, George J. 1729-40. 1903-80. *3214*

Mississippi, University of. Civil War. Historians. Wiley, Bell Irvin (obituary). ca 1926-80. *274*

—. Hemingway, William. Local Government. 1901-37. *3717*

—. History Teaching. Riley, Franklin L. Scholarship. 1897-1914. *1866*

Mississippi (Wayne County, Chickasawhay River). Counties. Petitions. 1808-09. *194*

Mississippi (West Point). Restorations. Waverly (house). 1852-1913. 1962-78. *1393*

Mississippi (Yazoo City). Fillmore, Millard. Letters. Prewett, Harriet Nelson. 1857-73. *3789*

Mississippi (Yazoo Valley). Federal aid. Flood control. Navigation, Inland. Whittington, Will M. 1873-1977. *2614*

Mississippi (Yazoo-Mississippi Delta). Plantations. ca 1860-1930. *3255*

Mississippians for Public Education. Public schools. School Integration. Whites. Women. 1960's. *2028*

Missouri. *See also* North Central States.

—. American Missionary Association. Blacks. Civil War. Education. 1862-65. *2428*

—. Arkansas. Brophy, Lawrence William. Movie theaters. Oklahoma. 1907-26. *1500*

—. Buildings. Elks Lodge. Louisiana Purchase Exposition (St. Louis, 1904). Oklahoma (El Reno). Preservation. 1904-79. *1395*

Missouri and North Arkansas Railroad. Arkansas (northern). Economic Growth. Railroads. Settlement. 1880-1920's. *2985*

Missouri (Cahokia site). Artifacts. Indians. Louisiana (Poverty Point site). Prehistory. *4137*

Missouri, Kansas, and Texas Railroad. Architecture. Oklahoma. Railroad stations. 1870-1970's. *1229*

—. Cattle raising. Oklahoma. Railroads. 1865-1972. *2998*

—. Labor. Oklahoma. Railroads. Texas. 1906-75. *3004*

—. Oklahoma Railroad Maintenance Authority. Pressure Groups. Railroads. 1906-73. *3000*

Missouri Volunteers, 1st. Florida. Okeechobee (battle). Seminole War, 2d. Taylor, Zachary. 1837. *4055*

Mitchell, Broadus. Economic history. Socialism. Textile Industry. 1910's-40's. *2635*

Mitchell, John P. Editors and Editing. Newspapers. Race Relations. Richmond *Planet*. Social Reform. Virginia. ca 1883-1929. *1616*

Mitchell, Margaret. Authors. 1900-49. *1007*

Mitchell, Margaret (*Gone with the Wind*). 1936-78. *456*

—. Cervantes, Miguel de (*Don Quixote*). Genteel tradition. Novels. Social Change. 1605-15. 1936. *443*

—. Civil War. Literary Criticism. Social Conditions. Tolstoy, Leo (*War and Peace*). 1863-1936. *2447*

—. Daily Life. Myths and Symbols. 1850-70. 1936. *1006*

—. Films. Harwell, Richard (review article). Letters. Novels. 1936-49. *1023*

—. Georgia (Atlanta). Novels. Scarlett O'Hara (fictional character). Social Change. Women. 1860-70. 1920-40. *440*

—. Novels. 1928-70. *963*

Mitchell, Morris R. Educational theory. Social Theory. 1920's-76. *1849*

Mitchell, Robert D. (review article). Agriculture. Economic development. Settlement. Virginia (Shenandoah Valley). 18c. 1977. *2754*

Mixon, Wayne. King, Richard H. Literature (review article). Ridgely, J. V. Rowe, Anne E. 19c-20c. 1978-80. *940*

Mizell, Terrence A. Horses. Personal Narratives. Tennessee. Trade. 1940's-70's. *1584*

Mizner, Addison. Architecture. Florida (Palm Beach). 1918-31. *1183*

—. Architecture. Florida (Palm Beach). Singer, Paris. 20c. *1256*

"Mobile hoard" (notes). Alabama. Numismatics. 1821-67. *2599*

Mobile homes. Business. Housing. Labor. Mechanization. Taylor Homes. 1972-79. *3181*

Mobility. *See* Geographic Mobility; Social Mobility.

Model Land Company. Flagler, Henry Morrison. Florida (St. Augustine). Real Estate Business. 1885-1920's. *2641*

Models. *See also* Methodology.

—. Agricultural labor. Industrialization. Slavery. 1800's. *2579*

—. Architecture. Material culture. Virginia. 1640's-1850's. *1377*

—. Baptists, Southern. Blacks. Metropolitan Areas. 1951-81. *2459*

—. Cheyenne Indians. Indians. Politics. Social Organization. Tribal government. 1800-75. *4002*

—. Coal. Economic Conditions. West Virginia. 1880-1930. *3122*

—. Political change. South Carolina. 1920-76. *3534*

—. Race Relations. Voting and Voting Behavior. Wallace, George C. 1968. *3828*

Modernism. Faulkner, William. Literary Criticism. 1915-60. *1112*

Modernization. *See also* Developing Nations; Economic Theory; Industrialization; Social Change.

—. Agriculture. Economic reform. Reform. ca 1865-1979. *2713*

—. Architecture. Preservation. South Carolina (Charleston). 1970's. *1249*

—. Bibliographies. Historiography. 19c. *239*

—. Cajuns. Daily life. Leisure. Louisiana. Social Customs. 1900-79. *499*

—. Crews, Harry. Literature. Perfection (concept). 1968-79. *1053*

—. Delaware. DuPont, Pierre S. Public Schools. State Government. Taxation. 1920-40. *1865*

Mohrbacher, Ellen Whitmore. Films. Oklahoma (Prague). Savoy Theatre. 1921-58. *1617*

Molton, Flora. Blacks. District of Columbia. Folk songs. Women. 1930's-70's. *1764*

Monetary exchange rates. Cotton. Economic conditions. Income. ca 1820-85. *2871*

Monetary Systems. Black Friday. Gold. Gould, Jay. New York. 1869-70. *2654*

Money. *See also* Banking; Capital; Foreign Exchange.

—. Economic Regulations. Exports. Maryland. Prices. Tobacco Inspection Act (1747). 1747. *2837*

Monopolies. *See also* Capitalism; Railroads.

—. France. Great Britain. International Trade. North America. Price, Jacob (review article). Tobacco. 17c-18c. *2716*

Monroe Auto Equipment Company. Georgia (Hartwell). Labor Unions and Organizations. United Automobile Workers of America. 1964-76. *3449*

Monroe Female College. Baptists. Daniell, David Gonto. Georgia. McCall, Moses N., Jr. Missions and Missionaries. Teachers. 1808-85. *2228*

Monroe, James. Historical Sites and Parks. James Monroe Museum and Memorial Library. Law. Virginia (Fredericksburg). 1786-1973. *312*

Montana. *See also* Western States.

—. Cheyenne Indians. Indians. Oklahoma. Petter, Rodolphe. Photographs. 1892-1947. *4175*

Montgomery *Advertiser*. Alabama. Attitudes. Hall, Grover Cleveland. Newspapers. 1888-1941. *448*

Montgomery *Herald*. Alabama. Blacks. Duke, Jesse C. Editors and Editing. Political Commentary. Republican Party. 1886-1916. *3650*

Monticello. Architecture. Delorme, Philibert. Jefferson, Thomas. Virginia. 1780's-90's. *1237*

—. Architecture. Virginia (Charlottesville). 1856. *1159*

—. Gardens. Jefferson, Thomas. Orchards. Restorations. Virginia. 1800-1977. *1286*

—. Jefferson, Thomas. Levy, Uriah Phillips. Virginia. 1809-1980. *1220*

—. Jefferson, Thomas. Photographs. Virginia (Charlottesville). 1770's-1826. *1268*

—. Jefferson, Thomas. Restorations. Virginia. 1978. *1384*

—. Restorations. Virginia (Charlottesville). 1826-1954. *1182*

Montpensier, Duc de (Antoine). Beaujolais, Count of. France. Louis Philippe. Travel. West Virginia (Charles Town, Harper's Ferry, Wheeling). 1797. *740*

Monuments. Cemeteries. Kentucky (Mayfield). Wooldridge, Henry C. 1899-1976. *1360*

—. Confederate Army. Myths and Symbols. Social Change. 1866-1910. *706*

—. Crawford, Thomas. Sculpture. Virginia (Richmond). Washington, George. 1784-1868. *1036*

—. Crockett, Davy. Tennessee (Trenton). 1790's-1836. 1923-68. *708*

—. District of Columbia. Sculpture. 1809-1974. *883*

—. Florida (St. Augustine). Fort Matanzas National Monument. 1820-1965. *8*

Monypenny, Alexander. Cherokee Indians. Diaries. Grant, James. Indian Wars. South Carolina. 1761. *4146*

Moon. Folklore. Kentucky. 1950-73. *1664*

Moon, Lottie. Baptists. Georgia (Cartersville). Secondary Education. 1870-1903. *2202*

Moonshining. Alcoholism. Kentucky. 1900's. *1414*

—. Folklore. Literature. Mullins, Mahala. Tennessee (Hancock County). 19c-20c. *1538*

—. Language. 1901-71. *1613*

Moore, Aaron McDuffie. Blacks. North Carolina (Durham). Philanthropy. Social reform. 1863-1923. *633*

Moore, G. Bedell. Lumber and Lumbering. Lutcher, Henry J. Sawmills. Texas, East. 1870-1930. *3040*

Moore, Janie Gilliard. Africa. Blacks. Georgia. Personal Narratives. Sea Islands. South Carolina. 1970-80. *1754*

# N

—. Abbot, John. Georgia (Savannah Valley). Illustrations. 1776-1840. *1022*

—. Physician-naturalists. South Carolina (Charleston). 18-19c. *2127*

Natural Resources. *See also* Conservation of Natural Resources; Fishing; Forests and Forestry; Power Resources; Soil Conservation; Wilderness.

—. Louisiana. Manufactures. Spanish moss. 19c-1980. *2563*

—. Louisiana, northern. Natural Gas. Oil Industry and Trade. 20c. *2586*

Nature Conservation. *See also* Wildlife Conservation.

—. Canals. Dismal Swamp. Lumber and Lumbering. North Carolina. Virginia. 1700-1976. *3295*

Naval Air Forces. *See also* Air Forces.

—. Florida. Miami, University of. Richmond Air Force Base. 1942-70. *2604*

—. Florida (Pensacola). Urbanization. 1900-45. *3861*

Naval Construction. *See* Shipbuilding.

Naval Engineering. *See* Marine Engineering.

Naval Vessels. *Augusta* (vessel). Georgia (Augusta). Silver services. 1928-80. *3851*

Navies. *See also* terms beginning with the word naval; Marine Engineering; Military; Navigation; Shipbuilding.

—. *Alleghany* (vessel). Memphis Navy Yard. Tennessee. 1845-69. *3853*

—. Armies. Carter, Samuel Powatan. Civil War. Military General Staff. *Seminole* (vessel). 1819-91. *3845*

—. Cattle rustling. Mexico. *Rio Bravo* (vessel). Rio Grande. Texas. 1840's-79. *3865*

—. Civil War. District of Columbia. Remey, "Molly" Mason. Women. 1845-1938. *694*

—. *Eclipse* (vessel). Escapes. Germany. Internment. *Kronprinz Wilhelm* (vessel). *Prinz Eital Friedrich* (vessel). Virginia (Norfolk). 1915. *3874*

—. Hambleton, John Needles. Hambleton, Samuel. Letters. Maryland. 1813-32. *3849*

—. House of Representatives. Illinois. Judges. Oklahoma (Muskogee). Thomas, John Robert. 1870's-1924. *3527*

Navigation. *See also* Lighthouses; Navies; Shipbuilding.

—. Map Drawing. Surveying. Virginia. 1612-1880's. *3313*

Navigation, Inland. *See also* Canals; Rivers.

—. Apalachicola River. Chattahoochee River. Flint River. 1828-1900. *3328*

—. Federal aid. Flood control. Mississippi (Yazoo Valley). Whittington, Will M. 1873-1977. *2614*

Neal, John. Art criticism. Maryland (Baltimore). Peale, Sarah. 1822-29. *829*

Neal, John R. Legal education. Tennessee, University of. 1893-1959. *1844*

Negroes. *See* Black Capitalism; Black Nationalism; Blacks; Discrimination; Freedmen; Mulattoes; Race Relations; Racism; Slavery.

Neighborhoods. Agee, James. Literature. Social Change. Tennessee (Knoxville). 1915-82. *788*

—. Architecture. East End Historical District. Preservation. Texas (Galveston). Victorian style. 1972-77. *1327*

—. Blacks. District of Columbia. Housing. Social Organization. Working Class. 1850-1970. *2549*

—. Business. Downtown areas. Economic Conditions. Maryland (Baltimore). Social Conditions. 1800-1980. *3174*

—. City Government. Maryland (Baltimore). Organizations. 1880-1979. *2889*

—. Cobb-Hill Street Community Association. Georgia (Athens). Historic Cobbham Foundation. Preservation. 1834-19. *1358*

—. Ethnic groups. Maryland (Baltimore). 1850-70. *571*

—. Geographic Mobility. Georgia (Atlanta). Greek Americans. Jews (German, Russian). 1880-1940. *3192*

—. Georgia (Atlanta). Inman Park Restoration, Inc. Preservation. 1880's. 1970-79. *1348*

Neiman-Marcus. Department stores. Fashion. Merchandising. Texas (Dallas). 1880-1970. *2936*

Nelson, Thomas A. R. Brownlow, William G. "Parson". Johnson, Andrew. State Politics. Tennessee. 1840-77. *3468*

Neoclassicism. Architecture. Florida (St. Augustine). 1775-99. *1275*

—. Arts and Crafts. Maryland (Baltimore). Social change. Wrought iron. 1810-60. *1411*

Neoorthodoxy. Protestantism. 1930's. *2345*

Nevin, John W. Adger, John B. Dabney, Robert Lewis. Hodge, Charles. Presbyterian Church. 1845-75. *2314*

New College. Colleges and Universities. Education, Experimental Methods. Florida (Sarasota). State Aid to Education. 1950's-75. *1855*

New Deal. Agricultural Policy. Association of Southern Commissioners of Agriculture. Cotton. Tennessee (Memphis). 1936-37. *2800*

—. Cherokee Indians. Federal Policy. Indians. North Carolina, western. 1930's. *4181*

—. Cotton Acreage Control Law (Texas, 1931). Crops. Long, Huey P. 1931-33. *2861*

—. Cumberland Homesteads. Fairfield Glade. Housing. Resettlement. Tennessee. 1934-80. *1353*

—. Democratic Party. Georgia. Roosevelt, Franklin D. Talmadge, Eugene. 1926-38. *3529*

—. Documents. Holt, Rush Dew. Senate. West Virginia. 1920-55. *3593*

—. Federal government. Howorth, Lucy Somerville. Mississippi. Somerville, Nellie Nugent. State Legislatures. 1923-57. *3629*

—. Resettlement Administration. Rural Development. Texas (Ropesville). 1933-43. *2745*

New Echota, Treaty of. Cherokee Indians. Federal Government. Indians. Ross, John. Watie, Stand. 1839. *3983*

New, Elmira Hudson. Folklore. North Carolina (Anson County). 1900-75. *1607*

New England. *See also* individual states.

—. Belles lettres. Simpson, Lewis P. (review article). 17c-20c. *923*

—. Cotton. Technology. Textile Industry. 1890-1970. *2963*

New Hampshire Covenant. Baptists, Southern. Brown, J. Newton. 1833-1972. *2255*

New Jersey (Salem). Glass and Glassmaking. Pennsylvania (Manheim). Stiegel, William. Virginia (Jamestown). Wistar, Casper. 18c. *3016*

New Mexico. *See also* Western States.

—. Baptists (Southern). Far Western States. Illinois. 1942-78. *2298*

New Orleans *Daily Picayune*. Louisiana. Newspapers. Nicholson, Eliza Jane. Poets. 1849-96. *1532*

New Orleans Historic District Landmarks Committee. Coliseum Square Association. Louisiana. Preservation. 1807-1978. *1403*

New Orleans Public Service Inc. Amalgamated Association of Street and Electric Railway Employees of America. Labor Unions and Organizations. Local Government. Louisiana. Public utilities. 1894-1929. *2575*

New Orleans *Times-Picayune*. Israel. Louisiana (New Orleans). News, foreign. Newspapers. 1973. *1528*

New Right. Baptists, Southern. Conservatism. Fundamentalism. Politics. Social Problems. 1964-82. *2530*

New School Synod. Ecclesiastical questions. Kentucky. Presbyterian Church. 1837-58. *2403*

New York. American Revolution. Congress. Few, William. Georgia. 1771-1828. *3795*

—. Black Friday. Gold. Gould, Jay. Monetary Systems. 1869-70. *2654*

—. Diaries. Frontier and Pioneer Life. Steele, J. D. Tennessee. Travel (accounts). 1821. *742*

New York City. Florida. Justice Department. Labor recruitment. Peonage. Quackenbos, Mary Grace. Turpentine industry. 1905-10. *3444*

—. Louisiana (New Orleans). Public health. 19c. *2121*

New York City (Manhattan). Apportionment. Blacks. Louisiana (New Orleans). Mississippi. 1962-76. *3732*

New Yorker Hotel. Architecture. Art Deco. Florida (Miami Beach). 1981. *1207*

Newcomb, Horace. Baptists, Southern. Personal Narratives. 1940's-70's. *2396*

Newcomb, John Lloyd. Virginia, University of. 1931-33. *1946*

Newfield, Morris. Alabama (Birmingham). Christianity. Ecumenism. Judaism. Social Reform. Temple Emanu-El. 1895-1940. *2244*

News, foreign. Israel. Louisiana (New Orleans). New Orleans *Times-Picayune*. Newspapers. 1973. *1528*

*News-Banner*. Brice, James Moffatt. Country Life. Editors and Editing. Newspapers. Personal narratives. Tennessee (Troy). 1879-1925. *1497*

Newspapers. *See also* Editors and Editing; Freedom of the Press; Journalism; Periodicals; Press; Publishers and Publishing; Reporters and Reporting.

—. Agricultural labor. Blacks. Immigration. Italian Americans. 1880-1915. *2839*

—. Alabama. Attitudes. Hall, Grover Cleveland. Montgomery *Advertiser*. 1888-1941. *448*

—. *American Eagle*. Elections. Florida (Lee County). Koreshan Unity (community). Progressive Liberty Party. Teed, Cyrus Reed. 1894-1908. *3683*

—. Arp, Bill (pseud. for Charles Henry Smith). Atlanta *Constitution*. Attitudes. Blacks. Georgia. 1878-1903. *1609*

—. Arp, Bill (pseud. for Charles Henry Smith). Georgia, northwestern. Humor. Language. Smith, Charles Henry. 1861-1903. *754*

—. *Augusta Chronicle*. Editors and Editing. Georgia. Loyless, Thomas W. 1903-26. *1456*

—. Austin *American-Statesman*. Cartoons and Caricatures. Civil Rights. Political Commentary. Sargent, Ben. Texas. 1977-78. *3833*

—. Baptists. Cherokee Georgia Baptist Convention. Georgia. *Landmark Banner and Cherokee Baptist*. 1859-64. *2281*

—. Baptists. Graves, James Robinson. *Tennessee Baptist*. 1820-93. *2457*

—. Baptists. Literature. *South Western Baptist*. Taliaferro, Hardin Edwards. 1810-75. *1106*

—. Blacks. *Free Speech*. Lynching. Tennessee (Memphis). Wells, Ida B. 1892. *1711*

—. Blacks. McCabe, Edward Preston. Migration, Internal. Oklahoma (Langston). 1850-1920. *3307*

—. Brice, James Moffatt. Country Life. Editors and Editing. *News-Banner*. Personal narratives. Tennessee (Troy). 1879-1925. *1497*

—. Bruce, Philip Alexander. Literary criticism. Richmond *Times*. 1889. *1065*

—. Capers, William. *Christian Advocate*. Letters-to-the-editor. Methodism. Slavery. 1854. 1875. *2422*

—. Cartoons and Caricatures. Politics. *Richmond Times-Dispatch*. Seibel, Frederick O. Virginia. 1926-68. *3798*

—. Catholic Church. Democratic Party. Irish Americans. *Kentucky Irish American*. 1898-1968. *1605*

—. *Cherokee Phoenix*. Ethnohistory. Indians. Scholars. 1820's. *4076*

—. Communications. North Carolina. Public Opinion. Raleigh *Star*. 1810. *1442*

—. Community participation. Harte, Houston. Texas (San Angelo). 1900's-72. *1458*

—. Cowan, Sara. Folklore. Greensboro *Weekly Courier*. Kentucky. Local history. 1968-74. *1587*

—. Editorials. Equal Rights Amendment. 1970-78. *3645*

—. Editors and Editing. Mitchell, John P. Race Relations. Richmond *Planet*. Social Reform. Virginia. ca 1883-1929. *1616*

—. Editors and Editing. North Carolina. 1736-1929. *1651*

—. Florida. Freedom of the Press. Supreme Court. 1901-74. *3636*

—. Foreign policy. South Carolina. 1890-1900. *3838*

—. French language. Louisiana. 1794-1860. *1430*

—. *Frontier Echo*. Pioneers. Publishers and Publishing. Robson, George W. Texas, northwestern. 1857-1918. *664*

—. Georgia. Indexes. Milledgeville *Southern Recorder*. 1820-1981. *9*

—. Israel. Louisiana (New Orleans). New Orleans *Times-Picayune*. News, foreign. 1973. *1528*

—. Literature. Race Relations. Sex. Smith, Lillian. 20c. *1021*

—. Louisiana. New Orleans *Daily Picayune*. Nicholson, Eliza Jane. Poets. 1849-96. *1532*

—. Louisiana (Lincoln Parish). 1873-1920's. *1558*

—. Louisiana (St. Joseph). *Tensas Gazette*. 1852-1974. *1452*

—. McGown, A. J. Presbyterian Church, Cumberland. Publishers and Publishing. *Texas Presbyterian*. 1846-73. *1653*

—. Methodist Episcopal Church. 1861-65. *2383*

—. Mississippi. Public Opinion. Reporters and Reporting. 1978. *3236*

—. Norfolk *Journal and Guide*. Race Relations. Virginia. Washington, Booker T. Young, Plummer B. 1904-20's. *1770*

Newsprint. Georgia. Herty, Charles Holmes. Pine trees. Scientific Experiments and Research. Turpentine. 1901-04. 1930-39. *2561*

—. Herty, Charles Holmes. Paper mills. Pine trees. Scientific Experiments and Research. 1927-40. *3068*

Newton, James D. Development. Florida (Fort Myers; Edison Park). 1926-80. *2912*

Nicholls State University. Louisiana. 1944-73. *1953*

Nicholson, David Bascom, III. Baptist Student Center. Education. Georgia (Athens). 1925-52. *1814*

Nicholson, Eliza Jane. Louisiana. New Orleans *Daily Picayune*. Newspapers. Poets. 1849-96. *1532*

—. Breckinridge, Mary. Frontier Nursing Service. Kentucky. 1925-65. *2119*

Nye, Edgar Wilson "Bill". Edwards, Harry Stillwell. Georgia. Lectures. Lyceum movement. Riley, James Whitcomb. 1888. *938*

—. Edwards, Harry Stillwell. Humorists. Lectures. Redpath Lyceum Bureau. Riley, James Whitcomb. 1888. *1556*

# O

Oak Ridge *Journal.* Army Corps of Engineers. Atomic energy. Journalism. Tennessee. 1943-49. *1409*

Oakland Cemetery. Architecture. Georgia (Atlanta). Historic Oakland Cemetery, Inc. Preservation. 1850-1979. *1366*

Oakland College. Colleges and Universities. Mississippi (Rodney). Presbyterian Church. 1830-71. *1936*

Obituaries. Authors. Historians. North Carolina. Reporters and Reporting. 1980-81. *1010*

O'Brien, Lucy Fulghum. Florida. Personal narratives. Reporters and Reporting. Tampa *Tribune.* 1935-50's. *1598*

O'Brien, Michael. Grantham, Dewey W. (review article). 1870-1979. *278*

Occupations. Agriculture. Students. 1970-79. *2797*

—. Blacks. Douglass, Frederick. Oceans. 19c. *3427*

—. Blacks. Geographic Mobility. Texas (Dallas). 1880-1910. *3215*

—. Blacks. High Schools. Whites. 1970's. *3429*

—. Blacks. Men. Migration, Internal. 1967. *2619*

—. Canton. Housing. Industry. Maryland (Baltimore; Canton). 1880-1930. *2906*

—. Regionalism. Slavery. Unitarianism. 1831-60. *2465*

Oceans. *See also* names of oceans and seas, e.g. Atlantic Ocean; Navigation; Storms.

—. Blacks. Douglass, Frederick. Occupations. 19c. *3427*

Ochsner, Alton. Louisiana (New Orleans). Matas, Rudolph. Medical Research. Personal Narratives. Surgery. 1927-52. *2155*

O'Connor, Flannery. Christianity. Literature. Solzhenitsyn, Alexander. Western nations. 1940's-75. *975*

—. Fiction. 1940's-64. *994*

—. Fiction. 1951-64. *959*

—. Literature. 20c. *974*

—. Short stories. Social classes. 1946-65. *1089*

O'Connor, Flannery (ancestry). Catholic Church. Family. Georgia. ca 1733-1949. *868*

O'Connor, Flannery (review article). Fitzgerald, Sally. Letters. 1955-64. *903*

O'Connor, Flannery (*Wise Blood*). Gordon, Caroline. Letters. Literary Criticism. 1951-64. *867*

Oconostota. Cherokee Indians. Documents. Indians. Kerlerec, Louis Billouart de. Military officers. 1761. *3981*

—. Cherokee Indians. Indian-White Relations. 1740's-83. *4015*

Octagon (house). Architecture. District of Columbia. Thornton, William. 1800. *1290*

Officeholding. County Government. Kentucky (Nicholas County). Local Politics. Sugg, John F. 1909-49. *3774*

—. Elections. Minorities. Texas (Galveston). 1895-1981. *3541*

Ogeechee Old Town (plantation). Georgia (Jefferson County). Plantations. 1540-1860. *2840*

Ohio. *See also* North Central States.

—. Daily Life. Georgia (Decatur). Letters-to-the-editor. Springfield *Weekly News.* Willard, Levi. 1826-64. 1876. *538*

Ohio (Cincinnati). Kentucky. Railroads. South Carolina (Charleston). 1835-39. *3127*

Ohio (Martins Ferry). Iron Industry. Laughlin Nail Works. Strikes. West Virginia (Wheeling). 1833-86. *3412*

Ohio Valley. Archives. Genealogy. West Virginia University Library (West Virginia and Regional History Collection). 1776-1983. *15*

—. Cherokee Indians. Delaware Indians. Indian Wars. Shawnee Indians. 1750's-80's. *4105*

Ohio Valley Trades and Labor Assembly. Bond issues. Carnegie, Andrew. Homestead Strike. Libraries. West Virginia (Wheeling). 1892-1911. *160*

—. Industrialization. Labor Unions and Organizations. West Virginia (Ohio County). 1882-1914. *3407*

Oil and Petroleum Products. *See also* Oil Industry and Trade.

—. Colleges and Universities. Endowments. Public lands. Texas A. & M. University. Texas, University of. 1923-40. *3084*

—. Conservation of Natural Resources. Economic Regulations. Oklahoma Corporation Commission. 1907-31. *2934*

—. Evil. Folklore. Kentucky. Prehistory-1829. *1413*

Oil fields. Daily Life. Texas (Permian Basin). Women. 1920's-30's. *3070*

Oil Industry and Trade. American Petroleum Institute. Pollution. Texas (Gulf Coast). 1900-70. *3082*

—. Architecture. Boomtowns. Houses, shotgun. Texas Panhandle. 1920-40. *1232*

—. Arkansas, southern. Louisiana, northern. Texas, east. 1900-35. *3013*

—. Boomtowns. Texas (Burkburnett). Wichita Falls and Northwestern Railway. 1902-40. *3001*

—. Conservation of Natural Resources. Murray, William J. Natural gas. Texas Railroad Commission. 1930-49. *3085*

—. Higgins, Pattillo. Lucas, Anthony F. Spindletop Oil Rush. Texas (Beaumont). 1901-30's. *3119*

—. Lafitte, Jean. Louisiana (Barataria area). Resorts. Slave Trade. Smuggling. Sugar. ca 1528-1980. *3330*

—. Louisiana. Strikes. Texas. 1917-18. *3415*

—. Louisiana, northern. Natural Gas. Natural Resources. 20c. *2586*

—. Mansions. Marland, Ernest W. Oklahoma (Ponca City). 1920's-75. *1170*

—. Photographs. Rundell, Walter, Jr. Texas. 1900-40. *3179*

—. Social Conditions. Texas (Otis Chalk). 1925-30's. *3032*

O'Kain, Dennis. Georgia (Savannah River area). Historic American Building Survey. Photographs. Richard B. Russell Dam. 1793-1927. *1400*

Okeechobee (battle). Florida. Missouri Volunteers, 1st. Seminole War, 2d. Taylor, Zachary. 1837. *4055*

Oklahoma. *See also* Indian Territory.

—. Acculturation. Davis, Alice Brown. Educators. Indian-White Relations. Seminole Indians. 1870-1935. *3912*

—. Adams-Onís Treaty (1819). Boundaries. Spain. Texas. 1819-1930. *3287*

—. Agricultural Technology and Research. Danne, Joseph. Genetics. Wheat. 1920-59. *2812*

—. Agriculture. Five Civilized Tribes. Indian Territory. 1840-1906. *3989*

—. Appalachia. Cherokee Indians. Georgia. Indian-White Relations. Ridge family. 1785-1907. *3967*

—. Archaeology. Excavations. 1830's-1915. *3222*

—. Architecture. Missouri, Kansas, and Texas Railroad. Railroad stations. 1870-1970's. *1229*

—. Archives, National. Chapman, Berlin Basil. Documents. Indians. Research. 1920's-60's. *39*

—. Arkansas. Brophy, Lawrence William. Missouri. Movie theaters. 1907-26. *1500*

—. Art. Bacone College (Art Department). Blue Eagle, Acee. Indians. 1935-80. *4174*

—. Artists. Indians. Painting. Social Customs. 1870's-1920. *988*

—. Assimilation. Cherokee Indians. Labor. Social organization. Prehistory-1975. *3911*

—. Ballenger, Tom Lee. Cherokee Indians. Historians. Indians. 1905-82. *3*

—. Baptists. Indians. Missions and Missionaries. Presbyterian Church. Seminole Indians. 1842-85. *4125*

—. Bibliographies. Blacks. 1880-1980. *392*

—. Bibliographies. Highways. Public Records. 1824-1981. *2939*

—. Bibliographies. Indians. Pioneers. 19c-1978. *120*

—. Birds. Wichita Mountains Wildlife Refuge. 1904-77. *3331*

—. Blacks. Colleges and Universities. Economic conditions. Langston University. McCabe, Edward Preston. Social Change. 1896-1982. *2079*

—. Brindley, Ethel Mae. Daily Life. 1889-1981. *511*

—. Cattle raising. Missouri, Kansas, and Texas Railway. Railroads. 1865-1972. *2998*

—. Cherokee Indians. Christie, Ned. Indian-White Relations. Keetoowah Society. Murder. Smith, Redbird. 1850-92. *3996*

—. Cherokee Indians. Foreman, Stephen. Georgia. Indians. Presbyterian Church. 1820's-81. *3960*

—. Cherokee Indians. Georgia. Indian Territory. Removals, forced. 1785-1865. *4004*

—. Cherokee Indians. Georgia. Indians. Leadership. Removals, forced. Ross, John. Tennessee. 1815-66. *4063*

—. Cherokee Indians. Indians. 1869-81. *4029*

—. Cherokee Indians. Indians. Northeastern Oklahoma State University (Cherokee Collection). Starr, Emmet. 1913-78. *4182*

—. Cherokee Indians. Indians. Religion. Rites and ceremonies. Prehistory-20c. *3905*

—. Cherokee Indians. Indians. Rogers, Clement V. Rogers, Will. 1832-90's. *4052*

—. Cherokee Indians. Indians. Vann, Joseph. 1820's-60's. *4039*

—. Cherokee Indians. Ross, John. 1790-1866. *4035*

—. Cheyenne Indians. Indians. Montana. Petter, Rodolphe. Photographs. 1892-1947. *4175*

—. Chickasaw Indians. Indian Territory. Removals, forced. 1800-65. *3940*

—. Choctaw Indians. Federal Policy. Indian Territory. Removals, forced. 1803-47. *4012*

—. Choctaw Indians. Historians. Wright, Muriel Hazel. 1889-1974. *3886*

—. Circuit riders. Frontier and Pioneer Life. German Americans. Lutheran Church (Missouri Synod). Texas. Wacker, Hermann Dietrich. 1847-1938. *2461*

—. Classics. Congregationalism. House, J. T. Kingfisher College. 1890-1922. *1893*

—. Congress. 1907-37. *3597*

—. Congress. Democratic Party. Leadership. Political power. 1945-72. *3598*

—. Courts. Indian Territory. Jurisdiction. Law. 1880-1917. *3887*

—. Creek Indians. Indians. Johnson, Grant. Law enforcement. Marshals, deputy. Texas. 1895-1906. *3820*

—. Democratic Party. McDougal, Myrtle Archer. Reform. Women. 1904-30's. *3635*

—. Dust Bowl. Erosion. Farmers. Migration, Internal. 1921-30's. *2784*

—. Ethnic groups. Europeans. Immigration. 1890-1920. *582*

—. Family. Interpersonal Relations. Rogers, Clement V. Rogers, Will. 1879-1911. *1633*

—. Films. 1910-70. *419*

—. Five Civilized Tribes. Historiography. Manifest Destiny. Removals, forced. 19c-20c. *3924*

—. Flags (State). Fluke, Mrs. George. 1911-41. *709*

—. Foreman, Carolyn Thomas. Foreman, Grant. Historians. 1897-1967. *68*

—. Fort Gibson. Restorations. 1824-1963. *3844*

—. Historians. Shirk, George. 1913-77. *691*

—. Historiography. Methodology. 1890-1930's. *254*

—. Impeachment. Judges. State Legislatures. Supreme courts (state). 1927-30. *3538*

—. Indians. Methodism. 1820-45. *4116*

—. Indians. Osage Indians. Social status. Women. 1870-1980. *3916*

—. Johnson, Edith. Reporters and Reporting. Women. 1908-61. *1455*

—. Journalism. Sanitary inspectors. Sturgeon, Sallie Lewis. Women. 1894-1930's. *547*

—. Labor. Missouri-Kansas-Texas Railroad. Railroads. Texas. 1906-75. *3004*

—. Landmarks. Preservation. 1913-79. *1222*

—. Prisons. Reform. 1910-67. *3531*

—. Railroads. 1866-1907. *2945*

—. Railroads. Rock Island Railroad. 1899-1937. *3047*

—. Railroads. Texas. Towns. Wichita Falls and Northwestern Railway. 1900-20. *3003*

—. Rivers. Transportation. 19c. *3223*

—. Shirk, George (obituary). Toponymy. 20c. *3217*

—. War. 1890-1968. *3850*

Oklahoma (Ardmore). Confederate Army. Pensions. Veterans Home. 1909-49. *3859*

Oklahoma (Ardmore; St. Philip's Church). Brooke, Francis Key. Carden, Joseph. Clergy. Episcopal Church, Protestant. 1893-1927. *2293*

Oklahoma (Big Salt Plain). Blackmon Salt Company. Salt and Salt Manufacturing. 1803-1980. *3243*

Oklahoma (Blackburn). Railroads. Settlement. Skinner, John. 1893-1910. *3230*

Oklahoma, central. Radio. 1920-30's. *1670*

Oklahoma (Cherokee Outlet). Cherokee Indians. Indian-White Relations. Land. 1893. *3939*

Oklahoma (Cherokee Strip; Kildare). Agriculture. Boomtowns. Settlement. 1893-1975. *2763*

Oklahoma Corporation Commission. Conservation of Natural Resources. Economic Regulations. Oil and Petroleum Products. 1907-31. *2934*

Oklahoma, eastern. Agriculture. Cotton. Sharecroppers. 1920-40. *2726*

—. Texas Road. 19c. *3270*

Oklahoma (El Reno). Buildings. Elks Lodge. Louisiana Purchase Exposition (St. Louis, 1904). Missouri. Preservation. 1904-79. *1395*

Oklahoma (Enid). Bass, Henry B. Business. Historians. Public services. 20c. *668*

Oklahoma Gas and Electric Company. Public Utilities. 1889-1904. *3129*

Oklahoma (Gibbon). Economic Development. 1890's-1945. *3296*

Oklahoma (Grady, Stephens counties). Boundaries. County Government. 1935-50. *3303*

—. Blacks. Employment. Industrialization. Social Mobility. 1860's-1974. *2772*

—. Blacks. Musicians. Social status. 1820's-50's. *1721*

—. Blacks. Page, Thomas Nelson (*In Ole Virginia*). 1829-60. *2767*

—. Boscobel Cottage. Louisiana (Ouachita Parish). Restorations. 1820-1978. *1227*

—. Brazil. Darwin, Charles. Hopley, Catherine. Slavery. Stereotypes. 1831-63. *729*

—. Bres, Jean (family). Breston Plantation House. Louisiana (Columbia area). Ouachita River. ca 1790-1866. *1390*

—. Business. Management. Profit. ca 1830-60. *2794*

—. Butler, Thomas (family). Documents. Landscaping. Louisiana State University, Department of Archives. 1768-1900. *1375*

—. Civil War. Harrison, Constance Cary. Novels. 1863-1911. *1045*

—. Classics. Elites. Europe. Virginia. 19c. *765*

—. Colbert, William Williams. Louisiana (Bienville Parish). 1849-90. *2692*

—. Commerce. Galt, James. Galt, William, Jr. Slavery. Virginia. 1800-76. *2734*

—. Cotton. Great Britain. Slavery. 17c-19c. *2753*

—. Crops. Georgia (Glynn County). Hopeton (plantation). 1818-52. *2689*

—. Daily life. Diaries. Slavery. Texas (Harrison County). Webster, John B. 1858-59. *2758*

—. Daily Life. Wives. 1780-1835. *539*

—. Diaries. Louisiana, southern. 1839-59. *554*

—. Documents. Phillips, Ulrich B. Research. Slavery. 1900-34. *2847*

—. Economic Conditions. Mandle, Jay R. Regionalism (review article). Thompson, Edgar T. Wright, Gavin. 1865-1978. *2580*

—. Economic Structure. Farming. Statistics. ca 1865-1910. *2773*

—. Economic Structure. Households. Social Organization. 1783-1865. *567*

—. Elites. Junkers. Land Tenure. Proslavery Sentiments. Prussia. 1800-61. *2678*

—. Elites. Recreation. Virginia. 1640's-1775. *1427*

—. Farms. Sugar. 1850's. *2835*

—. Faulkner, William ("The Bear"). Fiction. Mississippi (Lafayette County, Panola County, Yazoo Delta). Railroads. Wilderness. 19c-20c. *3186*

—. Films. Slaves. Stereotypes. 1800-65. 1958-78. *425*

—. Georgia. Labor. Rice. Slaves. 1820-80. *3371*

—. Georgia (Jefferson County). Ogeechee Old Town (plantation). 1540-1860. *2840*

—. Georgia (Savannah). Rice. South Carolina. Townhouses. 1800-1933. *2740*

—. Ideology (review article). Luraghi, Raimondo. Politics. Thornton, J. Miller, III. 1607-1860. 1970's. *2868*

—. Ironworks. North Carolina (Lincoln County). Slavery. Vesuvius Furnace. 1791-1876. *3124*

—. Jesuits. Maryland (St. Marys County). St. Inigoes Church. Slavery. 1806-1950. *2182*

—. Letterbooks. Raper, Robert. South Carolina. Trade. 1759-65. *2779*

—. Location. Louisiana. Sugar. 1742-1870. *3305*

—. Louisiana. Novels. Regionalism. Saxon, Lyle (*Children of Strangers*). 1920's-40's. *1092*

—. Louisiana (Minden). North Louisiana Historical Association. Perryman, Melvill Lucile Martin. 1876-1975. *29*

—. Mississippi (Yazoo-Mississippi Delta). ca 1860-1930. *3255*

—. Novels. Racism. Sex. Violence. 1970-79. *879*

—. Popes Creek plantation. Virginia. Washington, George. 1656-1982. *1372*

—. Race Relations. Social Organization. Thompson, Edgar T. (review article). 19c. 1975. *189*

—. Rice. South Carolina (Berkeley County; Limerick Plantation). 1683-1945. *1264*

—. Social status. Tutors. 1773-1860. *1853*

—. South Carolina (May River). Tombstones (inscriptions). 18c-1830's. *1536*

Planter class. Alabama. Merchants. Reconstruction. State Government. 1865-70's. *2866*

—. Contracts. Freedmen's Bureau. Sharecropping. 1865-68. *2842*

—. Social conditions. South Carolina (Charleston). 1860. *655*

—. South Carolina. Speeches. Trescot, William Henry. 1847-98. *3711*

Plants. Appalachia. Cherokee Indians. Folk Medicine. 1540-1977. *1578*

—. Cherokee Indians. Folklore. Indians. 1887-88. *4057*

—. Cherokee Indians. Food Consumption. Indians. 1975. *4183*

—. Friends, Society of. Settlement. Texas (Crosby County). 1877-1936. *3200*

—. Geography. Harper, Roland M. 1900-60. *849*

—. Mississippi. Names. 1930's-70's. *1437*

Plaster. District of Columbia. Giannetti, Bob. Giannetti, John. Restorations. 1935-80. *1113*

Playwrights. *See* Dramatists.

Pleasant Grove School. Elementary Education. Kentucky (Jefferson County). 1840-1949. *1420*

Pleasant Hill (community). Kentucky. Restorations. Shakers. 1805-1970's. *2212*

Pleasant, Ruffin G. Long, Huey P. Louisiana. Prisons. Uniforms. 1916-40. *3742*

Pluralism. Appalachia. Capitalism. Myths and Symbols. Values. 1880-1980. *470*

—. Levin, Louis H. Maryland. 1889-1923. *1860*

Plymouth Congregational Church. Blacks. Congregationalism. Kentucky (Louisville). 1877-1930. *2201*

Poe, Clarence Hamilton. Agricultural reform. Editors and Editing. Farmers. Periodicals. *Progressive Farmer*. 1899-1964. *2698*

—. Branson, Eugene C. Electric Power. North Carolina. Rural Electrification Administration. State Government. 1917-36. *2918*

Poe, Edgar Allan. Cemeteries. Death and Dying. Maryland (Baltimore). Washington College Hospital. 1849-1962. *1038*

—. Collections. Gimbel, Richard. Raven (manuscript). 1959-73. *905*

—. Cooke, Philip Pendleton. Letters. *Southern Literary Messenger*. 1847-49. *1095*

—. Fiction. 19c. *912*

—. Literary criticism. Symbolism in Literature. Wilbur, Richard. 1820's-49. 1959. *970*

—. Psychologists. Short stories. ca 1835-46. *1072*

Poetry. Agrarians. Handicapped. Warren, Robert Penn (interview). 1917-81. *860*

—. Alienation. 19c-20c. *832*

—. Anthologies. Hubbard, Addison. Owen, Guy. Williams, Mary C. 1928-79. *931*

—. Appalachia. Identity. Miller, Jim Wayne. Norman, Gurney. Politics. Webb, Jim. 1970-80. *1123*

—. Authorship. Georgia. Wilde, Richard Henry (*Hesperia: A Poem*). ca 1820's-47. *889*

—. Bibliographies. Jarrell, Randall. 1941-81. *968*

—. Blacks. Davis, Daniel Webster. Virginia (Richmond). 1895-1910. *667*

—. Blacks. Harper, Frances W. (Aunt Chloe poems). Women. 19c. *1742*

—. Blacks. Knight, Etheridge. 1968-80. *1741*

—. Blacks. Lilly, Octave, Jr. (obituary). 1930-60. *1730*

—. Blacks, free. Louisiana (New Orleans). 1845. *1737*

—. Cawein, Madison Julius. Germany. Kentucky. 1865-1914. *1032*

—. Damas, Leon. Georgia. Jenkins, James. Sea Islands. South Carolina. 1970-80. *1773*

—. Faulkner, William. 1921-24. *818*

—. Folk songs. Kentucky (Ohio County). Vigilante group. ca 1900-18. *1422*

—. Folklore. Tombstones. Virginia. 19c-1979. *1480*

—. Friends, Society of. North Carolina (Albemarle region). White, Henry. 1698. *2481*

—. Frost, Robert. Georgia, University of. 1935-63. *435*

—. Georgia. Hayne, Paul Hamilton (obituary). 1886. *937*

—. Horton, George Moses. North Carolina (Chapel Hill). Slaves. 1797-1884. *1745*

—. Norris, William A. Self-perception. West Virginia, north-central. 1770-1980's. *1108*

—. Warren, Robert Penn (interview). 1920's-78. *861*

Poets. Alabama. Henderson, Elbert Calvin (Bert). 1920's-74. *843*

—. Blacks. North Carolina. Women. 1975-80. *1122*

—. Creoles. Louisiana (New Orleans). 1845-70. *1736*

—. Jarrell, Randall. Suicide. 1914-65. *967*

—. Lewis, Janet. Personal Narratives. 1899-1982. *2300*

—. Louisiana. New Orleans *Daily Picayune*. Newspapers. Nicholson, Eliza Jane. 1849-96. *1532*

—. Mississippi. 19c-20c. *979*

—. Preston, Margaret Junkin. Women. 1840-97. *1062*

—. Tucker, St. George. Virginia. 1752-1827. *1004*

Point of Honor (home). Owen, Robert (family). Virginia (Lynchburg). 1830-1978. *665*

Police. *See also* Crime and Criminals; Criminal Law; Law Enforcement; Prisons.

—. Attitudes. Immigrants. Irish Americans. Know-Nothing Party. Louisiana (New Orleans). 1830-80. *3101*

—. Georgia (Atlanta). Political Corruption. 1890-1905. *3809*

Polish Americans. Arkansas (Marche). Personal Narratives. Sarna, Jan. Settlement. Social Customs. 1877-1977. *662*

Political activism. Education. Highlander Folk School. Horton, Myles. Tennessee. 1930-80. *1830*

—. Journalism. Labor. Louisiana (New Orleans). Personal Narratives. Rogers, Elizabeth Cousins. Rogers, Walter "Rog". 1940-82. *3585*

Political Attitudes. Alabama. House of Representatives. 1849-61. *3704*

—. Alabama (Birmingham). Huddleston, George, Sr. 1915-37. *3481*

—. Allin, John M. Civil rights. Clergy. Episcopal Church, Protestant. Mississippi. 1964-73. *2183*

—. American Revolution. Confederate States of America. 1861. *95*

—. Blacks. Florida. Reconstruction. Republican Party. Walls, Josiah T. 1867-85. *3660*

—. Domestic policy. North Carolina. Truman, Harry S. 1944-48. *3602*

—. Heyburn, Weldon B. Sectionalism. Senate. 1910. *3779*

—. Historiography. Key, V. O., Jr. Martin, Roscoe C. *Southern Politics* project. 1944-70. *3726*

—. North Carolina. Rural areas. Wallace, George C. 1920's-73. *3601*

Political Campaigns. *See also* Campaign Finance; Elections; Political Speeches; Primaries.

—. Alabama. Folsom, James E. 1933-46. *3595*

—. Elections (gubernatorial). Louisiana. Morrison, deLesseps S. 1951-52. *3607*

—. Kentucky. Political Speeches. 1790-1865. *3542*

—. Louisiana (Shreveport). Prohibition. 1950-52. *3724*

Political Campaigns (congressional). Allen, John Mills. Carmack, Edward Ward. Democratic Party. Patterson, Josiah. State Politics. Tennessee. 1893-1908. *3561*

—. Randolph, John (of Roanoke). Virginia. Voting and Voting Behavior. 1773-1833. *3653*

Political Campaigns (gubernatorial). Alabama. Folsom, James E. 1946. *3596*

—. Biography. McNutt, Alexander G. Mississippi. Paxton, Andrew Jackson. ca 1837-48. 1891. *3718*

Political Campaigns (presidential). Bryan, William Jennings. Delaware. Foreign Policy. Stevenson, Adlai E. (1835-1914). 1900. *3768*

—. Carter, Jimmy. Values. 1976. *3675*

—. Conservatism. Democratic Party. Kennedy, John F. 1956-60. *3667*

Political Campaigns (presidential, senatorial). Glass, Carter. Virginia. 1936. *3663*

Political Campaigns (vice-presidential). Democratic Party. Populism. Stevenson, Adlai E. (1835-1914). 1892. *3767*

Political candidates. City Politics. Elections. Georgia (Atlanta). Property. 1865-1935. *3810*

Political change. Attitudes. Blacks. Social Change. Whites. 1964-76. *700*

—. Blacks. 1945-75. *3627*

—. Blacks. City planning. Virginia (Richmond). 1945-75. *3118*

—. City government. Elections. Political representation. Voting Rights Act (US, 1965). 1979. *3669*

—. Economic development. Industry. Regionalism. 1970-80. *2574*

—. Maryland. Voting and Voting Behavior. 1872-1948. *3678*

—. Models. South Carolina. 1920-76. *3534*

—. State Politics. Tennessee. 1837-1976. *3639*

Political Commentary. Alabama. Blacks. Duke, Jesse C. Editors and Editing. Montgomery *Herald*. Republican Party. 1886-1916. *3650*

—. Austin *American-Statesman*. Cartoons and Caricatures. Civil Rights. Newspapers. Sargent, Ben. Texas. 1977-78. *3833*

—. Integration. Mississippi. State Politics. 1970-72. *3822*

Political conditions. 1865-1980. *3599*

—. Alabama (Mobile). Blacks. Bromberg, Frederick G. 1836-1908. *3781*

Political Corruption. *See also* Elections; Lobbying; Political Reform.

—. Arkansas. Davis, Jeff (1862-1913). 1898-1907. *3672*

—. Berry, Harry S. Tennessee (Nashville). Works Progress Administration. 1935-43. *3515*

—. Campaign finance. Election Laws. Maryland. 1954-74. *3553*

—. Cannon, James, Jr. Glass, Carter. Methodist Church. Virginia. 1909-34. *2409*

—. Coal Mines and Mining. Kentucky (Harlan, Bell counties). Labor Disputes. 1920-39. *3379*

—. Georgia (Atlanta). Police. 1890-1905. *3809*

Political economy. Architects. Development. Georgia (Atlanta). Peachtree Center Complex. Portman, John. Urban revitalization. 1960-80. *3017*

Political executions. Centennial Celebrations. Cuba. Florida. 1871. 1971. *3562*

Political Factions. *See also* Interest Groups; Lobbying.

—. Butler, Pierce M. Cherokee Indians. Foreman, James. Indian Territory. Murder. Watie, Stand. 1830-42. *4140*

—. Clay, Henry. Kentucky. State Politics. 1820-44. *3696*

—. Congress. Democratic Party. Woodward, C. Vann. 1873-97. *3622*

—. Democratic Party. Election Laws. Key, V. O., Jr. 1932-77. *3519*

—. Democratic Party. Key, V. O., Jr. 1932-79. *3520*

—. Democratic Party. Lea, Luke. Peay, Austin. Republican Party. State Government. Tennessee, East. 1922-32. *3674*

—. Democratic Party. Mississippi. 1965-68. *3780*

—. Democratic Party. Mississippi. Primaries (gubernatorial). 1927-75. *3665*

—. Elections (gubernatorial). 1920-80. *3493*

—. Georgia. Hoover, Herbert C. Patronage. Race Relations. Republican Party. 1928-32. *3588*

Political Leadership. Agriculture. Bracebridge Hall (plantation). Democratic Party. North Carolina. State Government. 1839-1900. *674*

—. Alabama. Attitudes. Blacks. Industrialization. Rural Development. Tennessee-Tombigbee Waterway. Whites. 1979. *2892*

—. Arkansas. Remmel, Harmon L. Republican Party. 1880-1913. *3759*

—. Arkansas (Jefferson County). Blacks. Havis, Ferdinand. Republican Party. 1846-1918. *3677*

—. Baptists. Georgia. State Politics. 1772-1823. *2342*

—. Bilbo, Theodore G. Mississippi. State Government. Whites. 1908-32. *3590*

—. Blacks. Developing nations. Elites. Mississippi. 1965-70. *3763*

—. Blacks. Economic Theory. Washington, Booker T. 1880-1915. *383*

—. Blacks. Elections. 1968-74. *3511*

—. Blacks. Historiography. Louisiana (New Orleans). Reconstruction. ca 1800-75. *3746*

—. Bossier, Pierre. Louisiana. 1838-45. *3801*

—. Bradford, Alexander Blackburn. Chivalry. Law. Military Service. ca 1820-73. *420*

—. Bushyhead, Dennis. Cherokee Indians. Corporations. Indian-White Relations. 1879-98. *4054*

—. Democratic Party. Ideology. Republican Party. Texas. 1972-74. *3713*

—. Dickson, Anna Mae. Race Relations. Social Organizations. Texas, east. 1930's-70's. *686*

—. Economic Conditions. Elites. Kentucky. Mountaineers. Social Organization. 1790-19c. *3532*

—. Economic Conditions. Historiography. ca 1865-1979. *2672*

—. Elites. Genovese, Eugene D. Historiography. North Carolina (Mecklenburg County). Woodward, C. Vann. 1850-80. *3729*

—. Farmers. Louisiana State Fair. Schuler, Charles. State Board of Agriculture. 1840-1911. *3736*

—. Florida (Polk County). Trammell, John W. 1882-1904. *3657*

—. Governors. Mississippi. State Legislatures. Wright, Fielding. 1927-38. *3632*

—. Indians. Seminole Indians. Social Change. 1858-1958. *3883*

—. Jackson, John Jay, Jr. (family). Law. West Virginia (Parkersburg). 1715-1847. *3476*

—. Reconstruction. Republican Party. Texas. ca 1850-77. *3477*

Political participation. Alienation. Arkansas. Blacks. Colleges and Universities. Tennessee. 1968-69. *2019*

—. Appalachian Studies. Social Classes. 20c. *354*

—. Attitudes. State legislators. Women. 1979. *3684*

—. Blacks. Cities. Florida (Jacksonville). 1887-1907. *3466*

—. Blacks. Civics. Curricula. 1970's. *2060*

—. Cities. Race. Social Classes. Voting and Voting Behavior. 1960-74. *3722*

—. Government. Maryland (Baltimore). Poor. 1969-70. *3357*

—. Mexican Americans. Race Relations. Social Change. Texas (Cameron County). Wells, James B. 1882-1920. *3471*

—. Mexican Americans. State Politics. Texas. -1973. *3700*

—. Texas. Women. 1910's-83. *3500*

Political Parties. *See also* names of political parties, e.g. Democratic Party, Republican Party, etc.; Campaign Finance; Elections; Political Campaigns; Primaries.

—. Attitudes. 1952-72. *3516*

—. Blacks. Sectionalism. 1830-1976. *3484*

—. Decisionmaking. State legislatures. 1789-1820. *3507*

—. Democratic Party. Elections. Louisiana. Primaries. 1952-64. *3817*

—. Florida. 1936-71. *3735*

—. Leadership. 1865-1973. *3815*

—. Primaries. 1927-79. *3836*

—. Race. 1952-72. *3486*

—. Race Relations. Social Status. 1952-72. *3577*

—. Texas (Harrison County). 1850-80. *3518*

Political Parties (review article). Bartley, Numan V. Graham, Hugh D. Seagull, Louis M. 1944-70's. *3743*

Political power. Alabama (Birmingham). Social Classes. 1821-1921. *3616*

—. Blacks. Decisionmaking. Desegregation. Teachers. Voting and Voting Behavior. 1950's-60's. *1996*

—. Church Finance. Protestant Churches. 1930's-75. *2450*

—. Congress. Democratic Party. Leadership. Oklahoma. 1945-72. *3598*

—. Economic conditions. Income. Social Classes. 1970's. *2587*

—. Farms. Land tenure. Racism. 1877-1915. *2774*

—. Governors. Louisiana. State Government. 1699-1974. *3554*

Political Protest. *See also* Civil Disobedience; Riots; Youth Movements.

—. Ballads. "Corrido de Gregorio Cortez" (ballad). "Discriminación a un Martir". Mexican Americans. Social change. Texas (Three River). 20c. *717*

—. Blacks. City Government. Maryland (Baltimore). Public schools. 1865-1900. *2084*

—. Blacks. Folk Songs. Shack bully (character). 1920's. *1724*

—. Refuse disposal. Toxic substances. 1981. *3837*

Political Protest (review article). Blacks. 1877-1978. *3690*

Political Reform. *See also* names of reform movements, e.g. Progressivism, etc.; Lobbying; Political Corruption.

—. Bossism. Colonel Effingham (fictional character). Crackers (faction). Democratic Party. Fleming, Berry (*Colonel Effingham's Raid*). Georgia (Augusta). 1943-50. *3528*

—. Carter, William Hodding, Jr. Editors and Editing. Mississippi. Race Relations. ca 1930-60. *3576*

—. City government. Progressivism. Texas (Galveston). 1890-1906. *3748*

—. Constitutions, State. Local government. South Carolina. 1895-1970's. *3467*

—. Delegates. Democratic Party. 1972. *3543*

—. Elections. Elites. Louisiana. Poor. Progressive Party. 1894-1921. *3769*

Political Representation. *See also* Representation.

—. Attitudes. South Carolina. 1776-1860. *3603*

—. City government. Elections. Political Change. Voting Rights Act (US, 1965). 1979. *3669*

—. Congress. District of Columbia. Social Conditions. 1800-1980. *3563*

Political Science. *See also* Government; Imperialism; Law; Legislation; Nationalism; Politics; Utopias.

—. Appalachia. Economic conditions. 1960's-70's. *44*

Political Speeches. *See also* Debates; Speeches.

—. Bibliographies. 1935-75. *3503*

—. Christianity. Civil religion. 1960's-70's. *3813*

—. Kentucky. Oratory. State Politics. 1780-1930. *3521*

—. Kentucky. Political Campaigns. 1790-1865. *3542*

Political systems. Blacks. Kousser, J. Morgan (review article). Suffrage. 1880-1910. 1974. *3473*

Political Theory. *See also* kinds of political theory, e.g. Democracy; Political Science.

—. Agrarians. Economic theory. Humanism. *I'll Take My Stand*. Religion. 1930. *3823*

—. Banking. Kentucky. 1806-22. *2632*

—. Government. Madison, James. Virginia. 1774-1817. *3479*

Politicians. Anti-Catholicism. France. Maryland. Protestants. 1750's. *2210*

—. Capitalism. Economic Policy. Kentucky. Labor. 1787-1890's. *2537*

—. Historians. Mississippi Historical Society. Perry, B. G. 1789-1974. *3738*

Politics. *See also* headings beginning with the word political; City Politics; Elections; Government; Intergovernmental Relations; Lobbying; Local Politics; Presidents; State Politics.

—. AFL-CIO (Committee on Political Education). 1943-75. *3433*

—. Agrarians. *I'll Take My Stand*. Literature. 1930-80. *901*

—. Agrarians. Literature. Proletarians. 1930-39. *3824*

—. Agriculture. Conservatism. Sloan, James F. South Carolina. 1840-1901. *718*

—. Appalachia. Civil War. Mountaineers. Regionalism. 1860-99. *715*

—. Appalachia. Identity. Miller, Jim Wayne. Norman, Gurney. Poetry. Webb, Jim. 1970-80. *1123*

—. Appalachian studies. Colleges and Universities. Interest Groups. 1978. *119*

—. Architecture. City Planning. District of Columbia. L'Enfant, Pierre Charles. Republicanism. 1783-1800. *1380*

—. Arkansas. Blacks. Constitutional conventions (state). Delegates. Reconstruction. 1868. *3762*

—. Arkansas. Elazar, Daniel. Immigration. Regionalism. Social Organization. 19c-1970's. *3314*

—. Arkansas (Little Rock). Blacks. Gibbs, Mifflin W. Republican Party. 1878-1915. *3547*

—. Army Corps of Engineers. Flood control. Mississippi River (lower). 1927-41. *3747*

—. Art. Free Southern Theater. Racism. 1960's-70's. *1757*

—. Assassination. Cherokee Indians. Foreman, James. Walker, John, Jr. 1820's-30's. *4019*

—. Aswell, James B. Educators. Louisiana. 1869-1931. *1861*

—. Attitudes. Religion. Social Conditions. ca 1800-61. *422*

—. Baptists. Bible. Theology. 1925-81. *2453*

—. Baptists. Conservatism. First Baptist Church (Fort Worth). Norris, J. Frank. Texas. 1900-50. *2377*

—. Baptists. Social Reform. 1976. *2306*

—. Baptists, Southern. Conservatism. Fundamentalism. New Right. Social Problems. 1964-82. *2530*

—. Baptists, Southern. Individualism. Social problems. 18c-1976. *2278*

—. Barksdale Air Force Base. Long, Huey P. Louisiana (Shreveport). State legislatures. 1923-33. *3862*

—. Barnwell, Joseph W. St. Cecilia Society. South Carolina (Charleston). Upper Classes. 1865-1930. *3641*

—. Blacks. Colleges and Universities. Segregation. Tennessee State University. Tennessee, University of. Whites. 1869-1977. *1862*

—. Blacks. Cotton, Dorothy. Personal narratives. Southern Christian Leadership Conference. 1960-82. *3816*

—. Blacks. Editors and Editing. Norfolk *Journal and Guide*. Virginia. Young, Plummer B. 1910-54. *677*

—. Blacks. Georgia (Atlanta). Jackson, Maynard. 1940's-74. *3694*

—. Blacks. Howard, Perry W. Mississippi. Republican Party. 1924-60. *3705*

—. Blacks. Louisiana, northern. Religion. 1865-77. *2284*

—. Blacks. Minorities. Voting Rights Act, 1965. 1965-75. *3517*

—. Campbell, Randolph B. Lowe, Richard G. Social Organization. Texas (review article). Wealth. 1830's-60. 1977. *642*

—. Cartoons and Caricatures. Newspapers. *Richmond Times-Dispatch*. Seibel, Frederick O. Virginia. 1926-68. *3798*

—. Chandler, Daniel Leon. Liberalism (review article). Race. Sosna, Morton. 1977. *117*

—. Cherokee Indians. Congress. Jackson, Andrew. Removals, forced. 1780-1838. *3991*

—. Cheyenne Indians. Indians. Models. Social Organization. Tribal government. 1800-75. *4002*

—. Confederate Army. Conservatism. Editors and Editing. Rogers, Robert Leonidas. Veterans. 1864-1927. *3555*

—. Conservatism. Economic Conditions. 1968-78. *3692*

—. Country Life. Georgia. Talmadge, Eugene. 1927-46. *3754*

—. Crump, Edward Hull. Key, V. O., Jr. (*Southern Politics*). McKellar, Kenneth D. Tennessee. 1920-50. *3685*

—. Duels. House of Representatives. Jackson, John George. Maryland (Bladensburg). Pearson, Joseph. 1805-12. *3508*

Priestley, James. Classical Studies. Cumberland College. Educators. Scholarship. 1774-1821. *290*
Primaries. *See also* Elections; Voting and Voting Behavior.
—. Blacks. Democratic Party. NAACP. Suffrage. Supreme Court. Texas. 1927-45. *3633*
—. Democratic Party. Elections. Louisiana. Political Parties. 1952-64. *3817*
—. Democratic Party. Mississippi. State Government. 1947-78. *3804*
—. Political Parties. 1927-79. *3836*
—. Republican Party. 1960-75. *3495*
Primaries (gubernatorial). Democratic Party. Mississippi. Political Factions. 1927-75. *3665*
—. Republican Party. State Politics. 1960-77. *3649*
Primary Education. *See* Elementary Education.
Primary sources. Civil War. Coups d'Etat. Ellet, Charles. Letters. Methodology. Military Organization. 1863. 1979. *221*
Primers. Cherokee Indians. Elementary Education. Fleming, John. Indian Territory. Missions and Missionaries. 1819-36. *4031*
Primitive Baptists. Georgia. 1835-87. *235*
Princess Anne Academy. Blacks. Colleges and Universities. Maryland (Somerset). 1890-1930. *2090*
Princeton University Library. Boundaries (disputes). Chew, Benjamin. Documents. Maps. Maryland. Mason-Dixon Line. Pennsylvania. 1731-68. *3338*
Printing. Cherokee Indians. Indians. Missions and Missionaries. Worcester, Samuel Austin. 1828-59. *4036*
Prints. Artists. Kentucky. Kentucky Stock Book. Livestock. 1837-41. *1042*
*Prinz Eital Friedrich* (vessel). *Eclipse* (vessel). Escapes. Germany. Internment. *Kronprinz Wilhelm* (vessel). Navies. Virginia (Norfolk). 1915. *3874*
Prisland, Marie. Adamic, Louis. Baraga, Frederick. Ethnic studies. Slovenian Americans. 1687-1975. *579*
Prisons. *See also* Crime and Criminals; Criminal Law; Police.
—. 1978. *3707*
—. Blacks. Labor. Tennessee. 1830-1915. *3775*
—. Capital Punishment. Construction. Ingle, Joe (interview). Legislation. Reform. Southern Coalition on Jails and Prisons. 1978. *3565*
—. Frontier and Pioneer Life. Preservation. Tennessee. ca 1860-1979. *3537*
—. Long, Huey P. Louisiana. Pleasant, Ruffin G. Uniforms. 1916-40. *3742*
—. Oklahoma. Reform. 1910-67. *3531*
—. Tennessee. Women. 1831-1979. *3611*
Private Schools. *See also* Church Schools.
—. Alabama (Lafayette). Desegregation. Public schools. 1966-70's. *2094*
—. Alabama (Selma). Dallas Academy. 1836-1962. *1845*
—. Beaufort Academy. Discrimination. Education, Finance. Public schools. South Carolina. 1974-80. *2039*
—. Blacks. Maryland (Baltimore). 1794-1860. *1997*
—. Mississippi. Public Schools. Residential segregation. -1973. *2035*
—. Protestantism. School Integration. 1970's. *2047*
—. Segregation. Virginia (Prince Edward County). 1954-73. *2083*
Private sector. Competition. Electric power. Prices. Public Utilities. Texas (Lubbock). 1916-81. *2907*
Produce. Agricultural Industry. Mississippi (Copiah County). 1870's-1940's. *2782*
—. Illinois Central Railroad. Mississippi. Railroads. 1880's-1940. *3043*
Productivity. Agricultural Labor. Cotton. Quantitative methods. 1850's-1900's. 1958-78. *2810*
—. Agriculture. Blacks. Education. Government. 1945-64. *2739*
—. Agriculture. Economic Conditions. Farms (tenant). 1850's-90's. *2820*
—. Cotton. Discrimination, Employment. Textile Industry. 1830's-60's. *3144*
—. Cotton. Farmers. Income. ca 1880-1910. *2706*
—. Economic Development. Income. 1865-70's. *2607*
—. Kentucky. Slavery. Tennessee. Tobacco. 1850-60. *2831*
Professional Education. *See also* Medical Education; Technical Education.
—. Blacks. Desegregation. Discrimination, Educational. Graduate schools. Lawsuits. North Carolina. 1930-51. *1974*
Professionalization. Baptists. Clergy. Theology. Virginia. 1760-90. *2423*

Professorships. English. Georgia (Macon). Literature. Wesleyan Female College. 1844-1973. *1840*
Profit. Business. Management. Plantations. ca 1830-60. *2794*
Profit sharing. Callahan, Patrick Henry. Industrial Relations. Kentucky. Louisville Varnish Company. 1908-40. *3388*
Profitability. Cattle drives. Kansas. Texas. 1865-85. *2581*
—. Industry. Investments. 1830-70. *2903*
Progress. Agrarians. *I'll Take My Stand.* 1930. 1980. *921*
—. Country Music. Mississippi. Music. 1930-78. *3202*
Progressive education. Alabama. Holtville School. 1920's-78. *1833*
—. Blacks. Depressions. 1930-45. *2004*
Progressive era. Baseball teams. City Politics. Ownership. ca 1877-1916. *1630*
—. City Government. Florida (Pensacola). Prostitution. Social Change. 1900-40. *626*
*Progressive Farmer.* Agricultural reform. Editors and Editing. Farmers. Periodicals. Poe, Clarence Hamilton. 1899-1964. *2698*
—. Country Life. Periodicals. Values. Women. 1930-40. *483*
Progressive Liberty Party. *American Eagle.* Elections. Florida (Lee County). Koreshan Unity (community). Newspapers. Teed, Cyrus Reed. 1894-1908. *3683*
Progressive Party. Elections. Elites. Louisiana. Political Reform. Poor. 1894-1921. *3769*
Progressivism. 1890-1920. *3600*
—. Agricultural experiment stations. Allen, Robert McDowell. Drugs. Food Adulteration and Inspection. Kentucky. Scovell, Melville Amasa. 1898-1916. *3826*
—. Arkansas. Democratic Party. Kirby, William Fosgate. Senate. Wilson, Woodrow. 1880's-1934. *3727*
—. Beckham, John C. W. Kentucky. McCreary, James B. State Government. Willson, Augustus E. 1899-1915. *3512*
—. Blacks. Discrimination, Educational. Disfranchisement. Middle Classes. North Carolina. Suffrage. Whites. 1880-1910. *2027*
—. Candler, Asa Griggs. Cities. Conservatism. Social Reform. ca 1900-20. *3115*
—. City government. Political Reform. Texas (Galveston). 1880-1906. *3748*
—. City Politics. Maryland (Baltimore). 1895-1911. *3539*
—. Crothers, Austin Lane. Governors. Maryland. 1904-12. *3513*
—. Kefauver, Estes. Senate Subcommittee on Antitrust and Monopoly. 1950's-60's. *3702*
—. Long, Huey P. Louisiana. Populism. State Government. 1891-1935. *3544*
Prohibition. Constitutional Amendments (18th). Dean Act (1919). State Legislatures. Texas. 1917-33. *3560*
—. Crime and Criminals. Louisiana (New Orleans). 1918-33. *3643*
—. Florida (Miami). Law Enforcement. Smuggling. 1896-1920. *3579*
—. Louisiana (Shreveport). Political campaigns. 1950-52. *3724*
Projectile points. Indians. North Carolina. South Carolina. Virginia. ca 10,000-5,000 BC. *4072*
—. Indians. Virginia (Virginia Beach; Great Neck). 810 BC-660. *4071*
Proletarians. Agrarians. Literature. Politics. 1930-39. *3824*
Proletariat. *See* Working Class.
Propaganda. *See also* Advertising; Public Opinion.
—. Exiles. Liberal Party. Mexican Americans. Mexico. Texas. Women. 1898-1910. *3832*
Property. *See also* Income.
—. Bertinatti, Eugenia Bate Bass. Estates. Italy. Tennessee. Travel. 1826-1906. *557*
—. Cherokee Indians. Christianity. Indian-White Relations. Missions and Missionaries. Social Change. Women. 19c. *4139*
—. City Politics. Elections. Georgia (Atlanta). Political candidates. 1865-1903. *3810*
—. Confiscations. Debt. Houses. Moratoriums. Texas. 1829-1921. *2611*
—. Economic Conditions. Local government. Urbanization. 1960's-70's. *3136*
—. Marriage. South Carolina. Women. 1730-1830. *659*
Propes, James Marlowe. Flat Creek Sacred Singers. Georgia (Gainesville). Personal narratives. Singing. 1900-81. *1686*
Proslavery Sentiments. *See also* Antislavery Sentiments.
—. Christianity. 1844-1977. *2355*

—. Elites. Junkers. Land Tenure. Plantations. Prussia. 1800-61. *2678*
—. Faust, Drew Gilpin (review article). Intellectuals. Psychology. 1840-60. 1978. *944*
—. Intellectuals. 1800-65. *864*
—. Literature. *Southern Quarterly Review.* States' rights. Whitaker, Daniel K. 1842-57. 1879-80. *980*
Prostitution. City Government. Florida (Pensacola). Progressive era. Social Change. 1900-40. *626*
—. Public policy. Social Reform. Texas (Austin). 1870-1915. *3642*
Protest Marches. *See* Political Protest.
Protestant Churches. *See also* names of churches, e.g. Methodist Church, etc.; Protestantism.
—. Alabama. Reconstruction. 1865-67. *2344*
—. Blacks. Clergy. ca 1800-65. *864*
—. Blacks. Georgia (Atlanta). Haven, Gilbert. Segregation. 1865-1906. *2397*
—. Church Finance. Political power. 1930's-75. *2450*
—. Converts. Evangelism. Louisiana (New Orleans). Slavery. 1800-61. *2418*
—. Desegregation. Korean War. Vietnam War. Whites. 1950-70. *2289*
—. Education. German Americans. Maryland (Frederick County). 1734-1800. *2340*
—. Feminism. Women. 1920's. *2181*
—. Georgia, southern. Gospel music. Singing. 1873-1978. *1649*
Protestantism. *See also* Evangelism; Fundamentalism.
—. Appalachia. Bibliographies. 1905-75. *2332*
—. Appalachia. Daily Life. 1788-1974. *2321*
—. Appalachia. Mountaineers. 1978. *2251*
—. Bates, Elisha. Boudinot, Elias (ca. 1803-39; *Poor Sarah).* Cherokee Indians. Indians. 1820's-39. *4128*
—. Bible. Folklore. Visions. 20c. *1417*
—. Blacks. Dance. Georgia. Music. Rites and Ceremonies. Sea Islands. South Carolina. 1970-80. *1769*
—. Byington, Cyrus. Choctaw Indians. Indians. Missions and Missionaries. Mississippi. 1820-68. *4115*
—. Camp meetings. Foster, Elizabeth Pyburn. Louisiana, Northern. Old Siloam Camp Ground. Personal Narratives. 19c. *1498*
—. Churches. Economic conditions. Location. Maryland (Baltimore). 1840-70. *2276*
—. Civil War. 1861-65. *2249*
—. Dabbs, James McBride. Historians. Race Relations. 1896-1970. *446*
—. Evangelism. Slavery. 18-19c. *2365*
—. Music. Religion. Walker, William. 1830-50. *2227*
—. Neoorthodoxy. 1930's. *2345*
—. North Carolina (Piedmont). 1890-1952. *3187*
—. Private schools. School Integration. 1970's. *2047*
—. Racism. 1885-90's. *2189*
Protestantism (review article). Caskey, Marie. Mathews, Donald G. Moorhead, James H. Reform. Walters, Ronald. 1830-80. 1976-78. *2231*
Protestants. Anti-Catholicism. France. Maryland. Politicians. 1750's. *2210*
Provincial Government. Church of England. North Carolina. Tryon, William. 1765-76. *2277*
Provost, Tessie. Blacks. Louisiana (New Orleans). Public schools. School Integration. 1960-79. *2101*
Prussia. Elites. Junkers. Land Tenure. Plantations. Proslavery Sentiments. 1800-61. *2678*
Psychohistory. Cash, Wilbur J. Dollard, John. Elkins, Stanley. Genovese, Eugene D. Taylor, William R. 1935-78. *305*
—. Georgia. State Politics. Watson, Thomas E. 1856-1922. *3572*
Psychologists. Poe, Edgar Allan. Short stories. ca 1835-46. *1072*
Psychology. *See also* Psychiatry; Social Psychology.
—. Colleges and Universities. Freeman, Ellis. Kentucky. Louisville, University of (Psychology Department). 1907-53. *1792*
—. Faust, Drew Gilpin (review article). Intellectuals. Proslavery Sentiments. 1840-60. 1978. *944*
—. Laboratories. Parrish, Celestia S. Randolph-Macon Woman's College. Titchener, Edward Bradford. Virginia (Lynchburg). 1893-1938. *1939*
Public awareness. Mississippi. Preservation. 1900-78. *3196*
Public Employees. American Federation of Labor. Appalachia. Industrial Relations. Tennessee Valley Authority. 1933-78. *2601*
Public Finance. Cherokee Indians. Indians. Removals, forced. Ross, John. Treaty of New Echota (1835). 1835-1906. *4062*

# R

Rabb, Maxwell M. Eisenhower, Dwight D. Faulkner, William. Foreign Relations. People-to-People Program (Writers' Group). State Department. UNESCO (National Commission). 1954-61. *809*

Rabbis. Assimilation. Geffen, Tobias. Georgia (Atlanta). Jews. 1903-70. *2336*

Rabinowitz, Howard N. Brownell, Blaine A. Goldfield, David R. Goldin, Claudia Dale. Harris, Carl V. Urbanization (review article). Watts, Eugene J. 1820-1980. *2950*

Raboteau, Albert J. Christianity (review article). Holifield, E. Brooks. Slavery. 1795-1860. *2204*

Race. Attitudes. Blacks. Breckenridge family. Elites. Kentucky. 1760-1935. *601*
—. Blacks. Jazz. Lyrics. Music. 20c. *1720*
—. Chandler, Daniel Leon. Liberalism (review article). Politics. Sosna, Morton. 1977. *117*
—. Cities. Political Participation. Social Classes. Voting and Voting Behavior. 1960-74. *3722*
—. Debates. Methodist Episcopal Church. Unification. Virginia. 1924-25. *2357*
—. Education, Finance. Louisiana. Public Schools. 1890-1910. *2036*
—. Political Parties. 1952-72. *3486*
—. Voting and Voting Behavior. Whites. 1952-68. *3617*

Race Relations. *See also* Acculturation; Busing; Discrimination; Emigration; Ethnology; Human Relations; Immigration; Indian-White Relations.
—. Abolition Movement. Freedmen. Labor. Slavery. 1830-63. *359*
—. Abolition movement. McPherson, James M. (review article). 1870's-1960's. 1976. *3739*
—. Alabama. Governors. Memoirs. 1923-55. *3548*
—. Arkansas. Blacks. Republican Party. 1867-1928. *3546*
—. Attitudes. Authors. Blacks. Faulkner, William. 1930's-79. *1116*
—. Attitudes. Great Britain. Travelers. ca 1865-1914. *752*
—. Baptists. First Baptist Church. Merry, Nelson. Tennessee (Nashville). 1810-65. *2462*
—. Baptists (Southern). Blacks. Emancipation. 1863-67. *2385*
—. Baptists (Southern). Blacks. Home Mission Board. 1845-1981. *2370*
—. Bible. Presbyterian Church, Southern. 1861-1980. *2460*
—. Blacks. Cakewalks. Dance. Satire. 1860-1910. *1714*
—. Blacks. Cheshire, Joseph Blount, Jr. Episcopal Church, Protestant. North Carolina. Paternalism. 1870-1932. *2275*
—. Blacks. Clergy. Colleges and Universities. Phillips, Daniel W. Roger Williams University. Tennessee (Nashville). 1867-1910. *1948*
—. Blacks. Florida. Law. Segregation. Social customs. 1865-1977. *3777*
—. Blacks. Football. High Schools. 1972-76. *2042*
—. Blacks. Immigrants. Italians. Louisiana. Sugarcane. 1880-1910. *2828*
—. Blacks. Immigration. Italian Americans. Louisiana. Sugarcane. 1880-1910. *2829*
—. Bratton, Theodore DuBose. Conference for Education in the South. Episcopal Church, Protestant. Mississippi. 1908. *2456*
—. Brotherhood of Timber Workers. Industrial Workers of the World. Louisiana. Lumber and Lumbering. Texas. 1910-13. *3401*
—. Brotherhood of Timber Workers. Louisiana, western. Lumber and Lumbering. Southern Lumber Operators' Association. Texas, east. 1911-13. *3402*
—. Cable, George Washington (*Grandissimes*). Fiction. Freedmen. Harris, Joel Chandler ("Free Joe and the Rest of the World"). Twain, Mark (*Huckleberry Finn*). 1880-84. *801*
—. Carter, William Hodding, Jr. Editors and Editing. Mississippi. Political Reform. ca 1930-60. *3576*
—. Chesnutt, Charles W. Fiction. Howells, William Dean. Washington, Booker T. 1890's-1910's. *1710*
—. Coincoin. Creoles. Family. Louisiana (Cane River, Natchitoches). Social status. 1767-20c. *632*
—. Comparative Studies. Fredrickson, George M. (review article). South Africa. 18c-20c. *473*
—. Conservatives. Historiography. 1865-1973. *362*
—. Courts. North Carolina. Phillips, Samuel Field. Republican Party. 1844-1903. *3709*
—. Criminal justice system. North Carolina. School Integration. Trials. Wilmington Ten. 1971-77. *2049*
—. Dabbs, James McBride. Historians. Protestantism. 1896-1970. *446*

—. Dickson, Anna Mae. Political Leadership. Social Organizations. Texas, east. 1930's-70's. *686*
—. Editors and Editing. Mitchell, John P. Newspapers. Richmond *Planet*. Social Reform. Virginia. ca 1883-1929. *1616*
—. Evangelicalism. Jones, Charles Colcock. Utopias. 1804-63. *2364*
—. Fisk University. Tennessee (Nashville). Youth Movements. 1909-26. *1918*
—. Folk Songs. Music. 1900-41. *1602*
—. Georgia. Hoover, Herbert C. Patronage. Political factions. Republican Party. 1928-32. *3588*
—. Historiography. Washington, Booker T. 1898-1972. *372*
—. International Longshoremen's Association. 1866-1920. *3037*
—. Knights of Labor. 1880-87. *3420*
—. Labor Unions and Organizations. Longshoremen. Louisiana (New Orleans). 1850's-1976. *3458*
—. Liberals. Myrdal, Gunnar (*An American Dilemma*). Whites. 1944-75. *279*
—. Literature. Newspapers. Sex. Smith, Lillian. 20c. *1021*
—. Mexican Americans. Political participation. Social Change. Texas (Cameron County). Wells, James B. 1882-1920. *3471*
—. Mexican Americans. Texas. 19c. *611*
—. Mississippi. 1900-78. *3242*
—. Mississippi. 1900-78. *3260*
—. Mississippi. Poverty. Public Opinion. 1900-78. *3197*
—. Mississippi. Public Opinion. Social Change. 1930-78. *3352*
—. Models. Voting and Voting Behavior. Wallace, George C. 1968. *3828*
—. Newspapers. Norfolk *Journal and Guide*. Virginia. Washington, Booker T. Young, Plummer B. 1904-20's. *1770*
—. North Carolina (Wilmington). Riots. 1898. 1971. *639*
—. Plantations. Social Organization. Thompson, Edgar T. (review article). 19c. 1975. *189*
—. Political parties. Social Status. 1952-72. *3577*
—. Populism. Suffrage. Washington, Booker T. 1877-1910. *3794*
—. Teachers. Tennessee. 1865-1920. *1993*

Race Relations Institutes. Fisk University. Johnson, Charles S. Tennessee (Nashville). 1942-56. *2003*

Rachal, William Munford Ellis (obituary). Editors and Editing. Historians. Virginia Historical Society. 1910-80. *355*

*Rachel Plummer's Narrative* (first edition). Books (editions). Captivity narratives. Indians (captivities). Texas. Yale University (Streeter Texas Collection). 1838-44. 1975-77. *898*

Racism. Africa. Industrial arts education. Pan-Africanism. 1879-1940. *2078*
—. Agricultural Labor. Economic Structure. Freedmen. Reconstruction. Texas. 1865-74. *2845*
—. Agriculture. Blacks. 1860-1910. *2879*
—. Alabama Sharecropper's Union. Blacks. Communist Party. Personal Narratives. Rosengarten, Theodore (review article). Shaw, Nate. 1890-1945. *3422*
—. American Revolution. Presbyterian Church. Slavery. 1750-1818. *2485*
—. Anthropology, cultural. Cherokee Indians. Indian-White Relations. Methodology. Social organization. Prehistory-1975. *3908*
—. Art. Free Southern Theater. Politics. 1960's-70's. *1757*
—. Attitudes. Old Dominion University. School Integration. Students. Virginia (Norfolk). 1978. *2062*
—. Aycock, Charles Brantley. Education. Governors. North Carolina. 1895-1912. *3757*
—. Baptists, Southern. Churches. Education. Reconstruction. 1865-76. *2474*
—. Black Studies. Historiography (review article). Phillips, Ulrich B. 1964-74. *367*
—. Blacks. Colleges and Universities. Fort Valley State College. Georgia (Peach County). *Hunnicutt et al. v. Burge et al.* (Georgia, 1972). School Integration. 1972-78. *1970*
—. Blacks. Education. English language. *Martin Luther King, Jr. Elementary School Children v. Ann Arbor School District Board* (Michigan, 1979). Social Classes. 1979. *2075*
—. Blacks. Genocide. Georgia (Atlanta). 20c. *3691*
—. Blacks. Minstrelsy. Social Status. 1854-75. *1640*
—. Blacks. Physicians. Social Reform. 1900-40. *2109*
—. Boles, John B. (review article). Evangelicalism. Religion. Smith, H. Shelton (review article). 1972. *2302*

—. Cable, George Washington. Louisiana (New Orleans). Novels. 19c. *434*
—. Cherokee Indians. Cultural identity. Indian-white relations. Social organization. ca 16c-1975. *3900*
—. Cherokee Indians. Freedmen. Indian Territory. 1839-88. *3985*
—. Civil War. Louisiana (New Orleans). Nationalism. Palmer, Benjamin Morgan. Secession. 1860-1902. *2419*
—. Coal Mines and Mining. Labor Unions and Organizations. Strikes. United Mine Workers of America. 1894-1920. *3450*
—. Cocking, Walter D. Georgia, University of. Holley, Joseph Winthrop. Talmadge, Eugene. 1941. *2057*
—. Comparative Studies. South Africa. 19c-20c. *404*
—. Convict labor. Economic Conditions. Georgia. 1868-1909. *3687*
—. Coulter, Ellis Merton. 1890-1979. *494*
—. Elites. Materialism. ca 1775-1974. *702*
—. Elitism. Spelling reform. 1973. *775*
—. Farms. Land tenure. Political power. 1877-1915. *2774*
—. Florida (Miami). Law Enforcement. Terrorism. 1896-1930. *3581*
—. Florida (Miami; Colored Town). 1896-1930. *3580*
—. Historiography. Woodward, C. Vann (*Tom Watson: Agrarian Rebel*). ca 1920-38. *257*
—. Indian-White Relations. Oklahoma, western. Stereotypes. 1967-71. *4178*
—. Labor Unions and Organizations. 1960's-70's. *3387*
—. Louisiana (Plaquemines Parish). Perez, Leander. Public Welfare. Social reform. 1919-69. *3646*
—. Morality. Myrdal, Gunnar. National Self-image. Social psychology. Virginia. 1944-70's. *430*
—. Myths and Symbols. Rhetoric. Washington, Booker T. ca 1895-1915. *382*
—. Novels. Plantations. Sex. Violence. 1970-79. *879*
—. Protestantism. 1885-90's. *2189*

Racism (review article). Blacks. 1780-1914. *576*

Radford, John Blair. Business. Physicians. Virginia. 1823-72. *2171*

Radicals and Radicalism. *See also* Political Reform; Social Reform.
—. Arkansas. Colleges and Universities. Commonwealth College. Education, Experimental Methods. Labor. Student activism. 1925-35. *1805*
—. Christianity. Fellowship of Southern Churchmen. Social Reform. 1934-57. *2360*
—. Christianity. Kester, Howard Anderson. 1921-41. *3693*
—. Civil Rights movement. Johnson, Lyndon B. Long, Huey P. 1920-70. *3821*
—. Conservatism. Ellender, Allen J. Hall, Covington. Louisiana. 1871-1972. *3487*
—. Education. Health services. Minorities. Southern Conference Education Fund. 1946-76. *1832*
—. Horton, Myles. Moyers, Bill. Personal Narratives. Tennessee (Chattanooga area). 1932-81. *1591*

Radio. Collins, Curley. Country music. Forman, Tex. Georgia (Atlanta). Musicians. Personal narratives. Pop Eckler and His Young'uns. 1936-42. *1470*
—. Communications Technology. Louisiana (New Orleans). Television. WWL (station). 1940-50. *1623*
—. Country Music. *Louisiana Hayride* (program). Music. 1948-54. *1673*
—. Country Music. Music. Old Time Country Radio Reunion. Tennessee (Jonesboro). 1979. *1434*
—. Country-Western Music. *Midday Merry Go-Round* (program). Music. Tennessee (Knoxville). 1921-41. *1647*
—. Federal Regulation. Henderson, William K. Louisiana (Shreveport). 1925-35. *1624*
—. Kentucky (Louisville). WHAS (station). 1922-42. *1431*
—. Oklahoma, central. 1920-30's. *1670*

Radoff, Morris Leon. Archives. Maryland Hall of Records. 1939-74. *288*

Ragtime. Blacks. Composers. Joplin, Scott. 1900-17. 1970's. *1727*

Railroad stations. Architecture. Civic pride. Economic Conditions. Urbanization. 1890-1920. *1172*
—. Architecture. Missouri, Kansas, and Texas Railroad. Oklahoma. 1870-1970's. *1229*
—. Architecture. Texas. 1890-1976. *1173*

Railroads. Accidents. Folklore. Ghosts. North Carolina (Maco). 19c-1973. *1650*
—. Acme, Red River and Northern Railroad. Gypsum mills. Lazarus, Samuel L. Texas (Hardeman County). 1890-1909. *2997*

—. Agriculture. Attitudes. Florida. Fruit and Fruit Crops. Settlement. 19c-1910. *2761*
—. Architecture. Cities. 1890-1920. *1171*
—. Arkansas. Louisiana and Arkansas Railway. 1898-1949. *2917*
—. Arkansas (northern). Economic Growth. Missouri and North Arkansas Railroad. Settlement. 1880-1920's. *2985*
—. Ball, Ed. DuPont estate. Florida East Coast Railway. Pepper, Claude. 1926-58. *3132*
—. Banking. Capital. Georgia Railroad and Banking Company. Taxation. 1833-1980. *3110*
—. Boll Weevil (locomotive). Percy, Walker (*Last Gentleman*). Social Change. 1930's-79. *3103*
—. Business. Florida (Jacksonville). 1865-1930. *2949*
—. Calvert, Robert. Economic Conditions. Houston and Texas Central Railway. Texas (Calvert). 1868-1918. *2970*
—. Carter, George Lafayette. Coal Mines and Mining. Iron Industry. 1877-1936. *3064*
—. Cattle raising. Missouri, Kansas, and Texas Railway. Oklahoma. 1865-1972. *2998*
—. Church Hill Tunnel. South Carolina (Richmond). 1872-1926. *2978*
—. Clinchfield Railroad. 1886-1924. *2954*
—. Clinchfield Railroad. Locomotives. Photographs. Steam power. 1887-1954. *2956*
—. Cohen, Mendes. Engineering. Maryland (Baltimore). 1847-1915. *2973*
—. Construction. Oklahoma panhandle. Settlement. 1890's-1931. *2999*
—. Cumberland Mountain. Tennessee (Cowan district). Tunnels. 1845-1975. *2895*
—. Daily Life. Florida (Boca Grande). 1885-1981. *3093*
—. Delaware (Wilmington). Economic Conditions. Philadelphia, Wilmington, and Baltimore Railroad. 19c-20c. *3109*
—. Development. Texas and Pacific Railroad. Texas (Martin County). 1881-1976. *3092*
—. Development. Texas and Pacific Railroad. Texas (Ward County). 1880-1910. *3089*
—. Discovery and Exploration. Indian Territory. Indian-White Relations. Whipple, Amiel Weeks. 1853. *3882*
—. Economic Conditions. 1830-60. *3150*
—. Economic conditions. Oklahoma panhandle. Territorial status. 1880's-1930's. *2966*
—. Economic Development. Florida Southern Railroad (Charlotte Harbor Division). 1884-1904. *3077*
—. Economic Development. Steamboats. Transportation, Commercial. Western States. 1811-60. *2981*
—. Faulkner, William ("The Bear"). Fiction. Mississippi (Lafayette County, Panola County, Yazoo Delta). Plantations. Wilderness. 19c-20c. *3186*
—. Florida East Coast Railway. Immigrants. Italian Americans. Labor recruitment. Padrone system. ca 1890-1901. *3435*
—. Georgia. 1915-78. *3049*
—. Georgia. Location. North Carolina. Planning. South Carolina. 1830-60. *3153*
—. Gould, Jay. Louisiana, northern. Mergers. Texas and Pacific Railroad. 1870-1914. *3050*
—. Henderson, C. C. Louisiana (Bernice). 1899-1910. *2897*
—. Illinois Central Railroad. Mississippi. Produce. 1880's-1940. *3043*
—. Illinois Central Railroad. *Mississippi* (locomotive). 1836-1979. *3158*
—. Industrialization. Oklahoma (Oklahoma City). Population. 1889-1939. *3051*
—. Kentucky. Ohio (Cincinnati). South Carolina (Charleston). 1835-39. *3127*
—. Labor. Missouri-Kansas-Texas Railroad. Oklahoma. Texas. 1906-75. *3004*
—. Literature. Music. 1830's-1970's. *2996*
—. Locomotives. Louisiana and Arkansas Railway. 1896-1929. *2955*
—. Louisa Railroad Company. Virginia. 1836-1980. *3142*
—. Louisiana (Algiers, Gretna). Mules. Zagel, Hermann. 1883-84. *753*
—. Louisiana, northern. 1851-84. *3027*
—. Mississippi. Southern Railroad. 1840-89. *3149*
—. Missouri-Kansas-Texas Railroad. Oklahoma Railroad Maintenance Authority. Pressure Groups. 1906-73. *3000*
—. Oklahoma. 1866-1907. *2945*
—. Oklahoma. Rock Island Railroad. 1899-1937. *3047*
—. Oklahoma. Texas. Towns. Wichita Falls and Northwestern Railway. 1900-20. *3003*
—. Oklahoma (Blackburn). Settlement. Skinner, John. 1893-1910. *3230*

—. Personal narratives. Smith, E. A. "Frog". 1896-1959. *1707*
—. Quanah, Acme and Pacific Railway. Texas. 1909-29. *3002*
—. Roanoke and Western. Virginia (Roanoke). 1881-1976. *2909*
—. South Carolina (Florence). Wilmington and Manchester Railroad Company. 1853-90. *3020*
—. Stagecoaches. Virginia (Caroline County). Woolfolk, John George. 1742-1846. *2962*
—. Tennessee Midland Railway. 1886-1981. *3091*
—. Texas. 1890-1920. *2977*
—. Texas (Dallas). 1843-73. *3100*
—. Virginia (Richmond, Petersburg, Norfolk). 1830's-1850's. *3130*
Raleigh *Star*. Communications. Newspapers. North Carolina. Public Opinion. 1810. *1442*
Ramée, Joseph Jacques. Architects. Calverton (estate). Long, Robert Cary, Sr. Maryland. 1815-72. *1310*
Ranches. Cattle brands. Texas (Borden County). 19c. *1580*
—. Explorers. Goodnight, Charles. Indians. Settlement. Texas (Palo Duro Canyon). 1541-1900. *3228*
Ranching. Architecture. Hispanic Americans. Texas, south. 1750-1900. *1336*
—. Architecture. Preservation. Texas Tech University. 1830-1900. *1302*
—. Cattle drives. Texas. 1820-70. *3015*
—. Cattle raising. Florida, southern. Land tenure. Settlement. 1840's-20c. *2790*
—. Lich, Balthasar. Lich, Elisabeth Scholl. Texas (Cypress Creek). 1845-1975. *615*
Randolph, A. Philip. Civil Rights (review article). 1910-70. *3583*
Randolph Field. Air Forces. Lahm, Frank Purdy. Military History. Texas. 1897-1963. *3872*
Randolph, John. Dawidoff, Robert (review article). Education. ca 1750-84. *762*
Randolph, John (of Roanoke). Political Campaigns (congressional). Virginia. Voting and Voting Behavior. 1773-1833. *3653*
Randolph, Mary (*Virginia Housewife*). Cookbooks. Virginia. 1762-1980. *1534*
Randolph, Vance. Ozark Mountains. Rayburn, Otto Ernest. Regionalism. Wilson, Charles Morrow. 1930-75. *833*
Randolph, W. C. N. Architecture. Virginia, University of. White, Stanford. 1896. *1397*
Randolph-Macon Woman's College. Laboratories. Parrish, Celestia S. Psychology. Titchener, Edward Bradford. Virginia (Lynchburg). 1893-1938. *1939*
Rankin, Jeannette. Feminism. Georgia. Peace Movements. 1924-73. *3623*
Rankin, John. Gasper River Meeting House. Kentucky (Logan County). McGready, James. Presbyterian Church. Revivals. 1798-1810. *2521*
Ransom, Harry Huntt (obituary). Texas, University of. 1922-76. *1935*
Ransom, John Crowe. Agrarianism. Debates. 1930-31. *2875*
—. Agrarians. Davidson, Donald. *I'll Take My Stand*. Tate, Allen. Values. Warren, Robert Penn. 1925-30. *3831*
—. Davidson, Donald. Rubin, Louis D. (review article). Tate, Allen. Warren, Robert Penn. 1920's-30's. 1978. *892*
—. Mississippi (Taylorsville). 1904-07. *1137*
Ransom, Roger L. Agriculture. Economic Development (review article). Freedmen. Sutch, Richard. 1865-1900. *2873*
—. Economic Conditions (review article). Mandle, Jay R. Sutch, Richard. Wiener, Jonathan M. 1850-1910. 1977-78. *3362*
Raper, Robert. Letterbooks. Plantations. South Carolina. Trade. 1759-65. *2779*
Rare Books. Lambdin, William. Mormons. Smith, Joseph (*Book of Commandments*). West Virginia (Wheeling). 1830-33. *2219*
Raven (manuscript). Collections. Gimbel, Richard. Poe, Edgar Allan. 1959-73. *905*
Ray, Cyrus N. Archaeology. Medicine (practice of). Texas (Abilene). 1909-66. *3231*
Ray, John. Blacks. Louisiana. Republican Party. Scalawags. ca 1836-88. *3818*
Rayburn, Otto Ernest. Ozark Mountains. Randolph, Vance. Regionalism. Wilson, Charles Morrow. 1930-75. *833*
Rays of Rhythm. Blacks. Holloway, Lou. Mississippi. Music. Personal narratives. Piney Woods School. 1940-49. *911*
Read, Opie. Kentucky. Literature. Tennessee. 1870's-1900's. *794*
Real Estate Business. Agriculture. Settlement. Soash, William Pulver. Texas Panhandle. 1905-43. *2724*

—. Flagler, Henry Morrison. Florida (St. Augustine). Model Land Company. 1885-1920's. *2641*
Realism. Historiography. Liberalism. Populism. Woodward, C. Vann. 1950-78. *306*
—. Literature. Romance. Satire. Simms, William Gilmore. ca 1825-70. *1127*
—. Stribling, Thomas Sigismund. 1920-46. *998*
Reapportionment. *See* Apportionment.
Rebellions. *See also* particular mutinies, insurrections, and rebellions by name, e.g. Kronstadt Mutiny, Warsaw ghetto uprising; Political Protest; Revolutionary Movements.
—. Boundaries. Mexico. Texas (Brownsville, Eagle Pass area). 1850-1900. *3204*
Recessions. *See also* Depressions.
—. Economic Development. Industry. Population. 1970-77. *2562*
Recipes. Cookbooks. Gunter, Bessie. Virginia (eastern shore). 1889-1935. *1485*
Reconstruction. *See also* Carpetbaggers; Confederate States of America; Emancipation; Freedmen; Ku Klux Klan.
—. Agricultural Labor. Economic Structure. Freedmen. Racism. Texas. 1865-74. *2845*
—. Alabama. Blacks. Haralson, J. Republican Party. Suffrage. 1867-82. *3771*
—. Alabama. Civil War. Livestock. 1850-1900. *2789*
—. Alabama. Civil War. Plantations. Women. 1850-70. *2864*
—. Alabama. Merchants. Planter class. State Government. 1865-70's. *2866*
—. Alabama. Protestant Churches. 1865-67. *2344*
—. American Missionary Association. Cardozo, Francis L. Education. Freedmen. South Carolina (Charleston). State Politics. 1865-70. *2059*
—. Arkansas. Blacks. Constitutional conventions (state). Delegates. Politics. 1868. *3762*
—. Baptists, Southern. Churches. Education. Racism. 1865-76. *2474*
—. Bibliographies. Civil War. Slavery. 1830-80. 1974. *196*
—. Blacks. Bruce, Blanche Kelso. Mississippi. Senate. 1875-81. *3688*
—. Blacks. Civil War. Slavery. Women. 19c. *3568*
—. Blacks. Dixon, Thomas (*Leopard's Spots*). Fiction. Stowe, Harriet Beecher (*Uncle Tom's Cabin*). 1850-1900. *1019*
—. Blacks. Federal Government. Public Schools (review article). Vaughn, William Preston. Warren, Donald R. 1865-76. 1974. *2086*
—. Blacks. Florida. Forest industries. Labor. 1860-1900. *3116*
—. Blacks. Florida. Political attitudes. Republican Party. Walls, Josiah T. 1867-85. *3660*
—. Blacks. Harris, Cicero. Harris, Robert. Harris, William. Teaching. 1864-70. *2091*
—. Blacks. Historiography. Louisiana (New Orleans). Political Leadership. ca 1800-75. *3746*
—. Blacks. House of Representatives. Lynch, John Roy. Mississippi. 1869-1939. *3488*
—. Blacks. Letters. Lynch, James. Methodist Episcopal Church. Mississippi. 1868-69. *2291*
—. Blacks. Republican Party. Southern States Convention. 1864-72. *3661*
—. Blacks, free. Civil Rights. Civil War. Louisiana. Military Service. 1850-90. *3857*
—. Butchart, Ronald E. Freedmen. Jones, Jacqueline. Teachers (review article). 1862-75. 1980. *2071*
—. Cherokee Indians. Indian Territory. 1865-70. *3993*
—. Chickasaw Indians. Choctaw Indians. Indians. Treaties. 1865-66. *4037*
—. Civil War. Cooke, Alistair. Historiography. Northerners. 1860-76. 20c. *275*
—. Civil War. Texas. ca 1861-69. *3612*
—. Civil War. Governors. Military General Staff. Smith, William "Extra Billy". Virginia Infantry, 49th. 1797-1887. *3506*
—. Cotton. Mississippi. Small farms. Tenancy. Whites. ca 1865-80. *2756*
—. DuBois, W. E. B. (*Black Reconstruction in America*). Historiography. Plagiarism. Wesley, Charles H. (*Negro Labor in the United States*). 1927-35. *386*
—. Economic Growth. Farming. Federal Government. Indians. Seminole Indians. Social conditions. 1865-70. *4108*
—. Economic structure. Florida (Duval County). Upper classes. 1850-70. *2591*
—. Elementary education. Florida. Peabody Fund. Segregation. 1869-76. *1856*
—. Freedmen. Homesteading and Homesteaders. Louisiana. 1865-83. *2806*
—. Freedmen's Bureau. History Teaching. Secondary Education. Textbooks. 1971-80. *376*
—. Historiography. 1865-83. 1973-76. *64*

—. Cherokee Indians. Indians. Ross, John. Treaty of New Echota (1835). 1839-46. *4082*

—. Cherokee Indians. Indian-White Relations. 1839-44. *3972*

—. Cherokee Indians. Indian-White Relations. Jackson, Andrew. 1835. *4141*

—. Cherokee Indians. Indian-White Relations. Jefferson, Thomas. Speeches. 1809. *4150*

—. Cherokee Indians. Indian-White Relations. Land. Treaties. 1791-1829. *4142*

—. Cherokee Indians. Indian-White Relations. Personal narratives. Ross, John. Tennessee. 1838-39. *3997*

—. Cherokee Indians. Indian-White Relations. Personal narratives. Scott, Winfield. 1838. *4091*

—. Cherokee Indians. Nonviolence. Ross, John. 1833-38. *3944*

—. Chickasaw Indians. Choctaw Indians. Financial settlements. Indians. Public Opinion. 1830-80. *4134*

—. Chickasaw Indians. Indian Territory. Oklahoma. 1800-65. *3940*

—. Choctaw Indians. Federal Policy. Indian Territory. Oklahoma. 1803-47. *4012*

—. Creek Indians. Indian Territory. Indian Wars. 1812-65. *4088*

—. Creek Indians. Indian Territory. Indian Wars. 1836. *4113*

—. Diseases. Indian Territory. Indian-White Relations. Medicine (practice of). 1830's-70's. *4007*

—. Five Civilized Tribes. Historiography. Manifest Destiny. Oklahoma. 19c-20c. *3924*

—. Florida. Indian Territory. Indian Wars. Osceola. Seminole Indians. 1800-60. *4124*

—. Indian Territory. Indian Wars. 1855-94. *3994*

Renggli, Rose (Mother Mary Beatrice). Arkansas (Jonesboro). Catholic Church. Missions and Missionaries. Olivetan Benedictine Sisters. 1847-1942. *2499*

Renoir, Jean. Daily Life. Films. *Southerner* (film). 1945-50. *485*

Reporters and Reporting. *See also* Editors and Editing; Journalism; Press.

—. Artists. Bruce, Edward Caledon. Virginia. 1847-1901. *1060*

—. Authors. Historians. North Carolina. Obituaries. 1980-81. *1010*

—. Florida. O'Brien, Lucy Fulghum. Personal narratives. Tampa *Tribune*. 1935-50's. *1598*

—. Johnson, Edith. Oklahoma. Women. 1908-61. *1455*

—. Mississippi. Newspapers. Public Opinion. 1978. *3236*

Representation. *See also* Political Representation.

—. Blacks. Cities. City councils. 1970's. *3721*

Republic of New Afrika. Agricultural cooperatives. Blacks. Mississippi. 1866-1974. *390*

Republican Party. 1940-74. *3606*

—. Alabama. Blacks. Duke, Jesse C. Editors and Editing. Montgomery *Herald*. Political Commentary. 1886-1916. *3650*

—. Alabama. Blacks. Haralson, J. Reconstruction. Suffrage. 1867-82. *3771*

—. Alabama (Mobile). Black Capitalism. Editors and Editing. Johnson, Andrew N. Tennessee (Nashville). 1890-1920. *1415*

—. Arkansas. Blacks. Race Relations. 1867-1928. *3546*

—. Arkansas. Political Leadership. Remmel, Harmon L. 1880-1913. *3759*

—. Arkansas (Jefferson County). Blacks. Havis, Ferdinand. Political Leadership. 1846-1918. *3677*

—. Arkansas (Little Rock). Blacks. Gibbs, Mifflin W. Politics. 1878-1915. *3547*

—. Blacks. City Government. Maryland (Baltimore). 1890-1931. *3604*

—. Blacks. Florida. Political attitudes. Reconstruction. Walls, Josiah T. 1867-85. *3660*

—. Blacks. Howard, Perry W. Mississippi. Politics. 1924-60. *3705*

—. Blacks. Louisiana. Ray, John. Scalawags. ca 1836-88. *3818*

—. Blacks. Reconstruction. Southern States Convention. 1864-72. *3661*

—. Courts. North Carolina. Phillips, Samuel Field. Race Relations. 1844-1903. *3709*

—. Democratic Party. Ideology. Political Leadership. Texas. 1972-74. *3713*

—. Democratic Party. Lea, Luke. Peay, Austin. Political Factions. State Government. Tennessee, East. 1922-32. *3674*

—. Democratic Party. Voting and Voting Behavior. 1952-76. *3608*

—. Elections (congressional). Middle classes. 1972-76. *3812*

—. Florida. Hoover, Herbert C. Patronage. State Politics. 1928-33. *3589*

—. Freedmen. Hartzell, Joseph C. Methodist Church. Missions and Missionaries. 1870-73. *2352*

—. Georgia. Harding, Warren G. Johnson, Henry Lincoln. Philips, John Louis. 1920-24. *3626*

—. Georgia. Hoover, Herbert C. Patronage. Political factions. Race Relations. 1928-32. *3588*

—. Oklahoma Territory. Settlement. 1890-1907. *3567*

—. Political Leadership. Reconstruction. Texas. ca 1850-77. *3477*

—. Primaries. 1960-75. *3495*

—. Primaries, gubernatorial. State Politics. 1960-77. *3649*

—. South Carolina (Greenville). Virginia (Richmond). Voting and Voting Behavior. 1972-74. *3465*

—. Voting and Voting Behavior. 1972-76. *3745*

Republicanism. Architecture. City Planning. District of Columbia. L'Enfant, Pierre Charles. Politics. 1783-1800. *1380*

—. Morality. Presbyterian Church. Revivals. 1825-60. *2351*

Research. *See also* Methodology.

—. Appalachia. Ballads. Personal Narratives. Williams, Cratis. 1930's. *1693*

—. Appalachian Studies. Women. 1890's-1981. *307*

—. Archives. Delaware. Economic history. Social history. 17c-19c. 1977. *18*

—. Archives. Maryland (Baltimore). Public Records. 1796-1980. *59*

—. Archives, National. Chapman, Berlin Basil. Documents. Indians. Oklahoma. 1920's-60's. *39*

—. Artifacts. Maryland Historical Society. Photographs. 1670-1981. *46*

—. Authors. Bibliographies. 1977. *324*

—. Baptists, Southern. Church History. 1607-1979. *2395*

—. Bibliographies. Florida. 1973. *327*

—. Bibliographies. Florida. Social Sciences. 1974-75. *328*

—. Blacks. Folklore. Sea Islands. 1975. *1776*

—. Blacks. Gullah (dialect). Sea Islands. 16c-1974. *379*

—. Documents. Laurens, Henry. South Carolina (Charleston). 18c. 1977. *253*

—. Documents. Phillips, Ulrich B. Plantations. Slavery. 1900-34. *2847*

—. Florida. Local History. St. Augustine Historical Society Library. 1972-77. *248*

—. Georgia. 18c-20c. *282*

—. Georgia Historical Society. Preservation. 1839-1979. *69*

—. Lexicology. *Linguistic Atlas of the Gulf States.* Regionalism. 1970's. *3290*

—. Louisiana. Oral history. 1936-79. *158*

—. Methodology. Photography. 19c-20c. *360*

—. Migration, Internal. 1910-60. *186*

Reserve Officers' Training Corps. Military training. Oklahoma State University. Preparedness. Veterans. Women Appointed for Volunteer Emergency Service. 1891-1951. *3868*

Reservoirs. *See also* Irrigation; Water Supply.

—. Louisiana (Cross Lake Reservoir, Shreveport). 1883-1926. *2596*

Resettlement. *See also* Removals, forced; Settlement.

—. Cumberland Homesteads. Fairfield Glade. Housing. New Deal. Tennessee. 1934-80. *1353*

Resettlement Administration. New Deal. Rural Development. Texas (Ropesville). 1933-43. *2745*

Residential patterns. Blacks. Georgia (Atlanta). Transportation. Women. 1910-40. *3157*

—. Industry. Maryland (Baltimore). Urbanization. Villages. 1880-1925. *2905*

—. Virginia (Fredericksburg). 1888. 1976. *3031*

Residential segregation. Cities. Italians. Louisiana (New Orleans). 20c. *622*

—. Mississippi. Private schools. Public Schools. -1973. *2035*

Resorts. *See also* Spas.

—. Architecture. Baldwin, Ephraim. Deer Park Hotel. Garrett, John Work. Maryland (Garrett County). 1873-1932. *1244*

—. Construction. 1740's-1982. *1262*

—. Cottages. North Carolina (Outer Banks; Nags Head). 1830-1977. *3195*

—. Fishing. Hunting. Virginia (Cobb's Island). 1839-96. *3252*

—. Lafitte, Jean. Louisiana (Barataria area). Oil Industry and Trade. Slave Trade. Smuggling. Sugar. ca 1528-1980. *3330*

—. Medical care. Water. 19c-20c. *2138*

—. Tennessee (Sumner County). Tyree Springs (spa). 1822-1940. *1323*

Restorations. *See also* Historical Sites and Parks; Preservation.

—. Agecroft Hall (manor). England (Lancashire). Furniture and Furnishings. Virginia (Richmond). 16c-17c. 1926. *1328*

—. Alabama. Eufaula Heritage Association. 1965-78. *203*

—. Architecture. Athens-Clarke Heritage Foundation. Georgia. 1967-79. *96*

—. Architecture. Churches. Gothic Revival Style. Holy Trinity Episcopal Church. Tennessee (Nashville). 1840's-1970's. *1300*

—. Architecture. Georgia. Housing. Savannah Landmark Rehabilitation Project, Inc. Victorian style. 1870's-1979. *1329*

—. Art Deco. Florida (Miami Beach). Historic Districts. ca 1925-81. *1160*

—. Artists. Louisiana (De Soto Parish). Saint Anne's Chapel. 1891-1975. *1267*

—. Boscobel Cottage. Louisiana (Ouachita Parish). Plantations. 1820-1978. *1227*

—. Bridges, covered. Georgia. Photographs. 19c. *1288*

—. Buildings. Georgia. Historic Columbus Foundation. 1966-78. *1270*

—. Buildings. Georgia (Columbus). 1970's. *1271*

—. Capitols. District of Columbia. Senate. 1810-1976. *125*

—. Caspiana Plantation ("Big House"). Hutchinson family. Louisiana (Shreveport). 1850-1978. *1370*

—. Custom House. Federal Government. Tennessee (Nashville). 1877-1977. *1330*

—. District of Columbia. Giannetti, Bob. Giannetti, John. Plaster. 1935-80. *1113*

—. District of Columbia. National Trust for Historic Preservation. 1785 Massachusetts Avenue (building). 1906-78. *1396*

—. Farms. Louisiana (Bienville Parish). Sylvan Retreat (house). 1848-1978. *1281*

—. Fort Gibson. Oklahoma. 1824-1963. *3844*

—. Fort Washington. Gun batteries. Maryland. 1885-1978. *1346*

—. Gardens. Jefferson, Thomas. Monticello. Orchards. Virginia. 1800-1977. *1286*

—. Georgia (Albany). Heritage Plaza. Thronateeska Heritage Foundation. 1974-79. *1266*

—. Georgia (Monroe). Housing. 1972-78. *1295*

—. Georgia (Thomasville). Housing. Presidents. Victorian style. 1870-1978. *1404*

—. German Americans. Henkel Square. Letters. Log cabins. Texas (Round Top). 1840's-83. *1405*

—. Historical Sites and Parks. Kentucky (Elizabethtown). Lincoln, Thomas. Log cabins. Thomas, Hardin. 1790. 1974. *1292*

—. Historical sites and parks. North Carolina (Halifax). 1759-1976. *3329*

—. Historical Sites and Parks. North Carolina (New Bern). Tryon Palace. 1767-70. 1975. *1236*

—. Houses. Leigh, Gilbert (residence). North Carolina (Edenton). 1759-1969. *1304*

—. Jefferson, Thomas. Monticello. Virginia. 1978. *1384*

—. Kentucky. Pleasant Hill (community). Shakers. 1805-1970's. *2212*

—. Log cabins. Louisiana (De Soto Parish). 1960-78. *1365*

—. Louisiana (New Orleans; Algiers Point, Lower Marigny). 1950-70. *1311*

—. Mississippi (West Point). Waverly (house). 1852-1913. 1962-78. *1393*

—. Monticello. Virginia (Charlottesville). 1826-1954. *1182*

—. Oklahoma State University. Old Central (building). 1889-1976. *1169*

—. Preservation. Virginia (Waterford). 1937-79. *256*

Retail trade. Assimilation. Cherokee Indians. Indians. Tribal politics. 1838-90. *3921*

—. Business. Jews. 1790-1960. *2649*

—. Goldsmith's (department store). Ottenheimer, Ike. Tennessee (Memphis). 1900-63. *2643*

Retrocession Act (1846). District of Columbia. Hunter, R. M. T. Territorial boundaries. Virginia (Alexandria, Arlington). 1789-1846. *3279*

Reunions. Blacks. Family. Homecomings. Kinship. North Carolina (Montgomery County). Rites and Ceremonies. 19c-1970's. *381*

—. Colleges and Universities. Louisiana (Mansfield). Mansfield Female College. Women. 1844-1930. 1974. *1920*

Revels, Hiram. Blacks. Mississippi. Public Opinion. Senate. 1870. *3680*

Revivals. *See also* Great Awakening.

—. Appalachia. Behavior. Theology. 1830-1980. *2417*

—. Appalachia. Granade, John Adam. Hymns. Methodist Church. 1800-07. *2320*

# S

Shawnee Indians. Cherokee Indians. Delaware Indians. Indian Wars. Ohio Valley. 1750's-80's. *4105*

Sheehan, Bernard W. Axtell, James. Indian-White Relations (review article). Kupperman, Karen. 1580-1770. *3949*

—. Indian-White Relations (review article). Kupperman, Karen Ordahl. Virginia. 1580-1640. 1980. *4093*

Sheftall family. Cemeteries. Georgia (Savannah). Jews. 1733-1979. *613*

Sheftall, Levi. American Revolution. Commerce. Georgia (Savannah). Jews. Memoirs. 1739-1809. *2470*

Shelby, Isaac. Chickasaw Indians. Indians (reservations). Jackson, Andrew. Land transfers. 1818. *3941*

—. Clark, George Rogers. Clay, Henry. Kentucky. Taylor, Zachary. 1775-1850. *3614*

Shellenberger, Jack H. Faulkner, William. Japan. Personal Narratives. Travel. US Information Service. 1955. *1051*

Shenandoah National Park. Virginia. 1924-36. *3319*

Sherburne, John H. Federal Government. Indians. Ross, John. Seminole War, 2d. 1832-38. *4060*

Sherwood Manor. Architecture. Land. Massachusetts (Talbot County). Tilghman, Lloyd. 1718-1823. *1316*

Shipbuilding. Chesapeake Bay. Skipjacks. *Willie L. Bennett* (vessel). 1899-1950's. *3025*

—. Mississippi (Pascagoula River). 1870's-1974. *3170*

Shipwrecks. Maritime archaeology. Methodology. Virginia (Portsmouth; Scott Creek). 1893-1982. *205*

Shirk, George. Historians. Oklahoma. 1913-77. *691*

Shirk, George (obituary). Oklahoma. Toponymy. 20c. *3217*

Shleppey, John W. Collections. Documents. Indian studies. Tulsa, University of (McFarlin Library). Worcester, Samuel Austin. 1820-1900. 1975-77. *4030*

Shoe stores. Edison Brothers Company. Georgia. Jews. 1910's-40's. *2551*

Short stories. Editors and Editing. Faulkner, William. Literary Criticism. 1919-32. *1005*

—. O'Connor, Flannery. Social classes. 1946-65. *1089*

—. Poe, Edgar Allan. Psychologists. ca 1835-46. *1072*

Shotgun houses. Architecture. Haiti. Louisiana (New Orleans). Nigeria. Yoruba. 18c-1974. *1379*

Shreveport Art Club. Arts. Louisiana. 1922-81. *995*

Shreveport City Railroad Company. Louisiana. Public transportation. Street railways. 1870-76. *3159*

Shrivenham American (Army) University. Music. Personal Narratives. Southwestern College. Tennessee (Memphis). Tuthill, Burnet Corwin. 1888-1973. *1100*

Shuck, Eliza G. Sexton. Baptists. China. Missions and Missionaries. 1844-51. *2326*

Shugg, Roger (review article). Class Struggle. Historiography. Louisiana. 1800-60. 1939-76. *296*

Shuptrine, Herbert. Dickey, James. Literature. Painting. 1975. *854*

Sibour, Jules Henri de. Architecture. District of Columbia. 1785 Massachusetts Avenue (building). 1872-1938. *1149*

Sierra Leone. *See also* Africa, West.

—. Choctaw Indians. Coal Mines and Mining. Indians. Italian Americans. Oklahoma (Krebs). 1875-1907. *3039*

Silicosis. Labor. Tunnels. Union Carbide and Carbon Corporation. West Virginia (Hawks Nest). 1930-69. *3456*

Silk industry. Georgia Corporation Trustees. 1751. *2639*

Silver mining. Texas (western). 1880-1942. *2927*

Silver services. *Augusta* (vessel). Georgia (Augusta). Naval Vessels. 1928-80. *3851*

Silversmithing. Delaware. 1728-1880. *2595*

Simcott, Mr. Peddie Academy. Personal Narratives. Teachers. Values. Virginia. Watterson, William Collins. 1965-71. *1875*

Simmons, Philip. Blacksmiths. South Carolina (Charleston). 1855-1979. *683*

Simmons, Robert (interview). Arts and Crafts. Bear grass rope. Mississippi (Lucedale). 1971. *1462*

Simms, William Gilmore. American Revolution. Heroes. Humor. Porgy (character). 1775-83. 1835-55. *846*

—. American Revolution. History. Novels. 1775-83. 1834-69. *891*

—. American Revolution. Literature. Romanticism. 1830's-70's. *815*

—. American Revolution. Loyalists. Novels. South Carolina. 1780-83. 19c. *913*

—. Appalachia. Literature. Myths and Symbols. 1847-50. *1055*

—. Authors. Editors and Editing. Regionalism. 1824-56. *1054*

—. Bibliographies. Fiction. 1825-70. *1082*

—. deSoto expedition. Historiography. Novels. Pickett, Albert J. 1539-42. 1842-60. *303*

—. Dramatists. Fiction. 1824-76. *852*

—. Editors and Editing. Greene, Nathanael. Johnson, William P. 1822. 1849. *1105*

—. Indians. Literature. 1850-80. *4008*

—. Literature. 1830-70. *920*

—. Literature. ca 1860's-80's. *1110*

—. Literature. Realism. Romance. Satire. ca 1825-70. *1127*

Simms, William Gilmore (review article). American Revolution. Novels. 1775-82. 19c. 1975. *1128*

Simms, William Gilmore (*Woodcraft*). Literature. 1852. *1111*

Simpson, James A. District of Columbia (Georgetown). Painting. Portraits. 1825-83. *894*

Simpson, Lewis P. (review article). Belles lettres. New England. 17c-20c. *923*

—. Literary themes. Pastoral ideal. Social Customs. 19c-20c. *1028*

Singal, Daniel Joseph (review article). Social Change. Values. 1919-45. *457*

Singer, Paris. Architecture. Florida (Palm Beach). Mizner, Addison. 20c. *1256*

Singing. Appalachia. Family. Ritchie, Jean (review essay). 1955-80. *1547*

—. Festivals. Music. Societies. West Virginia (Wheeling). 1855-1906. *1699*

—. Flat Creek Sacred Singers. Georgia (Gainesville). Personal narratives. Propes, James Marlowe. 1900-81. *1686*

—. Georgia, southern. Gospel music. Protestant churches. 1873-1978. *1649*

Singing Societies. German Americans. Music. Social classes. West Virginia (Wheeling). 1855-1961. *1700*

Sisters of St. Joseph. Catholic Church. Education. Florida (Ybor City). Missions and Missionaries. Poor. 1891-1943. *654*

Sisters of the Visitation. Cardome (residence). Catholic Church. Education. Kentucky (Scott County; Georgetown). Mount Admirabilis. 1875-1975. *1791*

Skidmore, Hubert. Appalachia. Capitalism. Economic Development. Novels. Social Change. 1936-38. *2571*

Skinner, John. Oklahoma (Blackburn). Railroads. Settlement. 1893-1910. *3230*

Skinner, John Stuart. *American Farmer*. Animal husbandry. Horse racing. Maryland. Periodicals. 1819-29. *1429*

Skinner, William (residence). Georgia (Augusta). 1767-1966. *1331*

Skipjacks. Chesapeake Bay. Shipbuilding. *Willie L. Bennett* (vessel). 1899-1950's. *3025*

Skipwith, Jean. Book Collecting. Virginia (Mecklenburg County). 1779-1826. *1*

Slash-and-burn cultivation. Agriculture. Appalachia. Ozark Mountains. Scotch Irish. 1750-1980. *2803*

Slate, Blance, Joseph G. Georgia (Rockmart). Parker, Charles Taylor. 1832-1978. *3276*

Slaughter, Marianne Marbury. Authors. Louisiana. 1860's-1928. *1013*

Slave Revolts. Blacks. Styron, William. Turner, Nat. 19c. 1960's-70's. *1121*

Slave Trade. Lafitte, Jean. Louisiana (Barataria area). Oil Industry and Trade. Resorts. Smuggling. Sugar. ca 1528-1980. *3330*

—. Old Slave Mart Museum. South Carolina (Charleston). 19c. *1215*

Slavery. *See also* Abolition Movement; Antislavery Sentiments; Emancipation; Freedmen; Proslavery Sentiments; Slave Trade.

—. Abolition Movement. Freedmen. Labor. Race relations. 1830-63. *359*

—. Africa. Arts and crafts. Blacks. Social Customs. 1800-1975. *1772*

—. Agricultural labor. Industrialization. Models. 1800's. *2579*

—. Agricultural Production. Wealth. 1860. *2802*

—. Alabama. Civil War. Family. Social Change. Whites. 1850-70. *504*

—. American Revolution. Presbyterian Church. Racism. 1750-1818. *2485*

—. Baptists. Bushyhead, Jesse. Cherokee Indians. Indians. Schisms. 1830-45. *2375*

—. Baptists (Southern). Clergy. Loveland, Anne C. (review article). Methodist Church. Presbyterian Church. 1800-60. *2246*

—. Behavior. Genovese, Eugene D. Gramsci, Antonio. Hegemony (concept). 1812-65. *405*

—. Bibliographies. Civil War. Reconstruction. 1830-80. 1974. *196*

—. Blacks. 1865-1940. *540*

—. Blacks. Civil War. Reconstruction. Women. 19c. *3568*

—. Blacks. Coincoin. Family. Louisiana (Metoyer). 1742-1850. *631*

—. Blacks. Documents. Social Conditions. 1774-1841. *406*

—. Blacks. Five Civilized Tribes. Indians. 1721-1835. *3988*

—. Blacks. Social Customs. 1800-1900. *401*

—. Brazil. Darwin, Charles. Hopley, Catherine. Plantations. Stereotypes. 1831-63. *729*

—. Capers, William. *Christian Advocate*. Letters-to-the-editor. Methodism. Newspapers. 1854. 1875. *2422*

—. Catholic Church. 1619-1860. *2379*

—. Choctaw Indians. Congregationalism. Harkins, Richard. Missions and Missionaries. Murder. 1858-59. *4044*

—. Christianity. Genovese, Eugene D. (review article). Millenarianism. 17c-1865. *2328*

—. Christianity (review article). Holifield, E. Brooks. Raboteau, Albert J. 1795-1860. *2204*

—. Church and State. Presbyterian Church. 1850-80. *2354*

—. Circuit riders. Jones, John Griffing. Methodism. Mississippi. 1821-88. *2381*

—. Civil War. Region. World view. 1850's-70's. *707*

—. Clapp, Theodore. Louisiana (New Orleans). Theology. Unitarianism. 1822-56. *2421*

—. Commerce. Galt, James. Galt, William, Jr. Plantations. Virginia. 1800-76. *2734*

—. Converts. Evangelism. Louisiana (New Orleans). Protestant Churches. 1800-61. *2418*

—. Cotton. 1820-1900. *2874*

—. Cotton. Great Britain. Plantations. 17c-19c. *2753*

—. Culture. Davis, Richard Beale (review article). Indians. Literature. 1585-1763. *825*

—. Daily life. Diaries. Plantations. Texas (Harrison County). Webster, John B. 1858-59. *2758*

—. Dance. Louisiana (New Orleans). Minstrelsy. Theater. 1820-65. *1477*

—. Documents. Phillips, Ulrich B. Plantations. Research. 1900-34. *2847*

—. Dodson, John George. Great Britain. Travel (accounts). 1853-54. *750*

—. Doub, Peter. Education. Methodist Episcopal Church. North Carolina. Women. 1796-1869. *2312*

—. DuBois, W. E. B. Historiography. Phillips, Ulrich B. ca 1620-1865. 1896-1940. *398*

—. Economic Conditions. Marxism. Social Organization. 17c-1860. *2573*

—. Education. Episcopal Church, Protestant. Louisiana (New Orleans). Polk, Leonidas. 1805-65. *2420*

—. Evangelism. Protestantism. 18-19c. *2365*

—. Finkelman, Paul. Hindus, Michael Stephen. Law (review article). 1767-1878. *3697*

—. Freehling, William W. Nullification. South Carolina. Tariff. 1832. 1966. *3489*

—. Genovese, Eugene D. Historiography. 1800-65. 1963-79. *394*

—. Historiography. 1956-74. *66*

—. Historiography. Phillips, Ulrich B. 1908-34. 1976. *62*

—. Historiography. Rhodes, James Ford (*History of the United States from the Compromise of 1850*). Wilson, Woodrow. ca 1890-1920. *276*

—. Ironworks. North Carolina (Lincoln County). Plantations. Vesuvius Furnace. 1791-1876. *3124*

—. Jesuits. Maryland (St. Marys County). Plantations. St. Inigoes Church. 1806-1950. *2182*

—. Kentucky. Productivity. Tennessee. Tobacco. 1850-60. *2831*

—. Lutheran Church. 1790-1865. *2400*

—. Music. Spirituals. ca 1700-1865. *1780*

—. Novels. 1824-60. *981*

—. Occupations. Regionalism. Unitarianism. 1831-60. *2465*

Slaves. Agricultural Labor. Floods. Plantations. South Carolina (Santee Delta). Storms. Towers. 18c-19c. *1175*

—. Agricultural Production. Arkansas (Yell County). Cotton. Farmers. ca 1850-59. *2804*

—. Blacks. *Gone with the Wind* (film). NAACP. Stereotypes. 1939-40. *479*

—. Deer hides. Indians. Trade. 1690-1715. *4026*

—. Federal Writers' Project. Musical instruments. Personal Narratives. 1829-60. 1935-39. *1748*

—. Films. Plantations. Stereotypes. 1800-65. 1958-78. *425*

—. Fur Trade. Indians. Social mobility. South Carolina. 1670-1719. *3929*

South Carolina (Greenville). Business. Chambers of Commerce. Nonunionization. 1970's. *3441*

—. Industry. Labor Unions and Organizations. Nonunionization. 1873-1979. *3447*

—. Republican Party. Virginia (Richmond). Voting and Voting Behavior. 1972-74. *3465*

*South Carolina Historical Magazine.* Periodicals. 1900-77. *299*

South Carolina Historical Society. Archival Catalogs and Inventories. Microfiche. 1752-1980. *223*

—. Historians. Waring, Joseph Ioor (obituary). 1897-1977. *620*

South Carolina (Johns Island). Blacks. Moving Star Hall. Sects, Religious. 18c-1970. *2226*

South Carolina (Marlboro County). Burials. Indians. Pee Dee Indians. ca 1716. *4003*

—. Medicine (practice of). 1760-1824. *2145*

South Carolina (May River). Plantations. Tombstones (inscriptions). 18c-1830's. *1536*

South Carolina (Purrysburg). Archaeology. Assimilation. Pottery. Swiss Americans. 1733-1820. 1979-80. *3259*

—. DuPont Cemetery. Inscriptions. Strobhar Cemetery. Tombstones. 1736-1872. *1542*

South Carolina (Richmond). Church Hill Tunnel. Railroads. 1872-1926. *2978*

South Carolina (Santee Delta). Agricultural Labor. Floods. Plantations. Slaves. Storms. Towers. 18c-19c. *1175*

South Carolina (Spartanburg). Curricula. Humanities. Wofford College. 1971-79. *1951*

South Carolina, University of. Brewer, Fisk Parsons. Higher education. Integration. 1873-76. *1954*

South Carolina (Walnut Grove Plantation). Tombstones (inscriptions). 1840-1955. *1448*

South Carolina (Williston). Bush Hill Cemetery. Epitaphs. 1835-1905. *1486*

South Florida, University of. Florida. Local history. Periodicals. Public history. *Tampa Bay History.* ca 1978-81. *195*

South, University of the. Architecture. Colleges and Universities. Episcopal Church, Protestant. Tennessee (Sewanee). 1857-1979. *1892*

*South Western Baptist.* Baptists. Literature. Newspapers. Taliaferro, Hardin Edwards. 1810-75. *1106*

Southall, John Wesley (family). Davis, Joseph H. (family). Methodist Church. North Carolina (Murfreesboro area). Wesleyan Female College. 1854-59. *1944*

Southeastern Baptist Theological Seminary. North Carolina. Southern Baptist Convention. Wake Forest College. 1945-51. *1938*

Southern and Western Theological Seminary. Abolition movement. Anderson, Isaac. Presbyterian Church. Tennessee (Maryville). 1819-50's. *2406*

Southern Baptist Convention. North Carolina. Southeastern Baptist Theological Seminary. Wake Forest College. 1945-51. *1938*

Southern Baptist Theological Seminary. Clergy. Denominationalism. Theology. 18c-1980. *2454*

Southern Baptist winter assembly grounds. Assassination. Baptists. Florida (Umatilla). Lincoln, Abraham. 1865. 1925-29. *2186*

Southern Christian Leadership Conference. Blacks. Citizenship Education Program. Georgia (McIntosh). 1960-80. *1978*

—. Blacks. Civil Rights. Clark, Septima. NAACP. South Carolina. Suffrage. Teaching. 1916-79. *2012*

—. Blacks. Cotton, Dorothy. Personal narratives. Politics. 1960-82. *3816*

Southern Coalition on Jails and Prisons. Capital Punishment. Construction. Ingle, Joe (interview). Legislation. Prisons. Reform. 1978. *3565*

Southern Conference Education Fund. Anti-Communist Movements. Louisiana (New Orleans). School Integration. Senate Internal Security Subcommittee. Williams, Aubrey W. 1954. *1859*

—. Education. Health services. Minorities. Radicals and Radicalism. 1946-76. *1832*

Southern Consumers Cooperative. Blacks. Economic development. 1963-83. *2560*

Southern Education Board. Episcopal Church, Protestant. Murphy, Edgar Gardner. Social reform. 1900-13. *2522*

Southern Educational Reporting Service. Blacks. Johnson, Charles S. Public schools. School Integration. Whites. 1954-60's. *2002*

*Southern Exposure.* Institute for Southern Studies (report). Periodicals. Social Conditions. 1979. *334*

Southern Farmers' Alliance. Agricultural Organizations. North Carolina. Women. ca 1880-1900. *2743*

—. Agriculture. McMath, Robert C., Jr. (review article). Populism. Social Organization. 1870's-80's. 1975. *2669*

—. Farmers. Methodology. 1884-90. *2836*

—. Leadership. Populism. 1890's. *3770*

Southern Female University. Alabama (Florence). Boosterism. Higher education. 1886-1909. *1829*

Southern gentlemen (concept). Confederate States of America. Stereotypes. 1829-60. 1974. *424*

—. Cooke, John Esten. Novels. Social Customs. Virginia. 1750-1870. *461*

—. Faulkner, William. Literature. 1924-42. *972*

—. Houston, Sam. Stereotypes. Texas. 1832-54. *481*

—. Humor. Noland, Charles Fenton Mercer. Periodicals. *Spirit of the Times.* 1836-44. *865*

Southern Historical Association. 1982. *164*

—. Hanna, Kathryn Trimmer Abby. Lonn, Ella. Massey, Mary Elizabeth. 1900-74. *353*

—. History. 1934-35. *246*

Southern Historical Association (38th Annual meeting). 1972. *213*

Southern Historical Association (40th annual meeting). 1974. *25*

Southern Historical Association (43d annual meeting). 1977. *34*

Southern Improvement Company. Alabama. Blacks. Farms (tenant). Social Reform. Virginia. 1900-20. *2668*

Southern lady (concept). Stereotypes. Women. 19c-20c. *492*

*Southern Literary Culture.* Bibliographies. Literature. 1948-79. *969*

*Southern Literary Messenger.* Cooke, Philip Pendleton. Letters. Poe, Edgar Allan. 1847-49. *1095*

Southern Literary Renaissance. Authors. Cabell, James Branch. Glasgow, Ellen. Virginia (Richmond). 1920's. *922*

—. Authors. Glasgow, Ellen. Southern Writers Conference. Virginia (Charlottesville). 1931. *1044*

—. Faulkner, William. Literature. ca 1929-60's. *1132*

—. Literature. 1920-60. *935*

Southern Lumber Operators' Association. Brotherhood of Timber Workers. Louisiana, western. Lumber and Lumbering. Race Relations. Texas, east. 1911-13. *3402*

*Southern Lumberman.* Horn, Stanley F. Industry. Lumber and Lumbering. Periodicals. Personal Narratives. Trade associations. 1908-33. *3006*

Southern Methodist University. Higher Education (review article). Nall, Kline A. Rushing, Jane G. Texas Tech University. Thomas, Mary. 1920-75. *1949*

Southern Oral History Program. North Carolina, University of. Oral history. 1973-76. *132*

Southern Pine Association. Lumber and lumbering. National Recovery Administration. 1933-35. *2964*

Southern Political Science Association. Academic freedom. Civil Rights. Educational Reform. 1928-79. *144*

*Southern Politics* project. Historiography. Key, V. O., Jr. Martin, Roscoe C. Political attitudes. 1944-70. *3726*

*Southern Quarterly Review.* Literature. Proslavery Sentiments. States' rights. Whitaker, Daniel K. 1842-57. 1879-80. *980*

Southern Railroad. Mississippi. Railroads. 1840-89. *3149*

*Southern Review.* Brooks, Cleanth. Literature. Louisiana State University. Periodicals. Warren, Robert Penn. 1925-42. *1090*

Southern Rural Action, Inc. Agricultural cooperatives. Blacks. Land tenure. Rural settlements. 1966-70's. *2687*

Southern Speech Communication Association. O'Neill, James Milton. *Quarterly of Public Speaking.* Speech. 1906-70. *771*

—. Speech. Winans, James A. 1900-56. *782*

Southern States Convention. Blacks. Reconstruction. Republican Party. 1864-72. *3661*

Southern Tenant Farmers' Union. Agrarians. Land reform. 1933-40. *2721*

Southern University. Blacks. Colleges and Universities. Louisiana (New Orleans). 1879-87. *1955*

Southern Writers Conference. Authors. Glasgow, Ellen. Southern Literary Renaissance. Virginia (Charlottesville). 1931. *1044*

*Southerner* (film). Daily Life. Films. Renoir, Jean. 1945-50. *485*

Southland College. Arkansas (Helena). Blacks. Colleges and Universities. Friends, Society of. 1866-1925. *2024*

Southwestern at Memphis College. Colleges and Universities. Tennessee (Memphis). 1848-1981. *1937*

Southwestern Baptist Theological Seminary (Fleming Library). Archival Catalogs and Inventories. Baptists. Blacks. Texas. 1875-1941. *2432*

Southwestern College. Music. Personal Narratives. Shrivenham American (Army) University. Tennessee (Memphis). Tuthill, Burnet Corwin. 1888-1973. *1100*

Southwestern State Normal School. Oklahoma (Weatherford). Teacher training. 1902-39. *1950*

Souvenirs. Florida (St. Augustine). 1840-1920. *1520*

Sovereignty. Cherokee Indians. Indians. Methodist Church. Missions and Missionaries. 1824-34. *4042*

Soybeans. Agricultural Production. Cotton. Economic Conditions. 1920's-75. *2714*

Spain. Adams-Onís Treaty (1819). Boundaries. Oklahoma. Texas. 1819-1930. *3287*

—. Cannons. Florida. 1786-1898. 1973. *3875*

—. Cherokee Indians. Indian Wars. Military Aid. 1790-94. *4145*

—. Florida. Indian-White Relations. Pelota (game). 1675-84. *3933*

—. Florida. Painting. Smith, James Calvert. 1821. 1879-1962. *826*

—. Fort San Fernando de las Barrancas. Maps. Tennessee (Memphis area). 1795-97. *3309*

—. France. Louisiana. Medicine (practice of). Pharmacy. 1717-1852. *2122*

—. Louisiana State University, Department of Archives and Manuscripts. Manuscripts. West Florida. 1763-1800. *45*

Spalding, Phinizy. Georgia (Augusta). Local history. Preservation. Sacred Heart Church. 1976-78. *1359*

Spalding, Thomas. Archaeology. Georgia (Sapelo Island). Sugar industry. ca 1795-1850's. 1976. *2700*

Spaniards. Latin Americans. Travel accounts. 1865-1950. *745*

Spanish. Florida (St. Augustine). Great Britain. Indians. Trade. 1700-83. *3965*

Spanish language. English language. Mexican Americans. Names (personal). Texas (El Paso). 1981. *703*

Spanish moss. Louisiana. Manufactures. Natural resources. 19c-1980. *2563*

Spanish-American War. Louisiana. Volunteer Armies. 1898. *3846*

Sparks, Chauncey. Alabama. Democratic Party. Elections, gubernatorial. Folsom, James E. Graves, Bibb. 1926-50. *3482*

Spas. Florida. 1840-1973. *3335*

—. Vacations. Virginia (Yellow Sulphur Springs). 1800-1923. *3350*

Special Interest Groups. *See* Lobbying; Political Factions; Pressure Groups.

Speculation. Brandreth, William C. Copper Mines and Mining. Cowles, Calvin J. North Carolina. 1854-89. *2911*

—. Flagler, Henry Morrison. Florida. Land. Miles, George. 1845-1910. *2884*

Speech. *See also* Dialects; Language; Linguistics; Rhetoric.

—. Bibliographies. Mass Media. Theater. 1975. *295*

—. Blacks. Whites. 1970-79. *763*

—. O'Neill, James Milton. *Quarterly of Public Speaking.* Southern Speech Communication Association. 1906-70. *771*

—. Southern Speech Communication Association. Winans, James A. 1900-56. *782*

Speech education. Bibliographies. Mass Media. Periodicals. Theater. 1977. *294*

Speech patterns. Georgia (central). Humor. Rural Settlements. 1800-99. *1643*

Speeches. *See also* Political Speeches.

—. Bibliographies. 1975-82. *21*

—. Blacks. DuBois, W. E. B. 1946. *370*

—. Boggs, Thomas Hale. Federal Bureau of Investigation. Hoover, J. Edgar. 1971. *3584*

—. Cherokee Indians. Indians. Removals, forced. Rhetoric. 1828-32. *4098*

—. Cherokee Indians. Indian-White Relations. Jefferson, Thomas. Removals, forced. 1809. *4150*

—. Delaware. Public schools. Segregation. Stewart, Theophilous G. 1882. *2030*

—. Educational reform. Myths and Symbols. Page, Walter Hines. Social Conditions. 1889-1914. *1817*

—. Faulkner, William. Literature. Nobel Prizes. 1950. *907*

—. Ladner, Heber. Mississippi. State Government. 1931-79. *3666*

—. Planter class. South Carolina. Trescot, William Henry. 1847-98. *3711*

Spelling reform. Elitism. Racism. 1973. *775*

—. Constitutions, State. Louisiana. Slidell, John. 1812-52. *3758*

—. Felton, Rebecca Latimer. Georgia. Politics. Senate. Women. 1860's-1922. *3755*

—. Gordon, Kate. Louisiana. Women. 1896-1918. *3587*

—. Kentucky (Louisville). Women. 1828-1920. *3605*

—. Paul, Alice. South Carolina. Women. ca 1891-1919. *3497*

—. Populism. Race relations. Washington, Booker T. 1877-1910. *3794*

Sugar. Agricultural Production. Congress. Economic Conditions. Louisiana. Subsidies. 1860-1930. *2833*

—. Agricultural Technology and Research. Economies of scale. Louisiana. Plantations. 1850's. *2834*

—. Farms. Plantations. 1850's. *2835*

—. Interstate Commerce Commission. Tennessee. Transportation. 1895-1925. *2946*

—. Lafitte, Jean. Louisiana (Barataria area). Oil Industry and Trade. Resorts. Slave Trade. Smuggling. ca 1528-1980. *3330*

—. Location. Louisiana. Plantations. 1742-1870. *3305*

Sugar industry. Agriculture. Blacks. Louisiana. Mechanization. 1865-1914. *2710*

—. Archaeology. Georgia (Sapelo Island). Spalding, Thomas. ca 1795-1850's. 1976. *2700*

—. Immigration. Italian Americans. Labor recruitment. 1880-1910. *2827*

Sugarcane. Agricultural Production. Climate. Land. Louisiana. 19c. *2738*

—. Blacks. Immigrants. Italians. Louisiana. Race Relations. 1880-1910. *2828*

—. Blacks. Immigration. Italian Americans. Louisiana. Race Relations. 1880-1910. *2829*

Sugg, John F. County Government. Kentucky (Nicholas County). Local Politics. Officeholding. 1909-49. *3774*

Suicide. Authors. North Carolina (Winston-Salem). Ricks, Peirson. 1908-53. *897*

—. Coal Mines and Mining. Harper, Larry. Labor Unions and Organizations. West Virginia (Stony Creek). 1940's-54. *3413*

—. Jarrell, Randall. Poets. 1914-65. *967*

Sullivan, Jordan James. Coca-Cola Company. Courts. Federal Regulation. Food and Drug Administration. Georgia. Massengill, S. E. Company. Tennessee. 1906-40. *3830*

Sullivan, Maud. Cisneros, Jose. Culture. Hertzog, Carl. Lea, Tom. Sonnichsen, C. L. Texas (El Paso). 1920's-75. *1000*

Sully, George Washington. Florida. Louisiana (New Orleans). Painting. 1829-39. *856*

Summers, Lewis Preston. Historians. Virginia (Washington County). 1890-1943. *23*

Sumter Historic Preservation Society. Georgia (Americus). Preservation. 1972-79. *131*

Sunday schools. Baptists (Southern). 1790-1900. *2366*

—. Baptists (Southern). 1891-1980. *2477*

—. Baptists, Southern. 1891-1980. *2507*

—. Baptists (Southern). 20c. *2239*

—. Baptists, Southern. 20c. *2271*

Sunday, William Ashley "Billy". Georgia (Atlanta). Revivals. 1917. *2196*

Superstitions. Childbirth. Folklore. Pregnancy. Tennessee (Chester County). 18c-1974. *1529*

Supreme Court. Arkansas. Bridges. *Charles River Bridge* v. *Warren Bridge* (US, 1837). Ferries. ca 1837-1940. *3550*

—. Blacks. *Brown* v. *Board of Education* (US, 1954). Discrimination, Educational. NAACP. Public schools. South Carolina (Clarendon County). 1948-54. *2026*

—. Blacks. Democratic Party. NAACP. Primaries. Suffrage. Texas. 1927-45. *3633*

—. Boundaries. Geography, historical. Georgia. Savannah River. South Carolina (Barnwell Island area). 18c. 1977. *3209*

—. Campbell, John Archibald. Jacksonianism. Lawyers. 1829-89. *3652*

—. Civil rights. Constitutional Amendments (14th). *Gitlow* v. *New York* (US, 1925). Sanford, Edward Terry. ca 1890-1930. *3668*

—. Florida. Freedom of the Press. Newspapers. 1901-74. *3636*

—. Jackson, Howell Edmunds. Politics. Tennessee. 1832-95. *3619*

—. Kentucky (Big Sandy Valley). Vinson, Frederick Moore. 1890-1953. *3625*

—. Reed, Stanley F. 1900-80. *3514*

Supreme courts (state). *Herold et al.* v. *Parish Board of School Directors et al.* (Louisiana, 1914). Louisiana. Religion in the Public Schools. 1913-15. *3712*

—. Impeachment. Judges. Oklahoma. State Legislatures. 1927-30. *3538*

—. Law. North Carolina. Public Schools. Segregation. Taxation. 1865-1954. *1968*

Surgery. Louisiana (New Orleans). Matas, Rudolph. Medical Research. Ochsner, Alton. Personal Narratives. 1927-52. *2155*

Surnames. Kentucky (Mammoth Cave region). Linguistics. 1775-1971. *784*

Surrender. Civil War. Confederate States of America. Indian Territory. Watie, Stand. 1865. *3927*

Surveying. Boundaries. Clark, John H. Maps. Texas (northwestern). 1858-62. *3324*

—. Frontier and Pioneer Life. Martin, Absalom. Military Service. West Virginia (Wheeling area). 1758-1802. *678*

—. Georgia, northeastern. Land grants. 1770's-1870's. *3239*

—. Map Drawing. Navigation. Virginia. 1612-1880's. *3313*

Surveys. 18c-19c. *3238*

—. Bridges, metal truss. Roads. Turnpikes. Virginia. 1725-1900. *1263*

Susquehanna and Tidewater Canal. Canals. Maryland. 1840-1902. *3108*

Susquehanna River. Chesapeake Bay. Delaware River. Industrialization. 1700-1865. *2935*

Sutch, Richard. Agriculture. Economic Development (review article). Freedmen. Ransom, Roger L. 1865-1900. *2873*

—. Economic Conditions (review article). Mandle, Jay R. Ransom, Roger L. Wiener, Jonathan M. 1850-1910. 1977-78. *3362*

Sutton, Maude Minish. Blue Ridge Mountains. Coffey, Ann. Folklore. Frank C. Brown Collection of North Carolina Folklore. North Carolina, western. 1920's-30's. *1611*

Sutton, Willis. Business. City Government. Georgia (Atlanta). Public Schools. 1921-43. *1854*

Swain County High School. Arts. Curricula. Forrister, Donald. North Carolina. Secondary Education. 1982. *1788*

Swamps. Cypress. Louisiana, southern. Lumber and Lumbering. Williams, Frank B. 1869-1929. *2925*

—. Cypress. Lumber and Lumbering. Pullboat logging. 1889-1961. *3035*

Sweden. Bremer, Fredrika. Letters. Travel (accounts). 1851. *747*

"Sweet Sally". Folk Songs. Virginia (Lunenburg County). 1825. 1973. *1408*

Swimming. Desegregation. Florida (St. Petersburg). 1930's-59. *3734*

Swiss Americans. Acculturation. Architecture. German Americans. German language. Virginia (Shenandoah Valley). 1720-1800. *1190*

—. Archaeology. Assimilation. Pottery. South Carolina (Purrysburg). 1733-1820. 1979-80. *3259*

Sylvan Retreat (house). Farms. Louisiana (Bienville Parish). Restorations. 1848-1978. *1281*

Sylvester, James Joseph. Colleges and Universities. Gilman, Daniel Coit. Johns Hopkins University. Letters. Maryland (Baltimore). Teaching. 1825-84. *1841*

Symbolism in Literature. Authors. Land. 1640-1970. *712*

—. Literary criticism. Poe, Edgar Allan. Wilbur, Richard. 1820's-49. 1959. *970*

Syncretism. Powhatan Indians. Social Customs. Virginia. 1607-1975. *3909*

Synods. *See* Councils and Synods.

# T

Tabb's Purchase (estate). Country Life. Farms, Tenant. Maryland. Tableware. 19c. *1581*

Tabert, Martin. Florida. Law. Peonage. Turpentine camps. 1923-50. *3445*

Tableware. Country Life. Farms, Tenant. Maryland. Tabb's Purchase (estate). 19c. *1581*

Tackett, Francis Marion. Kentucky, eastern. Music. Shape-note singing. Teachers. 1920-80. *1582*

Taft, William Howard. Court of Appeals. Harlan, John Marshall. Lurton, Horace H. Tennessee. 1897. *3741*

Taliaferro, Hardin Edwards. Baptists. Literature. Newspapers. *South Western Baptist*. 1810-75. *1106*

"Talking Trash". Folklore. Georgia (Okefenokee Swamp Rim). Men. Social Customs. 1966-72. *1468*

Talladega College. Alabama. Blacks. Colleges and Universities. Ethnicity. 1875-1980. *1972*

Talmadge, Eugene. Blacks. Cocking, Walter D. Georgia. Higher education. 1937-43. *1981*

—. Cocking, Walter D. Georgia, University of. Holley, Joseph Winthrop. Racism. 1941. *2057*

—. Country Life. Georgia. Politics. 1927-46. *3754*

—. Democratic Party. Georgia. New Deal. Roosevelt, Franklin D. 1926-38. *3529*

—. Georgia. National Recovery Administration. State Government. Strikes. Textile industry. 1934. *3370*

*Tampa Bay History*. Florida. Local history. Periodicals. Public history. South Florida, University of. ca 1978-81. *195*

Tampa *Tribune*. Florida. O'Brien, Lucy Fulghum. Personal narratives. Reporters and Reporting. 1935-50's. *1598*

Tank Warfare. *See* Armored Vehicles and Tank Warfare.

Tariff. *See also* Smuggling.

—. Cotton. Investments. Prices. Quantitative Methods. 1840-60. *2742*

—. Freehling, William W. Nullification. Slavery. South Carolina. 1832. 1966. *3489*

Tate, Allen. Agrarianism. Biography. Jackson, Thomas J. (Stonewall). 1927-28. *304*

—. Agrarians. Davidson, Donald. *I'll Take My Stand*. Ransom, John Crowe. Values. Warren, Robert Penn. 1925-30. *3831*

—. Authors. Davidson, Donald. Friendship. 1921-68. *838*

—. Bishop, John Peale. Friendship. Letters. 1931. *1135*

—. Davidson, Donald. Ransom, John Crowe. Rubin, Louis D. (review article). Warren, Robert Penn. 1920's-30's. 1978. *892*

—. History. Literature. Myths and Symbols. 1922-41. *128*

—. Letters. Literature. Tate, Caroline Gordon. 1925-37. *916*

—. Literature. 1918-45. *839*

—. Literature. 1920's-60's. *822*

Tate, Allen (tribute). Conservatism. Regionalism. Values. Western civilization. 1910's-79. *432*

Tate, Caroline Gordon. Letters. Literature. Tate, Allen. 1925-37. *916*

Tate homestead. Architecture. Georgia (Pickens County). 1920's-79. *1235*

Tate, Mitchell. Medicine, practice of. Preston, Francis (family). Virginia (Washington County). 1815-21. *2148*

Taverns. Cherokee Indians. Georgia. Highways. Indian-White Relations. Tennessee. 1800-25. *3956*

Tax lists. Virginia (Charles City County). 1782-87. *363*

Taxation. *See also* Tariff.

—. Alabama (Birmingham). Reform. Steel industry. 1871-1921. *3621*

—. Alabama (Fairhope). City Government. Michigan (Southfield). Pennsylvania (Pittsburgh). 1887-1973. *2896*

—. Banking. Capital. Georgia Railroad and Banking Company. Railroads. 1833-1980. *3110*

—. Chain stores. Depressions. ca 1925-40. *2633*

—. Chain stores. Government regulation. Kentucky. 1925-45. *3761*

—. Cherokee Indians. Federal government. Indian-White Relations. Tribal government. 1820's. *4041*

—. Delaware. DuPont, Pierre S. Modernization. Public Schools. State Government. 1920-40. *1865*

—. Education, Finance. School Integration. South Carolina. White flight. 1965-75. *2070*

—. Law. North Carolina. Public Schools. Segregation. Supreme courts (state). 1865-1954. *1968*

Taylor Homes. Business. Housing. Labor. Mechanization. Mobile homes. 1972-79. *3181*

Taylor, Sarah. Friends, Society of. Maryland (Baltimore). Medicine (practice of). 1823. *2113*

Taylor, William R. Cash, Wilbur J. Dollard, John. Elkins, Stanley. Genovese, Eugene D. Psychohistory. 1935-78. *305*

Taylor, Zachary. Clark, George Rogers. Clay, Henry. Kentucky. Shelby, Isaac. 1775-1850. *3614*

—. Florida. Missouri Volunteers, 1st. Okeechobee (battle). Seminole War, 2d. 1837. *4055*

Teacher Training. 1820-60. *1793*

—. Blacks. Bowie State College. Education, Finance. Maryland (Baltimore). 1866-1908. *1932*

—. Blacks. Chautauqua Society. Louisiana (Grambling, Ruston). 1890-1906. *1942*

—. Oklahoma (Weatherford). Southwestern State Normal School. 1902-39. *1950*

Teachers. *See also* College Teachers; Educators; Teaching.

—. Attitudes. North. 1770's-1865. *1880*

—. Attitudes. Strikes. 1979. *3389*

Tilghman, Lloyd. Architecture. Land. Massachusetts (Talbot County). Sherwood Manor. 1718-1823. *1316*

Tillman, Benjamin Ryan. Irby, John Laurens Manning. South Carolina. State Politics. 1854-1900. *3782*

Tilly, Dorothy. Civil rights. Georgia. Methodist Church. 1900's-70. *3772*

Timucuan Indians, Eastern. Agriculture. Florida. LeMoyne, Jacques. Painting. ca 1564-1620. *3947*

Titchener, Edward Bradford. Laboratories. Parrish, Celestia S. Psychology. Randolph-Macon Woman's College. Virginia (Lynchburg). 1893-1938. *1939*

Toasts. Men. Social Customs. Whites. 1966-78. *1544*

Tobacco. Agricultural Cooperatives. Bingham, Robert Worth. Marketing. Sapiro, Aaron. 1920's. *2709*

—. Agricultural Industry. 1970's. *2843*

—. Agricultural Production. Country Life. Industry. Mechanization. North Carolina, eastern. 1880's-1976. *2730*

—. Agricultural Production. Maryland (Eastern Shore). Plantations. ca 1700-50. *2686*

—. Cherokee Indians. Indians. Medicine. Rites and Ceremonies. 16c-1978. *3885*

—. Chesapeake Bay. Prices. 1618-60. *2791*

—. Church of England. Clergy. Virginia. Wages. 1750-70. *2311*

—. Cubans. Florida (Tampa). Labor Disputes. *Lector* (reader). Perez, Louis A., Jr. Personal Narratives. ca 1925-35. *3432*

—. Documents. Notarial Archives of Amsterdam and Rotterdam. Virginia. 1608-53. *2755*

—. Economic Conditions. Virginia. 1613-1732. *2663*

—. Economic Development. Maryland. Virginia. 1617-1730. *2792*

—. England (London). Trade. Virginia. 1614-40. *2808*

—. England (Winchcombe). Virginia. 16c-17c. *2727*

—. Farmers, yeoman. Income. Kentucky. Migration, Internal. Tennessee. 1850-60. *2832*

—. Federal Writers' Project. 1933-39. *2671*

—. France. Great Britain. International Trade. Monopolies. North America. Price, Jacob (review article). 17c-18c. *2716*

—. Kentucky. Productivity. Slavery. Tennessee. 1850-60. *2831*

Tobacco Inspection Act (1747). Economic Regulations. Exports. Maryland. Money. Prices. 1747. *2837*

Tobacco pipes. Indians. Maryland. St. John's (house). Terra-cotta. Virginia. 17c. *1526*

Tocqueville, Alexis de. Beaumont de la Bonniniéré, Gustave Auguste de. Travel Accounts. 1831-40. *727*

Tolomato Cemetery. Florida (St. Augustine). 1704-1876. *545*

Tolstoy, Leo (*War and Peace*). Civil War. Literary Criticism. Mitchell, Margaret (*Gone with the Wind*). Social Conditions. 1863-1936. *2447*

Tombstones. Baptists. Inscriptions. Louisiana (Bienville Parish). Mount Lebanon University. 1848-1976. *524*

—. Bibliographies. Cemeteries. Georgia Genealogical Society. Inscriptions. 1817-1946. *82*

—. Cemeteries. Inscriptions. Louisiana (Jackson Parish). Rural Settlements. 1845-1930's. *528*

—. DuPont Cemetery. Inscriptions. South Carolina (Purrysburg). Strobhar Cemetery. 1736-1872. *1542*

—. Ebenezer Lutheran Church. Inscriptions. Mount Bethel Baptist Church. South Carolina (Anderson County). 1856-1978. *1487*

—. Folk Art. Georgia (northern). 19c. *1466*

—. Folk art. German Americans. Harmony Methodist Church Cemetery. West Virginia (Jane Lew). 1827-55. *1659*

—. Folklore. Poetry. Virginia. 19c-1979. *1480*

—. Georgia. Iconography. Ideology. South Carolina. 18c-1850. *2290*

—. Hancock, Christopher Carson. Kentucky (Allen County). Stonecutting. Tennessee. 1878-1936. *1680*

—. Hermitage. Jackson, Andrew. Jackson, Rachel. Tennessee (Nashville). 1828-1976. *1166*

—. Inscriptions. Kentucky (Henry County). 1770-1970. *1545*

—. Inscriptions. Louisiana (Claiborne Parish). 1828-73. *525*

—. Inscriptions. Louisiana (De Soto Parish). 1843-1978. *530*

—. Inscriptions. Louisiana (Lincoln Parish). Pioneers. 19c-1973. *529*

—. Inscriptions. Louisiana (Morehouse Parish). Pioneers. 1844-1957. *527*

—. Inscriptions. Louisiana (Ouachita Parish). ca 1830-1920. *531*

—. Inscriptions. Louisiana (Union Parish). 1839-1970's. *526*

—. Inscriptions. Louisiana (Winn Parish). Populism. Socialism. 1852-1975. *523*

—. Inscriptions. West Virginia (West Liberty). 1786-1946. *635*

—. Tennessee, central. 1811-1964. *1185*

Tombstones (inscriptions). Alabama (Pike County). Genealogy. 1970-73. *337*

—. Plantations. South Carolina (May River). 18c-1830's. *1536*

—. South Carolina (Walnut Grove Plantation). 1840-1955. *1448*

Tomeh Indians. Alabama. French. Indians. Levasseur, Charles. Travel accounts. 1700. *4023*

*Tomorrow* (film). Daily Life. Films. 1920-40. 1972. *415*

Toombs, Henry J. Architecture. Georgia Warm Springs Foundation. Roosevelt, Franklin D. (residence). 1924-35. *1333*

Toomer, Jean. Authors. Blacks. Hurston, Zora Neale. Migration, Internal. 1860-1960. *374*

Toothaches. Alabama. Folk Medicine. Rural areas. 16c-20c. *1481*

Toponymy. Alabama. 1975. *3248*

—. Cities. Great Britain. Kentucky. 18c-1974. *3249*

—. Cities. Mississippi. 18c-19c. *3250*

—. Cities. Tennessee. 18c-20c. *3251*

—. Counties. South Carolina. 1672-1977. *3269*

—. Delaware (New Castle). 1638-1976. *3345*

—. Farms. Folklore. Kentucky (Butler, Warren Counties). Language. Stewart family. 1850-1978. *1595*

—. Florida (Norris Cut). Waterways. 1822-1905. *3207*

—. Folklore. Kentucky. Mountains. ca 1755-1850. *3206*

—. Friendship Airport. Land use. Maryland (Anne Arundel County, Baltimore). 1608-1972. *3218*

—. Georgia. Indians. -1973. *3891*

—. Indians. South Carolina. 17c-1977. *3289*

—. North Carolina (Ashe County). 1790's-1977. *3244*

—. Oklahoma. Shirk, George (obituary). 20c. *3217*

—. Oklahoma (Wichita Mountains). 1852-1978. *3281*

—. Politics. Social organization. Virginia. 17c-20c. *3274*

—. Tennessee River basin (upper). 1707-1954. *3277*

Torbert, James H. Blacks. Education. Fort Valley High and Industrial School. Georgia. 1897-1911. *1969*

Tougaloo College. Blacks. Mississippi (Jackson). 1869-1975. *1929*

Tourism. *See also* Resorts.

—. Appalachia. Discrimination. Ethnicity. Melungeons. Mountaineers. 19c-1970's. *412*

—. Cherokee Indians. Indian-White Relations. North Carolina. Western Carolina University. 1970's. *4162*

—. Civilian Conservation Corps. Land Tenure. Texas (Palo Duro Canyon State Park). 1906-66. *3293*

—. Flagler, Henry Morrison. Florida (Miami). Sewell, Everest G. 1895-1940. *3582*

—. Florida (Tampa Bay area). Photographs. Transportation. 1876-1922. *2947*

—. Florida (Tampa Bay area). Postcards. 1890's-1981. *2569*

—. Gary, Raymond. *Oklahoma Today*. Periodicals. Photography. Public Relations. 1956-81. *1472*

—. Myths and Symbols. 1960's-80's. *722*

Towers. Agricultural Labor. Floods. Plantations. Slaves. South Carolina (Santee Delta). Storms. 18c-19c. *1175*

Towles, Catharine. Alabama. Authors. Burton, Robert Wilton. Hooper, George W. ca 1850-1900. *908*

Townhouses. Georgia (Savannah). Plantations. Rice. South Carolina. 1800-1933. *2740*

Towns. Business. City Planning. Development. Indiana (Kingsport). North. 1880-1950. *1156*

—. Mississippi. 1770-1970. *3184*

—. Oklahoma. Railroads. Texas. Wichita Falls and Northwestern Railway. 1900-20. *3003*

—. Settlement. Ukraine (southern). 18c-19c. *2951*

Towns, small. Architecture. Economic Conditions. Mississippi. Natchez Pilgrimage of Homes. Preservation. 1900-80. *1219*

—. Migration, Internal. Population. Rural Development. 1970-80. *2544*

Townsend, George Alfred. Maryland (Gathland State Park). War Correspondents' Memorial. 1895-1978. *1231*

Toxic substances. Political Protest. Refuse disposal. 1981. *3837*

Toynbee, Arnold J. (*Study of History*). Appalachia. Great Britain. Somervell, D. C. 20c. *24*

Tractors. Agricultural Technology and Research. Cotton. Sharecroppers. 1915-60. *2798*

Trade. *See also* International Trade; Retail Trade; Tariff.

—. Agriculture. Industry. Urbanization. 18c. *2952*

—. American Revolution. Cherokee Indians. Indians. Military Strategy. Starr, Caleb. 1776. *4097*

—. Banking. Brown, Alexander. Business History. Maryland (Baltimore). Social change. ca 1800-34. *2553*

—. Barnard, George. Indians. Merchants. Pioneers. Texas (Waco). 1830-83. *2651*

—. Borderlands. Diplomacy. Mexico. 1858-1905. *2539*

—. Cherokee Indians (Overhill). Indian-White Relations. Tennessee (Monroe County). 1690-1760. *4086*

—. Creek Indians. Economic Conditions. Indian Wars. South Carolina. Yamassee War. 1710-15. *3992*

—. Deer hides. Indians. Slaves. 1690-1715. *4026*

—. Economic Conditions. South Carolina (Charleston). 1865-1979. *2617*

—. Economic Development. Identity. Louisiana (New Orleans). Mississippi River. Technology. 1850-1950. *2913*

—. England (London). Tobacco. Virginia. 1614-40. *2808*

—. Florida (St. Augustine). Great Britain. Indians. Spanish. 1700-83. *3965*

—. Horses. Mizell, Terrence A. Personal Narratives. Tennessee. 1940's-70's. *1584*

—. Letterbooks. Plantations. Raper, Robert. South Carolina. 1759-65. *2779*

Trade associations. Horn, Stanley F. Industry. Lumber and Lumbering. Periodicals. Personal Narratives. *Southern Lumberman*. 1908-33. *3006*

Trade Unions. *See* Labor Unions and Organizations.

Trading Posts. Deery, William. Historical Sites and Parks. Irish Americans. Tennessee (Blountville). 1795-1970's. *1192*

—. Florida (Everglades). Indian-White Relations. Seminole Indians. 1900-20. *4155*

Tradition. Episcopal Church, Protestant. Gailor, Thomas Frank. Lost Cause (theme). Nationalism. Rhetoric. Tennessee. University of the South. 1856-1935. *2524*

—. Indians. Paiute Indians. Personal Narratives. Social Change. Women. 1890's-1982. *4166*

—. Literature. Percy, William A. (*Lanterns on the Levee*). 1940's. *768*

Traditionalism. Cherokee Indians. Citizenship. North Carolina. Thomas, William Holland. 1838-66. *3973*

—. Cherokee Indians. Constitutions. Indians. 1800-27. *4077*

Traffic control. Arnold, H. H. Automobiles. Florida (Miami). 1896-1935. *3582*

Trammell, John W. Florida (Polk County). Political Leadership. 1882-1904. *3657*

Translating and Interpreting. Anticlericalism. Bible. Jefferson, Thomas. 1813-20. *2353*

Transportation. *See also* specific modes of transportation,, e.g. Automobiles, Ships, Buses, Trucks, Railroads, etc.; Bridges; Canals; Commerce; Navigation, Inland; Postal Service; Public Transportation; Roads; Waterways.

—. Arkansas (Buffalo Valley). Lead mining. Zinc mining. ca 1720-1930's. *3081*

—. Blacks. Georgia (Atlanta). Residential patterns. Women. 1910-40. *3157*

—. Economic conditions. Law. Maryland. 1820-40. *2540*

—. Ferries. North Carolina. 1700-1900. *3152*

—. Florida (Tampa Bay area). Photographs. Tourism. 1876-1922. *2947*

—. Interstate Commerce Commission. Sugar. Tennessee. 1895-1925. *2946*

—. Louisiana (Attakapas, Opelousas areas). Waterways. 19c. *3275*

—. Oklahoma. Rivers. 19c. *3223*

—. Sprague, Frank Julian. Trolleys. Virginia (Richmond). 1888-1973. *3053*

Transportation, Commercial. Economic Development. Railroads. Steamboats. Western States. 1811-60. *2981*

Transylvania University. American Revolution. Kentucky (Lexington). Medicine (practice of). Ridgely, Frederick. 1757-1824. *2124*

—. Colleges and Universities. Kentucky (Lexington). Science. 1799-1857. *1804*

Trappists. Holy Cross Abbey. Virginia (Shenandoah Valley). Wormeley Manor. 1744-1980. *2506*

—. Cotton. Mississippi. Reconstruction. Small farms. Tenancy. ca 1865-80. *2756*

—. Democratic Party. Generations. 1952-72. *3525*

—. Depressions. McCloud, Emma Gudger. Personal Narratives. Sharecroppers. 1916-79. *2780*

—. Desegregation. Korean War. Protestant churches. Vietnam War. 1950-70. *2289*

—. Fundamentalism. Gospel music. Music. Texas. 1930's. *2401*

—. Geography. Identity. 1973. *3304*

—. Human Relations. North Carolina. Regionalism. Stereotypes. 1971. *656*

—. Liberals. Myrdal, Gunnar (*An American Dilemma*). Race Relations. 1944-75. *279*

—. Literature. Poor. 20c. *3360*

—. Men. Social Customs. Toasts. 1966-78. *1544*

—. Mexican Americans. Migration. Social Conditions. Texas, south. 1850-1900. *2566*

—. Mississippians for Public Education. Public schools. School Integration. Women. 1960's. *2028*

—. Politics. Social Status. 1952-72. *3524*

—. Race. Voting and Voting Behavior. 1952-68. *3617*

Whiteside, Harriet Leonora Straw. Tennessee (Chattanooga). 1824-1903. *573*

Whitney, Eli. Industrial Technology. Inventors. Social change. 1792-1825. *2957*

Whitsitt Controversy. Baptists. Graves, James Robinson. Landmarks. 1850-1950. *2411*

Whittington, Will M. Federal aid. Flood control. Mississippi (Yazoo Valley). Navigation. Inland. 1873-1977. *2614*

Wichita Falls and Northwestern Railway. Boomtowns. Oil Industry and Trade. Texas (Burkburnett). 1902-40. *3001*

—. Oklahoma. Railroads. Texas. Towns. 1900-20. *3003*

Wichita Indians. Indians. Louisiana. Meteorites. Texas. 1808-26. *3978*

Wichita Mountains Wildlife Refuge. Birds. Oklahoma. 1904-77. *3331*

Wichita National Game Preserve. Buffalo. Game preserves. Oklahoma (Wichita Mountains). Rush, Franklin S. 18c-1923. *3232*

Wickham, John (residence). Architecture. Latrobe, B. Henry. Parris, Alexander. Virginia (Richmond). 1801-1827. *1399*

Wiener, Jonathan M. Economic Conditions (review article). Mandle, Jay R. Ransom, Roger L. Sutch, Richard. 1850-1910. 1977-78. *3362*

Wigfall, Louis T. Democratic Party. Elections (senatorial). States' Rights. Texas. 1859. *3670*

Wigg family. South Carolina. 1705-1860. *614*

Wight, Peter Bonnett. Architecture. Gothic Revival Style. Jacob, Thomas Prather. Kentucky (Louisville). 1866-92. *1253*

Wilbur, Richard. Literary criticism. Poe, Edgar Allan. Symbolism in Literature. 1820's-49. 1959. *970*

Wilde, Oscar. Aesthetics. Lectures. Travel. 1882. *738*

—. Decorative Arts. Georgia. Lectures. 1882. *939*

Wilde, Richard Henry (*Hesperia: A Poem*). Authorship. Georgia. Poetry. ca 1820's-47. *889*

Wilderness. *See also* Conservation of Natural Resources; Forests and Forestry; National Parks and Reserves.

—. Faulkner, William (*Big Woods*). Literary themes. 1934-55. *926*

—. Faulkner, William ("The Bear"). Fiction. Mississippi (Lafayette County, Panola County, Yazoo Delta). Plantations. Railroads. 19c-20c. *3186*

Wildlife Conservation. *See also* Forests and Forestry; National Parks and Reserves; Natural Resources.

—. Louisiana Gulf Coast Club. McIlhenny, Edward Avery. 1910-24. *3321*

Wiley, Bell Irvin (obituary). Civil War. Historians. ca 1930-80. *111*

—. Civil War. Historians. Mississippi, University of. ca 1926-80. *274*

Wiley College. Bands. Blacks. Colleges and Universities. Jazz. Morris, Kelso B. Music. Personal narratives. Texas (Marshall). 1925-35. *1756*

Wilkes, Jessie Hubert. Arkansas (Cave City). Folklore. Personal narratives. 1978. *772*

Willard, Levi. Daily Life. Georgia (Decatur). Letters-to-the-editor. Ohio. Springfield *Weekly News*. 1826-64. 1876. *538*

William and Mary, College of. Bellini, Carlo. Karzhavin, Fedor. Language. Virginia. 1773-1805. *1812*

—. Blair, James. Church of England. Church of Scotland. Virginia. 1679-1720. *2448*

—. Coats of arms. Seals, official. Virginia. 1690-1930. *1945*

—. Colleges and Universities. Dawson, William. Leadership. 1725-52. *1913*

—. Ewell, Benjamin Stoddert. Virginia (Williamsburg). 1854-88. *1912*

—. Law. Virginia (Williamsburg). Wythe, George. 1780-90. *1786*

Williams, Aubrey W. Anti-Communist Movements. Louisiana (New Orleans). School Integration. Senate Internal Security Subcommittee. Southern Conference Education Fund. 1954. *1859*

Williams, Chester L. Blacks. Florida. Sculpture. 1970's. *1713*

Williams, Claude. Labor Unions and Organizations. Leadership. People's Institute of Applied Religion. Williams, Joyce. 1940-75. *2494*

—. Social change. Williams, Joyce. 1930's-70's. *3725*

Williams, Cratis. Appalachia. Ballads. Personal Narratives. Research. 1930's. *1693*

Williams, Frank B. Cypress. Louisiana, southern. Lumber and Lumbering. Swamps. 1869-1929. *2925*

Williams, Jesse Wallace (tribute). Authors. Midwestern State University. Teachers. Texas (Wichita Falls). 20c. *982*

Williams, John. Billings, Dwight. Economic Development (review article). North Carolina. West Virginia. 1865-1900. *3121*

Williams, Joyce. Labor Unions and Organizations. Leadership. People's Institute of Applied Religion. Williams, Claude. 1940-75. *2494*

—. Social change. Williams, Claude. 1930's-70's. *3725*

Williams, Leonard. Humor (review article). Literature. Noland, Charles Fenton Mercer. West, James L. W., III. 1835-70. 1978-79. *2527*

Williams, Mary C. Anthologies. Hubbard, Addison. Owen, Guy. Poetry. 1928-79. *931*

Williams, Mildred M. Blacks. Education (review article). Engs, Robert Francis. Missions and Missionaries. Philanthropy. Prather, H. Leon, Sr. 1861-1968. *1965*

Williams, Robert Lee. Archives, National. Federal government. Foreman, Grant. Indians. Oklahoma Historical Society. 1934. *3894*

Williams, Tennessee (*Memoirs*). Drama. Family. ca 1919-75. *814*

*Willie L. Bennett* (vessel). Chesapeake Bay. Shipbuilding. Skipjacks. 1899-1950's. *3025*

Willingham, Calder. Novels. 1960-73. *1134*

Wills. Blacks. Church, Robert Reed, Sr. Tennessee (Memphis). Wealth. 1912. *630*

—. Blacks. Education. Maryland (Baltimore). Wells, Nelson. 1786-1908. *2056*

Wills, Bob. Country Music. Music. Texas Playboys. 1920-80. *1654*

Wills, Frank. Architecture. Episcopal Church, Protestant. Gothic Revival Style. Upjohn, Richard. 1835-60. *1319*

Willson, Augustus E. Beckham, John C. W. Kentucky. McCreary, James B. Progressivism. State Government. 1899-1915. *3512*

Willson, Jim. Florida. Friends of the Florida Seminoles. Seminole Indians. Willson, Minnie Moore. 1890-1930. *4168*

Willson, Minnie Moore. Florida. Friends of the Florida Seminoles. Seminole Indians. Willson, Jim. 1890-1930. *4168*

Willstown, Treaties of (1806). Cherokee Indians. Indians. Jefferson, Thomas. Removals, forced. Tennessee. 1794-1817. *4048*

Wilmington and Manchester Railroad Company. Railroads. South Carolina (Florence). 1853-90. *3020*

Wilmington Ten. Criminal justice system. North Carolina. Race Relations. School Integration. Trials. 1971-77. *2049*

Wilson, Charles Morrow. Ozark Mountains. Randolph, Vance. Rayburn, Otto Ernest. Regionalism. 1930-75. *833*

Wilson, Charles Reagan. Hill, Samuel S., Jr. Historiography. Loveland, Anne C. Religion (review article). 1941-81. *2206*

Wilson, Gordon. Archives. Folklore. Kentucky (Edmonson County). Linguistics. 1959-67. *1703*

Wilson, Joseph Ruggles. Presbyterian Church. 1844-1903. *2391*

Wilson, Louis Round. Chicago, University of (School of Library Science). Colleges and Universities. Librarians. North Carolina, University of, Chapel Hill. 1901-76. *267*

Wilson, William E. Alabama. Georgia. Photographs. Social Conditions. 1880-1905. *464*

Wilson, Woodrow. Arkansas. Brough, Charles Hillman. Democratic Party. State Politics. 1903-35. *3814*

—. Arkansas. Democratic Party. Kirby, William Fosgate. Progressivism. Senate. 1880's-1934. *3727*

—. Historiography. Rhodes, James Ford (*History of the United States from the Compromise of 1850*). Slavery. ca 1890-1920. *276*

Winans, James A. Southern Speech Communication Association. Speech. 1900-56. *782*

Winans, William. Louisiana (New Orleans). Methodist Church. 1813-14. *2313*

Windmills. Texas Panhandle. 1885-1929. *2670*

Windsor Hotel. Georgia (Americus). Norrman, Gottfried L. 1890-1980. *1168*

Winemaking. Fairchild Wine Vault. Oklahoma (Oklahoma City). 1890-1925. *1221*

Winfrey, Howess Dewey. Folklore. Kentucky (Cumberland County). Musicians. Social criticism. 1923-72. *1641*

Winter. Architecture. Cherokee Indians. Housing. Indians. Tennessee. Woodland culture. Prehistory. *3966*

Winterthur Museum (Henry Francis du Pont Collection). Delaware. Furniture and Furnishings. Museums. 1640-1840. *1600*

Winthrop College. Archival Catalogs and Inventories. Education. South Carolina. 1841-1978. *1891*

Winyah Indians. Artifacts. South Carolina (Georgetown County; Wachesaw Landing). Waccamaw Indians. 1600-1890. *4109*

Wirt, William. Rhetoric. Virginia. 19c. *1516*

Wisconsin. *See also* North Central States.

—. North Carolina. Quality of life. ca 1840-1975. *704*

Wistar, Casper. Glass and Glassmaking. New Jersey (Salem). Pennsylvania (Manheim). Stiegel, William. Virginia (Jamestown). 18c. *3016*

Witchcraft. *See also* Folklore.

—. Aged. Folklore. Poor. West Virginia. Women. 1975. *1583*

—. Bell, Kate. Tennessee (Adams). 19c. *1682*

—. Devil. Folklore. West Virginia. 1950-67. *1594*

Wittenberg, Judith Bryant. Bezzerides, A. L. Faulkner, William (review article). Literature. Minter, David. Stonum, Gary Lee. 20c. *880*

Wives. Daily Life. Plantations. 1780-1835. *539*

Wofford College. Curricula. Humanities. South Carolina (Spartanburg). 1971-79. *1951*

Wolf, Lucyann Davis (family). Cherokee Indians. Daily Life. Indians. Tennessee. 1900-35. *4179*

Wolfe, Thomas. Appalachia. Literature. 1900-38. *884*

—. Editors and Editing. Nowell, Elizabeth. 1933-58. *932*

—. Faulkner, William. 1920's-70. *1107*

—. Literature. North Carolina (Asheville). 1920-38. *1029*

—. Presbyterian Church. 1900-38. *2493*

Women. *See also* Feminism; Sex Discrimination; Wives.

—. Actors and Actresses. Films. 1939-71. *463*

—. Aged. Folklore. Poor. West Virginia. Witchcraft. 1975. *1583*

—. Agricultural Organizations. North Carolina. Southern Farmers' Alliance. ca 1880-1900. *2743*

—. Alabama. Civil War. Plantations. Reconstruction. 1850-70. *2864*

—. Alabama. Florence University for Women. Higher Education. 1890-1910. *1826*

—. Alabama. Physicians. 1828-1979. *687*

—. Alabama (Florence). Colleges and Universities. Florence University for Women. 1890-1911. *1827*

—. Alston, Mary Niven. Blacks. Cooper, Anna Haywood. Episcopal Church, Protestant. Higher education. Robertson, Isabella Gibson. 1875-1981. *1803*

—. Appalachia. Attitudes. Griffin, Susan. Kolodny, Annette. Land. Literature. 19c-20c. *1025*

—. Appalachian Studies. Research. 1890's-1981. *307*

—. Art. Emanuel, Anne. Georgia (Atlanta). Pon, Alyson. Stone, Scribenne. 1977-78. *1101*

—. Artists. 1979. *882*

—. Artists. Attitudes. Florida. 1979. *955*

—. Arts. 1735-1981. *866*

—. Astor, Nancy Langhorne. Great Britain. House of Commons. Virginia. 1897-1964. *605*

—. Athas, Daphne. Authors. Personal narratives. 1940-49. *793*

—. Attitudes. 1930's-70's. *471*

—. Attitudes. Political participation. State legislators. 1979. *3684*

—. Attitudes. Social Conditions. ca 1800-70. *409*

—. Authors. Blacks. Walker, Alice. 1960's-83. *1728*

—. Authors. Godwin, Gail. 1950's-83. *1017*

—. Authors. Harris, Corra. Periodicals. 1880's-1935. *1546*

—. Authors. King, Grace. 1877-1932. *1086*

# AUTHOR INDEX

## A

Abbott, Collamer M. 2533 3369
Abbott, Martin 496
Abbott, Shirley 409
Abel, Ernest L. 2663
Abernathy, Mollie C. 2181
Abney, Everett E. 1963 1964
Abraham, Mildred K. 1
Abramowitz, Alan I. 3464
Abrams, W. Amos 1406 1407 1408
Adams, David Wallace 1965 3918
Adams, Donald R., Jr. 2534 2882 2883
Adams, Emily S. 2
Adams, Frank 410
Adams, Katherine J. 32
Adams, Michael 411
Adams, Sherée L. 4023
Adamson, June 1409
Adkins, Howard G. 3183 3184
Adler, Leopold, II 1329
Agee, Hugh 1410
Agee, James 786
Agnew, Brad 3 3842 3919 4182
Agogino, George A. 2103
Agonito, Joseph 2182
Ahern, Wilbert H. 3920
Aiesi, Margaret 3465
Aiken, Charles S. 787 788 2664 3185 3186
Ainsley, W. Frank, Jr. 3187 3188
Akin, Edward N. 497 2884 3466
Albert, Harold E. 3467
Alder, Gale Shipman 1149
Aldrich, Duncan M. 3921
Aldrich, Mark 2665
Alexander, Mary 3922
Alexander, Robert L. 1150 1151 1411
Alexander, Thomas B. 3468
Alford, John J. 2535 3189
Algeo, Adele 498
Algeo, John 498
Allain, Mathé 499 1412
Allcott, John V. 1152 1153
Allen, H. David 503
Allen, John E. 3370
Allen, Margaret Sheffield 1413
Allen, Ruby 1414
Allen, Susan Emily 17
Allen, Tip H., Jr. 3665
Allen, Virginia A. 4007
Allen, William Rodney 789
Allin, Jean 4
Almaráz, Félix D., Jr. 5 6 7
Alonzo, Frank O. 3469 3470
Alsobrook, David E. 1415 1784
Alston, Lee J. 2666 2667
Alther, Lisa 412
Alvey, R. Gerard 1416
Alvis, Joel L., Jr. 2183
Ammerman, Nancy T. 2184
Ancelet, Barry Jean 1412
Anders, Evan 3471
Anders, Gary 3876
Anderson, Annette 1154
Anderson, George M. 500
Anderson, James D. 1966 2668
Anderson, N. E. 2803
Anderson, Solena 1708
Anderson-Green, Paula Hathaway 1417
Andrews, Andrea R. 2885
Andrews, Nathalie 1418
Andrews, William D. 1104
Andrews, William L. 1709 1710
Ansley, Fran 1419 2886 2887
Anthony, Allen 1420 2536 3190
Aptheker, Bettina 1711
Arana, Luis Rafael 8
Arbuckle, H. C., III 2104
Arendale, Marirose 3472

## B

Baas, Jacob C., Jr. 3476
Bachtel, Douglas C. 2892
Bacon, Lloyd 3354
Bacot, H. Parrott 1157
Baehr, Theodore, Jr. 10
Baer, Evelyn D. 1158
Baer, Hans A. 2188
Baggett, James Alex 3477
Bahr, Betsy 2893
Bailey, Fred A. 1785 1885
Bailey, Kenneth K. 2189 2190
Bailey, Kenneth R. 2894
Bailey, Raymond C. 2191
Bailey, Thomas E. 2895
Bails, Dale 2896
Baird, Keith E. 785 1774 1775
Baird, Nancy D. 2105 2106 2107
Baird, Reed M. 794
Baker, Eugene W. 1886
Baker, Liva 1786
Baker, Robert A. 2192 2193 2194
Baker, Russell P. 3191
Baker, T. Lindsay 2670
Baker, Tod A. 3465 3520 3608 3649 3665 3745 3836
Baker, Vaughan 501
Baldwin, Brooke 1714
Baldwin, John T., Jr. 2897 3478
Baldwin, Lewis V. 1715
Ball, Donald B. 1424 1425
Ball, Lynn 502
Ballenger, T. L. 3877
Banks, Alan J. 2537 2898 3373
Banks, Ann 2671
Banks, William N. 2899
Bankston, William B. 503
Banning, Lance 3479
Barber, Rims 3355
Barbera, Jack 415
Bardsley, Beverly J. 1787
Bargainnier, Earl F. 416 698 1426
Barge, Laura 795
Barham, Mack E. 3480
Barka, Norman F. 1187
Barnard, William D. 3481 3482
Barnes, Robert 2195
Barnett, C. Robert 1427
Barney, William L. 504
Barnidge, James L. 3483
Barnwell, John 1159
Barone, Thomas 1788
Barr, Alwyn 566
Barr, Debbie 2900
Barr, Stringfellow 1962
Barr, Susan M. 1789
Barrett, Clifton Waller 1887

Argersinger, Peter H. 2669 3473
Armentrout, Donald S. 2185
Armour, Robert A. 413
Armour, Rollin S. 2186
Arms, Valarie Meliotes 790
Armstrong, Dee A. 2888
Armstrong, Thomas F. 9 3371 3372
Arner, Robert D. 791
Arnez, Nancy L. 1967
Arnold, Joseph L. 2889 2890 3174 3474
Arnold, Marilyn 792
Aronson, David 1712
Arrington, Theodore S. 3475
Asbury, Eslie 1421
Ash, Stephen V. 1155
Ashby, Rickie Zayne 1422
Ashdown, Ellen A. 1713
Ashdown, Paul G. 2187
Atack, Jeremy 2891
Athas, Daphne 793
Aubey, Robert T. 2545
Auman, Dorothy Cole 1423
Austin, James C. 754
Austin, Wade 414
Ayers, Edward L. 1156

Barron, Hal Seth 755
Bartlett, Ellen 1160
Bartley, Numan V. 11 2672 3484
Barton, Josef J. 2673
Bateman, Fred 2901 2902 2903 3178
Batteau, Allen 756 757
Bauer, Craig A. 2538
Bauer, Mary 2108
Baulch, J. R. 3485
Bauman, Mark K. 505 2196 2197 2198
Baumstein, Paschal 1161
Baxley, Bennett 1428
Bayor, Ronald H. 3192
Beardsley, E. H. 2109
Beauchamp, Virginia Walcott 796
Beaver, Pat 3181
Beck, Earl R. 506
Beck, Paul Allen 3486
Beck, Tom 357
Beckwith, James P., Jr. 699
Becnel, Thomas 12 3487
Bederman, Sanford H. 597
Beeth, Howard 2199
Beezer, Bruce 1968
Begaye, Russell 3878
Beirne, D. Randall 2904 2905 2906
Bell, Brenda 1419 2886 2887
Bell, Frank C. 3488
Bell, Samuel E. 2539
Bellamy, Donnie D. 1969 1970 2674
Bellamy, Jan 2907
Benario, Herbert W. 1790
Bender, Thomas 2540
Bendixen, Alfred 797
Benham, Evelyn 3193
Bennett, James D. 798
Bennett, Patrick 13
Bennett, S. M. 799
Benson, Robert G. 800
Benton, Lee David 3923
Bergeron, Paul H. 3489
Berkove, Lawrence I. 801
Berman, Myron 2200
Bernard, Jacqueline 3374
Bernard, Richard M. 1871
Bernhard, Virginia 3356
Bernheim, Mark 417
Berrigan, Joseph R. 14
Berry, Benjamin D., Jr. 2201
Berry, Mary Frances 358
Berry, Mrs. John 2908
Berryman, Jack W. 1429
Bertho, Catherine 2541
Bertolino-Green, Dianne 2441
Bertoluzzi, Renitia 3889
Bethell, Thomas N. 2542 3375
Bettersworth, John K. 1888 1889
BeVard, Ginger 15
Bevins, Ann B. 1791
Bezou, James F. 1430
Bianchi, Diane 1706
Bickel, Minnette 16
Bickley, R. Bruce, Jr. 1147
Bildner, Robert 2675
Billings, Dwight B. 300 354 507 2543
Billings, Warren M. 3490
Billington, Monroe 3491
Bills, Robert 2047
Bilotta, James D. 3924
Bingham, Edgar 3194
Biola, Heather 1716
Birbalsingh, Frank M. 418
Birdwhistell, Terry L. 17 1431
Bishir, Catherine W. 1162 3195
Bishko, Lucretia Ramsey 2676
Bishop, Bill 3376
Bishop, David W. 1971
Bixby, Arthur M., Sr. 2909
Bixler, Ray H. 1792
Bjornseth, Dick 1163 2910
Black, Ann McMurry 802
Black, Earl 3492 3493 3495
Black, Margie 2202

Black, Merle 700 3494 3495
Black, Patti Carr 3196
Black, Watt L. 1793
Blackburn, Bob L. 177
Blair, John L. 2203
Blake, J. Herman 379
Blakely, Edward J. 2544
Blakemore, Robbie G. 1762
Bland, David H. 3496
Bland, Sidney R. 3497
Blaustein, Richard 1432 1433 1434 1435 1436
Blauvelt, Martha Tomhave 2204
Blazek, Ron 1794
Blend, Benay 3879
Bleser, Carol K. 353
Blevins, Kent B. 2205
Blicksilver, Jack 2545
Bloomer, John W. 803
Blosser, Susan Sokol 2911
Blotner, Joseph 804 805
Blumer, Thomas J. 3880 4153
Blunt, Ruth H. 976
Board, Prudy Taylor 2912
Bobbitt, Charles A. 3498
Bobbitt, Randy 179
Bodenhamer, David J. 3197
Bogardus, Carl R., Sr. 508
Bohmer, David A. 3499
Bohn, Thomas W. 419
Bolding, Gary 2913
Boles, Janet K. 3500
Boles, John B. 2206
Boling, T. Edward 2207
Boling, T. Edwin 2208
Bolsterli, Margaret Jones 701
Bolton, S. Charles 2209
Bonacich, Edna 359
Bonawit, Oby 509
Boney, Francis Nash 510 702 725 3843
Bonner, Judith Hopkins 806
Bonner, Thomas, Jr. 807
Bonnifield, Paul 2546 2677 3925
Boone, Robert 2787
Boozer, William 808
Borchert, James 360 2547 2548 2549
Born, Kate 3501
Bosha, Francis J. 809
Boston, Thomas D. 361
Bosworth, Timothy W. 2210
Boulding, Kenneth E. 2550
Bourdon, David 810
Bourke, Paul F. 3502
Bowden, Beryl 2644
Bowden, Thomas A. 18
Bowen, William R. 83
Bowers, Beth 19
Bowers, Thomas A. 1442
Bowles, Stephen E. 1443
Bowman, David 1164 1165
Bowman, Shearer Davis 2678
Boxerman, Burton Alan 2551
Boyce, Douglas W. 3926
Boyd, Joel D. 4152
Boydstun, Q. B. 3844
Boyer, Dorothy M. 187
Brabham, Robin 1890
Braden, Waldo W. 20 21 3503
Bradford, Danelle 1444
Bradford, M. E. 362 811 812
Bradford, Ronald W. 420
Bradley, Frank 363
Bradshaw, Ted K. 2544
Bragaw, Donald H. 2552
Braithwaite, Roland 1972
Branch, Edgar M. 758
Branch, Harold T. 2211
Brandmeyer, Gerard A. 1445
Brannan, Beverly W. 2914
Brans, Jo 813
Branscome, James 2915
Branson, Branley Allan 2212
Branton, Wiley A. 1973
Brantsaeter, Per L. 814
Bratton, Mary J. 2213
Breckinridge, John B. 3504

Breeden, James O. 2110 2111
Breibart, Solomon 2214
Bresnahan, Roger J. 815
Breton, Roland J.-L. 3264
Breton, Ronald J.-L. 3198
Brett, Jeanne M. 3398
Brewer, Krista 2679
Brewster, C. Ray 2215
Brigance, Fred W. 1166
Brindley, Esther E. 511
Brink, Betty 3837
Brinkman, Leonard W. 759
Brittain, James E. 1795
Broach, Claude U. 2216
Broadwell, Elizabeth Pell 816 817
Brodie, Fawn M. 512
Brodsky, Louis D. 818
Bromberg, Alan B. 3505 3506
Brooks, Bill 3837
Brooks, Cleanth 819
Brophy, William J. 2916
Broussard, James H. 3507
Broward, Robert C. 1167
Brown, A. E. 2917
Brown, Bahngrell W. 3199
Brown, Bubberson 569
Brown, Buster J. 3812
Brown, Catherine 513
Brown, D. Clayton 2112 2918
Brown, David J. 1168
Brown, Dorothy M. 22 94
Brown, Douglas Summers 23 514 2217
Brown, Elton Thomas 4152
Brown, Gayle Ann 3927
Brown, James S. 24
Brown, Kenny L. 1169 3377
Brown, Lawrence L. 2218
Brown, Lisle G. 2219
Brown, M. L. 3928
Brown, Martha Frances 2919
Brown, Pat 3200
Brown, Philip M. 3929
Brown, Richard Maxwell 25
Brown, Robert L. 1717
Brown, Stephen W. 3508
Brown, Steve 2721
Brown, Thomas 3509
Brown, Walter L. 26 27
Brown, William R. 2680
Browne, Gary L. 2553 2920 2921
Brownell, Blaine A. 2922 2923
Browning, Denise 1170
Bruccoli, Matthew J. 820
Bruce, Dickson D., Jr. 421 760 761
Brugger, Robert J. 422 515
Bruseth, James E. 4078
Bryant, Keith L., Jr. 516 1171 1172 1173
Bryce, Lynn 821
Buckles, Carol K. 1629
Buckley, Cathryn 1796
Buckley, Thomas E. 423
Buckner, Gladys 1174
Buffington, Robert 822
Buice, David 2220 3930 3931
Buker, George E. 2681 2924
Bulger, Peggy A. 1446 1447
Bull, Elias B. 1175
Bullock, Charles S., III 2080 3510 3511
Bunte, Pamela 4166
Burckel, Nicholas C. 3512 3513
Burger, Warren E. 3514
Burkette, Alice Gaillard 1448
Burkhardt, Sue Pope 1176
Burnett, John G. 3932
Burnett, Robert A. 517
Burns, Anna C. 2554 2925 2926
Burns, Augustus Marion, III 1602 1759 1974 2805
Burns, Robert Carter 3845
Burran, James A. 3515
Burrison, John A. 1449 1450 1451
Burt, Eleanor Bales 3201

# E

Earle, Carville V. 2952
Eason, Thomas 2570
Eaton, Clement 433 559 729
Eaton, Richard Bozman 434
Eberson, Frederick W. 2123 2124
Eckford, Elizabeth 2100
Edmonds, Katharine Spicer 1485
Edmonson, James H. 2953 3213
Edmunds, R. David 4054 4063
Edsall, Thomas B. 3553
Edson, William D. 2954 2955 2956
Edward, C. 2957
Edwards, Edwin W. 3554
Edwards, John Carver 3555
Edwards, Katharine Bush 1486 1487
Egerton, John 97 1900 1990 2100
Ehrenpreis, Anne Henry 730
Eidson, John Olin 435
Eiler, Lyntha Scott 1488
Eiler, Terry 1488
Einstein, Frank H. 98 2571
Eisterhold, John A. 2958 2959
Elder, Harris J. 560
Elifson, Kirk W. 2262
Elkins, Nancy F. 2263
Eller, Ronald D. 99 100 2960
Elliot, Jeffrey M. 391
Elliott, Jack D., Jr. 3214
Ellis, John 3556
Ellis, L. Tuffly 101 102 103 104 105 1901 2572
Ellis, M. Carolyn 3628
Ellis, William E. 2264 2265 2709 3388
Ellsworth, Linda V. 856
Ellsworth, Lucius F. 3953
Ellwanger, Walter H. 2266
Elusche, Michael 1991
Engelhardt, H. Tristram, Jr. 2125
Engerman, Stanley L. 2573 2662
Engerrand, Steven W. 3215
Englund, Donald R. 3954
Engstrom, Richard L. 3557 3558 3559
Enstam, Elizabeth York 561
Ernst, Joseph A. 2961 3182
Ernst, William 562 563
Ervin, Sam J., Jr. 564
Estall, Robert 2574
Ethridge, Harrison M. 3852
Ethridge, Robbie F. 3885
Eubanks, Ralph T. 20
Evans, David 1732
Evans, E. Raymond 1217 3955 3956 3957 3958 3959 3960 3961 4019
Evans, Frank B. 1812
Evans, Margaret B. 106
Evans, Teddy H. 2267 2268
Evans, Walker 786
Everett, Dianna 3560
Everhart, Frances B. 1902
Everman, H. E. 1813
Evitts, William J. 857
Ewan, Joseph W. 858 3962 3963
Ewers, John C. 3964
Ezell, Macel D. 1489

# F

Fairbanks, Charles H. 3965
Fairclough, Adam 2575
Falk, Leslie A. 2126
Falk, William W. 1992 3389
Fall, Ralph E. 2962
Fanning, Michael 731
Farbman, Michael 2576
Faries, Clyde J. 3561
Farley, Benjamin W. 436 859
Farley, Judith 1031
Farrell, David 860 861
Fasold, Ralph W. 763
Faucette, Shirley 437
Faulkner, Charles H. 3966

Faulkner, William 862 863
Faust, Drew Gilpin 864
Faust, Patricia L. 1218
Fazio, Michael 1219
Feagin, Joe R. 3517
Feder, Bernard 3967
Feest, Christian F. 3968 3969
Feinberg, Andrew 438
Feintuch, Burt 1490 1491 1492
Feldman, Paula R. 732
Feller, Irwin 2963
Fennell, Janice C. 9
Fenton, James I. 3216
Fenton, William N. 3970
Ferguson, Anne Williams 1903
Ferguson, Bobbie 2103
Ferguson, Clyde R. 3971
Ferguson, Henry N. 1220
Ferleger, Louis 2710
Ferm, Lois 2269
Fernandez, José B. 3562
Ferris, William 1733
Fetherling, Doug 733
Feucht, Oscar E. 2270
Fewkes, Charles K. 3217
Fickett, Laura J. 3390
Fickle, James E. 2964 3391 3392 3393
Fienberg, Lorne 865
Fifer, J. Valerie 3563
Figh, Margaret Gillis 1493
Filby, Vera Ruth 3218
Files, W. Dan 3564
Findlay, Stephen M. 3853
Fine, Elsa Honig 866
Finger, Bill 1494 2965 3565
Finger, John R. 3972 3973 3974
Fingerhut, Eugene R. 3566
Fink, Gary M. 3370 3378 3386 3394 3415 3426 3433 3438
Fiorato, Jacqueline 3975
Fischer, LeRoy H. 1169 1221 1222 1904 3219 3567 3886 3976 4152
Fisher, James S. 2711
Fisher, Stephen L. 1495
Fisher, Steve 107 108 2577 2712
Fishman, Walda Katz 565
Fitch, James E. 2271
Fite, Gilbert C. 2707 2713 2869
Fitzgerald, Martha H. 2578
Fitzgerald, Sally 867 868
Flaherty, David H. 109
Flanary, Sara E. Lewis 869
Flanders, Jane 870
Fleischauer, Carl 1488
Fleisig, Heywood 2579
Fleming, Cynthia Griggs 1993 1994
Fleming, John E. 3568
Fletcher, Charlotte 1905
Fletcher, Jesse C. 2272
Flores, Dan L. 3977 3978
Florestano, Patricia S. 3569
Florin, John W. 3187
Floyd, Fred 2966
Floyd, William Barrow 871
Flusche, Michael 872
Flynt, J. Wayne 2273 2274 3359
Flynt, Wayne 3570
Fogelson, Raymond D. 3979 4157 4158 4159
Foley, Douglas E. 3788
Folks, Jeffrey J. 873
Folmar, J. Kent 110
Ford, Jeanette W. 3887
Ford, Oliver 439
Foret, Michael J. 3980
Forkner, Ben 874
Forman, William H., Jr. 1496
Fornari, Harry D. 2714
Forrester, Rebel C. 1497
Foster, Elizabeth Pyburn 1498
Foster, Gaines M. 875 2275
Foster, Jim 107 3395
Foster, Robert L. 566
Fournier, Louise 3336
Foust, J. Brady 2715
Foust, James 2903

Fowler, Robert H. 111
Fox-Genovese, Elizabeth 440 567 2716
Fraas, Elizabeth 3220
France, Mary Duncan 3571
Franch, Michael S. 2276
Franklin, Robert L. 1814
Franklin, W. Neil 3981
Franks, Kenny A. 3982 3983
Frantz, Joe B. 112 568
Franzoni, Janet Brenner 3572
Frate, Dennis A. 2174
Frazier, Kitty 1995
Frederickson, Mary 3396 3573
Freedman, Alex S. 1499
Freeman, Richard B. 1996
Freeze, Gary 2277
French, Laurence 3888 3889 4160 4161 4162
French, Warren 441
Friedman, Lawrence J. 372
Friedmann, Harriet 2580
Friend, Llerena 113
Frisbie, Louise K. 1223
Frost, Roon 1224
Fry, Joseph A. 3574
Fugate, Robert 2967
Fuller, Justin 114
Fullerton, Eula 709

# G

Gaby, Donald C. 3221
Gaddy, C. Welton 2278
Gadsden, Sam 569
Gaffney, Floyd 1734
Gage, Duane 876
Gage, Patricia Anthony 2279 2968
Galant, Debbie 3575
Galenson, David W. 2581
Galishoff, Stuart 3556
Gallagher, Richard J. 3314
Gallaway, Lowell E. 3144
Gallman, Robert E. 2660 2717
Galloway, Patricia 3984
Galphin, Bruce 2969
Gamble, Robert A. 115 1225
Gamio, Manuel 570
Gammon, Tim 3985 3986
Gann, Daniel H. 2280
Ganong, Overton G. 1226
Ganschow, Thomas 513
García, Mario T. 3397
Gardien, Kent 2718
Gardner, Bettye 1997
Gardner, Booker T. 1998
Gardner, Don 943
Gardner, Lloyd 442
Gardner, Robert G. 1815 2281 2282 2283 3987
Garner, H. Hal 1227
Garner, John S. 2970
Garofalo, Charles 2971 2972
Garonzik, Joseph 571
Garrett, Franklin M. 116
Garrison, Bruce M. 3576
Garrison, Gail L. 877
Gass, W. Conrad 572
Gaston, Kay Baker 573
Gates, Paul W. 2719
Gatewood, Willard B., Jr. 117 2720
Gatlin, Douglas S. 3577
Gatton, John Spalding 878
Gaventa, John 118 119 2582
Gavins, Raymond 373
Gaw, Jerry L. 2284
Gayle, Addison, Jr. 374
Geary, Helen Brophy 1500
Geist, Christopher D. 879 3988
Geithman, David T. 3661
George, Angelo I. 1501
George, Paul S. 2583 3578 3579 3580 3581 3582
Gernes, Sonia 1500
Gerrard, Ginny 2285
Gershman, Carl 3583
Gerster, Patrick 734
Gettys, James W., Jr. 2531
Gettys, Marshall 3222
Gibb, Hugh R. 2973
Gibson, Arrell Morgan 120 3223

Gibson, Dirk Cameron 3584
Gibson, Gail 574
Gibson, George H. 764
Gidley, M. 880
Gifford, George Edmund, Jr. 881 2127
Gilbert, Dee 575 3585
Gilbert, G. D. 242
Gilbert, Gail R. 121
Gilbert, Jess 2721
Giles, James R. 1735
Giles, Michael W. 1999
Giles, Micheal W. 2000
Giliomee, Hermann B. 576
Gill, Harold B., Jr. 2128
Gillespie, Dorothy 882
Gillespie, Paul 2286
Gillespie, Robert Gill 3586
Gillette, Michael L. 375 2001
Gilley, B. H. 3587
Gilliam, Will D., Jr. 2287
Gilliland, Evelyn 2129
Gilmore, James Haynes 122
Gilpin, Patrick J. 2002 2003
Gilstrap, Lucille 2764
Ginzl, David J. 3588 3589
Giordano, Paolo 577
Giraud, Marcel 578
Giroux, Vincent A., Jr. 3590
Gitelman, H. M. 3176
Gizycki, Horst von 2288
Gobetz, Giles E. 579
Goddard, John H., Jr. 123
Godoy, Gustavo J. 3591
Gohdes, Clarence 765
Gold, Gérald L. 580 3224
Goldberg, Stephen B. 3398
Goldfarb, Stephen J. 2974
Goldfield, David Reed 2130 2975
Golding, Gordon 2289
Goldstein, Jonathan 3592
Gonzales, John Edmond 124 1531
Goode, James M. 883
Goode, Thomas H. 3593
Goodenow, Ronald K. 2004
Goodman, George J. 1906
Goodwin, Stephen 125
Goodwyn, Frank 443
Gordon, Avishag 1528
Gordon, Martin K. 3225
Gordon, Robert 1503
Gorman, Frederick J. E. 2290
Goudeau, John 581
Goudeau, Loretta 581
Gouger, James B. 2722
Gould, Alan B. 126
Gover, C. Jane 305
Grable, Stephen W. 2976
Gracy, David B., II 2723 2724
Graebner, Laura Baum 3989
Graf, LeRoy P. 127
Grafton, Carl 3594 3595 3596
Graham, Eleanor 541
Graham, Thomas 1228
Granquist, Charles L. 1384
Grant, C. L. 3990
Grant, Gerald 1962
Grant, H. Roger 1229 2977
Grant, Jim 3399
Grant, Philip A., Jr. 2725 3597 3598
Grantham, Dewey W. 3599 3600
Grantham, Nell 3837
Grasmick, Harold G. 3601
Gravely, William B. 2291 2292
Graves, Gregory R. 2726
Graves, Oliver Finley 1504
Gray, R. J. 128
Gray, Richard 884
Gray, Ricky Harold 1907
Gray, Sally M. 2293
Grayson, A. G. 3602
Green, Archie 129 1505
Green, Ben 3400
Green, Edward C. 2131
Green, George D. 115 3178
Green, Henry D. 1506
Green, James R. 3401
Green, Jesse C., Jr. 2294
Green, Jim 3402
Green, Joe L. 1816
Greenberg, Kenneth S. 3603

Greenberg, Mike 1230
Greene, Candace 3890
Greene, Clarence H. 885
Greene, Robert B. 1507
Greene, Suzanne Ellery 3604
Greenfield, Sidney M. 2545
Greenwalt, Mary Burgner 1231
Greer, Fred 3226
Greer, L. Sue 285
Gresdna, Doty 264
Gretlund, Jan Nordby 886 887 888
Grider, Sylvia Ann 1232
Griepentrog, Gary L. 2558
Griessman, B. Eugene 3227
Griffin, Keith H. 1817
Griffin, Roger A. 1908
Griffin, William W. 1022
Griggs, Walter E., Jr. 2978
Griggs, William C. 3228
Grimes, Michael D. 3389
Grinde, Donald 3991
Grob, Alan 1909
Groff, Patrick 376
Gronberg, Douglas C. 889
Groos, Seymour 890
Groth, Philip 2584
Groves, Paul A. 3061 3062
Gryski, Gerard S. 3684
Guerard, Albert J. 2979
Guermonprez, Jean H. 2585
Guertler, John T. 130
Guethlein, Carol 3605
Guevin, Bryan L. 4069
Guilds, John C. 891
Guillaume, Alfred J., Jr. 1736
Guillory, Ferrel 3606
Gundersen, Joan Rezner 2295 2296
Gunderson, Gerald 2660
Gurr, Steve 131 2132
Guthrie, Charles S. 1508
Guttenberg, Barnett 892
Guy, Duane F. 1509
Guy-Sheftall, Beverly 2005
Gwinn, Erna Ottl 1510 1511

# H

Haan, Richard L. 3992
Haas, Edward F. 3607
Habig, Marion A. 3229
Hackney, Sheldon 444
Haden, Courtney 1512
Hadley, Charles D. 3608 3609 3839
Hadsell, Richard M. 2980
Hager, Jean 3230
Hagerman, Edward 1910
Hagy, James William 1233 1234 3610
Hahn, H. George 893
Hahn, Nicolas Fischer 3611
Hair, William I. 2586
Haites, Erik F. 2981
Halan, Y. C. 1513
Halbrooks, G. Thomas 2297 2298
Hale, Douglas 582
Hale, Duane Kendall 2982 3231
Hale, Tony 1514 1515
Haley, Jack D. 3232
Haley, Kenneth C. 894
Hall, Bob 2299 2587 2983 3375 3447
Hall, H. Gaston 895
Hall, Jacquelyn Dowd 132
Hall, John Whitling 3233
Hall, Kermit L. 3612
Hall, Lark 1911
Hall, Larry D. 2693
Hall, Leon 2006
Hall, Linda B. 2936
Hall, Virginius Cornick, Jr. 133
Halliburton, R., Jr. 3613
Halliday, James 2727
Halsell, Willie D. 134 135
Halverson, Delia 1235
Hambrick, Keith S. 896
Hamer, Collin Bradfield, Jr. 136
Hamilton, Holman 3614
Hamilton, Howard 3522
Hamm, Keith E. 3615

# LIST OF PERIODICALS

## A

A.A.G. Bijdragen |Netherlands|
AAUP Bulletin (see Academe: Bulletin of the AAUP)
Academe: Bulletin of the AAUP
Administration & Society
Aerospace Historian
Afro-Americans in New York Life and History
Agricultural History
Alabama Historical Quarterly
Alabama Review
Amerasia Journal
American Antiquity (AIA)
American Archivist
American Bar Association Journal
American Behavioral Scientist
American Benedictine Review
American Economic Review
American Heritage
American Historical Review
American History Illustrated
American Indian Art Magazine
American Indian Quarterly: A Journal of
    Anthropology, History and Literature
American Jewish Archives
American Jewish Historical Quarterly (see
    American Jewish History)
American Jewish History
American Journal of Economics and Sociology
American Journal of Legal History
American Journal of Political Science
American Journal of Sociology
American Literary Realism, 1870-1910
American Literature
American Neptune
American Political Science Review
American Politics Quarterly
American Preservation
American Quarterly
American Scholar
American Sociological Review
American Speech
American Studies International
American Studies (Lawrence, KS)
American West
Americas: A Quarterly Review of Inter-American
    Cultural History (Academy of American
    Franciscan History)
Américas (Organization of American States)
Annales de la Recherche Urbaine |France|
Annals of Iowa
Annals of the American Academy of Political and
    Social Science
Annals of the Association of American Geographers
Annals of Wyoming
Annual Review of Jazz Studies
Anuario de Estudios Americanos |Spain|
Appalachian Journal
APT Bulletin |Canada|
Archives of Natural History |Great Britain|
Arizona and the West
Arizona Quarterly
Arkansas Archeologist
Arkansas Historical Quarterly
Armenian Review
Art & Antiques
Art in America
Arts in Society (ceased pub 1976)
Aztlán

## B

Baptist History and Heritage
Black Scholar
Blackwood's Magazine (ceased pub 1980) |Great
    Britain|
Bulletin of Bibliography
Bulletin of the History of Medicine
Business History |Great Britain|
Business History Review

## C

Cahiers de Géographie de Québec |Canada|
Canadian Review of American Studies |Canada|
Capitol Studies (see Congress & the Presidency)
Caribbean Quarterly |Jamaica|
Catholic Historical Review
Centennial Review
Change
Chesopiean
Chronicles of Oklahoma
Church History
Cithara

Civil Liberties Review (ceased pub 1979)
Civil War History
Civil War Times Illustrated
Comparative Studies in Society and History |Great
    Britain|
Concordia Historical Institute Quarterly
Congress & the Presidency: A Journal of Capital
    Studies
Contemporary Review |Great Britain|
Continuity
Crisis

## D

Daedalus
Daughters of the American Revolution Magazine
Delaware History
Development and Change |Netherlands|
Dhaka University Studies Part A |Bangladesh|
Dissent

## E

Early American Life
Early American Literature
East Tennessee Historical Society's Publications
Economic Geography
Education and Urban Society
Encounter
Environmental Review
Escribano
Espace, Populations, Sociétés |France|
Esprit |France|
Ethnic Groups
Ethnohistory
Explorations in Economic History

## F

Family Heritage (ceased pub 1979)
Feminist Studies
Fides et Historia
Film & History
Filson Club History Quarterly
Florida Historical Quarterly
Folklore Forum
Foreign Service Journal
Forest History (see Journal of Forest History)
Foundations: A Baptist Journal of History and
    Theology (superseded by American Baptist
    Quarterly)
Frankfurter Hefte |German Federal Republic|
Freedomways
French-American Review
Frontiers

## G

Geographical Review
Georgia Historical Quarterly
Georgia Life (ceased pub 1980)
Georgia Review
Government Publications Review: An International
    Journal of Issues and Information Resources
Great Plains Journal
Great Plains Quarterly
Greek Orthodox Theological Review
Guildhall Studies in London History (pub
    suspended 1981) |Great Britain|

## H

Harvard Educational Review
Harvard Library Bulletin
Hayes Historical Journal
Histoire |France|
Historia Mexicana |Mexico|
Historian
Historic Preservation
Historical Archaeology
Historical Journal |Great Britain|
Historical Journal of Massachusetts
Historical Journal of Western Massachusetts (see
    Historical Journal of Massachusetts)
Historical Magazine of the Protestant Episcopal
    Church
Historical Methods
Historical New Hampshire
Historical Reflections = Réflexions Historiques
    |Canada|
History and Theory
History of Education Quarterly
History Teacher
History Today |Great Britain|

Horizon
Human Organization

## I

Idaho Yesterdays
Indian Historian (see Wassaja: The Indian
    Historian)
Indian Journal of American Studies |India|
Indiana Folklore (ceased pub 1980)
Industrial Archaeology |Great Britain|
Inter-American Review of Bibliography = Revista
    Interamericana de Bibliografía
International Labor and Working Class History
International Social Science Journal |France|
Italian Americana

## J

Jednota Annual Furdek
JEMF Quarterly
Jewish Social Studies
Journal for the Scientific Study of Religion
Journal of African Studies
Journal of American Culture
Journal of American Ethnic History
Journal of American Folklore
Journal of American History
Journal of American Studies |Great Britain|
Journal of Black Studies
Journal of Cherokee Studies
Journal of Economic History
Journal of Ecumenical Studies
Journal of Ethnic Studies
Journal of European Economic History |Italy|
Journal of Family History: Studies in Family,
    Kinship, and Demography
Journal of Folklore Research
Journal of Forest History
Journal of Garden History |Great Britain|
Journal of Interdisciplinary History
Journal of Intergroup Relations
Journal of Jazz Studies (superseded by Annual
    Review of Jazz Studies)
Journal of Library History, Philosophy, &
    Comparative Librarianship
Journal of Mississippi History
Journal of Modern History
Journal of NAL Associates
Journal of Negro Education
Journal of Negro History
Journal of Political Economy
Journal of Political Science
Journal of Politics
Journal of Popular Culture
Journal of Popular Film and Television
Journal of Popular Film (see Journal of Popular
    Film and Television)
Journal of Presbyterian History
Journal of Religious History |Australia|
Journal of Social History
Journal of Social Issues
Journal of Southern History
Journal of Sport History
Journal of the Afro-American Historical &
    Genealogical Society
Journal of the Alabama Academy of Science
Journal of the American Planning Association
Journal of the Early Republic
Journal of the Folklore Institute (see Journal of
    Folklore Research)
Journal of the History of Medicine and Allied
    Sciences
Journal of the History of Sociology
Journal of the History of the Behavioral Sciences
Journal of the Society for the Bibliography of
    Natural History (see Archives of Natural
    History) |Great Britain|
Journal of the Society of Architectural Historians
Journal of the United Reformed Church History
    Society |Great Britain|
Journal of the West
Journal of the West Virginia Historical Association
Journal of Urban History
Journalism History
Journalism Quarterly
Judicature

## K

Kansas Historical Quarterly (superseded by Kansas
    History)
Kentucky Folklore Record: A Regional Journal of
    Folklore and Folklife
Keystone Folklore

# L

Labor History
Land Economics
Landscape
Liberal Education
Library Chronicle of the University of Texas at Austin
Lincoln Herald
Louisiana History
Louisiana Review = Revue de Louisiane (ceased pub 1982)
Louisiana Studies (see Southern Studies: An Interdisciplinary Journal of the South)

# M

Magazine Antiques
Mankind (suspended pub 1982)
Manuscripta
Marxist Perspectives (ceased pub 1980)
Maryland Historian
Maryland Historical Magazine
Massachusetts Review
Masterkey
Material Culture
Mennonite Life
Methodist History
Michael: On the History of the Jews in the Diaspora |Israel|
Mid-America
Midstream
Midwest Journal of Political Science (see American Journal of Political Science)
Midwest Quarterly
Midwestern Archivist
Military History of Texas and the Southwest
Miroir de l'Histoire |France|
Missionalia Hispanica |Spain|
Mississippi Quarterly
Missouri Historical Review
Missouri Historical Society. Bulletin (superseded by Gateway Heritage)
Modern Age
Modernist Studies: Literature and Culture 1920-1940 (ceased pub 1982) |Canada|
Monthly Labor Review

# N

Names
National Civic Review
National Parks and Conservation Magazine
Nautical Research Journal
Negro History Bulletin
New England Quarterly
New Scholar
New South (superseded by Southern Voices)
New York Folklore
New York Folklore Quarterly (superseded by New York Folklore)
New York History
Nineteenth Century
North Carolina Folklore Journal
North Carolina Historical Review
North Dakota Quarterly
North Louisiana Historical Association Journal
Novaia i Noveishaia Istoriia |Union of Soviet Socialist Republic|
Nuestro Tiempo (IHE) |Spain|

# O

Oral History Review

# P

Pacific Historian
Pacific Historical Review
Pacific Northwest Quarterly
Panhandle-Plains Historical Review
Papers of the Abraham Lincoln Association
Partisan Review
Past and Present |Great Britain|
Pennsylvania Folklife
Pennsylvania Heritage
Pennsylvania Magazine of History and Biography
Pennsylvania Mennonite Heritage
Permian Historical Annual
Perspectives in American History (ceased pub 1979)
Phylon
Pioneer America (see Material Culture)

Pioneer America Society Transactions
Plains Anthropologist
Plantation Society in the Americas
Policy Studies Journal
Political Science Quarterly
Polity
Present Tense
Princeton University Library Chronicle
Proceedings of the American Philosophical Society
Proceedings of the South Carolina Historical Association
Prologue: the Journal of the National Archives
Psychohistory Review
Public Historian
Public Interest
Public Opinion Quarterly
Publius

# Q

Quaker History
Quarterly Journal of Economics
Quarterly Journal of Speech
Quarterly Journal of the Library of Congress (ceased pub 1983)
Quarterly Review of Historical Studies |India|

# R

Radical America
Railroad History
Reason
Records of the American Catholic Historical Society of Philadelphia
Red River Valley Historical Review
Register of the Kentucky Historical Society
Religion in Life (ceased pub 1980)
Research in Economic History
Research Studies
Review (Fernand Braudel Center)
Review of Economics and Statistics
Review of Radical Political Economics
Reviews in American History
Revista de História (suspended pub 1977) |Brazil|
Revista de Historia Militar |Spain|
Revue de Louisiane-Louisiana Review (see Louisiana Review = Revue de Louisiane)
Revue d'Histoire de l'Amérique Française |Canada|
Revue Française d'Etudes Américaines |France|
Revue Internationale de Droit Comparé |France|
Richmond County History
Rocky Mountain Social Science Journal (see Social Science Journal)
RQ
Rural Sociology

# S

Samtiden |Norway|
San Jorge (see Sant Jordi) |Spain|
San José Studies
Science & Society
Scottish Geographical Magazine |Great Britain|
Shakaikeizaishigaku (Socio-Economic History) |Japan|
Signs: Journal of Women in Culture and Society
Smithsonian
Social Education
Social Forces
Social History = Histoire Sociale |Canada|
Social Policy
Social Problems
Social Research
Social Science History
Social Science Journal
Social Science Quarterly
Social Studies
Society
Sociological Analysis
Sociology and Social Research
Sociology of Education
Soundings (Nashville, TN)
South Atlantic Quarterly
South Carolina Historical Magazine
South Carolina Review
Southern Changes
Southern Economic Journal
Southern Exposure
Southern Folklore Quarterly
Southern Humanities Review
Southern Indian Studies
Southern Literary Journal

Southern Quarterly
Southern Review
Southern Speech Communication Journal
Southern Studies: An Interdisciplinary Journal of the South
Southwest Review
Southwestern Art (ceased pub 1978)
Southwestern Historical Quarterly
Spiegel Historiael |Netherlands|
State Government
Studies in History and Society (suspended pub 1977)
Studies in Romanticism
Studies in the American Renaissance
Supreme Court Historical Society Yearbook
Swiss American Historical Society Newsletter

# T

Tampa Bay History
Teachers College Record
Technology and Culture
Tennessee Folklore Society Bulletin
Tennessee Historical Quarterly
Tequesta
Terrae Incognitae
Texana (ceased pub 1974)
Texas Quarterly (ceased pub 1978)
Theatre Survey: The American Journal of Theatre History
Thought
Trends in History

# U

Ukrainian Quarterly
Umoja: A Scholarly Journal of Black Studies
United States Naval Institute Proceedings
Upper Ohio Valley Historical Review
Urban Affairs Quarterly
Urban Review
Urban Studies |Great Britain|

# V

Vermont History
Vie Française |Canada|
Viewpoints: Georgia Baptist History
Virginia Cavalcade
Virginia Magazine of History and Biography
Virginia Quarterly Review
Voprosy Istorii |Union of Soviet Socialist Republic|

# W

Washington Monthly
Wassaja: The Indian Historian (suspended pub 1980)
West Georgia College Review
West Georgia College Studies in the Social Sciences
West Tennessee Historical Society Papers
West Texas Historical Association Year Book (ceased pub)
West Virginia History
Western Folklore
Western Historical Quarterly
Western Humanities Review
Western Journal of Speech Communication
Western Political Quarterly
Western Review (ceased pub 1973)
Western Speech (see Western Journal of Speech Communication)
Western States Jewish Historical Quarterly (see Western States Jewish History)
Western States Jewish History
Westways
Wiener Beiträge zur Geschichte der Neuzeit |Austria|
William and Mary Quarterly
Wilson Library Bulletin
Winterthur Portfolio
Working Papers for a New Society (see Working Papers Magazine)
Working Papers from the Regional Economic History Research Center (suspended pub 1982)
Working Papers Magazine (suspended pub 1983)
Worldview

# Y

Yale University Library Gazette
Youth and Society

# LIST OF ABSTRACTERS

## A

Aimone, A. C.
Aldrich, R.
Andrew, J.
Athey, L. L.
Atkinson, J. L. B.

## B

Bailey, E. C.
Bamber, J.
Bassett, T. D. S.
Beaber, P. A.
Beck, P. J.
Bedford, W. B.
Beecher, L. N.
Beer, S.
Belles, A. G.
Benson, J. A.
Billigmeier, J. C.
Blaser, L. K.
Bobango, G. J.
Bolton, G. A.
Bowers, D. E.
Bradford, J. C.
Brewster, D. E.
Broussard, J. H.
Burckel, N. C.
Burns, H. M.
Buschen, J. J.
Bushnell, D.
Butchart, R. E.
Butcher, K.

## C

Calkin, H. L.
Cameron, D. D.
Campbell, E. R.
Chard, D. F.
Cimbala, D. J.
Cleyet, G. P.
Clive, A.
Coleman, J. S.
Coleman, P. J.
Colwell, J. L.
Conner, S. P.
Correia-Afonso, J.
Coutinho, J. V.
Crapster, B. L.
Crowe, J. C.
Crowther, K. N. T.
Curtis, G. H.

## D

D'Aniello, C. A.
Davis, D. G.
Dean, D. M.
Dewees, A. C.
Dibert, M. D.
Doyle, Sr. A.
Drysdale, A.
Dubay, R. W.

## E

Egerton, F. N.
Eid, L. V.
Eminhizer, E. E.
English, J. C.
Estes, K. W.

## F

Fahl, R. J.
Falk, J. D.
Farmerie, S. A.
Feingold, M.
Fenske, B. L.
Findling, J. E.
Fitzgerald, C. B.
Fox, G.
Frame, R. M., III
Frenkley, N.
Friedel, J. N.
Fulton, R. T.
Furdell, W. J.

## G

Gagnon, G. O.
Garland, A. N.
Gassner, J. S.
Geist, C. D.
Gillam, M. R.
Gilmont, K. E.
Glasrud, B. A.
Glovins, G. A.
Goerler, R. E.
Grant, C. L.
Grant, H. R.
Griswold del Castillo, R.
Groves, J. V.
Gunter, C. R.

## H

Harling, F. F.
Henderson, D. F.
Herrick, J. M.
Herstein, S. R.
Hillje, J. W.
Hinnebusch, P. D.
Hively, W. R.
Hoffman, A.
Holton, J. T.
Hough, C. M.
Huff, A. V.
Human, V. L.
Hurt, R. D.

## J

Jirran, R. J.
Johnson, B. D.
Johnson, E. D.
Johnson, E. S.
Johnson, L. F.
Jordan, D. P.
Judd, R. W.

## K

Kascus, M. A.
Kaufman, M.
Keller, R. A.
Kennedy, P. W.
Keyser, E. L.
Koppel, T.
Kuntz, N. A.

## L

Lambert, D. K.
Ledbetter, B. D.
Lederer, N.
Lee, J. M.
Leedom, J. W.
Legan, M. S.
Leonard, I. M.
Lewis, J. A.
Lifka, M. L.
Linkfield, T. P.
Lokken, R. N.
Lovin, H. T.
Lucas, M. B.

## M

Marks, H. S.
Marr, W. L.
McArthur, J. N.
McCarthy, E.
McCarthy, J. M.
McCarthy, M. M.
McGinnis, D.
McGinty, G. W.
McKinney, G. B.
McNeill, C. A.
Miller, R. M.
Moore, J.
Mtewa, M.
Mulligan, W. H.
Murdock, E. C.
Mycue, D. J.
Myres, S. L.

## N

Neville, G. L.
Neville, J. D.
Neville, R. G.

## O

Oaks, R. F.
Olbrich, W. L.
Olson, C. W.
Olson, G. L.
Osur, A. M.
Overbeck, J. A.

## P

Parker, H. M.
Patzwald, G.-A.
Paul, B. J.
Paul, J. F.
Pearson, S. C.
Petersen, P. L.
Pickens, D. K.
Piersen, W. D.
Porter, B. S.
Powell, J.
Powell, L. N.
Pragman, J. H.
Preece, C. A.
Puffer, K. J.
Pusateri, C. J.

## Q

Quinlivan, M. E.

## R

Read, C. J.
Reichardt, O. H.
Richardson, T. P.
Ritter, R. V.
Rockwood, D. S.
Rosenthal, F.
Russell, L.

## S

Sapper, N. G.
Sarna, J. D.
Sassoon, T.
Savitt, T. L.
Schmidt, D. S.
Schoonover, T. D.
Schroeder, G. R.
Schulz, C. B.
Schumacher, M.
Sherer, R. G.
Shergold, P. R.
Sicher, E. R.

Newton, C. A.
Nicholls, D. J.
Nielson, D. G.
Noble, R. E.
Novitsky, A. W.

Sirriyeh, E. M.
Sliwoski, R. S.
Smith, C. O.
Smith, D. L.
Smith, L. C.
Smith, T. W.
Solodkin, P. L.
Souby, A. R.
Sprague, S. S.
Stack, R. E.
Stickney, E. P.
Stoesen, A. R.
Street, J. B.
Street, N. J.
Strom, S. C.
Sweetland, J. H.

## T

Tate, M. L.
Taylorson, P. J.
Thacker, J. W.
Tomlinson, R. H.
Touchstone, D. B.
Travis, P.
Trickey, D. J.
Tull, J.

## U

Underwood, T. L.

## V

Velicer, L. F.
Verardo, D. R.
Vivian, J. F.

## W

Walker, W. T.
Ward, H. M.
Wasson, G. V.
Wechman, R. J.
Wendel, T. H.
Wentworth, M. J.
West, K. B.
Wiederrecht, A. E.
Wiegand, W. A.
Williams, J. W.
Wilson, M. T.
Woehrmann, P. J.
Wood, C. W.
Woodward, R. L.
Wyk, L. Van

## Y

Yanchisin, D. A.

## Z

Zabel, O. H.